DAMAGES

General Editor

*Simon Levene, MA (Cantab),
Barrister, 199 Strand*

© Simon Levene 2001

Published by
EMIS Professional Publishing Ltd
31–33 Stonehills House
Welwyn Garden City
Hertfordshire
AL8 6PU

ISBN 1 85811 264 8

All rights reserved. No part of this publication may be reproduced, stored in a retrieval system, or transmitted, in any form or by any means, electronic, mechanical, photocopying, recording or otherwise, without the prior permission of the publisher.

The moral right of the author has been asserted.

Typeset by Tracey Dabell and Stephen Theaker.

Cover design by Jane Conway.

Printed and bound in the UK by Antony Rowe Ltd, Bumper's Farm, Chippenham, Wiltshire.

CONTENTS

Table of cases	v
INTRODUCTION	lv
Appendix 1: Updating Awards in Line with Heil	lxi
Appendix 2: Checklist for General Damages	lxiv
USING THIS SERVICE	lxvii
SECTION 1.1	
INJURY CASES	1
1.1 General Injury	1
SECTION 1.2	
DAMAGE TO HEAD	7
1.2.1 Hair Loss	7
1.2.2 Headaches	11
1.2.3 Head Injury	23
SECTION 1.3	
DAMAGE TO SPINE	116
1.3.1 Neck Injury	116
SECTION 1.4	
DAMAGE TO UPPER LIMBS	252
1.4.1 Shoulder Injury	252
1.4.2 Arm or Wrist Injury	265
1.4.3 Arm or Wrist and Other Injury	282
1.4.4 Hand Injury	300
SECTION 1.5	
DAMAGE TO TRUNK	334
1.5.1 Chest Injury	334
1.5.2 Breast Injury	340

1.5.3 Buttock Injury	341
1.5.4 Abdominal Injury	342
1.5.5 Pelvis and Hip Injury	355

SECTION 1.6
DAMAGE TO LOWER LIMBS — 362
1.6.1 Leg or Ankle Injury	362

SECTION 1.7
PHYSICAL DAMAGE TO SKIN — 435
1.7.1 Burns	436
1.7.2 Needle Stick	441
1.7.3 Scarring	442

SECTION 1.8
SPECIFIC INJURIES — 461
1.8.1 Animal Bites	461
1.8.2 Amputation	462
1.8.3 Injury Resulting in Death	466
1.8.4 Poisoning and Medication Overdose	467
1.8.5 Paralysis	468
1.8.6 Sexual Abuse	474

SECTION 1.9
ONSET OF DISEASE — 497
1.9.1 Circulatory Disease	497
1.9.2 Failure to Diagnose	497
1.9.3 Gastro-intestinal Disease	499
1.9.4 Infectious Disease	499
1.9.5 Neurological Disease	500
1.9.6 Psychiatric Disease	501
1.9.7 Respiratory Disease	544
1.9.8 Skin Disease	557

INDEX — 561

TABLE OF CASES

A (a child) v Milupa Ltd [2000] 6 CL 202 500
A (a child) v Westminster Society For People With Learning Difficulties,
  Kemp & Kemp, PRC-019; [2000] 3 CL 184 508
A (a minor) v Ellwood, Kemp & Kemp, K2-122; [1999] CLY 1617 337
A (a minor) v Severn Trent Water plc, Kemp & Kemp, C6-020;
  [1999] CLY 1458 76
A (a minor) v Sullivan (1999) 99 (5) QR 8; Kemp & Kemp, K2-268;
  [1999] CLY 1595 196
A, M and T, Re, Kemp & Kemp, C4-046; [1994] CLY 1579 475
A, Re (1996) 96 (2) QR 5; Kemp & Kemp, H6-037/1; [1996] CLY 2268 307
A, Re, Kemp & Kemp, C4-254; [1992] CLY 1603 489
A, Re, Kemp & Kemp, I2-438; [1994] CLY 1682 403
AB, Re, Kemp & Kemp, C4-246; [1998] CLY 1514 487
Abbott, Re: Sub Nom. Abbott v Roebuck, Kemp & Kemp, H6-050/2;
  [1996] CLY 2320 259
Abram v St Helens Borough Council, Kemp & Kemp, F5-065/1;
  [1994] CLY 1641 354
Adams, Re, Kemp & Kemp, C3-010; [1990] CLY 1586 103
AH, Re, Kemp & Kemp, C4-214; [1997] CLY 1842 524
Ahmed v Aquamead [1995] CLY 1823 124
Aissani v HF Food Management (Holborn), Kemp & Kemp, F2-056;
  [1994] CLY 1634 543
AJR, Re, Kemp & Kemp, C4-049; [1992] CLY 1580 342
Akroyd v Patterson [1992] CLY 1737 264
Albrighton v Townscape Products, Kemp & Kemp, H5-021; [1993] CLY 1520 291
Alexander v HCC Tinsley and Son, Kemp & Kemp, H4-032; [1991] CLY 1426 306
Alford, Re, Kemp & Kemp, C2-038; [1994] CLY 1558 105
Aliseo v Edenborough [1991] CLY 1487 287
Alldis v Myer, Kemp & Kemp, E3-124/1; [1997] CLY 1939 232
Allin v City and Hackney HA [1996] Med LR 167; Kemp & Kemp,
  C4-080; [1996] CLY 2185 533
Allington, Re [1992] CLY 1629 85
Allsop v White [1992] CLY 1614 451
Almond v Britt-Waight, Kemp & Kemp, I3-027/1; [1995] CLY 1746 389
Alsbury v Care, Kemp & Kemp, E2-041; [1991] CLY 1398 136
Amatyakul v Olding, Kemp & Kemp, E2-080/3; [1998] CLY 1599 166
Ambler v Hepworth, Kemp & Kemp, F2-023; BPILS, I 344.1 [1992] CLY 1661 544

Anderson v Davies and Anderson [1993] PIQR Q87; Kemp & Kemp,
  C4-030; BPILS I225,305, XV 1007; [1992] CLY 1576 251
Anderton v Granulators Ltd, Kemp & Kemp, E2-015/1; [1999] CLY 1468 198
Andrew v Herbert and Neale, Kemp & Kemp, I4-036; [1996] CLY 2324 427
Angell v Brough, Kemp & Kemp, E2-116, K2-048; [1997] CLY 1911 180
Antony, Re, Kemp & Kemp, H5-011; [1990] CLY 1652 326
AP (a minor), Re, Kemp & Kemp, C4-222; [1991] CLY 1365 481
AP, Re, Kemp & Kemp, C4-209; [1991] CLY 1363 478
Appleton v JB Taxis, Kemp & Kemp, K2-038/1; [2000] 3 CL 185 205
Ara, Re [1997] CLY 1847 283
Archer & Archer v Leighton [1990] CLY 1709 509
Arkle, Re [1995] CLY 1660 103
Arkley v Alfred Ellis and Sons (Wakefield) [1990] CLY 1611 558
Armatrading, Re, Kemp & Kemp, K2-138; [1996] CLY 2342 428
Armstrong (a minor) v Gharhdagi, Kemp & Kemp, E2-115/2; [1998] CLY 1610 179
Armstrong v Scarborough HA (1999) 99 (3) QR 5; Kemp & Kemp, C2-037;
  [1999] CLY 1434 104
Arrighi v Brewers, Kemp & Kemp, K2-099; [1990] CLY 1683 265
Asghar, Re [1994] CLY 1547 1
Ashouri v Penfold, Kemp & Kemp, PRK-012; [2000] 2 CL 146 242
Ashton v Mortlock, Kemp & Kemp, E2-073/2; [1997] CLY 1903 162
Asperry Ltd v Rigg, Kemp & Kemp, E3-123; [1996] CLY 2327 232
AT, Re [1992] CLY 1602 483
ATA v Hellen [2000] 6 CL 182 137
Atkinson v Waring and Waring, Kemp & Kemp, K2-124; [1994] CLY 1722 371
Atkinson v Whittle, Kemp & Kemp, E2-048/3; [1999] CLY 1479 155
Attison, Re [1991] CLY 1394 69
Attwood v Booth, Kemp & Kemp, I2-521/3; [1996] CLY 2278 388
Attwood v Woodward, Kemp & Kemp, K2-176/2; [1999] CLY 1573 129
Atwal, Re, Kemp & Kemp, C4-045; [1992] CLY 1577 112
Aurckett v Smith, Kemp & Kemp, H7-018/1; [1992] CLY 1699 330
Avgerinos, Re (CICB Quantum: 1999), Kemp & Kemp, PRO-001[2000] 2 CL 144 85
Avola, Re, Kemp & Kemp, C6-074; [1992] CLY 1620 63
Aylesbury v Hale, Kemp & Kemp, D2-017; [1995] CLY 1691 69
Ayling v Davenport-Strange, Kemp & Kemp, E2-110; [1995] CLY 1715 231

B (a child) v Littlewoods plc, Kemp & Kemp, PRC-017; [2000] 3 CL 170 48
B (a minor) v Mitchell (1999) 99 (2) QR 7; Kemp & Kemp, K2-117/3;
  [1999] CLY 1598 297
B (a minor) v Pleasure and Leisure Corporation, Kemp & Kemp, PRI-004;
  [2000] 3 CL 182 390
B, Re [1992] CLY 1601 482
B, Re [1999] CLY 1439 476
B, Re [1999] CLY 1440 477
B, Re [1999] CLY 1451 480
B, Re, Kemp & Kemp, C4-220; [1991] CLY 1364 481
B, Re, Kemp & Kemp, C4-234; [1996] CLY 2196 484

B, Re, Kemp & Kemp, D2-042; [1994] CLY 1593 87
Babla v Patel, Kemp & Kemp, K2-253; [1990] CLY 1705 281
Back v Sharpe, Kemp & Kemp, B2-043; [1995] CLY 1658 404
Bahi v Rai, Kemp & Kemp, I3-016; [1996] CLY 2285 416
Bailey (Charles Andrew) v Gateway Food Markets, Kemp & Kemp,
  G2-038; [1994] CLY 1645 358
Bailey v Chemical Recoveries Ltd, Kemp & Kemp, C4-089; [1998] CLY 1534 34
Bailey v Knowsley, Kemp & Kemp, K2-145/1; [1998] CLY 1703 355
Bailey, Re [1991] CLY 1377 455
Baines (Onkar Singh) v Sherazia T/A A&S Autos, Kemp & Kemp, C4-124;
  [1997] CLY 2013 36
Baines v Spartan Sheffield Ltd, Kemp & Kemp, K2-249; [1996] CLY 2358 342
Baker (a minor) v Williams, Kemp & Kemp, B2-036/4; [1998] CLY 1499 60
Baker v Hunter, Kemp & Kemp, E3-099; [1993] CLY 1497 239
Baker v Tugwell, Kemp & Kemp, PRK-011, K2-208/4; [1998] CLY 1745 280
Bakhitiari (Leila) v The Zoological Society of London, Kemp & Kemp, H5-015;
  [1992] CLY 1689 326
Baldwin v Dilks [1993] CLY 1505 184
Baldwin v Wirral Borough Council, Kemp & Kemp, J3-020; [1991] CLY 1450 438
Baldwin, Re, Kemp & Kemp, B2-014; [1994] CLY 1551 110
Ball v Genge [1992] CLY 1757 189
Balli v Mahmood, Kemp & Kemp, K2-055/1; [1999] CLY 1566 539
Banfield, Re [1992] CLY 1709 455
Barber v Severn Trent Water [1995] CLY 1817 361
Barden v Jobquote, Kemp & Kemp, B2-011; [1993] CLY 1428 2
Barker v Ipswich Buses, Kemp & Kemp, E2-023; [1991] CLY 1396 149
Barker v North-West Water [1994] CLY 1649 261
Barker v Roberts, Kemp & Kemp, F2-050; [1997] CLY 1946 556
Barnes v Commissioner of Police for the Metropolis [1992] CLY 1781 264
Barnes v Kenmore Refrigeration Ltd, Kemp & Kemp, J3-039/1;
  [1997] CLY 2003 278
Barnes v Lunt and Motor Insurers Bureau, Kemp & Kemp, E2-081;
  [1996] CLY 2225 377
Barnett v Lintern, Kemp & Kemp, E2-055/2; [1998] CLY 1590 157
Barraclough v Saunders, Kemp & Kemp, L8-096; [1994] CLY 1752 345
Barrett v Cramp, Kemp & Kemp, E2-090/1; [1998] CLY 1600 168
Barrington v Glass Glover Group plc, Kemp & Kemp, E2-005/1;
  [1998] CLY 1577 116
Barry and Morgan v Williams and Jones [1996] CLY 2187 534
Barry v Evans [1996] CLY 2354 55
Barry v Guys and Dolls [1992] CLY 1624 10
Barsby v Harrison, Kemp & Kemp, PRK-010, J2-047; [1998] CLY 1754 415
Bartley v Liverpool City Council, Kemp & Kemp, I3-037; [1996] CLY 2329 414
Barton v Ali Raj Tandoori Takeaway [1992] CLY 1768 500
Barwise v Liverpool City Council, Kemp & Kemp, F2-067; [1996] CLY 2245 545
Bate v Department of Employment, Kemp & Kemp, E3-072;
  [1994] CLY 1604, 1625 137

Bateman v Industrial Orthopaedic Society (1998) 3 Medical Litigation 3;
  BPILS, XVII 1089; [1998] CLY 1762 498
Battle v Sharples [1994] CLY 1738 192
Batty, Re [1993] CLY 1475 84
Baughan v Paxton, Kemp & Kemp, 1-008/2; [1990] CLY 1698......................................191
Bawden v Gardner, Kemp & Kemp, B2-026/2; [1998] CLY 1497 362
Baynard v Manchester City Council, Kemp & Kemp, J2-024; [1998] CLY 1694 272
Baynham v Kenmore, Kemp & Kemp, PRJ-011, J2-049; [1998] CLY 1746 315
Baynton v ICI, Kemp & Kemp, C4-034; [1996] CLY 2183 523
Beacham v Shaw, Kemp & Kemp, E2-064/1/1; [1999] CLY 1474 159
Beal v Turner, Kemp & Kemp, K2-074; [1993] CLY 1560 313
Beales, Re, Kemp & Kemp, C2-052L; [1998] CLY 1495 109
Beavan v Derby City Transport, Kemp & Kemp, E2-078; [1997] CLY 1892 119
Beck v Bemrose, Kemp & Kemp, K2-251; [1991] CLY 1490 322
Bedford (a minor) v Dyson, Kemp & Kemp, B2-036/3; [1998] CLY 1498.......................33
Bedford v Ackworth Working Men's Club, Kemp & Kemp, K2-072;
  [1992] CLY 1736 295
Beecham v Wright, Kemp & Kemp, H2-028/1; [1996] CLY 2257 228
Begum, Re, Kemp & Kemp, I2-505; [1995] CLY 1744 383
Bell v Quinn, Kemp & Kemp, I2-522; [1993] CLY 1534 388
Bell v Wash, Kemp & Kemp, E3-120; [1990] CLY 1681...182
Bellovics v British Railways Board [1990] CLY 1584 25
Benn v G & F Joinery (Portsmouth), Kemp & Kemp, I4-021; [1993] CLY 1546............423
Bennet v Handford, Kemp & Kemp, E2-097; [1994] CLY 1614......................................172
Bennet v Notley, Kemp & Kemp, K2-022; [1999] CLY 1575 230
Bennett v British Coal, Kemp & Kemp, C6-002; [1995] CLY 1687 38
Bennett v Central Manchester Health Authority, Kemp & Kemp,
  A4-016/1; [1991] CLY 1334..97
Bennett v Newell, Kemp & Kemp, K2-232; [1991] CLY 1488 287
Bennett, Re, Kemp & Kemp, E2-025; [1992] CLY 1638 149
Bennett, Re, Kemp & Kemp, I3-020/2; [1993] CLY 1542...60
Benney v Carnon Consolidated Tin Mines [1993] PIQR Q7;
  Kemp & Kemp, C4-048; [1992] CLY 1579 502
Benson v Howard, Kemp & Kemp, E3-035; [1994] CLY 1622..236
Bent, Re, Kemp & Kemp, D2-047; [1991] CLY 1392 79
Bentley v Pushman, Kemp & Kemp, E3-115; [1993] CLY 1502 204
Berry & Loades v Roe, Kemp & Kemp, H2-031; [1993] CLY 1557 143
Berry v Pearce, Kemp & Kemp, K2-196; [1992] CLY 1764..147
Bettany v Harvey Plant [1992] CLY 1634...68
Bettridge v Hoque, Kemp & Kemp, E2-102/1/1; [1999] CLY 1579 203
Betts v Dolby, Kemp & Kemp, G2-028/2; [1997] CLY 1954 355
Bevan v Pannell, Kemp & Kemp, K2-264; [1998] CLY 1708 346
Bevan v South Wales Fire Service, Kemp & Kemp, K2-244/1; [2000] 5 CL 195 430
Beverley, Re [1992] CLY 1596..540
Bhatti (Mohinder) (1996) 96 (2) QR 7; Kemp & Kemp, K2-162; [1996] CLY 2343..........54
Bhatti, Re, Kemp & Kemp, C4-116; [1998] CLY 1538 539

Bhavsar, Re (CICB Quantum: 2000), Kemp & Kemp, E3-004/2/1;
[2000] 4 CL 153 211
Bhudia v Newman, Kemp & Kemp, K2-113; [1994] CLY 1720 370
Bidwell, Re, Kemp & Kemp, C4-093; [1996] CLY 2188 535
Bielby v Thorpe [1992] CLY 1753 459
Bigelow v Jones, Kemp & Kemp, K2-218; [1996] CLY 2355 234
Billington, Re, Kemp & Kemp, H1-104, H6-050; [1999] CLY 1605..............................313
Binney, Re, Kemp & Kemp, C4-119; [1994] CLY 1578 507
Bir v AL Dunn & Co, Kemp & Kemp, H5-023/1; [1993] CLY 1525...............................308
Bird v Husain, Re, Kemp & Kemp, E3-007; [1993] CLY 1486 212
Bird v Rixon, Kemp & Kemp, K2-020; [1996] CLY 2306 143
Birtwhistle, Re [1995] CLY 1680...60
Bispham v Central Nottinghamshire Health Authority, Kemp & Kemp,
E3-014; [1994] CLY 1620 214
Blackaller v Young [1992] CLY 1636 214
Blackwood v G D Bowes & Sons 1995] CLY 1759 384
Blakemore v College of St Mark and St John, Kemp & Kemp, I3-020;
[1993] CLY 1547 432
Blakey v Brown, Kemp & Kemp, K2-106; [1996] CLY 2331 435
Blanc v Baskerville, Kemp & Kemp, I2-515; [1992] CLY 1706 386
Blanche v Brown, Kemp & Kemp, H2-030; [1995] CLY 1724 258
Blenkiron v Turton, Kemp & Kemp, K1-100, K2-079/1; [1999] CLY 1597 5
Boisson v Mohommedi Studios [1992] CLY 1747 21
Boland v Corby Towage, Kemp & Kemp, PRH-006, H6-046/1; [1999] CLY 1506.........325
Bollard v Simmonds, Kemp & Kemp, E2-102/1; [1998] CLY 1604 173
Bond v West Midlands Travel, Kemp & Kemp, E2-060; [1996] CLY 2220 158
Bond, Re, Kemp & Kemp, H4-028; [1993] CLY 1521..295
Bonita Bryg v Fuji Television Network Inc, Kemp & Kemp, H2-017;
[1993] CLY 1512 254
Bonney v Radcliffe Infirmary NHS Trust, Kemp & Kemp, E3-087;
[1997] CLY 1934 225
Bonsor v Blake, Kemp & Kemp, H3-159; [1994] CLY 1651 269
Booth v Barruffo, Kemp & Kemp, E3-091; [1994] CLY 1606..138
Boother v British Railways Board [1992] CLY 1685...299
Bosah, Re, Kemp & Kemp, J5-013; [1992] CLY 1623..10
Bouchta v Swindon HA [1996] 7 Med LR 62; Kemp & Kemp, F4-020;
BPILS, XVII 1148,1297; [1996] CLY 2247..349
Bould v Wakefield Health Authority, Kemp & Kemp, A4-003/3;
[1994] CLY 1545 93
Boulton v Brammer and Logic Office Furniture, Kemp & Kemp, C2-049;
[1993] CLY 1441 108
Boundy v Valavanis, Kemp & Kemp, K2-112; [1997] CLY 2019 54
Bourne, Re, Kemp & Kemp, C4-126; [1997] CLY 2014 540
Bovenzi v Kettering Health Authority [1991] 2 Med LR 293; Kemp & Kemp,
F4-031; BPILS, XVII 1126; [1990] CLY 1642 347
Bowden v Lane (dec'd), Kemp & Kemp, A2-007, A2-105; [1990] CLY 1577..................472
Bowers, Re, Kemp & Kemp, H4-015; [1995] CLY 1730...289

Bowler v Smart, Kemp & Kemp, J2-032; [1993] CLY 1549 366
Boyce v Secur Scan (UK) Ltd, Kemp & Kemp, E2-123/2; [1999] CLY 1478..................181
BR, Re, Kemp & Kemp, C4-137; [1996] CLY 2199 495
Bradley v Farid [1995] CLY 1701 157
Bradley, Re [1992] CLY 1567 92
Bragg v Ford Motor Co. [1992] PIQR Q72; Kemp & Kemp, D3-022, D3-117;
  [1992] CLY 1635 70
Bragg v Ministry of Defence, Kemp & Kemp, H4-014/1; [1994] CLY 1654 268
Braham v Golding, Kemp & Kemp, E2-065/1; [1998] CLY 1595....................................160
Braithwaite v Latham, Kemp & Kemp, H4-017; BPILS, I 14; [1990] CLY 1649 299
Branch v Lowe, Kemp & Kemp, C5-051; [1990] CLY 1603 47
Breese v Darnton, Kemp & Kemp, I2-308; [1996] CLY 2275..382
Brelsford v British Railways Board [1993] CLY 1566 413
Brennan (a minor) v Howell, Kemp & Kemp, I2-539; [1998] CLY 1673.......................392
Brewer, Re [1997] CLY 1823 473
Brewis v GEC Alsthom, Kemp & Kemp, K2-214; [1994] CLY 1734..............................280
Brewster v Thamesway Bus Co., Kemp & Kemp, E2-032; [1995] CLY 1710 219
Bridges v Cornwall and Isles of Scilly Area Health Authority [1992] CLY 1618..............59
Bridle v Hammacott, Kemp & Kemp, J2-046; [1996] CLY 2296 459
Brinkworth v Payne, Kemp & Kemp, E2-096; [1996] CLY 2226 171
Britten v Haymills Holdings and Blencoes Scaffolding, Kemp & Kemp, I2-416;
  [1994] CLY 1679 399
Britton v Ivens, Kemp & Kemp, D2-048; [1994] CLY 1594..89
Brookes v T Elmes & Sons Ltd, Kemp & Kemp, K2-047; [1999] CLY 1596 258
Brookstein, Re, Kemp & Kemp, C4-121; [1991] CLY 1357 341
Brough v Carty, Kemp & Kemp, K2-113/1; [1998] CLY 1723 186
Brown and Brown v Childs, Kemp & Kemp, E3-116; [1996] CLY 2308 177
Brown v Gwent Health Authority, Kemp & Kemp, J4-018; [1995] CLY 1768 559
Brown v Hillier, Kemp & Kemp, K2-224; [1990] CLY 1699...265
Brown v Ledson and Billington, Kemp & Kemp, H2-026; [1995] CLY 1705 257
Brown v Newman [1992] CLY 1597..115
Brown v O'Brien [1992] CLY 1740 144
Brown v Saunders Valve Co Ltd, Kemp & Kemp, F2-049; [1998] CLY 1626................550
Brown, Re [1992] CLY 1688 294
Browning v Southampton and South West Hampshire Health Authority
  (1991) The Times, October 29; Kemp & Kemp, A4-017/1; [1992] CLY 1565.............100
Brownlie v Tate & Lyle, Kemp & Kemp, C4-105; [1993] CLY 1457 75
Broxson, Re, Kemp & Kemp, K2-194; [1995] CLY 1810 394
Bryan v Euroguard Ltd, Kemp & Kemp, C2-083; [1998] CLY 1537 35
Bryans v Mount Vernon and Watford Hospitals Trust, Kemp & Kemp, F5-058/1;
  [1999] CLY 1543 351
Bryson v Dwyer, Kemp & Kemp, E2-076; [1996] CLY 2224 140
Buck v Hamer, Kemp & Kemp, E2-046/1; [1998] CLY 1587 154
Buckland v Edward Thompson (a firm), Kemp & Kemp, J2-039; [1994] CLY 1707 50
Buckle v Brown, Kemp & Kemp, H2-034; [1998] CLY 1744 259
Budd v Bowditch, Kemp & Kemp, B2-004/2/3; [1998] CLY 1483 101
Bugden v Wills, Kemp & Kemp, E2-118; [1996] CLY 2316 544

Bullard v Thomas, Kemp & Kemp, E2-125; [1995] CLY 1788 126
Bunzl Transpotation v Bosdet, Kemp & Kemp, J6-072; [1991] CLY 1455.....................202
Burbridge v Argos Distribution plc, Kemp & Kemp, E2-102/1/2; [1998] CLY 1605 173
Burdiss v Redbridge London Borough Council, Kemp & Kemp, D2-035;
   [1994] CLY 1592 86
Burgess v Electricity Sports and Social Club, Kemp & Kemp, E3-117;
   [2000] 3 CL 175 231
Burgess v Hooper, Kemp & Kemp, K2-015; [1991] CLY 1360 286
Burgess v PD Stevens, Kemp & Kemp, H6-035; [1995] CLY 1735 329
Burgess, Re [1996] CLY 2170 114
Burgon, Re, Kemp & Kemp, J2-013; [1994] CLY 1692...267
Burke v Roy, Kemp & Kemp, E2-015; [1994] CLY 1600...117
Burleigh, Re, Kemp & Kemp, C2-076; [1993] CLY 1438 98
Burns (a minor) v Doncaster HA, Kemp & Kemp, F6-010; [1998] CLY 1760 498
Burns v Davies BPILS, VIII 54; [1999] CLY 1424 469
Burns, Re, Kemp & Kemp, F4-015; [1998] CLY 1540...348
Burrows v Kingston upon Hull City Council, Kemp & Kemp, H6-056;
   [2000] 4 CL 162 318
Burrows, Re, Kemp & Kemp, H4-015/2; [1993] CLY 1517...290
Burton v Daxner, Kemp & Kemp, C5-026; [1997] CLY 1870 40
Burton v Frigoscandia, Kemp & Kemp, K2-051; [1990] CLY 1676 404
Butler v Guildford Borough Council, Kemp & Kemp, E3-050, [1990] CLY 1631 219
Butler v Liverpool City Council, Kemp & Kemp, H6-024; [1993] CLY 1522 302
Butterfield v Clifford Williams & Son, Kemp & Kemp, H7-024; [1990] CLY 1660........320
Butters v Grimsby and Scunthorpe HA, Kemp & Kemp, F5-012/1; [1998] CLY 1630 ..350
Butterworth v Lumb, Kemp & Kemp, K2-103; [1991] CLY 1469 145
Byatt v British Coal, Kemp & Kemp, C4-062; [1991] CLY 1447 422
Byers v Brent LBC, Kemp & Kemp, H5-017; [1998] CLY 1645 267
Bygraves v London Borough of Southwark, Kemp & Kemp, F2-062;
   [1990] CLY 1640 546
Byrne [1993] CLY 1459..507
Byrne v Swan Moulinex, Kemp & Kemp, H3-106; [1995] CLY 1728 299

C (a child) v Leeds NHS Teaching National Trust, Kemp & Kemp, K2-253/1;
   [2000] 4 CL 160 297
C (a child) v Peers, Kemp & Kemp, K2-145/9; [2000] 4 CL 157 189
C (a child) v Taylor, Kemp & Kemp, PRC-012; [2000] 5 CL 177..................................44
C (a minor) v Chief Constable of Hampshire, Kemp & Kemp, C5-065;
   [1999] CLY 1462 51
C (a minor) v Kay (1999) 99(2) QR 7; Kemp & Kemp, J4-023/1; [1999] CLY 1524 452
C and L (minors), Re, Kemp & Kemp, C4-252; [1991] CLY 1375 484
C v S, Kemp & Kemp, C4-217; [1998] CLY 1508...480
C, Re [1992] CLY 1578 526
C, Re [1992] CLY 1584 40
C, Re [1992] CLY 1589 4
C, Re [1999] CLY 1450 525
C, Re, Kemp & Kemp, C4-212; [1996] CLY 2194...524

C, Re, Kemp & Kemp, C4-226; [1991] CLY 1348 518
C, Re, Kemp & Kemp, C4-227; [1991] CLY 1367 482
C, Re, Kemp & Kemp, C4-271; [1999] CLY 1445 493
C, Re, Kemp & Kemp, D2-021; [1995] CLY 1690 83
Calderbank v Lancashire County Council, Kemp & Kemp, F6-042/1;
 [1992] CLY 1667 343
Caley v Ideal Standard [1993] CLY 1580 372
Calford v Campbell, Kemp & Kemp, E2-054/2; [2000] 4 CL 145 156
Calvert v Greenfield, Kemp & Kemp, C4-091; [1993] CLY 1456 200
Camaish v Marske Machine Co, Kemp & Kemp, I2-421; [1994] CLY 1684 412
Cambridge v The Post Office, Kemp & Kemp, F6-012/1; [1993] CLY 1507 335
Cameron McCabe v Scottish Agricultural Industries [1993] CLY 1530 374
Campbell (a minor) v Nottingham City Council (1999) 99 (1) QR 8;
 Kemp & Kemp, K2-145/3; [1998] CLY 1704 435
Campbell, Re, Kemp & Kemp, D2-024; [1993] CLY 1474 ....lvii, 88
Camus v Williams, Kemp & Kemp, E2-016; [1997] CLY 1888 148
Canning v Roberts, Kemp & Kemp, E3-068; [1996] CLY 2234 223
Cantwell, Re, Kemp & Kemp, D2-037/1; [1999] CLY 1463 79
Caplin v Parkinson [1993] CLY 1586 27
Carlin, Re (1997) 97 (1) QR 3; Kemp & Kemp, B2-038/1[1997] CLY 1830 3
Carlisle v Chapman, Kemp & Kemp, K2-259; [1997] CLY 2021 430
Carlton v Ford Motor Co, Kemp & Kemp, K2-216; [1994] CLY 1735 372
Carnegie v Barkers (of Malton) Ltd, Kemp & Kemp, H1-104, H6-049/2/1;
 [1999] CLY 1507 312
Carpenter v Easton, Kemp & Kemp, C4-114; [1997] CLY 2008 507
Carr v IMI plc, Kemp & Kemp, K2-170/6; [1999] CLY 1609 371
Carr, Re, Kemp & Kemp, I2-439; [1994] CLY 1683 405
Carr, Re, Kemp & Kemp, I2-439; [1995] CLY 1756 403
Carrington, Re (CICB Quantum: 2000) [2000] 6 CL 188 58
Carroll, Re, Kemp & Kemp, C6-015; [1994] CLY 1589 49
Carron v Lion Plant Ltd, Kemp & Kemp, PRK-002, K2-117/2; [1998] CLY 1752 427
Carstairs, Re, Kemp & Kemp, E3-112; [1991] CLY 1406 229
Carter v Automobile Association, Kemp & Kemp, I2-313; [1998] CLY 1681 363
Cartmel v Anderson [1992] CLY 1630 505
Cartwright v British Telecommunications [1992] CLY 1678 263
Cartwright v Jones, Kemp & Kemp, C5-034; [1991] CLY 1380 450
Cartwright v Steetley [1992] CLY 1697 327
Carver v Queens Square Petroleum Ltd, Kemp & Kemp, I2-520/1;
 [1999] CLY 1512 365
Cashman v Westland Group plc, Kemp & Kemp, E3-067/1; [1998] CLY 1585 153
Cassel v Riverside Health Authority [1992] PIQR Q168; Kemp & Kemp,
 A4-001/1; BPILS, I 260.1, XV 14; [1990] CLY 1575 92
Cassidy v West Country Frozen Foods [1992] CLY 1654 248
Castens v Lecointe-Gayle, Kemp & Kemp, K2-118; [1993] CLY 1569 332
Castle, Re, Kemp & Kemp, B2-007; [1998] CLY 1493 282
Castle, Re, Kemp & Kemp, H3-150; [1995] CLY 1665 520
Catchpole, Re, Kemp & Kemp, K2-022; [1997] CLY 1975 310

Table of Cases

Cawthorne v Bennett, Kemp & Kemp, K2-255; [1994] CLY 1745 65
Chadwick v Cunningham [1993] CLY 1585 260
Chadwick v Ismail-Zade, Kemp & Kemp, K2-002; [1999] CLY 1551 141
Chamberlain v Esselte Dymo, Kemp & Kemp, G2-035/1; [1995] CLY 1721 357
Champion v Grimsby Health Authority, Kemp & Kemp, H3-160; [1992] CLY 1680 291
Chandler v Ward Meadows Plant, Kemp & Kemp, E3-060; [1994] CLY 1603 152
Chapman v Bennett, Kemp & Kemp, E3-004/2; [1998] CLY 1567 520
Chapman v British Rail Engineering , Kemp & Kemp, F6-048/1, K2-021;
  [1992] CLY 1669 344
Chapman v Sunderland Borough Council [1991] CLY 1486 320
Chapman, Re, Kemp & Kemp, D4-012/1; [1994] CLY 1596 66
Chappel v TDC Motor Factors, Kemp & Kemp, E3-040; [2000] 3 CL 174 247
Chappell v Chief Constable of Hertfordshire, Kemp & Kemp, E2-051;
  [1990] CLY 1619 155
Charalambous v Andreou, Kemp & Kemp, G2-030/1; [1990] CLY 1643 356
Charlton v AAH plc, Kemp & Kemp, K2-176/1; [1999] CLY 1559 129
Charnick v Russell, Kemp & Kemp, K2-271; [1997] CLY 1918 196
Chase v West Sussex CC [1996] CLY 2168 114
Chatham v Hinton Poultry, Kemp & Kemp, K2-070; [1992] CLY 1741 260
Cheston v Letkey, Kemp & Kemp, H2-027/3; [1999] CLY 1493 202
Cheung v Parry, Kemp & Kemp, K2-066; [1999] CLY 1587 181
Chhokran v Southampton and South-West Hampshire Health Authority,
  Kemp & Kemp, G2-042; [1993] CLY 1495 249
Cho v Fairlord (Wholesale Confectioners), Kemp & Kemp, E3-095;
  [1994] CLY 1627 226
Choudhary v Murtaza [1992] CLY 1671 359
Choudhery v Heathrow Airport Ltd, Kemp & Kemp, K2-004; [1996] CLY 2299 141
Choudhry v Jhangir, Kemp & Kemp, H3-164/3; [1997] CLY 1967 273
Christer, Re, Kemp & Kemp, C5-035; [1998] CLY 1554 43
Cinque v O'Donegan, Kemp & Kemp, E2-130/1; [1998] CLY 1701 21
Claringbold, Re, Kemp & Kemp, C4-100; [1990] CLY 1591 506
Clark v Allied Signal Ltd, Kemp & Kemp, E3-089/1; [1999] CLY 1489 238
Clark v Commissioner of Police of the Metropolis, Kemp & Kemp, E2-009;
  [1997] CLY 1898 197
Clark, Re, Kemp & Kemp, I3-071; [1996] CLY 2284 416
Clarke v Liverpool City Council, Kemp & Kemp, H3-170; [1996] CLY 2262 276
Clarke v South Yorkshire Transport Ltd [1998] PIQR Q104; Kemp & Kemp,
  G2-075; BPILS, I 127; [1998] CLY 1631 355
Clarke v Vauxhall Motors Ltd, Kemp & Kemp, J4-020; [1999] CLY 1532 559
Clarke, Re [1996] CLY 2169 114
Clay v McHugh, Kemp & Kemp, I2-420; [1993] CLY 1539 400
Clayton v Bank Cafe, Kemp & Kemp, E2-095/1; [1998] CLY 1582 120
Clayton v Liverpool City Council, Kemp & Kemp, I2-423; [1991] CLY 1440 409
Clear v Stephenson [1999] CLY 1516 362
Cleghorn v Stenna Offshore, Kemp & Kemp, I4-018; [1994] CLY 1687 409
Clements v Wake, Kemp & Kemp, I2-431; [1997] CLY 1985 410
Cliffe v Williams, Kemp & Kemp, K2-060; [1996] CLY 2317 180

Coates v Daneheath, Kemp & Kemp, K2-183; [1995] CLY 1807 191
Coggin v Portaway Minerals (Elton) Ltd, Kemp & Kemp, I3-079/1;
    [1999] CLY 1520 365
Cohen v Servi Group Travel SA, Kemp & Kemp, I3-025; [1996] CLY 2287 432
Cole v Birmingham City Council, Kemp & Kemp, E3-039; [1996] CLY 2230 218
Cole v Woodhall, Kemp & Kemp, K2-068; [1996] CLY 2319 182
Coles v Lewis [2000] 6 CL 198 421
Coles, Re, Kemp & Kemp, B2-004/2/1; [1996] CLY 2173 97
Collett (a minor) v Barlow, Kemp & Kemp, C4-108; [1997] CLY 1864 378
Collett v Bean, Kemp & Kemp, H3-168; [1999] CLY 1497 293
Collings v Cheshire CC, Kemp & Kemp, H6-053; [1996] CLY 2333 314
Collins and Dalton v Allen, Kemp & Kemp, E2-021; [1992] CLY 1639 148
Collins v Adwinkle, Kemp & Kemp, I2-309, I2-604; [1991] CLY 1433 382
Collins v Elks, Kemp & Kemp, E2-053; [1996] CLY 2219 118
Collins v Whip, Kemp & Kemp, E2-043/1; [1998] CLY 1586 199
Collins, Re, Kemp & Kemp, C6-004; [1994] CLY 1588 16
Colwill v Rodosthenous, Kemp & Kemp, H6-025; [1991] CLY 1428 327
Condra v Norcros, Kemp & Kemp, H6A-028; [1994] CLY 1665 304
Cook v Containership, Kemp & Kemp, H7-015/2; [1993] CLY 1529 306
Cook, Re [1992] CLY 1611 46
Cook, Re, Kemp & Kemp, I2-510; [1991] CLY 1435 364
Cooke and Rippin v Pruski, Kemp & Kemp, L5-011; [1992] CLY 1784 466
Cooke v Hawkins, Kemp & Kemp, E2-112; [1993] CLY 1484 178
Coombs v Roberts, Kemp & Kemp, K2-252; [1990] CLY 1700 340
Coombs v Warren, Kemp & Kemp, K2-170/5; [1999] CLY 1558 287
Coonan v Rashid & Rashid, Kemp & Kemp, E3-071; [1993] CLY 1492 248
Cooper (Michael) v Keylighting Products, Kemp & Kemp, K2-181;
    [1994] CLY 1732 317
Cooper v P & O Stena Line Ltd [1999] 1 Lloyd's Rep 734; (1999) The Times,
    February 8; Kemp & Kemp, E3-004/3; BPILS, VIII 76; [1999] CLY 1480 211
Cooper, Re, Kemp & Kemp, [1999] CLY 1483 236
Cooper, Re, Kemp & Kemp, C3-078; [1991] CLY 1339 111
Cooper, Re, Kemp & Kemp, C3-078; [1991] CLY 1344 90
Coots v Stead McAlpine & Co Ltd, Kemp & Kemp, E3-089/3; [2000] 4 CL 155 226
Cornbill v Turfsoil, Kemp & Kemp, I2-424; [1993] CLY 1540 400
Cornell v Green, Kemp & Kemp, C2-035; [1998] CLY 1485 104
Corner v Osment, Kemp & Kemp, E2-033/1; [2000] 5 CL 180 136
Corthorn v Foster, Kemp & Kemp, E2-058; [1990] CLY 1620 157
Costley (a minor) v Costley [1992] CLY 1731 448
Cotton v Freddie Martin (Scaffolding) Ltd, Kemp & Kemp, PRH-005;
    [1998] CLY 1638 254
Cotton v Navarro, Kemp & Kemp, K2-263; [1998] CLY 1741 196
Couch v Miotla, Kemp & Kemp, I2-440; [1997] CLY 1986 405
Coughlin v Montpellier Plant Hire, Kemp & Kemp, I2-502; [1993] CLY 1532 382
Coverdale v Suffolk HA, Kemp & Kemp, F4-022; [1997] CLY 1952 349
Cowan v Kitson Insulations [1992] PIQR Q19; Kemp & Kemp, F2-064, F2-110;
    BPILS I 42.1; [1992] CLY 1660 556

Cowan v Quotareed and R Mansell [1992] CLY 1560 87
Cox v Conway, Kemp & Kemp, PRK-002; [1999] CLY 1581 175
Cox v GKN Axles, Kemp & Kemp, H6-034; [1993] CLY 1523 465
Coyle v Gateshead Metropolitan Borough Council, Kemp & Kemp, I3-023;
    [1992] CLY 1723 450
Coyle, Re [1992] CLY 1593 325
Craddy, Re, Kemp & Kemp, K2-137; [1991] CLY 1473 337
Craggs v Rowan Hankinson Ltd, Kemp & Kemp, 2-515/1; [1998] CLY 1668 364
Craig (a minor) v Erdman Lewis Ltd, Kemp & Kemp, J2-048; [1998] CLY 1755 371
Crane v Oliver, Kemp & Kemp, C2-030; [1994] CLY 1550 103
Creedon v Grange Construction and Sehmis Builders Merchants,
    Kemp & Kemp, H2-021; [1993] CLY 1513 255
Creek v Petryszyn, Kemp & Kemp, PRK-008, K2-177/1; [1998] CLY 1735 146
Creighton v Estate of Dholakia (deceased), Kemp & Kemp, E2-034;
    [1996] CLY 2216 151
Cressey, Re, Kemp & Kemp, K2-117; [1992] CLY 1749 459
Crestwell v Windmill Housing Association, Kemp & Kemp, K2-036;
    [1994] CLY 1711 277
Crews v Harrison [1990] CLY 1625 172
Crilley v Koeppl, Kemp & Kemp, I4-022; [1991] CLY 1446 423
Crisp v Hare, Kemp & Kemp, J2-045; [1996] CLY 2295 278
Crolla, Re (CICB Quantum: 1999), Kemp & Kemp, C4-096; [2000] 2 CL 141 536
Crompton v Peacock; , Kemp & Kemp, C2-063; [1990] CLY 1581 501
Crompton v White [1992] CLY 1657 143
Croucher, Re, Kemp & Kemp, C4-043; [1997] CLY 1849 526
Crowson v Evans, Kemp & Kemp, E2-127; [1993] CLY 1564 183
Crump v Rickwood, Kemp & Kemp, E2-131; [1995] CLY 1798 127
Crutchley v Gazzard, Kemp & Kemp, K2-072; [1991] CLY 1480 372
CT, Re, Kemp & Kemp, J3-017; [1994] CLY 1698 444
Cuddy, Re, Kemp & Kemp, C30-71; [1996] CLY 2179 89
Cuke v O'Callaghan, Kemp & Kemp, K2-117/1; [1998] CLY 1722 21
Cummings v W Lucy & Co, Kemp & Kemp, B2-075; [1993] CLY 1431 375
Cummins v Wallace, Kemp & Kemp, K2-165; [1996] CLY 2344 189
Cunliffe v Murrell, Kemp & Kemp, F6-017; [1994] CLY 1724 337
Cunningham v Kensington & Chelsea and Westminster HA, Kemp & Kemp,
    C2-008; [1998] CLY 1480 96
Cunningham, Re, Kemp & Kemp, C4-129; [1990] CLY 1594 508
Curi v Colina, Kemp & Kemp, B2-008/1; [1998] CLY 1503 242
Curphy v Ward, Kemp & Kemp, H2-027/4; [1998] CLY 1637 257
Curry, Re, Kemp & Kemp, F6-013/1; [1995] CLY 1720 335
Curtis v Securicor, Kemp & Kemp, K2-061; [1995] CLY 1786 20
Cusack, Re, Kemp & Kemp, C5-028; [1997] CLY 1871 42
Cutts v Mackie, Kemp & Kemp, H7-013; [1996] CLY 2274 463
CW, Re, Kemp & Kemp, C4-208; [1995] CLY 1677 521

D (a minor) v Martin, Kemp & Kemp, I2-521/1; [1999] CLY 1515 377
D (a minor) v White, Kemp & Kemp, J2-018; [1999] CLY 1526 377

D (a minor), Re, Kemp & Kemp, C4-256; [1994] CLY 1582 490
D, Re, Kemp & Kemp, C4-248; [1998] CLY 1513...488
D and C, Re, Kemp & Kemp, C4-238; [1994] CLY 1581 485
D and D (minors), Re, Kemp & Kemp, C4-247; [1998] CLY 1512 487
D and K, Re, Kemp & Kemp, C4-282; [1998] CLY 1518 496
D, Re [1992] CLY 1581 59
Daden v Lowings, Kemp & Kemp, K2-067; [1990] CLY 1680 182
Daggart, Re, Kemp & Kemp, H3-165/3; [1996] CLY 2292 274
Dalby v Toogood [1992] CLY 1774 194
Daley v Harris, Kemp & Kemp, I2-427; [1996] CLY 2281 409
Daly v Newbold Domestic Appliances Ltd, Kemp & Kemp, J2-050;
   [1998] CLY 1756 280
Dan v Welsh and Rogers, Kemp & Kemp, E3-122; [1996] CLY 2323 232
Danbrogio v Knowsley Borough Council [1992] CLY 1775 78
Daniel v Valor Heating, Kemp & Kemp, H6-013; [1990] CLY 1654 300
Darby v Marconi Electronic Devices, Kemp & Kemp, C5-070; [1992] CLY 1615 126
Darmanin v Vauxhall Motors Ltd, Kemp & Kemp, J4-035; [1999] CLY 1612 426
Davey v MJF Precision Welding, Kemp & Kemp, I2-403; [1995] CLY 1757 379
Davies v Clarkson, Kemp & Kemp, PRB-001; [1999] CLY 1436 107
Davies v Dorman, Kemp & Kemp, K2-133; [1996] CLY 2340 128
Davies v Edmonds, Kemp & Kemp, K2-162/1; [1999] CLY 1556 540
Davies v Gravelle Plant Ltd, Kemp & Kemp, I2-521/1; [2000] 1 CL 122 388
Davies v Gwent Health Authority, Kemp & Kemp, J4-014; [1995] CLY 1765 558
Davies v London Borough of Bexley, Kemp & Kemp, I2-436; [1991] CLY 1441 366
Davies v Newalls Insulation Co., Kemp & Kemp, F2-071, [1990] CLY 1639 551
Davis v AG Barr plc, Kemp & Kemp, J3-036; [1999] CLY 1531......................................277
Davis v Cope, Kemp & Kemp, K2-125; [1994] CLY 1725 5
Davis v Cork [1995] CLY 1740 379
Davis v Gregg & Co (Knottingley) Ltd, Kemp & Kemp, J2-041; [1997] CLY 2011 336
Davis v Milborrow (No. 1), Kemp & Kemp, E2-085/1; [1997] CLY 1906 166
Davis, Re, Kemp & Kemp, H3-153; [1995] CLY 1726 298
Davis-Desmond v Islington LBC, Kemp & Kemp, H3-105/1; [1996] CLY 2259 292
Davison v Interspan Services Ltd [1999] CLY 1611 428
Davison v The Post Office, Kemp & Kemp, H2-022; [1992] CLY 1676.........................262
Dawson v West Yorkshire Police Authority, Kemp & Kemp, I2-426;
   [1995] CLY 1749 401
Dawson, Re, Kemp & Kemp, C5-049; [1996] CLY 2191 63
Day v Bell, Kemp & Kemp, C4-031; [1999] CLY 1449...523
DC, Re [1995] CLY 1667 542
De Smet v Gold, Kemp & Kemp, J5-001; [1998] CLY 1559 7
Dean v Wundpets Ltd, Kemp & Kemp, I2-538; [2000] 2 CL 148 392
Deeley v Western National, Kemp & Kemp, E2-094, E3-109; [1993] CLY 1501 203
Delaney, Re, Kemp & Kemp, C4-266; [1993] CLY 1454 535
Dennis v Brassett, Kemp & Kemp, E2-087; [1991] CLY 1400 167
Denny v Childs [1991] CLY 1358..26
Desborough v Carlisle City Council, Kemp & Kemp, E3-070; [1990] CLY 1634 223
Dewar, Re, Kemp & Kemp, C4-035; [1996] CLY 2182 524

Table of Cases xvii

Dewhurst, Re, Kemp & Kemp, C5-025; [1995] CLY 1681 532
DH, Re [1992] CLY 1679 265
Dickinson v Burton, Kemp & Kemp, C4-130; [1996] CLY 2336 517
Dickson v Bridge Hotel, Kemp & Kemp, K2-066/1; [1999] CLY 1564 442
Dingsdale v Jones and The Ministry of Defence, Kemp & Kemp, I3-026;
   [1993] CLY 1544 34
Dinsdale v Urban Firm, Kemp & Kemp, 13-023; [1994] CLY 1685 412
Dion v Mayhew, Kemp & Kemp, E2-107; [1994] CLY 1611, 1709 123
Dix v MG Engineering Services, Kemp & Kemp, H6-046/1; [1996] CLY 2271 457
Dixon, Re, Kemp & Kemp, C4-131; [1996] CLY 2347 518
DJH, Re, Kemp & Kemp, C4-028; [1999] CLY 1448 523
Dobson, Re, Kemp & Kemp, E3-010; [1996] CLY 2227 212
Doe v Markey, Kemp & Kemp, K2-064; [1993] CLY 1469 77
Doherty v Law, Kemp & Kemp, H4-041; [1998] CLY 1650 279
Doherty v Spreadbury, Kemp & Kemp, K2-042; [1997] CLY 1893 123
Dolton v Studley, Kemp & Kemp, K2-145; [1990] CLY 1689 188
Dominey v Amenco (Poole) Ltd, Kemp & Kemp, PRE-003; [1999] CLY 1482 235
Donald v Vince [1992] CLY 1710 381
Dooler, Re, Kemp & Kemp, K2-033; [1997] CLY 1998 257
Dooley v Machin [1997] CLY 2020 361
Dopson v Oscar Faber Group Ltd, Kemp & Kemp, K2-221/1; [1998] CLY 1737 130
Dordevic v Smith, Kemp & Kemp, C2-075; [1994] CLY 1577 90
Doughty v Brown and Federal Express (UK), Kemp & Kemp, E2-049;
   [1993] CLY 1480 200
Dow v Dow, Kemp & Kemp, I2-306; [1998] CLY 1683 411
Dowle v Graham, Kemp & Kemp, PRC-008; [2000] 3 CL 168 199
Downing v A&P Appledore (Falmouth) Ltd (1997) 97 (1) QR 5;
   Kemp & Kemp, E3-086; [1997] CLY 1933 225
Doyle v Cable, Kemp & Kemp, B1-100; [1996] CLY 2175 298
Doyle v Van Bruggen, Kemp & Kemp, H2-028/2; [1997] CLY 2006 172
Drummond, Re, Kemp & Kemp, B2-005/1; [1993] CLY 1424 28
Dryhurst v Dale, Kemp & Kemp, H4-027; [1999] CLY 1499 141
Dublin, Re (1997) 97 (1) QR 3; Kemp & Kemp, L8-220; [1997] CLY 2017 452
Ducker, Re, Kemp & Kemp, B2-030; [1999] CLY 1453 528
Dufaur v South East Kent Health Authority [1992] CLY 1649 244
Duff v Edge, Kemp & Kemp, E2-082; [1996] CLY 2300 141
Duff, Re, Kemp & Kemp, C4-082; [1992] CLY 1586 515
Duffin, Re, Kemp & Kemp, C4-102; [1991] CLY 1356 4
Duffy v First Choice Holidays & Flights Ltd [2000] 6 CL 201 500
Duke, Re, Kemp & Kemp, C4-204; [1995] CLY 1679 520
Duncan, Re [1991] CLY 1354 61
Dunkeyson v Kirklees MBC, Kemp & Kemp, B2-019; [1999] CLY 1519 414
Dunn v Durham County Council [1992] CLY 1652 217
Dunn v Rennoc, Kemp & Kemp, F6-016/1; [1997] CLY 2025 184
Durau v Evans [1996] PIQR Q18 lix
Durie v Liverpool City Council, Kemp & Kemp, K2-180; [1994] CLY 1731 346
Durose v Novaceta, Kemp & Kemp, C4-059; [1998] CLY 1531 438

Durrant v Macdonald [1992] PIQR Q76 Kemp & Kemp, E3-004, E3-200;
[1992] CLY 1648 210
Dyer (a minor) v Lambeth, Southwark and Lewisham HA, Kemp & Kemp,
A2-001; [1998] CLY 1478 95
Dyer v Burgess [1999] CLY 1456 47

E (a child) v Calderdale MBC [2000] 6 CL 197 370
E (a minor) v Greaves, Kemp & Kemp, I2-516/1; [1999] CLY 1514 376
E (a minor) v Hatton, Kemp & Kemp, I4-020; [1999] CLY 1523....................422
E, J, K and D (minors), Re, Kemp & Kemp, C4-224; [1990] CLY 1596 474
E, Re [1992] CLY 1730 436
E, Re, Kemp & Kemp, H6-038; [1993] CLY 1524 307
Eardley v North West Anglia Health Care NHS Trust, Kemp & Kemp,
E3-004/1; [1998] CLY 1613 250
Earlam v Hepworth Heating Ltd, Kemp & Kemp, D3-027/1, D3-118;
[1997] CLY 1878 71
Early v Thomas Ware & Sons, Kemp & Kemp, E3-009/1; [1998] CLY 1614 243
Eason v Brewster, Kemp & Kemp, K2-219; [1997] CLY 1978 320
Easton v Ellis, Kemp & Kemp, C4-026; [1998] CLY 1525 522
Eaton v British Coal Corporation, Kemp & Kemp, F6-048/2; [1995] CLY 1781............345
Eddleston v Sheffield HA, Kemp & Kemp, F2-051; [1991] CLY 1410 550
Edgar v I & M Adams (a firm), Kemp & Kemp, J3-043; [1994] CLY 1702 429
Edge v Calderwood, Kemp & Kemp, E2-037; [1997] CLY 1891 117
Edwards v Adams, Kemp & Kemp, E2-103; [1994] CLY 1615 122
Edwards v Blackmore, Kemp & Kemp, C6-072; [1995] CLY 1688..................454
Edwards v Dannimac, Kemp & Kemp, K2-126; [1994] CLY 1721 278
Edwards v Matthews, Kemp & Kemp, E2-083; [1995] CLY 1771 115
Edwards v Owen, Kemp & Kemp, K2-170/3; [1998] CLY 1748......................316
Edwards v Oxytech Services [1990] CLY 1713 197
Edwards v Pryce, Kemp & Kemp, PRK-007; [2000] 1 CL 129 188
Edwards v Walker [1992] CLY 1613 49
Edwards, Re [1992] CLY 1572...112
Elder v Sands, Kemp & Kemp, I2-419; [1997] CLY 1984 399
Elford v Ministry of Defence, Kemp & Kemp, F2-052; [1997] CLY 1945 556
Elgie v Hodges, Kemp & Kemp, B2-026/1/1; [1999] CLY 1429 32
Ellinger v Riverside Health Authority, Kemp & Kemp, H2-013; [1993] CLY 1511........252
Elliott, Re, Kemp & Kemp, F4-013; [1993] CLY 1508 347
Ellis v Butler, Kemp & Kemp, I2-430; [1996] CLY 2282 402
Ellis v Liverpool City Council, Kemp & Kemp, H6A-026; [1998] CLY 1658..................301
Ellis v Mainzer, Kemp & Kemp, J3-028; [1991] CLY 1451 439
Ellis v Rothen, Kemp & Kemp, I3-018; [1998] CLY 1684 34
Ellis v Soole, Kemp & Kemp, E2-134, K2-136; [1997] CLY 1914....................187
Elsdon, Re, Kemp & Kemp, C4-094; [1991] CLY 1353 450
Entwistle v Furniss & White (Foundries) Ltd, Kemp & Kemp, K2-209/4;
[1999] CLY 1606 319
Escott v Escott, Kemp & Kemp, J2-020; [1997] CLY 2000 365
Essex v Coventry Health Authority, Kemp & Kemp, E3-032; [1992] CLY 1651 217

Table of Cases

Evans v Dewsbury Civil Engineering (1996) 96 (4) QR 6; Kemp & Kemp, I3-028;
[1996] CLY 2288 390
Evans v Hafeez, Kemp & Kemp, I2-432; [1998] CLY 1678 402
Evans v Jibb, Kemp & Kemp, E2-141; [1995] CLY 1804 129
Evans v Mid Glamorgan Health Authority, Kemp & Kemp, C4-109;
[1992] CLY 1594 441
Evans v Ministry of Defence, Kemp & Kemp, I2-541; [1996] CLY 2311 392
Evans v Morton, Kemp & Kemp, E2-130/2; [1998] CLY 1702 21
Evans v Neath Borough Council, Kemp & Kemp, E3-024; [1994] CLY 1597 197
Evans, Re, Kemp & Kemp, C2-066; [1990] CLY 1613 15
Evans, Re, Kemp & Kemp, H6-014; [1994] CLY 1660 284
Evason v Merseyside Transport, Kemp & Kemp, I4-026; [1992] CLY 1720 418
Everard v Unigate Dairies [1990] CLY 1670 415

F (a minor) v Slater, Kemp & Kemp, C5-030; [2000] 1 CL 124 42
F, Re (CICB Quantum: 2000) [2000] 6 CL 185 485
F, Re, Kemp & Kemp, C2-021; [1997] CLY 1839 12
F, Re, Kemp & Kemp, C4-218; [1998] CLY 1507 480
F, Re, Kemp & Kemp, C4-258; [1996] CLY 2197 490
Fahy v Wolverhamton MBC and Banbury Windows Ltd, Kemp & Kemp,
H3-060; [1997] CLY 1964 288
Falck (Arthur) v Wilson [1992] CLY 1595 360
Falck (Constance) v Wilson [1992] CLY 1598 21
Fallon v Beaumont, Kemp & Kemp, J3-023, L7-021; [1994] CLY 1749 439
Farley, Re, Kemp & Kemp, C4-257; [1993] CLY 1461 490
Farley, Re, Kemp & Kemp, H2-020; [1991] CLY 1425 254
Farnan v Liverpool City Council, Kemp & Kemp, H7-019/1; [1995] CLY 1776 309
Farnborough v Davies, Kemp & Kemp, E2-040; [1993] CLY 1478 153
Farrell v Porn and Dunwoody [1990] CLY 1678 11
Farrelly v CourtauldsChemicals, Kemp & Kemp, PRK-010; [2000] 2 CL 143 37
Farrup, Re, Kemp & Kemp, J2-077; [1996] CLY 2200 40
Faulkner v Shah [1991] CLY 1424 295
Faulkner v Shamji [2000] 6 CL 192 182
Fawcett, Re, Kemp & Kemp, C2-041; [1991] CLY 1335 106
Fay v Hawes, Kemp & Kemp, J2-015; [1994] CLY 1693 376
Feeney v Littlewood [1992] CLY 1767 193
Fender v British Coal Corporation, Kemp & Kemp, F5-054; [1990] CLY 1641 501
Fendwick v Chief Constable of the South Yorkshire Police, Kemp & Kemp,
C4-078; [1993] CLY 1452 489
Fenton v A Camm, Kemp & Kemp, E2-059; [1991] CLY 1399 201
Fenton v Picktet [1992] CLY 1742 144
Fentum v William Baird plc, Kemp & Kemp, J4-022; [1999] CLY 1616 560
Ferguson v Covel, Kemp & Kemp, E2-054; [1997] CLY 1900 156
Fernley v Nei Control Systems Ltd, Kemp & Kemp, H6-055; [1998] CLY 1749 316
Finch v Langford [1995] CLY 1719 354
Finegold, Re, Kemp & Kemp, C4-016; [1992] CLY 1573 250
Finnigan v British Steel plc, Kemp & Kemp, K2-247; [1997] CLY 2004 441

Firth v Zanussi, Kemp & Kemp, C4-120; [1996] CLY 2193 539
Fish v David Brown Gear Industries [1992] CLY 1668 344
Fisher v Bandwidth Vehicles Rentals, Kemp & Kemp, E2-044; [1995] CLY 1699 153
Fisher v Darlington Insulation, Kemp & Kemp, F2-018/5, F2-027; [1994] CLY 1632 ..548
Fitzgerald v Smith, Kemp & Kemp, H2-029/1; [1999] CLY 1553 264
Fitzhugh, Re, Kemp & Kemp, C4-067; [1991] CLY 1350..357
Flaherty v Catley, Kemp & Kemp, K2-174; [1995] CLY 1803 128
Flegg v Reed [1992] CLY 1761 411
Fletcher, Re, Kemp & Kemp, C3-077; [1995] CLY 1666..14
Foley v Summerfield, Kemp & Kemp, K2-193; [1999] CLY 1568 9
Foot v Kenny Transport Ltd (1999) 99 (2) QR 6; Kemp & Kemp, I3-024/1;
  [1999] CLY 1513 452
Forbes v Scott Ltd, Kemp & Kemp, H7-013; [1998] CLY 1660 464
Ford v Clarbeston Ltd, Kemp & Kemp, F2-075; [1997] CLY 1947..................................557
Ford v Excotur SA, Kemp & Kemp, J2-014; [1992] CLY 1721 284
Ford v Large, Kemp & Kemp, H4-015; [1992] CLY 1563..34
Foreman v Saroya [1992] CLY 1739 499
Forkes v Norwich CC (1998) 98 (6) QR 8; Kemp & Kemp, J3-033;
  [1998] CLY 1689 425
Forrest (a minor) v Forrest, Kemp & Kemp, B2-023/1; [1995] CLY 1657 444
Forshaw v GEC [1990] CLY 1616..89
Foster v Appleton, Kemp & Kemp, H2-033; [1993] CLY 1553 259
Foster v British Waterways Board [1995] CLY 1753..402
Fotheringham v Murfitt and Scholey [1995] CLY 1663 451
Fowler v San, Kemp & Kemp, E2-136; [1993] CLY 1574..208
Fox v London Transport Executive, Kemp & Kemp, E3-094; [1990] CLY 1636 18
Fox v Slaughter, Kemp & Kemp, E2-084; [1996] CLY 2301..166
Fox v Thompson [1993] CLY 1538..398
Fradgley v Pontefract Hospitals NHS Trust, Kemp & Kemp, G2-031;
  [1997] CLY 1955 356
Francis v Neal, Kemp & Kemp, I2-527; [1990] CLY 1664 390
Francis v Padley (Poultry), Kemp & Kemp, H6-048; [1995] CLY 1737 312
Franklin v Challis, Kemp & Kemp, E2-093/1; [1998] CLY 1602 170
Franks v British Railways Board, Kemp & Kemp, E3-042; [1990] CLY 1632 247
Fraser v Doncaster MBC, Kemp & Kemp, H6-050/1; [1998] CLY 1656.........................466
Fraser v Lakeside Corp Ltd, Kemp & Kemp, I4-034; [1998] CLY 1691 426
Fraser v Southampton City Council, Kemp & Kemp, C6-007; [1995] CLY 1683 61
Frazer v Courtaulds [1990] CLY 1682..80
Free, Re [1992] CLY 1575 109
French, Re, Kemp & Kemp, C4-072; [1991] CLY 1351 376
French, Re, Kemp & Kemp, C5-011; [1993] CLY 1427 57
French, Re, Kemp & Kemp, D2-045/1; [1996] CLY 2213..62
Friar v Pickup, Kemp & Kemp, G2-032; [1993] CLY 1510...356
Frost v Furness, Kemp & Kemp, K2-245; [1997] CLY 1886 195
Frost v Palmer [1992] PIQR P14, [1993] PIQR Q14; Kemp & Kemp, I2-206,
  I2-605; BPILS, 191.1; [1993] CLY 1531..374
Frost v Yorkshire Water Authority [1991] CLY 1453 557

Fryer v Hussain, Kemp & Kemp, D4-018/2; [1995] CLY 1695...66
Fryer v Smith, Kemp & Kemp, H3-163; [1992] CLY 1681 449
Full, Re, Kemp & Kemp, C2-007; [1997] CLY 1833 12
Fuller v Haymills (Contractors) Ltd, Kemp & Kemp, I4-076; [1998] CLY 1687 431
Fulton v Turners (Southampton), Kemp & Kemp, E2-086; [1990] CLY 1624 166

G (a child) v Grindal [2000] 6 CL 186 76
G (a minor) v Calderdale MBC (1999) 99 (2) QR 7; Kemp & Kemp, H6-049/1;
 [1999] CLY 1603 458
G (a minor) v Croydon LBC, Kemp & Kemp, K2-208/1; [1997] CLY 1867....................55
G (a minor) v Leadstay Ltd, Kemp & Kemp, F5-064/1; [1997] CLY 1841....................115
G (A Minor), Re, Kemp & Kemp, C3-014; [1991] CLY 1336 107
G, Re [1993] CLY 1444 91
G, Re, Kemp & Kemp, B2-007/1; [1998] CLY 1494 373
G, Re, Kemp & Kemp, C4-200; [1993] CLY 1462..475
G, Re, Kemp & Kemp, C4-201; [1993] CLY 1460..475
Galloway v Hampshire County Council, Kemp & Kemp, H2-032; [1994] CLY 1713....259
Galloway, Re [1998] CLY 1657 315
Galvin v Beckerleg, Kemp & Kemp, K2-115; [1992] CLY 1750 241
Gambill (No 2), Re, Kemp & Kemp, C4-079L [1998] CLY 1532 533
Gambill (No. 1), Re, Kemp & Kemp, C4-064; [1997] CLY 1846 31
Gardner (a minor), Re, Kemp & Kemp, C4-054; [1998] CLY 1529 529
Gardner (John Lewis), Re, Kemp & Kemp, B2-009/1 J2-071; [1998] CLY 1504 338
Gardner (Michelle), Re, Kemp & Kemp, B2-009/1 J2-071; [1998] CLY 1541 445
Gardner v Epirotiki Steamship Co, Kemp & Kemp, C4-053; [1994] CLY 1572 528
Gardner v Mullins, Kemp & Kemp, E2-091; [1990] CLY 1622 169
Gargano, Re, Kemp & Kemp, I4-012; [1999] CLY 1521...420
Garraway v Buckinghamshire HA, Kemp & Kemp, J3-031, J3-033/1;
 [1996] CLY 2290 424
Garrett v British Airways, Kemp & Kemp, E3-055; [1997] CLY 1927 220
Garrett v Somerset County Council, Kemp & Kemp, J2-031; [1993] CLY 1548 366
Gauden v Durham County Council, Kemp & Kemp, E3-084; [1993] CLY 1493 225
Gaughan v Lucas Electrical, Kemp & Kemp, H8-012; [1993] CLY 1518 270
Gay v Dalgety, Kemp & Kemp, K2-017; [1991] CLY 1456...276
GB, RB and RP, Re, Kemp & Kemp, C4-228;[1997] CLY 1850......................................482
Gee v Bayes, Kemp & Kemp, E3-056; BPILS, I 84.1, 99; [1990] CLY 1633 220
Gee v Vantage Joinery, Kemp & Kemp, H7-013/1; [1994] CLY 1668 464
Gensale, Re [1996] CLY 2192 506
George v Groom, Kemp & Kemp, K2-026; [1994] CLY 1618 177
George v Ministry of Defence, Kemp & Kemp, PRI-003; [2000] 3 CL 183 422
George v Tipper [1995] CLY 1656 15
George v Tower Hamlets HA, Kemp & Kemp, F4-077; [1997] CLY 1951 348
Gerken v Fisher, Kemp & Kemp, K2-110; [1996] CLY 2332 145
Gibbs v Cowles and Cowles [1994] CLY 1658 326
Gibney, Re, Kemp & Kemp, C4-037; [1998] CLY 1527 524
Gibson and Hughes v Hodges, Kemp & Kemp, I2-517, I3-030; ; [1992] CLY 1707 387
Gibson and Hughes v Hodges, Kemp & Kemp, I2-517, I3-030; [1992] CLY 1735 35

Gilchrist, Re, Kemp & Kemp, E3-104; [1993] CLY 1499 140
Giles v Pontefract Health Authority, Kemp & Kemp, H2-014; [1994] CLY 1647 252
Giles, Re, Kemp & Kemp, C6-073; [1996] CLY 2202 47
Gill v Hughes, Kemp & Kemp, E3-088/1; [1998] CLY 1575 226
Gimblet v Swansea City Council, Kemp & Kemp, E2-041/1/2; [2000] 4 CL 151 118
Glassby, Re [1996] CLY 2164 105
Gleeson v Cardale Engineering [1994] CLY 1659 323
Glendinning v Powergen plc, Kemp & Kemp, F2-040; [1997] CLY 1943 555
Glorman v Ford Motor Co Ltd [1996] CLY 2272...304
Glover v Stuart, Kemp & Kemp, K2-145/2; [1999] CLY 1618 337
Goacher v Pearman, Kemp & Kemp, E2-038/1; [1998] CLY 1584..................................152
Goble v Airedale Hospitals NHS Trust, Kemp & Kemp, C2-078; [1999] CLY 1433..........99
Godfrey v Bernard Matthews plc, Kemp & Kemp, PRH-001; [1999] CLY 1498 266
Godfrey v Gnitrow Ltd, Kemp & Kemp, PRF-004; [1999] CLY 1537..............................549
Goff (a minor) v Broadland Properties Ltd, Kemp & Kemp, J2-040/2;
  [1998] CLY 1654 310
Goldberg v Hogger, Kemp & Kemp, K2-102/4; [1999] CLY 1590 185
Goldsmith, Re, Kemp & Kemp, E3-085; [1996] CLY 2235..249
Gomery v Archway Supplies, Kemp & Kemp, E3-062; [1996] CLY 2232 221
Good, Re, Kemp & Kemp, C5-077; [1999] CLY 1452 58
Goodall, Re (CICB Quantum: 1999) [2000] 3 CL 173 210
Goodenough v Dunlop Ltd, Kemp & Kemp, F2-058; [1996] CLY 2243 545
Goodman v Ministry of Defence, Kemp & Kemp, 12-275,F2-043/1;
  [1991] CLY 1412 551
Goodridge v Ferguson, Kemp & Kemp, C2-029; [1998] CLY 1484 102
Goodwill v Jewson Ltd, Kemp & Kemp, I3-027/3; [1997] CLY 1988 389
Goodwin v Fryer, Kemp & Kemp, B2-036/2; [1998] CLY 1500......................................237
Goodwin v GKN Sheepbridge Stokes Ltd [2000] 6 CL 200 433
Gornall v Yandell, Kemp & Kemp, PRE-011; [1999] CLY 1576 167
Gorry v Southern, Kemp & Kemp, K2-134; [1996] CLY 2341 394
Gott v McGrath, Kemp & Kemp, K2-047/1; [1999] CLY 1583 180
Goudie v Night Freight (East) Ltd, Kemp & Kemp, E2-071/1; [2000] 1 CL 121 139
Gough v Consolidated Beryllium Ceramics Ltd, Kemp & Kemp, F2-012/1;
  [1999] CLY 1533 510
Graham v Kelly (No. 1), Kemp & Kemp, E2-080/1; [1997] CLY 1904............................165
Graham, Re, Kemp & Kemp, K2-087; [1993] CLY 1565 340
Grainger v Howes, Kemp & Kemp, E2-080/2; [1997] CLY 1905 165
Grange, Re [1993] CLY 1455 505
Grant v Gregory, Kemp & Kemp, K2-209/3; [1999] CLY 1594 209
Grant v Hampshire County Council [1992] CLY 1766 55
Grant v Measor, Kemp & Kemp, K2-177; [1992] CLY 1756..462
Grantham v Gales, Kemp & Kemp, K2-233; [1991] CLY 1489 281
Gration v Wilkes [1994] CLY 1656..270
Gray v Gwent Health Authority, Kemp & Kemp, J4-017; [1995] CLY 1767 559
Grayson-Crowe v Ministry of Defence, Kemp & Kemp, F5-012/1; [1992] CLY 1663....351
Green v GM Buses, Kemp & Kemp, I2-428; [1994] CLY 1680...237
Green v Leicester CC [2000] 6 CL 196..312

Table of Cases

Green v MC PR Ltd, Kemp & Kemp, I4-037; [1996] CLY 2334 428
Green v Northern Foods plc, Kemp & Kemp, H5-023; [1997] CLY 1972 308
Green v Stewart, Kemp & Kemp, E2-139; [1995] CLY 1800 128
Green v Wilson, Kemp & Kemp, H2-011; [1990] CLY 1646 282
Green, Re, Kemp & Kemp, C4-063; [1994] CLY 1575 3
Greenfield v Jolley, Kemp & Kemp, K2-028; [1995] CLY 1779 310
Greenhall v Sunblest Bakeries, Kemp & Kemp, J3-037; [1994] CLY 1701 440
Greenhow v Rilmac Ltd, Kemp & Kemp, F2-073/1; [1999] CLY 1541 516
Greensides, Re, Kemp & Kemp, J2-035; [1993] CLY 1550 367
Greenwood v Newalls Insulation Co Ltd, Kemp & Kemp, F2-058/1; [1999] CLY 1538 513
Gregory (a minor) v Millington, Kemp & Kemp, C5-076; [1997] CLY 1869 39
Gregory, Re, Kemp & Kemp, C2-028; [1990] CLY 1585 501
Greig v South Wales Fire Service, Kemp & Kemp, K2-145/7; [2000] 5 CL 192 64
Grewal, Re, Kemp & Kemp, C2-032; [1993] CLY 1440 28
Gridley v Phillips, Kemp & Kemp, E2-067; [1996] CLY 2222 119
Griggs v Latus, Kemp & Kemp, H3-156; [1991] CLY 1423 267
Griggs v Olympic Holidays Ltd (No 1), Kemp & Kemp, C4-068; [1996] CLY 2184 531
Griggs v Olympic Holidays Ltd (No. 2), Kemp & Kemp, G2-037; [1996] CLY 2251 358
Grime v Manchester Airport [1992] CLY 1701 380
Groom v Ford Motor Company Ltd, Kemp & Kemp, K2-250; [1996] CLY 2359 407
Groom v RSM Fabrications Ltd, Kemp & Kemp, H6-025/1; [1999] CLY 1504 303
Groves v Pretty, Kemp & Kemp, K2-125/1; [1999] CLY 1592 186
Gudge v Milroy [2000] 6 CL 190 158
Guin, Re, Kemp & Kemp, C4-061; [1993] CLY 1450 486
Guthrie v Hampshire CC, Kemp & Kemp, H4-030; [1996] CLY 2265 295

H (a child) v Hillingdon HA [2000] 6 CL 184 96
H (a minor) v Bass plc, Kemp & Kemp, K2-056/1; [1999] CLY 1608 393
H (a minor) v Lincolnshire CC, Kemp & Kemp, C6-026; [1999] CLY 1459 77
H (a minor), Re [1999] CLY 1444 493
H (a minor), Re, Kemp & Kemp, B2-042/1; [1999] CLY 1552 91
H v Home Office, Kemp & Kemp, C4-263; [1999] CLY 1443 491
H v Nottinghamshire CC, Kemp & Kemp, C4-280; [1998] CLY 1520 496
H(a minor) v MHT Services Ltd, Kemp & Kemp, J3-034; [1999] CLY 1530 456
H, Re (1999) 99 (4) QR 8; Kemp & Kemp, C4-028; [1999] CLY 1547 476
H, Re [1991] CLY 1371 486
H, Re [1992] CLY 1587 535
H, Re [1999] CLY 1446 494
H, Re, Kemp & Kemp, A4-020; [1996] CLY 2166 14
H, Re, Kemp & Kemp, C4-240; [1997] CLY 1853 486
H, Re, Kemp & Kemp, C4-250; [1990] CLY 1599 488
H, Re, Kemp & Kemp, C4-261; [1998] CLY 1516 491
Hack v Heald, Kemp & Kemp, J2-012/1, J2-015; [1992] CLY 1722 447
Hadjiyianni v Craven, Kemp & Kemp, C6-005; [1996] CLY 2205 73
Hajid, Re, Kemp & Kemp, K2-203; [1997] CLY 1884 186
Hale v London Underground [1994] CLY 1569 522

Hales v Clark, Kemp & Kemp, K2-240; [1997] CLY 1916 194
Hall v Bolton MBC, Kemp & Kemp, H6-040; [1997] CLY 1974 330
Hall v Hampton, Kemp & Kemp, E3-052; [1996] CLY 2231 247
Hall v Staffs Moorlands District Council, Kemp & Kemp, F6-071;
    [1994] CLY 1643 342
Hall, Re [1992] CLY 1571 24
Hallam v Thompson, Kemp & Kemp, D3-018; [1995] CLY 1692 15
Hambis v Boon, Kemp & Kemp, PRK-001; [1999] CLY 1580 175
Hamer v North West Water Authority, Kemp & Kemp, E3-080; [1992] CLY 1655........224
Hamilton v Air Products and Saluveer, Kemp & Kemp, E2-047/1; [1997] CLY 1899 17
Hancock, Re, Kemp & Kemp, C3-072; [1998] CLY 1505 106
Handley v Morris Cohen (Underwear), Kemp & Kemp, C6-029; [1994] CLY 1590 78
Hanks v Courtaulds, Kemp & Kemp, K2-213; [1990] CLY 1696 320
Hanrahan v Home Office, Kemp & Kemp, PRI-005; [2000] 4 CL 164 419
Hanson v Moore, Kemp & Kemp, K2-145/4; [1998] CLY 1725......................................188
Hanwell v Bell and O'Neill, Kemp & Kemp, K2-010; [1995] CLY 1824 19
Harbidge v Earl, Kemp & Kemp, E2-095/3; [2000] 5 CL 181 171
Harcourt v Harper and Harper, Kemp & Kemp, K2-123; [1993] CLY 1568....................433
Hardcastle v Dodgshon, Kemp & Kemp, I2-504; [1994] CLY 1573.................................33
Harding v Basingstoke and Deane BC, Kemp & Kemp, H6-039; [2000] 4 CL 161 465
Harding, Re, Kemp & Kemp, B2-012; [1995] CLY 1655...108
Hardinges v Firstsell, Kemp & Kemp, I2-521; [1991] CLY 1445 366
Hardy v Daldorph, Kemp & Kemp, I2-412; [1990] CLY 1666 397
Harling v Huddersfield Health Authority, Kemp & Kemp, L8-150; [1992] CLY 1662 ..340
Harman v Coleburn, Kemp & Kemp, K2-072; [1996] CLY 2322....................................144
Harper v Wilson (t/a Royal Star Public House), Kemp & Kemp, H2-024/1;
    [1999] CLY 1492 262
Harper, Re, Kemp & Kemp, C5-019; [1993] CLY 1443 32
Harries v Collins, Kemp & Kemp, E2/102/1/3; [1998] CLY 1608 173
Harrington v Newham LBC, Kemp & Kemp, C6-006; [1998] CLY 1555........................74
Harris v Harris, Kemp & Kemp, I2-205; [1997] CLY 1982 379
Harris v Readymix Drypack, Kemp & Kemp, J4-013; [1994] CLY 1703 515
Harris v Rulfell, Kemp & Kemp, G2-044; [1991] CLY 1421..360
Harris, Re, Kemp & Kemp, C5-078; [1996] CLY 2204 39
Harrison v Crane, Kemp & Kemp, C2-057; [1991] CLY 1340 57
Harrison v Mo, Kemp & Kemp, K2-048/2; [1999] CLY 1585...179
Harrison v Pilkington Glass, Kemp & Kemp, H4-018; [1990] CLY 1651 271
Harrison, Re, Kemp & Kemp, B2-017; [1994] CLY 1552 30
Harrow-Bunn, Re, Kemp & Kemp, H2-018; [1990] CLY 1644 290
Hart v Cauldwell, Kemp & Kemp, K2-081; [1991] CLY 1462 206
Hart v Tenmat [1992] CLY 1776..519
Hart, Re, Kemp & Kemp, J3-012; [1991] CLY 1449 437
Hartfield v Green, Kemp & Kemp, K2-019; [1995] CLY 1778 276
Hartley v Postlethwaite, Kemp & Kemp, K2-169/1; [1997] CLY 1880 190
Harvey v Cadbury, Kemp & Kemp, I2-437; [1995] CLY 1755 403
Harvey v Fairscope, Kemp & Kemp, PRL-005; [1997] CLY 2022 467
Harvey, Re, Kemp & Kemp, H6/022; [1995] CLY 1733 301

Table of Cases

Hasan v Boots the Chemist plc, Kemp & Kemp, H3-169/1; [1997] CLY 1963 275
Hasselby v Waddington, Kemp & Kemp, K2-226; [1994] CLY 1743 338
Havill v Wilson, Kemp & Kemp, H4-030; [2000] 5 CL 187..138
Hawken v Apex Bodyworks Ltd, Kemp & Kemp, H4-015/1/1; [1998] CLY 1639 289
Hawkes v Garside, Kemp & Kemp, I2-302; [1998] CLY 1674 374
Hawkeswood v Lewis, Kemp & Kemp, E2-123; [1994] CLY 1612, 1714 126
Hawkins and Cadwaladr v Gator Tool Hire & Sales Ltd, Kemp & Kemp, J3-030;
 [1998] CLY 1697 439
Hawkins v London Fire and Civil Defence Authority, Kemp & Kemp, H2-021;
 [1994] CLY 1657 271
Hawkins, Re, Kemp & Kemp, C4-052; [1994] CLY 1570 527
Hawkins, Re, Kemp & Kemp, D2-028/1; [1995] CLY 1668 82
Hayes v Bass North [1991] CLY 1493..373
Hayes v Rickwood, Kemp & Kemp, E2-064; [1995] CLY 1713 227
Hazell v Taylor, Kemp & Kemp, K2-170/1; [1998] CLY 1729 190
Hazle v Platt, Kemp & Kemp, E2-128; [1994] CLY 1715 183
Healey v Hampshire County Council [1992] CLY 1783 343
Heap v Partridge, Kemp & Kemp, H4-018; [1998] CLY 1646 290
Heath v Berkshire Health Authority [1992] 3 Med LR 57; 8 BMLR 98;
 Kemp & Kemp, D4-018/1; BPILS, XVII 1184; CLY 1619 39
Heden v BPC Magazines (Leeds) Ltd, Kemp & Kemp, H3-165/1;
 [1997] CLY 1968 286
Heil v Rankin [2000] PIQR Q187 ....lv, lvii, lviii
Hemsley v Hesketh, Kemp & Kemp, K2-129; [1995] CLY 1796 187
Henderson v Watchorn, Kemp & Kemp, I2-418; [1990] CLY 1667...............................399
Hendy v Milton Keynes HA [1992] PIQR P281; [1992] 3 Med LR 119;
 Kemp & Kemp, F4-028; BPILS, XVII 1296; [1991] CLY 1420 350
Hepworth v Gotch, Kemp & Kemp, E2-061/2; [1998] CLY 1594 159
Heskey v GKN Sankey, Kemp & Kemp, K2-170; [1990] CLY 1693 12
Hewett v Chef & Brewer Ltd, Kemp & Kemp, C4-058; [1998] CLY 1542 324
Hewlett, Re, Kemp & Kemp, B2-015/1; [1997] CLY 1825 24
Hibberd (Lesley Ann), Re, Kemp & Kemp, E3-065; [1997] CLY 1929 222
Hickinson (a minor) v Chesterfield Transport Ltd, Kemp & Kemp, H6-049/1;
 [1998] CLY 1655 466
Hicks v Dunston, Kemp & Kemp, K2-230; [1994] CLY 1740 56
Hicks v Munley, Kemp & Kemp, I2-505/1; [1995] CLY 1743 383
Higgins, Re, Kemp & Kemp, C4-213; [1996] CLY 2195 479
Higton v Constance, Kemp & Kemp, F6-014; [1994] CLY 1681 139
Higton v Constance, Kemp & Kemp, F6-014; [1995] CLY 1754 139
Hill and McKay v BDL Contracts and Design [1994] CLY 1733 185
Hill v Arc (South Wales) Ltd, Kemp & Kemp, D3-014/1; [1998] CLY 1563 68
Hill v Barnsley MDC (1996) 96 (4) QR 7; Kemp & Kemp, I2-537; [1996] CLY 2294 456
Hill v Craven, Kemp & Kemp, E2-073; [1993] CLY 1482 162
Hill v Dudley Metropolitan Borough Council, Kemp & Kemp, H6-041;
 [1995] CLY 1774 276
Hill v Holmes, Kemp & Kemp, E3-110/1; [2000] 3 CL 178...229
Hill v Liverpool Health Authority, Kemp & Kemp, F5-058/1; [1994] CLY 1639............352

Hill, Re [1990] CLY 1715 415
Hillier v Karminski, Kemp & Kemp, E2-052; [1994] CLY 1605 137
Hinchliffe v Hill, Kemp & Kemp, E2-105; [1994] CLY 1708 176
Hind v Howel [1992] CLY 1773 193
Hinnigan v Jackson, Kemp & Kemp, E3-046; [1990] CLY 1629 135
Hirst (a minor) v Tameside and Glossop HA, Kemp & Kemp, L8-081;
    [1998] CLY 1758 498
Hirst, Re, Kemp & Kemp, K2-013; [1993] CLY 1458 506
Hitchcock v Wheeler, Kemp & Kemp, E2-114/1; [1998] CLY 1717 178
Hitchcock, Re, Kemp & Kemp, J2-014/1/1; [1996] CLY 2293 239
Hitchings v Gilbert, Kemp & Kemp, E2-048; [1993] CLY 1479......................................154
Hobart v McGiff and Stuart, Kemp & Kemp, J2-022; [1997] CLY 1995 451
Hockin and Willott v Bradley, Kemp & Kemp, K2-234; [1994] CLY 1744 186
Hodge, Re [1992] CLY 1625 82
Hodges v Lambeth LBC, Kemp & Kemp, E3-004; [1997] CLY 1923 245
Hodgkinson v Dutton, Kemp & Kemp, I2-513; [1995] CLY 1750..................................396
Hodgkiss v Brassett, Kemp & Kemp, K2-109; [1991] CLY 1470 336
Hodgson v Abrahams, Kemp & Kemp, E2-079; [1994] CLY 1610.................................165
Hogg v Smith and Forder, Kemp & Kemp, I2-507; [1992] CLY 1702 73
Holder v Williams, Kemp & Kemp, J5-011; [1993] CLY 1471 10
Holland v Wood, Kemp & Kemp, E2-010; [1994] CLY 1599 198
Hollands v GK Salter & Associates and O'Neill, Kemp & Kemp, E2-088/1;
    [1997] CLY 1907 120
Holloway, Re (CICB Quantum: 2000) [2000] 6 CL 189...38
Holmes v Leeds Health Authority [1992] CLY 1616 54
Holmes, Re, Kemp & Kemp, C5-046; [1998] CLY 1552...46
Holton, Re, Kemp & Kemp, H2-016; [1993] CLY 1515 134
Hones v Brown, Kemp & Kemp, E2-142; [1994] CLY 1739...193
Hook v Yattendon Estates, Kemp & Kemp, I4-025; [1994] CLY 1691 464
Hookings v Wiltshire County Council [1992] CLY 1682 278
Hooper v Young, Kemp & Kemp, F4-015/1, F4-024; [1995] CLY 1717 349
Hope v DC Leisure (Camberley) [1995] CLY 1718...353
Hope v Money [1990] CLY 1708 131
Hopgood v Homebase, Kemp & Kemp, C5-069; [1990] CLY 1679 52
Horesh v Ryman, Kemp & Kemp, K2-164; [1990] CLY 1692 233
Horne v Prescot (No 1) Ltd (1999) 99(2) QR 6; Kemp & Kemp, F2-063/1;
    [1999] CLY 1540 514
Hornigold v Taylor, Re, Kemp & Kemp, K2-159; [1993] CLY 1575...............................233
Hosen v Marsland, Kemp & Kemp, F3-015; [1994] CLY 1638.......................................348
Hosken, Re, Kemp & Kemp, A3-004; [1993] CLY 1421 470
Howard v British Coal Corporation, Kemp & Kemp, H5-014; [1991] CLY 1427 327
Howard v Rogers [1992] CLY 1780...373
Howard, Re, Kemp & Kemp, C6-010; [1991] CLY 1384...74
Howden v Suffolk County Council, Kemp & Kemp, E3-059; [1994] CLY 1624 219
Howe v DT Tarmacadam (1999) 99 (1) QR 8; Kemp & Kemp, I2-445;
    [1998] CLY 1680 406
Howe v Moore, Kemp & Kemp, I2-314; [1992] CLY 1704...385

Howell v Bolton Hospitals NHS Trust [1996] CLY 2325 517
Howell v Deans, Kemp & Kemp, E3-124; [1995] CLY 1794 127
Howell v J Lyons & Co (1998) 98 (6) QR 7; Kemp & Kemp, H5-026;
  [1998] CLY 1651 275
Hoy v Cole, Kemp & Kemp, K2-096; [1997] CLY 1895 146
Huber v Szender, Kemp & Kemp, E2-130; [1994] CLY 1716 206
Hudson, Re, Kemp & Kemp, F2-025; [1994] CLY 1631 334
Hughes (Ieuan Richard), Re, Kemp & Kemp, A2-008; [1994] CLY 1541 473
Hughes v Bloor [2000] 6 CL 203 207
Hughes v Doncaster Borough Council, Kemp & Kemp, K2-148; [1992] CLY 1759 460
Hughes v Eadon, Kemp & Kemp, D2-043/1; [1996] CLY 2212 87
Hughes v Hunt, Kemp & Kemp, K2/253/4; [2000] 4 CL 158 195
Hughes v St Helens MBC, Kemp & Kemp, PRH-004; [1999] CLY 1607 309
Hughes, Re, Kemp & Kemp, C5-053; [1992] CLY 1612 454
Huke v Shobbrook, Kemp & Kemp, E2-066; [1992] CLY 1641 119
Hulme (CICB Quantum: 2000), Kemp & Kemp, PRC-005; [2000] 4 CL 149 30
Humphries v Goodyear Great Britain, Kemp & Kemp, K2-178; [1993] CLY 1577 429
Humphries v HG Transport [1998] CLY 1721 185
Hunn v McFarlane, Kemp & Kemp, E2-063; [1997] CLY 1901 159
Hunt v Barnet, Kemp & Kemp, K2-146; [1991] CLY 1388 78
Hunt v Clancy, Kemp & Kemp, C4-118; [1990] CLY 1592 507
Hunt v Strudwick, Kemp & Kemp, H7-013/2; [1992] CLY 1698 328
Hunt v Unigate Dairies Ltd, Kemp & Kemp, E3-118; [1996] CLY 2363 250
Hunt, Re [1992] CLY 1755 468
Hunter v Deuchart, Kemp & Kemp, B2-016/1; [1998] CLY 1502 58
Huntingdon v Armstrong, Kemp & Kemp, E3-085/1; [1998] CLY 1618 138
Huntley v Atkins, Kemp & Kemp, I2-415; [1996] CLY 2280 261
Hurley, Re, Kemp & Kemp, I4-023; [1996] CLY 2291 432
Hussain v Nawaz, Kemp & Kemp, PRC-014; [2000] 4 CL 150 45
Hutchings v Jackson, Kemp & Kemp, K2-236; [1994] CLY 1742 325
Hutchinson v Abdalla, Kemp & Kemp, K2-032; [1997] CLY 2012 339
Hutton, Re [1999] CLY 1426 23
Huxter v Lock (1998) 98 (6) QR 8; Kemp & Kemp, I4-032; [1998] CLY 1690 433
Hyde v Clive Warcup Transport Ltd, Kemp & Kemp, PRK-008; [1999] CLY 1599 279
Hyland v George, Kemp & Kemp, E3-051; [1993] CLY 1490 247

I, L and S, Re, Kemp & Kemp, M4-052/1; [1998] CLY 1764 532
Ingless v Intransit (t/a Woodlands Medical Group (UK)) [1992] CLY 1729 458
Ingrasci v Greatwood, Kemp & Kemp, K2-268/2; [1998] CLY 1710 407
Inkersole, Re, Kemp & Kemp, C4-088; [1990] CLY 1590 505
Iqbal v Irfan, Kemp & Kemp, F5-067/1; [1994] CLY 1642 354
Iqubal v Amuah [1997] CLY 1937 226
Isaacs, Re, Kemp & Kemp, C4-057; [1995] CLY 1671 503
Ives, Re, Kemp & Kemp, C2-033; [1997] CLY 1836 13

J (a child) v Jones, Kemp & Kemp, PRC-022; [2000] 4 CL 169 23
J and N, Re, Kemp & Kemp, C4-225; [1990] CLY 1597 477

J, Re, Kemp & Kemp, C2-014; [1997] CLY 1822 474
J, Re, Kemp & Kemp, E2-004/1; [1997] CLY 1887 211
J, Re, Kemp & Kemp, H3-165/2; [1996] CLY 2260..273
Jachim and Martin v Barrett, Kemp & Kemp, K2-135; [1996] CLY 2338 128
Jackson & Jackson v Mourne [1990] CLY 1707 196
Jackson v Ikeda Hoover Ltd, Kemp & Kemp, K2-167; [1997] CLY 1868.........................80
Jackson v Sung, Kemp & Kemp, H4-023; [1992] CLY 1686..293
Jackson v Torquay Leisure Hotels, Kemp & Kemp, K2-088; [1991] CLY 1466 336
Jackson, Re (CICB Quantum: 1999), Kemp & Kemp, C5-064; [2000] 1 CL 120..............91
Jacobs v Corniche Helicopters, Kemp & Kemp, H5-015/2; [1999] CLY 1501 323
James (a minor) v Robertson, Kemp & Kemp, C5-054; [1998] CLY 1547........................19
James and Evand v Keenan [1990] CLY 1710 510
James v London Electricity plc, Kemp & Kemp, C4-042; [1998] CLY 1528 526
James v Oatley [1995] CLY 1813 314
James v Victoria Palace Theatre Ltd, Kemp & Kemp, H2-027/2; [1999] CLY 1495........263
James v Watker, Kemp & Kemp, K2-091; [1997] CLY 2018..360
Janardan v East Berkshire Health Authority [1990] 2 Med LR 1; Kemp & Kemp, A4-
    001/1, A4-109; BPILS, I 56, 58, 286.4, 286.7,582.4; XVII 1043; [1991] CLY 1333 471
Japal v Ford Motor Co., Kemp & Kemp, K2-084; [1990] CLY 1685 406
Jawando v Sphinx Hairdressing, Kemp & Kemp, J5-010; [1998] CLY 1558 9
Jefferies v Byrne, Kemp & Kemp, H4-029; [1999] CLY 1500..277
Jeffrey v Cape Insulation Ltd (1999) 99 (2) QR 5; Kemp & Kemp, F2-030/1;
    [1999] CLY 1536 511
Jenkins v Darlington Insulation Co., Kemp & Kemp, F2-024; [1991] CLY 1407 547
Jenkins, Re, Kemp & Kemp, C4-069; [1997] CLY 1856 531
Jennings v Cummins & Phillips, Kemp & Kemp, E2-018; [1997] CLY 1889 148
JH, Re, Kemp & Kemp, C2-026; [1994] CLY 1549 102
Jinks v Ramzan, Kemp & Kemp, K2-188; [1995] CLY 1808..260
JK, Re (1996) 96 (4) QB 3; Kemp & Kemp, K2-198; [1996] CLY 2353............................129
Jobling v Gala Leisure Ltd, Kemp & Kemp, K2-253/2; [1999] CLY 1572 73
John (Mark), Re, Kemp & Kemp, C2-067; [1997] CLY 1837...15
John Laing Construction and Whattam (Thomas) v Stickells (David)
    [1993] CLY 1582 12
Johnson v Baker, Kemp & Kemp, I3-035/1; [1996] CLY 2321..378
Johnson v British Railways Board, Kemp & Kemp, F2-048; [1998] CLY 1625 556
Johnson v Cawdor Industrial Holdings [1996] CLY 2239 553
Johnson v Doncaster Leisure Management, Kemp & Kemp, J3-032;
    [1994] CLY 1700 424
Johnson v Edwards, Kemp & Kemp, K2-014; [1995] CLY 1777 229
Johnson v Hill, Kemp & Kemp, K1-100, I2-126/1; [1999] CLY 1555 145
Johnson v Khan, Kemp & Kemp, E2-105/1; [1998] CLY 1620 176
Johnson v Pattenden, Kemp & Kemp, E2-115/1; [1998] CLY 1611 178
Johnson v Rogers, Kemp & Kemp, E2-029/1; [1999] CLY 1470 150
Johnson v Rolls Royce [1990] CLY 1672 418
Johnson v Sidaway, Kemp & Kemp, K2-270; [1997] CLY 1897......................................131
Johnston, Re, Kemp & Kemp, C4-086; [1995] CLY 1673 534
Jones (a minor) v Morgan, Kemp & Kemp, I2-540; [1996] CLY 2307............................392

Jones (a minor) v Wrexham CBC, Kemp & Kemp, I2-531; [1998] CLY 1669 391
Jones (SA), Re [1994] CLY 1571, 1699 445
Jones v Adams, Kemp & Kemp, E2-102/3; [1998] CLY 1607 173
Jones v Aderogba, Kemp & Kemp, K2-167/1; [1998] CLY 1705 371
Jones v Clwyd HA, Kemp & Kemp, I4-024; [1996] CLY 2289 423
Jones v Hicklin [1992] CLY 1703 384
Jones v Hones [1992] CLY 1732 359
Jones v Houlder Marine Drilling, Kemp & Kemp, I3-013; [1990] CLY 1671 416
Jones v Leadbitter, Kemp & Kemp, I2-530; [1994] CLY 1675 35
Jones v Liverpool City Council, Kemp & Kemp, E3-113; [1994] CLY 1628 250
Jones v Pandis [1993] CLY 1590..132
Jones v South Glamorgan HA [1997] CLY 1920 244
Jones v Swansea City Council, Kemp & Kemp, i2-509; [1998] CLY 1664...........385
Jones v Whitbread plc, Kemp & Kemp, E3-017/1; [1998] CLY 1615 244
Jones, Re, Kemp & Kemp, C6-019; [1990] CLY 1608..75
Joseph v Kaur, Kemp & Kemp, J3-042; [1993] CLY 1578 429
Joyce v Lucey, Kemp & Kemp, K2-166/1; [1998] CLY 1727 190
Joyce v Mumin, Kemp & Kemp, L2-052; [1994] CLY 1751 499
Judd, Re, Kemp & Kemp, C2-023; [1993] CLY 1439 101
Jukes v Ratcliff, Kemp & Kemp, C4-276; [1997] CLY 1844 540
JW, Re, Kemp & Kemp, C4-245; [1997] CLY 1855..487

K (a minor) v Tesco Stores Ltd, Kemp & Kemp, PRK-013; [2000] 1 CL 127 27
K v Hickman, Kemp & Kemp, PRC-003; [2000] 3 CL 162...................................28
K, Re [1991] CLY 1341 500
K, Re, Kemp & Kemp, C4-092; [1996] CLY 2198 493
K, Re, Kemp & Kemp, C4-243; [1997] CLY 1854 487
K, Re, Kemp & Kemp, C4-253; [1991] CLY 1372 488
Kahl v Rosencourt [1994] CLY 1607 159
Kalam v Khan, Kemp & Kemp, K2-224/1; [2000] 5 CL 194 193
Kasprzyk, Re, Kemp & Kemp, C5-027; [1991] CLY 1376...................................448
Kataria v Arpino, Kemp & Kemp, E2-139/1; [1998] CLY 1728 128
Kaur, Re, Kemp & Kemp, B2-004/2/3; [1999] CLY 1425 99
Kay (Jacqueline) v Convenience Foods, Kemp & Kemp, K2-150; [1994] CLY 1726 315
Kaylow v Kaylow, Kemp & Kemp, F6-015; [1994] CLY 1636 339
Kear v Torfaen Borough Council [1992] CLY 1724 453
Kearney v Calsonic Llanelli Radiators Ltd, Kemp & Kemp, D3-029/1;
  [1999] CLY 1466 72
Kee v Sharma (1999) 99 (2) QR 5; Kemp & Kemp, E2-123/3; [1999] CLY 1586............181
Keith, Re, Kemp & Kemp, K2-192; [1995] CLY 1806 518
Kelleher v Ford Motor Co [1995] CLY 1751..269
Kelly v Hemming, Kemp & Kemp, PRC-015; [2000] 3 CL 167 35
Kelly v The Post Office [1992] CLY 1650 245
Kemp v Burden (No 1), Kemp & Kemp, C4-128; [1998] CLY 1712....................517
Kemp v Burden (No 2), Kemp & Kemp, K2-224/2; [1998] CLY 1707 37
Kempster v Ashfield [2000] 6 CL 191...163
Kendal v Moxom, Kemp & Kemp, I2-544; [1996] CLY 2328..............................345

Kennedy and Kennedy v Berry, Kemp & Kemp, E2-123/1; [1998] CLY 1731 174
Kenny v Hewdon Stuart Crane Hire Ltd, Kemp & Kemp, G2-036; [1999] CLY 1509....357
Kent v Wakefield Metal Traders, Kemp & Kemp, F2-018; BPILS, I 133, III 17.2;
 [1990] CLY 1637 547
Kerr v Tudor Thomas Construction and Development Ltd, Kemp & Kemp,
 K2-245/1; [1997] CLY 1992..414
Khan (Arbab), Re, Kemp & Kemp, J2-017; [1997] CLY 1999...448
Khan v Bibb, Kemp & Kemp, E2-115/4; [1999] CLY 1585 179
Khan v Jones, Kemp & Kemp, C2-040; [1998] CLY 1487 106
Khan v Oldham, Kemp & Kemp, K2-170/2; [1998] CLY 1730 190
Khan v W&J Whitehead (Laisterdyke) Ltd, Kemp & Kemp, C4-112;
 [1996] CLY 2304 36
Kibbie v Bourdon, Kemp & Kemp, E2-087/1; [1999] CLY 1476 167
Kibble v Bond, Kemp & Kemp, E2-073/1; [1998] CLY 1596 162
Kilford v United Engineering Steels, Kemp & Kemp, K2-050; [1991] CLY 1459 313
King v Co-Steel Sheerness plc, Kemp & Kemp, I4-073; [1998] CLY 1686.....................431
King v Johnson, Kemp & Kemp, L8-097; [1994] CLY 1666, 1754..................................311
Kingsley v Moate, Kemp & Kemp, E2-135; [1994] CLY 1727 208
Kinsella v Jameson [1992] CLY 1751 186
Kirk v Laine Theatre Arts [1995] CLY 1712 216
Kitching v Tesco Stores, Kemp & Kemp, H4-026/1; [1995] CLY 1731 272
Knight [1992] CLY 1588 536
Knight and Gilbert v Hooper [1993] CLY 1584 196
Knight v Ford Motor Company, Kemp & Kemp, H6A-030; [1991] CLY 1429 309
Knight v Thamesdown Borough Council, Kemp & Kemp, H2-030; [1992] CLY 1677 ..258
Knight v Tower Hamlets Health Authority BPILS, XVIII 1088; [1994] CLY 1755..........467
Knott v Haden Maintenance Ltd, Kemp & Kemp, C4-012; [1998] CLY 1521 519
Kotecha v Harrow LBC [1995] CLY 1812 55
Kumar v Kumar, Kemp & Kemp, E3-027/1; [1998] CLY 1576......................................242
Kyei v Utility Tyre Services Ltd, Kemp & Kemp, D2-032/1; [1997] CLY 1876 86
Kyffin v Creighton [1996] CLY 2361 234

L (a child) v Berkshire HA [2000] 6 CL 183 95
L, Re (CICB Quantum: 1999), Kemp & Kemp, C4-274; [2000] 2 CL 142 494
L, Re (CICB Quantum: 2000), Kemp & Kemp, PRC-006; [2000] 5 CL 175 298
L, Re, Kemp & Kemp, A4-017; [1997] CLY 1821 471
L, Re, Kemp & Kemp, C4-223; [1991] CLY 1366 481
L, Re, Kemp & Kemp, C4-249; [1991] CLY 1374 488
Lago v John Williams of Cardiff, Kemp & Kemp, F6-051; [1991] CLY 1495 345
Lakhrissi, Re [1990] CLY 1673 334
Lamb v Alcan Speciality Extrusions, Kemp & Kemp, E2-071; [1995] CLY 1702...........161
Lamb v Turner, Kemp & Kemp, E2-133; [1996] CLY 2337 127
Lambert v Broun and Dixons Group [1992] CLY 1770 56
Lambert v Knowsley Metropolitan Borough Council, Kemp & Kemp, C5-043;
 [1993] CLY 1467 45
Lambeth v Williams (1997) 97 (4) QR 7; Kemp & Kemp, H3-059/1;
 [1997] CLY 1958 266

Table of Cases

Lamey v Wirral Health Authority, Kemp & Kemp, A4-015/1, A4-120;
[1993] CLY 1437 96
Lancaster v Birmingham City Council, Kemp & Kemp, C4-076; [1999] CLY 1438 504
Lane v Evans, Kemp & Kemp, D3-026; [1995] CLY 1694 71
Lane v Lucas & Avalon Surfacing, Kemp & Kemp, E2-048/1; [1998] CLY 1589 155
Lanera v Regan, Kemp & Kemp, i2-315; [1998] CLY 1667 386
Langden-Jones v Rossiter, Kemp & Kemp, K2-048/1; [1999] CLY 1591 142
Larcombe v Willis [1990] CLY 1695 280
Large v Ministry of Defence, Kemp & Kemp, 12-277,F2-076; [1991] CLY 1413............552
Laurie v Makepeace Universal (Killingworth), Kemp & Kemp, E3-033;
[1993] CLY 1489 215
Lavender v Foley [1992] CLY 1640...160
Lavender v Hayes, Kemp & Kemp, E2-093; [1991] CLY 1401 169
Laverick, Re [1992] CLY 1674...254
Lawrence v Bown & Bown [1991] CLY 1361 508
Lawrence v Scott Ltd, Kemp & Kemp, h7-022/1; [1998] CLY 1662 313
Lawrence v WW Martin (Thanet) Ltd, Kemp & Kemp, C4-025; [1998] CLY 1523.........502
Laws v British Railways Board [1994] CLY 1655 270
Lawson, Re, Kemp & Kemp, C2-034; [1998] CLY 1486 469
Lawson, Re, Kemp & Kemp, C4-021; [1997] CLY 1845 521
Laycock v Morrison (WM), Kemp & Kemp, D4-019; [1991] CLY 1381 66
Lazenby v Panayiotou [1992] CLY 1743 411
Le Gallou v Malorey [1997] CLY 1932 238
Lea v Baird, Kemp & Kemp, K2-189; [1995] CLY 1805 318
Leacock v Ward, Kemp & Kemp, E2-061/1; [1998] CLY 1593 158
Leadbeater (a minor) v Allied Domecq Ltd (1998) 98 (6) QR 8; Kemp & Kemp,
K2-108/2; [1998] CLY 1751...370
Leal v British Sugar, Kemp & Kemp, F2-043; [1990] CLY 1638........................547
Leatherland v Rissman, Kemp & Kemp, J2-030; [1997] CLY 1997 274
Leckie v TJ Hairdressers, Kemp & Kemp, J5-075; [1996] CLY 2210...................22
Ledgar v Kidd, Kemp & Kemp, E2-100/1; [1998] CLY 1603 172
Lee v Clark, Kemp & Kemp, C2-073; [1998] CLY 1501 33
Lee v Gough, Kemp & Kemp, C6-017; [1991] CLY 1385.....................................75
Lee v Liverpool City Council, Kemp & Kemp, H4-026/2; [1995] CLY 1732..................294
Leech v Ward, Waring and Leadbetter [1995] CLY 1708....................................218
Lemar (a minor) v Lloyds Chemists plc, Kemp & Kemp, J3-039/2; [1998] CLY 1696 ..440
Lennon v McDonald, Kemp & Kemp, H2-029; [1990] CLY 1645 258
Leonard v Niagara Holdings Ltd, Kemp & Kemp, B2-004/2/1; [1998] CLY 1492...........89
Lewis v BTR plc, Kemp & Kemp, PRD-003; [1999] CLY 1465 71
Lewis v Emmins [1995] CLY 1700 154
Lewis v Jukes, Kemp & Kemp, H3-164/2; [1995] CLY 1727 453
Lewis v Tesco Stores Ltd, Kemp & Kemp, G2-038/1; [1996] CLY 2252.........................253
Leyland, Re, Kemp & Kemp, C2-020; [1998] CLY 1482 100
Lill v Wakefield MDC, Kemp & Kemp, E3-031/1; [1997] CLY 1924 246
Linell v Draper, Kemp & Kemp, K2-265; [1991] CLY 1492 509
Lingard v C V Stubbs & Sons, Kemp & Kemp, D2-031; BPILS, IV 5594;
[1990] CLY 1614 85

xxxii *Damages*

Linsdell, Re, Kemp & Kemp, D2-025; [1990] CLY 1612 84
Litchfield v Flear, Kemp & Kemp, H2-027; [1990] CLY 1610 142
Little v VSEL Birkenhead Ltd, Kemp & Kemp, F2-049/1; [1998] CLY 1627 550
Littlefair v Turner, Kemp & Kemp, B2-042; [1993] CLY 1435 25
Littleford v Wood, Kemp & Kemp, K2-161; [1990] CLY 1691 11
Littlewort v Adams, Kemp & Kemp, K2-049; [1993] CLY 1559 205
Livesey (a minor) v Hammersmith and Fulham LBC, Kemp & Kemp,
  C5-042; [1998] CLY 1553 45
Lloyd v Simms, Kemp & Kemp, E3-078; [1996] CLY 2218 154
Lloyd, Re, Kemp & Kemp, C4-041; [1991] CLY 1347 525
Lloyd-Davies v Lyth, Kemp & Kemp, E2-047/2; [2000] 5 CL 185 199
Lo Sterzo (a minor) v Hopkins [1998] CLY 1732 183
Lobo v Hamilton, Kemp & Kemp, K2-254; [1993] CLY 1583 195
Locker, Re, Kemp & Kemp, C5-040; [1991] CLY 1382 44
Loft v Nottingham County Council, Kemp & Kemp, E3-023; [1994] CLY 1621 215
Lofthouse v North Tees Health Authority [1992] CLY 1664 352
Long v Cornwall County Council, Kemp & Kemp, H3-103; [1992] CLY 1684 291
Long, Re (CICB Quantum: 1999), Kemp & Kemp, C4-060; [2000] 1 CL 118 525
Longworth v Sunbeams Ltd, Kemp & Kemp, J3-035; [1997] CLY 2002 440
Lord v Alco Waste Management, Kemp & Kemp, E2-037/1; [1999] CLY 1485 221
Lord v Cryers, Kemp & Kemp, E2-095/1/1; [1999] CLY 1477 170
Lorimer, Re, Kemp & Kemp, C2-065; [1993] CLY 1446 67
Lorryman, Re [1994] CLY 1563 114
Loughran v London Buses, Kemp & Kemp, E2-029; [1993] CLY 1476 150
Lovatt v Linde Gas UK, Kemp & Kemp, D3-024; [1995] CLY 1693 70
Lovence, Re, Kemp & Kemp, C5-020; [1999] CLY 1527 39
Lowe v Baron Meats Ltd, Kemp & Kemp, K2-040; [1997] CLY 1987 404
Lowe v Convenience Foods [1992] CLY 1779 81
Lowe v Haskell, Kemp & Kemp, H3-058; [1997] CLY 1966 266
Lowe v Kapadia, Kemp & Kemp, E2-102; [1993] CLY 1556 121
Lower v British Broadcasting Corp., Kemp & Kemp, L3-075; [1991] CLY 1411 551
Lower v Hagland, Kemp & Kemp, C4-033; [1998] CLY 1526 31
Lucas v Lacey (No 1), Kemp & Kemp, E2-104; [1997] CLY 1908 175
Lucas v Sketchley plc, Kemp & Kemp, H6-049/2; [1998] CLY 1652 332
Lucas, Re, Kemp & Kemp, C2-071; [1993] CLY 1588 32
Lunney, Re, Kemp & Kemp, C2-047; [1994] CLY 1559 108
Lymer v Henson, Kemp & Kemp, C4-107; [1997] CLY 1863 202
Lynch, Re [1990] CLY 1602 42
Lyon v Chambers, Kemp & Kemp, E2-137; [1993] CLY 1572 146

M (a child) v Oraha, Kemp & Kemp, E2-130/1; [2000] 5 CL 193 176
M (a child), Re (CICB Quantum: 1999), Kemp & Kemp, PRC-007;
  [2000] 3 CL 165 530
M (a minor) v Brent and Harrow Health Authority, Kemp & Kemp, F5-059/1;
  [1999] CLY 1544 353
M (a minor) v De Koning, Kemp & Kemp, K2-161/1; [2000] 3 CL 180 316
M (a minor) v Debenhams plc, Kemp & Kemp, C5-060; [2000] 1 CL 128 26

M (a minor) v Snakes and Ladders Adventure Centres Ltd, Kemp & Kemp,
 H3-164/1; [1999] CLY 1496 292
M (a minor) v Sun World Ltd, Kemp & Kemp, K2-145/5, K1-100; [1999] CLY 1614 407
M, Re [1991] CLY 1369 483
M, Re [1995] CLY 1662 17
M, Re, Kemp & Kemp, C4-044; [1993] CLY 1447 481
M, Re, Kemp & Kemp, C4-229; [1997] CLY 1851 482
Mabbett v Mead, Kemp & Kemp, E2-062; [1996] CLY 2236 201
Mace v Brown, Kemp & Kemp, K2-171; [1991] CLY 1479 372
Macey v ORB Electrical Steels, Kemp & Kemp, K2-107; [1994] CLY 1719 232
Macey, Re, Kemp & Kemp, E2-036; [1997] CLY 1890 118
MacFarlane, Re [1995] CLY 1674 41
Mackel, Re, Kemp & Kemp, D2-037/2; [1997] CLY 1877 86
Mackie v Rogerson, Kemp & Kemp, F3-013/2; [1996] CLY 2186 533
MacLeod, Re [1992] CLY 1607 449
Macmillan v Seymour Plant Hire & Co [1992] CLY 1673 261
Maddison v Gandy, Kemp & Kemp, E3-108; [1993] CLY 1483 167
Maddox v George Fischer (Lincoln) [1994] CLY 1747 373
Mafe v Amin, Kemp & Kemp, C6-021; [1996] CLY 2206 76
Mahon v Lowley [1992] CLY 1738 393
Mahoney v Williams, Kemp & Kemp, E2-111; [1996] CLY 2310 178
Main v Birchmore, Kemp & Kemp, E3-111; [1995] CLY 1773 121
Malcolm v Commissioner of Police of the Metropolis, Kemp & Kemp,
 H2-027/1; [1999] CLY 1494 263
Mallett v Committee of the Hanney War Memorial Hall, Kemp & Kemp,
 H6-036/1; [1995] CLY 1736 329
Maloney v Liverpool City Council, Kemp & Kemp, J2-021; [1994] CLY 1694 271
Malpass v Berlei [1995] CLY 1819 321
Mamczynski v GM Buses (North) Ltd, Kemp & Kemp, E2-115/5; [2000] 5 CL 178 124
Mapley, Re, Kemp & Kemp, C2-039; [1994] CLY 1561, 1567 105
March v The Post Office [1990] CLY 1694 509
Marram v North Tees Health Authority [1992] CLY 1665 354
Marsh (a minor) v Igoe, Kemp & Kemp, C4-132; [1998] CLY 1713 508
Marsh v Ashton Corrugated (Midlands) Ltd, Kemp & Kemp, H6-038/1; [
 1997] CLY 1973 308
Marsh v Kirwen, Kemp & Kemp, E3-025; [1995] CLY 1707 216
Marshall v Lyon [1992] CLY 1769 194
Martin v Ainscough [1992] CLY 1637 134
Martin v Crane and Martin [1991] CLY 1444 417
Martin v Crane, Kemp & Kemp, I3-022, K2-168; [1991] CLY 1481 209
Martin v Imperial Chemical Industries plc, Kemp & Kemp, C6-030;
 [1996] CLY 2207 78
Martin v Imperial War Museum, Kemp & Kemp, K2-260; [1992] CLY 1777 81
Martin v Press Offshore, Kemp & Kemp, H5-022; [1993] CLY 1527 328
Martin v Sealey, Kemp & Kemp, C4-123; [1996] CLY 2335 538
Martin, Re (1996) 96 (1) QR 4; Kemp & Kemp, E2-003; [1996] CLY 2365 132
Martin, Re (CICB Quantum: 2000) [2000] 6 CL 187 40

Maslin v Sankey Jonchu, Kemp & Kemp, E3-067; [1993] CLY 1491..............................222
Mason v Car Collection Services, Kemp & Kemp, E3-119; [1996] CLY 2318 125
Mason v Norweb, Kemp & Kemp, E3-044; [1991] CLY 1395 135
Mason v Weeks [1995] CLY 1682..449
Masterson v Chemical Services, Fabrications & Erection Ltd, Kemp & Kemp,
    E3-003/1; [1998] CLY 1566..210
Mastin v Rotherham HA, Kemp & Kemp, PRH-008; [1999] CLY 1604 332
Matbey v Bayley, Kemp & Kemp, E2-085/2; [1998] CLY 1598 166
Mather v British Gas and Biggs and Wall & Co, Kemp & Kemp, I2-307;
    [1995] CLY 1742 381
Mather v British Gas and Biggs and Wall & Co, Kemp & Kemp, I2-307;
    [1994] CLY 1670 381
Matthews v Oldfield and Hawkins, Kemp & Kemp, K2-003; [1991] CLY 1342 25
Matthews v Strenglade, Kemp & Kemp, E2-030; [1991] CLY 1397 150
Matthews, Re, Kemp & Kemp, J2-044; [1995] CLY 1686..52
Mattinson v Ullah, Kemp & Kemp, E3-110; [1993] CLY 1500 228
Mawson v Harvey (1999) 99 (1) QR 7; Kemp & Kemp, E3-105; [1998] CLY 1617 227
Maxim v Indelicato, Kemp & Kemp, H6-027; [1994] CLY 1661 303
May v Essex County Council, Kemp & Kemp, C5-068; [1994] CLY 1585 458
Mayhew v Dacorum BC, Kemp & Kemp, E3-026; [1996] CLY 2229 245
McBride v Basildon &Thurrock Hospital NHS Trust, Kemp & Kemp, PRI-006;
    [2000] 4 CL 165 426
McCaffery v Lambeth London Borough Council, Kemp & Kemp, F2-078;
    [1994] CLY 1635 546
McCallion v Dodd, Kemp & Kemp, K2-153; [1995] CLY 1799 338
McCarthy v Abbott Insulation, Kemp & Kemp, F2-058/2; [1999] CLY 1539 513
McCarthy v British Gas, Kemp & Kemp, K2-130; [1995] CLY 1797 406
McCarthy v Davis, Kemp & Kemp, PR;-002; [2000] 5 CL 191 341
McCarthy, Re, Kemp & Kemp, C4-027; [1991] CLY 1346 2
McCausland v Khan, Kemp & Kemp, E2-106; [1994] CLY 1617 176
McClean v Boult [2000] 6 CL 199 418
McClean v Costa, Kemp & Kemp, I4-030; [1997] CLY 1994..425
McConnell v Welch, Kemp & Kemp, C2-026; [1992] CLY 1566......................................104
McConnell, Re, Kemp & Kemp, A2-006/3; [1994] CLY 1542 474
McDaid v Howletts and Port Lympne Estates Ltd, Kemp & Kemp, H3-012;
    [1996] CLY 2258 266
McDermot v Liverpool City Council [1992] CLY 1762 54
McDevitt v Rochford Mouldings Ltd, Kemp & Kemp, I4-028; [1998] CLY 1688 432
McDevitt, Re [1992] CLY 1726 455
McDonald v Niland, Kemp & Kemp, K2-152; [1994] CLY 1728 64
McDonald v Watson, Kemp & Kemp, I2-311; [1994] CLY 1671 363
McDonnell v Woodhouse and Jones (1995) The Times, May 25;
    Kemp & Kemp, F4-018; BPILS, XI 1947; [1995] CLY 1716 347
McEwan, Re [1992] CLY 1604 58
McFarlane v Clifford Smith & Buchanan, Kemp & Kemp, PRI-002;
    [2000] 5 CL 189 463
McGarragle, Re [1992] CLY 1590 4

Table of Cases

McGowan v Harrow HA, Kemp & Kemp, E3-016; [1991] CLY 1403 214
McGuffie, Re, Kemp & Kemp, C2-043; [1997] CLY 1840 107
McGuirk v Hardie and Atkinson, Kemp & Kemp, I2-525; [1990] CLY 1663 389
McHugh v Carlisle City Council, Kemp & Kemp, E3-034/1; [2000] 4 CL 154 246
McIlgrew v Devon County Council [1995] PIQR Q66; Kemp & Kemp,
    E3-008; BPILS, I 243; [1993] CLY 1487 243
McIlwee (a minor) v Zanussi Ltd, Kemp & Kemp, C4-120; [1998] CLY 1641 296
McKenna v Heron, Kemp & Kemp, C6-016; [1990] CLY 1607 75
McLafferty v London Borough of Southwark, Kemp & Kemp, I3-036;
    [1991] CLY 1464 369
McLaughlin v QDF Component [1995] CLY 1820 81
McLean, Re [1994] CLY 1663 331
McMaster v Prince Recycling Ltd, Kemp & Kemp, C5-047; [1999] CLY 1461 46
McNamara v Liverpool City Council, Kemp & Kemp, H6A-029; [1996] CLY 2273 305
McPherson v Shiasson, Kemp & Kemp, E2-076/4; [2000] 5 CL 184 164
McPherson, Re [1995] CLY 1669 529
McQuaide, Re [1991] CLY 1391 85
Mears v Kitsons Insulations, Kemp & Kemp, F2-079; [1991] CLY 1415 552
Medjoub (a minor) v Ayub, Kemp & Kemp, E2-080/4; [1998] CLY 1581 120
Medland, Re [1991] CLY 1378 457
Megarry v Torkmatic, Kemp & Kemp, E2-031; [1994] CLY 1602 150
Mehrlich v McLaughlin, Kemp & Kemp, K2-246; [1996] CLY 2357 321
Meletti v Lane, Kemp & Kemp, J4-021; [1999] CLY 1615 559
Melling v Liverpool City Council, Kemp & Kemp, K2-025; [1997] CLY 1981 392
Melton, Re, Kemp & Kemp, B2-003; [1992] CLY 1561 65
Mendoza, Re, Kemp & Kemp, C2-079; [1991] CLY 1494 18
Menhenott v Wiggins Teape Fine Papers, Kemp & Kemp, C5-024; [1992] CLY 1606 16
Merriot v Tiley [1992] CLY 1746 5
Messam v Macnamara, Kemp & Kemp, J5-005; [1995] CLY 1689 8
Messum, Re [1992] CLY 1728 457
Metcalf v GL Ord, Kemp & Kemp, K2-100; [1992] CLY 1744 184
Metcalf-Wood v Bradford's Building Supplies Ltd, Kemp & Kemp, PRE-006;
    [1999] CLY 1485 221
Michalski v Stabin Martin, Kemp & Kemp, E3-003; [1993] CLY 1429 471
Milan v West Glamorgan CC, Kemp & Kemp, H6-034/1; [1996] CLY 2270 306
Milbourne v William Press (Construction), Kemp & Kemp, E3-011;
    [1991] CLY 1402 234
Miles v Martyn, Kemp & Kemp, E2-092; [1990] CLY 1623 169
Miles v West Kent HA [1997] 8 Med LR 191; BPILS, XVII 1109; [1997] CLY 1949 499
Miller v Dythe, Kemp & Kemp, J2-019/1,J2-043; [1993] CLY 1552 341
Mills v British Rail Engineering Ltd. [1992] 1 PIQR Q130; Kemp & Kemp,
    F2-053, M2-075, M2-238; BPILS, I 238, 569.1, II 266; [1991] CLY 1497 555
Mills v Morris Motorcycles, Kemp & Kemp, H2-016; [1995] CLY 1723 253
Mills, Re, Kemp & Kemp,J2-012; [1995] CLY 1762 327
Milne v Mateus, Kemp & Kemp, K2-008; [1999] CLY 1577 203
Mirfin v Spencer Clark Metal Industries plc, Kemp & Kemp, H6A-026/1;
    [1998] CLY 1659 307

Misiri v Milner, Kemp & Kemp, K2-035; [1990] CLY 1593 26
Miskell (a minor) v Bennett (deceased), Kemp & Kemp, E2-113, K2-038;
  [1997] CLY 1910 204
Mitchel v Lewis, Kemp & Kemp, B2-039; [1992] CLY 1564 151
Mitchell (a minor) v Cheshire CC, Kemp & Kemp, H3-177; [1997] CLY 1962 275
Mitchell v Burkitt, Kemp & Kemp, C6-009; [1997] CLY 1874 74
Mitchell v Rivett, Kemp & Kemp, K2-169/2, PRK-006; [1998] CLY 1733 22
Mitchell v The Post Office (1996) 96 (1) QR 7; Kemp & Kemp, I3-034;
  [1996] CLY 2312 368
Mitchell, Re [1992] CLY 1605 84
Mitchem v Kefford, Kemp & Kemp, C5-048; [1990] CLY 1605 47
Mizon v Comcon International Ltd, Kemp & Kemp, C4-013; [2000] 1 CL 125 437
Mochan and Mochan v Paterson Candy Holst, Kemp & Kemp, E3-038;
  [1993] CLY 1498 216
Mohammed, Re, Kemp & Kemp, C3-013; [1995] CLY 1664 13
Molinari v Ministry of Defence [1994] PIQR Q33; Kemp & Kemp, L3-091;
  [1994] CLY 1756 497
Molyneux v Knowsley Borough Council, Kemp & Kemp, I3-032; [1994] CLY 1710 412
Moon v Lake, Kemp & Kemp, K2-217; [1990] CLY 1702 320
Mooney (a minor) v Sait, Kemp & Kemp, J2-024/1; [1998] CLY 1551 62
Moore (Christine), Re, Kemp & Kemp, F6-072; [1993] CLY 1451 489
Moore v Hopwood, Kemp & Kemp, E3-085/2; [1999] CLY 1472 200
Moore v Mauri Products Ltd, Kemp & Kemp, K2-195; [1996] CLY 2351 468
Moore v Ministry of Defence, Kemp & Kemp, F2-077; [1991] CLY 1414 552
Moore, Re, Kemp & Kemp, C3-016; [1994] CLY 1565 110
Moore, Re, Kemp & Kemp, D2-020/1; [1998] CLY 1562 81
Moores v Dixon, Kemp & Kemp, C4-122; [1991] CLY 1359 506
Morant v Amtico Co Ltd, Kemp & Kemp, H2-024/2; [1998] CLY 1634 256
Morgan v Inco Alloys [1990] CLY 1714 322
Morgan v Southampton City Council, Kemp & Kemp, H3-169; [1995] CLY 1729 300
Morley v Heating and Ventilating Services [1992] CLY 1734 397
Morley v Sussex Coastline Buses Ltd, Kemp & Kemp, K2-253/3; [2000] 5 CL 183 195
Morrell, Re, Kemp & Kemp, J3-019; [1995] CLY 1764 384
Morris v Coal Product Holdings Ltd, Kemp & Kemp, E2-112; [2000] 4 CL 167............123
Morris v The Post Office [1992] CLY 1765 6
Morrisey v Borderdown Communication Ltd, Kemp & Kemp, I4-029;
  [1999] CLY 1522 424
Morrisey v Khosa, Kemp & Kemp, E3-018; [1996] CLY 2254 235
Morrison v Bewise plc, Kemp & Kemp, J2-040/1; [1998] CLY 1550 50
Moseley v London Underground Ltd [1999] CLY 1467 133
Moulang v Morton, Kemp & Kemp, E2-072; [1996] CLY 2223 161
Mowbray v Federal Express (UK), Kemp & Kemp, K2-140; [1991] CLY 1474 208
Moyses v Cleveland Bridge & Engineering Co, Kemp & Kemp, G2-041;
  [1994] CLY 1646 401
MP, Re, Kemp & Kemp, C4-270; [1997] CLY 1859 493
MRR, Re, Kemp & Kemp, C4-239; [1997] CLY 1843 485
Muff, Re, Kemp & Kemp, H2-019; [1994] CLY 1648 256

Mulgrew v Upper Clyde Shipbuilders Ltd, Kemp & Kemp, F2-078; [1996] CLY 2238 ..553
Mulla v Blackburn, Hyndburn and Ribble Health Authority [1992] CLY 1683 289
Mullally v Mountney, Kemp & Kemp, I2-402; [1994] CLY 1676 283
Mullett v East London and City HA, Kemp & Kemp, H5-022/1; [1997] CLY 1971 273
Mulry v William Kenyon & Son [1992] PIQR Q24; Kemp & Kemp, F2-035,
  F2-109; BPILS, I 42.1; [1991] CLY 1408 549
Munson v Richardson [1990] CLY 1706 242
Murby v Derby City Transport, Kemp & Kemp, C4-020; [1994] CLY 1568 521
Murdoch v Allerdale Borough Council, Kemp & Kemp, I4-027; [1994] CLY 1688 423
Murphy and Murphy v Carroll [1994] CLY 1712 174
Murphy v Gosforth Park Care Homes Ltd, Kemp & Kemp, H6-054;
  [1997] CLY 1977 316
Murphy v Moywest Ltd, Kemp & Kemp, H7 022; [1998] CLY 1661..............................309
Murphy v Rowlands, Kemp & Kemp, K2-209/1; [1998] CLY 1706 147
Murray (a minor) v Knowsley BC, Kemp & Kemp, H4-029/1; [1998] CLY 1649 297
Murray v TJ & T K Williams, Kemp & Kemp, H7-015/1; [1995] CLY 1739 305
Murtagh, Re, Kemp & Kemp, H3-152; [1997] CLY 1959................................288
Musmar v Kalala, Kemp & Kemp, K2-030; [1999] CLY 1565 204
Mustard v Morris, formerly in Kemp and Kemp I2-106, 604, now referred to
  only in the Law Commission's Consultation Paper Damages for Personal
  Injury: Non-Pecuniary Loss (No. 140) at 2. 32 n. 127 lix
MVR, Re, Kemp & Kemp, J3-011/1; [1996] CLY 2297 436

N (a minor) v Yorkshire Water Services Ltd, Kemp & Kemp, H3-183;
  [1999] CLY 1601 296
N, Re (CICB Quantum: 2000), Kemp & Kemp, PRC-010; [2000] 5 CL 176 495
Narroway (Ian) v Pendleton (James), Kemp & Kemp, C2-005; [1994] CLY 1554............96
Narula v Prashar [1993] CLY 1551 63
Nelson v Ellis, Kemp & Kemp, E2-057; [1993] CLY 1481 18
Nelson v Nelson Taxis (Teesside), Kemp & Kemp, I2-543; [1990] CLY 1665 369
Nelson v Page [1990] CLY 1579 59
Neuman v White, Kemp & Kemp, H3-158; [1994] CLY 1650................................268
Newing v East Sussex County Council, Kemp & Kemp, H3-154; [1991] CLY 1422......288
Newman v Hampshire County Council, Kemp & Kemp, C6-018; [1992] CLY 1621 50
Newton v Whittaker, Kemp & Kemp, K2-058; [2000] 5 CL 182 125
Newton, Re [1990] CLY 1662 385
Nicholls v Yorkshire Water Services Ltd, Kemp & Kemp, I2-404; [1998] CLY 1682......408
Nicholls, Re, Kemp & Kemp, C2-011; [1997] CLY 1834 27
Nichols v Port Eynon Transport, Kemp & Kemp, K2-210; [1991] CLY 1485 319
Nicholson v Bolton [1990] CLY 1712 510
Nicholson v Hallamshire Construction [1992] CLY 1672................................253
Nicholson v Oakleaf Conservatories, Kemp & Kemp, K2-102; [1995] CLY 1814 126
Niftylift Ltd v Walker, Kemp & Kemp, K2-208/3; [1998] CLY 1743 233
Nixon, Re, Kemp & Kemp, J2-010; [1998] CLY 1524....................................522
Noblett v Webber, Kemp & Kemp, K2-228; [1994] CLY 1741 64
Noon v Princess Alice Hospice (1998) 98 (6) QR 7; Kemp & Kemp,
  H2-025/1/1; [1998] CLY 1636..256

Norman v Taylor, Kemp & Kemp, E3-114; [1994] CLY 1629 230
Norrington v Struth, Kemp & Kemp, E3-010; [1994] CLY 1609 160
Norton v Rentokil [1990] CLY 1661..380

O (a minor) v Great Ormond Street Hospital for Children NHS Trust,
   Kemp & Kemp, J3-020/1; [1999] CLY 1529 447
O (a minor) v Rowley, Kemp & Kemp, K2-251/1; [1999] CLY 1562 509
O (a minor), Re, Kemp & Kemp, C4-259; [1997] CLY 1865 490
O'Boyle v Laurence, Kemp & Kemp, C5-038; [1997] CLY 1930 222
O'Brien (a minor) v Worthing BC, Kemp & Kemp, C5-077; [1998] CLY 1549................53
O'Brien v Berol [1990] CLY 1653 302
O'Brien v Martin, Kemp & Kemp, E2-020; [1996] CLY 2215 148
O'Brien v Moyes & Mendip Music, Kemp & Kemp, C2-053; [1998] CLY 1489 109
O'Dell v Jarvis and Whitbread, Kemp & Kemp, H3-102; [1993] CLY 1516 289
O'Donnell v Shropshire CC, Kemp & Kemp, H5-020/1; [1996] CLY 2267 301
O'Donnell v South Bedfordshire Health Authority, Kemp & Kemp, A4-001/4;
   [1990] CLY 1578 472
O'Hanlon v Merseyside Passenger Transport Executive [1990] CLY 1704 56
O'Hare v Harrogate Borough Council and Coseley Contracts, Kemp & Kemp,
   C5-057; [1993] CLY 1468 48
O'Keefe v Harvey-Kemble, Kemp & Kemp, L8-151; [1998] CLY 1761 335
O'Keefe v Webb, Kemp & Kemp, A4-017/2; [1995] CLY 1659 13
O'Leary v Howlett, Kemp & Kemp, C2-075; [1998] CLY 1481 98
O'Neill v Matthew Brown plc, Kemp & Kemp, J2-026; [1997] CLY 1996.....................273
O'Toole (deceased) v Iarnrod Eireann Irish Rail, Kemp & Kemp, F2-026/1;
   [1999] CLY 1535 554
Oades v Park, Kemp & Kemp, E3-053; [1994] CLY 1623...248
Oake v Biddlecombe, Kemp & Kemp, G2-024; [1998] CLY 1632 355
Oakley, Re [1998] CLY 1759 367
Oboh, Re, Kemp & Kemp, C5-038; [1999] CLY 1528 43
Odd v Tesco Stores, Kemp & Kemp, F6-052; [1991] CLY 1472 346
Ogilvie v Heron, Kemp & Kemp, K2-166; [1996] CLY 2345 316
Ohene v Rymer, Kemp & Kemp, K2-209; [1995] CLY 1815 23
Okine, Re, Kemp & Kemp, D3-013; [1990] CLY 1617 67
Oldfield v Batterton, Kemp & Kemp, L8-099; [1994] CLY 1723, 1753 342
Oliver v Burton, Kemp & Kemp, E2-504/3; [2000] 4 CL 159 156
Oliver v Contract Fencing Services, Kemp & Kemp, K2-211; [1995] CLY 1816 319
Orchard v Phoenix Taxis, Kemp & Kemp, I2-516/2; [1999] CLY 1511 365
Orves, Re [1992] CLY 1631 79
Osborn v Madgwick, Kemp & Kemp, I2-417; [1994] CLY 1678 399
Ostling v Hastings, Kemp & Kemp, I2-413; [1998] CLY 1677......................................398
Ostrachowcha, Re, Kemp & Kemp, B2-026; [1996] CLY 2176.....................................68
Otalor v Chez Vicky Modern Hairdressing Salon, Kemp & Kemp, J5-009;
   [1998] CLY 1557 9
Owen v Grimsby and Cleethorpes Transport [1992] PIQR Q27; (1991) The Times,
   February 14; Kemp & Kemp, E3-040; BPILS, I 126; [1990] CLY 1630 246
Owen v Prior, Kemp & Kemp, PRK-057; [1997] CLY 1894 125

Table of Cases

Owen, Re, Kemp & Kemp, C2-042; [1999] CLY 1435 106
Owens v Express Food Group, Kemp & Kemp, D3-022/1; [1991] CLY 1393 69
Oxley v BCH Ltd, Kemp & Kemp, K2-207; [1997] CLY 1832 26

P (a child) v Hammersmith and Queen Charlotte's Special HA,
  Kemp & Kemp, PRC-001; [2000] 4 CL 146 94
P (a minor) v Hampshire CC, Kemp & Kemp, PRK-009; [1999] CLY 1613.....................53
P (a minor) v Humphries [1999] CLY 1460 43
P (a minor) v Meakin, Kemp & Kemp, I4-019; [1997] CLY 1993 431
P, Re, Kemp & Kemp, B2-003/3; [1996] CLY 2172...95
P, Re, Kemp & Kemp, C4-231; [1991] CLY 1368 483
P, Re, Kemp & Kemp, C4-235; [1997] CLY 1852 484
P, Re, Kemp & Kemp, C4-260; [1990] CLY 1600 491
P, Re, Kemp & Kemp, H6-046; [1992] CLY 1695 311
Pace v McLennan, Kemp & Kemp, E3-074; [1991] CLY 1404 220
Padley v Wing, Kemp & Kemp, K2-184; [1994] CLY 1729 147
Page v Luckett, Kemp & Kemp, E2-103/1; [1998] CLY 1609..174
Page v Smith [1996] 1 AC 155; [1996] PIQR P364; [1995] 2 WLR 644;
  [1995] 2 All ER 736; [1995] 2 Lloyd's Rep 95; [1995] PIQR P239;
  [1995] RTR 210; [1995] 23 LS Gaz R 33; (1995) 145 NLJ Rep 723, HL;
  Kemp & Kemp, L8-210; BPILS, I98.8, 98.17, 105.1, VIII 61, 3403 502
Pallant, Re, Kemp & Kemp, C2-045; [1998] CLY 1522 520
Pancovics v Daffy E2-059/1; [1998] CLY 1591..157
Pape v Cumbria County Council, Kemp & Kemp, J4-011; [1991] CLY 1452 557
Parkes v Chester HA (1997) 97 (4) QR 5; Kemp & Kemp, F4-014; [1997] CLY 1950 346
Parkes, Re [1992] CLY 1782 500
Parkinson v Longfield Care Homes, Kemp & Kemp, E3-106; [1995] CLY 1714 228
Parkinson v Trust House Forte [1993] CLY 1571 5
Parnham (a minor) v Metropolitan Housing Trust Ltd, Kemp & Kemp, 13-031;
  [1997] CLY 2007 391
Parrington v Marriot, Kemp & Kemp, C4-216; [1998] CLY 1509 479
Parslow, Re [1992] CLY 1713 408
Partington v Moore, Kemp & Kemp, I4-014; [1991] CLY 1434......................................395
Patel v Patel [1993] CLY 1589 468
Patterson v Midland Bank plc, Kemp & Kemp, PRI-007; [2000] 5 CL 190 406
Patterson v Whitbread and Company [1992] CLY 1696 457
Pattison, Re, Kemp & Kemp, C2-077; [1999] CLY 1432 99
Paul v Glickman (deceased), Kemp & Kemp, F5-018/1; [1999] CLY 1542 352
Paul v Payne, Kemp & Kemp, K2-046; [1995] CLY 1783...124
Pauley v London Borough of Southwark [1992] CLY 1694...330
Pawson v Neil, Kemp & Kemp, E2-126; [2000] 4 CL 156 182
Paxton v Newman, Kemp & Kemp, K2-238; [1995] CLY 1818 130
Payne v Jackson, Kemp & Kemp, I2-511; [1993] CLY 1533...385
Peach v Tesco Stores Ltd, Kemp & Kemp, i2-316; [1998] CLY 1665 387
Pearce v Abraham Shaw & Co, Kemp & Kemp, E2-119; [1995] CLY 1784 125
Pearce v Hampshire County Council, Kemp & Kemp, I2-526; [1991] CLY 1454 396
Pearce v Humpit Removals Ltd, Kemp & Kemp, EC-105/3; [2000] 3 CL 176................231

Pearson v British Midland Airways, Kemp & Kemp, C4-056; [1998] CLY 1530 529
Pearson, Re [1992] CLY 1628 84
Pedley v Timmins, Kemp & Kemp, E3-028; [1990] CLY 1628......................................134
Pegg v Denford Machine Tools, Kemp & Kemp, E2-028; [1993] CLY 1434 135
Pennell, Re, Kemp & Kemp, B2-041/1; [1996] CLY 2177 3
Pepperall v Memory Lane Cakes Ltd, Kemp & Kemp, K2-248/1; [2000] 4 CL 172 321
Pereira, Re, Kemp & Kemp, I2-425; [1995] CLY 1752 409
Perkins, Re, Kemp & Kemp, C6-001; [2000] 1 CL 119 29
Peskett and Peskett v Morris (No. 1), Kemp & Kemp, I3-029/1; [1996] CLY 2302..........49
Peskett and Peskett v Morris (No. 2), Kemp & Kemp, C2-082; [1996] CLY 2171 115
Peters v Robinson, Kemp & Kemp, B2-036/1; [1997] CLY 1828 417
Peters v Worthing District Health Authority, Kemp & Kemp, H6-049, K2-039;
  [1990] CLY 1675 331
Pheasant v Lowrey, Kemp & Kemp, I2-312; [1996] CLY 2276 363
Phillips (Marcus Timothy) v Southern Vectis, Kemp & Kemp, I4-033;
  [1994] CLY 1690 425
Phillips v Kannike-Martins Associates [1993] CLY 1470 9
Philpotts v Gheest Holdings [1991] CLY 1483 279
Phipps v Goldpasta, Kemp & Kemp, I3-029; [1994] CLY 1689 425
Pigott, Re, Kemp & Kemp, K2-111; [1996] CLY 2330 394
Pike v BWOC Ltd, Kemp & Kemp, E2-059/3; [1998] CLY 1592 158
Pinder v Hardings (FT) & Son, Kemp & Kemp, H7-018; [1991] CLY 1431 307
Piotrowsk, Re i (1996) 96 (4) QR 8' Kemp & Kemp, K2-163; [1996] CLY 2346 22
Pitman v Clarke, Kemp & Kemp, E3-096; [1993] CLY 1496 239
Pitt, Re, Kemp & Kemp, C2-061; [1993] CLY 1442 111
Pittham v North Glamorgan NHS Trust, Kemp & Kemp, K2-144/2; [1999] CLY 1571 ..80
Pittman v Perrier, Kemp & Kemp, C2-046; [1996] CLY 2165 24
Pitts (A Minor), Re [1992] CLY 1568 111
Pizzey v Ford Motor Co (1993) The Times, March 8; [1993] 17 LS Gaz R 46;
  Kemp & Kemp, I2-529; BPILS, XI 3590; [1994] CLY 1674..367
Plume v Mason Bros (Butchers) Ltd [2000] 6 CL 194 290
Podd v Ransomes and Napier, Kemp & Kemp, J3-021; [1994] CLY 1576 438
Poleon v Ramdhani, Kemp & Kemp, K2-245/2; [1998] CLY 1740 195
Poll v Mohammed, Kemp & Kemp, I2-433; [1999] CLY 1518 344
Pollard v Blackman, Kemp & Kemp, K2-015; [1995] CLY 1706..................................143
Pomfret v County Palatine Housing Society Ltd [1996] CLY 2250 384
Porter v United Parcels Services Ltd, Kemp & Kemp, E2-080/5; [1998] CLY 1580 120
Porter v Wilton Contracts Ltd, Kemp & Kemp, H6-036; [1999] CLY 1505................329
Potter, Re, Kemp & Kemp, C2-059; [1996] CLY 2167 14
Pottinger (a minor) v Bendigo Construction Ltd, Kemp & Kemp, J2-023;
  [1998] CLY 1693 272
Power v Kitchener [1990] CLY 1582 90
Pownall, Re, Kemp & Kemp, E2-101; [1993] CLY 1555..121
Prangley v National Power [1995] CLY 1809..317
Price v B H Components (Clwyd), Kemp & Kemp, K2-132 [1991] CLY 1476 208
Pritchard v Cumberland Motor Services Ltd, Kemp & Kemp, H3-155;
  [1997] CLY 1960 267

Proctor v Hussain, Kemp & Kemp, E2-035; [1996] CLY 2217 198
Pucci v Reigate and Banstead District Council, Kemp & Kemp, I2-406;
   [1992] CLY 1711 408
Pugh v Chesterfield Borough Council, Kemp & Kemp, K2-098; [1994] CLY 1717........341
Pullar v Aldi Stores Ltd, Kemp & Kemp, H6-023/1; [1999] CLY 1502 302
Pullen v Bird's Eye Walls, Kemp & Kemp, K2-202; [1995] CLY 1738 319
Purcell, Re [1992] CLY 1719 420
Purkis v Rehman, Kemp & Kemp, I3-016/1; [1997] CLY 1980 383
Purvis, Re, Kemp & Kemp, D4-018/3; [1998] CLY 1565 66
Pyke v Summers, Kemp & Kemp, 13-015; [1991] CLY 1442 416
Pyrah v Tickles Nightclub [1992] CLY 1670 358

R (a minor) v Bradmarr Joiners, Kemp & Kemp, C5-031; [1997] CLY 1872 42
R (a minor) v Calderdale MBC, Kemp & Kemp, K2-047/2; [1999] CLY 1600................296
R (a minor) v Mohamed, Kemp & Kemp, K2-066/2; [1999] CLY 1554...........................37
R (minors) v Putt, Kemp & Kemp, K2-248; [1999] CLY 1561 22
R and R, Re, Kemp & Kemp, C4-236; [1994] CLY 1580..484
R and S, Re, Kemp & Kemp, C4-103; [1998] CLY 1535 537
R v Gardner, Kemp & Kemp, PRL-001; [2000] 4 CL 166 467
R, Re (1996) Kemp & Kemp, J3-015; [1996] CLY 2180 437
R, Re [1992] CLY 1562 442
R, Re [1998] CLY 1519 496
R, Re [1999] CLY 1455 536
R, Re, Kemp & Kemp, C4-017; [1992] CLY 1574 541
R, Re, Kemp & Kemp, C4-215; [1990] CLY 1595 479
R, Re, Kemp & Kemp, C4-241; [1998] CLY 1511 486
Radley v Claremount Garments Ltd, Kemp & Kemp, K2-159/1; [1999] CLY 1525 371
Rafferty v Skelton, Kemp & Kemp, E2-095; [1994] CLY 1613.......................................170
Rafiq v Crendley (t/a Lewis Motor Repairs), Kemp & Kemp, H5-024;
   [1994] CLY 1664 310
Rahman, Re, Kemp & Kemp, C5-045; [1995] CLY 1685 46
Ralph v Smith [1990] CLY 1690 325
Ramsay v CICB, Kemp & Kemp, H3-167; [1994] CLY 1706 275
Ramsbottom v Novacki, Kemp & Kemp, J5-008; [1997] CLY 1875...................................8
Randall and Randall v England, Kemp & Kemp, E2-065; [1996] CLY 2221 152
Randall v Feredenzi and Tomlyn, Kemp & Kemp, E2-075; [1995] CLY 1704 140
Ranger, Re, Kemp & Kemp, C4-051; [1998] CLY 1539 88
Rathbone v Liverpool County Council, Kemp & Kemp, K2-121; [1992] CLY 1748......333
Ravenscroft v Clarke, Kemp & Kemp, F6-016; [1990] CLY 1677...................................340
Rayner, Re, Kemp & Kemp, J3-038; [1991] CLY 1461 369
Read v British Railways Board, Kemp & Kemp, D3-026/1; [1998] CLY 1564 71
Read, Re, Kemp & Kemp, A3-012; [1992] CLY 1559 470
RED, Re, Kemp & Kemp, C4-265; [1993] CLY 1463 492
Redfern, Re [1990] CLY 1615 88
Reed v Sunderland HA (1998) The Times, October 16, Kemp & Kemp,
   C4-019, F4-019/1; BPILS, I 41.8; [1998] CLY 1629..335
Rees v Hooper, Kemp & Kemp, E2-064/1; [1997] CLY 1902 201

Rees v Mabco (102) Ltd, Kemp & Kemp, IT-431; [1999] CLY 1534...............553
Rees v Walker [1992] CLY 1643 120
Reeves v Ford Motor Co, Kemp & Kemp, K2-215; [1994] CLY 1736 55
Reid v Chowdhury, Kemp & Kemp, K2-244; [1997] CLY 1991 414
Reid v Simpson, Kemp & Kemp, I3-072; [1993] CLY 1432 244
Reynolds v TNT (UK) Ltd, Kemp & Kemp, i2-310; [1998] CLY 1663 382
RH, Re [1991] CLY 1362 111
RH, Re, Kemp & Kemp, C2-054; [1998] CLY 1488 109
Rhodes v Soor, Kemp & Kemp, I2-535; [1998] CLY 1670 391
Rhodes v Watson, Kemp & Kemp, C3-015; [1993] CLY 1445 107
Rice v Garrett [1990] CLY 1697 192
Richards v Hampshire CC, Kemp & Kemp, H4-036; [2000] 5 CL 188 294
Richards v Jones, Kemp & Kemp, E2-097/1; [1998] CLY 1716 203
Richards v Prodger, Kemp & Kemp, E2-026/1; [1999] CLY 1469 149
Richardson v Davy Roll Co Ltd, Kemp & Kemp, I2-441; [1998] CLY 1679 405
Richardson v Dunning, Kemp & Kemp, E2-064/2; [1999] CLY 1475 160
Richardson v Durham County Council [1992] CLY 1675...............255
Riches v A E Timmins and Son [1992] CLY 1658 229
Richley v Cooper, Kemp & Kemp, I2-516; [1992] CLY 1716...............421
Ridley v Pattenden and Batchelor, Kemp & Kemp, C2-055; [1994] CLY 1560...............110
Rigby, Re [1992] CLY 1617 460
Rigby, Re, Kemp & Kemp, C5-022; [1998] CLY 1543 24
Riggs v East Dorset HA, Kemp & Kemp, F5-022; [1991] CLY 1417 353
Riley v AC Products (St Helens), Kemp & Kemp, M5-017/1; [1992] CLY 1785 38
Riley v Graham, Kemp & Kemp, E3-037; [1994] CLY 1553...............135
Ringer v Criddle, Kemp & Kemp, I3-027/2; [1995] CLY 1760...............419
Ritter v British Steel plc, Kemp & Kemp, K2-248/2; [2000] 4 CL 173...............321
RM (a person under disability) v Richards 99 (1) QR 6; Kemp & Kemp, E2-005/2; [1998] CLY 1578 116
Roberts v Hunt, Kemp & Kemp, H4-020/1; [1997] CLY 1969 293
Roberts v Kendrick [1992] CLY 1570 113
Roberts, Re, Kemp & Kemp, C2-025; [1997] CLY 1835 102
Roberts, Re, Kemp & Kemp, H3-164; [1994] CLY 1652 271
Roberts-Smith, Re, Kemp & Kemp, E3-081; [1995] CLY 1711 249
Robinson v Hart [1992] CLY 1609 44
Robinson v Taylor and Roger Clark Cars [1992] CLY 1687 293
Robinson, Re, Kemp & Kemp, C6-022; [1991] CLY 1386 76
Robson v Safeway plc, Kemp & Kemp, H6-038/2; [1998] CLY 1653...............308
Rodrigues v Woods, Kemp & Kemp, A4-015/2; [1994] CLY 1555 97
Rogers v Birdseye Wall's [1992] CLY 1700 277
Rogers v Birmingham City Council, Kemp & Kemp, E3-063; [1997] CLY 1928...............221
Rogers v Bromley LBC, Kemp & Kemp, K2-056/2; [1999] CLY 1570 63
Rogers v Dunkley, Kemp & Kemp, K2-190; [1991] CLY 1484 372
Rooker v Metro Cammell Ltd, Kemp & Kemp, F2-025/1; [1998] CLY 1622 554
Rooney v Palmer, Kemp & Kemp, E2-054/1; [1999] CLY 1473 156
Rosa v Charles, James and Ellington, Kemp & Kemp, J5-007; [1991] CLY 1390 8
Rosamund v TRW Valves, Kemp & Kemp, H6-042; [1990] CLY 1658 331

Table of Cases

Roseje v Lambourne, Kemp & Kemp, I2-532; [1995] CLY 1747 391
Rosingdale, Re, Kemp & Kemp, C5-058; [1999] CLY 1457 49
Ross v Bowbelle and Marchioness, Kemp & Kemp, C4-097; [1991] CLY 1355 537
Rothwell v Hodson, Kemp & Kemp, E2-077; [1994] CLY 1704.......................................164
Rothwell v Hodson, Kemp & Kemp, E2-077; [1995] CLY 1770.......................................165
Rothwell, Re, Kemp & Kemp, J3-014; [1994] CLY 1697 57
Rouse v Doncaster Metropolitan Borough Council, Kemp & Kemp, I3-035;
    [1994] CLY 1686 413
Routledge v Shires [1992] CLY 1666 234
Rowe v Waddington Technical Services [1990] CLY 1621..161
Rowland v Griffin, Kemp & Kemp, I2-317; [1997] CLY 1961 290
Rowland v Matthews, Kemp & Kemp, K2-201; [1997] CLY 1882 130
Rowland, Re, Kemp & Kemp, C5-052; [1990] CLY 1604 47
Roy v Greenline Carriers, Kemp & Kemp, E2-129/2; [1998] CLY 1720..........................183
Rubidge v Harvey, Kemp & Kemp, E2-109; [1996] CLY 2309 178
Rubins v Employment Office, Kemp & Kemp, L3-051; [1997] CLY 2023......................499
Rucastle v Cumberland Motor Services Ltd, Kemp & Kemp, H2-025;
    [1997] CLY 1956 257
Rudd v North Eastern Electricity Board [1992] CLY 1712 397
Ruparelia v Odedra, Kemp & Kemp, K2-239; [1998] CLY 1711 26
Rush v Mobil Oil Co Ltd, Kemp & Kemp, K2-208/2; [1998] CLY 1714 541
Rushton v Bairdwear, Kemp & Kemp, K2-179; [1993] CLY 1579 317
Rushton v Gee, Kemp & Kemp, PRC-002; [2000] 3 CL 177 136
Rushton v Jervis [2000] 4 CL 147..100
Russell v John Williams Foundaries, Kemp & Kemp, E3-126; [1994] CLY 1630............233
Russell v Nathan, Kemp & Kemp, E3-027/2[1998] CLY 1568 261
Rutherford v Wandsworth LBC, Kemp & Kemp, G2-041; [1998] CLY 1633.................359
Rutland v Ferguson, Kemp & Kemp, H3-054; [1998] CLY 1643 288
Rutter v Stevenage BC, Kemp & Kemp, 13-020/1; [1999] CLY 1517...............................285
Ryan v Trans Manche Link, Kemp & Kemp, I2-201/2; [1994] CLY 1669 462

S (a child) v Bloomfield, Kemp & Kemp, PRC-013; [2000] 3 CL 169 62
S (a child) v Forrester, Kemp & Kemp, PRC-004; [2000] 3 CL 163 29
S (a minor) v Calderdale MBC, Kemp & Kemp, K2-256; [1999] CLY 1563.....................56
S (a minor) v Glynn Webb Wallpapers, Kemp & Kemp, PRK-005; [1999] CLY 1610 427
S (a minor) v Hearnshaw, Kemp & Kemp, C4-081; [1999] CLY 1454 533
S (a minor) v Portsmouth and South EastHampshire HA, Kemp & Kemp, PRA-001;
    [2000] 1 CL 116 93
S (a minor) v Somerset HA, Kemp & Kemp, PRA-003; [1999] CLY 1546 94
S (a minor) v St Helier NHS Trust, Kemp & Kemp, J2-014/1; [1996] CLY 2201 19
S and B, Re, Kemp & Kemp, C4-210; [1999] CLY 1441 477
S v S [1998] CLY 1510..483
S, Re (CICB Quantum: 1999)(Sexual Abuse), Kemp & Kemp, PRC-011;
    [2000] 3 CL 164 494
S, Re [1991] CLY 1349 33
S, Re, Kemp & Kemp, C4-107; [1990] CLY 1601 496
S, Re, Kemp & Kemp, C4-264; [1999] CLY 1442 492

Sadler v Thomas, Kemp & Kemp, I2-407; [1991] CLY 1437 395
Saggers v Lee Valley Regional Park Authority, Kemp & Kemp, E3-082;
    [1990] CLY 1635 224
Saggu v Worrod, Kemp & Kemp, K2-029; [1995] CLY 1780 177
Salmon v SJT Stafford Ltd, Kemp & Kemp, K2-243; [1997] CLY 1917 194
Samler v Shaw, Kemp & Kemp, B2-004/1/1; [1999] CLY 1430 23
Sampson v Georgiou, Kemp & Kemp, I2-303; [1997] CLY 1979....................................381
Sams v Olley, Kemp & Kemp, H3-056; [1998] CLY 1644 283
Sanders, Re, Kemp & Kemp, C2-002; [1996] CLY 2163 497
Sanderson v Precision Engineering, Kemp & Kemp, H7-014/1; [1993] CLY 1528 328
Sandford v British Railways Board, Kemp & Kemp, PRF-001; [2000] 1 CL 126 552
Sandifer v Spanton, Kemp & Kemp, K2-120; [1992] CLY 1754.....................................207
Sangster v Kensington Building Services, Kemp & Kemp, K2-139; [1997] CLY 1913....187
Santos, Re, Kemp & Kemp, E2-038; [1995] CLY 1697 16
Sargent v Jeffs [1992] CLY 1758 188
Saunders v Hammersmith and Fulham LBC, Kemp & Kemp, E3-030/2;
    [1998] CLY 1570 236
Saunders, Re, Kemp & Kemp, C4-275; [1993] CLY 1464..494
Savage v ICI plc, Kemp & Kemp, F6-047/1; [1996] CLY 2248..343
Savage v Paramount, Kemp & Kemp, G2-043; [1995] CLY 1722 359
Savory v Birmingham, Kemp & Kemp, H3-155/2; [1996] CLY 2362 116
Sawford v Sabourn, Kemp & Kemp, C4-115; [1996] CLY 2305......................................174
Schembri, Re (CICB Quantum: 1999), Kemp & Kemp, PRI-001; [2000] 4 CL 163 462
Schooling v Bird, Kemp & Kemp, K2-092; [1996] CLY 2326..184
Scott v Gage, Kemp & Kemp, I2-409; [1997] CLY 1983 323
Scott v Higgins Potato Merchants, Kemp & Kemp, H6-044; [1993] CLY 1526..............465
Scott v Kennedy Construction Group Ltd [1996] CLY 2233 222
Scott v Miller, Kemp & Kemp, K2-274; [1998] CLY 1750 408
Scott v Theatre Royal (Plymouth) [1992] CLY 1718 412
Scourfield and British Gas plc v Gammon, Kemp & Kemp, K2-033;
    [1997] CLY 2010 231
SCP, Re [1992] CLY 1705 285
Sear v Stamford Pantomime Players [1991] CLY 1448 436
Seedin, Re, Kemp & Kemp, E2-011; [1994] CLY 1574 529
Segree v Shepherd [1992] CLY 1644...169
Severs v Dudley, Kemp & Kemp, K2-059; [1996] CLY 2314 180
Seymour v Passmore International, Kemp & Kemp, E3-090; [1994] CLY 1626 251
Sharkey v Cassar [1991] CLY 1432 380
Sharma (Harshed), Re, Kemp & Kemp, A4-004; [1997] CLY 1824 92
Sharp v MTL Trust Holdings, Kemp & Kemp, K2-131; [1995] CLY 1795 127
Sharpe v Woods, Kemp & Kemp, B2-002; [1994] CLY 1546 469
Shaw v Frost, Kemp & Kemp, E2-129; [1994] CLY 1619 206
Shaw v Grazette, Kemp & Kemp, D4-020; [1994] CLY 1586...52
Shaw v Wirral Health Authority [1993] 4 Med LR 275; Kemp & Kemp,
    H2-012; [1993] CLY 1514 132
Sheil v Chamberlain, Kemp & Kemp, E3-073; [1991] CLY 1405....................................224
Shenton v Christchurch Ski Centre [1996] CLY 2279 388

Shepherd v Iceland Group plc, Kemp & Kemp, E2-076/2; [1998] CLY 1536 538
Sheppard v Neville and Sagar, Kemp & Kemp, C4-117; [1992] CLY 1585 539
Shields v Liverpool School of Tropical Medicine [1992] CLY 1591................461
Shields v Vera [1995] CLY 1769 119
Shillington-Thorne v Stevens, Kemp & Kemp, C6-027; [1991] CLY 1387 78
Shimmin, Re, Kemp & Kemp, H5-019; [1992] CLY 1691 301
Shioda v Fitzgerald Light Ring [1992] CLY 1714 401
Shone v Rigby, Kemp & Kemp, C2-013; [1998] CLY 1491 98
Short v Mathewman [1991] CLY 1471................207
Short v Trustees of Yeovil Agricultural Society, Kemp & Kemp, I4-031;
    [2000] 1 CL 123 433
Silver v Ford Motor Company [1992] CLY 1778 27
Sim, Re, Kemp & Kemp, C5-061; [1995] CLY 1775 20
Simmonds v Smith, Kemp & Kemp, K2-085; [1991] CLY 1468................207
Simmonds, Re, Kemp & Kemp, C4-110; [1995] CLY 1675 538
Simmons, Re, Kemp & Kemp, F4-018, F4-019; [1991] CLY 1419 443
Simms v Walls, Kemp & Kemp, K2-160/1; [2000] 3 CL 186 209
Simon, Re [1994] CLY 1557................100
Simpkins v British Rail Engineering Ltd., Kemp & Kemp, F2-026;
    [1991] CLY 1496 554
Simpson v Grant, Kemp & Kemp, K2-145/8; [2000] 4 CL 171 189
Simpson v Liverpool City Council [1995] CLY 1791................393
Simpson, Re, Kemp & Kemp, C4-071; [1990] CLY 1589 503
Simson v Sutton, Kemp & Kemp, K2-170/7; [1999] CLY 1557 241
Sinfield v Department of Transport, Kemp & Kemp, i2-515/2; [1998] CLY 1666 364
Singh v Dhillon, Kemp & Kemp, H3-012/1; [1998] CLY 1642 282
Singh v M&N Contractors Ltd [2000] 6 CL 195 144
Singh, Re, Kemp & Kemp, C5-056; [1990] CLY 1606 19
Singh, Re, Kemp & Kemp, H6-032; [1996] CLY 2269 305
Singleton v Samor Electrical [1992] CLY 1745................440
Sivieri v Mills, Kemp & Kemp, E2-129/1; [1998] CLY 1719 183
SJY, Re, Kemp & Kemp, C4-267; [1998] CLY 1517 492
Skerry v Liverpool City Council [1992] CLY 1752................297
Skipp v Fisher, Kemp & Kemp, B2-035; [1991] CLY 1430 59
SKR, Re, Kemp & Kemp, C4-255; [1994] CLY 1583................504
Slater, Re, Kemp & Kemp, C4-050; [1993] CLY 1448................502
Slater, Re, Kemp & Kemp, K2-079; [1995] CLY 1789................260
Slimings v South Glamorgan Health Authority, Kemp & Kemp,
    C4-111; [1992] CLY 1592 441
Slotz Vending and Egleton v Avandero UK Ltd [1998] CLY 1635................256
Small v United Engineering Steels [1992] CLY 1771 430
Smee v Adye, Kemp & Kemp, B2-011/1; [1999] CLY 1427 2
Smith (Brynmor), Re, Kemp & Kemp, B2-031; [1997] CLY 1826 113
Smith (JG), Re, Kemp & Kemp, B2-021; [1994] CLY 1562................112
Smith (Natalie) v Miller [1992] CLY 1727 456
Smith v Advanced Plant, Kemp & Kemp, L7-024; [1994] CLY 1750................4

Smith v Ainger and O'Donnell (1990) The Times, 5 June; Kemp & Kemp,
  F3-012/1; BPILS, VIII 3005; XI4024; [1991] CLY 1416..133
Smith v Arcadia Group plc, Kemp & Kemp, PRE-005; [1999] CLY 1471 152
Smith v Baker and McKenzie, Kemp & Kemp, H8-013; [1994] CLY 1662 304
Smith v Beeline Buzz Co, Kemp & Kemp, PRE-012; [1999] CLY 1574 142
Smith v Blue Band Motors, Kemp & Kemp, K2-226; [1996] CLY 2356.........................281
Smith v Cape, Kemp & Kemp, F2-039; [1991] CLY 1409 549
Smith v Cottrell, Kemp & Kemp, K2-268; [1998] CLY 1709 65
Smith v Creedon and Yiasoumi, Kemp & Kemp, I2-534; [1993] CLY 1537 368
Smith v Dicks Eagle Insulation Ltd, Kemp & Kemp, F2-038; [1997] CLY 1942 555
Smith v Ellis [1992] CLY 1646 122
Smith v Halstead Plastics [1992] CLY 1690 300
Smith v Hurst, Kemp & Kemp, K2-082; [1991] CLY 1465..461
Smith v Jagger [1990] CLY 1668...400
Smith v Musso (t/a Ficarazzi), Kemp & Kemp, J5-004; [1991] CLY 1389 8
Smith v Salford HA [1994] 5 Med LR 321; 23 BMLR 137; BPILS, XI 9323;
  [1996] CLY 2214 471
Smith v Stickley, Kemp & Kemp, C4-090; [1997] CLY 1860 516
Smith v Warrington Health Authority, Kemp & Kemp, A4-004/1; BPILS,
  XVII 1258; [1994] CLY 1540...473
Smith, Re, Kemp & Kemp, B2-015; [1990] CLY 1580 83
Smith, Re, Kemp & Kemp, D2-022; [1992] CLY 1627 83
Smith, Re, Kemp & Kemp, I2-528; [1993] CLY 1536...390
Smith, Re, Kemp & Kemp, J5-072;[1993] CLY 1472 10
Smithies v Eatoughs, Kemp & Kemp, H4-025; [1990] CLY 1650 292
Snelling v Evans, Kemp & Kemp, K2-209/2; [1999] CLY 1602 280
SNH (a minor), Re, Kemp & Kemp, C4-268; [1994] CLY 1584 492
Socha v Gage, Kemp & Kemp, E2-085; [1995] CLY 1772 121
Sola v Royal Marsden Hospital, Kemp & Kemp, F2-047; [1997] CLY 1948..................545
Solanki v Land Rover (UK) Ltd, Kemp & Kemp, H4-025/1; [1996] CLY 2264 272
Sollis v Hughes, Hughes, Colson (T/A Byron Construction) and Broad,
  Kemp & Kemp, E3-043/1; [1997] CLY 1925..149
Somerset v Simpkin Machin & Co Ltd, Kemp & Kemp, F2-041; [1997] CLY 1944 550
Somwaru v London Electricity, Kemp & Kemp, C4-066; [1995] CLY 1670 531
Soper v Midland Rollmakers [1991] CLY 1491 281
Soudah v Villarreai, Kemp & Kemp, K2-227; [1993] CLY 1581.....................................333
Southeran v Singh, Kemp & Kemp, E2-141/1; [1998] CLY 1736 192
Southward v Peers Recovery, Kemp & Kemp, K2-097; [1997] CLY 1938 145
Southwell v Calderdale Metropolitan Borough Council, Kemp & Kemp,
  I2-422; [1993] CLY 1541..404
Southworth v Taberner, Kemp & Kemp, K2-199; [1997] CLY 1885 191
Sowerby v North Yorkshire CC [1996] CLY 2286 417
Spalding v NSS Newsagents and Avery, Kemp & Kemp, C4-015; [1998] CLY 1545 38
Spearman (Sandra Jean), Re, Kemp & Kemp, E2-008; [1994] CLY 1598 134
Speechly v Spencer, Kemp & Kemp, K2-016; [1990] CLY 1674.....................................368
Speed (a minor) v G & A Shipman, Kemp & Kemp, G2-045; [1998] CLY 1671 360
Spencer v Arco, Kemp & Kemp, F2-018/6, F2-028; [1996] CLY 2240 548

Spencer v BRB, Kemp & Kemp, H6-047; [1991] CLY 1457 311
Stanley v Rosewell, Kemp & Kemp, E2-139/2; [1997] CLY 1881 190
Stanley, Re [1992] CLY 1626 88
Stannard v Flanagan, Kemp & Kemp, E2-089; [1994] CLY 1705 168
Stansfield v Alexon Group t/a Mead Manufacturing, Kemp & Kemp, I4-038;
 [1995] CLY 1811 429
Stanton v St Helens and Knowsley Health Authority, Kemp & Kemp, F4-032;
 [1993] CLY 1509 350
Steadman v Gaffar, Kemp & Kemp, H2-020/1; [1996] CLY 2255 255
Steeksma v British Aerospace plc, Kemp & Kemp, I2-477; [1996] CLY 2352 407
Stephens & Stephens v Mander, Kemp & Kemp, C5-073; [1993] CLY 1570 53
Steveley v Harvey, Kemp & Kemp, K2-158; [1995] CLY 1802 394
Stevenson v Townsend, Kemp & Kemp, E3-095/1; [1998] CLY 1616 227
Steventon v Cotmor Tool and Presswork Co., Kemp & Kemp, C4-014;
 [1990] CLY 1587 322
Steward v Gates Hydraulics, Kemp & Kemp, I2-414; [1995] CLY 1748 398
Stewart-Davies v Sinton, Kemp & Kemp, PRK-011; [1999] CLY 1593 147
Stibbs v British Gas plc, Kemp & Kemp, L2-107; [1996] CLY 2364 468
Stimpson v Beevor Castings, Kemp & Kemp, H4-017/1; [1996] CLY 2263 269
Stimson v Williams, Kemp & Kemp, E2-132; [1996] CLY 2339 187
Stobbart v Ryan, Kemp & Kemp, L8-215; [1998] CLY 1757 199
Stock, Re, Kemp & Kemp, H3-164/1; [1998] CLY 1640 292
Stockley, Re, Kemp & Kemp, K2-144/1; [1998] CLY 1726 287
Stocks v Wadsworth, Kemp & Kemp, J3-018/1; [1997] CLY 2001 445
Stokes v Forestry Commission, Kemp & Kemp, I2-514/1; [1996] CLY 2277 386
Stokle, Re, Kemp & Kemp, J3-014/1; [1997] CLY 2005 437
Stone v Commissioner of Police of the Metropolis, Kemp & Kemp,
 PRE-001; [2000] 2 CL 145 213
Stone v Redair Mersey Agencies, Kemp & Kemp, F2-038/2, F2-066;
 [1996] CLY 2244 546
Stoneman, Re, Kemp & Kemp, C2-070; [1997] CLY 1838 113
Stonier, Re, Kemp & Kemp, E3-022; [1993] CLY 1488 215
Storey v Rae, Kemp & Kemp, I4-011; [1998] CLY 1692 431
Storfer v Yogaratnam 98 (6) QR 6; Kemp & Kemp, E2-091/1; [1998] CLY 1601 169
Stote v Anderson, Kemp & Kemp, H3-056/1; [1995] CLY 1725 443
Strainge v HO, Kemp & Kemp, E2-020/1; [1998] CLY 1583 148
Stratford v British Rail Engineering Ltd, Kemp & Kemp, F2-045; [1991] CLY 1498 555
Straughan v Scaife [1996] CLY 2350 361
Streatfield v Long, Kemp & Kemp, H6-033; [1990] CLY 1656 305
Streets v Direct Image Litho Services Ltd, Kemp & Kemp, H5-015/1;
 [1996] CLY 2266 326
Stride (A) v Lipscombe, Kemp & Kemp, E2-131/1, K2-205; [1997] CLY 1915 192
Stride (S) v Lipscombe, Kemp & Kemp, E2-131/1[1997] CLY 2015 146
Studd, Re, Kemp & Kemp, D2-020/2; [1996] CLY 2211 83
Sturley v Carmarthen Town Council, Kemp & Kemp, 13-027; [1998] CLY 1685 418
Styles v Liverpool City Council [1992] CLY 1622 77
Suffler v Bell, Kemp & Kemp, K2-151; [1995] CLY 1801 22

Suleman, Re, Kemp & Kemp, C2-069; [1995] CLY 1661 112
Sullivan v Massin-Smart, Kemp & Kemp, K2-224/1; [1998] CLY 1739 193
Sumners v Mid Downs HA and Brighton HA [1996] CLY 2366 349
Surdivall v K Walker Transport, Kemp & Kemp, E2-076/1; [1998] CLY 1597 163
Surrey v Manchester Health Commission, Kemp & Kemp, E3-114/1;
  [1998] CLY 1619 230
Sutcliffe v Heywood Williams Group plc, Kemp & Kemp, F2-035/1;
  [1998] CLY 1624 549
Suttle v Amec Process & Energy Ltd, Kemp & Kemp, E3-069/2; [1999] CLY 1488........136
Sutton v Ling, Kemp & Kemp, C2-077; [1999] CLY 1550 18
Swales, Re, Kemp & Kemp, C5-029; [1991] CLY 1379...70
Swan v Bush, Kemp & Kemp, E2-095/2; [1999] CLY 1578 171
Sweeney v South Tyneside Borough Council, Kemp & Kemp, 13-019;
  [1992] CLY 1717 417
Swift, Re, Kemp & Kemp, C4-018; [1996] CLY 2181 511
Swinhoe v Taylor and Mainline, Kemp & Kemp, I2-434; [1996] CLY 2283 403
Sykes, Re, Kemp & Kemp, H6-052; [1994] CLY 1667 314
Sylvester, Re, Kemp & Kemp, C5-021; [1992] CLY 1582 446
Szulc v Howard, Kemp & Kemp, C4-113; [1995] CLY 1676 544

T (a minor) v Luton & Dunstable Hospital NHS Trust, Kemp & Kemp,
  PRA-002; [1999] CLY 1545 93
T (a minor) v Moloney, Kemp & Kemp, K2-102/3; [1999] CLY 1588 185
T, G and J, Re, Kemp & Kemp, C4-036, M4-070; [1990] CLY 1588 501
T, Re [1999] CLY 1437 31
T, Re, Kemp & Kemp, C4-055; [1993] CLY 1449 68
T, Re, Kemp & Kemp, C4-251; [1991] CLY 1373 488
T, Re, Kemp & Kemp, C4-275; [1993] CLY 1465 495
Taiani v Hill, Kemp & Kemp, C5-067; [1994] CLY 1587 52
Tallentire, Re, Kemp & Kemp, F4-027; [1998] CLY 1621 3
Tansley, Re, Kemp & Kemp, A2-006/2; [1992] CLY 1557 472
Tate v West Cornwall and Isles of Scilly Health Authority, Kemp & Kemp,
  A3-008; [1994] CLY 1543 470
Taylor v Ansari, Kemp & Kemp, E2-120; [1996] CLY 2315 180
Taylor v IBC Vehicles Ltd [1999] CLY 1491 223
Taylor v IMI Yorkshire Imperial, Kemp & Kemp; H6-039; [1990] CLY 1657 330
Taylor v Orion Express Parcels [1992] CLY 1645 122
Taylor v R & S Thompson, Kemp & Kemp, PRE-019; [1995] CLY 1782 20
Taylor v The Post Office [1991] CLY 1475 333
Taylor v Turner, Kemp & Kemp, K2-230/1; [1998] CLY 1738 130
Taylor v Walkley, Meagher and Poll, Kemp & Kemp, I2-305; [1991] CLY 1438 395
Taylor, Re, Kemp & Kemp, C2-074; [1994] CLY 1564 17
Taylor, Re, Kemp & Kemp, D2-046/1; [1997] CLY 1866 48
Teague v Camden LBC, Kemp & Kemp, C4-077; [1997] CLY 1858................................532
Temelkowski v McMath, Kemp & Kemp, C6-071; [1998] CLY 1556...............................74
Thakar v Bakar, Kemp & Kemp, C4-084; [1991] CLY 1352 41
Thakerar v Pajman, Kemp & Kemp, E3-115/1; [1999] CLY 1486 230

Thatcher v Anders, Kemp & Kemp, K2-005; [1993] CLY 1436 405
Thirtle, Re, Kemp & Kemp, C2-050; [1991] CLY 1337 109
Thomas v Associated British Ports [1992] CLY 1653 237
Thomas v Booker Services, Kemp & Kemp, E3-088; [1993] CLY 1519 237
Thomas v Dewhirst, Kemp & Kemp, K2-221; [1994] CLY 1737 435
Thomas v Fury, Kemp & Kemp, E2-043; [1990] CLY 1618 153
Thomas v Hannon Robe, Kemp & Kemp, E2-117; [1996] CLY 2313 144
Thomas v Howmet Turbine (UK) Inc, Kemp & Kemp, H6-026; [1990] CLY 1655 302
Thomas v Stagecoach (South) Ltd, Kemp & Kemp, K2-102/5; [1999] CLY 1589 51
Thomas v West Glamorgan AHA, Kemp & Kemp, J4-076; [1996] CLY 2298 558
Thomas v West Midlands HA, Kemp & Kemp, F5-060; [1991] CLY 1418......................498
Thompson v British Railways Board, Kemp & Kemp, 13-017; [1991] CLY 1443 421
Thompson v Caradon Heating, Kemp & Kemp, K2-104; [1994] CLY 1718 427
Thompson v Chappell, Kemp & Kemp, K2-176; [1998] CLY 1734................................190
Thompson v Mersey Ferries, Kemp & Kemp, F2-075/1; [1998] CLY 1628 48
Thompson v Priest, Kemp & Kemp, E2-017; [1995] CLY 1698 530
Thompson v South Tees Area Health Authority, Kemp & Kemp, A4-003;
  BPILS, I 70.8, 286.6, 570.2, 593.3; [1990] CLY 1576 472
Thorogood, Re [1992] CLY 1725 228
Thorpe v Calderdale Metropolitan Borough Council, Kemp & Kemp, K2-075;
  [1993] CLY 1561 426
Thorpe v Hooper, Kemp & Kemp, A4-008; [1995] CLY 1654 94
Threlkeld v Northern Electric plc, Kemp & Kemp, PRD-002; [1999] CLY 1464 86
Thrul v Ray, Kemp & Kemp, B2-009/2; [1999] CLY 1508 29
Thurman v Wiltshire and Bath HA [1997] PIQR Q115; Kemp & Kemp,
  F5-012/1, F5-117; [1997] CLY 1953 351
Ticehurst v Spa Hotel (Goring), Kemp & Kemp, H6-037; [1992] CLY 1693 306
Tidy, Re [1995] CLY 1792 53
Tierney v Mavadia 98 (6) QR 6; Kemp & Kemp, E3-028/1; [1998] CLY 1569.................73
Tierney, Re, Kemp & Kemp, K2-182; [1994] CLY 1730 279
Tilley v Tucker, Kemp & Kemp, F2-020; [1997] CLY 1941..547
Tilson v Taylor, Kemp & Kemp, I2-408; [1994] CLY 1677...397
Timms v Buchanan, Kemp & Kemp, E2-015/2; [1999] CLY 1481 235
Tindale v Dowsett Engineering Construction Ltd, unreported, 2 December 1980 lx
Tiwana v Heir, Kemp & Kemp, K2-056; [1995] CLY 1785 124
Tiyur, Re [1992] CLY 1633 69
Todd, Re, Kemp & Kemp, J2-025; [1990] CLY 1609..453
Topham (a minor) v Acorn Fabrics, Kemp & Kemp, K2-208/5; [1998] CLY 1753 430
Topping v Ferranti Resin, Kemp & Kemp, I2-433; [1992] CLY 1715..............................402
Torrance, Re, Kemp & Kemp, H6-031/1; [1997] CLY 1970 304
Toulson v RS Bruce (Metals and Machinery), Kemp & Kemp, E3-005;
  [1993] CLY 1485 243
Towler v Ali, Kemp & Kemp, E2-103/2; [2000] 3 CL 172 122
Traverse v Nelson, Kemp & Kemp, C5-062; [1996] CLY 2203...50
Tree v Phillips, Kemp & Kemp, K2-027; [1997] CLY 1909...177
Treffrey v Smith, Kemp & Kemp, E3-027; [1997] CLY 1922 245

Tricker v Hoban and Trembath Services, Kemp & Kemp, B2-004/1;
[1994] CLY 1548 1
Trotter v Black, Kemp & Kemp, E2-022; [1994] CLY 1601 117
Troy v Ghosh, Kemp & Kemp, C5-044; [1991] CLY 1383 45
Truscott v Saipe, Kemp & Kemp, E2-055/1; [1997] CLY 1896......................118
Trushell v Gamblin & Robinson, Kemp & Kemp, J5-074; [1996] CLY 2209....................20
Tuckerman v Moy Park, Kemp & Kemp, K2-235; [1992] CLY 1772 130
Tunnicliffe v Wandlowsky, Kemp & Kemp, K2-147; [1993] CLY 1573 428
Turnbull v Kenneth, Kemp & Kemp, E3-017; [1996] CLY 2228 251
Turner v British Steel plc, Kemp & Kemp, K2-095; [1997] CLY 1976 332
Turner v Dale, Kemp & Kemp, K2-078; [1995] CLY 1763 369
Turner v Nei Parsons Ltd, Kemp & Kemp, D2-049; [1998] CLY 1560............80
Turner v NS Hair Treatment Clinic, Kemp & Kemp, J5-003; [1994] CLY 1591..................7
Turner v Owens Corning Fibreglass UK Ltd, Kemp & Kemp, E3-032/1;
[1998] CLY 1572 217
Turner v Sefton MBC, Kemp & Kemp, J2-023; [1998] CLY 1546 43
Twycross v Hilton, Kemp & Kemp, E2-093/1; [2000] 3 CL 179 170
Tylman v British Coal Corp, Kemp & Kemp, E3-083; [1993] CLY 1494.......224
Type v Merthyr Tydfil Borough Council, Kemp & Kemp, K2-086; [1990] CLY 1684....296
Tyrell-Wilson v Bostan, Kemp & Kemp, J2-034; [1994] CLY 1695 367
Tyrone v Broadfoot, Kemp & Kemp, K2-273; [1998] CLY 1742 131

U (a minor) v Living World Ltd, Kemp & Kemp, J2-049/1; [1999] CLY 1560 318
U (a minor) v Manchester City Council, Kemp & Kemp, C6-025; [1999] CLY 1569 77
Ullrich v Carlisle City Council, Kemp & Kemp, H2-025/2; [1997] CLY 1957 257
Upton v North Tees Health Authority, Kemp & Kemp, D3-011; [1992] CLY 1632 67
Urwin v Darlington Insulation, Kemp & Kemp, F2-059; [1996] CLY 2242 551
Uter v Williams, Kemp & Kemp, PRG-001; [2000] 3 CL 181 339
Utley v Parker, Kemp & Kemp, E2-076/3; [2000] 4 CL 152...........................164

V, Re, Kemp & Kemp, C4-011; [1993] CLY 1425 519
V, Re, Kemp & Kemp, C4-237; [1991] CLY 1370 485
Vango v Kettering General Hospital NHS Trust, Kemp & Kemp, E3-069/1;
[1998] CLY 1574 223
Vater v Dry Silver (in liquidation), Kemp & Kemp, E2-033; [1993] CLY 1477 151
Vaughan v BT Whelan, Kemp & Kemp, E2-033; [1998] CLY 1700 205
Vaughan v Moogan, Kemp & Kemp, D3-030; [1994] CLY 1595 72
Venn v Hitachi Consumer Products (UK) Ltd, Kemp & Kemp, F2-055;
[1996] CLY 2241 545
Veogent v Matrix Scaffolding, Kemp & Kemp, C4-104; [1996] CLY 2190 ...537
Verrier v London Borough of Islington [1992] CLY 1708 389
Vickerage v Rotherham MBC, Kemp & Kemp, E3-054; [1997] CLY 1926....220
Vincent v London Electricity, Kemp & Kemp, F2-044; [1994] CLY 1633 512
Vincent, Re, Kemp & Kemp, E3-015; [1990] CLY 1627 215
Vizor and Russell v Pilgrem, Kemp & Kemp, K2-080; [1991] CLY 1463 336
Vogwell v Cockbill, Kemp & Kemp, C2-024; [1991] CLY 1343 101
Voller v Smith, Kemp & Kemp, H3-171; [1990] CLY 1648 286

W (a child) v Classic Cuts, Kemp & Kemp, PRC-016; [2000] 3 CL 171 72
W (a minor) v Gloucestershire CC, Kemp & Kemp, PRH-005; [2000] 2 CL 147 331
W (a minor) v Kerry, Kemp & Kemp, PRC-018; [2000] 3 CL 166 25
W (a minor), Re, Kemp & Kemp, C4-278; [1997] CLY 1861 495
W (a minor), Re, Kemp & Kemp, C4-279; [1997] CLY 1862 495
W, Re (CICB Quantum: 1999), Re, Kemp & Kemp, C4-232; [2000] 1 CL 117 483
W, Re [1999] CLY 1428 65
W, Re, Kemp & Kemp, C4-015; [1991] CLY 1345 67
W, Re, Kemp & Kemp, K2-143; [1991] CLY 1477 64
W, Re, Kemp & Kemp, PRH-002, H3-160; [1999] CLY 1503 324
Waghorn v Buckland, Kemp & Kemp, K2-105; [1995] CLY 1793 370
Walchester v Chief Constable of Staffordshire, Kemp & Kemp, C2-078;
    [1999] CLY 1548 11
Wale v London Underground Ltd, Kemp & Kemp, E2-031/2; [2000] 5 CL 186 236
Walker (a minor) v Walker, Kemp & Kemp, F6-072/1; [1994] CLY 1637 343
Walker v BP Chemicals, Kemp & Kemp, J3-041; [1991] CLY 1482 441
Walker v Miricki [2000] 6 CL 193 179
Walkes (a minor) v Oxley, Kemp & Kemp, K2-238/1; [1998] CLY 1715 541
Waller and Waller v Canterbury and Thanet Health Authority, Kemp & Kemp,
    C4-085; [1993] CLY 1453 504
Walley v Linney [1990] CLY 1701 509
Wallis v Smith, Kemp & Kemp, K2-043; [1994] CLY 1696 368
Walsh v William Morrison Supermarket Ltd, Kemp & Kemp, K3-030/1;
    [1998] CLY 1571 246
Walsh, Re, Kemp & Kemp, C4-047; [1995] CLY 1672 527
Walters, Re [1992] CLY 1659 240
Wand v Gozuboyok, Kemp & Kemp, K2-044; [1992] CLY 1647 546
Warburton v Barrington, Kemp & Kemp, E2-137/1; [1997] CLY 1879 189
Warburton v Halliwell, Kemp & Kemp, E3-069; [1997] CLY 1931 248
Warby v Perkins, Kemp & Kemp, E2-048/2; [1998] CLY 1588 155
Ward v Batten & Stamford Asphalt Co Ltd, Kemp & Kemp, E3-087/1;
    [1997] CLY 1935 225
Ward v Lenscrafters EC Corp., Kemp & Kemp, B2-036; [1997] CLY 1827 217
Ward v Newalls Insulation Co Ltd [1998] 1 WLR 1722; [1998] 2 All ER 690;
    [1998] PIQR Q41; 95(15) LSG 32; 142 SJLB 103; (1998) The Times, March 5,
    Kemp & Kemp, F2-025/2 ; [1998] CLY 1623 548
Ward v Wakefield Health Authority, Kemp & Kemp, I2-542; [1993] CLY 1558 393
Warner (a minor), Re [1998] CLY 1561 79
Warren, Re, Kemp & Kemp, D2-019; [1993] CLY 1473 82
Washington, Re [1992] CLY 1610 62
Wasiuk v Auto Travel Ltd, Kemp & Kemp, PRK-003; [1999] CLY 1567 36
Waters (a minor) v North British Housing Association Ltd, Kemp & Kemp,
    C5-041; [1997] CLY 1873 44
Watford (a minor) v Tesco Stores Ltd, Kemp & Kemp, I2-536; [1998] CLY 1672 391
Watkinson v British Railways Board [1992] CLY 1733 378
Watkinson v Chief Constable of the West Midlands, Kemp & Kemp,
    K2-048/3; [2000] 4 CL 170 410

Watson (Linda), Re [1997] CLY 1921 214
Watson v CICB, Kemp & Kemp, B-026/1; E2-020; [1997] CLY 1848 526
Watson v Gray, Kemp & Kemp, I2-034; [1999] CLY 1510...375
Watson, Re, Kemp & Kemp, C4-083; [1998] CLY 1533 60
Watt (a minor) v Asda Stores Ltd, Kemp & Kemp, J2-040/3; [1998] CLY 1548 51
Watts, Re [1992] CLY 1583 514
Waudby v Humberside County Council, Kemp & Kemp, H6-50; [1990] CLY 1659......315
Waumsley v British Railways Board, Kemp & Kemp, K2-101; [1993] CLY 1567 413
Waxman v Scrivens, Kemp & Kemp, E3-013; [1997] CLY 1919 133
Waygood v Kane, Kemp & Kemp, E2-115; [1991] CLY 1458 205
Wayt v Swansea City Council, Kemp & Kemp, G2-039; [1996] CLY 2253 358
Weaver v Hocking, Kemp & Kemp, I2-506; [1991] CLY 1439...421
Webber v Bruton, Kemp & Kemp, C2-009; [1998] CLY 1490 87
Webster, Re, Kemp & Kemp, C5-033; [1998] CLY 1544..42
Weekes v Isebor, Kemp & Kemp, E2/102/2; [1998] CLY 1606.......................................173
Weeks v Williams and Lucas-Farley [1993] CLY 1503 240
Weinberger (a minor) v Jacobs, Kemp & Kemp, J3-016/1; [1998] CLY 1695 438
Weir v Smith, Kemp & Kemp, I2-514; [1994] CLY 1672 386
Welsh, Re, Kemp & Kemp, C6-028; [1993] CLY 1576 54
Wesley v Cobb (deceased), Kemp & Kemp, PRC-009; [2000] 5 CL 179 137
West (a minor) v Kerr, Kemp & Kemp, B2-018; [1998] CLY 1496....................................31
West v Campagnie, Kemp & Kemp, K2-002; [1995] CLY 1703 163
West v HSHT Clinic, Kemp & Kemp, J2-002; [1996] CLY 2208 7
West v Shephard [1965] AC 326 lix
Westmoquette v Dean, Kemp & Kemp, B2-003/1; [1998] CLY 1477 362
Whale v United Biscuits (UK), Kemp & Kemp, K2-090; [1991] CLY 1467 314
Whalley, Re, Kemp & Kemp, J2-019; [1993] CLY 1466 41
Whatley v Robson [1995] CLY 1822 407
Wheeler v Central Independent Television and John Frost Scenery,
    Kemp & Kemp, H6-030; [1995] CLY 1734 303
Whiddett v Phillips, Kemp & Kemp, K2-031; [1999] CLY 1582 204
White v Munir, Kemp & Kemp, H3-106/1; [1996] CLY 2261 274
White v Onions, Kemp & Kemp, E2-121, K2-065; [1997] CLY 1912 181
Whitehouse v Foster, Kemp & Kemp, E2-090; [1992] CLY 1642....................................168
Whiteside v Howes, Kemp & Kemp, B2-001; [1994] CLY 1544..92
Whiteside, Re [1995] CLY 1758 380
Whittaker v BBA Groups, Kemp & Kemp, F2-020/1; BPILS. I 366; [1995] CLY 1825....554
Whittaker v Gallagher, Kemp & Kemp, K2-268/1; [1998] CLY 1747 322
Whorton v British Coal, Kemp & Kemp, J3-029; [1993] CLY 1554 324
Wickens v Red Shift Theatre Co, Kemp & Kemp, H3-166; [1994] CLY 1653 274
Wilcock v John Mace Ltd, Kemp & Kemp, J6-013; [1997] CLY 2024 557
Wilcock, Re, Kemp & Kemp, C2-080; [1999] CLY 1549 11
Wild v Couvret, Kemp & Kemp, I3-027/5; [1993] CLY 1545 419
Wild, Re, Kemp & Kemp, H3-161; [1992] CLY 1692 285
Wilders v Peppers Ltd, Kemp & Kemp, G2-033; [1996] CLY 2249 356
Wilkie v Radcliffe Hospital NHS Trust, Kemp & Kemp, E3-043/2; [1998] CLY 1573 218
Wilkinson v Jones, Kemp & Kemp, A5-004; [1998] CLY 1479 95

Willett v North Bedfordshire Health Authority [1993] PIQR Q166;
　　Kemp & Kemp, A4-006/1, A4-119; BPILS, I 260.1; [1993] CLY 1422 94
Williams & Williams v Appleton, Kemp & Kemp, K2-073; [1993] CLY 1562................264
Williams v Bowen, Kemp & Kemp, E2-134/1; [1998] CLY 1724 188
Williams v Butcher, Kemp & Kemp, B2-036/4; [1998] CLY 1648 296
Williams v Clarkson, Kemp & Kemp, E3-089/2; [1999] CLY 1490 238
Williams v Doyle, Kemp & Kemp, B2-004/2/2; [1999] CLY 1431 98
Williams v Fisher, Kemp & Kemp, E2-014/1; [1998] CLY 1579......................................117
Williams v Griffiths, Kemp & Kemp, E2-108; [1994] CLY 1616 123
Williams v Gwent Health Authority, Kemp & Kemp, J4-015/1; [1995] CLY 1766 558
Williams v Parry (t/a "Animal Lovers"), Kemp & Kemp, E3-121; [1993] CLY 1563........37
Williams v Russell, Kemp & Kemp, K2-222; [1990] CLY 1703 434
Williams v Smith and Daniels, Kemp & Kemp, K2-063; [1997] CLY 1990....................413
Williams v Winstone Rollers, Kemp & Kemp, K2-160; [1991] CLY 1478 434
Williams, Re [1990] CLY 1583 91
Williams, Re, Kemp & Kemp, B2-004/3; [1996] CLY 2174 101
Williams/Thorne, Re, Kemp & Kemp, J2-012; [1995] CLY 1684 446
Willmore, Re, Kemp & Kemp, C2-031; [1996] CLY 2178 13
Wilson (David Michael), Re, Kemp & Kemp, K2-023; [1997] CLY 1989.......................419
Wilson and Wilson v Seagram Distillers plc, Kemp & Kemp, K2-200;
　　[1997] CLY 1883 192
Wilson v Anstey [1995] CLY 1709 218
Wilson v Busways Travel Services, Kemp & Kemp, I2-518; [1995] CLY 1745................387
Wilson v Carrick Carr & Garwood, Kemp & Kemp, L3-024; [1993] CLY 1543 420
Wilson v Clarke, Kemp & Kemp, E2-006; [1995] CLY 1696 213
Wilson v Fenlon, Kemp & Kemp, E2-140; [1996] CLY 2349 191
Wiltshire v Warwick DC, Kemp & Kemp, H3-172; [1998] CLY 1647 294
Winfield v J Lyons & Co Ltd, Kemp & Kemp, H7-023/1; [1996] CLY 2348 318
Wingrove v Ford Motor Co, Kemp & Kemp, F6-047/2; [1994] CLY 1644 344
Winn and Kwiatowski v Townend 98 (6) QR 6; Kemp & Kemp, E2-105/2;
　　[1998] CLY 1612 201
Winstanley v Case (JI) [1991] CLY 1460 241
Winstanley v Laithwaite, Kemp & Kemp, E2-108/2; [1998] CLY 1699 202
Winterbone v West Suffolk Health Authority, Kemp & Kemp, F5-023;
　　[1994] CLY 1640 350
Winterton, Re, Kemp & Kemp, C2-060; [1991] CLY 1338 30
Wolf v Anafield Builders, Kemp & Kemp, E2-005; [1990] CLY 1626 133
Wolfendon v James, Kemp & Kemp, E3-103; [1992] CLY 1656 162
Wood v British Railways, Kemp & Kemp, I2-519; [1994] CLY 1673 387
Wood v Cleaver [1994] CLY 1566 113
Wood v Draper [1992] CLY 1763 191
Woodhouse v Normanton, Kemp & Kemp, C2-084; [1997] CLY 2009...........................36
Wooding v Torbay District Council [1992] CLY 1558 473
Woods, Re, Kemp & Kemp, C4-099; [1996] CLY 2189 537
Worboys, Re, Kemp & Kemp, C5-032; [1992] CLY 1608 61
Worf v Heath-Qualters [1993] CLY 1430 90
Workman v Radcliffe, Kemp & Kemp, I2-520; [1991] CLY 1436 396

Worrall v Powergen plc [1999] PIQR P103; [1999] Lloyd's Rep Med 177;
  96(6) LSG 34; 99 (2) QR 8; (1999) The Times, February 10; Kemp & Kemp,
  F2-020/1, M2-056; BPILS, II 166.1, XI 3103, XV 33; [1999] CLY 1619 553
Worth v Worcester and District HA, Kemp & Kemp, E3-102; [1996] CLY 2237 227
Wray v Pardey, Kemp & Kemp, E2-059/2; E2-059/2; [1997] CLY 1936 238
Wright v Cole [1990] CLY 1711 131
Wright v Macclesfield Health Authority, Kemp & Kemp, I2-512;
  [1995] CLY 1761 364
Wright v Marina Developments Ltd, Kemp & Kemp, E3-110/1;
  [1998] CLY 1698 240
Wright v Ramsden, Kemp & Kemp, B2-009; [1993] CLY 1426 282
Wright v Serco Ltd, Kemp & Kemp, H2-016/2; [1997] CLY 1829 151
Wright, Willis, Short and Bottomer v Royal Doulton (UK) Ltd, Kemp & Kemp,
  H3102/2; [1997] CLY 1965 283
Wriglesworth v Doncaster HA, Kemp & Kemp, F3-013/1; [1996] CLY 2246 357
Wroe v Playforth, Kemp & Kemp, E2-120/1; [1998] CLY 1718 168

X, Re [1992] CLY 1599 478
X, Re [1992] CLY 1600 478
X, Re, Kemp & Kemp, C4-207; [1999] CLY 1447 478
X, Re, Kemp & Kemp, C4-244; [1990] CLY 1598 487

Y, Re, Kemp & Kemp, C4-211; [1995] CLY 1678 479
Yamoah v Woolworths plc, Kemp & Kemp, H2-020/2[1996] CLY 2256 255
Yates v Dowdeswell, Kemp & Kemp, E3-127; [1995] CLY 1821 131
Yates v Ford Motor Company, Kemp & Kemp, K2-175; [1992] CLY 1760 317
Young v Costello, Kemp & Kemp, E2-068; [1994] CLY 1608 161
Young v Griffin, Kemp & Kemp, K2-267; [1994] CLY 1746 281

Z (a child) v Greater Manchester Police Authority, Kemp & Kemp, PRC-021;
  [2000] 4 CL 168 12
Z, Re, Kemp & Kemp, C4-262; [1998] CLY 1515 491
Zammit v Stena Offshore Ltd, Kemp & Kemp, C4-070; [1997] CLY 1857 531

INTRODUCTION

PRELIMINARY

This book tries to do something new. It is an attempt to gather together all reported cases of general damages over the past ten years, update those awards both in line with inflation and with the Court of Appeal's decision in *Heil v Rankin* [2000] PIQR Q187, and provide an easy search mechanism, in book form, on disc, and updated regularly online. (For further information on using the disc, see page lxvii and the user instructions supplied with the disc at the back of the book.) In particular, we have tried to make it easy to search for cases in which the Claimants have suffered injuries to more than one part of the body – e.g. facial scarring and loss of a finger, or a whiplash injury and fractured ribs. We also take the Judicial Studies Board Guidelines into account. An attempt has been made to fit the majority of reported cases into the appropriate categories in the Guideline.

GENERAL DAMAGES

General damages, or damages for pain, suffering and loss of amenity, are awarded to a Claimant to compensate for physical or mental injury. In theory, "pain", "suffering" and "loss of amenity" are separate elements, and there will be some cases where there is, for example, loss of amenity but no pain or suffering, as where a Claimant is in a persistent vegetative state. In practice, however, "pain, suffering and loss of amenity" is a term of art. (See "The Elements of an Award" below.) General damages are conventional sums, fitted into a tariff whose top end is about £200,000, and in assessing such damages a court will have regard to the overall seriousness of the Claimant's loss of amenity, rather than to each individual symptom or injury.

SOURCES

The cases in this book have been decided by County Courts, the High Court, and the Court of Appeal, and the Criminal Injuries Compensation Authority. The reported authorities have been considered and categorised by the

Judicial Studies Board, whose Guidelines are an attempt to set out appropriate bands of damages in the light of the reported cases.

Not all cases are equally useful: sometimes Claimant's lawyers will report a case because it was exceptionally high, and sometimes Defendant's lawyers will report a case for the opposite reason. Sometimes an award will appear to be well above or below the appropriate Judicial Studies Board category, but though the award was a reasonable one in the circumstances, the report does not set out all those circumstances. In assessing the quantum of general damages in a case, it is therefore important not to look for the single authority in which the reported injuries come closest to the Claimant's: it is good practice to look at some of the higher and lower awards, to put your case into context.

THE JUDICIAL STUDIES BOARD GUIDELINES

The Judicial Studies Board first published its *Guidelines for the Assessment of General Damages in Personal Injury Cases* in 1992. The aim was set out in the introduction:

> "... whilst no two cases are ever precisely the same, justice requires that there be consistency between awards. The solution to this dilemma has lain in using the amount of damages awarded in reported cases as guidelines or markers and seeking to slot the particular case into the framework thus provided. That is easier stated than done, because reports of the framework cases are scattered over a variety of publications and not all the awards appear, from the sometimes brief reports, to be consistent with one another."

In the introduction to the 1996 edition the Editors said that:

> "The purpose of this guide is not to preach but rather to reflect the approach adopted by those who assess damages."

The *Guidelines* are a helpful first port of call, but again it is important to put them in context by looking at the reported authorities. Lord Woolf said in his introduction to the 1996 edition:

> "Usually it will be the starting off point rather than the last word on the appropriate award in any particular case ... it should be used not only because it is convenient to do so, but because due to the way in which it is compiled and because of its extensive use, it is the most reliable tool which up to now has been made available to courts up and down the land as to what is the correct range of damages for common classes of injuries."

Introduction   lvii

For example, at 4(A)(d) the *Guidelines* suggest a range of £28,000 to £33,000 for the loss of sight in one eye, though "the level of the award within the bracket will depend on age and cosmetic effect". In *Re Campbell* (*Kemp & Kemp* D2-024) the 25-year old female Claimant suffered severe alkaline burns to both eyes, leading to the loss of sight in one eye and permanent cosmetic deformity. She underwent a number of operations but was left permanently cosmetically deformed. She suffered a personality change, panic attacks, loss of confidence, sleeplessness and depression. Her lifestyle became severely limited. She was awarded £30,000 in September 1992, an award worth about £39,500 at today's rates.

It is the task of the Claimant's lawyers to ensure that the court is aware of all the relevant factors that may take the award out of the conventional range set out in the Guidelines. The Defendant is often at a disadvantage, not being able to assess those factors because he does not have direct access to the Claimant.

The Criminal Injuries Compensation Authority produces its own *Tariff of Injuries*, contained in its *Guide to the Criminal Injuries Compensation Scheme*. Both the 1996 edition, covering applications from 1 April 1996 to 31 March 2001, and the 2001 edition, relating to applications on or after 1 April 2001, can be found at www.cica.gov.uk.

UPDATING AWARDS

It is the duty of the judge to assess general damages in the "money of the day" – that is, at the date of trial and not of the injury. The Retail Price Index is used to update awards – but see also *Heil* v *Rankin*, below. In this book, all updating is done automatically, and cases put in the order of their present-day values as at February 2001. Users of the electronic service will be prompted to download an updated calculator with their monthly update in the days after the publication of the RPI. For more on how this works see the note on the Award Now function at page lxi. The Index is published in newspapers, in *Kemp & Kemp*, *Current Law*, and elsewhere. To update an award in line with the Index, multiply it by the *current* index figure, and then divide it by the index figure *for the month in which the award was originally made*. For example:

> In October 1990 a claimant was awarded £4,000 for a soft-tissue injury to the cervical spine. The RPI for that month stood at 130.30. To find the value of the award as at February 2000, when the RPI stood at 172.0:
>
> [172.0 x £4,000] ÷ 130.30 = £5,280

HEIL v RANKIN

On 23 March 2000 the Court of Appeal delivered its judgment in *Heil* v *Rankin*, and made significant adjustments to the levels of general damages. They considered a range of cases. For cases worth up to £10,000 on 23 March 2000 there was no increase. Awards worth £150,000 and above on that date were increased by one third. For awards between £10,000 and £150,000 there was a tapered increase.

Updating a pre-23 March 2000 case is therefore a three-part process:

1. Use the Retail Price Index to update the award from the date it was originally made to 23 March 2000.

2. If the updated award is worth £10,000 or more, increase it in line with *Heil* v *Rankin*. (At the end of this Introduction is a table for converting pre-*Heil* awards to their 23 March 2000 values.)

3. Use the Retail Price Index a second time to update the award from 23 March 2000 to date.

Further information regarding this process can be found in *Appendix 1*.

THE ELEMENTS OF AN AWARD

This section sets out the main factors that will influence a court in its assessment of general damages. It is not exhaustive, and both parties will want to check whether there are other factors that will significantly influence the award.

1. Pain and suffering
Where the period of suffering has been short – for example, where the Claimant died not long after the accident, either of his injuries or for some other cause – it may be important to emphasise this part of the injury.

2. Loss of amenity
If a Claimant had a particular interest or pleasure that his injuries have denied him (for example, deafness in a musician, or lameness in a sportsman) the Court can take this into account:

> "If there is loss of amenity apart from the obvious and normal loss inherent in the deprivation of the limb – if, for instance, the Plaintiff's

main interest in life was some sport or hobby from which he will in future be debarred, that too increases the assessment."

West v Shephard [1965] AC 326, 365

3. Previous state of health

This may be relevant where the Claimant was already ill at the time of the accident. The accident may have accelerated a pre-existing condition for a number of months or years, or it may have aggravated it for a while. The Claimant's previous condition is also a common feature of clinical negligence cases. It is important to bear in mind what the Court of Appeal said in *Mustard v Morris*,[1] where the Defendant argued that the damages for a seriously unfit Claimant should be lower than those for a healthy one:

> "An argument to the contrary might well be made. To impose upon a man who, though natural causes, has been made ill to a certain extent, very grave injuries such as were sustained in this Plaintiff and which reduce his capacity to bear natural ill health, is in my judgment more likely to increase than reduce damages."[2]

4. Multiple injuries

As we said above, the courts are concerned with a Claimant's *overall level of disability*. In *Durau v Evans* [1996] PIQR Q18 the Court of Appeal gave good guidance for multiple-injury cases:

> "To a limited extent, in a case where there are multiple injuries, the figures in the Judicial Studies Board table can help but I accept Mr Murphy's criticism of them that, where one has a multiplicity of injuries, it is necessary to take an overall view. The off-setting process may mean it is not possible to derive a great deal of benefit from that particular source. One then looks to see if anything can be gained from looking at a comparable award, if one is to be found, in another case. Even that may not prove to be a particularly fruitful source of inquiry. It may be necessary, if it be possible, to select what may be the most serious head of injury to see if a comparable award can be found in relation to that and, if so, build on it to allow for the other heads of injury which have been sustained by the Plaintiff in the instant case."

5. Loss of expectation of life

General damages are not awarded to compensate for a shortened life.[3]

6. Sex

In most claims the sex of the Claimant is irrelevant. There used to be a significant difference between the awards to men and women for facial scarring, but the emphasis now is more on the effect of the scarring on a particular Claimant. The possible effect of hip, pelvic, and low back injuries on women of childbearing age may be relevant.

7. Age
This is relatively unimportant, though awards to the very old may be slightly lower.

8. Circumstances of the accident
These are seldom relevant to the award (which is why they tend not to feature in the case summaries in this work). They may be relevant if they cause psychological or psychiatric harm.

9. Loss of leisure
If a Claimant has to work longer hours to earn the same income, the court can compensate him by an increase in general damages: see, for example, *Tindale v Dowsett Engineering Construction Ltd*,[4] where the Claimant was awarded approximately £3,500 at current rates for having to work ten hours a week longer for two years in order to earn the same income.

In *Appendix 2* there is a checklist to help both parties assess the impact of injuries on a Claimant.

References

1. Formerly in *Kemp and Kemp* 12-106, 604, now referred to only in the Law Commission's Consultation Paper *Damages for Personal Injury: Non-Pecuniary Loss* (No. 140) at 2. 32 n. 127.

2. Watkins LJ. (The author recently had an extreme case of a young autistic girl who was blind and deaf: her only known sources of pleasure were tactile, and in particular she appeared to derive particular pleasure from smearing herself with her own excrement. As a result of the Defendant's negligence the lower part of her body was permanently scarred, interfering even with this limited degree of amenity. How should the conventional damages for such scarring be adjusted in such a case?)

3. Administration of Justice Act 1982, s. 1(1)(a). But see s. 1(1)(b): "If the injured person's life has been reduced by the injuries, the court, in assessing damages in respect of pain and suffering caused by the injuries, shall take account of any suffering caused or likely to be caused to him by awareness that his expectation of life has been so reduced."

4. Unreported, Mustill J, 2 December 1980.

APPENDIX 1

UPDATING AWARDS IN LINE WITH *HEIL*

How the reported cases have been updated
There are three parts to this exercise:

1. Updated the award to 23 March 2000 using the Retail Price Index;
2. If the award was worth more than £10,000 on 23 March 2000, the formula below is applied. The table that follows does this exercise for you.
3. You now have the value of the award as at 23 March 2000: it must now be updated a second time, using the Retail Price Index.

How the formula works

1. Awards worth less than £10,000 on 23rd March 2000 are not changed.
2. From £10,000 to £150,000 (a range of £140,000) the uplift gradually increases from zero to one third.
3. Let us call the original (pre-*Heil*) award £A. The formula is:

$$£A + \left[{}^{(£A-10,000)}\!/_{420,000} \times £A \right]$$

The part in square brackets is the uplift.

To illustrate the formula in action, choose a case using the disc version of this book and choose to show the Award Now calculation. For ease of general reference, tables are provided in the pages following.

TABLE TO CONVERT PRE-*HEIL* AWARDS
INTO POST-*HEIL* AWARDS

OLD	NEW	OLD	NEW	OLD	NEW	OLD	NEW
<10,000	No change	30,000	31,428	50,000	54,761	70,000	79,999
11,000	11,026	31,000	32,550	51,000	55,978	71,000	81,311
12,000	12,057	32,000	33,676	52,000	57,200	72,000	82,628
13,000	13,092	33,000	34,807	53,000	58,426	73,000	83,950
14,000	14,133	34,000	35,942	54,000	59,657	74,000	85,276
15,000	15,178	35,000	37,083	55,000	60,892	75,000	86,607
16,000	16,228	36,000	38,228	56,000	62,133	76,000	87,942
17,000	17,283	37,000	39,378	57,000	63,378	77,000	89,283
18,000	18,342	38,000	40,533	58,000	64,628	78,000	90,629
19,000	19,407	39,000	41,692	59,000	65,883	79,000	91,979
20,000	20,476	40,000	42,857	60,000	67,142	80,000	93,333
21,000	21,549	41,000	44,026	61,000	68,407	81,000	94,693
22,000	22,628	42,000	45,199	62,000	69,676	82,000	96,057
23,000	23,711	43,000	46,378	63,000	70,949	83,000	97,426
24,000	24,799	44,000	47,561	64,000	72,228	84,000	98,800
25,000	25,892	45,000	48,749	65,000	73,511	85,000	100,179
26,000	26,990	46,000	49,942	66,000	74,799	86,000	101,562
27,000	28,092	47,000	51,140	67,000	76,092	87,000	102,945
28,000	29,199	48,000	52,342	68,000	77,390	88,000	104,343
29,000	30,311	49,000	53,549	69,000	78,692	89,000	105,740

Appendices

© *Simon Levene April 2001*

OLD	NEW	OLD	NEW	OLD	NEW	OLD	NEW
90,000	107,142	110,000	136,190	130,000	167,143	150,000	200,000
91,000	108,549	111,000	137,693	131,000	168,740	>150,000	Add $^1/_3$
92,000	109,961	112,000	139,200	132,000	170,343		
93,000	111,378	113,000	140,712	133,000	171,950		
94,000	112,800	114,000	142,229	134,000	173,562		
95,000	114,226	115,000	143,750	135,000	175,179		
96,000	115,657	116,000	142,276	136,000	176,800		
97,000	117,092	117,000	146,807	137,000	178,426		
98,000	118,533	118,000	148,343	138,000	180,057		
99,000	119,978	119,000	149,883	139,000	181,692		
100,000	121,428	120,000	151,428	140,000	183,333		
101,000	122,883	121,000	152,979	141,000	184,978		
102,000	124,342	122,000	154,533	142,000	186,628		
103,000	125,807	123,000	156,093	143,000	188,283		
104,000	127,276	124,000	157,657	144,000	189,942		
105,000	128,745	125,000	159,226	145,000	191,607		
106,000	130,229	126,000	160,800	146,000	193,276		
107,000	131,712	127,000	162,379	147,000	194,949		
108,000	133,200	128,000	163,962	148,000	196,628		
109,000	134,693	129,000	165,549	149,000	198,311		

APPENDIX 2

CHECKLIST FOR GENERAL DAMAGES

The following list is not exhaustive: it sets out many of the most common effects of injuries, and is intended as a guide for Claimants and Defendants to the factors that a court can take into account when assessing general damages.

1. The Injuries
   1. Nature of the injuries
   2. Treatment, and the Claimant's reaction to it
   3. Operations undergone
   4. Length of time in hospital
   5. Other therapies

2. Pain
   1. Continuous, Intermittent
   2. Severity
   3. How disabling
   4. What therapies help
   5. Does pain interrupt sleep

3. Mental effects (falling short of separate psychiatric injury)
   1. Fear
   2. Worry
   3. Embarrassment
   4. Withdrawing from society
   5. Distress at the thought of premature death
   6. Distress at the effect of the injuries on Claimant's family

4. Mobility
   1. Climbing ladders
   2. Climbing stairs

3. Walking on rough ground
4. Getting
    1. out of bed
    2. into and out of chairs
    3. into and out of the bath
    4. on and off the lavatory
5. Kneeling
6. Running
7. Sitting
8. Sleep (turning over in bed)
9. Squatting
10. Standing
11. Walking on uneven ground
12. Walking on a slope
13. Walking – distance

5. Hygiene
1. Grooming
2. Dressing
3. Bathing
4. Showering
5. Using the lavatory
6. Washing hair

6. Housework
1. Cleaning windows
2. Cooking
3. Dusting
4. Gardening
5. Hoovering
6. Ironing
7. Moving furniture
8. Painting and decorating
9. Putting objects into cupboards or on high shelves
10. Shopping

11. Washing up
12. Washing floors
13. Washing
14. Other DIY tasks

7. Other personal functions
1. Sexual dysfunction
2. Lifting children

8. Work
1. Cannot work at all
2. Cannot work full-time
3. Can do the same work, but it takes longer
4. Has to do a different job
5. Loss of enjoyment of work
6. Loss of holiday

9. Pastimes
1. Hobbies
2. Sports
3. Family outings

USING THIS SERVICE

To make best use of this product, the features of the electronic service should be used to aid searching and to make sure that the book text is as up to date as possible. The book will always be less up to date than the electronic service in terms of cases reported. However, in addition, awards on cases reported in the book can be updated by means of the electronic service. Accordingly we advise users of the book to use the book in conjunction with the disk.

FINDING YOUR WAY AROUND THE PAGE

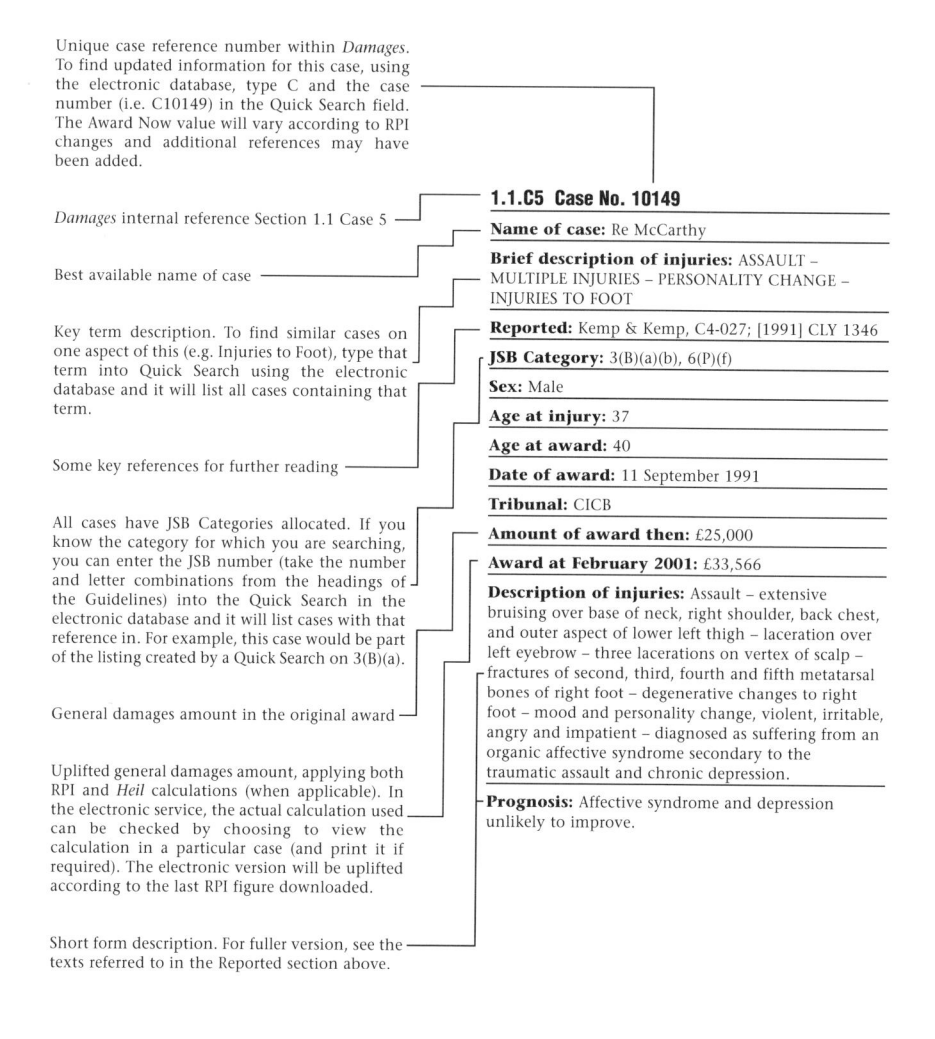

Unique case reference number within *Damages*. To find updated information for this case, using the electronic database, type C and the case number (i.e. C10149) in the Quick Search field. The Award Now value will vary according to RPI changes and additional references may have been added.

Damages internal reference Section 1.1 Case 5

Best available name of case

Key term description. To find similar cases on one aspect of this (e.g. Injuries to Foot), type that term into Quick Search using the electronic database and it will list all cases containing that term.

Some key references for further reading

All cases have JSB Categories allocated. If you know the category for which you are searching, you can enter the JSB number (take the number and letter combinations from the headings of the Guidelines) into the Quick Search in the electronic database and it will list cases with that reference in. For example, this case would be part of the listing created by a Quick Search on 3(B)(a).

General damages amount in the original award

Uplifted general damages amount, applying both RPI and *Heil* calculations (when applicable). In the electronic service, the actual calculation used can be checked by choosing to view the calculation in a particular case (and print it if required). The electronic version will be uplifted according to the last RPI figure downloaded.

Short form description. For fuller version, see the texts referred to in the Reported section above.

1.1.C5 Case No. 10149

Name of case: Re McCarthy

Brief description of injuries: ASSAULT – MULTIPLE INJURIES – PERSONALITY CHANGE – INJURIES TO FOOT

Reported: Kemp & Kemp, C4-027; [1991] CLY 1346

JSB Category: 3(B)(a)(b), 6(P)(f)

Sex: Male

Age at injury: 37

Age at award: 40

Date of award: 11 September 1991

Tribunal: CICB

Amount of award then: £25,000

Award at February 2001: £33,566

Description of injuries: Assault – extensive bruising over base of neck, right shoulder, back chest, and outer aspect of lower left thigh – laceration over left eyebrow – three lacerations on vertex of scalp – fractures of second, third, fourth and fifth metatarsal bones of right foot – degenerative changes to right foot – mood and personality change, violent, irritable, angry and impatient – diagnosed as suffering from an organic affective syndrome secondary to the traumatic assault and chronic depression.

Prognosis: Affective syndrome and depression unlikely to improve.

SECTION 1.1
INJURY CASES

1.1 GENERAL INJURY

1.1.C1 Case No. 10701

Name of case: Re Asghar

Brief description of injuries: MULTIPLE INJURIES – 2 STABBING ATTACKS – SEVERE ABDOMINAL AND PSYCHIATRIC SEQUELAE

Reported: [1994] CLY 1547

JSB Category: 5(D)(a); 3(B); 6(K)(c)(iii); 8

Sex: Male

Age at injury: 18

Age at award: 24

Date of award: 01 December 1993

Tribunal: CICB, London

Amount of award then: £100,000

Award at February 2001: £152,575

Description of injuries: Two separate stabbing attacks – first attack to chest – liver transfixed, causing massive haemorrhaging – condition critical for several weeks – renal failure – septicaemia – liver abscess, requiring surgical draining – permanent scarring to chest and stomach area – later hernia in laparotomy wound, successfully healed – second stabbing attack in leg by friend of first assailants – development of post-traumatic stress disorder – nightmares – insomnia – reversed sleep patterns – phobic anxiety – fear of leaving house, crowds and close physical contact – in-patient psychiatric treatment for 3 weeks, thereafter counselling and anti-depressants, but claimant did not keep up counselling due to feelings of hopelessness and lack of motivation – diet limited – now only able to consume small quantities of food – frequent vomiting.

Prognosis: Prognosis of almost continual pain in region of abdominal wound – will never fully recover physically – permanently unable to lift heavy weights – prospects of career in sports, particularly as martial arts instructor, at an end – symptoms of post-traumatic stress disorder ongoing at time of trial and prognosis uncertain – unlikely to be able to return to work for a further 2 to 3 years after date of trial due to psychiatric condition.

1.1.C2 Case No. 10702

Name of case: Tricker v Hoban and Trembath Services

Brief description of injuries: MULTIPLE MAJOR INJURIES – COMA 7 MONTHS – SERIOUS COGNITIVE DEFECTS – INABILITY TO LIVE INDEPENDENTLY

Reported: Kemp & Kemp, B2-004/1; [1994] CLY 1548

JSB Category: 2(A)(b); 4(A)(f); 5(I)(c); 6(C)(a), 6(K)(b)

Sex: Male

Age at injury: 18

Age at award: 26

Date of award: 14 February 1994

Tribunal: QBD

Amount of award then: £85,000

Award at February 2001: £125,112

Description of injuries: Motorcycle accident – severe injuries to head and internal organs and multiple fractures – in coma 7 months – ruptured aorta – ruptured bladder – torn rectum – fractures of both pubic rami – laceration of right groin – fracture of left femur requiring internal fixation – comminuted left and right tibial fractures requiring compression plates – emergency tracheostomy – massive blood transfusion for shock – various complications – discharge of sinus into left hip, necessitating removal of locking screw – deep, persistent infection of femur, necessitating excision of infected tissue – chronic osteomyelitis of left femur – 2 hamstring release operations – operation to remove 2 stones from penis – clawing of toes in both feet, and left foot drop – left temporal fracture extending to base of skull – diffuse injury to 2 cerebral hemispheres and brain stem – complete nerve palsy and left eye droop, double vision when left eye not closed – severe neuropsychological deficit – serious impairment of short- and long-term memory and cognitive function, one test putting claimant at level of 8 year old – poor verbal comprehension – slurred speech – impaired sense of smell – significant personality change; easily upset, prone to outbursts of temper, sometimes violent.

Prognosis: Claimant currently in rehabilitation centre, expected to remain there for 2 years – would thereafter need 2 live-in carers and case manager – permanently unable to return to pre-accident work.

Other points: Judge held that appropriate award was comparable with case of paraplegia.

1.1.C3 Case No. 10536

Name of case: Barden v Jobquote

Brief description of injuries: MULTIPLE FRACTURES – SEVERE PERMANENT DISABILITY

Reported: Kemp & Kemp, B2-011; [1993] CLY 1428

JSB Category: 5(A); 5(E); 5(K); 6(C)

Sex: Male

Age at injury: 54

Age at award: 58

Date of award: 09 December 1992

Tribunal: QBD

Amount of award then: £40,000

Award at February 2001: £53,943

Description of injuries: Crushed by road roller – displaced fracture of left clavicle – at least 7 rib fractures – surgical emphysema on right side – fractures of pubic rami extending into walls of acetabulum – wide diastasis of symphisis pubis – damage to sacro-iliac joint – lacerations to scrotum – impotence due to nerve and tissue damage – bi-lateral inguinal hernias – injuries were life threatening.

Prognosis: Severe and permanent disability – will never work again – walking aids and wheelchair always required – dependent on assistance from others.

1.1.C4 Case No. 11764

Name of case: Smee v Adye

Brief description of injuries: MULTIPLE INJURIES

Reported: Kemp & Kemp, B2-011/1; [1999] CLY 1427

JSB Category: 6(C)(a)(iii), 6(K)(b), 6(L)(b), 6(O); 7(A)(b), 7(B)(b); 8; 2(B)

Sex: Male

Age at injury: 39

Age at award: 43

Date of award: 29 March 1999

Tribunal: QBD

Amount of award then: £45,000

Award at February 2001: £51,229

Description of injuries: Minor brain injuries – tracheostomy – facial bone fractures – fracture dislocation of right hip and pubic rami – multiple fractures of right acetabulum – damage to right sciatic nerve – fractures in right foot – deep vein damage and chronic venous insufficiency in right leg, manifesting itself 2 years after accident, causing varicose veins, lipodermatosclerosis, atrophie blanche and intermittent ankle swelling – multiple scarring to face, arm, hip and knees – right leg shortened by injuries, requiring special shoes – use of right leg restricted and uncomfortable in all joints – pain experienced when lifting right forearm – abnormal sensation below right eye and difficulty clearing mucus caused by facial injuries – coughing and sinusitis worsened by cold or infections – multiple operations, 8 weeks in hospital, 6 weeks in rehabilitation and 8 months off work required – claimant unable to play sport, carry out heavy gardening or do DIY – restricted seating, driving long distances or prolonged sitting uncomfortable.

Prognosis: Osteoarthritis of hip expected hip replacement required at 55; operation will be technically demanding due to damage to hip and venous system – 30 per cent risk of venous ulceration in leg if bitten, knocked or left immobile, due to venous insufficiency – claimant likely to retire at 55 rather than 60.

1.1.C5 Case No. 10149

Name of case: Re McCarthy

Brief description of injuries: ASSAULT – MULTIPLE INJURIES – PERSONALITY CHANGE – INJURIES TO FOOT

Reported: Kemp & Kemp, C4-027; [1991] CLY 1346

JSB Category: 3(B)(a)(b), 6(P)(f)

Sex: Male

Age at injury: 37

Age at award: 40

Date of award: 11 September 1991

Tribunal: CICB

Amount of award then: £25,000

Award at February 2001: £33,566

Description of injuries: Assault – extensive bruising over base of neck, right shoulder, back chest, and outer aspect of lower left thigh – laceration over left eyebrow – three lacerations on vertex of scalp – fractures of second, third, fourth and fifth metatarsal bones of right foot – degenerative changes to right foot – mood and personality change, violent, irritable, angry and impatient – diagnosed as suffering from an organic affective syndrome secondary to the traumatic assault and chronic depression.

Prognosis: Affective syndrome and depression unlikely to improve.

1.1.C6 Case No. 10727

Name of case: Re Green

Brief description of injuries: MULTIPLE STAB WOUNDS – POST-TRAUMATIC STRESS DISORDER – CIRCA 8 YEARS

Reported: Kemp & Kemp, C4-063; [1994] CLY 1575

JSB Category: 3(B)

Sex: Male

Age at injury: 23

Age at award: 34

Date of award: 25 July 1994

Tribunal: CICB, London

Amount of award then: £12,500

Award at February 2001: £15,095

Description of injuries: Assault – claimant stabbed 11 times along left side of body from head to leg – admitted to intensive care; chest drain inserted and blood transfused; in hospital 9 days – development of traumatic neurosis – severe panic and phobic symptoms – social withdrawnness and isolation – nightmares – phobia of knives – avoidance of enclosed spaces, darkness, social situation and knives – 7 years after incident, attended consultant psychiatrist for period of 1 year – claimant free of all phobic and anxiety symptoms and nightmares by 1991 – actively seeking work at time of hearing.

1.1.C7 Case No. 11283

Name of case: Re Carlin

Brief description of injuries: INTERNAL ORGANS – MULTIPLE INJURIES – POST-TRAUMATIC STRESS DISORDER

Reported: (1997) 97 (1) QR 3; Kemp & Kemp, B2-038/1[1997] CLY 1830

JSB Category: 5(G)

Sex: Male

Age at injury: 26

Age at award: 29

Date of award: 06 November 1996

Tribunal: CICB, London

Amount of award then: £10,000

Award at February 2001: £11,201

Description of injuries: Stab wound went through the left kidney and renal artery – virtually transected the posterior wall of the aorta – through the posterior aspect of the vena cava – required 44 units of blood – at the time of the hearing a full recovery had been made.

Prognosis: The prognosis for post-traumatic stress disorder was guarded.

Other points: The recovery phase was slow and difficult – he suffered renal failure, two grand mal epileptic fits – sepsis and chest infections.

1.1.C8 Case No. 11619

Name of case: Re Tallentire

Brief description of injuries: STAB WOUNDS

Reported: Kemp & Kemp, F4-027; [1998] CLY 1621

JSB Category: 5(D)(b); 3(A)

Sex: Male

Age at injury: 41

Age at award: 44

Date of award: 18 April 1997

Tribunal: CICB, Durham

Amount of award then: £9,000

Award at February 2001: £9,904

Description of injuries: Life-threatening stab wounds to the chest, abdomen and bowel – after 2 years T suffered a small incisional hernia at the site of the laparotomy – cosmetically unsightly 15 inch keloid mid-line scar – untreated psychological problems gradually settled.

1.1.C9 Case No. 11086

Name of case: Re Pennell

Brief description of injuries: MULTIPLE STAB WOUNDS

Reported: Kemp & Kemp, B2-041/1; [1996] CLY 2177

JSB Category: 5(A)

Sex: Male

Age at injury: 19

Age at award: 22

Date of award: 13 September 1996

Tribunal: CICB, Cardiff

Amount of award then: £7,500

Award at February 2001: £8,388

Description of injuries: Stab wounds to the abdomen, back, arms, neck and head – continued to suffer spasms of abdominal pain.

Other points: Recommended psychiatric treatment was not taken up.

1.1.C10 Case No. 10159

Name of case: Re Duffin

Brief description of injuries: EXTENSIVE BRUISING AND ABRASIONS PSYCHOLOGICAL EFFECTS "ANALOGOUS TO RAPE"

Reported: Kemp & Kemp, C4-102; [1991] CLY 1356

JSB Category: 1(B); 6(K)(c)(iii), 6(B)(c)

Sex: Female

Age at injury: 22

Age at award: 25

Date of award: 25 January 1991

Tribunal: CICB

Amount of award then: £5,000

Award at February 2001: £6,605

Description of injuries: Assault by husband – extensive bruising and abrasions to neck legs and back – wore soft collar for a week – regular headaches – tightness around throat especially when nervous – refused surgery – minor scars on left knee – psychologically scarred – persistent nightmares – afraid to go out alone at night – does not trust men – refuses to allow any one to put hands near neck – frightened of further attack when husband released – case considered to be analogous to rape.

1.1.C11 Case No. 10898

Name of case: Smith v Advanced Plant

Brief description of injuries: MULTIPLE INJURIES – DEATH AFTER 13 DAYS

Reported: Kemp & Kemp, L7-024; [1994] CLY 1750

JSB Category:

Sex: Male

Age at injury: 60

Age at award: Deceased

Date of award: 11 August 1994

Tribunal: Woolwich County Court

Amount of award then: £5,500

Award at February 2001: £6,538

Description of injuries: Deceased fell 15ft from scaffolding – compound depressed fracture of skull – stable wedge fracture of seventh dorsal vertebra – fracture of upper border of right scapula – severe bruising injury to right side of chest wall – aggravation of pre-existing degeneration of lumbar spine – unconscious upon admission to hospital – connected to ventilator – compound depressed fracture of skull elevated – tracheostomy performed – painkillers and antibiotics – gradually weaned off ventilator – improvement such as to be transferred from intensive care to general ward after 10 days – chest injuries led to development of broncho-pneumonia – cardio-pulmonary arrest – claimant died of respiratory failure 13 days after accident – conscious for 10 days between accident and death, and had experienced pain over that period – chest injuries made breathing especially painful, which contributed to respiratory failure.

1.1.C12 Case No. 10334

Name of case: Re McGarragle

Brief description of injuries: IMPALED ON RAILINGS – BRUISING – ANXIETY – DEPRESSION

Reported: [1992] CLY 1590

JSB Category: 3(A)(c)

Sex: Male

Age at injury: –

Age at award: 57

Date of award: 25 October 1991

Tribunal: CICB, Glasgow

Amount of award then: £5,000

Award at February 2001: £6,366

Description of injuries: Impaled on iron railings – bruising on lower limbs and genital area.

Prognosis: Depression and anxiety, mood swings and loss of interest.

1.1.C13 Case No. 10333

Name of case: Re C

Brief description of injuries: PARENTAL ABUSE – MULTIPLE INJURIES – CIGARETTE BURNS

Reported: [1992] CLY 1589

JSB Category: 3(A)(c)

Sex: Female

Age at injury: 2 – 16 months

Age at award: 3 years 11months

Date of award: 05 May 1992

Tribunal: CICB, London

Amount of award then: £5,000

Award at February 2001: £6,174

Description of injuries: Parental abuse – spiral fracture of the left humerus at two months – three fractured ribs, cigarette burn to the back of the head, old bruising to the forearm, nose and fourth finger of the right hand and abnormally erupted upper teeth believed to be caused by trauma at six months – untreated ulcerated lesions typical of cigarette burns and thirty-eight bruises to various parts of the body caused by a spate of assaults.

Prognosis: Full recovery with minor scarring – subject to nightmares attributed to the previous assaults – dental prognosis good – 5% chance of post-traumatic epilepsy.

1.1.C14 Case No. 10873

Name of case: Davis v Cope

Brief description of injuries: BRUISING – CUTS – MISCELLANEOUS

Reported: Kemp & Kemp, K2-125; [1994] CLY 1725

JSB Category: (1): 2(B); 3(A); 6(D)(c); 7(B)(A)(iv) (2): 3(A); 6(F), 6(K)(c)(iii)

Sex: (1): Female (2): Female

Age at injury: (1)7;(2)3

Age at award: (1)11;(2)7

Date of award: 09 February 1994

Tribunal: Birmingham County Court

Amount of award then: £2,000

Award at February 2001: £2,421

Description of injuries: Two sisters, (1) and (2), passengers in car involved in road accident.(1): Bang on head (not causing unconsciousness) – cut to left side of face – broken glass in mouth – black eye – bruising to right shoulder – shaken – off school 2 days – sleep disturbance for 2 weeks – 5 months after accident, small piece of glass discharged from cut, leaving scar 12 x 2mm near left ear – claimant's face already scarred by dog bite.(2): Bruising to arms and legs – shaken and very upset – crying at night on a few occasions after the accident – full recovery within 2-3 weeks.

Other points: Award split – (1): £1,500 (2): £500

1.1.C15 Case No. 11933

Name of case: Blenkiron v Turton

Brief description of injuries: BRUISING – 12 MONTHS

Reported: Kemp & Kemp, K1-100, K2-079/1; [1999] CLY 1597

JSB Category: 5(A); 6(F), 6(L)(b)

Sex: Male

Age at injury: 46

Age at award: 49

Date of award: 21 June 1999

Tribunal: Hull County Court

Amount of award then: £2,250

Award at February 2001: £2,337

Description of injuries: Road accident – multiple contusions, in particular to chest, left (non-dominant) hand and forearm, right upper arm, both knees – claimant unable to take any time off work because self-employed – difficulties carrying out work for 3-4 months – gradual recovery over 12 months following accident.

Other points: Claimant argued that injuries he sustained were analogous to minor whiplash resolving after a year – this argument accepted by judge.

1.1.C16 Case No. 10675

Name of case: Parkinson v Trust House Forte

Brief description of injuries: SPRAIN – 9 MONTHS

Reported: [1993] CLY 1571

JSB Category: 6(M)(d)

Sex: Female

Age at injury: 45

Age at award: –

Date of award: 20 November 1992

Tribunal: Northampton County Court

Amount of award then: £1,300

Award at February 2001: £1,601

Description of injuries: Trip and fall on first day of holiday – severe sprain of ankle – holiday spent sitting down with leg raised and bandaged – ankle constantly painful for 2 weeks after return home – gradual return to work over 8 weeks – aching and swelling in ankle at end of day still occurring at that point – all pain completely subsided within 8 months of accident – swelling subsided after 9 months.

1.1.C17 Case No. 10490

Name of case: Merriot v Tiley

Brief description of injuries: BRUISING – HAEMATOLOGY TO THIGH

Reported: [1992] CLY 1746

JSB Category: 6(K)

Sex: Male

Age at injury: –

Age at award: 46

Date of award: 07 October 1992

Tribunal: Taunton County Court

Amount of award then: £1,050

Award at February 2001: £1,291

Description of injuries: Bruising to the right thigh – suffered a haematoma of the upper thigh area and walked with a limp for six weeks.

Prognosis: Prognosis was for a complete recovery.

1.1.C18 Case No. 10509

Name of case: Morris v The Post Office

Brief description of injuries: BRUISING – 2 MONTHS

Reported: [1992] CLY 1765

JSB Category: 6

Sex: Male

Age at injury: 37

Age at award: –

Date of award: 17 November 1992

Tribunal: Coventry County Court

Amount of award then: £541

Award at February 2001: £666

Description of injuries: Thrown off his motorcycle – bruising to the right shoulder, hip, knee and ankle.

Prognosis: Not fully fit for two-and-a-half months.

SECTION 1.2
DAMAGE TO HEAD

1.2.1 HAIR LOSS

1.2.1.C1 Case No. 11557

Name of case: De Smet v Gold

Brief description of injuries: HEAD – SCALP – HAIR

Reported: Kemp & Kemp, J5-001; [1998] CLY 1559

JSB Category: 7(B)(a); 9

Sex: Female

Age at injury: 26

Age at award: 28

Date of award: 19 November 1997

Tribunal: Brighton County Court

Amount of award then: £12,500

Award at February 2001: £13,573

Description of injuries: Full thickness burn to the scalp after bleaching treatment – painful in-patient remedial treatment required over 15 months – S suffered embarrassment over her appearance – 2.5 years after the accident S had still not fully recovered.

Prognosis: Prognosis was for full recovery.

1.2.1.C2 Case No. 11117

Name of case: West v HSHT Clinic

Brief description of injuries: HEAD – HAIR – FAILED HAIR REPLACEMENT TREATMENT

Reported: Kemp & Kemp, J2-002; [1996] CLY 2208

JSB Category: 9(a)

Sex: Male

Age at injury: 29

Age at award: 31

Date of award: 16 August 1995

Tribunal: Birmingham County Court

Amount of award then: £5,000

Award at February 2001: £5,737

Description of injuries: Failed hair replacement treatment – loss of replacement hair – some sensitivity of the scalp remained.

1.2.1.C3 Case No. 10743

Name of case: Turner v NS Hair Treatment Clinic

Brief description of injuries: HEAD – LOSS OF HAIR TRANSPLANT – SCARS TO SCALP

Reported: Kemp & Kemp, J5-003; [1994] CLY 1591

JSB Category: 9; 8

Sex: Male

Age at injury: 41

Age at award: 44

Date of award: 12 September 1994

Tribunal: Salford County Court

Amount of award then: £4,500

Award at February 2001: £5,338

Description of injuries: Claimant underwent artificial hair implant treatment involving injection of individual artificial hairs into scalp under local anaesthetic – during latter part of 15 session treatment, scalp became infected, but treatment continued, with only anti-dandruff shampoo being prescribed – scalp became increasingly painful – shortly after conclusion of treatment, hair implants fell out and infection remained, producing pus – severe embarrassment, leading to giving up of work and effective refusal to participate in social activities, resulting in breakdown of relationship with girlfriend – noticeable scarring and pitting to scalp – distinct ridge extending from hairline over scalp, some areas of which sensitive – confidence gradually improving at time of report – however, claimant still consistently wore hat when out in public and avoided bright lights, which highlighted scarring.

1.2.1.C4 Case No. 10192

Name of case: Smith v Musso (t/a Ficarazzi)

Brief description of injuries: HAIR DAMAGED BY A PERMANENT WAVE – WEDDING POSTPONED

Reported: Kemp & Kemp, J5-004; [1991] CLY 1389

JSB Category: 9(b)

Sex: Female

Age at injury: 27

Age at award: 29

Date of award: 04 December 1990

Tribunal: Westminster County Court

Amount of award then: £4,000

Award at February 2001: £5,296

Description of injuries: A "body-wave" perm damaged the hair which matted and fell out – caused distress due to approaching wedding day – S became obsessed with the appearance of her hair – S felt at a disadvantage at work as her appearance was important to inspire staff and clients with confidence – gained weight.

1.2.1.C5 Case No. 10938

Name of case: Messam v Macnamara

Brief description of injuries: HAIR LOSS – UNLIKELY TO MAKE FULL RECOVERY

Reported: Kemp & Kemp, J5-005; [1995] CLY 1689

JSB Category: 9(a)

Sex: Female

Age at injury: 51

Age at award: 54

Date of award: 02 August 1995

Tribunal: Bow County Court

Amount of award then: £4,500

Award at February 2001: £5,163

Description of injuries: Four days after having a permanent wave treatment at a salon, plaintiff's hair began to break off and fall out – within one month she had suffered extensive hair loss and a large part of scalp was visible – plaintiff was extremely distressed and embarrassed about her appearance – had numerous steaming and conditioning treatments which gradually improved condition of hair and encouraged hair growth so that she could wear braids to disguise hair loss – plaintiff's hair grew back slowly but not fully and she was unlikely to recover a full head of hair – always wore a scarf around her hairline to hide the loss of hair and also tied the braids on top of her head to hide hair loss on her scalp – remained extremely embarrassed and distressed when people noticed her hair loss – was unable to attend several large family functions as she was too embarrassed to allow her family to see her.

1.2.1.C6 Case No. 11327

Name of case: Ramsbottom v Novacki

Brief description of injuries: HEAD – HAIR LOSS

Reported: Kemp & Kemp, J5-008; [1997] CLY 1875

JSB Category: 9(a)

Sex: Female

Age at injury: 21

Age at award: 22

Date of award: 02 January 1997

Tribunal: Manchester County Court

Amount of award then: £4,000

Award at February 2001: £4,456

Description of injuries: Hair loss and damage after hair-straightening treatment – traumatic response to a distressing experience.

Prognosis: No long-term psychological distress – estimated 28 months for the hair to re-grow.

1.2.1.C7 Case No. 10193

Name of case: Rosa v Charles, James and Ellington

Brief description of injuries: HAIR DAMAGED BY A PERMANENT WAVE TREATMENT – 8-9 YEARS TO RE-GROW

Reported: Kemp & Kemp, J5-007; [1991] CLY 1390

JSB Category: 9(b)

Sex: Female

Age at injury: 35

Age at award: 36

Date of award: 08 October 1991

Tribunal: Bradford County Court

Amount of award then: £3,500

Award at February 2001: £4,456

Description of injuries: Hair damage caused by a permanent wave treatment – the hair broke off in handfuls – areas of stubble left at and near scalp level – the bulk of the hair was at varying lengths – the shafts dry and brittle – likely to break off – considerable embarrassment, anxiety and loss of confidence.

Prognosis: Poor prognosis for re-growth of the damaged hair – it would take eight or nine years to re-grow to its former length – hair was cut short very much against her wishes.

1.2.1.C8 Case No. 10577

Name of case: Phillips v Kannike-Martins Associates

Brief description of injuries: HAIR – PATCHY LOSS – CLAIMANT A MODEL

Reported: [1993] CLY 1470

JSB Category: 9

Sex: Female

Age at injury: 27

Age at award: -

Date of award: 29 October 1993

Tribunal: Central London County Court

Amount of award then: £3,500

Award at February 2001: £4,245

Description of injuries: Claimant professional model – hair straightening treatment caused breakage of hair to scalp level – hair loss in patches, mainly from back and side of head – described as looking like "mangy dog" – whole style of life affected – considerable stress – self-confidence destroyed – hair regrowing normally all over the scalp within 3 to 4 months of incident – only small amount of discomfort.

Prognosis: No permanent damage.

1.2.1.C9 Case No. 11555

Name of case: Otalor v Chez Vicky Modern Hairdressing Salon

Brief description of injuries: HEAD – HAIR

Reported: Kemp & Kemp, J5-009; [1998] CLY 1557

JSB Category: 9

Sex: Female

Age at injury: 17

Age at award: 19

Date of award: 13 July 1998

Tribunal: Wandsworth County Court

Amount of award then: £4,000

Award at February 2001: £4,221

Description of injuries: Loss of hair after bleaching – bald patches – maximum hair length of 7cm to 10 cm caused great embarrassment – 18 months for hair to grow long enough for hair extensions to be added – incident described as "a disastrous piece of hairdressing".

1.2.1.C10 Case No. 11556

Name of case: Jawando v Sphinx Hairdressing

Brief description of injuries: HEAD – HAIR

Reported: Kemp & Kemp, J5-010; [1998] CLY 1558

JSB Category: 9

Sex: Female

Age at injury: 26

Age at award: 27

Date of award: 16 July 1997

Tribunal: Manchester County Court

Amount of award then: £3,500

Award at February 2001: £3,822

Description of injuries: Damage to the hair during conditioning treatment – immediate unwanted cutting was carried out – hair crumbled when rubbed – loss of confidence and stress caused by the accident – after 26 months 1 inch of damaged hair remained to be grown out.

1.2.1.C11 Case No. 11904

Name of case: Foley v Summerfield

Brief description of injuries: HEAD – MINOR INJURY – HAIR

Reported: Kemp & Kemp, K2-193; [1999] CLY 1568

JSB Category: 2(B); 9

Sex: Male

Age at injury: 30

Age at award: 33

Date of award: 16 December 1998

Tribunal: Bromley County Court

Amount of award then: £3,500

Award at February 2001: £3,662

Description of injuries: Road accident – claimant struck head and sustained 2cm laceration to scalp – laceration closed with glue at hospital – claimant off work for 1 week – injury healed after 2 months – for the following year, claimant suffered occasional headaches and dizzy spells lasting up to 10 minutes at a time – laceration resulted in 2cm bald patch which failed to grow back; after 9 months, claimant sought medical attention for this and was prescribed steroid cream, which helped hair grow back successfully.

1.2.1.C12 Case No. 10578

Name of case: Holder v Williams
Brief description of injuries: HAIR – THINNING
Reported: Kemp & Kemp, J5-011; [1993] CLY 1471
JSB Category: 9
Sex: Female
Age at injury: 47
Age at award: -
Date of award: 08 June 1993
Tribunal: Wandsworth County Court
Amount of award then: £3,000
Award at February 2001: £3,660

Description of injuries: Hair – straightening treatment caused thinning – loss of all hair on back of head from top of ears to neck within 2 or 3 weeks of treatment – claimant embarrassed but did not "go to pieces" – immediately bought weave to cover area, but weave noticeable and uncomfortable – caused occasional headaches – caused problems with washing hair and swimming – necessary treatments for hair and weave had smell which claimant and boyfriend found unpleasant – weave worn for 1 year – hair had regrown by then but was still short – hair only regrew to full length 2 years after the incident.

1.2.1.C13 Case No. 10579

Name of case: Re Smith
Brief description of injuries: HAIR – PATCHES PULLED OUT
Reported: Kemp & Kemp, J5-072;[1993] CLY 1472
JSB Category: 9
Sex: Male
Age at injury: 30
Age at award: 33
Date of award: 15 December 1992
Tribunal: CICB
Amount of award then: £2,750
Award at February 2001: £3,398

Description of injuries: Police officer suffered violent attack while restraining prisoner – 2 large handfuls of hair pulled out of top of head – severe head pain lasting 2 weeks – some regrowth, taking 6 months, but claimant left with 2-inch – square bald patch on side of head at time of trial – patch very noticeable, itchy, irritated and more prone to sunburn – loss of self esteem and self-confidence – self-consciousness about patch – claimant using special hair – treatment shampoo, having some limited effect on regrowth.

1.2.1.C14 Case No. 10367

Name of case: Re Bosah
Brief description of injuries: LOSS OF HAIR
Reported: Kemp & Kemp, J5-013; [1992] CLY 1623
JSB Category: 9(b)
Sex: Female
Age at injury: 54
Age at award: 57
Date of award: 10 September 1992
Tribunal: CICB, Leeds
Amount of award then: £2,500
Award at February 2001: £3,085

Description of injuries: Frightening attack during which two handfuls of hair were pulled out leaving two one-inch bald patches – headaches for three months.

Prognosis: At the time of the hearing there was no significant re-growth – three-quarter inch patches clearly visible – loss of self-esteem and embarrassment.

1.2.1.C15 Case No. 10368

Name of case: Barry v Guys and Dolls
Brief description of injuries: DAMAGE TO HAIR
Reported: [1992] CLY 1624
JSB Category: 9(b)
Sex: Female
Age at injury: -
Age at award: 49
Date of award: 24 June 1992
Tribunal: Liverpool County Court
Amount of award then: £1,500
Award at February 2001: £1,852

Description of injuries: Hair damaged during tinting process – turned multi-coloured – dry, textureless and broken – could not be re-styled.

Prognosis: Continued to work and resumed social life within two weeks – hair presentable within six months.

1.2.2 HEADACHES

1.2.2.C1 Case No. 11884
Name of case: Walchester v Chief Constable of Staffordshire
Brief description of injuries: HEAD – MIGRAINE
Reported: Kemp & Kemp, C2-078; [1999] CLY 1548
JSB Category: 2(B)
Sex: Female
Age at injury: 25
Age at award: 29
Date of award: 04 December 1998
Tribunal: Stoke-on-Trent County Court
Amount of award then: £7,000
Award at February 2001: £7,324
Description of injuries: Claimant struck on head – swelling and cuts and bruises to left eye, eyebrow and nose, settling after 3 weeks – swelling of nose affected sinuses, which were painful for some time – persistent migraine headaches, lasting a couple of hours, occurring 1-3 times per week 4 years after the accident, causing blurred vision and impaired concentration.
Prognosis: Headaches would continue at rate of 1-2 per week for approximately 20 years – thereafter, claimant would have long-term tendency to headaches at a rate of one about every few months for the rest of her life.

1.2.2.C2 Case No. 11885
Name of case: Re Wilcock
Brief description of injuries: HEAD – MIGRAINE
Reported: Kemp & Kemp, C2-080; [1999] CLY 1549
JSB Category: 2(B)
Sex: Male
Age at injury: 32
Age at award: 36
Date of award: 15 January 1999
Tribunal: CICB, Nottingham
Amount of award then: £6,000
Award at February 2001: £6,316
Description of injuries: Claimant struck on head and face in assault – blurred vision and severe headache for 2 days; thereafter swift recovery from immediate effects – 1 week later, claimant began to suffer from migraines – diagnosis of post-traumatic migraine – migraines continued irregularly, on average 3 times per month – each attack would begin with visual disturbances and nausea before development of throbbing headache – attacks lasted 2-4 hours – painkillers gave some relief, but anti-migraine medication caused unacceptable levels of drowsiness – claimant forced to adapt his working practices in order to cope with attacks.
Other points: Sum included £800 for medication.

1.2.2.C3 Case No. 10050
Name of case: Farrell v Porn and Dunwoody
Brief description of injuries: HEADACHES, 6+ YEARS
Reported: [1990] CLY 1678
JSB Category: 2(B)
Sex: Male
Age at injury: 51
Age at award: 57
Date of award: 15 June 1990
Tribunal: Ilford County Court
Amount of award then: £2,000
Award at February 2001: £2,715
Description of injuries: Plaintiff fell down flight of stairs – sustained bump on back of head and cut above left eyebrow – not unconscious – headaches developed, occurring two or three times a week, lasting three or four hours – at time of trial headaches were not so severe or frequent.
Prognosis: No medical explanation why headaches have continued – regarded as genuine, but likely to resolve.

1.2.2.C4 Case No. 10051
Name of case: Littleford v Wood
Brief description of injuries: HEADACHES, 1 YEAR
Reported: Kemp & Kemp, K2-161; [1990] CLY 1691
JSB Category: 2(B)
Sex: Female
Age at injury: -
Age at award: 63
Date of award: 03 January 1990
Tribunal: Bradford County Court
Amount of award then: £1,000
Award at February 2001: £1,439
Description of injuries: Rear seat passenger in taxi which collided with kerb – sustained blow to side of head causing tenderness and swelling – headaches irregularly for one year after.

1.2.2.C5 Case No. 10052

Name of case: Heskey v GKN Sankey

Brief description of injuries: HEADACHES, 2 YEARS

Reported: Kemp & Kemp, K2-170; [1990] CLY 1693

JSB Category: 2(B)

Sex: Male

Age at injury: -

Age at award: 50

Date of award: 10 August 1990

Tribunal: Not stated

Amount of award then: £1,000

Award at February 2001: £1,343

Description of injuries: Struck on head by metal eye on end of wire rope – knocked to ground but did not lose consciousness – laceration to head above hair line resulting in tender scar – suffered with headaches – two years after accident still suffers headaches – scar tender when combing hair.

1.2.2.C6 Case No. 12025

Name of case: Z (a child) v Greater Manchester Police Authority

Brief description of injuries: HEAD – HEADACHES – 7 WEEKS

Reported: Kemp & Kemp, PRC-021; [2000] 4 CL 168

JSB Category: 2

Sex: Male

Age at injury: 9

Age at award: 10

Date of award: 16 November 1999

Tribunal: Skegness County Court

Amount of award then: £1,250

Award at February 2001: £1,290

Description of injuries: Sustained minor injuries in a traffic accident – a blow to the head caused headaches which lasted for seven weeks – laceration of the frenulum and nightmares which lasted seven days.

1.2.2.C7 Case No. 10686

Name of case: John Laing Construction and Whattam (Thomas) v Stickells (David)

Brief description of injuries: HEAD – HEADACHES

Reported: [1993] CLY 1582

JSB Category: 2(B)

Sex: Male

Age at injury: 35

Age at award: 38

Date of award: 18 August 1993

Tribunal: Reading County Court

Amount of award then: £750

Award at February 2001: £913

Description of injuries: Claimant struck head when involved in accident – headaches for 7 days – sleepless nights for 3 or 4 weeks, resulting in general tiredness and affecting ability to concentrate.

1.2.2.1
HEADACHES AND OTHER INJURY

1.2.2.1.C1 Case No. 11285

Name of case: Re Full

Brief description of injuries: HEAD – FRACTURED SKULL

Reported: Kemp & Kemp, C2-007; [1997] CLY 1833

JSB Category: 2(A)(b)

Sex: Male

Age at injury: 36

Age at award: 41

Date of award: 31 October 1996

Tribunal: CICB, Sale

Amount of award then: £90,000

Award at February 2001: £121,870

Description of injuries: Fractured skull – massive blood clot – fractured elbow – deafness in the right ear – frequency of micturition – inability to ejaculate properly – severe personality change and behavioural problems – required supervision for the daily acts of living – could manage his own affairs.

Prognosis: Six per cent chance of developing epilepsy.

1.2.2.1.C2 Case No. 11291

Name of case: Re F

Brief description of injuries: HEAD – BRAIN – LOSS OF SPEECH

Reported: Kemp & Kemp, C2-021; [1997] CLY 1839

JSB Category: 2(A)(c)(i)

Sex: Male

Age at injury: 43

Age at award: 52

Date of award: 06 May 1997

Tribunal: CICB, London

Amount of award then: £75,000

Award at February 2001: £96,018

Description of injuries: Three skull fractures – dysphasia left him almost incapable of speech – grand mal epilepsy not completely under control – was able to live independently – required approximately four hours per day supervision and domestic assistance.

Prognosis: No prospect of re-employment.

1.2.2.1.C3 Case No. 10908

Name of case: O'Keefe v Webb

Brief description of injuries: BRAIN DAMAGE – MENTAL AND PHYSICAL IMPAIRMENT – WILL NOT LIVE INDEPENDENTLY

Reported: Kemp & Kemp, A4-017/2; [1995] CLY 1659

JSB Category: 2(A)(c)(ii)

Sex: Male

Age at injury: 18

Age at award: 21

Date of award: 14 March 1995

Tribunal: QBD

Amount of award then: £65,000

Award at February 2001: £87,384

Description of injuries: Plaintiff suffered a very serious head injury and brain damage in road traffic accident – suffered a degree of intellectual impairment and memory loss – unable to walk unaided, and was left with markedly unco-ordinated and weak left leg – unable to run and had to give up sport, which he had enjoyed prior to the accident.

Prognosis: Would never be able to live independently and required constant supervision – would never be able to consider participation in competitive sport.

1.2.2.1.C4 Case No. 11087

Name of case: Re Willmore

Brief description of injuries: HEAD – SKULL – FRACTURE – BRAIN INJURY

Reported: Kemp & Kemp, C2-031; [1996] CLY 2178

JSB Category: 2(A)(c)

Sex: Male

Age at injury: 19

Age at award: 32

Date of award: 09 February 1996

Tribunal: CICB, York

Amount of award then: £60,000

Award at February 2001: £77,664

Description of injuries: Penetrating depressed fracture injured underlying brain.

Prognosis: He had significant difficulties with basic tasks – a permanent high risk of epilepsy – severely restricted in the type of work he could carry out.

1.2.2.1.C5 Case No. 11288

Name of case: Re Ives

Brief description of injuries: HEAD – SKULL FRACTURE – MEMORY AND PERSONALITY AFFECTED

Reported: Kemp & Kemp, C2-033; [1997] CLY 1836

JSB Category: 2(A)(d) 4(B)(b) 4(C)(b)

Sex: Male

Age at injury: 20

Age at award: 24

Date of award: 10 December 1996

Tribunal: CICB, London

Amount of award then: £60,000

Award at February 2001: £75,662

Description of injuries: Severe skull fracture – contusion to the brain – permanently deaf in the right ear and tinnitus – full loss of smell – partial loss of taste – subtle neurological deficits causing an impairment of memory and personality change.

Other points: He presented very well on superficial contact.

1.2.2.1.C6 Case No. 10913

Name of case: Re Mohammed

Brief description of injuries: HEAD INJURY – GRAND MAL EPILEPSY – DEPRESSION AND ANXIETY

Reported: Kemp & Kemp, C3-013; [1995] CLY 1664

JSB Category: 2(C)(a)

Sex: Female

Age at injury: 35

Age at award: 40

Date of award: 19 May 1995

Tribunal: CICB, Durham

Amount of award then: £50,000

Award at February 2001: £63,821

Description of injuries: Plaintiff attacked outside restaurant in May 1990 – suffered cuts and bruises to face and short period of unconsciousness following being repeatedly punched to head – detained in hospital for five days and subsequently diagnosed as epileptic following a first grand mal seizure in August 1990. She had no family history of seizures – subsequently complained of headaches and grand mal seizures once or twice a month – took anti-convulsant drugs which reduced frequency of attacks but seizures continued to occur without warning – seizures had resulted in applicant injuring herself, including a burn to her hand and a shoulder injury. The Board accepted the causation on the balance of probabilities and accepted that the seizures were grand mal and accepted that a high dosage of anti-convulsants were required to control seizures and that the medication caused problems with sleeping – the applicant could not consider returning to her pre-accident employment as a dress designer/machinist – since assault the applicant had become depressed and tense and suffered from headaches – was now a regular hospital attender and required someone to "keep an eye on her" – had lost confidence and independence and was now incontinent – at time of the award was heavily pregnant and an increased dosage had been necessary to avoid seizures during pregnancy.

1.2.2.1.C7 Case No. 11075

Name of case: Re H

Brief description of injuries: HEAD – SEVERE HEAD AND FACIAL INJURIES

Reported: Kemp & Kemp, A4-020; [1996] CLY 2166

JSB Category: 2(A)(c)

Sex: Male

Age at injury: 25

Age at award: 29

Date of award: 12 September 1996

Tribunal: CICB, Liverpool

Amount of award then: £40,000

Award at February 2001: £48,333

Description of injuries: Severe head and facial injuries – severe shoulder strain – multiple abrasions – post-traumatic stress disorder – severely impaired memory and intellect – 20 per cent reduction in IQ – personality changes – spasticity in one upper and both lower limbs – risk of epilepsy 5 per cant – probably unemployable.

1.2.2.1.C8 Case No. 10915

Name of case: Re Fletcher

Brief description of injuries: BRAIN DAMAGE – EPILEPSY – PERSONALITY CHANGE

Reported: Kemp & Kemp, C3-077; [1995] CLY 1666

JSB Category: 2(A)(c)(iii)

Sex: Male

Age at injury: 26

Age at award: 33

Date of award: 01 December 1994

Tribunal: CICB, London

Amount of award then: £35,000

Award at February 2001: £44,214

Description of injuries: Attacked after helping woman who was being attacked in the street – struck several times over head with hammer – wound healed leaving 3cm indentation over right temple – claimant was left with three long-term serious sequelae: headaches, epilepsy and personality change – experienced migrainous headaches three times a week, lasting from four hours to two days – only bedrest in a darkened, quiet room provided any relief – epilepsy manifested itself four years after attack and took the form of night seizures involving tongue-biting and incontinence – also suffered from short blackouts during the day – the fits occurred every three to four weeks – medication prescribed, which caused drowsiness, did not entirely control the condition – prior to assault claimant had led normal social life – as consequence of injury he became aggressive, moody, bad-tempered, depressed and, on occasions, violent – his girlfriend and daughter left him.

Prognosis: His medical condition would not improve – it was not possible for him to return to work as a motor mechanic or work with heavy machinery – his ability to work was restricted by his frequent debilitating headaches – his employment prospects were limited to menial labour with understanding employers.

1.2.2.1.C9 Case No. 11076

Name of case: Re Potter

Brief description of injuries: HEAD – BRAIN – SEVERE BRAIN DAMAGE

Reported: Kemp & Kemp, C2-059; [1996] CLY 2167

JSB Category: 2(A)(c)(iii)

Sex: Male

Age at injury: 18

Age at award: 25

Date of award: 04 October 1996

Tribunal: CICB, Nottingham

Amount of award then: £35,000

Award at February 2001: £41,780

Description of injuries: Devastating brain injury – haematomas.

Prognosis: At the time of the award it was anticipated that the psychotic illness would pass given appropriate therapy and abstention from alcohol – cutting grass and digging was considered to be at the limit of his intellectual ability.

1.2.2.1.C10 Case No. 10905

Name of case: George v Tipper

Brief description of injuries: HEAD INJURY – PERSONALITY CHANGE – FRACTURE OF TIBIA AND FIBULA

Reported: [1995] CLY 1656

JSB Category: 6(K)(b)(iii)

Sex: Male

Age at injury: 8

Age at award: 14

Date of award: 07 February 1995

Tribunal: Bristol County Court

Amount of award then: £25,000

Award at February 2001: £30,572

Description of injuries: Infant male injured while crossing a zebra pedestrian crossing – suffered a compound fracture to the right tibia and fibula – also suffered a wound to back of right thigh, multiple grazes to ankle and foot, cuts to right arm and a closed head injury – as result of head injury suffered behavioural problems, manifesting themselves in irritability and tendency to temper outbursts which occurred daily – given carbamazepine to control temper outbursts – suffered angulated displaced fracture of the distal third of the right tibia and fibula which united in almost anatomical position, although there was lack of 10 degrees flexion in the knee on right leg and some discomfort in right shin – left with a stable scar measuring 13cm in the posterior aspect of the right thigh, together with cosmetically acceptable scars on the right shin and the right forearm – possibility that head injury affected memory and concentration and that educational performance, which was below standard pre-accident, may have been affected.

Prognosis: Likely to need to remain on medication for several years.

1.2.2.1.C11 Case No. 10024

Name of case: Re Evans

Brief description of injuries: EYE INJURIES – DOUBLE VISION, HEADACHES

Reported: Kemp & Kemp, C2-066; [1990] CLY 1613

JSB Category: 4(A)

Sex: Male

Age at injury: 53

Age at award: 59

Date of award: 21 February 1990

Tribunal: CICB, Leeds

Amount of award then: £20,000

Award at February 2001: £29,847

Description of injuries: Injury to left pupil – bruise to right frontal area of head – ribs and abdomen tender after kick – double vision and headaches – diplopia, ameliorated by wearing left eye-patch.

Prognosis: Unable to resume employment, read or write, continue leisure activities – became morose – sex life impaired.

1.2.2.1.C12 Case No. 11289

Name of case: Re John (Mark)

Brief description of injuries: HEAD – BRAIN – CONCENTRATION AFFECTED

Reported: Kemp & Kemp, C2-067; [1997] CLY 1837

JSB Category: 2(A)(c)(iii)

Sex: Male

Age at injury: 17

Age at award: 25

Date of award: 18 February 1997

Tribunal: CICB, London

Amount of award then: £25,000

Award at February 2001: £28,875

Description of injuries: Serious head injury – moderate brain damage.

Prognosis: Possibility of epilepsy – permanent effects to concentration – only able to undertake semi-skilled or manual work.

Other points: The papers were not to be destroyed to cater for the possibility of the onset of epilepsy.

1.2.2.1.C13 Case No. 10941

Name of case: Hallam v Thompson

Brief description of injuries: SKULL – HAEMATOMA – INCREASED RISK OF EPILEPSY

Reported: Kemp & Kemp, D3-018; [1995] CLY 1692

JSB Category: 2(A)(d)

Sex: Male

Age at injury: 11

Age at award: 14

Date of award: 18 January 1995

Tribunal: Halifax County Court

Amount of award then: £15,000

Award at February 2001: £17,978

Description of injuries: Boy injured in road traffic accident on 26 March 1992 – scan showed left-sided parieto-temporal extradural haematoma with midline shift and effacement of left ventricle – emergency operation and haematoma was evacuated – plaintiff gradually recovered, was fully alert nine days after accident and was discharged from hospital 10 days after accident – after accident he was easily upset but six months after accident any personality change had completely resolved.

Prognosis: He was left with five per cent risk of developing epilepsy which would probably gradually reduce to one per cent risk three years after accident – at date of hearing he had no epilepsy or any other neurological symptoms and the only permanent effect of accident was conduction deafness in left ear.

1.2.2.1.C14 Case No. 10740

Name of case: Re Collins

Brief description of injuries: HEAD – JAW – HEADACHES

Reported: Kemp & Kemp, C6-004; [1994] CLY 1588

JSB Category: 7(A)(e)

Sex: Male

Age at injury: 36

Age at award: 40

Date of award: 17 December 1993

Tribunal: CICB, Manchester

Amount of award then: £12,500

Award at February 2001: £15,326

Description of injuries: Assault – claimant struck indiscriminately about head and body, sustaining whiplash injury, small cut to earlobe, soft-tissue damage to shoulder and, most seriously, injury left side of face and jaw – absent from work 4 weeks – complete recovery from all injuries except jaw injury – ongoing discomfort over left tempero-mandibular joint, despite physiotherapy – minor modifications to diet made to avoid excessive chewing – jaw pain associated with headaches – jaw "clicked" on occasions.

Prognosis: Prognosis of persisting discomfort indefinitely – 10 per cent chance of increased pain – less than 5 per cent chance of surgery becoming necessary.

1.2.2.1.C15 Case No. 10350

Name of case: Menhenott v Wiggins Teape Fine Papers

Brief description of injuries: SEVERELY BROKEN NOSE – HEADACHES

Reported: Kemp & Kemp, C5-024; [1992] CLY 1606

JSB Category: 7(A)(c)(i)

Sex: Male

Age at injury: 37

Age at award: 42

Date of award: 09 September 1992

Tribunal: Exeter County Court

Amount of award then: £9,500

Award at February 2001: £11,722

Description of injuries: Severe comminuted compound fracture of the nasal complex.

Prognosis: Scars of cosmetic surgery not particularly obvious – headaches not resolved by medication – extensive reconstruction work required – eleven weeks off work – continuous headaches immediately after the accident gradually reduced to several times a week.

1.2.2.1.C16 Case No. 10946

Name of case: Re Santos

Brief description of injuries: HEADACHES – INJURY TO ELBOW

Reported: Kemp & Kemp, E2-038; [1995] CLY 1697

JSB Category: 2(A)(d)

Sex: Male

Age at injury: 37

Age at award: 42

Date of award: 27 January 1995

Tribunal: CICB, Liverpool

Amount of award then: £9,000

Award at February 2001: £10,603

Description of injuries: Plaintiff sustained injuries as result of cast iron bath crashing through ceiling onto his head during employment as fireman – sustained injuries to neck, shoulder and right arm – X-rays did not reveal any fractures but cervical collar fitted – applicant sustained widespread soft-tissue injury in neck, shoulder and right arm and developed occipital headaches – underwent physiotherapy including traction and injections of cortisone which only partially alleviated symptoms – occipital head pains and aching in neck and right shoulder persisted – unable to continue in fire brigade even on light duties and was unable to play football and volleyball and could only swim at reduced capacity – experienced difficulties in vacuuming or carrying shopping because of pain and swelling in right elbow – sleep pattern disturbed – fell within small group whose condition progressed to chronicity – suffered from reduced libido as well as post-traumatic stress disorder which would take further 18 months from date of hearing to fade.

1.2.2.1.C17 Case No. 10717

Name of case: Re Taylor

Brief description of injuries: POST-CONCUSSION SYNDROME – HEADACHES

Reported: Kemp & Kemp, C2-074; [1994] CLY 1564

JSB Category: 2(A)(d)

Sex: Male

Age at injury: 37

Age at award: 41

Date of award: 28 June 1994

Tribunal: CICB, London

Amount of award then: £7,500

Award at February 2001: £8,915

Description of injuries: Claimant struck on head – no wound or loss of consciousness – headache developed later that day – 2.5 weeks later, headaches became violent and forced claimant to return from work overseas – post-concussion syndrome diagnosed – headaches continued for a year – accompanied by aggression, irritability, poor memory and poor concentration – significant depression over same period, with insomnia and easy loss of temper – occasional periods of excessive euphoria – mild phobia of filming in potentially dangerous situations – symptoms did not satisfy diagnostic criteria for post-traumatic stress disorder – business suffered over course of the 1 year period; claimant lived on income support – financial problems put strain on new marriage – at time of trial, claimant had founded new company and endeavouring to re-establish business.

1.2.2.1.C18 Case No. 11351

Name of case: Hamilton v Air Products and Saluveer

Brief description of injuries: NECK – WHIPLASH – HEADACHES

Reported: Kemp & Kemp, E2-047/1; [1997] CLY 1899

JSB Category: 6(A)(b)(i)

Sex: Female

Age at injury: 31

Age at award: 33

Date of award: 23 June 1997

Tribunal: Willesden County Court

Amount of award then: £8,000

Award at February 2001: £8,737

Description of injuries: Whiplash type injury to the neck – headaches and bruising.

Prognosis: Symptoms would be permanent – no improvement in the future – no prospect of deterioration.

1.2.2.1.C19 Case No. 10911

Name of case: Re M

Brief description of injuries: SKULL FRACTURE (NO BRAIN DAMAGE) – SCAR ON FOREHEAD

Reported: [1995] CLY 1662

JSB Category: 7(A)(b)

Sex: Female

Age at injury: 9

Age at award: 12

Date of award: 03 May 1995

Tribunal: Stoke-on-Trent County Court

Amount of award then: £7,500

Award at February 2001: £8,623

Description of injuries: Plaintiff was a back-seat passenger in stationary car which was hit whilst she was holding a golf club – golf club hit her on forehead, resulting in comminuted depressed fracture of the frontal bone in middle of forehead – underwent operation under general anaesthetic – laceration on forehead was extended and wound cleaned – depressed bone fragments removed and 1cm tear in dura was closed – one large bone fragment was replaced in skull and skin stitched – discharged five days later and managed to attend school two-and-a-half weeks later – since that time had no faints or blackouts and had not complained of headaches – left with permanent scar 5.5 cm long running down central forehead, between 1mm and 2mm wide – initially wore hair in fringe to conceal scar – it sometimes felt itchy and tingly and people did comment on the scar – had a period of post-traumatic amnesia of about 24 hours consistent with a moderately severe head injury – there must have been some slight contusional damage to the brain but there was no residual neurological deficit on examination.

Prognosis: Five months after operation there was 10 per cent risk of epilepsy – the risk of epilepsy fell to five per cent after two years – in eight years time the risk was expected to be in order of two per cent and that risk would persist throughout plaintiff's life – incidence of spontaneously occurring epilepsy in the general population is 0.7 per cent – a provisional award was made on the basis that she would not develop epilepsy.

1.2.2.1.C20 Case No. 10588

Name of case: Nelson v Ellis

Brief description of injuries: NECK – WHIPLASH – HEADACHES

Reported: Kemp & Kemp, E2-057; [1993] CLY 1481

JSB Category: 6(A)(b)

Sex: Male

Age at injury: 22

Age at award: 24

Date of award: 08 June 1993

Tribunal: Clerkenwell County Court

Amount of award then: £6,500

Award at February 2001: £7,929

Description of injuries: Moderately severe hyperextension whiplash injury in road accident – off duties (as police officer) for 2 months – hard collar worn at nights for 1 month – severe discomfort continued after return to work – headaches – at time of trial symptoms had subsided to intermittent pain of varying degrees; some weeks without pain, some with continuous pain – headaches also subsiding at time of trial.

Prognosis: Likelihood of cervical spondylosis in approximately 10 years – claimant rendered more vulnerable to neck injury, such injury being likely to make him unfit for duty in short term and have possible effects on long-term employability.

1.2.2.1.C21 Case No. 11886

Name of case: Sutton v Ling

Brief description of injuries: HEAD – MIGRAINE – WHIPLASH

Reported: Kemp & Kemp, C2-077; [1999] CLY 1550

JSB Category: 2(B); 6(A)(c); 3(A)

Sex: Female

Age at injury: 58

Age at award: 61

Date of award: 19 July 1999

Tribunal: Ipswich County Court

Amount of award then: £7,500

Award at February 2001: £7,813

Description of injuries: Claimant involved in road accident – scalp muscle contraction – headaches – migraines – whiplash injury to neck – adjustment disorder – acute stress reaction – migraines most serious injury – claimant suffered migraines up to 3 times each week, varying in duration but sometimes lasting more than a day; disabling and associated with vomiting – attacks so severe on occasions that claimant admitted to hospital or tended by GP – neck injury prevented claimant from standing up for long periods and caused pain on almost daily basis – acute stress reaction lasted for a few hours after the incident, and adjustment disorder, characterised by depression and anxiety, persisted for a few weeks – claimant's ability to sail, sew, decorate, garden and keep house had been significantly impaired, and consequently the quality of her retirement had been adversely affected.

Prognosis: Migraines would continue in the long term.

1.2.2.1.C22 Case No. 10076

Name of case: Fox v London Transport Executive

Brief description of injuries: BACK INJURY – HEADACHES – 10 YEARS

Reported: Kemp & Kemp, E3-094; [1990] CLY 1636

JSB Category: 6(B)

Sex: Female

Age at injury: 49

Age at award: 59

Date of award: 07 November 1989

Tribunal: Bromley County Court

Amount of award then: £5,000

Award at February 2001: £7,251

Description of injuries: Banged head and suffered brief spells of unconsciousness – whiplash injury to the cervical spine – headaches and neck pain up to 10 years after accident (intermittently) – injury to coccyx needing physiotherapy in lumbar region – for two to three years unable to do any heavy housework – slept badly and was unable to play with grandchildren.

Prognosis: Possibility of intermittent pain continuing.

1.2.2.1.C23 Case No. 10297

Name of case: Re Mendoza

Brief description of injuries: HEADACHES – 50% CHANCE OF SIGNIFICANT IMPROVEMENT

Reported: Kemp & Kemp, C2-079; [1991] CLY 1494

JSB Category: 2

Sex: Male

Age at injury: 42

Age at award: -

Date of award: 02 November 1990

Tribunal: CICB, London

Amount of award then: £5,000

Award at February 2001: £6,615

Description of injuries: Struck on the left side of the head and jaw during an assault – M developed post-traumatic migraine – no specific neurological abnormalities noted – headaches improved after taking analgesics – they persisted from between eight hours to three days.

Prognosis: M had a less than 50 per cent chance of significant improvement with treatment – 10 per cent chance that the headaches would continue indefinitely.

1.2.2.1.C24 Case No. 11110

Name of case: S (a minor) v St Helier NHS Trust
Brief description of injuries: HEAD – FACE – FORCEPS DAMAGE
Reported: Kemp & Kemp, J2-014/1; [1996] CLY 2201
JSB Category: 7(B)(a)(iv)
Sex: Female
Age at injury: Birth
Age at award: -
Date of award: 18 December 1995
Tribunal: Epsom County Court
Amount of award then: £5,000
Award at February 2001: £5,707
Description of injuries: Negligently applied forceps during birth caused injuries – multiple facial scars – permanent disfiguring scars – obvious cosmetic defect.
Other points: Corrective surgery not recommended – not assisted by make-up.

1.2.2.1.C25 Case No. 11545

Name of case: James (a minor) v Robertson
Brief description of injuries: FACE – SCAR – HEADACHES
Reported: Kemp & Kemp, C5-054; [1998] CLY 1547
JSB Category: 7(B)(b)(iii)
Sex: Male
Age at injury: 12
Age at award: 15
Date of award: 21 January 1998
Tribunal: Central London County Court
Amount of award then: £4,750
Award at February 2001: £5,122
Description of injuries: Deep laceration to the forehead requiring 6 stitches – headaches.
Prognosis: The scar had faded considerably – it represented a permanent cosmetic deformity – headaches would continue for 5 to 7 years after the date of the accident.

1.2.2.1.C26 Case No. 10044

Name of case: Re Singh
Brief description of injuries: BROKEN NOSE – 2 OPERATIONS – HEADACHES
Reported: Kemp & Kemp, C5-056; [1990] CLY 1606
JSB Category: 7(A)
Sex: Male
Age at injury: 39
Age at award: 44
Date of award: 31 January 1990
Tribunal: CICB
Amount of award then: £3,500
Award at February 2001: £5,038
Description of injuries: Suffered fractured nasal bone – after two corrective operations still suffered global headaches and nasal breathing difficulty.
Prognosis: Suffered symptoms particularly at night with sleep difficulties – symptoms might diminish with further surgery.

1.2.2.1.C27 Case No. 11070

Name of case: Hanwell v Bell and O'Neill
Brief description of injuries: HEAD – HAEMATOMA – CONTINUING HEADACHES
Reported: Kemp & Kemp, K2-010; [1995] CLY 1824
JSB Category: 2(B)
Sex: Male
Age at injury: 55
Age at award: 59
Date of award: 02 March 1995
Tribunal: Sheffield County Court
Amount of award then: £3,980
Award at February 2001: £4,641
Description of injuries: Boiler cleaner involved in road traffic accident – struck head at junction between the front windscreen and roof inside motor car – sustained a scalp haematoma near vertex – visited hospital on day of accident but was not detained – was in severe pain for next two days, thereafter he returned to work but did not undertake normal (heavy) duties – during next month suffered almost continuous headaches and was taking analgesics twice daily – for reasons unrelated to accident, did not return to pre-accident duties – marked improvement over next three years – at trial still suffering headaches, described as "tightness" at the front of head, usually in both temples – continued to take paracetamol at average rate of about 12 tablets per week – on each occasion, pain would last for up to four hours – felt that stress exacerbated condition and there was evidence of asymptomatic pre-disposition to stress before accident.
Prognosis: Medical evidence indicated that symptoms were now likely to be permanent.

1.2.2.1.C28 Case No. 11023

Name of case: Re Sim

Brief description of injuries: HEAD – FRACTURED NOSE AND FRONTAL BONE – HEADACHES

Reported: Kemp & Kemp, C5-061; [1995] CLY 1775

JSB Category: 2(B)

Sex: Male

Age at injury: 23

Age at award: 26

Date of award: 22 September 1995

Tribunal: CICB, York

Amount of award then: £3,500

Award at February 2001: £3,997

Description of injuries: Applicant travelling to football match when assaulted outside stadium by group of rival fans – kicked repeatedly whilst lying on the ground, and suffered fractured nose, slight chip fracture to skull over left eyebrow, and bruising to face and body – applicant remained conscious during and after attack, but he suffered concussion and felt extremely tired and nauseous for two days afterwards – off work two weeks – skull fracture did not require treatment – injuries resolved without leaving any cosmetic deficit, although he suffered post-traumatic headaches about once or twice a fortnight for two years following the assault – some obstruction of nasal airways occurred, partly attributable to nasal fracture, and partly to frequent secondary infections causing or aggravating an enlargement of his adenoid glands.

1.2.2.1.C29 Case No. 11030

Name of case: Taylor v R & S Thompson

Brief description of injuries: HEAD INJURY – DIZZINESS AND HEADACHES – 18 MONTHS

Reported: Kemp & Kemp, PRE-019; [1995] CLY 1782

JSB Category: 2(B)

Sex: Female

Age at injury: 23

Age at award: 27

Date of award: 01 December 1994

Tribunal: Mayor's and City County Court

Amount of award then: £3,000

Award at February 2001: £3,534

Description of injuries: Female traffic warden struck on head by metal clip which fell from some scaffolding – dazed for few moments and felt nauseous – had red mark on side of head – symptoms soon resolved but developed headaches soon thereafter – though these had largely settled couple of months later when she returned to light duties, they reoccurred occasionally for another 16 months, spoiling her particular pleasure of attending punk rock gigs – lost confidence and unable to walk streets in uniform until eight months after accident when she returned to full duties – had made full recovery after 18 months.

1.2.2.1.C30 Case No. 11034

Name of case: Curtis v Securicor

Brief description of injuries: HEAD INJURY – UNCONSCIOUSNESS – DETAINED IN HOSPITAL 7 DAYS

Reported: Kemp & Kemp, K2-061; [1995] CLY 1786

JSB Category: 2(B)

Sex: Male

Age at injury: 11

Age at award: 15

Date of award: 06 April 1995

Tribunal: Southampton County Court

Amount of award then: £2,400

Award at February 2001: £2,770

Description of injuries: Infant struck by van driven by employee of defendants as plaintiff attempted to cross road – because of impact was thrown onto windscreen which he smashed with his head – unconscious when ambulance arrived – during journey Southampton General Hospital became more conscious – was able to localise painful stimulus and make incomprehensible sounds – no cardiovascular problems – hard collar was applied to neck – following examination was admitted to neurological department where he underwent CT scan of head injury showed tiny lesion in deep white matter of left frontal lobe – also right parietal white matter lesion – other investigation included lateral cervical spine X-ray which showed no evidence of spinal fracture or instability – chest X-ray was clear – left fronto parietal scalp laceration was sutured – discharged from hospital approximately a week after being admitted – was reviewed by neurosurgical department some four months after accident when no specific problems were reported and was discharged fully from neurosurgical care – in addition to head injury sustained soft-tissue injuries to right hand together with some bruising to inguinal region.

1.2.2.1.C31 Case No. 11118

Name of case: Trushell v Gamblin & Robinson

Brief description of injuries: HEAD – HAIR – ALLERGIC REACTION TO HAIR COLOURANT

Reported: Kemp & Kemp, J5-074; [1996] CLY 2209

JSB Category: 9(b)

Sex: Female

Age at injury: 57

Age at award: 61

Date of award: 16 May 1996

Tribunal: Lincoln County Court

Amount of award then: £2,000

Award at February 2001: £2,250

Description of injuries: Allergic reaction and dermatitis following hair-colourant treatment – full recovery after twelve months.

1.2.2.1.C32 Case No. 10491

Name of case: Boisson v Mohommedi Studios

Brief description of injuries: INJURIES FROM SOLVENT INHALATION – HEADACHES, ETC.

Reported: [1992] CLY 1747

JSB Category:

Sex: Female

Age at injury: -

Age at award: 36

Date of award: 30 August 1991

Tribunal: Willesden County Court

Amount of award then: £1,650

Award at February 2001: £2,116

Description of injuries: Respiratory discomfort, headaches and soreness and digestive problems.

Prognosis: No permanent injury suffered.

1.2.2.1.C33 Case No. 11698

Name of case: Cinque v O'Donegan

Brief description of injuries: NECK – BACK – HEADACHES

Reported: Kemp & Kemp, E2-130/1; [1998] CLY 1701

JSB Category: 6(A)(c), 6(B)(c); 3(A)

Sex: Female

Age at injury: 32

Age at award: -

Date of award: 28 January 1998

Tribunal: Kingston County Court

Amount of award then: £1,850

Award at February 2001: £1,995

Description of injuries: Soft-tissue injuries to the neck, mid and low back – headaches – psychological injuries – residual pulling sensation to the neck.

1.2.2.1.C34 Case No. 11719

Name of case: Cuke v O'Callghan

Brief description of injuries: NECK – WHIPLASH – HEADACHES AND SHOCK

Reported: Kemp & Kemp, K2-117/1; [1998] CLY 1722

JSB Category: 6(A)(c)

Sex: Male

Age at injury: 41

Age at award: 42

Date of award: 02 June 1998

Tribunal: Central London County Court

Amount of award then: £1,800

Award at February 2001: £1,895

Description of injuries: Whiplash injury – small cut to the temple – headaches and shock.

Prognosis: Residual headaches would resolve over the following few months.

Other points: Award breakdown: £1,000 for whiplash; £500 for headaches and shock; £250 for the cut.

1.2.2.1.C35 Case No. 10342

Name of case: Falck (Constance) v Wilson

Brief description of injuries: DAILY HEADACHES – SHAKING HANDS – PERMANENT

Reported: [1992] CLY 1598

JSB Category: 3(A)(d)

Sex: Female

Age at injury: 61

Age at award: 64

Date of award: 18 March 1992

Tribunal: Huddersfield County Court

Amount of award then: £1,500

Award at February 2001: £1,887

Description of injuries: Knocked down while crossing the road – black eye, large lump to the back of the head, cracked ribs and swollen ankle – daily headaches partly relieved by paracetamol – reading, sewing and television affected – slightly shaking hands made sewing and delicate cooking impossible.

Prognosis: No improvement likely.

1.2.2.1.C36 Case No. 11699

Name of case: Evans v Morton

Brief description of injuries: NECK – HEADACHES – 4 MONTHS

Reported: Kemp & Kemp, E2-130/2; [1998] CLY 1702

JSB Category: 6(A)(c)

Sex: Male

Age at injury: 47

Age at award: 48

Date of award: 03 March 1998

Tribunal: Oxford County Court

Amount of award then: £1,675

Award at February 2001: £1,792

Description of injuries: Neck pain – no bony injury – headaches – within 4 months of the date of the accident symptoms were mild.

1.2.2.1.C37 Case No. 11119

Name of case: Leckie v TJ Hairdressers

Brief description of injuries: HEAD – SCALP – BURNS

Reported: Kemp & Kemp, J5-075; [1996] CLY 2210

JSB Category: 9(b)

Sex: Female

Age at injury: 32

Age at award: 35

Date of award: 19 July 1996

Tribunal: Neath and Port County Court

Amount of award then: £1,500

Award at February 2001: £1,693

Description of injuries: Superficial burns to the scalp – some hair loss – distress – full recovery from the injury – hair re-grown.

Other points: It was considered that distress and embarrassment were significant.

1.2.2.1.C38 Case No. 11047

Name of case: Suffler v Bell

Brief description of injuries: HEAD – BLOW TO HEAD – BRUISED AND JOLTED – 1 YEAR

Reported: Kemp & Kemp, K2-151; [1995] CLY 1801

JSB Category: 2(B)

Sex: Male

Age at injury: 28

Age at award: 28

Date of award: 02 March 1994

Tribunal: Birkenhead County Court

Amount of award then: £1,250

Award at February 2001: £1,509

Description of injuries: Plaintiff riding bicycle was struck by taxi – sustained blow to right temporal region of skull with no loss of consciousness, glass injury to cervical spine, scarring and jolting force to right shoulder and bruising to left knee, ankle and toes of left foot – at time of hearing, plaintiff had made full recovery from all physical injuries – bicycle was destroyed in accident.

1.2.2.1.C39 Case No. 11897

Name of case: R (minors) v Putt

Brief description of injuries: NECK – HEADACHES – ENURESIS – 2/6 WEEKS (2 CLAIMANTS)

Reported: Kemp & Kemp, K2-248; [1999] CLY 1561

JSB Category: (1): 6(A)(c); 5(I) (2): 6(A)(c); 5(I)

Sex: (1): Male (2): Female

Age at injury: (1):7;(2):5

Age at award: (1):8;(2):6

Date of award: 18 May 1999

Tribunal: Weymouth County Court

Amount of award then: £1,400

Award at February 2001: £1,454

Description of injuries: 2 claimants sustained minor injuries in road accident.(1): neck pain, resolving in a matter of weeks without residual effect – occasional headaches, continuing for 6 weeks after date of accident.(2): headaches – neck pain – enuresis – symptoms lasted approximately 2 weeks.Both claimants able to attend school and play all sports without any disruptions.

Other points: Award split: (1): £750 (2): £650

1.2.2.1.C40 Case No. 11254

Name of case: Re Piotrowski

Brief description of injuries: HEAD – FACE – LACERATIONS

Reported: (1996) 96 (4) QR 8' Kemp & Kemp, K2-163; [1996] CLY 2346

JSB Category: 7(B)(b)(v)

Sex: Male

Age at injury: 27

Age at award: -

Date of award: 21 March 1996

Tribunal: CICB, London

Amount of award then: £1,250

Award at February 2001: £1,419

Description of injuries: Lacerations to the face and head – grazed knuckles – shock – full recovery – faint scarring on the forehead remained.

1.2.2.1.C41 Case No. 11730

Name of case: Mitchell v Rivett

Brief description of injuries: NECK – WHIPLASH – HEADACHES

Reported: Kemp & Kemp, K2-169/2, PRK-006; [1998] CLY 1733

JSB Category: 6(A)(c)

Sex: Male

Age at injury: 23

Age at award: 24

Date of award: 10 November 1997

Tribunal: Southampton County Court

Amount of award then: £1,250

Award at February 2001: £1,347

Description of injuries: Headache and neck stiffness – whiplash injury was diagnosed – at the time of the hearing M had no neck symptoms – occasional headaches.

Other points: M suffered from pre-existing petit mal epilepsy – there was no adverse connection.

1.2.2.1.C42 Case No. 11061

Name of case: Ohene v Rymer

Brief description of injuries: HEAD – LACERATION TO SCALP -SHOCK

Reported: Kemp & Kemp, K2-209; [1995] CLY 1815

JSB Category: 2(B)

Sex: Female

Age at injury: 35

Age at award: 38

Date of award: 12 May 1995

Tribunal: Lambeth County Court

Amount of award then: £900

Award at February 2001: £1,035

Description of injuries: Teacher involved in road accident on mini-roundabout near school at which she taught – on impact thrown sideways and hit head against driver's door, sustaining laceration to scalp (over right occiput) which required six stitches and healed well – for first week after accident, until the stitches were removed, suffered pain around laceration and constant throbbing ache on other side of head – oral analgesia reduced pain but did not remove it completely – suffered shock as result of collision and had difficulty in sleeping for one week – for three months remained nervous about driving in general and in particular about the mini-roundabout which she had to use to get to and from her school – thereafter recovery complete.

1.2.2.1.C43 Case No. 12026

Name of case: J (a child) v Jones

Brief description of injuries: HEADACHES – SHOULDER – KNEE

Reported: Kemp & Kemp, PRC-022; [2000] 4 CL 169

JSB Category: 2(B)

Sex: Male

Age at injury: 14

Age at award: 15

Date of award: 23 November 1999

Tribunal: Uxbridge County Court

Amount of award then: £1,000

Award at February 2001: £1,032

Description of injuries: Knocked off his bicycle and dragged along by a car – grazing to the forehead, right arm and hand, right shoulder, right hip – superficial laceration to the left knee – severe headaches and aching to the shoulder and knee for two weeks.

Prognosis: He was expected to make a full recovery.

1.2.3 HEAD INJURY

1.2.3.C1 Case No. 11767

Name of case: Samler v Shaw

Brief description of injuries: HEAD – SEVERE BRAIN DAMAGE – INCONTINENCE

Reported: Kemp & Kemp, B2-004/1/1; [1999] CLY 1430

JSB Category: 2(A)(b); 6(A), 6(L)(a); 7

Sex: Female

Age at injury: 17

Age at award: 25

Date of award: 16 April 1999

Tribunal: QBD

Amount of award then: £90,000

Award at February 2001: £111,942

Description of injuries: Serious brain injuries – significant facial injuries – fractured neck – severe damage to kneecap necessitating removal – personality devastated as a result of brain injuries – loss of sense of smell – partial incontinence – loss of left field of vision in both eyes – claimant left highly vulnerable – 24-hour supervision required.

Prognosis: Very little prospect of improvement – claimant would never work again.

1.2.3.C2 Case No. 11763

Name of case: Re Hutton

Brief description of injuries: HEAD – VOICE – MULTIPLE INJURIES

Reported: [1999] CLY 1426

JSB Category: 2(A)(c); 5; 3(A)(b)

Sex: Male

Age at injury: 17

Age at award: 27

Date of award: 01 July 1999

Tribunal: CICB, Manchester

Amount of award then: £75,000

Award at February 2001: £90,505

Description of injuries: Motorcycle accident left claimant with poor voice production – only able to speak in a whisper – unable to make himself heard or understood in an emergency – scarcely intelligible to strangers – difficulty in coping with dusty environments – damage to left side of brain, causing difficulties with fine control in dominant right hand and weakness in right side – considerable and continuing psychological trauma after the accident – difficulties in trying to cope with aftermath – unable to return to former employment, and unable to undertake heavy tasks.

Prognosis: Problems with dusty environments and speech problems practically exclude claimant from any form of employment.

1.2.3.C3 Case No. 11074

Name of case: Pittman v Perrier

Brief description of injuries: HEAD – SERIOUS CLOSED HEAD INJURY

Reported: Kemp & Kemp, C2-046; [1996] CLY 2165

JSB Category: 2(A)(c)(ii)

Sex: Male

Age at injury: 22

Age at award: 26

Date of award: 01 July 1996

Tribunal: QBD

Amount of award then: £45,000

Award at February 2001: £55,591

Description of injuries: Serious closed head injury – unable to re-learn lost skills as carpenter – reclusive – marriage and family prospects diminished – capable of labouring work only.

1.2.3.C4 Case No. 10315

Name of case: Re Hall

Brief description of injuries: HEAD INJURY – EPILEPSY – INTELLECTUAL IMPAIRMENT

Reported: [1992] CLY 1571

JSB Category: 2(C)(a)

Sex: Male

Age at injury: 23

Age at award: 28

Date of award: 01 March 1992

Tribunal: CICB, Newcastle upon Tyne

Amount of award then: £37,500

Award at February 2001: £51,250

Description of injuries: Blow on the head causing unconsciousness and temporal lobe seizures.

Prognosis: Marked personality change – incomplete numbness of the right side – partial deafness – tended to shout – difficulty in running – could not play football – could not climb ladders or work at heights – intellectual impairment – difficulty in learning new tasks – poor memory – sexual difficulties – epileptic fits about occur every six to eight weeks.

1.2.3.C5 Case No. 11278

Name of case: Re Hewlett

Brief description of injuries: HEAD – SERIOUS INJURIES

Reported: Kemp & Kemp, B2-015/1; [1997] CLY 1825

JSB Category: 2(C)(iii)

Sex: Male

Age at injury: 19

Age at award: 25

Date of award: 16 January 1997

Tribunal: CICB

Amount of award then: £35,000

Award at February 2001: £41,606

Description of injuries: Serious head injuries – fractured skull – extradural haematoma – intracerebral and generalised brain swelling – post-traumatic amnesia lasting four weeks.

Prognosis: He would be left with permanently impaired balance – weakness to his left side – recurrent severe headaches – 15 per cent risk of post-traumatic epilepsy – agoraphobia and panic attacks which would disturb his sleep and balance.

Other points: Found work with the Benefits Agency – he had limited prospects of promotion due to his permanent injuries.

1.2.3.C6 Case No. 11541

Name of case: Re Rigby

Brief description of injuries: SKULL – DAMAGE TO THE INFRA-ORBITAL NERVE

Reported: Kemp & Kemp, C5-022; [1998] CLY 1543

JSB Category:

Sex: Male

Age at injury: 23

Age at award: 30

Date of award: 09 October 1997

Tribunal: CICB

Amount of award then: £12,500

Award at February 2001: £13,581

Description of injuries: Damage to the infra-orbital nerve following an attack – cryosurgery was carried out, and neurolysis under general anaesthetic – without warning claimant suffered regular bouts of sharp pain which were totally debilitating – unable to work for 4 years.

Prognosis: Prognosis poor – any improvement considered unlikely.

1.2.3.C7 Case No. 10005

Name of case: Bellovics v British Railways Board
Brief description of injuries: MINOR HEAD INJURY
Reported: [1990] CLY 1584
JSB Category: 2(B)
Sex: Male
Age at injury: 60
Age at award: 62
Date of award: 31 October 1990
Tribunal: Leeds County Court
Amount of award then: £4,500
Award at February 2001: £5,940

Description of injuries: Fell down staircase at Leeds City Station – transient unconsciousness – depressed fracture of left molar complex – bruising to face – minor injuries to teeth. Fully healed at time of trial – permanent thickening of scalp in region of left forehead – some impairment of concentration and recent memory likely to remain.

1.2.3.C8 Case No. 10145

Name of case: Matthews v Oldfield and Hawkins
Brief description of injuries: HEAD INJURY REQUIRING THREE STITCHES – BRUISING OVER KNEE
Reported: Kemp & Kemp, K2-003; [1991] CLY 1342
JSB Category: 2(B)
Sex: Male
Age at injury: -
Age at award: 41
Date of award: 06 December 1991
Tribunal: District Registry
Amount of award then: £4,500
Award at February 2001: £5,704

Description of injuries: Road accident – head injury requiring three stitches – also bruising over knee.

Prognosis: Six months after the accident there was little change – full recovery occurred by hearing, 20 months after accident.Other points

1.2.3.C9 Case No. 10542

Name of case: Littlefair v Turner
Brief description of injuries: HEAD – LACERATIONS
Reported: Kemp & Kemp, B2-042; [1993] CLY 1435
JSB Category: 7(A)(f); 6(B), 6(K)(c)(iii)
Sex: Female
Age at injury: 68
Age at award: 70
Date of award: 12 January 1993
Tribunal: Preston County Court
Amount of award then: £4,500
Award at February 2001: £5,613

Description of injuries: Lacerations to face, nose, mouth and scalp – loss of several teeth – soft-tissue injuries to back and legs – left thigh swollen for several weeks and ulcerations developed – ongoing pain in back and legs – unable to wear new dentures – assistance now required for shopping and housework – now terrified of traffic.

Prognosis: Age made improvement in residual symptoms unlikely.

1.2.3.C10 Case No. 11982

Name of case: W (a minor) v Kerry
Brief description of injuries: HEAD INJURY – EXTRADURAL HAEMATOMA
Reported: Kemp & Kemp, PRC-018; [2000] 3 CL 166
JSB Category: 2(A)(d)
Sex: Male
Age at injury: 5
Age at award: 7
Date of award: 24 November 1999
Tribunal: Norwich County Court
Amount of award then: £4,500
Award at February 2001: £4,643

Description of injuries: Another child jumped onto W's head from a roof at a party hosted by K – he collapsed two hours later – CT scan revealed an extra dural haematoma – emergency right parietal craniotomy to remove the blood clot.

Prognosis: No primary brain injury – no residual neurological deficit – the risk of epilepsy was diminishing progressively.

Other points: Provisional award with entitlement to return for further damages if epilepsy developed within eight years of the date of the accident.

1.2.3.C11 Case No. 11968

Name of case: M (a minor) v Debenhams PLC
Brief description of injuries: HEAD – BRUISING – SIX WEEKS
Reported: Kemp & Kemp, C5-060; [2000] 1 CL 128
JSB Category: 2(B)
Sex: Female
Age at injury: 7
Age at award: 11
Date of award: 19 August 1999
Tribunal: Cheltenham County Court
Amount of award then: £4,000
Award at February 2001: £4,157
Description of injuries: Racking fell off a shelf and hit M on the forehead near the hairline – haematoma but no laceration – bruising lasted a few days and headaches for about six weeks – no neurological deficit. Permanent slight scarring was more noticeable when she frowned.

1.2.3.C12 Case No. 11904

Award at February 2001: £3,662
See: 1.2.1.C11 for details

1.2.3.C13 Case No. 10014

Name of case: Misiri v Milner
Brief description of injuries: INJURIES TO HEAD
Reported: Kemp & Kemp, K2-035; [1990] CLY 1593
JSB Category: 3(A), 2(B)
Sex: Male
Age at injury: 3
Age at award: 4
Date of award: 03 September 1990
Tribunal: Maidstone District Registry
Amount of award then: £2,500
Award at February 2001: £3,326
Description of injuries: Struck on pedestrian crossing – fracture of left frontal bone – detained for 2 days observation – bruising over front of forehead and bridge of nose and bleeding from both nostrils – for nine months suffered from occasional nightmares with enuresis and loss of appetite – became much more clingy to his mother, who had to give up her part-time work to care for him.
Prognosis: Full recovery

1.2.3.C14 Case No. 10161

Name of case: Denny v Childs
Brief description of injuries: BLOW TO THE HEAD – BRUISING AND TENDERNESS – DIZZINESS – TEMPER OUTBURSTS
Reported: [1991] CLY 1358
JSB Category: 2(B)
Sex: Female
Age at injury: 74
Age at award: 76
Date of award: 03 March 1991
Tribunal: Romford County Court
Amount of award then: £2,500
Award at February 2001: £3,272
Description of injuries: Bang on the head from thrown crate – bruising and tenderness but no nerve damage – suffered dizzy spells – outbursts of temper – no longer liked going out alone – reduced to irritable and anxious person.

1.2.3.C15 Case No. 11284

Name of case: Oxley v BCH Ltd
Brief description of injuries: HEAD – LACERATION
Reported: Kemp & Kemp, K2-207; [1997] CLY 1832
JSB Category: 7(B)(b)(v)
Sex: Male
Age at injury: 53
Age at award: -
Date of award: 10 July 1997
Tribunal:
Amount of award then: £1,000
Award at February 2001: £1,092
Description of injuries: Struck by a heavy metal plate above the left eye – full recovery within five months of the date of the accident.
Other points: £4,000 on appeal reduced to £1,000

1.2.3.C16 Case No. 11708

Name of case: Ruparelia v Odedra
Brief description of injuries: HEAD – DIZZINESS – 1 WEEK
Reported: Kemp & Kemp, K2-239; [1998] CLY 1711
JSB Category: 2(B)
Sex: Female
Age at injury: 26
Age at award: 31
Date of award: 12 May 1998
Tribunal: Leicester County Court
Amount of award then: £800
Award at February 2001: £842
Description of injuries: Head hit windscreen – blurred vision and dizziness – dizziness lasted for 1 week – loss of driving confidence lasted for 1 month.

1.2.3.C17 Case No. 10522

Name of case: Silver v Ford Motor Company

Brief description of injuries: KNOCK ON THE HEAD – DAZED

Reported: [1992] CLY 1778

JSB Category: 2(B)

Sex: Male

Age at injury: 32

Age at award: 34

Date of award: 14 May 1992

Tribunal: Romford County Court

Amount of award then: £450

Award at February 2001: £556

Description of injuries: Dazed but not knocked out.

Prognosis: Fully recovered at the time of the trial.

1.2.3.C18 Case No. 11967

Name of case: K (a minor) v Tesco Stores Ltd

Brief description of injuries: HEAD – BRUISING – DIZZINESS – 1 WEEK

Reported: Kemp & Kemp, PRK-013; [2000] 1 CL 127

JSB Category:

Sex: Male

Age at injury: 7

Age at award: 9

Date of award: 07 October 1999

Tribunal: Uxbridge County Court

Amount of award then: £500

Award at February 2001: £517

Description of injuries: Injured when an automatic door failed to open – minor injuries including a graze over the left eyebrow, nausea, dizziness and headache – lasted one day. The bruise lasted one week.

1.2.3.C19 Case No. 10690

Name of case: Caplin v Parkinson

Brief description of injuries: HEAD – DIZZINESS

Reported: [1993] CLY 1586

JSB Category: 2(B)

Sex: Female

Age at injury: 11

Age at award: -

Date of award: 05 October 1993

Tribunal: Birkenhead County Court

Amount of award then: £250

Award at February 2001: £303

Description of injuries: Road accident – claimant, in back of car, struck head on seat in front – mild pain and tenderness to forehead but no bruising – dizziness – nausea – shaken by incident – physical injuries resolved within 2 weeks – remaining nervousness about travelling in back seat of cars and preference for front seat.

1.2.3.1 HEAD AND OTHER INJURY

1.2.3.1.C1 Case No. 11286

Name of case: Re Nicholls

Brief description of injuries: HEAD – SEVERE BRAIN DAMAGE – FRACTURED ARMS

Reported: Kemp & Kemp, C2-011; [1997] CLY 1834

JSB Category: 2(A)(a)

Sex: Female

Age at injury: 1 month

Age at award: 11

Date of award: 20 September 1996

Tribunal: CICB, London

Amount of award then: £85,000

Award at February 2001: £113,859

Description of injuries: Skull fractures and severe brain damage – fractured arms.

Prognosis: Required 24 hour care – life expectancy reduced to perhaps age 22.

Other points: Her adoptive parents wished to move to a warmer part of the country and into more suitable accommodation.

1.2.3.1.C2 Case No. 10532

Name of case: Re Drummond

Brief description of injuries: HEAD – CONCUSSION – MULTIPLE INJURIES

Reported: Kemp & Kemp, B2-005/1; [1993] CLY 1424

JSB Category: 2(B); 2(C); 3(A); 4(A)(f); 6(C), 6(D), 6(I); 5(A); 7(A); (B); 8

Sex: Male

Age at injury: -

Age at award: 46

Date of award: 26 March 1993

Tribunal: CICB

Amount of award then: £60,000

Award at February 2001: £85,115

Description of injuries: Concussion – severe fracture to left orbit and upper jaw, and muscular, tissue and skin – related injuries in left orbit area resulting in permanent diplopia – fracture of lower jaw – blood loss – tracheostomy necessitated by onset of pneumonia – severe contusion to left shoulder – fracture of left shoulder blade – severe contusions to left chest – 4 broken ribs – blood in abdomen requiring laparotomy – bruising to caecum – partial de-gloving of right hand – severe comminuted fracture to upper left thigh and base of trochanter – exacerbation of previously controlled epileptic fits – continuing physical disablement; crutches required for walking; restriction of movement in hip, leg and left shoulder – embarrassing facial and other scarring, and facial asymmetry – personality change (bad temper, irritability, frustration).

Prognosis: Domestic assistance and physical aids needed in future – car required for work and shopping – slight future risk of retinal detachment and abdominal adhesions.

Other points: Claimant lost pre-incident manual employment and was forced to take less satisfying clerical work – personality change contributed to collapse of marriage.

1.2.3.1.C3 Case No. 10547

Name of case: Re Grewal

Brief description of injuries: HEAD – DEPRESSION – LOSS OF SENSE OF SMELL

Reported: Kemp & Kemp, C2-032; [1993] CLY 1440

JSB Category: 2(A)(c), 2(C); 3(A); 4(C)(c)

Sex: Male

Age at injury: 29

Age at award: 37

Date of award: 25 March 1993

Tribunal: CICB

Amount of award then: £55,400

Award at February 2001: £77,046

Description of injuries: Assault – unconsciousness – large acute extradural blood clot – bruising to brain – hydrocephalus – personality change (irritable, aggressive; occasionally violent; emotional instability; depression; loss of confidence) – epilepsy – agoraphobia – loss of sense of smell – retrograde and post-traumatic amnesia – loss of concentration – loss of ability to read – loss of family and social life – diminished ability for self care physically – incontinence – sexual problems – psychological overlay – required 6 months in rehabilitation centre to try and lessen dependency on wife.

Prognosis: Will never be able to work again.

1.2.3.1.C4 Case No. 11978

Name of case: K v Hickman

Brief description of injuries: HEAD INJURY – COGNITIVE IMPAIRMENT PERSONALITY CHANGE

Reported: Kemp & Kemp, PRC-003; [2000] 3 CL 162

JSB Category: 2(A)(c)(ii)

Sex: Male

Age at injury: 65

Age at award: 70

Date of award: 18 October 1999

Tribunal: QBD

Amount of award then: £60,000

Award at February 2001: £69,462

Description of injuries: Knocked down by a car – skull fracture to the right side of the head – unconscious two weeks – unable to communicate for four weeks – right sub-dural haematoma – swelling of the right cerebral hemisphere – contusion to the left temporal lobe – post-traumatic amnesia of at least two weeks duration – injury caused cognitive impairment, memory loss and personality change – typical features of organic frontal lobe syndrome – mood swings, frustration, loss of interest in previous hobbies and obsessional behaviour – not physically aggressive – he could be argumentative, including accosting strangers with excessive and argumentative conversation.

Prognosis: Childlike dependency on his wife – unable to manage his own affairs – independent of personal care – required constant support, company and encouragement which was likely to be provided by his wife with regular respite care – 5 per cent risk of post-traumatic epilepsy.

1.2.3.1.C5 Case No. 11844

Name of case: Thrul v Ray

Brief description of injuries: HIP – REPLACEMENT – MINOR HEAD INJURY – CLAIMANT ALREADY HANDICAPPED

Reported: Kemp & Kemp, B2-009/2; [1999] CLY 1508

JSB Category: 6(C)(A)(i); 2(B); 7(A)(e)

Sex: Female

Age at injury: 28

Age at award: 38

Date of award: 27 November 1998

Tribunal: QBD

Amount of award then: £50,000

Award at February 2001: £57,445

Description of injuries: Minor head injuries – fractured jaw – bilateral hip dislocations and undisplaced fracture of left distal fibula – subsequent development of avascular necrosis of left femoral head, leading to hip replacement 4 years after accident – complications arising from hip replacement leading to a Girdlestone's excision arthroplasty the following year – as a result, claimant in constant pain – 3-inch shortening of left leg – confined to wheelchair – claimant's problems exacerbated by pre-existing medical history; social problems, low IQ, learning difficulties, several mental breakdowns, schizophrenia and depression – following the accident, claimant now resident some miles from family in one of the few care homes able to cope with such a combination of mental and physical difficulties (although it was agreed that the claimant would have needed residential care in any event).

Prognosis: Claimant's confinement to wheelchair permanent.

1.2.3.1.C6 Case No. 11959

Name of case: Re Perkins

Brief description of injuries: HEAD-MULTIPLE INJURIES – POST-TRAUMATIC STRESS SYNDROME

Reported: Kemp & Kemp, C6-001; [2000] 1 CL 119

JSB Category: 7(A)(d)(ii), 7(A)(e) and 3(A)(a)

Sex: Male

Age at injury: 39

Age at award: 43

Date of award: 11 August 1999

Tribunal: CICB, York

Amount of award then: £50,000

Award at February 2001: £57,020

Description of injuries: Attacked with an iron bar sustaining blows to the head, face and left arm – cuts to the head and face with a Stanley knife – in-patient for seven days – comminuted fracture of the right zygomatic arch – fixed with a titanium bone plate – his cheek ached in cold weather – fracture to the left mandibular condyle and an undisplaced fracture of the left mandibular parasymphysis – both were treated by the placement of bridle wire – mouth opening was decreased – difficulty in eating certain foods – slight tinnitus and deafness in the left ear – mild disability to the left forearm and hand – lacerations to both ears – the left ear almost severed – multiple deep lacerations to the scalp – injuries gave rise to post-traumatic stress syndrome consisting of severe memory impairment, severe headaches, mood changes, momentary feelings of disequilibrium, speech disturbance.

Prognosis: Eating difficulties were permanent – a scar from the coronal flap running from the apex of the of the right ear, across the top of the head to the apex of the left ear – two 1cm scars to the right cheek and another to the left – post-traumatic stress syndrome symptoms would be permanent – unsuitable for any form of employment.

1.2.3.1.C7 Case No. 11979

Name of case: S (a child) v Forrester

Brief description of injuries: HEAD INJURY – NERVE PALSY – EYESIGHT

Reported: Kemp & Kemp, PRC-004; [2000] 3 CL 163

JSB Category: 2(A)(c)(ii)

Sex: Male

Age at injury: 5

Age at award: 11

Date of award: 14 September 1999

Tribunal: QBD

Amount of award then: £40,000

Award at February 2001: £44,404

Description of injuries: A severe closed head injury in a traffic accident – brain damage, hemiparesis, damage to the right fourth and sixth cranial nerves causing nerve palsy and loss of binocular vision – S developed foot drop requiring orthosis and there was reduced co-ordination to the left arm and leg.

Prognosis: S would never be able to carry out work requiring fine manipulation of the upper limbs or heavy manual work – risk of epilepsy had fallen to 3 per cent and would reduce further – regular physiotherapy would continue to be required – the head injury had caused a degree of cognitive/intellectual impairment.

Other points: The court approved the abandonment of the claim for provisional damages.

1.2.3.1.C8 Case No. 12006

Name of case: Hulme (CICB Quantum: 2000)
Brief description of injuries: HEAD INJURY – DEPRESSION
Reported: Kemp & Kemp, PRC-005; [2000] 4 CL 149
JSB Category:
Sex: Female
Age at injury: 27
Age at award: 32
Date of award: 19 October 1999
Tribunal: CICB, Manchester
Amount of award then: £40,000
Award at February 2001: £44,318

Description of injuries: Severe head injury – compound fracture of the right parietal region – underlying extradural haematoma – needed neuro surgical intervention to elevate the fracture – anti-convulsants were prescribed – severe headaches (post-traumatic in nature) – sometimes accompanied by violent sickness – weak left side – flashbacks of the incident caused psychological distress – post-traumatic stress disorder – three months of counsel therapy – depressive episodes treated with anti-depressant drugs – H developed fears of glass windows, restaurants, being stalked and men who resembled her assailant.

Prognosis: It was found to be unlikely that H would ever return to her pre-accident level of employment – post-traumatic migraines would continue indefinitely – at increased risk of epilepsy – and at the time of the hearing H was only just recovering from her post-traumatic stress disorder.

1.2.3.1.C9 Case No. 10141

Name of case: Re Winterton
Brief description of injuries: SEVERE MEMORY IMPAIRMENT
Reported: Kemp & Kemp, C2-060; [1991] CLY 1338
JSB Category: 2(A)(c)
Sex: Male
Age at injury: 16
Age at award: 20
Date of award: 20 September 1991
Tribunal: CICB
Amount of award then: £30,000
Award at February 2001: £40,848

Description of injuries: Brain damage resulting from hypoxia (oxygen deprivation).

1.2.3.1.C10 Case No. 10706

Name of case: Re Harrison
Brief description of injuries: HEAD INJURY – PELVIC FRACTURES – SCARS – HEADACHES
Reported: Kemp & Kemp, B2-017; [1994] CLY 1552
JSB Category: 2(B); 6(C), 6(F)(c); 7(A)(f), 7(B)(a); 8
Sex: Female
Age at injury: 19
Age at award: 24
Date of award: 10 May 1994
Tribunal: CICB, Birmingham
Amount of award then: £27,500
Award at February 2001: £34,401

Description of injuries: Claimant deliberately run down by car – depressed fracture of frontal area of skull and bi-lateral peri-orbital haematomas – concussion – complete radial nerve palsy in right arm – fracture of shaft and neck of right humerus, fixed with pins, plates and screws – 4 broken teeth, 3 of which required replacement in particularly painful procedure – minor fracture of right interior pubic rami and sacral ala – lacerations to back of left leg above and below knee, covering area of 12 x 3 inches – numerous areas of scarring: 2 inch square depression in forehead despite exploration and surgical elevation of skull fracture; 20cm surgical scar down outside of right arm; scarring from lacerations on leg, all causing claimant embarrassment, especially the facial deformity, and preventing her from sunbathing and wearing short sleeved or short legged clothes – headaches, sometimes accompanied by nausea, 4 or 5 times per week – claimant perceived herself to be markedly less outgoing and more irritable and forgetful – anxiety about going out at night – nightmares – uncomfortable sensation at base of spine after sitting or standing for prolonged periods – right arm aches in cold weather.

Prognosis: Radial nerve palsy fully recovered, but permanent slightly restriction in movement in right shoulder – headaches expected to reduce in frequency over next 10 years, although remaining a permanent nuisance – back and shoulder problems likely to cause difficulty in holding down job, given claimant's few academic qualifications and limited past employment history.

1.2.3.1.C11 Case No. 11495

Name of case: West (a minor) v Kerr

Brief description of injuries: HEAD – SKULL – ARM – LEG

Reported: Kemp & Kemp, B2-018; [1998] CLY 1496

JSB Category: 2(A)(d); 6(F)(c), 6(K)(c)(i); 8

Sex: Female

Age at injury: 11

Age at award: 16

Date of award: 10 August 1998

Tribunal: Leicester County Court

Amount of award then: £31,000

Award at February 2001: £34,269

Description of injuries: Multiple injuries – fractures to the skull, arm and leg – contusion to the lung – bruising – significant residual scarring – generally good recovery from brain injury.

Prognosis: Symptoms were expected to resolve within 3 years of the date of the accident – at risk of episodes of lymphodema.

1.2.3.1.C12 Case No. 11298

Name of case: Re Gambill (No. 1)

Brief description of injuries: HEAD INJURY – POST-TRAUMATIC STRESS DISORDER

Reported: Kemp & Kemp, C4-064; [1997] CLY 1846

JSB Category: 3(B)(b)

Sex: Male

Age at injury: 35

Age at award: 39

Date of award: 12 August 1997

Tribunal: CICB, Liverpool

Amount of award then: £30,000

Award at February 2001: £34,251

Description of injuries: Severe head injuries – multiple skull fractures – post-traumatic stress disorder.

Prognosis: Prior to the hearing he was "still psychologically disabled" – deemed unlikely to make a full recovery.

Other points: Suffered a significant personality change – marriage breakdown – unable to work since the assault.

1.2.3.1.C13 Case No. 11524

Name of case: Lower v Hagland

Brief description of injuries: HEAD – JAW – SEVERE POST-TRAUMATIC STRESS DISORDER

Reported: Kemp & Kemp, C4-033; [1998] CLY 1526

JSB Category: 3(B)(a); 7(A)(e)

Sex: Female

Age at injury: 53

Age at award: 56

Date of award: 04 August 1997

Tribunal: Cardiff County Court

Amount of award then: £27,000

Award at February 2001: £30,603

Description of injuries: Jaw and facial injuries – post-traumatic stress disorder and travel phobia – pre-existing vulnerable disposition – long history of psychiatric illness – L's capacity to function severely diminished by post-traumatic stress disorder.

Prognosis: Unlikely to drive again – slow minor improvements expected in years to come.

1.2.3.1.C14 Case No. 11774

Name of case: Re T

Brief description of injuries: HEAD – PSYCHIATRIC DAMAGE – POST-TRAUMATIC STRESS DISORDER

Reported: [1999] CLY 1437

JSB Category: 2(B); 3(A); 6(B)(ii); 8

Sex: Male

Age at injury: 19

Age at award: 33

Date of award: 02 June 1998

Tribunal: CICB, London

Amount of award then: £25,000

Award at February 2001: £27,303

Description of injuries: Assault – injury to occipital lobe of brain (regarded as asymptomatic) – injury to back leading to chronic back pain, caused by tethering of the latissimus dorsi muscle contributing to spinal deformity (scoliosis of lumbo – sacral spine) – friction burns to face, chest, right iliac crest, back, right knee (requiring skin graft), ears (requiring reconstruction), and left ring finger (requiring skin graft, leaving permanent scarring, flexion deformity and sensitive neuroma) – 3 weeks of confusion – post-traumatic amnesia – some retrograde amnesia – moderately severe psychiatric damage – panic attacks – anxiety – social phobia – fear of travelling – moodiness – irritability – depression – difficulty sustaining relationships – some poor memory, regarded as psychiatric in origin and not related to injury to occipital lobe – phobic anxiety state an extreme handicap 6 years after assault; prescription of Prozac after 11 years diminished phobic symptoms and ended symptoms of clinical depression.

Prognosis: Claimant expected to be able to face rehabilitation and retraining after hearing – expected to have difficulties working with large numbers of people – signs indicative of a risk of temporal lobe epilepsy detected – back pain would render claimant unfit for manual work.

1.2.3.1.C15 Case No. 11766

Name of case: Elgie v Hodges

Brief description of injuries: HEAD – MULTIPLE INJURIES – POST-TRAUMATIC STRESS DISORDER

Reported: Kemp & Kemp, B2-026/1/1; [1999] CLY 1429

JSB Category: 3(A)(b); 2(B); 6(I)(q); 8; 9

Sex: Male

Age at injury: 18

Age at award: 22

Date of award: 05 May 1999

Tribunal: Lincoln County Court

Amount of award then: £23,000

Award at February 2001: £24,651

Description of injuries: Laceration to crown of head requiring 14 internal and 19 external stitches, and leaving bald spot on top of head – laceration to right hand, leaving minor scarring – fracture to proximal phalanx of right ring finger, requiring operation – serious psychological reaction to incident – severe shock of accident led to development of abnormally intense fear of travel – tension and anxiety when travelling as passenger – unable to overcome fear of learning to drive, hampering employment prospects on open labour market and opportunities for improving employment situation, and preventing fulfilment of ambition to join the police force – therapy had helped with fear of travelling as a passenger, but not with fear of driving.

Prognosis: Judge's finding that claimant 80 per cent likely to recover ability to drive – bald patch on head permanent.

Other points: Award comprised: physical injuries: £4,250; scarring: £3,750; psychological injury: £15,000.

1.2.3.1.C16 Case No. 10691

Name of case: Re Lucas

Brief description of injuries: HEAD – POST-CONCUSSION SYNDROME – 3 YEARS

Reported: Kemp & Kemp, C2-071; [1993] CLY 1588

JSB Category: 2(A)(d)

Sex: Male

Age at injury: 33

Age at award: 42

Date of award: 30 March 1993

Tribunal: CICB, Plymouth

Amount of award then: £17,500

Award at February 2001: £22,182

Description of injuries: Claimant assaulted – knocked to ground, struck head – loss of consciousness – no external or X-ray evidence of injury – discharged from hospital with headache and pain in neck – development of significant post-concussion syndrome, with characteristic associated symptoms – headaches, sometimes with associated nausea and numbness and pain across shoulders, essentially migrainous in character, occupying roughly half waking hours, lasting from 15 hours to several days, and occurring never more than 4 days apart – little relief from analgesics, tranquilisers or anti-migraine pills – impaired concentration and memory – generalised depression – personality change from placid and outgoing to aggressive and somewhat introverted – loss of interest in hobby – break-up of long-term relationship with girlfriend, who described him as "like a changed man" – off work for 13 months and thereafter unable to continue to work due to headaches – headaches persisting up until date of hearing.

Prognosis: Prognosis cautiously optimistic – some recovery anticipated, but symptoms expected to be still present for a further 3 years after the hearing.

1.2.3.1.C17 Case No. 10550

Name of case: Re Harper

Brief description of injuries: HEAD – FACE AND SKULL – POST-CONCUSSION SYNDROME

Reported: Kemp & Kemp, C5-019; [1993] CLY 1443

JSB Category: 2(B); 7(A)(d); 7(B)(b); 4(A)(h)

Sex: Male

Age at injury: 35

Age at award: 38

Date of award: 12 September 1993

Tribunal: CICB, South Sefton

Amount of award then: £15,000

Award at February 2001: £18,520

Description of injuries: Assault – fracture to left cheekbone – 2 black eyes – laceration to forehead (8 stitches) – bruising to neck and back – blurred vision for 1 year after assault – post-concussion syndrome, manifesting itself in depression – small scar on forehead which discolours in cold weather – post-concussion syndrome ongoing at time of trial – lost job as HGV driver and unable to find work at time of appeal.

1.2.3.1.C18 Case No. 10725

Name of case: Hardcastle v Dodgshon

Brief description of injuries: HEAD INJURY – POST-TRAUMATIC STRESS DISORDER – IRRITABILITY

Reported: Kemp & Kemp, I2-504; [1994] CLY 1573

JSB Category: 2(B); 3(B)(c); 4(C); 6(B), 6(K)(c)(ii); 7(A)(d)

Sex: Male

Age at injury: 46

Age at award: 49

Date of award: 23 September 1994

Tribunal: Torquay District Registry

Amount of award then: £15,000

Award at February 2001: £18,108

Description of injuries: Road accident – fracture of shaft of right femur, fixed with intramedullary nailing and uniting with slight shortening and external rotation – fractured cheekbone – head injury – alteration to shape of nose, altering sense of smell and requiring surgery – development of post-traumatic stress disorder, affecting claimant quite severely – consequent delay to physical recovery – some change in personality; irritability, short temper – unable to return to work for prolonged period – claimant also had pre-existing back condition, exacerbated by accident.

Prognosis: Symptoms of irritability and short temper likely to lessen with the passage of time – accident accelerated onset of back symptoms by 3-5 years.

1.2.3.1.C19 Case No. 11500

Name of case: Lee v Clark

Brief description of injuries: HEAD – LEG – FRACTURE – SHOULDER

Reported: Kemp & Kemp, C2-073; [1998] CLY 1501

JSB Category: 2(B); 5(A)(g); 6(B)(c), 6(C)(d), 6(F)(d)

Sex: Male

Age at injury: -

Age at award: -

Date of award: 24 April 1998

Tribunal: CA

Amount of award then: £15,000

Award at February 2001: £16,076

Description of injuries: Moderately severe concussive head injury – fractured rib and femur – dislocated shoulder – schizophrenia developed 3 years after the accident.

Prognosis: Permanent pain to the back and hip – loss of sensation to the right arm.

Other points: The judge decided that the onset of schizophrenia as a result of the accident was conjectural – but the award for physical injuries should be increased.

1.2.3.1.C20 Case No. 10152

Name of case: Re S

Brief description of injuries: LACERATIONS AND SWELLING TO HEAD AND FACE – TWO BLACK EYES – PAINFUL TEETH – POST-TRAUMATIC STRESS DISORDER

Reported: [1991] CLY 1349

JSB Category: 1(B)

Sex: Male

Age at injury: -

Age at award: -

Date of award: 23 October 1990

Tribunal: CICB

Amount of award then: £12,000

Award at February 2001: £16,048

Description of injuries: Assaulted – lacerations and swelling to head and face – two black eyes – painful teeth – memory and concentration affected – become withdrawn and snappy – somatic symptoms of anxiety, tension and palpitations.

Prognosis: Had not worked since assault apart from three weeks.

1.2.3.1.C21 Case No. 11497

Name of case: Bedford (a minor) v Dyson

Brief description of injuries: HEAD – MULTIPLE INJURIES – POST-TRAUMATIC STRESS DISORDER

Reported: Kemp & Kemp, B2-036/3; [1998] CLY 1498

JSB Category: 7(B)(b)(ii); 3(B)

Sex: Male

Age at injury: 12

Age at award: 15

Date of award: 27 April 1998

Tribunal: Wandsworth County Court

Amount of award then: £12,500

Award at February 2001: £13,316

Description of injuries: Multiple injuries to the head, face, teeth – significant degree of stress and anxiety – cosmetic surgery to the lip – soft-tissue injuries were resolved.

Prognosis: Most psychological effects should be overcome within 12 months of the date of the trial.

1.2.3.1.C22 Case No. 11681

Name of case: Ellis v Rothen

Brief description of injuries: ANKLE – HEAD INJURY

Reported: Kemp & Kemp, I3-018; [1998] CLY 1684

JSB Category: 6(M)(c); 2(B); 6(L)(b)(ii)

Sex: Female

Age at injury: 26

Age at award: 30

Date of award: 03 July 1998

Tribunal: Barnsley County Court

Amount of award then: £12,500

Award at February 2001: £13,282

Description of injuries: Bimalleolar fracture to the right ankle – contusion to the left knee – abrasions to the right arm – head injury involving post-traumatic amnesia.

Prognosis: 4 years after the accident psychiatric symptoms had reduced – prognosis was good.

1.2.3.1.C23 Case No. 11532

Name of case: Bailey v Chemical Recoveries Ltd

Brief description of injuries: HEAD – LACERATION – DEPRESSION

Reported: Kemp & Kemp, C4-089; [1998] CLY 1534

JSB Category: 3(A)(c); 7; 6(A)

Sex: Male

Age at injury: 50

Age at award: 54

Date of award: 15 May 1997

Tribunal: Bristol County Court

Amount of award then: £8,500

Award at February 2001: £9,318

Description of injuries: Head laceration requiring 14 stitches – pain and stiffness in the neck – severe recurrent depressive disorder triggered by the head and neck injuries – substantially full recovery.

Prognosis: B might be more prone to suffer psychiatric illness in the future.

1.2.3.1.C24 Case No. 10717

Award at February 2001: £8,915

See: 1.2.2.1.C17 for details

1.2.3.1.C25 Case No. 10308

Name of case: Ford v Large

Brief description of injuries: WRIST, NECK, HEAD – BRUISING – ANXIETY

Reported: Kemp & Kemp, H4-015; [1992] CLY 1563

JSB Category: 6(A)(c), 6(H)(c)

Sex: Female

Age at injury: 21

Age at award: 25

Date of award: 01 April 1992

Tribunal: Court of Appeal

Amount of award then: £6,500

Award at February 2001: £8,055

Description of injuries: Bruising to the wrist, neck, face and head.

Prognosis: Symptoms causing stiffness and pain waxed and waned – psychological damage resulting in extreme anxiety when driving or as a passenger – headaches, tension and exhaustion – injuries made work more difficult.

1.2.3.1.C26 Case No. 10648

Name of case: Dingsdale v Jones and The Ministry of Defence

Brief description of injuries: ANKLE – SPRAIN – HEAD INJURY

Reported: Kemp & Kemp, I3-026; [1993] CLY 1544

JSB Category: 6(M)(d); 2(B)

Sex: Male

Age at injury: 32

Age at award: 35

Date of award: 19 August 1993

Tribunal: Aldershot County Court

Amount of award then: £5,300

Award at February 2001: £6,452

Description of injuries: Knocked down by car – head injury with laceration of scalp, requiring 8 sutures – sprain of right ankle – 3 days off work (as Royal Marines sergeant), 2 months on light duties – recurrent severe headaches for 6 months, disturbing sleep for first 3 months – complete recovery from head injury – ankle requires bandaging regularly to prevent wobbling while running on uneven ground or skiing – able to pursue sporting interests without restriction.

Prognosis: Symptoms at date of trial permanent, but no risk of degeneration or osteoarthritis.

1.2.3.1.C27 Case No. 11983

Name of case: Kelly v Hemming

Brief description of injuries: HEAD INJURY – POST-TRAUMATIC STRESS DISORDER – POST-CONCUSSIONAL SYNDROME

Reported: Kemp & Kemp, PRC-015; [2000] 3 CL 167

JSB Category: 2(B) and 3B)(d)

Sex: Male

Age at injury: 22

Age at award: 26

Date of award: 22 April 1999

Tribunal: Slough County Court

Amount of award then: £5,000

Award at February 2001: £5,206

Description of injuries: Assault by two assailants – punched to the head and face – kicked in the head as he lay on the ground – lost consciousness – cut to the left eyebrow required stitches and later scarred – bruising to the right eye – severe abrasion to the left temporal and parietal parts of the head – in-patient for four days – after discharge there was clumsiness, slurred speech and poor co-ordination – post-traumatic stress disorder – post-concussional syndrome.

Prognosis: There had been clinical recovery of motor function within twelve months of the date of the accident – full recovery within eighteen months.

1.2.3.1.C28 Case No. 11535

Name of case: Bryan v Euroguard Ltd

Brief description of injuries: HEAD INJURY – POST-TRAUMATIC STRESS DISORDER

Reported: Kemp & Kemp, C2-083; [1998] CLY 1537

JSB Category: 2(B); 3(B)(c)

Sex: Male

Age at injury: 31

Age at award: 35

Date of award: 16 July 1998

Tribunal: Pontefract County Court

Amount of award then: £4,500

Award at February 2001: £4,748

Description of injuries: Excessive force was used against the claimant during an arrest – suffered a head laceration, post-concussion and headaches – dizziness – mild to moderate post-traumatic stress disorder – symptoms resolved after 8 months.

1.2.3.1.C29 Case No. 10826

Name of case: Jones v Leadbitter

Brief description of injuries: LEG – HEAD

Reported: Kemp & Kemp, I2-530; [1994] CLY 1675

JSB Category: 6(K)(c)(iii); 2(B)

Sex: Male

Age at injury: 15

Age at award: 17

Date of award: 07 July 1993

Tribunal: Southampton County Court

Amount of award then: £3,750

Award at February 2001: £4,584

Description of injuries: Road accident – loss of consciousness – closed fracture to shaft of right femur – fracture reduced and fixed by 8-hole compression plate; consequent 20cm operative scar – discharged from hospital after 8 days on crutches – physiotherapy prescribed – return to pre-accident activities 15 months after accident – occasional aching discomfort following exercise.

Prognosis: 1 per cent risk of developing epilepsy as result of being rendered unconscious – otherwise full recovery expected – surgical removal of plate in leg required at some point in future.

1.2.3.1.C30 Case No. 10479

Name of case: Gibson and Hughes v Hodges

Brief description of injuries: FRACTURED ANKLE – MINOR HEAD INJURY

Reported: Kemp & Kemp, I2-517, I3-030; [1992] CLY 1735

JSB Category: 6(M)(d)

Sex: Female

Age at injury: 67

Age at award: 72

Date of award: 30 January 1992

Tribunal: Chester County Court

Amount of award then: £3,500

Award at February 2001: £4,440

Description of injuries: Laceration to the scalp – three separate fractures to the right ankle – loss of consciousness and short period of amnesia.

Prognosis: No subsequent head injury complications.

1.2.3.1.C31 Case No. 11212

Name of case: Khan v W&J Whitehead (Laisterdyke) Ltd
Brief description of injuries: HEAD – DIZZINESS – ANKLE
Reported: Kemp & Kemp, C4-112; [1996] CLY 2304
JSB Category: 2(B) 3(A)(c)
Sex: Male
Age at injury: 56
Age at award: Died age 62 two years before the date of the hearing.
Date of award: 15 February 1996
Tribunal: Bradford County Court
Amount of award then: £3,800
Award at February 2001: £4,331
Description of injuries: Struck on the head – depression – dizziness causing him to fall down stairs – sustained an undisplaced fracture to the ankle – symptoms had resolved before his death – depression continuing beyond the date of the accident was attributed to other factors in his life.

1.2.3.1.C32 Case No. 11903

Name of case: Wasiuk v Auto Travel Ltd
Brief description of injuries: HEAD – POST-CONCUSSION SYNDROME – 3 YEARS
Reported: Kemp & Kemp, PRK-003; [1999] CLY 1567
JSB Category: 2(B)
Sex: Male
Age at injury: 37
Age at award: 40
Date of award: 20 July 1999
Tribunal: Chester County Court
Amount of award then: £3,500
Award at February 2001: £3,646
Description of injuries: Claimant struck head on exposed metal – momentary unconsciousness – profuse bleeding from injury site – daily bifrontal headaches for a number of weeks, reducing in frequency and severity over 16 months – diagnosis of post-concussion syndrome, manifesting itself in persistent angry thoughts, sleep disturbance, increased irritability and greater awareness of pain affecting head and neck – level of psychological distress assessed as mild to moderate for a period of 12 months after the accident – no continuing symptoms evident 3 years later.
Prognosis: No suggestion of any long-term sequelae.

1.2.3.1.C33 Case No. 11460

Name of case: Woodhouse v Normanton
Brief description of injuries: HEAD – ABRASIONS – LEG
Reported: Kemp & Kemp, C2-084; [1997] CLY 2009
JSB Category: 6(L)(b)(ii)
Sex: Male
Age at injury: 12
Age at award: 14
Date of award: 24 September 1997
Tribunal: Halifax County Court
Amount of award then: £3,300
Award at February 2001: £3,563
Description of injuries: Extensive abrasions to the head – bruising to the upper left thigh and both knees.
Prognosis: Permanent small bald patch to the scalp – of no great concern to him – left knee clicked after 25 minutes walking.

1.2.3.1.C34 Case No. 11464

Name of case: Baines (Onkar Singh) v Sherazia T/A A&S Autos
Brief description of injuries: HEAD – LEG – SOFT-TISSUE INJURY
Reported: Kemp & Kemp, C4-124; [1997] CLY 2013
JSB Category: 6(K)(c)(iii)
Sex: Male
Age at injury: 28
Age at award: 30
Date of award: 26 August 1997
Tribunal: Keighley County Court
Amount of award then: £2,700
Award at February 2001: £2,930
Description of injuries: Bruising to the head – significant soft-tissue injury to the thigh.
Prognosis: Discomfort after driving for a long time was expected to be permanent.

1.2.3.1.C35 Case No. 11890

Name of case: R (a minor) v Mohamed

Brief description of injuries: HEAD INJURY (6 WEEKS) – PSYCHOLOGICAL SYMPTOMS (2 YEARS)

Reported: Kemp & Kemp, K2-066/2; [1999] CLY 1554

JSB Category: 2(B); 3(A)(d)

Sex: Male

Age at injury: 5

Age at award: 8

Date of award: 21 July 1999

Tribunal: Slough County Court (infant settlement approval hearing)

Amount of award then: £2,500

Award at February 2001: £2,604

Description of injuries: Road accident – claimant thrown forward and sustained bruising and swelling to head – normal appearance of forehead restored after 3 weeks, tenderness resolved after 6 weeks – claimant emotionally traumatised – became excitable when travelling in family car – main symptom persistent secondary enuresis, lasting for 2 years and requiring specialist treatment.

1.2.3.1.C36 Case No. 10667

Name of case: Williams v Parry (t/a "Animal Lovers")

Brief description of injuries: LOW BACK – HEAD – LEG

Reported: Kemp & Kemp, E3-121; [1993] CLY 1563

JSB Category: 6(B)(c); 2(B); 6(K)(c)(iii)

Sex: Male

Age at injury: 52

Age at award: 53

Date of award: 09 June 1993

Tribunal: Cardiff County Court

Amount of award then: £2,000

Award at February 2001: £2,440

Description of injuries: Slip and fall, landing heavily on base of spine and right leg, and striking head on ground – severe pain and immediate return home – claimant obliged to lie on floor for 3 days – considerable pain in lower back and occasional occipital headaches related to pain in lower back, continuing for a number of weeks – exacerbation of pre-existing osteoarthritis of cervical spine – sciatic pain in right leg – development of slight limp – restriction of back movement at right sacro-iliac joint – degree of limitation of flexion and external rotation of right hip – symptoms resolved almost completely within 3 to 4 months.

Prognosis: No significant permanent problems.

1.2.3.1.C37 Case No. 11972

Name of case: Farrelly v CourtauldsChemicals

Brief description of injuries: HEAD – CONCUSSION – POST-TRAUMATIC SYNDROME OF HEADACHES

Reported: Kemp & Kemp, PRK-010; [2000] 2 CL 143

JSB Category: 3(A)(d)

Sex: Male

Age at injury: 36

Age at award: 39

Date of award: 11 August 1999

Tribunal: Nottingham County Court (McDuff J)

Amount of award then: £1,250

Award at February 2001: £1,299

Description of injuries: Suffered a blow to the forehead from a protruding shaft on a cutter bar – resulting graze did not bleed but was sutured – prescribed paracetamol for headaches immediately after the incident – suffered headaches two or three times per week – he took paracetamol on most days – F did not need to consult his GP – no time off work – concussion and post-traumatic syndrome to headaches was diagnosed.

Prognosis: Complete resolution was expected within three to six months of the date of the accident – there was no visible scar.

1.2.3.1.C38 Case No. 11704

Name of case: Kemp v Burden (No 2)

Brief description of injuries: HEAD – KNEE – ELBOW – 10 WEEKS

Reported: Kemp & Kemp, K2-224/2; [1998] CLY 1707

JSB Category: 6(G)(c), 6(L)(b)(ii); 2(B)

Sex: Male

Age at injury: 16

Age at award: 18

Date of award: 15 October 1997

Tribunal: Milton Keynes County Court

Amount of award then: £850

Award at February 2001: £917

Description of injuries: Bruised hand – cut knee and elbow – banged head – no physical symptoms within 10 weeks of the date of the accident.

1.2.3.1.C39 Case No. 10529

Name of case: Riley v AC Products (St Helens)

Brief description of injuries: SPINE FRACTURE AND HEAD INJURY CAUSING DEATH

Reported: Kemp & Kemp, M5-017/1; [1992] CLY 1785

JSB Category: 6(B)(a)(i)

Sex: Male

Age at injury: 18

Age at award: Deceased

Date of award: 28 September 1992

Tribunal: St Helens County Court

Amount of award then: £600

Award at February 2001: £740

Description of injuries: Fractured spine – multiple bruises and severe head injury.

1.2.3.2 FACIAL INJURY WITH OR WITHOUT FRACTURE

1.2.3.2.C1 Case No. 10936

Name of case: Bennett v British Coal

Brief description of injuries: SEVERE INJURY TO CHIN CAUSING PERMANENT SEVERE PAIN – MILD DEPRESSION

Reported: Kemp & Kemp, C6-002; [1995] CLY 1687

JSB Category: 7(B)(b)(i)

Sex: Male

Age at injury: 31

Age at award: 36

Date of award: 10 April 1995

Tribunal: Sheffield County Court

Amount of award then: £30,000

Award at February 2001: £36,602

Description of injuries: Plaintiff was involved in accident underground where a steel link under high tension snapped and embedded itself in plaintiff's chin – it was a difficult rescue and plaintiff sustained a gruesome injury which had appearance of "grotesque metal tusk" and could have been fatal – serious damage to mental branch of trigeminal nerve in jaw, with resulting continuous excruciating pain like toothache – treated in a pain clinic by first drugs, secondly psychotherapy and ultimately using TENS machine – pain was permanent but plaintiff had to some extent come to terms with it – in addition plaintiff had developed post-traumatic stress disorder and a mild to moderative depressive condition which caused him to be moody, aggressive and short-tempered – outdoor work was not practicable because this caused increased pain and TENS machine could not be used.

Prognosis: The pain and depression were mutually sustaining and likely to be permanent.

1.2.3.2.C2 Case No. 12059

Name of case: Re Holloway (CICB Quantum: 2000)

Brief description of injuries: FACE – SCARS – EAR

Reported: [2000] 6 CL 189

JSB Category: 7(B)(a)(ii)

Sex: Female

Age at injury: 32

Age at award: 40

Date of award: 02 February 2000

Tribunal: CICB, London

Amount of award then: £22,500

Award at February 2001: £23,799

Description of injuries: 40 per cent of the right ear bitten off – reconstructive surgery required over three years – ear section sewn on became infected and the tissue died – cartilage and skin from the left ear and neck were used in reconstruction – disfiguring and distressing scarring remained – sleep disturbance due to pain – 6.5 cm scar to the neck an 4.5cm scar behind the right ear were visible – small scar behind the left ear was hidden by hair – psychological effect was significant – hair washing was difficult – unable to wear ear-rings or sun-glasses – felt diminished by the disfigurement.

1.2.3.2.C3 Case No. 11543

Name of case: Spalding v NSS Newsagents and Avery

Brief description of injuries: HEAD – FACE – SCAR

Reported: Kemp & Kemp, C4-015; [1998] CLY 1545

JSB Category: 7(B)(a)

Sex: Female

Age at injury: 5

Age at award: 16

Date of award: 30 January 1997

Tribunal: Reading County Court

Amount of award then: £20,000

Award at February 2001: £22,906

Description of injuries: Large laceration to the forehead – running in a curved shape from the top of claimant's forehead and through the eyebrow – part of the eyebrow was destroyed – claimant left with a surprised look.

Prognosis: Cosmetic surgery might cause further distortion of the eyebrow.

1.2.3.2.C4 Case No. 11321

Name of case: Gregory (a minor) v Millington

Brief description of injuries: FACE – SEVERE SCARRING

Reported: Kemp & Kemp, C5-076; [1997] CLY 1869

JSB Category: 7(B)(b)(i)

Sex: Male

Age at injury: 4

Age at award: 7

Date of award: 12 March 1997

Tribunal: Tameside County Court

Amount of award then: £20,000

Award at February 2001: £22,751

Description of injuries: Dog bites to the face – required skin grafts and surgery.

Prognosis: Facial scarring described as "particularly severe" – he would face stresses due to his disfigurement in future years.

Other points: He was cheerful and outgoing – of considerable psychological robustness.

1.2.3.2.C5 Case No. 11113

Name of case: Re Harris

Brief description of injuries: FACE – NOSE BITTEN OFF

Reported: Kemp & Kemp, C5-078; [1996] CLY 2204

JSB Category: 7(B)(b)(i)

Sex: Male

Age at injury: 25

Age at award: 37

Date of award: 23 February 1996

Tribunal: CICB, London

Amount of award then: £17,000

Award at February 2001: £19,791

Description of injuries: Loss of the end of the nose – 3 cm by 2.5 cm – bitten off.

Prognosis: Facial scars visible at conversational distance – the nose might require further surgery at age 50 to 55.

1.2.3.2.C6 Case No. 11863

Name of case: Re Lovence

Brief description of injuries: SCARS – BACK AND FACE

Reported: Kemp & Kemp, C5-020; [1999] CLY 1527

JSB Category: 7(B)(b); 8

Sex: Male

Age at injury: 19

Age at award: 24

Date of award: 10 May 1999

Tribunal: CICB, London

Amount of award then: £15,000

Award at February 2001: £15,775

Description of injuries: Claimant stabbed in back and slashed in face during assault – 100 stitches required in back wound, 10 stitches in face wound – facial scar keloid, 0.25in wide, extending 4 inches between left lower lip and left earlobe – claimant self-conscious about facial scar; found that other people looked at him constantly in public, and felt he was regarded as an aggressor rather than a victim – scar caused problem when shaving – scar on back prominent and occasionally painful, and made claimant self-conscious when swimming – submissions made that lethargy, memory problems and depression experienced by the claimant a sign of psychiatric problems – Board viewed scarring as having had some psychological effect.

1.2.3.2.C7 Case No. 10740

Award at February 2001: £15,326

See: 1.2.2.1.C14 for details

1.2.3.2.C8 Case No. 10363

Name of case: Heath v Berkshire Health Authority

Brief description of injuries: TONGUE – DAMAGED NERVE – PARTIAL LOSS OF TASTE

Reported: [1992] 3 Med LR 57; 8 BMLR 98; Kemp & Kemp, D4-018/1; BPILS, XVII 1184; CLY 1619

JSB Category: 4(C)(d)

Sex: Female

Age at injury: 36

Age at award: 42

Date of award: 19 November 1992

Tribunal: QBD

Amount of award then: £12,000

Award at February 2001: £14,932

Description of injuries: Permanent taste loss of taste on the right side of the tongue – pins and needles of varying intensity – occasional pain in the right ear – after prolonged talking speech was affected – no longer able to read to her children – unable to eat on the right side of the mouth due to the risk of biting her tongue.

Prognosis: Permanent damage to the right lingual nerve.

1.2.3.2.C9 Case No. 10328

Name of case: Re C
Brief description of injuries: FACE – EYEBROW CUT – PTSD
Reported: [1992] CLY 1584
JSB Category: 3(B)(c)
Sex: Male
Age at injury: 35
Age at award: 39
Date of award: 18 June 1992
Tribunal: CICB, London
Amount of award then: £10,000
Award at February 2001: £12,409
Description of injuries: Knife held to his neck – head-butted – cut to the left eyebrow required six stitches – post-traumatic stress disorder.
Prognosis: Healed cut remained painful – still suffered from post-traumatic stress.
Other points: Originally awarded £1,250 but then increased to £10,000 on appeal.

1.2.3.2.C10 Case No. 11109

Name of case: Re Farrup
Brief description of injuries: HEAD – FACE – SCARS
Reported: Kemp & Kemp, J2-077; [1996] CLY 2200
JSB Category: 7(B)(b)(ii)
Sex: Male
Age at injury: 19
Age at award: 22
Date of award: 23 February 1996
Tribunal: CICB, Cardiff
Amount of award then: £10,000
Award at February 2001: £11,430
Description of injuries: Facial slash with a Stanley knife – thirty-eight stitches – permanent and extremely visible scar.
Other points: Moved out of London – withdrawn – no longer went out.

1.2.3.2.C11 Case No. 12057

Name of case: Re Martin (CICB Quantum: 2000)
Brief description of injuries: FACE – SCARS
Reported: [2000] 6 CL 187
JSB Category: 7(B)(b)(ii)
Sex: Male
Age at injury: 29
Age at award: 37
Date of award: 10 February 2000
Tribunal: CICB, Durham
Amount of award then: £11,000
Award at February 2001: £11,324
Description of injuries: Lacerations to the left forearm, left little finger and under the surface of the chin – lacerations explored and sutured under general anaesthetic – the scar became hypertrophic and required revision on two occasions – re-stitching also required – scar caused some embarrassment – 5cms below the submental region – 1.5cm maximum width – skin puckering at each end produced a bulge or fold – minor scars to the arm and finger.
Prognosis: No further improvement expected.

1.2.3.2.C12 Case No. 11322

Name of case: Burton v Daxner
Brief description of injuries: FACE – SEVERE SCARRING
Reported: Kemp & Kemp, C5-026; [1997] CLY 1870
JSB Category: 7(B)(b)(ii)
Sex: Male
Age at injury: 30
Age at award: 32
Date of award: 11 March 1997
Tribunal: Mansfield County Court
Amount of award then: £10,000
Award at February 2001: £11,091
Description of injuries: Facial lacerations – facial nerves severed – well healed scarring – damaged nerves imperfectly re-grown – permanent facial spasms were an embarrassment – painful palliative treatment being given.

1.2.3.2.C13 Case No. 10923

Name of case: Re MacFarlane

Brief description of injuries: FACIAL INJURIES FOLLOWING GLASSING – 113 STITCHES – DEPRESSION

Reported: [1995] CLY 1674

JSB Category: 3(B)(c)

Sex: Male

Age at injury: 20

Age at award: 30

Date of award: 08 December 1994

Tribunal: CICB, London

Amount of award then: £9,000

Award at February 2001: £10,603

Description of injuries: Victim of an unprovoked attack in a pub when a broken glass was pushed into his face – suffered v-shaped laceration to tip of nose, such that tip was almost amputated – also suffered full thickness lacerations to both lips and a laceration to the left cheek, which lacerations required 113 stitches – claimant was left with considerable scarring of which he was extremely conscious – scarring swelled, changed colour and became itchy and uncomfortable in summer months – lower left second incisor was chipped, the pulp was extirpated and the tooth restored – claimant attended the dentist many times and tooth restoration would have to be replaced about every five years – incident had profound effect on claimant – he became significantly more depressed and nervous and his self-esteem and confidence were significantly reduced – some of his symptoms were typical of those of post-traumatic stress disorder – he considered his failure to defend himself a sign of weakness and was distressed that his assailant was not charged and prosecuted, despite his identity being known – was absent from work for three weeks – after being back at work for four weeks he left his home, job and family and moved to Canvey Island where he would not be recognised – his father traced him after a year and coaxed him back to London and back to work another year after that – in his final year of his absence he applied for, but did not get, alternative employment.

Other points: The Board found that his departure from London was caused by effects of the attack but that he was fit and able to work between six months to one year after it.

1.2.3.2.C14 Case No. 10155

Name of case: Thakar v Bakar

Brief description of injuries: ASSAULT – LACERATIONS TO THE FACE – SCARRING

Reported: Kemp & Kemp, C4-084; [1991] CLY 1352

JSB Category: 7(B)(iv)

Sex: Female

Age at injury: 37

Age at award: 40

Date of award: 23 April 1991

Tribunal: Reading County Court

Amount of award then: £8,000

Award at February 2001: £10,338

Description of injuries: Assault – lacerations to the face – 5cm laceration to the left ulnar styloid (no damage to tendons or nerves) – bruising to neck and right arm – reactive depression of moderate severity – unable to go out or socialise – unable to trust people – vulnerable personality – suffering continuing pain in right arm, back and leg, felt to be result of depression – assault aggravated by unfounded imputations on her character – felt isolated within her community and continually sad.

Prognosis: Scars permanent, sensitive to touch but minimum cosmetic importance – psychiatric counselling for unspecified period – condition might improve once litigation over.

1.2.3.2.C15 Case No. 10573

Name of case: Re Whalley

Brief description of injuries: FACE – SCAR – SEVERE

Reported: Kemp & Kemp, J2-019; [1993] CLY 1466

JSB Category: 7(B)(b)(ii)

Sex: Male

Age at injury: 24

Age at award: 26

Date of award: 16 April 1993

Tribunal: CICB, Manchester

Amount of award then: £8,000

Award at February 2001: £9,787

Description of injuries: Claimant thrust through glass door – extensive scarring to forehead – 3 vertical scars measuring 5 to 6 cm each, with slight breaks in 2 of them, first in middle of forehead (scar numb in part), second towards left, third at left temple and running into hairline – also scar on bottom part of nose – at time of hearing scars changed colour depending on weather – caused claimant social embarrassment when meeting new people – scars could be said to be severe.

Prognosis: Symptom of discolouration likely to settle in the future, but scars beyond cosmetic repair, permanent and cannot be covered up or disguised.

1.2.3.2.C16 Case No. 11964

Name of case: F (a minor) v Slater

Brief description of injuries: FACE – LACERATIONS – SCARRING

Reported: Kemp & Kemp, C5-030; [2000] 1 CL 124

JSB Category: 7(B)(a)(iii)

Sex: Female

Age at injury: 2

Age at award: 4

Date of award: 14 September 1999

Tribunal: Blackpool County Court

Amount of award then: £9,000

Award at February 2001: £9,314

Description of injuries: Multiple lacerations to the right side of the forehead – F was bitten by a golden retriever – four scars measuring 16mm x 2mm, 10mm x 2mm, 3mm x 2mm and 5mm x 3mm – scarring became more noticeable when exposed to the sun.

Prognosis: Scars were permanent – could be concealed by cosmetics – could not be treated by plastic surgery.

1.2.3.2.C17 Case No. 11324

Name of case: R (a minor) v Bradmarr Joiners

Brief description of injuries: FACE – SCAR

Reported: Kemp & Kemp, C5-031; [1997] CLY 1872

JSB Category: 7(B)(a)(iii)

Sex: Female

Age at injury: 2

Age at award: -

Date of award: 23 June 1997

Tribunal: Workington County Court

Amount of award then: £8,500

Award at February 2001: £9,283

Description of injuries: Facial scarring – a scar over the nose being reddened and quite obvious – due to "trap door deformity" – minor psychiatric effects.

Prognosis: Spontaneous improvement within two years – z-plasty might be required in the future.

Other points: Award included an undefined element for the likelihood of a pretty girl becoming self-conscious of the scarring in adolescence.

1.2.3.2.C18 Case No. 11323

Name of case: Re Cusack

Brief description of injuries: FACE – SCARRING

Reported: Kemp & Kemp, C5-028; [1997] CLY 1871

JSB Category: 7(B)(b)(ii)

Sex: Male

Age at injury: 42

Age at award: -

Date of award: 15 July 1997

Tribunal: CICB, Birmingham

Amount of award then: £8,500

Award at February 2001: £9,283

Description of injuries: Significant lacerations requiring a large number of stitches – permanent and extensive scarring measuring three inches by two inches.

Other points: Lost confidence and motivation to get another job.

1.2.3.2.C19 Case No. 11542

Name of case: Re Webster

Brief description of injuries: SKULL – FACIAL FRACTURES

Reported: Kemp & Kemp, C5-033; [1998] CLY 1544

JSB Category: 7(A)(b)

Sex: Male

Age at injury: 21

Age at award: 24

Date of award: 23 April 1998

Tribunal: CICB, York

Amount of award then: £8,500

Award at February 2001: £8,991

Description of injuries: Fracture to the infra-orbital margin – depressed fracture of the malar bone – nasal fracture – small degree of facial numbness – minor scarring around the orbit had faded at time of trial.

1.2.3.2.C20 Case No. 10040

Name of case: Re Lynch

Brief description of injuries: BROKEN NOSE – SCARRING AROUND EYE

Reported: [1990] CLY 1602

JSB Category: 7(B); 7(A)

Sex: Male

Age at injury: 20

Age at award: 24

Date of award: 23 April 1990

Tribunal: CICB, London

Amount of award then: £6,500

Award at February 2001: £8,937

Description of injuries: Laceration to right side of head and undisplaced nasal fracture – skin grafts needed.

Prognosis: Left with noticeable and unsightly permanent scarring around right eye – attracts stares and embarrassing questions – scarring now well healed but cannot be improved further.

Other points: Operation needed to "hitch up" lower right eyelid.

1.2.3.2.C21 Case No. 11552

Name of case: Re Christer

Brief description of injuries: HEAD – NOSE

Reported: Kemp & Kemp, C5-035; [1998] CLY 1554

JSB Category: 7(A)(c)(i), 7(A)(f)

Sex: Male

Age at injury: 21

Age at award: 23

Date of award: 12 March 1998

Tribunal: CICB, Durham

Amount of award then: £8,000

Award at February 2001: £8,557

Description of injuries: Broken nose – 2 black eyes – bruising round the head – loss of a front tooth – attempt to pack his nose was unsuccessful – it was operated on under general anaesthetic – suffered from intermittent headaches for 1 year after the accident – plastic artificial tooth fitted – claimant suffered problems with breathing, particularly at night.

1.2.3.2.C22 Case No. 11797

Name of case: P (a minor) v Humphries

Brief description of injuries: HEAD – FACE – SCARS

Reported: [1999] CLY 1460

JSB Category: 7(B)(a)

Sex: Female

Age at injury: 9

Age at award: 11

Date of award: 13 November 1998

Tribunal: Bristol County Court (infant settlement approval hearing)

Amount of award then: £7,850

Award at February 2001: £8,213

Description of injuries: Claimant bitten on right cheek by dog – "V" – shaped scar measuring 8mm on one side and 4mm on the other – additional multiple scar tissue producing a small protruding lump about 3mm in diameter, accentuating the scar – claimant suffered significant teasing at school – evidence to the effect that claimant had suffered and continued to suffer psychological injury as a result of the attack and continued impact of facial scarring.

Prognosis: Scarring permanent.

1.2.3.2.C23 Case No. 11864

Name of case: Re Oboh

Brief description of injuries: FACE – SCARS

Reported: Kemp & Kemp, C5-038; [1999] CLY 1528

JSB Category: 7(B)(b); 8; 2(B)

Sex: Male

Age at injury: 45

Age at award: 48

Date of award: 13 March 1999

Tribunal: CICB, London

Amount of award then: £7,500

Award at February 2001: £7,861

Description of injuries: Claimant suffered burns to forehead, lips and left upper arm, dry cleaning solution squirted into eye and blows to head with chair leg and baseball bat during assault – 10 x 10cm scar on forehead, healing within 5 months and leaving faint scar only visible on close inspection – series of burns on left upper arm had all left permanent scars, one of which keloid in appearance, largest scar being 4cm long – post-concussion syndrome, manifesting itself in headaches, disturbed vision and anxiety.

1.2.3.2.C24 Case No. 11544

Name of case: Turner v Sefton MBC

Brief description of injuries: FACE – SCAR

Reported: Kemp & Kemp, J2-023; [1998] CLY 1546

JSB Category: 7(B)(a)(iii); 7(A)(f)

Sex: Female

Age at injury: 33

Age at award: 34

Date of award: 07 October 1997

Tribunal: Liverpool County Court

Amount of award then: £7,000

Award at February 2001: £7,549

Description of injuries: Multiple scars to the nose and face – loss of crowns on upper incisors.

Prognosis: The appearance of the scars would be improved by plastic surgery.

1.2.3.2.C25 Case No. 12033

Name of case: C (a child) v Taylor

Brief description of injuries: FACE – SCARRING

Reported: Kemp & Kemp, PRC-012; [2000] 5 CL 177

JSB Category: 7(B)(a)(iv)

Sex: Female

Age at injury: 4

Age at award: 10

Date of award: 12 January 2000

Tribunal: Nottingham County Court

Amount of award then: £7,000

Award at February 2001: £7,227

Description of injuries: Facial injuries in an attack by a dog – cuts around the area of the left eyebrow, the bridge of the nose, right cheek below the right eye, right nostril and right side of the mouth – wounds left scars representing obvious cosmetic defects – clear contour deformity under the right eye and to the mouth – surgical revision improved the appearance of the scars – psychological reaction of phobic anxiety in relation to animals and dogs in particular – bedwetting. The scars represented a barely noticeable cosmetic defect – fully recovered from the psychological reaction.

1.2.3.2.C26 Case No. 10353

Name of case: Robinson v Hart

Brief description of injuries: BROKEN NOSE – LOSS OF SENSE OF SMELL

Reported: [1992] CLY 1609

JSB Category: 7(A)(c)(i)

Sex: Male

Age at injury: 26

Age at award: 30

Date of award: 29 September 1992

Tribunal: Watford County Court

Amount of award then: £5,500

Award at February 2001: £6,786

Description of injuries: Fractured nasal bone with deviation to the left – loss of sense of smell.

Prognosis: Further surgery required to correct residual symptoms – to be done privately due to twelve-year NHS waiting list – the sense of smell might return after surgery.

1.2.3.2.C27 Case No. 10185

Name of case: Re Locker

Brief description of injuries: DISPLACED NASAL FRACTURE – 2 OPERATIONS

Reported: Kemp & Kemp, C5-040; [1991] CLY 1382

JSB Category: 7(A)(c)(i)

Sex: Male

Age at injury: 24

Age at award: 29

Date of award: 09 November 1990

Tribunal: CICB, London

Amount of award then: £5,000

Award at February 2001: £6,615

Description of injuries: Displaced nasal fracture during an assault – two operations were required.

Prognosis: The second operation vastly improved the airway and cosmetic appearance.

1.2.3.2.C28 Case No. 11325

Name of case: Waters (a minor) v North British Housing Association Ltd

Brief description of injuries: FACE – SCAR

Reported: Kemp & Kemp, C5-041; [1997] CLY 1873

JSB Category: 7(B)(a)(iv)

Sex: Female

Age at injury: 17months

Age at award: -

Date of award: 21 April 1997

Tribunal: Nottingham County Court

Amount of award then: £6,000

Award at February 2001: £6,603

Description of injuries: 1.5 cm laceration beneath the right nostril – scar 1.3cm

Prognosis: Scar will remain visible – could be improved with surgery.

Other points: Award included consideration for the likelihood of her becoming self-conscious of the scar in adolescence.

1.2.3.2.C29 Case No. 11551

Name of case: Livesey (a minor) v Hammersmith and Fulham LBC

Brief description of injuries: FACE – SCAR

Reported: Kemp & Kemp, C5-042; [1998] CLY 1553

JSB Category: 7(B)(a)(iv)

Sex: Female

Age at injury: 4

Age at award: 7

Date of award: 09 June 1998

Tribunal: West London County Court

Amount of award then: £6,000

Award at February 2001: £6,316

Description of injuries: Through and through laceration from the upper lip through the alar to the dorsum of the nose – medial cartilage displacement of the nose – claimant had not been teased.

Prognosis: A 13mm scar was prominent and might need revision – the second scar was settled and relatively inconspicuous.

1.2.3.2.C30 Case No. 10574

Name of case: Lambert v Knowsley Metropolitan Borough Council

Brief description of injuries: FACE – SCAR – HAIR LOSS FROM EYEBROW

Reported: Kemp & Kemp, C5-043; [1993] CLY 1467

JSB Category: 7(B)(a)(iii)

Sex: Female

Age at injury: 16

Age at award: 19

Date of award: 15 December 1992

Tribunal: Liverpool County Court

Amount of award then: £5,000

Award at February 2001: £6,178

Description of injuries: Trip on defective pavement and fall onto railings – laceration to brow requiring a number of micro – stitches and resulting in permanent scarring – central portion of scarring ran from medial aspect of left eyebrow horizontally towards mid – eyebrow and upwards in 2 places – scar 3.8 cm in length – pale at time of trial, but significant loss of hair from eyebrow where scar crossed it.

Prognosis: No way of solving loss of hair problem, and eyeshadow not satisfactory disguise – claimant's hope to be a model now lost.

1.2.3.2.C31 Case No. 12007

Name of case: Hussain v Nawaz

Brief description of injuries: FACE – LACERATIONS – SCARS

Reported: Kemp & Kemp, PRC-014; [2000] 4 CL 150

JSB Category: 7(B)(b)(iii)

Sex: Male

Age at injury: 29

Age at award: 32

Date of award: 25 November 1999

Tribunal: Derby County Court

Amount of award then: £5,850

Award at February 2001: £6,036

Description of injuries: Tripped and fell through glass doors – 35 sutures were required for bad lacerations to the chin and lip – unable to work for five weeks – a 3cm vertical scar from the lip to the chin – a 2cm horizontal scar along the underside of the lower lip – a 3cm in diameter circular scar to the chin – loss of sensation within the circular scar – embarrassing dribbling when H ate or drank. At the time of the hearing the first two scars had faded but were still visible at conversational distance – the third scar was the most cosmetically apparent and distorted the chin.

1.2.3.2.C32 Case No. 10186

Name of case: Troy v Ghosh

Brief description of injuries: FRACTURED NASAL BONES – 2 OPERATIONS

Reported: Kemp & Kemp, C5-044; [1991] CLY 1383

JSB Category: 7(A)(c)(i)

Sex: Male

Age at injury: 28

Age at award: -

Date of award: 02 January 1991

Tribunal: Edmonton County Court

Amount of award then: £4,500

Award at February 2001: £5,945

Description of injuries: Unprovoked attack – fractured nasal bones – two black eyes – deviation of the nasal bridge – required manipulation under general anaesthetic and a large splint for one week.

Prognosis: Some deviation of the nose to the left – further surgery was expected – loss of confidence when dealing with complaining customers.

1.2.3.2.C33 Case No. 10934

Name of case: Re Rahman

Brief description of injuries: FACIAL FRACTURE – OTHER FACIAL INJURIES – HEADACHES AND SHOOTING PAINS

Reported: Kemp & Kemp, C5-045; [1995] CLY 1685

JSB Category: 7(B)(b)(iii)

Sex: Male

Age at injury: 58

Age at award: 63

Date of award: 09 January 1995

Tribunal: CICB, London

Amount of award then: £5,000

Award at February 2001: £5,890

Description of injuries: Claimant was assaulted – suffered a fracture of right facial maxilla bone and bruising over nose, upper chest and thighs when struck four times with a tree stake – was in hospital for seven days and was unable to work for three months – left with permanent injuries, shooting pains in right cheek and pain in teeth on right-hand side of upper jaw and eye – eye hurt in sunlight – suffered from headaches each night which were treated with two paracetamols – there was a well-healed scar, only a portion of which was noticeable and a gap in the infra-orbital floor extending about 1cm – insensitivity and dysesthesia over right side of cheek were due to infraorbital nerve damage – further surgery was not recommended.

1.2.3.2.C34 Case No. 11550

Name of case: Re Holmes

Brief description of injuries: HEAD – NOSE

Reported: Kemp & Kemp, C5-046; [1998] CLY 1552

JSB Category: 7(A)(c)(i)

Sex: Male

Age at injury: 27

Age at award: 32

Date of award: 22 July 1998

Tribunal: CICB, Nottingham

Amount of award then: £5,500

Award at February 2001: £5,804

Description of injuries: Comminuted fracture of the nose required to be manipulated twice – deformity to both maxilla – breathing difficulty – sinus problems – breathing and shape of nose were much improved after reconstructive surgery – well healed scar to the rear of the ear, concealed by long hair.

1.2.3.2.C35 Case No. 11798

Name of case: McMaster v Prince Recycling Ltd

Brief description of injuries: HEAD – FACE – SCARS

Reported: Kemp & Kemp, C5-047; [1999] CLY 1461

JSB Category: 7(B)(b)

Sex: Male

Age at injury: 20

Age at award: 24

Date of award: 10 November 1998

Tribunal: Cambridge County Court

Amount of award then: £5,500

Award at February 2001: £5,754

Description of injuries: Claimant struck in right eye region in road accident, causing cuts which bled heavily and brief loss of consciousness – fracture of orbital rim – subsequent tethering and tightness of right eyelid, easing over time – vertical depressed scar on eyelid, extending about 1.5 cm from eyebrow, extending round lateral canthal region of eye to another scar 1.5 cm in length and 3 mm in width in mid part of lower eyelid – scars visibly apparent at conversational distances – claimant somewhat self-conscious about scarring.

Prognosis: Claimant expected to develop "notch" in upper eyelid as he grew older which could be improved with plastic surgery.

1.2.3.2.C36 Case No. 10355

Name of case: Re Cook

Brief description of injuries: BROKEN NOSE – SIGNIFICANT DEFORMITY

Reported: [1992] CLY 1611

JSB Category: 7(A)(c)(i)

Sex: Male

Age at injury: 23

Age at award: -

Date of award: 21 February 1992

Tribunal: CICB, Newcastle

Amount of award then: £4,500

Award at February 2001: £5,679

Description of injuries: Fracture of the nasal bones – deformity of the nose – superficial bruising and abrasions to the face – embarrassed by the significant cosmetic deformity.

Prognosis: Deformity only slightly improved by nasal reduction – ten minute episodic epistaxes occurred once or twice a month – continuing discomfort when breathing.

1.2.3.2.C37 Case No. 10043

Name of case: Mitchem v Kefford

Brief description of injuries: BROKEN NOSE – BRUISING

Reported: Kemp & Kemp, C5-048; [1990] CLY 1605

JSB Category: 7(B); 7(A)

Sex: Female

Age at injury: 22

Age at award: 27

Date of award: 22 March 1990

Tribunal: Dartford County Court

Amount of award then: £4,000

Award at February 2001: £5,667

Description of injuries: Broken nose at base of skull – bruising across right clavicle – bruising over the right groin and upper right thigh – double vision – frequent headaches.

Prognosis: Headaches likely to resolve themselves shortly.

1.2.3.2.C38 Case No. 10041

Name of case: Branch v Lowe

Brief description of injuries: FRACTURED CHEEKBONE

Reported: Kemp & Kemp, C5-051; [1990] CLY 1603

JSB Category: 7(A), 7(B)

Sex: Female

Age at injury: 23

Age at award: 26

Date of award: 09 November 1990

Tribunal: Huntingdon County Court

Amount of award then: £4,000

Award at February 2001: £5,292

Description of injuries: During assault was knocked unconscious – sustained displaced fracture of left zygoma and zygomatic arch – had paraesthesia over left infra-orbital nerve. Continues to suffer from shooting pains, occasional headaches – jaw clicks when eating, unable to eat anything tough – left eye is slightly lower than right – flattening of cheekbones.

Prognosis: Unlikely to be much improvement in symptoms.

1.2.3.2.C39 Case No. 10042

Name of case: Re Rowland

Brief description of injuries: INJURIES TO FACE AND HEAD – SCARRING

Reported: Kemp & Kemp, C5-052; [1990] CLY 1604

JSB Category: 7(B)

Sex: Male

Age at injury: 30

Age at award: 33

Date of award: 23 October 1990

Tribunal: Plymouth County Court

Amount of award then: £4,000

Award at February 2001: £5,280

Description of injuries: Numerous lacerations to head and face leaving scars – concussion caused headaches and discomfort for six months.

Prognosis: There will be no significant future disability.

1.2.3.2.C40 Case No. 11111

Name of case: Re Giles

Brief description of injuries: FACE – MULTIPLE CUTS

Reported: Kemp & Kemp, C6-073; [1996] CLY 2202

JSB Category: 7(B)(b)(iv)

Sex: Male

Age at injury: 23

Age at award: 26

Date of award: 22 February 1996

Tribunal: CICB, Trafford

Amount of award then: £4,500

Award at February 2001: £5,129

Description of injuries: Assault – multiple cuts and abrasions to the face – broken tooth – minor scars to the face – tooth crowned.

Other points: He went towards the trouble – the Board accepted that that this was partially explicable as he was employed as a barman.

1.2.3.2.C41 Case No. 11793

Name of case: Dyer v Burgess

Brief description of injuries: NOSE – FRACTURE

Reported: [1999] CLY 1456

JSB Category: 7(A)(c)

Sex: Female

Age at injury: 36

Age at award: 39

Date of award: 01 July 1999

Tribunal: Norwich County Court

Amount of award then: £4,850

Award at February 2001: £5,053

Description of injuries: Claimant suffered deviated fracture of nasal bone and extensive bruising around both eyes in assault – operation for reduction on nose – septoplasty undertaken 7 months later – also some mild frontal headaches – claimant left with very mild external deviation of nose and some minimal restriction of nasal airways – headaches had settled within 3 years of assault.

1.2.3.2.C42 Case No. 11318

Name of case: Re Taylor
Brief description of injuries: FACE – EYELID – SCAR
Reported: Kemp & Kemp, D2-046/1; [1997] CLY 1866
JSB Category: 7(B)(b)(iv)
Sex: Male
Age at injury: 17
Age at award: 20
Date of award: 21 April 1997
Tribunal: CICB
Amount of award then: £4,500
Award at February 2001: £4,952
Description of injuries: Fracture to the floor of the orbit – bruising to the eye and orbit – repair incision scar on the lower eyelid – some dyplopia with upward gaze – pain when blowing his nose.

1.2.3.2.C43 Case No. 10575

Name of case: O'Hare v Harrogate Borough Council and Coseley Contracts
Brief description of injuries: FACE-SCARS-CHILD TEASED AT SCHOOL
Reported: Kemp & Kemp, C5-057; [1993] CLY 1468
JSB Category: 7(B)(a)(iii)
Sex: Female
Age at injury: 6
Age at award: 9
Date of award: 10 December 1992
Tribunal: Harrogate County Court
Amount of award then: £4,000
Award at February 2001: £4,943
Description of injuries: Fall onto shards of roofing tile left in garden of claimant's family's council house – 2 cuts to left cheek, leaving permanent residual scarring – first scar on cheek oblique, 1 cm in length, up to 5 mm wide, pink, thickened, shiny surface, not tender – second scar 1 cm below left angle of plaintiff's mouth, 2 cm in length, pink, slightly thickened, not tender – claimant self-conscious about appearance and had been teased at school
Prognosis: First scar could be improved by excision to narrow, but not remove, it – second scar could not be improved by surgery

1.2.3.2.C44 Case No. 11986

Name of case: B (a child) v Littlewoods PLC
Brief description of injuries: FACE – EYEBROW – LACERATION
Reported: Kemp & Kemp, PRC-017; [2000] 3 CL 170
JSB Category: 7(B)(a)(iv)
Sex: Female
Age at injury: 4
Age at award: 5
Date of award: 19 October 1999
Tribunal: Cheltenham County Court
Amount of award then: £4,750
Award at February 2001: £4,907
Description of injuries: The frame of anew bicycle snapped while B was riding it – collision with metal railings caused a 7mm laceration to the margin of her left eyebrow and associated bruising – the wound was cleaned and closed with skin tape. The wound healed soundly – it was expected to leave a permanent scar.

1.2.3.2.C45 Case No. 11626

Name of case: Thompson v Mersey Ferries
Brief description of injuries: RESPIRATORY ORGANS – NOSE
Reported: Kemp & Kemp, F2-075/1; [1998] CLY 1628
JSB Category:
Sex: Male
Age at injury: 35
Age at award: 41
Date of award: 04 February 1998
Tribunal: Liverpool County Court
Amount of award then: £4,500
Award at February 2001: £4,828
Description of injuries: Nasal irritation – runny nose and eyes – headaches – felt as if T had a permanent cold.
Prognosis: Further improvement of symptoms was expected.

Damage to Head

1.2.3.2.C46 Case No. 11794

Name of case: Re Rosingdale
Brief description of injuries: NOSE – FRACTURE
Reported: Kemp & Kemp, C5-058; [1999] CLY 1457
JSB Category: 6(L)(b)(ii); 7(A)(c), 7(B)(a)
Sex: Female
Age at injury: 21
Age at award: 24
Date of award: 18 December 1998
Tribunal: CICB, York
Amount of award then: £4,500
Award at February 2001: £4,708
Description of injuries: Claimant awoke in hospital with injuries to nose, abrasions to face, neck and knee and laceration of upper lip, requiring 10 cosmetic stitches – 2 weeks later diagnosis of saddle deformity and fracture dislocation of cartilage of nose, causing obstruction of right airway – septoplastomy, washout and cautery to left interior turbinate undergone – further surgery undergone 10 months later, entailing submucosal resection and reduction of right middle turbinate – main effects of nasal injury lasted 12 months – continuing nasal pain in very cold temperatures.

Prognosis: Partial restriction of right airway permanent – remaining nasal deformity visually conspicuous, but aesthetic appearance could be improved by rhinoplasty.

1.2.3.2.C47 Case No. 11211

Name of case: Peskett and Peskett v Morris (No. 1)
Brief description of injuries: FACE – SCARS
Reported: Kemp & Kemp, I3-029/1; [1996] CLY 2302
JSB Category: 6(M)(d) 7(B)(b)(iv)
Sex: Male
Age at injury: 33
Age at award: 37
Date of award: 24 June 1996
Tribunal: Hove County Court
Amount of award then: £4,000
Award at February 2001: £4,497
Description of injuries: Fracture to the left medial malleolus – cuts and bruises.

Prognosis: Scars to the nose and chin were of no cosmetic significance – injuries were well healed within eighteen months of the date of the accident.

1.2.3.2.C48 Case No. 10741

Name of case: Re Carroll
Brief description of injuries: HEAD – JAW – FRACTURES
Reported: Kemp & Kemp, C6-015; [1994] CLY 1589
JSB Category: 7(A)(e)
Sex: Male
Age at injury: 28
Age at award: 30
Date of award: 14 September 1994
Tribunal: CICB, Birmingham
Amount of award then: £3,750
Award at February 2001: £4,448
Description of injuries: Assault – fractures through left body of mandible and neck of right condyle of mandible – operated on under general anaesthetic on day after attack – eyelet wires placed round various teeth in upper and lower jaw, and jaws wired shut for 3 weeks – good recovery, but some pain experienced on moving right condyle – lower bite-raising appliance constructed and worn for 3 months over lower teeth, helping to ease problem – at date of trial, minor cosmetic deformity visible in claimant's jawline – still some difficulty with loud "cracks" or "clicks" when chewing or yawning, and in bringing upper and lower jaw together.

1.2.3.2.C49 Case No. 10357

Name of case: Edwards v Walker
Brief description of injuries: FACE AND HANDS – CUTS AND BRUISES – 2 YEARS
Reported: [1992] CLY 1613
JSB Category: 7(B)(a)(vi)
Sex: Female
Age at injury: 17
Age at award: 20
Date of award: 08 June 1992
Tribunal: Derby County Court
Amount of award then: £3,500
Award at February 2001: £4,322
Description of injuries: Laceration to the lower lip – bruising to the forehead and both legs – small area of fat necrosis on lower left leg – ligamentous soft-tissue injuries to both hands – leg ached on standing – relieved by rest.

Prognosis: Symptoms likely to be resolved within two years – scars to the lip and leg caused embarrassment.

1.2.3.2.C50 Case No. 10857

Name of case: Buckland v Edward Thompson (a firm)
Brief description of injuries: FACE – SCAR
Reported: Kemp & Kemp, J2-039; [1994] CLY 1707
JSB Category: 7(B)(b)
Sex: Male
Age at injury: 2
Age at award: 4
Date of award: 08 June 1994
Tribunal: Mansfield County Court
Amount of award then: £3,500
Award at February 2001: £4,160
Description of injuries: Claimant fell into hole in garden – bruising, abrasions (friction burns) to right side of face, and nosebleed – abrasions healed, leaving residual facial blemishes – 2 small abrasion scars and area of whitish appearance below right eye, approximately 2 x 3 inches – area not significantly different from surrounding skin at date of hearing, but Recorder accepted that area would become more visible when claimant blushed or developed significant suntan, as some pigment cells had been destroyed.
Prognosis: Scars, though symptom – free, would be permanent.

1.2.3.2.C51 Case No. 11548

Name of case: Morrison v Bewise plc
Brief description of injuries: HEAD – FACE – SCARS
Reported: Kemp & Kemp, J2-040/1; [1998] CLY 1550
JSB Category: 7(B)(b)(iv); 7(A)(f)
Sex: Male
Age at injury: 4
Age at award: -
Date of award: 01 December 1997
Tribunal: Portsmouth County Court
Amount of award then: £3,750
Award at February 2001: £4,031
Description of injuries: 10cm laceration to the scalp – 2-3cm laceration to the face/upper lip – damage to incisor and canine teeth – lacerations were stitched – 2 incisors were removed.
Prognosis: Neither scar could be cosmetically improved – the 7cm forehead scar would be visible if M lost his hair when older.
Other points: Traumatic injuries to the developing teeth might affect their future growth, hence a provisional award.

1.2.3.2.C52 Case No. 11112

Name of case: Traverse v Nelson
Brief description of injuries: FACE – MULTIPLE CUTS
Reported: Kemp & Kemp, C5-062; [1996] CLY 2203
JSB Category: 7(B)(a)(iv)
Sex: Female
Age at injury: 8
Age at award: 9
Date of award: 26 July 1996
Tribunal: Salford County Court
Amount of award then: £3,500
Award at February 2001: £3,950
Description of injuries: Multiple cuts to the face – shock and anxiety – one permanent 13mm scar to the right cheek.

1.2.3.2.C53 Case No. 10365

Name of case: Newman v Hampshire County Council
Brief description of injuries: FACIAL INJURIES – LOSS OF TOOTH
Reported: Kemp & Kemp, C6-018; [1992] CLY 1621
JSB Category: 7(A)(f)(i)
Sex: Male
Age at injury: 15
Age at award: -
Date of award: 26 July 1992
Tribunal: Aldershot and Farnham County Court
Amount of award then: £3,100
Award at February 2001: £3,841
Description of injuries: Facial injuries – soft-tissue swelling of the chin with 1cm laceration – soft-tissue swelling and laceration of the lips – right incisor tooth missing – superficial abrasions to the right side of the neck – chin laceration closed with three sutures – grazes cleaned up – denture supplied to replace the missing tooth – later replaced by a Marylandbridge until teeth were fully grown.
Prognosis: Dentist was concerned about the long-term effects on the other front teeth which were discolouring – he advised that they might become non-vital as a result of the accident and require root treatment and crowning – dental treatment and the estimated cost of future dental work (at then current prices) £600.

Damage to Head

1.2.3.2.C54 Case No. 11799

Name of case: C (a minor) v Chief Constable of Hampshire

Brief description of injuries: HEAD – FACE – SCAR

Reported: Kemp & Kemp, C5-065; [1999] CLY 1462

JSB Category: 7(B)(b)

Sex: Male

Age at injury: 4

Age at award: 8

Date of award: 06 November 1998

Tribunal: Southampton County Court

Amount of award then: £3,500

Award at February 2001: £3,662

Description of injuries: Fall down stairs – 0.5cm laceration to left side of upper lip, principally involving the vermilion border and extending onto the skin surface of upper left lip; no stitches required – graze to chin – damage to deciduous upper left central and lateral incisors; both teeth partially intruded and displaced palatally, causing bleeding to surrounding gum area – unable to eat solid food for 2 weeks – fear arising from fall necessitated carrying claimant up and down stairs for 1 month; claimant also became withdrawn for about 1 month and was unable to ride bicycle for 4 months – scar on lip successfully revised surgically – residual very slight asymmetry of left upper lip with some associated slight thickening – some lumping still evident at trial – no serious damage to permanent upper left central and lateral incisors, but both sustained localised white spot to incisor edge of distal aspect of crown – white spots not unsightly and no treatment recommended.

Prognosis: No future problems envisaged in respect of scar.

Other points: Settlement figure.

1.2.3.2.C55 Case No. 11546

Name of case: Watt (a minor) v Asda Stores Ltd

Brief description of injuries: FACE – SCAR

Reported: Kemp & Kemp, J2-040/3; [1998] CLY 1548

JSB Category: 7(B)(a)(iv)

Sex: Female

Age at injury: 10

Age at award: 13

Date of award: 05 February 1998

Tribunal: Liverpool County Court

Amount of award then: £3,200

Award at February 2001: £3,434

Description of injuries: Laceration under the chin – 1.5cm curved scar under the chin.

Prognosis: The scar was permanent – could be hidden by make-up when older.

1.2.3.2.C56 Case No. 11925

Name of case: Thomas v Stagecoach (South) Ltd

Brief description of injuries: (1) NECK – WHIPLASH – BACK – 1 YEAR (2) FACE – CUTS – HEADACHES – 4 WEEKS

Reported: Kemp & Kemp, K2-102/5; [1999] CLY 1589

JSB Category: 6(A)(c), 6(B)(c); 7; 3(A)(d)

Sex: (1): Male (2): Female

Age at injury: 17

Age at award: 18

Date of award: 08 June 1999

Tribunal: Central London County Court

Amount of award then: £2,900

Award at February 2001: £3,012

Description of injuries: 2 claimants together in car involved in road accident.(1) moderately severe lower back strain – mild whiplash – driving – related stress – claimant had previously suffered from lower back pain, which was almost totally cured at the time of the accident – whiplash injury caused pain for 1 week, controlled by anti-inflammatory tablets, and claimant unable to continue at work – moderately severe lower back pain for 1 month – thereafter, pain recurring every couple of weeks for periods of 4-5 hours, making working or sitting in front of a computer difficult – 1 year later, back pain far less frequent, and tending to recur every 6-8 weeks – claimant had become a nervous driver after accident, especially in presence of HGVs, and also avoided the site of the accident for 3 months.(2) headache in immediate aftermath of accident, lasting 24 hours – multiple small cuts to hands and face from shattered windscreen, not requiring stitches and healing of their own accord – whiplash moderately severe for 1 week – full recovery within 4 weeks.

Other points: Award split: (1): £2,000 (2): £900

1.2.3.2.C57 Case No. 10739
Name of case: Taiani v Hill
Brief description of injuries: DEFORMITY TO NOSE
Reported: Kemp & Kemp, C5-067; [1994] CLY 1587
JSB Category: 7(B)(a)
Sex: Female
Age at injury: 37
Age at award: 41
Date of award: 04 May 1994
Tribunal: Milton Keynes County Court
Amount of award then: £2,500
Award at February 2001: £2,972

Description of injuries: Claimant punched in nose – 7cm laceration over bridge, and nosebleed – considerable swelling over bridge, bruising under eyes and headaches, lasting about a month – at date of trial 1cm scar over left side of bridge – obvious bony swelling, tender to touch – septum deviated internally to right side, causing some obstruction – increase in sinus-type symptoms.

Prognosis: Surgery possibly required to straighten septum and improve breathing.

1.2.3.2.C58 Case No. 10935
Name of case: Re Matthews
Brief description of injuries: SCARS TO CHIN, SCALP AND ARM – 26 STITCHES
Reported: Kemp & Kemp, J2-044; [1995] CLY 1686
JSB Category: 7(B)
Sex: Male
Age at injury: 30
Age at award: 34
Date of award: 10 January 1995
Tribunal: CICB, London
Amount of award then: £2,500
Award at February 2001: £2,945

Description of injuries: Struck on head and arm by broken bottle – sustained a 1cm laceration to scalp, a 4cm deep laceration to chin and a 5cm deep laceration to ulnar aspect of left forearm – was treated with 26 sutures to skin and a further four sutures to muscle within chin – spent three to four days in bed and suffered periodic headaches for four weeks – stayed off work for six weeks and suffered pain in arm for further four to six weeks following return to work – a glass fragment came out of injury to scalp after four weeks which then healed completely – left with 4cm curved red scar over chin which was noticeable at a distance of four feet – it caused difficulties when shaving and was more prominent when smiling or whistling – plaintiff was quite embarrassed about scar and did not socialise for six months after incident as a result – scar on arm was whitish in appearance – diminishing pin prick sensation over area of 9cm by 1cm distal to scar – both scars turned blue/orange in cold weather, the arm scar being particularly painful at such times. (The Board declined to follow the recommendations of the Judicial Studies Board.)

1.2.3.2.C59 Case No. 10738
Name of case: Shaw v Grazette
Brief description of injuries: BROKEN NOSE – SURGERY
Reported: Kemp & Kemp, D4-020; [1994] CLY 1586
JSB Category: 7(A)(c)
Sex: Female
Age at injury: 24
Age at award: -
Date of award: 07 January 1994
Tribunal: Croydon County Court
Amount of award then: £2,250
Award at February 2001: £2,739

Description of injuries: Claimant pillion passenger on motorcycle involved in collision – thrown to ground – displaced fracture of nose – also shaken, shocked, dazed and ankle slightly sprained – pain in nose for 3-4 months, thereafter ongoing sinus pain and breathing difficulty – slight deformity at site of injury caused maxillary sinusoid discomfort, and caused claimant some embarrassment – septo-rhinoplasty undertaken 15 months after incident, operation described by judge as "unpleasant, but not very unpleasant" – 3 days in hospital – severe pain and swelling, and 2 weeks of dressings and bruising in area consequent upon operation, recognised by judge as being worse for an attractive young woman – surgery successful, rectifying deformity and curing breathing difficulties – some residual nervousness as pillion passenger.

Other points: Judge held in this case that, given long wait for operation and 3 days spent in hospital, the relevant JSB guidelines were too low.

1.2.3.2.C60 Case No. 10134
Name of case: Hopgood v Homebase
Brief description of injuries: FACE – UNSIGHTLY SCAR – 5CM
Reported: Kemp & Kemp, C5-069; [1990] CLY 1679
JSB Category: 7(B)
Sex: Male
Age at injury: 4
Age at award: -
Date of award: 04 October 1990
Tribunal: Basingstoke County Court
Amount of award then: £2,000
Award at February 2001: £2,640

Description of injuries: Struck face against sheet of Contiboard – five cm laceration to cheek – wound healed but left unsightly scar 5 cm by 2 mm.

Prognosis: Scar likely to become less noticeable as plaintiff gets older – some permanent disfigurement.

Damage to Head

1.2.3.2.C61 Case No. 10674

Name of case: Stephens & Stephens v Mander

Brief description of injuries: (1) FACE – NOSEBLEEDS (2) NECK – WHIPLASH – 1 MONTH

Reported: Kemp & Kemp, C5-073; [1993] CLY 1570

JSB Category: (1): 7(A); 3(A)(d) (2): 6(A)(c); 5(A)

Sex: Both female (sisters)

Age at injury: (1):9;(2):6

Age at award: (1):10;(2):7

Date of award: 01 November 1993

Tribunal: Bristol County Court

Amount of award then: £2,050

Award at February 2001: £2,490

Description of injuries: Two sisters ((1) and (2)) passengers in vehicle involved in road accident.(1) Struck head on car seat in front – bruising to nose, left side of face, and left thigh – nose slightly deviated and swollen, but corrected itself within a few months, and bruising resolved reasonably soon – most serious injuries nosebleeds and psychological reaction – regular, heavy, easily provoked nosebleeds which caused distress – nose required cauterisation under local anaesthetic, operation described by judge as minor but "nasty" – symptoms of anxiety when travelling in cars – behavioural difficulties, cause of which suggested to be awareness of general family tensions arising from the accident – cauterisation resolved nosebleeds problem within a few weeks of the operation – anxiety in cars improving but still present at date of trial – behavioural difficulties resolved within 6 months.(2) Minor whiplash injury – anterior chest bruising from seatbelt – headaches and stiff neck for about a month – symptoms not sufficient to necessitate visit to doctor – symptoms largely resolved after 1 month.

Other points: Award split: (1) £1,400 (2): £650.

1.2.3.2.C62 Case No. 11547

Name of case: O'Brien (a minor) v Worthing BC

Brief description of injuries: FACE – SCAR

Reported: Kemp & Kemp, C5-077; [1998] CLY 1549

JSB Category: 7(B)(b)(iv)

Sex: Male

Age at injury: 4

Age at award: 6

Date of award: 09 October 1997

Tribunal: Southampton County Court

Amount of award then: £2,000

Award at February 2001: £2,157

Description of injuries: 1.5cm laceration under the chin – required 5 stitches – visible scarring – grazed elbow.

Prognosis: The scarring would fade, but would remain a permanent cosmetic deformity.

1.2.3.2.C63 Case No. 11949

Name of case: P (a minor) v Hampshire CC

Brief description of injuries: SCARS – FACIAL AND NON-FACIAL

Reported: Kemp & Kemp, PRK-009; [1999] CLY 1613

JSB Category: 7(B)(b)(iv); 8; 3(A)

Sex: Male

Age at injury: 11

Age at award: 12

Date of award: 03 March 1999

Tribunal: Portsmouth County Court

Amount of award then: £2,000

Award at February 2001: £2,096

Description of injuries: Electrical burns to hands – also some facial injuries, claimant having been thrown to ground by electric shock – detained in hospital overnight for observation – multiple pin – point burns to both hands, including 2 large ones – 2 grazes to right cheek – laceration to right upper lip, requiring stitches – heavy nosebleed – off school for 1 week; dizzy and unwell during that period – difficulty eating for 3 weeks – unable to participate in sports at school for 6 weeks after his return – grazes left faint scarring (cut to lip internal and scar not visible) – burns on hands left small scars; largest was on left thumb, measuring 2cm x 1cm – other scars unnoticeable – claimant also suffered anxiety and stress, which had resolved.

Prognosis: Facial scarring expected to disappear within 14 months – scar on thumb permanent, but would fade.

1.2.3.2.C64 Case No. 11038

Name of case: Re Tidy

Brief description of injuries: FACIAL – 3CM SCAR ACROSS CHEEK

Reported: [1995] CLY 1792

JSB Category: 7(B)(b)(iii)

Sex: Male

Age at injury: 21

Age at award: -

Date of award: 28 November 1994

Tribunal: CICB, London

Amount of award then: £1,750

Award at February 2001: £2,072

Description of injuries: Plaintiff assaulted with piece of wood measuring about 12in long and suffered 3cm laceration to right cheek and bruising to right eye and left arm – treated with three stitches to laceration and was prescribed antibiotics and painkillers – laceration resulted in permanent 3cm scar across right cheek and "drooping" of upper lip which had resolved itself at date of hearing – also left with general numbness over scarred area.

1.2.3.2.C65 Case No. 11469

Name of case: Boundy v Valavanis

Brief description of injuries: JAW – BRUISING – 11 MONTHS

Reported: Kemp & Kemp, K2-112; [1997] CLY 2019

JSB Category: 6(B)(c)

Sex: Male

Age at injury: 38

Age at award: 40

Date of award: 19 September 1996

Tribunal: Birkenhead County Court

Amount of award then: £1,750

Award at February 2001: £1,957

Description of injuries: Soft-tissue trauma to the mandibular joints – flexion injury to the spine – bruising to the ankle.

Prognosis: Symptom free within eleven months of the date of the accident.

1.2.3.2.C66 Case No. 11251

Name of case: Re Bhatti (Mohinder)

Brief description of injuries: FACE – LACERATION TO EYEBROW

Reported: (1996) 96 (2) QR 7; Kemp & Kemp, K2-162; [1996] CLY 2343

JSB Category: 7(B)(b)(v)

Sex: Male

Age at injury: 53

Age at award: -

Date of award: 23 February 1996

Tribunal: CICB

Amount of award then: £1,250

Award at February 2001: £1,425

Description of injuries: Laceration to the eyebrow – black eye – had become more anxious of customers – he had no time off work – left with a small scar.

1.2.3.2.C67 Case No. 10360

Name of case: Holmes v Leeds Health Authority

Brief description of injuries: FACE – BURN – 1CM X 1.5CM

Reported: [1992] CLY 1616

JSB Category: 8(v)

Sex: Female

Age at injury: 29

Age at award: 30

Date of award: 24 February 1992

Tribunal: Pontefract County Court

Amount of award then: £1,100

Award at February 2001: £1,388

Description of injuries: Burn to the upper lip – very sore and raw – 1 cm wide and 1 cm high – thin and white – did not cross vermilion border.

Prognosis: The scar could be seen at conversational distance causing embarrassment – could not be significantly improved by surgery.

1.2.3.2.C68 Case No. 10506

Name of case: McDermot v Liverpool City Council

Brief description of injuries: FRACTURED CHEEKBONE

Reported: [1992] CLY 1762

JSB Category: 7(B)(b)(v)

Sex: Male

Age at injury: 20

Age at award: 23

Date of award: 14 February 1992

Tribunal: Liverpool County Court

Amount of award then: £1,000

Award at February 2001: £1,262

Description of injuries: Fractured malar bone in the left cheek – slight grazing to the backs of the hands.

Prognosis: Scarring close to the hairline barely visible.

1.2.3.2.C69 Case No. 10680

Name of case: Re Welsh

Brief description of injuries: JAW – SOFT-TISSUE INJURY – MINOR RESIDUAL SYMPTOMS

Reported: Kemp & Kemp, C6-028; [1993] CLY 1576

JSB Category: 7(A)(e)

Sex: Male

Age at injury: 28

Age at award: 31

Date of award: 11 October 1993

Tribunal: CICB, Liverpool

Amount of award then: £1,000

Award at February 2001: £1,213

Description of injuries: Claimant punched on right side of face – swelling to jaw – damage to muscles associated with tempero-mandibular joint – no bony injury – difficulty eating, talking and sleeping for maximum of 7 weeks.

Prognosis: Still occasional discomfort when yawning or tired, described as being similar to cramp – this discomfort likely to be permanent.

Damage to Head

1.2.3.2.C70 Case No. 11262

Name of case: Barry v Evans

Brief description of injuries: FACE – EYELID – LACERATION

Reported: [1996] CLY 2354

JSB Category: 8(v)

Sex: Male

Age at injury: 5

Age at award: 6

Date of award: 02 October 1995

Tribunal: Cheltenham County Court

Amount of award then: £1,000

Award at February 2001: £1,148

Description of injuries: Laceration to the eyelid – swelling and bruising round the eye.

Prognosis: The scar to the eyelid would be scarcely visible over time – there would be no long-term legacy.

1.2.3.2.C71 Case No. 11319

Name of case: G (a minor) v Croydon LBC

Brief description of injuries: FACE – LACERATION

Reported: Kemp & Kemp, K2-208/1; [1997] CLY 1867

JSB Category: 7(B)(b)(v)

Sex: Male

Age at injury: 9

Age at award: 12

Date of award: 07 August 1997

Tribunal: Epsom County Court

Amount of award then: £1,000

Award at February 2001: £1,085

Description of injuries: Grazed and bruised cheek – no obvious laceration – badly shaken.

Prognosis: An almost invisible scar would completely disappear in time.

1.2.3.2.C72 Case No. 11058

Name of case: Kotecha v Harrow LBC

Brief description of injuries: FACIAL CUTS AND BRUISING – BACK DISCOMFORT (2-3 WEEKS)

Reported: [1995] CLY 1812

JSB Category:

Sex: Female

Age at injury: -

Age at award: -

Date of award: 12 April 1995

Tribunal: Willesden County Court

Amount of award then: £900

Award at February 2001: £1,039

Description of injuries: Bruising to cheek, forehead and thigh and tenderness to chest – bruising lasted about one week – had cut lip which cleared up after about two weeks – had back pain which interfered with preparation for exams and prevented her doing aerobics – this discomfort lasted for two to three weeks.

1.2.3.2.C73 Case No. 10510

Name of case: Grant v Hampshire County Council

Brief description of injuries: FACIAL BRUISING – 6 WEEKS

Reported: [1992] CLY 1766

JSB Category: 7(B)

Sex: Female

Age at injury: 78

Age at award: 79

Date of award: 24 January 1992

Tribunal: Winchester County Court

Amount of award then: £800

Award at February 2001: £1,015

Description of injuries: Black eye, bruised nose and chin – cuts and grazes to the hands and knees – wrenched back – unable to go out for six days until spectacles were replaced.

Prognosis: Injuries healed within two weeks after repair with steristrips.

1.2.3.2.C74 Case No. 10884

Name of case: Reeves v Ford Motor Co

Brief description of injuries: FACE – CHIN

Reported: Kemp & Kemp, K2-215; [1994] CLY 1736

JSB Category: 7

Sex: Male

Age at injury: 29

Age at award: 31

Date of award: 20 May 1994

Tribunal: Romford County Court

Amount of award then: £850

Award at February 2001: £1,010

Description of injuries: Claimant hit by forklift truck and fell to ground, striking chin – cut to chin – bruising, swelling and tenderness for 2-3 weeks – difficulty chewing food, washing and shaving for 4-5 days – small, tender lump formed at site of injury – lump took 2 years to resolve.

1.2.3.2.C75 Case No. 10514

Name of case: Lambert v Broun and Dixons Group
Brief description of injuries: FACIAL BRUISING – 4 MONTHS
Reported: [1992] CLY 1770
JSB Category: 7
Sex: Female
Age at injury: 53
Age at award: 56
Date of award: 11 November 1991
Tribunal: Hemel Hempstead County Court
Amount of award then: £750
Award at February 2001: £951
Description of injuries: Contusions to the forehead and around the right eye.
Prognosis: Full recovery within four months.

1.2.3.2.C76 Case No. 10888

Name of case: Hicks v Dunston
Brief description of injuries: NOSE – CUTS AND BRUISING
Reported: Kemp & Kemp, K2-230; [1994] CLY 1740
JSB Category: 7
Sex: Male
Age at injury: 52
Age at award: -
Date of award: 20 April 1994
Tribunal: Kingston-upon Hull County Court
Amount of award then: £750
Award at February 2001: £895
Description of injuries: Trip and fall, striking nose – skin stripped off one side of nose – small puncture wound, causing internal and external bleeding for 3-4 weeks – no time off work – full recovery – no residual scarring.

1.2.3.2.C77 Case No. 10135

Name of case: O'Hanlon v Merseyside Passenger Transport Executive
Brief description of injuries: FACE – SCALD – FULL RECOVERY
Reported: [1990] CLY 1704
JSB Category: 7(B)
Sex: Male
Age at injury: -
Age at award: -
Date of award: 21 June 1989
Tribunal: Not stated
Amount of award then: £500
Award at February 2001: £745
Description of injuries: Suffered extensive facial scalds when radiator cap blew off – off work 11 days – fully recovered with no residual scarring.

1.2.3.2.C78 Case No. 11899

Name of case: S (a minor) v Calderdale MBC
Brief description of injuries: FACE – GRAZING
Reported: Kemp & Kemp, K2-256; [1999] CLY 1563
JSB Category: 7
Sex: Female
Age at injury: 7
Age at award: 9
Date of award: 13 October 1998
Tribunal: Halifax County Court (infant settlement approval hearing)
Amount of award then: £550
Award at February 2001: £575
Description of injuries: Trip and fall – laceration and bruising to top lip – nose bleed – grazes to hands and knees – no damage to teeth.

1.2.3.2.1 Facial and other injury

1.2.3.2.1.C1 Case No. 10848

Name of case: Re Rothwell

Brief description of injuries: FACE – SCARS – DEPRESSION

Reported: Kemp & Kemp, J3-014; [1994] CLY 1697

JSB Category: 7(B)(b)(i); 8; 3(A)

Sex: Male

Age at injury: 16

Age at award: 20

Date of award: 02 August 1994

Tribunal: CICB, Durham

Amount of award then: £65,000

Award at February 2001: £89,339

Description of injuries: Claimant involved in horseplay at work involving YTS trainees throwing paint thinners over each other – claimant set alight with match – mixed depth burns to 36 per cent of body surface, including scalp, face, neck, chest, upper back and both upper limbs – in hospital 3 months – 4 operations during that time, causing severe pain for 9 months – 3 further operations required to release scar contractures to neck and hands – all scars, especially those to face, ears and head, major cosmetic disabilities – bald patch of 14 x 8cm on head – complete cessation of formerly busy social life and sporting activities – extremely severe depression, and unwillingness to receive treatment for it – no girlfriends since accident, and claimant considered himself unlikely to ever have one in future – claimant still visited one friend, but only after dark, so his appearance could not be seen – inability to sleep; claimant listened to radio all night to "shut things out" – constant fatigue – inability to hold pen, due to reduced grip – inability to sit in one position for any length of time – inability to cope with extremes of temperature.

Prognosis: At least 2 more scar contracture operations were likely to be required at date of hearing – prospects of ever working poor.

1.2.3.2.1.C2 Case No. 10535

Name of case: Re French

Brief description of injuries: FACE – SCAR – DEPRESSION

Reported: Kemp & Kemp, C5-011; [1993] CLY 1427

JSB Category: 7(B)(a); 8; 3(A)

Sex: Female

Age at injury: 17

Age at award: 20

Date of award: 07 July 1993

Tribunal: CICB

Amount of award then: £45,000

Award at February 2001: £60,755

Description of injuries: Deep multiple lacerations to the face, forehead and neck – laceration through upper eyelid and minor laceration to cornea – substantial lacerations to greater part of left leg leaving scarring and some restriction of movement – severe post-operative depression – severe self-consciousness, nervousness, self-image problems.

Prognosis: Permanent and disfiguring scarring to face and leg – facelift operation envisaged necessary – psychological support required for the foreseeable future.

Other points: Award reduced by 25 per cent by reason of conduct (CICS para 6(c)).

1.2.3.2.1.C3 Case No. 10143

Name of case: Harrison v Crane

Brief description of injuries: SEVERE FACIAL AND SKULL FRACTURES – MULTIPLE ABRASIONS AND BRUISES TO BODY AND FACE – MILD TO MODERATE TRAUMATIC BRAIN DAMAGE

Reported: Kemp & Kemp, C2-057; [1991] CLY 1340

JSB Category: 2(A)(c)

Sex: Male

Age at injury: 15

Age at award: 27

Date of award: 14 February 1991

Tribunal: QBD

Amount of award then: £30,000

Award at February 2001: £42,103

Description of injuries: Road accident – severe facial and skull fractures and multiple abrasions and bruises to the body and face – fracture of base of skull close to right petrous bone and extensive fracture of the skull base – fractures of ethmoid air cells of right maxillary antral floor – contusions to the right frontal lobe of brain and acute extradural haematoma under the right parieto occipital part of skull – outer wall of the right orbit fractured – right zygomatic arch fractured – lacerations over right eye – right supra-orbital ridge was displaced.

Prognosis: Loss of intellectual capacity – prospects of academic success diminished.

1.2.3.2.1.C4 Case No. 11501

Name of case: Hunter v Deuchart

Brief description of injuries: FACE – BURNS – LEG – FRACTURE

Reported: Kemp & Kemp, B2-016/1; [1998] CLY 1502

JSB Category: 7(B)(a)(i); 6(K)(c)(iii); 4(A)

Sex: Female

Age at injury: -

Age at award: -

Date of award: 29 June 1998

Tribunal: County Court

Amount of award then: £33,000

Award at February 2001: £36,723

Description of injuries: Severe acid burns – severe facial scarring – cornea scarring – comminuted fracture of the tibia – broken fibula – conscious of facial scars.

Prognosis: Claimant likely to suffer from arthritis in her leg.

1.2.3.2.1.C5 Case No. 10348

Name of case: Re McEwan

Brief description of injuries: SKULL FRACTURE – 10 INCH FACIAL INJURY – PSYCHIATRIC DISORDER

Reported: [1992] CLY 1604

JSB Category: 7(A)(b)

Sex: Male

Age at injury: 25

Age at award: 27

Date of award: 20 February 1992

Tribunal: CICB

Amount of award then: £25,000

Award at February 2001: £33,117

Description of injuries: Loss of consciousness – severe facial injuries including broken jaw, cheekbone and nose – fractured skull – ten cm knife wound to the cheek – scalp laceration – two broken teeth – psychological damage – appearance often caused him to be barred entry at places of entertainment – interruption to career and loss of promotion.

Prognosis: Continuing psychological disorder likely to improve. Prominently scarred.

1.2.3.2.1.C6 Case No. 12058

Name of case: Re Carrington (CICB Quantum: 2000)

Brief description of injuries: FACE – SCARS – PSYCHIATRIC DAMAGE

Reported: [2000] 6 CL 188

JSB Category: 7(B)(b)(ii), 3(B)

Sex: Male

Age at injury: 30

Age at award: 34

Date of award: 03 February 2000

Tribunal: CICB, York

Amount of award then: £23,500

Award at February 2001: £24,913

Description of injuries: Severely beaten and kicked in the head – undisplaced skull fracture and lacerations to the face and abdomen – headaches resolved within one year – very small increase in the risk of epilepsy – modest hearing loss caused 5 per cent disability – one tooth crown required and other teeth loosened – the crowned tooth became infected and required an apicectomy – post-traumatic stress disorder – nightmares and intrusive thoughts – suffered an enduring personality change – permanently lowered confidence – tooth still ached after four years – curved scar through the lip 4.5cm – longer scar to the cheek and neck improved by cosmetic surgery but remained prominent – significant psychological sequelae.

1.2.3.2.1.C7 Case No. 11789

Name of case: Re Good

Brief description of injuries: FACE – "GLASSING" – POST-TRAUMATIC STRESS DISORDER; FACIAL INJURIES

Reported: Kemp & Kemp, C5-077; [1999] CLY 1452

JSB Category: 3(B); 7(B)(b)

Sex: Male

Age at injury: 22

Age at award: 32

Date of award: 23 July 1998

Tribunal: CICB, London

Amount of award then: £20,000

Award at February 2001: £21,641

Description of injuries: Claimant had broken glass thrust into right side of face in the area of the cheek – significant lacerations, requiring a large number of stitches – considerable blood loss, requiring transfusion of 2 units of blood – damage to mandibular branch of right facial nerve – right parotid (saliva) duct severed – 2 significant scars, of 8 cm and 5 cm, across right side of applicant's face – right upper lip significantly weaker than left upper lip – over course of next 9 years, numerous follow – up surgical procedures undertaken, including unsuccessful revision of scars and partial parotidectomy – eating still difficult after 10 years; claimant unable to open mouth wide enough to eat after only a few mouthfuls of food, and act of eating caused severe pain in right side of face, lasting for over an hour – severe emotional trauma as result of attack – post-traumatic stress disorder – depression – very disturbed sleep – frequent nightmares – range of incapacitating anxieties – low self – esteem – social withdrawal – restricted lifestyle – claimant successfully set up own business, but forced to abandon it due to number of operation and tests he had to undergo.

Prognosis: Prognosis for psychological problems good – however, traumatic memories, anxiety and depression to be expected for a number of years to come.

1.2.3.2.1.C8 Case No. 10362

Name of case: Bridges v Cornwall and Isles of Scilly Area Health Authority

Brief description of injuries: FACIAL NERVE DAMAGE – HYPER-SENSITIVITY – SEX-LIFE AFFECTED

Reported: [1992] CLY 1618

JSB Category: 7(B)(a)(ii)

Sex: Female

Age at injury: 58

Age at award: 68

Date of award: 01 June 1991

Tribunal: Exeter District Registry

Amount of award then: £16,000

Award at February 2001: £21,015

Description of injuries: Surgical procedure to free the jaw (condylotomy) successful – damage to an artery caused heavy bleeding and nerve damage.

Prognosis: Loss of sensation in the left side of the face – intermittent itching and prickling – could not bear to be touched – cessation of sexual relations in the marriage – difficulty with liquids and semi-liquid food caused embarrassment.

1.2.3.2.1.C9 Case No. 10028

Name of case: Nelson v Page

Brief description of injuries: FRACTURED THORACIC VERTEBRA, EYE SOCKET, FACIAL SCAR.

Reported: [1990] CLY 1579

JSB Category: 6(B)

Sex: Male

Age at injury: 36

Age at award: 42

Date of award: 17 January 1990

Tribunal: Westminster County Court

Amount of award then: £11,000

Award at February 2001: £16,040

Description of injuries: 12th thoracic vertebra fractured – possible minor crushed fracture of 1st lumbar vertebra – fracture of ethmoid bone in the nose – blowout fracture of the floor of the left orbit – sprains of and bruising to both ankles – laceration to chin – unable to walk for 3 weeks – extensive physiotherapy for back and ankle injuries – nine months after accident was re-admitted to hospital for sub-mucous resection of left nasal airway – significant double vision for more than one year after accident – at time of trial, continuing double vision on upward gaze – sleep disturbed by back and ankle symptoms.

Prognosis: Back injury: almost complete recovery within one year of trial – facial injuries: some scarring which was noticeable but not disfiguring.

Other points: Underwent three operations.

1.2.3.2.1.C10 Case No. 10325

Name of case: Re D

Brief description of injuries: FACE – MULTIPLE FRACTURES

Reported: [1992] CLY 1581

JSB Category: 7(A)(c)(i), 7(A)(d)(i)

Sex: Male

Age at injury: 18

Age at award: 26

Date of award: 18 June 1992

Tribunal: CICB, Leicester

Amount of award then: £12,500

Award at February 2001: £15,622

Description of injuries: Fracture of the nasal bones with displacement to the left and inward collapse of the right side of the nose – comminuted displaced fracture of the lower rim of the orbit – extensive damage to two major nerves – extensive bruising of the face – studies resumed at a later date – caused qualification to be delayed for six years.

Prognosis: Sensitivity to light was resolved by the start of the hearing – further improvement in the facial numbness was unlikely to occur.

1.2.3.2.1.C11 Case No. 10233

Name of case: Skipp v Fisher

Brief description of injuries: MULTIPLE FACIAL INJURIES – LE FORT II TYPE – TRAUMATIC AMPUTATION OF TIP OF LEFT THUMB

Reported: Kemp & Kemp, B2-035; [1991] CLY 1430

JSB Category: 6(I)

Sex: Male

Age at injury: -

Age at award: 70

Date of award: 27 November 1990

Tribunal: Gloucester County Court

Amount of award then: £11,500

Award at February 2001: £15,393

Description of injuries: Multiple injuries in a motor cycle accident – lacerations to the mid line of the nose, above and below the left eye, comminuted fracture of the orbital floor involving the maxillary sinus and the naso-ethmoidal complex – fracture to the upper jaw of Le Fort II type – dislocation of the right wrist – traumatic amputation of the tip of the left thumb – underwent extensive maxillo-facial procedures – tracheostomy required.

Prognosis: Numbness and decreased sensation to the left side of the face – varying intensity in his sense of smell – made a good recovery – lost precision of grip in his left hand.

1.2.3.2.1.C12 Case No. 11498

Name of case: Baker (a minor) v Williams
Brief description of injuries: HEAD – FACE – LEG
Reported: Kemp & Kemp, B2-036/4; [1998] CLY 1499
JSB Category: 2(B); 7(B)(b)(ii); 6(K)(c)
Sex: Male
Age at injury: 10
Age at award: 14
Date of award: 27 April 1998
Tribunal: Winchester County Court
Amount of award then: £12,000
Award at February 2001: £12,767

Description of injuries: Multiple injuries – Glasgow coma scale 11 – fractured tibia and fibula – cuts to the face requiring stitches.

Prognosis: Permanent and significant facial scarring – could be improved by surgical revision – very small risk of epilepsy.

1.2.3.2.1.C13 Case No. 10929

Name of case: Re Birtwhistle
Brief description of injuries: FACIAL FRACTURES – POST-TRAUMATIC STRESS DISORDER – DEPRESSION
Reported: [1995] CLY 1680
JSB Category: 3(B)(c)
Sex: Male
Age at injury: 58
Age at award: 62
Date of award: 28 October 1994
Tribunal: CICB, Liverpool
Amount of award then: £10,000
Award at February 2001: £11,891

Description of injuries: Club steward was attacked by intruder with hammer – sustained depressed fracture of left zygoma, a fractured maxilla and fractured nose – elevation of zygoma proved unsuccessful and nose was manipulated, packed and plastered – applicant was left with left infra-orbital paraesthesia and this altered the sensation in left cheek – was unable completely to seal lips at left corner which meant he dribbled from time to time – in addition, suffered headaches and post-traumatic stress disorder with some mild depression – not a day passed without him recalling the incident. His confidence was affected.

1.2.3.2.1.C14 Case No. 11531

Name of case: Re Watson
Brief description of injuries: FACE – ANXIETY DEPRESSIVE SYNDROME
Reported: Kemp & Kemp, C4-083; [1998] CLY 1533
JSB Category: 7; 3(B)(c)
Sex: Female
Age at injury: 36
Age at award: 40
Date of award: 03 June 1998
Tribunal: CICB, London
Amount of award then: £10,000
Award at February 2001: £10,534

Description of injuries: Facial wound 1cm in length – agoraphobia and anxiety – anxiety depressive syndrome – at the time of the hearing claimant had made a full recovery.

1.2.3.2.1.C15 Case No. 10646

Name of case: Re Bennett
Brief description of injuries: ANKLE – FRACTURE – FACIAL DISFIGUREMENT
Reported: Kemp & Kemp, I3-020/2; [1993] CLY 1542
JSB Category: 6(M); 7(B)(b); 4(A)
Sex: Male
Age at injury: 32
Age at award: 36
Date of award: 11 October 1993
Tribunal: CICB, Birmingham
Amount of award then: £8,000
Award at February 2001: £9,704

Description of injuries: Assault – tri-malleolar fracture of left ankle – laceration of right eyelid from spectacles being kicked into face – widespread bruising and lacerations – returned to employment 5 weeks after attack – second fracture of same ankle 18 months later; cause uncertain, claimant's belief that it spontaneously "gave way" and refractured – at date of hearing, ankle still affected by residual pain and intermittent swelling – vision obscured in right eye, but uncertain as to how far assault responsible for this – scars round eyes had significant cosmetic effect and almost constantly irritated; some tenderness also evident – unable to drive for more than an hour, lift heavy weights, run, play football with children, garden or decorate – discharged from Territorial Army due to injuries, it having formerly been large part of claimant's life for 9 years – claimant ceased to go out socially, due to fear of being attacked – handicapped on labour market as unable to do heavy work or climb ladders – special mask required in occupation as welder due to the effect of ultraviolet light on eyes and scars.

Other points: Award included unspecified Smith v Manchester element.

1.2.3.2.1.C16 Case No. 10352

Name of case: Re Worboys

Brief description of injuries: BROKEN NOSE – FACIAL FRACTURES

Reported: Kemp & Kemp, C5-032; [1992] CLY 1608

JSB Category: 7(A)(c)(ii)

Sex: Male

Age at injury: 30

Age at award: 33

Date of award: 09 September 1992

Tribunal: CICB, London

Amount of award then: £7,500

Award at February 2001: £9,254

Description of injuries: Fracture to the nose and left zygoma with blow-out fracture to the lateral wall – double vision – traumatised pupil and retina – loosened upper teeth.

Prognosis: Avoidance of crowded places – fear of confrontations – scar affected by cold.

1.2.3.2.1.C17 Case No. 11542

Award at February 2001: £8,991

See: 1.2.3.2.C19 for details

1.2.3.2.1.C18 Case No. 10932

Name of case: Fraser v Southampton City Council

Brief description of injuries: FRACTURED JAW AND OTHER FACIAL AND DENTAL INJURIES – EXTENSIVE DENTAL AND SURGICAL TREATMENT

Reported: Kemp & Kemp, C6-007; [1995] CLY 1683

JSB Category: 7(A)(f)

Sex: Female

Age at injury: 7

Age at award: 11

Date of award: 15 November 1994

Tribunal: Southampton County Court

Amount of award then: £7,000

Award at February 2001: £8,286

Description of injuries: Fracture of plaintiff's jaw, a cut to her chin, a cut to lower lip and fracture of four front teeth – liability was not in dispute and the court were requested to approve a settlement reached with defendants – plaintiff sustained a fracture of the right mandibular condylar (jaw joint) with significant displacement of condylar head – further sustained a fracture of left mandibular condylar/ascending ramus – sustained a full laceration to chin measuring approximately 3cm; a full thickness laceration of mucosa of right lower lip, 5mm in length, a result of her upper teeth becoming imbedded in her lower lip; fractures of upper central incisors and upper right and upper left lateral incisors which involved only enamel of those teeth – laceration to chin was thoroughly explored and sutured under local anaesthetic – as a result of jaw fractures was unable to bring her teeth into normal occlusion – soft diet recommended – laceration of lower lip was not sutured – extensive dental surgery – a year or so after the accident she reported occasional pain over fracture site of jaw injuries – scar injury was apparent although not of such significance for surgical intervention – continued to experience a lump on lower lip as a result of bite by teeth – scar on chin measured 2cm and was visible to casual observer – fracture of jaw resolved satisfactorily – likelihood of development of degenerative joint disease in jaw was in region of 10 to 20 per cent – she underwent an extensive programme of dental treatment as both upper incisal teeth were dead as result of trauma and root development had stopped – treatment choices were either complete extraction and replacement or an attempt to root fill and close – latter option was followed – procedure required a number of visits over many months – treatment undertaken under local anaesthetic where both upper central incisural teeth were opened fully and a filling of the root canals commenced – canals were washed, dried and filled with hypocal – process was continued until the successful closure of open ends of the roots with a calcific dentine-like material achieved from whole of hollow internal passageways inside the tooth roots were sealed up using a gutta percha and a sealant – teeth should now be secure (66 per cent over 10 years) although it was never possible to predict which would fail – further treatment of teeth would be to restore their appearance using bonded composite filling material – there was no scope for crowns since the existing teeth and roots were but shells and would not really permit that type of restoration – treatment had been delayed due to chronic infections in both upper and central incisors and the plaintiff's own reluctance to attend the dentist.

1.2.3.2.1.C19 Case No. 10157

Name of case: Re Duncan

Brief description of injuries: BRUISING TO FACE AND BODY

Reported: [1991] CLY 1354

JSB Category: 7(B)(iv)

Sex: Male

Age at injury: 73

Age at award:

Date of award: 17 January 1991

Tribunal: CICB

Amount of award then: £5,500

Award at February 2001: £7,266

Description of injuries: Assault – bruising to face and body – cut requiring nine stitches to left eye socket – consequent subdural haematoma – in hospital for one-and-a-half months – suffered from confusion after the assault – became angry and depressed easily – range of activity decreased – unsteady on feet – housebound.

Prognosis: Unlikely to regain full strength and independence.

1.2.3.2.1.C20 Case No. 11985

Name of case: S (a child) v Bloomfield
Brief description of injuries: FACE – LACERATIONS – ANXIETY
Reported: Kemp & Kemp, PRC-013; [2000] 3 CL 169
JSB Category: 7(B)(b)(iv) and 3(A)
Sex: Male
Age at injury: 8
Age at award: 11
Date of award: 07 October 1999
Tribunal: Chichester County Court
Amount of award then: £6,750
Award at February 2001: £6,973

Description of injuries: Two deep 7mm lacerations from glass to the right cheek – wounds cleaned and stitched under general anaesthetic – a damaged nerve left S with a deformed smile – nerve damage was fully healed within five months of the accident – S suffered a nervous reaction – bad dreams and flashbacks – anxiety concerning his more seriously injured mother – an occasional twitch to the cheek developed which was said to be anxiety related .

Prognosis: S's twitch and his post-accident appearance led to teasing at school – general anxiety was expected to improve within years rather than months.

Other points: S disliked medical intervention so no further treatment was recommended.

1.2.3.2.1.C21 Case No. 11122

Name of case: Re French
Brief description of injuries: SKULL – FRACTURE OF THE RIGHT ORBIT
Reported: Kemp & Kemp, D2-045/1; [1996] CLY 2213
JSB Category: 7(A)(b)
Sex: Male
Age at injury: 31
Age at award: 34
Date of award: 08 November 1995
Tribunal: CICB, South Sefton
Amount of award then: £6,000
Award at February 2001: £6,889

Description of injuries: Fracture of the right orbit – sub-conjunctival haemorrhage.

Prognosis: Permanent cosmetic defect – noticeable at conversation distance.

Other points: Fracture not identified for two years.

1.2.3.2.1.C22 Case No. 11549

Name of case: Mooney (a minor) v Sait
Brief description of injuries: HEAD – FACE – SCAR – CLAVICLE
Reported: Kemp & Kemp, J2-024/1; [1998] CLY 1551
JSB Category: 7(B)(b); 6(D)(d)
Sex: Male
Age at injury: 8
Age at award: 12
Date of award: 26 November 1997
Tribunal: Torquay County Court
Amount of award then: £5,875
Award at February 2001: £6,331

Description of injuries: Lacerations to the forehead and scalp – fractured clavicle – serious bruising over the fracture site – tenderness and lumpiness of the forehead persisted – forehead scars were clearly visible.

Other points: The trauma of the accident was already taken into account – £1,750 was considered adequate for the fractured clavicle, with £4,125 for scarring/lacerations.

1.2.3.2.1.C23 Case No. 10354

Name of case: Re Washington
Brief description of injuries: FACIAL FRACTURES – DISFIGUREMENT – DRIBBLING
Reported: [1992] CLY 1610
JSB Category: 7(A)(d)(i)
Sex: Female
Age at injury: 31
Age at award: 36
Date of award: 03 June 1992
Tribunal: CICB, Birmingham
Amount of award then: £5,000
Award at February 2001: £6,174

Description of injuries: Fracture of the right cheekbone and damage to orbital floor – slight nerve damage to the face – numbness, tingling, some dribbling – twitching of the right eye – slight displacement of the right eye – slight scarring of the eye area.

Prognosis: Problems would be permanent – vision and hobbies unaffected.

1.2.3.2.1.C24 Case No. 11100

Name of case: Re Dawson

Brief description of injuries: HEAD – FRACTURED CHEEKBONE – DEPRESSION

Reported: Kemp & Kemp, C5-049; [1996] CLY 2191

JSB Category: 3(A)(c)

Sex: Male

Age at injury: 28

Age at award: 32

Date of award: 29 August 1996

Tribunal: CICB, Sale

Amount of award then: £5,000

Award at February 2001: £5,617

Description of injuries: Fractured cheek bone – mild depression.

Prognosis: Possibly fit for employment in 1996 – impossible to predict when symptoms would end.

1.2.3.2.1.C25 Case No. 11545

Award at February 2001: £5,122

See: 1.2.2.1.C25 for details

1.2.3.2.1.C26 Case No. 10044

Award at February 2001: £5,038

See: 1.2.2.1.C26 for details

1.2.3.2.1.C27 Case No. 10364

Name of case: Re Avola

Brief description of injuries: JAW – FRACTURES – CONTINUING DIFFICULTIES

Reported: Kemp & Kemp, C6-074; [1992] CLY 1620

JSB Category: 7(A)(e)(iii)

Sex: Male

Age at injury: 17

Age at award: 21

Date of award: 09 January 1992

Tribunal: CICB, London

Amount of award then: £3,750

Award at February 2001: £4,757

Description of injuries: Two fractures to the wisdom tooth area of the mandible.

Prognosis: Mandible wired for one month – diet of liquidised food at that time – mandible left permanently out of alignment – light cosmetic deformity – attended out-patient clinic for four months – at the time of the hearing jaws still clicked – difficulty in eating hard foods – pain-killers still required about once a month.

1.2.3.2.1.C28 Case No. 10655

Name of case: Narula v Prashar

Brief description of injuries: FACE – SCAR – SHOULDER

Reported: [1993] CLY 1551

JSB Category: 7(B)(a); 6(D)(c)

Sex: Female

Age at injury: 50

Age at award: 52

Date of award: 30 March 1993

Tribunal: Uxbridge County Court

Amount of award then: £3,250

Award at February 2001: £4,013

Description of injuries: Passenger in car involved in collision – 2 cuts to face, each 2 cm deep, requiring 10 stitches in total – one scar hidden behind hairline – other scar towards centre of forehead and visible – pain in right shoulder following accident, no bony injury evident in X-ray – headache, subsequently recurring, controlled by analgesics – dislike of and worry about scar in forehead; claimant also has pre-existing scar on other side of forehead – headaches continuing at date of trial – pain in shoulder evident during course of employment as packer during heavy work, and when doing housework; claimant no longer going swimming because of it.

1.2.3.2.1.C29 Case No. 11906

Name of case: Rogers v Bromley LBC

Brief description of injuries: FACIAL SCAR – PSYCHOLOGICAL REACTION (3 MONTHS)

Reported: Kemp & Kemp, K2-056/2; [1999] CLY 1570

JSB Category: 7(B)(a); 3(A)(d)

Sex: Female

Age at injury: 29

Age at award: 36

Date of award: 16 April 1999

Tribunal: Bromley County Court

Amount of award then: £2,750

Award at February 2001: £2,863

Description of injuries: Claimant already suffering from severe mental handicap, with mental age of 4, vocabulary of 50-100 words, prominent intention tremor and marked myopia – assaulted by fellow attendee at day care centre – 4 x 3cm inverted "V" – shaped scar through left eyebrow – emotional distress for 3 months – significantly increased incontinence – stubbornness – kicking and swearing at her nieces – loss of confidence – refusal to ride her bicycle, watch TV or listen to the radio.

Other points: Agreed settlement.

1.2.3.2.1.C30 Case No. 10280

Name of case: Re W

Brief description of injuries: MINOR CUTS AND SCARRING TO THE FACE – STITCHES – SCAR

Reported: Kemp & Kemp, K2-143; [1991] CLY 1477

JSB Category: 7(B)(b)(v)

Sex: Male

Age at injury: 24

Age at award: -

Date of award: 15 March 1991

Tribunal: CICB

Amount of award then: £1,250

Award at February 2001: £1,636

Description of injuries: Minor cuts and scarring to the face – unprovoked attack with a glass – short scars to the top lip and to the right cheek – the cheek was stitched.

Prognosis: Prominent scar to the cheek – inconvenient when shaving.

1.2.3.2.1.C31 Case No. 12048

Name of case: Greig v South Wales Fire Service

Brief description of injuries: FACE – BRUISING – CHEST AND ABDOMEN

Reported: Kemp & Kemp, K2-145/7; [2000] 5 CL 192

JSB Category:

Sex: Male

Age at injury: 41

Age at award: 43

Date of award: 19 January 2000

Tribunal: Cardiff County Court (North J)

Amount of award then: £1,500

Award at February 2001: £1,549

Description of injuries: Struck in the face, chest and abdomen by a fire hose – no internal injury – bilateral black eyes and blurred vision (nine days) – significant chest and abdomen pain for ten days with bed rest – slowly recovered – chest pain resolved in four months. Full recovery made within four months of the date of the accident.

1.2.3.2.1.C32 Case No. 10876

Name of case: McDonald v Niland

Brief description of injuries: HEAD – CHEEKBONE – ELBOWS AND KNEES

Reported: Kemp & Kemp, K2-152; [1994] CLY 1728

JSB Category: 7(A)(d)(iii); 6(G)(c), 6(L)(b)(ii)

Sex: Male

Age at injury: 15

Age at award: 18

Date of award: 07 April 1994

Tribunal: Southampton County Court

Amount of award then: £1,260

Award at February 2001: £1,503

Description of injuries: Claimant struck by car at pedestrian crossing – fracture to left cheekbone, with overlying graze – various bruises and grazes, including to right elbow and both knees – discharged from hospital same day – quiet and unsteady for a couple of days – swelling in cheek and around eye for about a week – claimant forced to miss last day of school celebrations – social life curtailed for a fortnight – concentration impaired in build up to GCSE exams – resumption of most activities after 2 weeks (except for sailing, which claimant unable to participate in for further 2 weeks) – full recovery after 6 weeks.

1.2.3.2.1.C33 Case No. 10889

Name of case: Noblett v Webber

Brief description of injuries: FACE – CUTS – BRUISES TO LEGS AND BODY

Reported: Kemp & Kemp, K2-228; [1994] CLY 1741

JSB Category: 7

Sex: Female

Age at injury: 18

Age at award: 21

Date of award: 21 February 1994

Tribunal: Preston County Court

Amount of award then: £750

Award at February 2001: £908

Description of injuries: Road accident – facial cuts – multiple bruises to legs and body – considerably shaken up – off work 1 week – enjoyment of Christmas festivities impaired – facial cuts healed completely, leaving no scarring whatsoever.

Other points: Additional award of £100 for loss of enjoyment of Christmas.

1.2.3.2.1.C34 Case No. 10893

Name of case: Cawthorne v Bennett

Brief description of injuries: FACE – THROAT, ARM AND LEG

Reported: Kemp & Kemp, K2-255; [1994] CLY 1745

JSB Category: 7; 8

Sex: Male

Age at injury: "middle-aged"

Age at award:

Date of award: 14 July 1994

Tribunal: Weston-super-Mare County Court

Amount of award then: £500

Award at February 2001: £597

Description of injuries: Claimant assaulted in his office premises – struck in face, causing large haematoma above and below right eye and 1in abrasion on right side of chin – attempt at strangulation, leaving 3 finger marks on left side of throat, 1 finger mark on right side of throat – 3in abrasion on right forearm – 3in abrasion on left flank – 3in abrasion on left thigh – half day off work – injuries healed completely except for very faint residual scarring at abrasion sites.

1.2.3.2.1.C35 Case No. 11706

Name of case: Smith v Cottrell

Brief description of injuries: CHEST – FACE – 2 MONTHS

Reported: Kemp & Kemp, K2-268; [1998] CLY 1709

JSB Category: 5(A); 7

Sex: Female

Age at injury: 21

Age at award: 24

Date of award: 09 December 1997

Tribunal: Birmingham County Court

Amount of award then: £100

Award at February 2001: £108

Description of injuries: Aching chest – cut to the forehead – symptoms resolved within 2 months of the date of the accident.

1.2.3.3 LOSS OF SMELL OR TASTE

1.2.3.3.C1 Case No. 10306

Name of case: Re Melton

Brief description of injuries: FACE – GUNSHOT INJURIES – SEVERE COSMETIC INJURIES – NO TASTE, SMELL, HEARING – BLIND IN ONE EYE

Reported: Kemp & Kemp, B2-003; [1992] CLY 1561

JSB Category: 4(A)(e), 4(C)(a)

Sex: Female

Age at injury: -

Age at award: 43

Date of award: 05 September 1992

Tribunal: CICB, London

Amount of award then: £100,000

Award at February 2001: £155,937

Description of injuries: Severe facial injuries to the mouth, ears, nose cheek and throat requiring extensive and on-going cosmetic surgery – severely deformed face – loss of taste, smell, speech, hearing and sight in left eye – unable to eat solid food, only liquids – subject to choking – psychological disturbance including panic attacks – depression – inability to cope socially – housebound – unable to sleep, converse or use telephone – suicidal with no hope for the future – post-traumatic stress.

Prognosis: In need of constant attendance.

1.2.3.3.C2 Case No. 11765

Name of case: Re W

Brief description of injuries: MULTIPLE INJURIES – LOSS OF TASTE AND SMELL – POST-TRAUMATIC STRESS DISORDER

Reported: [1999] CLY 1428

JSB Category: 2(A)(d); 3(B); 4(B)(c), 4(B)(d), 4(C); 6(I); 8

Sex: Female

Age at injury: 41

Age at award: 46

Date of award: 01 July 1999

Tribunal: CICB, London

Amount of award then: £40,000

Award at February 2001: £44,728

Description of injuries: Fracture to base of skull – on life support machine for 4 days – deficiency in memory – deafness in right ear – tinnitus and echo vibration in left ear – loss of sense of taste and smell – serious fractures to left index, middle and ring fingers, leaving left hand with very weak grip and little power – scarring to left forearm and behind right ear – post-traumatic stress disorder, lasting 4-5 years after assault – depression – cessation of sexual and social activity – group therapy and counselling prescribed – claimant required help with everyday tasks like shopping, and had been unable to return to work by date of hearing.

Prognosis: Loss of hearing, taste and smell all permanent – certainty of osteoarthritis developing in little finger and 50 per cent likelihood of it developing in ring finger – joint replacement in little finger, and also possibly ring finger, likely – claimant expected to return to part-time work about 5 years after assault, and anticipation of returning to full – time work about 6-12 months thereafter.

1.2.3.3.C3 Case No. 10748

Name of case: Re Chapman

Brief description of injuries: SENSES – TASTE, SMELL AND HEARING

Reported: Kemp & Kemp, D4-012/1; [1994] CLY 1596

JSB Category: 4(B)(d), 4(C)(b)

Sex: Male

Age at injury: 19

Age at award: 25

Date of award: 15 November 1993

Tribunal: CICB, London

Amount of award then: £22,500

Award at February 2001: £28,421

Description of injuries: Assault – claimant struck on rear left side of skull – discovered on ground, with blood and fluid flowing from ear – significant head injury – total loss of sense of smell – near complete loss of sense of taste – reduction in hearing capacity of 60 per cent, even after partially successful inner ear operation – suggestion that claimant suffering from headaches – due to loss of sense of smell, claimant had become obsessive about personal hygiene and cleanliness.

Prognosis: Prognosis of disabilities being permanent.

1.2.3.3.C4 Case No. 10944

Name of case: Fryer v Hussain

Brief description of injuries: PERMANENT PARTIAL LOSS OF SENSE OF SMELL

Reported: Kemp & Kemp, D4-018/2; [1995] CLY 1695

JSB Category: 4(C)(c)

Sex: Male

Age at injury: 35

Age at award: 39

Date of award: 14 March 1995

Tribunal: Preston County Court

Amount of award then: £13,000

Award at February 2001: £15,334

Description of injuries: Undisplaced fracture of nose, cuts and grazes, serious whiplash, dental injuries requiring treatment and permanent partial loss of smell and deviated nasal septum causing diminution in nasal airway – spent 11 days in hospital, 32 weeks in collar and had courses of physiotherapy and cranial osteopathy – nine weeks off work – cycling hobby impaired – could no longer smell sour milk or meat cooking on barbecue.

1.2.3.3.C5 Case No. 10363

Award at February 2001: £14,932

See: 1.2.3.2.C8 for details

1.2.3.3.C6 Case No. 11563

Name of case: Re Purvis

Brief description of injuries: SENSES – SENSE OF SMELL

Reported: Kemp & Kemp, D4-018/3; [1998] CLY 1565

JSB Category: 4(C)(c); 8

Sex: Male

Age at injury: 29

Age at award: 35

Date of award: 21 January 1998

Tribunal: CICB, Durham

Amount of award then: £13,000

Award at February 2001: £14,143

Description of injuries: Laceration to the back of the skull – depression and blunting of intellectual abilities lasted 18 months – severe loss of sense of smell – could identify 11 out of 40 different smells in tests – laceration healed well – scar completely covered by hair – further loss of smell 2 years after the first test.

1.2.3.3.C7 Case No. 10184

Name of case: Laycock v Morrison (WM)

Brief description of injuries: LOSS OF THE SENSES OF SMELL AND TASTE

Reported: Kemp & Kemp, D4-019; [1991] CLY 1381

JSB Category: 4(C)

Sex: Male

Age at injury: 76

Age at award: 79

Date of award: 21 August 1990

Tribunal: QBD

Amount of award then: £7,500

Award at February 2001: £10,070

Description of injuries: Fell on his face – serious bruising.

Prognosis: Loss of the senses of smell and taste.

1.2.3.3.C8 Case No. 10353

Award at February 2001: £6,786

See: 1.2.3.2.C26 for details

1.2.3.4 HEARING AND EAR DAMAGE

1.2.3.4.C1 Case No. 10376

Name of case: Upton v North Tees Health Authority
Brief description of injuries: TOTAL DEAFNESS
Reported: Kemp & Kemp, D3-011; [1992] CLY 1632
JSB Category: 4(B)(b)
Sex: Male
Age at injury: 13
Age at award: 22
Date of award: 28 February 1992
Tribunal: Newcastle upon Tyne High Court
Amount of award then: £50,000
Award at February 2001: £70,873
Description of injuries: Contracted meningitis – became totally deaf in both ears.

1.2.3.4.C2 Case No. 10148

Name of case: Re W
Brief description of injuries: TEMPORARY DEAFNESS – MILD TINNITUS – SERIOUS POST-TRAUMATIC STRESS DISORDER
Reported: Kemp & Kemp, C4-015; [1991] CLY 1345
JSB Category: 3(B)(b); 4(B)(d)(vi)
Sex: Female
Age at injury: 24
Age at award: 31
Date of award: 21 January 1991
Tribunal: CICB
Amount of award then: £40,000
Award at February 2001: £58,093
Description of injuries: Terrorist bomb attack – minor physical injuries – temporary deafness – permanent mild bilateral tinnitus – developed serious post-traumatic stress disorder resulting in anxiety, panic attacks, spastic colon, headaches and depression – medical retirement from police force – developed dependency on alcohol (considered to be part of post-traumatic stress disorder) and required number of periods at alcohol treatment centres – alcoholism led to difficulty in keeping jobs.
Prognosis: Guarded. Not drunk alcohol for nine months and would be able to work if could find employment but would need retraining.

1.2.3.4.C3 Case No. 10048

Name of case: Re Okine
Brief description of injuries: HEARING, TOTAL DEAFNESS – 3 BROKEN TEETH
Reported: Kemp & Kemp, D3-013; [1990] CLY 1617
JSB Category: 7(A); 4(B)
Sex: Female
Age at injury: 30
Age at award: 36
Date of award: 19 October 1990
Tribunal: CICB
Amount of award then: £30,000
Award at February 2001: £42,314
Description of injuries: Three broken teeth, a black eye, cuts to lip, knee and hands, bruising and severe deafness – suffers from headaches, loss of balance, impaired taste and loss of sensation in face.
Prognosis: Total deafness – unable to return to work as a telephonist.

1.2.3.4.C4 Case No. 10553

Name of case: Re Lorimer
Brief description of injuries: HEAD – HEARING – EYESIGHT – DEPRESSION
Reported: Kemp & Kemp, C2-065; [1993] CLY 1446
JSB Category: 2(A)(d); 3(A); 4(A), 4(B)(d)
Sex: Male
Age at injury: 40
Age at award: 46
Date of award: 06 September 1993
Tribunal: CICB
Amount of award then: £25,000
Award at February 2001: £31,722
Description of injuries: Struck on head with blunt instrument – fracture of left ulna and severe head injury – daily headaches aggravated by noise – eyesight impaired to the extent that close work impossible – tinnitus – serious personality change – forgetfulness – concentration problems – anxiety – irritability – depression – withdrawnness – lack of confidence – loss of interest in things previously enjoyed – depression continuing despite group therapy and medication – family life and parental life seriously impaired.
Prognosis: Rendered effectively unemployable.

1.2.3.4.C5 Case No. 10748

Award at February 2001: £28,421

See: 1.2.3.3.C3 for details

1.2.3.4.C6 Case No. 11085

Name of case: Re Ostrachowcha

Brief description of injuries: LEG – HEARING – TINNITUS – TEETH

Reported: Kemp & Kemp, B2-026; [1996] CLY 2176

JSB Category: 6(K)(b)(iv); 7(A)(f)(i)

Sex: Female

Age at injury: 62

Age at award: 67

Date of award: 19 April 1996

Tribunal: CICB, London

Amount of award then: £22,000

Award at February 2001: £25,640

Description of injuries: Compound fracture of the left tibia and fibula – tinnitus – loss of five teeth – mild depressive illness.

Prognosis: Symptoms were unlikely to improve.

Other points: Award increased on Appeal from £15,000.

1.2.3.4.C7 Case No. 11561

Name of case: Hill v Arc (South Wales) Ltd

Brief description of injuries: HEARING – TINNITUS – DEPRESSIVE ILLNESS

Reported: Kemp & Kemp, D3-014/1; [1998] CLY 1563

JSB Category: 4(B)(d); 3(A)

Sex: Male

Age at injury: 48

Age at award: 56

Date of award: 21 July 1998

Tribunal: Cardiff County Court

Amount of award then: £19,500

Award at February 2001: £21,074

Description of injuries: Constant severe tinnitus and hearing loss – significant depressive illness requiring continuous psychiatric treatment – H had to give up his pre-accident work – unable to tolerate loud noise or quiet.

Prognosis: Unlikely to be able to obtain and keep any employment – continuing severe depression.

1.2.3.4.C8 Case No. 10556

Name of case: Re T

Brief description of injuries: PSYCHIATRIC DAMAGE – HEARING LOSS

Reported: Kemp & Kemp, C4-055; [1993] CLY 1449

JSB Category: 3(B); 4(B)(d)

Sex: Male

Age at injury: 35

Age at award: 39

Date of award: 09 February 1993

Tribunal: CICB

Amount of award then: £15,000

Award at February 2001: £18,951

Description of injuries: Beaten up in affray – subsequent stress – related problems – post-traumatic stress disorder diagnosed – loss of consciousness on one occasion – hallucination – panic attacks – frustration – irritability – short-term memory and concentration very poor – disturbance of smell and taste – feelings of detachment or estrangement – lack of motivation – also some hearing loss in both ears – retired as unfit.

Prognosis: Hearing loss expected to worsen (from -15 to -30 dB) due to presbycusis at about age 65.

1.2.3.4.C9 Case No. 10378

Name of case: Bettany v Harvey Plant

Brief description of injuries: MINOR HEARING LOSS AND TINNITUS – WHIPLASH 2 YEARS

Reported: [1992] CLY 1634

JSB Category: 4(B)(d)(ii)

Sex: Male

Age at injury: 49

Age at award: 51

Date of award: 07 July 1992

Tribunal: Leicester County Court

Amount of award then: £15,000

Award at February 2001: £18,951

Description of injuries: Partial loss of hearing and tinnitus.

Prognosis: Permanent moderate to severe tinnitus – 3khz masked at 75 decibels narrow band marking – minor loss of hearing – whiplash injury exacerbated existing symptoms for two years.

Damage to Head

1.2.3.4.C10 Case No. 10377

Name of case: Re Tiyur

Brief description of injuries: DEAF IN ONE EAR – VERTIGO – TINNITUS

Reported: [1992] CLY 1633

JSB Category: 4(B)(c)

Sex: Male

Age at injury: 15

Age at award: 22

Date of award: 02 November 1992

Tribunal: CICB, Birmingham

Amount of award then: £15,000

Award at February 2001: £18,824

Description of injuries: Attacked with a welding rod – penetrated the left ear – total hearing loss in the left ear – three jobs lost through having to take time off due to symptoms of the assault.

Prognosis: Unable to work in noisy conditions due to symptoms of vertigo, tinnitus and nausea – unable to work at heights.

1.2.3.4.C11 Case No. 10196

Name of case: Owens v Express Food Group

Brief description of injuries: LOSS OF HEARING AND TINNITUS – LOSS OF 65-70 DB

Reported: Kemp & Kemp, D3-022/1; [1991] CLY 1393

JSB Category: 4(B)(d)(ii)

Sex: Male

Age at injury: -

Age at award: 56

Date of award: 31 January 1991

Tribunal: QBD

Amount of award then: £13,500

Award at February 2001: £18,151

Description of injuries: Exposure to industrial noise for many years – loss of 65dB in the right ear – 70dB in the left ear. The award was discounted by 25 per cent as one quarter of the disability arose from his working for other employers.

Prognosis: Constant severe tinnitus – disturbed sleep – difficulty in hearing in a crowded environment.

1.2.3.4.C12 Case No. 10940

Name of case: Aylesbury v Hale

Brief description of injuries: MODERATELY SEVERE TINNITUS

Reported: Kemp & Kemp, D2-017; [1995] CLY 1691

JSB Category: 4(B)(d)(i)

Sex: Female

Age at injury: 39

Age at award: 45

Date of award: 09 November 1994

Tribunal: Cardiff High Court

Amount of award then: £15,000

Award at February 2001: £18,069

Description of injuries: Plaintiff's car was hit from behind causing it to leave motorway and turn over – suffered a violent commotional head injury, although no actual blow – developed moderately severe tinnitus in left ear and mild associated vertigo – experienced ringing in ears which increased in intensity in times of stress or pressure – it was obtrusive and unlikely to improve – prior to accident plaintiff was self-employed proprietor of nursing home – accident affected her ability to run her business.

1.2.3.4.C13 Case No. 10197

Name of case: Re Attison

Brief description of injuries: ASSAULT FRACTURED SKULL – SEVERE HEARING LOSS IN ONE EAR – CONTINUOUS TINNITUS

Reported: [1991] CLY 1394

JSB Category: 4(B)(d)(i)

Sex: Male

Age at injury: 31

Age at award: 35

Date of award: 25 October 1990

Tribunal: CICB, Leeds

Amount of award then: £12,500

Award at February 2001: £16,742

Description of injuries: Assault – fractures to the parietal and temporal bones – serious damage to the cochlear and vestibular mechanisms – loss of consciousness – severe hearing loss in one ear – loss of balance for nine months after the date of the accident.

Prognosis: Hearing loss amounted to total loss in one ear – there is the prospect of further deterioration – occasional dizziness – almost continuous tinnitus – analgesics required in cold and windy weather.

1.2.3.4.C14 Case No. 10379

Name of case: Bragg v Ford Motor Co.

Brief description of injuries: CONSTANT MODERATE TINNITUS

Reported: [1992] PIQR Q72; Kemp & Kemp, D3-022, D3-117; [1992] CLY 1635

JSB Category: 4(B)(d)(ii)

Sex: Male

Age at injury: 37

Age at award: 47

Date of award: 04 February 1992

Tribunal: Swansea County Court

Amount of award then: £11,000

Award at February 2001: £14,000

Description of injuries: Permanent bi-lateral hearing loss – 12 decibels over 1,2,and 3 khz frequencies – 15 decibels over1, 2 and 4 khz – permanent tinnitus – high pitched whining or ringing – took longer to fall asleep.

Prognosis: Constant moderate tinnitus – constant high pitched whining/ringing sound in the ears – sleeping pattern affected.

1.2.3.4.C15 Case No. 10942

Name of case: Lovatt v Linde Gas UK

Brief description of injuries: MODERATELY SEVERE TINNITUS – HEARING LOSS – RISK OF DETERIORATION

Reported: Kemp & Kemp, D3-024; [1995] CLY 1693

JSB Category: 4(B)(d)(ii)

Sex: Male

Age at injury: 26

Age at award: 29

Date of award: 07 February 1995

Tribunal: Stoke on Trent County Court

Amount of award then: £10,000

Award at February 2001: £11,750

Description of injuries: Claimant was struck in left ear by a high pressured jet of hydrogen gas from a fractured pipe less than 1ft away – further exposed to "extremely loud" high pitched whistle from pipe for approximately five seconds until he could shut off valve – suffered small perforation of left tympanic membrane with bruising of anterior meatal skin – unable to hear in left ear at all immediately after the accident – ear was blocked with cotton wool and cream for approximately one month during which time plaintiff was very worried about permanent total/partial hearing loss – had recovered majority of hearing by end of two months following accident but suffered permanent loss of hearing at one, two and four kHz average 15 Db and at six and eight kHz of 50 to 60 Db – had difficulty in hearing in social situations or where there was background noise – wife complained that he played television too loud – had no time off work – tinnitus in left ear described as moderate to severe and as a constant "screeching" sound – had difficulty in getting to sleep and staying asleep.

Prognosis: There was 25 per cent risk of further deterioration over next 25-30 years – tinnitus was permanent and unlikely to decrease in severity.

1.2.3.4.C16 Case No. 10182

Name of case: Re Swales

Brief description of injuries: LOSS OF PART OF ONE EAR

Reported: Kemp & Kemp, C5-029; [1991] CLY 1379

JSB Category: 7(B)

Sex: Male

Age at injury: 22

Age at award: 24

Date of award: 31 May 1990

Tribunal: CICB, Newcastle

Amount of award then: £7,500

Award at February 2001: £10,222

Description of injuries: Unprovoked attack with loss of part of one ear – caused by a human bite – sensitivity to cold.

Prognosis: S had to leave his employment at a frozen food factory due to the sensitivity to cold.

1.2.3.4.C17 Case No. 10943

Name of case: Lane v Evans
Brief description of injuries: MILD TO MODERATE UNILATERAL DEAFNESS
Reported: Kemp & Kemp, D3-026; [1995] CLY 1694
JSB Category: 4(B)(d)(ii)
Sex: Female
Age at injury: 2
Age at award: 8
Date of award: 27 February 1995
Tribunal: Birmingham County Court
Amount of award then: £8,000
Award at February 2001: £9,367
Description of injuries: Passenger in road traffic accident – suffered fracture of skull, a left sided haemotympanum, one convulsion and balance was affected for 10 days – only lasting injury was "mild to moderate" unilateral deafness in left ear due to dislocation of ossicular chain – whilst deafness in left ear was on average 44 Db between 500 and 8,000 Hz, was described as hearing "generally well" – also suffered otitis media with effusion (glue ear) in both ears but this was not attributable to the accident.

Prognosis: Hearing loss would be permanent unless she underwent surgery (an ossiculoplasty) total cost of which would be £3,000 and which could not take place until her mid/late teens – operation had 70-85 per cent chance of returning her hearing to "near normal", but one per cent chance of causing a deterioration in hearing and in that event a risk of tinnitus.

1.2.3.4.C18 Case No. 11562

Name of case: Read v British Railways Board
Brief description of injuries: HEARING – TINNITUS
Reported: Kemp & Kemp, D3-026/1; [1998] CLY 1564
JSB Category: 4(B)(d)(ii)
Sex: Male
Age at injury: 20s-40's
Age at award: 51
Date of award: 20 October 1997
Tribunal: York County Court
Amount of award then: £8,500
Award at February 2001: £9,166
Description of injuries: Slight hearing loss – tinnitus was obtrusive in his daily life – condition relieved by playing music – claimant's sleep frequently affected.

1.2.3.4.C19 Case No. 11330

Name of case: Earlam v Hepworth Heating Ltd
Brief description of injuries: HEARING – SIGNIFICANT HEARING LOSS
Reported: Kemp & Kemp, D3-027/1, D3-118; [1997] CLY 1878
JSB Category: 4(B)(iv)
Sex: Male
Age at injury: 41
Age at award: 46
Date of award: 25 June 1996
Tribunal: Burton on Trent County Court
Amount of award then: £5,500
Award at February 2001: £6,183
Description of injuries: Significant hearing loss.

Prognosis: There was a fifty per cent chance that he would need a hearing aid at an earlier age than someone who did not suffer from noise induced deafness.

1.2.3.4.C20 Case No. 11802

Name of case: Lewis v BTR plc
Brief description of injuries: HEARING
Reported: Kemp & Kemp, PRD-003; [1999] CLY 1465
JSB Category: 4(B)(d)
Sex: Male
Age at injury: 35 onwards
Age at award: 42
Date of award: 27 May 1999
Tribunal: Merthyr Tydfil County Court
Amount of award then: £5,500
Award at February 2001: £5,713
Description of injuries: Claimant suffered high frequency sensorineural hearing loss in both ears as result of exposure to loud noise in his employment in a factory – claimant capable of hearing one – to – one conversations in quiet environments, but experienced difficulties when competing background noise present, eg when in groups or when shopping – required volume to be turned up high when watching TV – no tinnitus, but experienced occasional high – pitched whining – extent of hearing loss in left ear was 10dB at 1kHz, 15dB at 2kHz and 15dB at 3kHz – extent of hearing loss in right ear 20dB at 1kHz, 15dB at 2kHz and 15dB at 3kHz – binaural hearing loss averaged over 1, 2 and 3kHz was 13.33 – results characteristics of noise trauma.

Prognosis: Hearing loss permanent – expected to deteriorate slowly with age.

1.2.3.4.C21 Case No. 11987

Name of case: W (a child) v Classic Cuts

Brief description of injuries: EAR – ABSCESS

Reported: Kemp & Kemp, PRC-016; [2000] 3 CL 171

JSB Category: 7(B)(a)

Sex: Female

Age at injury: 11

Age at award: 12

Date of award: 07 October 1999

Tribunal: Kingston upon Hull County Court

Amount of award then: £4,850

Award at February 2001: £5,010

Description of injuries: Perichondritis and abscess formation was diagnosed following ear-piercing – swelling remained after intravenous anti-biotics – the ear was incised under general anaesthetic – a drain was inserted and the wound dressed – culture of the pus showed pseudomonas species – she was put on a course of Ciprofloxacin – loss of cartilage resulted in swelling of the upper pole and kinking to the helical rim – there was a 13mm vertical scar behind the ear – the ear remained tender to firm pressure and painful in the cold.

Prognosis: Residual symptoms were expected to subside – W remained self-conscious and would only wear her hair arranged to conceal her ear.

1.2.3.4.C22 Case No. 11803

Name of case: Kearney v Calsonic Llanelli Radiators Ltd

Brief description of injuries: HEARING

Reported: Kemp & Kemp, D3-029/1; [1999] CLY 1466

JSB Category: 4(B)(d)(iv)

Sex: Male

Age at injury: late 40s onwards

Age at award: 54

Date of award: 25 November 1998

Tribunal: Swansea County Court

Amount of award then: £3,500

Award at February 2001: £3,662

Description of injuries: Claimant had suffered from noise – induced hearing loss since late 40s – audiogram in 1994 showed binaural impairment averaged over 1, 2 and 3kHz at 9.3dB – subsequent deterioration in claimant's hearing due to factors other than noise – overall disability 6 per cent, and, if compared with the 50th centile (ie, the "average man"), this would suggest the amount of claimant's hearing loss due to noise exposure was 1 per cent – however, claimant's hearing loss in 8kHz range, where age – related hearing loss is usually most pronounced, was only 10dB, indicating that claimant's hearing loss at 1-3kHz should only be in the region of 1.5dB, in turn suggesting that balance of nearly 8dB loss at 1-3kHz was in fact due to noise exposure – counsel for claimant therefore suggested that claimant should be compared with 77th centile, not 50th – further, claimant's complaints (necessity of high volume settings when watching TV; failure to hear wife from another room; difficulty following conversations in crowded rooms unless speaker in line of sight; asking interlocutors to repeat themselves; occasional tinnitus and hyperacusis) were in line with problems in 4-6kHz range, where damage due to noise exposure is usually experienced.

1.2.3.4.C23 Case No. 10747

Name of case: Vaughan v Moogan

Brief description of injuries: SENSES – HEARING – TINNITUS

Reported: Kemp & Kemp, D3-030; [1994] CLY 1595

JSB Category: 4(B)(d)

Sex: Female

Age at injury: 47

Age at award: 49

Date of award: 29 April 1994

Tribunal: Harrogate County Court

Amount of award then: £2,250

Award at February 2001: £2,684

Description of injuries: Road accident – blow to side of head – development of tinnitus, described as being of mild degree, in form of low, buzzing sound – irregular attacks 4-5 times a week, lasting sometimes for minutes and other times for an entire day, triggered by electrical noises, such as washing machines or air conditioning, or by noise in crowded rooms – interference with social life – disruption to foreign holiday – lengthy attacks caused irritability and fractiousness and prevented sleep – no evidence of impaired hearing.

Prognosis: Tinnitus likely to continue indefinitely – however, symptomology likely to be eased by conclusion of proceedings.

1.2.3.4.C24 Case No. 11908

Name of case: Jobling v Gala Leisure Ltd

Brief description of injuries: HEARING – TEMPORARY LOSS

Reported: Kemp & Kemp, K2-253/2; [1999] CLY 1572

JSB Category: 4(B)

Sex: Female

Age at injury: 63

Age at award: 65

Date of award: 28 May 1999

Tribunal: Sunderland County Court

Amount of award then: £600

Award at February 2001: £623

Description of injuries: Claimant subjected to loud explosive noise – deaf in both ears immediately after the incident – hearing returned to right ear in 2-3 days and in left ear over an unspecified time – claimant had experienced some hearing loss in both ears prior to the accident – 7 months after accident, hearing had returned to its pre-accident level.

1.2.3.5 DENTAL INJURY

1.2.3.5.C1 Case No. 10048

Award at February 2001: £42,314

See: 1.2.3.4.C3 for details

1.2.3.5.C2 Case No. 11567

Name of case: Tierney v Mavadia

Brief description of injuries: SPINE – TEETH

Reported: 98 (6) QR 6; Kemp & Kemp, E3-028/1; [1998] CLY 1569

JSB Category: 6(B)(b), 7(A)(f)

Sex: Male

Age at injury: 45

Age at award: 51

Date of award: 01 July 1998

Tribunal: QBD

Amount of award then: £17,500

Award at February 2001: £18,822

Description of injuries: Injury to the cervical spine – loss of 3 teeth – diagnosed as 40 per cent disabled – experienced difficulty with physical activities in his daily life.

Prognosis: The prognosis was for no improvement.

Other points: Previous injuries had led to claimant's discharge from the Navy – disability assessed at 18 per cent – these injuries had resolved within a few months.

1.2.3.5.C3 Case No. 10446

Name of case: Hogg v Smith and Forder

Brief description of injuries: FEMUR FRACTURE – LOSS OF 3 TEETH

Reported: Kemp & Kemp, I2-507; [1992] CLY 1702

JSB Category: 6(K)(c)(i)

Sex: Male

Age at injury: 38

Age at award: 47

Date of award: 09 October 1992

Tribunal: Colchester County Court

Amount of award then: £14,000

Award at February 2001: £17,493

Description of injuries: Fracture of the shaft of the left femur – fractures to three of the front teeth – unfit for work for eight months – permanent shortening of the leg by two cms – some bowing of the femur – operational scarring.

Prognosis: Left with a permanent limp – registered as disabled

1.2.3.5.C4 Case No. 11114

Name of case: Hadjiyianni v Craven

Brief description of injuries: TEETH – NEGLIGENT DENTAL TREATMENT

Reported: Kemp & Kemp, C6-005; [1996] CLY 2205

JSB Category: 7(A)(f)(i)

Sex: Female

Age at injury: 47

Age at award: 51

Date of award: 16 February 1996

Tribunal: Clerkenwell County Court

Amount of award then: £10,000

Award at February 2001: £11,430

Description of injuries: Dental treatment carried out negligently and without consent.

Prognosis: The plaintiff would have continued difficulty in eating.

Other points: Award reflected the amount of remedial treatment required and the extent of the pain and suffering endured.

1.2.3.5.C5 Case No. 11553

Name of case: Harrington v Newham LBC

Brief description of injuries: TEETH – LOSS OF TWELVE TEETH

Reported: Kemp & Kemp, C6-006; [1998] CLY 1555

JSB Category: 7(A)(f)(i), 7(A)(e)(iii) (see "Other points")

Sex: Male

Age at injury: 56

Age at award: 61

Date of award: 04 August 1998

Tribunal: Romford County Court

Amount of award then: £10,000

Award at February 2001: £10,514

Description of injuries: Loss of 12 teeth – including all the incisors and upper canines – the only appropriate permanent treatment was with dentures – dentures uncomfortable.

Prognosis: Dentures would need to be replaced every 10 years.

Other points: There was some overlap with awards cited for a fractured jaw – difficulties with using the dentures went beyond the mere loss of teeth.

1.2.3.5.C6 Case No. 11326

Name of case: Mitchell v Burkitt

Brief description of injuries: TWO TEETH LOST

Reported: Kemp & Kemp, C6-009; [1997] CLY 1874

JSB Category: 7(A)(ii)

Sex: Male

Age at injury: 45

Age at award: 51

Date of award: 09 July 1997

Tribunal: Salford County Court

Amount of award then: £6,500

Award at February 2001: £7,098

Description of injuries: Removal of two front teeth as a result of negligence by the dental surgeon – extensive restorative dental treatment was required.

Other points: Required treatment was not available under the NHS.

1.2.3.5.C7 Case No. 10187

Name of case: Re Howard

Brief description of injuries: LOSS OF TWO TEETH – FRACTURED JAW – EXTENSIVE DENTAL TREATMENT

Reported: Kemp & Kemp, C6-010; [1991] CLY 1384

JSB Category: 7(A)(f)(i)

Sex: Male

Age at injury: 20

Age at award: 23

Date of award: 24 May 1991

Tribunal: CICB, Leeds

Amount of award then: £5,000

Award at February 2001: £6,442

Description of injuries: Loss of two teeth during an assault – fractures to three further teeth – bridges, pinning and crowns required over eighteen months (more than 20 appointments) – fractures to the jaw which was plated – had to stop playing rugby – off work for six weeks.

Prognosis: Two years after the date of the accident there was a limitation on opening the jaw and jaw movement – neither likely to improve – difficulty in eating.

1.2.3.5.C8 Case No. 11554

Name of case: Temelkowski v McMath

Brief description of injuries: TEETH – NEGLIGENT DENTAL TREATMENT

Reported: Kemp & Kemp, C6-071; [1998] CLY 1556

JSB Category: 7(A)(f)

Sex: Female

Age at injury: 14

Age at award: 21

Date of award: 03 September 1997

Tribunal: Bradford County Court

Amount of award then: £5,500

Award at February 2001: £5,938

Description of injuries: 5 years of unnecessary and negligent treatment to a front incisor – underwent apicectomy to repair the damage caused – claimant unable to eat hard or stringy type food using that particular tooth.

1.2.3.5.C9 Case No. 10564

Name of case: Brownlie v Tate & Lyle
Brief description of injuries: PSYCHIATRIC DAMAGE-DENTAL INJURIES
Reported: Kemp & Kemp, C4-105; [1993] CLY 1457
JSB Category: 3(A)(c); 7(A)(f)
Sex: Male
Age at injury: 14 months
Age at award: -
Date of award: 02 December 1992
Tribunal: Mayors of City of London County Court
Amount of award then: £4,250
Award at February 2001: £5,251
Description of injuries: Boy injured in road accident – suffered loss of 2 front teeth, but major injury moderate psychiatric damage – inconsolable for several days after accident – introversion – disturbed sleep patterns for 12 months – traffic phobia (invariably unsettled when travelling by car, nervous reaction to heavy vehicles, reluctance to play with toy cars).
Prognosis: Future vulnerability to stress, making necessity of psychiatric treatment at some point in later life more likely – adult teeth not affected by damage to milk teeth.

1.2.3.5.C10 Case No. 10045

Name of case: McKenna v Heron
Brief description of injuries: LOSS OF 4 TEETH
Reported: Kemp & Kemp, C6-016; [1990] CLY 1607
JSB Category: 7(A)
Sex: Female
Age at injury: 16
Age at award: 20
Date of award: 24 May 1990
Tribunal: Birkenhead County Court
Amount of award then: £3,000
Award at February 2001: £4,089
Description of injuries: Lost upper right and left central incisors, upper right lateral incisor and upper right canine.
Prognosis: Crown and bridge work required every 10 years from wear and tear.

1.2.3.5.C11 Case No. 10188

Name of case: Lee v Gough
Brief description of injuries: ASSAULT – LOSS OF FRONT TEETH
Reported: Kemp & Kemp, C6-017; [1991] CLY 1385
JSB Category: 7(A)(f)(i)
Sex: Female
Age at injury: 27
Age at award: 30
Date of award: 01 November 1991
Tribunal: Epsom County Court
Amount of award then: £3,200
Award at February 2001: £4,059
Description of injuries: Assault – punched in the mouth – loss of front teeth which were replaced by the plaintiff – splinted for two months – difficulty in eating – swelling to the mouth and gums led to disfigurement and loss of work opportunity.
Prognosis: The teeth would discolour in the future – crowns and posts would be required – slight change in appearance.

1.2.3.5.C12 Case No. 10046

Name of case: Re Jones
Brief description of injuries: LOSS OF 2 TEETH – SMALL SCAR ON EAR
Reported: Kemp & Kemp, C6-019; [1990] CLY 1608
JSB Category: 7(A); 7(B)
Sex: Male
Age at injury: 59
Age at award: -
Date of award: 16 January 1990
Tribunal: CICB
Amount of award then: £2,750
Award at February 2001: £3,958
Description of injuries: Laceration to left ear – two upper incisors loosened and therefore extracted.
Prognosis: Left with faint scar on left ear – needed dentures fitted.

1.2.3.5.C13 Case No. 11795

Name of case: A (a minor) v Severn Trent Water plc
Brief description of injuries: TEETH
Reported: Kemp & Kemp, C6-020; [1999] CLY 1458
JSB Category: 7(A)(f)
Sex: Male
Age at injury: 7
Age at award: 10
Date of award: 17 June 1998
Tribunal: Nottingham County Court
Amount of award then: £3,650
Award at February 2001: £3,842

Description of injuries: Slip and fall causing damage to upper right incisor, which was fractured just below gum level – subsequent X-rays revealed vertical fracture to root of tooth, necessitating extraction (which took 3 attempts to achieve under general anaesthetic) – claimant provided with single tooth denture, but outgrew it as such a rapid rate that it was difficult to retain without frequent replacement – consequently, remaining teeth encroached on space for upper right central incisor – claimant suffered little pain, but was aware of cosmetic deformity and became increasingly self-conscious about it – forced to give up modelling for children's clothing catalogue – occasional eating problems.

Prognosis: Orthodontic treatment necessary in the future to reposition encroaching teeth so that permanent replacement for missing incisor can be fitted when claimant approximately 17 years of age.

1.2.3.5.C14 Case No. 10365

Award at February 2001: £3,841

See: 1.2.3.2.C53 for details

1.2.3.5.C15 Case No. 11115

Name of case: Mafe v Amin
Brief description of injuries: TEETH – NEGLIGENT DENTAL TREATMENT
Reported: Kemp & Kemp, C6-021; [1996] CLY 2206
JSB Category: 7(A)(f)(i)
Sex: Male
Age at injury: -
Age at award: 62
Date of award: 29 March 1996
Tribunal: Willesden County Court
Amount of award then: £3,250
Award at February 2001: £3,690

Description of injuries: negligent dental treatment – five crowns fell out – three years of specialist repairs had to be carried out.

1.2.3.5.C16 Case No. 10189

Name of case: Re Robinson
Brief description of injuries: FRACTURED WISDOM TEETH – FRACTURE WIRED
Reported: Kemp & Kemp, C6-022; [1991] CLY 1386
JSB Category: 7(A)(f)(iv)
Sex: Female
Age at injury: 19
Age at award: 23
Date of award: 06 February 1991
Tribunal: CICB, Newcastle
Amount of award then: £2,750
Award at February 2001: £3,613

Description of injuries: Assault – fractures through partly erupted wisdom teeth – both lower teeth removed and the fracture site was wired under general anaesthetic – unable to eat food for six weeks until the fixation of teeth was released.

Prognosis: Possibility of the wires being removed in the future – full recovery.

1.2.3.5.C17 Case No. 12056

Name of case: G (a child) v Grindal
Brief description of injuries: TEETH
Reported: [2000] 6 CL 186
JSB Category: 7(A)(f)(ii)
Sex: Female
Age at injury: 8
Age at award: 10
Date of award: 14 December 1999
Tribunal: Nuneaton County Court
Amount of award then: £3,000
Award at February 2001: £3,084

Description of injuries: Facial and oral injuries suffered in a fall from her bicycle – front lower and upper teeth were loosened and sensitive – traumatic ulceration of the labial mucosa with "tattooing" – lower lip was extremely swollen – unable to open her mouth or to eat solids one week after the accident – six weeks later she was able to open her mouth but complained of clicking and discomfort.

Prognosis: At the time of the hearing it was expected that crowning and root treatment would be required in the future.

Other points: The award covered the anticipated cost of further dental treatment.

1.2.3.5.C18 Case No. 10576

Name of case: Doe v Markey

Brief description of injuries: TOOTH – ASSAULT – ANXIETY

Reported: Kemp & Kemp, K2-064; [1993] CLY 1469

JSB Category: 7(A)(f)(iii); 3(A)(d)

Sex: Male

Age at injury: 36

Age at award: 38

Date of award: 15 January 1993

Tribunal: Halifax County Court

Amount of award then: £2,150

Award at February 2001: £2,682

Description of injuries: Claimant struck in face – traumatic root fracture of upper left first premolar – tooth extracted and permanent bridge cemented in – scar on inner surface of upper left lip which claimant occasionally bit into – anxiety about driving alone, especially at night – exacerbation of pre-existing headache condition.

Prognosis: Bridge work of high standard but replacement expected sometime after about 15 years – longevity of 2 adjacent teeth prejudiced – headaches and anxiety thought likely to subside within a year of assault; considerable improvement at date of trial.

Other points: Award split: tooth £1,750; other items £400.

1.2.3.5.C19 Case No. 11905

Name of case: U (a minor) v Manchester City Council

Brief description of injuries: TEETH – 2 REMOVED – PSYCHOLOGICAL REACTION

Reported: Kemp & Kemp, C6-025; [1999] CLY 1569

JSB Category: 7(A)(f); 3(A)

Sex: Male

Age at injury: 2

Age at award: 4

Date of award: 06 July 1999

Tribunal: Manchester County Court

Amount of award then: £2,500

Award at February 2001: £2,604

Description of injuries: Trip and fall onto face – claimant required to have 2 lower teeth removed and laceration to lower gum treated by maxillo – facial specialist in hospital – pain in mouth for 6 months following accident – sleep pattern disturbed – bed-wetting – withdrawnness – refusal to eat solids for 3 weeks – painkillers required regularly for 3 weeks – start at nursery school delayed for 6 months until all symptoms settled.

Prognosis: Missing teeth, as first teeth, expected to be replaced by secondary dentition teeth – no long-term complications expected to arise from accident.

1.2.3.5.C20 Case No. 11796

Name of case: H (a minor) v Lincolnshire CC

Brief description of injuries: TEETH

Reported: Kemp & Kemp, C6-026; [1999] CLY 1459

JSB Category: 7(A)(f)

Sex: Male

Age at injury: 9

Age at award: 13

Date of award: 14 July 1998

Tribunal: Skegness County Court

Amount of award then: £2,400

Award at February 2001: £2,533

Description of injuries: Trip and fall – chipping damage to upper two front central incisors – acid etch retained composite restoration required, and repeated on a regular basis as a result of the teeth continuing to grow

Prognosis: Long-term prognosis good – right incisor would benefit from porcelain veneer or crown in future, in addition to regular acid etch composite restoration treatment, once it had stopped growing – both teeth would need checking to ensure that they did not become non-vital

1.2.3.5.C21 Case No. 10366

Name of case: Styles v Liverpool City Council

Brief description of injuries: LOSS OF TWO FRONT TEETH – SYMPTOMS 12 MONTHS

Reported: [1992] CLY 1622

JSB Category: 7 (A)(f)(ii)

Sex: Female

Age at injury: 28

Age at award: 30

Date of award: 14 February 1992

Tribunal: Liverpool County Court

Amount of award then: £2,000

Award at February 2001: £2,524

Description of injuries: Two upper incisors pushed back – bruising and abrasions to the face.

Prognosis: Temporary repairs carried out – two teeth subsequently removed – five unit bridge fitted – twelve months of pain and suffering – two extremely painful operations.

1.2.3.5.C22 Case No. 10190

Name of case: Shillington-Thorne v Stevens

Brief description of injuries: ASSAULT – DISLOCATION OF INCISORS – BRIDGE REQUIRED

Reported: Kemp & Kemp, C6-027; [1991] CLY 1387

JSB Category: 7(A)(f)(ii)

Sex: Male

Age at injury: 38

Age at award: 41

Date of award: 04 October 1991

Tribunal: Bromley County Court

Amount of award then: £1,750

Award at February 2001: £2,228

Description of injuries: Assault – head-butted in the face – dislocation of incisors – locking of the bite- soft-tissue injury to the to the inside of the lower lip – a very painful injury.

Prognosis: At the time of the hearing a bonded eight-denture bridge was required.

1.2.3.5.C23 Case No. 10191

Name of case: Hunt v Barnet

Brief description of injuries: TRIPLE ASSAULT – FRACTURES TO 2 FRONT TEETH

Reported: Kemp & Kemp, K2-146; [1991] CLY 1388

JSB Category: 7(A)

Sex: Male

Age at injury: 22

Age at award: 25

Date of award: 04 September 1991

Tribunal: Doncaster County Court

Amount of award then: £1,200

Award at February 2001: £1,533

Description of injuries: Assault on three occasions - minor bruising and discomfort on the first two – fractures to two front teeth on the third occasion – repair work carried out including a crown.

Prognosis: No long-term problems were expected.

1.2.3.5.C24 Case No. 10742

Name of case: Handley v Morris Cohen (Underwear)

Brief description of injuries: DAMAGE TO TEETH

Reported: Kemp & Kemp, C6-029; [1994] CLY 1590

JSB Category: 7(A)(f)

Sex: Female

Age at injury: 35

Age at award: 37

Date of award: 15 April 1994

Tribunal: Cardiff County Court

Amount of award then: £1,000

Award at February 2001: £1,193

Description of injuries: Slip and fall – struck face on ground – bridgework to front upper teeth fractured – teeth below bridge loosened and tender – severe pain from upper front teeth – small amount of soft-tissue damage to lips and chin – bridge temporarily repaired – abscess developed under upper left front tooth as result of trauma – tooth required root filling and subsequent course of antibiotics – new bridge constructed and fitted shortly afterwards.

Prognosis: Future problem with bridgework not anticipated – long-term prognosis good.

1.2.3.5.C25 Case No. 11116

Name of case: Martin v Imperial Chemical Industries PLC

Brief description of injuries: TEETH – 3 FRONT TEETH BROKEN

Reported: Kemp & Kemp, C6-030; [1996] CLY 2207

JSB Category: 7(A)(f)(i)

Sex: Male

Age at injury: 26

Age at award: -

Date of award: 25 January 1996

Tribunal: Doncaster County Court

Amount of award then: £1,000

Award at February 2001: £1,145

Description of injuries: Three front teeth broken – swollen lip.

Prognosis: Further treatment required.

1.2.3.5.C26 Case No. 10519

Name of case: Danbrogio v Knowsley Borough Council

Brief description of injuries: LOSS OF ONE TOOTH

Reported: [1992] CLY 1775

JSB Category: 6(A)(f)(iii)

Sex: Female

Age at injury: 18

Age at award: 19

Date of award: 22 June 1992

Tribunal: Liverpool County Court

Amount of award then: £650

Award at February 2001: £803

Description of injuries: Bruising and abrasions to the face – fractured upper right incisor – unable to eat or drink for two days due to pain – tooth required acid-etching type restoration – crown required.

Prognosis: Pain and bruising resolved within 3 weeks

1.2.3.6 EYE INJURY

1.2.3.6.C1 Case No. 11559

Name of case: Re Warner (a minor)

Brief description of injuries: EYE – PARTIAL LOSS OF VISION

Reported: [1998] CLY 1561

JSB Category: 4(A)(f)

Sex: Male

Age at injury: 8

Age at award: -

Date of award: 01 July 1997

Tribunal: CICB, York

Amount of award then: £22,500

Award at February 2001: £25,393

Description of injuries: Struck in the eye with a metal rod – retina repair required within 7 months.

Prognosis: 60 per cent loss of efficiency in the eye – cosmetic defect – risk of glaucoma and retinal detachment in the future.

1.2.3.6.C2 Case No. 11800

Name of case: Re Cantwell

Brief description of injuries: EYE – DAMAGE

Reported: Kemp & Kemp, D2-037/1; [1999] CLY 1463

JSB Category: 4(A)

Sex: Male

Age at injury: 31

Age at award: 39

Date of award: 22 October 1998

Tribunal: CICB, London

Amount of award then: £20,000

Award at February 2001: £21,434

Description of injuries: Left eye sprayed with alkali – left corneal epithelium completely lost – conjunctiva stained – corneal epithelium started to regrow, and vision initially improved – subsequent development of lipid infiltration into visual axis causing serious deterioration of vision – left penetrating keroplasty operation undergone – discovery of irreversible injury to limbal stem cell – development of cataract, also as a result of original injury – 6 years after incident, limbal stem allograft undertaken; 6 months later, left cataract extraction and intraocular lens implant also undergone – claimant left with visual acuity in left eye of only 6/60 – left eye caused considerable discomfort, aggravated by exposure to VDUs and and polluted environments frequently encountered in claimant's job – claimant feared he would also lose sight in right eye, having had a detached retina repaired in that eye 4 years previously – loss of confidence – fear of another assault – mood swings, affecting family life – unable to continue with swimming and all contact sports – restriction of previously busy and happy social life.

Prognosis: Improvement in left eye unlikely, and deterioration possible – loss of sight in right eye due to retinal problems not considered likely.

1.2.3.6.C3 Case No. 10375

Name of case: Re Orves

Brief description of injuries: MAJOR INJURY TO THE RIGHT EYE

Reported: [1992] CLY 1631

JSB Category: 4(A)(g)

Sex: Male

Age at injury: 52

Age at award: 54

Date of award: 05 November 1992

Tribunal: CICB, Birmingham

Amount of award then: £5,000

Award at February 2001: £6,156

Description of injuries: Major injury to the right eye – vitreous haemorrhage and two tears of the choroid layer – bruising to the back of the head and torso – mild post-traumatic stress disorder – pre-existing severe myopia.

Prognosis: Increased risk of retinal detachment to ten per cent, macular degeneration and further haemorrhage – residual debris left in vitreous body caused "floaters" in the eye on a daily basis.

1.2.3.6.C4 Case No. 10195

Name of case: Re Bent

Brief description of injuries: ASSAULT – INJURY TO THE EYE, TOOTH

Reported: Kemp & Kemp, D2-047; [1991] CLY 1392

JSB Category: 4(A)(h)

Sex: Male

Age at injury: 38

Age at award: 41

Date of award: 18 February 1991

Tribunal: CICB, Nottingham

Amount of award then: £3,750

Award at February 2001: £4,927

Description of injuries: Injuries to the nose, eye, tooth, finger and general bruising following a head-butting assault

Prognosis: Finger injury cleared within one year – nose felt bunged up – a back tooth required a post cap – vision in the right eye was not expected to improve or to deteriorate.

1.2.3.6.C5 Case No. 10058

Name of case: Frazer v Courtaulds
Brief description of injuries: EYES, EXPOSED TO CHEMICALS
Reported: [1990] CLY 1682
JSB Category: 4(A)
Sex: Male
Age at injury: 55
Age at award: 60
Date of award: 13 November 1990
Tribunal: Barrow-in-Furness County Court
Amount of award then: £1,750
Award at February 2001: £2,315

Description of injuries: Exposed to chlorine fumes – caused irritation and streaming of the eyes – continuing symptoms up to trial of kerato-conjunctivitis due to tear film deficiency – sensation as if grit in the eye – required use of eye drops and ointment daily.

Prognosis: The sensation of grit in the eye is likely to be permanent – increased susceptibility to infection.

1.2.3.6.C6 Case No. 11558

Name of case: Turner v Nei Parsons Ltd
Brief description of injuries: EYE – CATARACTS – 20-YEAR ACCELERATION
Reported: Kemp & Kemp, D2-049; [1998] CLY 1560
JSB Category: 4(A)(h)
Sex: Male
Age at injury: 50's
Age at award: 60
Date of award: 23 July 1997
Tribunal: Newcastle-upon-Tyne County Court
Amount of award then: £1,750
Award at February 2001: £1,911

Description of injuries: Heat cataracts due to exposure to infra-red radiation from red hot metal – cataracts were successfully operated on.

Prognosis: Judge concluded that T would have developed cataracts anyway – development had been accelerated by 20 years.

1.2.3.6.C7 Case No. 11907

Name of case: Pittham v North Glamorgan NHS Trust
Brief description of injuries: EYE – ONE-EYED CLAIMANT – MINOR DAMAGE TO REMAINING EYE
Reported: Kemp & Kemp, K2-144/2; [1999] CLY 1571
JSB Category: 4(A)(h); 3(A)(d)
Sex: Female
Age at injury: 55
Age at award: 57
Date of award: 22 March 1998
Tribunal: Cardiff County Court
Amount of award then: £1,500
Award at February 2001: £1,604

Description of injuries: Claimant, functionally one – eyed, had both eyes splashed with sanitising chemical solution – eyes rinsed at hospital; no further treatment deemed necessary – claimant anxious about significant consequences if functional eye was damaged – initial pain and discomfort in both eyes for 3 weeks – 4 months after injury, intermittent pain in outer angle of right eye with occasional watering – no evidence of chemical injury or any deficit in sight – occasional ongoing symptoms attributed to anxiety engendered by accident.

Prognosis: No permanent consequences.

Other points: Liability was not established; figure for general damages an indication by the judge of what he would have awarded.

1.2.3.6.C8 Case No. 11320

Name of case: Jackson v Ikeda Hoover Ltd
Brief description of injuries: EYE – CORNEA – SCRATCH
Reported: Kemp & Kemp, K2-167; [1997] CLY 1868
JSB Category: 4(A)(i)
Sex: Male
Age at injury: -
Age at award: 26
Date of award: 11 December 1996
Tribunal: Durham County Court
Amount of award then: £1,250
Award at February 2001: £1,392

Description of injuries: Scratch to the cornea – imperceptibly reduced vision in the right eye – full recovery within one week.

Prognosis: No likelihood of his sight deteriorating as a result of the injury.

Damage to Head

1.2.3.6.C9 Case No. 11066

Name of case: McLaughlin v QDF Component

Brief description of injuries: EYE – FOREIGN BODY – 3 WEEKS

Reported: [1995] CLY 1820

JSB Category: 4(A)(i)

Sex: Male

Age at injury: 40

Age at award: 44

Date of award: 17 November 1994

Tribunal: Derby County Court

Amount of award then: £600

Award at February 2001: £710

Description of injuries: Plaintiff injured when small metal rust ring produced by a grinding machine entered left eye – eye became irritated and following day plaintiff had trouble opening it – object was removed at hospital and he was given antibiotic ointment and mydriatic drops to put in eye – plaintiff wore patch over left eye and was concerned about effect it might have had on his eyesight – took no time off work – experienced pain in eye and had difficulty sleeping – within two-and-a-half to three weeks after accident eye had returned to normal with no residual disability.

1.2.3.6.C10 Case No. 10521

Name of case: Martin v Imperial War Museum

Brief description of injuries: MINOR EYE INJURY – FULL RECOVERY

Reported: Kemp & Kemp, K2-260; [1992] CLY 1777

JSB Category: 4(A)(i)

Sex: Male

Age at injury: -

Age at award: 34

Date of award: 20 May 1992

Tribunal: Mayor's and City of London County Court

Amount of award then: £450

Award at February 2001: £556

Description of injuries: Rusty metal the size of a pin-head entered the left eye.

Prognosis: Full recovery – did not cause any problems after it had been removed.

1.2.3.6.C11 Case No. 10523

Name of case: Lowe v Convenience Foods

Brief description of injuries: CHEMICAL BURN TO ONE EYE – RECOVERY 1 WEEK

Reported: [1992] CLY 1779

JSB Category: 4(A)(i)

Sex: Female

Age at injury: 31

Age at award: -

Date of award: 22 October 1992

Tribunal: Nottingham County Court

Amount of award then: £400

Award at February 2001: £492

Description of injuries: Chemical burn to the right eye and lips – burn totally healed within one week – no scarring or permanent defect – visual acuity returned to normal.

1.2.3.6.1 Eye Injury and other injury

1.2.3.6.1.C1 Case No. 11560

Name of case: Re Moore

Brief description of injuries: EYE – POST-TRAUMATIC STRESS DISORDER

Reported: Kemp & Kemp, D2-020/1; [1998] CLY 1562

JSB Category: 4(A)(e); 3(B)(a)

Sex: Male

Age at injury: 23

Age at award: 30

Date of award: 04 August 1998

Tribunal: CICB, London

Amount of award then: £55,000

Award at February 2001: £64,198

Description of injuries: Severe damage to the left eye – scarring – psychiatric injury – mild post-traumatic stress disorder – enduring personality change.

Prognosis: Prognosis was extremely pessimistic – not amenable to further treatment or help – no foreseeable employment in the future.

1.2.3.6.1.C2 Case No. 10917

Name of case: Re Hawkins

Brief description of injuries: MAJOR DEPRESSIVE ILLNESS – INJURY TO EYE

Reported: Kemp & Kemp, D2-028/1; [1995] CLY 1668

JSB Category: 3(B)(b)

Sex: Male

Age at injury: 18

Age at award: 29

Date of award: 11 September 1995

Tribunal: CICB Appeal

Amount of award then: £25,000

Award at February 2001: £29,773

Description of injuries: Attacked during course of employment as cinema steward by three youths – stabbed through left eye, sustaining a penetrating injury involving the retina – at time of assault was awaiting confirmation from RAF of an offer of service as an airframe mechanic – was engaged to be married and led normal social life – his life was devastated as a result of assault – the injury to left eye and retina was surgically repaired – attack caused him to withdraw his application to RAF – he was left wholly lacking in confidence and with a reduced motivation to socialise and mix with other people or engage in useful working activity – he experienced anxiety and depression, and was angry and frustrated at the non-apprehension of his assailants – at time of hearing, 10 years after original assault, he still suffered from violent nightmares and headaches, which occurred twice a week or more, usually lasting for several hours at a time – his relationship with his girlfriend deteriorated and the engagement was broken off – had not worked since assault – personality had changed and he had suffered and remained subject to moderately severe to severe post-traumatic stress disorder – despite surgical repair of left eye, he continued to complain of loss of vision – such loss had been diagnosed as functional, related to the psychological factors affecting him.

Prognosis: The early resolution of the application would alleviate some of these psychological factors, thereby restoring at least in part, the vision of the left eye, thereby enabling him to get back to work and find suitable employment.

1.2.3.6.2 Visual loss

1.2.3.6.2.C1 Case No. 10580

Name of case: Re Warren

Brief description of injuries: EYE – LOSS OF PRACTICALLY ALL VISION IN ONLY GOOD EYE

Reported: Kemp & Kemp, D2-019; [1993] CLY 1473

JSB Category: 4(A)(c)

Sex: Male

Age at injury: 22

Age at award: 25

Date of award: 22 February 1993

Tribunal: CICB, London

Amount of award then: £70,000

Award at February 2001: £102,218

Description of injuries: Claimant, having previously completely lost right eye in an assault at age 17, assaulted and struck in left eye with hard object – detachment of retina – visual acuity reduced to 6/36 – no peripheral vision – registered blind at time of hearing and unable to read, watch television, prepare meals or go out alone – heavily dependent on mother, sister and girlfriend – depression – frustration.

Prognosis: Prognosis poor – little success in learning to read Braille – prospects of finding employment again poor (claimant had always previously been in employment, having continued to lead an independent life after first assault).

1.2.3.6.2.C2 Case No. 10369

Name of case: Re Hodge

Brief description of injuries: LOSS OF ONE EYE – OTHER EYE "LAZY"

Reported: [1992] CLY 1625

JSB Category: 4(A)(c)(ii)

Sex: Female

Age at injury: 19

Age at award: 23

Date of award: 24 March 1992

Tribunal: CICB Durham

Amount of award then: £40,000

Award at February 2001: £55,036

Description of injuries: Kicked in the face – permanent blindness in the right eye – replaced by artificial eye.

Prognosis: The left eye was a lazy eye – had not improved beyond 6/18 – further improvement unlikely.

Other points: Award raised from £25,000.

1.2.3.6.2.C3 Case No. 11120

Name of case: Re Studd

Brief description of injuries: EYE – TOTAL BLINDNESS OF ONE EYE

Reported: Kemp & Kemp, D2-020/2; [1996] CLY 2211

JSB Category: 4(A)(c)(ii)

Sex: Male

Age at injury: 50

Age at award: 56

Date of award: 19 April 1996

Tribunal: CICB

Amount of award then: £40,000

Award at February 2001: £48,750

Description of injuries: Total blindness of the right eye – undisplaced fracture of the nose – blind in one eye – cataracts in the remaining eye – sight reduced by 80 per cent.

Other points: Plaintiff refused cataract operation in 1995.

1.2.3.6.2.C4 Case No. 10939

Name of case: Re C

Brief description of injuries: LOSS OF VISION IN ONE EYE – CONTINUING DISABILITY – POST-TRAUMATIC STRESS DISORDER

Reported: Kemp & Kemp, D2-021; [1995] CLY 1690

JSB Category: 4(A)(d)

Sex: Female

Age at injury: 23

Age at award: 32

Date of award: 15 March 1995

Tribunal: CICB, York Enterprise Centre

Amount of award then: £35,500

Award at February 2001: £44,405

Description of injuries: Plaintiff suffered terrifying injuries when hand-held distress flare hit her in left eye and then exploded – life blighted both physically and psychologically – effectively lost sight of left eye, suffering a traumatic cataract and severe retinal damage – left with double vision in left eye – attempts to wear an occlusive contact lens proved unsuccessful – also had shrunken eye, shattered eyebrow, fixed dilated pupil and divergent squint and eye could not properly close because of tethering of the skin – slight risk of glaucoma – had plastic surgery but continued to suffer severe cosmetic embarrassment – eye would run in cold weather – at time of injury applicant was some two months pregnant and was diagnosed as depressed and suffering from post-traumatic stress disorder of some significant degree.

1.2.3.6.2.C5 Case No. 10022

Name of case: Re Smith

Brief description of injuries: LOSS OF VISION IN ONE EYE

Reported: Kemp & Kemp, B2-015; [1990] CLY 1580

JSB Category: 4(A); 3(A)

Sex: Male

Age at injury: 13

Age at award: 21

Date of award: 16 February 1990

Tribunal: CICB, Manchester

Amount of award then: £27,500

Award at February 2001: £42,024

Description of injuries: Shot fired at left eye causing cataract – needed corrective surgery – loss of vision in left eye – shot in forehead and stomach – immense distress and anxiety from sexual assault. Effectively "one-eyed", with a squint in the left eye – severe psychological scarring.

1.2.3.6.2.C6 Case No. 10371

Name of case: Re Smith

Brief description of injuries: LOSS OF ONE EYE – DISCHARGE FROM SOCKET

Reported: Kemp & Kemp, D2-022; [1992] CLY 1627

JSB Category: 4(A)(d)

Sex: Male

Age at injury: 10

Age at award: 12

Date of award: 11 March 1992

Tribunal: CICB, Leicester

Amount of award then: £30,000

Award at February 2001: £40,170

Description of injuries: Shot in the right eye with an air rifle pellet – loss of eye – eye removed and prosthesis fitted.

Prognosis: Occasional purulent discharge from the right eye – left eye treated with topical steroids to prevent sympathetic ophthalmia .

1.2.3.6.2.C7 Case No. 10023

Name of case: Re Linsdell

Brief description of injuries: LOSS OF VISION IN ONE EYE

Reported: Kemp & Kemp, D2-025; [1990] CLY 1612

JSB Category: 4(A)

Sex: Male

Age at injury: -

Age at award: -

Date of award: 24 October 1990

Tribunal: CICB

Amount of award then: £25,000

Award at February 2001: £34,753

Description of injuries: Struck in the region of the left eye and stabbed in the chest – suffered deep wound affecting upper nasal orbit and frontal sinus – left eye had no perception of light and was bulging from orbit -deep wound to upper nasal orbit and frontal sinus.

Prognosis: The left eye would remain permanently blind, and the plaintiff would, with medical supervision, be an out-patient on an annual basis.

1.2.3.6.2.C8 Case No. 10349

Name of case: Re Mitchell

Brief description of injuries: LOSS OF SIGHT IN ONE EYE

Reported: [1992] CLY 1605

JSB Category: 4(A)(e); 7(A)(f)

Sex: Female

Age at injury: 47

Age at award: 50

Date of award: 24 April 1992

Tribunal: CICB

Amount of award then: £25,000

Award at February 2001: £32,479

Description of injuries: Ferocious attack causing effective loss of sight in the right eye – permanent four-inch scar between the chin and lower lip – permanent loosening of lower front teeth.

Prognosis: Continuing pain associated to loosened front teeth – reluctance to go out alone – nervous depression.

1.2.3.6.2.C9 Case No. 10372

Name of case: Re Pearson

Brief description of injuries: LOSS OF SIGHT OF ONE EYE

Reported: [1992] CLY 1628

JSB Category: 4(A)(e)

Sex: Male

Age at injury: 15

Age at award: 16

Date of award: 14 April 1992

Tribunal: CICB, Leeds

Amount of award then: £25,000

Award at February 2001: £32,479

Description of injuries: Shot in the eye with a metal staple – despite extensive treatment the eye was lost – loss of sight in one eye.

Prognosis: Possibility that the remaining eye might develop sympathetic ophthalmitis in the future.

1.2.3.6.2.C10 Case No. 10582

Name of case: Re Batty

Brief description of injuries: EYE – LOSS OF SIGHT IN ONE EYE – 40-50 PER CENT CHANCE OF LOSING EYE

Reported: [1993] CLY 1475

JSB Category: 4(A)(e)

Sex: Female

Age at injury: 9

Age at award: 20

Date of award: 10 December 1992

Tribunal: CICB, Leicester

Amount of award then: £25,000

Award at February 2001: £32,380

Description of injuries: Struck in right eye by projectile from catapult – total hyphaema and dense cataract in right eye – lensectomy under general anaesthetic – 11 months later, readmitted to hospital with persistent uveitis and secondary glaucoma – trabeculectomy and capsulectomy under anaesthetic – 5 years later, operation to insert Molteno tube into eye due to persistent glaucoma – subsequent inoperable detachment of retina – eye blind – frequently irritated, requiring topical treatment – recurrent episodes of inflammation.

Prognosis: 40 to 50 per cent risk of enucleation being required.

1.2.3.6.2.C11 Case No. 11973

Name of case: Re Avgerinos (CICB Quantum: 1999)

Brief description of injuries: SENSES – EYE – LOSS OF EYE

Reported: Kemp & Kemp, PRO-001[2000] 2 CL 144

JSB Category: 4(A)(d)

Sex: Male

Age at injury: 18

Age at award: 20

Date of award: 18 May 1999

Tribunal: CICB, Manchester

Amount of award then: £27,000

Award at February 2001: £29,209

Description of injuries: Loss of an eye following an air-rifle accident – sustained a nuclination of the right eye – immediate and continual blindness – the eye was removed immediately after the incident – hydroxy apatite implants were inserted into the eye socket – prescribed antibiotics – artificial eye fitted after six-and-a-half months – the eye caused A embarrassment and loss of confidence.

Prognosis: Recovery was good – plastic surgery might be required in the future – the eye would need replacing about every two years.

1.2.3.6.2.C12 Case No. 10194

Name of case: Re McQuaide

Brief description of injuries: ASSAULT – LOSS OF ONE EYE

Reported: [1991] CLY 1391

JSB Category: 4(A)(d)

Sex: Male

Age at injury: 25

Age at award: 29

Date of award: 31 October 1991

Tribunal: CICB, Birmingham

Amount of award then: £22,000

Award at February 2001: £29,172

Description of injuries: Unprovoked attack with an implement – stabbed in the eye – eye was surgically removed following failure to save it.

Prognosis: Prosthesis fell out occasionally causing embarrassment – some double vision – pain in a smoky atmosphere – loss of position in the labour market.

1.2.3.6.2.C13 Case No. 10025

Name of case: Lingard v C V Stubbs & Sons

Brief description of injuries: EYE – VISION IMPAIRED – SQUINT

Reported: Kemp & Kemp, D2-031; BPILS, IV 5594; [1990] CLY 1614

JSB Category: 4(A)

Sex: Male

Age at injury: 29

Age at award: 32

Date of award: 25 May 1990

Tribunal: QBD (Lincoln High Court)

Amount of award then: £20,000

Award at February 2001: £28,341

Description of injuries: Foreign body struck plaintiff in left eye, resulting in penetrating injury severely affecting eyesight and causing squint – plaintiff lost all vision in left eye and his binocularity – barely able to perceive light and detect hand movements.

Prognosis: Little or no prospect of improvement to vision or squint.

1.2.3.6.2.C14 Case No. 10373

Name of case: Re Allington

Brief description of injuries: RESTRICTED SIGHT IN ONE EYE – BROKEN NOSE

Reported: [1992] CLY 1629

JSB Category: 4(A)(f); 7(A)(c)(iv)

Sex: Male

Age at injury: 20

Age at award: 23

Date of award: 24 February 1992

Tribunal: CICB, Leeds

Amount of award then: £20,000

Award at February 2001: £26,122

Description of injuries: Violent assault – punched in the face – periorbital haematoma to the left eye – fractured nasal bone – restricted sight in one eye.

Prognosis: Sight in the left eye restricted to light and dark.

Other points: Award increased from £15,000.

1.2.3.6.2.C15 Case No. 11328

Name of case: Kyei v Utility Tyre Services Ltd
Brief description of injuries: EYE – LOSS OF ONE EYE
Reported: Kemp & Kemp, D2-032/1; [1997] CLY 1876
JSB Category: 4(A)(e)
Sex: Male
Age at injury: 31
Age at award: 36
Date of award: 01 July 1997
Tribunal:
Amount of award then: £23,000
Award at February 2001: £25,990
Description of injuries: 5mm piece of wire penetrated the left eye.
Prognosis: Permanent loss of vision – cosmetic defect – socially embarrassed

1.2.3.6.2.C16 Case No. 10744

Name of case: Burdiss v Redbridge London Borough Council
Brief description of injuries: SENSES – SIGHT – LOSS OF SIGHT IN ONE EYE
Reported: Kemp & Kemp, D2-035; [1994] CLY 1592
JSB Category: 4(A)(e)
Sex: Male
Age at injury: 26
Age at award: 29
Date of award: 30 June 1994
Tribunal: Central London County Court
Amount of award then: £19,500
Award at February 2001: £23,880
Description of injuries: Claimant butted in face by lamb – loss of all functional sight in right eye – occasional psychosomatic headaches – hobbies of motorcycling, pool, tennis, darts and football no longer pursued – intention of career change to tree surgeon, for which applicant already qualified, impossible due to lack of confidence in climbing – still in current employment (as countryside warden) and job reasonably secure, although some contraction in workforce likely to continue.
Prognosis: Plaintiff developing squint – 20 per cent chance of surgery being required.

1.2.3.6.2.C17 Case No. 11329

Name of case: Re Mackel
Brief description of injuries: EYE – IMPAIRED SIGHT IN ONE EYE
Reported: Kemp & Kemp, D2-037/2; [1997] CLY 1877
JSB Category: 4(A)(f)
Sex: Male
Age at injury: 25
Age at award: 30
Date of award: 16 April 1997
Tribunal: CICB, Durham
Amount of award then: £17,500
Award at February 2001: £19,665
Description of injuries: Fractured cheekbone – serious injuries to the left eye.
Prognosis: Permanent damage to the sight in the left eye – some loss of sensation to the cheek – two small scars.
Other points: When he came to renew his PSV licence in 2012 he would no longer qualify.

1.2.3.6.2.C18 Case No. 11801

Name of case: Threlkeld v Northern Electric plc
Brief description of injuries: EYE – LOSS OF VISION
Reported: Kemp & Kemp, PRD-002; [1999] CLY 1464
JSB Category: 4(A)(d)
Sex: Male
Age at injury: 43
Age at award: 47
Date of award: 17 June 1999
Tribunal: QBD
Amount of award then: £17,500
Award at February 2001: £18,513
Description of injuries: Severe penetrating injury to left eye – eye could not be saved; removed by enucleation, and prosthesis fitted – eye in question had previously been injured in 1976, leaving it able to see only shapes and blurred movements – however, loss of eye meant complete loss of left – sided field of vision and much – reduced ability to judge depths and distances, ending claimant's employment as JCB operator – claimant disappointed with quality and range of movement of prosthesis, leading him to wear tinted glasses and avoid social situations; desired further operation to improve appearance – off work 7 months, then found employment as labourer.

1.2.3.6.2.C19 Case No. 10745

Name of case: Re B

Brief description of injuries: SENSES – SIGHT – SEVERE DAMAGE TO SIGHT IN ONE EYE

Reported: Kemp & Kemp, D2-042; [1994] CLY 1593

JSB Category: 4(A)(f)

Sex: Female

Age at injury: 12

Age at award: 16

Date of award: 20 October 1994

Tribunal: CICB, Nottingham

Amount of award then: £12,500

Award at February 2001: £14,965

Description of injuries: Claimant struck in right eye by stone fired from catapult – abrasion to cornea – damage to retina – blood in anterior chamber – permanent impairment of vision in right eye, acuity reduced to 6/60 – defect unable to be corrected by contact lenses or spectacles – central field of vision in right eye almost completely obscured – claimant unable to play ball games because of inability to see ball and nervousness when things thrown at her – loss of confidence and decline in frequency of going out – reading tiring, requiring much effort and concentration.

Prognosis: No possibility of improvement – some doubts about ability to drive – award took no account of likelihood of glaucoma, cataract or retinal detachment, but file left open should any of those risks subsequently materialise.

1.2.3.6.2.C20 Case No. 11121

Name of case: Hughes v Eadon

Brief description of injuries: EYE – 10% LOSS OF VISION

Reported: Kemp & Kemp, D2-043/1; [1996] CLY 2212

JSB Category: 4(A)(g)

Sex: Female

Age at injury: 10

Age at award: 15

Date of award: 20 February 1996

Tribunal: Chester County Court

Amount of award then: £10,000

Award at February 2001: £11,430

Description of injuries: Lens damage by flying glass.

Prognosis: Further remedial treatment required at age 16 – reduction of 10 per cent of vision.

1.2.3.6.2.1 Visual loss and other injury

1.2.3.6.2.1.C1 Case No. 10305

Name of case: Cowan v Quotareed and R Mansell

Brief description of injuries: BRAIN DAMAGE – VERY SEVERE – LOSS OF SIGHT, TASTE AND SMELL – PERSONALITY CHANGE

Reported: [1992] CLY 1560

JSB Category: 2(A)(b); 4(A)(b), 4(C)(a)

Sex: Male

Age at injury: 31

Age at award: 38

Date of award: 20 November 1990

Tribunal: QBD

Amount of award then: £100,000

Award at February 2001: £169,963

Description of injuries: Extensive fractures of the skull – total loss of sight, taste and smell – brain damage with personality change – reduced memory, concentration and depression.

Prognosis: Requiring permanent care.

1.2.3.6.2.1.C2 Case No. 10306

Award at February 2001: £155,937

See: 1.2.3.3.C1 for details

1.2.3.6.2.1.C3 Case No. 11489

Name of case: Webber v Bruton

Brief description of injuries: HEAD – BRAIN DAMAGE – VISUAL IMPAIRMENT

Reported: Kemp & Kemp, C2-009; [1998] CLY 1490

JSB Category: 2(A)(b)

Sex: Male

Age at injury: 35

Age at award: 40

Date of award: 06 October 1997

Tribunal: QBD

Amount of award then: £90,000

Award at February 2001: £116,701

Description of injuries: Moderately severe brain damage – visual impairment – severe intellectual, cognitive and speech impairment – other injuries – loss of memory – claimant a danger to himself – required constant care and supervision in residential accommodation adapted to accommodate his professional carers.

Prognosis: Intellectual, cognitive and speech impairment all permanent – permanently unable to undertake more than the most basic care requirements.

Other points: Family care had proved too difficult to sustain in the long-term.

1.2.3.6.2.1.C4 Case No. 10370

Name of case: Re Stanley

Brief description of injuries: LOSS OF ONE EYE – FACIAL BURNS – POST-TRAUMATIC STRESS

Reported: [1992] CLY 1626

JSB Category: 4(A)(d) 2(B)(a)

Sex: Male

Age at injury: 41

Age at award: 46

Date of award: 19 June 1992

Tribunal: CICB, London

Amount of award then: £40,000

Award at February 2001: £53,900

Description of injuries: Acid thrown in the face – extensive facial burns and loss of one eye – post-traumatic stress disorder.

Prognosis: Cosmetic surgery in March 1988 to improve appearance – post-traumatic depressive neurosis – increased alcohol intake – had not worked since the attack and was unlikely to do so again.

1.2.3.6.2.1.C5 Case No. 11979

Award at February 2001: £44,404

See: 1.2.3.1.C7 for details

1.2.3.6.2.1.C6 Case No. 10581

Name of case: Re Campbell

Brief description of injuries: EYE – LOSS OF SIGHT IN ONE EYE – DEPRESSION

Reported: Kemp & Kemp, D2-024; [1993] CLY 1474

JSB Category: 4(A)(e); 7(B)(a); 3(A)

Sex: Female

Age at injury: 25

Age at award: 33

Date of award: 01 September 1992

Tribunal: CICB, London

Amount of award then: £30,000

Award at February 2001: £39,328

Description of injuries: Ammonia sprayed in face – severe alkaline burns – loss of sight in right eye – permanent cosmetic deformation – significant change in temperament – panic attacks – loss of confidence – sleeplessness – depression – onset of constant headaches – loss of jobs due to unsightly appearance – abandonment of participation in social and sporting activities, leading to extreme depression – stressful pregnancy as a result.

Prognosis: Disability permanent – side-effects ongoing.

1.2.3.6.2.1.C7 Case No. 10553

Award at February 2001: £31,722

See: 1.2.3.4.C4 for details

1.2.3.6.2.1.C8 Case No. 10024

Award at February 2001: £29,847

See: 1.2.2.1.C11 for details

1.2.3.6.2.1.C9 Case No. 11537

Name of case: Re Ranger

Brief description of injuries: POST-TRAUMATIC STRESS DISORDER – DOUBLE VISION

Reported: Kemp & Kemp, C4-051; [1998] CLY 1539

JSB Category: 3(B)(b); 4(A)

Sex: Male

Age at injury: 46

Age at award: 56

Date of award: 19 May 1998

Tribunal: CICB, London

Amount of award then: £20,000

Award at February 2001: £21,570

Description of injuries: Double and blurred vision – giddiness – headaches – cramp-like pain in the neck – diagnosed as 35 per cent disabled by DSS – moderately severe post-traumatic stress disorder – retired on medical grounds.

Prognosis: Claimant would not work again.

1.2.3.6.2.1.C10 Case No. 10047

Name of case: Re Redfern

Brief description of injuries: EYE, DOUBLE VISION – SCARRING TO CHEEK

Reported: [1990] CLY 1615

JSB Category: 7(B); 4(A)

Sex: Female

Age at injury: 23

Age at award: 26

Date of award: 23 October 1990

Tribunal: CICB, Leeds

Amount of award then: £13,000

Award at February 2001: £17,438

Description of injuries: Penetrating injury to the eye, including lacerated cornea, prolapsed iris and injury to conjunctiva – lacerations down left side of face.

Prognosis: Permanent double vision – risk of retinal detachment and cataracts – permanent obvious and ugly scar (6 by 1 or 2 cm) on left cheek.

1.2.3.6.2.1.C11 Case No. 10026

Name of case: Forshaw v GEC

Brief description of injuries: EYE, DOUBLE VISION – LEG AND CHEEK INJURIES

Reported: [1990] CLY 1616

JSB Category: 4(A), 8

Sex: Male

Age at injury: -

Age at award: -

Date of award: 15 November 1989

Tribunal: QBD

Amount of award then: £8,000

Award at February 2001: £11,602

Description of injuries: Injuries to the right eye and cheek, and also to right leg resulting in a haematoma. Double vision, compensated for by plaintiff having to turn his head – 5 cm surgical scar on right leg.

1.2.3.6.2.1.C12 Case No. 10746

Name of case: Britton v Ivens

Brief description of injuries: SENSES – SIGHT – DAMAGE TO SIGHT IN ONE EYE – DIZZINESS AND HEADACHES

Reported: Kemp & Kemp, D2-048; [1994] CLY 1594

JSB Category: 4(A)(g)

Sex: Male

Age at injury: 50

Age at award: 52

Date of award: 01 December 1993

Tribunal: Edmonton County Court

Amount of award then: £3,000

Award at February 2001: £3,636

Description of injuries: Assault – claimant punched in face, knocked to ground, then kicked and punched further in eye, face and ribs – extensive bruising round both eyes, temples, side of nose and ribs – laceration under right eye requiring 3 stitches – internal injury to right eye (macula oedema), resulting in permanent slight blurring of vision – special spectacles prescribed – dizziness, and headaches about twice a week, keeping claimant unemployed – spectacles improved but did not completely rectify condition – bruising took 3 weeks to resolve, during which time claimant unable to attend job interviews (claimant previously unemployed) or socialise.

1.2.3.7 SKULL FRACTURE

1.2.3.7.C1 Case No. 11491

Name of case: Leonard v Niagara Holdings Ltd

Brief description of injuries: HEAD – SKULL – FRACTURE

Reported: Kemp & Kemp, B2-004/2/1; [1998] CLY 1492

JSB Category: 2(A)(c); 5(A)(g); 6(D)(d); 6(K); 7(A)(b); 7(A)(f)

Sex: Female

Age at injury: 51

Age at award: 59

Date of award: 05 March 1998

Tribunal: QBD

Amount of award then: £75,000

Award at February 2001: £93,317

Description of injuries: Fractured skull – multiple fractures to the facial bones – severe damage to the teeth – fractures to the clavicle, ribs and leg total loss of vision in one eye – damage to hearing in one ear – tinnitus – reduced mental speed – small decrease in intellectual functioning – impaired motor speed – required care – unable to resume hobbies or work.

Prognosis: Mobility would deteriorate as claimant aged.

1.2.3.7.C2 Case No. 11088

Name of case: Re Cuddy

Brief description of injuries: HEAD – SKULL – SUSPECTED FRACTURE

Reported: Kemp & Kemp, C30-71; [1996] CLY 2179

JSB Category: 2(A)(c)(ii)

Sex: Female

Age at injury: 17

Age at award: 31

Date of award: 05 July 1995

Tribunal: CICB, London

Amount of award then: £55,000

Award at February 2001: £71,321

Description of injuries: Possible fracture of the skull.

Prognosis: Basically housebound and dependent on her husband – it was hoped that with new drugs and counselling she would be able to gain some independent social and domestic life.

Other points: Husband had to give up work to care for her.

1.2.3.7.C3 Case No. 10147

Name of case: Re Cooper

Brief description of injuries: FRACTURED SKULL – RISK OF GRAND MAL EPILEPSY

Reported: Kemp & Kemp, C3-078; [1991] CLY 1344

JSB Category: 2(A)(c)(ii/iii)

Sex: Male

Age at injury: 17

Age at award:

Date of award: 17 May 1991

Tribunal: CICB

Amount of award then: £30,000

Award at February 2001: £41,215

Description of injuries: Assault – sustained compound depressed fracture of left temporal bone – grand mal epilepsy attacks for 12-18 months – treated by anti-convulsants for two and a quarter years.

Prognosis: Probably 5 per cent risk of epilepsy in the future – light risk of early senile dementia – unlikely to perform more demanding job.

1.2.3.7.C4 Case No. 10538

Name of case: Worf v Heath-Qualters

Brief description of injuries: HEAD – MULTIPLE FRACTURES

Reported: [1993] CLY 1430

JSB Category: 2(B); 5(A); 6(K), 6(M)

Sex: Male

Age at injury: 41

Age at award: 45

Date of award: 15 December 1992

Tribunal: QBD

Amount of award then: £26,000

Award at February 2001: £33,768

Description of injuries: Head injuries – laceration of tongue with residual scarring – fractures of sternum and ribs – comminuted fractures of femur, tibia, fibula and ankle – unable to return to work as van driver – fit for light manual work but possible difficulties in obtaining employment.

Prognosis: Full recovery within 6 months except for continuing problems with leg injury, resulting in restrictions in walking, and no further improvement expected – significant chance of osteoarthritis in ankle.

1.2.3.7.C5 Case No. 10039

Name of case: Power v Kitchener

Brief description of injuries: FRACTURED FRONTAL BONE

Reported: [1990] CLY 1582

JSB Category: 7(B); 4(A)

Sex: Female

Age at injury: 19

Age at award: 23

Date of award: 06 April 1990

Tribunal: QBD

Amount of award then: £16,000

Award at February 2001: £22,603

Description of injuries: fractures to left frontal bone extending to left orbit and to left zygomatic complex – lacerations to left forehead and right ear. Left eye looks smaller than right – double vision at extremes of gaze – facial scarring of 3.5 cm and 1.5 cm scars over left eyebrow, 3 cm glabellar scar.

Prognosis: No improvement.

Other points: Plaintiff was embarrassed by appearance and wore her hair over left side of face.

1.2.3.7.C6 Case No. 10729

Name of case: Dordevic v Smith

Brief description of injuries: HEAD – FRACTURED SKULL – MINOR WHIPLASH – 2 YEARS' SERIOUS NERVOUS REACTION

Reported: Kemp & Kemp, C2-075; [1994] CLY 1577

JSB Category: 2(B); 3(A)(c); 6(A)(b), 6(K)(c)

Sex: Female

Age at injury: 36

Age at award: 40

Date of award: 17 June 1994

Tribunal: Central London County Court

Amount of award then: £7,250

Award at February 2001: £8,618

Description of injuries: Claimant struck by car – severe contusion to left thigh, symptomatic for 6 months – fractured skull, resulting in painful headaches for a few months – minor whiplash injury – claimant had psychological difficulties before accident (neurosis; extreme reaction to unhappy divorce and unwanted pregnancy; other issues) – "very serious nervous reaction" to accident, characterised by fear of crowds and public transport – physical recovery complete – psychological reaction lasted 2 years.

Other points: Award split: £3,750 orthopaedic; £3,500 psychiatric.

1.2.3.7.C7 Case No. 10004

Name of case: Re Williams
Brief description of injuries: SKULL FRACTURE
Reported: [1990] CLY 1583
JSB Category: 2(B)
Sex: Male
Age at injury: 10
Age at award: 15
Date of award: 04 May 1990
Tribunal: CICB, Cardiff
Amount of award then: £4,500
Award at February 2001: £6,133

Description of injuries: Hit on head by fishing weight – depressed pond fracture of skull with bruising and bleeding from the wound – operation successful but followed by Todd's palsy for two days – anti-convulsant medication administered for 15 months. Fracture completely healed – scar hidden by hair – advised since that he can now resume playing "contact" sports, but is wary of further head injury.

Prognosis: No improvement.

1.2.3.7.C8 Case No. 10551

Name of case: Re G
Brief description of injuries: SKULL – FRACTURE
Reported: [1993] CLY 1444
JSB Category: 2(B)
Sex: Male
Age at injury: 15
Age at award: -
Date of award: 24 August 1993
Tribunal: CICB, Liverpool
Amount of award then: £5,000
Award at February 2001: £6,086

Description of injuries: Struck with brick – 15 cm laceration above hairline – skull fracture beneath

Prognosis: Risk of developing epilepsy less than 1 per cent

Other points: In light of evidence to the effect that claimant was a difficult pupil at school (bullying, disruptive, abusive) and had police record for assault and theft, judge ruled that any personality change due to the blow was so mild as to be of no significance in assessing damages.

1.2.3.7.C9 Case No. 11888

Name of case: Re H (a minor)
Brief description of injuries: HEAD – FRACTURED SKULL – GOOD RECOVERY
Reported: Kemp & Kemp, B2-042/1; [1999] CLY 1552
JSB Category: 2(B); 4(A)(i); 5(A)(g); 6(F), 6(K)
Sex: Female
Age at injury: 3.5 months
Age at award: 5
Date of award: 21 July 1999
Tribunal: CICB, Plymouth
Amount of award then: £5,000
Award at February 2001: £5,209

Description of injuries: Claimant assaulted – multiple fractures to skull, left elbow, right femur, right tibia and ribs – subdural haemorrhage in left frontal region of skull – retinal haemorrhages in both eyes – various other bruises – admitted to hospital; condition described as moribund – discharged after 2.5 weeks on anti-convulsant medication; recovery over following 4 months, during which she appeared fragile and poorly – remarkable recovery by age of 12 months – investigations carried out for epilepsy and impairment of visual function, but no abnormalities revealed – 5 years after incident, only residual symptoms were occasional night terrors occurring every 3 weeks, sometimes several nights in a row, and possible moments of absence, not regarded as worrying – no treatment being sought for these residual symptoms.

1.2.3.7.C10 Case No. 11960

Name of case: Re Jackson (CICB Quantum: 1999)
Brief description of injuries: HEAD SKULL – FRACTURE
Reported: Kemp & Kemp, C5-064; [2000] 1 CL 120
JSB Category: 7(A)(d)(ii)
Sex: Male
Age at injury: 23
Age at award: 27
Date of award: 22 February 1999
Tribunal: CICB, York
Amount of award then: £3,500
Award at February 2001: £3,677

Description of injuries: Assault – fracture to the left zygotic arch – prescribed painkillers – severe pain for about three weeks – intermittent discomfort for a few months. The cheekbone healed within four months of the date of the accident without the need for operative treatment – a front incisor was abridged under general anaesthetic.

1.2.3.8 BRAIN DAMAGE WITH OR WITHOUT SKULL FRACTURE

1.2.3.8.C1 Case No. 10001

Name of case: Cassel v Riverside Health Authority

Brief description of injuries: VERY SEVERE BRAIN DAMAGE

Reported: [1992] PIQR Q168; Kemp & Kemp, A4-001/1; BPILS, I 260.1, XV 14; [1990] CLY 1575

JSB Category: 2(A)

Sex: Male

Age at injury: Birth

Age at award: 8

Date of award: 22 December 1990

Tribunal: QBD (CA)

Amount of award then: £1,198,130

Award at February 2001: £2,109,963

Description of injuries: Very severely brain damaged at birth. Would never grow up mentally.

Prognosis: No improvement.

1.2.3.8.C2 Case No. 11277

Name of case: Re Sharma (Harshed)

Brief description of injuries: HEAD – BRAIN – VERY SEVERE DAMAGE

Reported: Kemp & Kemp, A4-004; [1997] CLY 1824

JSB Category: 1(a)

Sex: Male

Age at injury: 27

Age at award: 30

Date of award: 12 February 1997

Tribunal: CICB, Birmingham

Amount of award then: £150,000

Award at February 2001: £221,381

Description of injuries: Very severe brain damage – blindness – able to follow commands – has a degree of insight – doubly incontinent – unable to walk – required 24-hour care.

Other points: Current care was in hospital – family intended to purchase a large house – pay for 24 hour care – provide love, affection and stimulation themselves.

1.2.3.8.C3 Case No. 10698

Name of case: Whiteside v Howes

Brief description of injuries: VERY SEVERE BRAIN DAMAGE – SEVERE PHYSICAL HANDICAPS – FULL CONSCIOUSNESS AND AWARENESS OF INJURIES – NORMAL LIFE EXPECTANCY

Reported: Kemp & Kemp, B2-001; [1994] CLY 1544

JSB Category: 2(A)(a); 5(A); 6(F), 6(K), 6(L); 7(B)(b)

Sex: Female

Age at injury: 18

Age at award: 25

Date of award: 11 February 1994

Tribunal: QBD

Amount of award then: £130,000

Award at February 2001: £211,327

Description of injuries: Road accident – severe closed head injury – diffuse cerebral bruising – right frontal haematoma – intraventricular haemorrhage – fracture of right humerus, lower left radius and ulna, right femur and left collarbone – injuries to chest, including tearing of right lung – lacerations over eye with residual scarring – in coma for 6 months, requiring tracheotomy, ventilator and nasogastric feeding – 5 operations undergone: lengthening of tendons in knee; radial osteotomy; excision of ulna – manipulation of right knee, left wrist and hip – unable to stand or walk – limited manual dexterity – unable to cry, laugh or speak – post-traumatic amnesia for 8 months – fully conscious and aware of situation – IQ slightly lowered, but claimant retains intelligence, with good sense of humour – dependent on others for all domestic and toilet activities, eating and drinking – continuing speech therapy.

Prognosis: Confinement to wheelchair permanent – permanent physiotherapy required – will never marry or have children – life expectancy unchanged at 79.

1.2.3.8.C4 Case No. 10312

Name of case: Re Bradley

Brief description of injuries: BRAIN DAMAGE – INTELLECTUALLY DISABLED – RIGHT HEMIPARESIS – PERSONALITY CHANGE

Reported: [1992] CLY 1567

JSB Category: 2(A)(c)(i)

Sex: Male

Age at injury: 26

Age at award: 34

Date of award: 15 January 1992

Tribunal: CICB

Amount of award then: £115,000

Award at February 2001: £191,999

Description of injuries: Closed head injury involving right hemiparesis and dysphasia – low density lesion of the left temporal lobe region – intellectually disabled – post-traumatic amnesia for four days after injury – speech and writing difficulties – significant personality changes – episodes of bad temper, impatience and depression – severe agoraphobia being treated at time of the trial.

Prognosis: Unlikely that he would be able to keep a job long-term.

Damage to Head

1.2.3.8.C5 Case No. 10699

Name of case: Bould v Wakefield Health Authority

Brief description of injuries: VERY SEVERE BRAIN DAMAGE – SEVERE PHYSICAL DISABILITY – MODERATELY SEVERE MENTAL DISABILITY – EPILEPSY

Reported: Kemp & Kemp, A4-003/3; [1994] CLY 1545

JSB Category: 2(A)(a)

Sex: Male

Age at injury: at birth

Age at award: 11

Date of award: 18 October 1993

Tribunal: Not stated

Amount of award then: £110,000

Award at February 2001: £171,752

Description of injuries: Negligent obstetric care – severe asphyxiation and brain damage at birth – severe cerebral palsy – moderately severe intellectual impairment – epilepsy – unable to walk any useful distance unaided – speech very indistinct – assistance with self-care required.

Prognosis: Would remain dependent on others – life expectancy 40 to 50 years.

1.2.3.8.C6 Case No. 10305

Award at February 2001: £169,963

See: 1.2.3.6.2.1.C1 for details

1.2.3.8.C7 Case No. 11881

Name of case: T (a minor) v Luton & Dunstable Hospital NHS Trust

Brief description of injuries: CEREBRAL PALSY

Reported: Kemp & Kemp, PRA-002; [1999] CLY 1545

JSB Category: 2(A)(a)

Sex: Male

Age at injury: At birth

Age at award: 5

Date of award: 23 November 1998

Tribunal: QBD (infant settlement approval hearing)

Amount of award then: £125,000

Award at February 2001: £167,534

Description of injuries: Claimant injured at birth during which placental abruption and type II heart decelerations went unnoticed – after eventual delivery by forceps, claimant had APGAR score of 1 at 1 minute and 4 at 5 minutes – claimant suffered severe stage II hypoxic ischaemic encephalopathy, leaving him with severe quadriplegic or distonic athetoid cerebral palsy, characterised by variable tone in the whole body as well as involuntary movement and spasm, particularly in lower limbs – visual handicap – speech limited to sounds for yes and no – claimant unable to sit unless supported – claimant believed to be intellectually undamaged and able to reach and swipe with hands to operate switches – grand mal epilepsy, requiring lifelong medication – recurrent chest infections and severe feeding problems, leading to gastrostomy feeding for almost 2 years – fixed deformities at both hips, with left dislocated and right partially subluxed, which would probably require surgery eventually.

Prognosis: Life expectancy of 25-30 years – 24-hour care required for rest of life.

1.2.3.8.C8 Case No. 11956

Name of case: S (a minor) v Portsmouth and South EastHampshire HA

Brief description of injuries: HEAD – CEREBRAL PALSY

Reported: Kemp & Kemp, PRA-001; [2000] 1 CL 116

JSB Category: 2(A)(a)

Sex: Male

Age at injury: Birth

Age at award: 8

Date of award: 30 July 1999

Tribunal: Court of Appeal

Amount of award then: £125,000

Award at February 2001: £166,654

Description of injuries: Failure by the hospital and midwife to recognise hypoglycaemia which caused irreversible brain damage shortly after birth – severe developmental retardation – mild spastic quadriplegic cerebral palsy – S had the mental age of a child aged between twelve and eighteen months – a limited degree of insight into the nature and extent of his disabilities – doubly incontinent – unable to walk, feed or care for himself – experienced severe difficulties with communication – epileptic seizures with daytime fits and tantrums and night time fits – whole life expectancy was 37years.

1.2.3.8.C9 Case No. 10531

Name of case: Willett v North Bedfordshire Health Authority

Brief description of injuries: QUADRIPLEGIA – SEVERE BRAIN DAMAGE

Reported: [1993] PIQR Q166; Kemp & Kemp, A4-006/1, A4-119; BPILS, I 260.1; [1993] CLY 1422

JSB Category: 1(a); 2(A)(a)

Sex: Female

Age at injury: Birth

Age at award: 6

Date of award: 13 November 1992

Tribunal: QBD

Amount of award then: £105,000

Award at February 2001: £165,158

Description of injuries: Inter-uterine infection and asphyxia at birth – spastic quadriplegia – cerebral palsy.

Prognosis: Life expectancy 30 years.

Other points: Negligence admitted for inter-uterine infection.

1.2.3.8.C10 Case No. 11882

Name of case: S (a minor) v Somerset HA

Brief description of injuries: CEREBRAL PALSY

Reported: Kemp & Kemp, PRA-003; [1999] CLY 1546

JSB Category: 2(A)(a)

Sex: Male

Age at injury: At birth

Age at award: 10

Date of award: 17 November 1998

Tribunal: QBD (infant settlement approval hearing)

Amount of award then: £120,000

Award at February 2001: £159,302

Description of injuries: Claimant born profoundly asphyxiated and with no signs of life; described as being flat with no movement and no heart rate – intubation attempted, initially without success – bag and mask ventilation given for approximately 2 minutes – intubation then successfully accomplished, and cardiac massage attempted – first heart rate heard after 5 minutes – subsequent APGAR scores were 4 at 5 minutes, 5 at 10 minutes and 6 at 20 minutes – claimant suffered from severe metabolic acidosis – claimant commenced convulsing within 3 hours; convulsions had continued throughout his life – claimant left severely disabled, suffering from motor developmental delay with cerebral palsy taking the form of an asymmetric tetraplegia – claimant displayed all neurological features of hypoxic ischaemic encephalopathy of moderate degree – pattern of cerebral palsy seen claimed to be consistent with its being a sequel to acute hypoxia.

1.2.3.8.C11 Case No. 12004

Name of case: P (a child) v Hammersmith and Queen Charlotte's Special HA

Brief description of injuries: BRAIN DAMAGE – SEVERE LEARNING DIFFICULTIES – INCONTINENCE

Reported: Kemp & Kemp, PRC-001; [2000] 4 CL 146

JSB Category: 2(A)(a)

Sex: Male

Age at injury: 1 day

Age at award: 14

Date of award: 29 January 2000

Tribunal: QBD

Amount of award then: £120,000

Award at February 2001: £156,720

Description of injuries: Severe brain damage following surgery to repair a congenital cardiac condition – the operation was successful but blood in the supporting cardiopulmonary bypass unit clotted resulting in multiple cerebral emboli which caused the brain damage – P suffered catastrophic injuries – right sided hemiparesis – severe spasticity to the right arm – less severe effect to the left leg – his sight was restricted to objects ahead of him (right homonymous hemianopia) and in an arc of 45 degrees to the left – severe learning difficulties – behavioural problems – lacked the ability to concentrate – he functioned at the level of a three year old – P was extremely disruptive and required intensive supervision or one-to-one care while awake – he had no concept of danger and was not readily biddable – he had limited speech, was incontinent of faeces.

Prognosis: There was no prospect of real improvement except to his behaviour as he grew older – his life expectancy was 25 years.

1.2.3.8.C12 Case No. 10903

Name of case: Thorpe v Hooper

Brief description of injuries: DEVASTATING BRAIN DAMAGE – 10 YEARS LIFE EXPECTANCY

Reported: Kemp & Kemp, A4-008; [1995] CLY 1654

JSB Category: 2(A)(b)

Sex: Male

Age at injury: 22

Age at award: 25

Date of award: 13 March 1995

Tribunal: QBD

Amount of award then: £105,500

Award at February 2001: £155,376

Description of injuries: Plaintiff suffered devastating brain injuries in road traffic accident – in coma for two weeks – was in persistent vegetative state – underwent several major surgical procedures – discharged from hospital after 11 months – his parents' home had been adapted for his special needs with grant aid.

Prognosis: Life expectation of a further 10 years.

1.2.3.8.C13 Case No. 11477

Name of case: Dyer (a minor) v Lambeth, Southwark and Lewisham HA

Brief description of injuries: HEAD – CEREBRAL PALSY – QUADRIPLEGIA

Reported: Kemp & Kemp, A2-001; [1998] CLY 1478

JSB Category: 1(a)

Sex: Male

Age at injury: birth

Age at award: 15

Date of award: 03 June 1998

Tribunal: QBD

Amount of award then: £115,000

Award at February 2001: £152,330

Description of injuries: Cerebral palsy of a quadriplegic type – confined to a wheelchair – needed assistance with most of the activities of daily life.

1.2.3.8.C14 Case No. 12053

Name of case: L (a child) v Berkshire HA

Brief description of injuries: BRAIN DAMAGE – CEREBRAL PALSY

Reported: [2000] 6 CL 183

JSB Category: 2(A)(a)

Sex: Male

Age at injury: 0

Age at award: 8

Date of award: 02 November 2000

Tribunal: QBD

Amount of award then: £145,000

Award at February 2001: £144,916

Description of injuries: Birth asphyxia resulting in cerebral palsy.

Prognosis: Life expectancy estimated at 28 by the defendant and 60 by the plaintiff.

1.2.3.8.C15 Case No. 11478

Name of case: Wilkinson v Jones

Brief description of injuries: HEAD – BRAIN DAMAGE

Reported: Kemp & Kemp, A5-004; [1998] CLY 1479

JSB Category: 2(A)(b)

Sex: Male

Age at injury: 17

Age at award: 22

Date of award: 01 December 1997

Tribunal: QBD

Amount of award then: £106,666

Award at February 2001: £142,586

Description of injuries: Severe damage to the left hemisphere of the brain with right hemiplegia – unsteady gait – limp – serious retrograde and post-traumatic amnesia – verbal and non-verbal functioning within the lowest 32 per cent of the population – anxiety – depression – behavioural problems – spastic right leg – epilepsy – loss of earning ability.

Prognosis: Future care needed.

Other points: Before the accident W was intellectually within the top 80 per cent of the population.

1.2.3.8.C16 Case No. 11081

Name of case: Re P

Brief description of injuries: HEAD – BRAIN – EPILEPSY

Reported: Kemp & Kemp, B2-003/3; [1996] CLY 2172

JSB Category: 1(b) and 4(A)

Sex: Male

Age at injury: 18

Age at award: 27

Date of award: 15 September 1995

Tribunal: CICB, London

Amount of award then: £100,000

Award at February 2001: £141,897

Description of injuries: Penetrating injury to the eye – haematoma to the brain – permanent left hemiplegia – epilepsy – following further education his job prospects had considerably increased.

Prognosis: His condition would not improve – life expectancy reduced by two to three years.

1.2.3.8.C17 Case No. 12054

Name of case: H (a child) v Hillingdon HA

Brief description of injuries: BRAIN DAMAGE – CEREBRAL PALSY

Reported: [2000] 6 CL 184

JSB Category: 2(A)(a)

Sex: Female

Age at injury: 0

Age at award: 8

Date of award: 13 April 2000

Tribunal: QBD

Amount of award then: £132,000

Award at February 2001: £133,474

Description of injuries: Birth asphyxia resulting in cerebral palsy and a severe form of epilepsy – epilepsy had a greater impact on her life than the cerebral palsy – steroid treatment caused obesity – learning capacity reduced – she was obliged to wear a helmet outside due to the drop attacks – reduced life expectancy – regular physiotherapy required.

Prognosis: She would progressively require computer and environmental aids – travel costs would be very high.

1.2.3.8.C18 Case No. 10708

Name of case: Narroway (Ian) v Pendleton (James)

Brief description of injuries: BRAIN DAMAGE – GROSS COGNITIVE DEFECTS – PERSONALITY CHANGE – INABILITY TO LIVE INDEPENDENTLY

Reported: Kemp & Kemp, C2-005; [1994] CLY 1554

JSB Category: 2(A)

Sex: Male

Age at injury: -

Age at award: 28

Date of award: 20 December 1993

Tribunal: Liverpool County Court

Amount of award then: £85,000

Award at February 2001: £125,323

Description of injuries: Road accident – major cranio-cerebral injury – several weeks (at least) of post-traumatic amnesia, indicating that significant sequelae virtually certain – neuropsychological examination – gross cognitive defects – impairment of intellectual ability – major impairment of memory and learning – personality change involving impulsiveness and outspokenness.

Prognosis: Claimant rendered unable to manage own affairs or live independently – will never work again.

1.2.3.8.C19 Case No. 11479

Name of case: Cunningham v Kensington & Chelsea and Westminster HA

Brief description of injuries: HEAD – SEVERE BRAIN DAMAGE – REASONABLE MOBILITY

Reported: Kemp & Kemp, C2-008; [1998] CLY 1480

JSB Category: 2(A)(b)

Sex: Female

Age at injury: 45

Age at award: 49

Date of award: 02 May 1997

Tribunal: QBD

Amount of award then: £90,000

Award at February 2001: £119,005

Description of injuries: Severe generalised brain damage following an overdose of insulin – attempted suicide – constant close supervision required – 24 hour care – no awareness of surroundings – fairly mobile – virtually no speech – doubly incontinent – 3 or 4 people required to bathe her – averse to water.

Other points: C was difficult to place in a caring institution – very unusual combination of mental and sensory deficit with reasonable mobility.

1.2.3.8.C20 Case No. 11489

Award at February 2001: £116,701

See: 1.2.3.6.2.1.C3 for details

1.2.3.8.C21 Case No. 10544

Name of case: Lamey v Wirral Health Authority

Brief description of injuries: HEAD – BRAIN DAMAGE – ANOXIA

Reported: Kemp & Kemp, A4-015/1, A4-120; [1993] CLY 1437

JSB Category: 2(A)(b)

Sex: Female

Age at injury: Birth

Age at award: 11

Date of award: 22 September 1993

Tribunal: Liverpool High Court

Amount of award then: £80,000

Award at February 2001: £116,580

Description of injuries: Anoxic brain damage at birth – mental age of 6 – physical clumsiness – asymmetry of the mouth – speech defect – uninhibited and hyperactive, unsafe without supervision – frustration and temper tantrums.

Prognosis: Life expectancy 52.5 years – will never be able to live independently, responsible adult company required at all times – will never be able to work for a living.

1.2.3.8.C22 Case No. 10709

Name of case: Rodrigues v Woods

Brief description of injuries: BRAIN DAMAGE – CEREBRAL ATROPHY – 24 HOUR CARE – FRACTURED PELVIS AND VERTEBRAE

Reported: Kemp & Kemp, A4-015/2; [1994] CLY 1555

JSB Category: 2(A); 6(B), 6(C)(d)

Sex: Female

Age at injury: 48

Age at award: 51

Date of award: 03 May 1994

Tribunal: QBD

Amount of award then: £80,000

Award at February 2001: £113,909

Description of injuries: Knocked down by car – cerebral atrophy – unable to use left arm and hand, severely limited use of left leg – severe cognitive defect, rated at borderline retarded – marked impairment of memory – significant attentional problems – inefficiency of information processing, with evidence of frontal lobe dysfunction – demanding behaviour, at times like that of a spoiled child – headaches – orthopaedic injuries: fractures of pelvis and minor fractures of vertebrae at S1 and transverse process of L5; all healed satisfactorily – 24 hour care required – level of care provided allowing claimant good quality of life.

Prognosis: No symptoms of epilepsy, but 10 per cent risk of development – possibility of reduced life expectancy.

Other points: Case manager and working care regime set up, allowing for respite care.

1.2.3.8.C23 Case No. 11286

Award at February 2001: £113,859

See: 1.2.3.1.C1 for details

1.2.3.8.C24 Case No. 10137

Name of case: Bennett v Central Manchester Health Authority

Brief description of injuries: VERY SEVERE BRAIN DAMAGE

Reported: Kemp & Kemp, A4-016/1; [1991] CLY 1334

JSB Category: 2(A)(a)

Sex: Female

Age at injury: 39

Age at award: 50

Date of award: 11 March 1991

Tribunal: High Court, Manchester

Amount of award then: £72,500

Award at February 2001: £113,636

Description of injuries: Air embolism during heart valve operation – bilateral brain damage – left hemiparesis and left hemianopia (restricted left field of vision) – reduced co-ordination – paranoid schizophrenia – improved with treatment but not completely resolved – liability to epileptic seizures.

Prognosis: Life expectancy not less than 10-12 years post trial.

1.2.3.8.C25 Case No. 11082

Name of case: Re Coles

Brief description of injuries: HEAD – BRAIN – CEREBRAL HYPOXIA – DEPRESSION

Reported: Kemp & Kemp, B2-004/2/1; [1996] CLY 2173

JSB Category: 2(A)(c)

Sex: Male

Age at injury: 18

Age at award: 27

Date of award: 07 December 1995

Tribunal: CICB, London

Amount of award then: £80,000

Award at February 2001: £108,567

Description of injuries: Shotgun injuries to the back – bilateral pneumothoraces – severe cerebral hypoxia.

Prognosis: No shortening of life expectancy – no prospect of improvement in physical or mental ability – higher than normal risk of epilepsy.

Other points: Post accident depression – attempted suicide.

1.2.3.8.C26 Case No. 11768

Name of case: Williams v Doyle

Brief description of injuries: HEAD – SEVERE BRAIN DAMAGE – IQ REDUCED – POST-TRAUMATIC STRESS DISORDER

Reported: Kemp & Kemp, B2-004/2/2; [1999] CLY 1431

JSB Category: 2(A)(b); 3(A), 3(B); 6(D)(d), 6(H), 6(K); 7(A)(e)

Sex: Male

Age at injury: 32

Age at award: 43

Date of award: 17 June 1998

Tribunal: Cardiff County Court

Amount of award then: £85,000

Award at February 2001: £106,006

Description of injuries: Severe and profound head injury – also fractured clavicle; fractured right radius; compound fracture to right tibia and fibula; bilateral fractures to mandible – decrease in IQ of 29 per cent – severe personality change – several suicide attempts involving drug overdoses (claimant had history of some drug abuse prior to accident) – persistent distressing auditory hallucinations involving voices from inanimate objects (eg razors) urging claimant to harm himself – depression – short-term memory limited; claimant unable to take overall care of himself, although still capable of feeding and clothing himself – slight speech impediment – recovery from physical injuries good after 11 years; claimant able to walk, albeit with slight limp and weakness down left side.

Prognosis: Full – time care, assistance and supervision required, as claimant a danger to himself if left alone.

1.2.3.8.C27 Case No. 11490

Name of case: Shone v Rigby

Brief description of injuries: HEAD – SKULL FRACTURE – SURGICAL REMOVAL OF PART OF BRAIN

Reported: Kemp & Kemp, C2-013; [1998] CLY 1491

JSB Category: 2(A)(c)

Sex: Male

Age at injury: 8

Age at award: 21

Date of award: 15 May 1998

Tribunal: QBD

Amount of award then: £85,000

Award at February 2001: £105,928

Description of injuries: Depressed fracture of the skull – ruptured dura with herniation – some of brain was surgically removed – claimant unable to maintain a conversation – incapable of managing his own affairs – intellectual deficit – required 10 hours of domestic help each week.

Prognosis: Likely to be out of work for one third of his working life, which would not extend beyond 45 – unlikely to be able to marry or drive.

1.2.3.8.C28 Case No. 11480

Name of case: O'Leary v Howlett

Brief description of injuries: HEAD – BRAIN DAMAGE – PERSONALITY CHANGE

Reported: Kemp & Kemp, C2-075; [1998] CLY 1481

JSB Category: 2(A)(c)(i)

Sex: Male

Age at injury: 35

Age at award: 41

Date of award: 30 September 1997

Tribunal: QBD

Amount of award then: £80,000

Award at February 2001: £101,714

Description of injuries: Severe closed head injury – probable fractures – bleeding from the ear – fracture of the tibial plateau – elbow lacerations – personality change – morose, sad and irritable – aggressive outbursts – considerable physical handicaps – unable to work – able to cope with domestic activities in shared accommodation with significant support from his family.

1.2.3.8.C29 Case No. 10545

Name of case: Re Burleigh

Brief description of injuries: HEAD – SEVERE BRAIN DAMAGE

Reported: Kemp & Kemp, C2-076; [1993] CLY 1438

JSB Category: 2(A)(b)

Sex: Male

Age at injury: 27

Age at award: 33

Date of award: 11 September 1992

Tribunal: CICB

Amount of award then: £70,000

Award at February 2001: £101,703

Description of injuries: Assault – stabbed up nose with snooker cue, penetrating brain – pituitary gland destroyed – serious brain damage – profound memory impairment – appetite dysfunction, leading to gross obesity – apathy – complete personality change (irritable, intolerant to noise, lack of confidence, self-pitying, impaired sex drive).

Prognosis: Hormone replacement therapy needed for life after destruction of pituitary gland – continuous care required, day and night.

1.2.3.8.C30 Case No. 11769

Name of case: Re Pattison

Brief description of injuries: HEAD – MODERATE BRAIN DAMAGE

Reported: Kemp & Kemp, C2-077; [1999] CLY 1432

JSB Category: 2(A)(c)(i), 2(C)

Sex: Male

Age at injury: 18

Age at award: 31

Date of award: 16 February 1998

Tribunal: CICB, Durham

Amount of award then: £80,000

Award at February 2001: £100,971

Description of injuries: Blows to head causing subarachnoid haemorrhage – development of epilepsy – right – sided hemiparesis, causing severe limp in right leg and spastic dominant right arm – associated dysphasia – impaired short-term memory.

Prognosis: No prospect of improvement – life expectancy reduced by 7-8 years – permanent care required for 3-4 hours per day to assist with meals, medication and household tasks.

Other points: Medical evidence suggested that a subarachnoid haemorrhage could have spontaneously developed in middle age due to a natural predisposition – claimant had been made a patient under the Court of Protection owing to a perceived inability to manage his own financial affairs – claimant had no academic qualifications and had never been employed.

1.2.3.8.C31 Case No. 11770

Name of case: Goble v Airedale Hospitals NHS Trust

Brief description of injuries: HEAD – FURTHER BRAIN DAMAGE – CLAIMANT ALREADY SUFFERING FROM CEREBRAL PALSY

Reported: Kemp & Kemp, C2-078; [1999] CLY 1433

JSB Category: 2(A)(c)(i)

Sex: Male

Age at injury: 40

Age at award: 44

Date of award: 27 July 1998

Tribunal: QBD

Amount of award then: £80,000

Award at February 2001: £99,018

Description of injuries: Claimant, resident with elderly parents, had suffered from cerebral palsy since birth with generally well – controlled epilepsy – no significant physical disabilities, quality of life described as "reasonable" – admitted to hospital with uncontrolled epilepsy – hospital, admittedly negligent, failed to administer anti-convulsant medication for 72 hours – resultant development of status epilepticus – severe brain damage – double incontinence – inability to walk – loss of previous, limited, communication skills – feeding by gastrostomy tube required.

Prognosis: Constant nursing care required – life expectancy assessed at maximum of 15 years.

Other points: Approved settlement

1.2.3.8.C32 Case No. 11762

Name of case: Re Kaur

Brief description of injuries: HEAD – EPILEPSY – POST-TRAUMATIC STRESS DISORDER – MULTIPLE SEVERE SYMPTOMS

Reported: Kemp & Kemp, B2-004/2/3; [1999] CLY 1425

JSB Category: 2(A)(c), 2(C)(a); 3(A), 3(B); 4(B)(d)(iii), 4(C)(d); 6(I)(w); 7(A)(e), 7(B)(a)

Sex: Female

Age at injury: 47

Age at award: 52

Date of award: 01 July 1999

Tribunal: CICB, Nottingham

Amount of award then: £80,000

Award at February 2001: £97,551

Description of injuries: Fractures to left petrous and zygomatic bones of skull and subdural haematoma on right-hand side – lower jaw fractured from left to right, requiring splint, and causing ongoing problems with pain and inability to eat hard foods – fracture to left thumb – profound and cosmetically significant motor neurone facial palsy to left side of face, caused by damage to cranial nerves – loss of taste in left-hand side of mouth – some perceptive deafness – some loss of sensation and power throughout left-hand side of body – development of epilepty attacks approximately 1 year after incident, involving seizures, loss of consciousness, limb shaking, urinary incontinence – attacks no more than 6 weeks apart, often more frequent – some grand mal seizures experienced, in which claimant injured herself on more than one occasion – development of depression – tearful episodes – fear of going outside – fear of strangers, especially men – virtually complete cessation of social life – disturbed sleep patterns – loss of libido – Prozac prescribed – some symptoms of post-traumatic stress disorder, including situational anxiety, avoidance behaviour, hypervigilance, preoccupation with assault, fear of recurrence – loss of cognitive function (difficulty in recollecting recent events, diminished powers of concentration, reduced problem – solving skills, slowed reaction times), attributed to structural brain damage – daily headaches.

Prognosis: No symptoms related to left – sided cranial nerve damage or structural brain damage expected to improve – epileptic symptoms not expected to improve.

1.2.3.8.C33 Case No. 10710

Name of case: Re Simon

Brief description of injuries: BRAIN DAMAGE – SPEECH, READING, WRITING AND CALCULATING AFFECTED – EPILEPSY

Reported: [1994] CLY 1557

JSB Category: 2(A), 2(C)

Sex: Male

Age at injury: 27

Age at award: 35

Date of award: 24 May 1994

Tribunal: CICB, Manchester

Amount of award then: £70,000

Award at February 2001: £97,365

Description of injuries: Assault with knife and crowbars – blow to head – multiple stab wounds to chest – heart stopped – left thoracotomy carried out – tracheostomy performed – vocal chords damaged, making speech difficult – severe brain damage, resulting in slow speech, inability of self-expression, difficulty with reading, writing and calculating – epileptic attacks, controlled by anti-convulsants.

Prognosis: Damage to vocal chords permanent.

1.2.3.8.C34 Case No. 12005

Name of case: Rushton v Jervis

Brief description of injuries: HEAD – DIFFUSE CEREBRAL INJURY

Reported: [2000] 4 CL 147

JSB Category: 2(A)(c)(i)

Sex: Male

Age at injury: 22

Age at award: 32

Date of award: 12 May 1999

Tribunal: QBD

Amount of award then: £80,000

Award at February 2001: £97,209

Description of injuries: Severe diffuse cerebral injury in a traffic accident – unconscious for 48 hours – a CT scan showed areas of haemorrhage in the right frontal lobe and the left temporal and occipital lobes – incontinent of urine – post-traumatic epilepsy developed – treated with anti-convulsant drugs – change of character – impaired memory and concentration – unsteady gait – right sided headaches – double vision when looking to the right or downwards – unable to choose appropriate clothing – dropped things and misjudged distances – generally clumsy – tired easily and was slow to respond – IQ reduced to 71-78.

Prognosis: R would never be able to work or lead an independent life without supervision – he would not make any further recovery.

1.2.3.8.C35 Case No. 11481

Name of case: Re Leyland

Brief description of injuries: HEAD – BRAIN INJURY

Reported: Kemp & Kemp, C2-020; [1998] CLY 1482

JSB Category: 2(A)(b)

Sex: Male

Age at injury: 20

Age at award: 24

Date of award: 27 March 1997

Tribunal: CICB, London

Amount of award then: £75,000

Award at February 2001: £97,098

Description of injuries: Major brain injury – affected cognitive function, speech and behaviour – 24 hour care for rest of life required.

Prognosis: Life expectancy reduced by 5 years.

Other points: Largest part of the award represented the cost of full time carers – supplemented by relief care and a case manager.

1.2.3.8.C36 Case No. 10310

Name of case: Browning v Southampton and South West Hampshire Health Authority

Brief description of injuries: BRAIN – CEREBRAL PALSY – COGNITIVE FACULTIES UNIMPAIRED

Reported: (1991) The Times, October 29; Kemp & Kemp, A4-017/1; [1992] CLY 1565

JSB Category: 2(A)(b)

Sex: Female

Age at injury: Birth

Age at award: 6

Date of award: 28 October 1991

Tribunal: QBD

Amount of award then: £65,000

Award at February 2001: £96,746

Description of injuries: Cerebral palsy – physical injuries caused by lack of oxygen at birth.

Prognosis: General disability – speech impairment – lacking fine finger movement and motor control causing feeding difficulties and necessitating specially adapted computer equipment – required physiotherapy – should achieve tertiary education and employment – would require the assistance of a nanny if she had children.

1.2.3.8.C37 Case No. 10546

Name of case: Re Judd
Brief description of injuries: HEAD – BRAIN DAMAGE
Reported: Kemp & Kemp, C2-023; [1993] CLY 1439
JSB Category: 2(A)(c), 2(C)(a); 4(A)
Sex: Female
Age at injury: 66
Age at award: 68
Date of award: 04 November 1992
Tribunal: CICB, Durham
Amount of award then: £65,000
Award at February 2001: £93,054

Description of injuries: Assault during burglary – loss of part of skull – significant damage to left occipital lobe and posterior of left parietal lobe of the brain – hemanopsia, restricting vision – dysphasia – retrograde amnesia – poor short-term memory – development of grand mal epilepsy – reliant on anti-convulsants – psychologically unable to spend nights alone, anxiety and confusion necessitating some day care also.

1.2.3.8.C38 Case No. 11482

Name of case: Budd v Bowditch
Brief description of injuries: HEAD – BRAIN DAMAGE – MULTIPLE FRACTURES
Reported: Kemp & Kemp, B2-004/2/3; [1998] CLY 1483
JSB Category: 2(A)(b); 5(A)(g); 6(D), 6(K), 6(M)
Sex: Male
Age at injury: 25
Age at award: 30
Date of award: 23 April 1998
Tribunal: Norwich County Court
Amount of award then: £75,000
Award at February 2001: £92,119

Description of injuries: Serious head injury – fractured scapula, fractured ribs – fractured right malleolus – compound fracture of the tibia and fibula – unable to manage his own affairs – needed at least 8 hours support and care every day.

Prognosis: Unlikely to be ever gainfully employed.

Other points: B lost a promising career in accountancy – possibly to partnership level.

1.2.3.8.C39 Case No. 11083

Name of case: Re Williams
Brief description of injuries: HEAD – BRAIN – BRAIN STEM INFARCT
Reported: Kemp & Kemp, B2-004/3; [1996] CLY 2174
JSB Category: 2(A)(c)
Sex: Male
Age at injury: 14
Age at award: 21
Date of award: 15 August 1996
Tribunal: CICB, Nottingham
Amount of award then: £70,000
Award at February 2001: £91,186

Description of injuries: Meningitis – septicaemia – brain stem infarct – substantially wheelchair bound – lived in his own accommodation – receiving mainly domestic assistance.

Prognosis: Vulnerable to losing his job – no promotion likely in his current job.

1.2.3.8.C40 Case No. 10146

Name of case: Vogwell v Cockbill
Brief description of injuries: SEVERE HEAD INJURY – GRAND MAL EPILEPSY – FRACTURED PELVIS, FEMUR – NEEDS CONSTANT CARE
Reported: Kemp & Kemp, C2-024; [1991] CLY 1343
JSB Category: 2(C)(a), 6(L)(c)(ii)
Sex: Female
Age at injury: 59
Age at award: 62
Date of award: 19 March 1991
Tribunal: QBD
Amount of award then: £60,000
Award at February 2001: £91,048

Description of injuries: Road accident – severe head injury with left sided extradural and subdural haematoma and left frontal contusion – contralateral mid-line shift requiring left fronto-temporal craniotomy and left frontal lobectomy – fracture of the pelvis – fracture of head of left femur – generalised bruising and abrasions – grand mal epileptic seizure five months after injury – neurologically, dysconjugate eye movements, marked weakness of left limbs with flexion contractures of the joints treated by soft-tissue release with excision of left femoral head.

Prognosis: Expected to return home with full-time care – completely dependent for assistance with toiletting, washing, dressing and bathing – frequently incontinent – could feed herself using right hand only – required constant supervision and support.

1.2.3.8.C41 Case No. 11287

Name of case: Re Roberts

Brief description of injuries: HEAD – INTELLECTUAL IMPAIRMENT

Reported: Kemp & Kemp, C2-025; [1997] CLY 1835

JSB Category: 2(A)(c)

Sex: Male

Age at injury: 31

Age at award: 37

Date of award: 27 February 1997

Tribunal: CICB, London

Amount of award then: £70,000

Award at February 2001: £89,893

Description of injuries: A severe blow to the head – intellectual impairment – behavioural change – displayed some features of psychogenic pain disorder – unable to return to his previous employment.

1.2.3.8.C42 Case No. 10703

Name of case: Re JH

Brief description of injuries: BRAIN DAMAGE AND MULTIPLE INJURIES – FRACTURED SKULL AND SPINE – SEXUAL DISINHIBITION – LEARNING DIFFICULTIES – PERMANENT "MINDER"

Reported: Kemp & Kemp, C2-026; [1994] CLY 1549

JSB Category: 2(A)(b); 6(B); 5(A)(g)

Sex: Female

Age at injury: 19

Age at award: 29

Date of award: 31 October 1994

Tribunal: CICB, York

Amount of award then: £65,000

Award at February 2001: £88,984

Description of injuries: Assault – fractured skull – fractured cervical spine – fractured ribs – severe head injury – unconscious and artificially ventilated when in hospital – consciousness improved 1 month later – 2 months later, claimant started to speak, but with poor memory – admitted to head injuries rehabilitation unit – ACT scan showed diffuse brain swelling and contusions of frontal and left temporal areas – severe brain damage evident from psychological testing – acquisition of new information difficult – retention and retrieval of information, particularly verbal, difficult – reduced speed of information processing – reduced ability to maintain control over thought processes – most significant disability a considerably reduced ability to make reflective judgments and impairment of awareness of socially appropriate behaviour – serious sexual disinhibition – claimant sexually exploited in a number of incidents, fear of claimant falling into prostitution – claimant given contraceptive injections – absconded with stranger during intensive rehabilitation and not found for several days – lack of awareness of own disabilities and grossly unrealistic expectations about future – claimant's personal safety in serious danger without external control – necessity of 24 hour one-to-one "minder"-type caring – parents having difficulty in caring for daughter, and own lives detrimentally affected.

Prognosis: Expectation of claimant being set up in her own home nearby within 6 months of date of trial.

1.2.3.8.C43 Case No. 11483

Name of case: Goodridge v Ferguson

Brief description of injuries: HEAD – BRAIN DAMAGE

Reported: Kemp & Kemp, C2-029; [1998] CLY 1484

JSB Category: 2(A)(c)

Sex: Male

Age at injury: 20

Age at award: 27

Date of award: 17 October 1997

Tribunal: QBD

Amount of award then: £67,000

Award at February 2001: £82,700

Description of injuries: Severe head injury – skull fractures – significant brain injury.

Prognosis: Deficits of memory and cognitive function would be permanent – also the characteristic elements of deficit in frontal lobe function – G would never be able to work on the open market – would not be able to live an independent life without supervision – would not be able to manage his affairs – he was fit and able to enjoy a long-standing relationship with a girl-friend.

1.2.3.8.C44 Case No. 10704

Name of case: Crane v Oliver

Brief description of injuries: SERIOUS HEAD INJURY – BRAIN DAMAGE – COGNITIVE DEFECTS – UNEMPLOYABLE – LONG-TERM SUPPORT NEEDED

Reported: Kemp & Kemp, C2-030; [1994] CLY 1550

JSB Category: 2(A)(c)

Sex: Male

Age at injury: 20

Age at award: 26

Date of award: 19 October 1994

Tribunal: Manchester High Court

Amount of award then: £60,000

Award at February 2001: £81,159

Description of injuries: Road accident – serious head injury and brain damage – full-scale IQ declined by 20 points – mild expressive language difficulties in naming and word-finding – difficulties in executive function relating to abstract thinking and planning – impaired concentration, tendency to tire easily – slurred speech – slow writing – personality profoundly affected – mild disinhibition – impaired social skills – difficulty foreseeing consequences of actions – double vision at first, but largely resolved 16 months before trial, except for recurrence when claimant tired – impaired cutaneous sensation over left side of face and left side of tongue, but still able to taste food, and sense of smell not affected – incoordination of all 4 limbs – claimant able to care for himself at home, and continue with some form of social life – susceptibility to bad influences and to persuasion into actions against his best interests.

Prognosis: Risk of post-traumatic epilepsy of 5 per cent – permanent difficulties in establishing close relationships, particularly with members of opposite sex, and reduced prospects of marriage – inability to deal with any responsibilities that might arise from fathering children – no prospect of ever gaining employment on open market – likely to remain easily distracted and have difficulties in learning and retaining new skills, thus limiting future activities and interests – long-term support in form of rehabilitation in a structured setting required.

1.2.3.8.C45 Case No. 10006

Name of case: Re Adams

Brief description of injuries: MODERATE BRAIN DAMAGE

Reported: Kemp & Kemp, C3-010; [1990] CLY 1586

JSB Category: 2(C)

Sex: Male

Age at injury: 21

Age at award: 28

Date of award: 30 October 1990

Tribunal: CICB

Amount of award then: £50,000

Award at February 2001: £74,585

Description of injuries: Struck on back of head by a shovel, causing severe epilepsy – IQ had declined nearly 20 points due to epilepsy – abilities declined dramatically.

Prognosis: Prone to serious fits for the rest of his life. No improvement.

1.2.3.8.C46 Case No. 10909

Name of case: Re Arkle

Brief description of injuries: BRAIN DAMAGE – SEVERE SHORT-TERM MEMORY LOSS – PHYSICAL IMPAIRMENT

Reported: [1995] CLY 1660

JSB Category: 2(A)(c)(ii)

Sex: Male

Age at injury: 19

Age at award: 25

Date of award: 15 December 1994

Tribunal: CICB, Durham

Amount of award then: £55,000

Award at February 2001: £73,038

Description of injuries: In assault suffered an occipital skull fracture with diffuse brain damage and contusion of right frontal lobe – was in coma for four weeks and in hospital for four months – suffered severe retrograde amnesia of at least two years' duration – also suffered profound and severe loss of short-term memory – was able to receive information but not retain it – after 15 minutes had no recall of any information received and forgot words after few seconds – would forget to change clothes or have baths – unable to cope with unfamiliar surroundings or people and lacked any facility to plan or organise life – before incident was in the average intelligence range but at the time of hearing his intellectual performance was worse than 85 per cent of his age group – underwent some personality change in that he became passive and lacked motivation – physical disabilities comprised lack of co-ordination in left arm and leg with mild ataxia of gait and marked loss of field of vision – had no vision in left side of left eye nor in left half of right eye – prior to incident worked as a junior technician with the RAF but was left permanently unable to pursue any form of employment – required constant monitoring and supervision by parents.

Prognosis: Would never be able to lead an independent existence and ultimately would require institutional care.

1.2.3.8.C47 Case No. 11484

Name of case: Cornell v Green

Brief description of injuries: HEAD – BRAIN DAMAGE – ARM

Reported: Kemp & Kemp, C2-035; [1998] CLY 1485

JSB Category: 2(A)(c)(ii); 6(F)

Sex: Male

Age at injury: 25

Age at award: -

Date of award: 20 March 1998

Tribunal: QBD

Amount of award then: £60,000

Award at February 2001: £72,253

Description of injuries: Arm injury – brain damage – damage had affected concentration, emotional control, sense of smell and taste, and aggression and concentration which had made claimant an excellent salesman.

Other points: Reduced to £60,000 from £87,500 under JSB Guidance. Though appeal reduced general damages, it increased the total award.

1.2.3.8.C48 Case No. 10311

Name of case: McConnell v Welch

Brief description of injuries: BRAIN DAMAGE – MAJOR INTELLECTUAL IMPAIRMENT – ABLE TO WORK – EPILEPSY

Reported: Kemp & Kemp, C2-026; [1992] CLY 1566

JSB Category: 2(A)(b)

Sex: Male

Age at injury: 21

Age at award: 30

Date of award: 16 December 1991

Tribunal: QBD

Amount of award then: £50,000

Award at February 2001: £71,229

Description of injuries: Major intellectual and personality impairment – sometimes verbally abusive and physically violent.

Prognosis: Requiring constant supervision and professional care in the future – epilepsy five years after the accident controlled by medication – currently able to fulfil an undemanding job – likely to be unemployed in the foreseeable future.

1.2.3.8.C49 Case No. 11771

Name of case: Armstrong v Scarborough HA

Brief description of injuries: HEAD – MODERATE BRAIN DAMAGE – EPILEPSY

Reported: (1999) 99 (3) QR 5; Kemp & Kemp, C2-037; [1999] CLY 1434

JSB Category: 2(A)(c), 2(C)(a)

Sex: Male

Age at injury: 12

Age at award: 23

Date of award: 01 July 1999

Tribunal: QBD

Amount of award then: £60,000

Award at February 2001: £70,127

Description of injuries: Claimant taken to hospital with penetrating injury to brain causing a compound depressed skull fracture with foreign bodies driven into left temporal lobe – initial treatment at hospital negligent; foreign objects not identified and antibiotics not administered – development of disorientation, dysphasia and left – sided hemiparesis 22 hours after admission – commencement of fits 30 hours after admission – foreign objects and locuted gas located in temporal lobe on transfer to second hospital; operation to evacuate necrotic brain revealed abscess formation and development of gas gangrene from clostridium perfringens – subsequent development of regular grand mal epilepsy; fits occasionally coming without warning, sometimes resulting in nasty injuries – recurrence of abscess, with accompanying severe headaches, 6 months after operation – cognitive functions also affected, exacerbating previous learning difficulties – inability to speak fluently – IQ limited to 91 – apathy, caused by medication – substantial memory deficit resulting in verbal retention of a 6 year old; reading age of 11; calculating ability of 8 year old – claimant left with very little insight into own condition.

Prognosis: Epilepsy would continue, only poorly controlled, throughout claimant's lifetime – permanent 3 per cent risk of recurrent abscess or meningitis, which deterioration might be serious, especially if not competently treated, and provisional damages therefore awarded.

1.2.3.8.C50 Case No. 11073

Name of case: Re Glassby

Brief description of injuries: SKULL FRACTURE – EPILEPSY

Reported: [1996] CLY 2164

JSB Category: 2(A)(c)(ii)

Sex: Male

Age at injury: 24

Age at award: 30

Date of award: 10 April 1996

Tribunal: CICB, London

Amount of award then: £55,000

Award at February 2001: £69,475

Description of injuries: Fracture of the skull – large temporal haematoma – respiratory failure – developed epilepsy.

Prognosis: Lived in his own home – managed his own affairs – poor short-term memory – reading and speech severely affected.

Other points: Previously a graduate trainee – prospects of a directorship – had a clear understanding of his condition.

1.2.3.8.C51 Case No. 10711

Name of case: Re Alford

Brief description of injuries: BRAIN DAMAGE – SPEECH AND LANGUAGE IMPAIRED – UNEMPLOYABLE – "PERSONAL LIFE DESTROYED"

Reported: Kemp & Kemp, C2-038; [1994] CLY 1558

JSB Category: 2(A), 2(C); 4(B)(d)

Sex: Male

Age at injury: 39

Age at award: 45

Date of award: 25 July 1994

Tribunal: CICB, Birmingham

Amount of award then: £50,000

Award at February 2001: £66,614

Description of injuries: Assault – fall over fence, landing on head on pavement 5ft below – considerable right – sided haematoma, causing compression of the brain – evidence of contusion to brain – considerable bruising over right eye and temporal area – development of epileptic fits, at date of hearing 2-3 fits in 12-month period – right-sided headaches – tinnitus – depression and irritability, leading to several admissions to psychiatric hospitals – speech and capacity for language significantly impaired – easily distracted – poor memory – psychiatric, psychological and psychometric testing concluded that claimant virtually unemployable – personal life destroyed, and marriage broken down.

Prognosis: Epilepsy treated with anti-convulsants, likely to continue – headaches and tinnitus likely to continue.

1.2.3.8.C52 Case No. 10714

Name of case: Re Mapley

Brief description of injuries: BRAIN DAMAGE – TEMPORAL LOBE DYSRHYTHMIA – IMPAIRED INTELLECTUAL FUNCTION – LONG-TERM MEDICATION

Reported: Kemp & Kemp, C2-039; [1994] CLY 1561, 1567

JSB Category: 2(A)(c)

Sex: Male

Age at injury: 25

Age at award: 36

Date of award: 23 August 1994

Tribunal: CICB, London

Amount of award then: £50,000

Award at February 2001: £66,252

Description of injuries: Police officer kicked in head during course of duties – unconscious several minutes, subsequent dizzy spells – able to continue in employment for over 2 years – subsequent diagnosis of temporal lobe dysrhythmia, stemming from assault – forced to retire – daily fits – mood swings – depression, with olfactory hallucinations – episodic feelings of depersonalisation – increasing paranoid ideas – episodic panic attacks – violence on little provocation – loss of independence, confidence and self esteem – long-term need to take anti-convulsants, with subsequent effect on libido – headaches – impaired intellectual function, including loss of memory, reduction in attention span, difficulty in retaining information and in forming precise speech – distress at post-incident behaviour led claimant to attempt sex change treatment and adopt female identity – claimant had reverted to male persona at time of trial.

Prognosis: Condition almost certainly permanent.

1.2.3.8.C53 Case No. 11504

Name of case: Re Hancock

Brief description of injuries: HEAD – GRAND MAL EPILEPSY

Reported: Kemp & Kemp, C3-072; [1998] CLY 1505

JSB Category: 2(A)(c)(ii); 3(B); 5(H)

Sex: Male

Age at injury: 20

Age at award: 32

Date of award: 12 January 1998

Tribunal: CICB, London

Amount of award then: £55,000

Award at February 2001: £66,098

Description of injuries: Grand mal epilepsy following an attack – post-traumatic stress disorder – irritable bowel syndrome – partial loss of vision – development of mytonia congenica – mobility limited to 50 yards – unable to work full-time.

Prognosis: Liable to experience seizures when ill – on daily medication for life – permanently impaired vision.

1.2.3.8.C54 Case No. 11486

Name of case: Khan v Jones

Brief description of injuries: HEAD – BRAIN DAMAGE

Reported: Kemp & Kemp, C2-040; [1998] CLY 1487

JSB Category: 2(A)(c)(ii)

Sex: Male

Age at injury: 13

Age at award: 18

Date of award: 20 October 1997

Tribunal: Bradford County Court

Amount of award then: £55,000

Award at February 2001: £66,098

Description of injuries: Moderate brain injury – significant personality change – IQ reduced to 55.

Prognosis: K would never work – would require long-term supervision but not nursing care.

1.2.3.8.C55 Case No. 10138

Name of case: Re Fawcett

Brief description of injuries: MULTIPLE SKULL INJURIES – EPILEPSY – DYSPHASIA – PERSONALITY CHANGE

Reported: Kemp & Kemp, C2-041; [1991] CLY 1335

JSB Category: 2(C)(a)

Sex: Female

Age at injury: 24

Age at award: 30

Date of award: 13 June 1991

Tribunal: CICB

Amount of award then: £45,000

Award at February 2001: £64,110

Description of injuries: Assault – attacked with an iron bar – coma for six days – discharged from hospital after three-and-a-half weeks – multiple fractures to vault of skull – grand mal epilepsy – moderate expressive and receptive dysphasia: problems in communication – frustration – personality change – temper tantrums – aggressive – grossly irresponsible with money.

Prognosis: Unlikely to be any further improvement.

1.2.3.8.C56 Case No. 11772

Name of case: Re Owen

Brief description of injuries: HEAD – MODERATE BRAIN DAMAGE – LOSS OF CO – ORDINATION

Reported: Kemp & Kemp, C2-042; [1999] CLY 1435

JSB Category: 2(A)(c)(ii)

Sex: Male

Age at injury: 25

Age at award: 30

Date of award: 23 April 1999

Tribunal: CICB, Liverpool

Amount of award then: £55,000

Award at February 2001: £63,544

Description of injuries: Severe closed head injuries – subdural haematoma – also left – sided pneumothorax, requiring ventricular drain and tracheostomy – some ophthalmic deficiencies (but vision generally reasonable) – dysarthric speech – gross impairment of short-term memory – major co-ordination problems on right side, with diminished motor skills, impaired balance and significant loss of confidence when outdoors – claimant found to be functioning significantly below pre-morbid level in neuropsychological assessment, a finding consistent with organic brain damage.

Prognosis: Neuropsychological deficiencies unlikely to improve, although greater independence could be achievable following attendance at rehabilitation clinic – claimant unlikely ever to work again, and would require care and assistance for remainder of life with basic domestic tasks (some degree of independence retained in relation to personal routine).

1.2.3.8.C57 Case No. 10139

Name of case: Re G (A Minor)

Brief description of injuries: FRACTURED SKULL – EPILEPTIC FITS

Reported: Kemp & Kemp, C3-014; [1991] CLY 1336

JSB Category: 2 (C)(a)

Sex: Female

Age at injury: 22 months

Age at award: 17 years

Date of award: 18 July 1991

Tribunal: Preston High Court

Amount of award then: £43,500

Award at February 2001: £61,877

Description of injuries: Car accident – skull fracture on both sides – epileptic fits controlled by anti-convulsants.

Prognosis: Anti-convulsants still being taken at date of hearing – diminished achievement – mental slowness – obesity.

1.2.3.8.C58 Case No. 11292

Name of case: Re McGuffie

Brief description of injuries: HEAD – BRAIN – EPILEPSY

Reported: Kemp & Kemp, C2-043; [1997] CLY 1840

JSB Category: 2(A)(c)(ii)

Sex: Male

Age at injury: 20

Age at award: 31

Date of award: 14 January 1997

Tribunal: CICB, Liverpool

Amount of award then: £50,000

Award at February 2001: £61,605

Description of injuries: Depressed fracture of the skull – epileptic seizures – at time of hearing epilepsy was well managed – he could manage most routine daily tasks with some supervision – no earning capacity.

Other points: Before the date of the accident his work record was negligible.

1.2.3.8.C59 Case No. 10552

Name of case: Rhodes v Watson

Brief description of injuries: HEAD – EPILEPSY

Reported: Kemp & Kemp, C3-015; [1993] CLY 1445

JSB Category: 2(C)

Sex: Male

Age at injury: 10 months

Age at award: 14

Date of award: 01 December 1992

Tribunal: High Court, Sheffield

Amount of award then: £45,000

Award at February 2001: £61,487

Description of injuries: Struck by car when baby – fractured skull – damage to right frontal lobe of brain – pulsatile swelling overlaying a growing fracture – shortening of left hand and leg, weakness in co-ordination – impaired cognitive skills (organisation, concentration) – development of minor epilepsy at age 5 onwards – first grand mal seizure at age 12 – generalised epilepsy probably developed – claimant tires easily – impairment of left arm and leg, along with impaired cognitive skills and risk of epilepsy, further restricts opportunities for employment in high unemployment area, but some chance of still obtaining work.

Prognosis: Permanent risk of partial or general epilepsy, but believed controllable by medication – remote risk of enlarging granuloma and porencephalic cyst in damaged area of brain.

1.2.3.8.C60 Case No. 11773

Name of case: Davies v Clarkson

Brief description of injuries: HEAD – MODERATE BRAIN DAMAGE – LOSS OF 20 IQ POINTS – COGNITIVE DEFECTS

Reported: Kemp & Kemp, PRB-001; [1999] CLY 1436

JSB Category: 2(A)(c)(ii); 6(D)(d), 6(L)(a)

Sex: Male

Age at injury: 28

Age at award: -

Date of award: 28 April 1999

Tribunal: QBD

Amount of award then: £50,000

Award at February 2001: £57,137

Description of injuries: Serious brain injury – displacement of left knee, requiring total knee replacement, and ruptured ligament in right knee, reducing walking range to 50 yards with a stick – fractured clavicle – brain damage resulting in loss of 20 IQ points – severe depression – severe headaches – deterioration of memory, causing difficulties in running of own business and leading to business's eventual collapse – personality change; sadness, aggression; bad – temperedness; frustration at inability to carry out tasks.

Prognosis: No prospect of recovery in cognitive abilities – no prospect of returning to employment at similar level to that prior to the accident, and only a slight prospect of being able to return to employment at all.

Other points: Award included unspecified amount for loss of congenial employment.

1.2.3.8.C61 Case No. 10712

Name of case: Re Lunney

Brief description of injuries: BRAIN DAMAGE – COGNITIVE IMPAIRMENT – POST-TRAUMATIC STRESS DISORDER – PERSONALITY CHANGE – INDEPENDENT, BUT NEEDS HELP

Reported: Kemp & Kemp, C2-047; [1994] CLY 1559

JSB Category: 2(A); 3(B); 7(A)

Sex: Male

Age at injury: 29

Age at award: 36

Date of award: 10 December 1993

Tribunal: CICB, London

Amount of award then: £40,000

Award at February 2001: £52,810

Description of injuries: Assault – significant head injury and fractured facial bone – loss of consciousness – 2 weeks' post-traumatic amnesia – severe damage to right hemisphere of brain, particularly right temporal lobe – cognitive impairment – memory, concentration, co-ordination and perception all damaged – balance affected – frequent headaches – personality change; easily frustrated, prone to aggressive outbursts – agoraphobia – lassitude – total loss of libido – symptoms of post-traumatic stress disorder; continuing nightmares, hallucinations – epileptic-type episodes of unclear diagnosis, causing disorientation, confusion and debilitation, rendering claimant unfit for activity for about 3 days per week – depression – loss of "drive" – lifestyle markedly restricted; able to live alone, but reliant for life on family for domestic assistance and supervision (eg with financial affairs).

Prognosis: Memory, concentration, coordination and perception all permanently affected – permanently unfit for work, even in a sheltered environment – sessions with clinical psychologist producing improvement in symptoms of post-traumatic stress disorder.

1.2.3.8.C62 Case No. 10904

Name of case: Re Harding

Brief description of injuries: HEAD INJURY – PERSONALITY CHANGE – MODERATELY SEVERE BACK INJURY

Reported: Kemp & Kemp, B2-012; [1995] CLY 1655

JSB Category: 2(A)(c)(iii)

Sex: Male

Age at injury: 57

Age at award: 63

Date of award: 07 March 1995

Tribunal: CICB, Plymouth

Amount of award then: £40,000

Award at February 2001: £50,605

Description of injuries: Prison officer sustained injuries arising from an assault in Her Majesty's Prison, Dartmoor – in the assault the applicant was punched in the head about five times, sustaining concussive head injury, resulting in post-traumatic amnesia in the order of 15 minutes to two hours – lower back also injured in the assault – no surgical treatment required for any of the injuries – lower back injury caused restriction on the physical work the applicant could carry out – he was unable to do heavy digging or lifting and was unable to decorate ceilings – his back was also prone to "giving out", and as a result he was confined to his bed for periods of up to a week – could no longer carry out lapidary – could no longer drink alcohol – experienced headaches – under pressure his mind went blank – lost temper when criticised or under pressure.

1.2.3.8.C63 Case No. 10548

Name of case: Boulton v Brammer and Logic Office Furniture

Brief description of injuries: HEAD – BRAIN DAMAGE – FRONTAL LOBE DAMAGE

Reported: Kemp & Kemp, C2-049; [1993] CLY 1441

JSB Category: 2(A)(c)

Sex: Male

Age at injury: 19

Age at award: 24

Date of award: 01 December 1992

Tribunal: Sheffield High Court

Amount of award then: £37,500

Award at February 2001: £50,237

Description of injuries: Frontal lobe damage as result of fractures to the tempero-parietal skull region – unconscious for 3 weeks – memory and concentration significantly impaired (faulty judgment; would not wash, shave or change clothes without prompting; attitudinal difficulties; inappropriate laughing and yawning; lack of awareness of own situation) – slight dysarthria – injuries to teeth and jaw – difficulties in lifting arms – frequent headaches.

Prognosis: "Minder" required as cannot safely be left alone – 5-10 per cent chance of epilepsy – sheltered work in the distant future only hope of employment.

1.2.3.8.C64 Case No. 10140

Name of case: Re Thirtle

Brief description of injuries: FRACTURED SKULL – PERMANENTLY DISABLED

Reported: Kemp & Kemp, C2-050; [1991] CLY 1337

JSB Category:

Sex: Male

Age at injury: 52

Age at award: 56

Date of award: 11 July 1991

Tribunal: CICB

Amount of award then: £35,000

Award at February 2001: £48,640

Description of injuries: Assault – large temporo-occipital fracture of left vault.

Prognosis: Significantly and permanently disabled – would never work again.

1.2.3.8.C65 Case No. 10319

Name of case: Re Free

Brief description of injuries: HEAD INJURY – SCHIZOPHRENIA – UNEMPLOYABLE

Reported: [1992] CLY 1575

JSB Category: 3(A)(a)

Sex: Male

Age at injury: 26

Age at award: -

Date of award: 27 April 1992

Tribunal: CICB

Amount of award then: £35,000

Award at February 2001: £46,724

Description of injuries: Severe injuries to the head – undisplaced fractures of the left zygote and tip of the nose – loss of three teeth – extensive bruising and abrasions – permanent schizophrenic type illness – mental impairment – ability to compare previous state with present sufferings causing frustration.

Prognosis: Unemployable – future deterioration in his condition likely to lead to an inability to live independently.

1.2.3.8.C66 Case No. 11494

Name of case: Re Beales

Brief description of injuries: HEAD – SKULL – COMPOUND FRACTURE – PERSONALITY CHANGE

Reported: Kemp & Kemp, C2-052L; [1998] CLY 1495

JSB Category: 2(A)(c)(iii)

Sex: Male

Age at injury: 25

Age at award: 36

Date of award: 03 November 1997

Tribunal: CICB, London

Amount of award then: £40,000

Award at February 2001: £46,413

Description of injuries: Large compound fracture to the skull – multiple intracranial haematomas – acute subdural haematomas – personality change – episodes of physical and verbal abuse – unemployment.

1.2.3.8.C67 Case No. 11488

Name of case: O'Brien v Moyes & Mendip Music

Brief description of injuries: HEAD – BRAIN DAMAGE – EPILEPSY

Reported: Kemp & Kemp, C2-053; [1998] CLY 1489

JSB Category: 2(A)(c), 2(C)

Sex: Male

Age at injury: 21

Age at award: 32

Date of award: 13 February 1998

Tribunal: QBD

Amount of award then: £40,000

Award at February 2001: £46,192

Description of injuries: Serious brain damage – epileptic attacks – claimant unable to undertake further training in his father's business.

Prognosis: Likely to be unemployed for 40 to 50 per cent of his working life.

Other points: Award unchallenged.

1.2.3.8.C68 Case No. 11487

Name of case: Re RH

Brief description of injuries: HEAD – BRAIN DAMAGE – EPILEPSY

Reported: Kemp & Kemp, C2-054; [1998] CLY 1488

JSB Category: 2(A)(c)(ii); 2(C)

Sex: Male

Age at injury: 40

Age at award: 46

Date of award: 11 March 1998

Tribunal: CICB

Amount of award then: £40,000

Award at February 2001: £46,036

Description of injuries: Assault – chronic subdural haematoma – dizziness – claimant had only worked for 1 week since the attack.

Prognosis: 90 per cent risk of late epilepsy which might be difficult to control – epilepsy would remain controlled by medication – only fit for sedentary work – dizziness unlikely to resolve.

1.2.3.8.C69 Case No. 10713

Name of case: Ridley v Pattenden and Batchelor

Brief description of injuries: BRAIN DAMAGE – PERSONALITY CHANGE – DETACHMENT AND WITHDRAWNNESS – LOSS OF LIBIDO – MEMORY UNIMPAIRED

Reported: Kemp & Kemp, C2-055; [1994] CLY 1560

JSB Category: 2(A)(c); 7

Sex: Male

Age at injury: 28

Age at award: 34

Date of award: 25 November 1993

Tribunal: QBD

Amount of award then: £35,000

Award at February 2001: £45,715

Description of injuries: Road accident – severe facial and head injuries – brain damage to frontal lobes – personality change from formerly gregarious, highly energetic and active person – lethargy – irritability – short-term memory loss – detachment and withdrawnness – loss of libido – complete cessation of formerly extensive, skilled DIY activities – memory unimpaired; thus able to continue in previous employment as skilled machinist and foreman at timber yard, and gain promotion.

Prognosis: Employment in any other job would be difficult to obtain and retain.

1.2.3.8.C70 Case No. 10705

Name of case: Re Baldwin

Brief description of injuries: BRAIN DAMAGE AND MULTIPLE INJURIES – ACUTE BACK INJURY – PETIT MAL EPILEPSY

Reported: Kemp & Kemp, B2-014; [1994] CLY 1551

JSB Category: 2(A)(d), 2(C)(b); 6(B)(b), 6(C), 6(H); 7(A)(c), 7(A)(f)

Sex: Male

Age at injury: 30

Age at award: 37

Date of award: 21 June 1994

Tribunal: CICB, London

Amount of award then: £35,000

Award at February 2001: £44,649

Description of injuries: Assault – injuries to head – injuries to lumbar and cervical spine, resulting in ongoing and continual, sometimes acute, back pain, rendering claimant unable to stand for any length of time or sit for prolonged periods – injuries to both hips – injuries to both wrists – deflected septum, causing ongoing breathing problems and snoring – 3 broken teeth, requiring extensive dental work – establishment of petit mal epilepsy, with seizures every 3 weeks or so, and one grand mal incident – loss of mental faculty, assessed at 20 per cent by psychiatrist – impaired memory – bouts of depression – occasional pain in right shoulder and back of head – unable to continue in previous employment (as telephone engineer) due to effects of injuries and fear of working at night; at date of trial, employed in (insecure) job as safety officer – unable to do heavy work, walk long distances, drive or pursue physical pastimes – general anxiety, heightened when out late at night or speaking to groups of people.

Prognosis: Ongoing symptoms relating to mental, back and nasal injuries unlikely to improve.

1.2.3.8.C71 Case No. 10718

Name of case: Re Moore

Brief description of injuries: HEAD – EPILEPSY – AGORAPHOBIA

Reported: Kemp & Kemp, C3-016; [1994] CLY 1565

JSB Category: 2(C)

Sex: Male

Age at injury: 52

Age at award: 61

Date of award: 18 October 1994

Tribunal: CICB, Nottingham

Amount of award then: £35,000

Award at February 2001: £44,480

Description of injuries: Assault – cuts and bruises to face – left sub – conjunctival haemorrhage – fall against panel of bus, striking head – subsequent grand mal epileptic seizure some months after attack, as a direct consequence of it – second seizure 1 month later – 3 seizures 3 months later – anti-convulsant therapy thereafter controlled seizures – development of agoraphobia, also as a result of the attack – claimant subsequently suffered stroke, unconnected to attack – claimant lost job as bus driver due to epilepsy – agoraphobia diminished claimant's social and family life.

Other points: Board declined to follow in full JSB recommendations relating to epilepsy. Award increased from £15,000.

1.2.3.8.C72 Case No. 10143

Award at February 2001: £42,103

See: 1.2.3.2.1.C3 for details

1.2.3.8.C73 Case No. 10165

Name of case: Re RH

Brief description of injuries: PSYCHOSOMATIC EPILEPSY

Reported: [1991] CLY 1362

JSB Category: 2(C)(b)

Sex: Female

Age at injury: 6-16

Age at award: -

Date of award: 11 April 1991

Tribunal: CICB

Amount of award then: £30,000

Award at February 2001: £41,347

Description of injuries: Sexually abused by father regularly (almost every day) from age six to sixteen – abuser involved digital interference including penetration – forced to masturbate father – no physical damage but had myoclonic epileptic fits at age 12 – psychological evidence suggested that these were not related to sexual abuse – at 15 suffered psychosomatic epileptic fits of increasing severity and frequency – psychological evidence showed psychosomatic epilepsy probably directly related to sexual abuse – commenced at time when suffering great deal of stress and conflict – at time of assessment no major seizures for one year .

Prognosis: Good: though she would be affected permanently in some ways.

1.2.3.8.C74 Case No. 10142

Name of case: Re Cooper

Brief description of injuries: COMPOUND DEPRESSED FRACTURE OF LEFT TEMPORAL BONE – GRAND MAL EPILEPSY

Reported: Kemp & Kemp, C3-078; [1991] CLY 1339

JSB Category: 2(C)(a)

Sex: Male

Age at injury: 17

Age at award: 22

Date of award: 17 May 1991

Tribunal: CICB

Amount of award then: £30,000

Award at February 2001: £41,215

Description of injuries: Assault – compound depressed fracture of left temporal bone – grand mal epilepsy for 12-18 months, anti-convulsant treatment for two-and-a-quarter years.

Prognosis: 5% risk of epilepsy in future; slight risk of early senile dementia.

1.2.3.8.C75 Case No. 10313

Name of case: Re Pitts (A Minor)

Brief description of injuries: SKULL – DEPRESSED COMPOUND FRACTURE – PROFOUNDLY HANDICAPPED

Reported: [1992] CLY 1568

JSB Category: 2(A)(b)

Sex: Male

Age at injury: 4

Age at award: 9

Date of award: 14 February 1992

Tribunal: CICB, Leeds

Amount of award then: £30,000

Award at February 2001: £40,296

Description of injuries: Depressed compound fracture of the skull and lacerations to the brain.

Prognosis: Profoundly handicapped – likelihood of developing epilepsy – catastrophic personality and intellectual changes – profound difficulty with academic work – virtually unable to read, write or cope with numbers and unlikely to improve significantly – likely to cause behavioural problems in the future.

1.2.3.8.C76 Case No. 10549

Name of case: Re Pitt

Brief description of injuries: HEAD – EPILEPSY – MEMORY LOSS – LOSS OF SENSE OF SMELL

Reported: Kemp & Kemp, C2-061; [1993] CLY 1442

JSB Category: 2(A)(c); 2(C)(c); 4(C)(c)

Sex: Male

Age at injury: 29

Age at award: 36

Date of award: 17 December 1992

Tribunal: CICB, London

Amount of award then: £30,000

Award at February 2001: £39,389

Description of injuries: Struck about head – front cerebral contusion to both sides of brain, especially the right – grand mal epileptic fit – unconscious for several days – left with considerable impairment due to damage to both anterior poles of the brain – subsequent blackouts – loss of sense of smell – significant memory impairment – development of explosive temper through frustration.

Prognosis: Unable to ever return to skilled employment (formerly an aircraft engineer), and probably unemployable.

1.2.3.8.C77 Case No. 10715

Name of case: Re Smith (JG)

Brief description of injuries: BRAIN DAMAGE; LOSS OF SENSES OF TASTE AND SMELL – PERSONALITY CHANGE – DEPRESSION – LOSS OF SEXUAL ACTIVITY

Reported: Kemp & Kemp, B2-021; [1994] CLY 1562

JSB Category: 2(A)(d); 4(B)(d), 4(C)(a); 3(A); 7(A)(d), 7(A)(e)

Sex: Male

Age at injury: 57

Age at award: 62

Date of award: 20 June 1994

Tribunal: CICB, London

Amount of award then: £25,000

Award at February 2001: £31,068

Description of injuries: Assault – struck on head with object – fractures to skull, cheekbone and jaw – perforated eardrum – fractures to skull surgically reduced – hearing loss and some tinnitus, disturbing sleep – loss of senses of taste and smell – balance affected – depression – personality change, with aggressive periods – cessation of all sexual activity – claimant unable to return to work – aggressive periods refractory to all treatment – no indication of significant intellectual impairment – loss of balance a regular occurrence, with possible consequences of injury.

1.2.3.8.C78 Case No. 10316

Name of case: Re Edwards

Brief description of injuries: HEAD INJURY – EPILEPSY – BACK PAIN

Reported: [1992] CLY 1572

JSB Category: 2(C)(b)

Sex: Male

Age at injury: 37

Age at award: 49

Date of award: 05 December 1991

Tribunal: CICB, Manchester

Amount of award then: £20,000

Award at February 2001: £26,244

Description of injuries: Struck on the back of the head with a brick – multiple cuts and bruises – fractured toe – 50% disability caused by post-traumatic epilepsy, post-traumatic stress disorder and persistent back pain.

Prognosis: Considerable mental and physical suffering – career impaired.

1.2.3.8.C79 Case No. 10321

Name of case: Re Atwal

Brief description of injuries: HEAD AND TRUNK – STAB WOUNDS – PRE-EXISTING DEPRESSION EXACERBATED

Reported: Kemp & Kemp, C4-045; [1992] CLY 1577

JSB Category: 3(B)(b)

Sex: Female

Age at injury: 28

Age at award: 31

Date of award: 25 September 1992

Tribunal: CICB, Birmingham

Amount of award then: £20,000

Award at February 2001: £25,510

Description of injuries: Twenty four superficial stab wounds to the body and face – possible fracture of two ribs – collapsed lung – noticeable scarring to the body – could no longer wear sari – barely noticeable scars to the face.

Prognosis: Pre-existing depression exacerbated by post-traumatic stress syndrome – panic attacks – could no longer continue working.

1.2.3.8.C80 Case No. 10910

Name of case: Re Suleman

Brief description of injuries: BRAIN DAMAGE – SIGNIFICANT LOSS OF MEMORY AND INTELLECT

Reported: Kemp & Kemp, C2-069; [1995] CLY 1661

JSB Category: 2(A)(c)(iii)

Sex: Male

Age at injury: 35

Age at award: 39

Date of award: 24 May 1995

Tribunal: CICB, London

Amount of award then: £20,000

Award at February 2001: £23,680

Description of injuries: Assaulted – assailant struck him on the head with axe four/five times, causing depressed skull fracture to left parietal region, resulting in dysphasia and weakness of right hand – whilst in hospital for two weeks, fracture was elevated, applicant given blood transfusion and dural tear repaired – at time of hearing, applicant suffered occasional headaches and some numbness in right hand – had sustained a significant loss of intellect and memory lapse – was physics graduate who had been teaching as school teacher before arriving in the UK – evidence suggested that he would have obtained a meaningful, reasonably paid job had assault not happened – instead, applicant was reduced to working as warehouse operative which involved package labelling.

Damage to Head

1.2.3.8.C81 Case No. 11290

Name of case: Re Stoneman

Brief description of injuries: HEAD – BRAIN – PERSONALITY AND COGNITIVE CHANGES

Reported: Kemp & Kemp, C2-070; [1997] CLY 1838

JSB Category: 2(A)(c)(iii)

Sex: Male

Age at injury: 30

Age at award: 36

Date of award: 25 February 1997

Tribunal: CICB, Cardiff

Amount of award then: £20,000

Award at February 2001: £22,813

Description of injuries: Fracture of the left temporal parietal bone – fractured nose – bilateral black eyes – split lip – a degree of brain damage affecting his personality, cognitive function and behaviour.

Other points: Relationships suffered – marriage broke down.

1.2.3.8.C82 Case No. 11279

Name of case: Re Smith (Brynmor)

Brief description of injuries: HEAD – MEMORY LOSS – MENTAL IMPAIRMENT

Reported: Kemp & Kemp, B2-031; [1997] CLY 1826

JSB Category: 2(c)(iii)

Sex: Male

Age at injury: 48

Age at award: 50

Date of award: 19 August 1997

Tribunal: CICB, Birmingham

Amount of award then: £17,500

Award at February 2001: £19,379

Description of injuries: Pre-and post-traumatic amnesia – loss of all eight upper front teeth – three broken ribs – deformed nose – 5 inch and 2 inch facial scars.

Prognosis: Permanent numbness in the scar areas – permanent short-term memory loss – slight reduction in his mental abilities – headaches likely to recur for the rest of his life.

Other points: Memory loss and mental impairment made working almost impossible.

1.2.3.8.C83 Case No. 10314

Name of case: Roberts v Kendrick

Brief description of injuries: SKULL AND RIB FRACTURES – SOME INTELLECTUAL IMPAIRMENT

Reported: [1992] CLY 1570

JSB Category: 2(A)(d)

Sex: Male

Age at injury: 8

Age at award: 15

Date of award: 16 December 1991

Tribunal: Wrexham District Registry

Amount of award then: £10,000

Award at February 2001: £12,748

Description of injuries: Occipital lacerations overlying a depressed skull fracture – concussion – right sided pneumothorax with fracture to the right seventh rib.

Prognosis: Full physical recovery with some intellectual impairment.

1.2.3.8.C84 Case No. 10719

Name of case: Wood v Cleaver

Brief description of injuries: HEAD – SKULL FRACTURE – SENSES OF SMELL AND TASTE IMPAIRED – 3-4 PER CENT RISK OF EPILEPSY

Reported: [1994] CLY 1566

JSB Category: 2(B); 4(C)

Sex: Male

Age at injury: 34

Age at award: 36

Date of award: 02 August 1993

Tribunal: Birkenhead County Court

Amount of award then: £10,000

Award at February 2001: £12,228

Description of injuries: Claimant knocked off bicycle by car – fracture to skull – severe concussion – unconscious 10-15 minutes – detained in hospital 8 days – feelings of confusion after discharge – difficulty focusing on objects for several months – frequent bouts of vertigo, brought on by sudden movement or change in position and lasting several minutes, decreasing in frequency by date of trial to gaps of several months between attacks – sense of smell greatly impaired, sense of taste reduced and distorted to point where previously pleasant flavours became disagreeable.

Prognosis: Increased risk of developing post-traumatic epilepsy, in the order of 3 to 4 per cent in February 1992 and decreasing thereafter until after 5 years risk would return to universal, standard 1.5 per cent.

Other points: Court held that risk of development of epilepsy sufficient to justify award of provisional damages under s 51 of County Courts Act 1984 – claimant would be entitled to return for further award if epilepsy did in fact develop within 5 years of 1992.

1.2.3.8.C85 Case No. 10716

Name of case: Re Lorryman

Brief description of injuries: BRAIN – MENINGITIS – COGNITIVE DEFECTS – AGGRESSION

Reported: [1994] CLY 1563

JSB Category: 2(A)(d); 4(C); 6(D)(c)

Sex: Male

Age at injury: 24

Age at award: 31

Date of award: 03 November 1993

Tribunal: CICB, York

Amount of award then: £10,000

Award at February 2001: £12,202

Description of injuries: Assault – significant head injury – amnesia – severe peri-orbital haematoma – conjunctive haemorrhage – tender maxilla and grazed right eyebrow – detained in hospital overnight and discharged – development of blurred vision and severe headaches later that day; development of restless and aggressive behaviour – CAT scan revealed swollen brain, fracture at base of skull, fluid in applicant's sinuses – diagnosis of bacterial or viral meningitis – lumbar puncture prescribed – 3 months after discharge from hospital, review noted impairment of senses, particularly taste and smell – weakened left deltoid muscle – general feeling of weakness – pain in head, right arm and shoulder – headaches 3 times per week – problems with blocked nose – impaired sensation on top of head – short-term memory problems – increased aggression – claimant unable to return to work for 6 months – 3 years after assault, problems with memory, sense of taste, sense of smell, weekly headaches, nose blockage, aggression and numbness at top of head still evident.

1.2.3.8.C86 Case No. 11077

Name of case: Chase v West Sussex CC

Brief description of injuries: HEAD – BRAIN – BRAIN DAMAGE

Reported: [1996] CLY 2168

JSB Category: 2(A)(d)

Sex: Male

Age at injury: 38

Age at award: 41

Date of award: 31 May 1996

Tribunal: Mayor's and City of London Court

Amount of award then: £8,000

Award at February 2001: £8,999

Description of injuries: Struck on the head – post-traumatic amnesia – post-traumatic migraine – in a reasonably secure job which did not require him to drive.

Prognosis: A slow improvement with complete recovery within five to six years of the trial was anticipated.

1.2.3.8.C87 Case No. 11079

Name of case: Re Burgess

Brief description of injuries: HEAD – BRAIN – BRAIN DAMAGE

Reported: [1996] CLY 2170

JSB Category: 2(A)(d)

Sex: Male

Age at injury: -

Age at award: -

Date of award: 19 February 1996

Tribunal: CICB, London

Amount of award then: £7,500

Award at February 2001: £8,549

Description of injuries: Systematic beating lasting several hours – Glasgow coma scale eight.

Prognosis: There would be some degree of long-term cognitive impairment – short-term memory deficiency.

1.2.3.8.C88 Case No. 11078

Name of case: Re Clarke

Brief description of injuries: HEAD – BRAIN – BRAIN DAMAGE

Reported: [1996] CLY 2169

JSB Category: 2(A)(d)

Sex: Male

Age at injury: 25

Age at award: 29

Date of award: 05 August 1996

Tribunal: CICB, York

Amount of award then: £7,500

Award at February 2001: £8,426

Description of injuries: Blows to the head – kicks to the back.

Prognosis: Memory disturbances and headaches were expected to continue for the rest of his life – becoming less frequent.**Prognosis:** The continuing symptoms would affect his ability to work.

1.2.3.8.C89 Case No. 11019

Name of case: Edwards v Matthews

Brief description of injuries: NECK – WHIPLASH – FULL RECOVERY AFTER 14 MONTHS – EXTRA 0.5-1% RISK OF EPILEPSY

Reported: Kemp & Kemp, E2-083; [1995] CLY 1771

JSB Category: 6(A)(c)

Sex: Male

Age at injury: 34

Age at award: 36

Date of award: 08 November 1994

Tribunal: Reading County Court

Amount of award then: £4,500

Award at February 2001: £5,327

Description of injuries: Plaintiff involved in road traffic accident – unconscious for about five minutes and suffered bruising to temple and knees which cleared up in five days – also sustained cervical whiplash injury and muscular strain in right shoulder which was severe for two weeks – absent from work for two weeks – had difficulty with everyday tasks such as bathing or washing his hair – for following three weeks, undertook only light duties at work and suffered constant nagging pain – after that pain became intermittent with some restriction of movement in shoulder – bi-weekly hobby of weightlifting was temporarily suspended because pain was provoked by strenuous activity and lifting heavy objects – had made full recovery by 14 months after accident and resumed weightlifting – accident happened day before plaintiff's annual leave was due to start and holidays had to be cancelled.

Prognosis: The chance of developing epilepsy was increased by 0.5-1 per cent, but chance of onset would diminish as time progressed returning to normal risk after five to 10 years.

1.2.3.8.C90 Case No. 11080

Name of case: Peskett and Peskett v Morris (No. 2)

Brief description of injuries: HEAD – BRAIN – BRAIN DAMAGE

Reported: Kemp & Kemp, C2-082; [1996] CLY 2171

JSB Category: 2(B)

Sex: Female

Age at injury: 31

Age at award: 35

Date of award: 24 June 1996

Tribunal: Hove County Court

Amount of award then: £4,250

Award at February 2001: £4,778

Description of injuries: Head injuries – post concussion syndrome – returned to her pre-accident condition twelve months after the accident.

1.2.3.8.C91 Case No. 11293

Name of case: G (a minor) v Leadstay Ltd

Brief description of injuries: HEAD – BRAIN – INCONTINENCE

Reported: Kemp & Kemp, F5-064/1; [1997] CLY 1841

JSB Category: 3(A)(c)

Sex: Male

Age at injury: 3

Age at award: 6

Date of award: 29 August 1997

Tribunal: Oldham County Court

Amount of award then: £4,000

Award at February 2001: £4,341

Description of injuries: Bruising chest injury – psychiatric enuresis – oppositional disorder.

Prognosis: Treatment for enuresis should cause improvement – oppositional disorder remained.

Other points: His mother suffered post-traumatic stress disorder after his accident – it reduced her ability to care for him.

1.2.3.8.C92 Case No. 10341

Name of case: Brown v Newman

Brief description of injuries: ANXIETY – HEADACHES – TWO YEARS

Reported: [1992] CLY 1597

JSB Category: 3(B)(d)

Sex: Male

Age at injury: 76

Age at award: 77

Date of award: 04 March 1992

Tribunal: Southend County Court

Amount of award then: £2,000

Award at February 2001: £2,516

Description of injuries: Head struck during traffic accident – headaches persisted for several months – loss of sleep – significant effects of anxiety in a man of this age – feelings of anger and indignation concerning the plight of his invalid wife should he have been more seriously injured.

Prognosis: Condition should be resolved within two years of the accident.

SECTION 1.3
DAMAGE TO SPINE

1.3.1 NECK INJURY

1.3.1.C1 Case No. 11575

Name of case: Barrington v Glass Glover Group plc

Brief description of injuries: NECK – DISLOCATION OF CERVICAL SPINE

Reported: Kemp & Kemp, E2-005/1; [1998] CLY 1577

JSB Category: 6(A)(a)(iii); 3(A)

Sex: Male

Age at injury: 45

Age at award: 50

Date of award: 01 May 1998

Tribunal: QBD

Amount of award then: £25,000

Award at February 2001: £27,286

Description of injuries: Unilateral dislocation of the sixth and seventh cervical vertebra – fracture of the seventh vertebra – post-traumatic anxiety neurosis, subsiding at time of hearing.

Prognosis: Traumatically induced degeneration – early retirement at 55-60 considered likely – unlikely to find work thereafter.

1.3.1.C2 Case No. 11576

Name of case: RM (a person under disability) v Richards

Brief description of injuries: NECK – CERVICAL SPINE – UNSTABLE JOINT

Reported: 99 (1) QR 6; Kemp & Kemp, E2-005/2; [1998] CLY 1578

JSB Category: 6(A)(a)(iii)

Sex: Female

Age at injury: 44

Age at award: 49

Date of award: 28 September 1998

Tribunal: Cardiff County Court

Amount of award then: £25,000

Award at February 2001: £27,128

Description of injuries: Injury to the neck at C4/5

Prognosis: Permanent kyphosis of the spine – bony union appeared to be unsound – claimant at risk of paralysis were she to suffer further significant injury.

Other points: Award included an unspecified sum for risk of future injury.

1.3.1.C3 Case No. 11269

Name of case: Savory v Birmingham

Brief description of injuries: NECK – WHIPLASH – AGGRAVATING PRE-EXISTING QUADRIPLEGIA – POST-TRAUMATIC STRESS DISORDER

Reported: Kemp & Kemp, H3-155/2; [1996] CLY 2362

JSB Category: 6(A)(a)(iii)

Sex: Female

Age at injury: 50

Age at award: 53

Date of award: 24 July 1996

Tribunal: Epsom County Court

Amount of award then: £16,500

Award at February 2001: £18,986

Description of injuries: Pre-existing quadriplegia aggravated by whiplash – post-traumatic stress disorder – she had all but lost her hard won independence – post-traumatic stress disorder was 90 per cent resolved at the time of the hearing.

Other points: Loss of amenity was much greater than would normally have arisen from such an injury.

Damage to Spine

1.3.1.C4 Case No. 11577

Name of case: Williams v Fisher

Brief description of injuries: NECK – INJURY

Reported: Kemp & Kemp, E2-014/1; [1998] CLY 1579

JSB Category: 6(A)(a)(iv)

Sex: Male

Age at injury: 53

Age at award: 59

Date of award: 13 March 1998

Tribunal: Brighton County Court

Amount of award then: £15,000

Award at February 2001: £16,343

Description of injuries: Injury to the cervical spine at C6/7 – C6/7 lesion with nerve root compression – affected the left forearm and middle 3 fingers.

1.3.1.C5 Case No. 10752

Name of case: Burke v Roy

Brief description of injuries: NECK – WRENCHING INJURY – 12-14 YEAR ACCELERATION

Reported: Kemp & Kemp, E2-015; [1994] CLY 1600

JSB Category: 6(A)(b)

Sex: Female

Age at injury: 26

Age at award: 33

Date of award: 26 November 1993

Tribunal: Manchester County Court

Amount of award then: £13,000

Award at February 2001: £15,996

Description of injuries: Road accident – wrenching injury to neck – contusion and superficial laceration to left knee – damage to capsular ligament of C5/C6 intervertebral disc – X-rays showed no bony injury, loss of cervical lordosis or generalised arthritic change, but minimal spondylotic lipping – however, MRI scan showed reduction of disc height and signal intensity of C5/C6 disc – disc thus no longer an effective "cushion" between vertebrae and symptoms a direct consequence of this – continuing, intermittent pain and stiffness in neck and shoulders, radiating into arm and wrist, usually on left side but sometimes on right – loss of strength in both sides; unable to carry anything heavy – occasional pins and needles in left hand – pain when driving long distances, and difficulty reversing car because of neck pain – also mild chondromalacia patella as a result of contusion to knee – intermittent pain and stiffness, knee occasionally gave way – claimant forced to give up horse riding, badminton, jazz dancing and water sports (swimming causing severe pain in neck).

Prognosis: Degenerative changes in disc accelerated by 12-14 years.

1.3.1.C6 Case No. 10753

Name of case: Trotter v Black

Brief description of injuries: NECK INJURY – PRE-EXISTING CONDITION – PERMANENT PAIN

Reported: Kemp & Kemp, E2-022; [1994] CLY 1601

JSB Category: 6(A)(b)

Sex: Female

Age at injury: 46

Age at award: 54

Date of award: 13 January 1994

Tribunal: Middlesbrough County Court

Amount of award then: £11,000

Award at February 2001: £13,489

Description of injuries: Road accident – whiplash injury to cervical spine – exacerbation of pre-existing, asymptomatic degenerative changes in spine – development of almost daily discomfort; painkillers regularly required and cervical collar worn almost every day – disruption of previously highly active lifestyle involving much aerobics, running, occasional golf and squash – claimant forced to abandon desire to become aerobics instructor – gardening and decorating activities and daily chores also affected.

Prognosis: Symptoms likely to be permanent – quality of life substantially changed.

1.3.1.C7 Case No. 11343

Name of case: Edge v Calderwood

Brief description of injuries: NECK – WRENCHING INJURY

Reported: Kemp & Kemp, E2-037; [1997] CLY 1891

JSB Category: 6(A)(b)(i)

Sex: Male

Age at injury: 38

Age at award: 41

Date of award: 17 September 1996

Tribunal:

Amount of award then: £10,000

Award at February 2001: £11,209

Description of injuries: Wrenching injury to the neck – symptoms amounting to post-traumatic stress disorder.

Prognosis: At time of hearing constant aching in the neck would be permanent.

Other points: After twelve months he could reasonably have sought treatment for his driving phobia.

1.3.1.C8 Case No. 11342

Name of case: Re Macey

Brief description of injuries: NECK – WHIPLASH – DISC DAMAGE

Reported: Kemp & Kemp, E2-036; [1997] CLY 1890

JSB Category: 6(A)(b)(i)

Sex: Male

Age at injury: 34

Age at award: 42

Date of award: 23 October 1996

Tribunal: CICB

Amount of award then: £10,000

Award at February 2001: £11,209

Description of injuries: Musculo-ligamentous damage to the neck – more permanent damage to the intervertebral discs – after two months of normal duties the symptoms deteriorated severely.

Prognosis: Symptoms of pain and stiffness were permanent.

Other points: Discharged from the police force – unable to drive for any distance.

1.3.1.C9 Case No. 11128

Name of case: Collins v Elks

Brief description of injuries: NECK – SOFT-TISSUE INJURY

Reported: Kemp & Kemp, E2-053; [1996] CLY 2219

JSB Category: 6(A)(b)(i)

Sex: Male

Age at injury: 39

Age at award: 44

Date of award: 04 June 1996

Tribunal: Hastings County Court

Amount of award then: £7,500

Award at February 2001: £8,431

Description of injuries: Soft-tissue injury to the neck – he would have been fit to resume his pre-accident work by May 1996.

Other points: Pain caused him to stop work altogether at the end of 1991 – thereafter pain improved.

1.3.1.C10 Case No. 11348

Name of case: Truscott v Saipe

Brief description of injuries: NECK – EXACERBATION OF PRE-EXISTING CONDITION

Reported: Kemp & Kemp, E2-055/1; [1997] CLY 1896

JSB Category: 6(A)(b)(ii)

Sex: Female

Age at injury: 48

Age at award: 52

Date of award: 18 September 1997

Tribunal: Leeds County Court

Amount of award then: £7,500

Award at February 2001: £8,098

Description of injuries: Injury to the neck – exacerbated pre-existing degenerative changes to the neck – painful symptoms to the lumbar spine.

Prognosis: Significant exacerbation of the pre-existing degenerative condition was permanent – likely to be at a permanent disadvantage in the labour market – back pain fully resolved at the time of her return to work.

Other points: Award reduced by £500 to reflect that she would have suffered some degree of exacerbation of the pre-existing condition.

1.3.1.C11 Case No. 12008

Name of case: Gimblet v Swansea City Council

Brief description of injuries: NECK – 5-9 YEARS

Reported: Kemp & Kemp, E2-041/1/2; [2000] 4 CL 151

JSB Category: 6(B)(b)(ii)

Sex: Male

Age at injury: 24

Age at award: 28

Date of award: 17 November 1999

Tribunal: Neath and Port Talbot County Court

Amount of award then: £6,750

Award at February 2001: £6,965

Description of injuries: A jarring soft-tissue injury to the neck and lower back – no bony injury was found – initially off work for four weeks, then for another six weeks over twelve months – eighteen months after the accident G was off work for another twenty three weeks – the pain diminished with physiotherapy.

Prognosis: Stiffness and intermittent severe pain was likely to continue for a period of five years – a risk of residual pain and discomfort continuing into the future.

Other points: Prior to the accident G had been a fit and active marathon runner.

1.3.1.C12 Case No. 10385

Name of case: Huke v Shobbrook

Brief description of injuries: NECK INJURY

Reported: Kemp & Kemp, E2-066; [1992] CLY 1641

JSB Category: 6(A)(b)(ii)

Sex: Female

Age at injury: 33

Age at award: 37

Date of award: 22 July 1992

Tribunal: Bristol County Court

Amount of award then: £5,250

Award at February 2001: £6,506

Description of injuries: Injury to the neck – cut to the temple – abrasion to the right elbow – activity level reduced for two or three months – was assured symptoms would resolve without treatment so did not seek further help until the end of 1988 – treated with osteopathy bi-monthly until early 1991.

Prognosis: There would be aching and stiffness of the neck for years to come.

1.3.1.C13 Case No. 11131

Name of case: Gridley v Phillips

Brief description of injuries: NECK – SOFT-TISSUE INJURY

Reported: Kemp & Kemp, E2-067; [1996] CLY 2222

JSB Category: 6(A)(c)

Sex: Female

Age at injury: 61

Age at award: 64

Date of award: 22 April 1996

Tribunal: Peterborough County Court

Amount of award then: £5,750

Award at February 2001: £6,481

Description of injuries: Typical soft-tissue injury to the neck – as the family driver she had been inconvenienced by the symptoms.

Prognosis: A "nuisance rather than disability" – unlikely to degenerate or to improve.

1.3.1.C14 Case No. 11344

Name of case: Beavan v Derby City Transport

Brief description of injuries: NECK – SOFT-TISSUE INJURY

Reported: Kemp & Kemp, E2-078; [1997] CLY 1892

JSB Category: 6(A)(b)(ii)

Sex: Male

Age at injury: 30

Age at award: 41

Date of award: 29 November 1996

Tribunal: Derby County Court

Amount of award then: £5,000

Award at February 2001: £5,588

Description of injuries: Soft-tissue injury to the neck – only five years of his symptoms could be attributed to the accident.

Other points: Further symptoms due to a pre-existing degenerative condition.

1.3.1.C15 Case No. 11017

Name of case: Shields v Vera

Brief description of injuries: NECK – WHIPLASH – SUBSTANTIAL RECOVERY WITHIN 2 YEARS

Reported: [1995] CLY 1769

JSB Category: 6(A)(c)

Sex: Female

Age at injury: 34

Age at award: 36

Date of award: 14 August 1995

Tribunal: Reading County Court

Amount of award then: £4,750

Award at February 2001: £5,450

Description of injuries: Plaintiff was knocked off roundabout by defendant and into path of oncoming traffic – sustained whiplash injury to neck, thoracic spine and lumbar spine – also developed pain in front of left hip and across left wrist – off work for six weeks – after that time she continued to suffer from minor residual symptoms, including pins and needles sensation down left arm and difficulty with lifting which persisted for about a year – also suffered from headaches which, though initially severe, gradually improved and resolved within two years – plaintiff suffered from nightmares, flashbacks and dizzy spells for about six months after accident – two years after accident she still suffered from pain between shoulder-blades, but only every two to three months, with episodes lasting for up to a day at a time.

Prognosis: There was expected to be very minor acceleration of degenerative changes in hip and neck in long term and plaintiff would be more susceptible to aches and pains in lower back – prognosis was for complete recovery within 30 months of accident.

1.3.1.C16 Case No. 11579

Name of case: Medjoub (a minor) v Ayub
Brief description of injuries: NECK – HEAD
Reported: Kemp & Kemp, E2-080/4; [1998] CLY 1581
JSB Category: 6(A)(b)(ii); 2(B)
Sex: Female
Age at injury: 15
Age at award: 17
Date of award: 02 March 1998
Tribunal: Nottingham County Court
Amount of award then: £5,000
Award at February 2001: £5,348
Description of injuries: Head, neck and back injuries – scalp laceration – at time of hearing recovery was almost complete.

1.3.1.C17 Case No. 11578

Name of case: Porter v United Parcels Services Ltd
Brief description of injuries: NECK – INJURY – THREE-YEAR ACCELERATION
Reported: Kemp & Kemp, E2-080/5; [1998] CLY 1580
JSB Category: 6(A)(b)(ii)
Sex: Male
Age at injury: 61
Age at award: 63
Date of award: 18 March 1998
Tribunal: Carlisle County Court
Amount of award then: £5,000
Award at February 2001: £5,348
Description of injuries: Injury to the cervical spine – pain and restricted movement to the neck and shoulders.
Prognosis: Pre-existing degenerative changes in his neck would have stopped P from working within 3 years in any event.

1.3.1.C18 Case No. 11359

Name of case: Hollands v GK Salter & Associates and O'Neill
Brief description of injuries: NECK – WHIPLASH – 3-YEAR ACCELERATION
Reported: Kemp & Kemp, E2-088/1; [1997] CLY 1907
JSB Category: 6(A)(b)(ii)
Sex: Female
Age at injury: 49
Age at award: 55
Date of award: 05 August 1997
Tribunal: Maidstone County Court
Amount of award then: £4,750
Award at February 2001: £5,155

Description of injuries: Exacerbation of an existing neck injury – discomfort radiating into the neck muscles – existing symptoms had been accelerated/exacerbated by three years.
Other points: Assistance required for domestic, household and gardening tasks was not needed before the accident.

1.3.1.C19 Case No. 10387

Name of case: Rees v Walker
Brief description of injuries: STIFF NECK
Reported: [1992] CLY 1643
JSB Category: 6(A)(b)(ii)
Sex: Female
Age at injury: 50
Age at award: 52
Date of award: 08 May 1992
Tribunal: Chester County Court
Amount of award then: £4,000
Award at February 2001: £4,939
Description of injuries: Stiffening of the neck – pain was aggravated by lifting nine months after the accident.

1.3.1.C20 Case No. 11580

Name of case: Clayton v Bank Cafe
Brief description of injuries: NECK – 10 MONTHS
Reported: Kemp & Kemp, E2-095/1; [1998] CLY 1582
JSB Category: 6(A)(b)(ii)
Sex: Female
Age at injury: 19
Age at award: 22
Date of award: 03 November 1997
Tribunal: Gwent County Court
Amount of award then: £4,500
Award at February 2001: £4,850
Description of injuries: Injury to the cervical spine – full recovery had been made within 10 months of the date of the accident.

1.3.1.C21 Case No. 11021

Name of case: Main v Birchmore

Brief description of injuries: NECK – WHIPLASH – USE OF HAND AFFECTED FOR 12 MONTHS – FULL RECOVERY 2 YEARS

Reported: Kemp & Kemp, E3-111; [1995] CLY 1773

JSB Category: 6(A)(c)

Sex: Female

Age at injury: 19

Age at award: 22

Date of award: 07 September 1995

Tribunal: Andover County Court

Amount of award then: £3,750

Award at February 2001: £4,283

Description of injuries: Plaintiff a classic whiplash injury to cervical spine in road traffic accident with pain radiating down left shoulder and arm – X-rayed and fitted with cervical collar – extensive physiotherapy and daily doses of strong painkillers failed to alleviate symptoms and studies at local technical college were adversely affected, particularly due to fact she could not write with left (dominant) hand for 12 months following accident due to pain – a dozen manipulations by osteopath nearly two years after accident helped considerably – by date of trial she had stopped taking painkillers and was left with only minor residual neck symptoms, which were, however, aggravated particularly if she tried to carry heavy items – all symptoms in relation to left arm and shoulder had resolved within two years of accident – trial judge took into account effect on ability to study in assessing the award.

1.3.1.C22 Case No. 10659

Name of case: Re Pownall

Brief description of injuries: NECK – PAIN – 2 YEARS

Reported: Kemp & Kemp, E2-101; [1993] CLY 1555

JSB Category: 6(A)(c)

Sex: Female

Age at injury: 36

Age at award: not given

Date of award: 25 August 1993

Tribunal: Preston County Court

Amount of award then: £3,500

Award at February 2001: £4,260

Description of injuries: Road accident – development of ache in neck, much more painful on following day and severe for first few weeks – X-rays negative; muscle relaxants, analgesics and collar prescribed – pain radiating through left shoulder into left forearm – frontal headaches on most days – disturbed sleep for 3.5 months – examination after 3 months; no restriction of movement but pain evident on lateral flexion and rotation to right – at time of trial, neck pain present almost every day, radiating into shoulder but no longer into arm – headaches more or less ceased – sleep no longer disturbed – range of movement full, but painful at extremes.

Prognosis: Full recovery expected within 16 to 22 months.

1.3.1.C23 Case No. 10660

Name of case: Lowe v Kapadia

Brief description of injuries: NECK – PAIN – 2 YEARS

Reported: Kemp & Kemp, E2-102; [1993] CLY 1556

JSB Category: 6(A)(c)

Sex: Female

Age at injury: 38

Age at award: 39

Date of award: 18 August 1993

Tribunal: Bury County Court

Amount of award then: £3,500

Award at February 2001: £4,260

Description of injuries: Road accident – subsequent pain in neck and back – headaches, attributable to referred pain from the neck, occurring 2 or 3 times per week – painkillers required daily – still able to carry out domestic chores, although longer time required to complete them – hobby of knitting restricted – apprehensive when driving.

Prognosis: Full recovery expected in 2 years from date of accident.

1.3.1.C24 Case No. 11020

Name of case: Socha v Gage

Brief description of injuries: NECK – SOFT-TISSUE INJURY – RECOVERY IN 2 YEARS

Reported: Kemp & Kemp, E2-085; [1995] CLY 1772

JSB Category: 6(A)(c)

Sex: Female

Age at injury: 57

Age at award: -

Date of award: 13 December 1994

Tribunal: Manchester County Court

Amount of award then: £3,590

Award at February 2001: £4,229

Description of injuries: Plaintiff injured in road traffic accident – sustained a soft-tissue injury to neck and minor laceration to left foot – experienced continuous headaches for first three months after accident, which gradually decreased in frequency over period of two years – plaintiff wore collar consistently for four months after accident – thereafter gradually reduced its use – plaintiff, a mobile home help, was unable to work at all for three months and was advised to take another three months' absence due to arduous nature of her work – in total plaintiff experienced significant pain, gradually reducing in intensity, over a period of two years – subsequently experienced very minor symptoms.

1.3.1.C25 Case No. 10767

Name of case: Edwards v Adams

Brief description of injuries: NECK – SOFT-TISSUE INJURY – 1-2 YEAR EXACERBATION OF PRE-EXISTING BUT ASYMPTOMATIC CONDITION

Reported: Kemp & Kemp, E2-103; [1994] CLY 1615

JSB Category: 6(A)(c)

Sex: Male

Age at injury: 54

Age at award: 57

Date of award: 14 December 1993

Tribunal: Harlow County Court

Amount of award then: £3,250

Award at February 2001: £3,939

Description of injuries: Accident in car park – soft-tissue injury to paraspinal muscles and ligamentous structures of cervical spine – moderate initial pain and discomfort – over course of next 2 years, development of episodic sharp pain – rotation and lateral flexion reduced by three-quarters – symptoms result of pre-existing, but previously asymptomatic, cervical spondylosis – inability to continue with hobbies of decorating and car maintenance – unable to use blackboard in job as senior college lecturer.

Prognosis: Symptoms of cervical spondylosis brought forward between 1 and 2 years by the accident.

1.3.1.C26 Case No. 10389

Name of case: Taylor v Orion Express Parcels

Brief description of injuries: NECK INJURY

Reported: [1992] CLY 1645

JSB Category: 6(A)(c)

Sex: Male

Age at injury: 42

Age at award: 43

Date of award: 21 January 1992

Tribunal: Manchester County Court

Amount of award then: £3,100

Award at February 2001: £3,932

Description of injuries: Injuries to the face, neck and thumbs – head thrown forward onto the steering wheel – bruising around eyes and over the bridge of the nose – some swelling to the forehead.

Prognosis: All symptoms were expected to resolve within sixteen months of the accident.

1.3.1.C27 Case No. 11988

Name of case: Towler v Ali

Brief description of injuries: NECK – 2 1/2 YEARS

Reported: Kemp & Kemp, E2-103/2; [2000] 3 CL 172

JSB Category: 6(A)(c)

Sex: Male

Age at injury: 41

Age at award: 44

Date of award: 14 October 1999

Tribunal: Clerkenwell County Court

Amount of award then: £3,750

Award at February 2001: £3,874

Description of injuries: Soft-tissue injury to the neck – visited hospital after four days – visited his GP a month later – T had to work shorter shifts for six months due to pain and stiffness – T's sex life and hobby were affected by the injury for a few months. The symptoms had improved two years and six months after the date of the accident.

1.3.1.C28 Case No. 10390

Name of case: Smith v Ellis

Brief description of injuries: NECK INJURY – STIFFNESS

Reported: [1992] CLY 1646

JSB Category: 6(A)(c)

Sex: Male

Age at injury: 23

Age at award: 25

Date of award: 22 June 1992

Tribunal: Pontefract County Court

Amount of award then: £3,000

Award at February 2001: £3,704

Description of injuries: Soreness to the neck – left paravertebral tenderness.

Prognosis: Restricted range of motion in the neck – surgical collar worn for four to five weeks – he occasionally received treatment from a works nurse involving massage with a spray. Unable to look downwards at work (butchery) – nine weeks absence from work.

1.3.1.C29 Case No. 10763

Name of case: Dion v Mayhew

Brief description of injuries: NECK – INJURY – FULL RECOVERY EXPECTED

Reported: Kemp & Kemp, E2-107; [1994] CLY 1611, 1709

JSB Category: 6(A)(c)

Sex: Female

Age at injury: 60

Age at award: -

Date of award: 18 July 1994

Tribunal: Preston County Court

Amount of award then: £3,000

Award at February 2001: £3,583

Description of injuries: Road accident – neck pain radiating into right shoulder, persisting 2-3 months – occipital headaches and pins and needles in right hand in mornings – inability to sleep for 4 nights – painkillers for several months – physiotherapy reduced symptoms to level of mild and intermittent pain during certain household activities – 10 per cent decrease in extension and right rotation of cervical spine.

Prognosis: Full recovery expected within 15 months of accident.

1.3.1.C30 Case No. 10768

Name of case: Williams v Griffiths

Brief description of injuries: NECK – INJURY – CONTINUING MINOR SYMPTOMS

Reported: Kemp & Kemp, E2-108; [1994] CLY 1616

JSB Category: 6(A)(c)

Sex: Male

Age at injury: 30

Age at award: 32

Date of award: 06 May 1994

Tribunal: Shrewsbury County Court

Amount of award then: £3,000

Award at February 2001: £3,566

Description of injuries: Road accident – claimant woke following day with considerable pain and stiffness in neck, lasting 7-10 days – sleep disturbance – considerable discomfort in course of carrying out duties as police officer, but no absence from work – 3 to 4 weeks of severe pain – gradual resolution of symptoms over next 6 months; pain experienced daily, about 75 per cent of the time, but described as being more of a nuisance than disabling – discomfort at extremes of flexional and rotational movements, particularly when turning to right – thereafter, pain and discomfort still experienced regularly, particularly towards end of day and after long periods of desk work.

Prognosis: Strong likelihood of minor residual symptoms remaining permanently.

1.3.1.C31 Case No. 12024

Name of case: Morris v Coal Product Holdings Ltd

Brief description of injuries: NECK – 18 MONTHS

Reported: Kemp & Kemp, E2-112; [2000] 4 CL 167

JSB Category: 6(A)(c)

Sex: Male

Age at injury: 37

Age at award: 40

Date of award: 24 November 1999

Tribunal: Barnsley County Court

Amount of award then: £3,300

Award at February 2001: £3,405

Description of injuries: M fell from machinery onto a coal pile some ten feet below – suffered a neck strain with slight scarring of the ligaments – lacerated wrist embedded with coal pigments – unable to work for two weeks – in considerable pain – disrupted sleep – Christmas ruined – prescribed analgesia – symptoms began to improve after three months. Residual symptoms resolved completely within eighteen months of the date of the accident.

1.3.1.C32 Case No. 11345

Name of case: Doherty v Spreadbury

Brief description of injuries: NECK – 21 MONTHS

Reported: Kemp & Kemp, K2-042; [1997] CLY 1893

JSB Category: 6(A)(b)(ii)

Sex: Female

Age at injury: 19

Age at award: 22

Date of award: 07 May 1997

Tribunal: Reading County Court

Amount of award then: £3,000

Award at February 2001: £3,289

Description of injuries: Pain in the neck immediately following a road accident – all symptoms had resolved within 20 to 21 months of the date of the accident

1.3.1.C33 Case No. 11069

Name of case: Ahmed v Aquamead

Brief description of injuries: THROAT AND MOUTH – OVERDOSE – SORE MOUTH AND NOSEBLEEDS

Reported: [1995] CLY 1823

JSB Category:

Sex: Male

Age at injury: 14

Age at award: 16

Date of award: 16 May 1995

Tribunal: Ilford County Court

Amount of award then: £2,750

Award at February 2001: £3,162

Description of injuries: Male suffered from acute lymphoblastic leukaemia – plaintiff's pharmacist wrongly directed him to take eight doses of methotrexate every day – appropriate dosage was eight doses a week – plaintiff received 12 doses of drug over 12 days and suffered initially from sore throat and mouth and nose bleeds – was unable to eat or swallow and was admitted to hospital – diagnosed as suffering from pancytopenia, i.e. severe anaemia, a very low platelet count and a very low white cell count – on examination plaintiff had dry cracked lips and large necrotic ulcers inside both cheeks and on his tongue – received intravenous antibiotics, platelet and blood transfusions and after seven days in hospital was discharged – on discharge it was noted that mouth ulcers were healing well and that he was eating and drinking.

1.3.1.C34 Case No. 11031

Name of case: Paul v Payne

Brief description of injuries: NECK – MILD WHIPLASH – LARGELY RESOLVED IN 2 WEEKS – OCCASIONAL TWINGES THEREAFTER

Reported: Kemp & Kemp, K2-046; [1995] CLY 1783

JSB Category: 6(A)(c)

Sex: Female

Age at injury: 37

Age at award: 38

Date of award: 03 February 1995

Tribunal: Epsom County Court

Amount of award then: £2,700

Award at February 2001: £3,161

Description of injuries: Plaintiff suffered mild whiplash injury to neck and pain in left shoulder in road traffic accident – during first week after accident unable to do any housework or shopping – symptoms improved in second week although she continued to suffer sleep disturbances and nightmares – throughout the two weeks she took analgesics regularly, following which symptoms largely resolved – twelve months after accident still suffered occasional twinges and stiffness in neck.

1.3.1.C35 Case No. 12034

Name of case: Mamczynski v GM Buses (North) Ltd

Brief description of injuries: NECK – 21 MONTHS

Reported: Kemp & Kemp, E2-115/5; [2000] 5 CL 178

JSB Category: 6(A)(c)

Sex: Female

Age at injury: 47

Age at award: 49

Date of award: 11 January 2000

Tribunal: Oldham County Court

Amount of award then: £3,000

Award at February 2001: £3,097

Description of injuries: Acute neck sprain to the right side of the neck – constant pain for about four weeks – thereafter intermittent pain radiating into the shoulder – difficulty in driving, writing, carrying – nervous in traffic.

Prognosis: She was expected to be symptoms-free within twenty-one months of the date of the accident – fully recovered within a short time of the hearing.

1.3.1.C36 Case No. 11033

Name of case: Tiwana v Heir

Brief description of injuries: NECK AND BACK – PAIN AND STIFFNESS – 12 MONTHS

Reported: Kemp & Kemp, K2-056; [1995] CLY 1785

JSB Category: 6(A)(c)

Sex: Female

Age at injury: 26

Age at award: -

Date of award: 18 April 1995

Tribunal: West Bromwich County Court

Amount of award then: £2,500

Award at February 2001: £2,886

Description of injuries: Plaintiff driver's car was hit by defendant's car on front offside of her vehicle – experienced constant pain and stiffness in neck, upper back, middle back and right shoulders for 10 days – suffered from torn muscles in upper back and spine – had intermittent pain for next 12 months, particularly when carrying heavy loads – plaintiff could not participate in main hobby of swimming for eight months and was nervous of driving for 12 months – almost complete recovery by date of hearing.

1.3.1.C37 Case No. 11032

Name of case: Pearce v Abraham Shaw & Co
Brief description of injuries: NECK AND SHOULDER PAIN – 2 YEARS
Reported: Kemp & Kemp, E2-119; [1995] CLY 1784
JSB Category: 6(A)(c)
Sex: Female
Age at injury: 15
Age at award: 16
Date of award: 08 August 1995
Tribunal: Halifax County Court
Amount of award then: £2,500
Award at February 2001: £2,869

Description of injuries: Schoolgirl struck by vehicle whilst pedestrian and attended Accident and Emergency Department of local hospital complaining of pain in neck and right shoulder – supplied with neck collar and absent from school for one week – had difficulty bathing and washing hair for few weeks after accident – keen horse rider and usually rode about five times a week – unable to ride at all for about three months, although at date of hearing she was riding without difficulty – six months after accident she still suffered some aching in shoulder and neck, which was aggravated by cold weather.

Prognosis: It was expected that aching in shoulder and neck would resolve over following six to 12 months.

1.3.1.C38 Case No. 11346

Name of case: Owen v Prior
Brief description of injuries: NECK – 16 MONTHS
Reported: Kemp & Kemp, PRK-057; [1997] CLY 1894
JSB Category: 6(A)(c)
Sex: Male
Age at injury: 18
Age at award: 19
Date of award: 28 May 1997
Tribunal: Wigan County Court
Amount of award then: £2,600
Award at February 2001: £2,850

Description of injuries: Acute neck sprain and soft-tissue injuries to the spine.

Prognosis: Full recovery was expected within sixteen months of the date of the accident.

1.3.1.C39 Case No. 12038

Name of case: Newton v Whittaker
Brief description of injuries: NECK – 2 YEARS
Reported: Kemp & Kemp, K2-058; [2000] 5 CL 182
JSB Category: 6(A)(c)
Sex: Male
Age at injury: 51
Age at award: 53
Date of award: 07 January 2000
Tribunal: Sheffield County Court (Hawksworth J)
Amount of award then: £2,750
Award at February 2001: £2,839

Description of injuries: A jerking action to the neck – significant pain radiating to the shoulder and arm for about four weeks – residual discomfort for up to two years after the accident. No time taken off work – one session of physiotherapy – about five visits to a chiropractor one year after the date of the accident.

1.3.1.C40 Case No. 11226

Name of case: Mason v Car Collection Services
Brief description of injuries: NECK – WHIPLASH – 10-11 MONTHS
Reported: Kemp & Kemp, E3-119; [1996] CLY 2318
JSB Category: 6(A)(c)
Sex: Female
Age at injury: 36
Age at award: 37
Date of award: 12 October 1995
Tribunal: Gloucester County Court
Amount of award then: £2,350
Award at February 2001: £2,698

Description of injuries: Acute whiplash to the cervical spine – tearing of the cervical muscles – exacerbation of pre-existing condition of the lumbar spine – neck symptoms were resolved within ten to eleven months of the date of the accident – back returned to normal within the same time span.

1.3.1.C41 Case No. 10764

Name of case: Hawkeswood v Lewis

Brief description of injuries: NECK – INJURY – PAIN FOR 12 WEEKS – DULL ACHING THEREAFTER

Reported: Kemp & Kemp, E2-123; [1994] CLY 1612, 1714

JSB Category: 6(A)(c)

Sex: Female

Age at injury: 19

Age at award: 21

Date of award: 24 June 1994

Tribunal: Chesterfield County Court

Amount of award then: £2,250

Award at February 2001: £2,674

Description of injuries: Road accident – soft-tissue injury to neck – physiotherapy and collar prescribed; off work 1 week – pain and discomfort for 12 months, exacerbated in course of work as keyboard operator – wish to stop driving, and pain when turning head when manoeuvring, led claimant to sell car – after initial 12-month period, pain manifested as dull ache at least once a week – able to return to work, but occasional pain and problems experienced while working.

Prognosis: Symptoms of dull ache likely to continue for foreseeable future.

1.3.1.C42 Case No. 11035

Name of case: Bullard v Thomas

Brief description of injuries: NECK AND SHOULDER – SYMPTOMS FOR 13 MONTHS

Reported: Kemp & Kemp, E2-125; [1995] CLY 1788

JSB Category: 6(A)(c)

Sex: Female

Age at injury: 52

Age at award: 53

Date of award: 20 September 1995

Tribunal: Barnet County Court

Amount of award then: £2,250

Award at February 2001: £2,570

Description of injuries: Plaintiff suffered jolting injury to neck causing soft-tissue strain and exacerbating pre-existing dormant degenerative disc condition – also suffered jarring injury to left shoulder area – for two weeks neck symptoms were particularly troublesome, thereafter improving although continuing to be troublesome on occasion – she also suffered general aches and pains for few days, intermittent paratheseae in left arm for four to six weeks and anxiety when driving – symptoms faded and settled in the course of 13 months.

1.3.1.C43 Case No. 10359

Name of case: Darby v Marconi Electronic Devices

Brief description of injuries: NECK – BURN

Reported: Kemp & Kemp, C5-070; [1992] CLY 1615

JSB Category: 8(v)

Sex: Female

Age at injury: 41

Age at award: 45

Date of award: 01 April 1992

Tribunal: Lincoln County Court

Amount of award then: £1,750

Award at February 2001: £2,169

Description of injuries: Hydrofluoric burn to the left side of the neck.

Prognosis: Discomfort from the burn for six months – embarrassed by the three-quarter inch scar which was clearly visible and not susceptible to masking with cosmetics.

1.3.1.C44 Case No. 11060

Name of case: Nicholson v Oakleaf Conservatories

Brief description of injuries: NECK AND CHEST – PAIN AND STIFFNESS – 1 YEAR

Reported: Kemp & Kemp, K2-102; [1995] CLY 1814

JSB Category: 6(A)(c)

Sex: Male

Age at injury: 48

Age at award: 49

Date of award: 05 May 1995

Tribunal: Leeds County Court

Amount of award then: £1,850

Award at February 2001: £2,127

Description of injuries: Plaintiff in road traffic – next day experienced pain and stiffness down left side of his neck and left shoulder girdle and visited his GP who examined him and diagnosed whiplash injury – was given non-steroidal anti-inflammatory drug for pain relief – did not take any time off work – work caused pain in neck and around shoulder – sleep was disturbed for two nights, restricted from playing golf and could not resume hobby of weight training – at time of trial, approximately one year later, symptoms had resolved themselves – however, experienced difficulty when playing golf and weight training.

Damage to Spine

1.3.1.C45 Case No. 11044

Name of case: Crump v Rickwood

Brief description of injuries: NECK – STIFFNESS FOR 5-6 MONTHS

Reported: Kemp & Kemp, E2-131; [1995] CLY 1798

JSB Category: 6(A)(c)

Sex: Male

Age at injury: 29

Age at award: 31

Date of award: 12 December 1994

Tribunal: Reading County Court

Amount of award then: £1,500

Award at February 2001: £1,767

Description of injuries: Male in road traffic accident suffered whiplash type injury and cut fingers when he raised his hands to prevent radio, which had separated itself from dashboard, hitting head – awoke next morning with very stiff neck and attended GP, who advised rest and prescribed analgesics – absent from work one week – for five to six months suffered slight pain in neck when driving for more than three hours, but his work as bus driver was not affected – pain required no treatment and complete recovery was made after six months – plaintiff had to use public transport for seven weeks which lengthened his journey by an hour-and-a-half, and had to curtail his hobby of fishing while being without a car.

1.3.1.C46 Case No. 11041

Name of case: Sharp v MTL Trust Holdings

Brief description of injuries: NECK – WHIPLASH (2 WEEKS) – PSORIASIS (3 MONTHS)

Reported: Kemp & Kemp, K2-131; [1995] CLY 1795

JSB Category: 6(A)(c)

Sex: Female

Age at injury: 44

Age at award: 45

Date of award: 19 June 1995

Tribunal: Liverpool County Court

Amount of award then: £1,500

Award at February 2001: £1,722

Description of injuries: Plaintiff driving along motorway when window of a bus was blown out and struck her motor car – made emergency stop with no collision with any other vehicle – suffered whiplash-type injury necessitating soft collar and additional pain-killing medication – pain continued for two to three months and then intermittently for further two months – sprained right ankle when braking – resolved after two weeks – suffered considerable shock and distress, causing flare up of psoriasis along hairline and two small patches on face – hair hid psoriasis along the hairline but it was uncomfortable when she brushed her hair – psoriasis normally affected knees and hands – psoriasis resolved after three months.

1.3.1.C47 Case No. 11040

Name of case: Howell v Deans

Brief description of injuries: NECK AND CHEST – SOFT-TISSUE INJURIES – 6 MONTHS

Reported: Kemp & Kemp, E3-124; [1995] CLY 1794

JSB Category: 6(A)(c)

Sex: Female

Age at injury: 24

Age at award: 26

Date of award: 22 September 1995

Tribunal: Redditch County Court

Amount of award then: £1,500

Award at February 2001: £1,713

Description of injuries: Female travelling as back-seat passenger with her seatbelt fastened when car was hit from behind – upper body jerked backwards and forwards and she was shocked and shaken – woke following morning with pains at back of neck, across front of chest and over lower back which got progressively worse, prompting visit to hospital two days after accident – diagnosed as having suffered: trauma to cervical spine leading to soft-tissue and ligamentous injury producing pain and stiffness of movement in neck; bruising to front of chest; ligamentous injury resulting in pain and restricted movements of lumbo-sacral spine – emotionally shaken and distressed by accident and injuries, and it took several days for emotional effects to disappear – wore soft collar support for four weeks and was given analgesics – two months after accident experienced pains over lower back if sitting for any length of time – plaintiff unable to carry out aerobic exercises for several weeks and had difficulty lifting stock in course of part-time job after accident – plaintiff had completely recovered within six months of accident.

1.3.1.C48 Case No. 11245

Name of case: Lamb v Turner

Brief description of injuries: NECK – 10 MONTHS

Reported: Kemp & Kemp, E2-133; [1996] CLY 2337

JSB Category: 6(A)(c)

Sex: Female

Age at injury: 39

Age at award: 40

Date of award: 06 March 1996

Tribunal: Tunbridge Wells County Court

Amount of award then: £1,500

Award at February 2001: £1,703

Description of injuries: Neck injury – no symptoms after ten months.

1.3.1.C49 Case No. 11246

Name of case: Jachim and Martin v Barrett

Brief description of injuries: NECK – 10 WEEKS

Reported: Kemp & Kemp, K2-135; [1996] CLY 2338

JSB Category: 6(A)(c)

Sex: Male

Age at injury: 62

Age at award: 64

Date of award: 01 October 1996

Tribunal: Manchester County Court

Amount of award then: £1,500

Award at February 2001: £1,678

Description of injuries: Lateral flexion soft-tissue neck injury – full recovery within ten weeks.

1.3.1.C50 Case No. 11248

Name of case: Davies v Dorman

Brief description of injuries: NECK – SOFT-TISSUE STRAIN – 12 MONTHS

Reported: Kemp & Kemp, K2-133; [1996] CLY 2340

JSB Category: 6(A)(c)

Sex: Male

Age at injury: 35

Age at award: 38

Date of award: 30 September 1996

Tribunal: Holywell County Court

Amount of award then: £1,500

Award at February 2001: £1,678

Description of injuries: Soft-tissue strain to the neck – jarring to the lower back – full recovery took place within twelve months of the date of the accident.

1.3.1.C51 Case No. 11046

Name of case: Green v Stewart

Brief description of injuries: NECK – WHIPLASH – 14 MONTHS

Reported: Kemp & Kemp, E2-139; [1995] CLY 1800

JSB Category: 6(A)(c)

Sex: Female

Age at injury: 64

Age at award: 67

Date of award: 15 March 1995

Tribunal: Burnley County Court

Amount of award then: £1,250

Award at February 2001: £1,458

Description of injuries: Plaintiff suffered whiplash injury in road traffic accident – developed an immediate headache – later that evening had pain in neck described as "burning sensation" – headache lasted for two days and neck pain two weeks – during two-week period plaintiff was able to continue her household tasks but noticed a "pulling sensation" in neck whilst hoovering – sleep was disturbed – took painkillers throughout the two weeks – thereafter symptoms gradually diminished – but experienced recurrent periods of pain, lasting for approximately two days on each occasion, for 14 months after accident.

1.3.1.C52 Case No. 11725

Name of case: Kataria v Arpino

Brief description of injuries: NECK

Reported: Kemp & Kemp, E2-139/1; [1998] CLY 1728

JSB Category: 6(A)(c)

Sex: Female

Age at injury: 33

Age at award: -

Date of award: 08 December 1997

Tribunal: Watford County Court

Amount of award then: £1,250

Award at February 2001: £1,344

Description of injuries: Stiffness to the neck – K still suffered the occasional twinge at date of hearing.

1.3.1.C53 Case No. 11049

Name of case: Flaherty v Catley

Brief description of injuries: NECK – WHIPLASH – 8 WEEKS

Reported: Kemp & Kemp, K2-174; [1995] CLY 1803

JSB Category: 6(A)(c)

Sex: Male

Age at injury: 32

Age at award: 33

Date of award: 11 May 1995

Tribunal: Birkenhead County Court

Amount of award then: £1,100

Award at February 2001: £1,265

Description of injuries: Plaintiff suffered whiplash injury – prescribed Ibuprofen Plus– was in severe pain for 7-10 days and some pain persisted in neck, particularly after using computer for long periods – residual symptoms resolved after another four to eight weeks – by time of assessment plaintiff had made full recovery from all physical injuries.

1.3.1.C54 Case No. 11895

Name of case: Charlton v AAH plc

Brief description of injuries: NECK – DISCOMFORT

Reported: Kemp & Kemp, K2-176/1; [1999] CLY 1559

JSB Category: 6(A)(c); 3(A)(d)

Sex: Male

Age at injury: 53

Age at award: 54

Date of award: 25 November 1998

Tribunal: Reading County Court

Amount of award then: £1,200

Award at February 2001: £1,255

Description of injuries: Considerable stiffness in neck immediately following road accident – discomfort at back of neck, resolving in a week – occasional symptoms persisting for 6 months; discomfort in neck after working at screen; monthly occipital headaches – on examination 3 months after accident, some discomfort noted at extremes of rotation – claimant disinclined to take drugs and did not take any analgesics – almost 2 years later, claimant still felt uncomfortable after watching television at an angle for any extended period – continuing pronounced wariness when driving.

1.3.1.C55 Case No. 11909

Name of case: Attwood v Woodward

Brief description of injuries: NECK INJURY – 1 YEAR

Reported: Kemp & Kemp, K2-176/2; [1999] CLY 1573

JSB Category: 6(A)(c)

Sex: Female

Age at injury: 17

Age at award: 22

Date of award: 11 December 1998

Tribunal: Southend County Court

Amount of award then: £1,200

Award at February 2001: £1,255

Description of injuries: Road accident – minor soft-tissue injury to neck, also bruising to upper part of right leg – head jolted from side to side by force of impact – claimant attended hospital later that day after developing headaches and feeling generally unwell – no physical injuries noted on examination, but claimant provided with collar; collar worn and analgesics taken for 10-14 days – acute phase of injury lasted no longer than 3 weeks – claimant suffered occasional grating in neck, a minor but continued inconvenience until she was involved in another road accident approximately 1 year later – claimant also noticed that neck became painful on sitting for an hour or more and symptoms were affected by colder weather – claimant did not take any time off work, and sporting hobbies not affected.

1.3.1.C56 Case No. 11050

Name of case: Evans v Jibb

Brief description of injuries: NECK – WHIPLASH – NECK, BACK, HEADACHES – 2 WEEKS

Reported: Kemp & Kemp, E2-141; [1995] CLY 1804

JSB Category: 6(A)(c)

Sex: Female

Age at injury: 33

Age at award: 34

Date of award: 16 October 1995

Tribunal: Bolton County Court

Amount of award then: £1,000

Award at February 2001: £1,148

Description of injuries: Plaintiff was front seat passenger a car involved in road traffic accident – car in which she was travelling was hit from behind whilst stationary – wearing seatbelt – neck ached straight away – taken to hospital and soft cervical collar was fitted and worn for four days – continuous headaches for about four days and then symptoms gradually eased until two weeks after date of accident when symptom free – had backache for one week and bruising to back of head where it hit headrest – pain was moderate.

1.3.1.C57 Case No. 11261

Name of case: Re JK

Brief description of injuries: NECK – BRUISING – CHIPPED TOOTH

Reported: (1996) 96 (4) QB 3; Kemp & Kemp, K2-198; [1996] CLY 2353

JSB Category: 2(B)

Sex: Female

Age at injury: 36

Age at award: 40

Date of award: 08 May 1996

Tribunal: CICB, London

Amount of award then: £1,000

Award at February 2001: £1,125

Description of injuries: Bruising to the neck and thighs – chip to a front tooth – head injury – no neurological sequelae.

Prognosis: A full recovery would be made.

Other points: She was not eligible for an award under the 1990 scheme – satisfied the criteria under the 1995 scheme.

1.3.1.C58 Case No. 11334

Name of case: Rowland v Matthews
Brief description of injuries: NECK – WHIPLASH – 5 DAYS
Reported: Kemp & Kemp, K2-201; [1997] CLY 1882
JSB Category: 6(A)(c)
Sex: Male
Age at injury: 33
Age at award: 34
Date of award: 02 January 1997
Tribunal: Stockport County Court
Amount of award then: £1,000
Award at February 2001: £1,114
Description of injuries: Minor whiplash type injury to the neck and shoulder – symptom-free after five days.

1.3.1.C59 Case No. 11734

Name of case: Dopson v Oscar Faber Group Ltd
Brief description of injuries: NECK – 5 MONTHS
Reported: Kemp & Kemp, K2-221/1; [1998] CLY 1737
JSB Category: 6(A)(c)
Sex: Female
Age at injury: 39
Age at award: 40
Date of award: 13 July 1998
Tribunal: Swindon County Court
Amount of award then: £900
Award at February 2001: £950
Description of injuries: Pain in neck – claimant generally shaken – all symptoms had fully resolved within 5 months of the date of the accident.

1.3.1.C60 Case No. 11735

Name of case: Taylor v Turner
Brief description of injuries: NECK – 4 MONTHS
Reported: Kemp & Kemp, K2-230/1; [1998] CLY 1738
JSB Category: 6(A)(c)
Sex: Male
Age at injury: 46
Age at award: 47
Date of award: 30 June 1998
Tribunal: Stoke on Trent County Court
Amount of award then: £850
Award at February 2001: £895
Description of injuries: Minor soft-tissue injuries to the cervical spine – 4 months after the date of the accident T had fully recovered.

1.3.1.C61 Case No. 10516

Name of case: Tuckerman v Moy Park
Brief description of injuries: CHOKING – SORE THROAT 3 DAYS
Reported: Kemp & Kemp, K2-235; [1992] CLY 1772
JSB Category:
Sex: Male
Age at injury: 19
Age at award: -
Date of award: 17 January 1992
Tribunal: Slough County Court
Amount of award then: £700
Award at February 2001: £888
Description of injuries: Choked on a two-inch long elastic band – suffered a sore throat for three days – remained anxious about swallowing a foreign object again.
Prognosis: No medical evidence.

1.3.1.C62 Case No. 11064

Name of case: Paxton v Newman
Brief description of injuries: NECK AND BACK – MINOR WHIPLASH – 2 WEEKS
Reported: Kemp & Kemp, K2-238; [1995] CLY 1818
JSB Category: 6(A)(c)
Sex: Male
Age at injury: 15
Age at award: 17
Date of award: 20 April 1995
Tribunal: Exeter County Court
Amount of award then: £750
Award at February 2001: £866
Description of injuries: In road traffic accident plaintiff minor whiplash injury – on day of accident, attended casualty department of local hospital, reporting pain in cervical spine and lower back – upon examination, was found to have full mobility in lumbar spine and no symptoms in legs – as result of accident, was unable to return to sporting activities at school for period of one week – moreover, some 10 days after accident, experienced pain in left side of lower back whilst jogging – subsequently attended local casualty department again and was advised to rest – refrained from any sporting activities for another two weeks – after two-week rest period, reported having no further problems with back or neck. was not expected to suffer any long term sequelae as a result of accident.

Damage to Spine

1.3.1.C63 Case No. 11067

Name of case: Yates v Dowdeswell

Brief description of injuries: NECK – WHIPLASH – 8 DAYS

Reported: Kemp & Kemp, E3-127; [1995] CLY 1821

JSB Category: 6(A)(c)

Sex: Female

Age at injury: 38

Age at award: 39

Date of award: 24 October 1995

Tribunal: Birkenhead County Court

Amount of award then: £500

Award at February 2001: £574

Description of injuries: Plaintiff involved in road traffic accident when her motorvehicle was struck in rear by another motorvehicle – sustained a flexion/hypertension injury to cervical spine, causing pain and stiffness – symptom-free after eight days – one day off work.

1.3.1.C64 Case No. 10129

Name of case: Hope v Money

Brief description of injuries: NECK – FRICTION BURN

Reported: [1990] CLY 1708

JSB Category: 6(A)

Sex: Male, female

Age at injury: 3.5;2.5

Age at award: -;-

Date of award: 26 September 1990

Tribunal: Basingstoke County Court

Amount of award then: £350

Award at February 2001: £466

Description of injuries: In road traffic accident boy suffered friction burn to left of his neck from seat strap – this healed without a scar within one week – his sleep became disrupted – girl bumped her head on seat but otherwise no obvious physical injuries – her sleep patterns became disrupted and there were bedwetting problems – both children seemed fully recovered by the date of the trial.

1.3.1.C65 Case No. 10130

Name of case: Wright v Cole

Brief description of injuries: NECK – STIFFNESS 2 WEEKS

Reported: [1990] CLY 1711

JSB Category: 6(A)

Sex: Male

Age at injury: 50

Age at award: 51

Date of award: 27 March 1990

Tribunal: Walsall County Court

Amount of award then: £200

Award at February 2001: £283

Description of injuries: After road traffic accident neck felt stiff – pain interrupted sleep for a week – chest bruising became apparent after four/five days – no time taken off work – neck stiffness resolved itself within fortnight of accident – no further problems.

1.3.1.C66 Case No. 11349

Name of case: Johnson v Sidaway

Brief description of injuries: NECK – 24 HOURS

Reported: Kemp & Kemp, K2-270; [1997] CLY 1897

JSB Category: 6(A)(c)

Sex: Male

Age at injury: 28

Age at award: -

Date of award: 13 May 1997

Tribunal: Gloucester County Court

Amount of award then: £250

Award at February 2001: £274

Description of injuries: Stiffness and mild discomfort to the neck – all symptoms had resolved within twenty-four hours of the accident.

1.3.1.C67 Case No. 11739

Name of case: Tyrone v Broadfoot

Brief description of injuries: NECK – 7 DAYS

Reported: Kemp & Kemp, K2-273; [1998] CLY 1742

JSB Category: 6(A)(c)

Sex: Male

Age at injury: Early twenties

Age at award:

Date of award: 16 January 1998

Tribunal: Rawtenstall County Court

Amount of award then: £200

Award at February 2001: £216

Description of injuries: Neck pain – shocked and shaken – pain lasted for about 1 week.

1.3.1.1 NECK AND OTHER INURY

1.3.1.1.C1 Case No. 11272

Name of case: Re Martin

Brief description of injuries: NECK – THROAT – TRACHEOSTOMY – DEPRESSION

Reported: (1996) 96 (1) QR 4; Kemp & Kemp, E2-003;[1996] CLY 2365

JSB Category: 5

Sex: Male

Age at injury: -

Age at award: 57

Date of award: 12 December 1995

Tribunal: CICB, London

Amount of award then: £55,000

Award at February 2001: £70,465

Description of injuries: Twenty seven stab wounds – most serious to the neck – psychological trauma – unable to breathe adequately without a tracheostomy tube – only able to speak very quietly – unable to resume his employment – severely depressed.

1.3.1.1.C2 Case No. 10619

Name of case: Shaw v Wirral Health Authority

Brief description of injuries: ARMS – BRACHIAL PLEXUS INJURY

Reported: [1993] 4 Med LR 275; Kemp & Kemp, H2-012; [1993] CLY 1514

JSB Category: 6(F)(a); 3(A)

Sex: Female

Age at injury: 49

Age at award: 53

Date of award: 05 February 1993

Tribunal: Liverpool High Court

Amount of award then: £45,000

Award at February 2001: £61,685

Description of injuries: Injury to nerves running from brachial plexus and cervical plexus affecting dominant right arm – winging of right scapula evident – lack of action of subscapular muscle – wasting of supraspinatus, infraspinatus and deltoid muscles in right shoulder – no activity in trapezius muscle – inability to carry out active movement in right arm or shoulder; arm immobile at side, dead weight of it causing constant background pain – also spasms of pain between shoulder blades, radiating to neck and waist, when either arm moved – right fingers swollen and spindly with reduced perfusion; skin cold to touch – function in left arm limited to light activities – misery and depression, feeling of having changed beyond recognition; undergoing psychological counselling – sleeping difficulties – self-care difficulties – social life severely affected to point of non-existence – retired on grounds of ill-health after accident – psychological counselling ongoing at time of trial.

Prognosis: Possibility of future treatment to improve useful function of left arm, and thus quality of life, has 60 per cent chance of success – no chance of improving movement in right arm.

1.3.1.1.C3 Case No. 10693

Name of case: Jones v Pandis

Brief description of injuries: SKIN – PSORIASIS – NECK

Reported: [1993] CLY 1590

JSB Category:

Sex: Female

Age at injury: 41

Age at award: 46

Date of award: 28 May 1993

Tribunal: Middlesbrough/Newcastle County Court

Amount of award then: £28,000

Award at February 2001: £36,034

Description of injuries: Road accident – soft-tissue injury to muscles and ligaments of neck – movement still very restricted 1 year after injury – some pain still virtually constant in neck and shoulder 22 months after injury – episodic pain, lasting up to 3 weeks but decreasing in frequency, present 4 years after incident and improving further by date of trial – development of psoriasis, apparent 6 months after accident and triggered by stress – initially affected palms – condition deteriorated just under 3 years later, spreading over feet and with outbreak of lesions all over skin – palms remained most seriously affected; difficulties observed at medical examination in moving hands – claimant kept working until date of trial, despite medical opinion that most people in similar situation would stop, due to love of the job and uncertainty over level of damages forthcoming – inability to pursue hobbies and activities, go out, carry out household tasks or read (due to pain involved in turning pages) – insomnia – inability to bear being cuddled by husband – foreign family holiday an ordeal, as unable to cope with heat or go swimming and forced to keep hands and feet covered.

Prognosis: Prognosis of development of exacerbations for many years – condition likely to be difficult to treat – possible necessity for potentially dangerous cyto-toxic drugs (which can cause bone marrow depression or acute liver failure – 20 per cent of patients have to stop taking such medication due to side effects) – prospects of ever finding alternative employment accepted by judge to be bleak.

Damage to Spine

1.3.1.1.C4 Case No. 10219

Name of case: Smith v Ainger and O'Donnell

Brief description of injuries: OESOPHAGUS – SEVERE DAMAGE

Reported: (1990) The Times, 5 June; Kemp & Kemp, F3-012/1; BPILS, VIII 3005; XI4024; [1991] CLY 1416

JSB Category: 5(D)(a)

Sex: Male

Age at injury: 18 months

Age at award: 6

Date of award: 08 July 1991

Tribunal: QBD

Amount of award then: £25,000

Award at February 2001: £33,780

Description of injuries: Severe damage to the oesophagus after swallowing a caustic fluid – multiple operations under full general endotracheal anaesthesia – made a good recovery from the operations but suffered "dumping".

Prognosis: S had learned how to control his symptoms through diet and sensible eating habits – halitosis would be a permanent problem.

1.3.1.1.C5 Case No. 10066

Name of case: Wolf v Anafield Builders

Brief description of injuries: SPINAL INJURY – FRACTURED VERTEBRA – RESIDUAL WEAKNESS

Reported: Kemp & Kemp, E2-005; [1990] CLY 1626

JSB Category: 6(B)

Sex: Female

Age at injury: 36

Age at award: 40

Date of award: 04 December 1989

Tribunal: Not stated

Amount of award then: £20,000

Award at February 2001: £30,222

Description of injuries: Sustained burst fracture of sixth cervical vertebra – close to tetraplegia but made remarkable recovery – left with residual weakness in left arm and fingers – pain in neck.

Prognosis: Head and neck tired easily with restricted motion – degenerative changes likely to develop rapidly at age 60 – hopes of having children (now at age 40) were uncertain.

1.3.1.1.C6 Case No. 11804

Name of case: Moseley v London Underground Ltd

Brief description of injuries: NECK – PROLAPSED DISC – DEPRESSION

Reported: [1999] CLY 1467

JSB Category: 6(A)(b); 3(A)

Sex: Male

Age at injury: 32

Age at award: 37

Date of award: 26 February 1999

Tribunal: QBD

Amount of award then: £25,000

Award at February 2001: £27,250

Description of injuries: Prolapsed invertebral disc at C3/C4 level; tearing of fibres allowing material to escape from C3/C4 and directly compress the spinal cord in localised areas, causing some irreversible damage – also disruption of disc base at C4/C5; not possible for one vertebra to be rotated on another without putting similar force on the one adjacent – anterior decompression and fusion undergone 4 months after accident; deemed successful – claimant able to walk, drive, climb stairs, dress himself, cook and go shopping, all with some stiffness and restriction of movement, after operation – chronic pain, varying in intensity – necessary to sleep on floor to ease back problems – only limited movement in cervical spine – claimant formerly very physically active and fit – initially regarded as physically fit for light work after operation, but unconnected heart problems emerging 5 years after accident further restricted employment options open to him – development of depressive illness – frustration with condition – boredom – headaches – variations in appetite – sleeping difficulties – withdrawnness – irritability – excessive drinking – loss of interest in things, long periods spent watching television.

Prognosis: Significantly increased risk of surgery being required in the future – finding of 70 per cent chance of improvement in psychological symptoms with treatment.

1.3.1.1.C7 Case No. 11371

Name of case: Waxman v Scrivens

Brief description of injuries: NECK – BACK – POST-TRAUMATIC STRESS DISORDER

Reported: Kemp & Kemp, E3-013; [1997] CLY 1919

JSB Category: 6(B)(b)(i)

Sex: Female

Age at injury: 36

Age at award: 40

Date of award: 04 April 1997

Tribunal: Lincoln County Court

Amount of award then: £22,220

Award at February 2001: £25,264

Description of injuries: Soft-tissue injuries to the cervical spine – disc degeneration – disk prolapse – lumbar segmental instability – post-traumatic stress disorder.

Prognosis: The accident exacerbated existing low back and right-sided sciatica – but caused the disc prolapse – post-traumatic stress disorder resolved within five months.

1.3.1.1.C8 Case No. 10620

Name of case: Re Holton

Brief description of injuries: ARM – BRACHIAL PLEXUS INJURY

Reported: Kemp & Kemp, H2-016; [1993] CLY 1515

JSB Category: 6(F)(b)

Sex: Female

Age at injury: 28

Age at award: 35

Date of award: 27 April 1993

Tribunal: CICB, Manchester

Amount of award then: £18,000

Award at February 2001: £22,626

Description of injuries: Assault – extensive soft-tissue injury to shoulder, particularly to left brachial nerve root – constant and permanent pain in left shoulder and upper arm to elbow – pain radiating into dominant left hand when arm used – "pins and needles" in fingers – weakened grip – limitation of arm movements away from body – active leisure activities seriously curtailed – traction, physiotherapy and manipulation required indefinitely, increasing in frequency as each session increased muscle adhesion and accelerated relapse – valium prescribed as muscle relaxant.

Prognosis: Assessed 15 per cent disabled for life and unfit for work – on waiting list for pain management clinic.

1.3.1.1.C9 Case No. 10750

Name of case: Re Spearman (Sandra Jean)

Brief description of injuries: NECK – INJURY – DEPRESSION

Reported: Kemp & Kemp, E2-008; [1994] CLY 1598

JSB Category: 6(A)(b); 3(A)

Sex: Female

Age at injury: 39

Age at award: 47

Date of award: 02 November 1993

Tribunal: CICB, Durham

Amount of award then: £17,500

Award at February 2001: £21,804

Description of injuries: Claimant, nurse, attempted to stop two patients fighting – arm trapped between them, sending immediate pain travelling up arm and into neck – diagnosis of soft-tissue injury to C5/C6 disc with distortion of root fibres – initial prognosis of recovery within 2 years – symptoms persisted – claimant considered for spinal fusion, but no demonstrable surgical lesion or abnormality detected, so operation not performed – claimant eventually retired from work, as unable to lift loads or keep arm raised for any length of time – depression caused by continuing symptoms – prescribed imipramine as anti-depressant and pain reliever – claimant considerably disabled, physically and psychologically, by incident; psychological symptoms arose out physical ones – chronic depressive symptoms diagnosed, including at least one major depressive episode – other medical evidence concurred that claimant not consciously exaggerating symptoms.

Other points: Settled on appeal.

1.3.1.1.C10 Case No. 10381

Name of case: Martin v Ainscough

Brief description of injuries: SEVERE NECK INJURY – PULMONARY EMBOLISM

Reported: [1992] CLY 1637

JSB Category: 6(A)(a)(vi)

Sex: Female

Age at injury: 28

Age at award: 30

Date of award: 20 November 1991

Tribunal: Milton Keynes District Registry

Amount of award then: £16,500

Award at February 2001: £21,452

Description of injuries: Fracture of the odontoid process of axis – four days after the accident she suffered a pulmonary embolism – required immobilisation in a halo brace for two months – complicated by sickness and recurrent infection – somi brace worn for three months – cervical collar worn for three months – at the time of trial continued to experience stiffness and aching neck – numbness, pins and needles – weakness of the right arm – frustration and irritability – post-traumatic stress disorder.

Prognosis: Full recovery anticipated due to being motivated to mend.

1.3.1.1.C11 Case No. 10068

Name of case: Pedley v Timmins

Brief description of injuries: SPINAL INJURY – FRACTURED VERTEBRA

Reported: Kemp & Kemp, E3-028; [1990] CLY 1628

JSB Category: 6(B)

Sex: Female

Age at injury: 17

Age at award: 21

Date of award: 16 July 1990

Tribunal: Cambridge District Registry

Amount of award then: £14,000

Award at February 2001: £19,379

Description of injuries: Crush fracture on the first lumbar vertebra. Experienced 85 per cent loss of height at L1 and 30 per cent forward angulation of T12 and L1 – difficulty lifting and bending.

1.3.1.1.C12 Case No. 10707

Name of case: Riley v Graham

Brief description of injuries: NECK – FRACTURED VERTEBRA – DAMAGE TO KNEES

Reported: Kemp & Kemp, E3-037; [1994] CLY 1553

JSB Category: 6(A)(c), 6(D)(c), 6(L)

Sex: Male

Age at injury: 30

Age at award: 33

Date of award: 05 November 1993

Tribunal: Carlisle County Court

Amount of award then: £12,000

Award at February 2001: £14,724

Description of injuries: Road accident – compression fracture of eighth thoracic vertebra – seatbelt bruising over left side of neck, left collarbone and anterior aspect of chest – significant contusion to knees, causing crepitus and probably damaging articular cartilage – unable to pursue former employment as bricklayer, but subsequent to accident had obtained alternative, but uncertain, employment (at proposed expansion of nuclear plant) – unable to carry out DIY and decorating.

Prognosis: Balance of probability that claimant would develop localised osteoarthritis in both knees.

1.3.1.1.C13 Case No. 10069

Name of case: Hinnigan v Jackson

Brief description of injuries: SPINAL INJURY – FRACTURED VERTEBRA – CONSTANT PAIN

Reported: Kemp & Kemp, E3-046; [1990] CLY 1629

JSB Category: 6(B)

Sex: Female

Age at injury: 38

Age at award: 42

Date of award: 22 November 1990

Tribunal: QBD

Amount of award then: £10,000

Award at February 2001: £13,324

Description of injuries: Compression fracture of second lumbar vertebra. In constant pain – could not lift things and housework impossible – returned to work but needs help with lifting.

1.3.1.1.C14 Case No. 10198

Name of case: Mason v Norweb

Brief description of injuries: SOFT-TISSUE INJURIES TO THE NECK AND LOWER BACK – "CONSIDERABLE NUISANCE"

Reported: Kemp & Kemp, E3-044; [1991] CLY 1395

JSB Category: 6(A)(b)(i)

Sex: Female

Age at injury: 39

Age at award: 41

Date of award: 06 February 1991

Tribunal: QBD

Amount of award then: £10,000

Award at February 2001: £13,230

Description of injuries: Soft-tissue injuries to the neck and lower back on falling into a hole – M would be able to continue nursing until retirement age.

Prognosis: There would be no spontaneous improvement in the future – symptoms would be a "considerable nuisance".

1.3.1.1.C15 Case No. 10541

Name of case: Pegg v Denford Machine Tools

Brief description of injuries: NECK – DAMAGE TO CERVICAL CORD – WRIST – POST-TRAUMATIC STRESS DISORDER

Reported: Kemp & Kemp, E2-028; [1993] CLY 1434

JSB Category: 6(A)(b), 6(B), 6(H)(d); 3(B)

Sex: Male

Age at injury: 39

Age at award: 46

Date of award: 06 January 1993

Tribunal: Huddersfield County Court

Amount of award then: £10,000

Award at February 2001: £12,538

Description of injuries: Traumatic injury to lower part of cervical cord causing permanent impairment of sensation (but not grip) in right index finger and thumb (claimant right – handed), numbness or impairment of sensation in left leg and foot and impairment of sensation in urethra during ejaculation – soft-tissue injury to neck – fracture of distal radius or severe sprain of left wrist – post-traumatic stress disorder – sexual activity less frequent – only light duties at work – tires more easily – loss of "zest for life".

Prognosis: Injury to neck expected to resolve shortly after trial – full recovery expected from wrist injury – overall loss of efficiency of 5-10 per cent.

1.3.1.1.C16 Case No. 12036

Name of case: Corner v Osment

Brief description of injuries: NECK – WHIPLASH – DEPRESSION

Reported: Kemp & Kemp, E2-033/1; [2000] 5 CL 180

JSB Category: 6(A)(c) and 3(A)(c) and 3(B)(c)

Sex: Male

Age at injury: 48

Age at award: 51

Date of award: 15 December 1999

Tribunal: Brentford County Court

Amount of award then: £11,250

Award at February 2001: £11,603

Description of injuries: Bruising to the lower left leg – subungual haematoma – temporary loss of the big toe nail – whiplash type injury to C5/6 and C6/7 with exacerbation of a previously subsided crico-thyroid injury – headaches and post-traumatic stress disorder – anxious depression – uncharacteristic episodes of uncontrollable aggression.

Prognosis: C had an "egg-shell personality with extensive psychosomatic problems prior to the accident" – symptoms had improved but could continue indefinitely.

1.3.1.1.C17 Case No. 11993

Name of case: Rushton v Gee

Brief description of injuries: NECK – BACK – 7-9 YEARS

Reported: Kemp & Kemp, PRC-002; [2000] 3 CL 177

JSB Category: 6(A)(b)(ii) and 6(B)(c)

Sex: Male

Age at injury: 27

Age at award: 31

Date of award: 05 November 1999

Tribunal: Salford County Court

Amount of award then: £10,000

Award at February 2001: £10,320

Description of injuries: Soft-tissue injuries to the neck and lower back – three years and six months after the date of the accident he was suffering daily background neck pain with exacerbations causing pain lasting up to two weeks – constant lower back pain "like a bad bruise" – it was aggravated by activity – unable to return to his sporting activities – pilates treatment relieved pain for a few days – it would have been needed two or three times per week – frequent headaches two or three times a day were relieved by paracetamol.

Prognosis: At the time of the hearing the prognosis was for gradual improvement over three to five years.

1.3.1.1.C18 Case No. 10201

Name of case: Alsbury v Care

Brief description of injuries: WRENCHING INJURY TO THE CERVICAL SPINE – RECOVERY DELAYED BY ASSAULT

Reported: Kemp & Kemp, E2-041; [1991] CLY 1398

JSB Category: 6(A)(b)(i)

Sex: Male

Age at injury: 37

Age at award: 42

Date of award: 06 June 1991

Tribunal: Exeter County Court

Amount of award then: £7,700

Award at February 2001: £9,876

Description of injuries: A wrenching injury to the cervical spine – soft-tissue injury – off work for four months in 1987 due to pain – while the assault was the cause of his retirement the traffic accident had caused unpleasant and painful injury.

Prognosis: Recovery was anticipated during 1989 – but a later assault exacerbated the neck condition causing him to be medically retired.

1.3.1.1.C19 Case No. 11824

Name of case: Suttle v Amec Process & Energy Ltd

Brief description of injuries: NECK – BACK – 5 YEAR ACCELERATION

Reported: Kemp & Kemp, E3-069/2; [1999] CLY 1488

JSB Category: 6(B)(b)(ii)

Sex: Male

Age at injury: 32

Age at award: 35

Date of award: 22 December 1998

Tribunal: Central London County Court

Amount of award then: £9,000

Award at February 2001: £9,416

Description of injuries: Soft-tissue injury to neck and lumbar spine – claimant had difficulty controlling head due to neck pain – pain occasionally radiated to shoulder – stiffness, causing difficulty when driving – no paraesthesia or numbness – physiotherapy prescribed for neck and back injuries – neck injury virtually resolved after 7 months, and completely at time of trial, but low back pain ongoing – occasional sleep disturbance – prolonged activity difficult, and activities limited – pain worsened during day, especially bad in evenings, and exacerbated by periods of prolonged sitting – bending and lifting not possible – analgesics required at least every other day – claimant unable to continue with the numerous sporting activities he participated in prior to the injury – X-rays revealed degenerative lumbo – sacral disc, pre-dating the accident; assessed to have been exacerbated by the accident by a period of 5 years.

1.3.1.1.C20 Case No. 10756

Name of case: Bate v Department of Employment

Brief description of injuries: NECK AND BACK – LIGAMENT STRAIN – CONTINUING SYMPTOMS

Reported: Kemp & Kemp, E3-072; [1994] CLY 1604, 1625

JSB Category: 6(A); 6(B)

Sex: Female

Age at injury: 24

Age at award: 28

Date of award: 01 October 1993

Tribunal: Liverpool County Court

Amount of award then: £7,500

Award at February 2001: £9,097

Description of injuries: Claimant passenger in lift that dropped 2 floors and stopped suddenly – chronic ligamentous strains to neck and back – off work 7 weeks – pain in lower back and neck, even after course of physiotherapy, movements still full – neck pain became more constant, aggravated by housework – 9 hours' household assistance per week required – continuing, intermittent lower back pain – inability to lift heavy weights – reluctance to sit or stand still for long periods – physical signs, however, described as "minimal".

Prognosis: Symptoms expected to be permanent – no deterioration expected.

1.3.1.1.C21 Case No. 12052

Name of case: ATA v Hellen

Brief description of injuries: NECK – SHOULDER – KNEE

Reported: [2000] 6 CL 182

JSB Category: 6(A)(b)(ii)

Sex: Male

Age at injury: 21

Age at award: 24

Date of award: 13 January 2000

Tribunal: Wandsworth County Court

Amount of award then: £8,500

Award at February 2001: £8,776

Description of injuries: Initial impairment of vision – stiffness and pain to the neck and shoulder – knee swelling required four aspirations – no broken bones – analgesics were prescribed – a course of physiotherapy was undertaken – three weeks off work – crutches required for a short period.

Prognosis: At the time of the hearing residual neck symptoms were an intermittent nuisance – full recovery likely within six months.

1.3.1.1.C22 Case No. 12035

Name of case: Wesley v Cobb (deceased)

Brief description of injuries: NECK – MAJOR DEPRESSIVE EPISODE

Reported: Kemp & Kemp, PRC-009; [2000] 5 CL 179

JSB Category: 6(A)(b)(ii) 3(A)

Sex: Female

Age at injury: 41

Age at award: 46

Date of award: 19 January 2000

Tribunal: Altrincham County Court

Amount of award then: £8,500

Award at February 2001: £8,776

Description of injuries: Neck strain – major depressive episode and traffic phobia. The accident accelerated a pre-existing degenerative condition by about four years – major depressive episode and traffic phobia lasted for about twenty months.

1.3.1.1.C23 Case No. 10757

Name of case: Hillier v Karminski

Brief description of injuries: NECK – PAIN – INJURIES TO RIBS AND WRIST – HEADACHES

Reported: Kemp & Kemp, E2-052; [1994] CLY 1605

JSB Category: 6(A)(b), 6(H); 5(A); 3(B)(c); 2(B)

Sex: Male

Age at injury: 71

Age at award: 73

Date of award: 03 March 1994

Tribunal: Dartford County Court

Amount of award then: £7,000

Award at February 2001: £8,449

Description of injuries: Road accident – bruising to ribs – lacerations to wrist – soft-tissue injury to neck – development of dull frontal headaches, fairly constant – pain in neck at extremities of movement – unpleasant burning sensation in neck – post-traumatic stress disorder, described as "moderate" – nightmares relating to accident 3 or 4 times a month – loss of enjoyment of, and sense of purpose in, life – rib and wrist injuries settled after 3 months.

Prognosis: Symptoms in neck expected to be permanent – prognosis regarding psychological symptoms unclear; some improvement 2 years after date of accident possible.

1.3.1.1.C24 Case No. 11616

Name of case: Huntingdon v Armstrong

Brief description of injuries: BACK – NECK – 2.5 YEARS

Reported: Kemp & Kemp, E3-085/1; [1998] CLY 1618

JSB Category: 6(B)(b)(ii); 6(A)

Sex: Female

Age at injury: 29

Age at award: 34

Date of award: 17 June 1998

Tribunal: Sunderland County Court

Amount of award then: £8,000

Award at February 2001: £8,421

Description of injuries: Accident – symptoms noted in the neck – symptoms in the back and leg were noticed 3 months after the accident – pain in the neck cleared up after 2.5 years.

Prognosis: Symptoms of back pain were likely to persist indefinitely.

Other points: H did not mention back and leg pain to her GP until 5 months after the accident.

1.3.1.1.C25 Case No. 10308

Award at February 2001: £8,055

See: 1.2.3.1.C25 for details

1.3.1.1.C26 Case No. 10758

Name of case: Booth v Barruffo

Brief description of injuries: NECK INJURY EXACERBATING PRE-EXISTING CONDITION – PSYCHOLOGICAL REACTION – OTHER INJURIES

Reported: Kemp & Kemp, E3-091; [1994] CLY 1606

JSB Category: 6(A)(b); 3(A)

Sex: Female

Age at injury: 44

Age at award: 47

Date of award: 18 August 1994

Tribunal: Oldham County Court

Amount of award then: £6,500

Award at February 2001: £7,726

Description of injuries: Road accident – hyperflexion injury to cervical spine – strain to ligaments of lower part of back – pain and greatly restricted movement for 2 months – 6 months after accident, pain present daily from late afternoon until night – especially severe in back and left side of neck, and across both shoulders – neck movement restricted at extremes – 16 months after accident, pain still present when playing tennis or doing housework – examination found pre-existing degenerative arthritis in spine – claimant forced to give up ballet and embroidery, and ski at a lower level than previously – driving painful after an hour – psychological damage, found by court to be significant additional factor – loss of confidence – depression – tendency to relive accident, and daily thoughts about it – nervousness in cars, both as driver and passenger – also injuries to chest, right foot and left knee – chest injury caused 6 weeks acute pain, especially when breathing deeply, and some difficulty getting out of bed – foot and knee bruised for 2 weeks – momentary pain and giving-way of knee experienced 16 months after accident – chest symptoms resolved after 6 weeks.

Prognosis: Neck symptoms found to be permanent – pre-existing condition found to have been accelerated by 5 years – improvement in anxiety state likely by about 20 months, but claimant not expected to be as relaxed as prior to accident.

1.3.1.1.C27 Case No. 12043

Name of case: Havill v Wilson

Brief description of injuries: WRIST – NECK

Reported: Kemp & Kemp, H4-030; [2000] 5 CL 187

JSB Category: 6(H)(c)

Sex: Female

Age at injury: 27

Age at award: 29

Date of award: 15 December 1999

Tribunal: Bournemouth County Court

Amount of award then: £6,750

Award at February 2001: £6,940

Description of injuries: Injuries to the neck and wrists in a traffic accident – pain in the neck for four months – subsided by six months – continued pain to the wrists – wore splints at night and sometimes in the day – unable to cope fully with her duties as mother and child-minder.

Prognosis: W had noticed some small improvement – it was accepted that the problems were permanent.

1.3.1.1.C28 Case No. 11002

Name of case: Higton v Constance

Brief description of injuries: KNEE AND NECK – EXTENSIVE BRUISING – KNEE PAINFUL AND WEAKENED

Reported: Kemp & Kemp, F6-014; [1995] CLY 1754

JSB Category: 6(L)(b)(ii)

Sex: Male

Age at injury: 32

Age at award: 35

Date of award: 17 November 1994

Tribunal: Mansfield County Court

Amount of award then: £5,750

Award at February 2001: £6,807

Description of injuries: Plaintiff's vehicle was struck head-on – sustained extensive seatbelt bruising, bruised chest from contact with steering wheel, bruising to both knees and lacerations to forehead and right leg – admitted to hospital where his abrasions were dressed – later discharged – on returning home became aware of pain in neck but did not see his GP or return to hospital – work as miner was unaffected save he was limited to light duties for seven days – chest remained painful for two months, and laceration on forehead healed, leaving faint 2cm vertical scar which was not visible to naked eye by date of assessment – 20 months after accident, discomfort in left knee had resolved but right knee and neck still caused him some discomfort most days, starting at base of neck and spreading across shoulders and between shoulder blades – he did not suffer any headaches – right knee was painful on poor surfaces underground and continuing difficulties were ascribed to damage to patello-femoral joint and to medial ligament – there was measured two-and-a-half centimetre wasting of right thigh and one-and-a-half centimetre wasting on right calf, causing restriction of mobility – by date of assessment neck symptoms had improved gradually but there was still discomfort on specific activities such as tending coal fire.

Prognosis: Prognosis for neck was for further improvement, albeit gradual – symptoms in right knee had not improved and were not expected to do so – would not be able to return to pre-accident hobby of running.

1.3.1.1.C29 Case No. 10832

Name of case: Higton v Constance

Brief description of injuries: KNEE – NECK

Reported: Kemp & Kemp, F6-014; [1994] CLY 1681

JSB Category: 6(L)(b), 6(A)(c), 5(A)

Sex: Male

Age at injury: 32

Age at award: 35

Date of award: 17 November 1994

Tribunal: Mansfield County Court

Amount of award then: £5,750

Award at February 2001: £6,807

Description of injuries: Road accident – extensive seatbelt bruising – bruising to chest from impact with steering wheel – bruising to both knees – lacerations to forehead and right leg, which eventually healed without visible scarring – subsequent development of neck pain – light duties at work (as miner) for 7 days – discomfort in left knee resolved, but that in right knee and neck did not – pain starting at base of neck and spreading across shoulders between shoulder blades; no headaches – right knee painful on poor surfaces underfoot; continuing difficulties ascribed to damage to patello-femoral joint and medial ligament – measured 2.5cm wasting of right thigh and 1.5cm wasting of right calf, restricting mobility.

Prognosis: Neck symptoms had improved gradually by date of trial, apart from discomfort upon specific movements, and prognosis of further, albeit gradual, improvement – knee symptoms had not improved and were not expected to – claimant forced to give up hobby of running.

1.3.1.1.C30 Case No. 11961

Name of case: Goudie v Night Freight (East) Ltd

Brief description of injuries: NECK – WHIPLASH – ARM

Reported: Kemp & Kemp, E2-071/1; [2000] 1 CL 121

JSB Category: 6(A)(b)(i)

Sex: Male

Age at injury: 34

Age at award: 36

Date of award: 20 October 1999

Tribunal: Ipswich County Court

Amount of award then: £6,000

Award at February 2001: £6,198

Description of injuries: Injured in a traffic accident – multiple small lacerations which resolved within a few weeks – soft-tissue injuries to the right wrist and forearm and a whiplash injury – the arm injury caused pain for three months – fully resolved at the time of the hearing – whiplash injury caused immediate pain to both sides of the neck, both shoulders and between the shoulder blades – constant pain and restriction of movement in those areas.

Prognosis: G would continue to suffer pain to the neck and shoulder blades.

1.3.1.1.C31 Case No. 10606

Name of case: Re Gilchrist

Brief description of injuries: NECK – BACK – 5 YEAR ACCELERATION

Reported: Kemp & Kemp, E3-104; [1993] CLY 1499

JSB Category: 6(A), 6(B)

Sex: Female

Age at injury: 54

Age at award: 56

Date of award: 15 March 1993

Tribunal: CICB, London

Amount of award then: £5,000

Award at February 2001: £6,174

Description of injuries: Kicked in small of back – jarring injuries to cervical and lumbar spine – pain and stiffness in neck – severe pain in back aggravated by stooping, bending and lifting – pain on bowel movements related to lumbar injury – off work 4.5 months – physiotherapy and lumbar traction required – full recovery from neck injury within 3 months – continuing stiffness and pain in lower back at time of hearing, requiring analgesics every few days – upright seats and lying on stomach in bed preferred – returned to work on restricted/lighter duties – unable to pursue keep fit classes.

Prognosis: Assault had accelerated by 5 years natural onset of pre-existing degenerative changes in lower back.

1.3.1.1.C32 Case No. 10953

Name of case: Randall v Feredenzi and Tomlyn

Brief description of injuries: SOFT-TISSUE INJURIES – THORAX – NECK – LOW BACK

Reported: Kemp & Kemp, E2-075; [1995] CLY 1704

JSB Category:

Sex: Female

Age at injury: 43

Age at award: 45

Date of award: 25 November 1994

Tribunal: Central London County Court

Amount of award then: £5,000

Award at February 2001: £5,919

Description of injuries: Plaintiff physically ejected from first defendant's nightclub, by bouncer, the second defendant – suffered torsion and compression strain of rib and thorax, consistent with attacker's weight coming down on rib cage – suffered ligamentous damage to lumbar spine, whiplash to cervical spine and wrist injury which was caused by her wrist being slammed in door of nightclub by bouncer – experienced pain in hip if she stood for more than three hours – she was an emotionally vulnerable person and suffered extreme emotional stress.

1.3.1.1.C33 Case No. 11133

Name of case: Bryson v Dwyer

Brief description of injuries: NECK – KNEE

Reported: Kemp & Kemp, E2-076; [1996] CLY 2224

JSB Category: 6(A)(b)(ii)

Sex: Female

Age at injury: 30

Age at award: 33

Date of award: 13 February 1995

Tribunal: Liverpool County Court

Amount of award then: £5,000

Award at February 2001: £5,854

Description of injuries: Neck and knee injuries – pre-existing knee pain – post-accident knee pain could be attributed to the accident for twelve months thereafter.

Prognosis: Intermittent neck pain expected to continue for the foreseeable future.

1.3.1.1.C34 Case No. 11887

Name of case: Chadwick v Ismail-Zade

Brief description of injuries: NECK – SHOULDER – HEADACHES

Reported: Kemp & Kemp, K2-002; [1999] CLY 1551

JSB Category: 6(A)(c), 6(D)(c), 6(C)(d); 2(B)

Sex: Female

Age at injury: 43

Age at award: 47

Date of award: 20 November 1998

Tribunal: Central London County Court

Amount of award then: £5,500

Award at February 2001: £5,754

Description of injuries: Claimant struck by car – only momentarily unconscious, if at all, but seriously disoriented; believed she had been seriously injured and thought she might die – admitted to hospital and kept in overnight – X-rays revealed no bony injury – left arm grazed, left shoulder and left hip extensively bruised; bruising resolved after 3 weeks and residual tenderness after 6 weeks – swelling to occipital region of head, but CT scan revealed no abnormality; swelling took 3 weeks to settle and remained tender for 3 months – claimant bedridden in days after accident, and unable to walk for first 24 hours due to bruising and acute neck pain – claimant and husband forced to abandon pre-planned 1-week holiday – thereafter, claimant unsettled by noise and sight of traffic, and would walk touching the nearest building; subsequently flew to family home in Turkey for 1 month of recuperation away from traffic noise – claimant's sleep disturbed by nightmares for 3 months; unable to work during that period – 4 years after accident, claimant still affected by pain in neck and shoulder on cold mornings; related occasional headaches lasting several hours continued.

Prognosis: Only a limited prospect of complete recovery from occasional recurring pain.

1.3.1.1.C35 Case No. 11208

Name of case: Choudhery v Heathrow Airport Ltd

Brief description of injuries: NECK – BODY – MULTIPLE BRUISING

Reported: Kemp & Kemp, K2-004; [1996] CLY 2299

JSB Category: 6(L)(b)(ii)

Sex: Male

Age at injury: 62

Age at award: 66

Date of award: 14 March 1996

Tribunal: Reading County Court

Amount of award then: £5,000

Award at February 2001: £5,677

Description of injuries: Bruising to the fingers, chest, knee and shin – neck strain.

Prognosis: Symptoms for upwards of two years were attributable to the accident – the knee sensitivity would remain permanent – other persisting symptoms were attributable to underlying arthritic changes associated with age.

1.3.1.1.C36 Case No. 11835

Name of case: Dryhurst v Dale

Brief description of injuries: WRIST – 2 YEARS – NECK

Reported: Kemp & Kemp, H4-027; [1999] CLY 1499

JSB Category: 6(H); 6(A)(c)

Sex: Female

Age at injury: 32

Age at award: 34

Date of award: 08 January 1998

Tribunal: Manchester County Court

Amount of award then: £5,000

Award at February 2001: £5,392

Description of injuries: Jarring injury to wrists and arms and wrenching injury to neck – significant aching and stiffness in neck for 3 weeks and general nuisance symptoms thereafter, resolving completely after 16 months – symptoms in both wrists considerable, causing claimant serious difficulties, particularly because she was a single parent with a 4-month-old baby – nagging ache in wrists and restricted movement – pain made lifting impossible – sling for 1 week, tubigrips and other bandages thereafter for 2-3 weeks – extensive assistance needed for first month; flexibility improved thereafter, but pain still present – sleep disturbance in first few days after accident – continuing anxiety and nervousness when driving – full recovery initially expected after 18 months, but 26 months after accident claimant still experiencing symptoms – diagnosis that symptoms attributable to the accident had lasted for 24 months, and that residual symptoms thereafter were constitutional in nature.

1.3.1.1.C37 Case No. 11209

Name of case: Duff v Edge

Brief description of injuries: NECK – LEG

Reported: Kemp & Kemp, E2-082; [1996] CLY 2300

JSB Category: 6(A)(c)

Sex: Female

Age at injury: 77

Age at award: 78

Date of award: 07 June 1996

Tribunal: Liverpool County Court

Amount of award then: £4,750

Award at February 2001: £5,340

Description of injuries: Injury to the neck and lower leg – bruising to the chest.

Prognosis: Full resolution was expected within eighteen months of the date of the accident.

1.3.1.1.C38 Case No. 10030

Name of case: Litchfield v Flear

Brief description of injuries: FRACTURE OF NECK OF HUMERUS

Reported: Kemp & Kemp, H2-027; [1990] CLY 1610

JSB Category: 6(L)

Sex: Female

Age at injury: 16

Age at award: 17

Date of award: 16 November 1990

Tribunal: Grimsby County Court

Amount of award then: £4,000

Award at February 2001: £5,292

Description of injuries: Fracture of surgical neck of humerus – laceration on left knee resulting in scar 1 and-a-quarter inches by 1 inch in size. Fracture healed fully with no complications.

Prognosis: Aching and discomfort will disappear within six months – scar will be a permanent blemish.

1.3.1.1.C39 Case No. 11910

Name of case: Smith v Beeline Buzz Co

Brief description of injuries: BACK – NECK – SEATBELT BRUISING – ANXIETY (2.5 YEARS)

Reported: Kemp & Kemp, PRE-012; [1999] CLY 1574

JSB Category: 6(A)(c), 6(B)(c); 5(A); 3(A)

Sex: Female

Age at injury: 32

Age at award: 37

Date of award: 26 July 1999

Tribunal: Dewsbury County Court

Amount of award then: £4,750

Award at February 2001: £4,949

Description of injuries: Road accident – most serious injury lumbo – sacral strain to lower back; complete recovery after 2.5 years – soft-tissue injuries to neck and chest, latter being caused by seatbelt at point of impact; both injuries clearing within 1 month of accident – claimant's pre-existing eczema exacerbated for 9-month period – claimant was 1 month pregnant at time of accident, and had an episode of bleeding 1 month after the accident; despite reassurances, claimant anxious about possible damage to foetus until she gave birth to healthy baby.

1.3.1.1.C40 Case No. 11927

Name of case: Langden-Jones v Rossiter

Brief description of injuries: (1) NECK – SHOULDER – 1 YEAR (2) WRIST – NECK – POST-TRAUMATIC STRESS DISORDER – 16 MONTHS

Reported: Kemp & Kemp, K2-048/1; [1999] CLY 1591

JSB Category: 6(A)(c), 6(D)(c), 6(H)(d); 3(B)(d)

Sex: (1) Female (2): Male

Age at injury: (1):22;(2):33

Age at award: (1):25;(2):37

Date of award: 14 April 1999

Tribunal: Northampton County Court

Amount of award then: £4,750

Award at February 2001: £4,946

Description of injuries: 2 claimants injured in road accident.(1) injuries to neck and right shoulder – pain on daily basis for 1 week; sleep disturbed during that period; intermittent pain for a further 4 weeks thereafter – 4 days off work – unable to drive for 4 weeks – symptoms largely subsided after 6 weeks; however, claimant had suffered substantial loss of amenity during that period, as she was a keen triathlete, and sporting and training activities had been disrupted (as were other activities like dancing) – claimant on light duties at work for that period – for about 1 year after accident, claimant still suffered from some occasional clicking or aching in shoulder, especially after weight training – full recovery.(2) sprain to dominant wrist – neck strain – bruising – post-traumatic stress disorder – in hospital 24 hours, bed rest for further 48 hours – 1 week off work – bruising cleared up uneventfully – neck painful for 5 months, and still slightly tender at 7 months – both wrist and neck injury caused problems at work for several months – wrist continued to crack and grind at 7 months, and 20 per cent restriction in flexion – full recovery from physical injuries within 1 year of accident – activities of golf and attending gym disrupted for 6 months – post-traumatic stress disorder consisted of some months of generalised sleep disturbance and distress, and a lasting inability to return to claimant's main hobby of motorcycling, which was a large part of his social life and holiday activities – counselling undergone, but claimant did not anticipate return to motorcycling – full recovery, apart from the fear of motorcycling, shortly after 16 months following the accident.

Prognosis: (2)'s neck expected to remain permanently vulnerable to future trauma.

Other points: Award split: (1): £1,750 (2): £3,000 (orthopaedic injuries: £2,250; PTSD: £750)

Damage to Spine

1.3.1.1.C41 Case No. 10955

Name of case: Pollard v Blackman

Brief description of injuries: NECK – LOW BACK – PANIC ATTACKS

Reported: Kemp & Kemp, K2-015; [1995] CLY 1706

JSB Category: 6(A)(b)(ii)

Sex: Female

Age at injury: 29

Age at award: 31

Date of award: 10 March 1995

Tribunal: Reading County Court

Amount of award then: £3,500

Award at February 2001: £4,081

Description of injuries: Plaintiff sustained injuries when car drove into rear of her car – given cervical collar which she wore intermittently for four weeks – underwent three painful courses of physiotherapy involving manipulations and all neck symptoms resolved within three to four weeks – plaintiff endured very severe headache for 72 hours after accident and found sleeping difficult for first few weeks – off work for two weeks – one week after accident, felt low backache which she described as being a "nuisance" – had to be more careful when gardening and doing household tasks and could not push younger child about in pushchair for number of months – sitting in one position for hour or so brought on symptoms which would then last for one to two hours – at date of assessment, symptoms were ongoing – did not take any analgesics as "not the pain-killer type" – very shaken and upset by accident – stress made her first two periods after accident very heavy and uncomfortable and caused her pain in her pelvic area; she saw her GP twice about this – for long time after accident, felt very nervous and panicky when driving – by date of assessment, was suffering from such panic attacks only on an occasional basis.

Prognosis: The prognosis was that the physical symptoms would resolve themselves 22 months after the accident – prognosis, made 10 months after accident, was that panic problem should settle in due course.

1.3.1.1.C42 Case No. 10401

Name of case: Crompton v White

Brief description of injuries: NECK AND BACK – 1-2 YEARS

Reported: [1992] CLY 1657

JSB Category: 6(B)(c)

Sex: Male

Age at injury: 37

Age at award: 38

Date of award: 05 October 1992

Tribunal: Wigan County Court

Amount of award then: £3,250

Award at February 2001: £3,996

Description of injuries: Torsional injury to the spine – pain in the back – badly shaken – by October 1991 felt intermittent pain and stiffness in the neck and low back pain requiring up to eight distalgesic tablets per day.

Prognosis: Much improved after a course of physiotherapy in December 1991 – largely symptom-free at the time of the hearing.

1.3.1.1.C43 Case No. 11214

Name of case: Bird v Rixon

Brief description of injuries: NECK – STRAIN

Reported: Kemp & Kemp, K2-020; [1996] CLY 2306

JSB Category: 6(A)(c)

Sex: Female

Age at injury: 34

Age at award: 35

Date of award: 15 December 1995

Tribunal: Ipswich County Court

Amount of award then: £3,250

Award at February 2001: £3,709

Description of injuries: Musculo-ligamentous strain to the neck.

Prognosis: Full recovery was expected to follow within a few months.

1.3.1.1.C44 Case No. 10661

Name of case: Berry & Loades v Roe

Brief description of injuries: SHOULDER – STRAIN – NECK AND LEG

Reported: Kemp & Kemp, H2-031; [1993] CLY 1557

JSB Category: 6(D)(c); 6(A)(c); 6(K)(c)(iii)

Sex: Male

Age at injury: 30

Age at award: 31

Date of award: 10 September 1993

Tribunal: Bromley County Court

Amount of award then: £3,000

Award at February 2001: £3,636

Description of injuries: Road accident – strain to left shoulder – sprain of neck – contusional injury to lower part of right leg – 7 weeks off work, 4 weeks of light duties thereafter – symptoms in neck and leg settled after a couple of weeks – pain persisted in shoulder, preventing claimant from pursuing hobby of weightlifting for 7 months – at date of hearing, pain still present after lifting and ability to lift heavier weights still restricted.

Prognosis: Aches and pains in shoulder expected to resolve completely over next 3 months.

1.3.1.1.C45 Case No. 11221

Name of case: Thomas v Hannon Robe
Brief description of injuries: NECK – ELBOW – SOFT-TISSUE INJURIES
Reported: Kemp & Kemp, E2-117; [1996] CLY 2313
JSB Category: 6(A)(c)
Sex: Male
Age at injury: 23
Age at award: 25
Date of award: 02 September 1996
Tribunal: Birmingham County Court
Amount of award then: £2,700
Award at February 2001: £3,020
Description of injuries: Strain to the soft-tissues of the neck and elbow – at time of hearing there was continued intermittent neck pain – particularly after having driven for a long time.
Other points: The judge noted that his job involved large amounts of travel.

1.3.1.1.C46 Case No. 12065

Name of case: Singh v M&N Contractors Ltd
Brief description of injuries: ELBOW – SOFT-TISSUE INJURY – NECK AND LOWER BACK
Reported: [2000] 6 CL 195
JSB Category: 6(A)(c) 6G(c)
Sex: Male
Age at injury: 20
Age at award: 21
Date of award: 17 February 2000
Tribunal: Bradford County Court
Amount of award then: £2,900
Award at February 2001: £2,978
Description of injuries: Whiplash and soft-tissue injuries to the neck and lower back – not insignificant blow to the left elbow caused further soft-tissue injuries – considerable pain subsided over a two month period – insomnia lasting several months – elbow healed within two months – minor stabbing pains persisted – flashbacks caused anxiety which persisted to the time of the trial.

1.3.1.1.C47 Case No. 10484

Name of case: Brown v O'Brien
Brief description of injuries: SOFT-TISSUE DAMAGE TO NECK AND ELBOW
Reported: [1992] CLY 1740
JSB Category:
Sex: Male
Age at injury: 38
Age at award: 41
Date of award: 27 October 1991
Tribunal: Birmingham County Court
Amount of award then: £2,200
Award at February 2001: £2,801
Description of injuries: Soft-tissue damage to the elbow and rear of neck – grazing to the shin – two bouts of nervous illness at three months and six months – away from work for four weeks.
Prognosis: Injuries healed well.

1.3.1.1.C48 Case No. 11230

Name of case: Harman v Coleburn
Brief description of injuries: NECK – BACK
Reported: Kemp & Kemp, K2-072; [1996] CLY 2322
JSB Category: 6(A)(c)
Sex: Female
Age at injury: 44
Age at award: 45
Date of award: 24 July 1996
Tribunal: Kingston upon Hull County Court
Amount of award then: £2,200
Award at February 2001: £2,483
Description of injuries: Injury to the neck – pain in the shoulder and lumbar region.
Prognosis: Full recovery to the back – it was expected that she would eventually become completely symptom free.

1.3.1.1.C49 Case No. 10486

Name of case: Fenton v Picktet
Brief description of injuries: NECK, SPINE AND KNEE INJURIES – RECOVERED IN 11 MONTHS
Reported: [1992] CLY 1742
JSB Category: 6(B)(c)
Sex: Female
Age at injury: 14
Age at award: 16
Date of award: 25 February 1992
Tribunal: Kingston upon Thames County Court
Amount of award then: £1,750
Award at February 2001: £2,208
Description of injuries: Injury to the cervical spine, left knee and thoraco-lumbar spine.
Prognosis: Full recovery by eleven months after the accident.

Damage to Spine

1.3.1.1.C50 Case No. 11390

Name of case: Southward v Peers Recovery

Brief description of injuries: NECK – BACK – 12 MONTHS

Reported: Kemp & Kemp, K2-097; [1997] CLY 1938

JSB Category: 6(B)(c)

Sex: Male

Age at injury: 46

Age at award: -

Date of award: 12 June 1997

Tribunal: Birkenhead County Court

Amount of award then: £2,000

Award at February 2001: £2,184

Description of injuries: Injury to the cervical and lumbar spine.

Prognosis: Experienced pain and suffering for twelve month after the date of the accident.

1.3.1.1.C51 Case No. 10272

Name of case: Butterworth v Lumb

Brief description of injuries: NECK PAIN – MULTIPLE BRUISES AND ABRASIONS – RECOVERY 18 MONTHS

Reported: Kemp & Kemp, K2-103; [1991] CLY 1469

JSB Category: 6(A)(c)

Sex: Female

Age at injury: 34

Age at award: 36

Date of award: 19 July 1991

Tribunal: Bradford County Court

Amount of award then: £1,600

Award at February 2001: £2,057

Description of injuries: Knocked off her bicycle – bruising to the right elbow, right great trochanter, right knee, and right ankle – abrasions to the right knee and ankle – a keen sportswoman, B's activities were curtailed.

Prognosis: No time off work – discomfort in the neck settled within eight months.

1.3.1.1.C52 Case No. 11698

Award at February 2001: £1,995

See: 1.2.2.1.C33 for details

1.3.1.1.C53 Case No. 11891

Name of case: Johnson v Hill

Brief description of injuries: NECK – HEADACHES – BRUISING PSYCHOLOGICAL REACTION

Reported: Kemp & Kemp, K1-100, I2-126/1; [1999] CLY 1555

JSB Category: 6(A)(c); 5(A); 3(A)(d)

Sex: Female

Age at injury: 45

Age at award: 45

Date of award: 02 August 1999

Tribunal: Manchester County Court

Amount of award then: £1,750

Award at February 2001: £1,819

Description of injuries: Road accident – seatbelt injury to chest, resolving over 5-day period – neck pain and headaches, resolving over next 9 months – no time off work, but restricted to light duties for 4 weeks – keep – fit and some domestic duties disturbed – some anxiety experienced when travelling by car.

1.3.1.1.C54 Case No. 11240

Name of case: Gerken v Fisher

Brief description of injuries: NECK – SHOULDER

Reported: Kemp & Kemp, K2-110; [1996] CLY 2332

JSB Category: 6(A)(c)

Sex: Male

Age at injury: 41

Age at award: 42

Date of award: 20 May 1996

Tribunal: Bury County Court

Amount of award then: £1,600

Award at February 2001: £1,800

Description of injuries: Neck and right shoulder injury – symptoms lasted for about seven-and-a-half-months.

1.3.1.1.C55 Case No. 11699

Award at February 2001: £1,792

See: 1.2.2.1.C36 for details

1.3.1.1.C56 Case No. 11466

Name of case: Stride (S) v Lipscombe

Brief description of injuries: NECK – CHEST – 3 MONTHS

Reported: Kemp & Kemp, E2-131/1[1997] CLY 2015

JSB Category: 6(A)(c)

Sex: Female

Age at injury: 67

Age at award: 68

Date of award: 01 July 1997

Tribunal: Central London County Court

Amount of award then: £1,600

Award at February 2001: £1,747

Description of injuries: Discomfort to the neck and chest.

Prognosis: Pain and suffering continued for three months – nervous when travelling in a car.

1.3.1.1.C57 Case No. 11347

Name of case: Hoy v Cole

Brief description of injuries: NECK – SHOULDER – BACK – 1 YEAR

Reported: Kemp & Kemp, K2-096; [1997] CLY 1895

JSB Category: 6(A)(c)

Sex: Male

Age at injury: 26

Age at award: 29

Date of award: 23 April 1997

Tribunal: Chelmsford County Court

Amount of award then: £1,495

Award at February 2001: £1,645

Description of injuries: Pain in the back, shoulder and neck – two weeks of severe pain – symptoms had resolved within one year of the date of the accident.

1.3.1.1.C58 Case No. 10676

Name of case: Lyon v Chambers

Brief description of injuries: NECK AND BACK – LIGAMENT SPRAIN – 8 WEEKS

Reported: Kemp & Kemp, E2-137; [1993] CLY 1572

JSB Category: 6(A)(c), 6(B)(c)

Sex: Female

Age at injury: 23

Age at award: 25

Date of award: 01 November 1993

Tribunal: Mayor's and City of London County Court

Amount of award then: £1,250

Award at February 2001: £1,518

Description of injuries: Road accident – soft-tissue injury to muscles and ligaments of neck and back – collar prescribed, worn continuously for 2 weeks and on occasions thereafter for 3 further weeks – 2 days off work in total – pain initially considerable, but lessened gradually – claimant fainted 2 days after accident while on way to physiotherapy appointment – some difficulty in looking down at computer screen for several weeks – driving difficult; claimant avoided doing so for 6 to 8 weeks – pain ceased altogether after 6 weeks – complete recovery after 8 weeks.

1.3.1.1.C59 Case No. 11897

Award at February 2001: £1,454

See: 1.2.2.1.C39 for details

1.3.1.1.C60 Case No. 11732

Name of case: Creek v Petryszyn

Brief description of injuries: NECK – WHIPLASH – PSYCHOLOGICAL REACTION – 3 MONTHS

Reported: Kemp & Kemp, PRK-008, K2-177/1; [1998] CLY 1735

JSB Category: 6(A)(c); 3(A)

Sex: Female

Age at injury: 28

Age at award: 29

Date of award: 11 September 1997

Tribunal: Reading County Court

Amount of award then: £1,150

Award at February 2001: £1,242

Description of injuries: Whiplash injury – cervical collar was prescribed – insomnia, flashbacks and nightmares – after 3 months all of the physical, and most of the psychological, sequelae had passed.

1.3.1.1.C61 Case No. 10877

Name of case: Padley v Wing

Brief description of injuries: NECK – ASTHMA ATTACK

Reported: Kemp & Kemp, K2-184; [1994] CLY 1729

JSB Category: 5(C); 6(A)(c), 6(I)(c)

Sex: Male

Age at injury: 4

Age at award: 5

Date of award: 25 May 1994

Tribunal: Leeds County Court

Amount of award then: £1,000

Award at February 2001: £1,189

Description of injuries: Road accident – superficial lacerations to fingers of right hand and bleeding – discomfort in neck – asthma attack resulting from trauma of accident – off school 1 week – nightmares about accident for 4 weeks – slight discomfort in neck in cold weather 11 months after accident – full recovery to lacerations – minor injuries to cervical spine of nuisance value only.

1.3.1.1.C62 Case No. 10508

Name of case: Berry v Pearce

Brief description of injuries: SPRAINED NECK AND BACK – 5-6 WEEKS

Reported: Kemp & Kemp, K2-196; [1992] CLY 1764

JSB Category: 6(B)(c)

Sex: Male

Age at injury: 37

Age at award: 39

Date of award: 27 March 1992

Tribunal: Southampton County Court

Amount of award then: £900

Award at February 2001: £1,132

Description of injuries: Contusion to the left ankle – acute sprain or strain of the neck and lumbar spine – exacerbating pre-existing low-level symptoms.

Prognosis: All symptoms settled within five to six weeks.

1.3.1.1.C63 Case No. 11703

Name of case: Murphy v Rowlands

Brief description of injuries: NECK – ASTHMA ATTACK – 4 MONTHS

Reported: Kemp & Kemp, K2-209/1; [1998] CLY 1706

JSB Category: 6(A)(c); 5(C)(e)

Sex: Female

Age at injury: 20

Age at award: 22

Date of award: 25 September 1998

Tribunal: Pontypridd County Court

Amount of award then: £1,000

Award at February 2001: £1,046

Description of injuries: Neck sprain – asthma attack – bruising to the neck and chest – fully recovered within 4 months of the date of the accident.

1.3.1.1.C64 Case No. 11929

Name of case: Stewart-Davies v Sinton

Brief description of injuries: NECK – WHIPLASH – PSYCHOLOGICAL REACTION – 3 MONTHS

Reported: Kemp & Kemp, PRK-011; [1999] CLY 1593

JSB Category: 6(A)(c); 3(A)(d)

Sex: Male

Age at injury: 33

Age at award: 34

Date of award: 11 August 1999

Tribunal: Cardiff County Court

Amount of award then: £1,000

Award at February 2001: £1,039

Description of injuries: Road accident – whiplash injury to neck – cervical collar worn for 1 week – neck pain moderate for 2 days, mild and intermittent over following month – discomfort while lying in bed, driving a car and at work – no associated headaches, but claimant upset and shocked – sleep disturbed for 2 nights – recurrent intrusive thoughts about accident – anxiety while travelling in car for 2 weeks – when assessed 4 months after accident, claimant had had no physical symptoms in preceding 3 months and had made a full psychological recovery – clinical examination of cervical spine was normal.

Other points: Judge noted that claimant was of a stoical disposition, but the accident had been an unpleasant experience.

1.3.1.1.C65 Case No. 10529

Award at February 2001: £740

See: 1.2.3.1.C39 for details

1.3.1.2 WHIPLASH

1.3.1.2.C1 Case No. 11269

Award at February 2001: £18,986

See: 1.3.1.C3 for details

1.3.1.2.C2 Case No. 11340

Name of case: Camus v Williams

Brief description of injuries: NECK – WHIPLASH – SEVERE

Reported: Kemp & Kemp, E2-016; [1997] CLY 1888

JSB Category: 6(A)(b)(i)

Sex: Female

Age at injury: 33

Age at award: 41

Date of award: 18 July 1996

Tribunal: QBD

Amount of award then: £13,750

Award at February 2001: £15,711

Description of injuries: Severe whiplash type soft-tissue injury – minor dental injury.

Prognosis: At time of the hearing continued pain requiring a TENS machine – symptoms were likely to continue into the future.

Other points: Her future earning capacity would not catch up completely.

1.3.1.2.C3 Case No. 11341

Name of case: Jennings v Cummins & Phillips

Brief description of injuries: NECK – WHIPLASH – FIBRO-MYALGIA

Reported: Kemp & Kemp, E2-018; [1997] CLY 1889

JSB Category: 6(A)(b)(i)

Sex: Male

Age at injury: 22

Age at award: 28

Date of award: 25 September 1996

Tribunal: Bournemouth County Court

Amount of award then: £13,500

Award at February 2001: £15,270

Description of injuries: Soft-tissue injuries to the neck and spine – developed chronic moderately severe fibro-myalgia – physically fit and mobile – full range of movement – no degenerative changes – symptoms of severe pain following physical activity.

1.3.1.2.C4 Case No. 11124

Name of case: O'Brien v Martin

Brief description of injuries: NECK – WHIPLASH

Reported: Kemp & Kemp, E2-020; [1996] CLY 2215

JSB Category: 6(A)(b)(i)

Sex: Female

Age at injury: 25

Age at award: 31

Date of award: 02 April 1996

Tribunal: Not stated

Amount of award then: £12,500

Award at February 2001: £14,217

Description of injuries: Whiplash injuries to the neck and low back.

Prognosis: At the time of the hearing some pain and stiffness remained – 30 per cent risk of developing premature osteoarthritis.

Other points: Injuries not devastating – the effect on her life was devastating.

1.3.1.2.C5 Case No. 11581

Name of case: Strainge v HO

Brief description of injuries: NECK – WHIPLASH – 10 YEARS

Reported: Kemp & Kemp, E2-020/1; [1998] CLY 1583

JSB Category: 6(A)(b)(i)

Sex: Male

Age at injury: 33

Age at award: -

Date of award: 16 January 1998

Tribunal: Mayor's and City of London County Court

Amount of award then: £13,000

Award at February 2001: £14,143

Description of injuries: Whiplash injury to the neck.

Prognosis: For 10 years, claimant would not be able to live his life as normal.

1.3.1.2.C6 Case No. 10383

Name of case: Collins and Dalton v Allen

Brief description of injuries: FAIRLY SEVERE WHIPLASH – PERMANENT SYMPTOMS

Reported: Kemp & Kemp, E2-021; [1992] CLY 1639

JSB Category: 6(A)(b)(i)

Sex: Male

Age at injury: 25

Age at award: 27

Date of award: 30 October 1991

Tribunal: Swindon County Court

Amount of award then: £11,000

Award at February 2001: £14,128

Description of injuries: Fairly severe whiplash injury – significant permanent disability – sleepless nights – discomfort in the neck and shoulders whilst driving – headaches – temporary inability to perform sexual intercourse – inability to play football – interruption to golfing.

Prognosis: Some prospect of there being a twenty five per cent decrease in symptoms.

1.3.1.2.C7 Case No. 11377

Name of case: Sollis v Hughes, Hughes, Colson (T/A Byron Construction) and Broad

Brief description of injuries: NECK – WHIPLASH – BACK

Reported: Kemp & Kemp, E3-043/1; [1997] CLY 1925

JSB Category: 6(B)(b)(ii)

Sex: Female

Age at injury: 17

Age at award: 22

Date of award: 18 December 1996

Tribunal: Pontyprid County Court

Amount of award then: £12,500

Award at February 2001: £14,045

Description of injuries: Whiplash type injury to the neck – injury to the lower back.

Prognosis: Back injuries appeared to be permanent – she had had to change her career plans as a result of the accident.

1.3.1.2.C8 Case No. 10199

Name of case: Barker v Ipswich Buses

Brief description of injuries: WHIPLASH TO THE NECK – PRE-EXISTING BACK INJURY EXACERBATED

Reported: Kemp & Kemp, E2-023; [1991] CLY 1396

JSB Category: 6(B)(b)(ii)

Sex: Female

Age at injury: 42

Age at award: 44

Date of award: 22 March 1991

Tribunal: Ipswich County Court

Amount of award then: £10,000

Award at February 2001: £13,178

Description of injuries: Accident caused whiplash type injury to the neck – exacerbated pre-existing back injury – 35 per cent of the back injury was caused by the accident.

Prognosis: Constant pain to the back and neck – the neck pain sometimes becoming excruciating – forced to retire to bed for the day about three times per week.

1.3.1.2.C9 Case No. 10382

Name of case: Re Bennett

Brief description of injuries: WHIPLASH – 5 YEAR ACCELERATION OF PRE-EXISTING CONDITION

Reported: Kemp & Kemp, E2-025; [1992] CLY 1638

JSB Category: 6(A)(b)(i)

Sex: Male

Age at injury: 60

Age at award: 62

Date of award: 02 September 1992

Tribunal: Tunbridge Wells County Court

Amount of award then: £10,500

Award at February 2001: £13,038

Description of injuries: Whiplash injury to the neck – wedge compression of the C7 vertebral body – severe seatbelt bruising – minor cuts and bruising to all limbs – pre-existing history of cervical spondylitis – pain free at the time of the accident – cervical collar for one month – continuing aching at the base of the neck and in the shoulder blades – increased stiffness and restriction of movement in the neck.

Prognosis: Accident aggravated the degenerative process by five years.

1.3.1.2.C10 Case No. 11806

Name of case: Richards v Prodger

Brief description of injuries: NECK – WHIPLASH

Reported: Kemp & Kemp, E2-026/1; [1999] CLY 1469

JSB Category: 6(A)(b)(i)

Sex: Female

Age at injury: 31

Age at award: 35

Date of award: 09 February 1999

Tribunal: Gloucester County Court

Amount of award then: £12,000

Award at February 2001: £12,679

Description of injuries: Whiplash injury to neck and lower back – severe pain in neck, back and legs on morning after accident; claimant remained in bed for 3 days – anti-inflammatory medication and physiotherapy prescribed; soft collar worn continuously for 6 months and intermittently thereafter – lower back symptoms completely resolved, as did onset of headaches after the accident – upper back problems persisting at time of trial – regular attacks of pain in upper back, particularly in winter, causing considerable discomfort often lasting several days and some pain in neck – pins and needles in right arm, affecting grip and interfering with sleep – claimant unable to continue with congenial employment as assistant at children's playgroup, owing to amount of lifting and bending required – judge found that claimant now only fit for light shop work.

Prognosis: Significant improvement in the future unlikely.

1.3.1.2.C11 Case No. 10583

Name of case: Loughran v London Buses
Brief description of injuries: NECK – WHIPLASH – SEVERE – DIZZINESS
Reported: Kemp & Kemp, E2-029; [1993] CLY 1476
JSB Category: 6(A)(b); 3(B)
Sex: Male
Age at injury: 45
Age at award: 48
Date of award: 09 September 1992
Tribunal: Clerkenwell County Court
Amount of award then: £10,000
Award at February 2001: £12,400

Description of injuries: Bus driver's vehicle struck by another from behind – thrown forward over wheel, then backward, striking head on rear bulkhead and losing consciousness – concussion – ongoing headaches – whiplash, categorised by judge as "severe" – dizzy spells caused by dysfunction of vestibular mechanism sustained in head injury – features of post-traumatic stress exacerbating injuries – previous history of underlying worries and depression.

1.3.1.2.C12 Case No. 11807

Name of case: Johnson v Rogers
Brief description of injuries: NECK – WHIPLASH – BACK
Reported: Kemp & Kemp, E2-029/1; [1999] CLY 1470
JSB Category: 6(A)(b)(i), 6(B)(c)
Sex: Female
Age at injury: 38
Age at award: 42
Date of award: 01 October 1998
Tribunal: Norwich County Court
Amount of award then: £11,750
Award at February 2001: £12,345

Description of injuries: Whiplash injury to neck – increasing stiffness in neck during course of same day – claimant "felt something go" on following day when reaching over to pick up child – bed rest for 4 days, with some improvement – ongoing pain in right shoulder – dizziness – 50 per cent decrease in neck movements – pain on rib springing experienced in thoracic spine – sleep affected – ongoing help required with shopping, gardening, DIY, child care, housework – claimant's life significantly interfered with.

Other points: Award comprised: neck: £10,500; back: £1,250.

1.3.1.2.C13 Case No. 10200

Name of case: Matthews v Strenglade
Brief description of injuries: A SEVERE WHIPLASH INJURY – 20 YEAR EXACERBATION OF SPONDYLOSIS

Reported: Kemp & Kemp, E2-030; [1991] CLY 1397
JSB Category: 6(B)(i)
Sex: Male
Age at injury: 32
Age at award: 36
Date of award: 31 July 1991
Tribunal: Kingston upon Thames County Court
Amount of award then: £9,500
Award at February 2001: £12,212

Description of injuries: A severe whiplash injury and activation of symptomless spondylosis – anxiety made him unable to return to his former work – unable to carry on with several jobs due to the continuing symptoms in the neck and shoulder.

Prognosis: He would remain unfit for work requiring heavy lifting and carrying – he would remain a more nervous driver.

Other points: It was unlikely that he would have suffered symptoms in his neck until into his fifties before the date of the accident.

1.3.1.2.C14 Case No. 10754

Name of case: Megarry v Torkmatic
Brief description of injuries: NECK – WHIPLASH
Reported: Kemp & Kemp, E2-031; [1994] CLY 1602
JSB Category: 6(A)(b)
Sex: Female
Age at injury: 37
Age at award: 47
Date of award: 22 October 1993
Tribunal: Not stated
Amount of award then: £10,000
Award at February 2001: £12,184

Description of injuries: Whiplash injury to neck – pain, stiffness, limitation of movement – symptoms continued 10 years, ongoing at date of trial, despite numerous treatments – neck collar still worn whenever travelling – inability to drive – inability to lift heavy weights – inability to pursue hobbies of gardening, dancing and bowling – also some symptoms in right hand and elbow – medical examination unable to find any bony or neurological deformity except for neck muscle spasm – suggestion of condition being an hysterical one – judge's finding that symptoms resulted from accident and, whether cause hysterical or not, symptoms very real for claimant.

Prognosis: Neck condition permanent – no deterioration to be expected.

Other points: Judge found that symptoms in right hand and elbow not attributable to accident, and that claimant would have been able to work full-time, albeit with difficulty, if only suffering from neck condition – claim for loss of earnings therefore dismissed.

1.3.1.2.C15 Case No. 11282

Name of case: Wright v Serco Ltd

Brief description of injuries: SHOULDER – NECK – WHIPLASH

Reported: Kemp & Kemp, H2-016/2; [1997] CLY 1829

JSB Category: 6(D)(d) 3(A)

Sex: Male

Age at injury: 38

Age at award: 43

Date of award: 14 October 1996

Tribunal:

Amount of award then: £10,750

Award at February 2001: £12,073

Description of injuries: Fractured clavicle with joint disruption – torn shoulder muscles – minor head injury – lateral whiplash – bruised ankle.

Prognosis: Neck injury accelerated a pre-existing cervical spondylosis by five years – minor discomfort in walking was likely to persist indefinitely – exhibited significant symptoms of depression two years after the date of the accident.

Other points: Left the Royal Air Force voluntarily.

1.3.1.2.C16 Case No. 10584

Name of case: Vater v Dry Silver (in liquidation)

Brief description of injuries: NECK – WHIPLASH – SEVERE

Reported: Kemp & Kemp, E2-033; [1993] CLY 1477

JSB Category: 6(A)(b)

Sex: Female

Age at injury: 35

Age at award: 42

Date of award: 25 May 1993

Tribunal: Pontypridd County Court

Amount of award then: £9,500

Award at February 2001: £11,580

Description of injuries: Whiplash injury to neck in road accident – immediate neck pain – collar fitted and worn for 6 months – thereafter small reduction in neck rotation in both directions, flexion and extension limited to about half former range – return to previous unemployment impossible, fit for sedentary work only – vulnerable to attacks of pain if head turned suddenly – symptoms sufficiently severe to disturb sleep on occasions – not capable of carrying out household duties or pursuing chief hobby of gardening – symptoms had not improved significantly in 6.5 years

1.3.1.2.C17 Case No. 11125

Name of case: Creighton v Estate of Dholakia (deceased)

Brief description of injuries: NECK – WHIPLASH

Reported: Kemp & Kemp, E2-034; [1996] CLY 2216

JSB Category: 6(A)(b)(i)

Sex: Male

Age at injury: 42

Age at award: 48

Date of award: 18 January 1996

Tribunal: Northampton County Court

Amount of award then: £10,000

Award at February 2001: £11,484

Description of injuries: Whiplash injuries to the neck and cervical spine – permanent pain and lack of movement in the neck – numbness and weakness in the left arm and hand – increasing lack of dexterity in the hand.

Other points: His career was dependent on his being able to use his hands.

1.3.1.2.C18 Case No. 11342

Award at February 2001: £11,209

See: 1.3.1.C8 for details

1.3.1.2.C19 Case No. 10309

Name of case: Mitchel v Lewis

Brief description of injuries: WHIPLASH – TWO YEARS

Reported: Kemp & Kemp, B2-039; [1992] CLY 1564

JSB Category: 6(A)(c)

Sex: Male

Age at injury: 51

Age at award: 52

Date of award: 14 August 1992

Tribunal: Birmingham County Court

Amount of award then: £9,000

Award at February 2001: £11,145

Description of injuries: Moderate whiplash – elbow bone dislodged – contusion of the knee.

Prognosis: Difficulty with driving, shaving, recreational walking and badminton likely to be resolved with physiotherapy. – likely to recover in 3-6 months.

1.3.1.2.C20 Case No. 10755

Name of case: Chandler v Ward Meadows Plant

Brief description of injuries: NECK – WHIPLASH – CONTINUING SIGNIFICANT SYMPTOMS

Reported: Kemp & Kemp, E3-060; [1994] CLY 1603

JSB Category: 6(A)(b)

Sex: Female

Age at injury: 41

Age at award: 44

Date of award: 18 April 1994

Tribunal: Carlisle County Court

Amount of award then: £9,000

Award at February 2001: £10,735

Description of injuries: Road accident – whiplash injuries to cervical spine – modest improvement in 3 years following accident, but many symptoms still present – regular painkiller consumption – inability to lift weights of over 25lb – inability to lift arms above shoulder level – ironing and hoovering only possible in short spells – discomfort on long car journeys – forced to give up keen interest in playing badminton.

Prognosis: Condition now static and unlikely to improve – judge's finding of very real losses of amenity.

1.3.1.2.C21 Case No. 11130

Name of case: Randall and Randall v England

Brief description of injuries: NECK – WHIPLASH

Reported: Kemp & Kemp, E2-065; [1996] CLY 2221

JSB Category: P1: 6(A)(b)(ii); P2: 6(A)(b)(ii)

Sex: P1 Female; P2 Male

Age at injury: P1:62;P2:36

Age at award: P1:64;P2:38

Date of award: 31 May 1996

Tribunal: Birmingham County Court

Amount of award then: £9,500

Award at February 2001: £10,687

Description of injuries: P1 whiplash type injury – of "moderate severity" – P1 pre-existing degenerative change in the cervical spine exaggerated by five years – P2 whiplash type injuries.

Prognosis: Minor neck pain likely to persist.

Other points: Award split – P1: £6,000; P2: £3,500.

1.3.1.2.C22 Case No. 11808

Name of case: Smith v Arcadia Group plc

Brief description of injuries: NECK – WHIPLASH

Reported: Kemp & Kemp, PRE-005; [1999] CLY 1471

JSB Category: 6(A)(b)

Sex: Male

Age at injury: 64

Age at award: 66

Date of award: 21 January 1999

Tribunal: Rawtenstall County Court

Amount of award then: £10,000

Award at February 2001: £10,534

Description of injuries: Whiplash injury to neck and some paraesthesia in left hand – cervical collar for 2-3 weeks – symptoms ongoing at time of trial, including considerable stiffness, symptoms deteriorating when sat with neck in bent position or when driving for longer than 30 minutes – difficulty in turning head to left when reversing car – claimant forced to suspend hobby of bowling for several months, and neck still problematic when playing at time of trial – regular pain at night, and "flare – ups" almost daily – initial numbness in middle finger of non-dominant left hand subsiding to occasional paraesthesia by time of trial – X-rays revealed degenerative changes in neck; accident said to have caused changes to occur rapidly over a 2-year period rather than slowly over a 10-year period, making a net acceleration of about 8 years.

Prognosis: Stiffness in neck likely to be permanent.

1.3.1.2.C23 Case No. 11582

Name of case: Goacher v Pearman

Brief description of injuries: NECK – WHIPLASH

Reported: Kemp & Kemp, E2-038/1; [1998] CLY 1584

JSB Category: 6(A)(b)(i)

Sex: Male

Age at injury: 39

Age at award: 44

Date of award: 13 May 1998

Tribunal: Swindon County Court

Amount of award then: £10,000

Award at February 2001: £10,527

Description of injuries: Whiplash injury to the neck and shoulders.

Prognosis: At the time of the hearing claimant had reached a plateau – further improvement was unlikely.

1.3.1.2.C24 Case No. 10585

Name of case: Farnborough v Davies

Brief description of injuries: NECK – WHIPLASH – SEVERE

Reported: Kemp & Kemp, E2-040; [1993] CLY 1478

JSB Category: 6(A)(b)

Sex: Female

Age at injury: 72

Age at award: 73

Date of award: 16 February 1993

Tribunal: Trowbridge County Court

Amount of award then: £8,000

Award at February 2001: £9,914

Description of injuries: Whiplash injury to neck in road accident – significant pain and stiffness in early stages, collar, painkillers and medication prescribed – 6 months later, extensive rotation of cervical spine reduced by 50 per cent, lateral flexion of cervical spine reduced by 25 per cent – all movements painful, severe episodes of pain radiating down left arm – no significant improvement at time of hearing – activities such as gardening, housework and voluntary work severely curtailed.

Prognosis: Long-term symptoms of aching and restriction of movement anticipated.

1.3.1.2.C25 Case No. 11583

Name of case: Cashman v Westland Group plc

Brief description of injuries: NECK – WHIPLASH – BACK

Reported: Kemp & Kemp, E3-067/1; [1998] CLY 1585

JSB Category: 6(A)(b)(i); 6(B)

Sex: Female

Age at injury: 34

Age at award: 38

Date of award: 21 May 1998

Tribunal: Central London County Court

Amount of award then: £9,200

Award at February 2001: £9,678

Description of injuries: Whiplash injury to the neck – soft-tissue injuries to the lumbar spine.

Prognosis: Recovery from the residual symptoms of continual discomfort was unlikely.

1.3.1.2.C26 Case No. 10032

Name of case: Thomas v Fury

Brief description of injuries: SEVERE WHIPLASH

Reported: Kemp & Kemp, E2-043; [1990] CLY 1618

JSB Category: 6(A)

Sex: Female

Age at injury: 39

Age at award: 42

Date of award: 06 March 1990

Tribunal: Cardiff County Court

Amount of award then: £6,500

Award at February 2001: £9,209

Description of injuries: Sustained severe whiplash.

Prognosis: No risk of osteoarthritic changes in future, but symptoms affect many aspects of plaintiff's life and cause great discomfort and pain.

1.3.1.2.C27 Case No. 10948

Name of case: Fisher v Bandwidth Vehicles Rentals

Brief description of injuries: WHIPLASH – PERMANENT DULL ACHING

Reported: Kemp & Kemp, E2-044; [1995] CLY 1699

JSB Category: 6(A)(b)(i)

Sex: Female

Age at injury: 43

Age at award: 44

Date of award: 27 September 1995

Tribunal: Reading County Court

Amount of award then: £8,000

Award at February 2001: £9,137

Description of injuries: Plaintiff involved in a rear end shunt road traffic accident – suffered whiplash injury to neck and shoulder – off work three days, suffered from unsettled sleep and headaches and was extremely stiff in three weeks immediately following accident – after three weeks noticed a gradual improvement although she took analgesics three times per week – plaintiff performed her own stretching exercises and had massage treatment for neck – nine months after accident was unable to carry shopping more than 200 yards and had difficulty turning head to reverse when driving – suffered discomfort on driving for more than 30 minutes and on working with a "mouse" for more than 30 minutes in her job as secretary – could only hoover for 10 minutes and iron for 15 minutes at a time but speed in doing household tasks had not been affected – plaintiff became more short-tempered when she was suffering from pain related to accident – only played tennis four times in summer after accident whereas she had played some three or four times per week prior to accident – hobby of aerobics was also restricted – had some nightmares following accident and became vigilant or aware of cars approaching from rear – ability to perform DIY activities had been affected, leading to expense as she had moved house and would have to pay others to perform various tasks. The district judge assessed that loss as part of her General Damages.

Prognosis: The prognosis was that the plaintiff would continue indefinitely to suffer dull aching sensations after moderately heavy exertions and would be susceptible to muscle strains in neck and shoulder.

1.3.1.2.C28 Case No. 11585

Name of case: Buck v Hamer

Brief description of injuries: NECK – WHIPLASH – BACK

Reported: Kemp & Kemp, E2-046/1; [1998] CLY 1587

JSB Category: 6(A)(b)(i); 6(B)

Sex: Female

Age at injury: 37

Age at award: 40

Date of award: 29 October 1998

Tribunal: Central London County Court

Amount of award then: £8,500

Award at February 2001: £8,888

Description of injuries: Whiplash injury to the neck and lumbar spine – any form of movement aggravated her pain.

Prognosis: B was expected to continue with a degree of disability for the rest of her life.

1.3.1.2.C29 Case No. 10949

Name of case: Lewis v Emmins

Brief description of injuries: WHIPLASH – CONTINUING SYMPTOMS

Reported: [1995] CLY 1700

JSB Category: 6(A)(b)(i)

Sex: Male

Age at injury: 38

Age at award: 40

Date of award: 20 December 1994

Tribunal: Reading County Court

Amount of award then: £7,500

Award at February 2001: £8,836

Description of injuries: Plaintiff suffered whiplash injury – wore collar for one month after accident which ruined enjoyment of Christmas – absent from work for two months – at time of assessment still experienced two main symptoms – neck stiffened up when cold or tired or if he had to stay in one position for any length of time, eg when driving – resultant pain referred down his neck to his shoulders – awoke about once a week with pins and needles and paraesthesia in one arm – occasional unguarded movement would also bring on pain – wary of lifting heavy objects.

Prognosis: The symptoms would be permanent.

1.3.1.2.C30 Case No. 11127

Name of case: Lloyd v Simms

Brief description of injuries: NECK – WHIPLASH

Reported: Kemp & Kemp, E3-078; [1996] CLY 2218

JSB Category: 6(A)(b)(i)

Sex: Female

Age at injury: 49

Age at award: 53

Date of award: 03 April 1996

Tribunal: Central London County Court

Amount of award then: £7,750

Award at February 2001: £8,735

Description of injuries: Whiplash injury to the neck and lower back.

Prognosis: The back and neck would always be vulnerable – some other symptoms were expected to resolve in a few years.

1.3.1.2.C31 Case No. 10586

Name of case: Hitchings v Gilbert

Brief description of injuries: NECK – WHIPLASH – 3-4 YEAR ACCELERATION – HOLIDAY SPOILED

Reported: Kemp & Kemp, E2-048; [1993] CLY 1479

JSB Category: 6(A)(b)

Sex: Female

Age at injury: late 40's

Age at award: -

Date of award: 12 February 1993

Tribunal: Bristol County Court

Amount of award then: £7,000

Award at February 2001: £8,674

Description of injuries: Whiplash injury to neck and bruising to right upper arm and shoulder in road accident – soft collar and analgesics prescribed – right shoulder and neck continued to be in pain – global weakness in shoulders due to pain – claimant had suffered from ankylosing spondylitis and inflammatory arthritis for 15 years – went on sea cruise soon after accident due to heavy financial penalty consequent upon cancellation – holiday "a disaster" due to pain arising from the accident – compensation for spoilt holiday factored into the award.

Prognosis: Symptoms suffered as consequence of accident likely to have occurred in 3 to 4 years in any event.

1.3.1.2.C32 Case No. 11586

Name of case: Warby v Perkins

Brief description of injuries: NECK – WHIPLASH – EXACERBATION OF PRE-EXISTING SPONDYLITIC CHANGES

Reported: Kemp & Kemp, E2-048/2; [1998] CLY 1588

JSB Category: 6(A)(b)(i)

Sex: Female

Age at injury: 50

Age at award: 55

Date of award: 29 October 1997

Tribunal: Luton County Court

Amount of award then: £8,000

Award at February 2001: £8,627

Description of injuries: Whiplash injury to the neck – exacerbation of pre-existing spondylitic changes – W was unfit for heavy work – lacked skill and inclination for lighter jobs.

Prognosis: Claimant unlikely, in view of her age, to find other work.

1.3.1.2.C33 Case No. 11587

Name of case: Lane v Lucas & Avalon Surfacing

Brief description of injuries: NECK – WHIPLASH

Reported: Kemp & Kemp, E2-048/1; [1998] CLY 1589

JSB Category: 6(A)(b)(i)

Sex: Male

Age at injury: 33

Age at award: 36

Date of award: 09 October 1997

Tribunal: Cardiff County Court

Amount of award then: £8,000

Award at February 2001: £8,627

Description of injuries: Whiplash injury to the cervical spine – jarring injury to the sacral spine.

Prognosis: Continuing intermittent pain was likely for the foreseeable future.

1.3.1.2.C34 Case No. 11816

Name of case: Atkinson v Whittle

Brief description of injuries: NECK – WHIPLASH – 4 YEAR ACCELERATION

Reported: Kemp & Kemp, E2-048/3; [1999] CLY 1479

JSB Category: 6(A)(b)

Sex: Male

Age at injury: 46

Age at award: 54

Date of award: 30 March 1998

Tribunal: QBD

Amount of award then: £8,000

Award at February 2001: £8,557

Description of injuries: Whiplash injury to cervical and lumbar spine – claimant had suffered regular and significant symptoms in lumbar spine for a number of years; accident caused minor degree of aggravation to these for 12 months – pre-existing but asymptomatic degenerative changes also discovered in neck – judge's finding that symptoms in neck had been accelerated by 4 years as a result of the accident – claimant suffered almost constant pain in neck after accident – medically retired from post as deputy head – claimant forced to give up playing clarinet and saxophone, at which he was accomplished.

Prognosis: Not stated

Other points: Judge took account of loss of congenial employment and music in award for general damages.

1.3.1.2.C35 Case No. 10033

Name of case: Chappell v Chief Constable of Hertfordshire

Brief description of injuries: WHIPLASH

Reported: Kemp & Kemp, E2-051; [1990] CLY 1619

JSB Category: 6(A)

Sex: Male

Age at injury: 33

Age at award: 35

Date of award: 30 March 1990

Tribunal: QBD

Amount of award then: £6,000

Award at February 2001: £8,501

Description of injuries: Whiplash.

Prognosis: Not expected to affect normal working capacity – bouts of pain expected from time to time in the future.

1.3.1.2.C36 Case No. 11352

Name of case: Ferguson v Covel
Brief description of injuries: NECK – WHIPLASH
Reported: Kemp & Kemp, E2-054; [1997] CLY 1900
JSB Category: 6(A)(b)(i)
Sex: Female
Age at injury: 25
Age at award: 29
Date of award: 11 November 1996
Tribunal: Birmingham County Court
Amount of award then: £7,500
Award at February 2001: £8,382
Description of injuries: Whiplash type injury to the neck – pain to the lumbar spine – return to physiotherapy after a second accident.
Prognosis: Continuing pain was unlikely to improve significantly.
Other points: The injury had affected her domestic life – her work with computers was uncomfortable.

1.3.1.2.C37 Case No. 11810

Name of case: Rooney v Palmer
Brief description of injuries: NECK – WHIPLASH
Reported: Kemp & Kemp, E2-054/1; [1999] CLY 1473
JSB Category: 6(A)(b)(i)
Sex: Male
Age at injury: 69
Age at award: 71
Date of award: 19 November 1998
Tribunal: Swindon County Court
Amount of award then: £8,000
Award at February 2001: £8,370
Description of injuries: Whiplash injury to neck – claimant took 4 days off work immediately after accident, and some occasional days off thereafter – 1 year after accident, evidence of loss of normal lordosis – range of movement in flexion very limited – lateral flexion to left restricted – rotary movement to left 45 degrees; to right 40 degrees – very marked right – sided paravertebral muscular tenderness at base of neck – 6 months later, lateral flexion to left only 30 per cent of normal, and lateral flexion to right only marginal – X-rays revealed degenerative change with loss of disc height at C5/C6 and C6/C7 with predominantly unco – vertebral osteophytosis – very slight retrolithasis at C5/C6, secondary to degenerative change – 2 years after accident, claimant still experiencing difficulties with personal hygiene activities and domestic chores like gardening and decorating – driving uncomfortable, but claimant continuing in employment as HGV driver.
Prognosis: Symptoms expected to settle within about 12 months of date of hearing.

1.3.1.2.C38 Case No. 12003

Name of case: Calford v Campbell
Brief description of injuries: NECK – WHIPLASH – 5 YEAR ANELESATION
Reported: Kemp & Kemp, E2-054/2; [2000] 4 CL 145
JSB Category: 6(A)(b)(i)
Sex: Male
Age at injury: 30
Age at award: 34
Date of award: 18 November 1999
Tribunal: Rawtenstall County Court
Amount of award then: £8,000
Award at February 2001: £8,254
Description of injuries: Whiplash aggravating pre-existing cervical spondylitic disease – stiff neck radiating down the right shoulder into the right arm with a heavy sensation – immediate numbness to the fifth finger of the right hand – advised to keep the arm in a sling for seven days – referred for physiotherapy – there was continuing pain despite using analgesics and anti-inflammatory drugs – two disc protrusions showed on an MRI scan – at least one had occurred as a result of the accident. The onset of neck pain was the direct result of the accident – medical evidence suggested a five year acceleration of the spondylitic process had taken place.

1.3.1.2.C39 Case No. 12016

Name of case: Oliver v Burton
Brief description of injuries: NECK – WHIPLASH – DISC PROLAPSE
Reported: Kemp & Kemp, E2-504/3; [2000] 4 CL 159
JSB Category: 6(B)(b)(ii)
Sex: Male
Age at injury: 32
Age at award: 35
Date of award: 13 December 1999
Tribunal: Newcastle upon Tyne County Court
Amount of award then: £8,000
Award at February 2001: £8,225
Description of injuries: A whiplash type injury to the spine below the neck – off work for one week – wore a soft collar for five days – took analgesics – six week course of physiotherapy – neck pain had resolved within twelve months of the date of the accident. Lower back injury caused minimal protrusion of L5/S1 disc – intermittent pain and stiffness to the lower back – brought on by driving and prolonged sitting.

1.3.1.2.C40 Case No. 11588

Name of case: Barnett v Lintern
Brief description of injuries: NECK – WHIPLASH
Reported: Kemp & Kemp, E2-055/2; [1998] CLY 1590
JSB Category: 6(A)(b)(i)
Sex: Female
Age at injury: 36
Age at award: 40
Date of award: 13 November 1997
Tribunal: Swindon County Court
Amount of award then: £7,500
Award at February 2001: £8,083
Description of injuries: Acute whiplash injury to the cervical spine – claimant a disadvantage in the labour market.
Prognosis: Symptoms were likely to persist for the foreseeable future.

1.3.1.2.C41 Case No. 10950

Name of case: Bradley v Farid
Brief description of injuries: WHIPLASH
Reported: [1995] CLY 1701
JSB Category: 6(A)(b)(i)
Sex: Male
Age at injury: 29
Age at award: 31
Date of award: 05 September 1994
Tribunal: Manchester County Court
Amount of award then: £6,750
Award at February 2001: £8,007
Description of injuries: Male suffered whiplash injury to neck and soft-tissue injury to back – wore a collar for 10 days and was off work as coach painter for five days – had continuing and permanent pain in neck which was particularly noticeable when lifting heavy objects such as scaffolding frames which he had to move during his work – at time of assessment he described pain to both sides of neck and across shoulders which was "steady" and exacerbated when lifting his children – suffered intermittent "knife-like" pain in back, especially when turning – main problem was, however, the neck.
Prognosis: There was no likelihood of spontaneous resolution and it was concluded that the symptoms would, therefore be permanent.

1.3.1.2.C42 Case No. 10034

Name of case: Corthorn v Foster
Brief description of injuries: WHIPLASH – KNEE INJURY
Reported: Kemp & Kemp, E2-058; [1990] CLY 1620
JSB Category: 6(A)
Sex: Male
Age at injury: 39
Age at award: 41
Date of award: 19 February 1990
Tribunal: Nottingham County Court
Amount of award then: £5,500
Award at February 2001: £7,870
Description of injuries: Whiplash-type injury in road accident – stiffness, soreness and limited manoeuvrability – continues to have occasional discomfort when neck stiffens-up and aches – knee also injured and causes pain when asked to kneel for more than 30 minutes.
Prognosis: If heavy duties are avoided neck symptoms are likely to clear up within the next year – pain in knee is alleviated by knee pads.

1.3.1.2.C43 Case No. 11589

Name of case: Pancovics v Daffy
Brief description of injuries: NECK – WHIPLASH
Reported: E2-059/1; [1998] CLY 1591
JSB Category: 6(A)(b)(i)
Sex: Female
Age at injury: 28
Age at award: 30
Date of award: 06 April 1998
Tribunal: Northampton County Court
Amount of award then: £7,250
Award at February 2001: £7,669
Description of injuries: Whiplash injury to the neck and to the cervical spine.
Prognosis: P had progressed as far as she was going to – regular pain affected most aspects of her life.

1.3.1.2.C44 Case No. 11590

Name of case: Pike v BWOC Ltd
Brief description of injuries: NECK – WHIPLASH
Reported: Kemp & Kemp, E2-059/3; [1998] CLY 1592
JSB Category: 6(A)(b)(i)
Sex: Female
Age at injury: 55
Age at award: 56
Date of award: 04 August 1998
Tribunal: Bridgwater County Court
Amount of award then: £7,250
Award at February 2001: £7,618

Description of injuries: Whiplash injury to the cervical spine – grazed knees – bruising to the right forearm, chest and shoulder.

Prognosis: Symptoms had improved to a limited extent – they would continue at much the same level – no risk of future deterioration.

1.3.1.2.C45 Case No. 12060

Name of case: Gudge v Milroy
Brief description of injuries: NECK – WHIPLASH
Reported: [2000] 6 CL 190
JSB Category: 6(A)(b)(i)
Sex: Female
Age at injury: 24
Age at award: 29
Date of award: 21 January 2000
Tribunal: Hitchin County Court
Amount of award then: £7,250
Award at February 2001: £7,485

Description of injuries: Severe whiplash injury to the neck – immediate pain to the neck and shoulders – restricted movement – disabling for two to three months – dizziness, headaches and sleep disturbance for four months – wore a collar for six weeks – unable to drive her work vehicle for two months – unable to compete in horse-riding events at a national level for the 1996 season – minor psychological symptoms caused by threats issued by the other driver before the arrival of the police.

Prognosis: Intermittent residual symptoms were likely to be permanent.

1.3.1.2.C46 Case No. 11129

Name of case: Bond v West Midlands Travel
Brief description of injuries: NECK – WHIPLASH – 5-YEAR ACCELERATION
Reported: Kemp & Kemp, E2-060; [1996] CLY 2220
JSB Category: 6(A)(b)(ii)
Sex: Female
Age at injury: 45
Age at award: 49
Date of award: 20 October 1995
Tribunal: Birmingham County Court
Amount of award then: £6,500
Award at February 2001: £7,463

Description of injuries: Whiplash type injury to the neck – accident had accelerated pre-existing cervical spondylosis by five years.

Other points: At the time of the accident pre-existing cervical spondylosis had been pain-free for twelve months.

1.3.1.2.C47 Case No. 11591

Name of case: Leacock v Ward
Brief description of injuries: NECK – WHIPLASH
Reported: Kemp & Kemp, E2-061/1; [1998] CLY 1593
JSB Category: 6(A)(b)(i)
Sex: Male
Age at injury: 26
Age at award: 29
Date of award: 02 April 1998
Tribunal: Central London County Court
Amount of award then: £7,000
Award at February 2001: £7,405

Description of injuries: Whiplash injury to the cervical spine – a second accident exacerbated the injuries of the first – prolonged symptoms of pain by up to 9 months.

Prognosis: A full recovery could not be anticipated – L was likely to continue to suffer symptoms.

1.3.1.2.C48 Case No. 10759

Name of case: Kahl v Rosencourt

Brief description of injuries: NECK – WHIPLASH – PERMANENT INJURIES

Reported: [1994] CLY 1607

JSB Category: 6(A)(b)

Sex: Male

Age at injury: 31

Age at award: 34

Date of award: 27 October 1994

Tribunal: Clerkenwell County Court

Amount of award then: £6,250

Award at February 2001: £7,404

Description of injuries: Claimant, police officer, involved in road accident – whiplash injury to neck – badly shaken – no time off work – immediate pain across top of shoulders and in neck – continuing symptoms of stiff neck in mornings approximately 4 days per week, with pain above scapulae, necessitating manipulation of neck which caused loud "cracking" noise; movement then enabled and pain in scapulae reduced – 50 per cent restriction in left rotation – lateral flexion to right resisted with pain, causing difficulty when driving – occasional twinges in lumbar spine, exacerbated by (frequent) surveillance work – claimant forced to abandon sports pursued prior to accident and take up swimming; symptoms exacerbated by swimming, however – claimant unable to opportunity of working in support group and firearms unit, due to reduced fitness.

Prognosis: Condition likely to be permanent – no likelihood of degeneration.

1.3.1.2.C49 Case No. 11592

Name of case: Hepworth v Gotch

Brief description of injuries: NECK – WHIPLASH – FIVE YEARS

Reported: Kemp & Kemp, E2-061/2; [1998] CLY 1594

JSB Category: 6(A)(b)(i); 3(A)

Sex: Female

Age at injury: 29

Age at award: 32

Date of award: 05 August 1998

Tribunal: Worcester County Court

Amount of award then: £7,000

Award at February 2001: £7,355

Description of injuries: Moderate/severe whiplash injury to the cervical spine – psychological reaction – anxiety state lasted 3 years.

Prognosis: All symptoms were likely to resolve within 4 years and 9 months of the date of the accident.

1.3.1.2.C50 Case No. 11353

Name of case: Hunn v McFarlane

Brief description of injuries: NECK – WHIPLASH

Reported: Kemp & Kemp, E2-063; [1997] CLY 1901

JSB Category: 6(A)(c)

Sex: Female

Age at injury: 36

Age at award: 38

Date of award: 01 June 1996

Tribunal: West London County Court

Amount of award then: £6,500

Award at February 2001: £7,307

Description of injuries: Whiplash type injury to the neck – unable to continue with her lifetime interest in caring for her horses for eighteen months.

Other points: Award was assessed as £3,500 for whiplash / £3,000 for loss of amenity.

1.3.1.2.C51 Case No. 11811

Name of case: Beacham v Shaw

Brief description of injuries: NECK – WHIPLASH

Reported: Kemp & Kemp, E2-064/1/1; [1999] CLY 1474

JSB Category: 6(A)(b)(i)

Sex: Male

Age at injury: 47

Age at award: 50

Date of award: 21 April 1999

Tribunal: Launceston County Court

Amount of award then: £6,750

Award at February 2001: £7,028

Description of injuries: Whiplash injury to neck – immediate pain – collar and analgesics prescribed – continuous dull ache in left side of neck and shoulder, aggravated by activity and sometimes disturbing sleep, ongoing for 2 years – thereafter, symptoms would be absent for a few weeks and then recur at their original level for about a week – at time of trial, claimant still suffering intermittent neck pain, occasional night waking and limitation in neck movement – underlying osteoporosis hindering recovery, but neck pain over and above that which would have otherwise been experienced – claimant already medically retired for an unrelated condition, but injuries would adversely affect his lifestyle and ability to find work.

Prognosis: Probability that a full recovery would not be made from effects of accident.

Other points: Judge considered claim to fall at the bottom of the JSB Guidelines for whiplash injuries of the more severe type.

1.3.1.2.C52 Case No. 10384

Name of case: Lavender v Foley
Brief description of injuries: WHIPLASH
Reported: [1992] CLY 1640
JSB Category: 6(A)(b)(ii)
Sex: Male
Age at injury: 32
Age at award: 39
Date of award: 10 July 1992
Tribunal: Wood Green Trial Centre
Amount of award then: £5,500
Award at February 2001: £6,816

Description of injuries: Whiplash injury resulting in soft-tissue injury – neck pain – forced to give up all sports.

1.3.1.2.C53 Case No. 11812

Name of case: Richardson v Dunning
Brief description of injuries: NECK – WHIPLASH
Reported: Kemp & Kemp, E2-064/2; [1999] CLY 1475
JSB Category: 6(A)(b)(ii)
Sex: Male
Age at injury: 65
Age at award: 67
Date of award: 01 July 1999
Tribunal: Bristol County Court
Amount of award then: £6,500
Award at February 2001: £6,772

Description of injuries: Whiplash injury – 12 sessions of physiotherapy – severe headaches, nausea and vomiting for first month after accident – severe neck pain with paraesthesia in fingertips and thumb of right hand for next 5 months – significant improvement after 11 months, but still constant symptoms ranging from discomfort to severe pain – neck movement restricted to only 25 per cent of expected range – further 14 sessions of physiotherapy resulted in significant improvement – 2 years after accident, neck movement increased to 50 per cent of expected range and symptoms of pain intermittent, but still occurring daily and aggravated by activity or static posture – claimant unable to decorate or do DIY, or turn head when reversing car – only able to participate in main pastime and social activity of ballroom dancing to a limited degree.

Prognosis: Restricted movement of neck and intermittent symptoms permanent.

1.3.1.2.C54 Case No. 11593

Name of case: Braham v Golding
Brief description of injuries: NECK – WHIPLASH
Reported: Kemp & Kemp, E2-065/1; [1998] CLY 1595
JSB Category: 6(A)(b)(i)
Sex: Female
Age at injury: 19
Age at award: 22
Date of award: 26 November 1997
Tribunal: Bow County Court
Amount of award then: £6,250
Award at February 2001: £6,736

Description of injuries: Soft-tissue injuries to the cervical spine – at the time of the accident B was still suffering from injuries of a previous accident.

Prognosis: Symptoms of the second accident were likely to continue for a number of years.

1.3.1.2.C55 Case No. 10761

Name of case: Norrington v Struth
Brief description of injuries: NECK – WHIPLASH – EXACERBATION OF SYMPTOMS FROM PREVIOUS NECK INJURY
Reported: Kemp & Kemp, E3-010; [1994] CLY 1609
JSB Category: 6(A)(b)
Sex: Male
Age at injury: 18
Age at award: 21
Date of award: 24 November 1993
Tribunal: Colchester and Clacton County Court
Amount of award then: £5,250
Award at February 2001: £6,377

Description of injuries: Road accident – whiplash injury to neck and lower thoracic spine; bruising to knees, chest and face – claimant had previously sustained whiplash injury to neck and upper thoracic spine in road accident 3 years previously, for which he was still receiving treatment at time of second accident – aggravation of neck symptoms – pain in lower thoracic spine – continuing intermittent pain and crepitus in neck – pain in lower thoracic and lumbar spine, exacerbated by prolonged sitting, driving, lifting and repeated bending, and affecting claimant's enjoyment of playing squash – pain in chest when stretching and breathing heavily.

Prognosis: No improvement in symptoms between accident at trial – however, claimant expected to recover.

Damage to Spine

1.3.1.2.C56 Case No. 10760

Name of case: Young v Costello

Brief description of injuries: NECK – WHIPLASH – 3-4 YEAR ACCELERATION OF PREVIOUSLY ASYMPTOMATIC CONDITION

Reported: Kemp & Kemp, E2-068; [1994] CLY 1608

JSB Category: 6(A)(b); 3(A)

Sex: Female

Age at injury: 68

Age at award: 70

Date of award: 02 November 1993

Tribunal: Oldham County Court

Amount of award then: £5,250

Award at February 2001: £6,377

Description of injuries: Whiplash injury – pain in neck, particularly on right side, radiating into shoulder and down arm; occasionally into back of right side of head – sleep interrupted – various household tasks hindered, taking much longer to complete – inability to carry heavy shopping bags – claimant had not ridden bicycle since accident – nervousness – irritability – claimant terrified when travelling by car, and somewhat of a nuisance to driver – X-rays revealed pre-existing but previously wholly asymptomatic cervical spondylitis.

Prognosis: Accident had precipitated spondylitic symptoms, accelerating onset by 3 to 4 years – symptoms likely to be present for rest of claimant's life.

1.3.1.2.C57 Case No. 10035

Name of case: Rowe v Waddington Technical Services

Brief description of injuries: WHIPLASH

Reported: [1990] CLY 1621

JSB Category: 6(A)

Sex: Female

Age at injury: 33

Age at award: 36

Date of award: 25 May 1989

Tribunal: QBD

Amount of award then: £4,250

Award at February 2001: £6,357

Description of injuries: Whiplash – minor concussion – dizziness – cuts and abrasions – suffered headaches and back pain – some spinal degeneration occurred.

Prognosis: Full recovery anticipated within six to twelve months.

1.3.1.2.C58 Case No. 10951

Name of case: Lamb v Alcan Speciality Extrusions

Brief description of injuries: WHIPLASH – CONTINUING STIFFNESS

Reported: Kemp & Kemp, E2-071; [1995] CLY 1702

JSB Category: 6(A)(b)(ii)

Sex: Male

Age at injury: 39

Age at award: 41

Date of award: 02 June 1995

Tribunal: Leeds County Court

Amount of award then: £5,500

Award at February 2001: £6,315

Description of injuries: Male furnace operator was injured when forklift truck he was driving was struck by another forklift – finished shift but awoke following day with pain and stiffness in neck – pain subsided, but significant stiffness, restriction of movement and some discomfort persisted to trial – plaintiff's main complaints at date of trial were of difficulty in driving due to inability to turn head; discomfort when watching sporting fixtures and inability to resume pre-accident hobby of darts – had not been absent from work at any time and had sought only limited medical attention, including physiotherapy which had provided only temporary relief.

Prognosis: Strong likelihood that stiffness and restriction of movement would continue indefinitely.

1.3.1.2.C59 Case No. 11132

Name of case: Moulang v Morton

Brief description of injuries: NECK – WHIPLASH

Reported: Kemp & Kemp, E2-072; [1996] CLY 2223

JSB Category: 6(A)(b)(ii)

Sex: Female

Age at injury: 29

Age at award: 32

Date of award: 16 April 1996

Tribunal: Gloucester County Court

Amount of award then: £5,500

Award at February 2001: £6,199

Description of injuries: Moderately severe whiplash injury to the neck – back more vulnerable.

Prognosis: A full recovery was unlikely – she would suffer intermittent lower back pain in the foreseeable future.

1.3.1.2.C60 Case No. 10400

Name of case: Wolfendon v James

Brief description of injuries: WHIPLASH INJURY – THREE YEARS

Reported: Kemp & Kemp, E3-103; [1992] CLY 1656

JSB Category: 6(B)(c)

Sex: Female

Age at injury: 17

Age at award: 19

Date of award: 08 April 1992

Tribunal: Blackpool County Court

Amount of award then: £5,000

Award at February 2001: £6,196

Description of injuries: Whiplash injury to the neck and lower back – one year after the accident there was still stiffness in the neck and lower back – worse after a heavy day – pins and needles sensation in her right arm – discomfort on bending and lifting – injuries were thought to be perpetuated by the nature of her work.

Prognosis: Discomfort was expected to continue for some months – no long term disability was anticipated.

1.3.1.2.C61 Case No. 10589

Name of case: Hill v Craven

Brief description of injuries: NECK – WHIPLASH – EXACERBATION OF PRE-EXISTING CONDITION

Reported: Kemp & Kemp, E2-073; [1993] CLY 1482

JSB Category: 6(A)(b)

Sex: Male

Age at injury: 56

Age at award: 58

Date of award: 10 July 1992

Tribunal: Bristol County Court

Amount of award then: £5,000

Award at February 2001: £6,196

Description of injuries: Whiplash injury to neck in road accident – cervical collar worn continuously for 4 days, claimant off work for 6 weeks – thereafter, neck pain after standing for more than 10 minutes – pain radiating up back of neck a couple of times each month – tingling sensation in arms a couple of times a week – exacerbation of cervical spondylitis condition pre-existent since 1974 – unable to garden or do DIY without pain – difficulty in walking more than a mile.

Prognosis: Claimant would not have been free of spondylitis symptoms if accident had not occurred, but exacerbation was to such an extent as to affect ability to work.

1.3.1.2.C62 Case No. 11594

Name of case: Kibble v Bond

Brief description of injuries: NECK – WHIPLASH – 3 YEARS

Reported: Kemp & Kemp, E2-073/1; [1998] CLY 1596

JSB Category: 6(A)(b)(ii)

Sex: Female

Age at injury: 23

Age at award: 26

Date of award: 30 July 1998

Tribunal: Central London County Court

Amount of award then: £5,750

Award at February 2001: £6,067

Description of injuries: Soft-tissue whiplash injury to the cervical spine.

Prognosis: K would make a full recovery within a short time of the trial

1.3.1.2.C63 Case No. 11355

Name of case: Ashton v Mortlock

Brief description of injuries: NECK – WHIPLASH

Reported: Kemp & Kemp, E2-073/2; [1997] CLY 1903

JSB Category: 6(A)(b)(ii)

Sex: Female

Age at injury: 21

Age at award: 25

Date of award: 28 April 1997

Tribunal: Plymouth County Court

Amount of award then: £5,500

Award at February 2001: £6,052

Description of injuries: Whiplash type injury requiring 52 physiotherapy sessions.

Prognosis: The neck injury was expected to have permanent effects – intermittent episodes of pain – vulnerable to trauma – giving birth to and carrying children would cause neck pain.

1.3.1.2.C64 Case No. 10952

Name of case: West v Campagnie

Brief description of injuries: WHIPLASH – FULL RECOVERY EXPECTED

Reported: Kemp & Kemp, K2-002; [1995] CLY 1703

JSB Category: 6(A)(b)(ii)

Sex: Male

Age at injury: 42

Age at award: -

Date of award: 18 October 1994

Tribunal: Reading County Court

Amount of award then: £5,000

Award at February 2001: £5,923

Description of injuries: Plaintiff was driver of stationary motor car when it was struck from behind by another motor car at speed – sustained blow to occiput and lost consciousness for a very short period of time – suffered whiplash injury to neck, hyperextension of fingers and wrist of left hand and injuries from seatbelt to right shoulder and front of chest. – required no time off work and took no painkillers but underwent nine sessions of physiotherapy – five months after accident, plaintiff was still suffering from frequent headaches which were sometimes severe and could become migrainous – had persistent pains in neck on movement and had intermittent paraesthesia in right arm which sometimes woke him at night – also suffered from pain and clicking in right shoulder – had sustained post-traumatic supraspinatus injury to shoulder – plaintiff's job involved considerable amount of driving and some lifting, activities which exacerbated symptoms but he chose to persevere in his job due to the poor economic climate – when examined five months after accident plaintiff had a reduced range of movement in neck and right shoulder – neck movements were stiff and there were areas of tenderness – injury affected enjoyment of hobbies of gardening and squash but only for short period – at date of hearing, he still suffered from headaches twice a week, some of them migrainous, neck pains when driving for long periods of time (which job required) and occasional clicking in shoulder.

Prognosis: Headaches and neck pain were expected to subside within about two-and-a-half years and his shoulder injury by about three years after date of accident – after that time plaintiff was not expected to have any residual symptoms or any increased risk of degenerative changes.

1.3.1.2.C65 Case No. 11595

Name of case: Surdivall v K Walker Transport

Brief description of injuries: NECK – WHIPLASH

Reported: Kemp & Kemp, E2-076/1; [1998] CLY 1597

JSB Category: 6(A)(b)(ii)

Sex: Male

Age at injury: 49

Age at award: 52

Date of award: 17 July 1998

Tribunal: Burnley County Court

Amount of award then: £5,500

Award at February 2001: £5,804

Description of injuries: Whiplash injury to the cervical spine.

Prognosis: The injury was not of the most serious type, but S would be left with some long-term troubles following the injury.

1.3.1.2.C66 Case No. 12061

Name of case: Kempster v Ashfield

Brief description of injuries: NECK – WHIPLASH

Reported: [2000] 6 CL 191

JSB Category: 6(A)(b)(ii)

Sex: Male

Age at injury: 41

Age at award: 45

Date of award: 11 November 1999

Tribunal: Southampton County Court

Amount of award then: £5,500

Award at February 2001: £5,675

Description of injuries: Whiplash injury to the neck – wore a collar for one week – analgesics prescribed for one week when the neck was noticeably painful – off work for one week – symptoms settled over six weeks – only minor symptoms remained when K turned his head.

Prognosis: A stiff neck in the mornings was likely to persist for the foreseeable future.

1.3.1.2.C67 Case No. 12009

Name of case: Utley v Parker

Brief description of injuries: NECK – WHIPLASH INJURIES TO THE CERVICAL SPINE

Reported: Kemp & Kemp, E2-076/3; [2000] 4 CL 152

JSB Category: 6(B)(c)

Sex: Male

Age at injury: 42

Age at award: 46

Date of award: 24 November 1999

Tribunal: Sheffield County Court

Amount of award then: £5,500

Award at February 2001: £5,675

Description of injuries: In a road traffic accident U suffered whiplash injuries to the cervical spine – off work for a total of six months over a three year period – symptoms improved between the date of the accident and the time of the hearing but some remained.

Prognosis: Pain to the neck occurred once or twice a month – it could last for several days at a time – his condition had stabilised and no further deterioration was expected – intermittent symptoms were expected to continue for the foreseeable future.

1.3.1.2.C68 Case No. 12040

Name of case: McPherson v Shiasson

Brief description of injuries: NECK – WHIPLASH – 3-4 YEARS

Reported: Kemp & Kemp, E2-076/4; [2000] 5 CL 184

JSB Category: 6(A)(b)(ii)

Sex: Male

Age at injury: 53

Age at award: 57

Date of award: 09 December 1999

Tribunal: Wakefield County Court

Amount of award then: £5,500

Award at February 2001: £5,655

Description of injuries: A whiplash injury to the neck – pain and dizziness – three physiotherapy treatments – nine months after the accident the pain became so severe that a further course of physiotherapy was undertaken – seven weeks off work – C changed his job to reduce the hours spent driving. At the time of the hearing C was symptom-free – he had resumed full-time work.

Other points: Episodes of pre-existing neck pain for eight years before the accident were treated with analgesics.

1.3.1.2.C69 Case No. 10854

Name of case: Rothwell v Hodson

Brief description of injuries: NECK – WHIPLASH – BACK

Reported: Kemp & Kemp, E2-077; [1994] CLY 1704

JSB Category: 6(A)(c), 6(B)(c)

Sex: Female

Age at injury: 19

Age at award: 22

Date of award: 04 November 1994

Tribunal: Horsham County Court

Amount of award then: £4,750

Award at February 2001: £5,623

Description of injuries: Road accident – whiplash injury to neck and lower back – no evidence of bony injury – collar prescribed, worn for 2 weeks; absent from work for that period – intermittent pain in centre of neck, especially when tired or after prolonged standing – also pain in lower back – symptoms settled, but started to return 6 months later after change of work, involving lifting heavy bags of money and long periods of sitting – at trial, neck pains minimal but pain evident in lower back when tired, bending or carrying weights – range of movement good.

Prognosis: All symptoms likely to disappear within a few years – no increased chance of arthritic change.

1.3.1.2.C70 Case No. 11018

Name of case: Rothwell v Hodson

Brief description of injuries: NECK – WHIPLASH – MINIMAL SYMPTOMS AFTER 3 YEARS – FULL RECOVERY EXPECTED

Reported: Kemp & Kemp, E2-077; [1995] CLY 1770

JSB Category: 6(A)(c)

Sex: Female

Age at injury: 19

Age at award: 22

Date of award: 04 November 1994

Tribunal: Horsham County Court

Amount of award then: £4,750

Award at February 2001: £5,623

Description of injuries: Plaintiff suffered whiplash injuries to neck and lower back – no evidence of bony injury. Soft collar fitted which she wore for two weeks while absent from work – suffered intermittent pain in centre of neck, especially when tired or she had been standing for too long, coupled with pain in lower back – after two weeks symptoms began to resolve themselves – had two physiotherapy sessions – symptoms settled, but after six months and change of work (involving lifting heavy bags of money and long periods of sitting) they started to return – at trial, neck pains were minimal but plaintiff still suffered pain across lower back when tired, bending or carrying weights, although range of movement was good.

Prognosis: All symptoms were likely to disappear within a few years with no increased chance of arthritic change.

1.3.1.2.C71 Case No. 10762

Name of case: Hodgson v Abrahams

Brief description of injuries: NECK – WHIPLASH – 5 YEAR ACCELERATION OF PRE-EXISTING CONDITION – INJURY TO SHOULDER

Reported: Kemp & Kemp, E2-079; [1994] CLY 1610

JSB Category: 6(A)(b), 6(D)

Sex: Male

Age at injury: 56

Age at award: 59

Date of award: 21 September 1994

Tribunal: Aldershot County Court

Amount of award then: £4,650

Award at February 2001: £5,516

Description of injuries: Road accident – moderate whiplash injury to cervical spine – soft-tissue injury to rotator cuff muscles in right shoulder – soft collar and analgesics prescribed; claimant took no time off work, as self-employed – 2.5 years after accident, ongoing mild discomfort in neck and 25 per cent reduction in movement; X-rays revealed pre-existing degenerative changes in spine – reduced shoulder movement and residual stiffness – mild paraesthesia to right hand due to nerve root irritation – hobbies (golf, gardening, DIY) curtailed.

Prognosis: Degenerative changes in cervical spine accelerated 5 years by the accident – ongoing symptoms unchanged but mild at time of trial; strenuous lifting or carrying would cause more severe pain to return.

1.3.1.2.C72 Case No. 11017

Award at February 2001: £5,450

See: 1.3.1.C15 for details

1.3.1.2.C73 Case No. 11356

Name of case: Graham v Kelly (No. 1)

Brief description of injuries: NECK – WHIPLASH

Reported: Kemp & Kemp, E2-080/1; [1997] CLY 1904

JSB Category: 6(A)(b)(ii)

Sex: Male

Age at injury: 34

Age at award: 37

Date of award: 18 September 1997

Tribunal: Aldershot and Farnham County Court

Amount of award then: £5,000

Award at February 2001: £5,399

Description of injuries: Moderate whiplash injury to the neck – 19 physiotherapy sessions.

Prognosis: Three years after the date of the accident it was expected that a full recovery would be made – unlikely that there would be late complications.

Other points: The judge deemed the plaintiff a stoical man who was "toughing it out".

1.3.1.2.C74 Case No. 11357

Name of case: Grainger v Howes

Brief description of injuries: NECK – WHIPLASH

Reported: Kemp & Kemp, E2-080/2; [1997] CLY 1905

JSB Category: 6(A)(b)(ii)

Sex: Female

Age at injury: 25

Age at award: 29

Date of award: 30 September 1997

Tribunal: Reading County Court

Amount of award then: £5,000

Award at February 2001: £5,399

Description of injuries: Chronic whiplash syndrome – back and neck pain – very shaken.

Prognosis: The residual affects of the injury were expected to be permanent – at increased vulnerability to further trauma.

Other points: Continuing symptoms were extremely minor – the judge put this down to the adjustments she had made to her life-style – injury at the upper end of the bracket.

1.3.1.2.C75 Case No. 11597

Name of case: Amatyakul v Olding

Brief description of injuries: NECK – WHIPLASH – 2 YEARS

Reported: Kemp & Kemp, E2-080/3; [1998] CLY 1599

JSB Category: 6(A)(b)(ii)

Sex: Female

Age at injury: 34

Age at award: 36

Date of award: 10 October 1997

Tribunal: Canterbury County Court

Amount of award then: £5,000

Award at February 2001: £5,392

Description of injuries: Whiplash injury to the cervical spine – neck pain and dizziness.

Prognosis: A full recovery was expected within 2 years of the date of the accident.

1.3.1.2.C76 Case No. 11210

Name of case: Fox v Slaughter

Brief description of injuries: NECK – WHIPLASH – 26 MONTHS

Reported: Kemp & Kemp, E2-084; [1996] CLY 2301

JSB Category: 6(A)(c)

Sex: Female

Age at injury: 27

Age at award: 28

Date of award: 23 October 1996

Tribunal: Milton Keynes County Court

Amount of award then: £4,750

Award at February 2001: £5,312

Description of injuries: Whiplash type injury.

Prognosis: Full recovery expected within twenty-six months of the date of the accident.

1.3.1.2.C77 Case No. 11358

Name of case: Davis v Milborrow (No. 1)

Brief description of injuries: NECK – WHIPLASH

Reported: Kemp & Kemp, E2-085/1; [1997] CLY 1906

JSB Category: 6(A)(b)(ii)

Sex: Male

Age at injury: 44

Age at award: 47

Date of award: 24 June 1997

Tribunal: Tunbridge Wells County Court

Amount of award then: £4,850

Award at February 2001: £5,297

Description of injuries: Most serious injury was a whiplash type injury to the neck – the injuries had substantially resolved at the time of the hearing.

1.3.1.2.C78 Case No. 11596

Name of case: Matbey v Bayley

Brief description of injuries: NECK – WHIPLASH

Reported: Kemp & Kemp, E2-085/2; [1998] CLY 1598

JSB Category: 6(A)(b)(ii)

Sex: Female

Age at injury: 29

Age at award: 33

Date of award: 27 July 1998

Tribunal: Southampton County Court

Amount of award then: £5,000

Award at February 2001: £5,276

Description of injuries: Whiplash injury to the cervical spine.

Prognosis: The residual disability could be permanent, or might resolve over a protracted period.

1.3.1.2.C79 Case No. 10038

Name of case: Fulton v Turners (Southampton)

Brief description of injuries: WHIPLASH – COLLAR FOR 10 WEEKS

Reported: Kemp & Kemp, E2-086; [1990] CLY 1624

JSB Category: 6(A)

Sex: Male

Age at injury: 53

Age at award: -

Date of award: 01 April 1989

Tribunal: Bristol County Court

Amount of award then: £3,500

Award at February 2001: £5,267

Description of injuries: Whiplash injury to neck – cervical collar needed for approximately 10 weeks – work impaired due to tightness in neck muscles – occasional dizziness and pins and needles

1.3.1.2.C80 Case No. 11813

Name of case: Kibbie v Bourdon

Brief description of injuries: NECK – WHIPLASH

Reported: Kemp & Kemp, E2-087/1; [1999] CLY 1476

JSB Category: 6(A)(b)(ii); 3(A)(d)

Sex: Female

Age at injury: 47

Age at award: 50

Date of award: 21 January 1999

Tribunal: Boston County Court

Amount of award then: £5,000

Award at February 2001: £5,263

Description of injuries: Whiplash injury to neck in road accident – development on following morning of severe pain and stiffness in neck and interscapular pain – 2 weeks off work required; soft collar and physiotherapy prescribed – gardening still impossible 6 months after accident – gradual diminution of symptoms over 3 years, after which claimant only experienced pain after over – exertion – also minor psychological injuries; disturbed sleep for 1 week and occasional flashbacks – nervousness when placed in situation similar to that in which accident occurred still evident after 3 years.

1.3.1.2.C81 Case No. 10203

Name of case: Dennis v Brassett

Brief description of injuries: WHIPLASH – SOME IMPROVEMENT AFTER 15 MONTHS

Reported: Kemp & Kemp, E2-087; [1991] CLY 1400

JSB Category: 6(A)(b)(ii)

Sex: Male

Age at injury: 35

Age at award: 37

Date of award: 14 February 1991

Tribunal: Bromley County Court (HHJ Spon-Smith)

Amount of award then: £4,000

Award at February 2001: £5,256

Description of injuries: Whiplash type injury to the neck – minor bruising to the chest – nerve-root damage caused pins and needles radiating to the left arm for several weeks – received physiotherapy for two months – improvement was slow – recovery did proceed after fifteen months.

Prognosis: Unable to resume playing football – D was still experiencing symptoms several times a week – his condition was improving.

1.3.1.2.C82 Case No. 11912

Name of case: Gornall v Yandell

Brief description of injuries: NECK – WHIPLASH – 1 YEAR WITH OCCASIONAL CONTINUING SYMPTOMS

Reported: Kemp & Kemp, PRE-011; [1999] CLY 1576

JSB Category: 6(A)(c)

Sex: Female

Age at injury: 32

Age at award: 35

Date of award: 10 May 1999

Tribunal: Hertford County Court

Amount of award then: £5,000

Award at February 2001: £5,193

Description of injuries: Road accident – whiplash injury to neck – claimant went to hospital and advised to take painkillers, which she did for some months – off work 1 week – symptoms thereafter at mild, occasionally moderate, level – headaches – pins and needles in arm – very nervous in traffic for 1 year – did not return to gym for 1 year – unable to resume swimming due to neck pain – 3 years after accident, claimant still experiencing symptoms about once a month.

Prognosis: Symptoms would resolve within 3 years of accident – increased vulnerability in neck for a period of about 5 years.

1.3.1.2.C83 Case No. 10590

Name of case: Maddison v Gandy

Brief description of injuries: NECK – WHIPLASH

Reported: Kemp & Kemp, E3-108; [1993] CLY 1483

JSB Category: 6(A)(b)

Sex: Female

Age at injury: 38

Age at award: 43

Date of award: 11 March 1993

Tribunal: Ilford County Court

Amount of award then: £4,200

Award at February 2001: £5,186

Description of injuries: Whiplash injury to neck and lower backache in road accident – immediate pain and stiffness in neck spreading to both shoulders – soft collar for 2 weeks, off work 3 weeks – subsequent pain and stiffness in back and neck exacerbated by cold weather or by sitting for long periods of time – neck pain or aching, not severe or debilitating, still present at time of hearing, worsening through over-exertion and spreading to shoulders and arm, causing subsequent headaches and preventing heavy lifting, knitting or gardening.

Prognosis: No further improvement anticipated – caution would need to be exercised in the future.

1.3.1.2.C84 Case No. 11715

Name of case: Wroe v Playforth
Brief description of injuries: NECK – WHIPLASH
Reported: Kemp & Kemp, E2-120/1; [1998] CLY 1718
JSB Category: 6(A)(c)
Sex: P1: Male P2: Female P3: Female
Age at injury: -
Age at award: P1:58;P2:56;P3:26
Date of award: 24 November 1997
Tribunal: Doncaster County Court
Amount of award then: £4,800
Award at February 2001: £5,173

Description of injuries: Whiplash injuries of varying severity – at the time of the hearing injuries to P1 had largely resolved – injuries to P2 and P3 had completely resolved.

Other points: Award split between applicants – P1: £2,500; P2: £1,500; P3: £800.

1.3.1.2.C85 Case No. 11359

Award at February 2001: £5,155

See: 1.3.1.C18 for details

1.3.1.2.C86 Case No. 10855

Name of case: Stannard v Flanagan
Brief description of injuries: NECK – WHIPLASH – 12-18 MONTHS
Reported: Kemp & Kemp, E2-089; [1994] CLY 1705
JSB Category: 6(A)(c)
Sex: Female
Age at injury: 22
Age at award: 24
Date of award: 17 December 1993
Tribunal: Andover County Court
Amount of award then: £4,250
Award at February 2001: £5,152

Description of injuries: Road accident – whiplash injury to neck – tenderness, stiffness and pain in neck muscles – dizziness and pain in back of head – tingling in both forearms – surgical collar worn for 2 months continually, and on occasions thereafter – off work 1 week – pain ongoing in neck 7 months after accident, aggravated by activity – occasional symptoms at work, necessitating lying on floor of office on one occasion – hobbies of dancing, jogging, cycling, tennis, swimming affected – claimant forced to cease aerobics altogether, and had not recommenced at date of trial – pain when standing prevented her from watching boyfriend play football – anti-inflammatories and physiotherapy prescribed – further aggravation of symptoms 14 months after accident not eased by anti-inflammatories – further physiotherapy and osteopathy – recovery from injuries made at a point sometime between 12 and 18 months after accident.

1.3.1.2.C87 Case No. 10386

Name of case: Whitehouse v Foster
Brief description of injuries: WHIPLASH INJURY
Reported: Kemp & Kemp, E2-090; [1992] CLY 1642
JSB Category: 6(A)(b)(ii)
Sex: Female
Age at injury: 34
Age at award: 37
Date of award: 10 September 1991
Tribunal: Birmingham District Registry
Amount of award then: £4,000
Award at February 2001: £5,111

Description of injuries: Whiplash injury – blow to the right temple.

Prognosis: No long term improvement or deterioration expected.

1.3.1.2.C88 Case No. 11598

Name of case: Barrett v Cramp
Brief description of injuries: NECK – WHIPLASH – 3 YEARS
Reported: Kemp & Kemp, E2-090/1; [1998] CLY 1600
JSB Category: 6(A)(b)(ii)
Sex: Male
Age at injury: 43
Age at award: 46
Date of award: 09 March 1998
Tribunal: Cardiff County Court
Amount of award then: £4,750
Award at February 2001: £5,081

Description of injuries: Whiplash injury to the cervical spine – neck pain and headaches.

Prognosis: Pre-existing spondylosis would have caused symptoms of the type suffered in the accident within 3 years at any event.

Damage to Spine

1.3.1.2.C89 Case No. 10036

Name of case: Gardner v Mullins

Brief description of injuries: WHIPLASH – BRUISING

Reported: Kemp & Kemp, E2-091; [1990] CLY 1622

JSB Category: 6(A)

Sex: Female

Age at injury: 55

Age at award: 57

Date of award: 20 August 1990

Tribunal: Epsom County Court

Amount of award then: £3,750

Award at February 2001: £5,035

Description of injuries: Suffered shock, pains in chest, pains in neck and bruising to both knees.

Prognosis: Symptoms likely to diminish – expected residual aching in neck from time to time – possible visit to osteopath needed in future.

1.3.1.2.C90 Case No. 11599

Name of case: Storfer v Yogaratnam

Brief description of injuries: NECK – WHIPLASH

Reported: 98 (6) QR 6; Kemp & Kemp, E2-091/1; [1998] CLY 1601

JSB Category: 6(A)(b)(ii)

Sex: Male

Age at injury: 35

Age at award: 39

Date of award: 01 July 1998

Tribunal: Reading County Court

Amount of award then: £4,750

Award at February 2001: £5,012

Description of injuries: Whiplash injury to the cervical spine – bruising – puncture wound.

Prognosis: Symptoms were likely to persist at current level, but would not deteriorate.

1.3.1.2.C91 Case No. 10037

Name of case: Miles v Martyn

Brief description of injuries: WHIPLASH – PRE-EXISTING BACK PROBLEM – 3-5 YEARS ACCELERATION

Reported: Kemp & Kemp, E2-092; [1990] CLY 1623

JSB Category: 6(A)

Sex: Male

Age at injury: 55

Age at award: 56

Date of award: 31 October 1990

Tribunal: QBD

Amount of award then: £3,750

Award at February 2001: £4,950

Description of injuries: Plaintiff sustained whiplash injury when his car was driven into from behind – neck began to ache 3 days after accident – one week off work – underwent osteopathy – prescribed a collar and analgesics – neck ached on turning head to left, aggravated by cold weather and draughts – gardening and car maintenance hobbies restricted, but partly by independent back trouble – pre-existing but symptomless cervical spondylitis diagnosed as cause of problem – considering plaintiff's age, symptoms probably brought on 3 to 5 years early and would continue.

1.3.1.2.C92 Case No. 10388

Name of case: Segree v Shepherd

Brief description of injuries: WHIPLASH – POSSIBLE PERMANENT VULNERABILITY

Reported: [1992] CLY 1644

JSB Category: 6(A)(b)(ii)

Sex: Male

Age at injury: 44

Age at award: 46

Date of award: 03 June 1992

Tribunal: Manchester County Court

Amount of award then: £4,000

Award at February 2001: £4,939

Description of injuries: Whiplash type injury to the neck and left shoulder – X-ray revealed a symptomatic degenerative changes at C5/C6.

Prognosis: Possible permanent vulnerability of the cervical spine.

1.3.1.2.C93 Case No. 10204

Name of case: Lavender v Hayes

Brief description of injuries: WHIPLASH – SYMPTOMS FOR 3+ YEARS

Reported: Kemp & Kemp, E2-093; [1991] CLY 1401

JSB Category: 6(A)(b)(ii)

Sex: Female

Age at injury: 25

Age at award: 28

Date of award: 01 February 1991

Tribunal: Birmingham County Court

Amount of award then: £3,750

Award at February 2001: £4,927

Description of injuries: Whiplash injury – with pain to the neck – accidental manipulation to the neck in a further accident in 1989 resulted in improvement to the symptoms.

Prognosis: The residual symptoms were likely to resolve shortly after the time of the hearing.

1.3.1.2.C94 Case No. 11995

Name of case: Twycross v Hilton
Brief description of injuries: NECK – WHIPLASH
Reported: Kemp & Kemp, E2-093/1; [2000] 3 CL 179
JSB Category: 6(A)(c)
Sex: Female
Age at injury: 43
Age at award: 46
Date of award: 17 November 1999
Tribunal: Lincoln County Court
Amount of award then: £4,750
Award at February 2001: £4,901

Description of injuries: A whiplash neck injury – immediate pain, headache and shock – wore a collar for two weeks, and on and off for a further two weeks – saw her GP twice over the following weeks – who prescribed painkillers – nine sessions of chiropractic treatment – symptoms improved over the first two months.

Prognosis: At the time of the hearing medical evidence was that the residual nuisance symptoms were permanent.

1.3.1.2.C95 Case No. 11600

Name of case: Franklin v Challis
Brief description of injuries: NECK – WHIPLASH
Reported: Kemp & Kemp, E2-093/1; [1998] CLY 1602
JSB Category: 6(A)(b)(ii)
Sex: Female
Age at injury: 31
Age at award: 34
Date of award: 12 August 1998
Tribunal: Yeovil County Court
Amount of award then: £4,650
Award at February 2001: £4,886

Description of injuries: Whiplash injury to the cervical spine – exacerbation of existing back pain – F was left with an uncomfortable neck which disabled her to a moderate but significant extent.

Prognosis: Symptoms were likely to remain the same in the future.

1.3.1.2.C96 Case No. 10765

Name of case: Rafferty v Skelton
Brief description of injuries: NECK – WHIPLASH – 12-18 MONTH EXACERBATION OF PRE-EXISTING SYMPTOMS OF DEGENERATIVE CHANGES
Reported: Kemp & Kemp, E2-095; [1994] CLY 1613
JSB Category: 6(A)(b)
Sex: Female
Age at injury: 51
Age at award: 54
Date of award: 14 January 1994
Tribunal: Middlesbrough County Court
Amount of award then: £4,000
Award at February 2001: £4,869

Description of injuries: Whiplash injury to cervical spine – collar and painkillers prescribed – off work 1 week – pain and discomfort continued for approximately 2 years, at which point claimant undertook course of physiotherapy – prior to accident, claimant already exhibiting symptoms of pre-existing cervical spondylosis in form of degenerative changes in neck – claimant able to continue in existing employment, but advised not to undertake tasks involving lifting or using arms above head height – discomfort in mornings – ability to undertake domestic chores, and sew, adversely affected.

Prognosis: Accident found to have advanced existing symptoms in neck by 12 to 18 months – symptoms permanent.

1.3.1.2.C97 Case No. 11814

Name of case: Lord v Cryers
Brief description of injuries: NECK – WHIPLASH
Reported: Kemp & Kemp, E2-095/1/1; [1999] CLY 1477
JSB Category: 6(A)(b)(ii)
Sex: Male
Age at injury: 59
Age at award: 61
Date of award: 22 March 1999
Tribunal: Bolton County Court
Amount of award then: £4,500
Award at February 2001: £4,717

Description of injuries: Jarring injury to neck and lumbar spine – stiffness in neck with intermittent pain – lateral rotation to right 50 per cent of normal; to left 75 per cent of normal – flexion and extension lost the last 30 per cent of normal – lumbar spine movements not restricted, but varying degrees of discomfort experienced on different movements – pre-existing, marked constitutional and degenerative changes in neck compatible with claimant's age and 40-year history of heavy manual labour – accident brought forward symptoms in back by 2-3 years, those in neck by 5-6 years.

Prognosis: Injuries permanent.

1.3.1.2.C98 Case No. 11914

Name of case: Swan v Bush

Brief description of injuries: WHIPLASH – ANXIETY – 2 YEARS (2 CLAIMANTS)

Reported: Kemp & Kemp, E2-095/2; [1999] CLY 1578

JSB Category: 6(A)(c); 3(A)(d)

Sex: (1): Male (2): Female

Age at injury: (1):37;(2):41

Age at award: (1):39;(2):44

Date of award: 22 December 1998

Tribunal: Cardiff County Court

Amount of award then: £4,500

Award at February 2001: £4,708

Description of injuries: 2 claimants, (1) and (2), sustained whiplash injuries to neck – (1) development of stiffness pain in neck, radiating to left shoulder and arm, shortly after accident, and associated headaches – claimant considerably inconvenienced in daily activities (working life not affected, as claimant unemployed) – painkillers prescribed – 8 months after accident, claimant still troubled by aching pain aggravated by neck movements and use of arms – 2 years after accident, claimant mildly symptomatic; outbreaks of neck pain after extended driving or heavy physical activities, constituting a nuisance rather than a disability, and relieved by painkilling tablets.(2) development of generalised aching in torso and neck – pain in neck radiating to right arm; claimant unable to work for 3 weeks – symptoms slowly improved thereafter, but claimant remained symptomatic when lifting, carrying or undertaking physical tasks – claimant nervous and apprehensive of travelling by car to the extent that she sold her own car and had not returned to driving – physical symptoms resolved completely within 2 years of the accident.

Prognosis: (1) Claimant's continuing symptoms would persist.

Other points: Sum awarded to each applicant.

1.3.1.2.C99 Case No. 12037

Name of case: Harbidge v Earl

Brief description of injuries: NECK – WHIPLASH – 2 YEARS

Reported: Kemp & Kemp, E2-095/3; [2000] 5 CL 181

JSB Category: 6(A)(b)(ii)

Sex: Female

Age at injury: 27

Age at award: 32

Date of award: 27 January 2000

Tribunal: Reading County Court

Amount of award then: £4,500

Award at February 2001: £4,646

Description of injuries: Soft-tissue whiplash injuries to the neck – holiday had to be cancelled – wore a cervical collar for several weeks – strong painkillers were prescribed – intensive physiotherapy as an in-patient – continued physiotherapy as an out-patient – aggravation of a previous back injury. H fully recovered from the effects of the injury within twenty four months of the date of the accident.

Other points: Account was taken of the long and intensive physiotherapy and the loss of enjoyment of the holiday.

1.3.1.2.C100 Case No. 11135

Name of case: Brinkworth v Payne

Brief description of injuries: NECK – WHIPLASH

Reported: Kemp & Kemp, E2-096; [1996] CLY 2226

JSB Category: 6(A)(b)(ii)

Sex: Female

Age at injury: 37

Age at award: 38

Date of award: 21 November 1995

Tribunal: Reading County Court

Amount of award then: £4,000

Award at February 2001: £4,593

Description of injuries: Whiplash injury to the neck – bruising to the chest.

Prognosis: Expected that she would be largely recovered within two years of the accident.

1.3.1.2.C101 Case No. 10766

Name of case: Bennet v Handford

Brief description of injuries: NECK – WHIPLASH – EXACERBATION OF PRE-EXISTING HEADACHE CONDITION

Reported: Kemp & Kemp, E2-097; [1994] CLY 1614

JSB Category: 6(A)(b)

Sex: Male

Age at injury: 29

Age at award: 32

Date of award: 12 January 1994

Tribunal: Telford County Court

Amount of award then: £3,750

Award at February 2001: £4,565

Description of injuries: Road accident – whiplash injury to neck – collar prescribed, worn continuously for 2 weeks and during the day for further 3 weeks – in constant pain, but took no time off work (as HGV mechanic), although unable to undertake full duties for 7 weeks and experienced difficulties, especially when adopting awkward positions – sleep disrupted – unable to pursue hobbies for 7 weeks – continuing constant neck ache and occasional shooting pains, aggravated by driving, reaching up or holding head in one position for more than 10 minutes – claimant had also, prior to the accident, suffered from vascular headaches since age 10, which had been decreasing in frequency – return of severe and frequent headaches for 12-18 months after accident, controlled only by strong painkillers, and sometimes lasting a whole week – social activities and work detrimentally affected – neck symptoms improving, although still some problems with work and sleeping, at date of trial – headaches still continuing at date of trial, but less frequently.

1.3.1.2.C102 Case No. 10065

Name of case: Crews v Harrison

Brief description of injuries: WHIPLASH – EXACERBATION AND ACCELERATION OF PRE-EXISTING CONDITION BY 3-5 YEARS

Reported: [1990] CLY 1625

JSB Category: 6(A)

Sex: Female

Age at injury: 45

Age at award: 47

Date of award: 16 August 1989

Tribunal: Plymouth County Court

Amount of award then: £3,000

Award at February 2001: £4,456

Description of injuries: Whiplash injury exacerbating pre-existing problems – was already attending orthopaedic clinic regularly.

Prognosis: Exacerbated the pre-existing problem by about 3-5 years – left with pain in upper dorsal spine radiating down the back, also chest pain.

1.3.1.2.C103 Case No. 11457

Name of case: Doyle v Van Bruggen

Brief description of injuries: NECK – WHIPLASH

Reported: Kemp & Kemp, H2-028/2; [1997] CLY 2006

JSB Category: 6(c)

Sex: Male

Age at injury: 36

Age at award: 38

Date of award: 06 May 1997

Tribunal: Central London County Court

Amount of award then: £4,000

Award at February 2001: £4,385

Description of injuries: Shock – minor soft-tissue injury to the cervical spine – ulnar nerve entrapment.

Prognosis: Ninety five per cent recovery – no long-term problems other than to the ulnar nerve.

1.3.1.2.C104 Case No. 11601

Name of case: Ledgar v Kidd

Brief description of injuries: NECK – WHIPLASH

Reported: Kemp & Kemp, E2-100/1; [1998] CLY 1603

JSB Category: 6(A)(b)(ii)

Sex: Female

Age at injury: 55

Age at award: 57

Date of award: 22 April 1998

Tribunal: Stoke on Trent County Court

Amount of award then: £4,100

Award at February 2001: £4,337

Description of injuries: Whiplash injury to the cervical spine – pain to the shoulders and upper limbs.

Prognosis: Intermittent symptoms would continue indefinitely, provoked by physical activity.

Damage to Spine

1.3.1.2.C105 Case No. 11021
Award at February 2001: £4,283
See: 1.3.1.C21 for details

1.3.1.2.C106 Case No. 11602
Name of case: Bollard v Simmonds
Brief description of injuries: NECK – WHIPLASH – 4 YEARS
Reported: Kemp & Kemp, E2-102/1; [1998] CLY 1604
JSB Category: 6(A)(c)
Sex: Female
Age at injury: 31
Age at award: 33
Date of award: 10 August 1998
Tribunal: Reading County Court
Amount of award then: £4,000
Award at February 2001: £4,203
Description of injuries: Whiplash injury to the cervical spine – mild sprain to the lumbar spine.
Prognosis: B would be asymptomatic within 2 years.
Other points: This was a special case with special loss of amenity – claimant awarded a higher level of damages for an injury of this severity.

1.3.1.2.C107 Case No. 11603
Name of case: Burbridge v Argos Distribution plc
Brief description of injuries: NECK – WHIPLASH – 4 YEARS
Reported: Kemp & Kemp, E2-102/1/2; [1998] CLY 1605
JSB Category: 6(A)(b)(ii)
Sex: Female
Age at injury: 23
Age at award: 27
Date of award: 20 April 1998
Tribunal: Bristol County Court
Amount of award then: £3,850
Award at February 2001: £4,073
Description of injuries: Whiplash injury to the neck – a minor injury.
Prognosis: The most minor of residual symptoms remained 4 years after the accident – these were likely to continue.
Other points: Early optimism of a complete recovery was not fulfilled.

1.3.1.2.C108 Case No. 11606
Name of case: Harries v Collins
Brief description of injuries: NECK – WHIPLASH – 2-3 YEARS
Reported: Kemp & Kemp, E2/102/1/3; [1998] CLY 1608
JSB Category: 6(A)(b)(ii)
Sex: Female
Age at injury: 39
Age at award: 42
Date of award: 12 March 1998
Tribunal: Cardiff County Court
Amount of award then: £3,750
Award at February 2001: £4,011
Description of injuries: Whiplash injury to the neck – aching and stiffness – numbness and weakness to the shoulders.
Prognosis: Accident related symptoms would resolve within 2 to 3 years of the date of the accident.

1.3.1.2.C109 Case No. 11604
Name of case: Weekes v Isebor
Brief description of injuries: NECK – WHIPLASH
Reported: Kemp & Kemp, E2/102/2; [1998] CLY 1606
JSB Category: 6(A)(b)(ii)
Sex: Female
Age at injury: 31
Age at award: 34
Date of award: 07 April 1998
Tribunal: Shoreditch County Court
Amount of award then: £3,750
Award at February 2001: £3,967
Description of injuries: Whiplash injury to the cervical spine – emotionally shaken and distraught – neck and shoulder pain – neck pain was described as aching 3 years after the date of the accident.

1.3.1.2.C110 Case No. 11605
Name of case: Jones v Adams
Brief description of injuries: NECK – WHIPLASH – 3 YEARS
Reported: Kemp & Kemp, E2-102/3; [1998] CLY 1607
JSB Category: 6(A)(b)(ii)
Sex: Female
Age at injury: 19
Age at award: 21
Date of award: 07 April 1998
Tribunal: Birkenhead County Court
Amount of award then: £3,750
Award at February 2001: £3,967
Description of injuries: Whiplash injury to the neck – constant discomfort for 2 years.
Prognosis: J would make a full recovery within 3 years of the date of the accident.

1.3.1.2.C111 Case No. 11728

Name of case: Kennedy and Kennedy v Berry

Brief description of injuries: NECK – WHIPLASH – 3 MONTHS – 10 MONTHS (2 CLAIMANTS)

Reported: Kemp & Kemp, E2-123/1; [1998] CLY 1731

JSB Category: 6(A)(c)

Sex: K1: Male / K2: Male

Age at injury: K1:19;K2:43

Age at award: K1:20;K2:44

Date of award: 11 September 1998

Tribunal: West London County Court

Amount of award then: £3,750

Award at February 2001: £3,923

Description of injuries: Accident – K1 developed neck pain and a headache – largely recovered within 3 month – K2's neck and shoulders became uncomfortable, requiring pain killers – grazed temple – largely recovered within 10 months of the date of the accident

Other points: Award split – K1: £1,250; K2: £2,500.

1.3.1.2.C112 Case No. 11607

Name of case: Page v Luckett

Brief description of injuries: NECK – WHIPLASH – 16 MONTHS

Reported: Kemp & Kemp, E2-103/1; [1998] CLY 1609

JSB Category: 6(A)(c)

Sex: Male

Age at injury: 33

Age at award: 34

Date of award: 10 September 1998

Tribunal: Milton Keynes County Court

Amount of award then: £3,750

Award at February 2001: £3,923

Description of injuries: Whiplash injury to the cervical spine – 99 per cent recovery within 16 months of the date of the accident.

1.3.1.2.C113 Case No. 11213

Name of case: Sawford v Sabourn

Brief description of injuries: NECK – WHIPLASH – 3 YEARS

Reported: Kemp & Kemp, C4-115; [1996] CLY 2305

JSB Category: 6(A)(b)(ii)

Sex: Female

Age at injury: 28

Age at award: 30

Date of award: 10 September 1996

Tribunal: Kingston County Court

Amount of award then: £3,500

Award at February 2001: £3,914

Description of injuries: Whiplash injury to the neck.

Prognosis: Injuries would be likely to be resolved within two-and-a-half to three years of the date of the accident.

1.3.1.2.C114 Case No. 10861

Name of case: Murphy and Murphy v Carroll

Brief description of injuries: NECK – WHIPLASH

Reported: [1994] CLY 1712

JSB Category: 6(A)(c)

Sex: (1): Male (2): Female (husband and wife)

Age at injury: -

Age at award: -

Date of award: 16 November 1994

Tribunal: Pontypridd County Court

Amount of award then: £3,300

Award at February 2001: £3,906

Description of injuries: Husband (1) and wife (2) sustained whiplash injuries in road accident.(1): Immediate burning sensation to neck – soft collar for 3-4 days – headaches and nagging pain in neck for 6-8 weeks – slight restriction in movement of neck to right, but no pain, at date of trial (2 years later) – no time off work, as considered injuries "trivial".(2): Immediate burning sensation to neck – soft collar for 2 days and intermittently thereafter – 2 days off college – sleep disturbance for 3-4 nights per month – nagging pain in neck; very little trouble in summer but worsening in winter and quite painful – symptoms much improved by date of assessment.

Prognosis: (2): expected to be symptom free within 4 months of hearing.

Other points: Award split – (1): £800 (2): £2,500

1.3.1.2.C115 Case No. 11916

Name of case: Hambis v Boon

Brief description of injuries: NECK – WHIPLASH – 80 PER CENT RECOVERY

Reported: Kemp & Kemp, PRK-001; [1999] CLY 1580

JSB Category: 6(A)(c)

Sex: Female

Age at injury: 24

Age at award: 27

Date of award: 04 August 1999

Tribunal: Oxford County Court

Amount of award then: £3,750

Award at February 2001: £3,897

Description of injuries: Road accident – soft-tissue injury to neck – pain and stiffness in neck and right shoulder – cervical collar and painkillers provided by GP – collar worn for 1 week, during which time claimant unable to return to work – restricted movement in neck for 1 month – sporting activities impossible for several months – 17 months after accident, claimant considered herself to have made an 80 per cent recovery, but still with pain in neck and shoulder – at time of trial, 3.5 years later, claimant still suffering intermittent discomfort in neck and right shoulder, particularly when studying hard; this caused pain and disrupted sleep – claimant took massage regularly and painkillers reluctantly, 2-3 times a year – judge accepted that claimant had come to live with her symptoms and that she viewed them as a nuisance.

Prognosis: No risk of further degeneration – claimant would eventually make full recovery from injuries.

1.3.1.2.C116 Case No. 11917

Name of case: Cox v Conway

Brief description of injuries: NECK – WHIPLASH – BACK – CIRCA 3 YEARS

Reported: Kemp & Kemp, PRK-002; [1999] CLY 1581

JSB Category: 6(A)(c), 6(B)(c)

Sex: Female

Age at injury: 33

Age at award: 35

Date of award: 06 August 1999

Tribunal: Bath County Court

Amount of award then: £3,750

Award at February 2001: £3,897

Description of injuries: Road accident – immediate pain in neck, worsening as day progressed and development of headache – symptoms in neck worsened, and lower back pain also developed – symptoms quite severe for first month; husband's help needed with housework and child care – only mild improvement after first month; physiotherapy prescribed, which assisted – claimant able to return to horse riding and gentle gym exercises after first month; initially worried about riding, but used a cushioned saddle and refrained from jumping – 1 year after accident, neck symptoms improving and medical evidence suggested that work or social activities no longer affected – back still causing problems after sitting for long periods and when looking after family – lumbar support purchased and physiotherapy exercises being performed – 2.5 years after accident, claimant still suffering from residual low back pain, although neck pain and headaches fully resolved – claimant had been anxious about driving for a period of time after the accident, but this had resolved by date of hearing.

Prognosis: Full recovery expected.

1.3.1.2.C117 Case No. 11360

Name of case: Lucas v Lacey (No 1)

Brief description of injuries: NECK – WHIPLASH – 2 YEARS

Reported: Kemp & Kemp, E2-104; [1997] CLY 1908

JSB Category: 6(A)(b)(ii)

Sex: Female

Age at injury: 47

Age at award: 49

Date of award: 24 March 1997

Tribunal: Wandsworth County Court

Amount of award then: £3,500

Award at February 2001: £3,874

Description of injuries: Whiplash injury to the neck.

Prognosis: Full recovery expected within 19 to 25 months of the date of the accident.

1.3.1.2.C118 Case No. 10858

Name of case: Hinchliffe v Hill
Brief description of injuries: NECK – WHIPLASH – BACK
Reported: Kemp & Kemp, E2-105; [1994] CLY 1708
JSB Category: 6(A)(c), 6(B)(c)
Sex: Female
Age at injury: 37
Age at award: 38
Date of award: 09 June 1994
Tribunal: Sheffield County Court
Amount of award then: £3,250
Award at February 2001: £3,863

Description of injuries: Road accident – whiplash injury to neck – flexion-type injury to lower lumbar spine – stress related abdominal pain and diarrhoea, lasting 1 week – off work 5.5 months – physiotherapy 5 months – cervical collar worn continually for 4 months – inability to do housework for 4-5 months, necessitating reliance on husband – back problem had resolved by date of trial, but neck problems ongoing, particularly after driving for any length of time – inability to resume hobbies of horse-riding and tennis.

Prognosis: All symptoms expected to be resolved within relatively short period of time.

1.3.1.2.C119 Case No. 11618

Name of case: Johnson v Khan
Brief description of injuries: NECK – WHIPLASH – BACK – 2 YEARS
Reported: Kemp & Kemp, E2-105/1; [1998] CLY 1620
JSB Category: 6(B)(c), 6(A)(c)
Sex: Female
Age at injury: 18
Age at award: 21
Date of award: 09 October 1997
Tribunal: Burnley County Court
Amount of award then: £3,500
Award at February 2001: £3,774

Description of injuries: Whiplash injury to the back and neck – neck injuries were resolved within 1 week – full recovery from the lumbar injuries within 23 months of the date of the accident.

1.3.1.2.C120 Case No. 12049

Name of case: M (a child) v Oraha
Brief description of injuries: NECK – WHIPLASH – 7 MONTHS
Reported: Kemp & Kemp, E2-130/1; [2000] 5 CL 193
JSB Category: 6(A)(c)
Sex: Female
Age at injury: M1:7;M2:11
Age at award: M1:10;M2:14
Date of award: 10 February 2000
Tribunal: Central London County Court
Amount of award then: £3,625
Award at February 2001: £3,722

Description of injuries: Whiplash injury with pain and stiffness suffered by M1 and M2 – analgesics prescribed – residual niggling problems five months after the date of the accident were more severe in M2. Fully resolved within seven months of the date of the accident.

Other points: Award split: £1,625 for M1; £2,000 for M2

1.3.1.2.C121 Case No. 10769

Name of case: McCausland v Khan
Brief description of injuries: NECK – WHIPLASH
Reported: Kemp & Kemp, E2-106; [1994] CLY 1617
JSB Category: 6(A)(c)
Sex: Female
Age at injury: 29
Age at award: 31
Date of award: 10 December 1993
Tribunal: St Albans County Court
Amount of award then: £3,000
Award at February 2001: £3,636

Description of injuries: Road accident – claimant shaken – whiplash injury to neck – pain and some difficulty in moving neck, worsening on following morning – examination revealed mild spasm of paracervical muscles, with loss of normal lordotic curve – tenderness over both left and right trapezius and sternocledidomastoid muscles – extension of cervical spine limited by 10 per cent – cervical collar worn, and claimant off work, for 3 weeks – intermittent symptoms still present at time of trial – nagging pain, usually in winter – increased difficulty in carrying shopping – increased nervousness when driving.

1.3.1.2.C122 Case No. 10770

Name of case: George v Groom
Brief description of injuries: NECK – WHIPLASH
Reported: Kemp & Kemp, K2-026; [1994] CLY 1618
JSB Category: 6(A)(c)
Sex: Female
Age at injury: 27
Age at award: -
Date of award: 15 May 1994
Tribunal: Nuneaton County Court
Amount of award then: £3,000
Award at February 2001: £3,566

Description of injuries: Whiplash injury to neck, troubling claimant for 3 days – intermittent discomfort in right shoulder blade at end of a day's work for about 6 months – thereafter, only residual symptom a painless click of right sterno-clavicular joint associated with some rotational movements in claimant's pre-accident hobby of aerobics.

Prognosis: Development of degenerative change in sterno-clavicular joint over 10-15 year period possible – claimant forced to cut down on aerobic exercise and abandon hobby of trampolining to avoid this possibility.

1.3.1.2.C123 Case No. 11216

Name of case: Brown and Brown v Childs
Brief description of injuries: NECK – WHIPLASH – 18 MONTHS
Reported: Kemp & Kemp, E3-116; [1996] CLY 2308
JSB Category: 6(A)(c)
Sex: Female
Age at injury: 29
Age at award: -
Date of award: 09 November 1995
Tribunal: Mayor's and City of London Court
Amount of award then: £3,100
Award at February 2001: £3,559

Description of injuries: Moderately severe whiplash injury to the cervical spine.

Prognosis: Full recovery was made within eighteen months of the date of the accident.

1.3.1.2.C124 Case No. 11361

Name of case: Tree v Phillips
Brief description of injuries: NECK – WHIPLASH – 18 MONTHS
Reported: Kemp & Kemp, K2-027; [1997] CLY 1909
JSB Category: 6(A)(b)(ii)
Sex: Male
Age at injury: 57
Age at award: 58
Date of award: 09 June 1997
Tribunal: Cardiff County Court
Amount of award then: £3,250
Award at February 2001: £3,549

Description of injuries: Whiplash type injuries to the neck – some initial lower back symptoms.

Prognosis: A full recovery within eighteen months of the date of the accident.

Other points: This was a case of real inconvenience and suffering.

1.3.1.2.C125 Case No. 11028

Name of case: Saggu v Worrod
Brief description of injuries: NECK – WHIPLASH – 2 YEARS
Reported: Kemp & Kemp, K2-029; [1995] CLY 1780
JSB Category: 6(A)(c)
Sex: Female
Age at injury: 30
Age at award: 32
Date of award: 10 January 1995
Tribunal: Walsall County Court
Amount of award then: £3,000
Award at February 2001: £3,534

Description of injuries: In road traffic accident plaintiff received minor blow to knees – shocked and distressed – needed to go straight home to bed but found she could not sleep – next day had quite bad neck pain radiating into right shoulder – went to GP and attended hospital – given four days off work but chose to go back early to assist in office re-organisation and necessary paperwork – knees recovered within few days – for about four months she was nervous in traffic and experienced difficulty in driving and writing reports at work – even after 15 months, neck pain was intermittent and occurred when carrying and performing household chores – still had full range of movement then but there was pain in extremes of all movements – it was anticipated that a full recovery would be made within two years of the collision.

1.3.1.2.C126 Case No. 11217

Name of case: Rubidge v Harvey
Brief description of injuries: NECK – WHIPLASH – 2 YEARS
Reported: Kemp & Kemp, E2-109; [1996] CLY 2309
JSB Category: 6(A)(c)
Sex: Male
Age at injury: 42
Age at award: 43
Date of award: 24 April 1995
Tribunal: Slough County Court
Amount of award then: £3,000
Award at February 2001: £3,463
Description of injuries: Whiplash injury to the neck.
Prognosis: Full recovery was expected within two years of the date of the accident.

1.3.1.2.C127 Case No. 11218

Name of case: Mahoney v Williams
Brief description of injuries: NECK – WHIPLASH – 18 MONTHS
Reported: Kemp & Kemp, E2-111; [1996] CLY 2310
JSB Category: 6(A)(c)
Sex: Female
Age at injury: 13
Age at award: 15
Date of award: 29 February 1996
Tribunal: Reading County Court
Amount of award then: £3,000
Award at February 2001: £3,419
Description of injuries: Whiplash type injury – superficial bruising.
Prognosis: Full recovery made within about eighteen months of the date of the accident.

1.3.1.2.C128 Case No. 10591

Name of case: Cooke v Hawkins
Brief description of injuries: NECK – WHIPLASH – 2 YEARS
Reported: Kemp & Kemp, E2-112; [1993] CLY 1484
JSB Category: 6(A)(c)
Sex: Male
Age at injury: 55
Age at award: 57
Date of award: 10 March 1993
Tribunal: Mansfield County Court
Amount of award then: £2,750
Award at February 2001: £3,396

Description of injuries: Whiplash injury to neck in road accident – previous severe injury to another part of back in 1977, since when claimant had not worked – initial severe pain, controlled with analgesics already prescribed for back problem – most pain subsiding 8 months after accident – three-quarter range neck movement present 8 months after accident, pain and muscle spasm if further rotation attempted – daily "clicking" in neck, causing short periods of pain – full recovery initially anticipated within 20 months – at 23 months "clicking" problem still evident and claimant cautious of sudden neck movement.
Prognosis: Small risk of long-term cervical spondylosis.

1.3.1.2.C129 Case No. 11714

Name of case: Hitchcock v Wheeler
Brief description of injuries: NECK – WHIPLASH – MINOR INJURIES
Reported: Kemp & Kemp, E2-114/1; [1998] CLY 1717
JSB Category: 6(A)(c)
Sex: Female
Age at injury: 20
Age at award: 23
Date of award: 07 January 1998
Tribunal: Leicester County Court
Amount of award then: £3,000
Award at February 2001: £3,235
Description of injuries: Soft-tissue whiplash injury to the neck – bruising, headaches, nervous condition, bitten tongue – physical symptoms had settled within 6 months.

1.3.1.2.C130 Case No. 11609

Name of case: Johnson v Pattenden
Brief description of injuries: NECK – WHIPLASH – 12 MONTHS
Reported: Kemp & Kemp, E2-115/1; [1998] CLY 1611
JSB Category: 6(A)(c)
Sex: Female
Age at injury: 26
Age at award: 27
Date of award: 12 February 1998
Tribunal: Cheltenham County Court
Amount of award then: £3,000
Award at February 2001: £3,219
Description of injuries: Moderate whiplash injury to the neck – pain and stiffness acute for 2 months.
Prognosis: Medical evidence predicted a full recovery within 12 months of the date of the accident.

Damage to Spine

1.3.1.2.C131 Case No. 12063

Name of case: Walker v Miricki
Brief description of injuries: NECK – WHIPLASH
Reported: [2000] 6 CL 193
JSB Category: 6(A)(c) 3A(d)
Sex: Female
Age at injury: 18
Age at award: 20
Date of award: 11 February 2000
Tribunal: Chesterfield County Court
Amount of award then: £3,115
Award at February 2001: £3,199
Description of injuries: Soft-tissue injury to the cervical spine – severe discomfort for one month – soft collar worn for two months – psychological reaction fell short of post-traumatic stress disorder – depression led W to take an overdose but there were pre-existing causes for the depression – full recovery within eighteen months of the date of the accident – some psychological difficulties resulting from the accident persisted two years later.

1.3.1.2.C132 Case No. 11031

Award at February 2001: £3,161
See: 1.3.1.C34 for details

1.3.1.2.C133 Case No. 11608

Name of case: Armstrong (a minor) v Gharhdagi
Brief description of injuries: NECK – WHIPLASH
Reported: Kemp & Kemp, E2-115/2; [1998] CLY 1610
JSB Category: 6(A)(c)
Sex: Male
Age at injury: 8
Age at award: 13
Date of award: 17 June 1998
Tribunal: Central London County Court
Amount of award then: £3,000
Award at February 2001: £3,158
Description of injuries: Whiplash injury to the neck – no bony injury.
Prognosis: Symptoms occasionally flared up – no long-term sequelae expected.

1.3.1.2.C134 Case No. 11920

Name of case: Harrison v Mo
Brief description of injuries: NECK – WHIPLASH – 2 YEARS
Reported: Kemp & Kemp, K2-048/2; [1999] CLY 1585
JSB Category: 6(A)(c)
Sex: Male
Age at injury: 21
Age at award: 22
Date of award: 22 October 1998
Tribunal: Bury County Court
Amount of award then: £3,000
Award at February 2001: £3,137
Description of injuries: Road accident – cervical whiplash injury – development of stiffness in neck later that day – pain and stiffness continuing 3 days later; medication and physiotherapy prescribed – 6 months later, claimant still suffering intermittent deep aches over postero – lateral aspect of cervical spine, extending outwards to shoulder girdles; pain most apparent first thing in morning – headaches, on average once a week – claimant avoided taking time off, except for physiotherapy, due to pride in his attendance record – at time of hearing, 1 year after accident, claimant still suffered mild intermittent symptoms of pain and stiffness, especially when playing sport, and had been unable to return to golf and football – claimant felt he had largely recovered.

1.3.1.2.C135 Case No. 11921

Name of case: Khan v Bibb
Brief description of injuries: NECK – WHIPLASH (1-1.5 YEARS)
Reported: Kemp & Kemp, E2-115/4; [1999] CLY 1585
JSB Category: 6(A)(c), 6(B)(c)
Sex: Male
Age at injury: 32
Age at award: 34
Date of award: 22 October 1998
Tribunal: Bury County Court
Amount of award then: £3,000
Award at February 2001: £3,137
Description of injuries: Road accident – whiplash injury to neck – wrenching injury to back – no fractures found in X-rays – claimant off work 4 weeks, then forced by financial constraints to return on reduced shifts – 6 weeks after accident, claimant still suffering pain in neck and back, especially at the end of a working shift – sleep pattern poor – claimant used analgesics as recommended by GP – full recovery was initially expected between 7 and 11 months, but at trial claimant indicated that it had taken a little longer.

1.3.1.2.C136 Case No. 11363

Name of case: Angell v Brough

Brief description of injuries: NECK – WHIPLASH

Reported: Kemp & Kemp, E2-116, K2-048; [1997] CLY 1911

JSB Category: 6(A)(c)

Sex: Male

Age at injury: 19

Age at award: 22

Date of award: 29 November 1996

Tribunal: Leeds County Court

Amount of award then: £2,800

Award at February 2001: £3,129

Description of injuries: Soft-tissue injury to the neck – whiplash.

Prognosis: Symptoms were almost entirely resolved at time of hearing.

1.3.1.2.C137 Case No. 11919

Name of case: Gott v McGrath

Brief description of injuries: NECK – WHIPLASH – BACK – 12 MONTHS

Reported: Kemp & Kemp, K2-047/1; [1999] CLY 1583

JSB Category: 6(A)(c); 6(B)(c)

Sex: Male

Age at injury: 51

Age at award: 55

Date of award: 14 July 1999

Tribunal: Southport County Court

Amount of award then: £3,000

Award at February 2001: £3,125

Description of injuries: Claimant suffered whiplash injury in road accident – following accident, claimant complained of severe neck pain for period of 2 months; pain continuing and becoming constant at a reduced level thereafter – pain in neck at extremes of lateral flexion – claimant only able to miss 2 days of work, because self-employed – Neck pain and overlying pain in lower back directly attributable to the accident for a period of 12 months – no acceleration of condition.

1.3.1.2.C138 Case No. 11223

Name of case: Taylor v Ansari

Brief description of injuries: NECK – WHIPLASH – BACK – 18 MONTHS

Reported: Kemp & Kemp, E2-120; [1996] CLY 2315

JSB Category: 6(A)(c)

Sex: Male

Age at injury: 20

Age at award: 25

Date of award: 23 February 1996

Tribunal: Bury County Court

Amount of award then: £2,500

Award at February 2001: £2,850

Description of injuries: Whiplash type injury to the neck – wrenching injury to the back.

Prognosis: A full recovery was expected within twelve to eighteen months of the date of the accident.

1.3.1.2.C139 Case No. 11222

Name of case: Severs v Dudley

Brief description of injuries: NECK – WHIPLASH – 15 MONTHS

Reported: Kemp & Kemp, K2-059; [1996] CLY 2314

JSB Category: 6(A)(c)

Sex: Male

Age at injury: 57

Age at award: -

Date of award: 19 August 1996

Tribunal: Bury County Court

Amount of award then: £2,500

Award at February 2001: £2,809

Description of injuries: Whiplash injury to the neck – of moderate severity.

Prognosis: A full recovery was expected within fifteen months of the date of the accident.

1.3.1.2.C140 Case No. 11225

Name of case: Cliffe v Williams

Brief description of injuries: NECK – WHIPLASH – 18 MONTHS

Reported: Kemp & Kemp, K2-060; [1996] CLY 2317

JSB Category: 6(A)(c)

Sex: Female

Age at injury: 17

Age at award: 20

Date of award: 02 September 1996

Tribunal: Warrington County Court

Amount of award then: £2,500

Award at February 2001: £2,796

Description of injuries: Whiplash type injury to the neck – sprain to the lower spine – full recovery was reached eighteen months after the accident.

1.3.1.2.C141 Case No. 11226

Award at February 2001: £2,698

See: 1.3.1.C40 for details

1.3.1.2.C142 Case No. 11364

Name of case: White v Onions

Brief description of injuries: NECK – WHIPLASH

Reported: Kemp & Kemp, E2-121, K2-065; [1997] CLY 1912

JSB Category: 6(A)(c)

Sex: Female

Age at injury: 21

Age at award: 22

Date of award: 26 November 1996

Tribunal: Exeter County Court

Amount of award then: £2,400

Award at February 2001: £2,682

Description of injuries: Whiplash type injury to the neck – required physiotherapy for several weeks.

Prognosis: Eleven months after the accident she still suffered pain in the neck and back.

1.3.1.2.C143 Case No. 11923

Name of case: Cheung v Parry

Brief description of injuries: NECK – WHIPLASH – BACK – 1-2 YEARS

Reported: Kemp & Kemp, K2-066; [1999] CLY 1587

JSB Category: 6(A)(c), 6(B)(c)

Sex: Female

Age at injury: 43

Age at award: 44

Date of award: 18 February 1999

Tribunal: St Helens County Court

Amount of award then: £2,500

Award at February 2001: £2,627

Description of injuries: Road accident – whiplash injury to cervical and lumbar spine – lower spine immediately became very stiff with muscle spasm; pain – killing injection administered in hospital – development of severe pain and stiffness to neck and lower spine for a few weeks, followed by less severe symptoms – symptoms aggravated by domestic activities – 6 weeks after accident, pain and stiffness to neck and lower spine still persisted – full range of movement to cervical spine, but flexion and rotation caused pain and discomfort – straight leg raising on both sides reduced by 20 per cent – 7 months after accident, neck and lower back improved but not fully recovered; movement of cervical spine caused only slight tightness, and straight leg raising full – claimant took no time off work, and hobbies and pastimes not affected – at date of hearing, claimant had recovered from symptoms in accordance with prognosis.

1.3.1.2.C144 Case No. 11815

Name of case: Boyce v Secur Scan (UK) Ltd

Brief description of injuries: NECK – WHIPLASH

Reported: Kemp & Kemp, E2-123/2; [1999] CLY 1478

JSB Category: 6(A)(c)

Sex: Male

Age at injury: 25

Age at award: 26

Date of award: 20 November 1998

Tribunal: Salisbury County Court

Amount of award then: £2,500

Award at February 2001: £2,616

Description of injuries: Relatively minor whiplash injury to neck – no immediate symptoms – development on following day of stiffness and discomfort including shoulder pain radiating to neck, continuing for 3 days – all symptoms except occasional discomfort in shoulder subsided after 1 month – complete recovery predicted after 2-3 months, but after 10 months discomfort still persisted in shoulder, exacerbated by lengthy periods of work and sporting activities, and forcing claimant to sleep on his back – 20 months after accident, some improvement in shoulder symptoms, though some difficulties still present; judge described ongoing symptoms as a "daily reminder".

1.3.1.2.C145 Case No. 11922

Name of case: Kee v Sharma

Brief description of injuries: NECK – WHIPLASH – LARGELY RECOVERED AFTER 21 MONTHS

Reported: (1999) 99 (2) QR 5; Kemp & Kemp, E2-123/3; [1999] CLY 1586

JSB Category: 6(A)(c)

Sex: Female

Age at injury: 57

Age at award: 59

Date of award: 01 July 1999

Tribunal: Brighton County Court

Amount of award then: £2,500

Award at February 2001: £2,604

Description of injuries: Road accident – 2 days later, claimant began to suffer stiffness in neck and associated occipital headaches – over next 2 weeks, neck became more painful and pain radiated towards right shoulder – whiplash injury diagnosed and paracetamol and physiotherapy (14 sessions in total) prescribed – most severe symptoms resolved within 6 weeks – 3 months after accident, persistent dull ache on right side still present, symptoms gradually diminishing – 21 months after accident, claimant only suffering occasional stiffness in neck after stressful day at work, which could be relieved by massage – symptoms had not affected work, but heavy housework and swimming had been impossible for approximately 3 months.

1.3.1.2.C146 Case No. 10110

Name of case: Daden v Lowings
Brief description of injuries: WHIPLASH – 4-6 MONTHS
Reported: Kemp & Kemp, K2-067; [1990] CLY 1680
JSB Category: 6(A)
Sex: Female
Age at injury: 29
Age at award: 31
Date of award: 05 January 1990
Tribunal: Bristol County Court
Amount of award then: £1,800
Award at February 2001: £2,591
Description of injuries: VDU operator was front seat passenger in motor vehicle struck from behind – whiplash injury to neck and back and attendant shock – cervical collar used for three weeks – off work three weeks – administered Robaxin 750 and stronger non-steroidal anti-inflammatory drugs – attended osteopath.
Prognosis: Residual problems would have resolved themselves some four to six months after the accident.

1.3.1.2.C147 Case No. 11227

Name of case: Cole v Woodhall
Brief description of injuries: NECK – WHIPLASH – 15 MONTHS
Reported: Kemp & Kemp, K2-068; [1996] CLY 2319
JSB Category: 6(A)(c)
Sex: Female
Age at injury: 29
Age at award: 31
Date of award: 25 August 1995
Tribunal: Birmingham County Court
Amount of award then: £2,250
Award at February 2001: £2,582
Description of injuries: Whiplash injury to the neck – full recovery took place within fifteen months of the date of the accident.

1.3.1.2.C148 Case No. 12013

Name of case: Pawson v Neil
Brief description of injuries: NECK – WHIPLASH – 18-20 MONTHS
Reported: Kemp & Kemp, E2-126; [2000] 4 CL 156
JSB Category: 6(B)(c)
Sex: Female
Age at injury: 36
Age at award: 37
Date of award: 16 December 1999
Tribunal: Torquay County Court
Amount of award then: £2,500
Award at February 2001: £2,570
Description of injuries: Traffic shunt caused a flexion extension injury to the cervical spine – painkillers required – two sessions of physiotherapy – there was some diminution of the symptoms within two weeks but thereafter they reached plateau.
Prognosis: P would become symptom free within eighteen to twenty months of the date of the accident.

1.3.1.2.C149 Case No. 12062

Name of case: Faulkner v Shamji
Brief description of injuries: NECK – WHIPLASH
Reported: [2000] 6 CL 192
JSB Category: 6(A)(c)
Sex: Male
Age at injury: 27
Age at award: 29
Date of award: 11 February 2000
Tribunal: Milton Keynes County Court
Amount of award then: £2,500
Award at February 2001: £2,567
Description of injuries: Sudden hyper-flexion injury to the cervical spine – severe pain for one week to ten days – gradual but impressive improvement over three months – physiotherapy thereafter led to a rapid improvement to F's symptoms – aching and discomfort was infrequent but affected F's ability to play golf.

1.3.1.2.C150 Case No. 10111

Name of case: Bell v Wash
Brief description of injuries: WHIPLASH – 7 MONTHS
Reported: Kemp & Kemp, E3-120; [1990] CLY 1681
JSB Category: 6(A)
Sex: Female
Age at injury: 32
Age at award: 34
Date of award: 28 November 1989
Tribunal: Grays Thurrock County Court
Amount of award then: £1,750
Award at February 2001: £2,538
Description of injuries: Neck pain and severe backache – marked bruising on left shoulder – unable to walk without severe pain – five weeks off work – on return to work intermittent pain in neck and back – difficulty with shopping or climbing stairs – had to wear flat shoes for seven months.
Prognosis: Seven months after accident symptoms had cleared – no residual injury.

1.3.1.2.C151 Case No. 10668

Name of case: Crowson v Evans

Brief description of injuries: NECK – WHIPLASH

Reported: Kemp & Kemp, E2-127; [1993] CLY 1564

JSB Category: 6(A)(c)

Sex: Male

Age at injury: 20

Age at award: 22

Date of award: 20 April 1993

Tribunal: Peterborough County Court

Amount of award then: £2,000

Award at February 2001: £2,447

Description of injuries: Road accident – whiplash injury to neck – development of severe stiffness on following day – cervical collar worn continuously for 1 week, on occasions during the following week – acute pain for 3 or 4 days, subsiding after 2 weeks – residual symptoms continued for a period of 13 to 14 months – claimant took no time off work, but only worked part-time.

1.3.1.2.C152 Case No. 10863

Name of case: Hazle v Platt

Brief description of injuries: NECK – WHIPLASH – 12 MONTHS

Reported: Kemp & Kemp, E2-128; [1994] CLY 1715

JSB Category: 6(A)(c)

Sex: Female

Age at injury: 19

Age at award: 21

Date of award: 04 February 1994

Tribunal: Portsmouth County Court

Amount of award then: £2,000

Award at February 2001: £2,421

Description of injuries: Whiplash injury to neck – considerable pain and disability for 2 weeks – collar for 2 weeks and painkillers prescribed – inability to work for 1 week – continuing pain interfered with job upon resumption – after 5 months, pain had lessened to the extent of only being present in second half of day after standing at work for any length of time – full recovery within 12 months of accident.

1.3.1.2.C153 Case No. 11716

Name of case: Sivieri v Mills

Brief description of injuries: NECK – WHIPLASH – 12-15 MONTHS

Reported: Kemp & Kemp, E2-129/1; [1998] CLY 1719

JSB Category: 6(A)(c)

Sex: Male

Age at injury: 36

Age at award: 38

Date of award: 16 February 1998

Tribunal: Rawtenstall County Court

Amount of award then: £2,250

Award at February 2001: £2,414

Description of injuries: Whiplash injury to the neck and shoulder – restricted movement and sleep disturbance – S had become symptom-free within 12-15 months of the date of the accident.

1.3.1.2.C154 Case No. 11717

Name of case: Roy v Greenline Carriers

Brief description of injuries: NECK – WHIPLASH

Reported: Kemp & Kemp, E2-129/2; [1998] CLY 1720

JSB Category: 6(A)(c)

Sex: Female

Age at injury: 26

Age at award: 29

Date of award: 18 May 1998

Tribunal: Nottingham County Court

Amount of award then: £2,250

Award at February 2001: £2,367

Description of injuries: Whiplash type injury to the cervical spine – pain and discomfort to the neck.

Prognosis: Full recovery expected.

1.3.1.2.C155 Case No. 11729

Name of case: Lo Sterzo (a minor) v Hopkins

Brief description of injuries: NECK – WHIPLASH

Reported: [1998] CLY 1732

JSB Category: 6(A)(c)

Sex: A: Female B: Female

Age at injury: A:13;B:9

Age at award: A:15;B:11

Date of award: 22 September 1998

Tribunal: West London County Court

Amount of award then: £2,250

Award at February 2001: £2,354

Description of injuries: Soft-tissue injuries to the necks of A and B

Prognosis: A and B both made a full recovery – no long-term problems anticipated

Other points: Award split – A: £1,250 B: £1,000

1.3.1.2.C156 Case No. 11234

Name of case: Schooling v Bird
Brief description of injuries: NECK – WHIPLASH – 12 MONTHS
Reported: Kemp & Kemp, K2-092; [1996] CLY 2326
JSB Category: 6(A)(c)
Sex: Female
Age at injury: 24
Age at award: 26
Date of award: 14 October 1996
Tribunal: Edmonton County Court
Amount of award then: £2,000
Award at February 2001: £2,237
Description of injuries: Whiplash type injury to the neck – strain to the shoulder – full recovery within ten to twelve months of the date of the accident.

1.3.1.2.C157 Case No. 10611

Name of case: Baldwin v Dilks
Brief description of injuries: NECK – WHIPLASH – 3 YEARS
Reported: [1993] CLY 1505
JSB Category: 6(A)(c)
Sex: Female
Age at injury: 39
Age at award: 42
Date of award: 05 February 1993
Tribunal: Eastbourne County Court
Amount of award then: £1,750
Award at February 2001: £2,169
Description of injuries: Road accident – whiplash injury to neck – soft collar, stiff neck for 3 weeks – unable to drive – mobility affected – hobbies restricted (swimming distance reduced; unable to knit) – still some discomfort in neck and shoulder at time of trial, worsening towards evening.

1.3.1.2.C158 Case No. 11475

Name of case: Dunn v Rennoc
Brief description of injuries: HEART – ANGINA ATTACK – WHIPLASH
Reported: Kemp & Kemp, F6-016/1; [1997] CLY 2025
JSB Category: 6(A)(c)
Sex: Male
Age at injury: 58
Age at award: 59
Date of award: 05 September 1997
Tribunal: Blackburn County Court
Amount of award then: £2,000
Award at February 2001: £2,159
Description of injuries: Angina attack – whiplash injury.
Prognosis: It had been a very frightening experience.
Other points: Award included £700 for whiplash injury.

1.3.1.2.C159 Case No. 10488

Name of case: Metcalf v GL Ord
Brief description of injuries: WHIPLASH – CONTINUING SYMPTOMS
Reported: Kemp & Kemp, K2-100; [1992] CLY 1744
JSB Category: 6(A)(c)
Sex: Male
Age at injury: 36
Age at award: 37
Date of award: 04 November 1992
Tribunal: Stockton on Tees County Court
Amount of award then: £1,750
Award at February 2001: £2,155
Description of injuries: Whiplash injury.
Prognosis: Six months after the accident there was still pain in the neck – present symptoms were not likely to change.

1.3.1.2.C160 Case No. 10881

Name of case: Hill and McKay v BDL Contracts and Design

Brief description of injuries: NECK – WHIPLASH

Reported: [1994] CLY 1733

JSB Category: (1): 6(A)(c) (2): 6(A)(c)

Sex: (1): Female (2): Female

Age at injury: (1)31;(2):26

Age at award: -

Date of award: 01 November 1993

Tribunal: Liverpool County Court

Amount of award then: £1,750

Award at February 2001: £2,126

Description of injuries: 2 claimants ((1) and (2)) involved in road accident when their vehicle was struck from rear.(1): Stiffness in neck – soft collar worn for 2 weeks – development of headaches in that period, later becoming intermittent – 1 week off work – unable to do housework for 2 weeks – symptom free after 1 month, except for continued nervousness about driving for a further 3-4 months.(2): Pain and stiffness in neck – soft collar worn for approximately 2 weeks – intermittent pain in neck over one month period – 1 week off work – symptoms resolved after 1 month, except for continued nervousness about driving or being a passenger for 3-4 months.

Prognosis: (Both claimants): Neither suffered any bony injury likely to result in long-term arthritic change or neurological trauma that could lead to permanent loss of function.

Other points: Award split: (1): £950 (2): £800

1.3.1.2.C161 Case No. 11924

Name of case: T (a minor) v Moloney

Brief description of injuries: NECK – WHIPLASH – 17 MONTHS

Reported: Kemp & Kemp, K2-102/3; [1999] CLY 1588

JSB Category: 6(A)(c)

Sex: Female

Age at injury: 15

Age at award: 17

Date of award: 13 April 1999

Tribunal: Nottingham County Court

Amount of award then: £2,000

Award at February 2001: £2,082

Description of injuries: Road accident – immediate pain in upper back; also pain in left knee – on following day, claimant awoke with significant pain and stiffness in neck and upper back – off school 2 days – cervical collar for 3 weeks – widespread discomfort across neck, upper back and back of shoulders during that time – condition gradually improved within 2 months of incident, but claimant remained unable to pursue hobby of dancing – 10 months after accident, claimant had recovered to a substantial degree – 17 months after accident, occasional twinges still experienced, but claimant otherwise regarded herself as fully recovered.

1.3.1.2.C162 Case No. 11926

Name of case: Goldberg v Hogger

Brief description of injuries: NECK – WHIPLASH – 2 YEARS

Reported: Kemp & Kemp, K2-102/4; [1999] CLY 1590

JSB Category: 6(A)(c)

Sex: Female

Age at injury: 19

Age at award: 21

Date of award: 19 May 1999

Tribunal: Reading County Court

Amount of award then: £2,000

Award at February 2001: £2,077

Description of injuries: Road accident – whiplash injury to neck – painkillers and neck collar prescribed – symptoms acute in first weeks, during which time collar worn continuously – significant symptoms of pain and stiffness for 2 months – thereafter, intermittent symptoms of neck pain brought on by sitting in one position for a protracted period of time (eg driving for longer than 2 hours) – symptoms interfered with some activities, eg aerobics, but initially expected to settle within 14 months of accident – however, over 2 years after accident, claimant continued to experience intermittent aching down left side of neck approximately once a fortnight – residual symptom a nuisance rather than a disability – no formal physiotherapy ever provided.

1.3.1.2.C163 Case No. 11718

Name of case: Humphries v HG Transport

Brief description of injuries: NECK – WHIPLASH – 6 WEEKS

Reported: [1998] CLY 1721

JSB Category: 6(A)(c)

Sex: Female

Age at injury: 22

Age at award: 25

Date of award: 17 June 1998

Tribunal: Sheffield County Court

Amount of award then: £1,900

Award at February 2001: £2,000

Description of injuries: Whiplash injury to the neck – symptoms resolved within 6 weeks of the date of the accident – claimant unable to care fully for her baby for that period.

1.3.1.2.C164 Case No. 11720

Name of case: Brough v Carty

Brief description of injuries: NECK – WHIPLASH – FIVE MONTHS

Reported: Kemp & Kemp, K2-113/1; [1998] CLY 1723

JSB Category: 6(A)(c)

Sex: Female

Age at injury: 31

Age at award: 32

Date of award: 11 November 1997

Tribunal: Barnet County Court

Amount of award then: £1,800

Award at February 2001: £1,940

Description of injuries: Classic whiplash type injury – severe pain – headaches – physical symptoms resolved within 5 months of the date of the accident.

1.3.1.2.C165 Case No. 11336

Name of case: Re Hajid

Brief description of injuries: NECK – WHIPLASH – 12 MONTHS/9 MONTHS

Reported: Kemp & Kemp, K2-203; [1997] CLY 1884

JSB Category: 6(A)(c)

Sex: P1 Female / P2 Male

Age at injury: -

Age at award: P1:44;P2:22

Date of award: 15 May 1997

Tribunal: Preston County Court

Amount of award then: £1,750

Award at February 2001: £1,918

Description of injuries: Both suffered minor multiple soft-tissue injuries – full recovery by P1 in twelve months and by P2 in nine months.

Other points: Award split: P1 £1,000; P2 £750.

1.3.1.2.C166 Case No. 10892

Name of case: Hockin and Willott v Bradley

Brief description of injuries: NECK – WHIPLASH (3 CLAIMANTS)

Reported: Kemp & Kemp, K2-234; [1994] CLY 1744

JSB Category: (all 3 claimants): 6(A)(c); (claimant (H), additionally): 6(M)(d)

Sex: All female

Age at injury: (H):32;(W):65;(O):1

Age at award: (H):33;(W):66;(O):2

Date of award: 12 September 1994

Tribunal: Stockport County Court

Amount of award then: £1,600

Award at February 2001: £1,898

Description of injuries: 3 claimants, (H), (W) and (O), involved in head-on road accident.(H): Whiplash injury to neck – pain in neck and ankles for 2 weeks – shock, exacerbated by having been in a similar accident on same stretch of road 2 years before – full recovery within 1 month.(W): Mild whiplash injury – painkillers prescribed – shock, but not to same extent as (H) – full recovery within 1 month.(O): 4 x 1.5cm area of bruising on neck, caused by restraining action of seatbelt – full recovery within 2 weeks.

Prognosis: (all claimants): no evidence of any long-term symptoms of permanent disability or neck pain.

Other points: Award split – (H): £750 (W): £550 (O): £300

1.3.1.2.C167 Case No. 10495

Name of case: Kinsella v Jameson

Brief description of injuries: WHIPLASH – 1-2 YEARS

Reported: [1992] CLY 1751

JSB Category: 6(A)(c)

Sex: Male

Age at injury: 44

Age at award: 45

Date of award: 20 May 1992

Tribunal: Birkenhead County Court

Amount of award then: £1,500

Award at February 2001: £1,852

Description of injuries: Whiplash injury to the neck – back sprain – moderate injuries.

Prognosis: Pain expected to disappear in the near future.

1.3.1.2.C168 Case No. 11928

Name of case: Groves v Pretty

Brief description of injuries: NECK – WHIPLASH – 10 MONTHS

Reported: Kemp & Kemp, K2-125/1; [1999] CLY 1592

JSB Category: 6(A)(c)

Sex: Male

Age at injury: 29

Age at award: 30

Date of award: 19 May 1999

Tribunal: Clerkenwell County Court

Amount of award then: £1,750

Award at February 2001: £1,818

Description of injuries: Road accident – minor whiplash injury – neck pain and stiffness extending predominantly to left shoulder, accompanied by headaches – symptoms significant for first 4 months following accident – symptoms resolved within 10 months – social life not affected, but marriage and postponed honeymoon was, in claimant's words, "somewhat subdued".

1.3.1.2.C169 Case No. 11042

Name of case: Hemsley v Hesketh
Brief description of injuries: NECK – WHIPLASH – 6 MONTHS
Reported: Kemp & Kemp, K2-129; [1995] CLY 1796
JSB Category: 6(A)(c)
Sex: Male
Age at injury: 39
Age at award: 40
Date of award: 07 March 1995
Tribunal: Blackpool County Court
Amount of award then: £1,500
Award at February 2001: £1,749
Description of injuries: Plaintiff's motor car struck from rear by defendant's vehicle – sustained hyperextension/flexion injury to cervical spine – suffered with constant ache in neck which meant he could not indulge in his hobbies of motorcycling, badminton and swimming – plumber – two weeks off work – pain lasted for around six months, thereafter no symptoms save for occasional cold-weather stiffness.

1.3.1.2.C170 Case No. 11041

Award at February 2001: £1,722
See: 1.3.1.C46 for details

1.3.1.2.C171 Case No. 11247

Name of case: Stimson v Williams
Brief description of injuries: NECK – WHIPLASH – 10 MONTHS
Reported: Kemp & Kemp, E2-132; [1996] CLY 2339
JSB Category: 6(A)(c)
Sex: Male
Age at injury: 73
Age at award: 74
Date of award: 28 September 1995
Tribunal: Birkenhead County Court
Amount of award then: £1,500
Award at February 2001: £1,713
Description of injuries: Whiplash type injury to the neck – jarring to the lower back – he was emotionally shaken – was symptom free after ten months.

1.3.1.2.C172 Case No. 11366

Name of case: Ellis v Soole
Brief description of injuries: NECK – WHIPLASH – 7 MONTHS
Reported: Kemp & Kemp, E2-134, K2-136; [1997] CLY 1914
JSB Category: 6(A)(c)
Sex: Female
Age at injury: 37
Age at award: 38
Date of award: 20 November 1996
Tribunal: Exeter County Court
Amount of award then: £1,500
Award at February 2001: £1,676
Description of injuries: Whiplash type injury.
Prognosis: Virtually fully recovered within seven months of the date of the accident.
Other points: The judge preferred the line of Crowson v Evans Kemp and Kemp E2-034.

1.3.1.2.C173 Case No. 11365

Name of case: Sangster v Kensington Building Services
Brief description of injuries: NECK – WHIPLASH – 6 MONTHS
Reported: Kemp & Kemp, K2-139; [1997] CLY 1913
JSB Category: 6(A)(c)
Sex: Male
Age at injury: 35
Age at award: 36
Date of award: 04 February 1997
Tribunal: Birkenhead County Court
Amount of award then: £1,500
Award at February 2001: £1,665
Description of injuries: Whiplash type injury to the neck.
Prognosis: Symptoms had resolved within six months of the date of the accident.

1.3.1.2.C174 Case No. 11969

Name of case: Edwards v Pryce

Brief description of injuries: NECK – WHIPLASH – 8 MONTHS

Reported: Kemp & Kemp, PRK-007; [2000] 1 CL 129

JSB Category: 6(A)(c)

Sex: Male

Age at injury: 18

Age at award: 20

Date of award: 23 August 1999

Tribunal: Liverpool County Court

Amount of award then: £1,600

Award at February 2001: £1,663

Description of injuries: A whiplash injury – pain to the posterior aspect of the neck and shoulders most of the time – intermittent thereafter – associated with activities like driving for 20 minutes or lifting objects at work – prescribed non-steroidal anti-inflammatory analgesics – no time off work as he was seeking a promotion – unable to enjoy his hobby at which he had represented his country. E's symptoms had been improving constantly over a period of eight months – after which time any residual problems had completely cleared up.

1.3.1.2.C175 Case No. 11721

Name of case: Williams v Bowen

Brief description of injuries: NECK – WHIPLASH – 12 MONTHS

Reported: Kemp & Kemp, E2-134/1; [1998] CLY 1724

JSB Category: 6(A)(c)

Sex: Male

Age at injury: 31

Age at award: 34

Date of award: 12 February 1998

Tribunal: Swansea County Court

Amount of award then: £1,500

Award at February 2001: £1,609

Description of injuries: Shock and neck pain – claimant continued work and rugby training – intermittent mild symptoms had fully resolved within 12 months of the date of the accident.

1.3.1.2.C176 Case No. 10115

Name of case: Dolton v Studley

Brief description of injuries: WHIPLASH – ONLY OCCASIONAL SYMPTOMS AFTER 6 MONTHS

Reported: Kemp & Kemp, K2-145; [1990] CLY 1689

JSB Category: 6(A)

Sex: Female

Age at injury: -

Age at award: -

Date of award: 02 April 1990

Tribunal: Weymouth County Court

Amount of award then: £1,150

Award at February 2001: £1,581

Description of injuries: Plaintiff's car was struck from behind whilst stationary causing whiplash injury to neck – absent from work as word processor operator for three weeks – suffered stiffness in shoulders and cervical spine with slight headaches – upon return to work employers had to provide special high-backed chair – six months after accident still suffered occasional pain at base of neck and top of spine – at date of trial still suffering occasional pain – no bone abnormality.

1.3.1.2.C177 Case No. 11722

Name of case: Hanson v Moore

Brief description of injuries: NECK – WHIPLASH – 8 MONTHS

Reported: Kemp & Kemp, K2-145/4; [1998] CLY 1725

JSB Category: 6(A)(c)

Sex: Male

Age at injury: 21

Age at award: 23

Date of award: 27 October 1998

Tribunal: Ipswich County Court

Amount of award then: £1,500

Award at February 2001: £1,568

Description of injuries: Whiplash neck injury – severe stiffness and aching.

Prognosis: Complete recovery within 8 months – no long-term sequelae were expected.

1.3.1.2.C178 Case No. 10502

Name of case: Sargent v Jeffs

Brief description of injuries: WHIPLASH – BACK PAIN – FULL RECOVERY

Reported: [1992] CLY 1758

JSB Category: 6(A)(c)

Sex: Female

Age at injury: 18

Age at award: 22

Date of award: 21 April 1992

Tribunal: Stafford County Court

Amount of award then: £1,250

Award at February 2001: £1,549

Description of injuries: Whiplash injury – caused pain to the neck, shoulders and back.

Prognosis: Lower back pain had gradually reduced by the time of the hearing.

1.3.1.2.C179 Case No. 12028

Name of case: Simpson v Grant

Brief description of injuries: NECK – WHIPLASH – 5 WEEKS

Reported: Kemp & Kemp, K2-145/8; [2000] 4 CL 171

JSB Category: 6(A)(c)

Sex: Male

Age at injury: 41

Age at award: 42

Date of award: 15 November 1999

Tribunal: Manchester County Court

Amount of award then: £1,500

Award at February 2001: £1,548

Description of injuries: A whiplash injury to the neck – advised to take painkilling relief – pain and discomfort lasted about five months. S sought no other medical treatment.

1.3.1.2.C180 Case No. 12014

Name of case: C (a child) v Peers

Brief description of injuries: NECK – WHIPLASH – 8 MONTHS

Reported: Kemp & Kemp, K2-145/9; [2000] 4 CL 157

JSB Category: 6(B)(c)

Sex: Female

Age at injury: 14

Age at award: 15

Date of award: 26 November 1999

Tribunal: Leicester County Court

Amount of award then: £1,500

Award at February 2001: £1,548

Description of injuries: Mild to moderate whiplash injury – pain to the back and stiff neck caused sleep disturbance – analgesics prescribed – for two weeks concentration was disturbed and PE was painful – five months after the date of the accident C still experienced discomfort.

Prognosis: Full recovery was likely within eight months of the date of the accident.

1.3.1.2.C181 Case No. 10501

Name of case: Ball v Genge

Brief description of injuries: WHIPLASH – 3 MONTHS

Reported: [1992] CLY 1757

JSB Category: 6(A)(c)

Sex: Female

Age at injury: 25

Age at award: 27

Date of award: 07 August 1992

Tribunal: Barnstable County Court

Amount of award then: £1,250

Award at February 2001: £1,548

Description of injuries: Whiplash injury to the neck.

Prognosis: There was full recovery within three months.

1.3.1.2.C182 Case No. 11331

Name of case: Warburton v Barrington

Brief description of injuries: NECK – WHIPLASH – BACK – 3 MONTHS

Reported: Kemp & Kemp, E2-137/1; [1997] CLY 1879

JSB Category: 6(A)(c)

Sex: Male

Age at injury: 32

Age at award: 36

Date of award: 22 August 1997

Tribunal: Blackburn County Court

Amount of award then: £1,400

Award at February 2001: £1,519

Description of injuries: Neck strain – lower back pain – symptoms appeared to settle within three months of the date of the accident.

1.3.1.2.C183 Case No. 11046

Award at February 2001: £1,458

See: 1.3.1.C51 for details

1.3.1.2.C184 Case No. 11252

Name of case: Cummins v Wallace

Brief description of injuries: NECK – WHIPLASH – 2 MONTHS

Reported: Kemp & Kemp, K2-165; [1996] CLY 2344

JSB Category: 6(A)(c)

Sex: Male

Age at injury: 31

Age at award: 34

Date of award: 17 July 1996

Tribunal: Birkenhead County Court

Amount of award then: £1,250

Award at February 2001: £1,411

Description of injuries: Whiplash injury to the neck – full recovery within two months of the date of the accident.

1.3.1.2.C185 Case No. 11724

Name of case: Joyce v Lucey

Brief description of injuries: NECK – WHIPLASH – 3 MONTHS

Reported: Kemp & Kemp, K2-166/1; [1998] CLY 1727

JSB Category: 6(A)(c)

Sex: Female

Age at injury: 19

Age at award: 21

Date of award: 26 January 1998

Tribunal: Watford County Court

Amount of award then: £1,300

Award at February 2001: £1,402

Description of injuries: Whiplash injury to the neck – pain and stiffness to the neck and shoulders – J made a good recovery within 3 months of the date of the accident.

1.3.1.2.C186 Case No. 11332

Name of case: Hartley v Postlethwaite

Brief description of injuries: NECK – WHIPLASH – 2 MONTHS

Reported: Kemp & Kemp, K2-169/1; [1997] CLY 1880

JSB Category: 6(A)(c)

Sex: Male

Age at injury: 29

Age at award: 30

Date of award: 19 August 1997

Tribunal: Leeds County Court

Amount of award then: £1,250

Award at February 2001: £1,356

Description of injuries: Minor whiplash injury to the neck – symptom-free after two months.

1.3.1.2.C187 Case No. 11727

Name of case: Khan v Oldham

Brief description of injuries: NECK – WHIPLASH – 4 MONTHS

Reported: Kemp & Kemp, K2-170/2; [1998] CLY 1730

JSB Category: 6(A)(c); 6(B)(c)

Sex: Male

Age at injury: 24

Age at award: 26

Date of award: 18 February 1998

Tribunal: Leeds County Court

Amount of award then: £1,250

Award at February 2001: £1,341

Description of injuries: Minor whiplash to the neck – lower back pain – bruised knees – full recovery made within 4 months of the date of the accident.

1.3.1.2.C188 Case No. 11726

Name of case: Hazell v Taylor

Brief description of injuries: NECK – WHIPLASH – 3 WEEKS

Reported: Kemp & Kemp, K2-170/1; [1998] CLY 1729

JSB Category: 6(A)(c)

Sex: Male

Age at injury: 18

Age at award: 20

Date of award: 11 February 1998

Tribunal: Milton Keynes County Court

Amount of award then: £1,250

Award at February 2001: £1,341

Description of injuries: Whiplash type injury to the neck – neck pain settled after 3 weeks – H remained a nervous passenger.

1.3.1.2.C189 Case No. 11333

Name of case: Stanley v Rosewell

Brief description of injuries: NECK – WHIPLASH – 3 MONTHS

Reported: Kemp & Kemp, E2-139/2; [1997] CLY 1881

JSB Category: 6(A)(c)

Sex: Female

Age at injury: 21

Age at award: 23

Date of award: 05 September 1997

Tribunal: Staines County Court

Amount of award then: £1,200

Award at February 2001: £1,296

Description of injuries: Stiff neck – limited range of movement – whiplash was diagnosed – full recovery within three months of the date of the accident.

1.3.1.2.C190 Case No. 11731

Name of case: Thompson v Chappell

Brief description of injuries: NECK – WHIPLASH – BACK – 5 WEEKS

Reported: Kemp & Kemp, K2-176; [1998] CLY 1734

JSB Category: 6(A)(c)

Sex: Female

Age at injury: 31

Age at award: 34

Date of award: 23 July 1998

Tribunal: Ilford County Court

Amount of award then: £1,200

Award at February 2001: £1,266

Description of injuries: Minor whiplash injury to the neck and upper back – T suffered pain and discomfort for about 5 weeks.

1.3.1.2.C191 Case No. 11049
Award at February 2001: £1,265
See: 1.3.1.C53 for details

1.3.1.2.C192 Case No. 10507
Name of case: Wood v Draper
Brief description of injuries: WHIPLASH – 3 MONTHS
Reported: [1992] CLY 1763
JSB Category: 6(A)(c)
Sex: Female
Age at injury: 49
Age at award: 52
Date of award: 26 March 1992
Tribunal: Gloucester County Court
Amount of award then: £1,000
Award at February 2001: £1,258
Description of injuries: Whiplash injury with associated bruising from the seat belt.
Prognosis: Whiplash injury disappeared over two to three months.

1.3.1.2.C193 Case No. 11053
Name of case: Coates v Daneheath
Brief description of injuries: NECK – WHIPLASH – 7 DAYS
Reported: Kemp & Kemp, K2-183; [1995] CLY 1807
JSB Category: 6(A)(c)
Sex: Male
Age at injury: 25
Age at award: 27
Date of award: 06 January 1994
Tribunal: Leeds County Court
Amount of award then: £1,000
Award at February 2001: £1,217
Description of injuries: Social worker was driver of vehicle which was struck from behind whilst stationary – head jerked forward and seat was broken – temporarily shocked and suffered from pain and stiffness – whiplash – pain and stiffness continued for seven days, thereafter symptom free.

1.3.1.2.C194 Case No. 11050
Award at February 2001: £1,148
See: 1.3.1.C56 for details

1.3.1.2.C195 Case No. 11257
Name of case: Wilson v Fenlon
Brief description of injuries: NECK – WHIPLASH – 3 MONTHS
Reported: Kemp & Kemp, E2-140; [1996] CLY 2349
JSB Category: 6(A)(c)
Sex: Female
Age at injury: 27
Age at award: -
Date of award: 17 August 1995
Tribunal: Birkenhead County Court
Amount of award then: £1,000
Award at February 2001: £1,147
Description of injuries: Whiplash type injury – symptom free within three months of the date of the accident.

1.3.1.2.C196 Case No. 10121
Name of case: Baughan v Paxton
Brief description of injuries: WHIPLASH – PRE-EXISTING CONDITION AGGRAVATED FOR 8 WEEKS
Reported: Kemp & Kemp, 1-008/2; [1990] CLY 1698
JSB Category: 6(A)
Sex: Male
Age at injury: 41
Age at award: 42
Date of award: 16 November 1990
Tribunal: Watford County Court
Amount of award then: £846
Award at February 2001: £1,119
Description of injuries: Driver involved in low impact collision sustained whiplash injury to neck – suffered pain and headaches over following weekend – cervical collar worn for four weeks – pain and headaches continued for next four weeks, accompanied by restriction in movement of neck – had pre-accident spondylosis of the neck which was aggravated by accident.

1.3.1.2.C197 Case No. 11337
Name of case: Southworth v Taberner
Brief description of injuries: NECK – WHIPLASH – 6 MONTHS
Reported: Kemp & Kemp, K2-199; [1997] CLY 1885
JSB Category: 6(A)(c)
Sex: Male
Age at injury: 24
Age at award: 27
Date of award: 21 November 1996
Tribunal: Chorley County Court
Amount of award then: £1,000
Award at February 2001: £1,118
Description of injuries: Minor whiplash injury to the neck – full recovery within six months of the date of the accident.

1.3.1.2.C198 Case No. 11334
Award at February 2001: £1,114
See: 1.3.1.C58 for details

1.3.1.2.C199 Case No. 11335
Name of case: Wilson and Wilson v Seagram Distillers PLC
Brief description of injuries: NECK – WHIPLASH – 3 WEEKS
Reported: Kemp & Kemp, K2-200; [1997] CLY 1883
JSB Category: 6(A)(c)
Sex: Female
Age at injury: 48
Age at award: 50
Date of award: 27 January 1997
Tribunal: Chester County Court
Amount of award then: £1,000
Award at February 2001: £1,114
Description of injuries: Minor whiplash type injury – symptoms had gone after three weeks.
Other points: Plaintiff did not see a doctor.

1.3.1.2.C200 Case No. 10120
Name of case: Rice v Garrett
Brief description of injuries: WHIPLASH – FULL RECOVERY 2 MONTHS – NIGHTMARES
Reported: [1990] CLY 1697
JSB Category: 6(A)
Sex: Female
Age at injury: 24
Age at award: -
Date of award: 30 October 1989
Tribunal: Southampton County Court
Amount of award then: £750
Award at February 2001: £1,098
Description of injuries: Injury in road accident – whiplash causing pain and discomfort to neck and right shoulder – suffered acute pain for one week – took analgesic tablets and was off work for three days – sleep disturbance from pain and nightmares – still suffered occasional nightmares at time of trial – full recovery from neck/shoulder symptoms after two months.

1.3.1.2.C201 Case No. 11367
Name of case: Stride (A) v Lipscombe
Brief description of injuries: NECK – WHIPLASH – 3 WEEKS
Reported: Kemp & Kemp, E2-131/1, K2-205; [1997] CLY 1915
JSB Category: 6(A)(c)
Sex: Male
Age at injury: 64
Age at award: 66
Date of award: 01 July 1997
Tribunal: Central London County Court
Amount of award then: £1,000
Award at February 2001: £1,092
Description of injuries: Strain to the neck.
Prognosis: Pain and suffering resolved within three weeks of the date of the accident.

1.3.1.2.C202 Case No. 11733
Name of case: Southeran v Singh
Brief description of injuries: NECK – WHIPLASH – 3 WEEKS
Reported: Kemp & Kemp, E2-141/1; [1998] CLY 1736
JSB Category: 6(A)(c)
Sex: Female
Age at injury: 39
Age at award: 40
Date of award: 07 January 1998
Tribunal: Leicester County Court
Amount of award then: £1,000
Award at February 2001: £1,078
Description of injuries: Minor whiplash injury to the neck – pain resolved within 3 weeks.

1.3.1.2.C203 Case No. 10886
Name of case: Battle v Sharples
Brief description of injuries: NECK – WHIPLASH
Reported: [1994] CLY 1738
JSB Category: 6(A)(c)
Sex: Female
Age at injury: 24
Age at award: 25
Date of award: 24 November 1993
Tribunal: Preston County Court
Amount of award then: £800
Award at February 2001: £972
Description of injuries: Minor whiplash injury to cervical spine – pain in neck radiating to shoulders – acute pain in first 3-7 day period – marked pain on movement of head – anti-inflammatory drugs for 2 weeks – disturbed sleep for 1 week – difficulty looking behind when driving – unable to exercise in gym for 2 months – otherwise fully recovered within 1 month.

Damage to Spine

1.3.1.2.C204 Case No. 10511

Name of case: Feeney v Littlewood
Brief description of injuries: WHIPLASH
Reported: [1992] CLY 1767
JSB Category: 6(A)(c)
Sex: Male
Age at injury: 19
Age at award: 21
Date of award: 12 March 1992
Tribunal: Liverpool County Court
Amount of award then: £750
Award at February 2001: £944

Description of injuries: Whiplash injury – shocked and shaken – pain and stiffness in the shoulders – pain and tenderness to the back of the head.

Prognosis: Full recovery within 5 months.

1.3.1.2.C205 Case No. 12050

Name of case: Kalam v Khan
Brief description of injuries: NECK – WHIPLASH – 2 MONTHS
Reported: Kemp & Kemp, K2-224/1; [2000] 5 CL 194
JSB Category: 6(A)(c)
Sex: Male
Age at injury: 23
Age at award: 24
Date of award: 04 February 2000
Tribunal: Nuneaton County Court
Amount of award then: £900
Award at February 2001: £924

Description of injuries: Soft-tissue whiplash injuries to the neck – strain to both wrists – two days off work – anti-inflamatories prescribed two weeks later. A full recovery within two months of the date of the accident.

1.3.1.2.C206 Case No. 11736

Name of case: Sullivan v Massin-Smart
Brief description of injuries: NECK – WHIPLASH – 3 WEEKS
Reported: Kemp & Kemp, K2-224/1; [1998] CLY 1739
JSB Category: 6(A)(c)
Sex: P1: Male P2: Female
Age at injury: -
Age at award: 26
Date of award: 07 October 1997
Tribunal: Sheffield County Court
Amount of award then: £850
Award at February 2001: £917

Description of injuries: P1 and P2 suffered whiplash injury to the neck – P2 was shocked and shaken – both were fully recovered within 3 weeks of the date of the accident.

Other points: Sum awarded to each applicant.

1.3.1.2.C207 Case No. 10887

Name of case: Hones v Brown
Brief description of injuries: NECK – WHIPLASH – BACK
Reported: Kemp & Kemp, E2-142; [1994] CLY 1739
JSB Category: 6(A)(c), 6(B)(c)
Sex: Male
Age at injury: 22
Age at award: 23
Date of award: 07 September 1994
Tribunal: Southend County Court
Amount of award then: £750
Award at February 2001: £890

Description of injuries: Road accident – relatively minor whiplash injury to neck and back – no immediate pain, but development of aching in neck and back on following morning – anti-inflammatories and rest prescribed – claimant attempted to return to work (as printer) after 2 days, but back pain made him unable to continue; sent home – finally returned to work after 8 days – aching symptoms in neck and back for 4 weeks; worse in first 2 weeks, gradually improving thereafter – at date of hearing, claimant still experiencing occasional twinges after a stressful day – claimant forced to miss remainder of 1993/94 football season (his hobby) – unable to swim until January 1994 – social life and relationship with girlfriend adversely affected over 4-week period.

Prognosis: Anticipated that claimant would be able to resume playing football in 1994 season.

1.3.1.2.C208 Case No. 10517

Name of case: Hind v Howel
Brief description of injuries: WHIPLASH – BRUISING-STIFFNESS
Reported: [1992] CLY 1773
JSB Category: 6(A)(c)
Sex: Male
Age at injury: -
Age at award: 36
Date of award: 19 February 1992
Tribunal: Nottingham County Court
Amount of award then: £700
Award at February 2001: £883

Description of injuries: Blow to the head and thigh – bruising for 2-3 weeks – stiffness and limitation of movement – no time off work.

Prognosis: Resolved after 5 weeks.

1.3.1.2.C209 Case No. 10513

Name of case: Marshall v Lyon

Brief description of injuries: WHIPLASH – OFF WORK 5 DAYS

Reported: [1992] CLY 1769

JSB Category: 6(A)(c)

Sex: Male

Age at injury: 61

Age at award: 62

Date of award: 29 April 1992

Tribunal: Cambridge County Court

Amount of award then: £700

Award at February 2001: £867

Description of injuries: Whiplash – unable to visit elderly mother who relied on his assistance at her home or to bring her to his own home for a visit.

Prognosis: Resumed work after five days – otherwise symptom free.

1.3.1.2.C210 Case No. 11064

Award at February 2001: £866

See: 1.3.1.C62 for details

1.3.1.2.C211 Case No. 11368

Name of case: Hales v Clark

Brief description of injuries: NECK – WHIPLASH

Reported: Kemp & Kemp, K2-240; [1997] CLY 1916

JSB Category: 6(A)(c)

Sex: P1 Female / P2 Female

Age at injury: -

Age at award: P1:43;P2:14

Date of award: 16 April 1997

Tribunal: Oxford County Court

Amount of award then: £750

Award at February 2001: £825

Description of injuries: Both plaintiffs suffered pain in the neck – extremely distressed.

Prognosis: No long-term sequelae.

Other points: Sum awarded to each applicant.

1.3.1.2.C212 Case No. 10518

Name of case: Dalby v Toogood

Brief description of injuries: WHIPLASH – CUTS AND BRUISING – FULL RECOVERY 3 WEEKS

Reported: [1992] CLY 1774

JSB Category: 6(A)(c)

Sex: Female

Age at injury: 20

Age at award: 21

Date of award: 21 November 1991

Tribunal: Northampton County Court

Amount of award then: £650

Award at February 2001: £824

Description of injuries: Bruising to the right shoulder and both knees – minor cut to the left hand – whiplash injury.

Prognosis: Bruises took three weeks to resolve- shoulder and neck pain ten days.

1.3.1.2.C213 Case No. 11369

Name of case: Salmon v SJT Stafford Ltd

Brief description of injuries: NECK – WHIPLASH – 1 WEEK

Reported: Kemp & Kemp, K2-243; [1997] CLY 1917

JSB Category: 6(A)(c)

Sex: Male

Age at injury: 28

Age at award: 29

Date of award: 21 May 1997

Tribunal: Altrincham County Court

Amount of award then: £750

Award at February 2001: £822

Description of injuries: Acute whiplash to the cervical spine – shocked and shaken.

Prognosis: Symptom free within one week of the date of the accident.

1.3.1.2.C214 Case No. 11338

Name of case: Frost v Furness

Brief description of injuries: NECK – WHIPLASH – 10 DAYS

Reported: Kemp & Kemp, K2-245; [1997] CLY 1886

JSB Category: 6(A)(c)

Sex: Male

Age at injury: Not stated

Age at award:

Date of award: 14 July 1997

Tribunal: Reading County Court

Amount of award then: £750

Award at February 2001: £819

Description of injuries: Soft-tissue whiplash injury – settled rapidly after ten days.

1.3.1.2.C215 Case No. 11737

Name of case: Poleon v Ramdhani

Brief description of injuries: NECK – WHIPLASH – 7 DAYS

Reported: Kemp & Kemp, K2-245/2; [1998] CLY 1740

JSB Category: 6(A)(c)

Sex: Female

Age at injury: 23

Age at award: 25

Date of award: 22 July 1998

Tribunal: Birmingham County Court

Amount of award then: £750

Award at February 2001: £791

Description of injuries: Whiplash injury to the neck – no continuing symptoms after 7 days.

Prognosis: No risk of future degeneration.

1.3.1.2.C216 Case No. 12015

Name of case: Hughes v Hunt

Brief description of injuries: NECK – WHIPLASH – 7-10 DAYS

Reported: Kemp & Kemp, K2/253/4; [2000] 4 CL 158

JSB Category: 6(A)(c)

Sex: Female

Age at injury: 30

Age at award: 31

Date of award: 13 December 1999

Tribunal: Epsom County Court

Amount of award then: £600

Award at February 2001: £617

Description of injuries: A minor whiplash type injury in a traffic accident – neck pain and headache – prescribed painkillers and a gel – no further treatment sought – no time off work – the worst of the pain lasted three days.

Prognosis: Symptoms had fully resolved within seven to ten days of the date of the accident.

1.3.1.2.C217 Case No. 12039

Name of case: Morley v Sussex Coastline Buses Ltd

Brief description of injuries: NECK – WHIPLASH – 3-4 WEEKS

Reported: Kemp & Kemp, K2-253/3; [2000] 5 CL 183

JSB Category: 6(A)(c)

Sex: Female

Age at injury: 54

Age at award: 56

Date of award: 09 December 1999

Tribunal: Southampton County Court

Amount of award then: £600

Award at February 2001: £617

Description of injuries: A whiplash type injury to the neck – severe for seven to ten days. Symptoms resolved completely within about 24 days of the date of the accident – enjoyment of Christmas festivities was affected.

1.3.1.2.C218 Case No. 10687

Name of case: Lobo v Hamilton

Brief description of injuries: NECK – WHIPLASH – 2 WEEKS

Reported: Kemp & Kemp, K2-254; [1993] CLY 1583

JSB Category: 6(A)(c)

Sex: Male

Age at injury: 20

Age at award: 21

Date of award: 17 August 1993

Tribunal: Reading County Court

Amount of award then: £500

Award at February 2001: £609

Description of injuries: Road accident – minor whiplash injury – slight stiffness in neck for a couple of weeks – prevented from pursuing leisure activity of weight training – no visit to doctor made or medication taken.

1.3.1.2.C219 Case No. 10128

Name of case: Jackson & Jackson v Mourne

Brief description of injuries: WHIPLASH – 2 WEEKS

Reported: [1990] CLY 1707

JSB Category: 6(A)

Sex: Female, Female

Age at injury: -;-

Age at award: 21;19

Date of award: 17 January 1990

Tribunal: Portsmouth County Court

Amount of award then: £400

Award at February 2001: £576

Description of injuries: Both plaintiffs received whiplash injury in road traffic accident – both had difficulty in raising and moving the head, and both suffered with stiff necks – both plaintiffs recovered fully after two weeks with no further symptoms.

1.3.1.2.C220 Case No. 11067

Award at February 2001: £574

See: 1.3.1.C63 for details

1.3.1.2.C221 Case No. 11738

Name of case: Cotton v Navarro

Brief description of injuries: NECK – WHIPLASH – 3 DAYS

Reported: Kemp & Kemp, K2-263; [1998] CLY 1741

JSB Category: 6(A)(c)

Sex: Male

Age at injury: middle-aged

Age at award:

Date of award: 06 July 1998

Tribunal: Romford County Court

Amount of award then: £500

Award at February 2001: £528

Description of injuries: Whiplash type injuries – symptoms resolved completely within 3 days of the date of the accident.

1.3.1.2.C222 Case No. 10688

Name of case: Knight and Gilbert v Hooper

Brief description of injuries: NECK – WHIPLASH – 2 WEEKS

Reported: [1993] CLY 1584

JSB Category: (both claimants): 6(A)(c)

Sex: (1): not stated (2): not stated

Age at injury: (1) 26;(2) 41

Age at award: -;-

Date of award: 14 October 1993

Tribunal: Reading County Court

Amount of award then: £400

Award at February 2001: £485

Description of injuries: Two claimants in car involved in road accident suffered similar injuries – stiff and painful necks for 4-5 days – residual symptoms for 2 weeks – loss of sleep for about 2 nights – discomfort when driving (which was part of both claimants' jobs) – first claimant took painkillers for a few days – neither visited doctor.

Other points: £400 is sum awarded to each claimant.

1.3.1.2.C223 Case No. 11931

Name of case: A (a minor) v Sullivan

Brief description of injuries: NECK – WHIPLASH – 10 DAYS

Reported: (1999) 99 (5) QR 8; Kemp & Kemp, K2-268; [1999] CLY 1595

JSB Category: 6(A)(c)

Sex: Female

Age at injury: 15

Age at award: 16

Date of award: 28 April 1999

Tribunal: Oxford County Court

Amount of award then: £450

Award at February 2001: £469

Description of injuries: Road accident – hyperextension injury to cervical spine, causing immediate mild pain – 4 days after accident, mild stiffness and discomfort, easing gradually – symptoms completely resolved within 10 days – claimant on holiday at time, so did not miss any school – sport or recreational activity not affected – no sleep disturbance or reduced confidence.

Prognosis: No long-term consequences anticipated.

1.3.1.2.C224 Case No. 11370

Name of case: Charnick v Russell

Brief description of injuries: NECK – WHIPLASH – 1 WEEK

Reported: Kemp & Kemp, K2-271; [1997] CLY 1918

JSB Category: 6(A)(c)

Sex: Male

Age at injury: Not stated.

Age at award:

Date of award: 13 May 1997

Tribunal: Tunbridge Wells County Court

Amount of award then: £250

Award at February 2001: £274

Description of injuries: Whiplash type injury.

Prognosis: Symptom free within one week of the date of the accident.

1.3.1.2.C225 Case No. 10131

Name of case: Edwards v Oxytech Services

Brief description of injuries: WHIPLASH – 2 MONTHS

Reported: [1990] CLY 1713

JSB Category: 6(A)

Sex: Male

Age at injury: 34

Age at award: 36

Date of award: 09 November 1990

Tribunal: Rotherham County Court

Amount of award then: £200

Award at February 2001: £265

Description of injuries: Van reversed into front of plaintiff's stationary vehicle – later that night suffered neck pain and stiffness – no time off work – did not consult GP – pain was gone after two months.

1.3.1.2.1 Whiplash and other injury

1.3.1.2.1.C1 Case No. 10749

Name of case: Evans v Neath Borough Council

Brief description of injuries: WHIPLASH – PRE-EXISTING SPINE CONDITION – POST-TRAUMATIC STRESS DISORDER

Reported: Kemp & Kemp, E3-024; [1994] CLY 1597

JSB Category: 6(A)(b); 3(B)

Sex: Male

Age at injury: 29

Age at award: 37

Date of award: 19 May 1994

Tribunal: Cardiff High Court

Amount of award then: £17,500

Award at February 2001: £21,315

Description of injuries: Road accident – whiplash injury to cervical spine – claimant already suffering from pre-existing condition to dorsal spine sustained in coal – mining accident 1 year before accident – as a result of accident, claimant suffered pain, discomfort and tenderness in spine at level C6 to C4, causing pain in head, neck, upper back and right arm – some symptoms of post-traumatic stress disorder – difficulty driving or walking distances – unable to do DIY – intermittent severe headaches sometimes forcing claimant to stay in bed – previously keen sportsman, but now only swimming possible – claimant took up sheltered employment 2 years after accident but was unable to continue and gave up after a year.

Prognosis: Claimant was unlikely ever to have returned to mining job, but could have returned to lighter manual work, prior to accident – however, disabilities would now prevent claimant from holding down any type of job – significant and permanent effect on quality of life.

1.3.1.2.1.C2 Case No. 11350

Name of case: Clark v Commissioner of Police of the Metropolis

Brief description of injuries: NECK – WHIPLASH – POST-TRAUMATIC STRESS DISORDER

Reported: Kemp & Kemp, E2-009; [1997] CLY 1898

JSB Category: 6(A)(b)(i) 3(B)(c)

Sex: Female

Age at injury: 45

Age at award: 50

Date of award: 10 January 1997

Tribunal: Ilford County Court

Amount of award then: £17,500

Award at February 2001: £19,917

Description of injuries: Whiplash type injury to the cervical spine – moderate post-traumatic stress disorder – all aspects of her domestic chores were affected – at time of hearing the neck showed little sign of improvement – remaining anxiety and depression was probably caused by the constant pain.

Prognosis: The contention that pre-existing degenerative change would have become symptomatic was rejected.

1.3.1.2.1.C3 Case No. 10751

Name of case: Holland v Wood
Brief description of injuries: NECK – SEVERE WHIPLASH – DEPRESSION
Reported: Kemp & Kemp, E2-010; [1994] CLY 1599
JSB Category: 6(A)(b); 3(A)
Sex: Female
Age at injury: 65
Age at award: 67
Date of award: 02 July 1993
Tribunal: Torquay County Court
Amount of award then: £15,000
Award at February 2001: £18,684

Description of injuries: Road accident – claimant's head struck car roof – severe pain deep within head, behind right eye – whiplash injury to spine – shock – examined and discharged from casualty – pain in posterior skull worsened – numbness in left side of face – tingling in left arm and fingers of left hand – cervical collar prescribed – pain became unbearable – cessation of physical activities (swimming, walking) – rest in hospital prescribed, bringing some improvement – eventually admitted to hospital for cervical spine manipulation under anaesthetic – development of post-concussional syndrome for 4 months after the accident – anxious – depressed – irritable – emotional – forgetful – change in formerly energetic and "happy-go-lucky" personality – intrusive thoughts about collision – anxiety about travelling – manipulation and subsequent physiotherapy greatly improved head and neck symptoms – full resumption of physical activities.

Prognosis: Intermittent residual discomfort in neck, posteriorly on left hand side, likely to continue permanently but not a major limitation or disability – further medical treatment possibly necessary – progressive deterioration not expected – prognosis of return to full, normal life within 7 months of date of hearing – judge, however, uncertain that claimant would make full psychological recovery and return to previous "sunny" disposition – found that both physical and psychiatric symptoms serious and significant.

1.3.1.2.1.C4 Case No. 11805

Name of case: Anderton v Granulators Ltd
Brief description of injuries: NECK – WHIPLASH – ECZEMA – DEPRESSION
Reported: Kemp & Kemp, E2-015/1; [1999] CLY 1468
JSB Category: 6(A)(b); 3(A); 4(A)
Sex: Male
Age at injury: 46
Age at award: 50
Date of award: 20 May 1998
Tribunal: Oldham County Court
Amount of award then: £15,000
Award at February 2001: £15,985

Description of injuries: Claimant suffered whiplash injury in road accident – immediate pain in neck – ongoing pain forced claimant to take 27 months off work over following 4.5-year period – development of eczema 12 weeks after accident – depression, originally caused by accident and making claimant vulnerable and unable to cope with problems at work, made severe by altercation at work 2 years later – eyesight also affected by accident, bringing forward need for glasses by 2 years.

Prognosis: Neck problems ongoing, and claimant likely to be forced to take similar periods of time off work in the future – claimant now likely to retire at 60, rather than 65.

1.3.1.2.1.C5 Case No. 11126

Name of case: Proctor v Hussain
Brief description of injuries: NECK – WHIPLASH – POST-TRAUMATIC STRESS DISORDER
Reported: Kemp & Kemp, E2-035; [1996] CLY 2217
JSB Category: 6(A)(b)(i)
Sex: Female
Age at injury: 44
Age at award: 48
Date of award: 25 March 1996
Tribunal: Stoke on Trent County Court
Amount of award then: £10,000
Award at February 2001: £11,384

Description of injuries: Lateral flexion injury to the cervical spine – mild post-traumatic stress disorder.

Prognosis: Mild/moderate symptoms in the neck unlikely to improve – psychological symptoms likely to improve with treatment.

Other points: Any exaggeration of symptoms was sub-conscious.

1.3.1.2.1.C6 Case No. 11584

Name of case: Collins v Whip

Brief description of injuries: NECK – WHIPLASH – THORACO-LUMBAR INJURY

Reported: Kemp & Kemp, E2-043/1; [1998] CLY 1586

JSB Category: 6(A)(b)(i); 6(B)

Sex: Female

Age at injury: 30

Age at award: 35

Date of award: 13 October 1997

Tribunal: Barnet County Court

Amount of award then: £8,500

Award at February 2001: £9,166

Description of injuries: Whiplash injury to the neck – thoraco-lumbar spine injury – bruises and contusions – bilateral shoulder injury – significant residual disability in view of invasion of daily life by pain.

Prognosis: There was a 20 per cent chance that surgery might be required within the next 10 years.

1.3.1.2.1.C7 Case No. 11754

Name of case: Stobbart v Ryan

Brief description of injuries: NECK – WHIPLASH – ME ACCELERATED BY FIVE YEARS

Reported: Kemp & Kemp, L8-215; [1998] CLY 1757

JSB Category: 6(B)(c)

Sex: Male

Age at injury: 24

Age at award: 28

Date of award: 07 October 1997

Tribunal: Ipswich County Court

Amount of award then: £8,500

Award at February 2001: £9,166

Description of injuries: Acute strain to both cervical and lumbar spine – 25 per cent reduction of movement in the lumbar spine – 5 per cent reduction of movement in the cervical spine – relapse of myalgic encephalomyelitis – symptoms were at an all-time high 18 months after the date of the accident.

Prognosis: Exacerbation of ME by 5 years.

1.3.1.2.1.C8 Case No. 11984

Name of case: Dowle v Graham

Brief description of injuries: NECK – WHIPLASH – POST CONCUSSIONAL DISORDER

Reported: Kemp & Kemp, PRC-008; [2000] 3 CL 168

JSB Category: 2(B) and 3(B)(c)

Sex: Male

Age at injury: Not stated

Age at award:

Date of award: 26 March 1999

Tribunal: Taunton County Court

Amount of award then: £8,500

Award at February 2001: £8,909

Description of injuries: A panel beater, D was struck on the head by a car falling off an hydraulic ramp – knocked unconscious – post-traumatic amnesia – sore neck and lump to the side of the head – whiplash type injury to the neck – one night in hospital – four weeks mainly in bed.

Prognosis: D's neck continued to be problematic.

1.3.1.2.1.C9 Case No. 11351

Award at February 2001: £8,737

See: 1.2.2.1.C18 for details

1.3.1.2.1.C10 Case No. 12041

Name of case: Lloyd-Davies v Lyth

Brief description of injuries: BACK – 5-7 YEAR ACCELERATION – NECK – WHIPLASH

Reported: Kemp & Kemp, E2-047/2; [2000] 5 CL 185

JSB Category: 6(B)(b)(ii)

Sex: Male

Age at injury: 38

Age at award: 41

Date of award: 09 February 2000

Tribunal: Chester County Court

Amount of award then: £8,500

Award at February 2001: £8,728

Description of injuries: A whiplash injury to the neck – neck pain resolved within six months of the date of the accident – lumbar back strain – remained the main symptom six months after the accident – X-rays revealed a pre-existing asymptomatic back condition which would have become symptomatic by the age of 45 – seatbelt bruising – bruising to both knees – pre-existing patello-femoral arthritic condition exacerbated. The accident accelerated the pre-existing lumbar spine symptoms by between five to seven years.

1.3.1.2.1.C11 Case No. 10563

Name of case: Calvert v Greenfield

Brief description of injuries: PSYCHIATRIC DAMAGE – WHIPLASH

Reported: Kemp & Kemp, C4-091; [1993] CLY 1456

JSB Category: 3(A)(c); 6(A)(c)

Sex: Female

Age at injury: 53

Age at award: 56

Date of award: 09 March 1993

Tribunal: Watford County Court

Amount of award then: £7,000

Award at February 2001: £8,643

Description of injuries: Car accident – claimant sustained mild to moderate whiplash injury – also experiencing depression similar to clinical depression, due to irrational grief reaction to loss of car – whiplash symptoms improved over 3 months, but then improvement ceased – still experiencing discomfort at time of trial.

Prognosis: Optimistic prognosis of complete recovery, but periodic episodes of pain in the future also possible.

1.3.1.2.1.C12 Case No. 10587

Name of case: Doughty v Brown and Federal Express (UK)

Brief description of injuries: NECK – WHIPLASH – BACK INJURY

Reported: Kemp & Kemp, E2-049; [1993] CLY 1480

JSB Category: 6(A)(b), 6(B)(b)

Sex: Male

Age at injury: 42

Age at award: 46

Date of award: 23 August 1993

Tribunal: Lincoln County Court

Amount of award then: £7,000

Award at February 2001: £8,521

Description of injuries: Whiplash injury to neck and thoracic and lumbar regions of spine in road accident – restriction of movement in cervical spine and considerable pain – restriction of movement and some discomfort in lower spine – claimant's symptoms exacerbated by anything involving holding arms out in front of him, eg driving, using blackboard, playing keyboards, using computer – unable to play racket sports, or carry out decorating, DIY or heavy gardening – interest in hawking curtailed.

Prognosis: Able to keep working as head teacher, but symptoms likely to continue indefinitely – no risk of late complications such as osteoarthritis.

1.3.1.2.1.C13 Case No. 11809

Name of case: Moore v Hopwood

Brief description of injuries: NECK – WHIPLASH – LUMBAR SPINE

Reported: Kemp & Kemp, E3-085/2; [1999] CLY 1472

JSB Category: 6(A)(b), 6(B)(b)(ii)

Sex: Male

Age at injury: 26

Age at award: 31

Date of award: 15 January 1999

Tribunal: Lincoln County Court

Amount of award then: £8,000

Award at February 2001: £8,421

Description of injuries: Whiplash injury to cervical and lumbar spine – symptoms acute immediately after accident, spoiling enjoyment of claimant's holiday – discomfort aggravated by claimant, a farmer, being unable to take any time off work, and by heavy manual nature of work – neck symptoms eased appreciably over 2 months, with occasional intermittent pain, mainly felt when lifting – lumbar spine discomfort particularly aggravated by work, affecting claimant's ability to perform tasks; only minor improvement achieved, and claimant purchased lumbar support to help ease discomfort – home and social life not otherwise affected.

Prognosis: Lumbar problems had become permanent by date of trial, and would not resolve whilst claimant continued working.

1.3.1.2.1.C14 Case No. 10588

Award at February 2001: £7,929

See: 1.2.2.1.C20 for details

1.3.1.2.1.C15 Case No. 11886

Award at February 2001: £7,813

See: 1.2.2.1.C21 for details

1.3.1.2.1.C16 Case No. 10202

Name of case: Fenton v A Camm

Brief description of injuries: WHIPLASH – MODERATELY SEVERE – HEADACHES – SEVERE FOR 3 WEEKS, THEN PERSISTED

Reported: Kemp & Kemp, E2-059; [1991] CLY 1399

JSB Category: 6A)(b)(i)

Sex: Male

Age at injury: 69

Age at award: 72

Date of award: 30 July 1991

Tribunal: Reading District Registry

Amount of award then: £6,000

Award at February 2001: £7,713

Description of injuries: A moderately severe whiplash injury – neck pain, headache, and weakness and pain to one arm – severe discomfort for three weeks – thereafter his condition stabilised.

Prognosis: At the time of the hearing weakness in his right arm caused him to have to give up gardening – the prognosis for headaches was optimistic.

1.3.1.2.1.C17 Case No. 11145

Name of case: Mabbett v Mead

Brief description of injuries: NECK – WHIPLASH – SHOULDER – POST-TRAUMATIC STRESS DISORDER

Reported: Kemp & Kemp, E2-062; [1996] CLY 2236

JSB Category: 6(B)(b)(ii)

Sex: Female

Age at injury: 17

Age at award: 19

Date of award: 25 July 1996

Tribunal: Watford County Court

Amount of award then: £6,500

Award at February 2001: £7,336

Description of injuries: Whiplash injuries to the neck – inter-scapular pain – mild recrudescence of post-traumatic stress disorder.

Prognosis: Condition likely to linger indefinitely – prognosis for recovery from the post-traumatic stress disorder was good.

Other points: Inter-scapular pain was a legacy from another road accident 28 months earlier.

1.3.1.2.1.C18 Case No. 11354

Name of case: Rees v Hooper

Brief description of injuries: NECK – WHIPLASH – KNEE

Reported: Kemp & Kemp, E2-064/1; [1997] CLY 1902

JSB Category: 6(A)(b)(i)

Sex: Male

Age at injury: 51

Age at award: 52

Date of award: 22 September 1997

Tribunal: Oxford County Court

Amount of award then: £6,500

Award at February 2001: £7,018

Description of injuries: Whiplash injury to the neck – bruising to the knee.

Prognosis: Symptoms could be expected to improve over the following ten months.

Other points: Impossible to tell if he would be one of the people who would continue to suffer symptoms beyond two years.

1.3.1.2.1.C19 Case No. 11610

Name of case: Winn and Kwiatowski v Townend

Brief description of injuries: NECK – WHIPLASH – ELBOW – 2 YEARS

Reported: 98 (6) QR 6; Kemp & Kemp, E2-105/2; [1998] CLY 1612

JSB Category: 6(A)(c), 6(G)

Sex: Female

Age at injury: W:47;K:48

Age at award: W:49;K:50

Date of award: 01 July 1998

Tribunal: York County Court

Amount of award then: £6,500

Award at February 2001: £6,859

Description of injuries: Whiplash injuries – W: soft-tissue injury to the neck and back and bruising – K: soft-tissue injuries to the neck – bruised elbow.

Prognosis: W: Recovery expected within 12 to 18 months of the date of the accident – K: a good recovery was expected within 18 months to 2 years of the date of the accident.

Other points: Award split between applicants – W: £3,000; K: £3,500.

1.3.1.2.1.C20 Case No. 11696

Name of case: Winstanley v Laithwaite

Brief description of injuries: NECK – WHIPLASH – POST-TRAUMATIC STRESS DISORDER

Reported: Kemp & Kemp, E2-108/2; [1998] CLY 1699

JSB Category: 6(A)(c), 3(B)(d); 5(A)

Sex: Female

Age at injury: 60

Age at award: -

Date of award: 02 February 1998

Tribunal: Altrincham County Court

Amount of award then: £5,750

Award at February 2001: £6,170

Description of injuries: Classic whiplash injury to the neck – soft-tissue injury to the back – shoulders – chest and abdominal wall musculature – post-traumatic stress disorder – complete recovery within 18 to 19 months of the date of the accident.

Other points: Award comprised £3,250 physical symptoms: £2,500 post-traumatic stress disorder.

1.3.1.2.1.C21 Case No. 10258

Name of case: Bunzl Transpotation v Bosdet

Brief description of injuries: WHIPLASH INJURY – AGGRAVATED PSORIASIS FOR 12 MONTHS

Reported: Kemp & Kemp, J6-072; [1991] CLY 1455

JSB Category: 6(A)(b)(ii)

Sex: Male

Age at injury: 28

Age at award: 32

Date of award: 21 June 1991

Tribunal: Romford County Court

Amount of award then: £4,500

Award at February 2001: £5,772

Description of injuries: Suffered a whiplash injury – pain in the neck and back when looking over his shoulder – headaches – shock of the accident aggravated psoriasis – PUVA treatment was unsuccessful – an unpleasant and embarrassing condition – affected his life considerably.

Prognosis: Pain and headaches were not permanent – taking "rather longer to settle down" – psoriasis cleared within twelve months of the date of the accident.

1.3.1.2.1.C22 Case No. 11829

Name of case: Cheston v Letkey

Brief description of injuries: NECK – WHIPLASH – SHOULDER

Reported: Kemp & Kemp, H2-027/3; [1999] CLY 1493

JSB Category: 6(A)(c), 6(D), 6(C)(d), 5(A)

Sex: Female

Age at injury: 27

Age at award: 32

Date of award: 19 April 1999

Tribunal: Kingston-upon-Thames County Court

Amount of award then: £5,000

Award at February 2001: £5,206

Description of injuries: Whiplash injury to neck, bruising to chest and pelvis – collar worn continuously for 4 weeks, 17-20 months physiotherapy over period of approximately 5 months – bruising to pelvis resolved after 2 weeks; bruising to chest resolved after 6 weeks – neck pain intermittent after 6 months – claimant left with injury affecting right shoulder in trapezius region – limitation of movement to the extent of 20 degrees in that area – claimant unable to work for 2 weeks or drive for 3 months, and did not pursue hobby of squash for 6 months – medical evidence deemed symptoms to have persisted for 3 years and 9 months from date of accident, but claimant still complained of pain in right shoulder at date of trial (claimant confined at trial to addressing her symptoms over the shorter period).

1.3.1.2.1.C23 Case No. 11315

Name of case: Lymer v Henson

Brief description of injuries: NECK – WHIPLASH – POST-TRAUMATIC STRESS DISORDER

Reported: Kemp & Kemp, C4-107; [1997] CLY 1863

JSB Category: 3(B)(c)

Sex: Female

Age at injury: 47

Age at award: 50

Date of award: 16 December 1996

Tribunal: Stoke on Trent County Court

Amount of award then: £4,500

Award at February 2001: £5,013

Description of injuries: Minor whiplash injury – exacerbation of her pre-existing phobic anxiety state – panic attacks.

Prognosis: It was expected that panic attacks would be under control within three years of the date of the accident.

1.3.1.2.1.C24 Case No. 11913

Name of case: Milne v Mateus

Brief description of injuries: NECK – WHIPLASH – BACK – 3 YEARS' DEPRESSION

Reported: Kemp & Kemp, K2-008; [1999] CLY 1577

JSB Category: 6(A)(c), 6(B)(c); 3(A)(d)

Sex: Female

Age at injury: 27

Age at award: 30

Date of award: 10 May 1999

Tribunal: Barnet County Court

Amount of award then: £4,750

Award at February 2001: £4,934

Description of injuries: Road accident – soft-tissue injuries to neck and lower back – initial treatment with cervical collar and physiotherapy – 1 year after accident, claimant still suffering continuous pain at back of neck and lumbar spine, together with monthly headaches – 3 years after accident, episodes of neck pain only occurring once every 3 or 4 months, and back pain only experienced occasionally, when ironing for more than 2 hours – claimant was vulnerable to depression and accident triggered an episode, but claimant no longer depressed at time of trial – claimant remained nervous when driving and had not driven on a motorway since the accident.

Prognosis: Full recovery expected within a further few months after trial.

1.3.1.2.1.C25 Case No. 10608

Name of case: Deeley v Western National

Brief description of injuries: NECK – WHIPLASH – SHOULDERS

Reported: Kemp & Kemp, E2-094, E3-109; [1993] CLY 1501

JSB Category: 6(A)

Sex: Male

Age at injury: 25

Age at award: 29

Date of award: 04 June 1993

Tribunal: Aldershot and Farnham County Court

Amount of award then: £4,000

Award at February 2001: £4,879

Description of injuries: Car accident – whiplash injury to cervical spine – off work for 1 week, collar for 2 weeks – constant pain between shoulders for 4 weeks – prolonged headaches for 2 months – thereafter, intermittent burning sensation and aching between shoulder blades for an hour in the morning and again in evening, aggravated by driving, using VDU and strenuous physical activity – hobbies affected, but not seriously so – symptoms lingering, though minor, at date of trial.

Prognosis: Cervical spine remained vulnerable – injury might contribute to very late development of degenerative changes in cervical spine.

1.3.1.2.1.C26 Case No. 11914

Award at February 2001: £4,708

See: 1.3.1.2.C98 for details

1.3.1.2.1.C27 Case No. 11713

Name of case: Richards v Jones

Brief description of injuries: NECK – WHIPLASH – KNEE – 2 YEARS

Reported: Kemp & Kemp, E2-097/1; [1998] CLY 1716

JSB Category: 6(A)(b)(ii); 6(L)(b)(ii)

Sex: Female

Age at injury: 20

Age at award: 22

Date of award: 03 August 1998

Tribunal: Cardiff County Court

Amount of award then: £4,250

Award at February 2001: £4,465

Description of injuries: Neck and knee injuries – pain and stiffness aggravated by activity.

Prognosis: Full recovery from whiplash expected within 2 years.

1.3.1.2.1.C28 Case No. 11915

Name of case: Bettridge v Hoque

Brief description of injuries: NECK – WHIPLASH – KNEE – 2-3 YEARS

Reported: Kemp & Kemp, E2-102/1/1; [1999] CLY 1579

JSB Category: 6(A)(c), 6(L)(b)(ii)

Sex: Male

Age at injury: 41

Age at award: 43

Date of award: 30 October 1998

Tribunal: Southampton County Court

Amount of award then: £4,000

Award at February 2001: £4,182

Description of injuries: Road accident – whiplash injury to neck – considerable bruising to knee – significant pain in early stages – painkillers, physiotherapy, ultrasound and acupuncture prescribed – off work 4 weeks; unable to undertake heavy lifting on his return – pain in knee gradually resolved over 6-week period – 8 months after accident, claimant found to have muscle spasm and pain on lateral rotation to left side – claimant still suffering from intermittent stiffness in neck approximately 2-3 times per month at trial, 2 years after accident.

Prognosis: Complete recovery expected within 2 years and 8 months of accident.

1.3.1.2.1.C29 Case No. 10609

Name of case: Bentley v Pushman

Brief description of injuries: NECK-WHIPLASH-2 YEARS-LOW BACK PAIN

Reported: Kemp & Kemp, E3-115; [1993] CLY 1502

JSB Category: 6(A)(c), 6(B), 6(H)

Sex: Female

Age at injury: 22

Age at award: 24

Date of award: 16 December 1992

Tribunal: Reading County Court

Amount of award then: £3,000

Award at February 2001: £3,707

Description of injuries: Whiplash injury to neck, causing pain for 3 weeks, necessitating collar, subsiding to occasional twinges and symptom free at time of trial – sprain to right wrist, causing pain for 5 weeks, necessitating elastic bandage support, also symptom free at time of trial – headaches for 3 weeks after accident – ligamentous sprain to lumbar region – ligamentous sprain to sacro-iliac joint – initial slight back pain exacerbated when claimant returned to aerobic classes – physiotherapy and lumbar support required – disturbed sleep – hobbies affected – low-back pain still evident at time of trial, particularly after strenuous activity and necessitating occasional massage/exercises.

Prognosis: Symptoms improving, expected to resolve within 2 to 3 years.

1.3.1.2.1.C30 Case No. 11901

Name of case: Musmar v Kalala

Brief description of injuries: WHIPLASH (1 YEAR) – SEATBELT BRUISING – PSYCHOLOGICAL REACTION (3 YEARS)

Reported: Kemp & Kemp, K2-030; [1999] CLY 1565

JSB Category: 6(A)(c); 5(A); 3(A), 3(B)

Sex: Male

Age at injury: 18

Age at award: 21

Date of award: 01 March 1999

Tribunal: Croydon County Court

Amount of award then: £3,350

Award at February 2001: £3,511

Description of injuries: Claimant involved in road accident – whiplash injury and seatbelt bruising, resolving within 1 week – Post-traumatic stress disorder for 1 month – phobic reaction to driving, continuing 3 years after the accident – claimant had tried once, unsuccessfully, to resume driving after the accident, but had not sought treatment, despite being advised to do so 11 months prior to trial.

1.3.1.2.1.C31 Case No. 11918

Name of case: Whiddett v Phillips

Brief description of injuries: NECK – WHIPLASH – BRUISING TO CHEST – 9 MONTHS

Reported: Kemp & Kemp, K2-031; [1999] CLY 1582

JSB Category: 6(A)(c); 5(A)

Sex: Male

Age at injury: 29

Age at award: 31

Date of award: 15 April 1999

Tribunal: Hertford County Court

Amount of award then: £3,250

Award at February 2001: £3,384

Description of injuries: Whiplash injury to neck – bruising to chest – painkillers prescribed – off work 1 week; thereafter, worked 1 day per week at home for the following 4 weeks, because of symptoms – chest bruising largely resolved after 4 weeks; neck injury on way to recovery – however, recurrence of pain in both areas following a particular period of activity 6 months after accident – hobbies affected for 6 months after accident – complete recovery within 9 months of accident.

1.3.1.2.1.C32 Case No. 11362

Name of case: Miskell (a minor) v Bennett (deceased)

Brief description of injuries: NECK – WHIPLASH – POST-TRAUMATIC STRESS DISORDER

Reported: Kemp & Kemp, E2-113, K2-038; [1997] CLY 1910

JSB Category: 6(A)(c)

Sex: Female

Age at injury: 14

Age at award: 16

Date of award: 25 March 1997

Tribunal: Manchester County Court

Amount of award then: £3,000

Award at February 2001: £3,320

Description of injuries: Wrenching injury to the shoulder joint – minor wrenching injury to the spine – bruises and abrasions.

Prognosis: She had recovered from the physical injuries within about six months – full recovery from the psychological effects were expected within two years of the date of the hearing.

1.3.1.2.1.C33 Case No. 12001

Name of case: Appleton v JB Taxis

Brief description of injuries: NECK – WHIPLASH – SHOULDER – 1 YEAR

Reported: Kemp & Kemp, K2-038/1; [2000] 3 CL 185

JSB Category: 6(A)(c)

Sex: Male

Age at injury: 19

Age at award: 21

Date of award: 22 September 1999

Tribunal: Bolton County Court

Amount of award then: £3,200

Award at February 2001: £3,312

Description of injuries: A whiplash injury to the neck and strain to the left shoulder – no treatment other than simple analgesics – off work for one week by which time the shoulder symptoms had resolved – recurrent discomfort and "locking" occasionally to the neck. Entirely symptom free within twelve months of the date of the accident.

1.3.1.2.1.C34 Case No. 10261

Name of case: Waygood v Kane

Brief description of injuries: WHIPLASH INJURY – RESIDUAL SYMPTOMS

Reported: Kemp & Kemp, E2-115; [1991] CLY 1458

JSB Category: 6(A)(c)

Sex: Female

Age at injury: 47

Age at award: 48

Date of award: 24 April 1991

Tribunal: QBD

Amount of award then: £2,500

Award at February 2001: £3,231

Description of injuries: A whiplash injury to the neck – localised pain in the right shoulder and neck – slightly diminished range of movement – analgesics.

Prognosis: W would probably not regain the full movement of her neck – driving, teaching and sports were affected.

1.3.1.2.1.C35 Case No. 11697

Name of case: Vaughan v BT Whelan

Brief description of injuries: NECK – WHIPLASH – THUMB

Reported: Kemp & Kemp, E2-033; [1998] CLY 1700

JSB Category: 6(A)(c), 6(I)(w)

Sex: Male

Age at injury: 24

Age at award: 27

Date of award: 15 September 1998

Tribunal: Southampton County Court

Amount of award then: £3,000

Award at February 2001: £3,139

Description of injuries: Whiplash injury to the neck – wrench to the right thumb.

Prognosis: 2 years after the date of the accident, full recovery was expected within a short time.

1.3.1.2.1.C36 Case No. 10663

Name of case: Littlewort v Adams

Brief description of injuries: NECK – WHIPLASH – KNEE CONDITION EXACERBATED

Reported: Kemp & Kemp, K2-049; [1993] CLY 1559

JSB Category: 6(A)(c); 6(L)(b)

Sex: Female

Age at injury: 43

Age at award: 45

Date of award: 12 October 1992

Tribunal: Rugby County Court

Amount of award then: £2,500

Award at February 2001: £3,074

Description of injuries: Road accident – whiplash injury to neck – collar and physiotherapy prescribed – off work 6 weeks – development of acute pain over sides of chest 5 months after accident – 2 sessions of painful thoracic spine manipulation required to relieve symptoms – movement of cervical spine restricted to two-thirds of normal in all directions 1 year after date of accident – sex life substantially restricted for 6 months – 15 months' exacerbation of pre-existing minor knee injury (clicking and mild swelling) – restriction of movement, stiffness and discomfort had subsided within 18 months – occasional aching persisting in left side of neck.

Prognosis: Prognosis of complete cessation of neck pain within 2 years from date of accident.

1.3.1.2.1.C37 Case No. 10771

Name of case: Shaw v Frost

Brief description of injuries: NECK – WHIPLASH TO PREVIOUSLY – INJURED NECK – POST-TRAUMATIC STRESS DISORDER

Reported: Kemp & Kemp, E2-129; [1994] CLY 1619

JSB Category: 6(A)(c); 3(B)(d)

Sex: Male

Age at injury: 33

Age at award: 35

Date of award: 07 February 1994

Tribunal: Burnley County Court

Amount of award then: £2,500

Award at February 2001: £3,026

Description of injuries: Claimant involved in minor road traffic accident – claimant had previously experienced 2 road accidents in past 4 years; on one occasion struck from the side and on the other by an articulated HGV – claimant still suffering from neck discomfort and anxiety at time of third collision – suffered whiplash injury in third collision, described as being at "bottom end" of scale of severity – pain on lateral flexion – stiffness on most days – neck particularly uncomfortable when driving – pain on any sharp movement to left – psychological injuries, having some of the elements of post-traumatic stress syndrome – nightmares – anxiety when driving – lack of concentration – fatigue – neck symptoms resulting from third collision would normally be expected to resolve within 6 months, but medical expectation was that pre-existing degenerative change would cause them to last 18 months from date of accident.

Other points: Psychological difficulties suggested to have lasted 12 months from date of accident – court found that first two accidents more likely cause of claimant's psychological difficulties and third accident not responsible for claimant's psychological symptoms at date of trial, it being more in the nature of an exacerbating factor. Award split: whiplash: £2,000; psychological injuries: £500.

1.3.1.2.1.C38 Case No. 11925

Award at February 2001: £3,012

See: 1.2.3.2.C56 for details

1.3.1.2.1.C39 Case No. 10674

Award at February 2001: £2,490

See: 1.2.3.2.C61 for details

1.3.1.2.1.C40 Case No. 10864

Name of case: Huber v Szender

Brief description of injuries: NECK – WHIPLASH – BACK – FINGER

Reported: Kemp & Kemp, E2-130; [1994] CLY 1716

JSB Category: 6(A)(c), 6(B)(c), 6(I)(q)

Sex: Male

Age at injury: 20

Age at award: 24

Date of award: 29 March 1994

Tribunal: Chorley County Court

Amount of award then: £1,950

Award at February 2001: £2,354

Description of injuries: Road accident – whiplash injury to neck – injury to lower back – fracture of terminal phalanx of ring finger – initial severe pain in neck and shoulders and restriction of movement in shoulders, persisting several weeks – shooting pain in back brought on by exertion – off work 5 weeks, only light duties possible on return – substantial recovery after 4 months, with only occasional twinge in back and ache in finger.

1.3.1.2.1.C41 Case No. 10265

Name of case: Hart v Cauldwell

Brief description of injuries: WHIPLASH – 15 MONTHS

Reported: Kemp & Kemp, K2-081; [1991] CLY 1462

JSB Category: 6(A)(c)

Sex: Female

Age at injury: 20

Age at award: -

Date of award: 03 May 1991

Tribunal: Ilkeston County Court

Amount of award then: £1,800

Award at February 2001: £2,319

Description of injuries: A whiplash type injury to the neck – wore a cervical collar for one week – headaches, uncomfortable pain and stiffness for one week – slow improvement.

Prognosis: All symptoms were resolved within fifteen months.

1.3.1.2.1.C42 Case No. 12073

Name of case: Hughes v Bloor
Brief description of injuries: NECK – WHIPLASH – CHEST
Reported: [2000] 6 CL 203
JSB Category: 6(A)(c)
Sex: Female
Age at injury: 25
Age at award: 27
Date of award: 14 December 1999
Tribunal: Birmingham County Court
Amount of award then: £2,200
Award at February 2001: £2,262

Description of injuries: S suffered a whiplash type injury and seatbelt injuries to the chest – given a soft collar to wear – constant pain and stiffness to the right side of the neck for three weeks – off work for five weeks – underwent ten sessions of physiotherapy – assistance with household chores required for three months – symptoms entirely resolved within eight months of the date of the accident – continued to suffer nervousness as a driver and a passenger for sixteen months.

Other points: 1301 of 13021301 of 130

1.3.1.2.1.C43 Case No. 10271

Name of case: Simmonds v Smith
Brief description of injuries: WHIPLASH INJURY TO THE NECK
Reported: Kemp & Kemp, K2-085; [1991] CLY 1468
JSB Category: 6(A)(c)
Sex: Male
Age at injury: -
Age at award: 54
Date of award: 09 April 1991
Tribunal: Trowbridge County Court
Amount of award then: £1,750
Award at February 2001: £2,261

Description of injuries: A whiplash injury to the neck – pain and stiffness lasted about six months – difficulty in rotating and elevating the head to the right.

Prognosis: At the time of the hearing present symptoms should resolve themselves in the near future.

1.3.1.2.1.C44 Case No. 10274

Name of case: Short v Mathewman
Brief description of injuries: WHIPLASH – 12 MONTHS
Reported: [1991] CLY 1471
JSB Category: 6(A)(c)
Sex: Male
Age at injury: 23
Age at award: 25
Date of award: 24 May 1991
Tribunal: Doncaster County Court
Amount of award then: £1,500
Award at February 2001: £1,933

Description of injuries: A whiplash injury to the neck – pain to the head and right shoulder – collar not worn – no time off work – some minor discomfort.

Prognosis: A full recovery within twelve months.

1.3.1.2.1.C45 Case No. 11719

Award at February 2001: £1,895

See: 1.2.2.1.C34 for details

1.3.1.2.1.C46 Case No. 10498

Name of case: Sandifer v Spanton
Brief description of injuries: WHIPLASH – 5 MONTHS
Reported: Kemp & Kemp, K2-120; [1992] CLY 1754
JSB Category: 6(A)(c)
Sex: Female
Age at injury: 31
Age at award: 32
Date of award: 29 July 1992
Tribunal: Reading County Court
Amount of award then: £1,500
Award at February 2001: £1,859

Description of injuries: Whiplash injury to the neck.

Prognosis: Full recovery five months after the accident.

1.3.1.2.1.C47 Case No. 10279

Name of case: Price v B H Components (Clwyd)
Brief description of injuries: WHIPLASH – 5 WEEKS
Reported: Kemp & Kemp, K2-132 [1991] CLY 1476
JSB Category: 6(A)(c)
Sex: Male
Age at injury: 15
Age at award: 15
Date of award: 08 June 1990
Tribunal: Shrewsbury District Registry
Amount of award then: £1,235
Award at February 2001: £1,677

Description of injuries: A whiplash injury to the neck – localised to the left – soft-tissue bruises to the left side of the chest – eight days lost from school during "mock" GCSE examinations – no evidence of impaired performance.

Prognosis: A full recovery made within five weeks of the date of the accident.

1.3.1.2.1.C48 Case No. 10277

Name of case: Mowbray v Federal Express (UK)
Brief description of injuries: WHIPLASH – 5 MONTHS
Reported: Kemp & Kemp, K2-140; [1991] CLY 1474
JSB Category: 6(A)(c)
Sex: Female
Age at injury: 28
Age at award: 29
Date of award: 28 January 1991
Tribunal: Slough County Court
Amount of award then: £1,250
Award at February 2001: £1,651

Description of injuries: A whiplash injury to the neck – pain and stiffness to the neck and shoulder – off work for two weeks – difficulty sleeping – wore a collar for two months – unable to drive for two to three months due to pain and psychological reaction.

Prognosis: Full recovery after five months.

1.3.1.2.1.C49 Case No. 10875

Name of case: Kingsley v Moate
Brief description of injuries: NECK – WHIPLASH – KNEE
Reported: Kemp & Kemp, E2-135; [1994] CLY 1727
JSB Category: 6(A)(c); 6(L)(b)
Sex: Male
Age at injury: 29
Age at award: 30
Date of award: 15 November 1994
Tribunal: Uxbridge County Court
Amount of award then: £1,350
Award at February 2001: £1,598

Description of injuries: Road accident – whiplash injury to neck – pain in back – pain and tenderness in right knee, with a patella tap – painkillers and soft collar prescribed – collar worn on daily basis for nearly 2 months – majority of symptoms resolved within 2 months – knee injury rather more permanent, with pain, especially after long walks, still evident at time of hearing – likelihood, however, that knee injury was exacerbated by a separate accident 2.5 months after the one in question.

1.3.1.2.1.C50 Case No. 10678

Name of case: Fowler v San
Brief description of injuries: NECK – WHIPLASH – LUMBAR SPINE – 3 MONTHS
Reported: Kemp & Kemp, E2-136; [1993] CLY 1574
JSB Category: 6(A)(c), 6(B)(c)
Sex: Male
Age at injury: 31
Age at award: 32
Date of award: 27 January 1993
Tribunal: Edmonton County Court
Amount of award then: £1,250
Award at February 2001: £1,559

Description of injuries: Side – on road traffic collision – graze to right temple – whiplash injury to neck – pain in and around neck and right shoulder – painkillers prescribed – 2 weeks later, subsequent complaint of continuing pain in right shoulder, pain in right lumbar region and occasional numbness and tingling in both legs – reduced mobility of lumbar spine and tenderness in right paravertebral muscle diagnosed – physiotherapy prescribed – unable to work (as chauffeur) for 8 weeks – virtually full recovery after 8 weeks – full recovery 3 weeks thereafter.

1.3.1.2.1.C51 Case No. 12002

Name of case: Simms v Walls

Brief description of injuries: NECK – WHIPLASH – SHOULDER – 12 WEEKS

Reported: Kemp & Kemp, K2-160/1; [2000] 3 CL 186

JSB Category: 6(A)(c)

Sex: Male

Age at injury: 27

Age at award: 29

Date of award: 12 October 1999

Tribunal: Southampton County Court

Amount of award then: £1,400

Award at February 2001: £1,446

Description of injuries: A whiplash type injury to the neck in a traffic accident – wore a collar for two days – two weeks off work – consistent pain for eight to nine weeks – loss of sleep for eight weeks. Full recovery within twelve weeks of the date of the accident.

Other points: Hobbies affected for about four weeks.

1.3.1.2.1.C52 Case No. 10284

Name of case: Martin v Crane

Brief description of injuries: WHIPLASH INJURY – 1 YEAR

Reported: Kemp & Kemp, I3-022, K2-168; [1991] CLY 1481

JSB Category: 6(A)(c)

Sex: Male

Age at injury: 56

Age at award: 60

Date of award: 15 April 1990

Tribunal: Brighton County Court

Amount of award then: £1,000

Award at February 2001: £1,375

Description of injuries: A whiplash injury – wore a collar for three months – prickly pain to the neck and back of the head.

Prognosis: The symptoms had completely cleared by the end of the year.

1.3.1.2.1.C53 Case No. 11730

Award at February 2001: £1,347

See: 1.2.2.1.C41 for details

1.3.1.2.1.C54 Case No. 11732

Award at February 2001: £1,242

See: 1.3.1.1.C60 for details

1.3.1.2.1.C55 Case No. 10120

Award at February 2001: £1,098

See: 1.3.1.2.C200 for details

1.3.1.2.1.C56 Case No. 11930

Name of case: Grant v Gregory

Brief description of injuries: NECK – WHIPLASH – BACK – PSYCHOLOGICAL

Reported: Kemp & Kemp, K2-209/3; [1999] CLY 1594

JSB Category: 6(A)(c), 6(B)(c); 3(A)(d)

Sex: Female

Age at injury: 21

Age at award: 22

Date of award: 15 April 1999

Tribunal: Birmingham County Court

Amount of award then: £1,000

Award at February 2001: £1,041

Description of injuries: Road accident – whiplash injuries to neck and lower back – shocked and shaken – stiffness in neck worsened overnight and remained severe for about a week – pain in lower back persisted for 2 weeks – headaches for 2 days after accident – situation specific anxiety diagnosed – physical symptoms resolved after 2 months, psychological problems continuing 16 months after accident – 1 week of study at university lost as a result of accident, but part-time employment not affected – anxiety about driving, but continued to drive regularly after the accident out of necessity, even though suffering from flashbacks.

Prognosis: Full recovery expected.

Other points: Award comprised physical injuries: £750; psychological injuries: £250.

1.3.1.2.1.C57 Case No. 11929

Award at February 2001: £1,039

See: 1.3.1.1.C64 for details

1.3.1.3 BACK INJURY

1.3.1.3.C1 Case No. 11564

Name of case: Masterson v Chemical Services, Fabrications & Erection Ltd

Brief description of injuries: SPINE – SPASTICITY

Reported: Kemp & Kemp, E3-003/1; [1998] CLY 1566

JSB Category: 6(B)(a)

Sex: Male

Age at injury: 44

Age at award: 51

Date of award: 20 March 1998

Tribunal: Bury County Court

Amount of award then: £40,000

Award at February 2001: £46,036

Description of injuries: Two separate disc lesions at C5/6 and L3/4 – pain in the lower back – notable spasticity in the legs – claimant required a wheelchair for all but the shortest walks – occasionally fell – unable to return to any form of work.

1.3.1.3.C2 Case No. 11989

Name of case: Re Goodall (CICB Quantum: 1999)

Brief description of injuries: BACK – SEVERE INJURY

Reported: [2000] 3 CL 173

JSB Category: 6(B)(a)

Sex: Male

Age at injury: 33

Age at award: 54

Date of award: 13 May 1999

Tribunal: CICB, London

Amount of award then: £40,000

Award at February 2001: £44,580

Description of injuries: A police dog-handler G had a lower back injury – major disc protrusion at L5/S1 – in-patient for five weeks – off work for seven months – acute pain in the lower back in 1985 forced him to transfer to the CID – numerous facet joint blocks gave temporary relief – underwent denervation – further operations left G with foot-drop, significant back pain, sciatica and sensory disturbance – he retired in 1987 – he continued to suffer continuous and acute pain – he would spend most of his time in bed and used a wheelchair – unable to transfer from his bed or his wheelchair without assistance – high dosages of morphine and other strong analgesics were prescribed – an epidural gave relief for one month but repeated epidurals were unsuccessful – G suffered a cardiac infarction – insertion of a spinal cord stimulator in April 1995 allowed him to be pain free – it did not alter the permanence of his condition. At the time of the assessment G was able to drive an adapted car and walk a maximum of fifteen yards if necessary.

Other points: The Board considered G had been through a traumatic and painful existence until the spinal cordstimulator was implanted.

1.3.1.3.C3 Case No. 10392

Name of case: Durrant v Macdonald

Brief description of injuries: SEVERE BACK INJURY – CONSTANT PAIN

Reported: [1992] PIQR Q76 Kemp & Kemp, E3-004, E3-200; [1992] CLY 1648

JSB Category: 6(B)(a)(ii)

Sex: Female

Age at injury: 29

Age at award: 34

Date of award: 28 January 1992

Tribunal: Birmingham District Registry

Amount of award then: £32,500

Award at February 2001: £44,204

Description of injuries: Knocked off her horse – landed on her head – forces were transmitted through the facet joints of the lumbar spine with damage to the joints and associated tissues – accident led directly to the breakdown of her marriage – tried every form of treatment to try to improve her condition (physiotherapy, traction, hydrotherapy and treatments by chiropractor and osteopath).

Prognosis: Seriously disabled and in constant pain – severe deconditioning syndrome – in need of constant treatment and attention.

1.3.1.3.C4 Case No. 12010

Name of case: Re Bhavsar (CICB Quantum: 2000)

Brief description of injuries: SPINE – SPINAL CORD INJURY – IMPOTENCE

Reported: Kemp & Kemp, E3-004/2/1; [2000] 4 CL 153

JSB Category: 6(B)(a)(ii)

Sex: Male

Age at injury: 40

Age at award: 46

Date of award: 25 November 1999

Tribunal: CICB, Manchester

Amount of award then: £37,500

Award at February 2001: £41,261

Description of injuries: B was stabbed in the back in the course of a robbery – very severe spinal cord injury caused nerve damage and loss of sensation to the right side from leg to nipple level – total loss of sexual function – Viagra was ineffective and had side effects – mobility was impaired and required crutches for walking – subject to sudden leg spasm with risk of falling – not incontinent, suffered urgency and frequency of micturition and constipation – wheelchair required for trips out – adaptations were required on his two-level home (stairs and upstairs bathroom).

Prognosis: No reduction in life expectancy – no prospect of improvement to his symptoms.

1.3.1.3.C5 Case No. 11339

Name of case: Re J

Brief description of injuries: SPINE – WRIST – "EXTREME DISCOMFORT" – DEPRESSION

Reported: Kemp & Kemp, E2-004/1; [1997] CLY 1887

JSB Category: 6(A)(a)(ii)

Sex: Female

Age at injury: 36

Age at award: 42

Date of award: 31 July 1997

Tribunal: CICB

Amount of award then: £30,000

Award at February 2001: £34,484

Description of injuries: Considerable physical injury – stab wounds – injured wrist – very significant soft-tissue injury to the spinal region – extensive resulting symptoms – at time of hearing she was in constant extreme discomfort – reactive depression – her earning capacity was very limited.

Other points: Depressed by her loss of career where she had been expected to progress at least to Chief Inspector by retirement age – limitations caused to her social and private life.

1.3.1.3.C6 Case No. 11817

Name of case: Cooper v P & O Stena Line Ltd

Brief description of injuries: BACK – SEVERE LOW BACK INJURY

Reported: [1999] 1 Lloyd's Rep 734; (1999) The Times, February 8; Kemp & Kemp, E3-004/3; BPILS, VIII 76; [1999] CLY 1480

JSB Category: 6(B)(a)(iii)

Sex: Male

Age at injury: 32

Age at award: 36

Date of award: 30 October 1998

Tribunal: QBD (Adm Ct)

Amount of award then: £30,000

Award at February 2001: £32,914

Description of injuries: Slip and fall, striking lower left back – severe pain in back and down left leg – initial investigations revealed no bony injury or spinal damage – subsequent diagnosis, 1 year later, of secondary fibromyalgia, a form of rheumatism – all attempts at pain relief unsuccessful after 4 years – severe pain in lower back extending down left leg to heel, exacerbated by walking – driving, sitting, standing and lying for long periods no longer possible; constant changing of position necessary – disturbed sleep, leading to moodiness and irritability – claimant unable to undertake any form of work – sex life adversely affected, just at the time at which claimant's wife had undergone major surgery to overcome a fertility problem as the couple sought to have a second child – claimant also forced to abandon home martial arts training and walking and swimming with daughter – stick required for walking – wife's assistance required for getting in and out of bed and washing lower body, and reliant on wife and friends to carry out home maintenance tasks – depression necessitating counselling by clinical psychologist.

Prognosis: Claimant would experience pain and disability for the foreseeable future, and remain unemployable.

1.3.1.3.C7 Case No. 10593

Name of case: Re Bird v Husain

Brief description of injuries: BACK – SOFT-TISSUE INJURY – CHRONIC PAIN

Reported: Kemp & Kemp, E3-007; [1993] CLY 1486

JSB Category: 6(B)

Sex: Female

Age at injury: 46

Age at award: -

Date of award: 06 July 1993

Tribunal: Leeds High Court

Amount of award then: £23,500

Award at February 2001: £29,968

Description of injuries: Claimant struck from behind by car – soft-tissue injuries to back and right foot – no fractures or bony injuries – development of chronic pain syndrome without recognised organic basis – claimant contended that back injury caused formation of, or hyper-irritation to pre-existing, trigger points, giving rise to local tenderness, chronic pain in back and predictable pattern of referred pain in legs – unable to return to employment, housework, leisure activities, sit for long periods or walk more than 200 yards – recommended to attend in-patient pain behaviour programme in hospital, but waiting list delayed admission for over 2 years – eventual attendance at programme improved condition – 6 months later, deterioration and re-activation of trigger points, possibly due to unconnected emotional problems – subsequent stabilisation, but with symptoms similar to those experienced prior to attending programme.

1.3.1.3.C8 Case No. 11136

Name of case: Re Dobson

Brief description of injuries: BACK

Reported: Kemp & Kemp, E3-010; [1996] CLY 2227

JSB Category: 6(B)(a)(iii)

Sex: Female

Age at injury: 21

Age at award: 28

Date of award: 04 July 1995

Tribunal: CICB, Manchester

Amount of award then: £22,500

Award at February 2001: £26,907

Description of injuries: Back injury in a fall – neck punched – leg kicked – unable to do housework – had to change occupation.

Prognosis: Disability in the back expected to continue.

1.3.1.3.C9 Case No. 10945

Name of case: Wilson v Clarke

Brief description of injuries: FRACTURES OF CERVICAL VERTEBRAE AND CLAVICLE – MODERATELY SEVERE ANXIETY

Reported: Kemp & Kemp, E2-006; [1995] CLY 1696

JSB Category: 6(A)(d)

Sex: Female

Age at injury: 39

Age at award: 44

Date of award: 15 December 1994

Tribunal: Colchester County Court

Amount of award then: £22,000

Award at February 2001: £26,866

Description of injuries: Plaintiff suffered fracture of right clavicle, severe lacerations at top of right ear and an unstable fracture of second cervical vertebra – traction for six weeks – given pain killers and some help in sleeping (throughout this period was subjected to "justifiable terror" that any movement of neck could lead to death) – cervical collar for one week – after further five weeks collar was replaced with soft collar, which was kept for four months until return to work – fracture of right clavicle was treated conservatively in sling and sutures for lacerations to her right ear – experienced some pain for a time with clavicle and was left with obvious bump – some minimal scarring to right ear – symptom-free within few months of accident – physical deformities caused some minor embarrassment – 14 weeks after accident, was still wearing soft collar – some limited restriction of movement of neck – plaintiff complained of tingling in fingers of both hands and aching sensation over brachium between shoulder and elbow of left arm – generally stiff both in back and hips – experiencing sore sensation at back of head over scalp where her head had rested on bed during traction – neurological examination of upper and lower limbs normal – no evidence of nerve compression as result of cervical spine injury – almost four years after accident, was still complaining of slight restriction of all movements in neck, with an aching pain in neck which increased as day wore on and radiated to both shoulders, particularly on left side – still suffering from irritation at the back of head – no abnormal neurological signs in upper limbs – medical evidence was that plaintiff was fortunate to be alive following life-threatening injuries with excellent recovery – some persisting discomfort in neck and restriction of movement, and symptoms were likely to become permanent – also suffered psychologically with fear that any movement would do permanent damage or kill her or leave her paralysed – fear continued during whole period she was in traction and later whilst in the stiff and soft collars – since accident, had continued to feel vulnerable to further accidents which (despite reassurance of doctors) she felt would inevitably be fatal – largely affected her either when driving or when passenger in car – when driving herself, took pains to avoid times when roads would be busy and would drive as carefully as she could – was even worse when a passenger, because she did not feel in control – was only prepared to travel with limited number of people in whom she had some confidence – she demonstrated "psychological manifestations of anxiety, manifested by extremely unpleasant feelings of fearfulness" but that she was expected to recover gradually from emotional distress over a period of years, although with possibility of some residual disability, particularly with regard to distress whilst being driven.

Prognosis: Medical evidence indicated plaintiff had now reached a plateau – there was no chance of any improvement but rather the possibility of some deterioration – plaintiff was likely to live a further 30 years or so with current pain, without any prospects of relief, and with possibility of position worsening – stiffness would increase over 15 to 20 years – no recovery from physical deformities of clavicle and ear but no additional symptoms were likely to develop.

1.3.1.3.C10 Case No. 11974

Name of case: Stone v Commissioner of Police of the Metropolis

Brief description of injuries: BACK – SEVERE SOFT-TISSUE INJURY

Reported: Kemp & Kemp, PRE-001; [2000] 2 CL 145

JSB Category: 6(B)(a)(iii)

Sex: Female

Age at injury: 23

Age at award: 28

Date of award: 15 September 1999

Tribunal: Milton Keynes County Court

Amount of award then: £25,000

Award at February 2001: £26,817

Description of injuries: Soft-tissue injury to the lower back – persistent and severe backache – no significant abnormalities revealed by X-rays, CT scans or MRI scans – unusual but not unknown for disabilities not to be revealed by presently available diagnostic tools – S's level of disability was assessed relying on her own account – unable to lift heavy weights or travel any distance without discomfort – walking limited to half a mile – unable to resume sporting activities – facet joint injections, physiotherapy, hydrotherapy, acupuncture, epidural and steroid injections failed to make any significant improvement. S had "substantial residual disability" – unable to return to work – no residual earning capacity – ability to enjoy motherhood and family life had been severely restricted.

1.3.1.3.C11 Case No. 10380

Name of case: Blackaller v Young

Brief description of injuries: SEVERE SPINAL INJURY

Reported: [1992] CLY 1636

JSB Category: 6(B)(a)(iii)

Sex: Male

Age at injury: 31

Age at award: 36

Date of award: 17 February 1992

Tribunal: Plymouth County Court

Amount of award then: £20,000

Award at February 2001: £26,122

Description of injuries: Whiplash soft-tissue injury to the cervical spine and lumbar spine – affected the lumbo-sacraldisc and left lower sacral nerve root – neck collar worn for two weeks – pain radiated to the knee – operation for removal of prolapsed intervertabral disc (July 1988) – disc surgery for lumbo-sacral disc prolapse (September 1990).

Prognosis: Continued pain after surgery – unable to continue with heavy work – unable to indulge in gardening, running and rugby.

1.3.1.3.C12 Case No. 10772

Name of case: Bispham v Central Nottinghamshire Health Authority

Brief description of injuries: BACK – INJURY TO ALREADY – VULNERABLE AREA OF SPINE – RETURN TO WORK UNLIKELY

Reported: Kemp & Kemp, E3-014; [1994] CLY 1620

JSB Category: 6(B)(b)

Sex: Female

Age at injury: 49

Age at award: 56

Date of award: 02 February 1994

Tribunal: QBD

Amount of award then: £20,000

Award at February 2001: £24,998

Description of injuries: Fall from stool – prolapsed intervertebral disc at L5/S1, leading to nerve root irritation – previous tear of disc annulus at same level 4 years earlier, causing slight narrowing of disc space and osteophytic lipping – some sciatica in following year – almost complete recovery made from earlier injuries – returned to work after most recent injury, but restricted movement and continued pain forced claimant to give up work; even light duties impossible – stick required to aid walking – pain in left leg necessitating painkillers – no longer able to go dancing – sex life affected – no longer able to do heavy housework, gardening and DIY.

Prognosis: Claimant unlikely ever to return to work.

1.3.1.3.C13 Case No. 10206

Name of case: McGowan v Harrow HA

Brief description of injuries: INJURY TO THE LOWER BACK – 40% DISABLED – CAREER WRECKED

Reported: Kemp & Kemp, E3-016; [1991] CLY 1403

JSB Category: 6(B)(a)(iii)

Sex: Female

Age at injury: 24

Age at award: 31

Date of award: 01 February 1991

Tribunal: QBD

Amount of award then: £17,500

Award at February 2001: £23,680

Description of injuries: Injury to the lower back – in traction for two weeks – in plaster for five-and-a-half weeks – physiotherapy treatments – no benefit gained from any treatment – two pregnancies had been difficult.

Prognosis: There was little prospect of recovery – her career had been wrecked – M was 40 per cent disabled.

1.3.1.3.C14 Case No. 11373

Name of case: Re Watson (Linda)

Brief description of injuries: BACK – CHRONIC COCCYDYNIA

Reported: [1997] CLY 1921

JSB Category: 6(B)(b)(iii)

Sex: Female

Age at injury: 27

Age at award: 38

Date of award: 29 January 1997

Tribunal: CICB, Durham

Amount of award then: £20,000

Award at February 2001: £22,906

Description of injuries: Injuries to the coccyx and lower back – chronic coccydynia.

Prognosis: At the time of the hearing she was limited in her ability to carry out domestic tasks – gardening – driving – sitting for any length of time.

1.3.1.3.C15 Case No. 10595

Name of case: Re Stonier

Brief description of injuries: BACK – LIGAMENT DAMAGE

Reported: Kemp & Kemp, E3-022; [1993] CLY 1488

JSB Category: 6(B)(b)

Sex: Male

Age at injury: 29

Age at award: 34

Date of award: 26 March 1993

Tribunal: CICB

Amount of award then: £17,500

Award at February 2001: £22,182

Description of injuries: Assault sustained in course of duties as police officer – lower back contusion with permanent damage to ligaments at bottom of spine – employment terminated – retired on medical pension, not working – unable to sit, walk or stand for long periods – unable to carry out heavy lifting or carrying.

1.3.1.3.C16 Case No. 10596

Name of case: Laurie v Makepeace Universal (Killingworth)

Brief description of injuries: BACK-FACET JOINT INJURY

Reported: Kemp & Kemp, E3-033; [1993] CLY 1489

JSB Category: 6(B)(b)

Sex: Female

Age at injury: 25

Age at award: 28

Date of award: 05 March 1993

Tribunal: Newcastle-upon-Tyne County Court

Amount of award then: £17,500

Award at February 2001: £22,182

Description of injuries: Trip and fall over open manhole while walking baby in pram – injury to lumbar region sustained in preventing baby falling from pram – immediate intense pain – diagnosis of facet joint injury resulting in permanently painful lower back movements – sleep disturbance – particularly painful second pregnancy – interference with ability to care for small children

Prognosis: Prognosis of persistent discomfort and pain – permanently unfit for pre-accident work as care assistant, unqualified for any other work – still fit for light work, retraining available after 6 months of registered unemployment

1.3.1.3.C17 Case No. 10773

Name of case: Loft v Nottingham County Council

Brief description of injuries: SPINE – 2 ACCIDENTS – CONTINUING PAIN AND STIFFNESS

Reported: Kemp & Kemp, E3-023; [1994] CLY 1621

JSB Category: 6(B)(b)

Sex: Male

Age at injury: 56 (first accident), 57 (second accident)

Age at award: 63

Date of award: 28 March 1994

Tribunal: Nottingham County Court

Amount of award then: £17,500

Award at February 2001: £21,660

Description of injuries: Claimant, school caretaker, involved in 2 accidents in course of employment – fall from ladder, sustaining back injuries – off work over 2 months – second, more serious accident 3 months after first; thrown across room by electric shock – muscular spasm and significant trauma to L4 and L5 discs, with rupture of annulus and classical disc prolapse – back painful and stiff – difficulty moving about, necessitating stick – discomfort and stiffness if in one position for any appreciable length of time – claimant had not worked since briefly returning to work after time of second accident – evidence of some psychological overlay, but not significant, and court concluded that claimant not malingering.

Other points: Evidence of spondylitic changes in spine pre-dating accident, but court found that claimant would have worked until age of 65 had accident not intervened.

1.3.1.3.C18 Case No. 10067

Name of case: Re Vincent

Brief description of injuries: INJURIES TO BACK – CONSTANT PAIN

Reported: Kemp & Kemp, E3-015; [1990] CLY 1627

JSB Category: 6(B)

Sex: Male

Age at injury: 45

Age at award: 50

Date of award: 26 June 1990

Tribunal: CICB

Amount of award then: £15,218

Award at February 2001: £21,163

Description of injuries: Police officer assaulted April 1985 – back injuries – history of lower back trouble requiring occasional physiotherapy and some short absence from work each year or so – in constant pain – takes pain killers every 3-4 months.

Prognosis: Suffered pain after lengthy sitting or driving – constantly guarding his back – unable to realise ambition of horticulture/land conservation.

1.3.1.3.C19 Case No. 10605

Name of case: Mochan and Mochan v Paterson Candy Holst

Brief description of injuries: BACK – CRUSH FRACTURE OF VERTEBRA

Reported: Kemp & Kemp, E3-038; [1993] CLY 1498

JSB Category: 6(B)(b)

Sex: One male, one female (husband and wife)

Age at injury: husband:48;wife:45

Age at award: husband:52;wife:49

Date of award: 29 October 1993

Tribunal: Lincoln County Court

Amount of award then: £17,000

Award at February 2001: £21,121

Description of injuries: Vehicle driven over open manhole cover at 60 mph.(Husband): soft-tissue injuries with damage to ligaments in lower back – pre-existing asymptomatic degenerative changes in lumbar region – off work 5 weeks – pain and discomfort in back exacerbated by activity – unable to sit for long periods of time – adapted to stiffness and limitations in sitting or activity, returned to work.(Wife): probable crush fracture at T12 – extreme pain for 1 year – continuing pain in lumbar region, more or less constant – aggravated by standing more than 20 to 30 minutes – unable to continue employment as hairdresser – light employment avoiding repetitive lifting, bending or prolonged standing possible.

Prognosis: (wife): symptoms unlikely to improve and might deteriorate.

Other points: Award split – husband: £5,000; wife: £12,000.

1.3.1.3.C20 Case No. 10956

Name of case: Marsh v Kirwen

Brief description of injuries: ACUTE LUMBAR STRAIN – CHRONIC PAIN

Reported: Kemp & Kemp, E3-025; [1995] CLY 1707

JSB Category: 6(B)(b)(i)

Sex: Male

Age at injury: 39

Age at award: 43

Date of award: 20 February 1995

Tribunal: Winchester District Registry

Amount of award then: £17,500

Award at February 2001: £20,981

Description of injuries: Service engineer fell on icy step when visiting defendant's home – lower back struck edge of step – sustained soft-tissue injury which was generally agreed to have been an acute lumbar ligament strain – left with chronic and permanent residual disability which would prevent him from carrying out any heavy lifting in future – back would remain "at risk" – had some depressive symptoms for about three years following accident – medical treatment included pain-killers, traction, two courses of physiotherapy, acupuncture, massage and visits to chiropractor – medically retired from previous employment, disadvantaged in labour market and any future employment was likely to be less remunerative than pre-accident occupation – plaintiff could not stand, sit or drive for periods of more than approximately one hour – sex life was affected and no longer able to do gardening.

1.3.1.3.C21 Case No. 10961

Name of case: Kirk v Laine Theatre Arts

Brief description of injuries: LOWER BACK AND GROIN – LOSS OF CAREER AS DANCER

Reported: [1995] CLY 1712

JSB Category: 6(B)(c)

Sex: Female

Age at injury: 17

Age at award: 23

Date of award: 10 March 1995

Tribunal: Nottingham County Court

Amount of award then: £16,000

Award at February 2001: £19,025

Description of injuries: Student at theatre arts college with ambition of becoming professional dancer – suffered from severe ligamentous and capsular strain in lower back and around the right thigh whilst performing a boxsplits exercise in jazz dancing class – felt immediate pain in groin and was unable to continue class – tried to carry on dancing for two weeks after accident but had to stop – one month after accident pain in lower back supervened that in groin – received treatment from physiotherapist and osteopath and took substantial rest during summer vacation – advised to walk with stick – tried returning to college after summer vacation but back and groin pain were too severe to allow her to dance and she had to leave – continued to experience significant symptoms as a result of injuries from which she would never fully recover – would never be able to dance professionally – would never be able to take part in sporting activities to any great extent without aggravating symptoms – no significant increase in disability was expected – had found employment as airline hostess. General Damages: £6,000. Loss of ability to follow chosen career as a dancer: £10,000. Total damages: £16,000.NB: Trial judge held that loss of ability to follow chosen career as professional dancer was very different from cases where damages had been awarded for inability to follow a congenial employment as a fireman or policeman – this was a case where a young girl from the age of eight had set her heart on becoming a professional dancer – she had spent her last years at school giving up her free time to pursue this aim – judge was satisfied that there was distinct possibility of her being a top dancer, bearing in mind evidence that only a minute number of girls reach such a level.

1.3.1.3.C22 Case No. 10395

Name of case: Essex v Coventry Health Authority

Brief description of injuries: MODERATELY SEVERE BACK INJURY – "EXCRUCIATING PAIN"

Reported: Kemp & Kemp, E3-032; [1992] CLY 1651

JSB Category: 6(B)(b)(ii)

Sex: Female

Age at injury: 39

Age at award: 47

Date of award: 31 July 1992

Tribunal: Coventry County Court

Amount of award then: £13,000

Award at February 2001: £16,331

Description of injuries: Moderately severe back injury caused by lifting. Injury happened in 1984 – caused excruciating pain in lower lumbar region – felt able to work where lifting, carrying, stooping or bending were not required.

Prognosis: Diagnosed in January 1988 as suffering from damaged lumbar nerve roots – in May 1991 she was able to walk for about a mile and a half – had retired on medical grounds in 1986.

1.3.1.3.C23 Case No. 11570

Name of case: Turner v Owens Corning Fibreglass UK Ltd

Brief description of injuries: BACK – ACUTE STRAIN

Reported: Kemp & Kemp, E3-032/1; [1998] CLY 1572

JSB Category: 6(B)(b)(i)

Sex: Male

Age at injury: 51

Age at award: 53

Date of award: 28 November 1997

Tribunal: County Court

Amount of award then: £14,500

Award at February 2001: £15,823

Description of injuries: Acute strain injury to the lumbar spine – minor injury to a lumbar disc – mobility in the lower back reduced to 50-70 per cent.

Prognosis: Constant nagging pain was permanent – no risk of further deterioration – claimant would be at a permanent disadvantage in the labour market.

1.3.1.3.C24 Case No. 10396

Name of case: Dunn v Durham County Council

Brief description of injuries: MODERATELY SEVERE BACK INJURY – SOME OVERLAY

Reported: [1992] CLY 1652

JSB Category: 6(B)(b)(ii)

Sex: Female

Age at injury: 30

Age at award: 35

Date of award: 12 June 1992

Tribunal: QBD

Amount of award then: £12,500

Award at February 2001: £15,622

Description of injuries: Injured back in fall from a bench.

Prognosis: Constant dull back pain aggravated by extended sitting and walking – orthopaedic opinion was divided on the possibility of facet joint injury, disc lesions or disc prolapse – agreed that there were signs of functional overlay – unfit for heavy work – able to pursue pre-accident hobbies of riding, badminton and dancing.

1.3.1.3.C25 Case No. 11280

Name of case: Ward v Lenscrafters EC Corp.

Brief description of injuries: BACK – SHOULDER

Reported: Kemp & Kemp, B2-036; [1997] CLY 1827

JSB Category: 6(B)(b)(ii) 6(D)(d)

Sex: Female

Age at injury: 55

Age at award: 59

Date of award: 08 May 1997

Tribunal: Brighton County Court

Amount of award then: £13,500

Award at February 2001: £14,957

Description of injuries: Strain to the lower back – rotor cuff injury to the left shoulder – left shin injury became ulcerated and required a skin graft – healing occurred more than three years after the date of the accident

Prognosis: Back and shoulder symptoms were likely to be permanent – shin was permanently vulnerable.

Other points: Her pre-existing condition made the injuries more significant – attracting a higher award.

1.3.1.3.C26 Case No. 11139

Name of case: Cole v Birmingham City Council
Brief description of injuries: LUMBAR SPINE – STRAIN
Reported: Kemp & Kemp, E3-039; [1996] CLY 2230
JSB Category: 6(B)(b)(ii)
Sex: Female
Age at injury: 48
Age at award: 53
Date of award: 09 September 1996
Tribunal: Birmingham County Court
Amount of award then: £13,000
Award at February 2001: £14,684
Description of injuries: Strain of the lumbar spine – permanently unfit for work as a care assistant.
Prognosis: Low back pain would continue indefinitely – requiring the use of pain killers.

1.3.1.3.C27 Case No. 10957

Name of case: Leech v Ward, Waring and Leadbetter
Brief description of injuries: BACK – FRACTURE OF 3 THORACIC VERTEBRAE – CHRONIC RESIDUAL SYMPTOMS
Reported: [1995] CLY 1708
JSB Category: 6(B)(b)(ii)
Sex: Male
Age at injury: 24
Age at award: 29
Date of award: 09 January 1995
Tribunal: Burton-upon-Trent County Court
Amount of award then: £12,000
Award at February 2001: £14,267
Description of injuries: Plaintiff injured in course of his work as steel erector – fell 30ft from partially constructed roof – sustained significant crush fractures of fifth, eighth and ninth thoracic vertebrae, as well as injury to right knee joint – in hospital for three weeks – made full recovery from knee injury, but back was tender over dorsal spine and suffered prolonged backache – also suffered from onset of psoriasis which was not present before accident – injury affected pre-accident sporting activities of football, cricket, squash and tennis – suffered occasional discomfort in night and whilst driving and bending – felt unable to walk more than half a mile and could not cope with difficult terrain – also distressed at significant weight gain – at time of trial, continued to experience chronic residual low back symptoms.

1.3.1.3.C28 Case No. 11571

Name of case: Wilkie v Radcliffe Hospital NHS Trust
Brief description of injuries: BACK – STRAIN
Reported: Kemp & Kemp, E3-043/2; [1998] CLY 1573
JSB Category: 6(B)(b)(ii)
Sex: Female
Age at injury: 33
Age at award: 36
Date of award: 09 January 1997
Tribunal: Central London County Court
Amount of award then: £12,500
Award at February 2001: £14,045
Description of injuries: Strain injury to the lumbar spine.
Prognosis: Permanent persisting mild pain to the lower back – claimant unable to return to clinical nursing.

1.3.1.3.C29 Case No. 10958

Name of case: Wilson v Anstey
Brief description of injuries: BACK – MODERATE – SIGNIFICANT RESIDUAL SYMPTOMS
Reported: [1995] CLY 1709
JSB Category: 6(B)(b)(ii)
Sex: Male
Age at injury: 21
Age at award: 23
Date of award: 15 August 1995
Tribunal: Tunbridge Wells County Court
Amount of award then: £11,500
Award at February 2001: £13,287
Description of injuries: Plaintiff involved in road traffic accident – suffered moderate soft-tissue injury to lumbar spine – was employed as bank sales analyst and job required sitting for long periods – suffered "background pain" almost constantly, and was rarely pain-free for any period – suffered periods of acute pain between one and three times a week depending on activities, which he treated with anti-inflammatory drugs – back "tightened up" about once a month, requiring physiotherapy – was not classed as disabled but injuries had considerable effect on his life – unable to lift heavy items and suffered embarrassment at asking work colleagues to do so for him – walking long distances caused pain – unable to sit for long periods and found driving and rail travel trying – had given up weight training and cycling – employer allowed him to work from home if necessary.
Prognosis: Medical opinion was that he was unlikely to make any recovery, but that there was some possibility of improvement late in life, towards the age of 60 – judge considered that injury was more serious at his age because he had been deprived of at least 10 years of physical activities which he would otherwise have been able to undertake.

1.3.1.3.C30 Case No. 10959

Name of case: Brewster v Thamesway Bus Co.

Brief description of injuries: BACK INJURY – 5-9 YEAR ACCELERATION

Reported: Kemp & Kemp, E2-032; [1995] CLY 1710

JSB Category: 6(B)(b)(ii)

Sex: Female

Age at injury: 51

Age at award: 54

Date of award: 06 March 1995

Tribunal: Hastings County Court

Amount of award then: £10,000

Award at February 2001: £11,701

Description of injuries: Plaintiff involved in road traffic accident – described as a stoic and sensible woman with symptomless but substantial pre-accident degenerative changes in cervical and lumbar spine – office worker who, prior to the accident, enjoyed squash, swimming, cycling and aerobics – accident was violent traffic collision in which bus struck side of her car – suffered whiplash injury to neck and soft-tissue strain to lower spine – experienced intense pain and discomfort in neck and back for six weeks, but was not prescribed a collar – neck symptoms largely resolved after about two-and-a-half years but there were persistent minor twinges which were likely to be permanent – back symptoms did not resolve – plaintiff suffered stiff and painful back on waking on most mornings – pain eased after moving about but constant dull ache remained – unable to sit for prolonged periods or drive long distances – sleep was disturbed – off work for six weeks, returned part-time for eight months but resigned because of inability to sit for long periods – required home help six hours per week – symptoms were aggravated because she was not advised to mobilise spine in early stages of recovery.

Prognosis: Medical opinion was that back condition was permanent and that she would have remained symptom-free in her back for five to nine years from date of accident if accident had not occurred.

1.3.1.3.C31 Case No. 10071

Name of case: Butler v Guildford Borough Council

Brief description of injuries: BACK INJURY – 10-YEAR ACCELERATION

Reported: Kemp & Kemp, E3-050, [1990] CLY 1631

JSB Category: 6(B)

Sex: Male

Age at injury: 46

Age at award: 51

Date of award: 24 April 1990

Tribunal: QBD

Amount of award then: £8,500

Award at February 2001: £11,687

Description of injuries: Sustained strain to lower back – aggravated by pre-existing degenerative back condition – accelerated his inability to continue in a heavy job by some 10 years. Suffers dull ache in right side of back – other movements of back restricted to half normal – straight leg raising a little restricted – unfit for work involving lifting, bending or any strain on the back.

1.3.1.3.C32 Case No. 10776

Name of case: Howden v Suffolk County Council

Brief description of injuries: BACK STRAIN – MODERATE PERMANENT LIMITATIONS – SCALDED ARM

Reported: Kemp & Kemp, E3-059; [1994] CLY 1624

JSB Category: 6(B)(b), 6(F)

Sex: Female

Age at injury: 52

Age at award: 57

Date of award: 16 February 1994

Tribunal: Ipswich County Court

Amount of award then: £9,500

Award at February 2001: £11,499

Description of injuries: Claimant sat on vandalised chair and fell – injury to back – claimant's coffee spilt onto right forearm, causing scald – scald caused some pain for a few hours, healing over next 4 months without significant cosmetic deformity – development of pain in lower back, worsening progressively over course of following week – 5 weeks off work (as part-time supermarket shelf filler) – lumbo-sacral strain diagnosed, leading to chronic lower backache exacerbated by all activity – capacity for tasks at work, household chores and leisure activities restricted; claimant gave up gardening and swimming due to difficulties in bending and moving legs, and took up form of badminton – continued at work despite pain for 4 further years, albeit with regular week-long breaks due to bouts of difficulty with back – claimant ultimately resigned on health grounds.

Prognosis: Strain regarded as permanent – consequent limitations on work and leisure activities also permanent – due to injury, lack of skills and age, claimant regarded as unlikely ever to find future employment.

Other points: Judge considered injuries to be at top end of scale for "moderate back injuries", but slight discount made on account of claimant's age. Award split: back injury: £9,000 scald: £500.

1.3.1.3.C33 Case No. 11378

Name of case: Vickerage v Rotherham MBC
Brief description of injuries: BACK – SOFT-TISSUE INJURIES – CONVERSION
Reported: Kemp & Kemp, E3-054; [1997] CLY 1926
JSB Category: 6(B)(c) 3(A)(b)
Sex: Female
Age at injury: 38
Age at award: 43
Date of award: 27 February 1997
Tribunal: Sheffield County Court
Amount of award then: £10,000
Award at February 2001: £11,120
Description of injuries: Soft-tissue injuries to the back – conversion hysteria.
Prognosis: Attendance at a pain clinic caused rapidly improving symptoms – she should be fit for part-time employment within twelve months of the date of the trial.
Other points: The judge held that the accident was the precipitating cause of her on-going condition.

1.3.1.3.C34 Case No. 11379

Name of case: Garrett v British Airways
Brief description of injuries: BACK – STRAIN
Reported: Kemp & Kemp, E3-055; [1997] CLY 1927
JSB Category: 6(B)(b)(ii)
Sex: Male
Age at injury: 27
Age at award: 31
Date of award: 12 March 1997
Tribunal: Wandsworth County Court
Amount of award then: £10,000
Award at February 2001: £11,091
Description of injuries: Severe lower back strain.
Prognosis: Retired on ill-health grounds in 1997 as a result of the back injury – his back would remain vulnerable.
Other points: Pain block might disguise the true vulnerability of the back.

1.3.1.3.C35 Case No. 10207

Name of case: Pace v McLennan
Brief description of injuries: NECK AND LUMBAR SPINE – SOFT-TISSUE INJURIES – HEADACHES – PERMANENT DISCOMFORT
Reported: Kemp & Kemp, E3-074; [1991] CLY 1404
JSB Category: 6(B)(b)(ii)
Sex: Female
Age at injury: 21
Age at award: 23
Date of award: 04 April 1991
Tribunal: Plymouth County Court
Amount of award then: £8,500
Award at February 2001: £10,984
Description of injuries: Soft-tissue injuries to the neck and lumbar spine – pain and migrainous headaches – disabilities limited the kind of work she could do within her chosen career.
Prognosis: At the time of the hearing the lumbar injury was causing constant discomfort which would be permanent – neck showed gradual improvement – risk of degenerative changes in 20 to 25years.

1.3.1.3.C36 Case No. 10073

Name of case: Gee v Bayes
Brief description of injuries: BACK INJURY – PRE-EXISTING CONDITION? – 10-YEAR ACCELERATION
Reported: Kemp & Kemp, E3-056; BPILS, I 84.1, 99; [1990] CLY 1633
JSB Category: 6(B)
Sex: Female
Age at injury: 38
Age at award: 46
Date of award: 20 October 1989
Tribunal: QBD
Amount of award then: £7,500
Award at February 2001: £10,979
Description of injuries: Suffered whiplash trauma to C5/C6 – but pre-existing congenital abnormality of upper cervical region (osodontoideum, in which odontoid process of C2 separated so no skeletal continuity with C1) seriously exacerbated by accident – instability present, revealed by the accident – spondylosis at C5/C6 to minor degree prior to trauma – spinal fusion of C1/C2 carried out, C5/C6 problem alleviated by treatment incidental to operation – five years later root irritation at C5/C6 returned – unable to cope with job – only able to do light part-time work – has difficulty with household chores – medical opinion that plaintiff would have suffered symptoms in middle age.

1.3.1.3.C37 Case No. 11821

Name of case: Lord v Alco Waste Management

Brief description of injuries: BACK

Reported: Kemp & Kemp, E2-037/1; [1999] CLY 1485

JSB Category: 6(B)(b)(ii)

Sex: Male

Age at injury: 25

Age at award: 30

Date of award: 28 January 1998

Tribunal: Carlisle County Court

Amount of award then: £10,000

Award at February 2001: £10,798

Description of injuries: Slip and fall, injuring neck and back – neck collar required for 6 weeks – off work almost 2 months – continuing intermittent back pain, worsening in winter months – approximately 3.5 years later, back injury aggravated when claimant attempted to change wheel on car – further 5 weeks off work – intermittent discomfort and sleep disturbance ongoing at time of trial – anti-inflammatories required on daily basis – claimant able to continue with work, but avoided heavy lifting.

1.3.1.3.C38 Case No. 11822

Name of case: Metcalf-Wood v Bradford's Building Supplies Ltd

Brief description of injuries: BACK – 5 YEAR ACCELERATION – DEPRESSION

Reported: Kemp & Kemp, PRE-006; [1999] CLY 1485

JSB Category: 6(B)(b)(ii); 3(A)

Sex: Male

Age at injury: 26

Age at award: 32

Date of award: 20 May 1999

Tribunal: Exeter County Court

Amount of award then: £10,000

Award at February 2001: £10,390

Description of injuries: Injury to lower back while lifting heavy load – immediate stabbing pain in back; thereafter, back pain and sciatic pain radiating into both legs, but mainly left leg – 2 abortive attempts to return to work; employment then terminated due to ill health 6 months after accident – claimant's spine already vulnerable due to a similar injury, suffered 16 months previously, from which he had recovered promptly – spinal fusion operation carried out 3 years after second accident, with minimal success – development of depression, partially attributable to injury and partly to other causes – claimant physically fit for light work, but depression had prevented him from taking any employment up; judge found that, absent the accident, claimant would have overcome his depression relating to the other events.

Prognosis: Claimant's back symptoms permanent – judge found that accident had caused an acceleration of claimant's underlying spinal problems, which would have taken hold in any event after 5 years – claimant no longer depressed 6 years after accident; expected to return to light work within 1 year of trial.

1.3.1.3.C39 Case No. 11141

Name of case: Gomery v Archway Supplies

Brief description of injuries: BACK

Reported: Kemp & Kemp, E3-062; [1996] CLY 2232

JSB Category: 6(B)(b)(ii)

Sex: Male

Age at injury: 52

Age at award: 57

Date of award: 12 April 1995

Tribunal: Gloucester County Court

Amount of award then: £9,000

Award at February 2001: £10,389

Description of injuries: Back injury – pain radiating into the groin – left leg gave way sometimes – he had not responded to treatment – substantial alteration to his lifestyle.

Prognosis: Unlikely to work again.

Other points: Worked for two months from the time of the accident – then employment was terminated.

1.3.1.3.C40 Case No. 11380

Name of case: Rogers v Birmingham City Council

Brief description of injuries: BACK – 5-YEAR ACCELERATION

Reported: Kemp & Kemp, E3-063; [1997] CLY 1928

JSB Category: 6(B)(b)(ii)

Sex: Male

Age at injury: 42

Age at award: 45

Date of award: 14 January 1997

Tribunal: Birmingham County Court

Amount of award then: £9,250

Award at February 2001: £10,304

Description of injuries: Injury to the lumbar spine – prolapse of an already degenerate lumbar disc.

Prognosis: The accident accelerated the effects of the pre-existing degenerate condition by a factor of five years.

1.3.1.3.C41 Case No. 11142

Name of case: Scott v Kennedy Construction Group Ltd

Brief description of injuries: BACK – LIGAMENT STRAIN

Reported: [1996] CLY 2233

JSB Category: 6(B)(b)(ii)

Sex: Female

Age at injury: 21

Age at award: 25

Date of award: 13 March 1996

Tribunal: Barnsley County Court

Amount of award then: £9,000

Award at February 2001: £10,218

Description of injuries: Ligamentous back strain – neck pain.

Prognosis: Symptoms would probably never leave her completely – there was a small chance of resolution in time.

Other points: Three stone weight gain since the accident worsened her condition.

1.3.1.3.C42 Case No. 11381

Name of case: Re Hibberd (Lesley Ann)

Brief description of injuries: BACK – 2.5 YEARS

Reported: Kemp & Kemp, E3-065; [1997] CLY 1929

JSB Category: 6(B)(b)(ii)

Sex: Female

Age at injury: 29

Age at award: -

Date of award: 11 March 1997

Tribunal: CICB, London

Amount of award then: £9,000

Award at February 2001: £9,961

Description of injuries: Injury to the lower back – back pain – nerve root entrapment of the thigh.

Prognosis: Almost complete recovery from the lower back problems within two-and-a-half years of the date of the accident – surgery greatly improved the trapped nerve symptoms.

Other points: Pre-existing asymptomatic spondylolithesis was irrelevant to her symptoms.

1.3.1.3.C43 Case No. 11382

Name of case: O'Boyle v Laurence

Brief description of injuries: BACK – SHOULDER – GROIN

Reported: Kemp & Kemp, C5-038; [1997] CLY 1930

JSB Category: 6(B)(b)(ii)

Sex: Male

Age at injury: 28

Age at award: 31

Date of award: 12 May 1997

Tribunal: Ilford County Court

Amount of award then: £9,000

Award at February 2001: £9,866

Description of injuries: Back, shoulder and groin pain.

Prognosis: Continuing tenderness of the neck and upper back – condition was expected to be permanent – participation in rugby, golf, riding and hunting was impossible as a result of the accident.

1.3.1.3.C44 Case No. 10598

Name of case: Maslin v Sankey Jonchu

Brief description of injuries: BACK – EXACERBATION OF PRE-EXISTING CONDITION

Reported: Kemp & Kemp, E3-067; [1993] CLY 1491

JSB Category: (6)(B)(b)(ii)

Sex: Male

Age at injury: 41

Age at award: 48

Date of award: 21 October 1993

Tribunal: Blackpool County Court

Amount of award then: £8,000

Award at February 2001: £9,704

Description of injuries: Claimant attempted to catch heavy object falling from lorry – lower back injury – acute symptoms and severe pain for 4 weeks – conflict of medical evidence but injury found to be mild to moderate prolapsed inter-vertebral disk – aggravation of similar, pre-existing injury which had thus far not affected claimant's ability to work – severe spasmodic pain in back, left buttock and leg, worsening in damp or cold weather – unable to stand or lift heavy objects – marked restriction of movement in lumbar spine with virtually no forward flexion.

Damage to Spine

1.3.1.3.C45 Case No. 11143

Name of case: Canning v Roberts

Brief description of injuries: BACK – 10-YEAR ACCELERATION

Reported: Kemp & Kemp, E3-068; [1996] CLY 2234

JSB Category: 6(B)(b)(ii)

Sex: Male

Age at injury: 54

Age at award: 58

Date of award: 03 July 1996

Tribunal: Wolverhampton County Court

Amount of award then: £8,500

Award at February 2001: £9,593

Description of injuries: Lower back injury – accelerated pre-existing back problem by 10 years.

Prognosis: His condition was not likely to get any worse – or to improve.

1.3.1.3.C46 Case No. 11572

Name of case: Vango v Kettering General Hospital NHS Trust

Brief description of injuries: BACK – STRAIN

Reported: Kemp & Kemp, E3-069/1; [1998] CLY 1574

JSB Category: 6(B)(b)(ii)

Sex: Female

Age at injury: 27

Age at award: 31

Date of award: 26 August 1998

Tribunal: Central London County Court

Amount of award then: £9,000

Award at February 2001: £9,456

Description of injuries: Muscular or ligamentous strain injury to the lumbar spine.

Prognosis: Constant background back pain exacerbated by exertion would be permanent.

1.3.1.3.C47 Case No. 11827

Name of case: Taylor v IBC Vehicles Ltd

Brief description of injuries: BACK

Reported: [1999] CLY 1491

JSB Category: 6(B)(b)(ii)

Sex: Male

Age at injury: 40

Age at award: 45

Date of award: 19 March 1999

Tribunal: CA

Amount of award then: £9,000

Award at February 2001: £9,433

Description of injuries: Claimant, who had been suffering from backache for a week before the accident, injured when lifting an object at work – severe sharp pain in back, radiating through left hip, causing him to collapse and almost faint; claimant dropped object and clutched at conveyor belt to stop himself falling – shooting pains in lower back – numbness from waist down – 2 weeks off work; 3 sessions of physiotherapy – moved to lighter duties at work – claimant applied for benefits 1 year after accident; assessed at 15 per cent disabled by Benefits Agency doctors – ability to bend from waist limited – symptoms expected to ease 3 years after accident, but they did not – movements generally restricted – activities limited – sleep disturbed – forced to abandon weight training, jogging, and occasional sporting activities – gardening, driving, shopping considerably restricted – claimant only able to be active for an hour at a time before requiring rest.

Prognosis: Claimant unlikely to recover from injury, and further deterioration in back likely – deterioration in back would make claimant more likely to lose current job – inability to lift heavy objects would in turn make finding other employment more difficult.

1.3.1.3.C48 Case No. 10074

Name of case: Desborough v Carlisle City Council

Brief description of injuries: BACK INJURY

Reported: Kemp & Kemp, E3-070; [1990] CLY 1634

JSB Category: 6(B)

Sex: Male

Age at injury: 37

Age at award: 40

Date of award: 22 January 1990

Tribunal: QBD

Amount of award then: £6,500

Award at February 2001: £9,356

Description of injuries: Pavior – suffered low back strain when he fell, hitting his back on kerb – back pain became chronic, exacerbated by heavy lifting and cold weather – due to injury left previous employment to start his own paving business – occasional need to "help out" not always possible due to back injury.

Prognosis: Would eventually be unable to do any lifting and would have to remain in an administrative role – business may suffer in the future.

1.3.1.3.C49 Case No. 10208

Name of case: Sheil v Chamberlain

Brief description of injuries: LUMBAR SPINE – WRENCHING INJURY – 5 YEAR ACCELERATION OF SPONDYLOSIS

Reported: Kemp & Kemp, E3-073; [1991] CLY 1405

JSB Category: 6(B)(b)(ii)

Sex: Male

Age at injury: 41

Age at award: 43

Date of award: 03 April 1991

Tribunal: Tameside County Court

Amount of award then: £7,000

Award at February 2001: £9,046

Description of injuries: Traffic accident caused discomfort to the neck and severe headaches for six to seven weeks – reducing further over the next twelve months – blunt trauma to the right knee caused soreness and stiffness for a few weeks – wrenching injury to the lumbar spine accelerated pre-existing mild lumbar spondylosis by five years – six weeks off work.

Prognosis: A builder, S had to modify the type he undertook.

1.3.1.3.C50 Case No. 10399

Name of case: Hamer v North West Water Authority

Brief description of injuries: JARRING INJURY – SPINE – PRE-EXISTING CONDITION

Reported: Kemp & Kemp, E3-080; [1992] CLY 1655

JSB Category: 6(B)(b)(ii)

Sex: Male

Age at injury: 35

Age at award: 44

Date of award: 22 September 1992

Tribunal: Burnley County Court

Amount of award then: £7,000

Award at February 2001: £8,637

Description of injuries: Jarring injury to the spine – X-rays showed considerable narrowing of the lumbo-sacral disc space – following the accident he had severe low back pain with limitation of movement – discomfort radiating down both legs – unable to walk for more than ten minutes – ability to stand restricted – could not run – had to avoid bending, heavy lifting and carrying tasks – some pre-existing intermittent low-back trouble – at the time of the accident he had not been experiencing any problems unless he exerted himself.

Prognosis: No significant improvement expected.

1.3.1.3.C51 Case No. 10075

Name of case: Saggers v Lee Valley Regional Park Authority

Brief description of injuries: BACK INJURY – MUCH IMPROVED AFTER 3 YEARS

Reported: Kemp & Kemp, E3-082; [1990] CLY 1635

JSB Category: 6(B)

Sex: Male

Age at injury: 55

Age at award: 59

Date of award: 15 November 1990

Tribunal: Court of Appeal

Amount of award then: £6,500

Award at February 2001: £8,600

Description of injuries: Injury to lower back may have damaged a disc – pain in sacroiliac region with some radiation down the sides.

Prognosis: Symptoms improved somewhat by 1988 (3 years after injury) – much improved by time of trial but still some lower back pain – possible bouts of more serious back pain.

1.3.1.3.C52 Case No. 10601

Name of case: Tylman v British Coal Corp

Brief description of injuries: BACK – 4 YEAR ACCELERATION

Reported: Kemp & Kemp, E3-083; [1993] CLY 1494

JSB Category: 6(B)(b)(ii)

Sex: Male

Age at injury: 36

Age at award: 41

Date of award: 19 July 1993

Tribunal: Liverpool High Court

Amount of award then: £7,000

Award at February 2001: £8,557

Description of injuries: Lower back injury sustained in course of duties as miner – early degenerative changes to lumbar spine – continuing discomfort in lumbar spine, radiating into left hip on walking and sometimes into right hip, exacerbated by bending – limited lateral flexion – tenderness in lower three-quarters of spine – X-rays revealed degenerative changes to much of spine.

Prognosis: Rendered unfit for employment in mining industry; however, degenerative changes to spine would have made it unlikely that claimant could have continued in industry much after age of 40.

1.3.1.3.C53 Case No. 10600

Name of case: Gauden v Durham County Council

Brief description of injuries: BACK – 10 YEAR ACCELERATION OF PRE-EXISTING CONDITION

Reported: Kemp & Kemp, E3-084; [1993] CLY 1493

JSB Category: 6(B)(b)(ii)

Sex: Male

Age at injury: 44

Age at award: 48

Date of award: 27 September 1993

Tribunal: Newcastle-upon-Tyne High Court

Amount of award then: £7,000

Award at February 2001: £8,485

Description of injuries: Agreed diagnosis of either strain of left sacro-iliac joint or slight lateral disc prolapse of lumbar spine – recurring pain in small of back, also brought on by prolonged sitting or walking – loss of both jobs – previous back injury, some symptoms of which were accelerated by the accident by 10 to 12 years – unable to participate in football or gardening – loss of earnings award anticipated 2 years until re-availability for employment.

Prognosis: Permanently unfit for work involving repetitive bending and lifting.

1.3.1.3.C54 Case No. 11385

Name of case: Downing v A&P Appledore (Falmouth) Ltd

Brief description of injuries: BACK – 5-7 YEAR ACCELERATION

Reported: (1997) 97 (1) QR 5; Kemp & Kemp, E3-086; [1997] CLY 1933

JSB Category: 6(B)(b)(ii)

Sex: Male

Age at injury: 55

Age at award: 60

Date of award: 19 September 1996

Tribunal: Truro County Court

Amount of award then: £7,500

Award at February 2001: £8,388

Description of injuries: Soft-tissue injury to the lumbar spine.

Prognosis: After the date of the accident he had constant lumbar pain – pre-existing degenerative lumbar spondylosis was made symptomatic by the accident – accelerated by five to seven years.

1.3.1.3.C55 Case No. 11386

Name of case: Bonney v Radcliffe Infirmary NHS Trust

Brief description of injuries: BACK – MUSCULAR TEAR

Reported: Kemp & Kemp, E3-087; [1997] CLY 1934

JSB Category: 6(B)(b)(ii)

Sex: Female

Age at injury: 31

Age at award: 35

Date of award: 03 February 1997

Tribunal: Wandsworth County Court

Amount of award then: £7,500

Award at February 2001: £8,323

Description of injuries: Muscular tear to the lumbar sacral area.

Prognosis: She would continue to suffer from intermittent low back pain indefinitely – she had a vulnerable back – heavy lifting would lead to injury.

1.3.1.3.C56 Case No. 11387

Name of case: Ward v Batten & Stamford Asphalt Co Ltd

Brief description of injuries: BACK – 10-YEAR ACCELERATION

Reported: Kemp & Kemp, E3-087/1; [1997] CLY 1935

JSB Category: 6(B)(b)(ii Injury to the lower back)

Sex: Female

Age at injury: 25

Age at award: 30

Date of award: 13 June 1997

Tribunal: Basingstoke County Court

Amount of award then: £7,500

Award at February 2001: £8,190

Description of injuries: Injury to the lower back – exacerbated pre-existing asymptomatic degenerative changes by a factor of ten years.

Prognosis: She would be left with mild continual pain – exacerbated by certain activities – unable to guard against the aggravation – would require an average eight to ten treatments per year.

Other points: It was unlikely that the back pain was caused by her pregnancy – unable to return to her pre-accident work as a dental nurse – she had obtained other employment.

1.3.1.3.C57 Case No. 11573

Name of case: Gill v Hughes

Brief description of injuries: BACK – SOFT-TISSUE INJURIES

Reported: Kemp & Kemp, E3-088/1; [1998] CLY 1575

JSB Category: 6(B)(b)(ii)

Sex: Male

Age at injury: 29

Age at award: 31

Date of award: 13 March 1998

Tribunal: Chester County Court

Amount of award then: £7,500

Award at February 2001: £8,022

Description of injuries: Soft-tissue injuries to the dorsal spine.

Prognosis: Claimant would continue to have a permanent degree of chronic discomfort from his back.

Other points: Inability to take part in sports caused weight gain.

1.3.1.3.C58 Case No. 12012

Name of case: Coots v Stead McAlpine & Co Ltd

Brief description of injuries: BACK – ACCELERATION OF PRE-EXISTING CONDITION

Reported: Kemp & Kemp, E3-089/3; [2000] 4 CL 155

JSB Category: 6(B)(b)(ii)

Sex: Male

Age at injury: 40

Age at award: 44

Date of award: 20 May 1999

Tribunal: Carlisle County Court

Amount of award then: £7,500

Award at February 2001: £7,790

Description of injuries: Tripped and fell causing a strain to the lumbar spine – aggravated pre-existing asymptomatic degenerative changes in the back – prescribed painkillers and rest – undertook a private course of physiotherapy.

Prognosis: Symptoms would continue indefinitely – they would not prevent him from continuing in his occupation until retirement age.

Other points: The accident had brought forward the on set of the symptoms but not significantly worsened them.

1.3.1.3.C59 Case No. 11389

Name of case: Iqubal v Amuah

Brief description of injuries: BACK – 3.5 YEARS

Reported: [1997] CLY 1937

JSB Category: 6(B)(c)

Sex: Male

Age at injury: 47

Age at award: 50

Date of award: 16 October 1996

Tribunal: Croydon County Court

Amount of award then: £6,500

Award at February 2001: £7,269

Description of injuries: Injury to the lumbar spine – suffered acute exacerbation of pre-existing significant degenerative changes at L4/5.

Prognosis: After three-and-a-half years the effects of the accident had subsided – the back was at the level it would have deteriorated to even had there been no accident.

Other points: He had almost recovered from the depression and anxiety caused by the accident.

1.3.1.3.C60 Case No. 10778

Name of case: Cho v Fairlord (Wholesale Confectioners)

Brief description of injuries: BACK – INJURY – CONTINUING PAIN AND VULNERABILITY

Reported: Kemp & Kemp, E3-095; [1994] CLY 1627

JSB Category: 6(B)(b)

Sex: Male

Age at injury: 26

Age at award: 30

Date of award: 29 April 1994

Tribunal: Bow County Court

Amount of award then: £6,000

Award at February 2001: £7,157

Description of injuries: Low-speed road accident – pain in lumbar spine 2 days after collision – soft-tissue injury diagnosed and painkillers prescribed – pain for 1 year after accident – daily discomfort upon waking – claimant played badminton to county and national level – back injury caused discomfort after matches and prevented claimant from competing at that level – formerly trained 3 times per week for 2-3 hours and played matches at weekends – at time of trial, only playing once a week and experiencing pain when bending and playing difficult shots.

Prognosis: Claimant likely to be in continued pain and discomfort – spine would probably remain vulnerable.

1.3.1.3.C61 Case No. 11614

Name of case: Stevenson v Townsend
Brief description of injuries: BACK
Reported: Kemp & Kemp, E3-095/1; [1998] CLY 1616
JSB Category: 6(B)(b)(ii)
Sex: Male
Age at injury: 48
Age at award: 51
Date of award: 28 April 1998
Tribunal: Nottingham County Court
Amount of award then: £6,750
Award at February 2001: £7,140

Description of injuries: Injury to the spine below neck – constant ache in back radiated to the buttocks and thighs – sitting or standing for a period of time was uncomfortable – residual symptoms of a constant dull ache – unable to do heavy work.

Prognosis: Claimant unlikely to experience any spontaneous improvement.

1.3.1.3.C62 Case No. 10962

Name of case: Hayes v Rickwood
Brief description of injuries: WHIPLASH (3 YEARS) – LOW BACK PAIN (18 MONTHS)
Reported: Kemp & Kemp, E2-064; [1995] CLY 1713
JSB Category: 6(B)(b)
Sex: Female
Age at injury: 34
Age at award: 36
Date of award: 12 December 1994
Tribunal: Reading County Court
Amount of award then: £6,000
Award at February 2001: £7,068

Description of injuries: Plaintiff was involved in road traffic accident and sustained whiplash type injury to cervical spine – taken to hospital but not detained – 24 hours after accident began to suffer pain in lower spine – some 10 years previously she suffered a prolapsed disc which at time of accident was asymptomatic – suffered acute pain for three weeks but after about five or six weeks condition had stabilised and remained the same until the time of trial – experienced sleepless nights for two weeks and took analgesics for 10 weeks – absent from work for 13 weeks because she would have suffered pain when using a keyboard and screen for more than 30 minutes if she had returned earlier – social life was severely curtailed for four weeks during which period she was unable to shop – plaintiff had given up step aerobic classes and her sex life had also suffered – household chores were also difficult for her.

Prognosis: The prognosis was that cervical pain would continue to get better and resolve itself into no more than a niggle some two-and-a-half to three-and-a-half years after accident and that back pain was merely an 18-month exacerbation.

1.3.1.3.C63 Case No. 11146

Name of case: Worth v Worcester and District HA
Brief description of injuries: BACK – 5-YEAR ACCELERATION
Reported: Kemp & Kemp, E3-102; [1996] CLY 2237
JSB Category: 6(B)(b)(ii)
Sex: Male
Age at injury: 32
Age at award: 39
Date of award: 19 April 1996
Tribunal: Birmingham County Court
Amount of award then: £5,500
Award at February 2001: £6,199

Description of injuries: Injury to the lumbar spine.

Prognosis: The accident brought forward by five years symptoms he would have suffered.

Other points: Pre-existing vulnerable back.

1.3.1.3.C64 Case No. 11615

Name of case: Mawson v Harvey
Brief description of injuries: BACK – 5-YEAR ACCELERATION
Reported: (1999) 99 (1) QR 7; Kemp & Kemp, E3-105; [1998] CLY 1617
JSB Category: 6(B)(c)
Sex: Male
Age at injury: 50
Age at award: 54
Date of award: 08 October 1998
Tribunal: Leeds County Court
Amount of award then: £5,750
Award at February 2001: £6,012

Description of injuries: Soft-tissue injury to the lower back – constant aching – intermittent pain after heavy activity.

Prognosis: Injury had aggravated and accelerated pre-existing degenerative changes by 5 years.

1.3.1.3.C65 Case No. 10963

Name of case: Parkinson v Longfield Care Homes

Brief description of injuries: SACRUM – LOW BACK – 3 YEAR ACCELERATION

Reported: Kemp & Kemp, E3-106; [1995] CLY 1714

JSB Category: 6(B)(b)

Sex: Female

Age at injury: 49

Age at award: 55

Date of award: 30 March 1996

Tribunal: Preston County Court

Amount of award then: £5,000

Award at February 2001: £5,677

Description of injuries: Care assistant at nursing home fell down stairs whilst working on night shift – suffered probable fracture of sacrum and considerable on-going pain in lumbar spine and left shoulder – had previous history of back complaints and had visited GP on number of occasions prior to accident, including a visit with regard to her left shoulder, just two months before accident – X-rays revealed significant degenerative change in both her cervical and lumbar spine, although these had not caused any time off work prior to accident – following accident was unable to return to work – although plaintiff failed to establish liability the judge found that the accident was entirely responsible for her symptoms for a period of 12 months after accident. Thereafter accident had increased the level of discomfort and accelerated the onset of degenerative changes by further two years (three years in total post-accident). Despite evidence of the plaintiff being stoical, the judge found she would have been forced to retire three years post-accident in any event due to an increasing level of symptoms.

1.3.1.3.C66 Case No. 10469

Name of case: Re Thorogood

Brief description of injuries: KNIFE WOUND DOWN LENGTH OF BACK – WELL HEALED

Reported: [1992] CLY 1725

JSB Category: 8

Sex: Male

Age at injury: 23

Age at award: 26

Date of award: 19 May 1992

Tribunal: CICB, London

Amount of award then: £4,500

Award at February 2001: £5,556

Description of injuries: Slashed with a Stanley knife from the base of the neck to the top of the buttocks.

Prognosis: Cut had healed well and was not very noticeable – slight embarrassment when taking off his shirt in public.

1.3.1.3.C67 Case No. 10607

Name of case: Mattinson v Ullah

Brief description of injuries: BACK – 2 YEARS

Reported: Kemp & Kemp, E3-110; [1993] CLY 1500

JSB Category: 6(B)

Sex: Male

Age at injury: 25

Age at award: 27

Date of award: 18 August 1993

Tribunal: Bury County Court

Amount of award then: £4,000

Award at February 2001: £4,869

Description of injuries: Car accident – pain in lower back, ongoing at date of trial for 2 or 3 hours in the morning, recurring thereafter, and when lifting – stiff and painful neck for 2 weeks.

Prognosis: Full recovery expected within 2 years of date of accident.

1.3.1.3.C68 Case No. 11166

Name of case: Beecham v Wright

Brief description of injuries: FIBROSITIS

Reported: Kemp & Kemp, H2-028/1; [1996] CLY 2257

JSB Category: 6(D)(b)

Sex: Male

Age at injury: 25

Age at award: 30

Date of award: 22 May 1995

Tribunal: Doncaster County Court

Amount of award then: £4,000

Award at February 2001: £4,599

Description of injuries: Fibrositis and stiffness resulting from injury – pain and tenderness.

1.3.1.3.C69 Case No. 11994

Name of case: Hill v Holmes

Brief description of injuries: BACK – SHOULDER – 18-20 MONTHS

Reported: Kemp & Kemp, E3-110/1; [2000] 3 CL 178

JSB Category: 6(B)(c)

Sex: Female

Age at injury: 46

Age at award: 49

Date of award: 09 September 1999

Tribunal: Reading County Court

Amount of award then: £4,250

Award at February 2001: £4,398

Description of injuries: Soft-tissue injuries to the lower back and dominant shoulder – after three weeks she attended the hospital for the second time – severe pain to the lumbar area radiating into the right leg – limited movement with discomfort to the shoulder and arm – physiotherapy proved to be limited benefit – six months after the accident a lumbar support was prescribed – practical and recreational activities remained restricted – assistance with housework was required – gained four stones in weight due to inactivity. Medical experts concluded that the accident caused the pain experienced for eighteen to twenty months.

1.3.1.3.C70 Case No. 11025

Name of case: Johnson v Edwards

Brief description of injuries: LOWER BACK – SLOW RECOVERY – MINOR WHIPLASH

Reported: Kemp & Kemp, K2-014; [1995] CLY 1777

JSB Category: 6(A)(c)

Sex: Male

Age at injury: 23

Age at award: 25

Date of award: 16 November 1993

Tribunal: Slough County Court

Amount of award then: £3,500

Award at February 2001: £4,251

Description of injuries: Plaintiff sustained whiplash injury to neck and back – anti-inflammatory medication was required but cervical collar not prescribed – neck problems lasted for about one month but back problems persisted, with episodes of aggravated symptoms – recovery was slow because of plaintiff's working activities, which included bending and climbing ladders or climbing into confined spaces – award was slightly more than considered appropriate by reference to Judicial Studies Board Guidelines because of this – full recovery was expected, to be assisted by short course of physiotherapy.

1.3.1.3.C71 Case No. 10402

Name of case: Riches v A E Timmins and Son

Brief description of injuries: LUMBAR SPINE – CONTINUING MINOR SYMPTOMS

Reported: [1992] CLY 1658

JSB Category: 6(B)(c)

Sex: Female

Age at injury: 45

Age at award: 47

Date of award: 11 May 1992

Tribunal: Southampton County Court

Amount of award then: £3,250

Award at February 2001: £4,013

Description of injuries: Strains to the neck and lumbar spine – no specific treatment – occasional analgesics – off work four weeks – intermittent discomfort – tenderness and slight limitation of movement to the neck – possibly suffered minor damage to a lumbar intervertebral disc.

Prognosis: Symptoms would improve but there would be continuing minor symptoms to the neck and lower back.

1.3.1.3.C72 Case No. 10209

Name of case: Re Carstairs

Brief description of injuries: INJURY TO THE LUMBAR SPINE – OFF SPORTS FOR 2 YEARS

Reported: Kemp & Kemp, E3-112; [1991] CLY 1406

JSB Category: 6(B)(c)

Sex: Male

Age at injury: 29

Age at award: -

Date of award: 24 October 1990

Tribunal: CICB, London

Amount of award then: £3,000

Award at February 2001: £3,960

Description of injuries: Injury to the lower back during an assault – off work for several weeks.

Prognosis: C's back continued to be painful – he was unable to do weight lifting at all or to play golf and football for two years.

Other points: Award increased from £500 on appeal.

1.3.1.3.C73 Case No. 10780

Name of case: Norman v Taylor

Brief description of injuries: BACK – INJURY – SYMPTOMS WORSE DURING PREGNANCY

Reported: Kemp & Kemp, E3-114; [1994] CLY 1629

JSB Category: 6(B)(c)

Sex: Female

Age at injury: 34

Age at award: 35

Date of award: 02 November 1993

Tribunal: Bristol County Court

Amount of award then: £3,250

Award at February 2001: £3,948

Description of injuries: Road accident – back pain for 2 days, developing into low back pain and right groin pain – low back pain worsened when walking – 1 month after accident, episode of acute back pain, persisting in some degree for 5 months – 6 months after accident, acute left and right sacro-iliac pain with bilateral groin pain, exacerbated by weight-bearing, remaining in one position and when moving; claimant unable to lift her 18-month-old child – claimant suffered from pre-existing disability of right leg being three-quarters-of-an-inch shorter than left leg, but no previous history of back pain – claimant suffered low back pain throughout second pregnancy, in contrast to first pregnancy, when no back pain experienced; passage of time left no doubt that pregnancy was intensifying symptoms – pain exacerbated by domestic chores and by claimant having to walk 4 miles per day, her car having been written off in the accident – physiotherapy having no long – lasting effect – chiropractic treatment undertaken by date of trial, with course of treatment recommended to continue for 9 more sessions.

1.3.1.3.C74 Case No. 11617

Name of case: Surrey v Manchester Health Commission

Brief description of injuries: BACK – 12-MONTH ACCELERATION

Reported: Kemp & Kemp, E3-114/1; [1998] CLY 1619

JSB Category: 6(B)(c)

Sex: Female

Age at injury: 54

Age at award: 58

Date of award: 10 September 1997

Tribunal: Manchester County Court

Amount of award then: £3,500

Award at February 2001: £3,779

Description of injuries: Injury to the back at work – S had to take early retirement after the accident.

Prognosis: Pre-existing back problems were accelerated by about 12 months.

1.3.1.3.C75 Case No. 11823

Name of case: Thakerar v Pajman

Brief description of injuries: BACK – 2 YEARS

Reported: Kemp & Kemp, E3-115/1; [1999] CLY 1486

JSB Category: 6(B)(c)

Sex: Male

Age at injury: 42

Age at award: 44

Date of award: 05 February 1999

Tribunal: Central London County Court

Amount of award then: £3,500

Award at February 2001: £3,677

Description of injuries: Musculo – ligamentous spinal column injuries, affecting lumbar spine – intense symptoms of pain and stiffness spreading down entire length of back – pins and needles in right foot – off work for 1 week; daily activities a struggle thereafter – sleep pattern disrupted for 5 months – 10 months after accident, back pain ongoing, requiring daily painkillers and anti-inflammatories – symptoms particularly bad in mornings – unable to sit for long periods – efficiency at work affected – deterioration in family life; claimant unable to play with his young children – considerable tenderness between L3 and L4 with lumbar curvature impaired by 25 per cent – residual pain persisting 18 months after accident.

Prognosis: Full recovery expected within 2 years of accident, with no anticipated complications.

1.3.1.3.C76 Case No. 11911

Name of case: Bennet v Notley

Brief description of injuries: BACK – 10 MONTH AGGRAVATION OF PRE-EXISTING CONDITION

Reported: Kemp & Kemp, K2-022; [1999] CLY 1575

JSB Category: 6(B)(c)

Sex: Male

Age at injury: 63

Age at award: 68

Date of award: 04 March 1999

Tribunal: Doncaster County Court

Amount of award then: £3,500

Award at February 2001: £3,668

Description of injuries: Claimant, who had a long history of serious back problems and had been claiming Sickness Benefit and Invalidity Benefit for continuously for 3 years prior to the incident, tripped and fell – aggravation of pre-existing injury, lasting for approximately 10 months, described by judge as severe and painful recurrence – claimant went on pre-planned touring holiday to Spain shortly after accident, but was unable to drive and was forced to obtain physiotherapy while abroad – physiotherapy continued for 5 more sessions in England on his return.

1.3.1.3.C77 Case No. 11992

Name of case: Pearce v Humpit Removals Ltd
Brief description of injuries: BACK – 3 YEARS
Reported: Kemp & Kemp, EC-105/3; [2000] 3 CL 176
JSB Category: 6(B)(c)
Sex: Female
Age at injury: 20
Age at award: –
Date of award: 13 October 1999
Tribunal: Reading County Court
Amount of award then: £3,500
Award at February 2001: £3,616
Description of injuries: Pain to the right knee, ankle, neck and low back following a collision – wore a neck collar for one week – the neck resolved in a further week – back pain was constant for one month before it became intermittent – it ached every morning, after prolonged driving or sitting and upon lifting – six sessions of physiotherapy about one year after the accident – the ache continued but was less intense. It was a cause of some inconvenience to her at the time of the hearing.
Prognosis: Full recovery likely within three years of the date of the accident.

1.3.1.3.C78 Case No. 10964

Name of case: Ayling v Davenport-Strange
Brief description of injuries: BACK PAIN – 2.5 YEARS – CONTINUING VULNERABILITY
Reported: Kemp & Kemp, E2-110; [1995] CLY 1715
JSB Category: 6(B)(b)
Sex: Female
Age at injury: 28
Age at award: 32
Date of award: 13 June 1995
Tribunal: Brighton County Court
Amount of award then: £3,000
Award at February 2001: £3,445
Description of injuries: Plaintiff suffered soft-tissue neck and thoracic spine injuries in rear-end road traffic collision – before accident she had one child, worked as project consultant with computers and enjoyed squash – three days off work and three weeks of acute neck and back symptoms – neck pain resolved within one month – had five months of disruption of work due to thoracic spine pain – treated by GP and had 10 sessions of osteopathy and six sessions of acupuncture – avoided squash for seven months – became pregnant within one year after accident and suffered moderate thoracic back pain during pregnancy as result of her injuries (she had no back pain during her first pregnancy) – lower back pain continued for two years and six months – it was aggravated when driving or sitting still for long periods of time or doing heavy lifting – thereafter was left with continuing vulnerability but otherwise symptoms resolved.

1.3.1.3.C79 Case No. 11461

Name of case: Scourfield and British Gas PLC v Gammon
Brief description of injuries: BACK – 18 MONTHS
Reported: Kemp & Kemp, K2-033; [1997] CLY 2010
JSB Category: 6(B)(c)
Sex: Female
Age at injury: 37
Age at award: -
Date of award: 03 December 1996
Tribunal: Haverfordwest County Court
Amount of award then: £3,000
Award at February 2001: £3,342
Description of injuries: Facet arthrosis syndrome – short-lived lumbar pain.
Prognosis: No long term complications were expected – eighteen months of pain was attributable to the accident.

1.3.1.3.C80 Case No. 11991

Name of case: Burgess v Electricity Sports and Social Club
Brief description of injuries: BACK – SOFT-TISSUE INJURY
Reported: Kemp & Kemp, E3-117; [2000] 3 CL 175
JSB Category: 6(B)(c)
Sex: Female
Age at injury: 60
Age at award: 63
Date of award: 13 October 1999
Tribunal: Cardiff County Court
Amount of award then: £3,000
Award at February 2001: £3,099
Description of injuries: A jarring soft-tissue injury to the lumbosacral spine in a fall to the floor while ballroom dancing – immediate pain and discomfort within the pelvis, lower spine and legs – sustained bruising – underwent physiotherapy – symptoms gradually improved.
Other points: An overseas holiday began a few days after the accident – aggravation of her symptoms ruined the trip. Unable to enjoy badminton, cycling and ballroom dancing.

1.3.1.3.C81 Case No. 11231

Name of case: Dan v Welsh and Rogers
Brief description of injuries: BACK – 18 MONTHS
Reported: Kemp & Kemp, E3-122; [1996] CLY 2323
JSB Category: 6(B)(c)
Sex: Male
Age at injury: 24
Age at award: 26
Date of award: 08 July 1996
Tribunal: Plymouth County Court
Amount of award then: £2,000
Award at February 2001: £2,257
Description of injuries: Soft-tissue injuries to the lumbar spine – the back was vulnerable to trauma – he was able to engage in light weight-lifting after eighteen months.

1.3.1.3.C82 Case No. 11235

Name of case: Asperry Ltd v Rigg
Brief description of injuries: BACK – SKIN – MULTIPLE GRAZES
Reported: Kemp & Kemp, E3-123; [1996] CLY 2327
JSB Category: 8(v)
Sex: Male
Age at injury: 20
Age at award: 22
Date of award: 14 February 1996
Tribunal: Leeds County Court
Amount of award then: £1,850
Award at February 2001: £2,109
Description of injuries: Deep graze to the back – grazes to the elbow and knee – circular one-inch scar on his back.
Prognosis: There was a possibility of permanent discomfort over the injured area of the lower lumbar spine upon direct pressure.

1.3.1.3.C83 Case No. 10867

Name of case: Macey v ORB Electrical Steels
Brief description of injuries: CHEST – BACK – BRUISES AND GRAZING
Reported: Kemp & Kemp, K2-107; [1994] CLY 1719
JSB Category: 5(A), 6(B)(c)
Sex: Male
Age at injury: 32
Age at award: 34
Date of award: 16 March 1994
Tribunal: Bristol County Court
Amount of award then: £1,650
Award at February 2001: £1,992
Description of injuries: Machine snagged claimant's clothes from behind and dragged him towards it – dragged for 20-30 seconds, during which time claimant in fear of life – colleague switched machine off and claimant extricated himself-extensive, deep bruising, and grazing, to back – claimant completed shift but did little work – subsequent development of pain in chest when driving home, where snagged clothes had pulled against his chest and caused bruising – GP signed claimant off work for 5 weeks – shock for 1-2 days – chest pains bad for 1 week and slackened thereafter, but pain still present on deep respiration – arm movements restricted by pain in chest; driving, and hobby of sea angling, impossible – difficulty getting dressed – pains subsided within 2 months – grazing to back, including one large patch over left shoulder, gradually healed, but left occasional itching, still evident 8 months later – full year until all symptoms had resolved.

1.3.1.3.C84 Case No. 11391

Name of case: Alldis v Myer
Brief description of injuries: BACK – 9-MONTH ACCELERATION
Reported: Kemp & Kemp, E3-124/1; [1997] CLY 1939
JSB Category: 6(B)(c)
Sex: Male
Age at injury: 50
Age at award: 53
Date of award: 20 June 1997
Tribunal: Central London County Court
Amount of award then: £1,500
Award at February 2001: £1,638
Description of injuries: Sustained soft-tissue strain to the lumbar spine.
Prognosis: The accident had caused exacerbation of a pre-existing back problem for nine months.

1.3.1.3.C85 Case No. 10679

Name of case: Re Hornigold v Taylor

Brief description of injuries: SPINE – JARRING INJURY – 5 MONTHS

Reported: Kemp & Kemp, K2-159; [1993] CLY 1575

JSB Category: 6(B)(c)

Sex: Male

Age at injury: 59

Age at award: 61

Date of award: 23 June 1993

Tribunal: Preston County Court

Amount of award then: £1,200

Award at February 2001: £1,464

Description of injuries: Jarring injury to axial skeleton, particularly lumbar spine – confined to bed 3 days – unable to drive 6 weeks – analgesics and painkilling injection prescribed – pre-existing back problem exacerbated – hobby of shooting interrupted – recovery to pre-accident levels of mobility within 5 months – still some persistent lumbar pain.

1.3.1.3.C86 Case No. 10117

Name of case: Horesh v Ryman

Brief description of injuries: BACK – MINOR INJURY – SOME RESIDUAL SYMPTOMS

Reported: Kemp & Kemp, K2-164; [1990] CLY 1692

JSB Category: 6(B)

Sex: Male

Age at injury: 23

Age at award: -

Date of award: 27 March 1990

Tribunal: Liverpool County Court

Amount of award then: £1,000

Award at February 2001: £1,417

Description of injuries: Sustained significant injury to back in road traffic accident – five weeks later complained of intermittent severe low back pain aggravated by standing, lifting and bending – gradual improvement thereafter, but 18 weeks after accident plaintiff complained of low back ache on heavy lifting, etc.

Prognosis: Plaintiff on the road to recovery but would still probably suffer occasional symptoms – would not be sufficient to cause permanent disability.

1.3.1.3.C87 Case No. 10781

Name of case: Russell v John Williams Foundaries

Brief description of injuries: BACK – INJURY – EXACERBATION OF PRE-EXISTING ASYMPTOMATIC CONDITION

Reported: Kemp & Kemp, E3-126; [1994] CLY 1630

JSB Category: 6(B)(c)

Sex: Male

Age at injury: 50

Age at award: 58

Date of award: 25 November 1993

Tribunal: Cardiff County Court

Amount of award then: £1,000

Award at February 2001: £1,215

Description of injuries: Claimant, worker in foundry, jumped 2-3 feet from platform to ground to avoid being splashed by molten metal – no pain at time, twinges of pain in back 2-3 days later – 3 months later, claimant immobilised by pain in lower back and rescued from home by neighbours – in hospital 3 weeks – surgery undertaken on extruded spinal disc 4 months later – extensive rehabilitative physiotherapy – further surgical intervention required after 6 months, providing only limited relief – medical evidence that claimant had been suffering from a pre-existing, asymptomatic degenerative back condition which had been accelerated by 6 months by the jarring associated with jump from platform.

Prognosis: Claimant rendered unfit to work.

1.3.1.3.C88 Case No. 11740

Name of case: Niftylift Ltd v Walker

Brief description of injuries: BACK – 8 WEEKS

Reported: Kemp & Kemp, K2-208/3; [1998] CLY 1743

JSB Category: 6(B)(c)

Sex: Male

Age at injury: 42

Age at award: 43

Date of award: 06 January 1998

Tribunal: Milton Keynes County Court

Amount of award then: £1,000

Award at February 2001: £1,078

Description of injuries: Soft-tissue injury to the lower back – aggravated a pre-existing back condition – return to pre-accident condition was attained 8 weeks after the date of the accident.

1.3.1.3.C89 Case No. 11263

Name of case: Bigelow v Jones

Brief description of injuries: BACK – 11 WEEKS

Reported: Kemp & Kemp, K2-218; [1996] CLY 2355

JSB Category: 6(B)(c)

Sex: Male

Age at injury: 34

Age at award: 35

Date of award: 03 October 1996

Tribunal: Birkenhead County Court

Amount of award then: £900

Award at February 2001: £1,007

Description of injuries: Jarring, jolting force to the spine – trauma – soft-tissue injury – symptom free within eleven weeks of the date of the accident.

1.3.1.3.C90 Case No. 11268

Name of case: Kyffin v Creighton

Brief description of injuries: BACK – 3 WEEKS

Reported: [1996] CLY 2361

JSB Category: 6(B)(c)

Sex: Not stated

Age at injury: 22

Age at award: 23

Date of award: 06 February 1996

Tribunal: Birkenhead County Court

Amount of award then: £500

Award at February 2001: £570

Description of injuries: Jarring, jolting force to the lumbar spine – a soft-tissue injury to the neck – symptoms were resolved within three weeks of the date of the accident.

1.3.1.3.1 Back and other injury

1.3.1.3.1.C1 Case No. 10410

Name of case: Routledge v Shires

Brief description of injuries: CANDA EQUINA LESION – LOSS OF BLADDER AND BOWEL FUNCTION – PAIN – DEPRESSION

Reported: [1992] CLY 1666

JSB Category: 5(I)(b), 5(H)(b)

Sex: Female

Age at injury: 30

Age at award: 37

Date of award: 22 May 1992

Tribunal: QBD

Amount of award then: £55,000

Award at February 2001: £77,046

Description of injuries: Negligent failure to recognise entral disc prolapse impinging on the cauda equina – suffered a cauda equina lesion resulting in injuries – injuries included loss of bladder and bowel control requiring permanent digital evacuation of the bowels – chronic pain in the back and back passage and frequent pain in the right buttock, leg and bladder which would continue – impaired sexual relations with her husband – depression, anxiety, loss of confidence and embarrassment – need for care would increase in about twenty years with progressive disability – small risk of bladder infection with ascending resulting in renal failure – plaintiff was the breadwinner after her husband suffered brain damage in1985 – her ability to carry on her previously successful practice was severely impeded.

Prognosis: Unable to do heavy lifting, shopping or heavy domestic tasks – needed extra help with the house and children – could not go hunting or skiing.

1.3.1.3.1.C2 Case No. 10904

Award at February 2001: £50,605

See: 1.2.3.8.C62 for details

1.3.1.3.1.C3 Case No. 12010

Award at February 2001: £41,261

See: 1.3.1.3.C4 for details

1.3.1.3.1.C4 Case No. 10205

Name of case: Milbourne v William Press (Construction)

Brief description of injuries: LIGAMENTOUS INJURY TO THE LOWER BACK – CATASTROPHIC EFFECT ON LIFE – DEPRESSION

Reported: Kemp & Kemp, E3-011; [1991] CLY 1402

JSB Category: 6(B)(a)(iii)

Sex: Female

Age at injury: 50

Age at award: 59

Date of award: 28 June 1991

Tribunal: QBD

Amount of award then: £20,000

Award at February 2001: £26,576

Description of injuries: A fall into an unguarded hole in the pavement – shock, general lacerations, pain and bruising to the left leg in particular – ligamentous injury to the lower back caused chronic low back pain – she was retired on grounds of ill health – M had not worked since- there was constant pain, immobility and depression and sleep disturbance.

Prognosis: The accident had had a catastrophic effect on her life – prognosis was poor – she was unlikely to experience any improvements.

1.3.1.3.1.C5 Case No. 10316

Award at February 2001: £26,244

See: 1.2.3.8.C78 for details

1.3.1.3.1.C6 Case No. 11371

Award at February 2001: £25,264

See: 1.3.1.1.C7 for details

1.3.1.3.1.C7 Case No. 11818

Name of case: Timms v Buchanan

Brief description of injuries: BACK – LEGS

Reported: Kemp & Kemp, E2-015/2; [1999] CLY 1481

JSB Category: 6(B)(b), 6(K)(c)(iii)

Sex: Female

Age at injury: 27

Age at award: 32

Date of award: 13 May 1999

Tribunal: Cambridge County Court

Amount of award then: £22,500

Award at February 2001: £24,086

Description of injuries: Injuries to neck, leg and back in road accident – injuries to neck and leg largely resolved – back symptoms fluctuated for 18 months, then major exacerbation, requiring surgery to remove part of L5/S1 disc – surgery ameliorated some symptoms but not others – claimant still significantly disabled at time of trial – help needed with housework and child care – only part-time work, in a sedentary job with flexible hours and a sympathetic employer, possible.

Prognosis: No prospect of improvement.

Other points: Claimant had experienced acute episode of back pain some months prior to accident, but judge found that this had ceased completely at the time of the trial, and that the accident was directly responsible for all symptoms experienced by the claimant thereafter.

1.3.1.3.1.C8 Case No. 11163

Name of case: Morrisey v Khosa

Brief description of injuries: BACK – ACUTE LUMBAR STRAIN – POST-TRAUMATIC STRESS DISORDER

Reported: Kemp & Kemp, E3-018; [1996] CLY 2254

JSB Category: 6(B)(b)(ii) and 3(B)(c)

Sex: Male

Age at injury: 30

Age at award: 33

Date of award: 18 September 1996

Tribunal: Central London County Court

Amount of award then: £20,000

Award at February 2001: £23,000

Description of injuries: Acute lumbar strain – post-traumatic stress disorder – painful shoulder.

Prognosis: He would always suffer a painful back – unlikely to work again – suffered recrudescence of phobic anxieties.

Other points: Before the accident there were only thirty people in the country who were more advanced than the plaintiff in Tibetan martial arts. The Recorder rejected the defendant's argument that there were so many imponderables in this case.

1.3.1.3.1.C9 Case No. 11819

Name of case: Dominey v Amenco (Poole) Ltd

Brief description of injuries: BACK – DEPRESSION

Reported: Kemp & Kemp, PRE-003; [1999] CLY 1482

JSB Category: 6(B)(b); 3(A)

Sex: Male

Age at injury: 41

Age at award: 47

Date of award: 16 February 1999

Tribunal: QBD

Amount of award then: £17,500

Award at February 2001: £18,737

Description of injuries: Fall down stairs – diagnosis 4 months later of disc protrusion at L4/5 – discectomy undergone; only partially successful, probably owing to development of fibrosis in disc space and around an adjacent nerve root – chronic low back pain and discomfort, radiating into left leg, aggravated by prolonged sitting, standing, walking or driving – bending, lifting, gardening, DIY, and golf impossible – help required with dressing and bathing – mood disorder (chronic depression, apathy, withdrawnness, sleep disturbance), largely resolved by counselling and medication by date of trial – claimant had history of low back and neck problems, requiring visits to chiropractor but not affecting work or social life, dating from road accident 13 years previously.

Prognosis: Claimant likely to have been forced to retire at 60 due to pre-existing back problems in any event – claimant retired as medically unfit 2 years after accident and had not worked since, but still regarded as being fit for part-time, and possibly full-time, semi-sedentary work.

1.3.1.3.1.C10 Case No. 11820

Name of case: Re Cooper
Brief description of injuries: BACK -DEPRESSION
Reported: Kemp & Kemp, [1999] CLY 1483
JSB Category: 6(B)(b); 3(A)
Sex: Male
Age at injury: 53
Age at award: 58
Date of award: 01 June 1999
Tribunal: CICB, Liverpool
Amount of award then: £17,500
Award at February 2001: £18,513

Description of injuries: Injuries to neck and lumbar spine – neck injury resolved after 12 months, except for slight restriction of movement at rotational extremes – strain to lumbar spine did not resolve; development of muscle guarding – constant pain, worsening after standing or sitting for a period of time ranging from 30 minutes at worst to a few hours at best – pain ongoing, despite physiotherapy and many other attempts to alleviate the pain – claimant attended pain management course – development of depression – frequent sleep disturbance; claimant often awoke with cramp – type pain in back, this being the most difficult aspect of his symptoms – domestic life restricted – claimant forced to abandon hobby of fishing – development of short – temperedness and irritability with family – marital relations difficult.

Prognosis: Diagnosis of pain continuing for rest of claimant's life – depression would only improve when physical situation improved.

1.3.1.3.1.C11 Case No. 11568

Name of case: Saunders v Hammersmith and Fulham LBC
Brief description of injuries: SPINE – DEPRESSION
Reported: Kemp & Kemp, E3-030/2; [1998] CLY 1570
JSB Category: 6(B)(b); 3(A)
Sex: Male
Age at injury: 24
Age at award: 32
Date of award: 29 January 1998
Tribunal: Central London County Court
Amount of award then: £16,500
Award at February 2001: £18,108

Description of injuries: Series of back injuries accelerated pre-existing isthmic spondylosis at L4/5 and L5/S1 – severe pain for 1 year – disabling pain thereafter – moderately severe depressive illness – mobility and social/hobby/sexual restrictions.

Other points: £3,000 for depression, £13,500 for injuries.

1.3.1.3.1.C12 Case No. 12042

Name of case: Wale v London Underground Ltd
Brief description of injuries: INTERNAL ORGANS – BLADDER – BACK INJURY
Reported: Kemp & Kemp, E2-031/2; [2000] 5 CL 186
JSB Category: 5(I)(c)
Sex: Female
Age at injury: 41
Age at award: 46
Date of award: 30 October 1998
Tribunal: Central London County Court
Amount of award then: £15,500
Award at February 2001: £16,433

Description of injuries: Fell downstairs at work – low back injury with low back pain – pre-existing degenerative disc disease would have progressed naturally – the fall had accelerated symptoms by about ten years – injury also caused an abnormality of the detrusor (bladder) muscle – bladder required emptying every hour during the day and two or three times at night – some incontinence.

Prognosis: W would never have normal bladder function again.

1.3.1.3.1.C13 Case No. 10774

Name of case: Benson v Howard
Brief description of injuries: BACK INJURY – FRACTURED PELVIS – 50 PER CENT LOSS OF GRIP IN RIGHT HAND
Reported: Kemp & Kemp, E3-035; [1994] CLY 1622
JSB Category: 6(B), 6(C), 6(I); 7(A)(f)(iv), 7(B)(b)
Sex: Male
Age at injury: 29
Age at award: 33
Date of award: 07 July 1994
Tribunal: Woolwich County Court
Amount of award then: £12,500
Award at February 2001: £15,095

Description of injuries: Claimant knocked off motorcycle – undisplaced fracture of pubic ramus – soft-tissue injuries to both hands and one ankle – broken molar – in hospital 7 days, off work 3 months; crutches required for a longer period – on return to work, development of increasing lower back pain and stiffness – loss of 50 per cent flexion in lumbar spine, with some restriction on rotation – also 50 per cent reduction of grip in right hand – inability to continue playing sports – main leisure activity of motorcycle riding seriously affected.

Prognosis: Restriction in spine movement permanent – future degenerative change likely due to lumbar scoliosis caused by the accident – reduction of grip in right hand also permanent.

1.3.1.3.1.C14 Case No. 10397

Name of case: Thomas v Associated British Ports

Brief description of injuries: MODERATELY SEVERE BACK INJURY – WHIPLASH

Reported: [1992] CLY 1653

JSB Category: 6(B)(b)(ii)

Sex: Male

Age at injury: 49

Age at award: 52

Date of award: 02 March 1992

Tribunal: Swansea County Court

Amount of award then: £11,000

Award at February 2001: £13,958

Description of injuries: Injury to the spine consisting of disruption to the intervertebral disc at the lumbo-sacral junction – with symptoms described as instability syndrome – whiplash injury – injury to the rotor cuff of his left shoulder – there was some adverse effect on sexual relations with his wife.

Prognosis: His back needed protection.

1.3.1.3.1.C15 Case No. 11499

Name of case: Goodwin v Fryer

Brief description of injuries: NECK – BACK – ARM – DEPRESSION

Reported: Kemp & Kemp, B2-036/2; [1998] CLY 1500

JSB Category: 6(A)(b)(ii), 6(B)(c), 6(L)(b)(ii); 3(A)(c)

Sex: Male

Age at injury: 48

Age at award: 53

Date of award: 17 August 1998

Tribunal: Tunbridge Wells County Court

Amount of award then: £13,000

Award at February 2001: £13,768

Description of injuries: Soft-tissue injuries to the arm, neck and lower back – exacerbated pre-existing degenerative capsulitis to the shoulders – chronic reactive depression – lower back developed into sciatica.

Prognosis: The neck would remain vulnerable – psychiatric illness and age would deter future employers.

Other points: Award breakdown: £8,000 for physical injuries £5,000 for depression.

1.3.1.3.1.C16 Case No. 10831

Name of case: Green v GM Buses

Brief description of injuries: KNEE – BACK

Reported: Kemp & Kemp, I2-428; [1994] CLY 1680

JSB Category: 6(L)(b), 6(B)(c), 6(K)(c)(iii), 6(M)(d); 2(B)

Sex: Female

Age at injury: 19

Age at award: 23

Date of award: 24 November 1993

Tribunal: Manchester County Court

Amount of award then: £8,500

Award at February 2001: £10,325

Description of injuries: Claimant knocked off bicycle – dazed but not rendered unconscious – soft-tissue injuries to knee (causing pain), calf and ankle of left leg, necessitating leg support for 8 months – also lower back pain for several months and frequent severe headaches for 12 months – return to work after 5 weeks – pain in knee aggravated by kneeling, lifting, climbing steps and sitting for long periods – return to pre-accident activities of tennis, dancing and aerobics after 8 months, but at lower frequency and level of attainment than before – attempt to take up new pastime of horse – riding failed due to pain in leg – discomfort when driving – full recovery from injuries to calf and ankle – knee pain, back pain and headaches still troubling claimant at time of trial.

Prognosis: Prognosis of some discomfort in knee for rest of claimant's life.

1.3.1.3.1.C17 Case No. 10624

Name of case: Thomas v Booker Services

Brief description of injuries: BACK – MILD ANXIETY – WRIST

Reported: Kemp & Kemp, E3-088; [1993] CLY 1519

JSB Category: 6(B); 3(A)(d); 6(H)

Sex: Female

Age at injury: 42

Age at award: -

Date of award: 03 December 1992

Tribunal: Swansea County Court

Amount of award then: £7,850

Award at February 2001: £9,700

Description of injuries: Claimant's vehicle struck by heavy object falling from lorry – minor sprain of right wrist, resolved completely in a few weeks – mild anxiety state (fear of driving and travelling in vehicles, especially in proximity to lorries) lasting 2 years – jolting injury to back exacerbating pre-existing but largely asymptomatic degenerative changes – dull continuous low backache.

Other points: Award breakdown: wrist: £350; anxiety state: £1,000; back: £6,500.

1.3.1.3.1.C18 Case No. 11384

Name of case: Le Gallou v Malorey
Brief description of injuries: BACK – CHRONIC PAIN
Reported: [1997] CLY 1932
JSB Category: 6(B)(b)(ii)
Sex: Male
Age at injury: 32
Age at award: -
Date of award: 01 July 1997
Tribunal:
Amount of award then: £8,000
Award at February 2001: £8,737
Description of injuries: Soft-tissue injuries to the elbow, wrist, leg, jaw and nose – neuro-praxia of the knee – lower back injury more muscular and ligamentous than skeletal.
Prognosis: Likely to be a chronic back sufferer – with permanent pain – in the light of his condition he would be unable to carry out manual work.
Other points: He was not qualified to do office work – likely to be at a permanent disadvantage in the labour market.

1.3.1.3.1.C19 Case No. 11825

Name of case: Clark v Allied Signal Ltd
Brief description of injuries: BACK – PAIN RADIATING INTO LEGS – 6 YEAR ACCELERATION
Reported: Kemp & Kemp, E3-089/1; [1999] CLY 1489
JSB Category: 6(B)(b)(ii)
Sex: Female
Age at injury: 44
Age at award: 47
Date of award: 14 August 1998
Tribunal: Carlisle County Court
Amount of award then: £7,500
Award at February 2001: £7,880
Description of injuries: Development of back pain in course of employment which included heavy lifting – back locked up while lifting on following day – co – drydamol, anti-inflammatories and rest prescribed – pain in lower back ongoing, radiating down left leg, causing limp and necessitating use of a stick; movements considerably limited – employment terminated 5 months after accident, since claimant could not return to work, and claimant unable to work since – claimant had pre-existing degenerative changes in spine and history of anxiety and depression – No evidence of treatment for back pain before injury.
Prognosis: Back symptoms accelerated by a period of 6 years.

1.3.1.3.1.C20 Case No. 11826

Name of case: Williams v Clarkson
Brief description of injuries: BACK – LUMBAR INSTABILITY SYNDROME – 6/7 YEAR ACCELERATION
Reported: Kemp & Kemp, E3-089/2; [1999] CLY 1490
JSB Category: 6(B)(b)(ii)
Sex: Male
Age at injury: 20
Age at award: 24
Date of award: 01 July 1999
Tribunal: Central London County Court
Amount of award then: £7,500
Award at February 2001: £7,813
Description of injuries: Strain to lumbo – sacral spine, sprained shoulder, soft-tissue injury to neck and sprained wrist – injuries to neck, shoulder and wrist resolved over a period of 5 weeks – some improvement in back injury, but claimant left with intermittent backache, particularly after prolonged sitting, squatting, lifting or exertion – claimant forced to give up football and swim less frequently – lumbar instability syndrome diagnosed – claimant advised to avoid heavy lumbar exertion – claimant gave up job as motorcycle mechanic, as heavy lifting involved, and opted to retrain.
Prognosis: Claimant would have developed lumbar instability syndrome within 6 or 7 years of the accident in any event.

1.3.1.3.1.C21 Case No. 11388

Name of case: Wray v Pardey
Brief description of injuries: BACK – WHIPLASH
Reported: Kemp & Kemp, E2-059/2; E2-059/2; [1997] CLY 1936
JSB Category: 6(B)(b)(ii)
Sex: Female
Age at injury: 32
Age at award: 36
Date of award: 01 July 1997
Tribunal: Newport, IOW County Court
Amount of award then: £7,000
Award at February 2001: £7,644
Description of injuries: Classic whiplash type injuries to the neck and lower back – required 15/12 sessions physiotherapy in 1993/1995.
Prognosis: Permanent tenderness in her back from C4 to T9.
Other points: Pain was aggravated when dealing with her own small children – and the physical demands of her job (primary school teacher).

1.3.1.3.1.C22 Case No. 10076

Award at February 2001: £7,251

See: 1.2.2.1.C22 for details

1.3.1.3.1.C23 Case No. 10603

Name of case: Pitman v Clarke

Brief description of injuries: BACK (1 YEAR'S ACCELERATION) – RIBS – HAEMATOMA

Reported: Kemp & Kemp, E3-096; [1993] CLY 1496

JSB Category: 6(B); 8; 5(A)(g)

Sex: Female

Age at injury: 40

Age at award: 44

Date of award: 20 May 1993

Tribunal: Court of Appeal

Amount of award then: £5,500

Award at February 2001: £6,704

Description of injuries: Road accident – 3 broken ribs – wrenching injury to already vulnerable spine, for which claimant had undergone successful laminectomy to alleviate, if not resolve, sciatica 6 months prior to accident – return of sciatica subsequent to accident – 5 weeks after accident, on return to work, persistent pain in groin and burning sensation in toes – dismissed from employment for failure to fulfil duties – haematoma in right groin area diagnosed – laparotomy necessitated, leaving permanent scar.

Prognosis: Trial judge accepted that accident had caused 1 year's acceleration in sciatica symptoms.

Other points: Court of Appeal upheld judge's finding on acceleration of symptoms – indicated award was generous, but not outside the bracket which applied to this kind of injury.

1.3.1.3.1.C24 Case No. 10604

Name of case: Baker v Hunter

Brief description of injuries: BACK – SUBSTANTIAL RECOVERY WITHIN 4 YEARS

Reported: Kemp & Kemp, E3-099; [1993] CLY 1497

JSB Category: 6(B)(c)

Sex: Male

Age at injury: 37

Age at award: 41

Date of award: 04 February 1993

Tribunal: Leeds County Court

Amount of award then: £5,250

Award at February 2001: £6,506

Description of injuries: Road accident – claimant's chest struck steering wheel, then thrown back so that head struck head restraint – pain across chest, especially in sternum, worse upon deep respiration – pain in neck and back of increasing severity, necessitating wearing of collar for 5 to 6 weeks – off work for 3.5 months initially, then subsequent periods of 2 weeks and 4 weeks – headaches – persistent slight weakness in neck, and occasional discomfort in back, preventing participation in hobby of tenpin bowling more than 3 years later – loss of confidence – claimant able to continue with employment as police officer seconded to coroner's office, but considered himself unable to return to active beat duties due to increased vulnerability to injury.

Prognosis: No long-term complications anticipated – further improvement likely – substantial if not full recovery within 4+ year period from incident.

1.3.1.3.1.C25 Case No. 10953

Award at February 2001: £5,919

See: 1.3.1.1.C32 for details

1.3.1.3.1.C26 Case No. 11202

Name of case: Re Hitchcock

Brief description of injuries: BACK – SCARS – PNEUMONIA

Reported: Kemp & Kemp, J2-014/1/1; [1996] CLY 2293

JSB Category: 8(iii)

Sex: Male

Age at injury: 24

Age at award: 27

Date of award: 10 June 1996

Tribunal: CICB, Nottingham

Amount of award then: £5,000

Award at February 2001: £5,621

Description of injuries: Stabbing to the upper right back – developed pneumonia – complicated by an infection of the pleural space – thoracotomy scar more than six inches long – scar remained sensitive.

1.3.1.3.1.C27 Case No. 11695

Name of case: Wright v Marina Developments Ltd
Brief description of injuries: BACK – HIP – HEEL
Reported: Kemp & Kemp, E3-110/1; [1998] CLY 1698
JSB Category: 6(B)(c), 6(C)(d), 6(O)(g)
Sex: Female
Age at injury: 23
Age at award: -
Date of award: 05 January 1998
Tribunal: Southampton County Court
Amount of award then: £4,000
Award at February 2001: £4,313

Description of injuries: Laceration to the heel – retained foreign body – swollen and sore knee – bruising to the left hip and lower back strain – most back and hip symptoms had resolved within 12 months.

Prognosis: No suggestion of long-term disability.

1.3.1.3.1.C28 Case No. 10955

Award at February 2001: £4,081

See: 1.3.1.1.C41 for details

1.3.1.3.1.C29 Case No. 10401

Award at February 2001: £3,996

See: 1.3.1.1.C42 for details

1.3.1.3.1.C30 Case No. 10610

Name of case: Weeks v Williams and Lucas-Farley
Brief description of injuries: BACK – PRE-EXISTING CONDITION – DEPRESSION
Reported: [1993] CLY 1503
JSB Category: 6(B); 3(A)(d)
Sex: Female
Age at injury: 57
Age at award: 63
Date of award: 22 January 1993
Tribunal: Barnstaple County Court
Amount of award then: £3,000
Award at February 2001: £3,742

Description of injuries: Claimant dragged along pavement while getting into taxicab that suddenly started moving – severe twisting injury to back, especially painful and stiff for 3 months, pain continuing to a lesser extent thereafter and with tendency to "flare up" – bruising to chest, causing ongoing tenderness in rib area – grazing to knee – claimant distressed by accident, suffered from depression for first 3 months, anti-depressants prescribed – sleep disturbance, exacerbated by inability to use bed and necessity of sleeping in chair – sexual relations ceased, partial cause of breakup of marriage – pre-existing arthritic condition in back, neither eased nor exacerbated by accident, also degenerating at this time, necessitating claimant's use of walking sticks and stairlift, and becoming the primary problem – back pain ongoing at time of trial, necessitating painkillers – judge held that accident 70 per cent responsible for this pain.

Prognosis: Medical evidence that tenderness in rib area would slowly diminish doubted by judge on evidence from claimant.

1.3.1.3.1.C31 Case No. 10403

Name of case: Re Walters
Brief description of injuries: LOWER BACK – HIP – OFF WORK 8 MONTHS
Reported: [1992] CLY 1659
JSB Category: 6(B)(c)
Sex: Female
Age at injury: 51
Age at award: 54
Date of award: 05 March 1992
Tribunal: CICB, Leeds
Amount of award then: £2,500
Award at February 2001: £3,146

Description of injuries: Injury to lower back and right hip – acute back pain – unable to move substantially for three months – rest and traction in hospital for two weeks – X-ray showed sciatica probably associated with mild prolapsed intervertebral disc – physiotherapy for five months – returned to work eight months after injury.

Prognosis: Still suffered intermittent and occasional back pain three years after the injury – unable to carry heavyweights.

1.3.1.3.1.C32 Case No. 10263

Name of case: Winstanley v Case (JI)

Brief description of injuries: LOWER BACK PAIN – OFF WORK 17 WEEKS

Reported: [1991] CLY 1460

JSB Category: 6(B)(c)

Sex: Male

Age at injury: -

Age at award: 42

Date of award: 06 December 1990

Tribunal: Doncaster County Court

Amount of award then: £2,200

Award at February 2001: £2,913

Description of injuries: Acute attack of lower back pain – his work entailed the carrying of 36lb weights in each hand for about 12 feet – the trip repeated about 70 times per day – required physiotherapy – off work for seventeen weeks.

Prognosis: Few physical signs – no serious long term problems.

1.3.1.3.1.C33 Case No. 11230

Award at February 2001: £2,483

See: 1.3.1.1.C48 for details

1.3.1.3.1.C34 Case No. 10667

Award at February 2001: £2,440

See: 1.2.3.1.C36 for details

1.3.1.3.1.C35 Case No. 11698

Award at February 2001: £1,995

See: 1.2.2.1.C33 for details

1.3.1.3.1.C36 Case No. 10494

Name of case: Galvin v Beckerleg

Brief description of injuries: LACERATION TO SHIN – BRUISING – BACK PAIN

Reported: Kemp & Kemp, K2-115; [1992] CLY 1750

JSB Category: 6(K)

Sex: Female

Age at injury: 49

Age at award: 51

Date of award: 13 September 1991

Tribunal: Welshpool and Newtown County Court

Amount of award then: £1,500

Award at February 2001: £1,917

Description of injuries: Laceration to the right shin – severe shock and distress – bruising and abrasions to the ankles, knees and hips – soft-tissue injuries to the spine – regular discomfort in the right hip and lower back remained a nuisance.

Prognosis: Good

1.3.1.3.1.C37 Case No. 11347

Award at February 2001: £1,645

See: 1.3.1.1.C57 for details

1.3.1.3.1.C38 Case No. 11893

Name of case: Simson v Sutton

Brief description of injuries: BACK – HIP – SOFT-TISSUE INJURIES – 7 MONTHS

Reported: Kemp & Kemp, K2-170/7; [1999] CLY 1557

JSB Category: 6(B)(c), 6(C)(d), 6(K), 6(L); 5(A)

Sex: Female

Age at injury: 31

Age at award: 33

Date of award: 03 June 1999

Tribunal: Stockport County Court

Amount of award then: £1,250

Award at February 2001: £1,298

Description of injuries: Road accident – superficial trauma to lower hip – soft-tissue injury to anterior chest wall – bruising to lower lumbar region – bruising to posterior aspect of right thigh and left aspect of both knees – injuries to hip and chest cleared within 1 week – injuries to thigh and knees lasted approximately 5 weeks, during which time it was painful to walk or sit down – injury to lower lumbar region, for which analgesics were taken periodically, cleared up within 7 months.

1.3.1.3.1.C39 Case No. 10508

Award at February 2001: £1,132

See: 1.3.1.1.C62 for details

1.3.1.3.1.C40 Case No. 11975

Name of case: Ashouri v Penfold

Brief description of injuries: BACK – WHIPLASH – THREE WEEKS

Reported: Kemp & Kemp, PRK-012; [2000] 2 CL 146

JSB Category: 6(B)(c)

Sex: Female

Age at injury: 36

Age at award: 48

Date of award: 22 October 1999

Tribunal: Southampton County Court

Amount of award then: £850

Award at February 2001: £878

Description of injuries: A minor whiplash injury – pain to the lower back and left sided sciatica – GP advised analgesics – pain persisted for three weeks – A suffered a general travel anxiety. Pain resolved fully within three weeks – psychological problems fully resolved within sixteen months of the date of the accident.

1.3.1.3.1.C41 Case No. 10127

Name of case: Munson v Richardson

Brief description of injuries: BACK – BRUISING – LEFT ARM AND SPRAINING OF RIGHT WRIST – RECOVERY 2 WEEKS

Reported: [1990] CLY 1706

JSB Category: 6(B), 6(F), 6(I)

Sex: Male

Age at injury: 37

Age at award: 38

Date of award: 02 July 1990

Tribunal: Southend County Court

Amount of award then: £400

Award at February 2001: £543

Description of injuries: In road traffic accident, suffered bruising and grazing to lower back, bruising to left arm and spraining to right wrist – pain to right wrist worsened – took one day off work – improvement rapid – two weeks after accident all injuries settled – no medical treatment received – no residual disability.

1.3.1.3.2 Back fracture and disc injury

1.3.1.3.2.C1 Case No. 11502

Name of case: Curi v Colina

Brief description of injuries: BACK – FRACTURE OF LUMBAR SPINE

Reported: Kemp & Kemp, B2-008/1; [1998] CLY 1503

JSB Category: 6(B); 5(A), 5(H)(c); 7(A)(f)

Sex: Female

Age at injury: 22

Age at award: -

Date of award: 14 October 1998

Tribunal: CA

Amount of award then: £55,000

Award at February 2001: £63,847

Description of injuries: Fracture dislocation of L1 and L2 – nerve root damage – ruptured bowel and pelvic abscess – pneumothorax – multiple facial lacerations – fractured teeth.

Prognosis: As a result of the accident C's present employment was expected to cease within 15 years.

1.3.1.3.2.C2 Case No. 11574

Name of case: Kumar v Kumar

Brief description of injuries: BACK – VERTEBRA – CRUSH FRACTURE

Reported: Kemp & Kemp, E3-027/1; [1998] CLY 1576

JSB Category: 6(B)(a)(iii)

Sex: Male

Age at injury: -

Age at award: -

Date of award: 29 October 1997

Tribunal: CA

Amount of award then: £30,000

Award at February 2001: £34,021

Description of injuries: Crush fracture to the twelfth thoracic vertebra – serious injury to the spinal ligaments.

Prognosis: Serious degenerative change to the lumbar region.

Other points: Award reduced from £41,401.

1.3.1.3.2.C3 Case No. 10592

Name of case: Toulson v RS Bruce (Metals and Machinery)

Brief description of injuries: BACK – FRACTURED VERTEBRAE – PERMANENT SYMPTOMS

Reported: Kemp & Kemp, E3-005; [1993] CLY 1485

JSB Category: 6(B)

Sex: Male

Age at injury: 25

Age at award: 34

Date of award: 29 July 1993

Tribunal: High Court, Sheffield

Amount of award then: £25,000

Award at February 2001: £32,011

Description of injuries: Half-ton metal flap folded down onto back of claimant – fracture dislocation of L5/S1 complex, with damage to posterior facets causing rotary deformity – avulsion fractures of transverse processes of L1-5 – remarkably good recovery from injuries that could have caused paraplegia, but permanent symptoms remained – slight rotary deformity (shoulders no longer parallel with hips) – movement in back limited to 50 per cent of normal – very slight limp – regular aches and pains in back exacerbated by exercise, driving or sitting for prolonged periods – active outdoor pursuits now largely curtailed – unable to return to job as skilled fitter, forced to take sedentary office job.

Prognosis: Some further deterioration expected – 50 per cent risk of increased back pain between ages of 40 and 45 – 10 per cent risk of spinal fusion – some aggravation of symptoms already evident by time of trial.

1.3.1.3.2.C4 Case No. 10066

Award at February 2001: £30,222

See: 1.3.1.1.C5 for details

1.3.1.3.2.C5 Case No. 10594

Name of case: McIlgrew v Devon County Council

Brief description of injuries: BACK – DAMAGED DISC – SEVERE INJURY

Reported: [1995] PIQR Q66; Kemp & Kemp, E3-008; BPILS, I 243; [1993] CLY 1487

JSB Category: 6(B), 8

Sex: Female

Age at injury: 23

Age at award: 29

Date of award: 22 October 1993

Tribunal: Exeter High Court

Amount of award then: £22,500

Award at February 2001: £28,379

Description of injuries: Severe low back pain through lifting – physiotherapy and osteopathy unsuccessful – epidural required – disc derangement of L5/S1 with annular tear – operation to insert carbon fibre device and bone graft from right iliac crest unsuccessful – claimant left with constant pain and restriction of movement – stick required for walking – sleep pattern disturbed – unable to sit for more than 1 hour, stoop, lift or continue with previous active pursuits – assistance required for heavy housework and shopping – sex life with husband severely interfered with – self-consciousness of 21 cm operation scar across stomach – at time of report claimant unemployed and unemployable.

Prognosis: Claimant hoping to have children – child bearing and birth would now be extremely painful – assistance with lifting children in early years also necessary – symptoms permanent.

1.3.1.3.2.C6 Case No. 11612

Name of case: Early v Thomas Ware & Sons

Brief description of injuries: BACK – DISC PROLAPSE

Reported: Kemp & Kemp, E3-009/1; [1998] CLY 1614

JSB Category: 6(B)(a)(iii)

Sex: Male

Age at injury: 50

Age at award: 54

Date of award: 06 January 1998

Tribunal: QBD

Amount of award then: £25,000

Award at February 2001: £28,011

Description of injuries: Prolapsed intervertebral disc at L5/S1 – constant low back pain and pain to the left leg – mobility was severely restricted.

Prognosis: E would not return to any form of gainful employment in the future.

1.3.1.3.2.C7 Case No. 11613

Name of case: Jones v Whitbread plc
Brief description of injuries: BACK – DISC PROLAPSE
Reported: Kemp & Kemp, E3-017/1; [1998] CLY 1615
JSB Category: 6(B)(a)(iii)
Sex: Male
Age at injury: 40
Age at award: 44
Date of award: 06 January 1998
Tribunal: QBD
Amount of award then: £21,000
Award at February 2001: £23,303

Description of injuries: Claimant suffered a prolapsed intervertebral disc at L5/S1 – removal of 2 substantial fragments gave considerable relief – pain to the right buttock, leg and calf and to the mid-back – constant pain 4 years after the accident.

Prognosis: Judge accepted that it was unlikely that claimant would work again, except in a hobby type job.

1.3.1.3.2.C8 Case No. 11372

Name of case: Jones v South Glamorgan HA
Brief description of injuries: BACK – PROLAPSED INTERVERTEBRAL DISC
Reported: [1997] CLY 1920
JSB Category: 6(B)(a)(iii)
Sex: Female
Age at injury: 35
Age at award: 46
Date of award: 19 April 1996
Tribunal: Cardiff County Court
Amount of award then: £20,000
Award at February 2001: £23,190

Description of injuries: Prolapsed intervertebral disc – soft-tissue injury to the dorso-lumbar junctions.

Prognosis: Ten years after the date of the accident there was continued pain – the accident had resulted in a disabling injury.

Other points: The judge accepted that there had not been any pre-accident constitutional back pain.

1.3.1.3.2.C9 Case No. 10540

Name of case: Reid v Simpson
Brief description of injuries: BACK – FRACTURED VERTEBRA – MULTIPLE INJURIES
Reported: Kemp & Kemp, I3-072; [1993] CLY 1432
JSB Category: 6(B)(b), 6(A)(c), 6(K)(c), 6(M); 5(A)(g)
Sex: Male
Age at injury: 34
Age at award: 38
Date of award: 22 October 1993
Tribunal: Bradford County Court
Amount of award then: £18,000
Award at February 2001: £22,425

Description of injuries: 7 rib fractures – undisplaced fracture of second lumbar vertebra – soft-tissue injuries to neck – large haematoma to left thigh requiring evacuation of 1.5 litres of blood – fracture dislocation of left ankle (requiring bone graft 12 months after accident as not healing) – now only doing limited, sedentary duties at work.

Prognosis: Permanently vulnerable to attacks of lumbar pain – 1 to 5 per cent risk of osteoarthritic change in ankle, diminishing over next 5 to 10 years.

1.3.1.3.2.C10 Case No. 10393

Name of case: Dufaur v South East Kent Health Authority
Brief description of injuries: SEVERE BACK INJURY – SEVERELY DISABLED – CAN ONLY WALK SLOWLY
Reported: [1992] CLY 1649
JSB Category: 6(B)(b)(i)
Sex: Female
Age at injury: 45
Age at award: 49
Date of award: 03 July 1992
Tribunal: Canterbury County Court
Amount of award then: £17,500
Award at February 2001: £22,266

Description of injuries: Disc lesion at L5/S1 level – the first sacral root "bulging partly sequestrated disc" was noted during operation – placed in a plaster jacket – slow undramatic improvement over the following two years – she could only walk slowly – pain-killers taken on a regular basis – suffered regular headaches.

Prognosis: Would remain severely disabled – in need of constant treatment and attention.

1.3.1.3.2.C11 Case No. 10394

Name of case: Kelly v The Post Office

Brief description of injuries: MODERATELY SEVERE BACKINJURY – DAMAGED DISC – SURGERY MIGHT HELP

Reported: [1992] CLY 1650

JSB Category: 6(B)(b)(i)

Sex: Male

Age at injury: 39

Age at award: 49

Date of award: 19 May 1992

Tribunal: QBD

Amount of award then: £17,500

Award at February 2001: £22,182

Description of injuries: Sustained damage to a lumbo-sacral disc including a minor protrusion – probable tear of the anulus. Unable to return to his pre-accident employment – unable to resume pre-accident hobbies.

Prognosis: He had lived with a distressing condition for along time – evidence given that there was a high degree of certainty that a bone graft operation would substantially relieve the symptoms he was suffering.

1.3.1.3.2.C12 Case No. 11138

Name of case: Mayhew v Dacorum BC

Brief description of injuries: BACK – PROLAPSED DISC – LEG – FOOT

Reported: Kemp & Kemp, E3-026; [1996] CLY 2229

JSB Category: 6(B)(a)(iii)

Sex: Female

Age at injury: 52

Age at award: 55

Date of award: 25 March 1996

Tribunal: Milton Keynes County Court

Amount of award then: £18,000

Award at February 2001: £20,923

Description of injuries: Prolapsed disk at L4/5 – nerve root irritation and herniation at L5/S1.

Prognosis: Permanent low back pain – border of the right foot and toes permanently numb – some minor improvement expected – disabilities permanent.

1.3.1.3.2.C13 Case No. 11374

Name of case: Treffrey v Smith

Brief description of injuries: BACK – VERTEBRAE – MULTIPLE FRACTURES

Reported: Kemp & Kemp, E3-027; [1997] CLY 1922

JSB Category: 6(B)(b)(i)

Sex: Female

Age at injury: 17

Age at award: 20

Date of award: 15 October 1996

Tribunal: Bodmin County Court

Amount of award then: £17,500

Award at February 2001: £19,998

Description of injuries: Multiple fractures to vertebrae and ribs – fractures to the fourth metacarpal and elbow.

Prognosis: Her back would always be vulnerable – osteoarthritis was almost a certainty in middle-age.

1.3.1.3.2.C14 Case No. 10068

Award at February 2001: £19,379

See: 1.3.1.1.C11 for details

1.3.1.3.2.C15 Case No. 11375

Name of case: Hodges v Lambeth LBC

Brief description of injuries: BACK – PROLAPSED DISC

Reported: Kemp & Kemp, E3-004; [1997] CLY 1923

JSB Category: 6(B)(b)(i)

Sex: Female

Age at injury: 36

Age at award: 42

Date of award: 09 January 1997

Tribunal: Central London County Court

Amount of award then: £16,000

Award at February 2001: £18,141

Description of injuries: Prolapsed disc in the lower spine – pain and suffering affected the ordinary quality of her life.

Prognosis: At the time of the hearing her condition was permanent – degenerative changes could improve or worsen her condition in the future.

1.3.1.3.2.C16 Case No. 11569

Name of case: Walsh v William Morrison Supermarket Ltd

Brief description of injuries: BACK – FRACTURE TO SPINE

Reported: Kemp & Kemp, K3-030/1; [1998] CLY 1571

JSB Category: 6(B)(b)(i)

Sex: Male

Age at injury: 39

Age at award: 43

Date of award: 30 September 1997

Tribunal: Worcester County Court

Amount of award then: £16,500

Award at February 2001: £18,131

Description of injuries: Fracture to the spine at L5 – unable to work full time – diagnosed as suffering from chronic back pain syndrome, a genuine condition which was unusually incapacitating.

Other points: Pre-existing back pain would not have prevented claimant from working to retirement age.

1.3.1.3.2.C17 Case No. 11376

Name of case: Lill v Wakefield MDC

Brief description of injuries: BACK – DISC PROLAPSE

Reported: Kemp & Kemp, E3-031/1; [1997] CLY 1924

JSB Category: 6(B)(b)(i)

Sex: Male

Age at injury: 24

Age at award: 32

Date of award: 12 September 1997

Tribunal: Pontefract County Court

Amount of award then: £16,000

Award at February 2001: £17,560

Description of injuries: Disc prolapse – depression and mood swings.

Prognosis: He remained vulnerable to further periods of pain – a further six to eighteen months of treatment with anti-depressant drugs – unable to return to heavy work.

Other points: No evidence of degeneration or back problems before the date of the accident.

1.3.1.3.2.C18 Case No. 12011

Name of case: McHugh v Carlisle City Council

Brief description of injuries: BACK – DISC DAMAGE

Reported: Kemp & Kemp, E3-034/1; [2000] 4 CL 154

JSB Category: 6(B)(b)(i)

Sex: Male

Age at injury: 29 and 32

Age at award: 34

Date of award: 26 July 1999

Tribunal: Carlisle County Court

Amount of award then: £14,500

Award at February 2001: £15,279

Description of injuries: M sustained injuries to his back on two occasions – lifting a kerbstone and slipping from a flatbed wagon – both accidents caused low back pain and sciatica.

Prognosis: M sustained a permanent back injury and was permanently unfit for heavy labouring – pre-existing degenerating back condition clouded the case – an operation might be needed in the future on the degenerating disc.

1.3.1.3.2.C19 Case No. 10070

Name of case: Owen v Grimsby and Cleethorpes Transport

Brief description of injuries: BACK INJURY – 3 FRACTURED VERTEBRAE – REASONABLE RECOVERY

Reported: [1992] PIQR Q27; (1991) The Times, February 14; Kemp & Kemp, E3-040; BPILS, I 126; [1990] CLY 1630

JSB Category: 6(B)

Sex: Male

Age at injury: 27

Age at award: 32

Date of award: 12 December 1989

Tribunal: Lincoln County Court

Amount of award then: £10,000

Award at February 2001: £14,622

Description of injuries: Undisplaced fracture of left transverse processes of second, third and fourth lumbar vertebrae – bruising and minor disc protrusion – virtually pain-free after 16 weeks – heavy lifting caused backache – numbness and pain in right thigh needing an operation to free trapped nerve – unfit for heavy lifting.

Prognosis: Possibility of condition improving.

1.3.1.3.2.C20 Case No. 11990

Name of case: Chappel v TDC Motor Factors
Brief description of injuries: BACK – PROLAPSED DISC
Reported: Kemp & Kemp, E3-040; [2000] 3 CL 174
JSB Category: 6(B)(b)(i)
Sex: Male
Age at injury: 34
Age at award: 37
Date of award: 01 November 1999
Tribunal: QBD
Amount of award then: £14,000
Award at February 2001: £14,588

Description of injuries: Pain to the area between the shoulder blades following a traffic accident – no neurological deficit – discharged from hospital with a soft collar – 14 day medical certificate for neck strain – pain in the neck and shoulders subsided but the low back pain became worse – relieved by anti-inflammatories – pain remained significant – referred for physiotherapy – suffered from intractable left-sided sciatica – disc prolapse of L4/L5 diagnosed – discectomy and lateral nerve root decompression was carried out. Two years later C still experienced some back pain which fluctuated daily – reluctant to take painkillers for fear of damaging the lumbar spine further.

Other points: Unable to play golf, play with his children or do jobs around the house.

1.3.1.3.2.C21 Case No. 10072

Name of case: Franks v British Railways Board
Brief description of injuries: BACK INJURY – WEDGING OF 2 VERTEBRAE
Reported: Kemp & Kemp, E3-042; [1990] CLY 1632
JSB Category: 6(B)
Sex: Male
Age at injury: -
Age at award: -
Date of award: 27 February 1990
Tribunal: Not stated
Amount of award then: £10,000
Award at February 2001: £14,446

Description of injuries: Lumbar spinal injury involving wedging of two vertebrae and soft-tissue damage – unable to continue employment – prolonged sitting or standing causes eventual discomfort.

1.3.1.3.2.C22 Case No. 10069

Award at February 2001: £13,324

See: 1.3.1.1.C13 for details

1.3.1.3.2.C23 Case No. 10597

Name of case: Hyland v George
Brief description of injuries: BACK – COMPRESSION FRACTURE OF VERTEBRA – FRACTURED STERNUM
Reported: Kemp & Kemp, E3-051; [1993] CLY 1490
JSB Category: 6(B)(b)
Sex: Male
Age at injury: 28
Age at award: 32
Date of award: 12 August 1993
Tribunal: Liverpool County Court
Amount of award then: £9,500
Award at February 2001: £11,564

Description of injuries: Claimant working in trench when sides collapsed and buried him under heavy weight of soil – fractured sternum – back injuries (compression fracture of T9, minor damage to upper border of T12) – minor twisting injury to neck – unable to do heavy lifting for 9 months – sternum recovered completely after 8 months, all pain and subsequent tenderness subsiding – neck injury also resolved – pain continuing in thoracic spine; claimant taking painkillers regularly.

Prognosis: Pain in lumbarsacral region expected to fully resolve – continuing discomfort in thoracic spine will be permanent, and aggravated by working with heavy weights.

1.3.1.3.2.C24 Case No. 11140

Name of case: Hall v Hampton
Brief description of injuries: BACK – DISC BULGE
Reported: Kemp & Kemp, E3-052; [1996] CLY 2231
JSB Category: 6(B)(b)(ii)
Sex: Female
Age at injury: 61
Age at award: 64
Date of award: 12 July 1996
Tribunal: Plymouth County Court
Amount of award then: £10,000
Award at February 2001: £11,315

Description of injuries: Right sided disk bulge at L4/5.

Prognosis: She was left with a vulnerable back – a significant nuisance – not disabling.

1.3.1.3.2.C25 Case No. 10775

Name of case: Oades v Park

Brief description of injuries: BACK – FRACTURE OF LUMBAR VERTEBRA – FULL RECOVERY EXPECTED

Reported: Kemp & Kemp, E3-053; [1994] CLY 1623

JSB Category: 6(B)(b)

Sex: Male

Age at injury: 18

Age at award: 20

Date of award: 21 October 1994

Tribunal: Slough County Court

Amount of award then: £9,500

Award at February 2001: £11,253

Description of injuries: Road accident – fracture of first lumbar vertebra, with 75 per cent loss of anterior vertebral body height – in hospital 15 days – open reduction and external fixation undertaken – spinal brace worn for 2.5 months – good recovery after 5 months.

Prognosis: Claimant would always suffer mild back pain – initial prognosis that claimant would be able to return to sporting pursuits of badminton and hockey within 1 year – however, 2 years after accident, claimant still experiencing regular sharp lower back pain and still unable to return to sporting activities – full recovery, apart from mild back pain, expected within "a short time".

1.3.1.3.2.C26 Case No. 10398

Name of case: Cassidy v West Country Frozen Foods

Brief description of injuries: SPINE – DAMAGED DISC

Reported: [1992] CLY 1654

JSB Category: 6(B)(b)(ii)

Sex: Female

Age at injury: 22

Age at award: 25

Date of award: 20 February 1992

Tribunal: Plymouth County Court

Amount of award then: £7,750

Award at February 2001: £9,780

Description of injuries: Twisted left leg – compressed spine – soft-tissue injury to the lower back – probable damage to a disc – knee injury cleared up quickly – previously a "fitness fanatic" – after the accident she restricted life and actions accordingly.

Prognosis: Back injury would be a handicap – not great but not too insignificant to be ignored – more risk of degenerative disease in 15-20 years time – she would suffer more back ache in pregnancy and while her children were young.

1.3.1.3.2.C27 Case No. 11383

Name of case: Warburton v Halliwell

Brief description of injuries: BACK – DISC PROTRUSION

Reported: Kemp & Kemp, E3-069; [1997] CLY 1931

JSB Category: 6(B)(b)(ii)

Sex: Male

Age at injury: 32

Age at award: 36

Date of award: 03 October 1996

Tribunal: Sheffield County Court

Amount of award then: £8,500

Award at February 2001: £9,506

Description of injuries: Pain and stiffness to the lower back – disc protrusion at L5/S1 – radial tear at L5.

Prognosis: There was no prospect of improvement in the symptoms.

Other points: Vulnerable to redundancy – thereafter at a disadvantage in the labour market due to his condition.

1.3.1.3.2.C28 Case No. 10599

Name of case: Coonan v Rashid & Rashid

Brief description of injuries: BACK – DISC PROLAPSE

Reported: Kemp & Kemp, E3-071; [1993] CLY 1492

JSB Category: 6(B)(b)

Sex: Female

Age at injury: 36

Age at award: 40

Date of award: 07 October 1993

Tribunal: Brentford County Court

Amount of award then: £7,500

Award at February 2001: £9,097

Description of injuries: Slip and fall in shower, twisting injury to lower back – pain in right knee, calf and coccyx, radiating into buttock – sciatica on right side – diagnosis of large inter-vertebral disc prolapse – operation to remove sequestrated disc – operation cured sciatica.

Prognosis: Back pain from prolonged sitting or exertion still existent at time of trial, also muscle spasm in buttocks and calf – these symptoms likely to continue for rest of claimant's life (still in protective corset 4 years after injury).

Other points: Claimant has also had long-term very serious hearing problem – in combination with these injuries, this has meant unemployment since time of incident – social life non-existent.

1.3.1.3.2.C29 Case No. 10960

Name of case: Re Roberts-Smith

Brief description of injuries: BACK INJURY – SURGERY TO REMOVE DISC – VULNERABLE SPINE

Reported: Kemp & Kemp, E3-081; [1995] CLY 1711

JSB Category: 6(B)(b)(ii)

Sex: Female

Age at injury: 27

Age at award: 30

Date of award: 05 June 1995

Tribunal: CICB, York

Amount of award then: £7,500

Award at February 2001: £8,611

Description of injuries: Group assistant at centre for care of mentally handicapped was injured when violent patient kicked her, causing her to collide with door handle – appellant suffered immediate low back pain and left work – rested for two days without improvement – went to see GP who initially advised further rest and pain-killers – one week after incident GP referred her to consultant orthopaedic surgeon who diagnosed a lumbar disc prolapse and left-sided sciatica – treated by traction for seven days without improvement, whereafter an MRI scan revealed central disc protrusion with extension to the left side at L5/S1 – laminectomy carried out in May 1992 and the plaintiff was discharged ten days later – operation was success in that appellant returned to work in November 1992 and was able to do light duties – residual symptoms were that she had lost reflex in right knee and ankle – immediately after operation had to wear support tights to assist circulation – no longer necessary because of exercise to thigh – continued to experience some nagging aches in back especially first thing in morning and last thing at night – could no longer walk long distances and had difficulty carrying same volume of shopping as she did before incident and household tasks such as vacuuming and washing up were difficult – had a well-healed post-operative scar about five inches in length at base of spine – pre-incident activities of karate and fitness exercises no longer possible – incident "precipitated the symptoms in a spine that was vulnerable to it".

1.3.1.3.2.C30 Case No. 11144

Name of case: Re Goldsmith

Brief description of injuries: BACK – PROLAPSED DISC

Reported: Kemp & Kemp, E3-085; [1996] CLY 2235

JSB Category: 6(B)(b)(ii)

Sex: Male

Age at injury: 50

Age at award: 55

Date of award: 01 July 1996

Tribunal: CICB

Amount of award then: £7,500

Award at February 2001: £8,465

Description of injuries: Low back injury – quite serious disc prolapse – 15 per cent disability – medically retired seven months after the accident – lifestyle affected.

Prognosis: Risk of arthritic change in the future.

Other points: Pre-existing condition had been pain-free for two years before the accident.

1.3.1.3.2.C31 Case No. 10602

Name of case: Chhokran v Southampton and South-West Hampshire Health Authority

Brief description of injuries: BACK – FRACTURED SACRUM/COCCYX

Reported: Kemp & Kemp, G2-042; [1993] CLY 1495

JSB Category: 6(B)(b)

Sex: Female

Age at injury: 37

Age at award: 41

Date of award: 20 July 1993

Tribunal: Willesden County Court

Amount of award then: £6,500

Award at February 2001: £7,946

Description of injuries: Slip and fall – displaced fracture of lower end of sacrum at sacro – coccygeal junction (unusual injury) – anterior displacement of first portion of coccyx – fracture healed – injury to coccyx still causing pain after sitting for prolonged period, rendering worship (at Sikh temple) painful and rendering – claimant able to continue in previous non-sedentary employment as catering assistant.

Prognosis: Pain after sitting for long periods will render claimant unfit for any sedentary work, if necessary or arising in the future.

1.3.1.3.2.C32 Case No. 10779

Name of case: Jones v Liverpool City Council

Brief description of injuries: BACK – DISC PROLAPSE

Reported: Kemp & Kemp, E3-113; [1994] CLY 1628

JSB Category: 6(B)(c)

Sex: Male

Age at injury: 30

Age at award: 33

Date of award: 30 November 1993

Tribunal: Liverpool County Court

Amount of award then: £3,250

Award at February 2001: £3,948

Description of injuries: Claimant, gardener, slipped over and twisted back at work – judge's finding of structural injury to lumbar spine, on balance of probabilities some damage to an intervertebral disc, probably a minor disc prolapse – claimant off work 11 weeks, and took painkillers and anti-inflammatory drugs – 2 "flare-ups", one 10 months after accident and one approximately 2 years after accident, the second involving 11 weeks off work, but exacerbated by an unrelated neck condition – some minor symptoms of discomfiture in back at time of trial.

Prognosis: Judge accepted that, 3 or 4 years from date of accident, claimant would be in no worse a position in relation to vulnerability in back than any other gardener doing heavy work.

1.3.1.3.2.C33 Case No. 11270

Name of case: Hunt v Unigate Dairies Ltd

Brief description of injuries: BACK – DISC PROLAPSE – 12 MONTH ACCELERATION

Reported: Kemp & Kemp, E3-118; [1996] CLY 2363

JSB Category: 2(B)(c)

Sex: Male

Age at injury: 29

Age at award: 33

Date of award: 24 May 1996

Tribunal: Swansea County Court

Amount of award then: £2,750

Award at February 2001: £3,094

Description of injuries: Traumatic prolapse of the lumbo-sacral disk – pre-existing back problems were accelerated by twelve months.

Prognosis: Pre-existing back problem would have put him out of heavy manual work within one year.

1.3.1.3.2.1 Back fracture, disc and other injury

1.3.1.3.2.1.C1 Case No. 10317

Name of case: Re Finegold

Brief description of injuries: SPINE – FRACTURE AND PARALYSIS – PARALYSIS OF LEG – HYSTERICAL CONVERSION

Reported: Kemp & Kemp, C4-016; [1992] CLY 1573

JSB Category: 6(K)(b)(ii)

Sex: Male

Age at injury: 33

Age at award: -

Date of award: 21 July 1992

Tribunal: CICB

Amount of award then: £40,000

Award at February 2001: £54,115

Description of injuries: Crush fracture to vertebra with sensory loss and paralysis of the right leg – subconscious mechanism causing an hysterical conversion or perpetuation – bladder weakness and frequency of micturition – loss of sensation during intercourse – stiff gait when walking.

Prognosis: Career impairment through having to leave the police force.

1.3.1.3.2.1.C2 Case No. 11611

Name of case: Eardley v North West Anglia Health Care NHS Trust

Brief description of injuries: BACK – DISC PROLAPSE – LOSS OF SEXUAL RELATIONS

Reported: Kemp & Kemp, E3-004/1; [1998] CLY 1613

JSB Category: 6(B)(a)(ii)

Sex: Female

Age at injury: 40

Age at award: 44

Date of award: 27 June 1997

Tribunal: QBD

Amount of award then: £37,000

Award at February 2001: £43,350

Description of injuries: Prolapse of L4/5 – damage to tissues and nerve roots – loss of sensitivity in the lower left leg – severe back pain and loss of function – no treatment resulted in lasting benefit.

Prognosis: E's condition was expected to be permanent – constant gnawing pain across her back and lower left leg – no prospect of returning to her job – unable to contemplate sexual relations – claimant faced a lonely future.

1.3.1.3.2.1.C3 Case No. 10320

Name of case: Anderson v Davies and Anderson

Brief description of injuries: SPINE – CRUSH FRACTURE – PTSD – MANIC DEPRESSION EXACERBATED

Reported: [1993] PIQR Q87; Kemp & Kemp, C4-030; BPILS I225,305, XV 1007; [1992] CLY 1576

JSB Category: 3(A)(a)

Sex: Male

Age at injury: 46

Age at award: 55

Date of award: 25 September 1992

Tribunal: QBD

Amount of award then: £25,000

Award at February 2001: £32,331

Description of injuries: T8 crush fracture to the spine – considerable bruising – nervous shock – post-traumatic stress disorder – initially suffered nightmares and hypochondriacle thoughts – developed into full-blown manic depression.

Prognosis: Loss of promising career – forced to give up lecturing post two years after the accident and private physiotherapy practice some time later – unlikely to return to economically viable work.

1.3.1.3.2.1.C4 Case No. 11137

Name of case: Turnbull v Kenneth

Brief description of injuries: BACK – COMPRESSION FRACTURE – WHIPLASH

Reported: Kemp & Kemp, E3-017; [1996] CLY 2228

JSB Category: 6(B)(a)(iii)

Sex: Male

Age at injury: 30

Age at award: 34

Date of award: 27 March 1996

Tribunal: QBD

Amount of award then: £20,000

Award at February 2001: £23,367

Description of injuries: Wedge compression fracture at L1 and whiplash injury to the cervical spine.

Prognosis: Intermittent lower back pain unlikely to be resolved – movement in the cervical spine reduced by 50 per cent – spine likely to become stiffer in the next 15 to 20 years – secondary facetal arthritis likely.

1.3.1.3.2.1.C5 Case No. 10028

Award at February 2001: £16,040

See: 1.2.3.2.1.C9 for details

1.3.1.3.2.1.C6 Case No. 10777

Name of case: Seymour v Passmore International

Brief description of injuries: BACK – DISC PROTRUSION – FLUCTUATING DISCOMFORT

Reported: Kemp & Kemp, E3-090; [1994] CLY 1626

JSB Category: 6(B)

Sex: Male

Age at injury: 42

Age at award: 46

Date of award: 14 June 1994

Tribunal: Maidstone County Court

Amount of award then: £6,500

Award at February 2001: £7,726

Description of injuries: Slip at work – small disc protrusion at L5/S1 – absent at work for number of short periods in following 14-week period – able to continue in work, with some discomfort, until made redundant 2 years later, then unemployed 18 months – company's fortunes fluctuated; claimant re-employed, then kept on by successor company when company folded, and still employed at time of trial.

Prognosis: Prognosis of fluctuating discomfort – however, if claimant careful with movement and posture, possibility of staying in full employment to retirement age – claimant would be handicapped to a certain extent on open labour market; certain tasks impossible for him to perform.

SECTION 1.4
DAMAGE TO UPPER LIMBS

1.4.1 SHOULDER INJURY

1.4.1.C1 Case No. 10616

Name of case: Ellinger v Riverside Health Authority

Brief description of injuries: SHOULDER – NERVE DAMAGE

Reported: Kemp & Kemp, H2-013; [1993] CLY 1511

JSB Category: 6(D)(a); 8

Sex: Female

Age at injury: 28

Age at award: 33

Date of award: 4 October 1992

Tribunal: QBD

Amount of award then: £30,000

Award at February 2001: £39,177

Description of injuries: Claimant, right – handed, suffered partial left accessory nerve lesion during negligently – performed minor operation to remove lump on neck – consequent wasting of left trapezius muscle – significant limitation of movement in left shoulder – difficulty in lifting weights with left arm – acute pain in left shoulder and neck, subsiding over 2 years to moderate ache, present almost continuously, and worsening with use of shoulder – sexual relations with husband painful – claimant keen sportswoman, unable to continue with nearly all the large number of outdoor activities pursued prior to injury – inability to perform many of the tasks required to care for baby, particularly lifting and carrying – cosmetic disability; shoulders now asymmetrical due to muscle wastage and 6 cm scar evident on neck from 2 subsequent (unsuccessful) operations to rectify damage.

Prognosis: Nanny and home help would now always be required – waterbed required to help sleep – work unaffected by injury, although pain experienced driving to and from office, using keyboard and carrying books – no prospect of improvement in condition.

1.4.1.C2 Case No. 10798

Name of case: Giles v Pontefract Health Authority

Brief description of injuries: SHOULDER – DYSTOCIA

Reported: Kemp & Kemp, H2-014; [1994] CLY 1647

JSB Category: 6(D)(a)

Sex: Male

Age at injury: at birth

Age at award: 9

Date of award: 23 June 1993

Tribunal: Leeds High Court

Amount of award then: £25,000

Award at February 2001: £31,938

Description of injuries: Dystocia of left shoulder at birth – consequent damage to brachial plexus – Duchenne Erb plexus paralysis – musculature of left shoulder and left side of chest less well developed than the right – left scapula 2-3cm higher than right – left arm thinner and less well – developed than right and unable to be elevated or abducted above 135 degrees – good elbow movement, but limited pronation or supination of arm – hand and finger movements good, but manoeuvring hand into right position to perform complex tasks difficult and often impossible – tendency to pass objects from left to right hand to be able to better manage them – difficulty holding fork in left hand – left arm held in abnormal posture when running; elbow flexed, arm internally rotated and forearm pronated – no sensory loss – significant cosmetic disability – some teasing at school.

Prognosis: Claimant coping well with everyday tasks (eg fastening own buttons), but injury permanent and no improvement expected – lifting heavy weights with both arms or deft bimanual tasks (or those requiring speed, such as keyboarding), would always be beyond him – fine manipulative tasks, when claimant could take time, still possible – range of social and sporting activities not open to him.

1.4.1.C3 Case No. 10972

Name of case: Mills v Morris Motorcycles

Brief description of injuries: SHOULDER – 90% LOSS OF MOVEMENT

Reported: Kemp & Kemp, H2-016; [1995] CLY 1723

JSB Category: 6(D)(a)

Sex: Male

Age at injury: 41

Age at award: 45

Date of award: 12 April 1994

Tribunal: Cardiff County Court

Amount of award then: £12,500

Award at February 2001: £15,073

Description of injuries: In road accident plaintiff suffered number of injuries, most serious of which was to right shoulder – also injured neck, lumbar spine, and left knee but over period of three to four months these injuries and discomfort therefrom became minimal – also lost and damaged number of teeth – shoulder injury left plaintiff with permanent partial incapacity together with considerable scar over right shoulder – also suffered fracture of right humerus involving insertion of rotator cuff muscles into humeral head – external rotation of shoulder was restricted, 90 per cent of movement having been lost – infraspinatus muscle over right shoulder was wasted and there was expected to be permanent restriction of movement in right shoulder which would restrict ability to carry out heavy work above head – unable to continue in pre-accident employment with MOD as airframe fitter.

1.4.1.C4 Case No. 10416

Name of case: Nicholson v Hallamshire Construction

Brief description of injuries: WRENCHING INJURY TO RIGHT SHOULDER

Reported: [1992] CLY 1672

JSB Category: 6(D)(a)

Sex: Male

Age at injury: 61

Age at award: 66

Date of award: 29 November 1991

Tribunal: Peterborough County Court

Amount of award then: £9,500

Award at February 2001: £12,050

Description of injuries: Violent wrenching injury to the shoulder with dislocation – intensive course of pain-killing injections – manipulation under general anaesthetic twice – diagnosis of traction lesion of the right shoulder, producing post-traumatic pericapsulitis of the shoulder.

Prognosis: Able to continue his work in a managerial capacity to retirement at age 65.

1.4.1.C5 Case No. 11161

Name of case: Lewis v Tesco Stores Ltd

Brief description of injuries: SHOULDER – TROCHANTERIC BURSITIS

Reported: Kemp & Kemp, G2-038/1; [1996] CLY 2252

JSB Category: 6(C)(c)

Sex: Female

Age at injury: 63

Age at award: 68

Date of award: 19 February 1996

Tribunal: Luton County Court

Amount of award then: £10,000

Award at February 2001: £11,430

Description of injuries: Wrenching injury to the right shoulder – severe bruising to the left hip – trochanteric bursitis – the shoulder had improved dramatically within ten months – hip worsened over five years.

Prognosis: She would continue to suffer from her disability for the rest of her life.

Other points: Her quality of life was significantly affected.

1.4.1.C6 Case No. 10617

Name of case: Bonita Bryg v Fuji Television Network Inc

Brief description of injuries: SHOULDER

Reported: Kemp & Kemp, H2-017; [1993] CLY 1512

JSB Category: 6(D)(a)

Sex: Female

Age at injury: 37

Age at award: 43

Date of award: 02 June 1993

Tribunal: Central London County Court

Amount of award then: £9,000

Award at February 2001: £10,979

Description of injuries: Claimant professional dancer in Japanese production of "Starlight Express" on roller skates – collision with another performer on stage, fall onto dominant right shoulder – severe pain, arm in sling for 3 weeks, painkilling injections – unable to dance at all for 3 weeks, thereafter largely restricted to teaching and supervising, not performing – unable to do some housework or dress herself, as unable to reach behind back – sexual relations adversely affected – depression from constant pain in shoulder – eventual referral to orthopaedic surgeon – diagnosis of fracture of front right acromion and subluxation of acromio – clavicular joint – decompression acromioplasty operation carried out – operation relieved many symptoms – minor difficulties still remaining; discomfort when reaching across body with right arm, inability to sleep on right side, ache occasionally radiating to neck, exacerbated by housework and driving.

Other points: Claimant at crucial point in career, at transition from dancer to assistant choreographer when injury occurred – special damages award reflected her inability to take up such post from time of injury (December 1987) until late 1991 – no award made for loss of publicity.

1.4.1.C7 Case No. 11636

Name of case: Cotton v Freddie Martin (Scaffolding) Ltd

Brief description of injuries: SHOULDER – SEVERE LIMITATION OF MOVEMENT

Reported: Kemp & Kemp, PRH-005; [1998] CLY 1638

JSB Category: 6(D)(a)

Sex: Male

Age at injury: 31

Age at award: –

Date of award: 01 July 1998

Tribunal: CA

Amount of award then: £10,000

Award at February 2001: £10,560

Description of injuries: Fractures of the insertion of shoulder muscles and shoulder joint – limited abduction to 70 degrees – forward flexion to 60 degrees – severely limited internal and external rotation.

1.4.1.C8 Case No. 10418

Name of case: Re Laverick

Brief description of injuries: RIGHT SHOULDER INJURY

Reported: [1992] CLY 1674

JSB Category: 6(D)(a)

Sex: Female

Age at injury: 40

Age at award: 43

Date of award: 15 July 1992

Tribunal: CICB Durham

Amount of award then: £7,500

Award at February 2001: £9,294

Description of injuries: Rotor cuff lesion to the right shoulder – upper arm stiff and painful – change in work required lifting which caused a relapse – right arm elevation restricted by ten degrees and still suffering from a dull ache in the shoulder at the time of the hearing.

Prognosis: Residual symptoms were unlikely to resolve completely.

1.4.1.C9 Case No. 10228

Name of case: Re Farley

Brief description of injuries: ASSAULT – ROTOR CUFF INJURY – LEFT SHOULDER – 20% DISABLED

Reported: Kemp & Kemp, H2-020; [1991] CLY 1425

JSB Category: 6(D)(a)

Sex: Male

Age at injury: 49

Age at award: 51

Date of award: 15 October 1990

Tribunal: CICB, Newcastle

Amount of award then: £6,500

Award at February 2001: £8,580

Description of injuries: Assault – rotor cuff injury to the left shoulder – great difficulty in raising the left arm from the side – assessed by the DSS as 20 per cent disabled for life – there was significant pre-accident degenerative change in the shoulder.

Prognosis: F would be able to continue in his work until age 60.

1.4.1.C10 Case No. 11164

Name of case: Steadman v Gaffar

Brief description of injuries: ARM – FRACTURE – SHOULDER

Reported: Kemp & Kemp, H2-020/1; [1996] CLY 2255

JSB Category: 6(F)(c)

Sex: Female

Age at injury: 63

Age at award: 68

Date of award: 10 April 1996

Tribunal: Croydon County Court

Amount of award then: £7,500

Award at February 2001: £8,453

Description of injuries: Fracture of the right humerus – dislocation of the right shoulder – continuing permanent problems with lifting – right handed but had to rely on her left hand more – no muscular wasting or neurological deficit.

1.4.1.C11 Case No. 10618

Name of case: Creedon v Grange Construction and Sehmis Builders Merchants

Brief description of injuries: SHOULDER – FRACTURED CLAVICLE AND SOFT-TISSUE INJURY TO SHOULDER

Reported: Kemp & Kemp, H2-021; [1993] CLY 1513

JSB Category: 6(D)(a), 6(D)(d)

Sex: Male

Age at injury: 41

Age at award: about 46

Date of award: 24 March 1993

Tribunal: Brentford County Court

Amount of award then: £6,500

Award at February 2001: £8,026

Description of injuries: Fall from motorcycle after skidding on sand left on road by defendants – loss of consciousness for a few minutes – right shoulder very painful and stiff – fracture of shaft of right clavicle and soft-tissue injury to shoulder diagnosed – right shoulder abduction limited to 150 degrees – extension and internal rotation limited to two-thirds of normal range – lump over clavicle on right side – clavicle healed well, but with callous formation – loss of movement in shoulder improved by time of trial; abduction practically full – evidence of crepitus, particularly in region of acromio-clavicular joint – limitation of movement and discomfort when putting hand behind back – residual stiffness in right shoulder – claimant's medical expert assessed loss of function in shoulder at 20 per cent in total.

1.4.1.C12 Case No. 11165

Name of case: Yamoah v Woolworths PLC

Brief description of injuries: SHOULDER – DISLOCATION

Reported: Kemp & Kemp, H2-020/2[1996] CLY 2256

JSB Category: 6(D)(a)

Sex: Male

Age at injury: 19

Age at award: 24

Date of award: 12 February 1996

Tribunal: Wandsworth County Court

Amount of award then: £7,000

Award at February 2001: £7,979

Description of injuries: Dislocated right shoulder.

Prognosis: Discomfort and difficulty with lifting was highly likely to be permanent – subject to the possibility of surgery which might or might not be successful, symptoms were likely to be permanent.

1.4.1.C13 Case No. 10419

Name of case: Richardson v Durham County Council

Brief description of injuries: SHOULDER INJURY – TEAR IN ROTOR CUFF – CONTINUING WEAKNESS

Reported: [1992] CLY 1675

JSB Category: 6(D)(a)

Sex: Female

Age at injury: 60

Age at award: 66

Date of award: 19 June 1992

Tribunal: Newcastle upon Tyne County Court

Amount of award then: £6,000

Award at February 2001: £7,408

Description of injuries: Tear in the rotor cuff – the acrimio-clavicular joint was divided, the rotor cuff decompressed and the coraco-acromial ligament was divided – hobby of dancing five nights a week no longer open to her – unable to perform heavier household tasks.

Prognosis: Medical opinion was divided as to whether the accident had afflicted a totally a symptomatic neck with degenerative changes – or whether slight neck restrictions were an indirect consequence of restricted movements in the shoulders.

1.4.1.C14 Case No. 11632

Name of case: Morant v Amtico Co Ltd
Brief description of injuries: SHOULDER – 10-YEAR ACCELERATION
Reported: Kemp & Kemp, H2-024/2; [1998] CLY 1634
JSB Category: 6(D)(b)
Sex: Male
Age at injury: 47
Age at award: 51
Date of award: 03 December 1997
Tribunal: Coventry County Court
Amount of award then: £6,250
Award at February 2001: £6,719
Description of injuries: Soft-tissue injury to the shoulder – reduction in the mobility of the shoulder – 20 per cent on abduction and 60 per cent on flexion – pre-existing spondylosis rendered symptomatic by the accident.
Prognosis: Spondylitic symptoms had been accelerated by up to 10 years.

1.4.1.C15 Case No. 11633

Name of case: Slotz Vending and Egleton v Avandero UK Ltd
Brief description of injuries: SHOULDER
Reported: [1998] CLY 1635
JSB Category: 6(D)(b)
Sex: Male
Age at injury: 34
Age at award: 35
Date of award: 01 July 1998
Tribunal: Reading County Court
Amount of award then: £6,000
Award at February 2001: £6,331
Description of injuries: Injury caused constant pain to the shoulder – audible crepitus – affected sleeping, lifting, getting out of chairs and sex life – within 7 months of the date of the accident symptoms largely resolved.
Prognosis: Residual symptoms would be permanent.

1.4.1.C16 Case No. 11634

Name of case: Noon v Princess Alice Hospice
Brief description of injuries: SHOULDER
Reported: (1998) 98 (6) QR 7; Kemp & Kemp, H2-025/1/1; [1998] CLY 1636
JSB Category: 6(D)(b)
Sex: Female
Age at injury: 88
Age at award: 90
Date of award: 01 July 1998
Tribunal: Epsom County Court
Amount of award then: £5,850
Award at February 2001: £6,173
Description of injuries: Blow to the left shoulder and back of the head – persistent tenderness – restricted movement.
Prognosis: Stiffness was effectively permanent.
Other points: Damages were discounted due to the age of the claimant.

1.4.1.C17 Case No. 10799

Name of case: Re Muff
Brief description of injuries: SHOULDER – DISLOCATION
Reported: Kemp & Kemp, H2-019; [1994] CLY 1648
JSB Category: 6(D)(a)
Sex: Male
Age at injury: 46
Age at award: 48
Date of award: 25 March 1994
Tribunal: CICB, York
Amount of award then: £5,000
Award at February 2001: £6,035
Description of injuries: Claimant assaulted by cohabitee of his estranged wife – anterior dislocation of left shoulder – shoulder immobilised with bandage for 3 weeks – thereafter, permanent sensation of discomfort, exacerbated by any form of heavy work; considerable difficulty caused to claimant as he was in manual employment – discomfort disrupted sleep – abduction limited to 10 degrees above horizontal.
Prognosis: Unlikely to be any further improvement – claimant's employment secure, but claimant gave evidence that he felt he would be at a disadvantage if placed on open labour market.
Other points: Award reduced from £7,500.

1.4.1.C18 Case No. 11407

Name of case: Rucastle v Cumberland Motor Services Ltd

Brief description of injuries: SHOULDER – BRUISING

Reported: Kemp & Kemp, H2-025; [1997] CLY 1956

JSB Category: 6(D)(b)

Sex: Male

Age at injury: 49

Age at award: 53

Date of award: 26 July 1996

Tribunal: Carlisle County Court

Amount of award then: £5,250

Award at February 2001: £5,925

Description of injuries: Bruising injury to the shoulder.

Prognosis: Pre-existing osteoarthritic changes were made symptomatic and accelerated by the injury.

Other points: If he lost his present work he would be at a permanent disadvantage in the labour market.

1.4.1.C19 Case No. 11408

Name of case: Ullrich v Carlisle City Council

Brief description of injuries: SHOULDER – DAMAGED CLAVICLE

Reported: Kemp & Kemp, H2-025/2; [1997] CLY 1957

JSB Category: 6(D)(b)

Sex: Male

Age at injury: 35

Age at award: 38

Date of award: 26 July 1996

Tribunal: Carlisle County Court

Amount of award then: £5,000

Award at February 2001: £5,643

Description of injuries: Damage to the capsule of the acromioclavicular joint – bruising to the deltoid muscle and rotor cuff.

Prognosis: At the time of the hearing there were some residual symptoms attributable to the accident.

1.4.1.C20 Case No. 10954

Name of case: Brown v Ledson and Billington

Brief description of injuries: SHOULDER – SPRAIN – MINOR NECK SYMPTOMS

Reported: Kemp & Kemp, H2-026; [1995] CLY 1705

JSB Category: 6(D)(b)

Sex: Male

Age at injury: 15

Age at award: 17

Date of award: 23 November 1994

Tribunal: Southport County Court

Amount of award then: £4,500

Award at February 2001: £5,327

Description of injuries: Plaintiff was front seat-passenger in motorvehicle involved in collision with motorcycle – suffered strain to right shoulder and neck, and bruising and swelling of right shoulder – bruising and swelling resolved quickly, but he wore a sling on and off for six weeks – plaintiff underwent course of physiotherapy for 10 weeks and later for further three weeks.

Prognosis: Permanent residual discomfort of a minor nature in the neck.

1.4.1.C21 Case No. 11449

Name of case: Re Dooler

Brief description of injuries: SHOULDER – SCAR

Reported: Kemp & Kemp, K2-033; [1997] CLY 1998

JSB Category: 8

Sex: Female

Age at injury: 11

Age at award: 14

Date of award: 02 April 1997

Tribunal: Doncaster County Court (Foster J)

Amount of award then: £4,500

Award at February 2001: £4,952

Description of injuries: Gravel lacerations to the shoulder – purple circular scar measuring 4.5cms in diameter – slight concave deformity due to fat loss beneath the scar.

Prognosis: No psychological sequelae – embarrassed by the scar – it was not felt to be suitable for scar revision surgery.

1.4.1.C22 Case No. 11635

Name of case: Curphy v Ward

Brief description of injuries: SHOULDER – ROTOR CUFF TEAR

Reported: Kemp & Kemp, H2-027/4; [1998] CLY 1637

JSB Category: 6(D)(b)

Sex: Male

Age at injury: 61

Age at award: 63

Date of award: 31 July 1997

Tribunal: Kendal County Court

Amount of award then: £4,500

Award at February 2001: £4,914

Description of injuries: Wrenching injury to the shoulder – probable tear of the rotor cuff.

Prognosis: Permanent residual disability – limited internal rotation of the arm – severe symptoms were not expected to ensue.

1.4.1.C23 Case No. 10421

Name of case: Knight v Thamesdown Borough Council

Brief description of injuries: DISLOCATION OF THE SHOULDER – NUMBNESS AND POOR GRIP – ALMOST COMPLETE RECOVERY

Reported: Kemp & Kemp, H2-030; [1992] CLY 1677

JSB Category: 6(D)(b)

Sex: Male

Age at injury: 35

Age at award: 40

Date of award: 02 November 1992

Tribunal: Swindon County Court

Amount of award then: £3,750

Award at February 2001: £4,617

Description of injuries: Dislocation of the right shoulder with an avulsion of the greater tuberosity – minor laceration to the left groin causing partial injury to the medial femoral cutaneous nerve – produced a varicole – off work for ten weeks – one year after the accident there was occasional pain every two or three months – numbness and poor grip in the right hand – still suffering minor discomfort at the time of the trial.

Prognosis: Small likelihood of recurrent dislocation – degenerative arthritis very unlikely.

1.4.1.C24 Case No. 10079

Name of case: Lennon v McDonald

Brief description of injuries: FROZEN SHOULDER

Reported: Kemp & Kemp, H2-029; [1990] CLY 1645

JSB Category: 6(D)

Sex: Female

Age at injury: 76

Age at award: 79

Date of award: 01 February 1990

Tribunal: Coventry County Court

Amount of award then: £2,750

Award at February 2001: £3,935

Description of injuries: Was thrown onto right shoulder, causing "frozen shoulder" from soft-tissue injury – made good recovery from minor injuries such as bruising and minor injuries to hips and ankle.

Prognosis: After three years still some stiffness and pain in shoulder – could not sleep on right side – could not carry weights or reach up with her right arm – continuing symptoms would gradually improve.

1.4.1.C25 Case No. 10973

Name of case: Blanche v Brown

Brief description of injuries: SHOULDER – SUBLUXATION – ALMOST FULL RECOVERY AFTER 3 MONTHS

Reported: Kemp & Kemp, H2-030; [1995] CLY 1724

JSB Category: 6(D)(c)

Sex: Male

Age at injury: 24

Age at award: 28

Date of award: 11 April 1995

Tribunal: Exeter County Court

Amount of award then: £3,250

Award at February 2001: £3,752

Description of injuries: In road traffic accident plaintiff suffered partial subluxation of right acromio-clavicular joint and some superficial grazing to shoulder and knees – not detained in hospital – right arm placed in sling which he wore for about a month after accident – unable to return to work as self-employed decorator and artexer for about five weeks – thereafter experienced some difficulty at work – "back to normal" after about three months save for some aching in right shoulder when working with arm above head – would generally recover from this very quickly if he held his arm by his side – no restriction of movement in shoulder.

Prognosis: The prognosis was that he would continue to suffer aching when working with arm above head, otherwise there were no residual symptoms – very small risk of developing increased symptoms due to future onset of arthritis – was left with noticeably prominent end of right clavicle.

1.4.1.C26 Case No. 11932

Name of case: Brookes v T Elmes & Sons Ltd

Brief description of injuries: SHOULDER – SOME PERMANENT EFFECTS

Reported: Kemp & Kemp, K2-047; [1999] CLY 1596

JSB Category: 6(D)(c)

Sex: Male

Age at injury: 29

Age at award: 33

Date of award: 25 February 1999

Tribunal: Luton County Court

Amount of award then: £3,000

Award at February 2001: £3,152

Description of injuries: Soft-tissue strain to right shoulder – arm placed in sling – claimant off work for 6 weeks – restricted to light duties on return; aware of niggling ache – 7 months later, reasonably good recovery, and improvement continuing – full recovery 14-15 months after accident – claimant's hobby of weightlifting restricted by injury – when claimant returned to weightlifting, 15 months after accident, he found his ability had been affected – claimant thus gave up weight training altogether, as he feared it would cause unequal weight distribution across his body.

Prognosis: No long-term disability.

1.4.1.C27 Case No. 10862

Name of case: Galloway v Hampshire County Council

Brief description of injuries: SHOULDER – CLAVICLE

Reported: Kemp & Kemp, H2-032; [1994] CLY 1713

JSB Category: 6(D)(d)

Sex: Male

Age at injury: 18

Age at award: 20

Date of award: 10 October 1994

Tribunal: Basingstoke County Court

Amount of award then: £2,500

Award at February 2001: £2,961

Description of injuries: Claimant fell off motorcycle due to uneven road surface – mid-shaft fracture of left (non-dominant) clavicle – some disruption of acromio-clavicular joint – arm in sling, and claimant off work, for 3 weeks – pain resolved after 8 weeks – discomfort when lying on left side for 6 months – minor residual deformity in middle of clavicle at fracture site.

Prognosis: No long-term disability or disadvantage on labour market expected – likelihood of continuing transient discomfort when leaning on left elbow for long periods.

1.4.1.C28 Case No. 10657

Name of case: Foster v Appleton

Brief description of injuries: SHOULDER – SCAR

Reported: Kemp & Kemp, H2-033; [1993] CLY 1553

JSB Category: 8

Sex: Male

Age at injury: 26

Age at award: 30

Date of award: 14 January 1993

Tribunal: Oldham County Court

Amount of award then: £2,250

Award at February 2001: £2,806

Description of injuries: Attacked by dog – laceration to left shoulder – 2 lacerations to left forearm – 2 lacerations to left thigh – permanent scarring – worst scar is on shoulder, upper part of scar being 1 cm broad and 4 cm long – claimant made substantial recovery from lacerations in 2 weeks – not particularly anxious about scarring – scar on shoulder associated with aching at end of hard day's work.

1.4.1.C29 Case No. 11741

Name of case: Buckle v Brown

Brief description of injuries: SHOULDER – COLLAR BONE

Reported: Kemp & Kemp, H2-034; [1998] CLY 1744

JSB Category: 6(D)(d); 5(A)

Sex: Female

Age at injury: 47

Age at award: 48

Date of award: 01 June 1998

Tribunal: Cardiff County Court

Amount of award then: £2,500

Award at February 2001: £2,632

Description of injuries: Fracture to the left clavicle – bruising to the chest.

Prognosis: Excellent prognosis – permanent bony lump at the site of the fracture would cause no functional difficulty.

1.4.1.C30 Case No. 11228

Name of case: Abbott, Re: Sub Nom. Abbott v Roebuck

Brief description of injuries: SHOULDER – TRAPEZIUM – POSSIBLE FRACTURE

Reported: Kemp & Kemp, H6-050/2; [1996] CLY 2320

JSB Category: 6(F)

Sex: Male

Age at injury: 18

Age at award: 22

Date of award: 10 October 1995

Tribunal: Bromley County Court

Amount of award then: £2,250

Award at February 2001: £2,583

Description of injuries: Changes suggestive of a fracture to the trapezium.

Prognosis: The on-going symptoms were expected to resolve in the following three to six months.

Other points: There was some doubt as to whether the trapezium had been fractured.

1.4.1.C31 Case No. 10485

Name of case: Chatham v Hinton Poultry

Brief description of injuries: SEVERE WRENCHING OF RIGHT SHOULDER

Reported: Kemp & Kemp, K2-070; [1992] CLY 1741

JSB Category: 6(D)(c)

Sex: Male

Age at injury: 25

Age at award: 26

Date of award: 09 October 1991

Tribunal: Bath County Court

Amount of award then: £2,000

Award at February 2001: £2,546

Description of injuries: Severe wrench injury to the right shoulder involving soft-tissue injuries.

Prognosis: Made a good recovery.

1.4.1.C32 Case No. 11036

Name of case: Re Slater

Brief description of injuries: SHOULDER – FRACTURED CLAVICLE – FULL RECOVERY

Reported: Kemp & Kemp, K2-079; [1995] CLY 1789

JSB Category: 6(D)(c)

Sex: Female

Age at injury: 3

Age at award: 5

Date of award: 27 February 1995

Tribunal: Aylesbury County Court

Amount of award then: £2,000

Award at February 2001: £2,342

Description of injuries: Claimant injured in road traffic accident and sustained fracture of mid-shaft of right clavicle – wore a collar and cuff sling for approximately three weeks and was given analgesic tablets – missed weeks of nursery school as result of accident – had made full recovery from physical injury within six weeks from accident and at date of assessment fracture had completely united with no bump or cosmetic disfigurement – unlikely that there would be any complications in respect of injury – mother and next friend of infant gave evidence that for four to five months following accident infant had been hysterical and upset when she had to travel in motor car and had suffered nightmares.

1.4.1.C33 Case No. 11054

Name of case: Jinks v Ramzan

Brief description of injuries: SHOULDER AND THUMBS – BRUISING – 2 WEEKS

Reported: Kemp & Kemp, K2-188; [1995] CLY 1808

JSB Category: 6(D), 6(I)

Sex: Male

Age at injury: 19

Age at award: 21

Date of award: 14 February 1995

Tribunal: Newport (Gwent) County Court

Amount of award then: £1,000

Award at February 2001: £1,171

Description of injuries: Plaintiff involved in collision with defendant's motor car which threw him from motorcycle, over roof of motor car and onto ground – plaintiff was immediately taken to hospital as he was suffering from severe pain in left shoulder and right thumb – at hospital it was noted that movement of both these joints were limited – plaintiff was also suffering from painful left ankle and had sustained a cut to lower inside lip and minor abrasions to left side of body – no history of concussion was noted and there was no bony injury – off work two weeks, after which symptoms completely resolved – injuries relatively minor.

1.4.1.C34 Case No. 10689

Name of case: Chadwick v Cunningham

Brief description of injuries: CHEST – SHOULDERS – SEATBELT BRUISING – 2 WEEKS

Reported: [1993] CLY 1585

JSB Category: 5(A); 6(D)(c)

Sex: Female

Age at injury: 24

Age at award: 25

Date of award: 08 August 1993

Tribunal: Scunthorpe County Court

Amount of award then: £350

Award at February 2001: £426

Description of injuries: Road accident – tenderness in left and right shoulders and sternum caused by seatbelt bruising – full movement in all limbs upon examination – claimant refrained from swimming or aerobics for 2 weeks – 1 day off work, light duties for 2 weeks – no medication prescribed – all symptoms resolved within 2 weeks.

1.4.1.1 SHOULDER AND OTHER INJURY

1.4.1.1.C1 Case No. 10619

Award at February 2001: £61,685

See: 1.3.1.1.C2 for details

1.4.1.1.C2 Case No. 10620

Award at February 2001: £22,626

See: 1.3.1.1.C8 for details

1.4.1.1.C3 Case No. 10800

Name of case: Barker v North-West Water

Brief description of injuries: ARM – SHOULDER – PSYCHOLOGICAL REACTION

Reported: [1994] CLY 1649

JSB Category: 6(D), 6(F); 3(A)

Sex: Female

Age at injury: 67

Age at award: 69

Date of award: 01 June 1994

Tribunal: Liverpool County Court

Amount of award then: £17,500

Award at February 2001: £21,315

Description of injuries: Claimant, right-handed, tripped and fell – serious crush injury to upper part of right humerus, described as very comminuted fracture – head of humerus crushed into neck and upper shaft of bone – arm immobilised in collar and cuff for 5 weeks – inability to shower or dress self for 6 months – inability to resume hobby of knitting for 1 year – excellent recovery in that fracture healed; but humeral head had rotated through about 50 degrees and was misaligned – continual dull ache in shoulder, becoming sharp pain if used for any length of time – right shoulder movements restricted to half those of left shoulder, severely hindering lifestyle – grip in right hand reduced; claimant unable to carry objects of any weight, eg shopping – post-traumatic stress disorder – total loss of confidence – inability to be alone for more than a few minutes without suffering anxiety – irritability – bad temperedness – claimant withdrew from previously active social life; only going out when accompanied by husband and even then being preoccupied with looking at the ground.

Prognosis: Limits in movement of shoulder permanent.

1.4.1.1.C4 Case No. 11566

Name of case: Russell v Nathan

Brief description of injuries: SPINE – SHOULDER

Reported: Kemp & Kemp, E3-027/2[1998] CLY 1568

JSB Category: 6(B)(b)(i), 6(D)(c)

Sex: Male

Age at injury: 41

Age at award: 53

Date of award: 14 July 1997

Tribunal: QBD

Amount of award then: £17,500

Award at February 2001: £19,507

Description of injuries: Crush fractures to T12 and L1 – minor shoulder injury – injury to both knees – judge found that the major part of R's residual symptoms related to the accident.

Prognosis: Symptoms would not change.

1.4.1.1.C5 Case No. 11189

Name of case: Huntley v Atkins

Brief description of injuries: KNEE – LACERATIONS – SHOULDER

Reported: Kemp & Kemp, I2-415; [1996] CLY 2280

JSB Category: 6(L)(a)(iii)

Sex: Female

Age at injury: 27

Age at award: 31

Date of award: 17 September 1996

Tribunal: Tunbridge Well County Court

Amount of award then: £16,000

Award at February 2001: £18,214

Description of injuries: Severe lacerations to both knees – fractured clavicle – cut lip.

Prognosis: Unlikely to improve – possibility of arthritis in 20-30 years – extensive scarring to the knees – hip operation result was excellent.

1.4.1.1.C6 Case No. 11500

Award at February 2001: £16,076

See: 1.2.3.1.C19 for details

1.4.1.1.C7 Case No. 10417

Name of case: Macmillan v Seymour Plant Hire & Co

Brief description of injuries: RIGHT WRIST FRACTURE – ARTHRITIS OF SHOULDER

Reported: [1992] CLY 1673

JSB Category: 6(D)(a) and 6(H)(d)

Sex: Male

Age at injury: 54

Age at award: 57

Date of award: 15 July 1992

Tribunal: Carlisle County Court

Amount of award then: £12,000

Award at February 2001: £15,032

Description of injuries: Fracture of the distal ulna on the right wrist – there was new bone formation – loss of 20% supination – shoulder badly bruised – developed peri-arthritis of the shoulder – permanent restriction limited to only two-thirds movement in the shoulder – moderate disability – future disability to the wrist was expected to be minor – no loss of weakness in the grip.

Prognosis: Moderate permanent disability.

Other points: Award comprised of £8,000 for wrist and £4000 for shoulder.

1.4.1.1.C8 Case No. 11280
Award at February 2001: £14,957

See: 1.3.1.3.C25 for details

1.4.1.1.C9 Case No. 11382
Award at February 2001: £9,866

See: 1.3.1.3.C43 for details

1.4.1.1.C10 Case No. 12052
Award at February 2001: £8,776

See: 1.3.1.1.C21 for details

1.4.1.1.C11 Case No. 10420
Name of case: Davison v The Post Office

Brief description of injuries: WHIPLASH – SHOULDER INJURY – DISLOCATED TOE – SHOULDER SYMPTOMS CONTINUED

Reported: Kemp & Kemp, H2-022; [1992] CLY 1676

JSB Category: 6(D)(b)

Sex: Female

Age at injury: 46

Age at award: 49

Date of award: 11 March 1992

Tribunal: Sheffield County Court

Amount of award then: £6,000

Award at February 2001: £7,549

Description of injuries: Sustained whiplash injury to the neck – traumatic capsulitis of the right shoulder creating restriction of movement of internal rotation – dislocation of the little toe – the neck injury necessitated the use of a collar and physiotherapy – at the time of the hearing there was full recovery from the toe and whiplash injuries

Prognosis: Continuing loss of movement and minor discomfort in relation to the shoulder was accepted as permanent.

1.4.1.1.C12 Case No. 11145
Award at February 2001: £7,336

See: 1.3.1.2.1.C17 for details

1.4.1.1.C13 Case No. 11828
Name of case: Harper v Wilson (t/a Royal Star Public House)

Brief description of injuries: SHOULDER AND KNEE – SCAR

Reported: Kemp & Kemp, H2-024/1; [1999] CLY 1492

JSB Category: 6(D), 6(L)(b)(ii); 8

Sex: Female

Age at injury: 40

Age at award: 43

Date of award: 26 October 1998

Tribunal: Mayor's and City of London County Court

Amount of award then: £6,500

Award at February 2001: £6,796

Description of injuries: Trip and fall onto right hand, right shoulder and left knee – knee sore for 6 weeks before settling, during which time claimant had difficulty kneeling – range of movement in right shoulder reduced – arm placed in sling – symptoms continuing after 2 months – decompression operation on right shoulder performed – arm in sling for 6 weeks; physiotherapy for 11 months; off work 17 months – claimant returned to work, initially part-time, as a secretary, having previously been a PA to a partner in the firm – 3 years after accident, range of movement in shoulder still slightly restricted, and aching still developing after shopping or ironing – claimant felt unable to return to hobby of tennis – operation left 8 cm scar on shoulder, leading claimant to avoid wearing sleeveless dresses.

Prognosis: Symptoms in shoulder and scar both permanent.

1.4.1.1.C14 Case No. 11549
Award at February 2001: £6,331

See: 1.2.3.2.1.C22 for details

1.4.1.1.C15 Case No. 11830

Name of case: Malcolm v Commissioner of Police of the Metropolis

Brief description of injuries: SHOULDER – WRIST – 5 YEARS

Reported: Kemp & Kemp, H2-027/1; [1999] CLY 1494

JSB Category: 6(D)(b), 6(H)(d)

Sex: Female

Age at injury: 53

Age at award: 56

Date of award: 24 February 1999

Tribunal: QBD

Amount of award then: £5,000

Award at February 2001: £5,254

Description of injuries: Injuries to shoulder and wrist sustained when claimant wrenched arm free from being trapped in lift door – soft-tissue injuries diagnosed and tubigrip support prescribed for wrist; physiotherapy for 3 months – off work 8 weeks; after 3 months back at work, a further 10 weeks off required – right wrist swollen, but with full and pain free movement, 7 months after accident – obvious wasting of right deltoid muscles – 20 degree restriction of movement in internal and external rotation of shoulder – soreness when using computers; difficulties with domestic chores; difficulties getting in and out of bath – diagnosis of adhesive capsulitis (frozen shoulder) – injection and further physiotherapy prescribed – 2 years after accident, considerable improvement, with no visible wasting; but wrist still swollen, movement in shoulder still limited and computer use, shopping and decorating still limited.

Prognosis: Gradual recovery continuing – full recovery expected within 2 years of date of trial.

Other points: Agreed settlement.

1.4.1.1.C16 Case No. 11831

Name of case: James v Victoria Palace Theatre Ltd

Brief description of injuries: SHOULDER – 2 YEAR ACCELERATION – FINGERS

Reported: Kemp & Kemp, H2-027/2; [1999] CLY 1495

JSB Category: 6(D)(b), 6(I)

Sex: Male

Age at injury: 64

Age at award: 67

Date of award: 24 March 1999

Tribunal: Wandsworth County Court

Amount of award then: £5,000

Award at February 2001: £5,241

Description of injuries: Slip and fall onto right, dominant, side – injury to right shoulder – sprain to 2 fingers on right hand – sprain to finger slow to resolve; swollen for about 18 months, and some continuing reduced grip – rotator cuff of right shoulder had pre-existing degenerative changes, symptomatic 14 years earlier but since resolved – pain in shoulder increased in days following accident – analgesics and physiotherapy prescribed – pain improved over 18 months, but claimant unable to resume original employment – intermittent pain and stiffness ongoing – raising arm caused significant pain.

Prognosis: Accident had advanced pre-existing condition in shoulder by 1-2 years; claimant would not have been able to pursue original job beyond age of 67 in any event.

1.4.1.1.C17 Case No. 11829

Award at February 2001: £5,206

See: 1.3.1.2.1.C22 for details

1.4.1.1.C18 Case No. 10422

Name of case: Cartwright v British Telecommunications

Brief description of injuries: BROKEN COLLAR BONE – WHIPLASH – 20 MONTHS

Reported: [1992] CLY 1678

JSB Category: 6(D)(d)

Sex: Male

Age at injury: 23

Age at award: 28

Date of award: 30 January 1992

Tribunal: Manchester County Court

Amount of award then: £4,000

Award at February 2001: £5,074

Description of injuries: Fractured left clavicle – contusion to the left leg – concussion with short period of post-traumatic amnesia – whiplash injury to the neck – off work for twenty months – fracture failed to unite – permanent non-union of the clavicle with slight cosmetic deformity without physical functional handicap – good recovery within twenty months.

Prognosis: Continuing aches in the shoulder were not functionally disabling.

1.4.1.1.C19 Case No. 10608

Award at February 2001: £4,879

See: 1.3.1.2.1.C25 for details

1.4.1.1.C20 Case No. 11994

Award at February 2001: £4,398

See: 1.3.1.3.C69 for details

1.4.1.1.C21 Case No. 11889

Name of case: Fitzgerald v Smith

Brief description of injuries: SHOULDER – FRACTURE – SPRAINED ANKLES

Reported: Kemp & Kemp, H2-029/1; [1999] CLY 1553

JSB Category: 6(D)(b); 6(M)(d)

Sex: Male

Age at injury: 32

Age at award: 33

Date of award: 10 March 1999

Tribunal: Tunbridge Wells County Court

Amount of award then: £3,600

Award at February 2001: £3,773

Description of injuries: Impacted fracture of glenoid in shoulder – badly sprained lateral ligaments of both ankles – abrasions over left shin – mobilised – left arm placed in sling – claimant unable to lie down for 1 month after accident due to spasms of intercostal muscles when he tried to do so – off work 12 weeks – fracture had healed completely by time of trial, but still some residual stiffness of ankles, expected to clear up within 1 year – claimant forced to give up job as motor mechanic, as unable to lift heavy objects, and had retrained.

1.4.1.1.C22 Case No. 10481

Name of case: Akroyd v Patterson

Brief description of injuries: FRACTURED RIGHT CLAVICLE AND LEFT WRIST – FULL RECOVERY 8 MONTHS

Reported: [1992] CLY 1737

JSB Category: 6(D)(d) 6(H)(e)

Sex: Male

Age at injury: 27

Age at award: 29

Date of award: 28 July 1992

Tribunal: Bradford County Court

Amount of award then: £3,000

Award at February 2001: £3,718

Description of injuries: Fractured right clavicle and left wrist – stiffness of the shoulder present four months after the accident – unable to do weight-lifting for eight months.

Prognosis: Some cosmetic damage likely to disappear within two years of the accident.

1.4.1.1.C23 Case No. 10661

Award at February 2001: £3,636

See: 1.3.1.1.C44 for details

1.4.1.1.C24 Case No. 12001

Award at February 2001: £3,312

See: 1.3.1.2.1.C33 for details

1.4.1.1.C25 Case No. 10525

Name of case: Barnes v Commissioner of Police for the Metropolis

Brief description of injuries: DOUBLE FRACTURE OF THE CLAVICLE – POLICE ASSAULT

Reported: [1992] CLY 1781

JSB Category: 6(D)(d)

Sex: Male

Age at injury: 20

Age at award: 27

Date of award: 13 May 1992

Tribunal: Croydon County Court

Amount of award then: £2,500

Award at February 2001: £3,087

Description of injuries: Double fracture to the clavicle – assaulted by one or more police officers on one or more occasions – more serious assault was being struck with an implement – probably a truncheon.

Prognosis: Injury left a bony prominence – surgery to remove the prominence was ruled out.

1.4.1.1.C26 Case No. 10666

Name of case: Williams & Williams v Appleton

Brief description of injuries: SHOULDER – BACK – SOFT-TISSUE INJURIES

Reported: Kemp & Kemp, K2-073; [1993] CLY 1562

JSB Category: 6(B)(c), 6(D)(c)

Sex: Male

Age at injury: 20

Age at award: 22

Date of award: 01 February 1993

Tribunal: Southampton County Court

Amount of award then: £2,000

Award at February 2001: £2,478

Description of injuries: Road accident – soft-tissue injuries to left shoulder and back; both aching and stiff – shoulder symptomatic for 1 week – aching and stiffness in lower back intermittent after 2 weeks – no lifting at work for 2 weeks – did not play football for 4 weeks – occasional back symptoms thereafter, particularly after sport and in morning – some discomfort when sitting at work as telephone receptionist – 15 months after accident, 20 per cent restriction in forward flexion of lower back – at time of trial, claimant completing course of hydrotherapy and had made almost full recovery – judge's finding of no serious residual symptoms.

1.4.1.1.C27 Case No. 10112

Name of case: Arrighi v Brewers

Brief description of injuries: KNEE, SHOULDER AND FOOT – HEAVY BRUISING – RECOVERY IN 1 YEAR

Reported: Kemp & Kemp, K2-099; [1990] CLY 1683

JSB Category: 6(A), 6(D) & 6(O)

Sex: Male

Age at injury: 29

Age at award: 31

Date of award: 19 November 1990

Tribunal: Dartford County Court

Amount of award then: £1,650

Award at February 2001: £2,183

Description of injuries: In motorcycle accident plaintiff sustained heavy bruising to left knee, right shoulder and left foot – shoulder recovered in three weeks – foot settled after five weeks, but caused occasional twinges for another year – knee largely resolved after two weeks, though still caused mild discomfort – off work for four days.

1.4.1.1.C28 Case No. 11240

Award at February 2001: £1,800

See: 1.3.1.1.C54 for details

1.4.1.1.C29 Case No. 12002

Award at February 2001: £1,446

See: 1.3.1.2.1.C51 for details

1.4.1.1.C30 Case No. 12026

Award at February 2001: £1,032

See: 1.2.2.1.C43 for details

1.4.1.1.C31 Case No. 10122

Name of case: Brown v Hillier

Brief description of injuries: DOG BITE – LEFT ARM – RIGHT SHOULDER – TRIVIAL SCAR

Reported: Kemp & Kemp, K2-224; [1990] CLY 1699

JSB Category: 6(F)

Sex: Male

Age at injury: 28

Age at award: 29

Date of award: 20 November 1990

Tribunal: Newport, Isle of Wight County Court

Amount of award then: £700

Award at February 2001: £926

Description of injuries: Attacked by alsation dog and bitten on left forearm and right shoulderblade – lacerations cleaned and anti-tetanus injection administered, plus one week's course of antibiotics – continuing pain for one week – left with permanent scar on dorsal aspect of forearm and scar below tip of right scapula – did not constitute significant cosmetic disability.

1.4.2 ARM OR WRIST INJURY

1.4.2.C1 Case No. 10423

Name of case: Re DH

Brief description of injuries: LOSS OF USE OF RIGHT ARM

Reported: [1992] CLY 1679

JSB Category: 6(F)(a)

Sex: Male

Age at injury: 40

Age at award: 45

Date of award: 17 September 1991

Tribunal: CICB, London

Amount of award then: £50,000

Award at February 2001: £71,889

Description of injuries: Gunshot wounds to the dominant right arm – vein grafts required to save the arm – skin grafts and an unsuccessful muscle graft using muscle from the back.

Prognosis: Left with a virtually useless right arm – no likelihood of improvement – constant agonising pain below the elbow was resistant to any form of treatment or medication – little chance of improvement – depressive illness and post-traumatic stress disorder with poor prognosis almost entirely due to the incident – there was scarring to the arm and back caused by skin and muscle grafts.

1.4.2.C2 Case No. 11167

Name of case: McDaid v Howletts and Port Lympne Estates Ltd

Brief description of injuries: ARM – AMPUTATION

Reported: Kemp & Kemp, H3-012; [1996] CLY 2258

JSB Category: 6(E)(b)(ii)

Sex: Male

Age at injury: 2

Age at award: 9

Date of award: 17 May 1996

Tribunal: QBD

Amount of award then: £55,000

Award at February 2001: £69,322

Description of injuries: Traumatic amputation below the left shoulder – moderate post-traumatic stress disorder.

Prognosis: Further operations would be required – stump too short to enable a prosthesis to be worn – future disadvantage on the labour market.

1.4.2.C3 Case No. 11834

Name of case: Godfrey v Bernard Matthews plc

Brief description of injuries: ARM – WORK – RELATED UPPER LIMB DISORDER

Reported: Kemp & Kemp, PRH-001; [1999] CLY 1498

JSB Category: 6(J)

Sex: Male

Age at injury: 38

Age at award: 44

Date of award: 21 June 1999

Tribunal: Norwich County Court

Amount of award then: £45,000

Award at February 2001: £50,719

Description of injuries: Claimant worked for 3 months scraping glutinous detritus off 800-1,000 food preparation trays per day – no training, supervision or job rotation – no proper working surface provided; claimant therefore wrapped left arm round trays and clutched them to his chest with left wrist flexed – development of pain and stiffness in left hand, found by judge to be tendinitis – later development of reflex sympathetic distrophy, found by judge to be secondary to the tendonitis – claimant's wrist stiff and hand practically immobile and still moderately painful – "swan neck" deformities in fingers – hand and arm useless; light one – handed tasks still possible, but two – handed tasks (eg slicing bread) required assistance.

Prognosis: Prospects of recovery negligible – claimant therefore unemployable.

1.4.2.C4 Case No. 11417

Name of case: Lowe v Haskell

Brief description of injuries: WRIST

Reported: Kemp & Kemp, H3-058; [1997] CLY 1966

JSB Category: 6(H)(b)

Sex: Male

Age at injury: 26

Age at award: 31

Date of award: 12 March 1997

Tribunal: Colchester County Court

Amount of award then: £22,500

Award at February 2001: £25,756

Description of injuries: Fractures to the femur and to radius and ulna of both arms.

Prognosis: Permanent significant diminution of stamina and flexibility of the right wrist – 70 per cent probability of osteoarthritis developing – very high likelihood that he would be unable to continue the kind of work he did at the trial in 15 years time.

Other points: He was product engineer involved in highly skilled manual work.

1.4.2.C5 Case No. 11409

Name of case: Lambeth v Williams

Brief description of injuries: ELBOW – DEFORMITY

Reported: (1997) 97 (4) QR 7; Kemp & Kemp, H3-059/1; [1997] CLY 1958

JSB Category: 6(G)(a)

Sex: Male

Age at injury: 50

Age at award: 59

Date of award: 11 April 1997

Tribunal: QBD

Amount of award then: £22,500

Award at February 2001: £25,600

Description of injuries: Required open reduction of the elbow after a fall from a roof.

Prognosis: Considerable deformity of the left upper limb – 22cm scar – 3cm shortening of the humerus – no longer capable of heavy work.

1.4.2.C6 Case No. 11643

Name of case: Byers v Brent LBC

Brief description of injuries: WRIST – REFLEX SYMPATHETIC DYSTROPHY

Reported: Kemp & Kemp, H5-017; [1998] CLY 1645

JSB Category: 6(H)

Sex: Female

Age at injury: 25

Age at award: 31

Date of award: 24 April 1998

Tribunal: QBD

Amount of award then: £20,000

Award at February 2001: £21,695

Description of injuries: Reflex sympathetic dystrophy – chronic pain syndrome – residual RSD – wrist was of little use.

Prognosis: Small chance of some reduction in pain and increase in mobility.

Other points: Claimant unable to consider returning to her professional music career in any capacity.

1.4.2.C7 Case No. 11411

Name of case: Pritchard v Cumberland Motor Services Ltd

Brief description of injuries: ARM – SERIOUS INJURY

Reported: Kemp & Kemp, H3-155; [1997] CLY 1960

JSB Category: 6(F)(b)

Sex: Female

Age at injury: 44

Age at award: 48

Date of award: 02 August 1996

Tribunal: Carlisle County Court

Amount of award then: £17,500

Award at February 2001: £20,094

Description of injuries: Serious injury to the right dominant arm – residual scar after unsuccessful surgery to excise the head of the radius.

Prognosis: Unable to continue her employment – or do any heavy manual work – it was unlikely that there would be any improvement in her range of movement – or in the power of her grip.

Other points: She lost her PSV licence – she was at a permanent disadvantage in the labour market.

1.4.2.C8 Case No. 10226

Name of case: Griggs v Latus

Brief description of injuries: INJURIES TO ARM AT SITE OF PREVIOUS FRACTURE

Reported: Kemp & Kemp, H3-156; [1991] CLY 1423

JSB Category: 6(F)(c)

Sex: Male

Age at injury: 48

Age at award: –

Date of award: 01 October 1990

Tribunal: King's Lynn County Court

Amount of award then: £12,000

Award at February 2001: £16,048

Description of injuries: G received injuries to his arm – the plate holding a previous injury in place was broken in the accident.

1.4.2.C9 Case No. 10843

Name of case: Re Burgon

Brief description of injuries: ARM – SCARS – HAND

Reported: Kemp & Kemp, J2-013; [1994] CLY 1692

JSB Category: 6(F), 6(I); 8

Sex: Male

Age at injury: 43

Age at award: 48

Date of award: 11 February 1994

Tribunal: CICB, Durham

Amount of award then: £12,500

Award at February 2001: £15,304

Description of injuries: Severe shotgun wound to left, dominant, arm – shotgun wound to right hand – reconstructive surgery carried out using skin grafts from thigh – scarring well consolidated but unsightly – 2 further operative treatments to improve scarring – in-patient 3 weeks, off work 2 months, finally discharged from out-patient care after 4 years – grotesque scarring on left forearm, leading to upper arm, covering an area of 15 x 10cm, with linear scar running 15cm into upper arm through elbow; unsightly and embarrassing to claimant – extensive scarring at donor site on thigh covering 75 x 20cm, small part of which particularly unsightly and noticeable – claimant unable to wear short sleeved shirts or shorts – area over scars numb – 75-80 per cent loss of feeling in left hand, although functional mobility good and writing still possible – no continuing pain, but constant pins and needles in arm.

Prognosis: No further improvement expected – likelihood of some further operative treatment becoming necessary from time to time as further pellets came to surface.

1.4.2.C10 Case No. 10805

Name of case: Bragg v Ministry of Defence
Brief description of injuries: WRIST
Reported: Kemp & Kemp, H4-014/1; [1994] CLY 1654
JSB Category: 6(H)(b)
Sex: Male
Age at injury: 30
Age at award: 34
Date of award: 23 June 1993
Tribunal: Whitehaven County Court
Amount of award then: £12,000
Award at February 2001: £14,790

Description of injuries: Claimant, soldier at time of incident, fell from Army lorry – minor injury to face – compound fractures of radius and ulna at left, non-dominant, wrist – fractures fixed with wires, in plaster 5 weeks – wires removed after 2 months – 3 years later, examination revealed bones had healed solidly, with good, but not perfect, alignment – some distortion of wrist joint – some evidence of disruption to ligaments – some weakness of grip in left hand – up to 50 per cent loss in normal movement of wrist – wrist tender, and painful on passive manipulation – continuing sleep disturbance due to discomfort in wrist, particularly after heavy day's work – some stiffness in morning – symptoms of discomfort deteriorating; claimant had moved from non-prescription painkillers to prescribed, stronger painkillers at date of trial – active sporting career ended by injury – hobby of gardening restricted – difficulty in driving any car without automatic transmission and power steering – inhibited in fully partaking in boisterous activities with children.

Prognosis: Deterioration in condition expected – judge found that need for surgical stiffening of the wrist within 5-10 years a "probability" in light of deterioration of symptoms already evident – such surgery might involve bone graft taken from pelvis, requiring 2 weeks as in – patient, immobilisation of arm in plaster for 4-5 months and convalescence of 9-12 months – injury to face only slightly tender 3 years after accident.

1.4.2.C11 Case No. 10801

Name of case: Neuman v White
Brief description of injuries: ARM – ELBOW – SCARS
Reported: Kemp & Kemp, H3-158; [1994] CLY 1650
JSB Category: 6(G)(b); 8
Sex: Female
Age at injury: 24
Age at award: 29
Date of award: 16 May 1994
Tribunal: QBD
Amount of award then: £12,000
Award at February 2001: £14,398

Description of injuries: Fall from horse onto left (non-dominant) arm – fracture dislocation to left radial head; also bruising to left leg and hip which resolved within a couple of days – fracture reduced under general anaesthetic and fixed using wires and plate – shoulder-to-wrist plaster for 10 weeks, backslab for a further month – 5 months physiotherapy – second operation to remove wires – 7 months after fall, third operation to release radial head and increase movement in elbow – remaining occasional pain along outside of elbow after heavy lifting, prolonged use of elbow or in cold or damp weather – some sleep disturbance due to pain – inability to carry heavy items – some loss of supination – 3.25 inch scar remaining; claimant conscious of it and wore long sleeves in summer to hide it.

Prognosis: Remaining symptoms unlikely to improve – 25 per cent increase in risk of development of arthritis in elbow over next 20-30 years.

1.4.2.C12 Case No. 10999

Name of case: Kelleher v Ford Motor Co

Brief description of injuries: FRACTURE OF WRIST, INJURY TO NECK AND KNEE – CONTINUOUS ACHING IN WRIST AND KNEE

Reported: [1995] CLY 1751

JSB Category:

Sex: Male

Age at injury: 59

Age at award: 61

Date of award: 02 December 1994

Tribunal: Romford County Court

Amount of award then: £10,000

Award at February 2001: £11,823

Description of injuries: Plaintiff tripped over wire and fell – suffered left scaphoid fracture, jolting injury to neck and blow to right knee – absent from work for 13 weeks, had his wrist in plaster for nine weeks and knee strapped-up for nine weeks – had 22 sessions of physiotherapy to neck and knee between October 1993 and July 1994 – eight months after accident complained of occasional stiff neck and painful left shoulder on lifting – left wrist was also painful on stressing and lifting and knee was painful when going up stairs or lifting heavy objects – walking distance became limited also – five months thereafter he complained of some difficulty in left hand when playing piano, and his hobby of country and western dancing was compromised – some weakness of grip in left hand and slightly tender anatomical snuff box at base of thumb – plaintiff was slightly tender at lower pole of kneecap – identified as chondromalacia patellae which would normally be expected to subside within 12 to 18 months of accident, however plaintiff's obesity militated against any rapid progress in knee joint – tenderness in neck was probably due to degenerative changes, though no long-term disability was anticipated – at date of trial still stiffness in neck in mornings which wore off later in day – still experiencing pain in knee, had difficulty with stairs and prolonged periods of standing caused aching and swelling – plaintiff's wrist ached and he woke at night because of symptoms. The judge accepted the plaintiff's medical expert's evidence that although there could be further improvement in the six to seven months after trial the plaintiff would never return to his pre-accident state.

Prognosis: The judge accepted plaintiff's medical expert's evidence that although there could be further improvement in six to seven months after trial plaintiff would never return to pre-accident state.

1.4.2.C13 Case No. 11172

Name of case: Stimpson v Beevor Castings

Brief description of injuries: ARM – CARPAL TUNNEL SYNDROME

Reported: Kemp & Kemp, H4-017/1; [1996] CLY 2263

JSB Category: 6(J)(d)

Sex: Male

Age at injury: 30

Age at award: 36

Date of award: 14 October 1996

Tribunal: Lincoln County Court

Amount of award then: £10,500

Award at February 2001: £11,785

Description of injuries: Bilateral carpal tunnel syndrome.

Prognosis: After surgery the prognosis was excellent.

1.4.2.C14 Case No. 10802

Name of case: Bonsor v Blake

Brief description of injuries: ARM – HAND

Reported: Kemp & Kemp, H3-159; [1994] CLY 1651

JSB Category: 6(F), 6(I)

Sex: Female

Age at injury: 62

Age at award: 67

Date of award: 28 May 1993

Tribunal: Poole County Court

Amount of award then: £9,500

Award at February 2001: £11,580

Description of injuries: Fall down steps – serious spiral comminuted fracture of head of humerus in dominant right arm – shock and pain – tight bandage and sling for 1 month – physiotherapy – difficulty in dressing and combing hair – numbness in 4 fingers of right hand due to residual nerve damage, causing problems when picking up small items.

Prognosis: Curtailment of (previously prolific) hobby of knitting – no longer able to enjoy swimming – unable to lift heavy items.

1.4.2.C15 Case No. 10806

Name of case: Laws v British Railways Board

Brief description of injuries: WRIST – POST-TRAUMATIC TENOSYNOVITIS

Reported: [1994] CLY 1655

JSB Category: 6(H); 6(J)

Sex: Female

Age at injury: 51

Age at award: 56

Date of award: 14 December 1993

Tribunal: Newcastle-upon-Tyne High Court

Amount of award then: £9,000

Award at February 2001: £10,909

Description of injuries: Fracture of radial styloid, and mild to moderate strain of ligaments, of left wrist – acceleration of onset of pre-existing, asymptomatic arthritic changes in wrist by at least 10 years – development of post-traumatic tenosynovitis – initial treatment with plaster cast – when tenosynovitis diagnosed, physiotherapy prescribed – numerous other treatments undergone – De Quervains decompression performed, to little effect – further operation relieved symptoms of tenosynovitis considerably, though not completely – ongoing pain at base of thumb, index finger and second metacarpal on daily basis, exacerbated by very cold or very hot weather – inability to do heavy housework or heavy gardening – tendency to drop things – inability to pick up grandchildren – symptoms described by judge as "real discomfort" – claimant regularly made use of wrist brace to try to alleviate symptoms.

Prognosis: Symptoms continuing and permanent, resulting in very real change in circumstances.

1.4.2.C16 Case No. 10807

Name of case: Gration v Wilkes

Brief description of injuries: WRIST

Reported: [1994] CLY 1656

JSB Category: 6(H)(c)

Sex: Female

Age at injury: 51

Age at award: 56

Date of award: 08 September 1994

Tribunal: North Shields County Court

Amount of award then: £9,000

Award at February 2001: £10,676

Description of injuries: Claimant injured when taxi pulled away from kerb with her coat shut in door – swelling and tenderness to right elbow, left thumb and left knee and cut to mouth; symptoms settled within 5-6 weeks of accident – most serious injury soft-tissue injury to right, dominant, wrist – arm in sling for 3 weeks – 7 months after accident, wrist still in plaster and wrist support and receiving physiotherapy and steroid injection treatment – 2 years later, symptoms still ongoing – further investigation revealed tenosynovitis of the extensor carpi ulnaris and probable rupture of triangular cartilage within wrist – further steroid injection brought short-term relief – 3 years after accident, surgery undergone to excise pisiform bone where it was noted that there was degenerative change between that and adjacent hamate bone caused directly by accident – loss of movement of between 5 and 8 degrees – power in wrist reduced to about 80 per cent of normal – at time of trial, claimant still suffering from ache in wrist exacerbated by certain activities such as shopping, cooking, knitting, housework and writing – no significant change in claimant's symptoms, despite diminutions from time to time.

Prognosis: Surgery had made no long-term significant difference to symptoms – risk of minor deteriorations in wrist, but unlikely that any more functional loss would result.

Other points: Award split: wrist: £8,000, other injuries: £1,000.

1.4.2.C17 Case No. 10623

Name of case: Gaughan v Lucas Electrical

Brief description of injuries: WRIST – TENOSYNOVITIS – "ALMOST ONE HANDED" AT WORK

Reported: Kemp & Kemp, H8-012; [1993] CLY 1518

JSB Category: 6(J)(a)

Sex: Female

Age at injury: 26

Age at award: 33

Date of award: 26 November 1992

Tribunal: Manchester High Court

Amount of award then: £8,500

Award at February 2001: £10,465

Description of injuries: Claimant assembler at electrical plant, operating jig – jig replaced with new one that did not function correctly – increased manual gripping and twisting required by claimant to assemble components – development of severe pain in left wrist – tenosynovitis diagnosed – physiotherapy and cast prescribed – returned to work and assigned to same faulty jig – recurrence of symptoms – aggravation and pain on stretching and resisted contraction of forearm extensor muscles – squeeze grip and muscle power in hand and arm moderately weak, claimant frequently dropped objects in left hand – inability to lift or carry heavy items – difficulty carrying out household tasks – painkilling injections necessary – scarring at site of injections, loss of subcutaneous fat and prominence of veins, measuring 3 inches by 1 inch at back of central and distal regions of left forearm.

Prognosis: Tenosynovitis showing no signs of improvement and none expected – claimant retired from job soon after symptoms developed and had not worked since – significantly handicapped in labour market; for that purpose could be regarded as almost "one handed and one armed" – household tasks would continue to be difficult.

1.4.2.C18 Case No. 10845

Name of case: Maloney v Liverpool City Council

Brief description of injuries: ARM – SCAR

Reported: Kemp & Kemp, J2-021; [1994] CLY 1694

JSB Category: 8

Sex: Female

Age at injury: 9

Age at award: 10

Date of award: 21 October 1993

Tribunal: Liverpool County Court

Amount of award then: £8,000

Award at February 2001: £9,704

Description of injuries: Claimant fell into boating lake in public park, landing on serrated metal fence – severe laceration to inside of left arm – consequent raised and lumpy scar with prominent suture scars, measuring 8 x 1cm – loss of sensation for distance of 9cm below scar – claimant embarrassed by scar in public, particularly during sporting activities.

Prognosis: Revision of scar possible through operation to improve appearance, but scar would always amount to a significant cosmetic disability – loss of sensation permanent.

1.4.2.C19 Case No. 10803

Name of case: Re Roberts

Brief description of injuries: ARM – ELBOW

Reported: Kemp & Kemp, H3-164; [1994] CLY 1652

JSB Category: 6(F); 6(G)

Sex: Male

Age at injury: 32

Age at award: –

Date of award: 19 November 1993

Tribunal: CICB, Cardiff

Amount of award then: £7,500

Award at February 2001: £9,110

Description of injuries: Claimant struck on arm with iron bar – displacement of ulna – fracture of radial head near elbow – fracture plated; arm placed in plaster for 2 weeks – unable to return to work (as HGV driver) for 9 months, at which point he was made redundant – right arm remained uncomfortable and weak – 5.5 years after attack, bone graft operation undergone.

Prognosis: Arm improved following operation – good function anticipated, albeit with some aching.

1.4.2.C20 Case No. 10084

Name of case: Harrison v Pilkington Glass

Brief description of injuries: WRIST – RADIAL NERVE DIVIDED – SCAR

Reported: Kemp & Kemp, H4-018; [1990] CLY 1651

JSB Category: 6(H)

Sex: Male

Age at injury: 51

Age at award: 58

Date of award: 16 May 1990

Tribunal: St Helens County Court

Amount of award then: £6,000

Award at February 2001: £8,177

Description of injuries: Wrist cut by glass – radial sensory nerve completely divided – nerve and damaged tendons repaired – wrist bore a permanent scar – permanent reduction in span between thumb and hand – wrist extension and grip strength was weakened.

1.4.2.C21 Case No. 10808

Name of case: Hawkins v London Fire and Civil Defence Authority

Brief description of injuries: WRIST – 3.5 YEAR ACCELERATION OF OSTEOARTHRITIS

Reported: Kemp & Kemp, H2-021; [1994] CLY 1657

JSB Category: 6(H)(c)

Sex: Male

Age at injury: 52

Age at award: 56

Date of award: 21 April 1994

Tribunal: Mayor's and City County Court

Amount of award then: £6,500

Award at February 2001: £7,753

Description of injuries: Crushing injury to right wrist – pre-existing, moderately severe, but asymptomatic, bilateral osteoarthritis – symptoms of arthritis accelerated – injury not in itself serious, but aggravation of osteoarthritis made wrist painful upon activity – driving, and use of knife and fork, unaffected, but writing for more than 10 minutes made wrist very painful and stiff – inability to dig, forcing giving up of allotment – window cleaning, car repair, jogging and gardening now also impossible – hobby of bowls affected – judge held that arthritis would have become symptomatic by date of trial in any event – no damages therefore awarded for pain and suffering or loss of amenity and services after that date.

Prognosis: Symptoms of arthritis accelerated by 3 years 7 months.

1.4.2.C22 Case No. 11690

Name of case: Pottinger (a minor) v Bendigo Construction Ltd

Brief description of injuries: ARM – SCAR

Reported: Kemp & Kemp, J2-023; [1998] CLY 1693

JSB Category: 8

Sex: Male

Age at injury: 14

Age at award: 17

Date of award: 07 April 1998

Tribunal: Nottingham County Court

Amount of award then: £7,000

Award at February 2001: £7,405

Description of injuries: Laceration to the right forearm – 5cm scar with obvious suture marks – scar width of 1cm – 7cm area of altered sensation around the scar – at the time of the hearing symptoms had resolved completely.

1.4.2.C23 Case No. 11173

Name of case: Solanki v Land Rover (UK) Ltd

Brief description of injuries: ARM – DE QUERVAINS TENOSYNOVITIS

Reported: Kemp & Kemp, H4-025/1; [1996] CLY 2264

JSB Category: 6(J)(b)

Sex: Male

Age at injury: 49

Age at award: 52

Date of award: 05 March 1996

Tribunal: Birmingham County Court

Amount of award then: £6,000

Award at February 2001: £6,812

Description of injuries: Sustained traumatic De Quervains tenosynovitis.

Prognosis: An increased possibility of surgery to alleviate the symptoms.

1.4.2.C24 Case No. 11691

Name of case: Baynard v Manchester City Council

Brief description of injuries: ARM – SCAR

Reported: Kemp & Kemp, J2-024; [1998] CLY 1694

JSB Category: 8

Sex: Female

Age at injury: 15

Age at award: 17

Date of award: 05 December 1997

Tribunal: Manchester County Court

Amount of award then: £6,000

Award at February 2001: £6,450

Description of injuries: Cut to the right forearm – claimant embarrassed by resultant scar, which was 7.5cm by 0.5cm scar, shiny, raised, firm, and obvious at a distance.

1.4.2.C25 Case No. 10980

Name of case: Kitching v Tesco Stores

Brief description of injuries: WRIST – SOFT-TISSUE INJURY – CONTINUING PAIN

Reported: Kemp & Kemp, H4-026/1; [1995] CLY 1731

JSB Category: 6(H)(c)

Sex: Female

Age at injury: 22

Age at award: 26

Date of award: 24 August 1995

Tribunal: Leeds County Court

Amount of award then: £5,500

Award at February 2001: £6,311

Description of injuries: Plaintiff, right-handed, injured in course of employment as grocery assistant when she put out hands to prevent cases of soft drinks from toppling over onto her – sustained severe soft-tissue injury/sprain to right, dominant, wrist causing damage to capsule lining of wrist joint – was required to wear plaster cast for nearly four months and was off work throughout that period – was then fitted with wrist brace – upon return to work could only carry out light duties – by date of trial had still not returned to previous duties – continuous pain in wrist for eight months after accident – thereafter experienced pain radiating along forearm whenever she tried to carry out strenuous tasks using right arm – some pain on extremes of movement – pain caused difficulties in carrying out normal household tasks and with writing – unable to continue hobby of swimming for some time and it had interfered with writing to pen-friends – some improvement in symptoms as result of taking painkillers which she still took at date of trial.

Prognosis: Her disability and symptoms of pain were likely to be permanent, although there was a possibility of some improvement over course of time.

1.4.2.C26 Case No. 11422

Name of case: Mullett v East London and City HA

Brief description of injuries: WRIST – INJURY – NEGLIGENT TREATMENT

Reported: Kemp & Kemp, H5-022/1; [1997] CLY 1971

JSB Category: 6(I)

Sex: Female

Age at injury: 13

Age at award: 23

Date of award: 16 May 1997

Tribunal: Central London County Court

Amount of award then: £5,750

Award at February 2001: £6,303

Description of injuries: Minor wrist injury treated by negligently performed steroid injection – caused excruciating pain – mottling and bruising – formation of plaque-like lesions – wasted tissue – sensitivity to changes in temperature.

Prognosis: Results of guanethidine blocks was successful – cosmetic appearance of successful skin grafts described as "unsightly" – sensitivity to sunlight remained.

1.4.2.C27 Case No. 11418

Name of case: Choudhry v Jhangir

Brief description of injuries: WRIST

Reported: Kemp & Kemp, H3-164/3; [1997] CLY 1967

JSB Category: 6(H)(d)

Sex: Male

Age at injury: 21

Age at award: 24

Date of award: 24 September 1997

Tribunal: Leeds County Court

Amount of award then: £5,500

Award at February 2001: £5,938

Description of injuries: Comminuted fracture of the radius – avulsion of the tip of the ulnar styloid.

Prognosis: Minor permanent restriction of wrist movement – 10 per cent chance of developing arthritis within the next 10 to 20 years.

Other points: At the time of the hearing he had not achieved his previous high standards in martial arts, keeping fit and weightlifting.

1.4.2.C28 Case No. 11447

Name of case: O'Neill v Matthew Brown PLC

Brief description of injuries: ARM – SCAR

Reported: Kemp & Kemp, J2-026; [1997] CLY 1996

JSB Category: 8

Sex: Male

Age at injury: 28

Age at award: 30

Date of award: 22 October 1996

Tribunal: Accrington County Court

Amount of award then: £5,250

Award at February 2001: £5,871

Description of injuries: Severe lacerations to the underside of the arm – L-shaped wound 14cms by 3cms required 25 to 30 stitches.

Prognosis: The scar was obvious – painful if knocked or sun-burnt – otherwise a full recovery had been made.

1.4.2.C29 Case No. 11169

Name of case: Re J

Brief description of injuries: ARM – TENDON DAMAGE

Reported: Kemp & Kemp, H3-165/2; [1996] CLY 2260

JSB Category: 6(F)

Sex: Female

Age at injury: 20

Age at award: 23

Date of award: 21 November 1995

Tribunal: CICB, Glasgow

Amount of award then: £5,000

Award at February 2001: £5,741

Description of injuries: Stabbed in the left arm – 50 per cent division of the flexor digitorum superficialis – markedly less power in the injured arm.

Prognosis: Prominent and permanent scarring to arm.

Other points: Attack was not reported to the police for one month – damages reduced.

1.4.2.C30 Case No. 11201

Name of case: Re Daggart

Brief description of injuries: ABUSE – ARM – SCARS – DAMAGE TO EAR

Reported: Kemp & Kemp, H3-165/3; [1996] CLY 2292

JSB Category: 8(iv)

Sex: Male

Age at injury: 10-14

Age at award: 17

Date of award: 26 January 1996

Tribunal: CICB, Durham

Amount of award then: £5,000

Award at February 2001: £5,726

Description of injuries: Cut to the arm – should have been stitched – scar to the right ear-drum in the form of a barotramua caused by repeated blows to the right ear.

Prognosis: No suggestion of any permanent damage to hearing – 4cm scar to the arm

Other points: Removal from the care of his mother and step-father had alleviated any major psychological problems.

1.4.2.C31 Case No. 11448

Name of case: Leatherland v Rissman

Brief description of injuries: ARM – SCAR

Reported: Kemp & Kemp, J2-030; [1997] CLY 1997

JSB Category: 8

Sex: Male

Age at injury: 30

Age at award: 32

Date of award: 07 February 1997

Tribunal: Norwich County Court

Amount of award then: £5,000

Award at February 2001: £5,548

Description of injuries: Extensive soft-tissue lacerations to the back, arm and elbow – friction burns/abrasions to the buttock and forearm – bruising to a leg.

Prognosis: Injuries healed – a hypertrophic F-shaped scar on the upper arm measuring 10 cms by 2cms at its widest point – scarring would not diminish in size – its appearance would improve within nineteen months of the date of the accident.

1.4.2.C32 Case No. 10804

Name of case: Wickens v Red Shift Theatre Co

Brief description of injuries: ARM – TENOSYNOVITIS

Reported: Kemp & Kemp, H3-166; [1994] CLY 1653

JSB Category: 6(J)(c)

Sex: Female

Age at injury: 30

Age at award: 32

Date of award: 25 November 1993

Tribunal: Central London County Court

Amount of award then: £4,500

Award at February 2001: £5,466

Description of injuries: Claimant, actress, lifted heavy and bulky scenery in awkward manner and with poor posture – development of tenosynovitis in biceps tendon of dominant right arm and inflammation of tendons of rotator cuff in right shoulder – initial pain in upper right arm – later development of more severe stiffness of shoulder and neck – dressing, reaching behind back, writing, washing and drying hair, leaning on right hand, all difficult – objects dropped from right hand on occasions – some interference to sleep – 2 steroid injections to shoulder – at date of trial, claimant still forced to avoid heavy lifting or violent activity with right arm – claimant had adapted to use left arm for some tasks, eg vacuuming and shopping – ongoing pain and discomfort when sleeping on right side and shoulder – slightly uncomfortable "jarring" when arm brought down from abducted position – avoidance of auditioning for parts involving strenuous activity.

Prognosis: General acceptance of there being excellent prospects for full recovery.

1.4.2.C33 Case No. 11170

Name of case: White v Munir

Brief description of injuries: ARM – ULNA NERVE

Reported: Kemp & Kemp, H3-106/1; [1996] CLY 2261

JSB Category: 6(G)(c)

Sex: Female

Age at injury: 54

Age at award: 58

Date of award: 15 May 1996

Tribunal: Reading County Court

Amount of award then: £4,750

Award at February 2001: £5,343

Description of injuries: Injury to the ulna nerve – mild anxiety – only able to drive 10 miles or so – sufficient for shopping and visits to the family.

1.4.2.C34 Case No. 11413

Name of case: Mitchell (a minor) v Cheshire CC

Brief description of injuries: ARM – INJURY TO ARMPIT

Reported: Kemp & Kemp, H3-177; [1997] CLY 1962

JSB Category: 6(F)(d)

Sex: Male

Age at injury: 10

Age at award: 12

Date of award: 22 January 1997

Tribunal: Liverpool County Court

Amount of award then: £4,750

Award at February 2001: £5,291

Description of injuries: Injury to the armpit axillary area – penetrating one or two inches into the axillary fold.

Prognosis: V-shaped scar – six cms by four cms – hypertrophic and keloid – restricted movement to the shoulder – further surgery might be required.

1.4.2.C35 Case No. 10856

Name of case: Ramsay v CICB

Brief description of injuries: ARM – WRIST – OTHER MINOR INJURIES

Reported: Kemp & Kemp, H3-167; [1994] CLY 1706

JSB Category: 6(F), 6(H)

Sex: Male

Age at injury: 25

Age at award: 28

Date of award: 09 February 1994

Tribunal: CICB, Manchester

Amount of award then: £4,000

Award at February 2001: £4,842

Description of injuries: Claimant, police officer, attempted to make arrest in course of his duties – most serious injury a twisting injury to left arm and wrist – 2 head-butts, causing bruising injury to centre of forehead and laceration to right eyebrow – bite, breaking skin, to back of right shoulder – off work 2 weeks – pain in wrist for 2 weeks – some loss of use and grip for next year – cut to right eyebrow needed 2 stitches – bite left nasty weal on shoulder, which was stiff and painful for a few weeks – arm injury took 2 years in total to settle completely.

Prognosis: Cut to eyebrow left very slight scar, not raised or discoloured.

1.4.2.C36 Case No. 11649

Name of case: Howell v J Lyons & Co

Brief description of injuries: WRIST – CARPAL TUNNEL SYNDROME – 18 MONTHS

Reported: (1998) 98 (6) QR 7; Kemp & Kemp, H5-026; [1998] CLY 1651

JSB Category: 6(J)(d)

Sex: Female

Age at injury: 41

Age at award: 44

Date of award: 01 July 1998

Tribunal: Barnsley County Court

Amount of award then: £4,500

Award at February 2001: £4,748

Description of injuries: Crush injury to the fingers – carpal tunnel syndrome required 2 operations – H's symptoms resolved within 18 months of the date of the accident.

1.4.2.C37 Case No. 11414

Name of case: Hasan v Boots the Chemist PLC

Brief description of injuries: ARM – SOFT-TISSUE INJURY – 18 MONTHS

Reported: Kemp & Kemp, H3-169/1; [1997] CLY 1963

JSB Category: 6(F)(d)

Sex: Female

Age at injury: 21

Age at award: 23

Date of award: 05 September 1997

Tribunal: Central London County Court

Amount of award then: £4,000

Award at February 2001: £4,319

Description of injuries: Significant soft-tissue injury to the arm – caused the symptoms – pain caused erratic attendance at work.

Prognosis: Significant pain had been suffered for a period of eighteen months.

Other points: The plaintiff had a lower pain threshold than most people.

1.4.2.C38 Case No. 11022

Name of case: Hill v Dudley Metropolitan Borough Council

Brief description of injuries: WRIST – GREENSTICK FRACTURE – EXCELLENT RECOVERY

Reported: Kemp & Kemp, H6-041; [1995] CLY 1774

JSB Category: 6(H)(d)

Sex: Male

Age at injury: 13

Age at award: 14

Date of award: 13 March 1995

Tribunal: Stourbridge County Court

Amount of award then: £3,500

Award at February 2001: £4,081

Description of injuries: Greenstick fracture of left wrist at lower metaphysis of radius with slight dorsal angulation – manipulation of left wrist was attempted under intravenous sedation and wrist was immobilised in plaster cast – the following day plaintiff complained of pain in right wrist and X-ray of wrist revealed minor greenstick fracture of distal radius metaphysis – treated by splintage in crepe bandage – two days later left wrist was manipulated under general anaesthetic and plaster cast reapplied which was left on for two weeks – plaintiff spent two days in hospital and was discharged from fracture clinic eight weeks after accident – plaintiff missed school for three days, could not play violin or piano for eight weeks and could not participate in sporting activities for three months – made excellent recovery from injuries and both fractures united soundly without deformity.

1.4.2.C39 Case No. 11171

Name of case: Clarke v Liverpool City Council

Brief description of injuries: ELBOW – FRACTURES TO BOTH ELBOWS

Reported: Kemp & Kemp, H3-170; [1996] CLY 2262

JSB Category: 6(F)(d)

Sex: Female

Age at injury: 34

Age at award: 35

Date of award: 06 November 1995

Tribunal: Liverpool County Court

Amount of award then: £3,500

Award at February 2001: £4,019

Description of injuries: Fractures to the head of the radius of both arms – fractures united soundly.

Prognosis: Remote possibility of arthritis in the next 25-30 years.

1.4.2.C40 Case No. 10259

Name of case: Gay v Dalgety

Brief description of injuries: ELBOW – CRACK FRACTURE- RECOVERY IN 1 YEAR

Reported: Kemp & Kemp, K2-017; [1991] CLY 1456

JSB Category: 6(G)(c)

Sex: Female

Age at injury: 57

Age at award: –

Date of award: 12 April 1991

Tribunal: Wisbech County Court

Amount of award then: £3,000

Award at February 2001: £3,877

Description of injuries: A crack fracture of the lateral aspect of the radial head – seven weeks before the arm could be straightened comfortably – tenderness and restriction of movement for a year.

Prognosis: Aching and weakness was likely to resolve in time – no risk of osteoarthritis.

1.4.2.C41 Case No. 11026

Name of case: Hartfield v Green

Brief description of injuries: LACERATION TO ARM; SCARS – LOWER BACK PAIN FOR 6 MONTHS – SPOILED HOLIDAY

Reported: Kemp & Kemp, K2-019; [1995] CLY 1778

JSB Category: 6(F)

Sex: Female

Age at injury: 28

Age at award: 30

Date of award: 15 June 1995

Tribunal: Mayor's and City of London County Court

Amount of award then: £3,250

Award at February 2001: £3,732

Description of injuries: Plaintiff sustained lacerations to left arm and soft-tissue injuries to neck and back in road traffic accident – taken to hospital but discharged same day – unable to work for two weeks – judge considered cosmetic and physical aspects of plaintiff's injuries separately – pieces of glass had to be removed from arm and wounds required sixteen stitches – left with five or six small pinkish scars on upper arm as well as several smaller white scars – would fade to certain extent but would always be visible – plaintiff was embarrassed by them and felt unable to wear short-sleeved dresses or tops – neck injury resolved within month of accident – judge considered most significant physical effects of accident to be back pain (which lasted for some six months and for which plaintiff had six sessions of physiotherapy) and difficulty in sleeping for two weeks – he also had regard to acute pain that went with presence of glass in plaintiff's arm – plaintiff was keen sportswoman who played badminton at league level and also hockey – had been on way to France for active holiday at time accident occurred and when she was able to take replacement holiday later in year it was of necessity much more sedentary – judge placed specific emphasis on restriction on plaintiff's ability to enjoy hobbies for some months and on loss of her chosen type of holiday.

1.4.2.C42 Case No. 11836

Name of case: Jefferies v Byrne

Brief description of injuries: WRIST – CONTINUING MINOR SYMPTOMS

Reported: Kemp & Kemp, H4-029; [1999] CLY 1500

JSB Category: 6(H)

Sex: Male

Age at injury: 51

Age at award: 53

Date of award: 15 February 1999

Tribunal: Basingstoke County Court

Amount of award then: £3,250

Award at February 2001: £3,415

Description of injuries: Severe sprain to right, dominant wrist in road accident – claimant went on pre-planned holiday 1 month after accident; enjoyment of holiday impaired by pain and discomfort in wrist – claimant attended GP on return; suspicion of scaphoid fracture ruled out by X-rays – 3 months of severe discomfort – claimant had problems dressing – forced to employ cleaner and gardener – claimant's job necessitated a lot of driving; claimant initially only able to turn ignition key with left hand, and found steering uncomfortable – symptoms also exacerbated by carrying briefcase and shaking hands – occasional embarrassment caused – improvement after 6 months; symptoms only occurring once a week after prolonged or heavy use – further improvement 2 years after accident, but claimant still somewhat limited in heavy activities and prone to occasional bouts of aching.

1.4.2.C43 Case No. 10444

Name of case: Rogers v Birdseye Wall's

Brief description of injuries: BILATERAL TENOSYNOVITIS

Reported: [1992] CLY 1700

JSB Category: 6(J)(a)

Sex: Female

Age at injury: 50

Age at award: 55

Date of award: 03 June 1992

Tribunal: Sheffield County Court

Amount of award then: £2,750

Award at February 2001: £3,396

Description of injuries: Acute traumatic tenosynovitis – symptoms developed in one hand then in the other – symptoms ceased by 1988 – did not resume employment as a process worker for fear of recurrence.

Prognosis: Symptoms ceased by April 1988 – plaintiff feared recurrence.

1.4.2.C44 Case No. 10860

Name of case: Crestwell v Windmill Housing Association

Brief description of injuries: WRIST – 9 MONTHS

Reported: Kemp & Kemp, K2-036; [1994] CLY 1711

JSB Category: 6(H)(d)

Sex: Male

Age at injury: 4

Age at award: 6

Date of award: 28 February 1994

Tribunal: Lancaster County Court

Amount of award then: £2,750

Award at February 2001: £3,329

Description of injuries: Fracture of distal forearm bones and displacement of radius (but not ulna) in left, non-dominant, wrist – manipulation under general anaesthetic – detained in hospital overnight – long arm plaster for 4 weeks, tubigrip bandage thereafter – disturbed sleep for several weeks – difficulty with certain activities, such as riding bicycle, toilet functions, dressing, for 2-3 months after plaster removed – necessity of re-learning these tasks.

Prognosis: Full recovery within 9 months of accident.

1.4.2.C45 Case No. 11867

Name of case: Davis v AG Barr plc

Brief description of injuries: ARM – SCAR

Reported: Kemp & Kemp, J3-036; [1999] CLY 1531

JSB Category: 8

Sex: Female

Age at injury: 32

Age at award: 34

Date of award: 17 March 1999

Tribunal: Mansfield County Court

Amount of award then: £3,000

Award at February 2001: £3,144

Description of injuries: Burn to inner aspect of right, dominant, forearm – area blistered and scabbed over next few days; surrounding area of forearm became red and painful for more than a week – initial injury healed after 6 weeks – claimant left with round mark on palmar aspect of right mid forearm approximately 3cm in diameter, reasonably faint, but noticeable, with no scarring of overlying skin; described in medical report as "somewhat encircled with a post-inflammatory pigmentation which made the mark more defined" – claimant's skin tanned easily, but scar would not tan at all, always remaining white; claimant complained of odd sensation in scar area in the summer – no tethering by skin to any underlying tissues – judge found that claimant continued to be troubled by the scar, and that it was uncomfortable.

1.4.2.C46 Case No. 10426

Name of case: Hookings v Wiltshire County Council
Brief description of injuries: DOG BITE TO RIGHT ARM – OCCASIONAL SENSATION IN WOUND
Reported: [1992] CLY 1682
JSB Category: 6(F)(d)
Sex: Male
Age at injury: 28
Age at award: 31
Date of award: 20 May 1992
Tribunal: Swindon County Court
Amount of award then: £2,500
Award at February 2001: £3,087
Description of injuries: Dog bite causing deep puncture wound to the right upper arm – dressings required on alternate days until it was stitched – off work three weeks – light duties ten days.
Prognosis: Occasional electric shock sensation likely to continue in the foreseeable future.

1.4.2.C47 Case No. 11204

Name of case: Crisp v Hare
Brief description of injuries: ARM – SCARS
Reported: Kemp & Kemp, J2-045; [1996] CLY 2295
JSB Category: 8(iv)
Sex: Male
Age at injury: 15
Age at award: 23
Date of award: 13 November 1995
Tribunal: Cardiff County Court
Amount of award then: £2,250
Award at February 2001: £2,583
Description of injuries: Dog bites to the left hand, wrist, elbow and thigh.
Prognosis: Scarring was "not prominent but visible" – developed a phobia to dogs that was unlikely to be resolved.

1.4.2.C48 Case No. 11454

Name of case: Barnes v Kenmore Refrigeration Ltd
Brief description of injuries: ARM – BURNS
Reported: Kemp & Kemp, J3-039/1; [1997] CLY 2003
JSB Category: 8
Sex: Male
Age at injury: 49
Age at award: 51
Date of award: 15 May 1997
Tribunal: Leeds County Court
Amount of award then: £2,250
Award at February 2001: £2,467
Description of injuries: Burns to the inside of the right arm.
Prognosis: A Y-shaped scar – arms 10cms and 8cms – darkish in colour – not tender.

1.4.2.C49 Case No. 10869

Name of case: Edwards v Dannimac
Brief description of injuries: WRIST – BRUISING
Reported: Kemp & Kemp, K2-126; [1994] CLY 1721
JSB Category: 5(H)
Sex: Female
Age at injury: 24
Age at award: 26
Date of award: 28 March 1994
Tribunal: Manchester County Court
Amount of award then: £1,500
Award at February 2001: £1,811
Description of injuries: Sprain to left, non-dominant, wrist, which judge accepted was correctly described as "severe", rather than "moderate" – also some bruising to arms and lower back, which resolved within a few weeks – claimant 4 months pregnant and was concerned about a possible miscarriage, but this did not occur – no swelling of wrist, but swelling to fingers – unable to take time off work, which involved lifting items, due to financial need; assisted by colleagues where necessary – over following 2 years, claimant aware of wrist's inability to bear the load being carried on 40-50 occasions – intermittent pain over this period, but steadily decreasing in frequency – claimant almost symptom – free for 12 months leading up to date of hearing – however, some tingling in wrist and fingers in cold weather.

1.4.2.C50 Case No. 11935

Name of case: Hyde v Clive Warcup Transport Ltd

Brief description of injuries: ELBOW – SOFT-TISSUE INJURY – 12 MONTHS

Reported: Kemp & Kemp, PRK-008; [1999] CLY 1599

JSB Category: 6(G)(c)

Sex: Male

Age at injury: 52

Age at award: 54

Date of award: 17 June 1999

Tribunal: Preston County Court

Amount of award then: £1,500

Award at February 2001: £1,558

Description of injuries: Strain to outer side of left elbow – tenderness in "tennis elbow" area, but no evidence of trouble or damage within the elbow joint cavity – continuous pain for 3 months – thereafter, intermittent symptoms subsiding within a period of 12 months from date of accident – time off work not required, but claimant unable to continue hobby of mountain climbing, and elbow hurt when using keyboard.

1.4.2.C51 Case No. 11648

Name of case: Doherty v Law

Brief description of injuries: WRIST – STRAIN – 3 YEARS

Reported: Kemp & Kemp, H4-041; [1998] CLY 1650

JSB Category: 6(H)(d)

Sex: Male

Age at injury: 39

Age at award: 42

Date of award: 06 July 1998

Tribunal: Barnsley County Court

Amount of award then: £1,300

Award at February 2001: £1,372

Description of injuries: Strain to the left wrist – local tenderness – marked swelling and pain.

Prognosis: Medical evidence was that remaining symptoms would disappear within 3 years of the date of the accident.

1.4.2.C52 Case No. 10878

Name of case: Re Tierney

Brief description of injuries: ARM – BITE AND CUT – FEAR OF HIV

Reported: Kemp & Kemp, K2-182; [1994] CLY 1730

JSB Category: 6(F); 8; 3(A)

Sex: Male

Age at injury: 30

Age at award: 33

Date of award: 18 January 1994

Tribunal: CICB, Manchester

Amount of award then: £1,000

Award at February 2001: £1,217

Description of injuries: Claimant, police officer, injured in course of making arrest – bite to back of right arm, breaking skin – violent struggle – cut to arm on broken glass of window of police car, requiring stitches – bruising round bite mark, taking 2-3 weeks to heal completely – 1cm scar from glass wound on right upper arm, obliquely transverse across left elbow; not raised or deformed, no tenderness or sensory disturbance – tetanus injection carried out at hospital – anxiety about catching HIV virus or associated disease, as assailant was known drug user – claimant fully counselled by medical practitioners – anxiety overcome in full.

1.4.2.C53 Case No. 10286

Name of case: Philpotts v Gheest Holdings

Brief description of injuries: INFECTED OLECRANON BURSITIS -LEFT ELBOW

Reported: [1991] CLY 1483

JSB Category: 6(G)(c)

Sex: Male

Age at injury: 28

Age at award: 31

Date of award: 07 March 1991

Tribunal: Lincoln County Court

Amount of award then: £900

Award at February 2001: £1,178

Description of injuries: Injury to the left elbow – an infected olecranon bursitis developed – treated with anti-biotics and a sling – developed an allergic reaction to the anti-biotics – off work for two weeks.

Prognosis: P was left with a continuing area of sensitivity at the back of the elbow.

1.4.2.C54 Case No. 10118

Name of case: Larcombe v Willis
Brief description of injuries: ELBOW – TENDER SCAR
Reported: [1990] CLY 1695
JSB Category: 6(G)
Sex: Male
Age at injury: –
Age at award: –
Date of award: 30 June 1989
Tribunal: Chepstow County Court
Amount of award then: £750
Award at February 2001: £1,118
Description of injuries: Fell off motorcycle whilst swerving to avoid defendant's car – sustained abrasions to elbow leaving scar on inner aspect – slight tenderness in the scar on palpation – stiffness in cold weather.

1.4.2.C55 Case No. 11742

Name of case: Baker v Tugwell
Brief description of injuries: ARM – 8 WEEKS
Reported: Kemp & Kemp, PRK-011, K2-208/4; [1998] CLY 1745
JSB Category: 6(F)
Sex: Female
Age at injury: 17
Age at award: 19
Date of award: 11 November 1997
Tribunal: Bath County Court
Amount of award then: £1,000
Award at February 2001: £1,078
Description of injuries: Shock – muscular tenderness to the arm – sleep disturbance – symptoms were fully resolved within 8 weeks of the date of the accident.

1.4.2.C56 Case No. 11938

Name of case: Snelling v Evans
Brief description of injuries: WRIST – SPRAIN – 3 MONTHS
Reported: Kemp & Kemp, K2-209/2; [1999] CLY 1602
JSB Category: 6(H)(d)
Sex: Male
Age at injury: 22
Age at award: 23
Date of award: 07 April 1999
Tribunal: Leeds County Court
Amount of award then: £1,000
Award at February 2001: £1,041

Description of injuries: Sprain to left, non-dominant, wrist – immediate pain – support bandage provided at hospital; painkillers taken for 2-3 weeks – wrist continued to be uncomfortable with restricted movement and recurrent swelling – claimant returned to hospital 2 weeks after accident; provided with wrist splint, which was worn for 6-7 weeks – several weeks of marked discomfort before wrist settled over a period of 3 months – claimant then returned to hobby of weight training – no time off work – claimant also suffered grazed left knee, which settled over a period of a few days.

1.4.2.C57 Case No. 11753

Name of case: Daly v Newbold Domestic Appliances Ltd
Brief description of injuries: ARM – SCARS
Reported: Kemp & Kemp, J2-050; [1998] CLY 1756
JSB Category: 8
Sex: Male
Age at injury: 34
Age at award: 36
Date of award: 05 November 1997
Tribunal: Warrington County Court
Amount of award then: £950
Award at February 2001: £1,024
Description of injuries: 2 deep lacerations to the left arm – at time of hearing 1 scar was not particularly conspicuous – the other scar was unnoticeable – residual itch was a small nuisance.

1.4.2.C58 Case No. 10882

Name of case: Brewis v GEC Alsthom
Brief description of injuries: ARM – SCAR
Reported: Kemp & Kemp, K2-214; [1994] CLY 1734
JSB Category: 6(F); 8
Sex: Female
Age at injury: 58
Age at award: 60
Date of award: 19 August 1994
Tribunal: Wolverhampton County Court
Amount of award then: £850
Award at February 2001: £1,010
Description of injuries: 3 small fragments of wire embedded in claimant's arm following a wire breakage in the course of her employment as coilwinder – 2 fragments removed – third fragment required excision under local anaesthetic 2 months after accident – pain and swelling at wound site for 3 months – residual 2cm scar on left forearm – no time taken off work – no functional disability from wound – scar visible, but not embarrassing.

1.4.2.C59 Case No. 11264

Name of case: Smith v Blue Band Motors
Brief description of injuries: ARM – ABRASION
Reported: Kemp & Kemp, K2-226; [1996] CLY 2356
JSB Category: 3(A)(d)
Sex: Male
Age at injury: 2
Age at award: 4
Date of award: 18 September 1995
Tribunal: Stourbridge County Court
Amount of award then: £850
Award at February 2001: £971

Description of injuries: Small superficial abrasion to the arm – distressed and disturbed – all symptoms appeared to have abated within twelve months of the date of the accident.

1.4.2.C60 Case No. 10292

Name of case: Grantham v Gales
Brief description of injuries: RIGHT ARM – BRUISING – 5 MONTHS
Reported: Kemp & Kemp, K2-233; [1991] CLY 1489
JSB Category: 6
Sex: Male
Age at injury: 22
Age at award: 23
Date of award: 23 October 1991
Tribunal: Doncaster County Court
Amount of award then: £700
Award at February 2001: £891

Description of injuries: Bruising to the right upper arm in a traffic accident – G wore strapping for one week – painkillers – off work for two weeks.

Prognosis: A virtually full recovery within five months of the date of the accident.

1.4.2.C61 Case No. 10126

Name of case: Babla v Patel
Brief description of injuries: BURN TO LEFT FOREARM – RECOVERY 5 MONTHS
Reported: Kemp & Kemp, K2-253; [1990] CLY 1705
JSB Category: 6(F)
Sex: Male
Age at injury: 2
Age at award: 4
Date of award: 08 February 1990
Tribunal: Leicester County Court
Amount of award then: £450
Award at February 2001: £644

Description of injuries: Plaintiff at nursery school – burn to left forearm two inches by one inch in size, cause unknown – hospital applied Flamazine dressing – fully recovered from scarring within five months.

1.4.2.C62 Case No. 10294

Name of case: Soper v Midland Rollmakers
Brief description of injuries: RIGHT ARM – SOFT-TISSUE INJURY – 2 WEEKS
Reported: [1991] CLY 1491
JSB Category: 6
Sex: Male
Age at injury: 33
Age at award: 38
Date of award: 13 February 1991
Tribunal: Chester County Court
Amount of award then: £450
Award at February 2001: £591

Description of injuries: Soft-tissue bruising to the right arm and elbow – unable to move the arm for four to five days – stiff elbow for ten days – two weeks off work (one week coincided with the works holiday).

Prognosis: On return to work S was symptom free.

1.4.2.C63 Case No. 10894

Name of case: Young v Griffin
Brief description of injuries: ARM – BRUISES AND GRAZING
Reported: Kemp & Kemp, K2-267; [1994] CLY 1746
JSB Category: 6(F), 6(G)(c)
Sex: Male
Age at injury: 18
Age at award: 20
Date of award: 09 December 1993
Tribunal: Birmingham County Court
Amount of award then: £400
Award at February 2001: £485

Description of injuries: Claimant knocked off bicycle – bruising, grazing, tenderness and swelling to left elbow and forearm – arm in sling for 1 week – limited movement in elbow for 3-4 weeks – no time off work – symptom – free after 4 weeks and able to return to hobby of cycling.

1.4.3 ARM OR WRIST AND OTHER INJURY

1.4.3.C1 Case No. 11286
Award at February 2001: £113,859
See: 1.2.3.1.C1 for details

1.4.3.C2 Case No. 10080
Name of case: Green v Wilson
Brief description of injuries: ABOVE-ELBOW AMPUTATION OF LEFT ARM
Reported: Kemp & Kemp, H2-011; [1990] CLY 1646
JSB Category: 6(E)
Sex: Male
Age at injury: 23
Age at award: 27
Date of award: 23 November 1990
Tribunal: QBD
Amount of award then: £55,000
Award at February 2001: £83,380

Description of injuries: Suffered right brachial plexus injury from avulsion of the cervical cord resulting in flail right arm – after repair of subclavian artery no sign of neurological activity – extensive intercostal nerve transplant – pinning of the shoulder joints – amputation of right arm leaving upper third of upper arm – developed severe phantom limb pain.

Prognosis: After five operations he was still unrelieved – his disability had cost him his career.

1.4.3.C3 Case No. 11640
Name of case: Singh v Dhillon
Brief description of injuries: ARM AMPUTATION
Reported: Kemp & Kemp, H3-012/1; [1998] CLY 1642
JSB Category: 6(E)(b)(iii); 3(B)
Sex: Male
Age at injury: 46
Age at award: 55
Date of award: 23 April 1998
Tribunal: QBD
Amount of award then: £65,000
Award at February 2001: £78,142

Description of injuries: After suffering crush, burn and degloving injuries the left arm was surgically amputated below the elbow – permanent residual pain was constant – chronic post-traumatic stress disorder, not susceptible to treatment – judge found that claimant had lost everything he held most dear.

Prognosis: Claimant was probably unemployable.

1.4.3.C4 Case No. 11492
Name of case: Re Castle
Brief description of injuries: ARMS – LEG – POST-TRAUMATIC STRESS DISORDER
Reported: Kemp & Kemp, B2-007; [1998] CLY 1493
JSB Category: 6(F)(b), 6(K)(b)(iv); 3(B)(b); 4(B)(d)
Sex: Male
Age at injury: 27
Age at award: 36
Date of award: 14 July 1998
Tribunal: CICB, London
Amount of award then: £65,000
Award at February 2001: £77,922

Description of injuries: Multiple crush injuries to the arms and leg – burns to the back – tinnitus – post-traumatic stress disorder, a significant problem – loss of physical fitness and ability to play instruments, a very deep loss.

1.4.3.C5 Case No. 11484
Award at February 2001: £72,253
See: 1.2.3.8.C47 for details

1.4.3.C6 Case No. 10534
Name of case: Wright v Ramsden
Brief description of injuries: ARM – PARALYSIS – PERSONALITY CHANGE
Reported: Kemp & Kemp, B2-009; [1993] CLY 1426
JSB Category: 6(F)(a), 6(H), 6(K)
Sex: Male
Age at injury: 34
Age at award: 40
Date of award: 08 January 1993
Tribunal: Sheffield High Court
Amount of award then: £45,000
Award at February 2001: £62,136

Description of injuries: Left brachial plexus lesion resulting in almost complete paralysis of left arm, leaving it wasted and almost entirely numb – burning pain (causalgia) in left hand and forearm – fractured left femur – comminuted fracture of left fibula – comminuted and displaced fracture of right distal radius – fractured left upper humerus – some personality change (irritability, bad temper, depression) – left leg shortened when healed with reduced flexion – sexual difficulties.

Prognosis: Now virtually unemployable (as welder) and only 10 per cent chance of finding future work of any kind, further improvement unlikely – now wholly dependent on right arm, but right wrist injury resulted in reduced dorsiflexion (osteoarthritis likely).

1.4.3.C7 Case No. 10619

Award at February 2001: £61,685

See: 1.3.1.1.C2 for details

1.4.3.C8 Case No. 10827

Name of case: Mullally v Mountney

Brief description of injuries: KNEE – WRIST

Reported: Kemp & Kemp, I2-402; [1994] CLY 1676

JSB Category: 6(L)(a), 6(H)(c),8

Sex: Male

Age at injury: 31

Age at award: 37

Date of award: 28 April 1994

Tribunal: Southend County Court

Amount of award then: £35,000

Award at February 2001: £44,817

Description of injuries: Motorcycle accident – injuries to left knee and right wrist – comminuted displaced intra-articular fracture of left proximal tibia – comminuted displaced intra-articular fracture of right distal radius and ulna – 4 weeks in hospital – wrist manipulation under general anaesthetic – open reduction, elevation and bone graft (from right iliac crest) on knee – cast brace attached to knee and left for 2 years 6 months – knee unable to bear weight for first 4 months – unable to work for 7 months – knee suffering continuing and serious symptoms at time of trial – inability to run, ride bicycle or kneel on left knee – 20 per cent loss of flexion – swelling after activity – muscle wasting – 3 scars, of 21cm, 8cm and 1cm – donor site had 9cm scar and was lumpy and tender to lie upon – wrist retained lumpy swelling on distal end of ulna – pronation reduced by 10 degrees, palmar flexion by 20 degrees – full grip remained in hand.

Prognosis: Prognosis of wrist symptoms being permanent – knee already degenerating at time of trial; osteoarthritis a certainty at some stage – arthroscopy, debridement and lavage certainly required within 2-3 years and tibial osteotomy within 5 years – knee replacement eventually required.

1.4.3.C9 Case No. 11416

Name of case: Wright, Willis, Short and Bottomer v Royal Doulton (UK) Ltd

Brief description of injuries: ELBOW – GOLFER'S ELBOW – TENOSYNOVITIS

Reported: Kemp & Kemp, H3102/2; [1997] CLY 1965

JSB Category: 6(J)(b)

Sex: Male

Age at injury: B:41;W1:51;W2:47;S:24

Age at award: B:46;W1:56;W2:52;S:29

Date of award: 16 May 1996

Tribunal: Derby County Court

Amount of award then: £32,500

Award at February 2001: £38,805

Description of injuries: Recognised upper limb disorders as a result of their employment – golfer's elbow (B, W1 and W2) – tenosynovitis (W2 and S).

Prognosis: Unable to perform heavy repetitive work – at a future disadvantage in the labour market.

Other points: Award split – B: £8,000; W1: £7,500; W2: £9,000; S: £8,000

1.4.3.C10 Case No. 11642

Name of case: Sams v Olley

Brief description of injuries: ARM – SEVERE INJURY – SPLEEN REMOVED

Reported: Kemp & Kemp, H3-056; [1998] CLY 1644

JSB Category: 6(F)(b); 5(J), 5(A)(g), 5(K)

Sex: Male

Age at injury: 29

Age at award: 34

Date of award: 18 January 1998

Tribunal: QBD

Amount of award then: £33,000

Award at February 2001: £37,691

Description of injuries: Moderately severe multiple injuries – compound fracture to the left ulna and haemothorax – associated fractured ribs – significant haemorrhage and removal of the spleen – 2 hernia operations.

Prognosis: Permanent disability of the left arm – 30 to 40 per cent risk of developing post-traumatic osteoarthritis within 10 years – permanent need to take prophylactic antibiotics.

1.4.3.C11 Case No. 11299

Name of case: Re Ara

Brief description of injuries: ARM – POST-TRAUMATIC STRESS DISORDER

Reported: [1997] CLY 1847

JSB Category: 3(B)(b)

Sex: Female

Age at injury: 25

Age at award: 29

Date of award: 18 February 1997

Tribunal: CICB, Manchester

Amount of award then: £30,000

Award at February 2001: £35,081

Description of injuries: Multiple stab wounds – damage to the left ulnar nerve – moderate post-traumatic stress disorder.

Prognosis: She would never recover completely from the trauma – at a permanent disadvantage in the labour market.

Other points: Injury to the left hand prevented her from performing a number of manual tasks.

1.4.3.C12 Case No. 11495
Award at February 2001: £34,269

See: 1.2.3.1.C11 for details

1.4.3.C13 Case No. 10620
Award at February 2001: £22,626

See: 1.3.1.1.C8 for details

1.4.3.C14 Case No. 10800
Award at February 2001: £21,315

See: 1.4.1.1.C3 for details

1.4.3.C15 Case No. 10811
Name of case: Re Evans

Brief description of injuries: ARM – HAND – TRAUMATIC OSTEODYSTROPHY

Reported: Kemp & Kemp, H6-014; [1994] CLY 1660

JSB Category: 6(I)

Sex: Female

Age at injury: 51

Age at award: 58

Date of award: 18 August 1994

Tribunal: CICB, Manchester

Amount of award then: £15,000

Award at February 2001: £18,147

Description of injuries: Claimant mugged – shoulder bag wrenched from grasp – injuries to shoulder, wrist and fingers of dominant right arm – immediate swelling and pain in hand and wrist – return to work (in bank) after 2 weeks, but typing and shorthand difficult – 6 months after attack, general puffiness and stiffness in third, fourth and fifth proximal interphalangeal joints – second, third and fourth metacarpo-phalangeal joints tender and restricted – considerable flexion deformities in fingers – claimant unable to spread hand – grip poor – diagnosis of traumatic osteodystrophy (Sudek's Atrophy) – physiotherapy, exercise and oral cortico-steroids prescribed – some improvement, but problems continued, necessitating use of ice packs for up to 2 hours at end of working day to control swelling – early retirement on medical grounds 2 years after attack – some improvement after retirement – still severe difficulties in carrying out household chores and carrying objects in right hand – knitting, ironing and sewing problematic – writing for any length of time impossible – claimant expert pistol and rifle shot, and showed dogs around the country, but forced to abandon these hobbies – claimant also advanced driver, but driving any other than short distances now painful and stressful, and large padded steering wheel required – at date of hearing, claimant had little or no use of middle, ring and fifth fingers of right hand – constant pain, requiring daily painkillers, in little finger and forearm – still unable to stretch hand or make fist – grip still poor.

1.4.3.C16 Case No. 10417
Award at February 2001: £15,032

See: 1.4.1.1.C7 for details

1.4.3.C17 Case No. 10465
Name of case: Ford v Excotur SA

Brief description of injuries: MULTIPLE LACERATIONS TO THE LEG, ARM AND CHEST – 75 STITCHES – MINOR SCARRING

Reported: Kemp & Kemp, J2-014; [1992] CLY 1721

JSB Category: 8

Sex: Male

Age at injury: 20

Age at award: 28

Date of award: 21 October 1992

Tribunal: Central London County Court

Amount of award then: £12,000

Award at February 2001: £14,910

Description of injuries: Lacerations with subsequent scarring – three lacerations to the right leg – one laceration to the back of the right arm – laceration over the top of the right shoulder girdle – small laceration to the anterior chest wall – 75 stitches required in all.

Prognosis: Well healed – not unsightly – still suffered pain in the right shin which was symptomatic of a neuroma and required further surgery – scars caused some embarrassment.

1.4.3.C18 Case No. 11499
Award at February 2001: £13,768

See: 1.3.1.3.1.C15 for details

1.4.3.C19 Case No. 10449

Name of case: Re SCP

Brief description of injuries: LEG AND ELBOW – AXE WOUNDS – WALKING LIMITED

Reported: [1992] CLY 1705

JSB Category: 6(K)

Sex: Male

Age at injury: 22

Age at award: 24

Date of award: 04 November 1992

Tribunal: CICB, Birmingham

Amount of award then: £10,000

Award at February 2001: £12,372

Description of injuries: Cut scalp – axe wound to the elbow causing division of the right triceps – axe wound to the knee causing division of the right patella tendon – machete stab wound to the upper thigh, leaving an exit wound and just missing the femoral artery – off work for thirteen weeks – thigh wound was herniated and required an operation – he had to take rests at work – unable to walk long distances or play football.

Prognosis: Operation anticipated to deal with herniated thigh wound.

1.4.3.C20 Case No. 11853

Name of case: Rutter v Stevenage BC

Brief description of injuries: KNEE – 2.5 YEAR ACCELERATION – WRIST

Reported: Kemp & Kemp, 13-020/1; [1999] CLY 1517

JSB Category: 6(L)(b), 6(H)(d), 6(M)

Sex: Female

Age at injury: 50

Age at award: 52

Date of award: 17 November 1998

Tribunal: Central London County Court

Amount of award then: £9,500

Award at February 2001: £9,939

Description of injuries: Trip and fall – forced inversion injury, resulting in fracture of left lateral malleolus in ankle, avulsion fracture to palmar aspect of one of the carpal bones in dominant right wrist and blow to right knee, exacerbating pre-existing patellofemoral crepitus – ankle injury placed in back slab for 5 days, plaster cast for 6 weeks thereafter – wrist placed in splint – combination of injuries meant that claimant was unable to use crutches for 3 weeks and confined to a relative's home with a downstairs toilet – crutches thereafter for a month, stick for 4 months – off work 8 weeks – physiotherapy for 12 weeks – 2 years after accident, claimant still suffering occasional aching in ankle, especially in mornings or during cold weather – twinges in wrist when wordprocessing or communicating in sign language at work – knee symptoms worsening, with pain on bending, inability to kneel or squat and difficulty in managing stairs.

Prognosis: Wrist and ankle symptoms expected to resolve entirely within 1 year – accident had accelerated knee symptoms by 2 years and 6 months.

1.4.3.C21 Case No. 10624

Award at February 2001: £9,700

See: 1.3.1.3.1.C17 for details

1.4.3.C22 Case No. 10436

Name of case: Re Wild

Brief description of injuries: RIGHT HAND AND FOREARM – MULTIPLE INJURIES – STAB TO CHEST

Reported: Kemp & Kemp, H3-161; [1992] CLY 1692

JSB Category: 6(I)(k)

Sex: Male

Age at injury: 21

Age at award: 25

Date of award: 30 October 1992

Tribunal: CICB, Leeds

Amount of award then: £7,750

Award at February 2001: £9,528

Description of injuries: Stab injuries to the right posterior chest – deep transverse laceration over the ulnar aspect of the right forearm – flexor carpi ulnari and flexor digitorum subliminus muscles and ulna nerve were all divided – repairs carried out – limitation in the extension of the fingers – weakness in the grip – particularly between the thumb and fingers.

Prognosis: Unlikely there would be any improvement in the anaesthesia of the hand and lower forearm – expected the wound would ease in time.

1.4.3.C23 Case No. 11164

Award at February 2001: £8,453

See: 1.4.1.C10 for details

1.4.3.C24 Case No. 10308

Award at February 2001: £8,055

See: 1.2.3.1.C25 for details

1.4.3.C25 Case No. 12043

Award at February 2001: £6,940

See: 1.3.1.1.C27 for details

1.4.3.C26 Case No. 10081

Name of case: Voller v Smith

Brief description of injuries: DOG BITE – LEFT ARM – CONTINUING SYMPTOMS

Reported: Kemp & Kemp, H3-171; [1990] CLY 1648

JSB Category: 6(F)

Sex: Female

Age at injury: 70

Age at award: 77

Date of award: 09 April 1990

Tribunal: Brentford County Court

Amount of award then: £4,250

Award at February 2001: £5,843

Description of injuries: Suffered two bites on the non-dominant left forearm – one large bite of 5 by 3 cm on ulnar aspect of forearm with tissue loss and the other produced a small abrasion on the radial aspect of forearm – suffered pain on gripping, pain in left side of cheek on drinking hot liquids, and aching of whole of left arm – suffered constant pain in arm and hand with tingling in little and ring finger radiating up to the upper arm and shoulder – unable to carry heavy weights with left arm – restricted movement and stiffness in left shoulder, and also in little and ring fingers of left hand.

1.4.3.C27 Case No. 11419

Name of case: Heden v BPC Magazines (Leeds) Ltd

Brief description of injuries: WRIST – KNEE

Reported: Kemp & Kemp, H3-165/1; [1997] CLY 1968

JSB Category: 6(H)(d) 6(K)(c)(iii)

Sex: Male

Age at injury: 52

Age at award: 53

Date of award: 20 March 1997

Tribunal: Bradford County Court

Amount of award then: £5,200

Award at February 2001: £5,755

Description of injuries: Fracture to the radius – laceration to the knee.

Prognosis: Fully functional wrist – subject to short intermittent aching – scarring to the knee.

1.4.3.C28 Case No. 11835

Award at February 2001: £5,392

See: 1.3.1.1.C36 for details

1.4.3.C29 Case No. 11830

Award at February 2001: £5,254

See: 1.4.1.1.C15 for details

1.4.3.C30 Case No. 11927

Award at February 2001: £4,946

See: 1.3.1.1.C40 for details

1.4.3.C31 Case No. 11221

Award at February 2001: £3,020

See: 1.3.1.1.C45 for details

1.4.3.C32 Case No. 12065

Award at February 2001: £2,978

See: 1.3.1.1.C46 for details

1.4.3.C33 Case No. 10484

Award at February 2001: £2,801

See: 1.3.1.1.C47 for details

1.4.3.C34 Case No. 10163

Name of case: Burgess v Hooper

Brief description of injuries: DOG BITE – LACERATIONS TO ARM -PHOBIA OF DOGS

Reported: Kemp & Kemp, K2-015; [1991] CLY 1360

JSB Category: 6(F)(c)

Sex: Male

Age at injury: 47

Age at award: –

Date of award: 04 June 1991

Tribunal: Sunderland County Court

Amount of award then: £2,000

Award at February 2001: £2,565

Description of injuries: Bitten twice by Alsatian dog – lacerations to arm – off work for two weeks – small scars on right side of the forearm – two other insignificant scars on right flank – nightmares acute in first few weeks but continued sporadically since – phobia of dogs mainly focused on Alsatians – acute anxiety symptoms-some features of post-traumatic stress disorder as recurrent nightmares and psychological distress.

Prognosis: Nightmares and reminder reaction expected to subside-phobic avoidance of Alsatians expected to settle more slowly, likely to remain present for rest of life.

1.4.3.C35 Case No. 11723

Name of case: Re Stockley

Brief description of injuries: NECK – ARM

Reported: Kemp & Kemp, K2-144/1; [1998] CLY 1726

JSB Category: 6(A)(c), 6(F)

Sex: Female

Age at injury: 41

Age at award: 42

Date of award: 08 October 1997

Tribunal: Luton County Court

Amount of award then: £1,500

Award at February 2001: £1,618

Description of injuries: Neck pain radiating into the shoulder and arm.

Prognosis: A full recovery was made – no long-term problems were expected.

1.4.3.C36 Case No. 10876

Award at February 2001: £1,503

See: 1.2.3.2.1.C32 for details

1.4.3.C37 Case No. 11894

Name of case: Coombs v Warren

Brief description of injuries: WRISTS – KNEES – MINOR INJURIES – 3 MONTHS

Reported: Kemp & Kemp, K2-170/5; [1999] CLY 1558

JSB Category: 6(H)(d), 6(M)(d), 6(B)(c)

Sex: Male

Age at injury: 28

Age at award: 28

Date of award: 03 November 1998

Tribunal: Bridgwater County Court

Amount of award then: £1,250

Award at February 2001: £1,308

Description of injuries: Road accident – minor bruising to knees – minor ache in wrists – development of mid – lumbar muscular pain 2 days later – sleep disruption; on 5 occasions claimant forced to sleep on floor; at other times, claimant would wake early in bed with pain and move to the floor – pain at worst in morning, easing to an ache after walking around – claimant only consulted GP after 10 weeks, in the mistaken expectation that the pain would resolve – painkillers prescribed and symptoms wore off 4 weeks later – no time off work, but claimant consciously avoided the occasional lifting he was required to do at work – duration of symptoms found to be 3 months – judge found that there was only minimal disruption to lifestyle overall, but sleep disruption and being "slowed down" at work were "a nuisance".

1.4.3.C38 Case No. 10122

Award at February 2001: £926

See: 1.4.1.1.C31 for details

1.4.3.C39 Case No. 11704

Award at February 2001: £917

See: 1.2.3.1.C38 for details

1.4.3.C40 Case No. 10290

Name of case: Aliseo v Edenborough

Brief description of injuries: LEGS AND ARMS – BRUISING AND LACERATIONS

Reported: [1991] CLY 1487

JSB Category: 6(K)(c)(iii)

Sex: Male

Age at injury: 19

Age at award: 22

Date of award: 03 April 1991

Tribunal: Epsom County Court

Amount of award then: £700

Award at February 2001: £905

Description of injuries: A motorcycle accident – A had a deep four inch laceration to the left thigh into muscles – heavy bruising to the buttocks – light bruising to the elbow and leg – required eight sutures – stiff neck for two weeks – two migraines.

Prognosis: Full recovery.

1.4.3.C41 Case No. 10291

Name of case: Bennett v Newell

Brief description of injuries: FACE AND WRIST – FIRST DEGREE SUPERFICIAL BURNS

Reported: Kemp & Kemp, K2-232; [1991] CLY 1488

JSB Category: 7(B)(b)(v)

Sex: Male

Age at injury: 45

Age at award: –

Date of award: 15 October 1991

Tribunal: Dudley County Court

Amount of award then: £700

Award at February 2001: £891

Description of injuries: First degree superficial burns to the face and wrist – moustache and eyebrow largely burnt off – treated with sprays but not detained in hospital – upset and irritable for three months – feelings of fear when contemplating how much more serious the accident could have been.

Prognosis: Full recovery.

1.4.3.C42 Case No. 10893
Award at February 2001: £597
See: 1.2.3.2.1.C34 for details

1.4.3.C43 Case No. 10127
Award at February 2001: £543
See: 1.3.1.3.1.C41 for details

1.4.3.1 ARM OR WRIST FRACTURE

1.4.3.1.C1 Case No. 11641
Name of case: Rutland v Ferguson
Brief description of injuries: ARM – FRACTURE
Reported: Kemp & Kemp, H3-054; [1998] CLY 1643
JSB Category: 6(F)(a)
Sex: Male
Age at injury: 49
Age at award: 53
Date of award: 12 November 1997
Tribunal: QBD
Amount of award then: £45,000
Award at February 2001: £52,824
Description of injuries: Compound fracture of the left radius and ulna – extensive muscular degloving and compromised vascularity – lower arm extremely deformed.
Prognosis: R was effectively a one-armed man – he would not work again.

1.4.3.1.C2 Case No. 11410
Name of case: Re Murtagh
Brief description of injuries: ELBOW – FRACTURE
Reported: Kemp & Kemp, H3-152; [1997] CLY 1959
JSB Category: 6(F)(b)
Sex: Male
Age at injury: 44
Age at award: 48
Date of award: 11 March 1997
Tribunal: CICB, Carlisle
Amount of award then: £20,000
Award at February 2001: £22,751
Description of injuries: Comminuted fracture of the distal end of the shaft of the humerus.
Prognosis: Permanent loss of extension and flexion of the elbow – permanent loss of pronation and supination of the forearm.
Other points: Unable to return to painting and decorating – or to do any heavy manual work.

1.4.3.1.C3 Case No. 10225
Name of case: Newing v East Sussex County Council
Brief description of injuries: FRACTURE TO RIGHT HUMERUS – SERIOUS RESIDUAL DISABILITY
Reported: Kemp & Kemp, H3-154; [1991] CLY 1422
JSB Category: 6(F)(c)
Sex: Male
Age at injury: 8
Age at award: 12
Date of award: 29 August 1991
Tribunal: Brighton County Court
Amount of award then: £16,500
Award at February 2001: £21,703
Description of injuries: Serious injury to the dominant right arm – fracture to the lower end of the humerus – the fracture was manipulated under general anaesthesia – the fracture was found to be displaced eight days later – re-manipulated and stabilised using a percutaneous Kirschner wire – a third operation was required which significantly improved the range of movement.
Prognosis: Complete loss of supination with significant loss of dexterity in the hand – this is not likely to improve – significant loss of extension in the elbow so that it never straightens and is noticeably injured – N will be unable to take part in very vigorous activities – a small scar 2cms in length – an 11cm scar is 2cms at its widest point being both red and obvious on the posterior aspect of the elbow – a moderately severe cosmetic defect. Award was approved by the judge on the basis of no admission of liability.

1.4.3.1.C4 Case No. 11415
Name of case: Fahy v Wolverhamton MBC and Banbury Windows Ltd
Brief description of injuries: ARM – ELBOW – SEVERE FRACTURES
Reported: Kemp & Kemp, H3-060; [1997] CLY 1964
JSB Category: 6(G)(b)
Sex: Female
Age at injury: 50
Age at award: -
Date of award: 17 September 1996
Tribunal: Birmingham County Court
Amount of award then: £18,000
Award at February 2001: £20,596
Description of injuries: Severe fracture, dislocation to the elbow comminuted fracture of the radius – fracture of the humerus – vascular injury – significant threat to her left arm.
Prognosis: Extensive scarring in the elbow region – and donor grafting site – limitation in movement – a little pain.
Other points: Needed some assistance to perform household tasks – and in dressing and hair-washing.

1.4.3.1.C5 Case No. 10427

Name of case: Mulla v Blackburn, Hyndburn and Ribble Health Authority

Brief description of injuries: FRACTURE OF LEFT ARM – DEFORMITY – PERMANENT LOSS OF USE

Reported: [1992] CLY 1683

JSB Category: 6(G)(b)

Sex: Male

Age at injury: 5

Age at award: 11

Date of award: 26 September 1991

Tribunal: Blackburn County Court

Amount of award then: £12,500

Award at February 2001: £16,188

Description of injuries: Supracondylar fracture of the left arm immediately above the elbow joint – fracture was manipulated – staff failure to observe the fracture subsequently slip caused a further operation to be required to correct deformity in the elbow in June 1987 – a persisting, ugly "gun-stock" deformity to the left elbow and four-inch scar on the outer aspect remained – handicapped in the use of the left arm – further osteotomy operation scheduled to be carried out in his teens to remove cosmetic deformity.

Prognosis: Unlikely to be any improvement in functional disability.

1.4.3.1.C6 Case No. 10621

Name of case: O'Dell v Jarvis and Whitbread

Brief description of injuries: ELBOW – FRACTURE – SEVERE

Reported: Kemp & Kemp, H3-102; [1993] CLY 1516

JSB Category: 6(G)(b); 8

Sex: Male

Age at injury: 26

Age at award: 35

Date of award: 03 June 1993

Tribunal: Luton County Court

Amount of award then: £12,000

Award at February 2001: £14,790

Description of injuries: Fall – severe and displaced fracture of left (non-dominant) elbow – fracture reduced and fixed with wires under general anaesthetic – arm in plaster for 19 days, claimant off work (as lorry driver) for 3 months – subsequent infection of wound – subsequent occasional, but increasingly rare, episodes of pain in elbow – loss of 50 per cent extension and flexion – aching in mornings – 15 cm scar – claimant coping well with work on return, felt that arm had regained full strength.

Prognosis: Early osteoarthritic changes evident at time of trial – condition would steadily deteriorate – possibility of operative fusion of elbow or replacement of joint – deterioration would lessen claimant's ability to continue working as lorry driver.

1.4.3.1.C7 Case No. 10979

Name of case: Re Bowers

Brief description of injuries: ARM – FRACTURE - REDUCED MOVEMENT IN WRIST

Reported: Kemp & Kemp, H4-015; [1995] CLY 1730

JSB Category: 6(F)(c)

Sex: Female

Age at injury: 15

Age at award: 19

Date of award: 13 January 1995

Tribunal: CICB, York

Amount of award then: £11,995

Award at February 2001: £14,259

Description of injuries: Plaintiff pushed off wall in an unprovoked attack, sustaining fracture of distal radius and an ulna styloid fracture to left (non-dominant) wrist – fractures were initially placed in plaster of Paris back slab for six weeks – ulna styloid fracture did not unite and lay in displaced position at time of hearing – at that time applicant had reduced range of movements in left wrist and left hand grip strength was markedly reduced – fine crepitus was noted on forearm rotation – applicant had difficulties holding or lifting anything in left hand, opening door handles and other day-to-day activities – wrist condition expected to be permanent.

Prognosis: There was risk of an arthroscopy of wrist proving necessary in future and of further surgery thereafter – also a risk of painful post-traumatic osteoarthritis.

1.4.3.1.C8 Case No. 11637

Name of case: Hawken v Apex Bodyworks Ltd

Brief description of injuries: ARM – CRUSH – FRACTURE

Reported: Kemp & Kemp, H4-015/1/1; [1998] CLY 1639

JSB Category: 6(F)(c)

Sex: Male

Age at injury: 57

Age at award: 60

Date of award: 16 October 1997

Tribunal: Portsmouth County Court

Amount of award then: £12,000

Award at February 2001: £13,024

Description of injuries: Crushed arm – Galleazzi fracture and dislocation of the left forearm – post-operative nerve compression required decompression operation – unsightly 10 cm scar – wrist movements limited by 50 per cent – numbness and weakness of grip.

Prognosis: Scar, restriction of movement, numbness and weakness of grip all likely to be permanent.

1.4.3.1.C9 Case No. 10622

Name of case: Re Burrows
Brief description of injuries: WRIST – FRACTURE – INCOMPLETE RECOVERY
Reported: Kemp & Kemp, H4-015/2; [1993] CLY 1517
JSB Category: 6(H)
Sex: Female
Age at injury: 46
Age at award: 51
Date of award: 01 March 1993
Tribunal: CICB, Leicester
Amount of award then: £10,000
Award at February 2001: £12,409
Description of injuries: Social worker kicked by disturbed child – scaphoid fracture to right wrist – fracture did not unite properly – continuing disability in dominant right hand.

1.4.3.1.C10 Case No. 11644

Name of case: Heap v Partridge
Brief description of injuries: WRIST – FRACTURE FAILED TO UNITE
Reported: Kemp & Kemp, H4-018; [1998] CLY 1646
JSB Category: 6(H)(c)
Sex: Male
Age at injury: 20
Age at award: 25
Date of award: 19 March 1998
Tribunal: Tunbridge Wells County Court
Amount of award then: £11,000
Award at February 2001: £11,809
Description of injuries: Severely comminuted fracture of the wrist – claimant left with angulation of the wrist – ulna did not unite.
Prognosis: There was divided opinion concerning the outcome of further operative treatment.
Other points: H was determined to have the further treatment.

1.4.3.1.C11 Case No. 10078

Name of case: Re Harrow-Bunn
Brief description of injuries: FRACTURE OF LEFT HUMERUS
Reported: Kemp & Kemp, H2-018; [1990] CLY 1644
JSB Category: 6(D)
Sex: Female
Age at injury: 64
Age at award: 67
Date of award: 27 July 1990
Tribunal: CICB, Manchester
Amount of award then: £8,000
Award at February 2001: £10,852
Description of injuries: Comminuted fractured neck of non-dominant left humerus – bruising down left side – initially very painful – restricted movement.
Prognosis: Shoulder joint replacement possible if pain increases.

1.4.3.1.C12 Case No. 11412

Name of case: Rowland v Griffin
Brief description of injuries: ARM – FRACTURE
Reported: Kemp & Kemp, I2-317; [1997] CLY 1961
JSB Category: 6(F)(c)
Sex: Female
Age at injury: 78
Age at award: 80
Date of award: 02 July 1997
Tribunal: Central London County Court
Amount of award then: £9,500
Award at February 2001: £10,375
Description of injuries: Comminuted fracture of the humerus – fractured pubic ramus.
Prognosis: Permanent serious restriction of movement in the left shoulder – serious and disabling accident – would affect the rest of her life.
Other points: Restriction in movement was only 50% attributable to the accident.

1.4.3.1.C13 Case No. 12064

Name of case: Plume v Mason Bros (Butchers) Ltd
Brief description of injuries: ELBOW – FRACTURE
Reported: [2000] 6 CL 194
JSB Category: 6(G)(b)
Sex: Male
Age at injury: 45
Age at award: 48
Date of award: 20 January 2000
Tribunal: Burton upon Trent County Court
Amount of award then: £10,000
Award at February 2001: £10,327
Description of injuries: Type ll fracture of the radial head of the right elbow – wore a sling and underwent physiotherapy – sleeping difficulty for three months – supination limited to 40 per cent – unable to straighten the arm – secondary capsular tightness – onset of mild osteoarthritis.

1.4.3.1.C14 Case No. 10424

Name of case: Champion v Grimsby Health Authority

Brief description of injuries: FRACTURE OF LEFT ULNA – UNTREATED – CONTINUING PAIN – LOSS OF FUNCTION

Reported: Kemp & Kemp, H3-160; [1992] CLY 1680

JSB Category: 6(F)(d)

Sex: Female

Age at injury: –

Age at award: 20

Date of award: 10 July 1992

Tribunal: High Court, Nottingham

Amount of award then: £8,000

Award at February 2001: £9,914

Description of injuries: Monteggia fracture of the left ulna – hospital treated the fracture to the ulna – failed to diagnose the dislocation of the head of the radius until February 1980 – by then too late to treat it – decision taken not to operate at that stage – there had been no problems of pain or loss of function until after a period of rapid growth at age 13 – pain continued until physical maturity – had the dislocation been treated at the time of the accident there should have been complete recovery.

Prognosis: No risk of arthritis – no chance of improvement.

1.4.3.1.C15 Case No. 10428

Name of case: Long v Cornwall County Council

Brief description of injuries: FRACTURE OF LEFT ELBOW – SOME LOSS OF MOVEMENT – OSTEOARTHRITIS

Reported: Kemp & Kemp, H3-103; [1992] CLY 1684

JSB Category: 6(G)(b)

Sex: Female

Age at injury: 46

Age at award: 49

Date of award: 06 October 1992

Tribunal: Truro County Court

Amount of award then: £8,000

Award at February 2001: £9,836

Description of injuries: Severe fracture of the left olecranon (tip of the elbow) – open reduction and internal fixation – some fragments of bone removed – arm was in plaster for ten weeks – away from work for six months – further operation to remove fixation wires – unable to fully straighten the arm – only 90% flex.

Prognosis: Osteoarthritis likely to develop in the future.

1.4.3.1.C16 Case No. 10625

Name of case: Albrighton v Townscape Products

Brief description of injuries: WRIST – FRACTURE – BONE GRAFT

Reported: Kemp & Kemp, H5-021; [1993] CLY 1520

JSB Category: 6(H)(c)

Sex: Male

Age at injury: 27

Age at award: 32

Date of award: 16 June 1993

Tribunal: Mansfield County Court

Amount of award then: £7,500

Award at February 2001: £9,149

Description of injuries: Steel bollard fell on dorsum of right (dominant) hand – fracture of scaphoid in right wrist – scaphoid plaster for 12 weeks – fracture did not unite – operation to insert bone graft – fracture united after further 3 months in plaster – slight restriction in wrist movement, weakened grip and aching on heavy lifting still evident at time of trial – unable to return to hobbies of boxing, tennis and weightlifting.

Prognosis: Chances of early osteoarthritic deterioration assessed at 20 per cent over next 5-10 years.

1.4.3.1.C17 Case No. 11832

Name of case: M (a minor) v Snakes and Ladders Adventure Centres Ltd

Brief description of injuries: ARM – FRACTURE – SCAR

Reported: Kemp & Kemp, H3-164/1; [1999] CLY 1496

JSB Category: 6(F); 8

Sex: Male

Age at injury: 4

Age at award: 7

Date of award: 08 September 1998

Tribunal: Shoreditch County Court (infant settlement approval hearing)

Amount of award then: £8,500

Award at February 2001: £8,893

Description of injuries: Fall and subsequent trampling on bouncy castle – monteggia fracture of left, dominant, arm, comprising a displaced fracture of ulna shaft with dislocation of radial head in direction of displacement – claimant taken to hospital, where ulna fracture identified in X-ray but displacement of radial head went undiagnosed on 4 occasions – 10 weeks after accident, displacement of radial head finally diagnosed, by which time ulna shaft had united but radial head was still dislocated – medical evidence that, had radial head displacement been diagnosed straightaway, non-operative closed manipulation of the ulna and radial head would probably have been adequate treatment – delay in diagnosis made that treatment now unlikely to succeed – osteotomy of ulna with fixation with kirschner wire and reduction of radial head under general anaesthetic undertaken, with pin being removed 2 months later – claimant recovered full function in left arm – claimant left with 12cm scar on elbow.

Other points: £5,000 against owner of facility; £3,500 against hospital where claimant treated.

1.4.3.1.C18 Case No. 11168

Name of case: Davis-Desmond v Islington LBC

Brief description of injuries: ARM – FRACTURE

Reported: Kemp & Kemp, H3-105/1; [1996] CLY 2259

JSB Category: 6(F)(d)

Sex: Male

Age at injury: 33

Age at award: 34

Date of award: 22 April 1996

Tribunal: Central London County Court

Amount of award then: £7,500

Award at February 2001: £8,453

Description of injuries: Displaced fracture of the left arm – severe bruising to the left hip.

Prognosis: The left elbow would always be a little weak and ache after strenuous activity – there was a 25 per cent chance of progressive osteoarthritic change.

1.4.3.1.C19 Case No. 10083

Name of case: Smithies v Eatoughs

Brief description of injuries: LEFT WRIST – FRACTURE – RESIDUAL SYMPTOMS

Reported: Kemp & Kemp, H4-025; [1990] CLY 1650

JSB Category: 6(H)

Sex: Male

Age at injury: 63

Age at award: –

Date of award: 19 September 1990

Tribunal: Not stated

Amount of award then: £6,000

Award at February 2001: £7,981

Description of injuries: Comminuted fracture of left lower radius at wrist joint – fracture united but with residual displacement causing discomfort and definite restriction of movement, particularly in supination – hand turned only as far as the vertical position – power of grip was diminished and plaintiff could not carry heavy weights.

1.4.3.1.C20 Case No. 11638

Name of case: Re Stock

Brief description of injuries: ARM – FRACTURE

Reported: Kemp & Kemp, H3-164/1; [1998] CLY 1640

JSB Category: 6(F)(d)

Sex: Male

Age at injury: 26

Age at award: 28

Date of award: 24 April 1998

Tribunal: CICB, Birmingham

Amount of award then: £7,500

Award at February 2001: £7,934

Description of injuries: Simple fracture of the left forearm – plate inserted.

Prognosis: Arm was likely to remain plated indefinitely – 10 to 15 per cent movement restriction would be permanent.

1.4.3.1.C21 Case No. 11420

Name of case: Roberts v Hunt
Brief description of injuries: WRIST – FRACTURE
Reported: Kemp & Kemp, H4-020/1; [1997] CLY 1969
JSB Category: 6(H)(c)
Sex: Female
Age at injury: 45
Age at award: 50
Date of award: 08 January 1997
Tribunal: Norwich County Court
Amount of award then: £7,000
Award at February 2001: £7,798

Description of injuries: Fracture to the radial styloid – dislocation of the radio-carpal joint upper rotor cuff tear – dysfunction of the median nerve to the wrist and hand.

Prognosis: Wrist discomfort would be permanent – degenerative changes over the next 20 to 30 years.

1.4.3.1.C22 Case No. 10430

Name of case: Jackson v Sung
Brief description of injuries: FRACTURED LEFT WRIST – AMBIDEXTROUS
Reported: Kemp & Kemp, H4-023; [1992] CLY 1686
JSB Category: 6(H)(c)
Sex: Male
Age at injury: 32
Age at award: 34
Date of award: 27 July 1992
Tribunal: Reading County Court
Amount of award then: £6,000
Award at February 2001: £7,435

Description of injuries: Fracture dislocation and moderate degree of comminution to left wrist – numbness to the fingers of the left hand – above-elbow plaster for two weeks – below-elbow plaster for a further three weeks – return to work eleven weeks after the accident in spite of pain – continuing pain required pain-killers – he was effectively ambidextrous and used left and right hands equally at work – worked more slowly than before.

Prognosis: Secondary degenerative changes probable.

1.4.3.1.C23 Case No. 11833

Name of case: Collett v Bean
Brief description of injuries: ARM – FRACTURE – SCAR
Reported: Kemp & Kemp, H3-168; [1999] CLY 1497
JSB Category: 6(F); 8
Sex: Male
Age at injury: 22
Age at award: 26
Date of award: 20 May 1999
Tribunal: Wandsworth County Court
Amount of award then: £7,000
Award at February 2001: £7,271

Description of injuries: Fracture of right humerus – plate and screws inserted into arm – claimant in plaster 1 month, off work 2 months, unable to drive for 3 months – after acute phase of recovery, arm continued to ache on heavy lifting and during cold weather – post-operative scar, 19cm long by 1cm wide, from elbow to just below shoulder, causing claimant embarrassment when questioned about it – full movement and function restored in arm – claimant became police officer, and arm only caused occasional inconvenience.

Prognosis: No increased risk of arthritis in arm – metalwork in arm very unlikely to be removed.

1.4.3.1.C24 Case No. 10431

Name of case: Robinson v Taylor and Roger Clark Cars
Brief description of injuries: FRACTURED RIGHT WRIST – REDUCED MOVEMENT
Reported: [1992] CLY 1687
JSB Category: 6(H)(d)
Sex: Male
Age at injury: 29
Age at award: 31
Date of award: 13 September 1991
Tribunal: Leicester County Court
Amount of award then: £4,750
Award at February 2001: £6,070

Description of injuries: Severely displaced fracture of the lower right radius – involved the articular surface of the radio-carpal joint and disrupted the inferior radio-ulna joint. At the time of the trial symptoms included pain on lifting and pain in the wrist on flexion – deformity on the flexor aspect of the wrist – loss of dorsal prominence of the lower end of the ulna – pronation was virtually full – supination three-quarters.

Prognosis: Unlikely to develop significant arthritis in the wrist during his working life.

1.4.3.1.C25 Case No. 11645

Name of case: Wiltshire v Warwick DC

Brief description of injuries: WRIST – SMITH FRACTURE

Reported: Kemp & Kemp, H3-172; [1998] CLY 1647

JSB Category: 6(H)

Sex: Female

Age at injury: 62

Age at award: 65

Date of award: 11 May 1998

Tribunal: Warwick County Court

Amount of award then: £5,500

Award at February 2001: £5,786

Description of injuries: Smith-type fracture to the wrist – minor lacerations to the face.

Prognosis: Continuing discomfort and stiffness was likely to persist – no further improvement to W's condition was expected.

1.4.3.1.C26 Case No. 10981

Name of case: Lee v Liverpool City Council

Brief description of injuries: WRIST – COLLES' FRACTURE AND DUPUYTREN'S CONTRACTURE – 10% DISABILITY

Reported: Kemp & Kemp, H4-026/2; [1995] CLY 1732

JSB Category: 6(H)(c)

Sex: Female

Age at injury: 68

Age at award: 71

Date of award: 19 June 1995

Tribunal: Liverpool County Court

Amount of award then: £5,000

Award at February 2001: £5,741

Description of injuries: Plaintiff tripped on defective paving stone – sustained a Colles' fracture to right dominant wrist and minor laceration to chin – also diagnosed as suffering from Dupuytren's contracture of right palmar tissues due to fall – fracture was reset and two stitches were made to chin laceration under general anaesthetic next day – was in hospital for two days and in plaster for six weeks – cared for by daughter for three months until she was able to return home – three-and-a-half years after accident she still required daily assistance from her home help/ daughter with shopping and housework – was left with 10 per cent permanent disability in overall flexion of wrist and was unable to perform any tasks with right hand, such as washing, without pain.

Prognosis: There was no risk of arthritis – suffered from an overall lack of confidence and was unable to carry out former pastimes such as knitting and sewing – medical reports expressed view that she was suffering from "a permanent and considerable disability in quality of her lifestyle".

1.4.3.1.C27 Case No. 10432

Name of case: Re Brown

Brief description of injuries: FRACTURED LEFT WRIST – WEAKENED GRIP

Reported: [1992] CLY 1688

JSB Category: 6(H)(d)

Sex: Female

Age at injury: 68

Age at award: 70

Date of award: 21 April 1992

Tribunal: Liverpool County Court

Amount of award then: £4,500

Award at February 2001: £5,576

Description of injuries: Colles fracture of the left wrist (not dominant) – bruised knees and cut to the right ankle – wrist manipulated under anaesthetic – set in plaster – remanipulated and set two weeks later – in plaster for seven weeks – flexion reduced – grip significantly weaker.

Prognosis: Disability likely to be permanent.

1.4.3.1.C28 Case No. 12044

Name of case: Richards v Hampshire CC

Brief description of injuries: WRIST – FRACTURE – 20 MONTHS

Reported: Kemp & Kemp, H4-036; [2000] 5 CL 188

JSB Category: 6(H)(d)

Sex: Male

Age at injury: 35

Age at award: 39

Date of award: 28 January 2000

Tribunal: Portsmouth County Court

Amount of award then: £5,000

Award at February 2001: £5,162

Description of injuries: Fracture to the base of the radial styloid – plaster for six weeks – painkillers on a daily basis – unable to return to work for four months – the stiff and painful wrist resulted in a significant disability – basic physiotherapy for four months.

Prognosis: It took twenty months to regain normal function – slightly increased risk of developing osteoarthritis in the left radio-carpal joints within five to ten years.

Other points: A fit and active man – he had been unable to follow his normal sporting hobbies.

1.4.3.1.C29 Case No. 10480

Name of case: Bedford v Ackworth Working Men's Club

Brief description of injuries: FRACTURE OF RIGHT ARM – RECOVERY 2 YEARS

Reported: Kemp & Kemp, K2-072; [1992] CLY 1736

JSB Category: 6(F)

Sex: Female

Age at injury: 59

Age at award: 62

Date of award: 02 January 1992

Tribunal: Pontefract County Court

Amount of award then: £3,500

Award at February 2001: £4,440

Description of injuries: Fracture to the greater tuberosity of the right humerus. Some interference with household tasks during recovery period.

Prognosis: Full recovery two years after the accident

1.4.3.1.C30 Case No. 10626

Name of case: Re Bond

Brief description of injuries: WRIST – FRACTURE

Reported: Kemp & Kemp, H4-028; [1993] CLY 1521

JSB Category: 6(H)(d)

Sex: Male

Age at injury: 37

Age at award: 42

Date of award: 04 August 1993

Tribunal: CICB, London

Amount of award then: £3,500

Award at February 2001: £4,260

Description of injuries: Claimant police officer in specialist crowd control unit at football match – disturbance in crowd – claimant threatened with violence, struck first blow – blow caused fractured dislocation at junction of claimant's right wrist (carpus) and hand at base of fourth and fifth metacarpals – off work 2 months – discomfort in hand for 2 years, particularly if pressurised (eg by shaking hands) – slight swelling of hand, not particularly noticeable.

Prognosis: Small risk of post-traumatic osteoarthritis which could cause aching in later life.

1.4.3.1.C31 Case No. 10227

Name of case: Faulkner v Shah

Brief description of injuries: OLECRANON FRACTURE – RIGHT ARM

Reported: [1991] CLY 1424

JSB Category: 6(F)(d)

Sex: Female

Age at injury: 55

Age at award: 59

Date of award: 01 July 1991

Tribunal: Edmonton County Court

Amount of award then: £3,250

Award at February 2001: £4,178

Description of injuries: Tripped and fell – suffered an undisplaced olecranon fracture to her right arm – backslab plaster extended from the knuckles to above the elbow – in plaster for seven weeks – some stiffness in the shoulder.

Prognosis: At the time of the hearing G was suffering from a lack of full range of movement – the right elbow suffered from slight but palpable and visible irregularity of the right radial head – aching discomfort with continued activities like window cleaning.

1.4.3.1.C32 Case No. 11174

Name of case: Guthrie v Hampshire CC

Brief description of injuries: WRIST – COLLES FRACTURE

Reported: Kemp & Kemp, H4-030; [1996] CLY 2265

JSB Category: 6(H)(e)

Sex: Male

Age at injury: 21

Age at award: 27

Date of award: 10 August 1995

Tribunal: Not stated

Amount of award then: £3,500

Award at February 2001: £4,016

Description of injuries: Comminuted fracture of the distal end of the radius – Colles fracture – lacerations to the lower body.

Prognosis: There were no functional problems with the wrist – scarring to the lower body.

1.4.3.1.C33 Case No. 11646

Name of case: Williams v Butcher
Brief description of injuries: WRIST – FRACTURE
Reported: Kemp & Kemp, B2-036/4; [1998] CLY 1648
JSB Category: 6(H)(d)
Sex: Female
Age at injury: 61
Age at award: 64
Date of award: 06 October 1997
Tribunal: Blackwood County Court
Amount of award then: £3,500
Award at February 2001: £3,774
Description of injuries: Undisplaced crack fracture to the right distal radius – bruising and swelling to the face and nose – continuing difficulty with heavy lifting – full recovery made.

1.4.3.1.C34 Case No. 11639

Name of case: McIlwee (a minor) v Zanussi Ltd
Brief description of injuries: ARM – FRACTURE
Reported: Kemp & Kemp, C4-120; [1998] CLY 1641
JSB Category: 6(F)(d)
Sex: Male
Age at injury: 5
Age at award: 8
Date of award: 03 March 1998
Tribunal: Newbury County Court
Amount of award then: £3,220
Award at February 2001: £3,444
Description of injuries: Spiral fracture to the supracondylar region of the humerus – at the time of the hearing full recovery had taken place.

1.4.3.1.C35 Case No. 11936

Name of case: R (a minor) v Calderdale MBC
Brief description of injuries: WRIST – GREENSTICK FRACTURE
Reported: Kemp & Kemp, K2-047/2; [1999] CLY 1600
JSB Category: 6(H)(e)
Sex: Male
Age at injury: 9
Age at award: 12
Date of award: 16 July 1999
Tribunal: Halifax County Court (infant settlement approval hearing)
Amount of award then: £3,000
Award at February 2001: £3,125
Description of injuries: Greenstick fracture to radius in left wrist – wrist in pain for approximately 1 month – fracture united, but with some angulation, causing a slight deformity – also some slight restriction in pronation and supination – over 18 months, deformity gradually disappeared and was not visible by date of hearing; no restriction in movement – claimant's enjoyment of summer holiday immediately after accident considerably reduced.
Other points: Agreed settlement

1.4.3.1.C36 Case No. 11937

Name of case: N (a minor) v Yorkshire Water Services Ltd
Brief description of injuries: WRIST – GREENSTICK FRACTURE
Reported: Kemp & Kemp, H3-183; [1999] CLY 1601
JSB Category: 6(H)(e)
Sex: Male
Age at injury: 4
Age at award: 6
Date of award: 22 March 1999
Tribunal: Halifax County Court (infant settlement approval hearing)
Amount of award then: £2,500
Award at February 2001: £2,620
Description of injuries: Greenstick fracture to lower end of radius of left wrist – also nosebleed and abrasion to nose – plaster back slab applied to wrist, in place 4 weeks – fracture healed satisfactorily – claimant did not miss any schooling as a result of the incident.
Other points: Agreed settlement

1.4.3.1.C37 Case No. 10113

Name of case: Type v Merthyr Tydfil Borough Council
Brief description of injuries: LEFT HUMERUS AND RADIUS – FRACTURES – HEALED 3 MONTHS
Reported: Kemp & Kemp, K2-086; [1990] CLY 1684
JSB Category: 6(F)
Sex: Male
Age at injury: 11
Age at award: 13
Date of award: 27 March 1990
Tribunal: Merthyr Tydfil County Court
Amount of award then: £1,600
Award at February 2001: £2,267
Description of injuries: Fall from tree in park – compound fracture of both bones of left forearm – set under general anaesthetic and plaster cast applied – full recovery 12 weeks after accident – plaintiff subsequently wary of playing in park or near trees.

1.4.3.1.C38 Case No. 11647

Name of case: Murray (a minor) v Knowsley BC

Brief description of injuries: WRIST – FRACTURE – 6 WEEKS

Reported: Kemp & Kemp, H4-029/1; [1998] CLY 1649

JSB Category: 6(H)(d)

Sex: Male

Age at injury: 12

Age at award: 14

Date of award: 20 May 1998

Tribunal: Liverpool County Court

Amount of award then: £2,000

Award at February 2001: £2,104

Description of injuries: Greenstick fracture of the right dominant wrist – full movement of the wrist achieved and discomfort settled within 6 weeks of the date of the accident.

1.4.3.1.C39 Case No. 10496

Name of case: Skerry v Liverpool City Council

Brief description of injuries: FRACTURED WRISTS – PLASTER FOR 13 DAYS

Reported: [1992] CLY 1752

JSB Category: 6(H)(c)

Sex: Male

Age at injury: 12

Age at award: –

Date of award: 08 January 1992

Tribunal: Liverpool County Court

Amount of award then: £1,500

Award at February 2001: £1,903

Description of injuries: Fractures to both wrists – both wrists in elbow casts for eighteen days – unable to look after himself without help.

Prognosis: Full recovery within 3 months.

1.4.3.1.C40 Case No. 11934

Name of case: B (a minor) v Mitchell

Brief description of injuries: ARM – FRACTURE – 3 MONTHS

Reported: (1999) 99 (2) QR 7; Kemp & Kemp, K2-117/3; [1999] CLY 1598

JSB Category: 6(F)(d)

Sex: Male

Age at injury: 9

Age at award: 13

Date of award: 01 July 1999

Tribunal: Doncaster County Court

Amount of award then: £1,800

Award at February 2001: £1,875

Description of injuries: Fractures to non-dominant left arm – fractures manipulated and placed in cast – cast removed after 8 weeks and 2 weeks of physiotherapy followed – while arm in plaster, claimant unable to dress, bathe or carry out similar basic functions without assistance from parents – claimant unable to take part in PE lessons for 3 months after returning to school from summer holidays – fractures united in excellent positions.

Prognosis: No long-term problems anticipated.

1.4.3.1.C41 Case No. 12017

Name of case: C (a child) v Leeds NHS Teaching National Trust

Brief description of injuries: ARM – FRACTURE – LATE DIAGNOSIS

Reported: Kemp & Kemp, K2-253/1; [2000] 4 CL 160

JSB Category: 6

Sex: Female

Age at injury: 21 months

Age at award: 4

Date of award: 07 January 1998

Tribunal: Leeds County Court

Amount of award then: £600

Award at February 2001: £647

Description of injuries: Late diagnosis of a mid-shaft fracture to the right radius with some slight angulation – early callus formation on the ulna and some plastic deformation as opposed to a complete fracture – above elbow slab for nineteen days. C made a full and complete recovery.

Other points: Had diagnosis been made at the initial visit to hospital C would have been spared ten days of pain and discomfort.

1.4.3.2 ARM OR WRIST FRACTURE AND OTHER INJURY

1.4.3.2.C1 Case No. 11084

Name of case: Doyle v Cable

Brief description of injuries: ARM – LEG – MULTIPLE FRACTURES

Reported: Kemp & Kemp, B1-100; [1996] CLY 2175

JSB Category: 6(K)(b)(ii)

Sex: Male

Age at injury: 20

Age at award: 28

Date of award: 24 June 1996

Tribunal: Newcastle upon Tyne County Court

Amount of award then: £33,000

Award at February 2001: £39,423

Description of injuries: Fractures to the right radius, surgical neck of the right humerus, right femur, right tibia and fibula.

Prognosis: Within ten to fifteen years of the accident remedial surgery to the knee would be required – raised insole to the shoe required for the rest of his life.

Other points: The judge accepted that his value in the labour market was very substantially reduced.

1.4.3.2.C2 Case No. 12031

Name of case: Re L (CICB Quantum: 2000)

Brief description of injuries: ARM – FRACTURES – JAW

Reported: Kemp & Kemp, PRC-006; [2000] 5 CL 175

JSB Category: 6(F)(c) 7(A)(e)

Sex: Male

Age at injury: 61

Age at award: 67

Date of award: 27 January 2000

Tribunal: CICB

Amount of award then: £22,500

Award at February 2001: £23,934

Description of injuries: Fracture dislocation of the right elbow – dislocation of the radius at the elbow – fracture of the ulna – displaced fracture of the mandible in two places – laceration to the left ear – facial lacerations – minor head injury. Persistent discomfort to the left side of the jaw – difficulty eating – sleep disturbance – poor short term memory.

1.4.3.2.C3 Case No. 10975

Name of case: Re Davis

Brief description of injuries: RIGHT ARM – LEFT ELBOW – PERMANENT PAIN AND LOSS OF FUNCTION

Reported: Kemp & Kemp, H3-153; [1995] CLY 1726

JSB Category: 6(F)(b)

Sex: Male

Age at injury: 29

Age at award: 34

Date of award: 22 May 1995

Tribunal: CICB, London

Amount of award then: £20,000

Award at February 2001: £23,680

Description of injuries: Plaintiff injured when attacked with wooden club in September 1989 – suffered closed fracture of radius of right forearm and very comminuted displaced intra-articular fracture of olecranon of left elbow in addition to bruising and pain over chest, back and arms – underwent operation under general anaesthetic – radius of right arm was reduced and fixed with metal plate and screws, and left elbow was immobilised in plaster of Paris cast – applicant was kept in hospital for about three weeks and had continuing treatment from fracture clinic for nearly a year – long surgical scar to right forearm – suffered pain in right arm on waking up which increased with use and necessitatetd taking four painkillers per day – pain radiated to right shoulder with pins and needles and weakness to right hand; supination was only three-quarters normal, and grip power was reduced due to pain – pain on posterior aspect of left elbow, a lot of stiffness and an inability to fully straighten; grip power was reduced; supination was only two-thirds normal, flexion and extension lacked 40 degrees and there was damage to articular cartilage – pain on any heavy lifting in left side of chest with tenderness over 10th and 11th ribs – suffered increasing pain in back with tenderness over spinous processes – may have been aggravated by injury – deeply depressed and very reluctant to go out at night alone – left elbow showed irregularity and had mal-united, and prognosis was that he would definitely suffer osteo-arthritis in future. Lifting weights caused pain and accelerated the rate of development of osteoarthritis – would not be able to return to job as carpenter – suffered from dyslexia, and only job he knew was carpentry.

Prognosis: Disability was permanent and would get worse, giving him more pain and limitations.

1.4.3.2.C4 Case No. 10429

Name of case: Boother v British Railways Board

Brief description of injuries: FRACTURE OF RIGHT WRIST – BROKEN NOSE – PERMANENT ACHING DEFORMITY OF WRIST – REDUCED GRIP

Reported: [1992] CLY 1685

JSB Category: 6(H)(c)

Sex: Female

Age at injury: 58

Age at award: 65

Date of award: 18 February 1992

Tribunal: Wandsworth County Court

Amount of award then: £9,500

Award at February 2001: £11,988

Description of injuries: Colles fracture of the right (dominant) wrist – fracture of the nose – bruising to the knee – wrist fracture manipulated under anaesthetic and splinted in plaster – in plaster for six weeks – six weeks physiotherapy – away from work for seven months – fractured nose exacerbated pre-existing nasal blockage – manipulated under anaesthetic in December 1985.

Prognosis: Constant aching of the wrist with slight deformity – reduction of grip by 40% – permanent pain, deformity and limitation of movement.

1.4.3.2.C5 Case No. 10082

Name of case: Braithwaite v Latham

Brief description of injuries: RIGHT WRIST FRACTURE – FEMUR FRACTURE

Reported: Kemp & Kemp, H4-017; BPILS, I 14; [1990] CLY 1649

JSB Category: 6(H)

Sex: Male

Age at injury: 24

Age at award: 27

Date of award: 22 May 1990

Tribunal: QBD

Amount of award then: £5,500

Award at February 2001: £7,496

Description of injuries: Comminuted fracture of right wrist involving distal articular surface of the radius and styloid process of the ulna – undisplaced fractures to bases of fourth and fifth metacarpals of right hand – fracture at junction of middle and upper third of right femur – 35 degrees of palmar flexion lost from wrist – slight permanent restriction in flexion of right knee and some scarring to right thigh – pain and discomfort in both fracture sites in cold weather.

Prognosis: Risk of osteoarthritis in wrist in long term

1.4.3.2.C6 Case No. 10977

Name of case: Byrne v Swan Moulinex

Brief description of injuries: ELBOW – "TENNIS ELBOW" – SOME CONTINUING LIMITATION

Reported: Kemp & Kemp, H3-106; [1995] CLY 1728

JSB Category: 6(F)(d)

Sex: Female

Age at injury: 50

Age at award: 55

Date of award: 27 March 1995

Tribunal: Birmingham County Court

Amount of award then: £5,000

Award at February 2001: £5,831

Description of injuries: Plaintiff was working on assembly line at defendants' factory – after more than a year she developed symptoms of pain and discomfort in right arm – did not report problem but subsequently attended hospital – employers allowed her to continue to perform repetitive manual work from about July 1990 until she gave up work in October 1990, having seen her GP – during this time she was in some pain which subsided during weekends – GP described this as classic tennis elbow – after giving up work in October 1990, symptoms gradually subsided and was able to return to work for different employers in February 1991 – after 12 months symptoms recurred – it was held that these symptoms were caused by damage done in summer of 1990 when plaintiff was allowed to go on working with defendants – had to give up second job and had not worked since – now suffered from significant disability in right arm – not in pain and was able to do some of her housework but work involving gripping and demanding activity of right arm had to be carried out by her daughter.

1.4.3.2.C7 Case No. 10978

Name of case: Morgan v Southampton City Council

Brief description of injuries: ARM – FRACTURE – ELBOW MOVEMENT LIMITED

Reported: Kemp & Kemp, H3-169; [1995] CLY 1729

JSB Category: 6(F)(d)

Sex: Female

Age at injury: 7

Age at award: 10

Date of award: 27 September 1995

Tribunal: Southampton County Court

Amount of award then: £3,850

Award at February 2001: £4,397

Description of injuries: Sustained an injury to her right, non-dominant, arm – also sustained supracondylar fracture of right humerus – taken to hospital and admitted overnight – next day, under general anaesthetic, fracture was realigned and arm was placed in back slab and rested in sling – remained as in-patient for three days – later seen in fracture clinic roughly once a fortnight for about six weeks – was away from school for three weeks – 11 months after injury had occasional aches and pains in arm but nevertheless had been able to use it normally – had full range of extension of right elbow but flexion was reduced by 20 degrees compared to left side – 10 degree varus deformity of right elbow and there was also visible deformity of elbow – review of X-rays indicated overall an excellent alignment of fracture site – two years after accident plaintiff still reported occasional aches and pains in right elbow – she again had a full range of extension – flexion of right elbow was reduced by 10 degrees – there was just less than 10 degrees of varus deformity but there was no longer a visible deformity of elbow joint – slight but definite improvement in range of movement.

Prognosis: Prognosis was that as plaintiff continued to grow continuing improvements would occur – likelihood was that by time she reached maturity she would have no significant deformity of right elbow.

1.4.3.2.C8 Case No. 10481

Award at February 2001: £3,718

See: 1.4.1.1.C22 for details

1.4.4 HAND INJURY

1.4.4.C1 Case No. 10087

Name of case: Daniel v Valor Heating

Brief description of injuries: RIGHT HAND CRUSHED – SEVERE LIMITATION OF MOVEMENT

Reported: Kemp & Kemp, H6-013; [1990] CLY 1654

JSB Category: 6(I)

Sex: Female

Age at injury: –

Age at award: 48

Date of award: 09 February 1990

Tribunal: Manchester

Amount of award then: £34,803

Award at February 2001: £54,398

Description of injuries: Right dominant hand was crushed by unguarded machine – ring and little fingers amputated with part of the palm – limited movement in metacarpo-phalangeal joint of middle finger – although thumb and index finger unharmed, there was gross diminution of grip and dexterity – unable to manage any lifting with injured hand – embarrassed by disfigurement.

Prognosis: Discomfort in palm at site of neuroma likely to be permanent.

1.4.4.C2 Case No. 10434

Name of case: Smith v Halstead Plastics

Brief description of injuries: AMPUTATION OF THE RIGHT INDEX FINGER – MUSCLE NERVE DAMAGE – VERY UNSIGHTLY

Reported: [1992] CLY 1690

JSB Category: 6(I)(d)

Sex: Male

Age at injury: 22

Age at award: 27

Date of award: 16 April 1992

Tribunal: Colchester and Clacton County Court

Amount of award then: £22,500

Award at February 2001: £29,030

Description of injuries: Laceration of palm with severe damage to the thenar muscles – division of flexor pollicis tendon – exposure of the median nerve and several flexor tendons – major salvage surgery – damaged thenar muscles removed – amputation of the index finger – its skin and tendons used to improve web between thumb and fingers and movement of the thumb.

Prognosis: Hand very unsightly – assessed as 50% disabled – could hold a steering wheel.

1.4.4.C3 Case No. 10435

Name of case: Re Shimmin

Brief description of injuries: SEVERE INJURY TO RIGHT HAND – HAND VIRTUALLY USELESS

Reported: Kemp & Kemp, H5-019; [1992] CLY 1691

JSB Category: 6(I)(f)

Sex: Female

Age at injury: 58

Age at award: 60

Date of award: 08 March 1991

Tribunal: CICB, Newcastle upon Tyne

Amount of award then: £17,500

Award at February 2001: £23,586

Description of injuries: Severe injuries to the palm and flexor aspect of the dominant right hand – division of the flexor tendons to all the fingers – exploratory operation – followed by repair operation on tendons and nerves – third operation when tendons dehisced – it was found to be unrepairable – silastic rods inserted into the fingers as a preliminary for tendon grafting – but grafting was not a viable proposition.

Prognosis: Fingers unusable – unable to make any great use of the right hand.

1.4.4.C4 Case No. 11656

Name of case: Ellis v Liverpool City Council

Brief description of injuries: FINGERS – VIBRATION WHITE FINGER

Reported: Kemp & Kemp, H6A-026; [1998] CLY 1658

JSB Category: 6(I)(y)(i)

Sex: Male

Age at injury: 30

Age at award: 42

Date of award: 27 March 1998

Tribunal: Manchester County Court

Amount of award then: £15,000

Award at February 2001: £16,263

Description of injuries: Hand arm vibration syndrome – sensori-neural symptoms placed at stage 3SN or late 2SN – vascular symptoms between stage 2 and 3 – affecting all digits of each hand – E was found unfit for work outside – lacked aptitude for clerical side of storekeeping – unsuited to lifting cold metal objects.

1.4.4.C5 Case No. 10982

Name of case: Re Harvey

Brief description of injuries: HAND – LACERATION – 50 SUTURES – 15% DISABILITY

Reported: Kemp & Kemp, H6/022; [1995] CLY 1733

JSB Category: 6(I)(f)

Sex: Male

Age at injury: 25

Age at award: 30

Date of award: 31 March 1995

Tribunal: CICB, Liverpool

Amount of award then: £10,000

Award at February 2001: £11,701

Description of injuries: Right-handed male suffered laceration to left hand when protecting face from glass or bottle thrust towards him – laceration extended from just the wrist to base of cleft and between little and ring fingers – operation was performed under general anaesthetic with about 50 sutures inserted – last 10 degrees of extension of metacarpo-phalangeal and proximal interphalangeal joints of middle and ring fingers were lost, but was able to extend the index and little fingers fully and had normal function of thumb – was able to clench left hand into fist but not quite able to tuck in tips of little and ring fingers as on right hand – had impaired sensation of adjacent sides of middle and ring fingers with hypersensitivity at base of palm and wrist – power of grip was weak – tended to drop things and was unable to lift heavy objects – level of permanent disability was assessed at 15 per cent – incident precipitated post-traumatic stress disorder with reluctance to go out socially – underwent treatment for about four months.

Prognosis: Hopeful.

1.4.4.C6 Case No. 11176

Name of case: O'Donnell v Shropshire CC

Brief description of injuries: HAND – SEVERE CUTS

Reported: Kemp & Kemp, H5-020/1; [1996] CLY 2267

JSB Category: 6(I)

Sex: Female

Age at injury: 10

Age at award: 13

Date of award: 11 September 1996

Tribunal: Shrewsbury County Court

Amount of award then: £10,000

Award at February 2001: £11,209

Description of injuries: Severe cut to the left hand – total division of the ulna nerve – division of the flexor carpi-ulnaris tendon to the little finger and also the palmaris longus – permanent long scar – permanent weakness and clumsiness in the hand.

1.4.4.C7 Case No. 11838

Name of case: Pullar v Aldi Stores Ltd

Brief description of injuries: HAND – DAMAGE TO NERVES AND TENDONS

Reported: Kemp & Kemp, H6-023/1; [1999] CLY 1502

JSB Category: 6(I)(h), 6(I)(u)

Sex: Female

Age at injury: 41

Age at award: 42

Date of award: 11 February 1999

Tribunal: QBD

Amount of award then: £10,000

Award at February 2001: £10,514

Description of injuries: Severe laceration between thumb and index finger of left, non-dominant hand – flexor tendon of index finger severed; likewise digital nerves, mainly on thumb side – subsequent scarring and adhesion impinging on tendons – continuing pain and loss of sensation in finger, which was practically immobile – assistance required at home and claimant unable to live normal life without hindrance.

Prognosis: Future surgery recommended to attempt to free tendons from lesions and restore movement in index finger – failing that, procedure to replace tendon necessary – likelihood of success in both cases rated at 60 per cent – amputation of index finger possible last resort, but this might not relieve continuing pain or achieve a good cosmetic result.

1.4.4.C8 Case No. 10086

Name of case: O'Brien v Berol

Brief description of injuries: LEFT HAND – STAB – NEUROMA – HAND ALMOST USELESS

Reported: [1990] CLY 1653

JSB Category: 6(I)

Sex: Female

Age at injury: 30

Age at award: 34

Date of award: 22 November 1988

Tribunal: Norwich County Court

Amount of award then: £6,500

Award at February 2001: £10,164

Description of injuries: Stabbed the palm of her left, non-dominant, hand, dividing digital nerve to index and middle fingers – a neuroma formed which resisted treatment – hand was almost useless due to the exquisite tenderness and sensitivity in the palm.

1.4.4.C9 Case No. 10627

Name of case: Butler v Liverpool City Council

Brief description of injuries: FINGERS – VIBRATION WHITE FINGER

Reported: Kemp & Kemp, H6-024; [1993] CLY 1522

JSB Category: 6(I)(y)(ii)

Sex: Female

Age at injury: 52-64

Age at award: 68

Date of award: 02 October 1992

Tribunal: Liverpool District Registry

Amount of award then: £8,000

Award at February 2001: £9,836

Description of injuries: Claimant had operated floor – buffing machines for 12 years in capacity as school cleaner – vibration white finger assessed at stage 3 on Taylor-Pelmear Scale – symptoms occurring irrespective of ambient temperature – all fingers except thumbs blanched to proximal interphalangeal joints – persistent tingling in affected digits – grip progressively impaired – significant impact upon domestic activities – unable to carry out household duties – unable to continue hobbies of hairdressing and knitting.

1.4.4.C10 Case No. 10088

Name of case: Thomas v Howmet Turbine (UK) Inc

Brief description of injuries: RIGHT INDEX FINGER – SEVERE LACERATIONS

Reported: Kemp & Kemp, H6-026; [1990] CLY 1655

JSB Category: 6(I)

Sex: Male

Age at injury: 40

Age at award: 44

Date of award: 24 July 1990

Tribunal: QBD

Amount of award then: £7,000

Award at February 2001: £9,495

Description of injuries: Severe laceration to the right index finger, involving tendons and the bone – finger remains stiff and is unable to grip small tools – writing is affected – plaintiff tends to drop things – no useful movement in the finger – dorsal aspect is particularly sensitive, especially in cold weather – zigzag scar extending from mid-shaft region of the proximal phalanx across proximal interphalangeal joint – grip of hand affected.

Prognosis: Degenerative changes may occur in interphalangeal joint, but this will probably not be very serious – unable to return pre-accident work – some disadvantage on open labour market.

1.4.4.C11 Case No. 11840

Name of case: Groom v RSM Fabrications Ltd

Brief description of injuries: HAND – DEPRESSION

Reported: Kemp & Kemp, H6-025/1; [1999] CLY 1504

JSB Category: 6(I); 3(A)

Sex: Male

Age at injury: 36

Age at award: 42

Date of award: 01 July 1999

Tribunal: Gloucester County Court

Amount of award then: £9,000

Award at February 2001: £9,376

Description of injuries: Fractures to base of fourth and fifth metacarpals of non-dominant left hand – persistent pain, leading to carpo – metacarpal fusion operation and arthrodesis operation – claimant found to have been unable to pursue his manual employment as a result of the injury for 3 years, and would have been able to return to light manual work after that had it not been for unrelated problems with his shoulder – claimant in fragile psychological state at time of accident – 6 years after accident, claimant suffered from moderately severe depression, mild agoraphobia, mild panic disorder, general low self – esteem, anhedonia, and fixation on his disability – accident a material contribution to claimant's depressed mental state, but there were other, unrelated, relevant factors, such as redundancy – claimant found to be psychologically unfit for work at time of trial.

1.4.4.C12 Case No. 10812

Name of case: Maxim v Indelicato

Brief description of injuries: HAND – MULTIPLE INJURIES

Reported: Kemp & Kemp, H6-027; [1994] CLY 1661

JSB Category: 6(I); 6(H)(e)

Sex: Female

Age at injury: 36

Age at award: 38

Date of award: 24 May 1994

Tribunal: Milton Keynes County Court

Amount of award then: £7,500

Award at February 2001: £8,915

Description of injuries: Claimant involved in road accident – vehicle struck bollard, overturned and landed on roof – claimant left hanging upside – down for 45 minutes while being freed from wreckage – minor head injury – colles fracture to lower radius of right, dominant, wrist – severed extensor tendon in right index finger – abrasions on back of right ring, middle and index fingers – piece of glass embedded in right palm – wrist in plaster 6 weeks – fingers in splints 4-5 weeks – absent from work 5 weeks – unable to drive or resume hobby of cycling for 9 weeks – hand stiff and grip weak for 6 months – everyday tasks, such as cooking, eating, dressing and housework, problematic – other hobbies of sewing and knitting also difficult – sleep disturbed – minor scarring to fingers – near full recovery made after 6 months – some loss of grip, mild discomfort in fingers and slight loss of manual dexterity (index finger flexion reduced to 90 degrees) still present.

Other points: Award breakdown: finger: £4,000; wrist fracture: £2,500; shock: £1,000.

1.4.4.C13 Case No. 10983

Name of case: Wheeler v Central Independent Television and John Frost Scenery

Brief description of injuries: HAND – CRUSH INJURY TO 2 FINGERS – CONTINUING SYMPTOMS

Reported: Kemp & Kemp, H6-030; [1995] CLY 1734

JSB Category: 6(I)(f)

Sex: Male

Age at injury: 44

Age at award: –

Date of award: 03 January 1995

Tribunal: Nottingham County Court

Amount of award then: £7,500

Award at February 2001: £8,836

Description of injuries: Plaintiff employed as scenery and props man by defendants suffered crush injury to index, middle and ring fingers of right non-dominant hand – compound fractures of distal phalanges of middle and ring fingers with damage to nail beds and subungual haematoma of index finger – off work for six weeks – middle and ring fingertips healed a position of curving backwards – ridging of ring finger nail and marked ridging of middle finger nail – plaintiff was embarrassed by appearance of fingertips and nail – inco-ordination of fingertips meant that he had great difficulty tying knots, a task frequently required in his work – had aching discomfort in fingers after heavy work and in cold weather – fingertips were sore if knocked – had been able to continue with work despite difficulties.

Prognosis: The accident had brought forward by five years pre-existing but symptomless osteoarthritis in finger joints, and as result at age 60-65 would suffer some lack of dexterity in fingers.

1.4.4.C14 Case No. 10813

Name of case: Smith v Baker and McKenzie
Brief description of injuries: HAND – TENOSYNOVITIS
Reported: Kemp & Kemp, H8-013; [1994] CLY 1662
JSB Category: 6(J)
Sex: Female
Age at injury: mid-to-late 20s
Age at award: –
Date of award: 11 April 1994
Tribunal: Mayor's and City of London County Court
Amount of award then: £7,250
Award at February 2001: £8,648

Description of injuries: Claimant worked as legal secretary – claimed to be given no break from typing – in May 1990, development of stiffness in left fingers and pain and numbness across knuckles, and, later, wrist, of left hand – high-pressure typing caused left hand to become stiff, painful and difficult to move, resulting in an inability to perform certain household tasks – bursting of ganglion – pain continued to worsen thereafter – claimant advised to stop typing and go on leave in June 1990 – diagnosis by consultant rheumatologist of adhesions, forming between May and September 1990, leading to low-grade tenosynovitis affecting wrist extensor tendons, without diffuse upper limb pain – some symptoms continued at date of trial.

1.4.4.C15 Case No. 11181

Name of case: Glorman v Ford Motor Co Ltd
Brief description of injuries: FINGER – VIBRATION WHITE FINGER
Reported: [1996] CLY 2272
JSB Category: 6(I)(y)(iii)
Sex: Male
Age at injury: 44
Age at award: 52
Date of award: 10 May 1996
Tribunal: Liverpool County Court
Amount of award then: £7,500
Award at February 2001: £8,437

Description of injuries: Vibration white finger – stage II/III on the Taylor Pelmear scale – all fingers subject to blanching to the palmar crease – even in summer.

Prognosis: Interference in his life – loss of dexterity and grip – no difficulty with current work duties – he was handicapped in the labour market.

1.4.4.C16 Case No. 10816

Name of case: Condra v Norcros
Brief description of injuries: HAND – VIBRATION WHITE FINGER
Reported: Kemp & Kemp, H6A-028; [1994] CLY 1665
JSB Category: 6(I)(y)
Sex: Male
Age at injury: 14-year period
Age at award: 68
Date of award: 02 July 1993
Tribunal: Liverpool County Court
Amount of award then: £6,750
Award at February 2001: £8,252

Description of injuries: Claimant employed as window fixer and glazier – drilling using Hilti gun and impact gun for up to 2 hours daily – development of vibration white finger at stage II of Taylor-Pelmear Scale – little and ring fingers of right hand, and ring, middle and index fingers on left hand, affected – claimant's ability to decorate seriously affected – hobbies of golf and swimming curtailed.

1.4.4.C17 Case No. 11421

Name of case: Re Torrance
Brief description of injuries: FINGER – TENDON DAMAGE
Reported: Kemp & Kemp, H6-031/1; [1997] CLY 1970
JSB Category: 6(I)(k)
Sex: Male
Age at injury: –
Age at award: 33
Date of award: 24 July 1997
Tribunal: CICB Nottingham
Amount of award then: £7,500
Award at February 2001: £8,190

Description of injuries: Damage to the flexor tendons of the ring finger – a fortnight after repair an accidental knock and extension ruptured one tendon – lengthened the other.

Prognosis: Finger healed with fixed flexion contracture of 50 degrees – finger frequently "caught" – plaintiff reluctant to have the finger amputated – at a future disadvantage in the labour market.

1.4.4.C18 Case No. 11178

Name of case: Re Singh

Brief description of injuries: FINGER – AMPUTATION

Reported: Kemp & Kemp, H6-032; [1996] CLY 2269

JSB Category: 6(I)(o)

Sex: Female

Age at injury: 50

Age at award: 54

Date of award: 21 March 1996

Tribunal: CICB, Torquay

Amount of award then: £7,000

Award at February 2001: £7,947

Description of injuries: Dislocated middle and ring fingers of the left hand – boutonniere deformity diagnosed – ray amputation of the ring finger – three operations were required – suffered reduced grip and discomfort in cold weather – she was not overly troubled by the cosmetic defect – able to continue to work.

1.4.4.C19 Case No. 11182

Name of case: McNamara v Liverpool City Council

Brief description of injuries: FINGER – VIBRATION WHITE FINGER

Reported: Kemp & Kemp, H6A-029; [1996] CLY 2273

JSB Category: 6(I)(y)(iii)

Sex: Male

Age at injury: 26

Age at award: 41

Date of award: 25 March 1996

Tribunal: Liverpool County Court

Amount of award then: £6,000

Award at February 2001: £6,812

Description of injuries: Vibration white finger – stage III on the Taylor Pelmear scale.

Prognosis: Plaintiff was not at a substantial disadvantage in the labour market – dexterity had been permanently affected.

Other points: The judge found that comparison with awards for this condition, and other types of injury were not helpful – each case must be assessed in terms of severity.

1.4.4.C20 Case No. 10089

Name of case: Streatfield v Long

Brief description of injuries: LEFT MIDDLE FINGER – CRUSHED

Reported: Kemp & Kemp, H6-033; [1990] CLY 1656

JSB Category: 6(I)

Sex: Male

Age at injury: 22

Age at award: 25

Date of award: 01 May 1990

Tribunal: Norwich

Amount of award then: £4,950

Award at February 2001: £6,746

Description of injuries: Crushing injury to distal segment of left middle finger requiring amputation of that segment – stump hypersensitive to touch, the lightest pressure causing pain – unable to carry out heavy tasks with left hand – power of grip reduced – manipulation of small objects more difficult – feeling of tightness over tip of stump – self-conscious of appearance.

1.4.4.C21 Case No. 10988

Name of case: Murray v TJ & T K Williams

Brief description of injuries: HAND – CRUSH INJURY TO THUMB – RESTRICTION OF MOVEMENT

Reported: Kemp & Kemp, H7-015/1; [1995] CLY 1739

JSB Category: 6(I)(u)

Sex: Male

Age at injury: 39

Age at award: 41

Date of award: 16 December 1994

Tribunal: Manchester County Court

Amount of award then: £5,500

Award at February 2001: £6,479

Description of injuries: Right-handed male was former truck operator who suffered crushing injury and fracture to left thumb – taken to hospital and underwent operation to excise dirty and dead skin – sutures inserted and K-wires put across fractures – plaintiff was inpatient for two-and-a-half days – K-wires removed four weeks later and plaster of Paris cast encasing left thumb was left on for five weeks – plaintiff was off work for three months following accident and returned only to light duties – nearly three years after accident plaintiff's left thumb ached often and was sometimes swollen – still experienced shooting pain which was particularly acute in cold weather – left thumb was scarred and there was decreased sensation from tip down to level of interphalangeal joint – distal phalanx of thumb was splayed out clinically – great restriction of active and passive movement with particularly decreased range of movement from inter-phalangeal joint – medical evidence did not predict that plaintiff was at significantly increased risk of developing osteo-arthritis – thumb was "obvious" and plaintiff was therefore very aware and embarrassed by it – it tended to stick out and plaintiff frequently knocked it – plaintiff had difficulty picking up smaller items with left hand and doing up buttons – could not make a fist with his left hand.

1.4.4.C22 Case No. 10229

Name of case: Alexander v HCC Tinsley and Son
Brief description of injuries: CARPAL TUNNEL SYNDROME – BOTH HANDS – 2 OPERATIONS
Reported: Kemp & Kemp, H4-032; [1991] CLY 1426
JSB Category: 6(H)(d)
Sex: Female
Age at injury: 45
Age at award: 49
Date of award: 15 October 1991
Tribunal: Norwich County Court
Amount of award then: £5,000
Award at February 2001: £6,366

Description of injuries: Wrist injury – developed tingling in the hands – sensation of pins and needles, numbness and pain – diagnosed as carpal tunnel syndrome – underwent a relief operation on the right wrist in 1987 and the left in 1988. The judge did not accept that the injury was a result of A's work – it was a naturally occurring spontaneous carpal tunnel syndrome in a lady in her middle years.

Prognosis: Slight residual pain to the right hand.

1.4.4.C23 Case No. 11179

Name of case: Milan v West Glamorgan CC
Brief description of injuries: FINGER – LIGAMENT DAMAGE
Reported: Kemp & Kemp, H6-034/1; [1996] CLY 2270
JSB Category: 6(I)
Sex: Male
Age at injury: 9
Age at award: 14
Date of award: 09 March 1995
Tribunal: Swansea County Court
Amount of award then: £5,250
Award at February 2001: £6,122

Description of injuries: Damaged profundus and superficialis tendons of the right little finger – not diagnosed and repaired until nine weeks later – operation scar to the hand – three 2cm operation scars to the right forearm.

Prognosis: 75-80 per cent chance of full recovery had the injury been recognised when first treated – slight chance of the tendons not growing as he got older.

1.4.4.C24 Case No. 10634

Name of case: Cook v Containership
Brief description of injuries: THUMB – CRUSH INJURY
Reported: Kemp & Kemp, H7-015/2; [1993] CLY 1529
JSB Category: 6(I)(u)
Sex: Male
Age at injury: 50
Age at award: 52
Date of award: 08 June 1993
Tribunal: Middlesbrough County Court
Amount of award then: £5,000
Award at February 2001: £6,099

Description of injuries: "Very nasty" crush injury to thumb of dominant hand – comminuted fracture – rotational deformity of distal part of proximal phalanx – lacerations – altered sensation on back of thumb due to damage of radial nerve – gross restriction of flexion – some lack of hypertension – claimant given up darts; experiencing difficulties with holding pen or knife, fastening buttons, tying shoelaces.

Prognosis: Possibility of accelerated osteoarthritic changes assessed at 20-30 per cent – strong possibility of fusion of inter-phalangeal joint.

1.4.4.C25 Case No. 10437

Name of case: Ticehurst v Spa Hotel (Goring)
Brief description of injuries: AMPUTATION OF RIGHT LITTLE FINGER
Reported: Kemp & Kemp, H6-037; [1992] CLY 1693
JSB Category: 6(I)(m)
Sex: Male
Age at injury: 16
Age at award: 25
Date of award: 10 October 1991
Tribunal: Tunbridge Wells County Court
Amount of award then: £4,500
Award at February 2001: £5,729

Description of injuries: Right little finger cut – flexor tendon divided.

Prognosis: Repair failed to heal – finger removed eight months after the accident leaving a short stump and two scars – grip reduced by fifteen per cent.

1.4.4.C26 Case No. 11177

Name of case: Re A

Brief description of injuries: HAND – DISLOCATION – NERVE DAMAGE

Reported: (1996) 96 (2) QR 5; Kemp & Kemp, H6-037/1; [1996] CLY 2268

JSB Category: 6(I)(h)(i)

Sex: Male

Age at injury: 41

Age at award: 44

Date of award: 12 March 1996

Tribunal: CICB, London

Amount of award then: £5,000

Award at February 2001: £5,677

Description of injuries: Dislocated right lunate bone – median nerve damage – difficulty in forming a full fist and an ordinary grip – affected applicant's work – cosmetically unattractive index finger.

1.4.4.C27 Case No. 10234

Name of case: Pinder v Hardings (FT) & Son

Brief description of injuries: FRACTURED NON-DOMINANT THUMB – NAIL DEFORMED

Reported: Kemp & Kemp, H7-018; [1991] CLY 1431

JSB Category: 6(I)(u)

Sex: Male

Age at injury: 29

Age at award: 34

Date of award: 19 February 1991

Tribunal: QBD

Amount of award then: £4,250

Award at February 2001: £5,584

Description of injuries: Compound fracture to the distal phalanx of the not dominant left thumb – partial shearing off of the nail bed and loss of half the nail – lacerations to the middle and ring fingers – seventeen weeks off work.

Prognosis: Nail bed slow to heal – deformed nail – permanent slight restriction in the movement of the interphalangeal joint.

1.4.4.C28 Case No. 10629

Name of case: Re E

Brief description of injuries: FINGER – MIDDLE FINGER – LOSS OF TIP

Reported: Kemp & Kemp, H6-038; [1993] CLY 1524

JSB Category: 6(I); 3(A)(d)

Sex: Male

Age at injury: 21 months

Age at award: 3

Date of award: 29 September 1993

Tribunal: Newbury County Court

Amount of award then: £4,500

Award at February 2001: £5,455

Description of injuries: Infant caught middle finger in heavy fire door, severing top 0.5 cm of finger tip, including nail and some bone – shock – attempt to sew back tip of finger failed – great personal distress for 6-9 months; previously placid child nervous and screamed whenever approached – sleep very disturbed for 6 months.

Prognosis: Finger expected to be permanently shortened, and nail deformed into shape of talon, making it difficult to trim – permanent bump on side of finger – sensitivity to cold and slight loss of dexterity also expected – no functional disability expected – psychological problems largely resolved by date of trial.

Other points: Judge took into account effect of cosmetic defect on claimant as he grew older when assessing award.

1.4.4.C29 Case No. 11657

Name of case: Mirfin v Spencer Clark Metal Industries plc

Brief description of injuries: FINGERS – VIBRATION WHITE FINGER

Reported: Kemp & Kemp, H6A-026/1; [1998] CLY 1659

JSB Category: 6(I)(y)(iii)

Sex: Male

Age at injury: 45

Age at award: 51

Date of award: 15 October 1997

Tribunal: Barnsley County Court

Amount of award then: £5,000

Award at February 2001: £5,392

Description of injuries: Vibration white finger affecting the first and second fingers and the tips of the thumbs of both hands – degree of disability on border between stages II and III on the Taylor-Pelmear scale.

1.4.4.C30 Case No. 11423

Name of case: Green v Northern Foods PLC
Brief description of injuries: FINGERS – SOFT-TISSUE INJURIES
Reported: Kemp & Kemp, H5-023; [1997] CLY 1972
JSB Category: 6(I)(h)
Sex: Female
Age at injury: 48
Age at award: 51
Date of award: 27 February 1997
Tribunal: Sheffield County Court
Amount of award then: £4,500
Award at February 2001: £4,994
Description of injuries: Soft-tissue injuries to the fingers – twelve sessions of physiotherapy required.
Prognosis: Permanent dysfunction in the index and middle fingers – unable to make a tight fist – at a permanent disadvantage in the labour market.

1.4.4.C31 Case No. 11424

Name of case: Marsh v Ashton Corrugated (Midlands) Ltd
Brief description of injuries: FINGER – TIP – TRAUMATIC AMPUTATION
Reported: Kemp & Kemp, H6-038/1; [1997] CLY 1973
JSB Category: 6(I)(k)
Sex: Male
Age at injury: 44
Age at award: 50
Date of award: 09 June 1997
Tribunal: Leeds County Court
Amount of award then: £4,500
Award at February 2001: £4,914
Description of injuries: Traumatic amputation of the fingertip – fracture of the top phalanx – persisting whiteness, numbness and cold intolerance.
Prognosis: Suffering from a disability which could affect his future job prospects

1.4.4.C32 Case No. 10630

Name of case: Bir v AL Dunn & Co
Brief description of injuries: FINGER – VIBRATION WHITE FINGER
Reported: Kemp & Kemp, H5-023/1; [1993] CLY 1525
JSB Category: 6(I)(y)(iii)
Sex: Male
Age at injury: ongoing since 21
Age at award: 48
Date of award: 17 June 1993
Tribunal: Coventry County Court
Amount of award then: £4,000
Award at February 2001: £4,879
Description of injuries: Claimant employed as fettler since 1966 and exposed to vibration in that employment – development of cold – induced episodic blanching to all digits of both hands – diagnosis of hand/arm vibration syndrome – regular attacks in winter months – occasional attacks in summer – loss of sensation in digits until heat applied, causing "pins and needles" sensation – condition measured at stage 2 on Taylor-Pelmear scale, 2(R)5/2(L)5 vascular and 1SN neurological on Stockholm scale.
Prognosis: Exposure to vibration is ongoing – symptoms likely to continue and increase in severity.

1.4.4.C33 Case No. 11651

Name of case: Robson v Safeway plc
Brief description of injuries: FINGER – CRUSH INJURY
Reported: Kemp & Kemp, H6-038/2; [1998] CLY 1653
JSB Category: 6(I)(i)
Sex: Male
Age at injury: 52
Age at award: 55
Date of award: 18 June 1998
Tribunal: Newcastle upon Tyne County Court
Amount of award then: £4,600
Award at February 2001: £4,842
Description of injuries: Crush injury and loss of pulp substance to the index finger – pain in cold weather.
Prognosis: Scars and permanent loss of sensation in the finger.

1.4.4.C34 Case No. 10232

Name of case: Knight v Ford Motor Company

Brief description of injuries: VIBRATION "WHITE FINGER"

Reported: Kemp & Kemp, H6A-030; [1991] CLY 1429

JSB Category: 6(K)(y)(iii)

Sex: Male

Age at injury: 38

Age at award: 41

Date of award: 06 September 1991

Tribunal: Liverpool County Court

Amount of award then: £3,400

Award at February 2001: £4,345

Description of injuries: Vibration induced "white finger" – Taylor and Palmear Stage II with blanching, numbness and tingling in all eight fingers during cold weather.

Prognosis: No difficulty with his new duties at work – no substantial risk of disadvantage in the labour market.

1.4.4.C35 Case No. 11024

Name of case: Farnan v Liverpool City Council

Brief description of injuries: HAND – FRACTURE OF THUMB – SURGERY – ALMOST COMPLETE RECOVERY

Reported: Kemp & Kemp, H7-019/1; [1995] CLY 1776

JSB Category: 6(I)(w)

Sex: Male

Age at injury: 37

Age at award: 39

Date of award: 27 February 1995

Tribunal: Liverpool County Court

Amount of award then: £3,500

Award at February 2001: £4,098

Description of injuries: Plaintiff tripped on damaged pavement area and fell onto outstretched right hand – suffered displaced fracture of head and neck of proximal phalanx of right thumb – reduction took place under general anaesthetic with small screw – two K-wires were placed through head of proximal phalanx in case of further fracturing – screw and wires were removed as day patient and he underwent physiotherapy – left with 1.75in dorsal scar and a 1 in radial scar – scars were described by trial judge as "not ugly" – had no residual discomfort and was left with minimal restriction with which he would be able to cope.

Prognosis: There would be probable development of osteoarthritis but this would only involve "some additional discomfort".

1.4.4.C36 Case No. 11943

Name of case: Hughes v St Helens MBC

Brief description of injuries: THUMB – TENDON DAMAGE – 3 YEARS

Reported: Kemp & Kemp, PRH-004; [1999] CLY 1607

JSB Category: 6(I); 8

Sex: Male

Age at injury: about 30

Age at award: –

Date of award: 22 April 1999

Tribunal: St Helens County Court

Amount of award then: £3,750

Award at February 2001: £3,904

Description of injuries: Deep laceration to base of thumb, severing 2 tendons – operation under general anaesthetic to repair damaged tendons; thumb then immobilised for 6 weeks in moulded splint before claimant started to undergo physiotherapy – claimant unemployed at time of accident, but certified as unfit for work for 7 weeks – pain, aching and altered sensation along ulnar side of thumb – full functional recovery approximately 6 months after accident, but scarring to base of thumb and tendency to ache in cold and wet weather

Prognosis: Aching expected to resolve over the course of 3 winters following accident.

Other points: Liability not established – general damages figure only an indication by judge of what he would have awarded.

1.4.4.C37 Case No. 11659

Name of case: Murphy v Moywest Ltd

Brief description of injuries: THUMB – RUPTURED LIGAMENT TO LEFT THUMB

Reported: Kemp & Kemp, H7 022; [1998] CLY 1661

JSB Category: 6(I)(w)

Sex: Female

Age at injury: 43

Age at award: 45

Date of award: 25 September 1997

Tribunal: Liverpool County Court

Amount of award then: £3,500

Award at February 2001: £3,779

Description of injuries: Rupture to the ulna collateral ligament to the left thumb – bruising to the leg – at time of hearing there was occasional slight discomfort in the thumb.

1.4.4.C38 Case No. 11652

Name of case: Goff (a minor) v Broadland Properties Ltd

Brief description of injuries: FINGERS – LACERATIONS

Reported: Kemp & Kemp, J2-040/2; [1998] CLY 1654

JSB Category: 6(I)

Sex: Male

Age at injury: 5

Age at award: 7

Date of award: 04 March 1998

Tribunal: Portsmouth County Court

Amount of award then: £3,500

Award at February 2001: £3,744

Description of injuries: Lacerations to the right ring and middle fingers – full thickness skin graft required for both fingers – laceration to the outer canthus of an eye – 2 scars on the fingers – slight flexion in the joints.

1.4.4.C39 Case No. 11426

Name of case: Re Catchpole

Brief description of injuries: FINGER – DISLOCATION

Reported: Kemp & Kemp, K2-022; [1997] CLY 1975

JSB Category: 6(I)

Sex: Male

Age at injury: 41

Age at award: 45

Date of award: 14 August 1996

Tribunal: CICB, London

Amount of award then: £3,250

Award at February 2001: £3,651

Description of injuries: Dislocated little finger – swollen ring finger on the right hand.

Prognosis: Deformed ring finger – "Z" shaped – mallet deformity of the little finger – little residual deformity – no increased risk of osteoarthritis.

1.4.4.C40 Case No. 10815

Name of case: Rafiq v Crendley (t/a Lewis Motor Repairs)

Brief description of injuries: HAND – DIVIDED NERVE

Reported: Kemp & Kemp, H5-024; [1994] CLY 1664

JSB Category: 6(I)

Sex: Male

Age at injury: 38

Age at award: 40

Date of award: 18 November 1993

Tribunal: Stourbridge County Court

Amount of award then: £3,000

Award at February 2001: £3,644

Description of injuries: Claimant sustained deep gash to palm of right, dominant, hand when metal file driven into it by sudden collapse of defective car jack – initially regarded as modest injury – 4 days later, operation undergone to explore and repair divided digital nerve – off work 7 weeks – ongoing stiffness and tingling in index finger, reduced sensation to ulnar aspect of that finger, stiffness in thumb and reduced power of grip – claimant returned to work.

Prognosis: Claimant left with mild but permanent scarring, symptomatic and functional problems.

1.4.4.C41 Case No. 11027

Name of case: Greenfield v Jolley

Brief description of injuries: DOG BITES TO HAND, KNEE AND CALF – SCARS – DISTURBED SLEEP

Reported: Kemp & Kemp, K2-028; [1995] CLY 1779

JSB Category: 6(K)(c)(iii)

Sex: Female

Age at injury: 56

Age at award: 58

Date of award: 20 January 1995

Tribunal: Blackburn County Court

Amount of award then: £3,051

Award at February 2001: £3,594

Description of injuries: Plaintiff bitten by Alsatian/Labrador cross dog – left with three areas of scarring: (1) two tiny scars to left hand with small lumps about 5mm in diameter; (2) "V" shaped scar to outer aspect of left leg just below knee; and (3) a small scar to front of left calf area approximately 10mm in length – also tiny puncture wound to back of left leg which had fully healed by time of trial, no longer visible – scars to hand were barely visible although lumps could be palpated – two larger scars to left leg were visible at conversation distance – also slight swelling of calf area of left leg which emanated from dog bites in question – plaintiff had been extremely shaken and upset by bites – off work for four weeks following incident and had only worn a skirt on one occasion since being bitten (prior to biting incident plaintiff often wore skirts) – bites made plaintiff extremely anxious – she tended to stay indoors and avoided taking own dogs for anything longer than walks of minimum length – plaintiff's sleep was disturbed following accident, with nightmares several times a night – at date of trial, plaintiff's sleep continued to be disturbed at least once a week – plaintiff had had and continued to have nightmares in which she dreamt of dog in question leaping at her face as had happened in incident.

Other points: Wallis v Smith (Kemp & Kemp, 61056) & Burgess v Hooper ([1991] CLY 1360) considered. Award made on basis that physical and psychological aspects of case combined to make this a more frightening incident to plaintiff than reported in other two cases.

1.4.4.C42 Case No. 10817

Name of case: King v Johnson

Brief description of injuries: FINGER

Reported: Kemp & Kemp, L8-097; [1994] CLY 1666, 1754

JSB Category: 6(I); 8

Sex: Female

Age at injury: 68

Age at award: 71

Date of award: 22 June 1994

Tribunal: Nottingham County Court

Amount of award then: £3,000

Award at February 2001: £3,566

Description of injuries: Claimant bitten on middle finger of dominant right hand by dog – claimant lived alone, but self-care impossible for 6 weeks – unable to undertake shopping and housework – finger unable to be exposed to water; washing therefore difficult – poor grip, leading to difficulties opening jars and frequent dropping of objects – attempts to compensate by improving dexterity of left hand problematic – finger especially uncomfortable in cold weather – scarring – restricted movement – forced abandonment of hobby of knitting.

Prognosis: Condition likely to be permanent.

1.4.4.C43 Case No. 10439

Name of case: Re P

Brief description of injuries: CRUSH INJURY TO TWO RIGHT FINGERS – RESIDUAL STIFFNESS – RISK OF ARTHRITIS

Reported: Kemp & Kemp, H6-046; [1992] CLY 1695

JSB Category: 6(I)(q)

Sex: Male

Age at injury: 45

Age at award: 48

Date of award: 21 October 1992

Tribunal: CICB, Cardiff

Amount of award then: £2,750

Award at February 2001: £3,381

Description of injuries: Crush injury to the fourth and fifth fingers of the right dominant hand – splints applied to the fingers – at the time of the hearing fingers remained stiff and painful – unable to fully straighten the fingers.

Prognosis: 20% deformity and loss of grip expected to be permanent – risk of arthritis.

1.4.4.C44 Case No. 10260

Name of case: Spencer v BRB

Brief description of injuries: FINGER LACERATION – RECOVERY 3 YEARS

Reported: Kemp & Kemp, H6-047; [1991] CLY 1457

JSB Category: 6(I)

Sex: Male

Age at injury: –

Age at award: 24

Date of award: 16 May 1991

Tribunal: Wakefield County Court

Amount of award then: £2,600

Award at February 2001: £3,350

Description of injuries: Distally based flap laceration to the pulp of the terminal segment of the dominant right index finger – repaired under general anaesthetic.

Prognosis: Left with a raised area of thickened skin like a blister – residual occasional pain should resolve within three years and six months of the date of the accident.

1.4.4.C45 Case No. 10986

Name of case: Francis v Padley (Poultry)

Brief description of injuries: HAND – "MALLET FINGER" INJURY – RESIDUAL CLUMSINESS

Reported: Kemp & Kemp, H6-048; [1995] CLY 1737

JSB Category: 6(I)(l)

Sex: Female

Age at injury: 58

Age at award: 60

Date of award: 20 February 1995

Tribunal: King's Lynn County Court

Amount of award then: £2,850

Award at February 2001: £3,337

Description of injuries: Plaintiff suffered crush injury to right ring finger when it was trapped under metal shelf loaded with cooked chicken – she did not realise initial extent of injury because hands were very cold at time – awoke next morning to find right ring finger extremely painful and tender – it also drooped from end joint into flexed position and she was unable to straighten it actively – immediately consulted GP who referred her to local hospital where finger was examined and X-rayed – diagnosed as suffering from "mallet finger" injury – injured finger was placed in plastic splint which remained in place for following six weeks – when splint was removed plaintiff undertook course of physiotherapy – pain then returned and end joint of finger resumed previous drooping position – consequently she wore splint for further two weeks – plaintiff was able to return to work in November 1992 having been off work for four months and one week – between then and date of trial she had been off work for number of odd days due to swelling in injured finger and pain – at time of trial plaintiff could not make full fist with dominant right hand and therefore suffered a significant loss of grip – finger still drooped and tended to catch on objects when using her right hand, causing extreme pain – injury also caused plaintiff difficulties when carrying out normal household chores and gardening – unable to apply any pressure on injured finger, thus finding it very difficult to carry shopping or suitcases – when she did have to do this, she was only able to use two fingers and thumb to grip handles.

Prognosis: These symptoms were likely to continue indefinitely.

1.4.4.C46 Case No. 11843

Name of case: Carnegie v Barkers (of Malton) Ltd

Brief description of injuries: FINGERS – TENDON DAMAGE

Reported: Kemp & Kemp, H1-104, H6-049/2/1; [1999] CLY 1507

JSB Category: 6(I)(h)

Sex: Male

Age at injury: 30

Age at award: 32

Date of award: 23 July 1999

Tribunal: York County Court

Amount of award then: £3,000

Award at February 2001: £3,125

Description of injuries: Deep laceration to index finger of non-dominant left hand – flexor profundus tendon severed – damage to radial nerve – tendon surgically repaired – off work 6 weeks, light duties for 2 further weeks; lower arm in plaster 14 days – movement in distal interphalangeal joint at first severely restricted, but significant and steady improvement thereafter – 2 years after accident, claimant still unable to make a proper fist and grip still weakened – finger still hypersensitive to cold and almost insensitive to fine touch and heat.

Prognosis: Some further improvement expected, but symptoms permanent.

1.4.4.C47 Case No. 12066

Name of case: Green v Leicester CC

Brief description of injuries: HAND – RAT BITE

Reported: [2000] 6 CL 196

JSB Category: 6(I)

Sex: Male

Age at injury: 42

Age at award: 45

Date of award: 26 January 2000

Tribunal: Mansfield County Court

Amount of award then: £3,000

Award at February 2001: £3,097

Description of injuries: Rat bite to the web between the right thumb and index finger through protective gloves – G did not contract Weil's Disease – unable to work for twelve weeks – hand was useless for the first six weeks – painful, red and swollen – disturbed sleep for two weeks – occasional numbness and tingling to the whole arm – physiotherapy and electro-magnetic therapy required.

Prognosis: Residual occasional aching and swelling in cold weather and after heavy work were expected to resolve.

1.4.4.C48 Case No. 10262

Name of case: Kilford v United Engineering Steels

Brief description of injuries: RIGHT MIDDLE AND RING FINGERS – CRUSH INJURY

Reported: Kemp & Kemp, K2-050; [1991] CLY 1459

JSB Category: 6(I)

Sex: Male

Age at injury: 45

Age at award: 47

Date of award: 12 November 1990

Tribunal: Walsall County Court

Amount of award then: £2,250

Award at February 2001: £2,977

Description of injuries: Crush injury to the tips of the middle and ring fingers of the right hand – bleeding around the nails required drilling – swelling and bruising to both fingers.

Prognosis: Residual cramp, numbness, difficulty in lifting small objects were likely to resolve shortly.

1.4.4.C49 Case No. 11941

Name of case: Re Billington

Brief description of injuries: FINGER – TENDON DAMAGE – PERMANENT RESTRICTION

Reported: Kemp & Kemp, H1-104, H6-050; [1999] CLY 1605

JSB Category: 6(I)

Sex: Male

Age at injury: 49

Age at award: 53

Date of award: 16 April 1999

Tribunal: CICB, York

Amount of award then: £2,750

Award at February 2001: £2,863

Description of injuries: Injury to little finger of left, non-dominant, hand – X-rays revealed torn extensor tendon on back of end joint of little finger – finger placed in mallet splint for 6 weeks – at time of hearing, claimant had lost last 10 per cent of extension to distal interphalangeal joint – finger permanently displaced, resulting in a loss of grip and inability to lift heavy objects – claimant no longer able to accompany daughter on guitar.

Prognosis: Symptoms unlikely to improve.

1.4.4.C50 Case No. 11660

Name of case: Lawrence v Scott Ltd

Brief description of injuries: THUMB – CRUSH INJURY

Reported: Kemp & Kemp, h7-022/1; [1998] CLY 1662

JSB Category: 6(I)(w)

Sex: Male

Age at injury: 44

Age at award: 47

Date of award: 20 January 1998

Tribunal: Central London County Court

Amount of award then: £2,500

Award at February 2001: £2,696

Description of injuries: Crushing injury to the thumb – fractured terminal phalanx.

Prognosis: Permanent slight deformity to the pulp of the thumb.

1.4.4.C51 Case No. 10664

Name of case: Beal v Turner

Brief description of injuries: HAND – DOG BITE

Reported: Kemp & Kemp, K2-074; [1993] CLY 1560

JSB Category: 6(I); 3(A)(d)

Sex: Female

Age at injury: 34

Age at award: 38

Date of award: 19 August 1992

Tribunal: Slough County Court

Amount of award then: £2,000

Award at February 2001: £2,477

Description of injuries: Dog bite – deep puncture wound to palm of left hand – back of hand swollen and badly bruised – interference with sensation in hand for 6 weeks; severe pins and needles, weak and painful grip – unable to cut up food or wash own hair during this period – unable to work in capacity as piano teacher for 6 months – further period of time required before previous standard of playing attained, and personal and job satisfaction in piano – playing diminished for a further period – nightmares – nervousness of dogs – desire to wear heavy clothing and gloves in the summer following the attack – at date of hearing (4 years after incident), 2 tiny marks still on palm – otherwise effectively recovered.

1.4.4.C52 Case No. 10818

Name of case: Re Sykes

Brief description of injuries: FINGER

Reported: Kemp & Kemp, H6-052; [1994] CLY 1667

JSB Category: 6(I)

Sex: Female

Age at injury: 33

Age at award: 35

Date of award: 18 July 1994

Tribunal: CICB, York

Amount of award then: £2,000

Award at February 2001: £2,389

Description of injuries: Claimant, nurse in psychiatric unit, attempted to restrain violent patient from assault – twisting injury to left ring finger, causing immediate pain, swelling and bruising – finger became immobile – X-rays revealed snapped severed tendon and avulsion of chip of bone from base of terminal phalanx – finger put in splint – off work 6 weeks – ongoing symptoms of weakened grip, difficulty bending finger, and dull pain in cold weather lasting several hours – hobby of dog training severely restricted.

Prognosis: Symptoms not likely to improve.

1.4.4.C53 Case No. 10270

Name of case: Whale v United Biscuits (UK)

Brief description of injuries: FRACTURE OF THE LEFT MIDDLE FINGER- ALLERGIC REACTION TO MEDICATION

Reported: Kemp & Kemp, K2-090; [1991] CLY 1467

JSB Category: 6(I)(q)

Sex: Male

Age at injury: Not stated

Age at award:

Date of award: 12 February 1991

Tribunal: Willesden County Court

Amount of award then: £1,750

Award at February 2001: £2,299

Description of injuries: The middle fingers of both hands became trapped in the chain drive of a conveyor belt – lacerations to both fingers – fracture of the middle phalanx of the left middle finger – W developed a reaction to the prescribed antibiotics – rash and blisters to the body and face – off work for seventeen weeks – holiday to Singapore was ruined.

Prognosis: Made a good recovery – minor degree of impaired flexion to the middle left finger.

1.4.4.C54 Case No. 11059

Name of case: James v Oatley

Brief description of injuries: HAND AND THIGH – DOG BITE – SCARS – POST-TRAUMATIC STRESS DISORDER

Reported: [1995] CLY 1813

JSB Category: 6(I)

Sex: Male

Age at injury: 52

Age at award: –

Date of award: 16 August 1995

Tribunal: Cambourne and Redruth County Court

Amount of award then: £1,800

Award at February 2001: £2,065

Description of injuries: Plaintiff attacked by two Bull Mastiff dogs – sustained puncture wounds to left hand, and puncture wounds and haematoma to left thigh – wounds to hand occasioned loss of use, pain and discomfort for two to three weeks – thereafter full recovery, with no noticeable scarring – secondary infection in thigh, treated with antibiotics, caused peeling and cracking of skin of palms of hands and soles of feet – lost the use of his leg for two to three weeks, with further discomfort for five weeks – unable to work for two months – thigh was permanently scarred – suffered post-traumatic stress syndrome, manifested in interrupted sleep and nightmares, treated with Diazepam – previous fear of dogs had increased and remained greater than it had been before attack.

1.4.4.C55 Case No. 11241

Name of case: Collings v Cheshire CC

Brief description of injuries: FINGERS – PARTIAL AMPUTATIONS TO TWO FINGERS

Reported: Kemp & Kemp, H6-053; [1996] CLY 2333

JSB Category: 6(I)

Sex: Male

Age at injury: 12

Age at award: 15

Date of award: 01 October 1996

Tribunal: Holywell County Court

Amount of award then: £1,750

Award at February 2001: £1,957

Description of injuries: Partial amputations to the middle and ring fingers of the left hand – fingers were replaced with butterfly stitches – there was loss of sensation in the fingers and difficulty with grip.

Prognosis: Symptoms were expected to resolve gradually over the next few years.

1.4.4.C56 Case No. 11655

Name of case: Re Galloway

Brief description of injuries: FINGERS – RUPTURED TENDON

Reported: [1998] CLY 1657

JSB Category: 6(I)

Sex: Female

Age at injury: 47

Age at award: 51

Date of award: 13 May 1998

Tribunal: CICB, York

Amount of award then: £1,750

Award at February 2001: £1,841

Description of injuries: Rupture of the extensor tendon of the little finger.

Prognosis: Permanent small flexion deformity of the inter-phalangeal joint by 15 degrees.

1.4.4.C57 Case No. 11743

Name of case: Baynham v Kenmore

Brief description of injuries: HAND – LACERATION

Reported: Kemp & Kemp, PRJ-011, J2-049; [1998] CLY 1746

JSB Category: 6(I)

Sex: Male

Age at injury: 34

Age at award: 35

Date of award: 15 December 1997

Tribunal: Leeds County Court

Amount of award then: £1,600

Award at February 2001: £1,720

Description of injuries: Laceration to the interosseous space to the left hand – minor bruising to the shin.

Prognosis: A reasonable recovery was anticipated within 2 years of the date of the accident.

1.4.4.C58 Case No. 10874

Name of case: Kay (Jacqueline) v Convenience Foods

Brief description of injuries: FINGERS – CRUSH INJURIES

Reported: Kemp & Kemp, K2-150; [1994] CLY 1726

JSB Category: 7(I)

Sex: Female

Age at injury: 44

Age at award: 46

Date of award: 28 October 1993

Tribunal: Sheffield County Court

Amount of award then: £1,250

Award at February 2001: £1,516

Description of injuries: Crush injury to all fingers of left, non-dominant, hand when hand caught and drawn into conveyor belt at work – cut to left ring finger – swelling and bruising to all fingers, particularly index and middle – claimant attended medical centre at work but took no time off, transferring to alternative job not requiring use of left hand – pain and discomfort in fingers, ongoing 3 months after incident – spasms of pain in index finger – at date of trial, still problems with gripping and twisting with left hand – occasional painkillers required – discomfort in fingers following prolonged use – symptoms described by claimant as nagging and intermittent.

Prognosis: Prognosis that symptoms should have resolved themselves within 2.5 years of date of accident.

1.4.4.C59 Case No. 10092

Name of case: Waudby v Humberside County Council

Brief description of injuries: LEFT RING FINGER – SPLINTER – CONTINUING TENDERNESS

Reported: Kemp & Kemp, H6-50; [1990] CLY 1659

JSB Category: 6(I)

Sex: Female

Age at injury: 54

Age at award: 57

Date of award: 06 December 1989

Tribunal: Hull County Court

Amount of award then: £1,000

Award at February 2001: £1,448

Description of injuries: Splinter of wood penetrated dorsal aspect of left ring finger – plaintiff extracted splinter of length 0.375 of an inch – exploratory operation was performed two days later, but no foreign body was found – four days later plaintiff extracted a further piece of wood 0.75 of an inch in length – continued discomfort and persistent thickening over the base of the proximal phalanx and metacarpo-phalangeal joint – tenderness remained and the skin pruric – scaly area on dorsal surface, with pinkish minor cosmetic blemish – at extreme distal end of left ring finger, below the nail edge, was a small area of blunting, sensitive to touch and pin prick.

1.4.4.C60 Case No. 11996

Name of case: M (a minor) v De Koning
Brief description of injuries: HAND – BRUISING
Reported: Kemp & Kemp, K2-161/1; [2000] 3 CL 180
JSB Category: 6
Sex: Male
Age at injury: 11
Age at award: 13
Date of award: 16 November 1999
Tribunal: Halifax County Court
Amount of award then: £1,400
Award at February 2001: £1,445
Description of injuries: A hand was trapped between metal bars at the side of a conveyor belt on a fairground ride – bruising and tenderness to the hand – fracture to the left fifth metacarpal – plaster cast was applied and the left arm placed in a sling – plaster was removed three weeks later – no schooling missed as the accident occurred in the holidays. Discharged from hospital with no further treatment.
Other points: Enjoyment of Christmas holiday was severely disrupted.

1.4.4.C61 Case No. 11253

Name of case: Ogilvie v Heron
Brief description of injuries: HAND – NECK – ANKLE – 1 MONTH
Reported: Kemp & Kemp, K2-166; [1996] CLY 2345
JSB Category: 6(M)(d)
Sex: Male
Age at injury: 22
Age at award: 23
Date of award: 23 July 1996
Tribunal: Croydon County Court
Amount of award then: £1,250
Award at February 2001: £1,411
Description of injuries: Injuries to the hand, neck and ankle – fully resolved within one month of the date of the accident.

1.4.4.C62 Case No. 11428

Name of case: Murphy v Gosforth Park Care Homes Ltd
Brief description of injuries: THUMB – LACERATION
Reported: Kemp & Kemp, H6-054; [1997] CLY 1977
JSB Category: 6(I)(x)
Sex: Female
Age at injury: 50
Age at award: 54
Date of award: 25 July 1997
Tribunal: Newcastle upon Tyne County Court
Amount of award then: £1,250
Award at February 2001: £1,365
Description of injuries: Laceration to the base of the thumb.
Prognosis: Non adherent scar – of no cosmetic significance.

1.4.4.C63 Case No. 11746

Name of case: Fernley v Nei Control Systems Ltd
Brief description of injuries: FINGERS – LACERATION
Reported: Kemp & Kemp, H6-055; [1998] CLY 1749
JSB Category: 6(I)
Sex: Male
Age at injury: 44
Age at award: 46
Date of award: 19 March 1998
Tribunal: Manchester County Court
Amount of award then: £1,250
Award at February 2001: £1,337
Description of injuries: Deep laceration to the dorsum of the index finger – no reduction of function – pins and needles felt at the site 4 years after the date of the accident.

1.4.4.C64 Case No. 11745

Name of case: Edwards v Owen
Brief description of injuries: FINGERS – 8 WEEKS
Reported: Kemp & Kemp, K2-170/3; [1998] CLY 1748
JSB Category: 6(I)
Sex: Male
Age at injury: 34
Age at award: –
Date of award: 17 June 1998
Tribunal: Medway County Court
Amount of award then: £1,250
Award at February 2001: £1,316
Description of injuries: Dog bite injury to the index finger – split nail and bleeding – wound took 8 weeks to heal – diminished sensation at the finger tip for 2 years.

1.4.4.C65 Case No. 10504

Name of case: Yates v Ford Motor Company

Brief description of injuries: CRUSHED RIGHT FINGERS – VIRTUALLY FULL RECOVERY

Reported: Kemp & Kemp, K2-175; [1992] CLY 1760

JSB Category: 6

Sex: Male

Age at injury: 63

Age at award: 64

Date of award: 06 February 1992

Tribunal: Birmingham County Court

Amount of award then: £1,000

Award at February 2001: £1,262

Description of injuries: Crushing injury to the ring and middle fingers of the right hand.

Prognosis: No residual symptoms save for a clicking of the middle joint of the middle finger.

1.4.4.C66 Case No. 10683

Name of case: Rushton v Bairdwear

Brief description of injuries: HAND – CRUSH INJURY

Reported: Kemp & Kemp, K2-179; [1993] CLY 1579

JSB Category: 6(I)

Sex: Female

Age at injury: 25

Age at award: 26

Date of award: 02 April 1993

Tribunal: Birmingham County Court

Amount of award then: £1,000

Award at February 2001: £1,223

Description of injuries: Right (dominant) hand crushed between shelf and a trolley pushed by claimant and colleague – 3 days off work with swelling in hand – swelling subsided thereafter, but continuing difficulty in moving fingers – great inconvenience, inability to do housework and sleep disturbance – movement in hand and fingers improved after 5 weeks.

1.4.4.C67 Case No. 10880

Name of case: Cooper (Michael) v Keylighting Products

Brief description of injuries: HAND – LACERATION

Reported: Kemp & Kemp, K2-181; [1994] CLY 1732

JSB Category: 6(I); 8

Sex: Male

Age at injury: 45

Age at award: –

Date of award: 11 January 1994

Tribunal: Leeds County Court

Amount of award then: £1,000

Award at February 2001: £1,217

Description of injuries: Laceration to palm of right, dominant, hand – 4 stitches, dressing and tetanus booster required – claimant went on family holiday to Tenerife 3 days later (separate award of £750 made for loss of enjoyment of holiday) – enjoyment of holiday substantially impaired due to need to keep wound clean, preventing swimming with children – attendance at local doctors required for changing of dressings and removal of stitches – 2.5cm scar across palm – claimant's grip returned to normal after 2 weeks – able to resume work after holiday – some remaining occasional discomfort.

1.4.4.C68 Case No. 11055

Name of case: Prangley v National Power

Brief description of injuries: HAND – CRUSH FRACTURE TO RIGHT LITTLE FINGER – 1 YEAR

Reported: [1995] CLY 1809

JSB Category: 6(I)(q)

Sex: Male

Age at injury: 35

Age at award: 39

Date of award: 21 February 1995

Tribunal: Cardiff County Court

Amount of award then: £1,000

Award at February 2001: £1,171

Description of injuries: Male suffered crush fracture to terminal phalanx of right little finger, when his hand struck the door frame of ash hopper – skin on finger was split and it was bleeding – plaintiff attended hospital where finger was cleaned and dressed – unable to work for four weeks, his right hand being difficult to use – all discomfort ceased within one year of accident, leaving only well-healed fine scar which was only visible on very close inspection.

1.4.4.C69 Case No. 11896

Name of case: U (a minor) v Living World Ltd

Brief description of injuries: HAND – SCAR AND DISCOMFORT

Reported: Kemp & Kemp, J2-049/1; [1999] CLY 1560

JSB Category: 6(I); 8

Sex: Male

Age at injury: 4

Age at award: 6

Date of award: 15 June 1998

Tribunal: Leeds County Court

Amount of award then: £1,100

Award at February 2001: £1,158

Description of injuries: Laceration to right wrist and palm – wound 3cm in length, affecting ulnar side of wrist and hypothenar eminence – treated by approximating skin edges with steristrips – wound re-dressed 5 days later, and subsequently dressed by mother for approximately 6 weeks – scar, measuring 1cm x 3mm, on right wrist – underlying muscles and nerves not damaged – claimant continued to suffer occasional discomfort at site of scar when it was knocked, in cold conditions, or when hand had been rested on a hard surface, eg when writing – injured area appeared discoloured in cold conditions – claimant, who suffered from cerebral palsy, appeared to have been right-handed, but now preferred left hand for holding pens and crayons.

Prognosis: Scar permanent – any continuing symptoms of discolouration or discomfort expected to clear up within 2 years and 6 months of accident.

1.4.4.C70 Case No. 11051

Name of case: Lea v Baird

Brief description of injuries: HAND – NEEDLE THROUGH NAIL OF INDEX FINGER

Reported: Kemp & Kemp, K2-189; [1995] CLY 1805

JSB Category: 6(I)

Sex: Female

Age at injury: 38

Age at award: 41

Date of award: 28 April 1995

Tribunal: Manchester County Court

Amount of award then: £1,000

Award at February 2001: £1,154

Description of injuries: Sewing machinist, right hand dominant – needle went through nail into and through left index finger – needle remained penetrating finger until she was taken to hospital where needle and nail were removed under ring block – tiny fragment of metal was retained in finger as it was too small to remove – injury extremely painful – off work one week – after three weeks finger was largely comfortable for majority of time and she had made 95 per cent recovery – some sensitivity in cold weather persisted and there was faint mark on pad of finger where needle protruded – nail regrew in "flaky manner" for three months but when it had grown out fully it was of normal appearance.

1.4.4.C71 Case No. 12019

Name of case: Burrows v Kingston upon Hull City Council

Brief description of injuries: FINGER – PUNCTURE WOUND

Reported: Kemp & Kemp, H6-056; [2000] 4 CL 162

JSB Category: 6(I)(q)

Sex: Male

Age at injury: 22

Age at award: 25

Date of award: 23 November 1999

Tribunal: Nottingham County Court

Amount of award then: £1,100

Award at February 2001: £1,135

Description of injuries: B was supplied with a faulty tool which slipped on two occasions penetrating the index finger to the left non – dominant hand – bleeding was treated with plasters – a lump developed under the skin – it proved to be a cyst unconnected with the accident, which required excision under general anaesthetic. Symptoms resolved after the excision was carried out.

1.4.4.C72 Case No. 11256

Name of case: Winfield v J Lyons & Co Ltd

Brief description of injuries: THUMB – LACERATION

Reported: Kemp & Kemp, H7-023/1; [1996] CLY 2348

JSB Category: 6(I)(x)

Sex: Female

Age at injury: 45

Age at award: 47

Date of award: 30 April 1996

Tribunal: Barnsley County Court

Amount of award then: £1,000

Award at February 2001: £1,127

Description of injuries: Laceration to the thumb.

Prognosis: Symptoms would clear within three years of the date of the accident.

1.4.4.C73 Case No. 10987

Name of case: Pullen v Bird's Eye Walls

Brief description of injuries: HAND – INJURY TO LITTLE FINGER AND NAIL

Reported: Kemp & Kemp, K2-202; [1995] CLY 1738

JSB Category: 6(I)(n)

Sex: Female

Age at injury: 41

Age at award: 43

Date of award: 17 March 1995

Tribunal: Hull County Court

Amount of award then: £950

Award at February 2001: £1,108

Description of injuries: Right-handed process worker sustained injury to little finger of right hand when it became caught in conveyor belt – suffered extremely painful soft-tissue injury to right little finger and nail – two unsuccessful attempts were made by doctors to remove nail under local anaesthetic, causing plaintiff further extreme pain – nail was subsequently repaired with adhesive – plaintiff was unable to use right hand and was absent from work for three weeks, during which time injured finger was acutely painful - for six weeks she found it difficult to use right hand to fasten buttons, laces etc. – unable to drive car for three weeks – leisure activities were curtailed for six weeks – there was permanent incomplete re-attachment of nail bed – injured finger would be sensitive to cold for 18 to 24 months after accident.

1.4.4.C74 Case No. 11942

Name of case: Entwistle v Furniss & White (Foundries) Ltd

Brief description of injuries: FINGER – CRUSH INJURY

Reported: Kemp & Kemp, K2-209/4; [1999] CLY 1606

JSB Category: 6(I)

Sex: Male

Age at injury: 33

Age at award: 37

Date of award: 15 April 1999

Tribunal: Reading County Court

Amount of award then: £1,000

Award at February 2001: £1,041

Description of injuries: Crushing injury to little finger of right, dominant, hand – claimant discouraged from taking sick leave and had no time off work – 2 days later, X-rays revealed fracture – wound became infected; nail had to be removed – claimant in extreme pain for 9 days – unable to go cycling or attend gym for 4 weeks.

1.4.4.C75 Case No. 11062

Name of case: Oliver v Contract Fencing Services

Brief description of injuries: HAND AND FOOT – CUT TO INDEX FINGER – 3 WEEKS

Reported: Kemp & Kemp, K2-211; [1995] CLY 1816

JSB Category: 6(I)

Sex: Male

Age at injury: 3

Age at award: 6

Date of award: 19 April 1995

Tribunal: Liverpool County Court

Amount of award then: £900

Award at February 2001: £1,039

Description of injuries: Infant male was injured when fence post fell over onto him – suffered cut to left index finger, requiring six stitches, and bruising to left foot – plaintiff unable to bear weight on left foot for one week but both injuries were fully resolved within three weeks of accident – some very slight scarring to finger but this was considered to be of no cosmetic significance.

1.4.4.C76 Case No. 10288

Name of case: Nichols v Port Eynon Transport

Brief description of injuries: STRAIN TO THE LEFT THUMB – 15MONTHS

Reported: Kemp & Kemp, K2-210; [1991] CLY 1485

JSB Category: 6(I)(w)

Sex: Male

Age at injury: –

Age at award: –

Date of award: 08 April 1991

Tribunal: Swansea County Court

Amount of award then: £800

Award at February 2001: £1,034

Description of injuries: Strain to the left thumb – initially extremely painful – off work for three days – returned in a supervisory capacity – N wore a sling for seven days – strapping for up to five months.

Prognosis: A full recovery after fifteen months.

1.4.4.C77 Case No. 10119

Name of case: Hanks v Courtaulds

Brief description of injuries: RIGHT MIDDLE FINGER – LACERATION – OFF WORK ONE WEEK

Reported: Kemp & Kemp, K2-213; [1990] CLY 1696

JSB Category: 6(I)

Sex: Male

Age at injury: 49

Age at award: 53

Date of award: 16 July 1990

Tribunal: Lincoln County Court

Amount of award then: £750

Award at February 2001: £1,017

Description of injuries: Crushing injury at work – deep laceration and contusion to terminal phalanx of right middle finger – butterfly closure – septic wound treated with antibiotics – absent from work one week – well healed half-inch scar – minimal alteration of sensation – normal nail growth – full range of movement and grip unaffected.

1.4.4.C78 Case No. 10124

Name of case: Moon v Lake

Brief description of injuries: LEFT THUMB – 5 PUNCTURE WOUNDS – RECOVERY 1 MONTH

Reported: Kemp & Kemp, K2-217; [1990] CLY 1702

JSB Category: 6(I)

Sex: Male

Age at injury: 38

Age at award: 38

Date of award: 17 January 1990

Tribunal: Glasgow Sheriff Court

Amount of award then: £700

Award at February 2001: £1,008

Description of injuries: Suffered five puncture wounds with surrounding bruising and soft-tissue swelling over the back and base of the left thumb – scratches over lower third of left leg – anti-tetanus administered – absent from work for one week – wounds healed within two weeks – some stiffness which took another fortnight to resolve – left with two small scars on left thumb and two small scars on the left leg.

1.4.4.C79 Case No. 11429

Name of case: Eason v Brewster

Brief description of injuries: FINGER – LACERATION

Reported: Kemp & Kemp, K2-219; [1997] CLY 1978

JSB Category: 6(I)

Sex: Female

Age at injury: 6

Age at award: 8

Date of award: 08 November 1996

Tribunal: Halifax County Court

Amount of award then: £900

Award at February 2001: £1,006

Description of injuries: Small laceration to the little finger.

Prognosis: Scar 0.5cm long – of cosmetic significance only.

1.4.4.C80 Case No. 10289

Name of case: Chapman v Sunderland Borough Council

Brief description of injuries: BRUISED HAND

Reported: [1991] CLY 1486

JSB Category: 6

Sex: Male

Age at injury: 29

Age at award: 30

Date of award: 20 December 1990

Tribunal: Sunderland County Court

Amount of award then: £750

Award at February 2001: £993

Description of injuries: C tripped over a gulley drain – he had pain along the dorsum of the fifth metacarpal of the left hand – bruised and painful for four weeks.

Prognosis: Full recovery.

1.4.4.C81 Case No. 10093

Name of case: Butterfield v Clifford Williams & Son

Brief description of injuries: LEFT THUMB – SPLINTER – PAIN FOR 2 MONTHS

Reported: Kemp & Kemp, H7-024; [1990] CLY 1660

JSB Category: 6(I)

Sex: Female

Age at injury: 48

Age at award: 50

Date of award: 08 December 1989

Tribunal: Telford County Court

Amount of award then: £650

Award at February 2001: £941

Description of injuries: Splinter under nail of left non-dominant thumb – GP could not remove it – finally removed under local anaesthetic at hospital – severe pain for two weeks – diminishing pain for two months – occasional pins and needles and cold weather pain.

1.4.4.C82 Case No. 11065

Name of case: Malpass v Berlei

Brief description of injuries: HAND – NEEDLE EMBEDDED IN MIDDLE FINGER

Reported: [1995] CLY 1819

JSB Category: 6(I)

Sex: Female

Age at injury: 48

Age at award: 51

Date of award: 21 December 1994

Tribunal: Cardiff County Court

Amount of award then: £750

Award at February 2001: £884

Description of injuries: Plaintiff suffered accident in course of employment when guard on sewing machine broke and needle penetrated the middle finger of her left (non-dominant) hand and snapped off – taken to hospital and piece of needle removed from finger under local anaesthetic – course of antibiotics was supplied and tetanus immunisation injection was administered – X-rays revealed a minuscule piece of needle remained embedded in finger – plaintiff returned to work immediately and had no time off – suffered pain, swelling and bruising in finger for two weeks – after that suffered occasional discomfort for eight months in form of tingling sensation when pressure was applied to tip of finger – prognosis was that she would either become asymptomatic or that her symptoms would be minimal – by date of assessment she remained symptomatic but her symptoms were minimal.

Prognosis: As a result of piece of needle remaining embedded in finger, there was remote possibility of future infection which, if it occurred, would probably result in inflammation and abscess which would necessitate antibiotic treatment lasting from few days to three to four weeks.

1.4.4.C83 Case No. 11265

Name of case: Mehrlich v McLaughlin

Brief description of injuries: HAND – DOG BITE

Reported: Kemp & Kemp, K2-246; [1996] CLY 2357

JSB Category: 6(I)

Sex: Male

Age at injury: 22

Age at award: 25

Date of award: 07 May 1996

Tribunal: Bristol County Court

Amount of award then: £700

Award at February 2001: £787

Description of injuries: Dog bite to the hand – minor grazing – at time of trial a 1cm scar was scarcely visible

1.4.4.C84 Case No. 12029

Name of case: Pepperall v Memory Lane Cakes Ltd

Brief description of injuries: HAND – CRUSH INJURY

Reported: Kemp & Kemp, K2-248/1; [2000] 4 CL 172

JSB Category: 6

Sex: Female

Age at injury: 24

Age at award: 26

Date of award: 19 November 1999

Tribunal: Cardiff County Court

Amount of award then: £750

Award at February 2001: £774

Description of injuries: A crush injury to the left hand – it jammed between a bakery trolley and a metal bar – bad bruising – an abrasion to the left middle finger – no bony injury – wore strapping for seven days – considerable discomfort and inconvenience for four to six weeks.

Prognosis: It was anticipated that symptoms would settle entirely within six months of the date of the accident.

1.4.4.C85 Case No. 12030

Name of case: Ritter v British Steel plc

Brief description of injuries: HAND – BURN

Reported: Kemp & Kemp, K2-248/2; [2000] 4 CL 173

JSB Category: 6

Sex: Male

Age at injury: 45

Age at award: 50

Date of award: 26 November 1999

Tribunal: Cardiff County Court

Amount of award then: £750

Award at February 2001: £774

Description of injuries: A burn injury to the back of the right hand – the burnt area blistered and required dressings – it took five weeks to heal – the skin kept breaking causing pain and discomfort. R made a complete recovery with full movement to the hand – no residual scarring – there were no continuing difficulties.

1.4.4.C86 Case No. 10293

Name of case: Beck v Bemrose

Brief description of injuries: RIGHT HAND BRUISING

Reported: Kemp & Kemp, K2-251; [1991] CLY 1490

JSB Category: 6

Sex: Female

Age at injury: 36

Age at award: 39

Date of award: 24 July 1991

Tribunal: Derby County Court

Amount of award then: £600

Award at February 2001: £771

Description of injuries: Hand was bruised and swollen after becoming trapped in a conveyor belt at her place of work – cold water to reduce the swelling – painkillers – abrasions to the ulna border of the right hand – no time off work.

Prognosis: No damage to the deeper structures – no body injury.

1.4.4.C87 Case No. 11744

Name of case: Whittaker v Gallagher

Brief description of injuries: HAND – CRUSH INJURY – 6 WEEKS

Reported: Kemp & Kemp, K2-268/1; [1998] CLY 1747

JSB Category: 6(I)

Sex: Female

Age at injury: 50

Age at award: 51

Date of award: 22 December 1997

Tribunal: Rawtenstall County Court

Amount of award then: £350

Award at February 2001: £376

Description of injuries: Crushing injury to the left hand – pain and swelling – knuckles cut and bruised – cuts healed in 4 weeks – bruising subsided in 6 weeks.

1.4.4.C88 Case No. 10132

Name of case: Morgan v Inco Alloys

Brief description of injuries: RIGHT MIDDLE FINGER – PAIN FOR 3 DAYS

Reported: [1990] CLY 1714

JSB Category: 6(I)

Sex: Male

Age at injury: 22

Age at award: –

Date of award: 21 February 1990

Tribunal: Hereford County Court

Amount of award then: £0

Award at February 2001: £0

Description of injuries: In course of employment, plaintiff removed die guard from machine, dropping it onto his right hand, trapping the tip of his right middle finger under the guard – finger remained painful for three days – returned to his previous occupation.

1.4.4.1 HAND AND OTHER INJURY

1.4.4.1.C1 Case No. 10029

Name of case: Steventon v Cotmor Tool and Presswork Co.

Brief description of injuries: 3 FINGERS AMPUTATED – POST-TRAUMATIC STRESS DISORDER – ENURESIS

Reported: Kemp & Kemp, C4-014; [1990] CLY 1587

JSB Category: 6(I); 3(B)

Sex: Female

Age at injury: –

Age at award: 25

Date of award: 13 March 1990

Tribunal: QBD

Amount of award then: £40,000

Award at February 2001: £62,810

Description of injuries: Amputations through proximal phalanges index and middle finger and distal joint of ring finger of non-dominant hand – moderate post-traumatic stress reaction – enuresis.

1.4.4.1.C2 Case No. 11837

Name of case: Jacobs v Corniche Helicopters

Brief description of injuries: HAND – SEVERE INJURY – DEPRESSION

Reported: Kemp & Kemp, H5-015/2; [1999] CLY 1501

JSB Category: 6(I)(e); 3(B)(d); 5(A)(g); 8

Sex: Female

Age at injury: 36

Age at award: 41

Date of award: 08 February 1999

Tribunal: QBD

Amount of award then: £30,000

Award at February 2001: £33,087

Description of injuries: Severe injuries to dominant right hand in helicopter accident – 8 bone fractures of fingers and wrist – 11 separate operative procedures over 5 years required – tip of ring finger amputated – skin graft – bone fusions – gross loss of function in hand; now an "assist hand" – pinch grip and power significantly reduced – everyday functions, including driving, limited – resultant gross cosmetic defect – hot and cold sensitivity – 5 years after accident, secondary degenerative changes in some joints already apparent – also cracked ribs, mild post-traumatic stress and clinical depression, all resolved by time of trial – claimant unable to continue in her previous job.

Prognosis: Future treatment, including bone fusions and nerve end reduction, required, resulting in some improvement in level of pain at cost of further loss of function – only limited part-time work possible in future.

1.4.4.1.C3 Case No. 11434

Name of case: Scott v Gage

Brief description of injuries: KNEE – THUMB – SCARS

Reported: Kemp & Kemp, I2-409; [1997] CLY 1983

JSB Category: 6(L)(a)(iii)

Sex: Female

Age at injury: 21

Age at award: 25

Date of award: 16 September 1997

Tribunal: Colchester County Court

Amount of award then: £26,000

Award at February 2001: £29,241

Description of injuries: Knee injuries – compression fracture – ligament rupture damage to the meniscus – lacerations to the face – fracture of a front tooth – severe ligamentous rupture of the thumb.

Prognosis: Permanent valgus deformity to the knee – laxity pain and stiffness – scarring – 50 per cent risk of knee replacement after 20 years – minor facial scarring.

Other points: Awarded as follows: tooth £1,500 / thumb £6,000 / knee £18,000 / scarring £3,500 (discounted to £26,000 for overlap).

1.4.4.1.C4 Case No. 10810

Name of case: Gleeson v Cardale Engineering

Brief description of injuries: HAND – 4 FINGERS AMPUTATED AND REATTACHED – POST-TRAUMATIC STRESS DISORDER

Reported: [1994] CLY 1659

JSB Category: 6(I)(e); 3(B)

Sex: Male

Age at injury: 29

Age at award: 32

Date of award: 10 November 1993

Tribunal: Not stated

Amount of award then: £22,500

Award at February 2001: £28,421

Description of injuries: Claimant caught left, non-dominant, hand in circular saw at work – 4 fingers severed at shafts of metacarpals – damage to flexor aspect of thumb – highly successful microsurgery undertaken to reattach amputated fingers, with internal fixture of metacarpals, and repair damaged arteries, veins and nerves – later, successful, tendon transplant operation – sensation in hand almost normal – inability to make tight fist – lack of fine manipulative skill – stiffness – aching in cold weather – claimant's hand had sufficient grip to be able to drive car with manual gear change (judge's finding) – post-traumatic stress disorder – nightmares – disturbed sleep – hyper-vigilance – reactive depression.

Prognosis: Symptoms of post-traumatic stress likely to diminish after end of litigation (judge's finding).

1.4.4.1.C5 Case No. 10811

Award at February 2001: £18,147

See: 1.4.3.C15 for details

1.4.4.1.C6 Case No. 11540

Name of case: Hewett v Chef & Brewer Ltd

Brief description of injuries: HAND – BURNS – POST-TRAUMATIC STRESS – BURNS

Reported: Kemp & Kemp, C4-058; [1998] CLY 1542

JSB Category: 8; 3(B)(c)

Sex: Male

Age at injury: 41

Age at award: 45

Date of award: 20 November 1997

Tribunal: Norwich County Court

Amount of award then: £15,000

Award at February 2001: £16,390

Description of injuries: Full thickness electrocution burn to the left hand – 6cm by 3cm scar requiring 2 skin grafts – post-traumatic stress disorder of a very severe nature – "made claimant's life hell".

Prognosis: Claimant still not entirely symptom-free at the time of the hearing, but symptoms likely to clear up in the near future.

Other points: Claimant's marriage breakdown was accepted as being caused solely by his PTSD. Award breakdown: £5,500 for physical injury; £9,500 for PTSD.

1.4.4.1.C7 Case No. 10843

Award at February 2001: £15,304

See: 1.4.2.C9 for details

1.4.4.1.C8 Case No. 10802

Award at February 2001: £11,580

See: 1.4.2.C14 for details

1.4.4.1.C9 Case No. 11839

Name of case: Re W

Brief description of injuries: HAND – ELBOW

Reported: Kemp & Kemp, PRH-002, H3-160; [1999] CLY 1503

JSB Category: 6(G)(c), 6(I)

Sex: Male

Age at injury: 25

Age at award: 27

Date of award: 22 July 1999

Tribunal: CICB, Plymouth

Amount of award then: £10,000

Award at February 2001: £10,423

Description of injuries: Glass laceration to non-dominant left elbow and 100 per cent cut of ulnar nerve and 2 tendons of fourth and fifth fingers of left hand – nerve and tendons reattached surgically – claimant unable to work for 35 weeks – 2 years after incident, persisting ulnar claw deformity of left hand and weakness of grip, making use of power tools in claimant's employment difficult – constant numbness and tingling – cold intolerance.

Prognosis: Further remedial surgery not recommended.

1.4.4.1.C10 Case No. 10436

Award at February 2001: £9,528

See: 1.4.3.C22 for details

1.4.4.1.C11 Case No. 10658

Name of case: Whorton v British Coal

Brief description of injuries: LEG AND HAND – BURNS

Reported: Kemp & Kemp, J3-029; [1993] CLY 1554

JSB Category: 8

Sex: Male

Age at injury: 11

Age at award: 13

Date of award: 25 March 1993

Tribunal: Doncaster County Court

Amount of award then: £6,000

Award at February 2001: £7,408

Description of injuries: Fall into heap of colliery spoil that had been subjected to heat and combustion – burns to left hand and waist and circumferential burn to lower part of left leg – skin grafts performed on left calf (area of 7 cm) and left thigh (12 x 10 cm) – 5 x 4 cm scar on volar aspect of right wrist, white and completely flat – claimant still experienced pain if kicked in grafted area while playing sports – some itchiness from grafted area – donor site on left thigh flat and difficult to see – grafting on left leg had settled in well and would not constitute any more than fairly minor cosmetic blemish – claimant not concerned by its cosmetic appearance.

1.4.4.1.C12 Case No. 11831

Award at February 2001: £5,241

See: 1.4.1.1.C16 for details

1.4.4.1.C13 Case No. 10357

Award at February 2001: £4,322

See: 1.2.3.2.C49 for details

1.4.4.1.C14 Case No. 10337

Name of case: Re Coyle

Brief description of injuries: RIGHT THUMB – LACERATION – 8 STITCHES – DEPRESSION

Reported: [1992] CLY 1593

JSB Category: 3(A)(c)

Sex: Female

Age at injury: –

Age at award: 61

Date of award: 18 April 1991

Tribunal: CICB, Glasgow

Amount of award then: £3,000

Award at February 2001: £3,877

Description of injuries: Laceration to the base of the right thumb requiring eight stitches – diagnosed as suffering from an anxiety and depressive reaction of such severity as to impair her ability to control her emotions.

1.4.4.1.C15 Case No. 11842

Name of case: Boland v Corby Towage

Brief description of injuries: FINGERS – KNEE – TOE

Reported: Kemp & Kemp, PRH-006, H6-046/1; [1999] CLY 1506

JSB Category: 6(I)(l), 6(L)(b)(ii), 6(P)(e)

Sex: Male

Age at injury: 56

Age at award: 59

Date of award: 21 April 1999

Tribunal: Liverpool County Court

Amount of award then: £3,250

Award at February 2001: £3,384

Description of injuries: Injury to ring and middle fingers of dominant left hand, bruising and wrenching injury to left knee and contusion to left great toe – knee injury recovered within 1 month – nail lost from great toe, but otherwise little ongoing difficulty – tip of left ring finger degloved, requiring skin graft – ring finger left three – eighths of an inch shorter than that on right hand, and sensitive if knocked – nail clawed and unable to be cut by scissors – middle finger also badly bruised, and some loss of movement in next – to – end joint, but not of functional significance.

Prognosis: Symptoms in fingers all permanent.

1.4.4.1.C16 Case No. 10116

Name of case: Ralph v Smith

Brief description of injuries: KNEE – BURSITIS – BRUISED HANDS

Reported: [1990] CLY 1690

JSB Category: 6(I) & 6(L)

Sex: Male

Age at injury: 17

Age at award: 20

Date of award: 22 June 1990

Tribunal: Exeter County Court

Amount of award then: £1,100

Award at February 2001: £1,493

Description of injuries: Plaintiff's motorcycle in collision with car – sustained bruising to right thumb and left little finger – right knee injury later diagnosed as mild pre-patellar post-traumatic bursitis – no evidence of bone injury – off work for two weeks – still had occasional symptoms at date of trial, but symptoms not major.

1.4.4.1.C17 Case No. 10890

Name of case: Hutchings v Jackson

Brief description of injuries: FINGER – BRUISING TO THIGH

Reported: Kemp & Kemp, K2-236; [1994] CLY 1742

JSB Category: 6(I), 6(K)(c)(iii)

Sex: Male

Age at injury: 17

Age at award: 19

Date of award: 13 October 1994

Tribunal: Bournemouth County Court

Amount of award then: £750

Award at February 2001: £888

Description of injuries: Claimant thrown from motorcycle – deep laceration to little finger of right, non-dominant, hand – 3 stitches, painkillers and tetanus injection required – bruising to left thigh – off work 1 week – light duties for 4 months thereafter – full recovery 5 months after incident – injuries described by judge as minor, but not trivial.

1.4.4.2 HAND FRACTURE

1.4.4.2.C1 Case No. 10085
Name of case: Re Antony
Brief description of injuries: SERIOUS HAND INJURIES – LEFT THUMB SEVERED
Reported: Kemp & Kemp, H5-011; [1990] CLY 1652
JSB Category: 6(I)
Sex: Male
Age at injury: 47
Age at award: 53
Date of award: 11 August 1989
Tribunal: CICB, London
Amount of award then: £45,000
Award at February 2001: £75,662

Description of injuries: Attacked by man with Samurai sword – blow to head, cutting scalp from top of head to eyebrow – deep laceration from base of right thumb to fourth web space – deep slash across palm of right hand damaging bones, nerves, arteries, muscles and tendons, which were severed to each finger – thumb of left hand severed below first joint – right hand left with extensive scarring, and no feeling to thumb – feeling almost totally absent in first three fingers – no movement to thumb – little movement to first and second fingers – unable to grip between thumb and fingers – only able to pick up paper by gripping third and little finger together.

1.4.4.2.C2 Case No. 10809
Name of case: Gibbs v Cowles and Cowles
Brief description of injuries: HAND – LOSS OF 2 FINGERS
Reported: [1994] CLY 1658
JSB Category: 6(I)(e)
Sex: Male
Age at injury: 23
Age at award: 26
Date of award: 04 May 1994
Tribunal: Bristol High Court
Amount of award then: £32,000
Award at February 2001: £40,504

Description of injuries: Claimant's left (non-dominant) hand came into contact with cutters on spindle moulder – mutilating hand injury – complete amputation of middle finger through metacarpo-phalangeal joint – complete amputation through proximal phalanx of ring finger – K-wires fitted and bone grafts made – rotary osteotomy of index finger undergone 17 months after accident – comminuted compound fracture of proximal phalanx and metacarpal of index finger, which was left hanging off and was sewn back on – lacerations to little finger resulting in skin loss – traverse fracture through distal phalanx of thumb – claimant severely incapacitated – cosmetic deformity to hand, with index finger curved,

stiff, with rotary abnormality of 30 degrees and restricted range of movement – claimant still experiencing cold intolerance, numbness and stiffness to index finger in bad weather in winter at time of trial – unable to return to previous employment – unemployed at date of trial.

1.4.4.2.C3 Case No. 10433
Name of case: Bakhitiari (Leila) v The Zoological Society of London
Brief description of injuries: LOSS OF 3 FINGERS ON LEFT HAND – MARRIAGE PROSPECTS AFFECTED
Reported: Kemp & Kemp, H5-015; [1992] CLY 1689
JSB Category: 6(I)(d)
Sex: Female
Age at injury: 2
Age at award: 10
Date of award: 05 December 1991
Tribunal: QBD
Amount of award then: £30,000
Award at February 2001: £40,490

Description of injuries: Index, middle and ring fingers of left hand completely severed – lost tip of the little finger – plastic surgery left an unsightly stump with bulky skin-flap – groin scar which could not be completely hidden with two-piece bathing costume.

Prognosis: The child was born in this country of Iranian parents – account had to be taken of the revulsion with which the injury would be viewed in Iran – affecting the girl's marriage prospects.

1.4.4.2.C4 Case No. 11175
Name of case: Streets v Direct Image Litho Services Ltd
Brief description of injuries: HAND – AMPUTATION OF THE HAND
Reported: Kemp & Kemp, H5-015/1; [1996] CLY 2266
JSB Category: 6(I)(c)
Sex: Male
Age at injury: 20
Age at award: 24
Date of award: 17 November 1995
Tribunal: QBD
Amount of award then: £30,000
Award at February 2001: £36,392

Description of injuries: Traumatic amputation of the right hand – the hand was re-attached under micro-surgery – at the time of the hearing the wrist was scarred and the hand had a "clawed" appearance – able to pinch between the thumb and forefinger – could not carry heavy things in the left hand.

Other points: He was at a serious disadvantage in the labour market – retraining not practical or possible.

1.4.4.2.C5 Case No. 10230

Name of case: Howard v British Coal Corporation

Brief description of injuries: AMPUTATION OF ALL FINGERS OF LEFT HAND

Reported: Kemp & Kemp, H5-014; [1991] CLY 1427

JSB Category: 6(I)

Sex: Male

Age at injury: 36

Age at award: 42

Date of award: 05 March 1991

Tribunal: QBD Sheffield

Amount of award then: £19,000

Award at February 2001: £25,720

Description of injuries: Severe crushing injury to the left hand – hand trapped for five minutes – traumatic amputation of all fingers – complete loss of middle and index fingers, about half the ring finger and tip of little finger – one week in hospital undergoing surgery – underwent a course of physiotherapy until May 1986.

Prognosis: Unable to play the saxophone – difficulty with shoe laces, buttons, snooker – scarring represents a severe cosmetic blemish – at a permanent disadvantage in the labour market.

Other points: Plaintiff thought he could work as a welder – the judge commented that it was one thing to think a disabled man could do a job, but another to persuade a prospective employer.

1.4.4.2.C6 Case No. 11010

Name of case: Re Mills

Brief description of injuries: HAND – MULTIPLE INJURIES – MIDDLE FINGER SHORTENED

Reported: Kemp & Kemp,J2-012; [1995] CLY 1762

JSB Category: 6(I)(e)

Sex: Female

Age at injury: 33

Age at award: 38

Date of award: 31 January 1995

Tribunal: CICB, London

Amount of award then: £15,000

Award at February 2001: £17,978

Description of injuries: Plaintiff suffered gun shot wound to right (dominant) hand – suffered soft-tissue injury and loss on ulnar aspect of hand – terminal phalanx of middle finger was shortened and deformed – muscle damage and division of ulnar artery, nerve and flexor carpi ulnaris tendon – injury repaired under general anaesthetic – large skin defect of palm was covered with skin flap from back of forearm – remained as in-patient for one month and as out-patient for almost three years – left with long surgical scar running obliquely from above lateral aspect of right elbow down dorsum of forearm to medial border of wrist – wrist and proximal part of palm on medial side there was black patch of grafted skin running in band about an inch wide and three inches long from midline of palm and wrist to medial border of wrist – scars were obvious and she always wore long sleeves to cover them – loss of sensation over palm and some motor deficit impairing, in particular, finer movements of hand – as result she was no longer able to sew, carry heavy shopping, do her hair or type (she had been legal secretary at time of accident), although she continued to be employed in alternative capacity until her employers closed down.

1.4.4.2.C7 Case No. 10441

Name of case: Cartwright v Steetley

Brief description of injuries: AMPUTATION OF TOP JOINT OF LEFT THUMB

Reported: [1992] CLY 1697

JSB Category: 6(I)(t)

Sex: Male

Age at injury: 21

Age at award: 25

Date of award: 19 May 1992

Tribunal: Stoke County Court

Amount of award then: £8,000

Award at February 2001: £9,878

Description of injuries: Clean amputation of the left thumb through the proximal phalanx – loss of nail, nail-bed, and terminal joint.

Prognosis: Weakness of grip fifty per cent – unable to do heavy work or work at heights – stump painful – obvious cosmetic effect – assessed as 20 per cent disabled.

1.4.4.2.C8 Case No. 10231

Name of case: Colwill v Rodosthenous

Brief description of injuries: AMPUTATION OF TIPS OF NON-DOMINANT MIDDLE AND RING FINGERS

Reported: Kemp & Kemp, H6-025; [1991] CLY 1428

JSB Category: 6(I)(k)

Sex: Male

Age at injury: 24

Age at award: –

Date of award: 19 April 1991

Tribunal: Plymouth County Court

Amount of award then: £7,500

Award at February 2001: £9,692

Description of injuries: Traumatic amputation of the tips of the middle and ring fingers of the non dominant right hand at the terminal phalanx – fingers trimmed under general anaesthetic – neuroma on the ring finger excised under general anaesthetic as a day case.

Prognosis: Slight loss of dexterity – increased sensitivity was expected to decrease in time – grip a little weaker – tendency to drop things.

1.4.4.2.C9 Case No. 10442

Name of case: Hunt v Strudwick
Brief description of injuries: RIGHT THUMB FRACTURE – DEGENERATIVE CHANGES
Reported: Kemp & Kemp, H7-013/2; [1992] CLY 1698
JSB Category: 6(I)(t)
Sex: Male
Age at injury: 24
Age at award: 28
Date of award: 21 August 1992
Tribunal: Tunbridge Wells County Court
Amount of award then: £6,500
Award at February 2001: £8,049

Description of injuries: Fracture of the trapezium – initially suffered chest pain and pain at the base of the first and second metacarpals in the right dominant hand – laceration under the chin – no fracture found until three-and-a-half years later – there was rapid recovery from all except the thumb injury – discovery of fracture accounted for the continuing symptoms – pain in the base of the thumb – affected his work as a motorcycle mechanic – some reduction in grip – early osteoarthritic changes were present in the trapezio-metacarpal joint.

Prognosis: Pain and difficulty at work would increase over the next ten years.

1.4.4.2.C10 Case No. 10633

Name of case: Sanderson v Precision Engineering
Brief description of injuries: THUMB – FRACTURE
Reported: Kemp & Kemp, H7-014/1; [1993] CLY 1528
JSB Category: 6(I)(u)
Sex: Male
Age at injury: 50
Age at award: 54
Date of award: 02 February 1993
Tribunal: Preston County Court
Amount of award then: £5,250
Award at February 2001: £6,506

Description of injuries: Right (non-dominant) thumb trapped in machinery – compound comminuted fracture – laceration to base of thumb, on palmar and dorsal aspects, involving web space – digital nerve avulsed – tendon damaged – deformation of thumb when compared with left thumb – scarring – joint movements restricted – loss of sensation in tip – unable to play snooker – work not affected.

Prognosis: Dull ache in thumb, impaired pinch grip and scarring expected to be permanent.

1.4.4.2.C11 Case No. 10632

Name of case: Martin v Press Offshore
Brief description of injuries: THUMB – FRACTURE
Reported: Kemp & Kemp, H5-022; [1993] CLY 1527
JSB Category: 6(I)(u)
Sex: Male
Age at injury: 32
Age at award: 34
Date of award: 24 March 1993
Tribunal: Newcastle-upon-Tyne County Court
Amount of award then: £5,250
Award at February 2001: £6,482

Description of injuries: Trip – Bennett's fracture of first metacarpal bone involving carpo-metacarpal joint of thumb of dominant right hand – in plaster 6-7 weeks, off work over 5 months – loss of pre-accident dexterity – counting money, writing, tightening spanners, weapons handling for Territorial Army and flyfishing all difficult – inner glove needed to prevent hand becoming excessively cold and stiff at work (as scaffolder) – unable to lift or balance heavy/lengthy scaffolding with right hand or do weightlifting.

Prognosis: Should be able to continue work as scaffolder without difficulty for 10-12 years from June 1991, after which osteoarthritic change in joint at base of thumb would make climbing scaffolding unsafe – light work possible thereafter if available.

1.4.4.2.C12 Case No. 10984

Name of case: Burgess v PD Stevens

Brief description of injuries: HAND – AMPUTATION OF LITTLE FINGER

Reported: Kemp & Kemp, H6-035; [1995] CLY 1735

JSB Category: 6(I)(m)

Sex: Male

Age at injury: 16

Age at award: 18

Date of award: 24 January 1995

Tribunal: Market Drayton County Court

Amount of award then: £5,000

Award at February 2001: £5,890

Description of injuries: Plaintiff's little finger on left hand was crushed between hammer and part of vehicle – initially treated with wires and splint – roughly one month after accident, little finger was part amputated through proximal phalanx – off work five weeks and on returning was initially limited to light work – had further time off work in respect of injury – his main concern was that he had to give up playing rugby because he was frightened of knocking the finger – finger ached in cold weather and tip of finger was quite sensitive – there was loss of cylinder grip of between 20 per cent to 25 per cent but no risk of further complications.

Prognosis: Plaintiff had taken up work in light engineering and would remain a manual worker – had come to terms with injury although was concerned about appearance of hand – dexterity in existing work was affected.

1.4.4.2.C13 Case No. 10985

Name of case: Mallett v Committee of the Hanney War Memorial Hall

Brief description of injuries: HAND – LOSS OF TIP OF INDEX FINGER – NAIL DISTORTED

Reported: Kemp & Kemp, H6-036/1; [1995] CLY 1736

JSB Category: 6(I)(i)

Sex: Female

Age at injury: 8

Age at award: 9

Date of award: 25 April 1995

Tribunal: Oxford County Court

Amount of award then: £5,000

Award at February 2001: £5,772

Description of injuries: Minor suffered crush injury when left (non-dominant) index finger was trapped in door during function at defendant's premises – plaintiff was treated at hospital where fingertip was explored under general anaesthesia – examination revealed loss of pulp tissue, laceration of nail bed and fracture of finger – free skin graft was carried out but did not take – further skin graft from left buttock was carried out after fortnight and this did take – plaintiff was reluctant to look at finger and preferred to keep it bandaged even when that was no longer beneficial –

advised to see clinical psychologist but family moved out of area before appointment could be arranged – move appeared to resolve her anxieties – injury affected plaintiff's horse riding for three months and recorder playing for six months.

Prognosis: The prognosis at date of hearing was that fingernail would be curved and prone to infection – finger had been slightly shortened and there was slight loss of grip and dexterity – beaked nail might be improved by further operation if infections were to persist – no risk of long-term deformity other than to nail.

1.4.4.2.C14 Case No. 11841

Name of case: Porter v Wilton Contracts Ltd

Brief description of injuries: FINGER – LOSS OF TIP

Reported: Kemp & Kemp, H6-036; [1999] CLY 1505

JSB Category: 6(I)(h)

Sex: Male

Age at injury: 27

Age at award: 31

Date of award: 01 July 1999

Tribunal: Woolwich County Court

Amount of award then: £5,500

Award at February 2001: £5,730

Description of injuries: Traumatic amputation of tip of right, dominant, index finger to the extent of 1.25cm – stump debrided and sutured under general anaesthetic – 6 weeks of healing and 2-week course of physiotherapy required – claimant off work for 10 months, and unable to find a job thereafter for a further 11 months, having lost his original job; judge found period of unemployment to be reasonable in the circumstances – claimant learned over time to regain manual dexterity – increased sensitivity at tip of stump, some cold sensitivity and some stiffness – these symptoms found to represent a 5 per cent disability.

Prognosis: Symptoms permanent.

1.4.4.2.C15 Case No. 10438

Name of case: Pauley v London Borough of Southwark

Brief description of injuries: FRACTURES OF LEFT FINGER AND THUMB

Reported: [1992] CLY 1694

JSB Category: 6(I)(l)

Sex: Female

Age at injury: 58

Age at award: 61

Date of award: 04 February 1992

Tribunal: Bloomsbury County Court

Amount of award then: £4,250

Award at February 2001: £5,363

Description of injuries: Displaced fracture of the proximal phalanx of the left ring finger and left thumb – grazes and bruises to the hands and legs – ring finger internally fixed – both hands immobilised for four weeks – swelling, pain and stiffness to the right thumb worsened with the onset of reflex osteodystrophy which gradually settled.

Prognosis: Some residuary weakness of grip and slight lack of dexterity.

1.4.4.2.C16 Case No. 10443

Name of case: Aurckett v Smith

Brief description of injuries: LEFT THUMB FRACTURE – MINOR DISABILITY – 50% CHANCE OF OSTEOARTHRITIS

Reported: Kemp & Kemp, H7-018/1; [1992] CLY 1699

JSB Category: 6(I)

Sex: Male

Age at injury: 17

Age at award: 19

Date of award: 03 April 1992

Tribunal: Derby District Registry

Amount of award then: £4,000

Award at February 2001: £4,957

Description of injuries: Bennet's Fracture – dislocation of the base of the left thumb – concussion – twisting and bruising to the right shoulder – sprained right ankle.

Prognosis: At the time of the hearing the injury was described as being a continuing disability of a relatively minor nature with some interference with his work – risk of osteoarthritis developing put at fifty per cent.

1.4.4.2.C17 Case No. 10090

Name of case: Taylor v IMI Yorkshire Imperial

Brief description of injuries: RIGHT LITTLE FINGER FRACTURED

Reported: Kemp & Kemp; H6-039; [1990] CLY 1657

JSB Category: 6(I)

Sex: Male

Age at injury: 20s

Age at award: 20s plus 5

Date of award: 13 July 1989

Tribunal: Leeds County Court

Amount of award then: £3,000

Award at February 2001: £4,468

Description of injuries: Compound fracture to the terminal phalanx of right little finger – aching in finger in cold weather, which would ease in time but would never fully cease.

Prognosis: Jarring or knocking of the hand causes pain which would eventually pass – loss of sensation in finger with pain on pressure affecting power of grip – there is a permanent altered sensation which would cause minor difficulties – distal phalanx was a little bulbous – plaintiff found remaining scar ugly.

1.4.4.2.C18 Case No. 11425

Name of case: Hall v Bolton MBC

Brief description of injuries: FINGERS – FRACTURES TO TWO FINGERS

Reported: Kemp & Kemp, H6-040; [1997] CLY 1974

JSB Category: 6(I)

Sex: Female

Age at injury: 12

Age at award: 21

Date of award: 13 January 1997

Tribunal: Bolton County Court

Amount of award then: £4,000

Award at February 2001: £4,456

Description of injuries: Fractures to the middle and ring fingers – abrasions to the face.

Prognosis: Slight loss of movement – unable to make a tight fist – finger would not straighten – future improvement unlikely.

1.4.4.2.C19 Case No. 10091

Name of case: Rosamund v TRW Valves

Brief description of injuries: RIGHT MIDDLE FINGER – LOSS OF TIP

Reported: Kemp & Kemp, H6-042; [1990] CLY 1658

JSB Category: 6(I)

Sex: Female

Age at injury: –

Age at award: 49

Date of award: 24 January 1990

Tribunal: Bromwich County Court

Amount of award then: £2,750

Award at February 2001: £3,958

Description of injuries: Sustained a partial loss of tip of pulp of right dominant middle finger – required skin graft.

Prognosis: Left with scarred finger, slightly abnormal in shape – continuing symptoms of a feeling of loss of grip in right hand – control of small items lost – tightness in finger – intermittent shooting pains when using hand – aching in cold and hot conditions.

1.4.4.2.C20 Case No. 10814

Name of case: Re McLean

Brief description of injuries: HAND – FRACTURE

Reported: [1994] CLY 1663

JSB Category: 6(I)

Sex: Male

Age at injury: 27

Age at award: 29

Date of award: 15 December 1993

Tribunal: CICB, Birmingham

Amount of award then: £3,000

Award at February 2001: £3,636

Description of injuries: Oblique fracture through shaft of third metacarpal of left (non-dominant) hand – hand uncomfortable and swollen – off work 1 week – hand strapped for 3 weeks – 20-30 minutes exercise per day for 8-9 months required to restore pre-incident strength – claimant being considered for selection to Great Britain karate team at time of incident – injury and 4 months' disruption to training programme rendered him unavailable for selection – on resumption of training, hand occasionally became stiff, swollen and achy – medical examination 23 months after injury – hand appeared normal – however, claimant conscious of hand's tendency to react adversely, and had been unable to regain his former proficiency.

Other points: Board indicated that award would have been "substantially less" had it not been for the loss of amenity

1.4.4.2.C21 Case No. 11976

Name of case: W (a minor) v Gloucestershire CC

Brief description of injuries: FINGER – LOSS OF TIP

Reported: Kemp & Kemp, PRH-005; [2000] 2 CL 147

JSB Category: 6(I)(n)

Sex: Female

Age at injury: 6

Age at award: 8

Date of award: 10 September 1999

Tribunal: Cheltenham County Court

Amount of award then: £3,500

Award at February 2001: £3,622

Description of injuries: Crushed tip of the little finger on her left non-dominant hand – the bone extruded – treated with dressings and anti-biotics – protuberant end of the distal phalanx was removed by a bone nibbler under general anaesthetic – nearly 1cm of the little finger was lost – the nail growth curled around the end of her finger – W found the injury and treatment very distressing for about nine months.

1.4.4.2.C22 Case No. 10107

Name of case: Peters v Worthing District Health Authority

Brief description of injuries: RIGHT FIRST FINGER – FRACTURE

Reported: Kemp & Kemp, H6-049, K2-039; [1990] CLY 1675

JSB Category: 6(I)

Sex: Male

Age at injury: 48

Age at award: 50

Date of award: 12 October 1990

Tribunal: Worthing County Court

Amount of award then: £2,500

Award at February 2001: £3,300

Description of injuries: Sustained crush injury to right hand resulting in spiral fracture of first metacarpal, and considerable soft-tissue swelling and bruising – fracture united soundly – had pain and fear of machinery involved for about 10 months

Prognosis: Limitation of movement at metacarpal join was insignificant – osteoarthritis unlikely to develop as result of injury.

1.4.4.2.C23 Case No. 11650

Name of case: Lucas v Sketchley plc
Brief description of injuries: HAND – FINGERS – FRACTURES
Reported: Kemp & Kemp, H6-049/2; [1998] CLY 1652
JSB Category: 6(I)
Sex: Male
Age at injury: 60
Age at award: 63
Date of award: 19 June 1998
Tribunal: Worcester County Court
Amount of award then: £3,000
Award at February 2001: £3,158
Description of injuries: Open fractures to the middle and ring fingers with deep pulp lacerations – cold intolerance – a feeling of weakness of grip.Condition

1.4.4.2.C24 Case No. 11940

Name of case: Mastin v Rotherham HA
Brief description of injuries: FINGER – LOSS OF TIP
Reported: Kemp & Kemp, PRH-008; [1999] CLY 1604
JSB Category: 6(I); 8
Sex: Female
Age at injury: 43
Age at award: 45
Date of award: 14 April 1999
Tribunal: Doncaster County Court
Amount of award then: £2,750
Award at February 2001: £2,863
Description of injuries: Circumferential partial amputation of tip of pulp of (unspecified) finger of left non-dominant hand – immediate pain and blood loss – finger sutured under general anaesthetic – arm put in sling – stitches removed 1 week later; steristrips applied – wound continued to ooze and remain painful; painkillers taken regularly over course of next week or so – off work about 5 weeks – housework, washing hair and child care difficult over that time – light duties only undertaken for a time after returning to work – claimant left with scarring, although only a minor cosmetic disability, a slight pointing and shortening of the finger, and cold sensitivity.

Prognosis: Scarring permanent – cold sensitivity expected to settle in time.

1.4.4.2.C25 Case No. 11427

Name of case: Turner v British Steel PLC
Brief description of injuries: FINGER – FRACTURE
Reported: Kemp & Kemp, K2-095; [1997] CLY 1976
JSB Category: 6(I)(q)
Sex: Male
Age at injury: 30's
Age at award:
Date of award: 11 December 1996
Tribunal: Cardiff County Court
Amount of award then: £2,000
Award at February 2001: £2,228
Description of injuries: Fracture of the right little finger – pain and discomfort – loss of the nail..

Prognosis: Permanent symptoms amounted to a nuisance.

1.4.4.2.C26 Case No. 10673

Name of case: Castens v Lecointe-Gayle
Brief description of injuries: THUMB – FRACTURE
Reported: Kemp & Kemp, K2-118; [1993] CLY 1569
JSB Category: 6(I)(w)
Sex: Male
Age at injury: 23
Age at award: 24
Date of award: 19 February 1993
Tribunal: Bristol County Court
Amount of award then: £1,500
Award at February 2001: £1,859
Description of injuries: Knocked off motorcycle – fractured proximal phalanx of left (non-dominant) thumb – ring block inserted, thumb manipulated and plaster applied – position of thumb not satisfactory – further manipulation carried out under general anaesthetic – plaster thumb spica applied – plaster removed 1 month later – no residual pain and tenderness, but slight restriction of movement – full recovery 5 weeks after removal of plaster, 9 weeks after accident.

1.4.4.2.C27 Case No. 10492

Name of case: Rathbone v Liverpool County Council

Brief description of injuries: RIGHT INDEX FINGER – FLAKE FRACTURE

Reported: Kemp & Kemp, K2-121; [1992] CLY 1748

JSB Category: 6(I)(q)

Sex: Male

Age at injury: 23

Age at award: 25

Date of award: 02 October 1992

Tribunal: Liverpool County Court

Amount of award then: £1,500

Award at February 2001: £1,844

Description of injuries: Cut right index finger – avulsed flake of bone – one-inch scar round the middle joint of the finger – thickening of the proximal inter phalangeal joint.

Prognosis: Symptoms had resolved after 20 months.

1.4.4.2.C28 Case No. 10278

Name of case: Taylor v The Post Office

Brief description of injuries: CRACK FRACTURES TO THE MIDDLE AND RING FINGERS

Reported: [1991] CLY 1475

JSB Category: 6(I)

Sex: Female

Age at injury: 43

Age at award: 47

Date of award: 22 March 1991

Tribunal: Shoreditch County Court

Amount of award then: £1,250

Award at February 2001: £1,636

Description of injuries: Crack fractures to the middle and ring fingers – soreness and swelling – T's fingers were strapped – given a sling – off work for five weeks.

Prognosis: At the time of the hearing the hand became sore if immersed in hot water – a degree of swelling prevented her from wearing her wedding and other rings.

1.4.4.2.C29 Case No. 10685

Name of case: Soudah v Villarreai

Brief description of injuries: HAND – FRACTURE – 3 MONTHS

Reported: Kemp & Kemp, K2-227; [1993] CLY 1581

JSB Category: 6(I)(q)

Sex: Male

Age at injury: 26

Age at award: –

Date of award: 06 September 1993

Tribunal: Central London County Court

Amount of award then: £750

Award at February 2001: £909

Description of injuries: Road accident – displacement fracture to fourth metacarpal of left (non-dominant) hand – severe pain and swelling – shock – nausea – manipulation under local anaesthetic – hand in plaster for 6 weeks – unable to drive or participate in sports; generally incapacitated in domestic life.

Prognosis: Full recovery within 3 months of removal of plaster cast.

SECTION 1.5
DAMAGE TO TRUNK

1.5.C1 Case No. 10321
Award at February 2001: £25,510

See: 1.2.3.8.C79 for details

1.5.C2 Case No. 11283
Award at February 2001: £11,201

See: 1.1.C7 for details

1.5.C3 Case No. 10105
Name of case: Re Lakhrissi

Brief description of injuries: TRUNK AND LEG – STABBINGS – 38 STITCHES

Reported: [1990] CLY 1673

JSB Category:

Sex: Female

Age at injury: 38

Age at award: 43

Date of award: 17 July 1990

Tribunal: CICB

Amount of award then: £3,750

Award at February 2001: £5,087

Description of injuries: Multiple stab wound with penknife in neck, shoulder, chest, abdomen and leg requiring 38 stitches – assailant also attempted strangulation – no injuries to internal organs – hospital treatment for three weeks.

Prognosis: Substantial recovery by date of assessment – unable to carry heavy shopping with stabbed arm – still takes painkillers for pain in leg from stab wound.

1.5.1 CHEST INJURY

1.5.1.C1 Case No. 10782
Name of case: Re Hudson

Brief description of injuries: INTERNAL ORGANS – HEART – STAB WOUND – PERMANENT CARDIAC IMPAIRMENT

Reported: Kemp & Kemp, F2-025; [1994] CLY 1631

JSB Category: 5(A)(b)

Sex: Male

Age at injury: 16

Age at award: 21

Date of award: 11 November 1994

Tribunal: CICB, Birmingham

Amount of award then: £37,500

Award at February 2001: £47,928

Description of injuries: Assault – claimant stabbed with knife through heart at junction of right and left ventricles in extra-ventricular sulcus – cardiac arrest and resuscitation – thoracotomy performed – initially good post-operative recovery – 5 months later, complaint of effort dyspnoea – cardiac catheterisation required – left ventricular impairment, believed to be due to generalised hypoxic damage associated with cardiac arrest and resuscitation rather than stab wound itself – shortness of breath on moderate exertion – tightness in chest on walking – discomfort to left side over thoracotomy scar – resting electrocardiogram showed reduction in R waves in anterior leads with biphasic T waves over leads V4-V6 – exercise test undertaken over 3 years later – claimant exercised for 9.5 minutes, stopping at level 4 of standard Bruce protocol with shortness of breath and general exhaustion; blood pressure rose from 120-160 systolic.

Prognosis: Cardiac impairment would continue – unlikely to be any improvement – possibility of further deterioration due to further dilation in size of cardiac chamber and loss of function – claimant forbidden to undertake manual work – long-term survival adversely affected – at least 20 per cent chance of overt cardiac failure within 5 years of test in December 1992; 5-year survival rate in the region of 50-60 per cent – chances of surviving next 10 years put at 80-85 per cent – possibility of retraining for, and obtaining, some lighter work in future.

1.5.1.C2 Case No. 11627

Name of case: Reed v Sunderland HA

Brief description of injuries: INTERNAL ORGANS – UNDIAGNOSED TWISTED AND HERNIATED SMALL INTESTINE

Reported: (1998) The Times, October 16, Kemp & Kemp, C4-019, F4-019/1; BPILS, I 41.8; [1998] CLY 1629

JSB Category: 5(H)(b)

Sex: Female

Age at injury: 18

Age at award: 27

Date of award: 01 July 1997

Tribunal: Newcastle upon Tyne County Court

Amount of award then: £35,000

Award at February 2001: £40,717

Description of injuries: Undiagnosed twisted and herniated small intestine – necessitated the removal of 131cm of necrotic small intestine and 33cm of necrotic large intestine – severe problems with diarrhoea – mixed affective disorder.

Prognosis: Claimant unlikely to ever obtain gainful employment.

1.5.1.C3 Case No. 11758

Name of case: O'Keefe v Harvey-Kemble

Brief description of injuries: CHEST – BREAST

Reported: Kemp & Kemp, L8-151; [1998] CLY 1761

JSB Category: 5(A)

Sex: Female

Age at injury: 28

Age at award: 34

Date of award: 24 April 1998

Tribunal: CA

Amount of award then: £13,500

Award at February 2001: £14,417

Description of injuries: Haematoma following bilateral breast augmentation – encapsulation of the implants – a further 5 operations were required to achieve symmetry – satisfactory result achieved.

Prognosis: A satisfactory result was achieved.

Other points: O was distressed by failure to properly advise her about the risks inherent in the surgery – failure to assess her aspirations as to the eventual bust size.

1.5.1.C4 Case No. 10612

Name of case: Cambridge v The Post Office

Brief description of injuries: LUNGS – PNEUMOTHORAX – SURGERY REQUIRED

Reported: Kemp & Kemp, F6-012/1; [1993] CLY 1507

JSB Category: 5(B)(f); 8

Sex: Male

Age at injury: 57

Age at award: 62

Date of award: 22 January 1993

Tribunal: Nottingham County Court

Amount of award then: £7,500

Award at February 2001: £9,355

Description of injuries: Left pneumothorax suffered while lifting heavy weight – treated with simple aspiration using needle and local anaesthetic – partial recurrence – thoracotomy and pleurectomy performed – number of large cysts discovered and removed – lung surgically stapled to chest wall to avoid any recurrence – consequent major operation scar on left chest wall that claimant felt was embarrassing and unsightly – some aching and pain in chest and slight breathlessness still experienced at time of trial – first instance judge characterised symptoms as continuing, though slight.

Prognosis: Good recovery from surgery – no recurrence experienced at time of trial and virtually no risk of future recurrence – able to continue to undertake almost every aspect of former job.

1.5.1.C5 Case No. 10969

Name of case: Re Curry

Brief description of injuries: CHEST AND ABDOMEN – SCARS

Reported: Kemp & Kemp, F6-013/1; [1995] CLY 1720

JSB Category: 5(A)(d)

Sex: Male

Age at injury: 25

Age at award: 28

Date of award: 24 May 1995

Tribunal: CICB

Amount of award then: £6,500

Award at February 2001: £7,473

Description of injuries: Plaintiff suffered two stab wounds to chest – assailant used knife with narrow blade four inches long – on arrival at hospital applicant bled heavily and was in shock – was treated initially with infusion and transfusion and was then taken to theatre – underwent left thoracotomy and laparotomy, the latter involving division of diaphragm – chest drains were inserted – no direct damage to heart, lungs or intra-abdominal organs – remained in intensive care for 12 hours followed by 12 days as in-patient – discharged from out-patients some three-and-a-half months after attack having made good recovery, although further rehabilitation was required to regain full fitness – permanent extensive scars to stomach and left side of chest.

1.5.1.C6 Case No. 10603

Award at February 2001: £6,704

See: 1.3.1.3.1.C23 for details

1.5.1.C7 Case No. 11462

Name of case: Davis v Gregg & Co (Knottingley) Ltd
Brief description of injuries: CHEST – BRUISING AND ABRASIONS
Reported: Kemp & Kemp, J2-041; [1997] CLY 2011
JSB Category: 6(K)(c)(iii)
Sex: Male
Age at injury: 26
Age at award: 29
Date of award: 09 January 1997
Tribunal: Bradford County Court
Amount of award then: £3,000
Award at February 2001: £3,342

Description of injuries: Severe chest wall bruising – abrasion to the right shin – burn injury to the left forearm.

Prognosis: Chest pain resolved – flat, permanent scar to the shin – visible from ten feet.

Other points: Slipped into a hole in a metal walkway – avoided falling into a bottle-grinding machine below.

1.5.1.C8 Case No. 10266

Name of case: Vizor and Russell v Pilgrem
Brief description of injuries: FRACTURED STERNUM AND 6TH THORACIC VERTEBRA – RECOVERY 6 WEEKS
Reported: Kemp & Kemp, K2-080; [1991] CLY 1463
JSB Category: 6(B)
Sex: Female
Age at injury: 50
Age at award: –
Date of award: 05 December 1990
Tribunal: Oxford County Court
Amount of award then: £1,750
Award at February 2001: £2,317

Description of injuries: Seatbelt injuries – undisplaced fracture to the sternum – fracture of the sixth thoracic vertebra – bruising to the right thigh – very painful injury.

Prognosis: All symptoms fully resolved within six weeks.

1.5.1.C9 Case No. 10269

Name of case: Jackson v Torquay Leisure Hotels
Brief description of injuries: 3 BROKEN RIBS
Reported: Kemp & Kemp, K2-088; [1991] CLY 1466
JSB Category:
Sex: Male
Age at injury: 55
Age at award: –
Date of award: 13 August 1991
Tribunal: Torquay County Court
Amount of award then: £1,750
Award at February 2001: £2,245

Description of injuries: J fell when a bath mat slipped from under him – he suffered three broken ribs – six days in hospital – slept in a chair for six months – required painkillers – holiday was spoiled as the accident occurred on the first day.

Prognosis: No effect upon his pre-accident sedentary life-style.

1.5.1.C10 Case No. 10273

Name of case: Hodgkiss v Brassett
Brief description of injuries: FRACTURED RIB – ALMOST FULL RECOVERY AFTER 19 MONTHS
Reported: Kemp & Kemp, K2-109; [1991] CLY 1470
JSB Category:
Sex: Male
Age at injury: 40
Age at award: 43
Date of award: 14 February 1991
Tribunal: Bromley County Court
Amount of award then: £1,500
Award at February 2001: £1,971

Description of injuries: A fracture of the ninth rib – bruised chest – breathing difficult – great pain – rest advised for several weeks – after four months the chest felt sore and tender – substantial improvement by nineteen months.

Prognosis: At the time of the hearing H reported no continuing symptoms except after particularly strenuous exertion.

1.5.1.C11 Case No. 11953

Name of case: A (a minor) v Ellwood
Brief description of injuries: CHEST – STERNUM
Reported: Kemp & Kemp, K2-122; [1999] CLY 1617
JSB Category: 5(A); 6(K)(c)(iii); 3(A)
Sex: Male
Age at injury: 15
Age at award: 16
Date of award: 15 January 1999
Tribunal: Bury St Edmunds County Court
Amount of award then: £1,750
Award at February 2001: £1,842
Description of injuries: Road accident – cracked sternum – seatbelt bruising – bruised shin – chest injury uncomfortable for 1 week, and pain continued for 3 weeks, resolving within 6 weeks – claimant very able sportsman, but unable to partake in sporting activities for approximately 5 weeks – accident occurred during holidays, so claimant did not miss any time at school – claimant became a rather nervous car passenger as a result of accident.

1.5.1.C12 Case No. 10872

Name of case: Cunliffe v Murrell
Brief description of injuries: CHEST – DISLOCATED RIB
Reported: Kemp & Kemp, F6-017; [1994] CLY 1724
JSB Category: 5(A)(g)
Sex: Female
Age at injury: 40
Age at award: –
Date of award: 17 January 1994
Tribunal: Tunbridge Wells County Court
Amount of award then: £1,500
Award at February 2001: £1,826
Description of injuries: Claimant knocked from horse in road accident – dislocation of costochondral junction of left ninth rib – initial marked pain, especially when lying in certain positions, lifting heavy objects and driving – pain easing to moderate ache over 5-week period – claimant unable to pursue horse-riding for some months – almost full recovery after 13 weeks.

Prognosis: Increased chance of further dislocation and slight thickening in region of injury.

1.5.1.C13 Case No. 10276

Name of case: Re Craddy
Brief description of injuries: INJURY TO THE RIBS AND STERNUM – RECOVERY 2 MONTHS
Reported: Kemp & Kemp, K2-137; [1991] CLY 1473
JSB Category:
Sex: Male
Age at injury: 41
Age at award: 43
Date of award: 06 September 1990
Tribunal: CICB, Newcastle
Amount of award then: £1,305
Award at February 2001: £1,736
Description of injuries: Injury to the ribs and right side of the sternum – crack fracture of the rib could not be ruled out – off work for four weeks – quite severe pain reduced over eight weeks.

Prognosis: Virtually full recovery after two months – residual pain described as "a minimal and rare discomfort".

1.5.1.C14 Case No. 11954

Name of case: Glover v Stuart
Brief description of injuries: CHEST – STERNUM
Reported: Kemp & Kemp, K2-145/2; [1999] CLY 1618
JSB Category: 5(A)
Sex: Female
Age at injury: 67
Age at award: 68
Date of award: 11 January 1999
Tribunal: Exeter County Court
Amount of award then: £1,500
Award at February 2001: £1,579
Description of injuries: Seatbelt bruising to sternum, right breast and right side of chest as far as waist – bruising caused difficulty in breathing – claimant asthmatic, using both inhaler and acupuncture (smoker, but less than 10 cigarettes per day) – claimant unable to do housework following accident for 7 weeks – unable to wear bra for 2-3 months – difficulty in performing tasks requiring proper use of right arm, eg dressing, reaching up, and chores in general – asthmatic condition worsened by accident and caused delayed response to acupuncture treatment – claimant recovered after 7 months.

1.5.1.C15 Case No. 11045

Name of case: McCallion v Dodd

Brief description of injuries: CHEST – SOFT-TISSUE DAMAGE – 5 MONTHS

Reported: Kemp & Kemp, K2-153; [1995] CLY 1799

JSB Category: 5(A)(g)

Sex: Male

Age at injury: 32

Age at award: 34

Date of award: 03 April 1995

Tribunal: Bristol County Court

Amount of award then: £1,300

Award at February 2001: £1,501

Description of injuries: Self-employed construction contractor sustained soft-tissue damage to rib cage and shoulder area together with possible injury to cervical spine, complicated by restraining effect of seatbelt, in road traffic accident – attended hospital but was not detained – suffered severe chest pain for five days following accident – was given analgesics, anti-inflammatories and antibiotics – breathing became affected and over this period complained of wheezing – thereafter developed additional pain radiating into left side of chest and down left side of abdomen, described as "shooting pain" – acute pains resolved over next four weeks although he was unable to work during this period – as a result of chest pain, had disturbed sleep for six weeks which led to feeling of exhaustion during the day – all symptoms were resolved within five months of accident.

1.5.1.C16 Case No. 10891

Name of case: Hasselby v Waddington

Brief description of injuries: CHEST – BRUISING – MINOR ABRASIONS TO SHIN

Reported: Kemp & Kemp, K2-226; [1994] CLY 1743

JSB Category: 5(A); 6(K)(c)(iii)

Sex: Male

Age at injury: 63

Age at award: 65

Date of award: 17 January 1994

Tribunal: Leeds County Court

Amount of award then: £750

Award at February 2001: £913

Description of injuries: Road accident – seatbelt bruising to chest – minor abrasions to shin – slight restriction in movement of arms – 2 days off work – full recovery within 2 months – claimant had to rely on friends and public transport while car off road for 10 weeks – great inconvenience to claimant and family.

1.5.1.1 CHEST AND OTHER INJURY

1.5.1.1.C1 Case No. 11503

Name of case: Re Gardner (John Lewis)

Brief description of injuries: CHEST – KNIFE WOUNDS – POST-TRAUMATIC STRESS DISORDER

Reported: Kemp & Kemp, B2-009/1 J2-071; [1998] CLY 1504

JSB Category: 5(A)(d), 5(D)(b), 5(H)(c); 3(B)(a)

Sex: Male

Age at injury: 39

Age at award: –

Date of award: 19 February 1998

Tribunal: CICB, Durham

Amount of award then: £50,000

Award at February 2001: £59,083

Description of injuries: Knife wounds to the chest and abdominal wall – pneumothorax and small intestine prolapse – penetration of the peritoneal cavity – laceration of the small bowel – severe post-traumatic stress disorder – scarring – complete physical recovery – other symptoms thought to be manifestations of psychiatric illness.

Prognosis: G would never work again.

1.5.1.1.C2 Case No. 10436

Award at February 2001: £9,528

See: 1.4.3.C22 for details

1.5.1.1.C3 Case No. 10787

Name of case: Kaylow v Kaylow

Brief description of injuries: LUNG – PUNCTURE – MINOR FRACTURES TO JAW, RIBS

Reported: Kemp & Kemp, F6-015; [1994] CLY 1636

JSB Category: 5(A)(f), 5(A)(g); 7(A)(e)

Sex: Male

Age at injury: 9

Age at award: 10

Date of award: 15 August 1994

Tribunal: Rugby County Court

Amount of award then: £2,500

Award at February 2001: £2,972

Description of injuries: Road accident – claimant asleep and wearing seatbelt when accident occurred – multiple left side rib fractures – puncture of lung – immediate severe chest pain and breathing difficulties – lung drained at roadside – in intensive care for 3 days with abdominal drainage, and chest drain in place 4 days – also fracture to ramus and condyle of left side of mandible; allowed to heal spontaneously – discharged after 5 days – chest pain and distress for 3 weeks, absent from school – unable to play football for 3 months – no psychological aspect – broken ribs healed satisfactorily – 2 small scars from chest and peritoneal insertions.

Prognosis: No long-term sequelae.

1.5.1.1.C4 Case No. 11466

Award at February 2001: £1,747

See: 1.3.1.1.C56 for details

1.5.1.1.C5 Case No. 10689

Award at February 2001: £426

See: 1.4.1.C34 for details

1.5.1.2 CHEST FRACTURE

1.5.1.2.C1 Case No. 10314

Award at February 2001: £12,748

See: 1.2.3.8.C83 for details

1.5.1.2.C2 Case No. 11997

Name of case: Uter v Williams

Brief description of injuries: CHEST – FRACTURED STERNUM – TROCHANTERIC BURSITIS

Reported: Kemp & Kemp, PRG-001; [2000] 3 CL 181

JSB Category: 6(C)

Sex: Female

Age at injury: 58

Age at award: 62

Date of award: 21 October 1999

Tribunal: Bristol County Court

Amount of award then: £7,000

Award at February 2001: £7,231

Description of injuries: Fractured sternum and multiple bruising in a traffic accident – prescribed painkillers and physiotherapy – severe chest pain for six weeks gradually subsided – continuing pain to the right hip and buttock was diagnosed as trochanteric bursitis – five months later mobility was markedly restricted – daily painkillers required – unable to return to work for one year – symptoms gradually improved up to the time of the hearing when she still had aching to the buttock but not sharp pain.

Prognosis: There might be slight improvement – little change was likely in the near future.

1.5.1.2.C3 Case No. 11463

Name of case: Hutchinson v Abdalla

Brief description of injuries: RIBS – SHOULDER – MULTIPLE FRACTURES – 12 – 14 MONTHS

Reported: Kemp & Kemp, K2-032; [1997] CLY 2012

JSB Category: 6(D)(c)

Sex: Male

Age at injury: 57

Age at award: 59

Date of award: 11 November 1996

Tribunal: Central London County Court

Amount of award then: £3,000

Award at February 2001: £3,353

Description of injuries: Fractured two ribs – left shoulder blade – left clavicle

Prognosis: Fully recovered within 12 to 14 months of the date of the accident – future degenerative changes unlikely.

1.5.1.2.C4 Case No. 10109

Name of case: Ravenscroft v Clarke
Brief description of injuries: STERNUM – FRACTURE – MINOR RESIDUAL SYMPTOMS
Reported: Kemp & Kemp, F6-016; [1990] CLY 1677
JSB Category:
Sex: Male
Age at injury: 27
Age at award: 30
Date of award: 06 April 1990
Tribunal: Birmingham County Court
Amount of award then: £2,000
Award at February 2001: £2,750
Description of injuries: Police officer acting as observer in police car during chase – rammed twice by defendant's vehicle and shunted into crash barriers – sustained fracture of sternum and suffered pain in chest and stomach – no treatment necessary.
Prognosis: Pain gradually diminished over five to six weeks – occasional tightness in chest when on motorcycle duty or prolonged holding of riot shield – these complaints likely to be permanent.

1.5.1.2.C5 Case No. 10669

Name of case: Re Graham
Brief description of injuries: RIB – FRACTURE
Reported: Kemp & Kemp, K2-087; [1993] CLY 1565
JSB Category: 5(A)(g)
Sex: Male
Age at injury: 34
Age at award: 36
Date of award: 25 August 1993
Tribunal: CICB, Liverpool
Amount of award then: £1,850
Award at February 2001: £2,252
Description of injuries: Police officer sustained fall in pursuit of suspect – fracture of twelfth rib – considerable pain for first 4 weeks – off work 8 weeks in total – at date of hearing, occasional dull ache still evident at site of injury after strenuous exercise.
Prognosis: Residual symptoms may not resolve.

1.5.1.2.C6 Case No. 10123

Name of case: Coombs v Roberts
Brief description of injuries: RIBS – HAIRLINE CRACK
Reported: Kemp & Kemp, K2-252; [1990] CLY 1700
JSB Category: 6(A)
Sex: Female
Age at injury: 68
Age at award: 69
Date of award: 23 August 1990
Tribunal: Swindon County Court
Amount of award then: £1,218
Award at February 2001: £1,635
Description of injuries: Plaintiff suffered bruising and suspected hairline crack to her ribs – prescribed Coproximol – difficulty sleeping for three weeks – suffered loss of enjoyment on holiday due to pain.

1.5.2 BREAST INJURY

1.5.2.C1 Case No. 10406

Name of case: Harling v Huddersfield Health Authority
Brief description of injuries: BREAST – UNNECESSARY MASTECTOMY
Reported: Kemp & Kemp, L8-150; [1992] CLY 1662
JSB Category: 5(A)(b)
Sex: Female
Age at injury: 45
Age at award: 53
Date of award: 01 February 1992
Tribunal: Leeds District Registry
Amount of award then: £36,400
Award at February 2001: £49,759
Description of injuries: Unnecessary mastectomy of the left breast – depression, anxiety, frustration and embarrassment – florid plasma cell mastitis was wrongly diagnosed as cancer without any histological evidence of malignancy – the left breast was removed – subsequently five operations were performed to reconstruct the left breast and reduce the size of the right breast – the left breast was badly disfigured – the right breast moderately so – there had been considerable septic complications in both breasts from the series of operations.
Prognosis: Further surgery was unlikely to produce a worthwhile improvement.

1.5.2.C2 Case No. 12047

Name of case: McCarthy v Davis

Brief description of injuries: BREAST – RUPTURE OF IMPLANT

Reported: Kemp & Kemp, PR;-002; [2000] 5 CL 191

JSB Category: 5(A)

Sex: Female

Age at injury: 33

Age at award: 36

Date of award: 19 January 2000

Tribunal: Reading County Court

Amount of award then: £6,500

Award at February 2001: £6,711

Description of injuries: Rupture of a right breast implant – discomfort in the right breast – within weeks it had become reduced and distorted – placed on waiting list for surgery – it was carried out 11 months after the accident – in hospital for one week. Implant was replaced.

Other points: Damages reflected the 11 month wait for surgery – discomfort and embarrassment.

1.5.2.C3 Case No. 10160

Name of case: Re Brookstein

Brief description of injuries: LACERATIONS – WOUND TO RIGHT BREAST- MODERATE PSYCHOLOGICAL SYMPTOMS

Reported: Kemp & Kemp, C4-121; [1991] CLY 1357

JSB Category: 6(G)(c), 6(A)(c)

Sex: Male

Age at injury: 39

Age at award: 41

Date of award: 21 June 1991

Tribunal: CICB

Amount of award then: £2,500

Award at February 2001: £3,207

Description of injuries: Assault and robbery – one inch laceration above right elbow – five inch laceration to back of neck – small puncture wound to right breast – small laceration to right ear – applicant of vulnerable disposition – suffering from epilepsy – at time of hearing suffering from loss of confidence – subject to vivid flashbacks – nervous about going out at night.

Prognosis: Complete recovery made from physical injuries apart from scarring to right arm and back of neck – other symptoms gradually improving.

1.5.3 BUTTOCK INJURY

1.5.3.C1 Case No. 10656

Name of case: Miller v Dythe

Brief description of injuries: BUTTOCKS – SCAR – PSYCHOLOGICAL REACTION

Reported: Kemp & Kemp, J2-019/1,J2-043; [1993] CLY 1552

JSB Category: 8; 3(A)(d)

Sex: Female

Age at injury: 14

Age at award: 17

Date of award: 14 May 1993

Tribunal: Lambeth County Court

Amount of award then: £2,500

Award at February 2001: £3,047

Description of injuries: Attacked by dog – bitten on buttocks, chased along road and bitten on buttocks again – unable to sit properly or return to school for 2 weeks – 3 keloidal scars; two about 2 inches long, one about half an inch in diameter – development of nightmares and fear of dogs – exacerbation of eczema due to emotional disturbance in weeks following incident – nightmares still recurring occasionally at time of trial.

Prognosis: Fear of dogs may be permanent.

1.5.3.C2 Case No. 10865

Name of case: Pugh v Chesterfield Borough Council

Brief description of injuries: BUTTOCKS – ABSCESS

Reported: Kemp & Kemp, K2-098; [1994] CLY 1717

JSB Category:

Sex: Male

Age at injury: 31

Age at award: 35

Date of award: 23 November 1993

Tribunal: Derby County Court

Amount of award then: £1,800

Award at February 2001: £2,186

Description of injuries: Claimant lifted by heavy chain used to close large gate, and struck lower back against wall – bruising and discomfort – development of "nasty and painful" traumatic abscess at top of cleft of buttocks, regularly discharging pus – daily dressing required – no response to antibiotics – sleep disturbance – inability to sit or work properly for 4 months – hobbies of swimming and horse-riding affected – abscess eventually excised under general anaesthetic 3 months after accident – slight discomfort following excision.

Prognosis: Full recovery otherwise expected.

1.5.3.C3 Case No. 10871

Name of case: Oldfield v Batterton

Brief description of injuries: BUTTOCKS – DOG BITE

Reported: Kemp & Kemp, L8-099; [1994] CLY 1723, 1753

JSB Category: 3(A)(d)

Sex: Male

Age at injury: 6

Age at award: 8

Date of award: 20 June 1994

Tribunal: St Helens County Court

Amount of award then: £1,500

Award at February 2001: £1,783

Description of injuries: Claimant, playing in garden of empty house, attacked by rottweiler that had escaped from neighbouring property – bites to buttocks – abrasions to chest wall, sustained during escape over fence – claimant distressed by incident – wounds took 2 weeks to heal and left no scars – claimant left with fear of dogs, only partially overcome by date of hearing.

Other points: Approved settlement.

1.5.3.C4 Case No. 11266

Name of case: Baines v Spartan Sheffield Ltd

Brief description of injuries: BUTTOCK – SOFT-TISSUE INJURY – 12 WEEKS

Reported: Kemp & Kemp, K2-249; [1996] CLY 2358

JSB Category: 6(B)(c)

Sex: Male

Age at injury: –

Age at award: 56

Date of award: 26 June 1996

Tribunal: Sheffield County Court

Amount of award then: £650

Award at February 2001: £731

Description of injuries: Soft-tissue injury to the buttock – symptoms attributable to the accident were completely resolved within twelve weeks.

1.5.4 ABDOMINAL INJURY

1.5.4.C1 Case No. 10324

Name of case: Re AJR

Brief description of injuries: LIVER – STAB – PTSD

Reported: Kemp & Kemp, C4-049; [1992] CLY 1580

JSB Category: 3(A)(b)

Sex: Male

Age at injury: 26

Age at award: 31

Date of award: 19 March 1992

Tribunal: CICB, Liverpool

Amount of award then: £17,500

Award at February 2001: £22,625

Description of injuries: Ten inch stab wound penetrating the diaphragm to the liver – post-traumatic stress disorder – extensive scarring from original wound, operative procedures and drain-holes – embarrassed about personal appearance – panic attacks, flash-backs and anxiety induced excessive drinking and food bingeing gaining four stones in weight – irritable and aggressive – withdrawn, tense and sullen.

Prognosis: Anticipated that symptoms would improve in time.

1.5.4.C2 Case No. 12042

Award at February 2001: £16,433

See: 1.3.1.3.1.C12 for details

1.5.4.C3 Case No. 10794

Name of case: Hall v Staffs Moorlands District Council

Brief description of injuries: INTERNAL ORGANS – SPLEEN, KIDNEY AND BOWELS

Reported: Kemp & Kemp, F6-071; [1994] CLY 1643

JSB Category: 5(G), 5(H), 5(J)

Sex: Male

Age at injury: 15

Age at award: 19

Date of award: 01 December 1993

Tribunal: Stoke County Court

Amount of award then: £12,000

Award at February 2001: £14,693

Description of injuries: Fall from climbing frame onto raised concrete kerb – internal injury to spleen; spleen removed – renal damage destroyed part of left kidney, though remaining part still functioned – surgery necessary to treat these injuries caused adhesions from which claimant suffered repeated attacks of pain – further surgery performed to remove loop of strangulated bowel, repaired with end-to-end anastomosis – healthy appendix also removed because pain initially diagnosed as appendicitis.

Prognosis: Removal of spleen would lead to small but significant risk of infection carrying some risk to life – long-term risk of further intestinal obstructions which might possibly require further surgery.

1.5.4.C4 Case No. 11283

Award at February 2001: £11,201

See: 1.1.C7 for details

1.5.4.C5 Case No. 10788

Name of case: Walker (a minor) v Walker

Brief description of injuries: INTERNAL ORGANS – SPLEEN – SPLENECTOMY – MINOR HEAD INJURY

Reported: Kemp & Kemp, F6-072/1; [1994] CLY 1637

JSB Category: 5(J)(a); 2(B)

Sex: Female

Age at injury: 8

Age at award: 10

Date of award: 23 June 1994

Tribunal: Chelmsford County Court

Amount of award then: £9,000

Award at February 2001: £10,698

Description of injuries: Road accident – abdominal injury necessitating splenectomy – haematoma and laceration to front of head – period of retrograde amnesia – daily headaches, diminishing to a frequency of every 7-10 days – absent from school 5 weeks; thereafter attended on half-daily basis for 6 months – increased frequency of colds, resulting in time off school.

Prognosis: Lifelong risk of developing post-splenectomy infection – antibiotics necessary for rest of life – repeat pneumococcal vaccines every 5-10 years – abdominal surgery almost certain to lead to adhesions, which could lead to intestinal obstructions requiring surgery – head injury not expected to cause any long-term disability or deterioration.

1.5.4.C6 Case No. 10411

Name of case: Calderbank v Lancashire County Council

Brief description of injuries: INGUINAL HERNIA – OFF WORK 6 MONTHS

Reported: Kemp & Kemp, F6-042/1; [1992] CLY 1667

JSB Category: 5(K)(b)

Sex: Male

Age at injury: 46

Age at award: 48

Date of award: 23 May 1991

Tribunal: Manchester County Court

Amount of award then: £6,000

Award at February 2001: £7,730

Description of injuries: Right inguinal hernia of the direct type following a fall at work as a fireman – planned surgical repair four weeks later was cancelled – re-admitted two weeks later when repair was effected – in-patient for one week as a result of severe pain developing in the left loin requiring analgesics – off work for twenty-five weeks – followed by five weeks of light work – apprehensive about the possibility of recurring hernia.

Prognosis: Left with some pain in the groin.

1.5.4.C7 Case No. 10527

Name of case: Healey v Hampshire County Council

Brief description of injuries: PANCREATITIS – BRUISING TO TRUNK – POSSIBLE PROLONGED PAIN

Reported: [1992] CLY 1783

JSB Category:

Sex: Female

Age at injury: 60

Age at award: 62

Date of award: 27 April 1992

Tribunal: Southampton County Court

Amount of award then: £6,000

Award at February 2001: £7,435

Description of injuries: Severe blow and bruising to the abdomen, chest and rib cartilages – traumatic pacreatitis was a possible consequence – forced to give up her job – unable to return to work.

Prognosis: The prognosis was for prolonged pain – possibly indefinitely.

1.5.4.C8 Case No. 11157

Name of case: Savage v ICI PLC

Brief description of injuries: HERNIA

Reported: Kemp & Kemp, F6-047/1; [1996] CLY 2248

JSB Category: 5(K)(c)

Sex: Male

Age at injury: 47

Age at award: 50

Date of award: 06 January 1995

Tribunal: Middlesborough County Court

Amount of award then: £4,500

Award at February 2001: £5,301

Description of injuries: Right inguinal hernia – required surgery.

Prognosis: Stable – no likelihood of improving or worsening.

Other points: The case fell between the two brackets for uncomplicated inguinal hernia.

1.5.4.C9 Case No. 10412

Name of case: Fish v David Brown Gear Industries

Brief description of injuries: INGUINAL HERNIA – REPAIRED AFTER 4 YEARS

Reported: [1992] CLY 1668

JSB Category: 5(K)(b)

Sex: Male

Age at injury: 58

Age at award: 65

Date of award: 10 June 1991

Tribunal: Huddersfield County Court

Amount of award then: £3,750

Award at February 2001: £4,810

Description of injuries: Right inguinal hernia following lifting activity at work – initially suffered a severe burning sensation in the right groin – worsened with movement – two days later noticed a gurgling sensation in the right groin – again worsened with movement and associated with an indigestion type pain – a few months later a lump appeared in the right groin.

Prognosis: Diagnosed inguinal hernia was repaired August 1988 – post-operative progress was satisfactory.

1.5.4.C10 Case No. 10795

Name of case: Wingrove v Ford Motor Co

Brief description of injuries: HERNIA

Reported: Kemp & Kemp, F6-047/2; [1994] CLY 1644

JSB Category: 5(K)

Sex: Male

Age at injury: 61

Age at award: 64

Date of award: 15 June 1994

Tribunal: Wood Green County Court

Amount of award then: £3,750

Award at February 2001: £4,457

Description of injuries: Claimant attempted to lift barrel that, unknown to him, was full of liquid – suffered right – sided indirect inguinal hernia – advised by doctor to wear truss for 6 months – claimant returned to work during that period – hernia operation then performed – claimant off work 15 weeks – claimant returned to work with no recurring problems – symptom free at date of trial, but avoiding heavy lifting.

1.5.4.C11 Case No. 10413

Name of case: Chapman v British Rail Engineering

Brief description of injuries: INGUINAL HERNIA – REPAIRED AFTER 2.5 MONTHS

Reported: Kemp & Kemp, F6-048/1, K2-021; [1992] CLY 1669

JSB Category: 5(K)

Sex: Male

Age at injury: 26

Age at award: 34

Date of award: 07 October 1992

Tribunal: Derby County Court

Amount of award then: £3,000

Award at February 2001: £3,688

Description of injuries: Suffered a right-sided inguinal hernia when moving a heavy weight – he discovered a lump in the right groin that evening – operative intervention advised – operation was performed two-and-a-half months later – off work for six weeks – returned to full duties gradually.

Prognosis: Recovery was without complication.

1.5.4.C12 Case No. 11854

Name of case: Poll v Mohammed

Brief description of injuries: KNEE – ABDOMEN – SOFT-TISSUE INJURIES

Reported: Kemp & Kemp, I2-433; [1999] CLY 1518

JSB Category: 6(L)(b); 5(A)

Sex: Male

Age at injury: 59

Age at award: 61

Date of award: 29 September 1998

Tribunal: Redditch County Court

Amount of award then: £3,500

Award at February 2001: £3,662

Description of injuries: Soft-tissue injuries to abdominal wall, painful for about a week and resolving thereafter – soft-tissue injuries to left knee – development of acute pain in knee, with associated slight swelling, lasting for about 1 month after accident – continuing symptoms of pain and stiffness thereafter – 2 years after accident, occasional aches and pains still present, particularly on exertion, and at the end of most working days – painkillers required 2 or 3 times a week – driving in heavy traffic difficult – claimant no longer able to pursue hobby of cycling – car maintenance, DIY and gardening more problematic – discomfort after walking further than 1 mile – knee not unstable and had not given way.

Prognosis: Accident deemed to have bought forward symptoms of previously asymptomatic osteoarthritis in knee by 3-5 years.

1.5.4.C13 Case No. 10900

Name of case: Barraclough v Saunders

Brief description of injuries: STOMACH – DOG BITES – OTHER INJURIES

Reported: Kemp & Kemp, L8-096; [1994] CLY 1752

JSB Category: 6(F), 6(H); 8

Sex: Male

Age at injury: 40

Age at award: 44

Date of award: 06 April 1994

Tribunal: Bradford County Court

Amount of award then: £3,000

Award at February 2001: £3,578

Description of injuries: Claimant attacked by Alsatian dog; attack lasting a matter of seconds – bites to stomach, left wrist, right forearm and left buttock – left wrist lacerated, puncture wounds to other areas – wrist wounds treated and debrided under local anaesthetic, described as a very painful procedure – 2 visits to hospital, 6 to GP – extensive bruising to left wrist, forearm and abdomen – claimant unable to work (as self-employed model maker) for 5 weeks – pain and discomfort almost entirely resolved after 6 months, but remaining small areas of scarring to left wrist, abdomen and left buttock – scarring described as "minor" and "not disfiguring", and claimant not caused any embarrassment by it – claimant still wary of large dogs and frightened of alsatians at date of trial, but not frightened by smaller dogs, and kept one himself.

1.5.4.C14 Case No. 11029

Name of case: Eaton v British Coal Corporation

Brief description of injuries: INGUINAL HERNIA – SURGERY — FULL RECOVERY

Reported: Kemp & Kemp, F6-048/2; [1995] CLY 1781

JSB Category: 5(K)(c)

Sex: Female

Age at injury: 46

Age at award: 50

Date of award: 06 December 1994

Tribunal: Stafford County Court

Amount of award then: £3,000

Award at February 2001: £3,534

Description of injuries: Plaintiff suffered small right-sided inguinal hernia when lifting tea urn which weighed 35lb – continued working a canteen assistant until operation to repair hernia six months later – refrained from heavy lifting for 15 weeks following operation and felt pain for approximately one month afterwards – made full recovery save for slight tingling sensation around incision area.

1.5.4.C15 Case No. 11236

Name of case: Kendal v Moxom

Brief description of injuries: GROIN – MINOR ABRASIONS – MUSCLE TEAR

Reported: Kemp & Kemp, I2-544; [1996] CLY 2328

JSB Category: 6(O)(g)

Sex: Male

Age at injury: 33

Age at award: 35

Date of award: 11 March 1996

Tribunal: Reading County Court

Amount of award then: £1,850

Award at February 2001: £2,100

Description of injuries: Minor abrasions – immediate pain to the groin and thigh – muscle tear.

Prognosis: Ache expected to clear up within twenty-six months of the date of the accident with no long-term sequelae.

1.5.4.C16 Case No. 10298

Name of case: Lago v John Williams of Cardiff

Brief description of injuries: HERNIA

Reported: Kemp & Kemp, F6-051; [1991] CLY 1495

JSB Category: 5(K)(c)

Sex: Male

Age at injury: 57

Age at award: 64

Date of award: 14 December 1990

Tribunal: Cardiff County Court

Amount of award then: £1,500

Award at February 2001: £1,986

Description of injuries: Indirect inguinal hernia as a result of lifting six castings of 121lb in weight – accustomed to lifting 95lbs – L was not warned of the increased weight – hernia repair in March 1984 – L suffered from a congenital defect which rendered him prone to sustain inguinal hernia which was unknown to him or his employer – irrespective of his congenital defect 121lbs was too heavy a weight for a man of his age to lift on his own.

Prognosis: Trouble-free since June 1984.

Other points: Award reduced from £2,000.

1.5.4.C17 Case No. 10275

Name of case: Odd v Tesco Stores

Brief description of injuries: FEMORAL HERNIA – FULL RECOVERY

Reported: Kemp & Kemp, F6-052; [1991] CLY 1472

JSB Category: 5(K)(c)

Sex: Male

Age at injury: 31

Age at award: –

Date of award: 31 January 1991

Tribunal: Doncaster County Court

Amount of award then: £1,500

Award at February 2001: £1,982

Description of injuries: Left sided femoral hernia – severe pain in the left groin – light duties until hernia repair operation – one month off work – four months of light duties.

Prognosis: O made a complete and uneventful recovery.

1.5.4.C18 Case No. 10879

Name of case: Durie v Liverpool City Council

Brief description of injuries: ABDOMEN – BRUISING – CLAIMANT PREGNANT

Reported: Kemp & Kemp, K2-180; [1994] CLY 1731

JSB Category: 5(F); 6(L)(B)(ii); 3(A)

Sex: Female

Age at injury: 23

Age at award: –

Date of award: 20 January 1994

Tribunal: Liverpool County Court

Amount of award then: £1,000

Award at February 2001: £1,217

Description of injuries: Claimant, 7 months pregnant with first child, tripped and fell – bruising to knees and abdomen, resolving after 3 days – anxiety, despite reassurances from hospital, about possible resultant damage to foetus – healthy baby delivered 10 weeks after accident.

1.5.4.C19 Case No. 11705

Name of case: Bevan v Pannell

Brief description of injuries: ABDOMEN – BRUISING – 10 DAYS

Reported: Kemp & Kemp, K2-264; [1998] CLY 1708

JSB Category:

Sex: Male

Age at injury: 30

Age at award: 31

Date of award: 03 August 1998

Tribunal: Swindon County Court

Amount of award then: £500

Award at February 2001: £525

Description of injuries: Traumatic compression – subcutaneous bruising to the scrotum and lower abdomen – bruising settled within 10 days or so of the date of the accident.

1.5.4.1 BOWEL INJURY

1.5.4.1.C1 Case No. 11401

Name of case: Parkes v Chester HA

Brief description of injuries: INTERNAL ORGANS – BOWEL – FAECAL INCONTINENCE

Reported: (1997) 97 (4) QR 5; Kemp & Kemp, F4-014; [1997] CLY 1950

JSB Category: 5(H)(a)

Sex: Female

Age at injury: 47

Age at award: 55

Date of award: 22 April 1997

Tribunal: Chester County Court

Amount of award then: £40,000

Award at February 2001: £47,487

Description of injuries: Lord's procedure (anal stretch) without explanation of the risks – internal sphincter damage.

Prognosis: Faecal incontinence which would worsen over time – colostomy would be required in five years – substantial pain – unable to leave the house for about two days each week due to leakage.

1.5.4.1.C2 Case No. 10613

Name of case: Re Elliott

Brief description of injuries: INTESTINES – PUNCTURE – TEMPORARY COLOSTOMY

Reported: Kemp & Kemp, F4-013; [1993] CLY 1508

JSB Category: 5(D); 3(A); 8

Sex: Male

Age at injury: 27

Age at award: 29

Date of award: 14 December 1992

Tribunal: CICB, London

Amount of award then: £30,000

Award at February 2001: £39,389

Description of injuries: Unprovoked knife attack by stranger – single stab wound to abdomen, claimant initially not expected to survive – damage to small and large intestine – emergency loop colostomy performed, reversed 1 month later – development of fistula, with periodic discharge and weeping for a time – possibility of future complications from stitch abscess – mid-line laparotomy scar, unsightly scarring at colostomy site, scar from initial puncture wound – degree of psychological disturbance in the form of persistent thinking about the incident, inhibiting ability to concentrate and learn – 31 days in hospital and 17 weeks off work in total – normal bowel function restored within 2 years of attack.

Prognosis: Employment prospects restricted by lack of confidence in lifting weights, aggravated by pre-existing back problem.

1.5.4.1.C3 Case No. 10965

Name of case: McDonnell v Woodhouse and Jones

Brief description of injuries: PERFORATED COLON – TEMPORARY COLOSTOMY – CONTINUING BOWEL PROBLEMS

Reported: (1995) The Times, May 25; Kemp & Kemp, F4-018; BPILS, XI 1947; [1995] CLY 1716

JSB Category: 5(H)

Sex: Male

Age at injury: 17

Age at award: 26

Date of award: 10 April 1995

Tribunal: QBD

Amount of award then: £27,500

Award at February 2001: £33,339

Description of injuries: Perforation of right side of colon – also suffered lacerations to forehead, knee and groin, which required suturing and left plaintiff with scars – perforated colon necessitated a laparotomy, followed by construction of colostomy on right side – there was considerable contamination of peritoneal cavity – in hospital for eight days – readmitted on 18 July 1986 with abdominal pain, vomiting and diarrhoea, which was thought to be secondary to a viral infection – colostomy was successfully – had "made a quite good recovery although he has had a very unpleasant time and remains substantially disabled ... The initial shock, realisation of his injuries, the manipulation of his external bag and accompanying details all had a considerable effect on him." – colostomy caused him pain: his skin became very raw and sore and sometimes he would have accidents which were unpleasant and messy – unsightly scars at incision sites of both laparotomy and colostomy – there was mid-line scar at site of laparotomy which was six-and-a-half inches long and one inch in diameter, and which continued to be associated with pain – also herniation at this incision – colostomy scar itself was much less unsightly, however there was disfiguring and embarrassing bulge due to herniation at this incision – these incisions were likely to require two separate operations in future – substantial digestive problems: urgency and frequency of bowel action – unable to digest greasy and spicy foods – enjoyment of life and self-confidence were affected, particularly in relations with women – suffered pain on heavy lifting and had been advised to refrain from work of heavy nature – could no longer follow his desired career of tunnel mining, and was limited to work of a light nature – was a man who had a natural bent for heavy work in construction industry and this would have given him great satisfaction.

1.5.4.1.C4 Case No. 10064

Name of case: Bovenzi v Kettering Health Authority

Brief description of injuries: MEDICAL NEGLIGENCE – BOWEL INJURY

Reported: [1991] 2 Med LR 293; Kemp & Kemp, F4-031; BPILS, XVII 1126; [1990] CLY 1642

JSB Category: 5(H)

Sex: Female

Age at injury: 31

Age at award: 36

Date of award: 19 October 1990

Tribunal: QBD

Amount of award then: £6,000

Award at February 2001: £7,920

Description of injuries: Admitted to hospital of defendant for a D & C – during course of curettage, forceps perforated uterus and some small bowel was pulled down into the uterus – laparotomy performed immediately – 11 inches of small bowel removed. Difficulty with bowel movements – feared constipation – unable to have sexual intercourse for about six months – scar from laparotomy about 1 inch wide and thick.

1.5.4.1.1 Bowell and other injury

1.5.4.1.1.C1 Case No. 11642

Award at February 2001: £37,691

See: 1.4.3.C10 for details

1.5.4.1.1.C2 Case No. 10794

Award at February 2001: £14,693

See: 1.5.4.C3 for details

1.5.4.1.1.C3 Case No. 10789

Name of case: Hosen v Marsland

Brief description of injuries: DIGESTIVE SYSTEM – GASTRO-OESOPHAGAL REFLUX

Reported: Kemp & Kemp, F3-015; [1994] CLY 1638

JSB Category: 5(D)(b)

Sex: Male

Age at injury: 45

Age at award: 50

Date of award: 18 April 1994

Tribunal: Truro County Court

Amount of award then: £7,500

Award at February 2001: £8,946

Description of injuries: Road accident – severe bruising to anterior chest wall, considerable pain for 5-6 weeks – immediate symptoms largely resolved, except for occasional aching when bending or lifting and discomfort when turning head while driving – emergence of new injury a short while after accident – gastro-oesophagal reflux, causing significant and intrusive indigestion and heartburn on continual basis – symptoms aggravated by lifting, bending and inappropriate diet – sleep disturbance due to necessity of maintaining upright posture – claimant forced to abandon hobby of deep – sea fishing, and no longer able to drive taxis for a living, as doing so aggravated symptoms – considerable medication required to control symptoms – weight gain due to enforced inactivity.

Prognosis: Medical evidence restricted, but judge accepted that condition likely to continue for some years, and possibly indefinitely – judge also found that claimant could and should lose weight to try to alleviate the symptoms.

1.5.4.2 KIDNEY AND BLADDER

1.5.4.2.C1 Case No. 11538

Name of case: Re Burns

Brief description of injuries: INTERNAL ORGANS – KIDNEY – NEPHRECTOMY – POST-TRAUMATIC STRESS DISORDER

Reported: Kemp & Kemp, F4-015; [1998] CLY 1540

JSB Category: 5(G)(c); 3(B)(a)

Sex: Male

Age at injury: 40

Age at award: 47

Date of award: 02 December 1997

Tribunal: CICB, York

Amount of award then: £35,000

Award at February 2001: £40,029

Description of injuries: Loss of a kidney due to stabbing injury – post-traumatic affective state – full-scale panic attacks – the incident played on his mind all day and every day.

Prognosis: Slow improvements were expected – only relatively stress-free part-time work would be possible – suffering from residual symptoms would continue.

1.5.4.2.C2 Case No. 11402

Name of case: George v Tower Hamlets HA

Brief description of injuries: INTERNAL ORGANS – BLADDER

Reported: Kemp & Kemp, F4-077; [1997] CLY 1951

JSB Category: 5(I)(b)

Sex: Female

Age at injury: 41

Age at award: 47

Date of award: 26 March 1996

Tribunal: QBD

Amount of award then: £30,000

Award at February 2001: £35,954

Description of injuries: Repair to a re-opened abdominal hysterectomy wound – stress incontinence and gross urge treated by two unsuccessful Stamey colposuspension operations – much improved after Burch colposuspension was carried out – suffered depressive syndrome.

Prognosis: There would be no further improvement in remaining urinary problems – need to wear incontinence pads – suffer drain of energy – poor sleep pattern – repression of sexual function – with treatment 30 per cent improvement in her mental state was expected.

1.5.4.2.C3 Case No. 11156

Name of case: Bouchta v Swindon HA

Brief description of injuries: INTERNAL ORGANS – KIDNEY DAMAGE

Reported: [1996] 7 Med LR 62; Kemp & Kemp, F4-020; BPILS, XVII 1148,1297; [1996] CLY 2247

JSB Category: 5(G)(c)

Sex: Female

Age at injury: 41

Age at award: 45

Date of award: 01 September 1995

Tribunal: Wandsworth County Court

Amount of award then: £25,000

Award at February 2001: £29,773

Description of injuries: Kidney damage caused by a blocked ureter following an hysterectomy – damage caused by the negligence of the surgeon.

Other points: The plaintiff has to prove that the defendant's explanation of the injury is not a good one.

1.5.4.2.C4 Case No. 11403

Name of case: Coverdale v Suffolk HA

Brief description of injuries: INTERNAL ORGANS – BLADDER

Reported: Kemp & Kemp, F4-022; [1997] CLY 1952

JSB Category: 5(I)(b)

Sex: Female

Age at injury: –

Age at award: 53

Date of award: 25 November 1996

Tribunal: Norwich County Court

Amount of award then: £20,000

Award at February 2001: £22,984

Description of injuries: Incontinence caused by prolapse of the vaginal wall following a successful hysterectomy – RAZ colposuspension repair over-corrected – rectocele – cystocele – posterior and anterior vaginal repair – psychological effects of the injuries.

Prognosis: Permanent self-catheterisation and manual bowel evacuation required – regular urinary tract infections.

1.5.4.2.C5 Case No. 10966

Name of case: Hooper v Young

Brief description of injuries: KIDNEY

Reported: Kemp & Kemp, F4-015/1, F4-024; [1995] CLY 1717

JSB Category: 5(G)(c)

Sex: Female

Age at injury: 38

Age at award: 42

Date of award: 09 November 1994

Tribunal: Not stated

Amount of award then: £17,500

Award at February 2001: £21,223

Description of injuries: Plaintiff underwent routine hysterectomy in 1990 after history of pre-menstrual syndrome – suffered vomiting and severe back pain after operation – there was severe constriction of left ureter with hydronephrosis of left kidney, which was probably caused by stitch too close to left ureter – had to have second repair operation a week later and was discharged after 12 days – was readmitted to hospital with vomiting and left loin pain a month later, and this time a nephrostomy was performed – discharged three weeks later – following day was readmitted with suspected kidney infection and spent eight days in hospital – suffered depression.

Prognosis: The prognosis was that depression would continue to respond to psychotherapy.

1.5.4.2.C6 Case No. 11273

Name of case: Sumners v Mid Downs HA and Brighton HA

Brief description of injuries: INTERNAL ORGANS – KIDNEY – CANCER

Reported: [1996] CLY 2366

JSB Category: 5

Sex: Male

Age at injury: 41

Age at award: 51

Date of award: 25 January 1996

Tribunal: QBD

Amount of award then: £17,000

Award at February 2001: £19,887

Description of injuries: Kidney transplant from a donor with fatal colon cancer – cancer developed – twelve months after removal of the kidney cancer had gone – no clinical psychological condition – subsequent successful transplant – at the time of the trial the plaintiff was physically well.

Other points: The judge said it was "a unique case" – the award was based on consideration of the overall picture.

1.5.4.2.C7 Case No. 10223

Name of case: Hendy v Milton Keynes HA
Brief description of injuries: MEDICAL NEGLIGENCE -HYDRONEPHROSIS – FURTHER SURGERY NEEDED
Reported: [1992] PIQR P281; [1992] 3 Med LR 119; Kemp & Kemp, F4-028; BPILS, XVII 1296; [1991] CLY 1420
JSB Category: 5(I)
Sex: Female
Age at injury: –
Age at award: 51
Date of award: 15 July 1991
Tribunal: QBD
Amount of award then: £7,500
Award at February 2001: £9,641
Description of injuries: Hydronephrosis of the right kidney, urethra – vaginal fistula with leakage of urine from the vagina and urinary tract infection during a routine hysterectomy – repair operation and reimplantation of the urethra into the bladder performed one month later.
Prognosis: No further pre-menstrual problems – permanent incontinence in the form of a permanent dribble – aching bladder when full – frequency of micturition – H had to get up three or four times every night to empty her bladder – wore incontinence pads – underwear required changing at least three times daily. Increased psychological stress for five years.

1.5.4.2.C8 Case No. 10614

Name of case: Stanton v St Helens and Knowsley Health Authority
Brief description of injuries: BLADDER – PROLAPSE – RISK OF RECURRENCE
Reported: Kemp & Kemp, F4-032; [1993] CLY 1509
JSB Category: 6(I)
Sex: Female
Age at injury: 41
Age at award: 50
Date of award: 05 February 1993
Tribunal: Liverpool County Court
Amount of award then: £6,000
Award at February 2001: £7,435
Description of injuries: Prolapse of bladder and urethra as a result of lifting – discomfort for 2 months until anterior colporrhaphy performed – complication of retention of urine, requiring catheterisation – subsequent attacks of cystitis and urgency of voiding – cystoscopy performed.
Prognosis: Risk of recurrence through heavy lifting, chronic coughing or constipation.

1.5.4.2.C9 Case No. 10791

Name of case: Winterbone v West Suffolk Health Authority
Brief description of injuries: BLADDER – FISTULA
Reported: Kemp & Kemp, F5-023; [1994] CLY 1640
JSB Category: 5(I)(c); 8
Sex: Female
Age at injury: –
Age at award: 44
Date of award: 01 November 1993
Tribunal: Cambridge County Court
Amount of award then: £4,500
Award at February 2001: £5,466
Description of injuries: Claimant underwent surgery to remove ovarian cyst – also, correctly, womb, ovaries and fallopian tubes removed – 7 days after operation, claimant suddenly developed total incontinence of bladder – 2 months later, diagnosis of vesica-vaginal fistula – further month's delay to allow maximum recovery of tissues from first operation before corrective surgery undertaken – considerable discomfort and inconvenience suffered in that period – continuous catheterisation – abstinence from sexual intercourse – social embarrassment – post-operative scarring greater, due to need for second operation – second operation successful – claimant experienced some further discomfort and irritation for a few weeks after repair.

1.5.4.3 REPRODUCTIVE ORGANS

1.5.4.3.C1 Case No. 11628

Name of case: Butters v Grimsby and Scunthorpe HA
Brief description of injuries: REPRODUCTIVE ORGANS (FEMALE)
Reported: Kemp & Kemp, F5-012/1; [1998] CLY 1630
JSB Category: 5(F)(a)
Sex: Female
Age at injury: –
Age at award: –
Date of award: 12 January 1998
Tribunal: CA
Amount of award then: £60,000
Award at February 2001: £72,920
Description of injuries: Injuries to the reproductive organs during a medical procedure following childbirth – secondary amenorrhoea, multiple adhesions – Ascherman's Syndrome – 2 miscarriages and hysterectomy – further corrective and investigative surgery.
Prognosis: Further treatment might be required in the future.
Other points: £5,000 added to the original award of £55,000

1.5.4.3.C2 Case No. 11404

Name of case: Thurman v Wiltshire and Bath HA

Brief description of injuries: REPRODUCTIVE ORGANS – FEMALE – FAILURE TO DIAGNOSE CERVICAL CANCER

Reported: [1997] PIQR Q115; Kemp & Kemp, F5-012/1, F5-117; [1997] CLY 1953

JSB Category: 5(F)(a)

Sex: Female

Age at injury: 29

Age at award: 33

Date of award: 04 February 1997

Tribunal: QBD

Amount of award then: £50,000

Award at February 2001: £61,340

Description of injuries: Failure to diagnose cervical cancer – termination of pregnancy – total hysterectomy.

Prognosis: Scarring – the need for hormone replacement therapy – inability to have children – deformed and shortened vagina – otherwise the prognosis was good.

Other points: Application was made for a provisional award – with a right to re-apply.

1.5.4.3.C3 Case No. 10407

Name of case: Grayson-Crowe v Ministry of Defence

Brief description of injuries: UNAUTHORISED HYSTERECTOMY AND DEPRESSION

Reported: Kemp & Kemp, F5-012/1; [1992] CLY 1663

JSB Category: 5(F)(a)

Sex: Female

Age at injury: 30

Age at award: 35

Date of award: 30 June 1992

Tribunal: QBD

Amount of award then: £35,000

Award at February 2001: £46,541

Description of injuries: Unauthorised hysterectomy – claimant was referred to an army obstetrician suffering prolonged, heavy and irregular bleeding and suspected fibroids – admitted to the British Military Hospital, Hanover for a D&C and minor exploratory surgery – one very large and several smaller fibroids found in her otherwise healthy uterus – healthy ovaries and tubes – the uterus was removed –found out that a hysterectomy had been performed when she overheard nurses discussing her case – no permission had been given (or would have been given) for this procedure – the fibroids were found to be non-cancerous she was unable to reconcile herself to the fact that she would not be able to have children – she became withdrawn, depressed and reclusive.

Prognosis: In 1991 she was suffering from severe symptoms of depressive illness including anhedonia, sleep disturbance, loss of appetite and social phobias – she avoided former friends who had children.

1.5.4.3.C4 Case No. 11879

Name of case: Bryans v Mount Vernon and Watford Hospitals Trust

Brief description of injuries: REPRODUCTIVE ORGANS – MALE

Reported: Kemp & Kemp, F5-058/1; [1999] CLY 1543

JSB Category: 5(E); 3(A)

Sex: Male

Age at injury: 57

Age at award: 62

Date of award: 05 February 1999

Tribunal: Central London County Court

Amount of award then: £40,000

Award at February 2001: £45,145

Description of injuries: Claimant had suffered from cancer of the penis and had undergone partial penectomy, amputating glans and 2cm of shaft – reconstructive surgery, involving fashioning a neo – prepuce, reconstructing the foreskin, had been cosmetically excellent and claimant had, unusually, been able to regain normal sexual function and control urinary flow – gradual deterioration in urinary function was diagnosed as probably being to stenosis at end of neo – prepuce, and claimant consented to meatal dilatation operation – in course of procedure, surgeon, admittedly negligently, without consent and unnecessarily, excised whole of neo – prepuce, removing 2.5in in length and leaving only 1in in length – further cosmetic surgery made necessary by this procedure, the result of which largely resolved the cosmetic disability, but no more – claimant no longer able to urinate standing up, and more likely to wet himself or clothing when urinating sitting down – personality change and serious degree of mental disturbance (but falling short of psychiatric illness such as post-traumatic stress disorder) – claimant unable to have sexual relations, for largely psychogenic reasons – penis now less stable – damage to cutaneous nerves, causing persisting loss of sensation.

Prognosis: No sign of likely resolution of symptoms of loss of sensation, although some improvement possible – prospect of regaining normal sexual function assessed at no more than 25 per cent, and even then claimant would be unlikely to return to same level of sexual activity.

Other points: Without the negligent surgery, the risk that neo – prepuce would have had to have been removed at some point during the remainder of claimant's active sex life was no more than 10-15 per cent; judge did not accept that the case was one of accelerated total impotence.

1.5.4.3.C5 Case No. 10790

Name of case: Hill v Liverpool Health Authority

Brief description of injuries: REPRODUCTIVE ORGANS (MALE)

Reported: Kemp & Kemp, F5-058/1; [1994] CLY 1639

JSB Category: 5(E)(a)

Sex: Male

Age at injury: 35

Age at award: 43

Date of award: 10 December 1993

Tribunal: Manchester High Court

Amount of award then: £22,500

Award at February 2001: £28,358

Description of injuries: Claimant underwent vasectomy – complications necessitating further surgery – in course of further surgery, blood supply to left testicle negligently cut off – testicle became devitalised – problem not immediately recognised; claimant left with open wound on side of scrotum, painful, foul-smelling and discharging dead tissue – operation to clean wound – pain and discharge continued – left testicle finally surgically removed – physical recovery good – cosmetic deformity of only having 1 testicle resulted in claimant no longer going swimming with children due to embarrassment in changing rooms – unwillingness, found to be reasonable, to have prosthesis fitted – severe psychological reaction; loss of testicle described as dominating claimant's life – feelings of incompleteness and sexual inadequacy – gradually increasing sexual impotence; inability to have sexual intercourse – strain to marriage; claimant irritable, sarcastic and hurtful to wife – unwillingness, not found to be unreasonable, to undergo psychosexual counselling.

Prognosis: Judge found that marriage would probably survive and claimant's unhappiness at his position would lessen with time – only a possibility of claimant recovering ability to have sexual intercourse.

1.5.4.3.C6 Case No. 11878

Name of case: Paul v Glickman (deceased)

Brief description of injuries: REPRODUCTIVE ORGANS – FEMALE – 9 YEARS' INFERTILITY

Reported: Kemp & Kemp, F5-018/1; [1999] CLY 1542

JSB Category: 5(F)(b); 3(A)

Sex: Female

Age at injury: 35

Age at award: 41

Date of award: 21 January 1999

Tribunal: Central London County Court

Amount of award then: £16,500

Award at February 2001: £17,659

Description of injuries: Claimant, having had 2 children, had 2 intra-uterine contraceptive devices (IUCDs) inserted in 1978 – claimant had always planned to have 6 children in all; attempts to conceive in 1984 unsuccessful – GP had negligently advised claimant that IUCDs had been expelled – claimant underwent a number of investigative procedures – claimant increasingly worried that she was permanently infertile – in 1992, IUCDs discovered, still in situ, and removed – on discovering cause of 9-year period of infertility, claimant became moderately depressed for about 8 months, and unable to work, until discovering that she was pregnant – claimant mildly and intermittently depressed for about 1 year thereafter – claimant had had 3 children, in addition to first 2, by time of trial and was pregnant with her sixth.

Other points: Award breakdown: loss of amenity at being infertile for 9 years when claimant wanted children, and anxiety that condition was permanent: £7,500; pain and suffering associated with investigative procedures: £4,000; depression for a period of approximately 21 months: £5,000.

1.5.4.3.C7 Case No. 10408

Name of case: Lofthouse v North Tees Health Authority

Brief description of injuries: PERINEUM – INJURED IN CHILDBIRTH – 4 OPERATIONS

Reported: [1992] CLY 1664

JSB Category: 5(F)(b)

Sex: Female

Age at injury: 24

Age at award: 28

Date of award: 09 April 1992

Tribunal: QBD

Amount of award then: £10,500

Award at February 2001: £13,096

Description of injuries: Perineum torn during childbirth – the perineum was stitched too tightly so that sexual intercourse was impossible because of pain and restriction in size of the introitus.

Prognosis: A further four operations were needed to refashion the perineum over the next two years.

1.5.4.3.C8 Case No. 11880

Name of case: M (a minor) v Brent and Harrow Health Authority

Brief description of injuries: REPRODUCTIVE ORGANS – MALE – LOSS OF ONE TESTICLE

Reported: Kemp & Kemp, F5-059/1; [1999] CLY 1544

JSB Category: 5(E)

Sex: Male

Age at injury: 1 month

Age at award: 5

Date of award: 29 July 1998

Tribunal: Central London County Court (infant settlement approval hearing)

Amount of award then: £10,000

Award at February 2001: £10,560

Description of injuries: Claimant suffered right inguinal scrotal hernia – due to negligent delay, it became necessary to remove the right testicle, which could have been saved.

Prognosis: Significant risk that claimant would be subfertile as a result of loss of testicle – since loss occurred at such a young age, claimant unlikely to choose to have a prosthesis inserted, and likely to adapt well to his loss – future counselling for psychosexual problems therefore probably unnecessary.

Other points: General damages of £10,000 agreed, and including an element to reflect a chance of incurring the cost of prosthesis insertion in future.

1.5.4.3.C9 Case No. 10220

Name of case: Riggs v East Dorset HA

Brief description of injuries: INFERTILITY

Reported: Kemp & Kemp, F5-022; [1991] CLY 1417

JSB Category: 5(F)

Sex: Female

Age at injury: 19

Age at award: 25

Date of award: 25 October 1990

Tribunal: QBD

Amount of award then: £7,500

Award at February 2001: £9,900

Description of injuries: Late diagnosis of an ectopic pregnancy – laparotomy and excision of both fallopian tubes.

Prognosis: Rendered infertile except by invitro fertilisation.

1.5.4.3.C10 Case No. 10967

Name of case: Hope v DC Leisure (Camberley)

Brief description of injuries: REPRODUCTIVE ORGANS – MALE – DEGLOVING OF PENIS

Reported: [1995] CLY 1718

JSB Category:

Sex: Male

Age at injury: 7

Age at award: 10

Date of award: 05 May 1995

Tribunal: Guildford County Court

Amount of award then: £8,000

Award at February 2001: £9,198

Description of injuries: Laceration to right side of scrotum and complete degloving injury to distal two thirds of penis – skin was retrieved, trimmed and replaced as graft over penile shaft – excellent take was achieved and he was discharged – readmitted three weeks later for scabbed areas to be debrided under general anaesthetic and thereafter recovery was uneventful apart from psychological disturbance that manifested itself in nocturnal bed-wetting lasting few months – admitted and examined under general anaesthetic a year later when, apart from minor cosmetic damage, penis was found to have made a full functional recovery with no evidence of metal stenosis – artificial erection test showed no abnormal curvature of penis. The district judge approved an agreed award for general damages.

Prognosis: Prognosis was excellent with no foreseeable problems to future sex life or fertility – only lasting effects were minimal scarring and mild asymmetry of foreskin.

1.5.4.3.C11 Case No. 10409

Name of case: Marram v North Tees Health Authority

Brief description of injuries: VESICO-VAGINAL FISTULAR – REPAIRED AFTER 4-AND-A-HALF MONTHS' INCONTINENCE

Reported: [1992] CLY 1665

JSB Category: 5(I)(c)

Sex: Female

Age at injury: 26

Age at award: 32

Date of award: 09 March 1992

Tribunal: Stockton on Tees County Court

Amount of award then: £5,000

Award at February 2001: £6,291

Description of injuries: Vesico-vaginal fistula following total hysterectomy and removal of left cystic ovary – on discharge from hospital she appeared to be voiding satisfactorily – immediately became incontinent of urine – a catheter was inserted but failed to control the leak satisfactorily – underwent acytoscopic examination – decision taken for the catheter to remain in place for three months before further surgery was attempted – further cytoscopic examination five weeks later after she experienced pain with the catheter – supra-pubic catheter inserted – full continence was not achieved with the catheters – suffered from smell, excoriation of the vulva and the need to wear pads – a third cytoscopic examination was carried out before surgical closure of the fistula four-and-a-half months after it had developed.

Prognosis: The plaintiff could not lead a normal life.

1.5.4.3.C12 Case No. 10968

Name of case: Finch v Langford

Brief description of injuries: REPRODUCTIVE ORGANS – MALE – DOG BITE TO PENIS

Reported: [1995] CLY 1719

JSB Category:

Sex: Male

Age at injury: 24

Age at award: 29

Date of award: 02 December 1994

Tribunal: Blackburn County Court

Amount of award then: £4,500

Award at February 2001: £5,301

Description of injuries: Male postman attacked and bitten by Alsatian dog – suffered bite to glans penis which bled persistently – wound was cleaned under general anaesthetic and three stitches inserted in a laceration measuring 0.5cm – was left with small residual scar – suffered pain when penis was erect and did not have sexual intercourse for three months – absent from work for one month and suffered embarrassment and psychological trauma – while scar was not openly apparent he was acutely aware of it in periods of intimacy – also two superficial lacerations on undersurface of foreskin.

1.5.4.3.C13 Case No. 10792

Name of case: Abram v St Helens Borough Council

Brief description of injuries: REPRODUCTIVE ORGANS (MALE)

Reported: Kemp & Kemp, F5-065/1; [1994] CLY 1641

JSB Category: 5(E)

Sex: Male

Age at injury: 26

Age at award: 28

Date of award: 28 July 1994

Tribunal: Liverpool County Court

Amount of award then: £3,500

Award at February 2001: £4,181

Description of injuries: Claimant thrown off motorcycle by pot – hole, slid into wall – crushing injury to right groin – grazing to left iliac crest and both knees – contusions to left side of rib cage – development of severe pain in groin on night after accident – admitted to hospital – collection of blood around right testicle (traumatic haematocele) discovered – operation performed to evacuate blood – in hospital for 1 week – scrotal support worn for 4 weeks – antibiotics prescribed – no further difficulties since taking antibiotics – still occasional aching in testicle at time of trial.

Prognosis: Possibility of occasional minor symptoms occurring throughout claimant's life.

1.5.4.3.C14 Case No. 10793

Name of case: Iqbal v Irfan

Brief description of injuries: REPRODUCTIVE ORGANS – UNSUCCESSFUL CIRCUMCISION

Reported: Kemp & Kemp, F5-067/1; [1994] CLY 1642

JSB Category: 5(E)

Sex: Male

Age at injury: 7 months

Age at award: –

Date of award: 03 June 1994

Tribunal: Croydon County Court

Amount of award then: £2,000

Award at February 2001: £2,377

Description of injuries: Claimant underwent circumcision at hands of defendant – foreskin left substantially intact – claimant left with phimosis and pinhole meatus in foreskin through which urethra and glans could not be seen – acute wound infection (swelling, pyrexia, persistent difficulty passing urine), but no evidence that this caused by alleged poor hygiene practices – circumcision successfully re-done 6 months later.

Prognosis: No long-term physical or psychological sequelae.

1.5.4.3.C15 Case No. 11700

Name of case: Bailey v Knowsley

Brief description of injuries: REPRODUCTIVE ORGANS – FEMALE – BRUISING

Reported: Kemp & Kemp, K2-145/1; [1998] CLY 1703

JSB Category:

Sex: Female

Age at injury: 27

Age at award: 29

Date of award: 23 June 1998

Tribunal: Liverpool County Court

Amount of award then: £1,500

Award at February 2001: £1,579

Description of injuries: Severe bruising and swelling to the vulval area – pain and discomfort settled in 2 months – unable to have sexual intercourse for 4 months.

1.5.5 PELVIS AND HIP INJURY

1.5.5.C1 Case No. 10146

Award at February 2001: £91,048

See: 1.2.3.8.C40 for details

1.5.5.C2 Case No. 11844

Award at February 2001: £57,445

See: 1.2.3.1.C5 for details

1.5.5.C3 Case No. 11629

Name of case: Clarke v South Yorkshire Transport Ltd

Brief description of injuries: PELVIS – CRUSH INJURY

Reported: [1998] PIQR Q104; Kemp & Kemp, G2-075; BPILS, I 127; [1998] CLY 1631

JSB Category: 6(C)(a); 5(C)

Sex: Female

Age at injury: –

Age at award: 62

Date of award: 01 July 1998

Tribunal: CA

Amount of award then: £47,500

Award at February 2001: £54,787

Description of injuries: Severe crush injury to the pelvis – mobility difficulty – urine incontinence (4.5 years) – restricted movement to the neck and shoulders – one leg shortened – exacerbated asthma.

Other points: Award reduced from £55,000

1.5.5.C4 Case No. 11630

Name of case: Oake v Biddlecombe

Brief description of injuries: PELVIS – FRACTURE – UNSTABLE UNION

Reported: Kemp & Kemp, G2-024; [1998] CLY 1632

JSB Category: 6(C)(a)(ii)

Sex: Female

Age at injury: 36

Age at award: 39

Date of award: 11 May 1998

Tribunal: QBD

Amount of award then: £32,500

Award at February 2001: £36,101

Description of injuries: Dislocation of the right sacro-iliac joint – fractures to the left inferior and superior pubic rami and transverse process at L5 – unstable and un-united pelvis – claimant left with pronounced limp – unable to return to any work.

Prognosis: Condition was permanent.

Other points: Fractures were not diagnosed at the time of the accident due to x-rays being done using an abdominal shield, which obscured them.

1.5.5.C5 Case No. 11405

Name of case: Betts v Dolby

Brief description of injuries: HIP – FRACTURE

Reported: Kemp & Kemp, G2-028/2; [1997] CLY 1954

JSB Category: 6(C)(a)(iii)

Sex: Male

Age at injury: 30

Age at award: 35

Date of award: 06 November 1996

Tribunal: Nottingham County Court

Amount of award then: £22,500

Award at February 2001: £26,022

Description of injuries: Severe fracture of the hip joint – puncture wound to the buttock – abrasions to the arms – laceration to the head – chipped molar – soft-tissue injury to the shoulder.

Prognosis: Hip replacement required in eight to ten years – revision surgery thirteen to fourteen years thereafter.

1.5.5.C6 Case No. 10077

Name of case: Charalambous v Andreou

Brief description of injuries: PELVIS – FRACTURE – HIP REPLACEMENT

Reported: Kemp & Kemp, G2-030/1; [1990] CLY 1643

JSB Category: 6(C)

Sex: Female

Age at injury: 52

Age at award: 55

Date of award: 09 February 1990

Tribunal: Westminster County Court

Amount of award then: £16,000

Award at February 2001: £23,572

Description of injuries: Severely comminuted fracture of left side of pelvis, extending down into acetabulum.

Prognosis: Left leg one-and-a-half cm shorter than right – 25 cm scar down upper thigh – pain in groin and thigh when active – hip replacement expected at age 60.

1.5.5.C7 Case No. 11406

Name of case: Fradgley v Pontefract Hospitals NHS Trust

Brief description of injuries: HIP – FRACTURE – REPLACEMENT

Reported: Kemp & Kemp, G2-031; [1997] CLY 1955

JSB Category: 5(C)(a)(iii)

Sex: Female

Age at injury: 70

Age at award: 74

Date of award: 14 May 1997

Tribunal: Leeds County Court

Amount of award then: £20,000

Award at February 2001: £22,523

Description of injuries: Fractured head to the femur following hip replacement surgery – deep-vein thrombosis – anxiety precipitated a phobia concerning spiders – further surgery to repair the fracture.

Prognosis: There was a fifty to seventy-five per cent chance that a further revision operation would be required within four years – the prospects for this surgery were not good – she could become confined to a wheelchair.

1.5.5.C8 Case No. 10615

Name of case: Friar v Pickup

Brief description of injuries: PELVIS – FRACTURE

Reported: Kemp & Kemp, G2-032; [1993] CLY 1510

JSB Category: 6(C)(b)

Sex: Male

Age at injury: 24

Age at award: 28

Date of award: 16 October 1992

Tribunal: Bradford County Court

Amount of award then: £15,000

Award at February 2001: £18,795

Description of injuries: Trapped under wheel of HGV for 10-15 minutes – severe fractures to inferior and superior pubic rami on left side – wound to perineum – immobilised for 10 weeks in pelvic sling with legs supported in frame – pelvic abscess – jaundice – urinary – tract infection deep vein thrombosis in left leg – mild depression – resumed work as driver in just under 2 years – continuing difficulties with running, carrying heavy weights, climbing ladders, walking further than 2 miles – swelling and discomfort in left leg.

Prognosis: Increased risk of developing deep – vein thrombosis as a result of future trauma or surgery.

1.5.5.C9 Case No. 11158

Name of case: Wilders v Peppers Ltd

Brief description of injuries: HIP – OSTEOARTHRITIC DEGENERATION – 10-YEAR ACCELERATION

Reported: Kemp & Kemp, G2-033; [1996] CLY 2249

JSB Category: 6(C)(a)(iii)

Sex: Male

Age at injury: 44

Age at award: 47

Date of award: 28 March 1996

Tribunal: QBD

Amount of award then: £16,000

Award at February 2001: £18,502

Description of injuries: Osteoarthritic degeneration of both hips.

Prognosis: Pre-existing symptomless osteoarthritic degeneration of both hips brought forward by ten years – replacement hip joints would be required in the future.

Other points: There would be increasing loss of mobility and pain in the years before 2004.

1.5.5.C10 Case No. 10970

Name of case: Chamberlain v Esselte Dymo

Brief description of injuries: FRACTURED PELVIS – DAMAGED EURETHRA – IMPERFECT URINARY STREAM

Reported: Kemp & Kemp, G2-035/1; [1995] CLY 1721

JSB Category: 6(C)(b)

Sex: Male

Age at injury: 21

Age at award: 26

Date of award: 17 February 1995

Tribunal: Central London Trial Centre

Amount of award then: £13,000

Award at February 2001: £15,399

Description of injuries: Plaintiff sustained fractured pelvis and ruptured urethra when he was trapped under heavy pallet at work – on arrival at hospital he was found to have fractured both superior pubic rami and probably to have fractured the left interior pubic ramus – in attempting to urinate was able only to pass blood – a supra-pubic catheter was passed to drain the bladder – remained in hospital as in-patient for 10 days and was thereafter mobilised with zimmer frame and crutches – fractured pelvis healed well and did not require surgery, but there were two operations on urethra, each of which necessitated a three-week stay as in-patient – first operation was about a month after accident – urethra, which was found to have narrowed at injury site, was enlarged to enable a catheter to be passed – this operation was not successful and so, about eight months after accident, second operation was performed whereby urethra was successfully reconstructed – after operation plaintiff had imperfect urinary stream, with some spraying, but this gradually improved – loss of sexual function for about ten months after accident – also he suffered relatively minor knee problem which responded well to physiotherapy – not fit for work until about 20 months after accident.

Prognosis: His recovery was complete save for slight deformity of his penis on erection, which would be permanent.

1.5.5.C11 Case No. 10774

Award at February 2001: £15,095

See: 1.3.1.3.1.C13 for details

1.5.5.C12 Case No. 11845

Name of case: Kenny v Hewdon Stuart Crane Hire Ltd

Brief description of injuries: PELVIS – FRACTURE

Reported: Kemp & Kemp, G2-036; [1999] CLY 1509

JSB Category: 6(C)(b)

Sex: Male

Age at injury: 57

Age at award: 60

Date of award: 25 September 1998

Tribunal: Central London County Court

Amount of award then: £14,000

Award at February 2001: £14,799

Description of injuries: Fractures to right superior and inferior pubic rami and strain of soft-tissues of one sacro-iliac joint – claimant in hospital for 5 days, tended at home for 1 week, on crutches 6 weeks and off work 3 months before returning to previous employment – 3 years after accident, claimant still suffering discomfort and occasional pain in right buttock and groin, sometimes radiating down right leg, and occasional lower spine stiffness in the morning; painkillers sometimes taken – pain exacerbated by walking and sitting in soft chairs.

1.5.5.C13 Case No. 10153

Name of case: Re Fitzhugh

Brief description of injuries: SEVERE TRIMALLEOLAR FRACTURE AND DISLOCATION OF LEFT ANKLE – OFF WORK 22 MONTHS

Reported: Kemp & Kemp, C4-067; [1991] CLY 1350

JSB Category: 6(M)(b)

Sex: Male

Age at injury: 33

Age at award: 37

Date of award: 11 February 1991

Tribunal: CICB

Amount of award then: £10,750

Award at February 2001: £14,254

Description of injuries: Assault – severe trimalleolar fracture and dislocation of left ankle, treated by open reduction internal fixation wire screws and plate – unable to bear weight for 18 weeks – depressive illness and attempted suicide – short tempered – psychogenic pains in left ankle – away from work for 22 months – difficulty driving and climbing stairs.

1.5.5.C14 Case No. 11155

Name of case: Wriglesworth v Doncaster HA

Brief description of injuries: PELVIS – ABSCESS

Reported: Kemp & Kemp, F3-013/1; [1996] CLY 2246

JSB Category: 5(D)(b)

Sex: Female

Age at injury: 46

Age at award: 52

Date of award: 27 September 1996

Tribunal: Sheffield County Court

Amount of award then: £12,500

Award at February 2001: £14,102

Description of injuries: Undiagnosed pelvic abscess – permanent abdominal problems – excessive flatulence – loose bowels – embarrassing bowel sounds.

1.5.5.C15 Case No. 11160

Name of case: Griggs v Olympic Holidays Ltd (No. 2)

Brief description of injuries: HIP – FRACTURES – MULTIPLE FRACTURES

Reported: Kemp & Kemp, G2-037; [1996] CLY 2251

JSB Category: 6(C)(b)

Sex: Male

Age at injury: 50

Age at award: 53

Date of award: 29 July 1996

Tribunal: Lincoln County Court

Amount of award then: £12,000

Award at February 2001: £13,649

Description of injuries: Fractures to the pubic rami – right radius – right fifth metacarpal – subluxation of the right sacroiliac joint – at the time of the hearing the wrist was painless – largely recovered from the pelvic injury – little finger was slightly bent.

Prognosis: Could develop arthritis in wrist in ten years time.

Other points: He was not handicapped in the labour market.

1.5.5.C16 Case No. 10414

Name of case: Pyrah v Tickles Nightclub

Brief description of injuries: FRACTURE OF THE HIP – CONTINUING PAIN AND STIFFNESS – PRE-EXISTING INTESTINAL REABSOBTION SYNDROME EXACERBATED

Reported: [1992] CLY 1670

JSB Category: 6(C)(c)

Sex: Male

Age at injury: 60

Age at award: 61

Date of award: 15 July 1992

Tribunal: Bradford District Registry

Amount of award then: £10,000

Award at February 2001: £12,456

Description of injuries: Displaced intertrochanteric fracture of the right hip in fall at work. Pin and plate inserted to reduce and fix the fracture – intermittent pain and stiffness in the hip continued – unable to do gardening, DIY or drive long distances – used a stick for long walks – left with a nine-inch long operation scar.

Prognosis: Swelling and redness expected to subside – no risk of arthritic change.

1.5.5.C17 Case No. 10796

Name of case: Bailey (Charles Andrew) v Gateway Food Markets

Brief description of injuries: HIPS – DAMAGE TO PREVIOUS REPLACEMENT

Reported: Kemp & Kemp, G2-038; [1994] CLY 1645

JSB Category: 6(C)(c)

Sex: Male

Age at injury: 29

Age at award: 31

Date of award: 27 October 1993

Tribunal: Sheffield County Court

Amount of award then: £10,000

Award at February 2001: £12,184

Description of injuries: Claimant suffered from renal failure and poor bone texture, previous failure of bone circulation having necessitated a hip replacement – slipped on grapes on supermarket floor and fell – fracture of left hip – catastrophic failure of hip replacement, necessitating emergency second replacement in "non-controlled" situation, 5-6 years earlier than non-emergency second replacement was envisaged – over 4 weeks in hospital, returned to work on crutches thereafter hip able to bear weight after 6 months – pain and suffering consequent upon emergency procedure greater than would have been the case under controlled conditions; and period of time on crutches and period of disability similarly longer.

Prognosis: Claimant made remarkable recovery from emergency procedure, but results of operation far from optimal; third hip replacement likely to be required within a maximum of 15 years – necessity for right hip replacement advanced by a period of approximately 1 year.

Other points: Pain and suffering from fracture itself, together with pain, suffering and loss of mobility as a result of advanced second hip replacement, taken into account in awarding damages.

1.5.5.C18 Case No. 11162

Name of case: Wayt v Swansea City Council

Brief description of injuries: HIP – FRACTURE

Reported: Kemp & Kemp, G2-039; [1996] CLY 2253

JSB Category: 6(C)(c)

Sex: Male

Age at injury: 46

Age at award: 52

Date of award: 15 February 1996

Tribunal: Swansea County Court

Amount of award then: £9,375

Award at February 2001: £10,686

Description of injuries: Fracture of the left subcapital hip – injury happened when he slipped on a negligently prepared dance floor.

Prognosis: Expected to suffer permanent slight discomfort around the hip area.

1.5.5.C19 Case No. 11631

Name of case: Rutherford v Wandsworth LBC
Brief description of injuries: HIP – FRACTURE
Reported: Kemp & Kemp, G2-041; [1998] CLY 1633
JSB Category: 6(C)(c)
Sex: Female
Age at injury: 71
Age at award: 75
Date of award: 17 July 1998
Tribunal: Wandsworth County Court
Amount of award then: £10,000
Award at February 2001: £10,560
Description of injuries: Displaced sub-capital fracture to the right hip – constant discomfort to the hip – restricted mobility.
Prognosis: Discomfort in the right hip and a limp were permanent.

1.5.5.C20 Case No. 10415

Name of case: Choudhary v Murtaza
Brief description of injuries: FRACTURE OF THE PUBIC RAMUS
Reported: [1992] CLY 1671
JSB Category: 6(C)(d)
Sex: Female
Age at injury: 19
Age at award: 23
Date of award: 08 April 1992
Tribunal: Rochdale County Court
Amount of award then: £5,500
Award at February 2001: £6,816
Description of injuries: Displaced fracture through the inferior and superior pubic ramus – in hospital for two weeks – thereafter used two walking sticks for six weeks – one walking stick for a further two months – severe pain in the first six weeks – gradually subsided to occasional pain – unable to drive for four months.
Prognosis: Full recovery expected.

1.5.5.C21 Case No. 10476

Name of case: Jones v Hones
Brief description of injuries: BRUISING – WHIPLASH – NEED FOR HIP REPLACEMENT ACCELERATED
Reported: [1992] CLY 1732
JSB Category: 6(C)(d)
Sex: Male
Age at injury: 42
Age at award: 43
Date of award: 02 November 1992
Tribunal: Blackpool County Court
Amount of award then: £5,500
Award at February 2001: £6,772
Description of injuries: Multiple minor injuries – bruising to the left temple, chest, both feet and ankles – whiplash injury to the neck – injury to the right hip which exacerbated pre-existing osteo-arthritic changes.
Prognosis: At the time of the hearing there were continuing problems with the hip – the need for hip replacement had been accelerated by about eighteen months to two years.

1.5.5.C22 Case No. 10971

Name of case: Savage v Paramount
Brief description of injuries: PELVIS – FRACTURE
Reported: Kemp & Kemp, G2-043; [1995] CLY 1722
JSB Category: 6(C)(d)
Sex: Male
Age at injury: 35
Age at award: 39
Date of award: 20 June 1995
Tribunal: Dartford County Court
Amount of award then: £5,000
Award at February 2001: £5,741
Description of injuries: Plaintiff suffered an undisplaced fracture of the pelvis in the region of the ischium, with associated maximum tenderness of left ischial tuberosity, in road traffic accident and was admitted to hospital as inpatient for two days – sexual activity was precluded for four months thereafter and plaintiff stopped participating in weekly football games – did not return to sporting activity – plaintiff was on crutches, non-weight bearing, for a month and returned to work ten weeks after accident – heavy physical work, such as was required by his job as water pump engineer, aggravated pain in back.
Prognosis: Medical prognosis was that fracture was unlikely to cause future complications and plaintiff's back would settle in time with loss of weight and attention to posture.

1.5.5.C23 Case No. 10224

Name of case: Harris v Rulfell

Brief description of injuries: PELVIS – FRACTURE OF THE SYMPHYSIS PUBIS – FULL RECOVERY IN 13 MONTHS

Reported: Kemp & Kemp, G2-044; [1991] CLY 1421

JSB Category: 6(C)(d)

Sex: Male

Age at injury: 28

Age at award: 32

Date of award: 13 February 1991

Tribunal: Westminster County Court

Amount of award then: £3,500

Award at February 2001: £4,599

Description of injuries: Knocked down by a cab – minor cerebral concussion – fracture separation of the symphysis pubis – small laceration to the back of the head – abrasions to the left shoulder and chin. There was severe tenderness to the symphysis pubis and both pubic rami.

Prognosis: Full recovery within thirteen months of the date of the accident.

1.5.5.C24 Case No. 11695

Award at February 2001: £4,313

See: 1.3.1.3.1.C27 for details

1.5.5.C25 Case No. 11669

Name of case: Speed (a minor) v G & A Shipman

Brief description of injuries: PELVIS – SEVERE FRACTURE

Reported: Kemp & Kemp, G2-045; [1998] CLY 1671

JSB Category: 6(C)(d)

Sex: Male

Age at injury: 8

Age at award: 10

Date of award: 15 May 1998

Tribunal: Skegness County Court

Amount of award then: £4,000

Award at February 2001: £4,208

Description of injuries: Severe fracture of the pelvis – shock and bleeding – friction type burn.

Prognosis: Full recovery made with no long-term problems anticipated.

1.5.5.C26 Case No. 10403

Award at February 2001: £3,146

See: 1.3.1.3.1.C31 for details

1.5.5.C27 Case No. 10339

Name of case: Falck (Arthur) v Wilson

Brief description of injuries: HIP – BRUISING – LOSS OF CONFIDENCE

Reported: [1992] CLY 1595

JSB Category: 3(A)(d)

Sex: Male

Age at injury: 66

Age at award: 69

Date of award: 18 March 1992

Tribunal: CICB

Amount of award then: £2,500

Award at February 2001: £3,146

Description of injuries: Knocked down while crossing the road – pain in thigh and hip for three years to date of hearing – unable to walk unaided for any distance – loss of confidence – pre-existing vertigo and instability while walking worsened – housebound for three months after the accident and rarely ventured out thereafter – no longer able to drive.

1.5.5.C28 Case No. 11468

Name of case: James v Watker

Brief description of injuries: HIP – 9 MONTHS

Reported: Kemp & Kemp, K2-091; [1997] CLY 2018

JSB Category: 6(c)(d)

Sex: Male

Age at injury: 25

Age at award: 27

Date of award: 20 September 1996

Tribunal:

Amount of award then: £2,000

Award at February 2001: £2,237

Description of injuries: Multiple bruises and grazes – damaged joint capsule – hip.

Prognosis: Full recovery within nine months of the date of the accident.

1.5.5.C29 Case No. 11893

Award at February 2001: £1,298

See: 1.3.1.3.1.C38 for details

1.5.5.C30 Case No. 11258

Name of case: Straughan v Scaife

Brief description of injuries: HIP – BRUISING

Reported: [1996] CLY 2350

JSB Category: 6(C)(d)

Sex: Female

Age at injury: 33

Age at award: 35

Date of award: 23 February 1996

Tribunal: Aldershot County Court

Amount of award then: £1,000

Award at February 2001: £1,140

Description of injuries: Pain and bruising to the hip and lower abdomen – symptoms fully resolved at the time of the hearing.

Other points: Plaintiff was four months pregnant at the time of the accident – she felt concern for her unborn child.

1.5.5.C31 Case No. 11063

Name of case: Barber v Severn Trent Water

Brief description of injuries: PELVIS AND THIGH – BRUISING AND ABRASIONS TO INNER THIGH, PERINEUM, VAGINA – 2 MONTHS

Reported: [1995] CLY 1817

JSB Category: 6(C)(d)

Sex: Female

Age at injury: 4

Age at award: 7

Date of award: 21 September 1995

Tribunal: Birmingham County Court

Amount of award then: £750

Award at February 2001: £857

Description of injuries: Female involved in accident in which left leg disappeared into hole in road containing either a water tap or fire hydrant belonging to defendants – suffered "straddle" injuries to her upper inner thigh, perineum and vagina, with bruising to urethra and slight bleeding resulting from muscle tear – for a week had great difficulty and severe pain on passing water and walked with a limp – pain settled after a week – however, incontinent of urine on occasions during the day for up to six to eight weeks following the accident.

1.5.5.C32 Case No. 11470

Name of case: Dooley v Machin

Brief description of injuries: HIP – ANXIETY – 3 MONTHS

Reported: [1997] CLY 2020

JSB Category: 6(C)(d)

Sex: Female

Age at injury: 20

Age at award: –

Date of award: 22 April 1997

Tribunal: Birkenhead County Court

Amount of award then: £500

Award at February 2001: £550

Description of injuries: Bruised hip – anxiety when driving.

Prognosis: Hip settled in three weeks – anxiety lasted about three months.

SECTION 1.6
DAMAGE TO LOWER LIMBS

1.6.1 LEG OR ANKLE INJURY

1.6.1.C1 Case No. 11476

Name of case: Westmoquette v Dean

Brief description of injuries: LEGS – DOUBLE AMPUTATION – ARM – AMPUTATION

Reported: Kemp & Kemp, B2-003/1; [1998] CLY 1477

JSB Category: 6(K)(a)(i), 6(E)(a)(iii)

Sex: Female

Age at injury: 45

Age at award: 48

Date of award: 03 April 1998

Tribunal: QBD

Amount of award then: £115,000

Award at February 2001: £153,249

Description of injuries: Above knee amputations of both legs – below elbow amputation of the left arm – fractured mandible and mandibular condyle and maxilla, femur – burns to face and thigh.

Prognosis: Remarkable psychological recovery – additional care would be required in the future.

1.6.1.C2 Case No. 11852

Name of case: Clear v Stephenson

Brief description of injuries: KNEE – SEVERE INJURY

Reported: [1999] CLY 1516

JSB Category: 6(L)(a)

Sex: Male

Age at injury: 46

Age at award: 49

Date of award: 01 July 1999

Tribunal: Peterborough County Court

Amount of award then: £30,000

Award at February 2001: £32,787

Description of injuries: Comminuted fracture of tibial plateau and lateral condyle of left knee – medial collateral ligament strain – minor abrasions – knee reconstructed under general anaesthetic, including insertion of plate and screws – in hospital 11 days; on 2 crutches for 12 weeks and 1 crutch or stick over following 2 months – unable to work for 7 months (claimant self – employed) – plate and screws later removed, providing some pain relief – at time of trial, claimant unable to run, climb ladders, squat or kneel; knee ached generally and occasionally gave a "clunking" sensation – constant pain and occasional severe stabbing pains in back of knee – knee stiffened in morning or after sitting – walking range limited to 1 mile, after which rest required – DIY, home and car maintenance now beyond claimant – claimant forced to abandon motorcycle riding and required car with automatic transmission; driving long distances painful in any event – claimant returned to self – employment, working 40 hours per week, but less productive than before, and income reduced by 50 to 67 per cent.

Prognosis: Claimant had made considerable effort with rehabilitative exercises, but symptoms at time of trial would be permanent – probable that knee replacement surgery would be required in 10 years' time, providing relief from pain in knee, but after which claimant would be unable to continue in self – employment.

1.6.1.C3 Case No. 11496

Name of case: Bawden v Gardner

Brief description of injuries: LEG – SEVERE INJURIES

Reported: Kemp & Kemp, B2-026/2; [1998] CLY 1497

JSB Category: 6(C)(c), 6(M)(c)

Sex: Male

Age at injury: 25

Age at award: 33

Date of award: 29 July 1998

Tribunal: Central London County Court

Amount of award then: £22,000

Award at February 2001: £23,919

Description of injuries: Multiple injuries – leg and ankle – total of 8 operations required.

Prognosis: Likely to be osteoarthritic change in claimant's ankle in his 40s – arthrodesis operation in his 50s.

1.6.1.C4 Case No. 10822

Name of case: McDonald v Watson

Brief description of injuries: LEG – ANKLE

Reported: Kemp & Kemp, I2-311; [1994] CLY 1671

JSB Category: 6(K)(b), 6(M), 6(D)(c), 6(L)(b); 8

Sex: Female

Age at injury: 31

Age at award: 38

Date of award: 11 January 1994

Tribunal: Leeds County Court

Amount of award then: £15,000

Award at February 2001: £18,601

Description of injuries: Claimant knocked down by motorcycle – transverse comminuted fracture of left tibia and fibula – crack fracture to greater tuberosity of left shoulder, causing residual pain and stiffness for 6 months before recovering fully – strain to medial collateral ligament of right knee, causing pain behind kneecap for 1 year and further, minor pain for a year or two after that – abrasions to face, chin, forehead, left arm, wrist, knuckles, left leg, foot; all healing fully, with no residual scarring – rendered unconscious for a time, with some blurred vision in left eye for short period, which spontaneously resolved – 3 weeks in hospital – union of leg fracture slow – external fixator, held by 4 pins, in position for 1 year – 18 months after accident, leg weak; foot swollen, painful and discoloured – limp-stick required for walking – limited, painful inversion of foot (but full movement of ankle and knee) – 4 pinholes in shin where fixator removed – housework and swimming by now possible, but walking limited to duration of 20 minutes – 2 years after accident, symptoms greatly improved – limp gone and stick no longer required – foot movement still limited but no longer painful – considerable fading of scars – loss of congenial employment as nurse in geriatric ward – claimant left with residual symptoms – dull ache in ankle, exacerbated by prolonged walking or standing – minor scarring from pinholes in shin, described as not a significant disfigurement – development of flat foot deformity in left foot, causing loss of movement in foot and pain – difficulty in walking over rough ground.

Prognosis: Residual symptoms would be permanent.

1.6.1.C5 Case No. 11185

Name of case: Pheasant v Lowrey

Brief description of injuries: LEG – SEVERE SOFT-TISSUE INJURIES

Reported: Kemp & Kemp, I2-312; [1996] CLY 2276

JSB Category: 6(K)(c)(iii)

Sex: Male

Age at injury: 32

Age at award: 34

Date of award: 21 May 1996

Tribunal: Chichester County Court

Amount of award then: £16,000

Award at February 2001: £18,326

Description of injuries: Severe soft-tissue injuries to the thigh, groin and calf – injury to the medial meniscus in the left knee – work and social life affected.

Prognosis: Pre-existing degenerative condition of the right knee would have similarly limited his capacity for work and sport within ten years.

1.6.1.C6 Case No. 11678

Name of case: Carter v Automobile Association

Brief description of injuries: LEGS – CRUSH INJURY

Reported: Kemp & Kemp, I2-313; [1998] CLY 1681

JSB Category: 6(K)(b)(iv)

Sex: Female

Age at injury: 37

Age at award: 39

Date of award: 20 January 1998

Tribunal: Leicester County Court

Amount of award then: £14,000

Award at February 2001: £15,269

Description of injuries: Crush injury to the legs – tense haematoma to both legs above the knee joint – extensive bruising to both legs from mid-thigh to heel – at the time of the hearing C had fully recovered from injury to the left leg.

Prognosis: Permanent residual hypersensitivity to the right leg – no later complications were expected.

Other points: The judge found that post-traumatic stress disorder added nothing to the condition in which C found herself.

1.6.1.C7 Case No. 10238

Name of case: Re Cook

Brief description of injuries: SEVERE SOFT-TISSUE INJURIES TO THE LEFT KNEE, SHIN AND CALF – SCARRING

Reported: Kemp & Kemp, I2-510; [1991] CLY 1435

JSB Category: 6(K)(c)

Sex: Male

Age at injury: 24

Age at award: 25

Date of award: 18 October 1990

Tribunal: Cambridge District Registry

Amount of award then: £10,000

Award at February 2001: £13,292

Description of injuries: Severe soft-tissue injuries to the left knee, shin and calf – laceration to the right elbow and grazing to the left – the leg was cleaned, debrided and dressed under general anaesthetic – split skin graft from the left thigh – reaction to anti-biotics spread to the skin graft.

Prognosis: Extensive scarring to the knee, shin and calf – vulnerable to damage – swelling and discomfort of the leg after activity – no improvement likely – unable to resume contact sports.

1.6.1.C8 Case No. 11009

Name of case: Wright v Macclesfield Health Authority

Brief description of injuries: LEG – NEGLIGENTLY TREATED INJURY – "REASONABLE RECOVERY", BUT ACTIVELY LIMITED

Reported: Kemp & Kemp, I2-512; [1995] CLY 1761

JSB Category: 6(K)(c)(i)

Sex: Male

Age at injury: 21

Age at award: 25

Date of award: 14 March 1995

Tribunal: Altrincham County Court

Amount of award then: £10,000

Award at February 2001: £11,701

Description of injuries: Plaintiff sustained soft-tissue injury to his left leg during course of game of rugby which led to development of compartment syndrome – negligently treated by defendants who failed to carry out surgery which would have led to resolution of condition and good recovery with no neurovascular problems although he would have been left with surgical scar and some muscle protrusion – as result of failure to treat him, plaintiff suffered complete foot drop – walked with crutches for six weeks and then with drop foot splint for six months which restricted his mobility very severely – made reasonable recovery although had some residual loss of inversion and eversion of ankle – could walk normally, although was unable to jog for more than mile – could not now play rugby or squash and inability to participate in these activities caused him great distress.

Prognosis: Prior to the accident the plaintiff was a very proficient sportsman, playing competitive rugby to a high standard. There was no likelihood of future deterioration.

1.6.1.C9 Case No. 11666

Name of case: Craggs v Rowan Hankinson Ltd

Brief description of injuries: LEG – SOFT-TISSUE INJURIES

Reported: Kemp & Kemp, 2-515/1; [1998] CLY 1668

JSB Category: 6(K)(c)

Sex: Male

Age at injury: 44

Age at award: 49

Date of award: 22 October 1997

Tribunal: Newcastle upon Tyne County Court

Amount of award then: £10,000

Award at February 2001: £10,798

Description of injuries: Soft-tissue injuries to the lower right leg – reduced sensation – altered sensation and allodynia over the area of the right shin.

Prognosis: Real risk that claimant would be unable to work at some point in the future.

Other points: Claimant a resourceful and well motivated man – self-employed.

1.6.1.C10 Case No. 11664

Name of case: Sinfield v Department of Transport

Brief description of injuries: LEG – PUNCTURED VEIN – ULCER

Reported: Kemp & Kemp, i2-515/2; [1998] CLY 1666

JSB Category: 6(K)(c); 8

Sex: Male

Age at injury: 46

Age at award: 51

Date of award: 02 March 1998

Tribunal: Central London County Court

Amount of award then: £10,000

Award at February 2001: £10,709

Description of injuries: Punctured vein to the lower right leg – wound measured 1cm by 1cm – pre-existing venous incompetence – vulnerable to ulceration and DVTs – the wound failed to heal and developed an ulcer 2 inches in diameter – suffered a DVT to the right leg requiring hospitalisation.

Prognosis: Permanent discolouration of the right shin measured 17cm by 12cm – caused the claimant embarrassment.

1.6.1.C11 Case No. 11847

Name of case: Orchard v Phoenix Taxis

Brief description of injuries: LEG – SCAR

Reported: Kemp & Kemp, I2-516/2; [1999] CLY 1511

JSB Category: 6(K)(c)(i); 8

Sex: Male

Age at injury: 24

Age at award: 29

Date of award: 17 February 1999

Tribunal: Newcastle-upon-Tyne County Court

Amount of award then: £10,000

Award at February 2001: £10,514

Description of injuries: Compound comminuted fracture of right tibia and fibula in distal third – also soft-tissue injuries to hand and arm – fracture reduced under general anaesthetic with skeletal traction; intramedullary nail inserted into tibia – claimant in hospital 5 days; readmitted for a further 4 days 2 weeks later after complaining of an infection – below – knee plaster for 13 weeks initially, then a further 8 weeks the following year when nail removed – intensive physiotherapy – sound union of bone did not occur until 18 months after the accident – claimant complained of requiring a walking stick and that knee occasionally "gave way" – 5 years after accident, prescription analgesics required every day and claimant unable to kneel, although squatting possible claimant – unable to resume pastimes of Thai boxing and football – claimant unemployed at time of accident and had remained so in the intervening years until trial – residual problems described as "inconvenient" rather than "functional" – also scarring over patella and ankle, not of the worst sort, but altered configuration of limb embarrassing to claimant.

Prognosis: Problems with leg permanent – osteoarthritis not likely.

1.6.1.C12 Case No. 11856

Name of case: Coggin v Portaway Minerals (Elton) Ltd

Brief description of injuries: LEG – ACHILLES TENDON

Reported: Kemp & Kemp, I3-079/1; [1999] CLY 1520

JSB Category: 6(N)(c)

Sex: Male

Age at injury: 17

Age at award: 21

Date of award: 03 March 1999

Tribunal: Buxton County Court

Amount of award then: £10,000

Award at February 2001: £10,488

Description of injuries: 80 per cent division of Achilles tendon – repair successful – residual weakness and limitation of movement in ankle, and proneness to swelling – claimant forced to cease all active sports – difficulty walking on rough ground – heavy manual work no longer possible.

Prognosis: Not stated

1.6.1.C13 Case No. 11451

Name of case: Escott v Escott

Brief description of injuries: LEG – SCAR

Reported: Kemp & Kemp, J2-020; [1997] CLY 2000

JSB Category: 8

Sex: Female

Age at injury: 16

Age at award: 26

Date of award: 20 November 1996

Tribunal: Newport County Court

Amount of award then: £8,750

Award at February 2001: £9,779

Description of injuries: Superficial grazes and bruising to the head, face wrist and thigh – two lacerations which extended deep into the facia of the muscle of the calf.

Prognosis: The scarring was an obvious, considerable and permanent cosmetic defect – caused considerable embarrassment – no prospect of further improvement.

1.6.1.C14 Case No. 11848

Name of case: Carver v Queens Square Petroleum Ltd

Brief description of injuries: LEG – SCAR

Reported: Kemp & Kemp, I2-520/1; [1999] CLY 1512

JSB Category: 6(K)(c); 8

Sex: Male

Age at injury: 52

Age at award: 57

Date of award: 15 June 1998

Tribunal: Kingston-upon-Hull County Court

Amount of award then: £8,000

Award at February 2001: £8,421

Description of injuries: Basal fracture to left neck of femur – fracture surgically reduced and fixed with metal plate and screws – 18 cm scar on left thigh – in hospital 10 days; on crutches or in wheelchair for 3 months to preserve hip joint; off work 4.5 months – continuing discomfort when seated for long periods of time (eg when driving) – left thigh 1 cm shorter than right, and some muscle wasting – unable to pursue hobby of dancing or approximately 1 year.

Prognosis: Future surgery required to remove metalwork at some stage, but not imminent – assessment of 10-15 per cent increase in risk of developing osteoarthritis.

1.6.1.C15 Case No. 10248

Name of case: Hardinges v Firstsell

Brief description of injuries: ANKLE – FRACTURE – 2 OPERATIONS

Reported: Kemp & Kemp, I2-521; [1991] CLY 1445

JSB Category: 6(M)

Sex: Male

Age at injury: 26

Age at award: 29

Date of award: 03 April 1991

Tribunal: Harlow County Court

Amount of award then: £6,500

Award at February 2001: £8,400

Description of injuries: Fracture of the lower end of the right leg involving medial and lateral malleoli – bruising to the shoulder and chest – operation for open reduction of fractures – lower end of the tibia held together with screws – fibula held with plate and screws – below-knee plaster for seven weeks – five weeks physiotherapy – off work for five months and a further four weeks when the plate and screws were removed.

Prognosis: Range of movement now seemed excellent – two scars on the outer ankle – one scar on the inner ankle – slight increase in the chance of developing arthritis in the joint.

1.6.1.C16 Case No. 10244

Name of case: Davies v London Borough of Bexley

Brief description of injuries: DAMAGED CARTILAGE TO THE KNEE – WALKING LIMITED TO TWO MILES – 3 YEARS OF SYMPTOMS

Reported: Kemp & Kemp, I2-436; [1991] CLY 1441

JSB Category: 6(L)(b)(ii)

Sex: Female

Age at injury: 49

Age at award: Deceased

Date of award: 14 March 1991

Tribunal: Medway County Court

Amount of award then: £5,000

Award at February 2001: £6,545

Description of injuries: Fall onto the right knee – damaged cartilage lining the back of the knee – plaster cylinder for two weeks – off work for three months – died of unrelated causes three years after the accident.

Prognosis: Unable to walk more than two miles – knee gave way two or three times each week – continuing pain was slowly increasing in intensity.

1.6.1.C17 Case No. 10652

Name of case: Garrett v Somerset County Council

Brief description of injuries: LEG – LACERATION – SCAR

Reported: Kemp & Kemp, J2-031; [1993] CLY 1548

JSB Category: 8

Sex: Male

Age at injury: 12

Age at award: 14

Date of award: 28 October 1992

Tribunal: Taunton County Court

Amount of award then: £4,500

Award at February 2001: £5,533

Description of injuries: Shin struck on concealed angle iron – wound cleaned and stitched under general anaesthetic – foot in slab in hospital for 9 days – unable to play rugby, hockey, football, or use drum kit, for 6 months – scarring in form of inverted "V" on front of right shin – visible 2 years later from distance of 25 feet – described by judge as significant cosmetic disability – holiday ruined.

Prognosis: Shin pads now required to prevent further injury scar had broken open in past; risk of recurrence if knocked hard.

1.6.1.C18 Case No. 10653

Name of case: Bowler v Smart

Brief description of injuries: LEG – DOG BITE – SCAR

Reported: Kemp & Kemp, J2-032; [1993] CLY 1549

JSB Category: 8; 3(A)(d)

Sex: Male

Age at injury: 5

Age at award: 6

Date of award: 08 February 1993

Tribunal: Pontefract County Court

Amount of award then: £4,000

Award at February 2001: £4,957

Description of injuries: Attacked by dog – bitten on inner leg, above right knee, knocked to the ground and dragged – large amount of skin lost – at hospital, wound debrided and skin graft performed – skin taken from anterior aspect of right thigh – 7 x 4 cm scar on inner aspect of right thigh, just above knee, where wound occurred; skin graft of 3 x 2 cm at centre of scar; entire scar slightly depressed, contour deformity permanent – 6 x 6 cm scar on anterior aspect of right thigh where donor skin removed, lower 1 cm of which redder and hypertrophic – nightmares for 6 months, waking up crying.

Prognosis: Wound scar becoming paler and flatter with time, expected to improve further – donor site scar healed well, most of it expected to fade with time, but reddened area would remain permanent and noticeable – claimant now keeping well away from dogs, but adopting sensible, matter-of-fact attitude to incident – nightmares now ceased – claimant aware of disfiguring aspect to scar, but thought not uppermost in his mind.

1.6.1.C19 Case No. 10825

Name of case: Pizzey v Ford Motor Co

Brief description of injuries: LEG – FIBROUS LUMP

Reported: (1993) The Times, March 8; [1993] 17 LS Gaz R 46; Kemp & Kemp, I2-529; BPILS, XI 3590; [1994] CLY 1674

JSB Category: 6(K)(c)(iii)

Sex: Male

Age at injury: 61

Age at award: 69

Date of award: 25 October 1993

Tribunal: Bow County Court

Amount of award then: £4,000

Award at February 2001: £4,852

Description of injuries: Claimant struck on shin by crowbar falling from above – painful lump and bruise quickly appeared – injury did not fade, but became hard fibrous lump which increased in size, hardened, discoloured and remained painful when struck – almost impossible for claimant to avoid striking the lump at work – lump eventually excised 2 years later in 2 operations, incompletely in first operation and then completely in second operation, requiring a skin graft – claimant had understandable fears that lump might be some form of malignant growth – court found that there was no pre-existing tumour, and that all pain, suffering and absence from work were caused by the accident.

1.6.1.C20 Case No. 11756

Name of case: Re Oakley

Brief description of injuries: LEG – CAUSALGIA

Reported: [1998] CLY 1759

JSB Category: 6(K)(c)(iii)

Sex: Female

Age at injury: 54

Age at award: 58

Date of award: 13 February 1998

Tribunal: CICB, London

Amount of award then: £4,500

Award at February 2001: £4,828

Description of injuries: Causalgic syndrome following minor trauma – burning pain to the left buttock and leg.

Prognosis: The burning symptoms would continue indefinitely.

1.6.1.C21 Case No. 10846

Name of case: Tyrell-Wilson v Bostan

Brief description of injuries: LEG – SCAR

Reported: Kemp & Kemp, J2-034; [1994] CLY 1695

JSB Category: 8

Sex: Female

Age at injury: 11

Age at award: 13

Date of award: 20 May 1994

Tribunal: Bradford County Court

Amount of award then: £4,000

Award at February 2001: £4,755

Description of injuries: Claimant fell 6ft down unguarded, unlit pavement light – cuts to right leg in pre-tibial region – wounds dressed and required to be covered for 3.5 weeks, during which time claimant unable to bath and shower properly – pain and itching to injury site, ongoing to date of trial – claimant left with 3 scars in pre-tibial region on middle third of lower leg – lateral scar 6cm long, narrow and pale – central scar 7cm long and 5mm wide, deep brown in colour and therefore obvious – medial scar 4cm long and faint – claimant very conscious of and embarrassed about scars – unwilling to wear skirt unless she had to, and then only with dark tights – tracksuit bottoms worn for PE – unwillingness to go swimming, which claimant had previously enjoyed – itching in leg continual in hot summer months.

Prognosis: Prognosis that central scar would remain a noticeable blemish – judge found that scarring had had a very serious and debilitating impact on claimant.

1.6.1.C22 Case No. 10654

Name of case: Re Greensides

Brief description of injuries: LEG – SCAR

Reported: Kemp & Kemp, J2-035; [1993] CLY 1550

JSB Category: 8

Sex: Female

Age at injury: 23

Age at award: –

Date of award: 20 October 1993

Tribunal: Bath County Court

Amount of award then: £3,750

Award at February 2001: £4,549

Description of injuries: Claimant underwent electrolysis treatment to remove "thread veins" at knee and thigh level, involving multiple needle penetrations, causing acute discomfort and occasional bleeding – no warning of possible adverse consequences of treatment – development of thick scarring at some of the treated areas – scars initially purplish – red and itchy – slowly becoming paler, flatter and more comfortable – claimant left with white, shiny scarred areas, easily visible at conversational distances – psychological reaction of disappointment in failure of treatment, desire to conceal matter from boyfriend and self-consciousness about scarred areas.

Prognosis: Scars not amenable to surgery and likely to be permanent – improvement not expected – scars unlikely to tan in sunlight and thus likely to be more noticeable in summer – cosmetic camouflage not practicable.

1.6.1.C23 Case No. 10641

Name of case: Smith v Creedon and Yiasoumi

Brief description of injuries: LEGS – SOFT-TISSUE INJURIES

Reported: Kemp & Kemp, I2-534; [1993] CLY 1537

JSB Category: 6(K)(c)(iii)

Sex: Female

Age at injury: 55

Age at award: 59

Date of award: 01 March 1993

Tribunal: Peterborough County Court

Amount of award then: £3,500

Award at February 2001: £4,322

Description of injuries: Fall down flight of stairs – large lacerations to both shins with raised skin flaps – flaps reattached – plaintiff in hospital 10 days – remaining 12cm distally-based flap wound with 25cm surrounding scar on each leg – pain in left shin, swelling in left foot towards end of day – right shin uncomfortable but not as bad.

Prognosis: No long term complications expected, but flaps slightly more vulnerable than previously.

1.6.1.C24 Case No. 10106

Name of case: Speechly v Spencer

Brief description of injuries: HAEMATOMA OF LACERATION ON LEFT THIGH

Reported: Kemp & Kemp, K2-016; [1990] CLY 1674

JSB Category: 6(K)

Sex: Female

Age at injury: 41

Age at award: 43

Date of award: 07 September 1990

Tribunal: Bournemouth District Registry

Amount of award then: £3,000

Award at February 2001: £3,991

Description of injuries: Knocked off moped, receiving five-inch contused laceration across front of left thigh, and abrasions to left knee and lower right leg – wound cleaned and sutured in hospital – developed haematoma on wound, requiring 18 sessions of mega-pulse and ultrasonic therapy – injury continued to cause some discomfort on sitting and impaired hobbies of walking and dancing – barely visible scar at date of hearing.

1.6.1.C25 Case No. 10847

Name of case: Wallis v Smith

Brief description of injuries: LEG – SCAR

Reported: Kemp & Kemp, K2-043; [1994] CLY 1696

JSB Category: 8

Sex: Male

Age at injury: 69

Age at award: 70

Date of award: 22 April 1994

Tribunal: Salford County Court

Amount of award then: £2,750

Award at February 2001: £3,280

Description of injuries: Claimant bitten on left leg by alsatian dog, and left with 3 scars – 3 x 0.5cm depressed area of skin, 30cm below inner aspect of knee joint, due to absence of subcutaneous fat; quality of skin good and not a particularly obvious or embarrassing defect – heavy pigmented area of 7 x 4cm in mid-line of front of tibia surrounding "U" – shaped scar with medial limb of 2cm and lateral limb of 2cm, making a "flap" 2cm in length; skin satisfactorily healed, but with a white scaly scar, and reduced sensation around flap – 2cm scaly, depressed, pigmented area at site of satisfactorily healed puncture wound.

Prognosis: Areas of pigmentation would not change significantly and would be permanent features – skin in those areas would continue to be more vulnerable to trauma than claimant's normal skin, being inferior in texture and strength.

1.6.1.C26 Case No. 11220

Name of case: Mitchell v The Post Office

Brief description of injuries: LEG – WOUND

Reported: (1996) 96 (1) QR 7; Kemp & Kemp, I3-034; [1996] CLY 2312

JSB Category: 6(K)(c)(iii)

Sex: Male

Age at injury: 53

Age at award: 57

Date of award: 06 December 1995

Tribunal: Bristol County Court

Amount of award then: £2,750

Award at February 2001: £3,139

Description of injuries: Open wound and bruising to the leg.

Prognosis: All symptoms were likely to resolve eventually – on-going symptoms described as "mild".

1.6.1.C27 Case No. 10098

Name of case: Nelson v Nelson Taxis (Teesside)

Brief description of injuries: LEG – SEVERE BRUISING

Reported: Kemp & Kemp, I2-543; [1990] CLY 1665

JSB Category: 6(K)

Sex: Female

Age at injury: 78

Age at award: 79

Date of award: 25 September 1990

Tribunal: Middlesbrough County Court

Amount of award then: £2,200

Award at February 2001: £2,927

Description of injuries: Severe bruising to left leg below knee – bruising to right hip – cut to right foot – shock – housebound for two months – significant swelling in left leg and aching in right hip when lying on right side and getting on and off buses (up to date of trial).

1.6.1.C28 Case No. 10264

Name of case: Re Rayner

Brief description of injuries: ACID BURNS TO THE LEGS – FULL RECOVERY 15 MONTHS

Reported: Kemp & Kemp, J3-038; [1991] CLY 1461

JSB Category: 8

Sex: Female

Age at injury: 44

Age at award: –

Date of award: 18 July 1991

Tribunal: CICB

Amount of award then: £2,000

Award at February 2001: £2,571

Description of injuries: Assault – the backs of the top of both legs were sprayed with industrial oven cleaner containing acid – four hospital visits for dressings – considerable pain for ten days – unable to ride her bicycle for one year.

Prognosis: Scarring faded completely within thirty months.

1.6.1.C29 Case No. 11011

Name of case: Turner v Dale

Brief description of injuries: THIGH – DEEP LACERATION – SCAR

Reported: Kemp & Kemp, K2-078; [1995] CLY 1763

JSB Category: 6(K)(c)(ii)

Sex: Female

Age at injury: 42

Age at award: 45

Date of award: 06 January 1995

Tribunal: Chesterfield County Court

Amount of award then: £2,000

Award at February 2001: £2,356

Description of injuries: Plaintiff sustained deep laceration on posterior left thigh as result of sitting on toilet which had jagged broken edge – wound bled profusely and she was taken to hospital where it was sutured with seven stitches under local anaesthetic – roughly two weeks later wound became inflamed and antibiotics were prescribed – off work for 10 days and had difficulties sitting down or sleeping on back for some six to eight weeks afterwards – left with permanent scar measuring 3cm by 2mm which itched from time to time – was conscious of scar and no longer wore shorts or exposed that part of her leg to sun – remained nervous of using any toilet other than her own and always checked the rim for damage.

1.6.1.C30 Case No. 10267

Name of case: McLafferty v London Borough of Southwark

Brief description of injuries: SEVERE LIGAMENTOUS STRAIN TO THE LEFT ANKLE – SOME RESIDUAL WEAKNESS

Reported: Kemp & Kemp, I3-036; [1991] CLY 1464

JSB Category: 6(M)(d)

Sex: Female

Age at injury: 52

Age at award: –

Date of award: 15 March 1991

Tribunal: Lambeth County Court

Amount of award then: £1,750

Award at February 2001: £2,291

Description of injuries: Severe ligamentous strain to the left ankle – swelling – advised rest – prescribed painkillers and liniment – after five weeks able to get around reasonably normally.

Prognosis: At the time of the hearing the ankle was slightly weakened – inclined to give way – some aching after a full day of work.

1.6.1.C31 Case No. 12067

Name of case: E (a child) v Calderdale MBC

Brief description of injuries: LEG – LACERATION – SCAR

Reported: [2000] 6 CL 197

JSB Category: 6(K)(c)(iii)

Sex: Male

Age at injury: 10

Age at award: 13

Date of award: 05 January 2000

Tribunal: Halifax County Court

Amount of award then: £2,000

Award at February 2001: £2,065

Description of injuries: Injury caused in a fall over a piece of stone or concrete hidden by grass – 3cm laceration to the right tibia – laceration was cleaned and closed using steri-strips – re-dressed nine days later – required antibiotics and a further dressing the next day due to inflammation and discharge of the wound – a very unsightly scar 2.5cm by 0.5cm remained but was expected to improve – at time of the hearing the scar was pale and not readily visible – no functional problems with the leg.

1.6.1.C32 Case No. 11059

Award at February 2001: £2,065

See: 1.4.4.C54 for details

1.6.1.C33 Case No. 11039

Name of case: Waghorn v Buckland

Brief description of injuries: ARM AND THIGH – DOG BITES – WOUND INFECTED – RECOVERY 2 WEEKS

Reported: Kemp & Kemp, K2-105; [1995] CLY 1793

JSB Category: 6(F)

Sex: Female

Age at injury: 26

Age at award: 30

Date of award: 02 May 1995

Tribunal: Slough County Court

Amount of award then: £1,750

Award at February 2001: £2,012

Description of injuries: Plaintiff sustained bite to left forearm and puncture wound to left thigh from Alsatian cross-breed dog – left forearm wound cleaned and sutured with two stitches and tetanus toxcid booster was given – wound became infected and course of antibiotics were prescribed – off work 10 days – injuries had largely healed after two weeks but left forearm wound remained tender to pressure for about one year.

Prognosis: A small scar her forearm and red mark on her thigh remained.

1.6.1.C34 Case No. 11748

Name of case: Leadbeater (a minor) v Allied Domecq Ltd

Brief description of injuries: ANKLE – 9 MONTHS

Reported: (1998) 98 (6) QR 8; Kemp & Kemp, K2-108/2; [1998] CLY 1751

JSB Category: 6(M)(d)

Sex: Female

Age at injury: 9

Age at award: 10

Date of award: 01 July 1998

Tribunal: Halifax County Court

Amount of award then: £1,850

Award at February 2001: £1,952

Description of injuries: Severe ligamentous strain to the ankle – full recovery achieved within 9 months of the date of the accident.

1.6.1.C35 Case No. 10868

Name of case: Bhudia v Newman

Brief description of injuries: LEG – DOG BITE – PHOBIA

Reported: Kemp & Kemp, K2-113; [1994] CLY 1720

JSB Category: 6(K)(c)(iii); 3(A); 8

Sex: Female

Age at injury: 27

Age at award: –

Date of award: 17 November 1993

Tribunal: Willesden County Court

Amount of award then: £1,600

Award at February 2001: £1,944

Description of injuries: Claimant, out walking dog, herself attacked by another dog – dog restrained by owner, but escaped and attacked again – 2 bite wounds to right thigh, one an elongated tear of skin 2 in long – 2 bite marks to left thigh – shock – wounds healed 7 months later – left thigh constantly painful and slightly swollen – 2 discoloured scars – claimant suffered from phobia of dogs – unable to walk near vicinity of attack for fear of recurrence.

Prognosis: Scars permanent.

1.6.1.C36 Case No. 11752

Name of case: Craig (a minor) v Erdman Lewis Ltd
Brief description of injuries: LEG – SCAR
Reported: Kemp & Kemp, J2-048; [1998] CLY 1755
JSB Category: 8
Sex: Female
Age at injury: 7
Age at award: 10
Date of award: 29 June 1998
Tribunal: Nottingham County Court
Amount of award then: £1,750
Award at February 2001: £1,842
Description of injuries: Laceration to the shin – scar 1.5cm by 1.2cm, described as a minimal cosmetic defect.

1.6.1.C37 Case No. 10870

Name of case: Atkinson v Waring and Waring
Brief description of injuries: LEG – DOG BITE – SCAR
Reported: Kemp & Kemp, K2-124; [1994] CLY 1722
JSB Category: 6(K)(c)(iii); 8
Sex: Male
Age at injury: 30
Age at award: –
Date of award: 14 October 1993
Tribunal: Bradford County Court
Amount of award then: £1,500
Award at February 2001: £1,819
Description of injuries: Dog bite to lower leg – laceration approximately 3cm in length – off work 1 week – throbbing pain for several weeks after return to work, subsequently resolving completely – brown, flat, elliptical scar 3cm x 7mm on outer aspect of left calf – hobbies of boxing and rugby league unaffected.
Prognosis: Scar unlikely to improve further, but this of little concern to claimant.

1.6.1.C38 Case No. 11861

Name of case: Radley v Claremount Garments Ltd
Brief description of injuries: LEG – SCAR
Reported: Kemp & Kemp, K2-159/1; [1999] CLY 1525
JSB Category: 8
Sex: Female
Age at injury: 34
Age at award: 37
Date of award: 04 November 1998
Tribunal: Leeds County Court
Amount of award then: £1,400
Award at February 2001: £1,465

Description of injuries: Laceration to lateral aspect of left thigh – dressed for 3 days; uncovered healing thereafter – bruising settled within 4-5 weeks – injury did not cause claimant to be absent from work, or interfere with any hobbies or pastimes – 12 months after accident, mature, linear, flat, pigmented scar measuring 2cm, noticeable when claimant went swimming or wore shorts for 2 years after incident – contrary to initial prognosis, scar had continued to improve and had virtually disappeared 3 years after accident.

1.6.1.C39 Case No. 11702

Name of case: Jones v Aderogba
Brief description of injuries: LEG – GRAZING
Reported: Kemp & Kemp, K2-167/1; [1998] CLY 1705
JSB Category: 6(K)(c)(iii); 8
Sex: Male
Age at injury: 32
Age at award: 33
Date of award: 27 February 1998
Tribunal: Maidstone County Court
Amount of award then: £1,300
Award at February 2001: £1,395
Description of injuries: Grazed right knee – bruised left shin – shock – 1 year after the date of the accident 2 small scars remained.

1.6.1.C40 Case No. 11945

Name of case: Carr v IMI plc
Brief description of injuries: LEG – THIGH
Reported: Kemp & Kemp, K2-170/6; [1999] CLY 1609
JSB Category: 6(K)(c)(iii)
Sex: Female
Age at injury: 34
Age at award: 35
Date of award: 25 March 1999
Tribunal: Northampton County Court
Amount of award then: £1,250
Award at February 2001: £1,310
Description of injuries: Severe bruise to right thigh – claimant shocked and shaken, and leg unable to bear weight – painkillers prescribed at hospital – on following morning, top of right leg extremely stiff; pain across whole upper, outer part of thigh – hobble and limp for first 2 days; mobility improved thereafter – aching and bruising had only completely disappeared after 2 weeks – claimant left with slight lump in right outer thigh, which was tender and gave rise to painful "pulling" sensation, after walking for 15-20 minutes – 15 months after accident, claimant still had resolving haematoma in muscle of right quadriceps, about 10cm above right knee, and about the diameter of a 10 pence piece; power unaffected.
Prognosis: Full recovery expected within a further 9 months.

1.6.1.C41 Case No. 10282

Name of case: Mace v Brown

Brief description of injuries: LESION TO THE LOWER LEFT LEG – WHIPLASH – 3 WEEKS

Reported: Kemp & Kemp, K2-171; [1991] CLY 1479

JSB Category: 6(K)(c)(iii)

Sex: Male

Age at injury: 40

Age at award: 42

Date of award: 17 April 1991

Tribunal: Norwich County Court

Amount of award then: £1,000

Award at February 2001: £1,292

Description of injuries: A lesion to the lower left leg – whiplash injury – painful symptoms were resolved within about three weeks of the date of the accident.

Prognosis: Residual aching in the leg was a nuisance – neck problem had resolved.

1.6.1.C42 Case No. 10283

Name of case: Crutchley v Gazzard

Brief description of injuries: BRUISING TO THE LEGS AND ANKLE – 1 MONTH

Reported: Kemp & Kemp, K2-072; [1991] CLY 1480

JSB Category: 6(K)(c)(iii)

Sex: Male

Age at injury: 22

Age at award: –

Date of award: 28 June 1991

Tribunal: Burton-on-Trent County Court

Amount of award then: £1,000

Award at February 2001: £1,283

Description of injuries: Bruising to the inner thighs and right shin – minor laceration – bruising and swelling to the right ankle – headaches.

Prognosis: Symptoms generally cleared by three to four weeks – there was some residual weakness to the right ankle.

1.6.1.C43 Case No. 10287

Name of case: Rogers v Dunkley

Brief description of injuries: LEG AND FOOT – GRAZES AND ABRASIONS

Reported: Kemp & Kemp, K2-190; [1991] CLY 1484

JSB Category: 6(K)(c)(iii)

Sex: Male

Age at injury: 16

Age at award: –

Date of award: 01 December 1990

Tribunal: Northampton County Court

Amount of award then: £850

Award at February 2001: £1,125

Description of injuries: Deep graze measuring 5cms by 3cms over the right patella – small abrasions to the left knee, left leg and right foot.

Prognosis: Unable to work for one week – or to play squash for three weeks.

1.6.1.C44 Case No. 10883

Name of case: Carlton v Ford Motor Co

Brief description of injuries: LEG

Reported: Kemp & Kemp, K2-216; [1994] CLY 1735

JSB Category: 6(K)(c)(iii)

Sex: Male

Age at injury: 29

Age at award: 32

Date of award: 30 September 1994

Tribunal: Romford County Court

Amount of award then: £850

Award at February 2001: £1,008

Description of injuries: Claimant struck on shin by car door falling from its mounting frame – 0.5in cut – bruising and swelling – no stitches required – leg quite painful – 1 week off work – return to normal duties thereafter, but pain in leg continued for 2 weeks – symptoms lasted 3 weeks in all – unable to drive, walk with young daughter, or play football – full recovery after 3 weeks – claimant lost his place in his football team for a further 2 weeks after 3-week period, making 5 weeks in all without football.

1.6.1.C45 Case No. 10684

Name of case: Caley v Ideal Standard

Brief description of injuries: LEGS – BRUISING

Reported: [1993] CLY 1580

JSB Category: 6(K)(c)(iii)

Sex: Male

Age at injury: 39

Age at award: 41

Date of award: 27 July 1993

Tribunal: Kingston-upon-Hull County Court

Amount of award then: £800

Award at February 2001: £978

Description of injuries: Right leg trapped between conveyor belt and control panel – bruising and stiffness to right and left legs – cream and painkilling tablets prescribed – aches and pains for 3 weeks – bruising to legs for 4 weeks – fully recovered within 4 weeks of accident – no time taken off work.

1.6.1.C46 Case No. 11063
Award at February 2001: £857
See: 1.5.5.C31 for details

1.6.1.C47 Case No. 10524
Name of case: Howard v Rogers
Brief description of injuries: THIGH – BRUISING
Reported: [1992] CLY 1780
JSB Category:
Sex: Male
Age at injury: 18
Age at award: –
Date of award: 02 January 1992
Tribunal: Chorley County Court
Amount of award then: £350
Award at February 2001: £444
Description of injuries: Soft-tissue contusion to the right thigh and groin – discharged home with analgesia – soreness continued for about two weeks.

1.6.1.C48 Case No. 10296
Name of case: Hayes v Bass North
Brief description of injuries: ANKLE – LIGAMENTOUS STRAIN
Reported: [1991] CLY 1493
JSB Category: 6(M)(d)
Sex: Male
Age at injury: 49
Age at award: 51
Date of award: 28 January 1991
Tribunal: Liverpool County Court
Amount of award then: £300
Award at February 2001: £396
Description of injuries: Ligamentous strain to the lateral ligament of the right ankle – painful, swollen and bruised – applied strapping for two weeks – nervous and lost confidence outside – eight-and-a-half months later there was slight swelling.
Prognosis: Slight puffiness might remain in the long term.

1.6.1.C49 Case No. 10895
Name of case: Maddox v George Fischer (Lincoln)
Brief description of injuries: LEG – LACERATION
Reported: [1994] CLY 1747
JSB Category: 6(K)(c)(iii)
Sex: Male
Age at injury: 50
Age at award: 52
Date of award: 17 May 1994
Tribunal: Lincoln County Court
Amount of award then: £250
Award at February 2001: £297
Description of injuries: Claimant struck shin on protuberance in bin at work – laceration, requiring stitches – wound sore for about 10 days – swelling for some weeks – stitches removed after 2 weeks – no time off work – soreness in shin suffered for some time after accident.

1.6.1.1 LEG AND OTHER INJURY

1.6.1.1.C1 Case No. 11492
Award at February 2001: £77,922
See: 1.4.3.C4 for details

1.6.1.1.C2 Case No. 11493
Name of case: Re G
Brief description of injuries: LEGS – SEVERE INJURIES – POST-TRAUMATIC STRESS DISORDER
Reported: Kemp & Kemp, B2-007/1; [1998] CLY 1494
JSB Category: 6(K)(b)(i); 3(B)
Sex: Female
Age at injury: 22
Age at award: 27
Date of award: 24 March 1998
Tribunal: CICB, London
Amount of award then: £60,000
Award at February 2001: £72,253
Description of injuries: Terrorist attack – shrapnel wounds to the legs – compound comminuted fractures to the leg – degloving of soft-tissues – both legs seriously disfigured – required complex surgical revision – perforated eardrum – post-traumatic stress disorder.
Prognosis: Some hearing loss was permanent.

1.6.1.1.C3 Case No. 10635

Name of case: Cameron McCabe v Scottish Agricultural Industries

Brief description of injuries: LEGS – SEVERE CRUSH INJURIES – WHEELCHAIR

Reported: [1993] CLY 1530

JSB Category: 6(K)(b)(i)

Sex: Male

Age at injury: 30

Age at award: 36

Date of award: 01 February 1993

Tribunal: Carlisle High Court

Amount of award then: £50,000

Award at February 2001: £69,434

Description of injuries: Legs crushed by industrial locomotive – compound fracture of right tibia and fibula – compound fracture of left tibia and fibula – fracture of left and right medial tibial condyle – cross union between tibia and united fibula – gross deformity of articular surfaces – division of musculo-cutaneous nerve left calf – in-patient 6 months, returned home in wheelchair – walking range limited to 200 yards; stairs difficult; severe residual pain – symptoms of clinical depression.

Prognosis: Due to osteoarthritis, claimant likely to need wheelchair at some stage between June 1994 and June 1996 – special accommodation likely to be needed – total knee replacement necessary, ideally in 10 years time, but claimant unlikely to be able to take advantage of such an operation due to physical and mental incapacitation.

Other points: Claimant would have been likely to retire at 62 in any event, as had been epileptic since age of 7.

1.6.1.1.C4 Case No. 11672

Name of case: Hawkes v Garside

Brief description of injuries: LEG – SEVERE INJURY – OSTEOMYELITIS

Reported: Kemp & Kemp, I2-302; [1998] CLY 1674

JSB Category: 6(K)(b)(ii)

Sex: Female

Age at injury: 61

Age at award: 67

Date of award: 06 November 1997

Tribunal: QBD

Amount of award then: £35,000

Award at February 2001: £40,138

Description of injuries: Petrochanteric fracture to the upper left femur – midshaft fracture of the left femur – lacerations to the right leg – abscess developed at the site which required an emergency operation – chronic osteomyelitis was diagnosed in June 1994 – wound remained liable to infection – often purulent fluid was emitted.

Prognosis: Severely disabled – claimant wheelchair bound for most of the time.

1.6.1.1.C5 Case No. 10636

Name of case: Frost v Palmer

Brief description of injuries: LEG – SEVERE INJURIES – DEPRESSION

Reported: [1992] PIQR P14, [1993] PIQR Q14; Kemp & Kemp, I2-206, I2-605; BPILS, 191.1; [1993] CLY 1531

JSB Category: 6(K)(b); 3(A)(d)

Sex: Male

Age at injury: 31

Age at award: 39

Date of award: 15 October 1992

Tribunal: Court of Appeal

Amount of award then: £28,000

Award at February 2001: £36,367

Description of injuries: Road traffic accident – severe injuries to lower left leg and knee, including multiple fractures of left tibia and fibula – 10 operations required – leg saved, but greatly disfigured – shortening – restriction of movement – unstable knee – period of reactive depression – pain and discomfort still evident at date of trial – some tolerance for weight-bearing activities.

Prognosis: Future osteoarthritic changes virtually certain.

Other points: Award reduced on appeal from £37,000.

1.6.1.1.C6 Case No. 10539

Name of case: Cummings v W Lucy & Co

Brief description of injuries: LEG INJURY (SEVERE) – MULTIPLE INJURIES – POST-TRAUMATIC STRESS DISORDER

Reported: Kemp & Kemp, B2-075; [1993] CLY 1431

JSB Category: 6(K)(b), 6(B), 6(C); 3(B); 8

Sex: Male

Age at injury: 27

Age at award: 33

Date of award: 19 October 1993

Tribunal: QBD

Amount of award then: £21,500

Award at February 2001: £27,043

Description of injuries: Vehicle overturned into stream after collision – claimant trapped by legs and lower abdomen, head held above water by colleagues for 40 minutes – closed fracture of right tibia requiring fibulotomy and intra medullary nail – comminuted fracture of sacrum – fracture to right pubic ramus resulting in scarring, indentation and numbness in left thigh – hesitancy of micturition – post-traumatic stress disorder – returned to work in more sedentary job.

Prognosis: Assessed 15 per cent disabled for life – permanent low back pain.

Other points: Award of £21,500 included £1,500 separate award for PTSD.

1.6.1.1.C7 Case No. 11846

Name of case: Watson v Gray

Brief description of injuries: LEG INJURY – PROFESSIONAL FOOTBALLER – DEPRESSION

Reported: Kemp & Kemp, I2-034; [1999] CLY 1510

JSB Category: 6(K)(b)(iv) (see "Other points"); 3(A)(d)

Sex: Male

Age at injury: 25

Age at award: 28

Date of award: 07 May 1999

Tribunal: QBD

Amount of award then: £25,000

Award at February 2001: £26,920

Description of injuries: Claimant, First Division professional footballer, injured during course of match – comminuted transverse fracture of tibia and fibula – fracture surgically repaired with plate and screws on same day, and butterfly wedge of bone discarded – in hospital 5 days – physiotherapy beginning thereafter – partial weight-bearing after 4 months; metalwork removed from leg after 6 months – development of hernia on lateral aspect of fibula, requiring operation and disrupting rehabilitation – anger and depression for several months, for which claimant received counselling – good functional recovery – small (6mm) discrepancy in leg lengths – despite fears that his football career would be ended, claimant available for selection 18 months after incident – however, remaining muscle scarring in right leg increased tendency of foot to pronate – experts in agreement that speed and sharpness essential at this high level of sport now missing – claimant also lacked confidence when tackling and being tackled, and unable to perform to his previous levels – judge found that claimant's football career had been blighted and that he had been deprived of a chance to play the sport at the highest level.

Prognosis: Claimant likely to end football career in lower professional leagues at greatly reduced income, and premature retirement likely – no increased risk of premature arthritis.

Other points: Injury fell within the description in category 6(K)(b)(iv) of the JSB Guidelines, but general damages figure reflected the enhanced loss of amenity to a professional footballer of such an injury, together with loss of congenial employment as a result of likely early retirement.

1.6.1.1.C8 Case No. 11085

Award at February 2001: £25,640

See: 1.2.3.4.C6 for details

1.6.1.1.C9 Case No. 11818

Award at February 2001: £24,086

See: 1.3.1.3.1.C7 for details

1.6.1.1.C10 Case No. 11500

Award at February 2001: £16,076

See: 1.2.3.1.C19 for details

1.6.1.1.C11 Case No. 10153

Award at February 2001: £14,254

See: 1.5.5.C13 for details

1.6.1.1.C12 Case No. 10154

Name of case: Re French

Brief description of injuries: SHOT IN BOTH THIGHS – OFF WORK FOR 8 MONTHS

Reported: Kemp & Kemp, C4-072; [1991] CLY 1351

JSB Category: 6(K)(c)

Sex: Male

Age at injury: –

Age at award: 41

Date of award: 04 February 1991

Tribunal: CICB

Amount of award then: £10,000

Award at February 2001: £13,230

Description of injuries: Assault – shot in both thighs by single bullet – permanent scarring and loss of tissue at entry and exit wounds – psychological damage – become very depressed and anxious – absent from work eight months – in hospital two weeks – continues to suffer stiffness and aching in both thighs – can no longer cycle or play tennis – avoids crowds – receives counselling – continuing fear of meeting public.

1.6.1.1.C13 Case No. 11498

Award at February 2001: £12,767

See: 1.2.3.2.1.C12 for details

1.6.1.1.C14 Case No. 10449

Award at February 2001: £12,372

See: 1.4.3.C19 for details

1.6.1.1.C15 Case No. 10844

Name of case: Fay v Hawes

Brief description of injuries: LEG – SCARS – ECZEMA

Reported: Kemp & Kemp, J2-015; [1994] CLY 1693

JSB Category: 8

Sex: Female

Age at injury: 79

Age at award: 81

Date of award: 01 August 1994

Tribunal: Norwich County Court

Amount of award then: £10,000

Award at February 2001: £11,933

Description of injuries: Claimant struck on right calf by storage heater falling from wall – 2-hour operation to debride wound and make split skin graft from substantial donor site on thigh of same leg – claimant recollected 3 painful injections and removal of skin from leg before anaesthetic took effect – full thickness loss of skin at wound site of 15 x 5cm, covering part of Achilles tendon – 5 days in hospital – 16 very painful dressing changes – 6 visits to out-patients and 11 visits from GP thereafter – graft twice broke down through infection – development of eczema, caused by antibiotics, still evident at date of trial – claimant forced to sleep downstairs on sofa and required daughter's help for everyday tasks – scar unpleasant, but not noticeable under support tights; claimant not unduly concerned – skin over scar sensitive; only washable by dripping water over it – claimant concerned about striking it when shopping – twice daily cream applications required to render skin sufficiently supple to allow mobility – tendency of skin to tether to underlying tendon, making plantar flexion of ankle difficult – stair climbing consequently affected – prevention or restriction in upkeep of garden, previously tended unaided – walking range restricted from 3 miles to 1.5 miles – only light housework possible.

1.6.1.1.C16 Case No. 10026

Award at February 2001: £11,602

See: 1.2.3.6.2.1.C11 for details

1.6.1.1.C17 Case No. 11850

Name of case: E (a minor) v Greaves

Brief description of injuries: LEG – SCARS – PSYCHOLOGICAL REACTION

Reported: Kemp & Kemp, I2-516/1; [1999] CLY 1514

JSB Category: 6(K)(c); 3(A)(d); 8

Sex: Male

Age at injury: 5 years 10 months

Age at award: 7 years 10 months

Date of award: 16 June 1998

Tribunal: Pontefract County Court

Amount of award then: £10,000

Award at February 2001: £10,534

Description of injuries: Fracture to upper tibia and fibula of left leg – friction burns, with some degloving to lower left leg and some exposed bone at ankle; grazes to elbow and right knee – fracture reduced under anaesthetic – leg in plaster for 1 month, subsequently in lightweight case for a further 6 weeks – skin graft required for burns – scarring to left leg measured at 23 cm x 8 cm where skin grafted and 14cm x 9cm at donor site on right thigh; slightly rough, but not particularly discoloured – some psychological disturbance; claimant became quiet and withdrawn; nightmares; initial nervousness about roads; wanting to stay in bed – claimant not conscious of scarring.

Prognosis: No ongoing typical problems psychologically; claimant expected to recover without the need for counselling.

1.6.1.1.C18 Case No. 11862

Name of case: D (a minor) v White

Brief description of injuries: LEG – SCARS – PSYCHIATRIC DAMAGE

Reported: Kemp & Kemp, J2-018; [1999] CLY 1526

JSB Category: 8; 3(A)

Sex: Female

Age at injury: 6

Age at award: 9

Date of award: 27 April 1999

Tribunal: Sunderland County Court (infant settlement approval hearing)

Amount of award then: £10,000

Award at February 2001: £10,417

Description of injuries: Multiple dog bite injuries to left lower leg, leaving 15 puncture wounds – X-rays revealed several tiny flakes of bone elevated from anterior surface of tibia, necessitating surgery under general anaesthetic – claimant left with 4 small round scars measuring 0.5-0.75cm in diameter and circular area of scarring 1.5cm in diameter on medial side of mid – calf – 2 small rounded scars on lateral side of upper part of calf – oval scar measuring 1.5 x 1cm on lateral aspect of knee – oval scar measuring 2 x 1cm on proximal part of lateral aspect of lower leg – 2.5 x 1cm scar situated vertically on proximal part of lateral aspect of lower leg, with another scar 1 x 0.5cm just posterior to it – 3 small scars close together on lateral aspect of lower leg – no skin sensation impairment or neurological damage – nightmares for first 6 months after attack – anxiety whenever seeing a dog; helped by claimant's family getting their own dog.

Prognosis: Psychiatric evidence anticipated that claimant would become more self-conscious about scarring as she got older – plastic surgery in the future would improve, but not completely remove, the appearance of the scarring

1.6.1.1.C19 Case No. 11851

Name of case: D (a minor) v Martin

Brief description of injuries: LEG – SCAR – POST-TRAUMATIC STRESS DISORDER

Reported: Kemp & Kemp, I2-521/1; [1999] CLY 1515

JSB Category: 6(K)(c)

Sex: Female

Age at injury: 6

Age at award: 9

Date of award: 19 July 1999

Tribunal: Swindon County Court (infant settlement approval hearing)

Amount of award then: £8,000

Award at February 2001: £8,334

Description of injuries: Claimant struck by car – closed fracture to left tibia and fibula – 3 days in hospital; fracture manipulated under general anaesthetic and full – leg cast fitted – after 10 weeks, cast removed and replaced with knee – to – toe cast, worn for 10 weeks – some concern over slight in – toeing when walking and slight shortening of leg, but both matters resolved naturally as claimant continued to grow – faint 7cm scar on left tibial crest – regular bad dreams over 2-year period, flashbacks and increased aggression; mild post-traumatic stress disorder diagnosed – short course of therapy at hospital prescribed, and dreams had virtually completely resolved within 3 years of the accident.

1.6.1.1.C20 Case No. 11825

Award at February 2001: £7,880

See: 1.3.1.3.1.C19 for details

1.6.1.1.C21 Case No. 10658

Award at February 2001: £7,408

See: 1.4.4.1.C11 for details

1.6.1.1.C22 Case No. 11134

Name of case: Barnes v Lunt and Motor Insurers Bureau

Brief description of injuries: NECK – WHIPLASH – LEG

Reported: Kemp & Kemp, E2-081; [1996] CLY 2225

JSB Category: 6(A)(b)(ii)

Sex: Female

Age at injury: 25

Age at award: 28

Date of award: 31 May 1996

Tribunal: Ammanford County Court

Amount of award then: £4,750

Award at February 2001: £5,343

Description of injuries: Acute soft-tissue whiplash injury – leg pain.

Prognosis: Full recovery expected in three to three-and-a-half-years.

1.6.1.1.C23 Case No. 11209

Award at February 2001: £5,340

See: 1.3.1.1.C37 for details

1.6.1.1.C24 Case No. 10105

Award at February 2001: £5,087

See: 1.5.C3 for details

1.6.1.1.C25 Case No. 10477

Name of case: Watkinson v British Railways Board

Brief description of injuries: MINOR INJURIES – CRUSH INJURY TO LEG – MILD PTSD

Reported: [1992] CLY 1733

JSB Category:

Sex: Male

Age at injury: 49

Age at award: 52

Date of award: 19 August 1992

Tribunal: Nottingham County Court

Amount of award then: £3,800

Award at February 2001: £4,706

Description of injuries: Localised crush injury and mild post-traumatic stress disorder – absent from work for two weeks – difficulties in using the leg for ten weeks after the accident – effects of the accident and associated stress disrupted his way of life away from work – disturbed sleeping pattern – bouts of anxiety.

Prognosis: The prognosis was good.

1.6.1.1.C26 Case No. 11316

Name of case: Collett (a minor) v Barlow

Brief description of injuries: THIGH – WOUND – POST-TRAUMATIC STRESS DISORDER

Reported: Kemp & Kemp, C4-108; [1997] CLY 1864

JSB Category: 3(B)(c)

Sex: Male

Age at injury: 8

Age at award: 10

Date of award: 10 April 1997

Tribunal: Redditch County Court

Amount of award then: £4,250

Award at February 2001: £4,677

Description of injuries: Attack by a dog – large gaping wound to his thigh – three superficial wounds – post-traumatic stress disorder.

Prognosis: With a course of psychotherapy he would fully regain his previous level of psychological functioning.

1.6.1.1.C27 Case No. 10826

Award at February 2001: £4,584

See: 1.2.3.1.C29 for details

1.6.1.1.C28 Case No. 11229

Name of case: Johnson v Baker

Brief description of injuries: FOOT – LIGAMENT STRAIN – GROIN

Reported: Kemp & Kemp, I3-035/1; [1996] CLY 2321

JSB Category: 6(O)(g)

Sex: Male

Age at injury: 29

Age at award: 30

Date of award: 30 September 1996

Tribunal: Birmingham County Court

Amount of award then: £2,250

Award at February 2001: £2,516

Description of injuries: Severe bruising and ligament strain to the foot – groin strain.

Prognosis: Medical evidence suggested that symptoms would subside after five months.

1.6.1.1.C29 Case No. 10667

Award at February 2001: £2,440

See: 1.2.3.1.C36 for details

1.6.1.1.C30 Case No. 10494

Award at February 2001: £1,917

See: 1.3.1.3.1.C36 for details

1.6.1.1.C31 Case No. 10890

Award at February 2001: £888

See: 1.4.4.1.C17 for details

1.6.1.1.C32 Case No. 10893

Award at February 2001: £597

See: 1.2.3.2.1.C34 for details

1.6.1.2 LEG FRACTURE

1.6.1.2.C1 Case No. 10989

Name of case: Davis v Cork

Brief description of injuries: LEG – TRAUMATIC AMPUTATION THROUGH LOWER LEG

Reported: [1995] CLY 1740

JSB Category: 6(K)(a)(iv)

Sex: Male

Age at injury: 39

Age at award: 45

Date of award: 18 November 1994

Tribunal: Not stated

Amount of award then: £45,000

Award at February 2001: £58,616

Description of injuries: Plaintiff struck by motorcycle which was being pursued by police – suffered traumatic amputation of distal half of left leg – conscious throughout and in severe pain – under epidural anaesthetic he underwent wound debridement – four days later tibia was refashioned leaving four-and-a-half inches to allow for closure of skin and application of prosthesis – remained in hospital for four weeks – surgical stocking was fitted in order to shrink stump – with shrinkage there were six successive replacements of prosthesis – plaintiff was left with tenderness of stump, 15° of fixed flexion deformity of knee, pain across back of leg, thigh and hip joint, phantom symptoms, disfigurement and pain in right knee as result of favouring the left leg – it was likely that pain in both knees would worsen – before accident, plaintiff was very fit and active man who enjoyed cycling, walking, cricket and dancing and was keen on DIY – after accident could only enjoy pre-accident hobbies and carry out DIY at low level – social life was also greatly inhibited.

1.6.1.2.C2 Case No. 11433

Name of case: Harris v Harris

Brief description of injuries: LEG – AMPUTATION

Reported: Kemp & Kemp, I2-205; [1997] CLY 1982

JSB Category: 6(K)(a)(iv)

Sex: Male

Age at injury: 3

Age at award: 9

Date of award: 12 July 1996

Tribunal: QBD

Amount of award then: £42,000

Award at February 2001: £51,510

Description of injuries: Amputation below the knee after unsatisfactory healing.

Prognosis: NHS prosthesis was unsatisfactory – fitted with the American "flex-foot" prosthesis.

Other points: Future prosthesis costs calculated on a multiplier of 28.

1.6.1.2.C3 Case No. 11005

Name of case: Davey v MJF Precision Welding

Brief description of injuries: LEG – MULTIPLE FRACTURES – SIGNIFICANT RESIDUAL DISABILITY

Reported: Kemp & Kemp, I2-403; [1995] CLY 1757

JSB Category: 6(K)(b)(ii)

Sex: Male

Age at injury: 49

Age at award: 55

Date of award: 06 February 1995

Tribunal: Portsmouth County Court

Amount of award then: £35,000

Award at February 2001: £43,920

Description of injuries: Plaintiff employed as fabricated welder by defendant – plaintiff suffered serious leg injuries following a fall from wall where he was undertaking welding operation – plaintiff suffered comminuted fracture of lower shaft of left femur involving left knee joint, fracture of left patella and bi-malleolar fracture of right ankle – fracture of femur was pinned and put in traction – initial treatment comprised manipulating it under anaesthetic and supporting it with plaster back slab – right ankle was subsequently internally fixed – after two weeks plaintiff had good range of movement in ankle and with help from machine was able to bend his left knee passively – movement was beginning to return there – a month after accident cast brace was applied to left leg to allow plaintiff to mobilise – he was discharged from hospital on 5 January 1990, some seven-and-a-half weeks after accident – plaster cast was removed from left leg after about four months – plaintiff continued to have major problems with right ankle and left knee – right ankle was painful at time of trial – metal plates had been removed from ankle but with little reduction in pain – ankle felt stiff and was swollen – left knee had remained static for three years preceding trial – was in continuous pain but especially felt it when standing or walking, could only stand for short periods – could not kneel or climb steps and was unable to do home decorating – could not ride bicycle and could only drive short distances – had to keep knee elevated for most of time and if he sat with it bent for any period pain became worse – could not play golf or judo and walking was restricted for which he used stick – fracture of left femur had united with reasonable alignment – left knee would require replacement by artificial knee joint within five to ten years – there were already degenerative changes in left knee – had permanent loss of movement at right ankle joint – slight risk of osteo-arthritis developing in ankle joint – was substantially disabled as both legs were affected.

1.6.1.2.C4 Case No. 10094

Name of case: Norton v Rentokil

Brief description of injuries: FEMUR – FRACTURE – BOWING

Reported: [1990] CLY 1661

JSB Category: 6(K)

Sex: Male

Age at injury: 19

Age at award: 23

Date of award: 30 June 1989

Tribunal: QBD

Amount of award then: £22,500

Award at February 2001: £35,359

Description of injuries: Fracture of mid-shaft of left femur – fracture healed with one inch shortening to leg – fifteen degrees of medial rotation and obvious bowing – pain in leg – pain in lower back resolved by using shoe raise – crepitus behind kneecap.

Prognosis: Slight risk of patellectomy in future – risk of osteoarthritis in knee and ankle.

1.6.1.2.C5 Case No. 11006

Name of case: Re Whiteside

Brief description of injuries: LEG – FRACTURED TIBIA AND FIBULA – PERMANENT DISABILITY

Reported: [1995] CLY 1758

JSB Category: 6(K)(b)(ii)

Sex: Male

Age at injury: 32

Age at award: 34

Date of award: 06 December 1994

Tribunal: CICB, Durham

Amount of award then: £28,000

Award at February 2001: £34,737

Description of injuries: Plaintiff was victim of unprovoked attack – suffered break to left tibia and fibula above ankle – good surgical results were achieved with intra-medullary nail and two screws – injury to ulnar nerve during operation to insert the nail and screws had largely resolved by date of hearing – it was anticipated that further operation would probably be necessary to remove the screws – plaintiff also suffered mild post-traumatic stress syndrome – absent from work for 12 weeks and could bear weight on leg after three weeks – no muscle wasting – surgical scarring on upper calf and anterior aspect of ankle – no risk of arthritis – left with permanent discomfort in knee with "clicking" and strain on ankle which had set 10° in valgus, interfering with plaintiff's ability to carry out his work as self-employed window blind fitter – plaintiff's hopes of becoming showjumper were dashed.

1.6.1.2.C6 Case No. 10235

Name of case: Sharkey v Cassar

Brief description of injuries: COMMINUTED DISPLACED FRACTURE OF FEMUR – LIMITATION OF MOVEMENT – SCARRING

Reported: [1991] CLY 1432

JSB Category: 6(K)(b)(ii)

Sex: Female

Age at injury: –

Age at award: 45

Date of award: 05 November 1990

Tribunal: CA

Amount of award then: £22,500

Award at February 2001: £31,126

Description of injuries: Comminuted fracture of the right femur with gross displacement of fragments – initially secured by screws, subsequently reinforced with two Gallenaugh plates – loss of several front teeth – abrasions and minor lacerations.

Prognosis: Permanent shortening of the leg by a quarter inch – limited flexion of the knee – permanent modest limitation of right foot and ankle movement and use of a stick or crutch to aid walking – grossly disfiguring 12 inch scar to the outside of the leg – osteoarthritis of the knee cap would require surgery in 15 to 20 years.

Other points: Award increased at appeal from £18,000.

1.6.1.2.C7 Case No. 10445

Name of case: Grime v Manchester Airport

Brief description of injuries: TIBIA FRACTURE-OSTEOARTHRITIS

Reported: [1992] CLY 1701

JSB Category: 6(K)(b)(iii)

Sex: Female

Age at injury: 49

Age at award: 52

Date of award: 18 November 1992

Tribunal: QBD

Amount of award then: £23,000

Award at February 2001: £29,513

Description of injuries: Depressed fracture of the lateral tibial plateau of the right leg – fracture reunited leaving a one cm depression in the articular surface of the plateau.

Prognosis: Expected the injury would cause osteoarthritis within ten years of the date of the accident.

1.6.1.2.C8 Case No. 11430

Name of case: Sampson v Georgiou

Brief description of injuries: LEG – FRACTURE – 3 – 4 INCH SHORTENING

Reported: Kemp & Kemp, I2-303; [1997] CLY 1979

JSB Category: 6(K)(b)(ii)

Sex: Male

Age at injury: 28

Age at award: 34

Date of award: 22 April 1997

Tribunal:

Amount of award then: £25,000

Award at February 2001: £28,620

Description of injuries: Comminuted fracture of the tibia and fibula – laceration to the leg – fracture did not unite – bone graft.

Prognosis: Three to four inch shortening to the leg – slightly limited foot movement.

Other points: Plaintiff was not psychologically well equipped to deal with the injuries

1.6.1.2.C9 Case No. 10454

Name of case: Donald v Vince

Brief description of injuries: TIBIA FRACTURE – CONTINUING SIGNIFICANT DISABILITY

Reported: [1992] CLY 1710

JSB Category: 6(K)

Sex: Female

Age at injury: 23

Age at award: 28

Date of award: 29 April 1992

Tribunal: Slough County Court

Amount of award then: £21,000

Award at February 2001: £26,982

Description of injuries: Fracture to the lateral tibial plateau of the left leg – in traction for one month – non-weight bearing for two months – physiotherapy for about six months – there had been no significant improvement since then – unable to walk further than half a mile or stand for more than ten minutes without suffering pain – unable to lift heavy items – could only drive a car with automatic transmission – occasionally the knee gave way and had to be manipulated – some valgus deformity of the knee and wasting of the left quadriceps – there were degenerative changes present at the time of the hearing.

Prognosis: Further operative treatment was likely to be required in about ten years time.

1.6.1.2.C10 Case No. 10990

Name of case: Mather v British Gas and Biggs and Wall & Co

Brief description of injuries: LEG – FRACTURE OF TIBIA AND FIBULA – LEG SHORTENED BY 2CM

Reported: Kemp & Kemp, I2-307; [1995] CLY 1742

JSB Category: 6(K)(b)(ii)

Sex: Male

Age at injury: 41

Age at award: 46

Date of award: 28 June 1994

Tribunal: Southend County Court

Amount of award then: £20,000

Award at February 2001: £24,525

Description of injuries: Plaintiff fell into trench in course of his work – suffered serious injury to right leg, with fractures to tibia and fibula – set by external fixator, the track of which became infected – when fractures finally united, leg was 2cm shorter than other, and plaintiff had to wear built-up shoe – plaintiff, a workshop manager for local district council, was absent from work for more than 18 months following accident.

1.6.1.2.C11 Case No. 10821

Name of case: Mather v British Gas and Biggs and Wall & Co

Brief description of injuries: LEG – SERIOUS FRACTURE

Reported: Kemp & Kemp, I2-307; [1994] CLY 1670

JSB Category: 6(K)(b)

Sex: Male

Age at injury: 41

Age at award: 46

Date of award: 28 June 1994

Tribunal: Southend County Court

Amount of award then: £20,000

Award at February 2001: £24,525

Description of injuries: Fall into trench – serious injury to right leg; fractures to tibia and fibula – fractures set by external fixator, track of which became infected – when fractures finally united, leg was 2 cm shorter than the left – built-up shoe required – off work 18 months – very successful alternative employment (as Day Care organiser for elderly) found – claimant suffering some continuing disability; found to be partly due to an earlier injury.

1.6.1.2.C12 Case No. 11184

Name of case: Breese v Darnton
Brief description of injuries: LEG – MULTIPLE FRACTURES
Reported: Kemp & Kemp, I2-308; [1996] CLY 2275
JSB Category: 6(K)(b)(iii)
Sex: Male
Age at injury: 16
Age at award: 19
Date of award: 26 January 1996
Tribunal: Southampton County Court
Amount of award then: £20,000
Award at February 2001: £23,580
Description of injuries: Compound fracture of the femur – compound fracture of the tibia – stress fracture of the lower end of the fibula.
Prognosis: Continuing symptoms would be permanent – they amounted to only a minor nuisance.

1.6.1.2.C13 Case No. 10236

Name of case: Collins v Adwinkle
Brief description of injuries: COMMINUTED FRACTURES TO THE TIBIA AND FIBULA – LEG SHORTENED – WALKING LIMITED
Reported: Kemp & Kemp, I2-309, I2-604; [1991] CLY 1433
JSB Category: 6(K)(b)(iv)
Sex: Male
Age at injury: 62
Age at award: –
Date of award: 18 October 1991
Tribunal: Nottingham County Court
Amount of award then: £17,500
Award at February 2001: £22,906
Description of injuries: Comminuted fractures to the right lower tibia and fibula – required seven operations under general anaesthetic over two-and-a-half years.
Prognosis: Right leg shortened by 1.5cm to 2cms – unable to walk more than two miles – permanent slight limp.

1.6.1.2.C14 Case No. 11661

Name of case: Reynolds v TNT (UK) Ltd
Brief description of injuries: LEG – FRACTURE
Reported: Kemp & Kemp, i2-310; [1998] CLY 1663
JSB Category: 6(K)(b)(iii)
Sex: Male
Age at injury: 81
Age at award: 83
Date of award: 08 July 1998
Tribunal: Dudley County Court
Amount of award then: £18,500
Award at February 2001: £19,945
Description of injuries: Comminuted fracture to the lower right tibia and fibula in 3 places – 2cm shortening of the right leg – varus deformity of the tibia by 15 degrees – 30 degree loss of flexion in the ankle – 6 punctate scars from the pins – walking range reduced to 200 yards   required the use of a stick – too nervous to drive as a result of the accident.

1.6.1.2.C15 Case No. 10637

Name of case: Coughlin v Montpellier Plant Hire
Brief description of injuries: LEG – FRACTURES
Reported: Kemp & Kemp, I2-502; [1993] CLY 1532
JSB Category: 6(K)(b)(iii); 8
Sex: Male
Age at injury: 28
Age at award: 32
Date of award: 04 December 1992
Tribunal: Harrogate County Court
Amount of award then: £15,000
Award at February 2001: £18,894
Description of injuries: Motorcycle accident – grossly comminuted compound fractures of right tibia and fibula – detained in hospital 3 weeks – fixator and screws applied – accidental re-fracture, requiring new screws and skin graft – no union after 6 months – insertion of intramedullary nail required – union developed – 2 subsequent operations to remove screws – substantial scarring of leg, referred to by judge as "verging on the horrific" – claimant resumed work 18 months after accident.
Prognosis: Right leg permanently rotated to substantial extent – possible late onset of osteoarthritis 10 years after accident.

1.6.1.2.C16 Case No. 10992

Name of case: Re Begum

Brief description of injuries: LEG – FRACTURE OF TIBIA – 1CM OF SHORTENING, AND BOWING OF LEG – DEPRESSION – POST-TRAUMATIC STRESS DISORDER

Reported: Kemp & Kemp, I2-505; [1995] CLY 1744

JSB Category: 6(K)(b)(iv)

Sex: Female

Age at injury: 26

Age at award: 30

Date of award: 28 February 1995

Tribunal: CICB, Birmingham

Amount of award then: £15,000

Award at February 2001: £17,864

Description of injuries: Plaintiff subjected to violent assault by her brother-in-law who beat her about her lower legs with iron bar – at time of assault she was five-and-a-half months pregnant – sustained an open fracture of her left tibia together with cuts to both legs and bruising – in hospital her wounds were debrided and fracture manipulated under general anaesthetic – in hospital for three weeks – leg was put in plaster for seven months – caused her some difficulties during childbirth – until some four months after plaster was removed she was dependant upon husband and he had to wash and bathe her, whilst caring for their young children and carrying out all household tasks – fracture healed well but there was a 1cm shortening of leg and a remaining 15° bow to the leg – now walked with limp which in turn placed stress upon abdomen and caused further pain – continued to suffer intermittent pain at fracture site and was only able to walk short distances with aid of walking stick – required assistance with shopping and heavier household chores – fracture site was more painful in cold weather and she generally felt the cold more in that leg – as result of attack and her injuries, she suffered from depression and was diagnosed as suffering from post-traumatic stress disorder – fearful of leaving house and suffered from disturbed sleep, for which she took medication.

1.6.1.2.C17 Case No. 11431

Name of case: Purkis v Rehman

Brief description of injuries: LEG – FRACTURE – ANKLE

Reported: Kemp & Kemp, I3-016/1; [1997] CLY 1980

JSB Category: 6(K)(b)(iv)

Sex: Male

Age at injury: 40

Age at award: 43

Date of award: 25 September 1997

Tribunal: Hull County Court

Amount of award then: £16,000

Award at February 2001: £17,560

Description of injuries: Fractures to the tibia and fibula – involving the articular surface of the ankle joint – degenerative changes in the joint.

Prognosis: Significant restrictions in ankle movement – osteoarthritic changes expected to continue – unlikely to be able to continue his work until age 65.

Other points: Unpredictable rate of deterioration.

1.6.1.2.C18 Case No. 10991

Name of case: Hicks v Munley

Brief description of injuries: LEG – FRACTURES OF FIBULA AND ANKLE – RESIDUAL ACHING AND STIFFNESS – SCARS

Reported: Kemp & Kemp, I2-505/1; [1995] CLY 1743

JSB Category: 6(K)(b)(iv)

Sex: Male

Age at injury: 19

Age at award: 21

Date of award: 24 October 1995

Tribunal: Birkenhead County Court

Amount of award then: £15,000

Award at February 2001: £17,503

Description of injuries: Plaintiff's motorcycle was in collision with motorvehicle – plaintiff sustained fracture to right fibula; a fracture dislocation to right ankle; deep lacerations to outer aspect of right thigh; and abrasions to left knee – admitted to hospital from accident scene where he had surgery to his right ankle with internal fixation of lateral malleolar – thigh wound was debrided and initially left open, though later was closed in secondary procedure – detained in hospital for 10 days and leg was put in plaster – removed after 10 weeks – plaintiff was on crutches for that period- metalwork in right leg was removed in 1994 – by May 1995 full function had returned to left leg – residual scarring to left thigh, ankle and shin – right leg still ached occasionally, particularly if he stood for long periods – there was some slight residual stiffness in right ankle but he had returned to full-time employment – scarring to the right thigh was permanent but no later complications to the ankle were anticipated.

1.6.1.2.C19 Case No. 11012

Name of case: Re Morrell

Brief description of injuries: LEGS – 15% BURNS – SCARS

Reported: Kemp & Kemp, J3-019; [1995] CLY 1764

JSB Category: 6(K)(b)(iv)

Sex: Male

Age at injury: 10

Age at award: 16

Date of award: 28 September 1995

Tribunal: CICB, Liverpool

Amount of award then: £15,000

Award at February 2001: £17,407

Description of injuries: Plaintiff suffered extensive circumferential burns to both legs following incident when aerosol can was thrown towards him and exploded on contact, causing his trousers to catch fire – circumferential burns to both legs extended to approximately 15 per cent of body surface from just above knee to ankle, although burns did not extend completely around left leg – two operations were performed, one where burns were desloughed and second operation with skin grafts being taken from both thighs – applicant made good functional recovery although, at date of hearing, continued to experience some discomfort in cold weather and skin was susceptible to breakdown if knocked – applicant was left with extensive obvious scarring to both legs of which he was very self-conscious – would not wear shorts or go swimming.

1.6.1.2.C20 Case No. 10447

Name of case: Jones v Hicklin

Brief description of injuries: SERIOUS TIBIA AND FIBULA FRACTURE

Reported: [1992] CLY 1703

JSB Category: 6(K)(c)(i)

Sex: Male

Age at injury: 61

Age at award: –

Date of award: 01 November 1991

Tribunal: Liverpool County Court

Amount of award then: £12,000

Award at February 2001: £15,399

Description of injuries: Serious fracture of the tibia and fibula – fracture manipulated under anaesthetic – bone graft performed – complications occurred – in plaster for nine months

Prognosis: Acceleration of pre-existing arthritis to the knee – used a walking stick all the time.

1.6.1.2.C21 Case No. 11007

Name of case: Blackwood v G D Bowes & Sons

Brief description of injuries: ANKLE – FRACTURE – LIMITATION OF MOVEMENT

Reported: 1995] CLY 1759

JSB Category: 6(M)(c)

Sex: Male

Age at injury: 18

Age at award: 21

Date of award: 09 December 1994

Tribunal: Norwich County Court

Amount of award then: £12,000

Award at February 2001: £14,267

Description of injuries: Plaintiff injured by a fork lift truck – sustained fracture of neck of left talus, involving ankle and sub-taloid joints, which were surgically repaired – was still working for defendant at date of trial as trainee plumber – experienced continuing pain at date of trial, especially after heavy exertion and in cold damp weather – was no longer able to pursue his pre-accident sporting activities of athletics (at which he had been an area 800m champion) and badminton.

Prognosis: Inversion/eversion of left foot was very restricted and there was 24 per cent risk of subtaloid arthritis in 15 years' time, possibly necessitating arthrodesis.

1.6.1.2.C22 Case No. 11159

Name of case: Pomfret v County Palatine Housing Society Ltd

Brief description of injuries: LEG – FRACTURE – HIP

Reported: [1996] CLY 2250

JSB Category: 6(K)(c)(ii) and 6(C)(d)

Sex: Male

Age at injury: 51

Age at award: 55

Date of award: 23 February 1996

Tribunal: Bury County Court

Amount of award then: £12,000

Award at February 2001: £13,789

Description of injuries: Trochanteric fracture of the left femur – lack of 10 degrees of flexion in the hip joint – minor terminal restriction on rotation.

Prognosis: Good recovery was made – no likelihood of deterioration – would be able to continue working until retirement age.

1.6.1.2.C23 Case No. 11662

Name of case: Jones v Swansea City Council

Brief description of injuries: LEG – FRACTURE – SCAR – BACK

Reported: Kemp & Kemp, i2-509; [1998] CLY 1664

JSB Category: 6(K)(c)(i), 6(B)(b)(ii); 8

Sex: Female

Age at injury: 56

Age at award: 60

Date of award: 03 March 1998

Tribunal: Swansea County Court

Amount of award then: £12,500

Award at February 2001: £13,469

Description of injuries: Closed fracture to the distal ends of the shafts of the left tibia and fibula – pre-existing low back pain became constant – operation to remove the plate 2.5 years later – ongoing symptoms at the fracture site caused J to limp – constant pain to her back and buttock prevented her from working.

Prognosis: Permanent disfiguring scar.

1.6.1.2.C24 Case No. 10095

Name of case: Re Newton

Brief description of injuries: FEMUR – FRACTURE – RESIDUAL SYMPTOMS

Reported: [1990] CLY 1662

JSB Category: 6(K)

Sex: Male

Age at injury: 18

Age at award: 25

Date of award: 11 September 1989

Tribunal: CICB, Manchester

Amount of award then: £9,000

Award at February 2001: £13,276

Description of injuries: Innocent bystander when fighting broke out in public house – sustained fractured right femur (had broken same bone in same place in road accident six months previously) – slight leg shortening – slight limitation of knee flexion – disadvantage only for very heavy manual work but not for moderate manual work.

1.6.1.2.C25 Case No. 10448

Name of case: Howe v Moore

Brief description of injuries: SERIOUS FRACTURE TO TIBIA AND FIBULA

Reported: Kemp & Kemp, I2-314; [1992] CLY 1704

JSB Category: 6(K)(c)(i)

Sex: Male

Age at injury: 17

Age at award: 20

Date of award: 16 September 1992

Tribunal: Ipswich County Court

Amount of award then: £10,000

Award at February 2001: £12,400

Description of injuries: Comminuted fracture of the right lower leg tibia and fibula – obstructed circulation to the right foot – lacerations and grazes – almost lost the right foot – away from work for five months.

Prognosis: 20 per cent risk of that he would develop aching and stiffness in the ankle – boots with good ankle support might be required.

1.6.1.2.C26 Case No. 10638

Name of case: Payne v Jackson

Brief description of injuries: LEG – FRACTURES

Reported: Kemp & Kemp, I2-511; [1993] CLY 1533

JSB Category: 6(K)(c); 8

Sex: Male

Age at injury: 22

Age at award: 26

Date of award: 20 April 1993

Tribunal: Basingstoke County Court

Amount of award then: £10,000

Award at February 2001: £12,290

Description of injuries: Claimant struck by motorcycle – knocked unconscious – fractures of lower third tibia and fibula – traction pin inserted in left heel – fracture found to be unstable – screws and plate inserted in subsequent operation – off work 5.5 months initially, further 4.5 months in 1991 after removal of screws and plate – 20cm scar on leg, with some absence of sensation at one point, described by judge as "very unpleasant and very noticeable" and a "serious cosmetic blemish" – near full range of movement regained 5 months after accident, sporting activities possible with discomfort – by August 1991 wound healed well and plaintiff walked without limp – by date of trial, some residual aching on damp days and after circuit training – 0.5cm wasting of leg – otherwise excellent muscle tone and orthopaedically excellent functional result achieved.

Prognosis: No risk of osteoarthritis.

1.6.1.2.C27 Case No. 10823

Name of case: Weir v Smith

Brief description of injuries: LEG – FRACTURE – SCAR

Reported: Kemp & Kemp, I2-514; [1994] CLY 1672

JSB Category: 6(K)(c); 8

Sex: Male

Age at injury: 21

Age at award: 24

Date of award: 20 July 1994

Tribunal: Bath County Court

Amount of award then: £9,500

Award at February 2001: £11,347

Description of injuries: Claimant's van struck by car fleeing police pursuit – trapped in van 45 minutes – fracture to lower right femur – also abrasion to right forehead, friction burn to side of neck and small laceration to left knee – fracture internally fixed with dynamic condular screw plate – 2 post-operative blood transfusions required due to anaemia – hinged cast brace fitted to leg – non-weight-bearing crutches provided – knee flexion 140 degrees – off work 5.5 months – second operation carried out 15 months after accident to remove internal fixation – claimant unable to walk for 3 weeks thereafter, off work for further 2 months – 30cm scar on right thigh, running on lateral aspect to just below kneecap, numb but sensitive to touch.

Prognosis: Right leg expected to remain weaker than left by about 15-20 per cent – right knee expected to be weaker than left by 10 per cent – no limp or unusual gait – otherwise recovery substantially complete – returned to work as self-employed market trader, with some lifting and heavy work – possible necessity of changing employment at some future stage.

1.6.1.2.C28 Case No. 11186

Name of case: Stokes v Forestry Commission

Brief description of injuries: LEG – COMPOUND FRACTURES

Reported: Kemp & Kemp, I2-514/1; [1996] CLY 2277

JSB Category: 6(K)(c)(i)

Sex: Female

Age at injury: 33

Age at award: 36

Date of award: 25 June 1996

Tribunal: Swansea County Court

Amount of award then: £10,000

Award at February 2001: £11,269

Description of injuries: Compound fracture of the right tibia and fibula – at the time of the trial mobility was affected – she walked with a stick outside the house – there was surgical scarring.

Prognosis: Further surgery required – intermittent pain was likely to be permanent.

1.6.1.2.C29 Case No. 10450

Name of case: Blanc v Baskerville

Brief description of injuries: TIBIA AND FIBULA – SEVERE FRACTURE WHICH FAILED TO UNITE

Reported: Kemp & Kemp, I2-515; [1992] CLY 1706

JSB Category: 6(K)(c)(i)

Sex: Male

Age at injury: 52

Age at award: 55

Date of award: 23 July 1992

Tribunal: Kingston County Court

Amount of award then: £9,000

Award at February 2001: £11,153

Description of injuries: Severely displaced comminuted fracture of the junction of the middle and lower third of the right tibia and fibula.

Prognosis: The right leg was shortened by half an inch – fibula's failure to unite was permanent – symptoms of discomfort were likely to persist.

1.6.1.2.C30 Case No. 11665

Name of case: Lanera v Regan

Brief description of injuries: LEG – FRACTURED LEFT TIBIA AND FIBULA

Reported: Kemp & Kemp, i2-315; [1998] CLY 1667

JSB Category: 6(K)(c)(i); 8

Sex: Female

Age at injury: 58

Age at award: 63

Date of award: 17 October 1997

Tribunal: Halifax County Court

Amount of award then: £10,000

Award at February 2001: £10,798

Description of injuries: Fractured right tibia and fibula in 2 places – rotational movement of the left foot slightly restricted by a two-thirds range – bruising to the head and shoulder – discolouration to the left leg – claimant required 2 sticks to walk at all times – required more assistance.

Prognosis: L's level of independence was diminished by 25 per cent – disability was permanent.

1.6.1.2.C31 Case No. 11663

Name of case: Peach v Tesco Stores Ltd
Brief description of injuries: LEG – FRACTURED FEMUR – 7 MONTHS
Reported: Kemp & Kemp, i2-316; [1998] CLY 1665
JSB Category: 6(K)(c)(i)
Sex: Female
Age at injury: 65
Age at award: 67
Date of award: 24 July 1998
Tribunal: Oxford County Court
Amount of award then: £10,000
Award at February 2001: £10,560

Description of injuries: Fractured right femur at the tip of a prosthesis fitted 2 years earlier – required a plate, screws and bone graft – within 7 months of the date of the accident P had returned to her pre-injury state – she walked with a limp – there were 2 well healed scars.

1.6.1.2.C32 Case No. 10451

Name of case: Gibson and Hughes v Hodges
Brief description of injuries: TIBIA AND FIBULA – FRACTURE – LEG SHORTENED BY 1.5 CM
Reported: Kemp & Kemp, I2-517, I3-030; ; [1992] CLY 1707
JSB Category: 6(K)(c)(i)
Sex: Male
Age at injury: 66
Age at award: 71
Date of award: 30 January 1992
Tribunal: Chester County Court
Amount of award then: £8,000
Award at February 2001: £10,147

Description of injuries: Closed displaces fractures of the shafts of the left tibia and fibula – graze to the right shoulder and laceration to the scalp.

Prognosis: The leg was shortened by 1.5 cm requiring use of built-up shoes – general alignment good – permanent 10% restriction of upward motion of the left ankle – walking range was curtailed.

1.6.1.2.C33 Case No. 10993

Name of case: Wilson v Busways Travel Services
Brief description of injuries: LEG – DEBRIDING AND SOFT-TISSUE INJURIES – PLASTIC SURGERY
Reported: Kemp & Kemp, I2-518; [1995] CLY 1745
JSB Category: 6(K)(c)
Sex: Female
Age at injury: 10
Age at award: 13

Date of award: 01 March 1995
Tribunal: Newcastle upon Tyne
Amount of award then: £8,250
Award at February 2001: £9,620

Description of injuries: Plaintiff emerged from school and made her way to nearest bus stop in order to take bus home – bus driver failed to notice plaintiff attempting to enter bus and closed doors upon her right leg trapping if from knee to ankle – bus started to pull away and plaintiff was pulled hopping along side of bus – she banged on door to attract driver's attention but bus increased speed – she fell to ground and was dragged along for short distance and her left leg became trapped under wheel of bus – in Newcastle General Hospital it was confirmed that she had received no bony injuries to leg – she did receive avulsion injury of area of skin on distal part of inner aspect of thigh and abrasion of lateral aspect of lower leg – operation was performed upon plaintiff during which non-viable skin and subcutaneous tissue was excised from thigh wound, haematoma was evacuated and superficial damage to vastus medialis muscle was repaired – plaintiff's leg was in plaster back slab for two weeks – thereafter she attended plastic surgery department for dressings and physiotherapy until all areas soundly healed and she was fully mobile again – discharged from further attendance at hospital on 2 March 1992 – in September 1993 further operation of cosmetic nature was undertaken upon scar – at the time approval was given to settlement, plaintiff was left with fairly noticeable blemish – however, she had regained self-confidence, was no longer embarrassed about scar and had recovered.

1.6.1.2.C34 Case No. 10824

Name of case: Wood v British Railways
Brief description of injuries: LEG – RE-FRACTURE
Reported: Kemp & Kemp, I2-519; [1994] CLY 1673
JSB Category: 6(K)(c)
Sex: Male
Age at injury: 34
Age at award: 37
Date of award: 29 October 1993
Tribunal: Mayor's and City County Court, London
Amount of award then: £7,500
Award at February 2001: £9,097

Description of injuries: Slip down concrete steps – re-fracture of shaft of right femur, previously fractured 13 years ago and internally fixed by "Kunscher" nail and metal plate, leaving no abnormal weakness – Kunscher nail bent in accident – operation performed and new nail inserted – no complications – total of 5 weeks off work – nail later removed in further operation – good recovery – no shortening of leg and normal walking ability regained – slight ache in thigh when walking a lot.

Prognosis: Very slight external rotational deformity, of no functional significance and giving rise to no increased risk of osteoarthritis of hip and knee.

1.6.1.2.C35 Case No. 11962

Name of case: Davies v Gravelle Plant Ltd
Brief description of injuries: LEG – FRACTURE
Reported: Kemp & Kemp, I2-521/1; [2000] 1 CL 122
JSB Category: 6((K)(c)(i)
Sex: Male
Age at injury: 18
Age at award: 23
Date of award: 01 July 1999
Tribunal: Swansea County Court
Amount of award then: £8,000
Award at February 2001: £8,334

Description of injuries: The lower left leg became trapped between two metal structures, one a mechanical digger – two undisplaced segmental fractures to the lower left tibia just above the ankle – below knee plaster for eight weeks – within ten weeks of the removal of the plaster there was discomfort and instability of the ankle caused by lateral ligament laxity – trauma to the left tibia aggravated a pre-existing injury.

Prognosis: Corrective surgery would be necessary.

1.6.1.2.C36 Case No. 11188

Name of case: Shenton v Christchurch Ski Centre
Brief description of injuries: LEG – FRACTURE
Reported: [1996] CLY 2279
JSB Category: 6(K)(c)(iii)
Sex: Male
Age at injury: 4
Age at award: 7
Date of award: 01 July 1996
Tribunal: Poole County Court
Amount of award then: £7,000
Award at February 2001: £7,900

Description of injuries: Comminuted fracture of the tibial metaphysis – growth plate of the shin – full recovery at the time of the hearing.

Prognosis: Risk of damage to the growth plate causing angulation to the shin bone in his teenage years which would need surgery – possible risk to his employment prospects if the damage occurred – and osteoarthritis – permission to restore an application for further damages within ten years.

1.6.1.2.C37 Case No. 11187

Name of case: Attwood v Booth
Brief description of injuries: LEG – FRACTURES
Reported: Kemp & Kemp, I2-521/3; [1996] CLY 2278
JSB Category: 6(K)(c)(i)
Sex: Male
Age at injury: 54
Age at award: 58
Date of award: 03 July 1996
Tribunal: Coventry County Court
Amount of award then: £7,000
Award at February 2001: £7,900

Description of injuries: Fracture of the left tibia – transverse fracture of the fibula – pain in the knee was found to be a five-year acceleration of a pre-existing degenerative change – reasonable recovery had been made.

1.6.1.2.C38 Case No. 10639

Name of case: Bell v Quinn
Brief description of injuries: LEG FRACTURES
Reported: Kemp & Kemp, I2-522; [1993] CLY 1534
JSB Category: 6(K)(c)
Sex: Male
Age at injury: 38
Age at award: 42
Date of award: 15 September 1993
Tribunal: Coventry County Court
Amount of award then: £6,500
Award at February 2001: £7,879

Description of injuries: Struck by car – comminuted fractures of right tibia and fibula – undisplaced crack fracture higher up right tibia – in hospital 5 days, off work 31 weeks – knocked unconscious briefly in accident – 3 inch laceration to parietal region of skull – right leg now a quarter of an inch shorter, but no limp – stiffness in cold weather still present at time of trial – only jogging now possible, running long distances impossible; claimant thus forced to give up football – laceration to head healed well with no cosmetic effect.

1.6.1.2.C39 Case No. 10096

Name of case: McGuirk v Hardie and Atkinson

Brief description of injuries: TIBIA AND FIBULA – FRACTURE – RECOVERY 2.5 YEARS

Reported: Kemp & Kemp, I2-525; [1990] CLY 1663

JSB Category: 6(K)

Sex: Male

Age at injury: 21

Age at award: –

Date of award: 28 February 1990

Tribunal: Barrow-in-Furness County Court

Amount of award then: £5,000

Award at February 2001: £7,155

Description of injuries: Transverse fracture of right tibia and fibula in the distal thirds with slight comminution – open wound of left knee – bruising to back – pulmonary embolism – fractures soundly united but with some angulation and half-an-inch shortening – complaints of tiredness and aching continued for about two-and-a-half years, after which full recovery.

1.6.1.2.C40 Case No. 10452

Name of case: Verrier v London Borough of Islington

Brief description of injuries: MULTIPLE LEG FRACTURES – PRE-EXISTING PARAPLEGIA

Reported: [1992] CLY 1708

JSB Category: 6(K)(c)(ii)

Sex: Female

Age at injury: 85

Age at award: 86

Date of award: 16 September 1992

Tribunal: Westminster County Court

Amount of award then: £5,000

Award at February 2001: £6,169

Description of injuries: Fractured left tibia – fractured right ankle – supra condular fracture of the right femur – an uneventful recovery – virtually housebound for one year after the accident.

Prognosis: Suffering intermittent pain – pre-existing paraplegia – wheelchair-bound with no use to her legs at all.

1.6.1.2.C41 Case No. 10994

Name of case: Almond v Britt-Waight

Brief description of injuries: LEG – FRACTURED HEELBONE – OCCASIONAL RESIDUAL PAIN

Reported: Kemp & Kemp, I3-027/1; [1995] CLY 1746

JSB Category: 6(K)(c)

Sex: Male

Age at injury: 25

Age at award: 30

Date of award: 29 March 1995

Tribunal: Halifax County Court

Amount of award then: £5,250

Award at February 2001: £6,122

Description of injuries: In road traffic accident plaintiff sustained double fracture of right os calcis (one slightly displaced and comminuted) which extended into subtalar joint – was in hospital two days with leg elevated and packed in ice – used crutches for about three weeks – when swelling was reduced below-knee plaster was applied for further three weeks, after which plaintiff was mobilised with walking stick – he returned to work as electronics engineer seven weeks after accident and full duties two-and-a-half months after accident – plaintiff undertook high level of sporting activity prior to accident – unable to cycle for four months and returned to other hobbies such as running, climbing and fell walking nearly a year after accident whereupon he was aware of significant pain requiring a course of physiotherapy – a stable and final state was reached a year-and-a-half after accident – experienced occasional pain lasting up to an hour in right heel after performing high levels of sporting activity but this did not prevent him taking part – eversion of ankle movement was limited by five degrees and small lump on back of heel caused discomfort on wearing ordinary shoes.

Prognosis: These continuing symptoms would not affect his employment prospects but would intrude on his high level of sporting activity – there was long-term risk, assessed at 10%, of plaintiff developing symptomatic osteoarthritis in ankle joint.

1.6.1.2.C42 Case No. 11439

Name of case: Goodwill v Jewson Ltd

Brief description of injuries: LEG – FRACTURES

Reported: Kemp & Kemp, I3-027/3; [1997] CLY 1988

JSB Category: 6(K)(c)(ii)

Sex: Male

Age at injury: 17

Age at award: 20

Date of award: 04 April 1997

Tribunal: Darlington County Court

Amount of award then: £5,150

Award at February 2001: £5,667

Description of injuries: Fractures to the tibia and fibula – two courses of physiotherapy required.

Prognosis: A sound body union was achieved – no long term problems were anticipated.

1.6.1.2.C43 Case No. 10097

Name of case: Francis v Neal

Brief description of injuries: FEMUR – FRACTURE – SLIGHT LIMP

Reported: Kemp & Kemp, I2-527; [1990] CLY 1664

JSB Category: 6(K)

Sex: Male

Age at injury: 2

Age at award: 6

Date of award: 08 March 1990

Tribunal: Not stated

Amount of award then: £4,000

Award at February 2001: £5,667

Description of injuries: Child in pushchair hit by oncoming motorcycle on pedestrian crossing – serious fracture to the right femur – slight limp when tired for a considerable time – still runs awkwardly.

1.6.1.2.C44 Case No. 11998

Name of case: B (a minor) v Pleasure and Leisure Corporation

Brief description of injuries: LEG – FRACTURE

Reported: Kemp & Kemp, PRI-004; [2000] 3 CL 182

JSB Category: 6(A)(c)(ii)

Sex: Male

Age at injury: 14

Age at award: 16

Date of award: 16 November 1999

Tribunal: Skegness County Court

Amount of award then: £5,250

Award at February 2001: £5,417

Description of injuries: B was struck in the back by a go-kart as he was about to get into another one – transverse fracture to the right tibia and fibula – manipulation under general anaesthetic – in hospital for two days – the leg was in plaster for a total of twelve weeks – off school for the September/December term and had to re-sit the whole of that academic year – due to the injury B was unable to join the armed forces as he had hoped.

Prognosis: B would have complete resolution within twenty one months of the date of the accident.

1.6.1.2.C45 Case No. 11197

Name of case: Evans v Dewsbury Civil Engineering

Brief description of injuries: ANKLE – SEVERE STRAIN

Reported: (1996) 96 (4) QR 6; Kemp & Kemp, I3-028; [1996] CLY 2288

JSB Category: 6(M)(d)

Sex: Male

Age at injury: 19

Age at award: 24

Date of award: 10 May 1996

Tribunal: West Bromwich County Court

Amount of award then: £4,500

Award at February 2001: £5,062

Description of injuries: Severe ankle strain – partial tear of the lateral ligament.

Prognosis: Functional instability – ankle gave way every three months – not expected to improve.

1.6.1.2.C46 Case No. 10640

Name of case: Re Smith

Brief description of injuries: LEG – FRACTURE

Reported: Kemp & Kemp, I2-528; [1993] CLY 1536

JSB Category: 6(K)(c)(iii)

Sex: Male

Age at injury: 24

Age at award: –

Date of award: 01 February 1993

Tribunal: CICB, Liverpool

Amount of award then: £4,000

Award at February 2001: £4,957

Description of injuries: Police officer vaulted over 5-foot fence in pursuit of suspect, but 11-foot drop on other side – slightly comminuted fracture of left tibia and fibula – in hospital for 1 week, off work 6 months – full duties resumed after 8 months – complete recovery except for slight impaired sensation over small area of foot.

Other points: Claimant did not look over fence before vaulting – initial application refused by single member – on appeal, held that claimant was taking an exceptional risk within the scheme.

1.6.1.2.C47 Case No. 10995

Name of case: Roseje v Lambourne

Brief description of injuries: LEG – CRACK FRACTURE OF TIBIA – FULL RECOVERY IN 8 MONTHS

Reported: Kemp & Kemp, I2-532; [1995] CLY 1747

JSB Category: 6(K)(c)(iii)

Sex: Male

Age at injury: 17

Age at award: 21

Date of award: 22 September 1995

Tribunal: Hastings County Court

Amount of award then: £4,000

Award at February 2001: £4,568

Description of injuries: Plaintiff was victim of "nasty" assault by defendant in which he was struck on upper shin with crow bar causing crack fracture of tibia below knee without displacement of bone fragments – long leg cast from mid-thigh to toes was applied but plaintiff not detained in hospital – leg was in plaster for two-and-a-half months and plaintiff had to use crutches for three-and-a-half months – plaintiff was unable to play sports, enjoy social activities or drive and his college entrance was delayed – full recovery after eight months, apart from occasional pain and stiffness and burning sensation after exercise – the district judge stated that the injury was at the top of the scale for simple fractures of this kind and applied an uplift for the circumstances of the assault.

1.6.1.2.C48 Case No. 11667

Name of case: Jones (a minor) v Wrexham CBC

Brief description of injuries: LEG – FRACTURED TIBIA

Reported: Kemp & Kemp, I2-531; [1998] CLY 1669

JSB Category: 6(K)(c)(iii)

Sex: Male

Age at injury: 4

Age at award: 6

Date of award: 24 June 1998

Tribunal: Wrexham County Court

Amount of award then: £4,250

Award at February 2001: £4,474

Description of injuries: Undisplaced spiral fracture to the mid third of the right tibia – claimant symptom-free within 2 months of the date of the accident.

1.6.1.2.C49 Case No. 11668

Name of case: Rhodes v Soor

Brief description of injuries: LEG – FRACTURE

Reported: Kemp & Kemp, I2-535; [1998] CLY 1670

JSB Category: 6(K)(c)(iii); 6(D)

Sex: Male

Age at injury: 37

Age at award: 42

Date of award: 06 April 1998

Tribunal: Willesden County Court

Amount of award then: £4,000

Award at February 2001: £4,231

Description of injuries: Simple closed fracture of the head of the right fibula – headaches – painful shoulder – full recovery made within 10 months of the date of the accident.

1.6.1.2.C50 Case No. 11458

Name of case: Parnham (a minor) v Metropolitan Housing Trust Ltd

Brief description of injuries: LEG – AVULSION FRACTURE

Reported: Kemp & Kemp, 13-031; [1997] CLY 2007

JSB Category: 6(K)(c)(iii)

Sex: Male

Age at injury: 14

Age at award: -

Date of award: 18 July 1997

Tribunal: Nottingham County Court

Amount of award then: £3,750

Award at February 2001: £4,095

Description of injuries: Avulsion fracture – a fragment of bone of the fibula – ligament tear to the ankle.

Prognosis: No risk of any long term consequences.

1.6.1.2.C51 Case No. 11670

Name of case: Watford (a minor) v Tesco Stores Ltd

Brief description of injuries: LEG – SPIRAL FRACTURE

Reported: Kemp & Kemp, I2-536; [1998] CLY 1672

JSB Category: 6(K)(c)(iii)

Sex: Male

Age at injury: 2

Age at award: 5

Date of award: 07 May 1998

Tribunal: Uxbridge County Court

Amount of award then: £3,850

Award at February 2001: £4,050

Description of injuries: Spiral fracture to the left tibia – full recovery made within 3 months of the date of the accident.

1.6.1.2.C52 Case No. 11977

Name of case: Dean v Wundpets Ltd

Brief description of injuries: LEG – FRACTURE – 18 MONTHS

Reported: Kemp & Kemp, I2-538; [2000] 2 CL 148

JSB Category: 6(K)(c)(iii)

Sex: Male

Age at injury: 22

Age at award: 24

Date of award: 16 September 1999

Tribunal: Cheltenham County Court

Amount of award then: £3,600

Award at February 2001: £3,726

Description of injuries: Fracture to the lower fibula and puncture wound above the lateral malleolus – below knee plaster was applied – in-patient for two days due to weeping wound – plaster case remained for six weeks – absent from work for approximately seven weeks.

Prognosis: Some slight twinges of pain six months after the accident expected to fully resolve within eighteen months of the date of the accident – scar behind the right malleolus was a quarter of an inch by an eighth of an inch.

1.6.1.2.C53 Case No. 11671

Name of case: Brennan (a minor) v Howell

Brief description of injuries: LEG – GREENSTICK FRACTURES TO THE LEG

Reported: Kemp & Kemp, I2-539; [1998] CLY 1673

JSB Category: 6(K)(c)(iii)

Sex: Female

Age at injury: 3

Age at award: 4

Date of award: 29 October 1998

Tribunal: Tunbridge Wells County Court

Amount of award then: £3,500

Award at February 2001: £3,660

Description of injuries: Angulated greenstick fractures of the tibia and fibula of the right leg.

Prognosis: At the time of the hearing residual symptoms were expected to resolve within 1 month.

1.6.1.2.C54 Case No. 11215

Name of case: Jones (a minor) v Morgan

Brief description of injuries: LEG – FRACTURE

Reported: Kemp & Kemp, I2-540; [1996] CLY 2307

JSB Category: 6(K)(c)(iii)

Sex: Male

Age at injury: 4

Age at award: 8

Date of award: 09 September 1996

Tribunal: Worcester County Court

Amount of award then: £3,250

Award at February 2001: £3,635

Description of injuries: Mid-shaft fracture to the tibia and fibula.

Prognosis: At the time of the hearing he had made an excellent recovery – no anticipated residual problems.

Other points: Award reduced from JSB guideline amount – this was a young boy whose inconvenience was perhaps somewhat less than might be the case for someone older.

1.6.1.2.C55 Case No. 11432

Name of case: Melling v Liverpool City Council

Brief description of injuries: LEG – FRACTURE – 4 MONTHS

Reported: Kemp & Kemp, K2-025; [1997] CLY 1981

JSB Category: 6(K)(c)(iii)

Sex: Male

Age at injury: 30

Age at award: 31

Date of award: 25 April 1997

Tribunal:

Amount of award then: £3,250

Award at February 2001: £3,576

Description of injuries: Fractured fibula.

Prognosis: Full recovery after four months.

1.6.1.2.C56 Case No. 11219

Name of case: Evans v Ministry of Defence

Brief description of injuries: LEG – FRACTURE

Reported: Kemp & Kemp, I2-541; [1996] CLY 2311

JSB Category: 6(K)(c)(iii)

Sex: Female

Age at injury: 4 months

Age at award: –

Date of award: 10 May 1996

Tribunal: York County Court

Amount of award then: £3,000

Award at February 2001: £3,375

Description of injuries: Fracture of the right femur with minimal displacement.

Prognosis: There was no residual deformity.

1.6.1.2.C57 Case No. 10662

Name of case: Ward v Wakefield Health Authority

Brief description of injuries: LEG – FRACTURE – DELAY IN DIAGNOSIS

Reported: Kemp & Kemp, I2-542; [1993] CLY 1558

JSB Category: 6(K)(c)

Sex: Female

Age at injury: 92

Age at award: –

Date of award: 22 July 1993

Tribunal: Leeds County Court

Amount of award then: £2,700

Award at February 2001: £3,301

Description of injuries: Undisplaced inter-trochanteric fracture of left femur – failure to diagnose fracture at hospital – claimant referred to geriatric mobilisation ward and attempts made to persuade her to use leg for 3 days – discharged home – continual pain and discomfort – visit by consultant, whose handling of leg caused traumatic discomfort – fracture became displaced – correct diagnosis made after 17 days – nails inserted to repair fracture – delayed diagnosis prolonged recovery by 3 months.

Other points: Award calculated as £100 per day for first 17 days, plus £1,000 for prolonged recovery.

1.6.1.2.C58 Case No. 11944

Name of case: H (a minor) v Bass plc

Brief description of injuries: LEG – FRACTURE OF TIBIA – FULL RECOVERY

Reported: Kemp & Kemp, K2-056/1; [1999] CLY 1608

JSB Category: 6(K)(c)(iii)

Sex: Male

Age at injury: 3

Age at award: 6

Date of award: 25 March 1999

Tribunal: Eastbourne County Court (infant settlement approval hearing)

Amount of award then: £2,750

Award at February 2001: £2,882

Description of injuries: Salter type II fracture of distal tibial metaphysis – initial treatment with below – the – knee walking plaster, with claimant asked to remain non-weight-bearing for 2 weeks – plaster removed after further 2 weeks – 6 weeks later, at final clinical review, claimant described as "entirely normal" – even though no significant displacement of tibial epiphysis, there had been a risk initially that subsequent bone growth would be affected – 2.5 years later, X-rays revealed that position of epiphysis was normal and that risk could be discounted.

Prognosis: No further problems expected.

1.6.1.2.C59 Case No. 10482

Name of case: Mahon v Lowley

Brief description of injuries: FRACTURED TIBIA – ALMOST FULL RECOVERY 8 MONTHS

Reported: [1992] CLY 1738

JSB Category: 6(F)(d)

Sex: Male

Age at injury: 37

Age at award: 39

Date of award: 28 April 1992

Tribunal: Bradford County Court

Amount of award then: £2,250

Award at February 2001: £2,788

Description of injuries: Undisplaced fracture of the medial tibial condyle.

Prognosis: Expected to make a full recovery within eight months of the accident – still experienced twinges and pain at the time of the hearing.

1.6.1.2.C60 Case No. 11037

Name of case: Simpson v Liverpool City Council

Brief description of injuries: ANKLE – SEVERE STRAIN – 2 MONTHS

Reported: [1995] CLY 1791

JSB Category: 6(M)(d)

Sex: Female

Age at injury: 32

Age at award: 36

Date of award: 09 March 1995

Tribunal: Liverpool County Court

Amount of award then: £1,800

Award at February 2001: £2,099

Description of injuries: Plaintiff fell due to defective paving stone – foot was placed on edge of hole and twisted over – suffered severe strain to right ankle and was on crutches for about six weeks and off work for about seven or eight weeks – Judge found that "after eight weeks there was no great problem" and any continuing discomfort was "not significant" – plaintiff accepted that she had substantially recovered at end of this period but complained of continuing occasional discomfort – could have been resolved with an injection but had not sought such an injection – judge was unable to accept plaintiff's explanation for such failure to have injection.

1.6.1.2.C61 Case No. 11238

Name of case: Re Pigott

Brief description of injuries: LEGS – DOG BITES

Reported: Kemp & Kemp, K2-111; [1996] CLY 2330

JSB Category: 8(v)

Sex: Male

Age at injury: –

Age at award: –

Date of award: 05 August 1996

Tribunal: York County Court

Amount of award then: £1,750

Award at February 2001: £1,966

Description of injuries: Dog bites to both legs.

Prognosis: Three small permanent depressed scars were expected to fade.

1.6.1.2.C62 Case No. 11249

Name of case: Gorry v Southern

Brief description of injuries: LEG – SEVERE BRUISING – 10 MONTHS

Reported: Kemp & Kemp, K2-134; [1996] CLY 2341

JSB Category: 6(K)(c)(iii)

Sex: Male

Age at injury: 20

Age at award: 23

Date of award: 06 September 1996

Tribunal: St Helens County Court

Amount of award then: £1,500

Award at February 2001: £1,678

Description of injuries: Severe bruising to the left calf – minor bruising and abrasions to the right shoulder – shock – symptoms fully settled within ten months of the date of the accident.

1.6.1.2.C63 Case No. 11048

Name of case: Steveley v Harvey

Brief description of injuries: LEG – DOG BITE TO THIGH – PAIN 10 WEEKS

Reported: Kemp & Kemp, K2-158; [1995] CLY 1802

JSB Category: 6(K)(c)(iii)

Sex: Male

Age at injury: 34

Age at award: –

Date of award: 22 November 1994

Tribunal: Chelmsford County Court

Amount of award then: £1,250

Award at February 2001: £1,480

Description of injuries: Male chef bitten by German Shepherd dog – suffered puncture wounds and lacerations to right arm and both legs, the most significant being to thigh, where dog had bitten and vigorously shaken plaintiff's leg – wounds became infected, causing swelling, and were treated with antibiotics – also given tetanus injection – blood clots formed in right leg, causing aching and discomfort for 10 weeks – absent from work for two weeks – slight scarring remained, but this was hardly visible.

1.6.1.2.C64 Case No. 11056

Name of case: Re Broxson

Brief description of injuries: LEG – HAEMATOMA (3 DAYS) – BRUISING (8 WEEKS)

Reported: Kemp & Kemp, K2-194; [1995] CLY 1810

JSB Category: 6(K)(c)(iii)

Sex: Male

Age at injury: 35

Age at award: 38

Date of award: 16 October 1995

Tribunal: CICB, Durham

Amount of award then: £1,000

Award at February 2001: £1,148

Description of injuries: Policeman back-kicked twice on his right shin by youth – suffered considerable bruising and swelling to the front and side of right leg, extending from knee to ankle – a haematoma developed in right calf and he experienced a loss of sensation in region of right shin – ordered to leave work four days after assault and instructed by police surgeon to rest for four days with his right leg elevated – plaintiff was off work for five days and restricted to light duties for six weeks – experienced pain in right leg for six weeks and walked with limp for two weeks immediately following assault – haematoma had gone within three days – bruising lasted eight weeks – advice given to plaintiff by police surgeon had caused him and his wife considerable worry – at date of hearing still experienced loss of sensation in an area approximately the size of a five pence piece.

1.6.1.2.1 Leg fracture and other injury

1.6.1.2.1.C1 Case No. 11084

Award at February 2001: £39,423

See: 1.4.3.2.C1 for details

1.6.1.2.1.C2 Case No. 10241

Name of case: Taylor v Walkley, Meagher and Poll

Brief description of injuries: FRACTURED FEMUR AND KNEE CAP – 70% RISK OF ARTHRITIS IN KNEE

Reported: Kemp & Kemp, I2-305; [1991] CLY 1438

JSB Category: 6(L)(a)(iii) 6(K)

Sex: Female

Age at injury: 31

Age at award: 36

Date of award: 20 November 1991

Tribunal: Cheltenham County Court

Amount of award then: £20,000

Award at February 2001: £26,265

Description of injuries: Severe comminuted fracture to the left femur – compound fracture to the left knee cap – deep wounding and soft-tissue loss to the left calf – muscular damage to the left hip – broken scapula – lacerations to the face and hands.

Prognosis: At the time of the hearing the knee gave way unpredictably – T could walk only for 15 minutes before tiring – improvement not expected – 70 per cent risk of osteoarthritis of the knee within 10 to 20 years – permanent muscular injury to the hip was extremely detrimental to sexual intercourse – severe scarring to the hip knee and calf – significant psychological trauma since the accident.

1.6.1.2.1.C3 Case No. 10240

Name of case: Sadler v Thomas

Brief description of injuries: COMPOUND FRACTURE OF THE RIGHT TIBIA – KNEE REPLACEMENT

Reported: Kemp & Kemp, I2-407; [1991] CLY 1437

JSB Category: 6(L)(a)(iii) 6(K)

Sex: Male

Age at injury: 19

Age at award: 26

Date of award: 19 December 1990

Tribunal: Winchester County Court

Amount of award then: £17,017

Award at February 2001: £23,180

Description of injuries: Compound fracture of the right tibia – minor grazing to the forehead, shoulder and right foot – the fracture healed uneventfully – S developed symptoms in his knee – arthroscopy revealed severe degenerative change and gross cartilage destruction – total knee replacement required.

Prognosis: A further knee replacement would be required in about 10 years – unable to return to pre-accident employment on a building site – required re-training.

1.6.1.2.1.C4 Case No. 10237

Name of case: Partington v Moore

Brief description of injuries: FRACTURE TO THE TIBIA AND ULNA – PARTIAL AMPUTATION OF THE BIG TOE

Reported: Kemp & Kemp, I4-014; [1991] CLY 1434

JSB Category: 6(K)(c) 6(F)(d) 6(P)

Sex: Female

Age at injury: 18

Age at award: 24

Date of award: 31 January 1991

Tribunal: QBD

Amount of award then: £15,000

Award at February 2001: £20,259

Description of injuries: Fracture to the tibia and ulna – cuts to the left hand, wrist and knee – compound fracture of the big toe necessitating partial amputation – arm in plaster for twelve days – metal plate in the leg – in thigh to toe plaster for three months – plate removed thirty three months later.

Prognosis: At the time of the hearing there was no functional disability – good recovery – toe remained a cosmetic disability – scar to the front of the leg was noticeable – a matter of distress to the plaintiff who no longer swam and wore dark tights or jeans.

1.6.1.2.1.C5 Case No. 10446

Award at February 2001: £17,493

See: 1.2.3.5.C3 for details

1.6.1.2.1.C6 Case No. 10998

Name of case: Hodgkinson v Dutton

Brief description of injuries: LEG – FRACTURE OF FEMUR AND ANKLE – 5-YEAR ACCELERATION OF KNEE SYMPTOMS

Reported: Kemp & Kemp, I2-513; [1995] CLY 1750

JSB Category: 6(L)(b)(i)

Sex: Male

Age at injury: 61

Age at award: 65

Date of award: 31 March 1995

Tribunal: Stoke on Trent County Court

Amount of award then: £10,000

Award at February 2001: £11,701

Description of injuries: Plaintiff knocked from motorcycle – suffered injuries to left leg including fracture of femoral condyle and bi-malleolar fracture of ankle – plaintiff needed arthroscopy of left knee and knee fracture was then fixed with screws (which were removed over three years later) – ankle fracture was treated by immobilisation in plaster – initial period off work of seven months – he was able to return to work but work as estate worker/gardener was only possible because of employers' sympathetic attitude and because fellow employees were willing to undertake heavier tasks and in particular those involving any climbing, squatting or jumping down for him – plaintiff's knee remained lax – there was stiffness and occasional swelling in knee although relatively little pain – ankle substantially healed although there was some slight stiffness – progression of symptoms in knee was expected to lead to knee replacement in about 10 years – however, a knee replacement would have happened at some point in future in any event because of pre-existing asymptomatic degenerative condition – accident had brought forward such symptoms and necessity for knee replacement by period of five years – plaintiff was made redundant for reasons unconnected with injury but because of injuries was then unable to seek further work because of limitations imposed by injuries.

1.6.1.2.1.C7 Case No. 10239

Name of case: Workman v Radcliffe

Brief description of injuries: FRACTURES OF THE RIGHT TIBIA AND FIBULA AND RIGHT SECOND KNUCKLE

Reported: Kemp & Kemp, I2-520; [1991] CLY 1436

JSB Category: 6(K)(c)(iii)

Sex: Male

Age at injury: 22

Age at award: 26

Date of award: 29 April 1991

Tribunal: Doncaster District Registry

Amount of award then: £7,000

Award at February 2001: £9,046

Description of injuries: Dragged 100 yards under a vehicle – displaced closed comminuted fractures of the right tibia and fibula – closed comminuted fracture of the dominant right hand second knuckle – abrasions to the knees, elbow and lumbar area – plate and screws applied to the serious leg fracture. Missed four-and-a-half months from work and another six weeks when the plate was removed – unable to resume contact sports.

Prognosis: At the time of the hearing good recovery to "near normal".

1.6.1.2.1.C8 Case No. 10082

Award at February 2001: £7,496

See: 1.4.3.2.C5 for details

1.6.1.2.1.C9 Case No. 10257

Name of case: Pearce v Hampshire County Council

Brief description of injuries: FRACTURED FEMUR AND CLAVICLE – FULL RECOVERY

Reported: Kemp & Kemp, I2-526; [1991] CLY 1454

JSB Category: 6(D)(d); 6(K)(c)(iii)

Sex: Male

Age at injury: 12

Age at award: 15

Date of award: 13 June 1991

Tribunal: Southampton County Court

Amount of award then: £5,400

Award at February 2001: £6,926

Description of injuries: Knocked down and run over by a trailer – mid-shaft fracture to the femur with displacement – fracture of the left clavicle – minor injuries to the head, ear and mouth – treated as an hospital inpatient for seven weeks.

Prognosis: Fully recovered and playing competitive games.

1.6.1.2.1.C10 Case No. 10478

Name of case: Morley v Heating and Ventilating Services

Brief description of injuries: FIBULAR FRACTURE – PULMONARY EMBOLISM

Reported: [1992] CLY 1734

JSB Category: 6(K)(c)(iii)

Sex: Female

Age at injury: 67

Age at award: 72

Date of award: 06 May 1992

Tribunal: Nottingham County Court

Amount of award then: £3,600

Award at February 2001: £4,445

Description of injuries: Spiral fracture to the left distal fibula and injury to the middle finger.

Prognosis: Three months after the accident a pre-existing pulmonary embolism was activated – almost full recovery

1.6.1.3 KNEE INJURY

1.6.1.3.C1 Case No. 10828

Name of case: Tilson v Taylor

Brief description of injuries: KNEE REPLACEMENT

Reported: Kemp & Kemp, I2-408; [1994] CLY 1677

JSB Category: 6(L)(a)

Sex: Male

Age at injury: 39

Age at award: 44

Date of award: 12 November 1993

Tribunal: Not stated

Amount of award then: £25,000

Award at February 2001: £31,794

Description of injuries: Road accident – blow to knee – appearance of swelling after 2 days – blood aspirated from knee in hospital – claimant continued to be hampered in work as self-employed television repairer/installer, being unable to climb ladders and thus undertake aerial and (lucrative) satellite dish installations – extensive physiotherapy – arthroscopy in June 1990 showed loss of articular cartilage in medial femoral condyle; loose cartilage trimmed – further arthroscopy in June 1992 showed cartilage damage and loose fat pad – subsequent MRI scan confirmed full thickness articular loss – high tibial osteotomy immediately required; had not taken place by date of trial – claimant in considerable pain, requiring painkillers – no limp, but walking restricted to a quarter of a mile – swelling and giving-way of knee from time to time – knee brace worn to help with instability of knee – claimant still working full - time, and able to drive, but not safe to work on ladders – impossible for claimant to play football with his 2 sons, and difficult to walk dog – unable to clean windows or carry out DIY at home.

Prognosis: Tibial osteotomy yet to be performed – knee replacement required within 10 years, and further knee replacement 10-15 years thereafter – pain expected to be alleviated to some extent by operations – claimant never likely to be able to use ladders safely, with consequent adverse effect on business.

1.6.1.3.C2 Case No. 10099

Name of case: Hardy v Daldorph

Brief description of injuries: INJURY TO KNEE – TWO OPERATIONS

Reported: Kemp & Kemp, I2-412; [1990] CLY 1666

JSB Category: 6(L)

Sex: Female

Age at injury: 23

Age at award: 26

Date of award: 15 February 1990

Tribunal: QBD

Amount of award then: £17,500

Award at February 2001: £25,906

Description of injuries: Injury to left knee – two operations performed – in-patient for three weeks, in plaster for five weeks – physiotherapy for nine months – unable to work for 14.5 months – general loss of agility, making working at height dangerous.

Prognosis: Plaintiff's cruciate ligament stretched – occasional pain and swelling which will require analgesics – no future loss of earnings.

1.6.1.3.C3 Case No. 10456

Name of case: Rudd v North Eastern Electricity Board

Brief description of injuries: INJURED KNEE – REPLACEMENT IN 5 YEARS

Reported: [1992] CLY 1712

JSB Category: 6(K)(a)(iii)

Sex: Male

Age at injury: 42

Age at award: 50

Date of award: 08 July 1992

Tribunal: Newcastle upon Tyne County Court

Amount of award then: £20,000

Award at February 2001: £25,625

Description of injuries: Seriously injured the left knee at work – impeded in his mobility and walking – at age 50 it was unlikely that he would be able to return to any gainful employment.

Prognosis: Osteoarthritic changes in the left knee which continued to progress – total knee replacement would be required in five years.

1.6.1.3.C4 Case No. 11674

Name of case: Ostling v Hastings
Brief description of injuries: KNEE
Reported: Kemp & Kemp, I2-413; [1998] CLY 1677
JSB Category: 6(L)(a)(iii), 6(H); 8
Sex: Male
Age at injury: 23
Age at award: 28
Date of award: 14 November 1997
Tribunal: Guildford County Court
Amount of award then: £20,000
Award at February 2001: £22,124

Description of injuries: Injuries to both knees, left wrist and buttock – extensive wound around the patella of the right knee extending into the knee joint – 80 per cent disruption to the quadriceps tendon – subsequent development of clicking in stiff right knee.

Prognosis: Scars to both knees (10in and 1.5in) – permanent restriction on bending – slight risk of osteoarthritis – possibility of patellectomy in the future.

Other points: O had been an elite rower – he had potential to make the 1996 Great Britain Olympic squad – the judge found he had lost 6 years of elite rowing.

1.6.1.3.C5 Case No. 10996

Name of case: Steward v Gates Hydraulics
Brief description of injuries: KNEE – SERIOUS INJURY – 2 OPERATIONS – NOW CONSTANT PAIN, WALKS WITH STICK
Reported: Kemp & Kemp, I2-414; [1995] CLY 1748
JSB Category: 6(L)(a)(iii)
Sex: Female
Age at injury: 32
Age at award: 38
Date of award: 28 November 1994
Tribunal: Peterborough County Court
Amount of award then: £17,500
Award at February 2001: £21,223

Description of injuries: Plaintiff injured right knee on pedestal of her desk at work in April 1989 causing lasting damage to knee – a lateral release procedure operation was performed – in hospital for 48 hours – thereafter able to walk without stick – returned to work in April 1990 – suffered increasingly severe pain after return to work with marked retro-patella tenderness and crepitus and was provided with strong painkilling drugs – due to lack of progress she was admitted to hospital in June 1990 for arthrotomy of right knee which confirmed marked chondral degeneration over medial pole of patella with blister-like lesion over medial part of patella – the abnormal articular cartilage was excised and a 32mm carbon patch inserted into retropatella surface – in hospital for four days – absent from work 23 weeks between February 1990 and July 1990 – at date of trial, plaintiff walked with stick, found difficulty in climbing and descending stairs and suffered severe pain if right leg was accidently knocked – was in constant pain in cold weather, could no longer kneel down or squat, had limited sexual activity and could no longer enjoy gymnastics, netball, swimming and walking – unable to lift bulky objects like vacuum cleaners, dig garden, drive car, wear high heels or get up and down quickly – was able to hold down clerical job similar to her employment prior to accident.

1.6.1.3.C6 Case No. 10642

Name of case: Fox v Thompson
Brief description of injuries: KNEE – FRACTURED KNEECAPS
Reported: [1993] CLY 1538
JSB Category: 6(L)(a)
Sex: Male
Age at injury: 32
Age at award: 35
Date of award: 13 April 1993
Tribunal: Whitehaven County Court
Amount of award then: £16,000
Award at February 2001: £20,001

Description of injuries: Slip and fall on patch of oil at work – broken kneecap – off work 3 months – return to work, eventually at 70 per cent of original capacity – subsequent development of osteoarthrosis – claimant forced to less demanding duties – unable to kneel, squat or climb.

Prognosis: Patellectomy would be necessary.

1.6.1.3.C7 Case No. 10830

Name of case: Britten v Haymills Holdings and Blencoes Scaffolding

Brief description of injuries: KNEE

Reported: Kemp & Kemp, I2-416; [1994] CLY 1679

JSB Category: 6(L)(a)

Sex: Male

Age at injury: 60

Age at award: 63

Date of award: 25 March 1994

Tribunal: Bath County Court

Amount of award then: £14,000

Award at February 2001: £17,162

Description of injuries: Fall from roof onto protruding scaffolding pole 3ft below – complete disruption of attachment of patella tendon from lower pole of right patella – immediate admission to hospital – patella tendon reattached and protected with figure-of-eight tension band wire – discharged after 8 days on crutches – returned 8 months later for removal of tension band wire – 14cm scar on front of knee – at date of trial, ongoing pain over anterio-lateral aspect of knee when using stairs or getting down to or up from the ground – stiffness in morning – painkillers taken daily, knee described as being like a "sledgehammer" when walking; swelling after walking – running, climbing and crouching no longer possible – driving only possible for short distances – gardening problematic.

1.6.1.3.C8 Case No. 10829

Name of case: Osborn v Madgwick

Brief description of injuries: KNEE – OSTEOARTHRITIS

Reported: Kemp & Kemp, I2-417; [1994] CLY 1678

JSB Category: 6(L)(a); 8

Sex: Male

Age at injury: 41

Age at award: 49

Date of award: 11 May 1994

Tribunal: Central London County Court

Amount of award then: £14,000

Award at February 2001: £16,891

Description of injuries: Motorcycle accident – posterior cruciate ligament in right knee torn from its insertion at top of tibia – operation to refix ligament with screw, leaving 12 cm scar – in hospital 12 days, on crutches 2 months, off work 4.5 months – successful return to previous manual employment, despite pain of varying levels, sometimes "unbearable", and unwillingness to take analgesics – pain exacerbated by hard work and damp weather – mild limp – tendency of leg to give way without warning, sometimes causing claimant to fall – small fragment of bone in joint necessitated arthroscopy – further 6 weeks off work – no longer able to ride motorcycle – hobbies of fishing and snooker restricted – able to walk 1 mile on level ground, 0.5 mile on rough ground.

Prognosis: Osteoarthritis already developed, but progress slow – prior to injury, claimant would have worked to age of 59 or 60; accident expected to force retirement at 55 – combination of age and disability would cause problems in finding further employment.

1.6.1.3.C9 Case No. 10100

Name of case: Henderson v Watchorn

Brief description of injuries: KNEE – DAMAGE – SURGERY – DEGENERATIVE CHANGES

Reported: Kemp & Kemp, I2-418; [1990] CLY 1667

JSB Category: 6(M); 6(L)

Sex: Male

Age at injury: 23

Age at award: 27

Date of award: 07 June 1990

Tribunal: Westminster County Court

Amount of award then: £12,000

Award at February 2001: £16,521

Description of injuries: Police officer riding motorcycle which collided with car – injury to ankle, right knee and bruising to buttock – ankle injury though to be primarily ligamentous affecting the lateral side, although possible hairline fracture – damage to the underside of the kneecap – loose chunks and flaps of cartilage surgically removed – unable to walk due to pain and swelling, crutches being necessary for four weeks – severe damage to the patella.

Prognosis: Severe osteoarthritis of the patello-femoral joint could be expected to occur within five to 10 years.

1.6.1.3.C10 Case No. 11435

Name of case: Elder v Sands

Brief description of injuries: KNEE – EXTENSIVE SOFT-TISSUE DAMAGE

Reported: Kemp & Kemp, I2-419; [1997] CLY 1984

JSB Category: 6(L)(a)(iii)

Sex: Female

Age at injury: 32

Age at award: 38

Date of award: 02 February 1997

Tribunal: Chelmsford County Court

Amount of award then: £14,000

Award at February 2001: £15,728

Description of injuries: Widespread bruising and injury to the knee – articular cartilage damage in all departments.

Prognosis: Symptoms likely to persist indefinitely – likely to develop arthritis within five to ten years of the trial.

1.6.1.3.C11 Case No. 10643

Name of case: Clay v McHugh

Brief description of injuries: KNEE – CHRONDROMALACIA PATELLAE

Reported: Kemp & Kemp, I2-420; [1993] CLY 1539

JSB Category: 6(L)(a)

Sex: Male

Age at injury: 18

Age at award: 24

Date of award: 08 September 1993

Tribunal: Stockport County Court

Amount of award then: £12,500

Award at February 2001: £15,326

Description of injuries: Serious injury to left knee resulting in chrondromalacia patellae – also head injury involving loss of consciousness, injury to ankle and various soft-tissue injuries, from which complete recovery made – 3 years 9 months after accident, arthroscopy and capsular release performed – degenerative changes present, caused by accident – claimant unable to run or play squash as he had previously – discomfort when lifting and knee tired at end of day.

Prognosis: Further degeneration likely – 25 per cent chance of removal of kneecap being necessary and early retirement at age of 60 – permanently restricted movement in left knee.

Other points: Youth of claimant and loss of enjoyment of sporting activities factored into general damages.

1.6.1.3.C12 Case No. 10101

Name of case: Smith v Jagger

Brief description of injuries: INJURY TO BOTH KNEES – SURGERY – DEGENERATIVE CHANGES

Reported: [1990] CLY 1668

JSB Category: 6(L)

Sex: Male

Age at injury: –

Age at award: 31

Date of award: 04 December 1989

Tribunal: QBD

Amount of award then: £8,500

Award at February 2001: £12,306

Description of injuries: Struck by a car just above the knees and pinned against a fridge in a filling station – low back injury which improved considerably within 16 months – plaintiff had pre-existing symptomless chondromalacia in both knees which would not have troubled him, but for the accident, until his 40s or 50s – sustained torn cartilage in right knee, which was eventually removed following an arthroscopy.

Prognosis: Knee was now much improved and would be relatively trouble-free within five to 10 years – left knee arthroscopy not so successful, with the probability of arthritis developing within five to 10 years.

1.6.1.3.C13 Case No. 10644

Name of case: Cornbill v Turfsoil

Brief description of injuries: KNEE – CHRONDROMALACIA PATELLAE

Reported: Kemp & Kemp, I2-424; [1993] CLY 1540

JSB Category: 6(L)(a)

Sex: Male

Age at injury: 18

Age at award: 22

Date of award: 21 September 1993

Tribunal: Plymouth County Court

Amount of award then: £10,000

Award at February 2001: £12,176

Description of injuries: Fall into uncovered pit – injuries to both knees – extreme tenderness of left patella – stiff in mornings – occasionally gave way – exercise impossible, sports brace required to stabilise knee – chrondromalacia patellae in left knee diagnosed – minor symptoms in right knee – claimant medically discharged from Navy – unable to carry out any job requiring squatting or prolonged standing – by time of trial plaintiff could play badminton with sports brace and walk up to 1.5 miles without brace.

Prognosis: Significant risk of degenerative changes in left knee in 25 years' time.

1.6.1.3.C14 Case No. 10997

Name of case: Dawson v West Yorkshire Police Authority

Brief description of injuries: KNEE – TEAR OF MENISCUS – 5 YEARS ACCELERATION

Reported: Kemp & Kemp, I2-426; [1995] CLY 1749

JSB Category: 6(L)(b)(i)

Sex: Male

Age at injury: 29

Age at award: 32

Date of award: 16 November 1994

Tribunal: Wakefield County Court

Amount of award then: £10,000

Award at February 2001: £11,883

Description of injuries: Police officer slipped on gymnasium floor – sustained bucket handle tear of medial meniscus of right knee, together with total disruption of anterior cruciate ligament – knee was left unstable and he underwent Leeds Keo Ligament surgery, a prosthetic replacement for ligament, in April 1991 – within 12 months ligament was functioning satisfactorily – plaintiff was previously extremely fit with active sporting life – was a keen marathon runner and was proficient at most sports, including rugby – impact of accident was enough to deny plaintiff his sporting life, making it difficult for him to keep fit – had intermittent pain from right knee and discomfort and limitation of movement which led to reduction in amenities – judge accepted three years' loss of amenity generally – in 1985 plaintiff injured right knee playing rugby, from which partial meniscectomy was performed – he returned to full duties and full sporting activities without discomfort.

Prognosis: The judge, however, accepted that as result of combination of injuries, degenerative changes were likely to result – plaintiff was found to be vulnerable to leaving his employment as police sergeant five years earlier than would have been the case had December 1990 accident not occurred – the judge took into consideration increased risk of damage to career and effects of further slackening of ligament of knee and accepted there had been five years' acceleration of underlying condition.

1.6.1.3.C15 Case No. 10458

Name of case: Shioda v Fitzgerald Light Ring

Brief description of injuries: KNEE INJURY – PRE-EXISTING DEGENERATIVE CHANGES – ABILITY TO WALK AND STAND LIMITED

Reported: [1992] CLY 1714

JSB Category: 6(K)(b)(i)

Sex: Male

Age at injury: 50

Age at award: 56

Date of award: 26 November 1991

Tribunal: Exeter District Registry

Amount of award then: £9,000

Award at February 2001: £11,416

Description of injuries: Fell on the right knee – pre-existing degenerative wear was already occurring in the knee following an earlier accident – plaintiff had to wear a leg brace – thigh muscle became seriously wasted – physiotherapy was not successful – had a moderate limp – able to stand for only 20 minutes – able to walk only 20 yards with leg brace and crutches – it was felt that there was considerable emotional overlay delaying his recovery.

Prognosis: 10% disabled.

1.6.1.3.C16 Case No. 10797

Name of case: Moyses v Cleveland Bridge & Engineering Co

Brief description of injuries: KNEE – CRUSH INJURY – ACCELERATION OF ARTHRITIS

Reported: Kemp & Kemp, G2-041; [1994] CLY 1646

JSB Category: 6(L)(b), 6(C)

Sex: Male

Age at injury: 55

Age at award: 58

Date of award: 02 March 1994

Tribunal: Sheffield County Court

Amount of award then: £7,500

Award at February 2001: £9,053

Description of injuries: Crush injury to left knee – immediate pain – traumatic effusion to knee and haemarthrosis, necessitating aspiration – crutches initially prescribed; used for 2 weeks – weight-bearing using stick thereafter – development of pain and stiffness in left hip about 3 months after accident, in right hip about 12 months after accident – pre-existing osteoarthritic changes in both hips rendered symptomatic as a direct result of accident – continuing pain and restriction of movement in both hips and left knee – claimant formerly physically active, but physical activity now restricted – stick still required for walking at time of trial – claimant had not returned to work at time of trial.

Prognosis: Pain in hips and knee likely to vary in intensity but all likely to worsen in time – onset of condition in hips accelerated by approximately 5 years in case of left hip and approximately 3.5 years in case of right hip.

1.6.1.3.C17 Case No. 11191

Name of case: Ellis v Butler

Brief description of injuries: KNEE – RECOVERY IN 3-4 YEARS

Reported: Kemp & Kemp, I2-430; [1996] CLY 2282

JSB Category: 6(L)(b)(ii)

Sex: Male

Age at injury: 30

Age at award: 34

Date of award: 08 May 1996

Tribunal: Aldershot County Court

Amount of award then: £7,900

Award at February 2001: £8,887

Description of injuries: Injury to the knee – patello-femoral irritability and crepitus – resisted all attempts to cure it – seatbelt bruising – post-traumatic stress disorder.

Prognosis: Discomfort in the knee likely to be permanent – increased irritability was expected to resolve almost completely within 3-4 years.

1.6.1.3.C18 Case No. 11001

Name of case: Foster v British Waterways Board

Brief description of injuries: KNEE – BRUISING – OCCASIONAL INSTABILITY

Reported: [1995] CLY 1753

JSB Category: 6(L)(b)(i)

Sex: Male

Age at injury: 43

Age at award: 50

Date of award: 06 January 1995

Tribunal: Derby County Court

Amount of award then: £7,500

Award at February 2001: £8,836

Description of injuries: At work, plaintiff sustained severe bruising to right knee, calf and ankle, minor fracture of anterior end of left eighth rib and bruising to right shoulder – a full recovery from ankle, calf, rib and shoulder injuries within few weeks, but as result of knee injury suffered significant ligamentous instability – at time of trial, leg still gave way on occasion and was painful upon sustained exertion and in cold weather.

Prognosis: There was five per cent chance of surgery to knee before age of 65 which would be attributable to accident – plaintiff also suffered from symptoms of low back pain and sciatica, unrelated to accident, which would increase in future, and as a result of which the Smith v Manchester award was significantly reduced.

1.6.1.3.C19 Case No. 11675

Name of case: Evans v Hafeez

Brief description of injuries: KNEE

Reported: Kemp & Kemp, I2-432; [1998] CLY 1678

JSB Category: 6(L)(b)(i)

Sex: Female

Age at injury: 54

Age at award: 57

Date of award: 20 January 1998

Tribunal: Mayor's and City of London County Court

Amount of award then: £7,500

Award at February 2001: £8,088

Description of injuries: Knee injury requiring arthroscopy – pain in the knee most of the time – worse in cold weather – E had to change to lighter duties at work – pre-existing degeneration had been asymptomatic.

1.6.1.3.C20 Case No. 10459

Name of case: Topping v Ferranti Resin

Brief description of injuries: KNEE INJURY – AGGRAVATION OF PRE-EXISTING CONDITION

Reported: Kemp & Kemp, I2-433; [1992] CLY 1715

JSB Category: 6(K)(b)(ii)

Sex: Male

Age at injury: 33

Age at award: 36

Date of award: 11 December 1991

Tribunal: Newcastle District Registry

Amount of award then: £5,500

Award at February 2001: £6,971

Description of injuries: Knee injured in a fall from a ladder – plaintiff had been a keen sportsman and had played football professionally – unable to return to these activities. History of lateral meniscectomy in the right knee ten years previously – symptomless at the time of the accident.

Prognosis: Aggravation and an acceleration of degenerative changes in the knee joint.

1.6.1.3.C21 Case No. 11192

Name of case: Swinhoe v Taylor and Mainline

Brief description of injuries: KNEE

Reported: Kemp & Kemp, I2-434; [1996] CLY 2283

JSB Category: 6(L)(b)(ii)

Sex: Male

Age at injury: 37

Age at award: 39

Date of award: 19 March 1996

Tribunal: Sheffield County Court

Amount of award then: £6,000

Award at February 2001: £6,812

Description of injuries: Lesion to the joint surface in the right patella.

Prognosis: Degenerative changes in the knee were progressive – significant risk that his ability to continue driving buses would be impaired in 10 years time.

1.6.1.3.C22 Case No. 11003

Name of case: Harvey v Cadbury

Brief description of injuries: KNEE – 5-10 YEARS ACCELERATION OF UNDERLYING ARTHRITIS

Reported: Kemp & Kemp, I2-437; [1995] CLY 1755

JSB Category: 6(L)(b)(ii)

Sex: Male

Age at injury: 62

Age at award: 66

Date of award: 24 February 1995

Tribunal: Bristol County Court

Amount of award then: £5,500

Award at February 2001: £6,440

Description of injuries: Contusion injury to left knee – absent from work for initial period of three weeks – after return had further two weeks off work – plaintiff rested knee, applied cold compress and was prescribed pain-killers and cream to apply to knee – suffered acute pain in knee for three months – had underlying arthritis in his left retro-patella region which was asymptomatic prior to accident – after initial acute pain plaintiff experienced dull toothache-like pain in knee as result of arthritis – plaintiff was restricted in walking long distances, doing DIY and gardening.

Prognosis: But for accident would have continued to be asymptomatic for period of five to 10 years after accident – it was not anticipated that degree of pain experienced would increase.

1.6.1.3.C23 Case No. 10833

Name of case: Re A

Brief description of injuries: KNEE

Reported: Kemp & Kemp, I2-438; [1994] CLY 1682

JSB Category: 6(L)(b)

Sex: Male

Age at injury: 33

Age at award: 37

Date of award: 10 June 1994

Tribunal: CICB, London

Amount of award then: £5,000

Award at February 2001: £5,943

Description of injuries: Prison officer assaulted in line of duty – injury to right knee – problems with knee ongoing 15 months after assault – discovery of mild degenerative changes in articular cartilage in both patello-femoral aspect of knee joint and lateral compartment, and partial tear of anterior cruciate ligament – physiotherapy prescribed – knee still caused much discomfort.

Prognosis: Surgery might be necessary in future.

1.6.1.3.C24 Case No. 11004

Name of case: Re Carr

Brief description of injuries: KNEE – INJURY TO CARTILAGE – KNEE PAINFUL – MODERATE RISK OF ARTHRITIS

Reported: Kemp & Kemp, I2-439; [1995] CLY 1756

JSB Category: 6(L)(b)(ii)

Sex: Female

Age at injury: 33

Age at award: 39

Date of award: 28 October 1994

Tribunal: CICB

Amount of award then: £5,000

Award at February 2001: £5,923

Description of injuries: Postwoman was on duty in sorting office during armed robbery – was pushed to ground and landed on right knee – suffered niggling and throbbing pain when sitting or standing for long periods and knee was painful after walking short distances – occasionally knee gave way – arthroscopy carried out in 1992 and revealed injury to cartilage on lateral femoral condyle of right knee – no surgery necessary but there was moderate risk of arthritis occurring with no foreseeable improvement – sporting hobbies were curtailed by incident.

1.6.1.3.C29 Case No. 10645

Name of case: Southwell v Calderdale Metropolitan Borough Council

Brief description of injuries: KNEE – DEEP LACERATION – FULL RECOVERY

Reported: Kemp & Kemp, I2-422; [1993] CLY 1541

JSB Category: 6(L)(b)(ii), 8

Sex: Male

Age at injury: 9

Age at award: 10

Date of award: 23 August 1993

Tribunal: Halifax County Court

Amount of award then: £4,000

Award at February 2001: £4,869

Description of injuries: Slip and fall against gate – deep laceration on lateral aspect of right knee – 1 night in hospital, 5 weeks as out-patient – unable to exercise for some months – 7 months after accident, still occasional pain in scar region, approximately once a week for approximately 2 hours – 11cm inverted "V" – shaped scar on lateral aspect of knee.

Prognosis: Full recovery, but scar is permanent.

1.6.1.3.C30 Case No. 10907

Name of case: Back v Sharpe

Brief description of injuries: KNEE – SOFT-TISSUE INJURY – ACHING AND STIFFNESS – MINOR INJURIES

Reported: Kemp & Kemp, B2-043; [1995] CLY 1658

JSB Category: 6(L)(b)(ii)

Sex: Male

Age at injury: 31

Age at award: 33

Date of award: 02 March 1995

Tribunal: Dartford County Court

Amount of award then: £4,000

Award at February 2001: £4,664

Description of injuries: Plaintiff involved in road traffic accident when he was knocked off his motorcycle by the defendant's car – sustained minor multiple injuries: grazing to the left shoulder; mild contusion of the left elbow; a laceration across the front of the left knee; contusion of the left elbow; severe bruising and contusion of the left knee and left upper tibia with probable bruising to bone in the form of a subperiostal haematoma – most serious injury was to knee – was away from work for five weeks – complained of frequent sharp pains in knee when kneeling, stiffening of knee if held for too long in the same position and discomfort in the medial side of the knee when attempting to jog – stiffening of knee caused discomfort at work and the sharp pain resulting from pressure on the knee caused discomfort during sexual intercourse – pain in the left shoulder and elbow settled quickly but the symptoms associated with the knee injury still persisted at the date of the hearing.

1.6.1.3.C31 Case No. 11438

Name of case: Lowe v Baron Meats Ltd

Brief description of injuries: KNEE – SPRAIN

Reported: Kemp & Kemp, K2-040; [1997] CLY 1987

JSB Category: 6(L)(b)(ii)

Sex: Male

Age at injury: 25

Age at award: 30

Date of award: 18 April 1997

Tribunal: Nottingham County Court

Amount of award then: £3,000

Award at February 2001: £3,301

Description of injuries: Severely twisted the right knee – sprain injury – re-injured three weeks later.

Prognosis: The strain to the soft-tissues of the knee was significantly aggravated by the later incident.

1.6.1.3.C32 Case No. 10108

Name of case: Burton v Frigoscandia

Brief description of injuries: KNEE – SUBLUXATION – FULL RECOVERY EXPECTED

Reported: Kemp & Kemp, K2-051; [1990] CLY 1676

JSB Category: 6(L)

Sex: Male

Age at injury: 37

Age at award: –

Date of award: 31 October 1990

Tribunal: King's Lynn County Court

Amount of award then: £2,250

Award at February 2001: £2,970

Description of injuries: Suffered spontaneous lateral subluxation of right patella whilst lifting leg to avoid obstruction whilst helping to carry 3 cwt piece of machinery – on stretcher the subluxation spontaneously reduced – plaster of Paris cast applied, which was removed after two weeks – underwent physiotherapy for a period – experienced some continued aching in knee during cold or damp weather – these symptoms decreased during ensuing months.

Prognosis: Full recovery anticipated.

1.6.1.3.C25 Case No. 10834

Name of case: Re Carr
Brief description of injuries: KNEE
Reported: Kemp & Kemp, I2-439; [1994] CLY 1683
JSB Category: 6(L)(b)
Sex: Female
Age at injury: 33
Age at award: 39
Date of award: 28 October 1994
Tribunal: CICB
Amount of award then: £5,000
Award at February 2001: £5,923

Description of injuries: Claimant thrown to ground during armed robbery of postal sorting office – landed on right knee – niggling or throbbing pain when sitting or standing for long periods – knee painful after walking short distances – knee occasionally gave way – arthroscopy revealed injury to cartilage on lateral femoral condyle – sporting hobbies curtailed by incident – surgery not required.

Prognosis: Moderate risk of arthritis developing, with no foreseeable improvement.

1.6.1.3.C26 Case No. 11437

Name of case: Couch v Miotla
Brief description of injuries: KNEES – SOFT-TISSUE INJURIES
Reported: Kemp & Kemp, I2-440; [1997] CLY 1986
JSB Category: 6(L)(b)(ii)
Sex: Male
Age at injury: 57
Age at award: 60
Date of award: 04 February 1997
Tribunal: Wandsworth County Court
Amount of award then: £5,000
Award at February 2001: £5,548

Description of injuries: Soft-tissue injury to both knees.

Prognosis: Permanent lasting injuries were of mild degree.

1.6.1.3.C27 Case No. 10543

Name of case: Thatcher v Anders
Brief description of injuries: KNEE-MULTIPLE SOFT-TISSUE INJURIES
Reported: Kemp & Kemp, K2-005; [1993] CLY 1436
JSB Category: 6(L)(b),; 6(A)(c), 6(B)(c), 6(D)(c), 6(G)(c)
Sex: Male
Age at injury: 23
Age at award: 24
Date of award: 23 November 1992
Tribunal: Edmonton County Court
Amount of award then: £4,500
Award at February 2001: £5,540

Description of injuries: Soft-tissue injuries to neck, shoulder, elbow, back and knee (including damage to anterior cruciate ligament).

Prognosis: Recovered from neck and elbow injuries – substantial improvement in shoulder and back anticipated – knee injury would restrict participation in sports involving running, contact or twisting in the future.

1.6.1.3.C28 Case No. 11676

Name of case: Richardson v Davy Roll Co Ltd
Brief description of injuries: KNEE – FRACTURE OF PATELLA
Reported: Kemp & Kemp, I2-441; [1998] CLY 1679
JSB Category: 6(L)(b)(ii)
Sex: Male
Age at injury: 49
Age at award: 51
Date of award: 10 June 1998
Tribunal: Newcastle upon Tyne County Court
Amount of award then: £5,000
Award at February 2001: £5,263

Description of injuries: Vertical undisplaced fracture of the right patella.

Prognosis: All symptoms would resolve within 3 to 4 years of the date of the accident.

1.6.1.3.C33 Case No. 11677

Name of case: Howe v DT Tarmacadam

Brief description of injuries: KNEE – SOFT-TISSUE INJURY

Reported: (1999) 99 (1) QR 8; Kemp & Kemp, I2-445; [1998] CLY 1680

JSB Category: 6(L)(b)(ii)

Sex: Male

Age at injury: 51

Age at award: 54

Date of award: 25 August 1998

Tribunal: Bristol County Court

Amount of award then: £2,750

Award at February 2001: £2,889

Description of injuries: Blow to the patella causing soft-tissue injury to the knee – required aspiration.

Prognosis: Residual symptoms, of nuisance value, were permanent.

1.6.1.3.C34 Case No. 12046

Name of case: Patterson v Midland Bank PLC

Brief description of injuries: KNEE – 6 – 8 MONTH ACCELERATION

Reported: Kemp & Kemp, PRI-007; [2000] 5 CL 190

JSB Category: 6(L)(b)(ii)

Sex: Male

Age at injury: 52

Age at award: 55

Date of award: 31 January 2000

Tribunal: Pontefract County Court

Amount of award then: £2,250

Award at February 2001: £2,323

Description of injuries: A mild whiplash injury which subsided within 24 hours – impact injury to the left knee immediately swelled – pain for five months controlled by painkillers – pre-existing degenerative condition was asymptomatic before the accident – discomfort especially in cold weather – it was agreed that the accident had accelerated the symptoms by about six to eight months.

Prognosis: At the time of the hearing the knee was continuing to deteriorate.

1.6.1.3.C35 Case No. 10114

Name of case: Japal v Ford Motor Co.

Brief description of injuries: KNEE INJURIES – MINOR

Reported: Kemp & Kemp, K2-084; [1990] CLY 1685

JSB Category: 6(L)

Sex: Male

Age at injury: 32

Age at award: 33

Date of award: 21 February 1990

Tribunal: Romford County Court

Amount of award then: £1,600

Award at February 2001: £2,290

Description of injuries: Assembly worker, hit on back of knees by car shunted forward on assembly line – knees trapped between two cars – pain at front of both knees with bruising behind them

1.6.1.3.C36 Case No. 11043

Name of case: McCarthy v British Gas

Brief description of injuries: KNEE – "BRUISED BONE SYNDROME" TO BOTH KNEES – RECOVERY IN 16 MONTHS

Reported: Kemp & Kemp, K2-130; [1995] CLY 1797

JSB Category: 6(L)(b)(ii)

Sex: Male

Age at injury: 4

Age at award: 6

Date of award: 28 April 1995

Tribunal: Exeter County Court

Amount of award then: £1,500

Award at February 2001: £1,732

Description of injuries: P sustained injuries to both knees when he tripped over board which was covering a hole in pavement – although P sustained no fracture, both knees, and specifically knee-caps, sustained direct blow which resulted in "bruised bone syndrome", involving problems with patella articular cartilage and underlying bone – injury was exacerbated by the fact that, shortly before the accident, P had sustained fracture of right tibia and had broken right femur – infliction of "bruised bone syndrome" set P back in terms of recovery from earlier accidents and resumption of usual daily activities – had difficulty in walking and was unable to ride bike.

Prognosis: In normal circumstances, P would have been expected to have made full recovery within a matter of a few months – however, because P was diabetic, it took up to 16 months for injuries to settle – P was very unlikely to suffer from any long-term consequences as a result of accident.

1.6.1.3.C37 Case No. 11950

Name of case: M (a minor) v Sun World Ltd
Brief description of injuries: SCAR – KNEE
Reported: Kemp & Kemp, K2-145/5, K1-100; [1999] CLY 1614
JSB Category: 8
Sex: Male
Age at injury: 5
Age at award: 7
Date of award: 19 July 1999
Tribunal: Cheltenham County Court (infant settlement approval hearing)
Amount of award then: £1,500
Award at February 2001: £1,563
Description of injuries: 1.5cm vertical gash on right kneecap – 3 stitches inserted at hospital – subsequent treatment, covering a 4-month period, required at hospital in England because of delayed recovery due to infection – no time off school, but claimant could not participate in PE lessons for 2 weeks – claimant left with soundly – healed scar approximately 15mm x 5mm.
Prognosis: Scar likely to be permanent but of minimal cosmetic effect.

1.6.1.3.C38 Case No. 11260

Name of case: Steeksma v British Aerospace PLC
Brief description of injuries: KNEE – SWELLING – 4 WEEKS
Reported: Kemp & Kemp, I2-477; [1996] CLY 2352
JSB Category: 6(L)(b)(ii)
Sex: Male
Age at injury: 29
Age at award: 34
Date of award: 16 May 1996
Tribunal: Leeds County Court
Amount of award then: £1,000
Award at February 2001: £1,125
Description of injuries: Contusion to the left knee with swelling – symptoms gone after four weeks.

1.6.1.3.C39 Case No. 11267

Name of case: Groom v Ford Motor Company Ltd
Brief description of injuries: KNEE – SWELLING – 12 WEEKS
Reported: Kemp & Kemp, K2-250; [1996] CLY 2359
JSB Category: 6(L)(b)(ii)
Sex: Male
Age at injury: 34
Age at award: 37
Date of award: 28 August 1996
Tribunal: Romford County Court
Amount of award then: £600
Award at February 2001: £674
Description of injuries: Large swelling of the patella – back to full fitness after twelve weeks.

1.6.1.3.C40 Case No. 11707

Name of case: Ingrasci v Greatwood
Brief description of injuries: KNEE – CUTS
Reported: Kemp & Kemp, K2-268/2; [1998] CLY 1710
JSB Category: 6(L)(b)(ii)
Sex: Female
Age at injury: 27
Age at award: 29
Date of award: 07 April 1998
Tribunal: Kingston upon Thames County Court
Amount of award then: £300
Award at February 2001: £317
Description of injuries: 10 or 11 small gashes to the left knee – cuts had healed within a few weeks.

1.6.1.3.C41 Case No. 11068

Name of case: Whatley v Robson
Brief description of injuries: KNEE – DOG BITE – MINOR PUNCTURE WOUND
Reported: [1995] CLY 1822
JSB Category: 6(L)(b)(ii)
Sex: Male
Age at injury: 50
Age at award: 53
Date of award: 12 September 1995
Tribunal: Salisbury County Court
Amount of award then: £200
Award at February 2001: £228
Description of injuries: Male postman was delivering mail to defendant when he was bitten by Welsh springer spaniel resulting in small puncture wound to left knee and localised bruising – no stitches or dressing were required but he received anti-tetanus immunisation – took no time off work and there was no residual pain or scarring.

1.6.1.3.C42 Case No. 11747

Name of case: Scott v Miller

Brief description of injuries: KNEE – 7 DAYS

Reported: Kemp & Kemp, K2-274; [1998] CLY 1750

JSB Category: 6(L)(d)(ii)

Sex: Female

Age at injury: 37

Age at award: 39

Date of award: 24 July 1998

Tribunal: Harlow County Court

Amount of award then: £200

Award at February 2001: £211

Description of injuries: Painful knee – no bruising – fully resolved within 7 days.

1.6.1.3.1 Knee and other injury

1.6.1.3.1.C1 Case No. 11679

Name of case: Nicholls v Yorkshire Water Services Ltd

Brief description of injuries: KNEE – FRACTURE – PSORIASIS

Reported: Kemp & Kemp, I2-404; [1998] CLY 1682

JSB Category: 6(L)(b)

Sex: Female

Age at injury: 25

Age at award: 30

Date of award: 08 July 1998

Tribunal: Pontefract County Court

Amount of award then: £35,000

Award at February 2001: £39,233

Description of injuries: Fractured tibial plateau to the left knee – moderate to severe symptoms gradually became worse – stress over the injury caused psoriasis to spread over most of claimant's head and body requiring hospitalisation.

Prognosis: Psoriasis was never likely to be cured – a marked cosmetic deformity.

Other points: The knee injury and the skin condition were discrete injuries – no overlap as far as damages were concerned.

1.6.1.3.1.C2 Case No. 10455

Name of case: Pucci v Reigate and Banstead District Council

Brief description of injuries: FRACTURE DISLOCATION OF KNEE – 3 OPERATIONS – KNEE BRACE – GENERAL DEPRESSION

Reported: Kemp & Kemp, I2-406; [1992] CLY 1711

JSB Category: 6(K)(b)(iii)

Sex: Female

Age at injury: 26

Age at award: 31

Date of award: 21 October 1991

Tribunal: QBD

Amount of award then: £27,500

Award at February 2001: £37,034

Description of injuries: Fracture dislocation of the left knee – fractures of weight-bearing surface of the tibia – and rupture of a number of knee ligaments – suffered severe reactive depression requiring in-patient treatment – this deepened her depression – knee brace worn – degenerative changes manifesting in the knee.

Prognosis: Two further operations required which were hoped to bring about improvements for a few years – future deterioration expected and knee replacement or arthrodesis of the knee would be inevitable – psychiatric counselling was to continue for two years.

1.6.1.3.1.C3 Case No. 11434

Award at February 2001: £29,241

See: 1.4.4.1.C3 for details

1.6.1.3.1.C4 Case No. 10457

Name of case: Re Parslow

Brief description of injuries: KNEE FRACTURE – 4 OPERATIONS – CHRONIC PAIN – DEPRESSION

Reported: [1992] CLY 1713

JSB Category: 6(K)(a)(iii)

Sex: Male

Age at injury: 37

Age at award: 45

Date of award: 21 September 1992

Tribunal: CICB, Birmingham

Amount of award then: £20,000

Award at February 2001: £25,510

Description of injuries: Cracked fracture of the tibial eminence – two chondral flaps on the medial femoral chondyle had been partially knocked off – surgically removed – underwent three arthroscopies – left knee had markedly reduced range of movement – constant pain in the knee made worse by sitting for long periods – pain on walking more than 20 yards – enforced immobility and chronic pain caused development of a depressive illness – therapy for the illness was tried and failed.

Prognosis: He would always have continuing severe pain in that knee – medically retired in May 1987 – assessed at 30 per cent disability.

1.6.1.3.1.C5 Case No. 11189

Award at February 2001: £18,214

See: 1.4.1.1.C5 for details

1.6.1.3.1.C6 Case No. 10838

Name of case: Cleghorn v Stenna Offshore

Brief description of injuries: KNEE – EXACERBATION – FOOT

Reported: Kemp & Kemp, I4-018; [1994] CLY 1687

JSB Category: 6(L), 6(O), 6(B)

Sex: Male

Age at injury: 39

Age at award: 44

Date of award: 17 December 1993

Tribunal: Whitehaven County Court

Amount of award then: £12,500

Award at February 2001: £15,326

Description of injuries: Claimant, North Sea diver, fell 12ft through open hatch – fracture of 3 metatarsals in foot – exacerbation of pre-existing weakness in knee – on crutches 3 months – fractures did not unite for over a year – development of backache 13 months after accident due to uneven gait caused by use of crutches and subsequent use of stick – claimant had not worked since accident – residual disabilities of aching and stiffness causing limitation of movement.

Prognosis: Trouble from knee expected to be permanent.

1.6.1.3.1.C7 Case No. 10243

Name of case: Clayton v Liverpool City Council

Brief description of injuries: FRACTURED KNEE CAP – NOW WALKS WITH STICKS

Reported: Kemp & Kemp, I2-423; [1991] CLY 1440

JSB Category: 6(L)

Sex: Female

Age at injury: 59

Age at award: 63

Date of award: 12 February 1991

Tribunal: Liverpool County Court

Amount of award then: £10,000

Award at February 2001: £13,230

Description of injuries: Fracture to the right knee cap – leg plaster for 6 weeks – physiotherapy – grating and pain in both knees. Pre-accident C suffered from a congenital deformity – osteoarthritis to both knees – this had not given rise to any symptoms.

Prognosis: The injury made a considerable difference to her mobility – walked with two sticks – dependant on assistance for shopping and other tasks.

1.6.1.3.1.C8 Case No. 11000

Name of case: Re Pereira

Brief description of injuries: KNEE – DISRUPTED LIGAMENT – 2 OPERATIONS – ANXIETY

Reported: Kemp & Kemp, I2-425; [1995] CLY 1752

JSB Category: 6(L)(b)(i)

Sex: Male

Age at injury: 47

Age at award: 49

Date of award: 18 October 1994

Tribunal: CICB; London

Amount of award then: £10,000

Award at February 2001: £11,891

Description of injuries: Plaintiff was victim of unprovoked attack while performing as singer in public house – attacked by number of assailants, in course of which he was told he would be killed – suffered disruptive knee ligament and was hospitalised for three days – knee remained in plaster for two weeks – after three months had second operation to remove wire that had been inserted in knee – received physiotherapy for three months after attack and was absent from work for five months – left with 14cm operational scar above knee – two years after attack was still suffering some discomfort and restriction of movement in knee – as result of attack, he unable to continue working as entertainer in public houses and was limited to doing private functions – suffered generally from anxiety and loss of confidence and avoided going out in evenings.

Prognosis: Expert evidence was that these fears were likely to subside over a period of several years.

1.6.1.3.1.C9 Case No. 11190

Name of case: Daley v Harris

Brief description of injuries: KNEE – ARTHRITIS ACCELERATED BY 15 YEARS – OTHER INJURIES

Reported: Kemp & Kemp, I2-427; [1996] CLY 2281

JSB Category: 6(L)(b)(ii)

Sex: Male

Age at injury: 55

Age at award: 60

Date of award: 03 April 1996

Tribunal: Mayor's and City of London Court

Amount of award then: £10,000

Award at February 2001: £11,298

Description of injuries: Injuries to the right knee, back, elbow, head and groin.

Prognosis: Arthroscopy and physiotherapy required within six months – it was likely he would have to retire two years early.

Other points: Pre-existing asymptomatic arthritis of the knee accelerated by 12-15 years.

1.6.1.3.1.C10 Case No. 10831
Award at February 2001: £10,325
See: 1.3.1.3.1.C16 for details

1.6.1.3.1.C11 Case No. 12052
Award at February 2001: £8,776
See: 1.3.1.1.C21 for details

1.6.1.3.1.C12 Case No. 11436
Name of case: Clements v Wake
Brief description of injuries: FOOT – FRACTURE – KNEE
Reported: Kemp & Kemp, I2-431; [1997] CLY 1985
JSB Category: 6(O)(f)
Sex: Female
Age at injury: 22
Age at award: 25
Date of award: 10 February 1997
Tribunal: Canterbury County Court
Amount of award then: £7,500
Award at February 2001: £8,323
Description of injuries: Fractures to the foot – strain injury to the right knee – relatively mild post-traumatic stress disorder.
Prognosis: Permanent slight instability of the knee – increased risk of arthritis – treatment consisting of 6 to 10 sessions of cognitive behavioural therapy required.

1.6.1.3.1.C13 Case No. 11002
Award at February 2001: £6,807
See: 1.3.1.1.C28 for details

1.6.1.3.1.C14 Case No. 10832
Award at February 2001: £6,807
See: 1.3.1.1.C29 for details

1.6.1.3.1.C15 Case No. 11828
Award at February 2001: £6,796
See: 1.4.1.1.C13 for details

1.6.1.3.1.C16 Case No. 11133
Award at February 2001: £5,854
See: 1.3.1.1.C33 for details

1.6.1.3.1.C17 Case No. 11419
Award at February 2001: £5,755
See: 1.4.3.C27 for details

1.6.1.3.1.C18 Case No. 11854
Award at February 2001: £3,662
See: 1.5.4.C12 for details

1.6.1.3.1.C19 Case No. 11842
Award at February 2001: £3,384
See: 1.4.4.1.C15 for details

1.6.1.3.1.C20 Case No. 12027
Name of case: Watkinson v Chief Constable of the West Midlands
Brief description of injuries: KNEE – EXTENSIVE ABRASIONS – ANXIETY
Reported: Kemp & Kemp, K2-048/3; [2000] 4 CL 170
JSB Category: 6(K)(c)(iii)
Sex: Female
Age at injury: 22
Age at award: 26
Date of award: 08 December 1999
Tribunal: Leicester County Court
Amount of award then: £3,000
Award at February 2001: £3,084
Description of injuries: Knocked to the ground then stood upon by a police horse – extensive abrasions to her left knee – grazes to her shin – bruising to the calf where the horse stood on her – stiff and painful for six weeks – mild post-traumatic stress disorder – nightmares – scared of horses – anxious in police presence. At the time of the hearing there was gradual recovery – minor symptoms of anxiety persisted.
Other points: W was breast-feeding at the time of the accident – her milk dried up.

1.6.1.3.1.C21 Case No. 10486
Award at February 2001: £2,208
See: 1.3.1.1.C49 for details

1.6.1.3.1.C22 Case No. 10112
Award at February 2001: £2,183
See: 1.4.1.1.C27 for details

1.6.1.3.1.C23 Case No. 10487

Name of case: Lazenby v Panayiotou

Brief description of injuries: SOFT-TISSUE INJURY TO THE KNEE – SOME SHOCK

Reported: [1992] CLY 1743

JSB Category: 6(K)

Sex: Male

Age at injury: 20

Age at award: 24

Date of award: 13 October 1992

Tribunal: Edmonton County Court

Amount of award then: £1,750

Award at February 2001: £2,152

Description of injuries: Bad soft-tissue injury to the left knee and abrasions to both legs – no longer able to use his motorcycle.

Prognosis: Made a full recovery from his physical injuries – suffered shock and some psychological injury.

1.6.1.3.1.C24 Case No. 10876

Award at February 2001: £1,503

See: 1.2.3.2.1.C32 for details

1.6.1.3.1.C25 Case No. 11894

Award at February 2001: £1,308

See: 1.4.3.C37 for details

1.6.1.3.1.C26 Case No. 10505

Name of case: Flegg v Reed

Brief description of injuries: BRUISED KNEE – SHOCK

Reported: [1992] CLY 1761

JSB Category: 6(L)(b)(ii)

Sex: Female

Age at injury: 21

Age at award: 22

Date of award: 23 June 1992

Tribunal: Milton Keynes County Court

Amount of award then: £1,000

Award at February 2001: £1,235

Description of injuries: Badly bruised knee – shock – some psychological injury – nervous when driving and as a passenger after the accident.

Prognosis: No medical advice sought – no medical report.

1.6.1.3.1.C27 Case No. 12026

Award at February 2001: £1,032

See: 1.2.2.1.C43 for details

1.6.1.3.1.C28 Case No. 11704

Award at February 2001: £917

See: 1.2.3.1.C38 for details

1.6.1.4 ANKLE INJURY

1.6.1.4.C1 Case No. 11680

Name of case: Dow v Dow

Brief description of injuries: ANKLE

Reported: Kemp & Kemp, I2-306; [1998] CLY 1683

JSB Category: 6(M)(b)

Sex: Male

Age at injury: 41

Age at award: 48

Date of award: 27 March 1998

Tribunal: QBD

Amount of award then: £23,000

Award at February 2001: £25,427

Description of injuries: Comminuted fracture to the left tibia extending into the ankle joint – flake fracture to the lateral malleolus.

Prognosis: The chances of success of a subtalar fusion were estimated at 50 per cent – D would be at a permanent disadvantage in the labour market.

1.6.1.4.C2 Case No. 10835

Name of case: Camaish v Marske Machine Co
Brief description of injuries: ANKLE
Reported: Kemp & Kemp, I2-421; [1994] CLY 1684
JSB Category: 6(M)(c)
Sex: Male
Age at injury: 52
Age at award: 53
Date of award: 19 September 1994
Tribunal: Newcastle-upon-Tyne County Court
Amount of award then: £12,000
Award at February 2001: £14,369

Description of injuries: Compound comminuted fracture of left os calcis, laceration to ankle and wrenching injury to left knee – in hospital 2 weeks – ankle manipulated under general anaesthetic – walking restricted to 0.75 mile without stick – aching in ankle, ongoing at time of trial – unable to return to hobby of dancing – hobby of singing restricted, as only able to stand for 30 minutes at a time when performing – unable to return to former job as fitter, but able to take on lighter work avoiding climbing and walking for long periods or over rough ground – awarded 15 per cent assessment for industrial injuries benefit for life.

1.6.1.4.C3 Case No. 10836

Name of case: Dinsdale v Urban Firm
Brief description of injuries: ANKLE
Reported: Kemp & Kemp, I3-023; [1994] CLY 1685
JSB Category: 6(M)(c)
Sex: Female
Age at injury: 51
Age at award: 52
Date of award: 28 September 1993
Tribunal: Liverpool County Court
Amount of award then: £6,500
Award at February 2001: £7,879

Description of injuries: Claimant turned left ankle – crack fracture of navicular bone – fracture united satisfactorily, but with some irregularity to articular surface – 8 months in plaster; 2 months physiotherapy thereafter – post-traumatic degenerative change in ankle – disuse osteoporosis, causing discomfort.

Prognosis: Discomfort from osteoporosis permanent – residual disability no more than 5 per cent.

1.6.1.4.C4 Case No. 10462

Name of case: Scott v Theatre Royal (Plymouth)
Brief description of injuries: SEVERE ANKLE SPRAIN – CONTINUING PAIN
Reported: [1992] CLY 1718
JSB Category: 6(M)(d)
Sex: Female
Age at injury: 39
Age at award: 44
Date of award: 21 September 1992
Tribunal: Central London County Court
Amount of award then: £5,000
Award at February 2001: £6,169

Description of injuries: severe sprain of the anterior talo-fibular ligament of the right ankle.

Prognosis: At the time of the trial there was still a continuous dull ache in the ankle – as a result of the accident she would never be able to return to dancing, her chosen career.

1.6.1.4.C5 Case No. 10859

Name of case: Molyneux v Knowsley Borough Council
Brief description of injuries: ANKLE – ACHILLES TENDON – 12 MONTHS
Reported: Kemp & Kemp, I3-032; [1994] CLY 1710
JSB Category: 6(M)(d)
Sex: Male
Age at injury: 22
Age at award: 24
Date of award: 03 August 1994
Tribunal: Liverpool County Court
Amount of award then: £3,000
Award at February 2001: £3,566

Description of injuries: Partial rupture of right Achilles tendon – in hospital 3 days while tendon surgically repaired – plastercast for 3 weeks – metal brace for 8 weeks – crutches throughout that time – claimant able to walk unaided after 3 months, and run with reasonable comfort after 9 months – resumed training for hobby of amateur boxing after 12 months, taking part in first contest since accident 2 months later.

1.6.1.4.C6 Case No. 10837

Name of case: Rouse v Doncaster Metropolitan Borough Council
Brief description of injuries: ANKLE
Reported: Kemp & Kemp, I3-035; [1994] CLY 1686
JSB Category: 6(M)(d)
Sex: Male
Age at injury: 39
Age at award: 43
Date of award: 26 April 1994
Tribunal: Doncaster County Court
Amount of award then: £2,500
Award at February 2001: £2,982
Description of injuries: Claimant sat on chair, which collapsed – small flake fracture and severe strain of ligaments in dorsal aspect of left ankle – ankle bandaged for 3 months, claimant off work for that period – 4 months after accident, pain in ankle after walking, running or prolonged standing – some sleep disturbance – physiotherapy and hydrocortisone injection administered – symptoms improved and gradually subsided – at time of trial, minimal residual disability in that ankle painful after prolonged standing and uncomfortable in cold and damp weather.
Prognosis: Residual symptoms not expected to improve further – no future degeneration expected.

1.6.1.4.C7 Case No. 11441

Name of case: Williams v Smith and Daniels
Brief description of injuries: ANKLE – STRAIN
Reported: Kemp & Kemp, K2-063; [1997] CLY 1990
JSB Category: 6(M)(d)
Sex: Male
Age at injury: 38
Age at award: 39
Date of award: 17 June 1997
Tribunal: Blackpool County Court
Amount of award then: £2,500
Award at February 2001: £2,730
Description of injuries: Ankle injuries – medial and lateral ligamentous strain – possible chip fracture of the ankle.
Prognosis: At the time of the hearing aching and stiffness had almost completely resolved.

1.6.1.4.C8 Case No. 10670

Name of case: Brelsford v British Railways Board
Brief description of injuries: ANKLE – SPRAIN
Reported: [1993] CLY 1566
JSB Category: 6(M)(d)
Sex: Female
Age at injury: 35
Age at award: 37
Date of award: 18 January 1993
Tribunal: Derby County Court
Amount of award then: £1,850
Award at February 2001: £2,307
Description of injuries: Slip – sprain of left ankle – off work 2 weeks – limp for further 4 weeks – temporary residual weakness in ankle – ankle gave way on 4 subsequent occasions, without further injury – claimant unable to wear her customary high heeled shoes, as pain in left ankle developed after half an hour.
Prognosis: Prognosis of full recovery within 26 months of the accident.

1.6.1.4.C9 Case No. 10671

Name of case: Waumsley v British Railways Board
Brief description of injuries: ANKLE – SPRAIN – 18 MONTHS
Reported: Kemp & Kemp, K2-101; [1993] CLY 1567
JSB Category: 6(M)(d)
Sex: Female
Age at injury: 29
Age at award: 31
Date of award: 23 November 1992
Tribunal: Nottingham County Court
Amount of award then: £1,750
Award at February 2001: £2,155
Description of injuries: Step into hole and fall – sprain of right ankle and partial tear to lateral ligament – immediate swelling, bruising and pain – unable to work for 2 weeks, returned to normal duties thereafter – elasticated bandage for 6 months – discomfort persisted for 18 months – complete recovery after 18 months.
Prognosis: Prognosis of no long-term complications.

1.6.1.4.C10 Case No. 11237

Name of case: Bartley v Liverpool City Council
Brief description of injuries: ANKLE – LIGAMENT
Reported: Kemp & Kemp, I3-037; [1996] CLY 2329
JSB Category: 6(M)(d)
Sex: Male
Age at injury: 48
Age at award: 49
Date of award: 30 April 1996
Tribunal: Liverpool County Court
Amount of award then: £1,750
Award at February 2001: £1,972
Description of injuries: Plantar flexion strain – torn ligamentous fibres in the ankle – significant symptoms in the ankle were experienced for nine months.

1.6.1.4.C11 Case No. 11442

Name of case: Reid v Chowdhury
Brief description of injuries: ANKLE – SPRAIN – 6 – 8 WEEKS
Reported: Kemp & Kemp, K2-244; [1997] CLY 1991
JSB Category: 6(M)(d)
Sex: Female
Age at injury: 21
Age at award: 23
Date of award: 12 May 1997
Tribunal: Liverpool County Court
Amount of award then: £750
Award at February 2001: £822
Description of injuries: Wrenching inversion sprain to the soft-tissues of the ankle.
Prognosis: Full recovery after six to eight weeks.

1.6.1.4.C12 Case No. 11443

Name of case: Kerr v Tudor Thomas Construction and Development Ltd
Brief description of injuries: ANKLE
Reported: Kemp & Kemp, K2-245/1; [1997] CLY 1992
JSB Category: 6(M)(d)
Sex: Male
Age at injury: 11
Age at award: 14
Date of award: 15 September 1997
Tribunal: Aberdare County Court
Amount of award then: £750
Award at February 2001: £810
Description of injuries: Bruising to the leg and ankle and the chest wall – no bony injury – six sessions of physiotherapy were required.
Prognosis: Off school for one month – unable to do physical education for five weeks.

1.6.1.4.1 Ankle and other injury

1.6.1.4.1.C1 Case No. 11855

Name of case: Dunkeyson v Kirklees MBC
Brief description of injuries: ELBOW – ANKLE – LIMITATION OF MOVEMENT – SCAR
Reported: Kemp & Kemp, B2-019; [1999] CLY 1519
JSB Category: 6(G), 6(M)(c); 8
Sex: Female
Age at injury: 12
Age at award: 18
Date of award: 14 October 1998
Tribunal: Huddersfield County Court
Amount of award then: £27,500
Award at February 2001: £29,997
Description of injuries: Fracture dislocation of non-dominant left elbow – severe fracture dislocation of left ankle – elbow and ankle manipulated at hospital, initially without anaesthetic, as claimant had recently eaten – elbow reduction satisfactory, but open reduction and internal fixation required on ankle – claimant in hospital 6 weeks, on crutches for a further 6 weeks – school and daily living activities restricted thereafter – left elbow obviously deformed; 40 degree reduction in extension – movement in ankle restricted; unable to walk more than a mile without swelling and discomfort – unable to wear flat shoes, or walk on rough ground without stumbling – claimant now unable to play tennis or badminton – "noticeable and significant" scarring to ankle.
Prognosis: Risk of developing late ulnar neuritis, possibly requiring transposition of the ulnar nerve, within 15-20 years – 10 per cent risk of degenerative change in elbow – ankle arthrodesis operation required within 10 years.

Damage to Lower Limbs

1.6.1.4.1.C2 Case No. 10102

Name of case: Everard v Unigate Dairies
Brief description of injuries: CATASTROPHIC ANKLE INJURIES
Reported: [1990] CLY 1670
JSB Category: 6(M)
Sex: Male
Age at injury: 17
Age at award: 23
Date of award: 01 November 1989
Tribunal: Not stated
Amount of award then: £18,000
Award at February 2001: £27,072
Description of injuries: Plaintiff's motor cycle collided with milk float – sustained catastrophic ankle injuries, referred to as "rudder bar" injuries and minor crack fracture of his left radius – left ankle sustained compound fracture dislocation of the talus – right ankle sustained compound fracture of the distal tibia – constant ache in both ankles at time of trial, plus increasing pain in both ankles on walking – pain exacerbated by cold weather – analgesics necessary two to three times a day.
Prognosis: Over the next two to three years there would be little change, but over the following 10 to 15 years there would be considerable degeneration of both ankle joints – employed as caretaker in a school, but employment range considerably reduced.

1.6.1.4.1.C3 Case No. 10822

Award at February 2001: £18,601
See: 1.6.1.C4 for details

1.6.1.4.1.C4 Case No. 11681

Award at February 2001: £13,282
See: 1.2.3.1.C22 for details

1.6.1.4.1.C5 Case No. 10648

Award at February 2001: £6,452
See: 1.2.3.1.C26 for details

1.6.1.4.1.C6 Case No. 11889

Award at February 2001: £3,773
See: 1.4.1.1.C21 for details

1.6.1.4.1.C7 Case No. 11751

Name of case: Barsby v Harrison
Brief description of injuries: ANKLE – SCARS
Reported: Kemp & Kemp, PRK-010, J2-047; [1998] CLY 1754
JSB Category: 8; 6(C)(d), 6(K)(c)(iii), 6(M)(d)
Sex: Male
Age at injury: 46
Age at award: 48
Date of award: 26 January 1998
Tribunal: Derby County Court
Amount of award then: £1,750
Award at February 2001: £1,887
Description of injuries: Bruising to both legs and the left hip – grazing to both ankles and the left shin.
Prognosis: Small superficial scars on both ankles – permanent faint 3 inch scar to the shin.

1.6.1.4.1.C8 Case No. 10133

Name of case: Re Hill
Brief description of injuries: ANKLE LACERATION – FOUR STITCHES – MINOR DISCOMFORT
Reported: [1990] CLY 1715
JSB Category: 6(M)
Sex: Female
Age at injury: 57
Age at award: –
Date of award: 23 November 1990
Tribunal: CICB, Leeds
Amount of award then: £750
Award at February 2001: £992
Description of injuries: Plaintiff was domestic help in hospital – patient threw plate which hit plaintiff causing laceration to left ankle (1 cm by 1.5 cm) and leg – four stitches required – off work two weeks – scar remains tender and gives minor discomfort, especially in cold weather.

1.6.1.4.2 Ankle fracture

1.6.1.4.2.C1 Case No. 11193

Name of case: Re Clark

Brief description of injuries: ANKLE – FRACTURE DISLOCATION

Reported: Kemp & Kemp, I3-071; [1996] CLY 2284

JSB Category: 6(M)(b)

Sex: Male

Age at injury: 23

Age at award: 28

Date of award: 05 November 1996

Tribunal: CICB, Durham

Amount of award then: £20,000

Award at February 2001: £22,984

Description of injuries: Assault – fracture dislocation of the left ankle.

Prognosis: Symptoms were unlikely to improve – fusion was expected to be required within five years – unable to return to his previous work.

Other points: His condition was wholly due to the assault.

1.6.1.4.2.C2 Case No. 10103

Name of case: Jones v Houlder Marine Drilling

Brief description of injuries: ANKLE – FRACTURES – 2 OPERATIONS

Reported: Kemp & Kemp, I3-013; [1990] CLY 1671

JSB Category: 6(M)

Sex: Male

Age at injury: –

Age at award: 37

Date of award: 28 July 1990

Tribunal: Teesside Crown Court

Amount of award then: £16,000

Award at February 2001: £22,284

Description of injuries: Fractures of the midshaft of left fibula and fracture of left ankle – underwent operation affixing two screws on inner aspect and a plate with four screws on outer aspect of ankle – infection developed at fracture site – further operation performed to remove plate and screws four months after accident.

Prognosis: Continuing stiffness and weakness in left ankle and foot and restriction in ankle movement – can continue his job as painter for the present – arthritis will gradually develop in the ankle and within 10-12 years an arthrodesis of the ankle will be required – operational scars to lower left leg remain.

1.6.1.4.2.C3 Case No. 10245

Name of case: Pyke v Summers

Brief description of injuries: ANKLE – SEVERE TRIMALLEOLAR FRACTURE – 9 OPERATIONS – FIT FOR SEDENTARY WORK ONLY

Reported: Kemp & Kemp, 13-015; [1991] CLY 1442

JSB Category: 6(M)(b)

Sex: Female

Age at injury: 46

Age at award: 53

Date of award: 30 April 1991

Tribunal: QBD

Amount of award then: £15,000

Award at February 2001: £19,798

Description of injuries: Fell at work – severe trimalleolar fracture dislocation of the right ankle – internal fixation under general anaesthetic – two years later osteoarthritis required arthrodesis – ankle failed to settle – P was in plaster for most of the following twelve months – prolonged immobilisation led to degenerative change in mid-tarsal and sub-talar joints – nine procedures under general anaesthetic – referred to a pain clinic in 1989 – received anti-depressants and a series of guanethidine blocks.

Prognosis: Permanently unfit to return to pre-accident employment – she had recovered sufficiently to seek sedentary work as a cashier in a supermarket – she had come to terms with the pain.

1.6.1.4.2.C4 Case No. 11194

Name of case: Bahi v Rai

Brief description of injuries: ANKLE – FRACTURE

Reported: Kemp & Kemp, 13-016; [1996] CLY 2285

JSB Category: 6(M)(c)

Sex: Female

Age at injury: 24

Age at award: 27

Date of award: 30 August 1996

Tribunal: Birmingham County Court

Amount of award then: £16,000

Award at February 2001: £18,300

Description of injuries: Fractured right ankle.

Prognosis: Restricted movement likely to be permanent – unable to resume her pre-accident employment – scarring "not unsightly".

1.6.1.4.2.C5 Case No. 11431

Award at February 2001: £17,560

See: 1.6.1.2.C17 for details

1.6.1.4.2.C6 Case No. 11195

Name of case: Sowerby v North Yorkshire CC
Brief description of injuries: ANKLE – FRACTURE
Reported: [1996] CLY 2286
JSB Category: 6(M)(b)
Sex: Male
Age at injury: 29
Age at award: 32
Date of award: 19 October 1995
Tribunal: Newcastle upon Tyne County Court
Amount of award then: £12,500
Award at February 2001: £14,491
Description of injuries: Serious injury to the right ankle – slight injury to the knee.
Prognosis: At the age of 55 he would be unable to continue with his work – permanent loss of dorsiflexion – probable development of arthritis – intermittent pain and discomfort for the foreseeable future.
Other points: The fracture was not a typical ankle fracture.

1.6.1.4.2.C7 Case No. 11281

Name of case: Peters v Robinson
Brief description of injuries: ANKLE – FOOT – FRACTURES AND LACERATIONS
Reported: Kemp & Kemp, B2-036/1; [1997] CLY 1828
JSB Category: 6(M)(c)
Sex: Male
Age at injury: 26
Age at award: 33
Date of award: 27 January 1997
Tribunal: QBD
Amount of award then: £12,500
Award at February 2001: £14,045
Description of injuries: Avulsion fracture of the right ankle – severe soft-tissue injuries – fractures of the right big toe involving the interphalangeal joint – compound fracture of the right ring finger – laceration to the right arm – unable to return to his work for six months.
Prognosis: Likely to continue to suffer pain inn the right ankle.

1.6.1.4.2.C8 Case No. 10461

Name of case: Sweeney v South Tyneside Borough Council
Brief description of injuries: FRACTURED ANKLE – CONTINUING PAIN AND STIFFNESS
Reported: Kemp & Kemp, 13-019; [1992] CLY 1717
JSB Category: 6(M)(c)
Sex: Female
Age at injury: 41
Age at award: –
Date of award: 24 October 1991
Tribunal: Durham County Court
Amount of award then: £8,500
Award at February 2001: £10,822
Description of injuries: Potts' fracture to the left ankle – injury described as serious with non-union of the medial malleolus and some slight residual subluxation – prognosis was poor and it was unlikely the ankle would improve further and return to normal.
Prognosis: She would probably develop some arthritis in the ankle joint.

1.6.1.4.2.C9 Case No. 10247

Name of case: Martin v Crane and Martin
Brief description of injuries: ANKLE FRACTURE
Reported: [1991] CLY 1444
JSB Category: 6(M)(c)
Sex: Female
Age at injury: 68
Age at award: 72
Date of award: 15 May 1991
Tribunal: Brighton County Court
Amount of award then: £7,000
Award at February 2001: £9,019
Description of injuries: Traffic accident – fracture of the medial malleolus of the right ankle – knocked unconscious -cut lip – bruising to the face and abdomen – two operations under general anaesthetic – below knee plaster cast – post operative concussional syndrome – headaches.
Prognosis: Symptoms described as permanent.

1.6.1.4.2.C10 Case No. 12069

Name of case: McClean v Boult
Brief description of injuries: ANKLE – FRACTURE
Reported: [2000] 6 CL 199
JSB Category: 6(M)(c)
Sex: Male
Age at injury: 67
Age at award: 70
Date of award: 15 February 2000
Tribunal: Lambeth County Court
Amount of award then: £7,500
Award at February 2001: £7,701

Description of injuries: Bi-malleolar fracture of the right ankle – severe displacement of the ankle joint with some fragmentation of the tibia and fibula – internal fixation under general anaesthetic using a plate and seven screws – leg was elevated on a Braun frame – antibiotics prescribed – below-knee cast was applied for four weeks – severe pain for four weeks and unable to go out for four months – pre-existing social services home help had to be increased from two days per week to daily.

Prognosis: Walking range was reduced to half an hour – osteoarthritis in the ankle was likely to deteriorate.

1.6.1.4.2.C11 Case No. 10464

Name of case: Evason v Merseyside Transport
Brief description of injuries: FRACTURED ANKLE
Reported: Kemp & Kemp, I4-026; [1992] CLY 1720
JSB Category: 6(O)(g)
Sex: Female
Age at injury: 50
Age at award: 53
Date of award: 22 July 1992
Tribunal: Liverpool County Court
Amount of award then: £6,000
Award at February 2001: £7,435

Description of injuries: Fracture dislocation of the left foot.

Prognosis: At the time of the hearing a little persisting deformity remained in the tarso-metatarsal area.

1.6.1.4.2.C12 Case No. 11682

Name of case: Sturley v Carmarthen Town Council
Brief description of injuries: ANKLE – FRACTURE – 16 MONTHS
Reported: Kemp & Kemp, 13-027; [1998] CLY 1685
JSB Category: 6(L)(d); 6(D)(c)
Sex: Male
Age at injury: 49
Age at award: 52
Date of award: 05 February 1998
Tribunal: Swansea County Court
Amount of award then: £6,000
Award at February 2001: £6,438

Description of injuries: Fractured ankle with displacement – bruising to the right shoulder – full range of movement achieved within 16 months of the date of the accident.

1.6.1.4.2.C13 Case No. 10104

Name of case: Johnson v Rolls Royce
Brief description of injuries: ANKLE – FRACTURE – WALKS WITH LIMP
Reported: [1990] CLY 1672
JSB Category: 6(M)
Sex: Male
Age at injury: 55
Age at award: 59
Date of award: 21 November 1989
Tribunal: Court of Appeal
Amount of award then: £4,250
Award at February 2001: £6,164

Description of injuries: Slipped in car park due to employer's policy of not treating car park -sustained fracture/subluxation of left ankle – admitted to hospital where he received intravenous analgesia and sedation – off work 24 weeks – suffered recognised but unusual complication of pulmonary embolus on lung coming from injured ankle, and prescribed Warfarin – still suffers discomfort when walking on uneven ground three years on – reduction in sub-talar flexion and continuing slight discomfort in ankle – slight limp noticed by colleagues.

1.6.1.4.2.C14 Case No. 11008

Name of case: Ringer v Criddle

Brief description of injuries: ANKLE – MODERATE SOFT-TISSUE INJURY AND PROBABLE FRACTURE – RESIDUAL SWELLING AND ACHING

Reported: Kemp & Kemp, I3-027/2; [1995] CLY 1760

JSB Category: 6(M)(d)

Sex: Male

Age at injury: 49

Age at award: 53

Date of award: 03 February 1995

Tribunal: Colchester County Court

Amount of award then: £5,000

Award at February 2001: £5,854

Description of injuries: Plaintiff struck by car over left ankle and sustained long laceration running along medial side of ankle which was sutured – wound became infected and swollen – X-rays carried out two months after accident revealed some fragments described as being "probably bone" near heel – plaintiff was off work for 10 weeks by which stage wound had healed well – plaintiff suffered continuing symptoms with serious swelling in ankle necessitating wearing of tubigrip bandage during waking hours – also suffered from numbness in inner heel, sole of foot and big toe – scar of 3in across back of heel which tended to rub on shoes.

Prognosis: These problems had persisted to the date of trial, some three-and-a-half years after the accident, and were likely to be permanent.

1.6.1.4.2.C15 Case No. 10649

Name of case: Wild v Couvret

Brief description of injuries: ANKLE – FRACTURE

Reported: Kemp & Kemp, I3-027/5; [1993] CLY 1545

JSB Category: 6(M)(d)

Sex: Female

Age at injury: 12

Age at award: 15

Date of award: 01 March 1993

Tribunal: Bow County Court

Amount of award then: £4,500

Award at February 2001: £5,556

Description of injuries: Struck by car – fracture to lower tibia in right ankle – medial malleolus replaced and fixed with wires – in plaster for 2 months, on sticks for 2 more – permanent 6 cm scar over medial malleolus – was unable to ice skate or ballet dance for 18 months – now fully recovered, except for aching in ankle and empurpling of scar in cold weather.

1.6.1.4.2.C16 Case No. 12021

Name of case: Hanrahan v Home Office

Brief description of injuries: ANKLE – FRACTURE – UNSTABLE JOINT

Reported: Kemp & Kemp, PRI-005; [2000] 4 CL 164

JSB Category: 6(M)(d)

Sex: Male

Age at injury: 38

Age at award: 43

Date of award: 10 December 1999

Tribunal: Leeds County Court

Amount of award then: £4,000

Award at February 2001: £4,112

Description of injuries: H fell into a hole twisting his left ankle – it became immediately swollen and painful – a minor evulsion flake fracture at the tip of the left malleolus and injury to the left lateral ligament and the left capsule was diagnosed – H wore an aircast splint for one month – physiotherapy treatment followed – further investigation found that the lateral ligament had been stretched and rendered partly deficient – it was not susceptible to treatment.

Prognosis: Permanent moderate instability of the ankle joint – the residual symptoms did not affect his work.

1.6.1.4.2.C17 Case No. 11440

Name of case: Re Wilson (David Michael)

Brief description of injuries: ANKLE – FRACTURE

Reported: Kemp & Kemp, K2-023; [1997] CLY 1989

JSB Category: 6(M)(d)

Sex: Male

Age at injury: 39

Age at award: 43

Date of award: 29 October 1996

Tribunal: CICB

Amount of award then: £3,250

Award at February 2001: £3,635

Description of injuries: Fractured ankle.

Prognosis: Off work for about ten weeks – light duties for four weeks.

1.6.1.4.2.1.C5 Case No. 10647

Name of case: Wilson v Carrick Carr & Garwood

Brief description of injuries: ANKLE – FRACTURE – SEVERE LOSS OF CONFIDENCE

Reported: Kemp & Kemp, L3-024; [1993] CLY 1543

JSB Category: 6(M); 3(A)

Sex: Female

Age at injury: 76

Age at award: 79

Date of award: 03 March 1993

Tribunal: Hull County Court

Amount of award then: £6,000

Award at February 2001: £7,408

Description of injuries: Trip and fall – displaced bimalleolar fracture of right ankle – oblique fracture through medial malleolus – fracture through lateral malleolus, approx 3 cm proximal to the ankle joint – In plaster 6 weeks – pressure sore had developed, healed within 2 weeks – 4 months after accident, patient able to bear weight; persistent swelling but no localised tenderness – 16 months later, claimant complained that ankle tended to give way and become painful after walking any distance – gait slow, with antalgic limp, using a stick – reduced dorsiflexion – general mobility greatly reduced – severe loss of confidence – claimant no longer went out, became dependent on relatives for shopping and company – development of gross pitting oedema, caused by inactivity and sitting for long periods – signs of osteoarthritis in right ankle, unlikely to have been caused by accident – overriding factor in disability was loss of confidence.

Prognosis: Condition stabilised – no further deterioration expected.

1.6.1.5 FOOT INJURY

1.6.1.5.C1 Case No. 11857

Name of case: Re Gargano

Brief description of injuries: FEET – OS CALCIS (BILATERAL)

Reported: Kemp & Kemp, I4-012; [1999] CLY 1521

JSB Category: 6(O)(d)

Sex: Female

Age at injury: 19

Age at award: 28

Date of award: 22 July 1998

Tribunal: CICB, London

Amount of award then: £26,000

Award at February 2001: £28,536

Description of injuries: Comminuted crush fractures to os calcis in both feet, with fracture lines extending into the upper articular surfaces of os calcis where it forms the subtalar joint – also lacerations on right buttock and inner aspect of right upper thigh and laceration with loss of skin and pulp on tip of right index finger – fractures to heel bones extremely painful – in hospital 1 month, on 2 sticks for 3 months, 1 stick thereafter for a further few months – 9 years after incident, constant aches and pains in heels – unable to walk fast or for as long as 10 minutes – unable to do much housework or child care – unable to stand on tiptoe for any length of time, hop or squat fully – dorsiflexion to neutral in right ankle and to 5 degrees beyond neutral in left ankle; plantar flexion approximately 20 degrees and 15 degrees respectively – complete loss of inversion and eversion in left foot and only a few degrees in the right – talo – calcaneal arthritis present in both sides; claimant had been advised to undergo bilateral talo – calcaneal fusion, but had decided to delay procedure until all her children were at school.

1.6.1.5.C2 Case No. 10463

Name of case: Re Purcell

Brief description of injuries: SHOTGUN WOUNDS TO THE FOOT – CONTINUING PAIN AND DIFFICULTY IN WALKING

Reported: [1992] CLY 1719

JSB Category: 6(O)(e)

Sex: Female

Age at injury: 17

Age at award: 22

Date of award: 27 July 1992

Tribunal: CICB

Amount of award then: £12,500

Award at February 2001: £15,681

Description of injuries: Gunshot wounds to the feet – at least fifty shotgun pellets in each foot – at the time of the hearing she was still unemployed but the Board considered that she would be able to work in the future.

Prognosis: She had undergone an operation to remove pellets – some still remained embedded in the feet – further operations required – unable to work – suffered pain and difficulty in walking.

1.6.1.4.2.C18 Case No. 12068

Name of case: Coles v Lewis
Brief description of injuries: ANKLE – FRACTURE
Reported: [2000] 6 CL 198
JSB Category: 6(M)(d)
Sex: Male
Age at injury: 40
Age at award: 41
Date of award: 10 February 2000
Tribunal: Swansea County Court
Amount of award then: £3,500
Award at February 2001: £3,594

Description of injuries: Fractured lateral malleolus of the right ankle – plaster immobilisation required for six weeks – worked on light duties during this period – some discomfort persisted in cold weather.

Prognosis: Full recovery likely within twelve to eighteen months of the date of the accident.

1.6.1.4.2.1 Ankle fracture and other injury

1.6.1.4.2.1.C1 Case No. 10242

Name of case: Weaver v Hocking
Brief description of injuries: FRACTURED ANKLE AND NOSE – DAMAGE TO THE KNEE
Reported: Kemp & Kemp, I2-506; [1991] CLY 1439
JSB Category: 6(M)
Sex: Male
Age at injury: 39
Age at award: 46
Date of award: 24 April 1991
Tribunal: QBD
Amount of award then: £13,000
Award at February 2001: £17,058

Description of injuries: Bruises to the right leg – broken nose – dislocated ankle – large laceration to the left knee exposing the quadriceps tendon – damage to the gastrocnemius muscle – torn lateral popliteal nerve – fracture of the medial malleolus in the left ankle – ankle fracture was displaced several months later requiring internal fixation.

Prognosis: Fit for part time work within eighteen months of the accident – accepted that he could not work full time due to pain in the left foot – unable to referee at football matches or to garden.

1.6.1.4.2.1.C2 Case No. 10246

Name of case: Thompson v British Railways Board
Brief description of injuries: BIMALLEOLAR FRACTURE
Reported: Kemp & Kemp, 13-017; [1991] CLY 1443
JSB Category: 6(M)(c)
Sex: Male
Age at injury: 41
Age at award: 50
Date of award: 19 November 1991
Tribunal: QBD
Amount of award then: £12,500
Award at February 2001: £16,064

Description of injuries: Bimalleolar fracture to the right ankle – manipulated and fixed with a screw – in plaster for several weeks – underwent a course of physiotherapy. Ceased work in 1985 due to the injury and a pre-existing degenerative condition to his knee - suffered symptoms to the ankle and knee as well as problems with a shoulder.

Prognosis: T's condition was stable – some risk of osteoarthritis leading to deterioration.

1.6.1.4.2.1.C3 Case No. 10460

Name of case: Richley v Cooper
Brief description of injuries: FRACTURED ANKLE – ACTIVE LIFESTYLE SEVERELY RESTRICTED – WHIPLASH
Reported: Kemp & Kemp, I2-516; [1992] CLY 1716
JSB Category: 6(M)(c)
Sex: Female
Age at injury: 43
Age at award: 47
Date of award: 25 August 1992
Tribunal: Derby County Court
Amount of award then: £9,200
Award at February 2001: £11,392

Description of injuries: Trimalleolar Potts' fracture with considerable displacement of the talus out of the right ankle – fracture of the right fibula shaft – whiplash injury to the neck – ligamentous strain of the left ring finger – ankle fractures united soundly with good but not complete movement returning – embarrassing scars remained over the ankle where the metalwork had been fixed – her active lifestyle had been severely restricted.

Prognosis: Slightly increased risk of the onset of osteoarthritis in later life.

1.6.1.4.2.1.C4 Case No. 10646

Award at February 2001: £9,704

See: 1.2.3.2.1.C15 for details

1.6.1.5.C3 Case No. 10250

Name of case: Byatt v British Coal

Brief description of injuries: BIG TOE DISLOCATION

Reported: Kemp & Kemp, C4-062; [1991] CLY 1447

JSB Category: 6(P)(e)

Sex: Female

Age at injury: –

Age at award: 54

Date of award: 25 July 1991

Tribunal: Sheffield County Court

Amount of award then: £12,000

Award at February 2001: £15,614

Description of injuries: Dislocation to the right big toe – plaster applied – stiff and painful for three months – continuing pain and restriction – agility greatly reduced – at about age 60 B was likely to require arthrodesis which would reduce the pain but involve a further four to six months disability – prior thereto slow and progressive deterioration – post-traumatic stress syndrome complicated by domestic tragedies.

Prognosis: Held to be robust enough to work through therapy – likely to recover sufficient confidence to drive a car and travel as a passenger – surgery to defunction the toe at about age 60.

1.6.1.5.C4 Case No. 11859

Name of case: E (a minor) v Hatton

Brief description of injuries: TOES – CONTINUING LIMITATION

Reported: Kemp & Kemp, I4-020; [1999] CLY 1523

JSB Category: 6(P)

Sex: Male

Age at injury: 13

Age at award: 14

Date of award: 27 October 1998

Tribunal: Torquay and Newton Abbot County Court

Amount of award then: £10,000

Award at February 2001: £10,462

Description of injuries: Compound fracture of great left toe in go – karting accident – open reduction and fixation of fracture using K – wires – in hospital for 10 days, during which time claimant suffered sleep disturbance, toe became blackened, and persistent pins and needles developed in left little toe, which also became discoloured – below – knee plaster fitted and blister on great toe incised 9 days after accident – 27 days after accident, area of slough, piece of bone and some K – wires removed from great toe, and area of dead skin around little toe also removed – 37 days after accident, terminal phalanx, nail bed and nail of little toe amputated, causing claimant psychological distress; 4 operations in all performed – claimant off school 3 months, during which time normal routine seriously curtailed – left foot had to be kept elevated and dry throughout – pain – inability to bear weight – stiffness and swelling – inability to carry out normal activities such as bathing – disturbed sleep and anxiety about car travel – full weight bearing possible after 4.5 months, but elevation continued – claimant, keen sportsman, unable to play any sports for 6 months – recovery after approximately 1 year, though with natural arthrodesis of great toe – no limp – sprinting speed slightly reduced – little toe shortened, with no nail – stiff, bent great toe with scarring – area of some scarring on foot.

Prognosis: No significant long-term sequelae.

Other points: Judge considered that proper quantum evaluation would have been general damages of £10,000 plus £1,000 special damages, but approval was given to overall settlement of £10,000 in light of dispute over liability and early settlement.

1.6.1.5.C5 Case No. 11999

Name of case: George v Ministry of Defence

Brief description of injuries: FOOT – CONTAMINATED WOUND – BONE GRAFT

Reported: Kemp & Kemp, PRI-003; [2000] 3 CL 183

JSB Category: 6(O)

Sex: Male

Age at injury: 29

Age at award: 34

Date of award: 08 October 1999

Tribunal: Manchester County Court

Amount of award then: £10,000

Award at February 2001: £10,333

Description of injuries: A penetrating wound to the foot which was contaminated by the boot – the foot was cleaned and debrided – it became swollen and the cuboid bone was found to be diseased – at a sixth operation a bone graft was required from the hip – the foot arch collapsed – residual symptoms included painful scarring – throbbing pain – disturbed sleep – inability to take normal weight on the right foot – limited walking and standing – a limp – being resolute, G had managed to complete his combat training – there was some doubt about whether he would be able to complete his full army career or be promoted to sergeant.

1.6.1.5.C6 Case No. 10650

Name of case: Benn v G & F Joinery (Portsmouth)

Brief description of injuries: FEET – SOFT-TISSUE INJURIES – SIGNIFICANT LIMITATIONS

Reported: Kemp & Kemp, I4-021; [1993] CLY 1546

JSB Category: 6(O); 6(M)

Sex: Male

Age at injury: 52

Age at award: 57

Date of award: 10 February 1993

Tribunal: Southampton County Court

Amount of award then: £8,000

Award at February 2001: £9,914

Description of injuries: Fall into hole – soft-tissue injury to plantar aspect of left foot – soft-tissue injury in region of right Achilles' tendon – soft-tissue injury to rear of right lateral malleolus – immediate pain and tenderness in both feet – ability to walk, stand for long periods or play sports restricted – some resultant depression from time to time – left foot improved greatly at time of trial following surgical intervention to remove bony spur; only minor, continuous discomfort and some restriction of movement – right ankle still painful despite medical treatment; surgical intervention not likely to prove successful – at time of trial, claimant still unable to stand for long periods, play sports, walk more than half a mile or without a stick, or undertake physical tasks in course of work as publican.

Prognosis: Condition not expected to improve or deteriorate.

1.6.1.5.C7 Case No. 10249

Name of case: Crilley v Koeppl

Brief description of injuries: FOOT INJURIES – HAEMATOMA

Reported: Kemp & Kemp, I4-022; [1991] CLY 1446

JSB Category: 6(O)(g)

Sex: Female

Age at injury: 22

Age at award: 27

Date of award: 04 September 1991

Tribunal: Middlesbrough County Court

Amount of award then: £7,500

Award at February 2001: £9,584

Description of injuries: Severe soft-tissue bruises to the foot which developed into an haematoma – became fibrous – ten weeks on crutches, then a walking stick.

Prognosis: Swelling, tightening feeling and discomfort should gradually abate with time – swelling across the upper part of the foot was described as not serious but of some significance.

1.6.1.5.C8 Case No. 11198

Name of case: Jones v Clwyd HA

Brief description of injuries: FOOT – ABSCESS

Reported: Kemp & Kemp, I4-024; [1996] CLY 2289

JSB Category: 6(P)(c)

Sex: Female

Age at injury: 48

Age at award: 52

Date of award: 05 February 1996

Tribunal: Birmingham County Court

Amount of award then: £8,000

Award at February 2001: £9,119

Description of injuries: Negligent treatment of an abscess on the web between the toes.

Prognosis: Limp likely to be permanent – a degree of pressure and hence pain was unavoidable.

Other points: It was admitted that she should have been admitted immediately for emergency surgery under general anaesthetic.

1.6.1.5.C9 Case No. 10839

Name of case: Murdoch v Allerdale Borough Council

Brief description of injuries: FOOT

Reported: Kemp & Kemp, I4-027; [1994] CLY 1688

JSB Category: 6(O)(g)

Sex: Male

Age at injury: 4

Age at award: 7

Date of award: 14 July 1994

Tribunal: Carlisle County Court

Amount of award then: £6,000

Award at February 2001: £7,167

Description of injuries: Claimant's right foot run over by tractor mower – laceration around lateral border of right foot – three-quarter circumferential laceration (reducing blood supply), compound fracture of proximal phalanx (with some loss of bone substance), and complete division of extensor tendon mechanism, of fifth toe; ongoing symptoms of Raynaud's Phenomenon in toe thereafter – small laceration on base of fourth toe on plantar aspect – alopecia areata arising from shock and trauma – aching in cold weather – no functional deficit arising from injury – full recovery, including recovery from alopecia symptoms, by date of trial.

Prognosis: Continuing fear of loud machinery.

1.6.1.5.C10 Case No. 11199

Name of case: Garraway v Buckinghamshire HA
Brief description of injuries: FOOT – BURN
Reported: Kemp & Kemp, J3-031, J3-033/1; [1996] CLY 2290
JSB Category: 6(O)(g)
Sex: Male
Age at injury: Under 1 week
Age at award: –
Date of award: 21 February 1996
Tribunal: Slough County Court
Amount of award then: £4,500
Award at February 2001: £5,129

Description of injuries: Foot burn – immersed in water that was too hot.

Prognosis: Left little toe smaller than the right – continuing deformity "slight" – 50 per cent chance of further surgery being required.

Other points: Neither greater nor lesser damages were awarded than would have been awarded for an older child.

1.6.1.5.C11 Case No. 11858

Name of case: Morrisey v Borderdown Communication Ltd
Brief description of injuries: FOOT
Reported: Kemp & Kemp, I4-029; [1999] CLY 1522
JSB Category: 6(O)(g)
Sex: Female
Age at injury: 69
Age at award: 72
Date of award: 25 August 1999
Tribunal: Northampton County Court
Amount of award then: £4,750
Award at February 2001: £4,937

Description of injuries: Fracture to fifth metatarsal bone of left foot – bedrest for 4-5 days before going to hospital – below – knee plaster for first 3 weeks – severe pain for 4 weeks; claimant only able to mobilise with assistance of Zimmer frame, forced to sleep downstairs and required care from her adult daughters – knee plaster caused discomfort in knee for 2-3 months following accident – mobilisation improved somewhat after 8 weeks, but stairs difficult and some care still required from family – 3 months after accident, claimant complained of discomfort on outer side of foot, reduced walking distance, occasional limp, reduction in agility and being unable to wear high – heeled shoes – at date of trial, further improvement evident, but claimant still suffering occasional discomfort in foot, difficulty in managing stairs and swelling in ankle after walking for more than 2-3 hours – claimant unable to return to hobby of Irish dancing – ongoing limitations attributable to arthritis which was not accident-related.

Prognosis: Some further improvement possible, but full recovery not anticipated – 20 per cent risk of arthritis over next 5-10 years.

1.6.1.5.C12 Case No. 10850

Name of case: Johnson v Doncaster Leisure Management
Brief description of injuries: FOOT – BURNS
Reported: Kemp & Kemp, J3-032; [1994] CLY 1700
JSB Category: 8
Sex: Male
Age at injury: 24
Age at award: 25
Date of award: 01 February 1994
Tribunal: Leeds County Court
Amount of award then: £4,000
Award at February 2001: £4,842

Description of injuries: Extensive, full thickness chemical burns to dorsum of right foot when cleaning floor – pain and severe swelling – daily attendance at hospital 2 weeks, every other day for following month – foot unable to bear weight for 2 months – pain in foot upon contact with any object – sleep affected – claimant unable to wear any shoe or sock, thus preventing him from returning to work for 3 months – still occasional pain at time of trial – scarring to foot embarrassed claimant, who had therefore not returned to his hobby of swimming by date of trial.

Prognosis: Symptoms would resolve entirely with time.

1.6.1.5.C13 Case No. 10840

Name of case: Phipps v Goldpasta

Brief description of injuries: FOOT – DAMAGE TO PREVIOUSLY – INJURED FOOT

Reported: Kemp & Kemp, I3-029; [1994] CLY 1689

JSB Category: 6(O)(g)

Sex: Female

Age at injury: 48

Age at award: 50

Date of award: 16 May 1994

Tribunal: Ilford County Court

Amount of award then: £4,000

Award at February 2001: £4,755

Description of injuries: Claimant, suffering ongoing symptoms, from a previous fall, of subtalar fusion in right ankle, staple on dorsum of right foot, equinus deformity and low back pain (from disc protrusion and chronic degenerative changes), tripped and fell on crack in shop forecourt – staple in right foot broken – foot placed in plaster for 7 weeks – broken staple removed 11 weeks after accident – full recovery from symptoms associated with broken staple, but ongoing pain in foot movement – necessity for return to walking on 2 crutches, having previously progressed to being able to walk with just a stick (and sometimes, briefly, unaided) after previous fall – osteoarthritic changes, previously asymptomatic, in foot – also wrenching injury to knee, causing localised tenderness 7 months after accident.

Prognosis: Second fall had accelerated symptoms of osteoarthritic change in foot by 2-3 years – pain caused by changes would have increased over next 10 years in any event.

1.6.1.5.C14 Case No. 11686

Name of case: Forkes v Norwich CC

Brief description of injuries: FOOT – SCALD – 3.5 YEARS

Reported: (1998) 98 (6) QR 8; Kemp & Kemp, J3-033; [1998] CLY 1689

JSB Category: 6(O)(g)

Sex: Male

Age at injury: 36

Age at award: 40

Date of award: 01 July 1998

Tribunal: Norwich County Court

Amount of award then: £4,200

Award at February 2001: £4,432

Description of injuries: Scalded sole of the left foot – through the full thickness of skin over the ball of the foot – healing affected by infection requiring antibiotics – residual pain ongoing 3.5 years after the date of the accident.

1.6.1.5.C15 Case No. 11445

Name of case: McClean v Costa

Brief description of injuries: TOES – ARTHRITIS

Reported: Kemp & Kemp, I4-030; [1997] CLY 1994

JSB Category: 6(P)(e)

Sex: Male

Age at injury: 23

Age at award: 25

Date of award: 09 January 1997

Tribunal: Brentford County Court

Amount of award then: £3,848

Award at February 2001: £4,287

Description of injuries: Painful swelling of the toes – minor cuts to the shin.

Prognosis: Pre-existing Hallux Valgus deformity – the likely onset of arthritic changes was advanced by ten years.

1.6.1.5.C16 Case No. 10841

Name of case: Phillips (Marcus Timothy) v Southern Vectis

Brief description of injuries: FOOT

Reported: Kemp & Kemp, I4-033; [1994] CLY 1690

JSB Category: 6(O)(g)

Sex: Male

Age at injury: 16

Age at award: 20

Date of award: 28 October 1993

Tribunal: Southampton County Court

Amount of award then: £3,000

Award at February 2001: £3,639

Description of injuries: Claimant attempted to cross road, realised bus was turning into street and tried to step back – bus's back wheel ran over claimant's right foot – fractures through base of proximal phalanges of fourth and fifth toes – fracture through neck of proximal phalanx of third toe – skin of heel partially degloved – in hospital 5 days – discharged on crutches – some weight-bearing possible 1 month after discharge – some sharp pain experienced – residual sensation of no "padding" under foot, ongoing at date of trial.

Prognosis: No severe functional disability, but mild disability, of nuisance value, would be permanent – no residual disability from heel – no risk of degenerative arthritis.

1.6.1.5.C17 Case No. 11688

Name of case: Fraser v Lakeside Corp Ltd

Brief description of injuries: FOOT – PLANTAR FASCIITIS

Reported: Kemp & Kemp, I4-034; [1998] CLY 1691

JSB Category: 6(O)(g)

Sex: Male

Age at injury: 29

Age at award: 33

Date of award: 08 April 1998

Tribunal: Newcastle upon Tyne County Court

Amount of award then: £3,250

Award at February 2001: £3,438

Description of injuries: Cut hand – knee pain – injury to the plantar structures of the heel caused by plantar fasciitis.

Prognosis: F had made a full recovery at the time of the hearing – no further problems were expected.

1.6.1.5.C18 Case No. 11948

Name of case: Darmanin v Vauxhall Motors Ltd

Brief description of injuries: TOE – HAEMATOMA

Reported: Kemp & Kemp, J4-035; [1999] CLY 1612

JSB Category: 6(P)(e)

Sex: Female

Age at injury: 44

Age at award: 48

Date of award: 12 January 1999

Tribunal: Luton County Court

Amount of award then: £3,000

Award at February 2001: £3,158

Description of injuries: Undisplaced fracture of terminal phalanx of left big toe – development of haematoma under nail; nail pierced to allow release of blood – off work 2 weeks – dressings changed regularly for 3-4 weeks – nail lost after approximately 6 weeks – toe painful for 8 weeks; claimant wore trainers for that period – nail fell off a second time some time later; when it grew back, nail was thick and deformed; cosmetic effect "not significant, but could not be ignored" – claimant made good recovery from fracture, but still suffered from residual aching from time to time in cold weather.

Prognosis: Deformity to nail would be permanent.

1.6.1.5.C19 Case No. 12022

Name of case: McBride v Basildon &Thurrock Hospital NHS Trust

Brief description of injuries: FEET – TOES – WRONG SURGICAL PROCEDURE PERFORMED

Reported: Kemp & Kemp, PRI-006; [2000] 4 CL 165

JSB Category: 6(P)(e)

Sex: Male

Age at injury: 35

Age at award: 38

Date of award: 02 December 1999

Tribunal: Southend County Court

Amount of award then: £3,000

Award at February 2001: £3,084

Description of injuries: Suffered the wrong surgical procedure to the second and fourth toes to the right foot – the FETTS operation was correctly carried out on the third and fifth toes to the right foot as well as being incorrectly carried out to the second and fourth toes. M experienced the usual three to six months pain for such an operation.

Other points: The judge took into consideration the pain, suffering and loss of amenity suffered after the operation would have been experienced had only the necessary treatment been carried out.

1.6.1.5.C20 Case No. 10665

Name of case: Thorpe v Calderdale Metropolitan Borough Council

Brief description of injuries: FOOT – SOFT-TISSUE INJURY

Reported: Kemp & Kemp, K2-075; [1993] CLY 1561

JSB Category: 6(O)(g)

Sex: Female

Age at injury: 37

Age at award: 40

Date of award: 29 April 1993

Tribunal: Halifax County Court

Amount of award then: £2,000

Award at February 2001: £2,447

Description of injuries: Fall from stepped kerb – injury to right foot – no bony injury – crutches used for 7 weeks, 4 days – evidence given of disruption of enjoyment of Christmas holiday – pain in foot continued after coming off crutches, but gradually reduced – evidence given that claimant unable to wear closed shoes, as these caused pain in the foot.

1.6.1.5.C21 Case No. 11232

Name of case: Andrew v Herbert and Neale
Brief description of injuries: FOOT – CUT
Reported: Kemp & Kemp, I4-036; [1996] CLY 2324
JSB Category: 6(O)(g)
Sex: Male
Age at injury: 24
Age at award: 28
Date of award: 07 May 1996
Tribunal: Plymouth County Court
Amount of award then: £2,000
Award at February 2001: £2,250

Description of injuries: A shard of glass penetrated the foot – about four weeks post accident a piece of plastic extruded from the foot – wound left a small scar.

Other points: He was obliged to wear a dry suit in the months following the accident in pursuance of his degree course – suffered pain putting on and wearing the suit.

1.6.1.5.C22 Case No. 11946

Name of case: S (a minor) v Glynn Webb Wallpapers
Brief description of injuries: FOOT – BRUISING
Reported: Kemp & Kemp, PRK-005; [1999] CLY 1610
JSB Category: 6(O)(g)
Sex: Male
Age at injury: 8 years 5 months
Age at award: 9
Date of award: 15 September 1998
Tribunal: Halifax County Court (infant settlement approval hearing)
Amount of award then: £2,000
Award at February 2001: £2,092

Description of injuries: Claimant's foot struck by heavy falling object – some bruising, lasting for a few weeks, but no bony injury apparent from X-rays – tubigrip bandage and crutches supplied; bandage worn for 1 week – claimant off school for 1 week – difficulty walking for 2 weeks – 6 months after accident, some aching still experienced after walking distances in excess of 1 mile.

Prognosis: Aching expected to subside within 3 months of hearing.

1.6.1.5.C23 Case No. 10866

Name of case: Thompson v Caradon Heating
Brief description of injuries: FOOT – 4-5 WEEKS
Reported: Kemp & Kemp, K2-104; [1994] CLY 1718
JSB Category: 6(O)(g); 6(P)(e)
Sex: Male
Age at injury: 32
Age at award: 34
Date of award: 17 May 1994
Tribunal: Kingston-upon-Hull County Court
Amount of award then: £1,700
Award at February 2001: £2,021

Description of injuries: Claimant slipped in shower block and struck left foot on concrete step – contusions to second, third and fourth toes – soft-tissue injury to base of fifth metatarsal – associated abrasions – X-rays revealed no fracture – abrasions dressed and painkillers prescribed – claimant unable to join family for first week of holiday; unable to participate in leisure activities during second week due to pain in foot – unable to play football for 7 weeks – light duties for 2.5 weeks on return to work after holiday – effectively full recovery after 4-5 weeks, apart from occasional pain in second toe and inability to play football for a further 2 weeks.

1.6.1.5.C24 Case No. 11749

Name of case: Carron v Lion Plant Ltd
Brief description of injuries: FOOT – SEVERE BRUISING – 18 MONTHS
Reported: Kemp & Kemp, PRK-002, K2-117/2; [1998] CLY 1752
JSB Category: 6(O)(g)
Sex: Male
Age at injury: 24
Age at award: 28
Date of award: 18 November 1997
Tribunal: Liverpool County Court
Amount of award then: £1,750
Award at February 2001: £1,886

Description of injuries: Severe bruising injury to the foot – plaster cast for 3 days – full recovery made within 18 months of date of accident.

1.6.1.5.C25 Case No. 11242

Name of case: Green v MC PR Ltd
Brief description of injuries: FOOT – 10 MONTHS
Reported: Kemp & Kemp, I4-037; [1996] CLY 2334
JSB Category: 6(O)(g)
Sex: Female
Age at injury: 46
Age at award: 47
Date of award: 16 February 1996
Tribunal: Bow County Court
Amount of award then: £1,500
Award at February 2001: £1,710
Description of injuries: Foot was injured when a heavy fire extinguisher fell on it – a ganglion developed at the injury site – swelling subsided after ten months.
Prognosis: Residual symptoms were expected to subside.

1.6.1.5.C26 Case No. 11947

Name of case: Davison v Interspan Services Ltd
Brief description of injuries: FOOT
Reported: [1999] CLY 1611
JSB Category: 6(O)(g)
Sex: Male
Age at injury: 54
Age at award: 56
Date of award: 01 July 1999
Tribunal: King's Lynn County Court
Amount of award then: £1,600
Award at February 2001: £1,667
Description of injuries: Injury to inner side of right heel – immediate excruciating pain – unable to bear weight – ice packs and bandages applied, but heel became swollen and claimant taken to hospital – X-rays revealed no bony injury – claimant on crutches for 2 weeks, and was able to return to work a week later – at trial, 2 years after accident, claimant's heel still ached in cold weather or after spending a long time on his feet – claimant was unable to garden or walk dog for 4 weeks following accident, but no problems after that.

1.6.1.5.C27 Case No. 11250

Name of case: Re Armatrading
Brief description of injuries: FOOT – DOG BITE – SCAR
Reported: Kemp & Kemp, K2-138; [1996] CLY 2342
JSB Category: 6(O)(g)
Sex: Male
Age at injury: 33
Age at award: 37
Date of award: 03 June 1996
Tribunal: CICB
Amount of award then: £1,480
Award at February 2001: £1,664
Description of injuries: Dog bite to the heel of the left foot – four stitches required – left with permanent vertical scar of 5cms.

1.6.1.5.C28 Case No. 10677

Name of case: Tunnicliffe v Wandlowsky
Brief description of injuries: FOOT – SOFT-TISSUE INJURIES
Reported: Kemp & Kemp, K2-147; [1993] CLY 1573
JSB Category: 6(O)(g); 5(A)
Sex: Female
Age at injury: 21
Age at award: 23
Date of award: 09 June 1993
Tribunal: Hitchin County Court
Amount of award then: £1,250
Award at February 2001: £1,525
Description of injuries: Road accident – soft-tissue injuries to right side of chest and right foot – elasticated bandage and crutches prescribed for foot, but pain in chest precluded use of crutches for first week; claimant thus immobile for that time – absent 1 week from full-time course and 2 weeks from part-time job as barmaid – pain in chest resolved within 3 weeks – full mobility achieved in 4 weeks – at date of trial, symptoms of aching and tenderness over dorsum of right foot, exacerbated by cold weather, still evident, but improving – no effect on lifestyle.
Prognosis: Aching in foot expected to resolve gradually.

1.6.1.5.C29 Case No. 10681

Name of case: Humphries v Goodyear Great Britain

Brief description of injuries: FOOT – SOFT-TISSUE INJURY – 3-4 MONTHS

Reported: Kemp & Kemp, K2-178; [1993] CLY 1577

JSB Category: 6(O)(g), 6(M)(d); 8

Sex: Male

Age at injury: 28

Age at award: 29

Date of award: 19 October 1992

Tribunal: Wolverhampton County Court

Amount of award then: £1,000

Award at February 2001: £1,229

Description of injuries: Claimant dragged over drum of his tyre building machine when it suddenly started up – mild bruising to right side of body – more severe bruising to right foot and ankle – 2 days of considerable pain, especially in right ankle, interrupting sleep – light duties at work for 2.5 weeks – leg swollen for 3-4 weeks, causing considerable discomfort – leg felt insecure – claimant unable to play with young daughter or do gardening for 3 or 4 months – half inch long pink scar above and behind medial malleolus – claimant back to normal after 3 or 4 months.

Prognosis: Scar minor disfigurement which would improve with time.

1.6.1.5.C30 Case No. 10682

Name of case: Joseph v Kaur

Brief description of injuries: FOOT – BURNS – 2 MONTHS

Reported: Kemp & Kemp, J3-042; [1993] CLY 1578

JSB Category: 6(M)(d), 6(O)(d)

Sex: Male

Age at injury: 44

Age at award: 48

Date of award: 20 May 1993

Tribunal: Leeds County Court

Amount of award then: £1,000

Award at February 2001: £1,219

Description of injuries: Road accident – partial thickness burns to right foot from boiling water escaping from vehicle's engine cooling system – excitement of pre-existing but otherwise quiescent osteo-chondrites of navicular bone of right ankle – burns dressed and eventually blistered – considerable discomfort, and difficulty in walking and driving – blow to ankle slow to resolve, elastic bandage and analgesics eventually prescribed – full recovery with no long-term sequelae within 2 months of accident.

1.6.1.5.C31 Case No. 10852

Name of case: Edgar v I & M Adams (a firm)

Brief description of injuries: FOOT – SCAR

Reported: Kemp & Kemp, J3-043; [1994] CLY 1702

JSB Category: 8

Sex: Female

Age at injury: 17

Age at award: 19

Date of award: 30 November 1993

Tribunal: Stoke-on-Trent County Court

Amount of award then: £1,000

Award at February 2001: £1,215

Description of injuries: Boiling water spilt onto claimant's right foot – severe pain and blistering to upper part of foot – unable to bear weight on right foot for 1 week – off work 10 days – burns healed within 4 weeks – scarring to foot visible at date of trial, but not a serious cosmetic blemish – residual tenderness in foot, lasting about a year.

1.6.1.5.C32 Case No. 11057

Name of case: Stansfield v Alexon Group t/a Mead Manufacturing

Brief description of injuries: FOOT – BRUISING AND LACERATION

Reported: Kemp & Kemp, I4-038; [1995] CLY 1811

JSB Category: 6(P)(e)

Sex: Female

Age at injury: 30

Age at award: 33

Date of award: 22 February 1995

Tribunal: Cardiff County Court

Amount of award then: £950

Award at February 2001: £1,112

Description of injuries: Claimant suffered bruising and loop two-and-a-half centimetre laceration to top of left big toe when she slipped on piece of cloth and struck her toe on sewing machine – attended hospital where wound was cleaned and closed with butterfly stitches – did not lose any time from work – wound covered and dressed for four weeks – tenderness and discomfort lasted for approximately six months – scar remained obvious but of no cosmetic significance.

1.6.1.5.C33 Case No. 11750

Name of case: Topham (a minor) v Acorn Fabrics
Brief description of injuries: FOOT – POSSIBLE FRACTURE
Reported: Kemp & Kemp, K2-208/5; [1998] CLY 1753
JSB Category: 6(O)(g)
Sex: Female
Age at injury: 2
Age at award: 4
Date of award: 14 November 1997
Tribunal: Halifax County Court
Amount of award then: £1,000
Award at February 2001: £1,078
Description of injuries: Injury to the foot – not X-rayed – extreme pain – full recovery.
Other points: It was possible that the foot had been fractured – it could not be proved.

1.6.1.5.C34 Case No. 10515

Name of case: Small v United Engineering Steels
Brief description of injuries: BRUISED FOOT – 4 WEEKS
Reported: [1992] CLY 1771
JSB Category: 6
Sex: Male
Age at injury: 48
Age at award: 51
Date of award: 05 February 1992
Tribunal: Walsall County Court
Amount of award then: £750
Award at February 2001: £946
Description of injuries: Bruising to the top of the foot.
Prognosis: Some pain persisted for four weeks.

1.6.1.5.C35 Case No. 12051

Name of case: Bevan v South Wales Fire Service
Brief description of injuries: FOOT – BRUISING
Reported: Kemp & Kemp, K2-244/1; [2000] 5 CL 195
JSB Category: 6(O)(g)
Sex: Male
Age at injury: 27
Age at award: 29
Date of award: 19 January 2000
Tribunal: Cardiff County Court
Amount of award then: £800
Award at February 2001: £826
Description of injuries: Soft-tissue injury to the foot when it was struck by a fire hose – very swollen and bruised – provided with crutches – unable to weight bear for two weeks – gradual improvement thereafter.
Prognosis: A full resolution was expected within a short period.

1.6.1.5.C36 Case No. 11471

Name of case: Carlisle v Chapman
Brief description of injuries: FOOT – BRUISING – 2 WEEKS
Reported: Kemp & Kemp, K2-259; [1997] CLY 2021
JSB Category: 6(P)(e)
Sex: Male
Age at injury: 26
Age at award: -
Date of award: 11 November 1996
Tribunal: Medway County Court
Amount of award then: £500
Award at February 2001: £559
Description of injuries: Bruising to the right side of the body and leg – soft-tissue injury to the big toe.
Prognosis: Foot was painful for ten days – bruising lasted for two weeks.
Other points: No medical attention sought.

1.6.1.5.1 Foot and other

1.6.1.5.1.C1 Case No. 10838

Award at February 2001: £15,326
See: 1.6.1.3.1.C6 for details

1.6.1.5.1.C2 Case No. 11695

Award at February 2001: £4,313
See: 1.3.1.3.1.C27 for details

1.6.1.5.1.C3 Case No. 11842

Award at February 2001: £3,384
See: 1.4.4.1.C15 for details

1.6.1.5.1.C4 Case No. 10112

Award at February 2001: £2,183
See: 1.4.1.1.C27 for details

1.6.1.5.2 Foot fracture

1.6.1.5.2.C1 Case No. 11689

Name of case: Storey v Rae

Brief description of injuries: TOES – ALL TOES ON ONE FOOT AMPUTATED – MULTIPLE FRACTURES

Reported: Kemp & Kemp, I4-011; [1998] CLY 1692

JSB Category: 6(P)(a), 6(D)(d), 6(K), 6(M)

Sex: Female

Age at injury: 33

Age at award: 37

Date of award: 13 February 1998

Tribunal: QBD

Amount of award then: £28,500

Award at February 2001: £32,031

Description of injuries: Fractures to the clavicle, right tibia, right malleolus, right toes – the toes became gangrenous and had to be amputated – claimant still fit for light or sedentary work – able to walk and drive.

1.6.1.5.2.C2 Case No. 11683

Name of case: King v Co-Steel Sheerness plc

Brief description of injuries: FEET – FRACTURES TO BOTH FEET

Reported: Kemp & Kemp, I4-073; [1998] CLY 1686

JSB Category: 6(O)(d)

Sex: Male

Age at injury: 55

Age at award: 58

Date of award: 09 July 1998

Tribunal: Clerkenwell County Court

Amount of award then: £20,000

Award at February 2001: £21,641

Description of injuries: Comminuted fractures to the calcaneum of each foot – loss of natural Bohler's angle on both feet.

Prognosis: Progressive degenerative arthritis in both talo-calcaneal joints – K would have to give up employment at the age of 62.

1.6.1.5.2.C3 Case No. 11684

Name of case: Fuller v Haymills (Contractors) Ltd

Brief description of injuries: FOOT – FRACTURE – PSYCHOLOGICAL EFFECTS

Reported: Kemp & Kemp, I4-076; [1998] CLY 1687

JSB Category: 6(O)(e); 3(A)

Sex: Male

Age at injury: 44

Age at award: 47

Date of award: 26 September 1997

Tribunal: Peterborough County Court

Amount of award then: £15,000

Award at February 2001: £16,422

Description of injuries: Fracture to the right calcaneus – fracture to the right zygomatic arch – depression caused by financial worries after the accident.

Prognosis: Permanent problems in heel – 30 per cent chance that an operation to fuse the ankle would be carried out.

Other points: F suffered a major collapse of morale.

1.6.1.5.2.C4 Case No. 11444

Name of case: P (a minor) v Meakin

Brief description of injuries: FOOT – FRACTURE

Reported: Kemp & Kemp, I4-019; [1997] CLY 1993

JSB Category: 6(O)(f)

Sex: Female

Age at injury: 12

Age at award: 16

Date of award: 13 November 1996

Tribunal: Slough County Court

Amount of award then: £13,500

Award at February 2001: £15,259

Description of injuries: Crush injury to the left foot – fractures to four metatarsals – one displaced – one metatarsal dislocation – greenstick fracture of the collarbone.

Prognosis: Permanent disabilities were: stiffness – periodic pain – noticeable bony prominence on the bridge of the foot – second toe raised above the others – no risk of osteoarthritis.

Other points: Conscious of the appearance of the foot – difficult to buy court shoes..

1.6.1.5.2.C5 Case No. 10651

Name of case: Blakemore v College of St Mark and St John

Brief description of injuries: FOOT – FRACTURE – CONTINUING LIMITATIONS

Reported: Kemp & Kemp, I3-020; [1993] CLY 1547

JSB Category: 6(O)

Sex: Female

Age at injury: 33

Age at award: 37

Date of award: 26 October 1993

Tribunal: Plymouth County Court

Amount of award then: £8,000

Award at February 2001: £9,704

Description of injuries: Fall – slightly displaced fracture of left of calcis – no surgery required – off work 2 months – persistent residual disability in the form of episodic swelling in hot weather and continuing aching in cold weather, at end of working day, after walking more than half a mile or driving long distances – walking on uneven ground difficult – inability to wear high heels – inability to play ball games with children or ice skate – average consumption of 10 painkilling tablets per month – support bandage sometimes required – some restriction of leisure and social activities – earning capacity not restricted.

Prognosis: Subtalar and mid-tarsal movements permanently restricted to 75 per cent of normal – all symptoms expected to be permanent – no risk of osteoarthritic changes and degenerative changes in longer term.

1.6.1.5.2.C6 Case No. 11200

Name of case: Re Hurley

Brief description of injuries: FOOT – CRUSH INJURY – MULTIPLE FRACTURES

Reported: Kemp & Kemp, I4-023; [1996] CLY 2291

JSB Category: 6(P)(c)

Sex: Male

Age at injury: 58

Age at award: 61

Date of award: 08 May 1996

Tribunal: Liverpool County Court

Amount of award then: £8,500

Award at February 2001: £9,562

Description of injuries: Crush injury to the right foot – burst laceration to the great toe – fracture of the second toe – comminuted fracture of the great toe – post-traumatic arthritis developed as a result of the accident – unable to return to his pre-accident work.

1.6.1.5.2.C7 Case No. 11196

Name of case: Cohen v Servi Group Travel SA

Brief description of injuries: TOE – FRACTURE

Reported: Kemp & Kemp, I3-025; [1996] CLY 2287

JSB Category: 6(P)(e)

Sex: Female

Age at injury: 45

Age at award: –

Date of award: 12 June 1996

Tribunal: QBD

Amount of award then: £6,000

Award at February 2001: £6,745

Description of injuries: Fractured toe – badly bruised ankle – damaged collateral ligament – unable to wear ordinary heeled shoes – ankle continued to give way.

1.6.1.5.2.C8 Case No. 11685

Name of case: McDevitt v Rochford Mouldings Ltd

Brief description of injuries: FOOT – FRACTURED METATARSALS

Reported: Kemp & Kemp, I4-028; [1998] CLY 1688

JSB Category: 6(O)(g)

Sex: Male

Age at injury: 26

Age at award: 30

Date of award: 19 October 1998

Tribunal: Southend County Court

Amount of award then: £5,000

Award at February 2001: £5,228

Description of injuries: Obviously displaced fractures to the second, third and fourth metatarsals to the left foot – foot not deformed – continuing symptoms of pain and aching.

1.6.1.5.2.C9 Case No. 12070

Name of case: Goodwin v GKN Sheepbridge Stokes Ltd
Brief description of injuries: FEET – FRACTURED METATARSALS
Reported: [2000] 6 CL 200
JSB Category: 6(O)(e)
Sex: Male
Age at injury: 31
Age at award: 34
Date of award: 10 January 2000
Tribunal: Chesterfield County Court
Amount of award then: £4,300
Award at February 2001: £4,439

Description of injuries: Undisplaced fractures to the base of the second and third metatarsals of the right foot – in plaster for three weeks – G underwent a course of physiotherapy – away from work for seven months – an arch support was fitted – well healed within eighteen months of the date of the accident.

Prognosis: Persisting minor symptoms were expected to be permanent at a slight disadvantage in the labour market.

Other points: A claim for a Smith v Manchester award was rejected.

1.6.1.5.2.C10 Case No. 11963

Name of case: Short v Trustees of Yeovil Agricultural Society
Brief description of injuries: FOOT – FRACTURE OF NAVICULAR
Reported: Kemp & Kemp, I4-031; [2000] 1 CL 123
JSB Category: 6(M)(d)
Sex: Female
Age at injury: 26
Age at award: 28
Date of award: 24 September 1999
Tribunal: Yeovil County Court
Amount of award then: £4,000
Award at February 2001: £4,140

Description of injuries: S tripped and fell in a rabbit hole – immediate pain and swelling to the ankle – an avulsion fracture to the navicular (tarsal) bone – an initial back cast was replaced within two days by a below knee backslab – mobilised with physiotherapy – S improved quite rapidly – pain and swelling had largely settled within three months of the date of the accident.

Prognosis: No long term risk of degeneration.

1.6.1.5.2.C11 Case No. 11687

Name of case: Huxter v Lock
Brief description of injuries: FOOT – FRACTURED METATARSALS
Reported: (1998) 98 (6) QR 8; Kemp & Kemp, I4-032; [1998] CLY 1690
JSB Category: 6(O)(g)
Sex: Male
Age at injury: 21
Age at award: 24
Date of award: 26 June 1998
Tribunal: Weymouth County Court
Amount of award then: £3,500
Award at February 2001: £3,684

Description of injuries: Fractures to the third and fourth metatarsals of the right foot.

Prognosis: Permanent slight deformity – minimal symptoms described as a nuisance.

1.6.1.5.2.C12 Case No. 10672

Name of case: Harcourt v Harper and Harper
Brief description of injuries: FOOT – FRACTURE – FULL RECOVERY
Reported: Kemp & Kemp, K2-123; [1993] CLY 1568
JSB Category: 6(O)(g)
Sex: Female
Age at injury: 3
Age at award: 5
Date of award: 06 August 1993
Tribunal: Chesterfield County Court
Amount of award then: £1,500
Award at February 2001: £1,826

Description of injuries: Left foot struck by bricks falling from wall – crack fracture of shaft of first metatarsal – complete plaster cast applied, allowing claimant to walk, removed after 2 weeks – residual swelling for about 2 months after accident.

Prognosis: Excellent recovery with no long-term complications.

1.6.1.5.2.C13 Case No. 10281

Name of case: Williams v Winstone Rollers

Brief description of injuries: FRACTURE TO THE LITTLE TOE

Reported: Kemp & Kemp, K2-160; [1991] CLY 1478

JSB Category: 6(P)(e)

Sex: Male

Age at injury: 49

Age at award: 52

Date of award: 25 January 1991

Tribunal: Blackwood County Court

Amount of award then: £1,100

Award at February 2001: £1,453

Description of injuries: Moderate contusion of the soft-tissue of the left little toe – fracture at the proximal phalanx – treated with toe-strapping – symptoms almost settled after six weeks.

Prognosis: A nasty injury from which the plaintiff had fully recovered.

1.6.1.5.2.C14 Case No. 10125

Name of case: Williams v Russell

Brief description of injuries: LITTLE TOE – FRACTURE

Reported: Kemp & Kemp, K2-222; [1990] CLY 1703

JSB Category: 6(O)

Sex: Male

Age at injury: 22

Age at award: 23

Date of award: 19 January 1990

Tribunal: Wrexham County Court

Amount of award then: £650

Award at February 2001: £936

Description of injuries: In avoidance of car struck his left foot against metal gatestop – undisplaced fracture to base of proximal phalanx of fifth toe – initial period of pain, some nausea and difficulty in walking lasting five days.

Prognosis: Full recovery and no long-term consequences.

1.6.1.5.2.1 Foot fracture and other injury

1.6.1.5.2.1.C1 Case No. 11281

Award at February 2001: £14,045

See: 1.6.1.4.2.C7 for details

1.6.1.5.2.1.C2 Case No. 11436

Award at February 2001: £8,323

See: 1.6.1.3.1.C12 for details

SECTION 1.7
PHYSICAL DAMAGE TO SKIN

1.7.C1 Case No. 11239

Name of case: Blakey v Brown

Brief description of injuries: SKIN – SCRATCHES, BITES AND BRUISES

Reported: Kemp & Kemp, K2-106; [1996] CLY 2331

JSB Category:

Sex: Male

Age at injury: 10 months

Age at award: 2

Date of award: 30 January 1996

Tribunal: Bow County Court

Amount of award then: £1,750

Award at February 2001: £2,004

Description of injuries: Scratches, bites and bruises – possibly caused by another child – at time of the hearing an area of discolouration had faded – it was not to be permanent.

Other points: A plaster cast was removed from his right wrist when X-rays showed there was no fracture.

1.7.C2 Case No. 11701

Name of case: Campbell (a minor) v Nottingham City Council

Brief description of injuries: SKIN – GRAZING – TRUNK

Reported: (1999) 99 (1) QR 8; Kemp & Kemp, K2-145/3; [1998] CLY 1704

JSB Category: 8; 3(A)

Sex: Male

Age at injury: 7

Age at award: 9

Date of award: 28 September 1998

Tribunal: Nottingham County Court

Amount of award then: £1,500

Award at February 2001: £1,569

Description of injuries: Grazes to the rib cage, back, shoulder and hip – nightmares – bed-wetting – resultant pale areas of skin to the back and shoulder were barely noticeable – psychological consequences were resolved in a couple of months.

1.7.C3 Case No. 10885

Name of case: Thomas v Dewhirst

Brief description of injuries: SKIN – FLEA BITES – MINOR SCARS

Reported: Kemp & Kemp, K2-221; [1994] CLY 1737

JSB Category: 8

Sex: Female

Age at injury: 25

Age at award: -

Date of award: 14 March 1994

Tribunal: Sunderland County Court

Amount of award then: £800

Award at February 2001: £966

Description of injuries: Claimant bitten twice by flea just above right ankle while working at defendant's premises – bites blistered, causing some pain beneath the skin lasting for a few days – blisters lanced and required dressing – wounds healed within a couple of weeks – 2 areas of partial pigmentation remaining, approximately 1cm in diameter – pigmented areas only visible when claimant suntanned – practically invisible to naked eye.

Other points: Award included £300 for cosmetic injury.

1.7.1 BURNS

1.7.1.C1 Case No. 11206

Name of case: Re MVR
Brief description of injuries: SKIN – 45% BURNS
Reported: Kemp & Kemp, J3-011/1; [1996] CLY 2297
JSB Category: 7(B)(a)
Sex: Female
Age at injury: 42
Age at award: 50
Date of award: 11 September 1996
Tribunal: Not stated
Amount of award then: £85,000
Award at February 2001: £113,859

Description of injuries: 45 per cent burns – 15 per cent full thickness – 23 per cent multiple thickness the rest partial thickness – post-traumatic stress disorder.

Prognosis: Likely to need further correctional operations for the rest of her life – suffered acute embarrassment and distress at her appearance and its effect on other people – at risk of suicide – unable to get a job – she was unlikely to have retired at the usual age before the accident.

Other points: Ambulance was not called until the next day.

1.7.1.C2 Case No. 10474

Name of case: Re E
Brief description of injuries: 42% BURNS – SEVERE DEPRESSION
Reported: [1992] CLY 1730
JSB Category: 7(B)(a)(i)
Sex: Female
Age at injury: 42
Age at award: 46
Date of award: 07 October 1992
Tribunal: CICB, London
Amount of award then: £75,000
Award at February 2001: £109,834

Description of injuries: Suffered 42 per cent burns – head, neck, arms, hands, back and chest – respiratory burns – injuries caused by her husband having poured turpentine over her head and igniting it.

Prognosis: She had a bald patch 15 cm by 11 cm – loss of the pinnae of both ears – four months in hospital – several operations – difficulty in fine finger movements – teeth damaged by fire – all fillings had to be replaced under general anaesthetic due to difficulty in opening her mouth – had to sleep in a collar – eyes not burnt but it was difficult to read and to concentrate – very sensitive about her appearance – developed agoraphobia and anxiety – depression caused by her inability to fulfil emotional and sexual needs led to two suicide attempts – unable to enjoy dancing, swimming, sunbathing or holidays abroad – remained susceptible to infections.

1.7.1.C3 Case No. 10251

Name of case: Sear v Stamford Pantomime Players
Brief description of injuries: BURNS – 60%
Reported: [1991] CLY 1448
JSB Category: 8
Sex: Female
Age at injury: 9
Age at award: 20
Date of award: 15 January 1991
Tribunal: QBD
Amount of award then: £65,000
Award at February 2001: £101,012

Description of injuries: Severe burns in which 60 per cent of the skin surface was destroyed – affected the chin, lower two thirds of the trunk, right arm, legs and buttocks – particularly severe burning round the vulva and perineum – most of the face and breasts escaped – in hospital for four-and-a-half months – skin grafts and agonisingly painful dressings in between – S's survival was in doubt – incontinent of faeces until July 1986 – had to wear a helmet and elastic body and leg stockings at night to control scarring – her parents support was essential.

Prognosis: Perineal scarring causes some discomfort during sexual intercourse – suffers psychological problems in her sexual relations – at a disadvantage in the labour market and will lose earnings when undergoing further corrective treatment to the scars – inhibited in her social life and inability to wear normal clothes – most sport is denied her.

1.7.1.C4 Case No. 10252

Name of case: Re Hart
Brief description of injuries: BURNS – 40%
Reported: Kemp & Kemp, J3-012; [1991] CLY 1449
JSB Category: 8
Sex: Female
Age at injury: 42
Age at award: 52
Date of award: 27 September 1991
Tribunal: CICB, Manchester
Amount of award then: £65,000
Award at February 2001: £97,166

Description of injuries: Assault – H's former husband poured petrol over her and set it alight – hospital in-patient for five months – full thickness 40 per cent burns to the upper half of the trunk, arms, face and neck – three major skin grafts – further seven operations between May 1982 and June 1990 – movements to the neck and right shoulder painful – family reaction was difficult to cope with – children were teased at school about her scarring – extreme embarrassment at the scarring – unable to get her hands behind her back – difficulty in opening her mouth through scar contracture – some hair loss – loss of one ear – burn injury described as "most grievous".

Prognosis: H could have expected to work for about ten years before the accident – she was virtually unemployable – feelings of frustration, self-consciousness, anxiety, irritability and missed family life during hospitalisation.

1.7.1.C5 Case No. 11456

Name of case: Re Stokle
Brief description of injuries: SKIN – BURNS – 40%
Reported: Kemp & Kemp, J3-014/1; [1997] CLY 2005
JSB Category: 8
Sex: Male
Age at injury: 32
Age at award: 38
Date of award: 28 August 1997
Tribunal: CICB, London
Amount of award then: £70,000
Award at February 2001: £87,605

Description of injuries: Full thickness burns to 40 per cent of the upper body – including face, neck, upper limbs and dominant right hand – eight episodes of surgery – whiplash.

Prognosis: Chronic low back pain – hoarseness – hearing loss – prone to blistering and overheating – damaged skin needed protection from the sun – unrealistic to expect him to work in the future.

1.7.1.C6 Case No. 11089

Name of case: Re R (1996)
Brief description of injuries: SKIN – ACID BURNS – SCARS
Reported: Kemp & Kemp, J3-015; [1996] CLY 2180
JSB Category: 7(B)(a)(i)
Sex: Female
Age at injury: 18
Age at award: 29
Date of award: 11 July 1996
Tribunal: CICB, Bath
Amount of award then: £60,000
Award at February 2001: £76,793

Description of injuries: Full thickness skin acid burns to the mouth, chin, neck and chest.

Prognosis: No further improvement to the scarring was likely – had suffered a marked personality change.

Other points: Rejected by prospective employers – marriage broke down.

1.7.1.C7 Case No. 11965

Name of case: Mizon v Comcon International Ltd
Brief description of injuries: SKIN – HANDS – BURNS – ALCOHOLISM
Reported: Kemp & Kemp, C4-013; [2000] 1 CL 125
JSB Category: 8 and 3(B)(a)
Sex: Male
Age at injury: 55
Age at award: 62
Date of award: 19 August 1999
Tribunal: Kingston upon Hull County Court (Bowers J)
Amount of award then: £55,000
Award at February 2001: £63,416

Description of injuries: M was trapped in the flaming engine room of a merchant vessel when the engine exploded at sea – full thickness burns to the face, hands and forearms – skin grafts were carried out – three further operations to the hands to relieve contractures over the following years – scarring to the face was not obvious – he was very self-conscious about his hands and arms – family carried out cooking, cleaning and personal services on a daily basis – post-traumatic stress disorder with mixed anxiety and depression – a fixed phobic anxiety about being trapped indoors – M became alcohol dependent and short tempered with no interests and few friends. M's hands were severely scarred and clawed – with considerable loss of abduction and adduction – he got no benefit from counselling – he was unfit for work.

1.7.1.C8 Case No. 11692

Name of case: Weinberger (a minor) v Jacobs

Brief description of injuries: SKIN – SCALDING – 23 PER CENT

Reported: Kemp & Kemp, J3-016/1; [1998] CLY 1695

JSB Category: 8

Sex: Male

Age at injury: 16 months

Age at award: 3

Date of award: 15 January 1998

Tribunal: Luton County Court

Amount of award then: £25,650

Award at February 2001: £28,784

Description of injuries: Boiling water scald of 23 per cent of body surface and area scale – face, neck, upper chest, right arm and both hands – required split skin grafts to 14 per cent body surface.

Prognosis: Permanent extensive disfiguring scars – most were not amenable to surgical revision.

Other points: Approved settlement.

1.7.1.C9 Case No. 10253

Name of case: Baldwin v Wirral Borough Council

Brief description of injuries: BURNS – BACK

Reported: Kemp & Kemp, J3-020; [1991] CLY 1450

JSB Category: 8

Sex: Male

Age at injury: 17

Age at award: 23

Date of award: 20 March 1991

Tribunal: Liverpool County Court

Amount of award then: £13,000

Award at February 2001: £17,287

Description of injuries: Severe full thickness burns to the back – hospital in-patient for four weeks – major skin grafting under general anaesthetic.

Prognosis: Very ugly scarring covering a large part of his back – embarrassed to strip to the waist in public or to go swimming – extensive skin graft scars to his thighs – the sun caused itching – scarring had not reduced B's working capacity.

Other points: B said "It takes me a long time to tell a girl about the scarring, and when I do usually I don't see her again."

1.7.1.C10 Case No. 11529

Name of case: Durose v Novaceta

Brief description of injuries: SKIN – ELECTRICAL BURNS – DEPRESSION

Reported: Kemp & Kemp, C4-059; [1998] CLY 1531

JSB Category: 3(A)(b)

Sex: Male

Age at injury: 50

Age at award: 52

Date of award: 03 December 1997

Tribunal: Nottingham County Court

Amount of award then: £15,000

Award at February 2001: £16,347

Description of injuries: Electrocution burns to the hand – pain in the arm, hand and hip – claimant became reactively depressed – low confidence, self esteem and motivation.

Prognosis: Symptoms were acknowledged to be permanent – counselling and job seeking might take about 4.5 years.

1.7.1.C11 Case No. 10728

Name of case: Podd v Ransomes and Napier

Brief description of injuries: SKIN – 8-9 PER CENT BURNS – POST-TRAUMATIC STRESS DISORDER – DEPRESSION

Reported: Kemp & Kemp, J3-021; [1994] CLY 1576

JSB Category: 7(B); 3(A), 3(B); 8

Sex: Male

Age at injury: 35

Age at award: 42

Date of award: 04 November 1993

Tribunal: Colchester County Court

Amount of award then: £12,000

Award at February 2001: £14,724

Description of injuries: Leaking gas ignited while claimant changing gas canisters – canisters exploded in "quite horrific" accident – claimant burnt on face, hands and back, 8-9 per cent of surface area of skin – 7 days in hospital; burns sufficiently superficial for careful home nursing thereafter – return to work after 16 weeks – initial shock at accident, both at what had occurred and because of mistaken conviction that colleague had been killed in accident – development of reactive depression thereafter – inability to sleep – undue irritability – occasional breaking – down in tears – depression symptoms gradually improved, and resolved about 2 years after the accident – slight scarring to burnt areas, not readily noticeable at time of hearing.

Prognosis: Some sensation of tightness in skin on back of hands expected in cold weather.

Other points: General damages a single award for both physical and psychological damage – judge considered there to be an apparent shortage of reported cases in which physical injuries had healed quickly but left a longer term psychological problem.

1.7.1.C12 Case No. 10897

Name of case: Fallon v Beaumont

Brief description of injuries: BURNS – 65 PER CENT – DEATH AFTER 30 DAYS

Reported: Kemp & Kemp, J3-023, L7-021; [1994] CLY 1749

JSB Category:

Sex: Male

Age at injury: 22

Age at award: deceased

Date of award: 16 December 1993

Tribunal: Leeds County Court

Amount of award then: £10,000

Award at February 2001: £12,176

Description of injuries: High – speed road accident – deceased trapped in burning car until arrival of emergency services – no evidence of loss of consciousness during that period – conscious and breathing spontaneously upon arrival at hospital – 65 per cent burns (50 per cent total thickness, 15 per cent partial thickness) – medical evidence of extreme pain from partial burns, but no "pain" as such from total thickness burns, as sensory nerve endings would have been completely destroyed – activity around deceased upon arrival at hospital would have given him significant insight into gravity of his condition – endotracheal tube passed; claimant resisted, and had to be sedated – deceased not expected to survive night of accident – attended by priest; evidence that deceased aware of this – ventilation continued for 12 days, during which deceased's level of consciousness varied between deep anaesthesia and light sedation, when it was possible for him to understand words spoken to him – attempts made to wean deceased off ventilator for 2 days, at which time there were periods of spontaneous breathing and full consciousness – in third week after accident, renal functions deteriorated – dialysis commenced – ventilation via tracheostomy – skin grafts undertaken – from this time on, deceased had periods of partial awareness, decreasing in frequency over final days of life – died 30 days after accident from bleeding into the lungs (haemoptysis) caused by smoke inhalation – severe burns a contributory factor.

1.7.1.C13 Case No. 10254

Name of case: Ellis v Mainzer

Brief description of injuries: SEVERE CHEMICAL BURNS TO THE KNEES

Reported: Kemp & Kemp, J3-028; [1991] CLY 1451

JSB Category: 8

Sex: Male

Age at injury: 26

Age at award: 29

Date of award: 06 February 1991

Tribunal: Wigan District Registry

Amount of award then: £6,000

Award at February 2001: £7,884

Description of injuries: Severe chemical burns to the knees – knelt in cement – treated by dressings – no skin grafts due to imprisonment four weeks after the date of the accident – conservative treatment continued in prison – E has significant scarring to the knees – avoids kneeling – skin over the knees is very thin and sensitive – medical opinion is to the effect that E should undergo excision of scar tissue and remodelling of the skin over the knees – surgery should improve symptoms.

Prognosis: Able to resume work in the building industry – sensitivity will always be abnormal.

1.7.1.C14 Case No. 11694

Name of case: Hawkins and Cadwaladr v Gator Tool Hire & Sales Ltd

Brief description of injuries: SKIN – BURNS – 73 PER CENT – DEATH AFTER 14 DAYS

Reported: Kemp & Kemp, J3-030; [1998] CLY 1697

JSB Category:

Sex: Male

Age at injury: 22

Age at award: Deceased

Date of award: 01 May 1998

Tribunal: Blackwood County Court

Amount of award then: £5,000

Award at February 2001: £5,260

Description of injuries: Full thickness 73 per cent burns – partial thickness burns – inhalation injury with swelling to the throat and chemical burns below the vocal chords – breathing difficulties and pain – died after 14 days.

1.7.1.C15 Case No. 11453

Name of case: Longworth v Sunbeams Ltd

Brief description of injuries: SKIN – ULTRA-VIOLET BURNS

Reported: Kemp & Kemp, J3-035; [1997] CLY 2002

JSB Category: 8

Sex: Female

Age at injury: Not stated

Age at award:

Date of award: 20 June 1997

Tribunal: Reading County Court

Amount of award then: £3,750

Award at February 2001: £4,095

Description of injuries: Excessive ultra-violet radiation burns – reddening progressing to blistering to the legs – soreness over the back.

Prognosis: Residual red mark about the size of a matchbox caused embarrassment – continued to suffer some pain.

Other points: At the time of the hearing she continued to use sun-beds – she had considerable exposure to sunbeds in the past.

1.7.1.C16 Case No. 10851

Name of case: Greenhall v Sunblest Bakeries

Brief description of injuries: SKIN – BURNS TO BUTTOCK AND THIGH

Reported: Kemp & Kemp, J3-037; [1994] CLY 1701

JSB Category: 8

Sex: Male

Age at injury: 19

Age at award: 22

Date of award: 13 April 1994

Tribunal: Stoke-on-Trent County Court

Amount of award then: £2,500

Award at February 2001: £2,982

Description of injuries: Alkaline cleaning solution penetrated claimant's overalls – chemical burns to right buttock and inner thigh – area turned black and was extremely painful – burns dressed, with twice-weekly changes, for a month, skin cream applied for 6 months thereafter – pain initially considerable, especially when sitting down – sleep affected – superficial scarring remaining over an area of 6 x 9cm – painful rubbing necessitated wearing of shorts under trousers – sporting activities curtailed for 2 months – return to work on part-time basis after 5 weeks, full-time again after 3 months.

1.7.1.C17 Case No. 11693

Name of case: Lemar (a minor) v Lloyds Chemists plc

Brief description of injuries: SKIN – BURNS – PHOTO TOXIC REACTION – 4 MONTHS

Reported: Kemp & Kemp, J3-039/2; [1998] CLY 1696

JSB Category: 8

Sex: Female

Age at injury: 6

Age at award: 9

Date of award: 27 October 1997

Tribunal: Basingstoke County Court

Amount of award then: £2,250

Award at February 2001: £2,426

Description of injuries: Photo toxic reaction following the application of suntan lotion – ten 2cm-3cm blisters treated in hospital – erythema on unblistered areas of her back – 4 months after the injury the skin had healed fully – no residual damage.

1.7.1.C18 Case No. 10489

Name of case: Singleton v Samor Electrical

Brief description of injuries: BURNS – LEG – FADED OVER ONE YEAR

Reported: [1992] CLY 1745

JSB Category: 8

Sex: Male

Age at injury: 24

Age at award: 27

Date of award: 20 July 1992

Tribunal: Bradford County Court

Amount of award then: £1,750

Award at February 2001: £2,169

Description of injuries: Concrete burns to the right and left lower legs.

Prognosis: Scarring over the Achilles tendon area (about the size of a hand) faded over a year.

1.7.1.C19 Case No. 10285

Name of case: Walker v BP Chemicals

Brief description of injuries: ACID BURN TO THE LOWER BACK

Reported: Kemp & Kemp, J3-041; [1991] CLY 1482

JSB Category:

Sex: Male

Age at injury: 24

Age at award: -

Date of award: 11 September 1991

Tribunal: Hull County Court

Amount of award then: £1,000

Award at February 2001: £1,278

Description of injuries: Acid burn to the lower back – pain for thirty-six hours – healed after one week – left with a hyper pigmented discoid area measuring 5cms by 3cms – slight hyper-sensitivity to the same area.

Prognosis: Inability of the area to attract a sun-tan – effects were expected to diminish within six months.

1.7.1.C20 Case No. 11455

Name of case: Finnigan v British Steel PLC

Brief description of injuries: HAND – BURNS

Reported: Kemp & Kemp, K2-247; [1997] CLY 2004

JSB Category: 8

Sex: Male

Age at injury: 28

Age at award: 31

Date of award: 04 March 1997

Tribunal: Middlesborough County Court

Amount of award then: £700

Award at February 2001: £775

Description of injuries: Burn to the back of the left hand – not dominant.

Prognosis: Residual scar 1.5cms by 1cm – no neurological deficit or vascular innervation.

1.7.2 NEEDLE STICK

1.7.2.C1 Case No. 10338

Name of case: Evans v Mid Glamorgan Health Authority

Brief description of injuries: NEEDLE STICK FROM HYPODERMIC – SEVERE PTSD

Reported: Kemp & Kemp, C4-109; [1992] CLY 1594

JSB Category: 3(B)(c)

Sex: Female

Age at injury: 38

Age at award: 39

Date of award: 26 August 1992

Tribunal: Cardiff County Court

Amount of award then: £3,750

Award at February 2001: £4,644

Description of injuries: Finger punctured by a hypodermic needle used on a hepatitis B patient causing fairly severe post-traumatic stress syndrome.

Prognosis: Full recovery expected in the next few years.

1.7.2.C2 Case No. 10336

Name of case: Slimings v South Glamorgan Health Authority

Brief description of injuries: NEEDLE STICK FROM HYPODERMIC – FEAR OF AIDS

Reported: Kemp & Kemp, C4-111; [1992] CLY 1592

JSB Category: 3(A)(c)

Sex: Female

Age at injury: 55

Age at award: 60

Date of award: 15 July 1992

Tribunal: QBD

Amount of award then: £3,500

Award at February 2001: £4,337

Description of injuries: Finger punctured by a hypodermic needle wrongly placed in an incineration bag – plaintiff was informed that the needle had been used on a patient suffering from Hepatitis B – until favourable test results were received she feared that she would contract either hepatitis or HIV and die of AIDS.

Prognosis: No lasting injury.

1.7.2.C3 Case No. 11900

Name of case: Dickson v Bridge Hotel

Brief description of injuries: PSYCHOLOGICAL – REACTION TO NEEDLE STICK INJURY

Reported: Kemp & Kemp, K2-066/1; [1999] CLY 1564

JSB Category: 3(A)

Sex: Male

Age at injury: 27

Age at award: 30

Date of award: 25 March 1999

Tribunal: Whitehaven County Court

Amount of award then: £2,500

Award at February 2001: £2,620

Description of injuries: Claimant pricked himself on used hypodermic needle – fear of having contracted hepatitis B or HIV – number of tests undergone to discount contraction of either condition – course of immunisation against hepatitis – 4 months after injury, it was considered to be highly unlikely that claimant had contracted either condition, but he required reassurance until a year after the accident, when the final results of the tests were known – during that period, claimant irritable and upset – severe psychological trauma diagnosed for 5 months – period of serious worry and lingering concern for further 7 months – relationship between claimant and his wife adversely affected; claimant slept downstairs on a couch for fear he might infect her – claimant lost opportunity of going to Australia for 12-month working holiday, because of need for ongoing tests – judge found that fear of infection with either disease was a very considerable one and should not be underestimated.

1.7.3 SCARRING

1.7.3.C1 Case No. 10848

Award at February 2001: £89,339

See: 1.2.3.2.1.C1 for details

1.7.3.C2 Case No. 10307

Name of case: Re R

Brief description of injuries: MULTIPLE INJURIES TO HEAD – VAGINA, ANUS – LOSS OF BALANCE, TASTE, SMELL – UNSIGHTLY SCARRING

Reported: [1992] CLY 1562

JSB Category: 2(A)(b); 4(C)(c/d)

Sex: Female

Age at injury: 52

Age at award: 58

Date of award: 17 January 1992

Tribunal: CICB, Manchester

Amount of award then: £60,000

Award at February 2001: £87,796

Description of injuries: Lacerations and bruising to the face, scalp, vagina and anal canal – loss of several teeth – severe bilateral haematoma injury to both eyes – significant loss of balance, taste and smell – multiple bruising and grazing – ataxia during sudden movement with tendency to fall – loss of senses of taste and smell and of libido – significant personality change to being withdrawn and insular with mood-swings and long periods of silence – unsightly scarring of the scalp only partially concealed by hair.

Prognosis: Devastating disability requiring long term hospital care.

1.7.3.C3 Case No. 11089

Award at February 2001: £76,793

See: 1.7.1.C6 for details

1.7.3.C4 Case No. 10535

Award at February 2001: £60,755

See: 1.2.3.2.1.C2 for details

1.7.3.C5 Case No. 10974

Name of case: Stote v Anderson

Brief description of injuries: ARM – PERMANENT SIGNIFICANT DAMAGE – SCARS

Reported: Kemp & Kemp, H3-056/1; [1995] CLY 1725

JSB Category: 6(F)(b)

Sex: Male

Age at injury: 17

Age at award: 22

Date of award: 20 December 1994

Tribunal: Bournemouth District Registry

Amount of award then: £30,000

Award at February 2001: £37,413

Description of injuries: Plaintiff injured with chainsaw resulting in comminuted fracture of mid-shaft of left, non-dominant, humerus with serious vascular and nerve damage – had emergency operation in which biceps muscles were excised and fracture reduced – attempts were made at vascular reconstruction – later infections to wound required further operations and fitting of an external fixator – had six skin grafts or associated operations – after four months serious consideration was given to amputation but, following further operation to remove infected graft tissue and general cleaning of wound site, plaintiff's condition started to improve – plaintiff thereafter made remarkable progress and discharged from hospital six months after accident – after one year plaintiff's condition had stabilised – left with permanent functional and cosmetic disabilities – had severe wasting to upper arm with minimal strength and limited rotation of arm – considerable scarring to wound site and graft donor sites on both thighs – plaintiff unable to continue with previous employment as plumber and was severely handicapped on labour market.

1.7.3.C6 Case No. 10706

Award at February 2001: £34,401

See: 1.2.3.1.C10 for details

1.7.3.C7 Case No. 10235

Award at February 2001: £31,126

See: 1.6.1.2.C6 for details

1.7.3.C8 Case No. 10222

Name of case: Re Simmons

Brief description of injuries: ASSAULT – LOSS OF ONE KIDNEY – SCAR TO THE STOMACH

Reported: Kemp & Kemp, F4-018, F4-019; [1991] CLY 1419

JSB Category: 5(G)(c)

Sex: Male

Age at injury: 25

Age at award: 27

Date of award: 14 May 1991

Tribunal: CICB, Newcastle

Amount of award then: £22,500

Award at February 2001: £30,257

Description of injuries: Assault – stab wounds to the abdomen, chest and back – loss of one kidney – infection developed following a laparotomy – hospitalised for three months – then needed to have the wound cleaned and dressed at doctor's surgery every day for one month. Registered as unfit for work for seven months.

Prognosis: The scar to the stomach wound was unsightly – others caused no problem – S remained nervous of opening the door to strangers.

1.7.3.C9 Case No. 11855

Award at February 2001: £29,997

See: 1.6.1.4.1.C1 for details

1.7.3.C10 Case No. 11434

Award at February 2001: £29,241

See: 1.4.4.1.C3 for details

1.7.3.C11 Case No. 10906

Name of case: Forrest (a minor) v Forrest

Brief description of injuries: LEG – LOSS OF TOE – 4 YEARS POST-TRAUMATIC STRESS DISORDER – FACIAL SCAR

Reported: Kemp & Kemp, B2-023/1; [1995] CLY 1657

JSB Category: 6(K)(b)(iii)

Sex: Female

Age at injury: 7

Age at award: 12

Date of award: 08 March 1995

Tribunal: Middlesborough County Court

Amount of award then: £23,500

Award at February 2001: £28,502

Description of injuries: Plaintiff involved in road traffic accident – sustained double fracture to left femur, four lacerations to face measuring between 1.5 and 3cm, a 2 cm scar to left upper arm, amputation of the terminal phalanx of second toe and damage to upper left central incisor tooth which was now discoloured – treatment of fractures was by way of insertion of a traction pin through the upper tibia and traction for eight weeks – underwent extensive physiotherapy – facial lacerations cleaned and sutured – further suffered post-traumatic stress disorder which was particularly bad for up to four years – plaintiff left with permanent scarring to face and two unsightly scars to knee measuring 7cm and 5.5cm – at date of hearing was continuing to complain of an intermittent ache to fracture site, particularly in cold weather – although there was a 1cm shortening of leg, which could be satisfactorily made up by an insole raise, she made a good functional recovery.

1.7.3.C13 Case No. 10849

Name of case: Re CT

Brief description of injuries: SKIN – SCARS – EMOTIONAL DISORDER

Reported: Kemp & Kemp, J3-017; [1994] CLY 1698

JSB Category: 8; 3(A)

Sex: Male

Age at injury: 26 months

Age at award: 12

Date of award: 31 January 1994

Tribunal: CICB, London

Amount of award then: £20,000

Award at February 2001: £25,147

Description of injuries: Claimant placed in scalding bath and left there by mother, having been beaten with a stick and slapped – burns to 14 per cent of body, also subconjunctival haematoma, bruising to left ear and upper lip, scratches to face and cheek – placed on IV resuscitation – urethral catheter – convulsions, probably due to pyrexia – deep burns to both legs, de-sloughed and grafted – cystourethroscopy carried out; 5 different catheters passed in same month – discharged after 2 months – 3 years later, tight skin on dorsum of right foot released by skin graft and toes fixed with K-wires and skewers – release of burn contractures on left foot – UTI and URTI problems, with intermittent abdominal pain and pain on micturition for a year – 10 years later, further cystourethroscopy performed, and stricture of urethra at tip of penis discovered, causative of the original period of catheterisation – 10 operative procedures in all, 8 under general anaesthetic – episodes of bed-wetting ongoing to date of hearing – extensive scarring to hands, one arm, both legs, feet and toes – some toes blackened and deformed – limitation of movement in fingers and toes – application of cream necessary to protect skin, which had altered texture, colour and elasticity – pain in feet after long walks – skin became puffy and sticky in hot conditions – self-consciousness about scars, which claimant kept covered during sport, and reluctance to go swimming – considerable bullying and taunting, causing unhappiness and disruption at various schools – claimant intelligent, but markedly behind in schooling – evidence of emotional disorder: nightmares, obsessional thoughts about mother, periods of depression.

Prognosis: Claimant's ambition was to play professional basketball or to work as motor mechanic – difficulty with hands when in contact with motor oil and grime likely to hinder this.

1.7.3.C14 Case No. 11539

Name of case: Re Gardner (Michelle)

Brief description of injuries: SKIN – SCARS – POST-TRAUMATIC STRESS DISORDER

Reported: Kemp & Kemp, B2-009/1 J2-071; [1998] CLY 1541

JSB Category: 8; 3(B)(b)

Sex: Female

Age at injury: 29

Age at award: -

Date of award: 19 February 1998

Tribunal: CICB, Durham

Amount of award then: £22,500

Award at February 2001: £24,926

Description of injuries: Multiple knife wounds to an arm and breast – disfiguring and distressing scarring – post-traumatic stress disorder.

Prognosis: Poor prognosis – claimant's condition was linked to the condition of her husband – she had returned to less well paid work.

1.7.3.C15 Case No. 12058

Award at February 2001: £24,913

See: 1.2.3.2.1.C6 for details

1.7.3.C16 Case No. 12059

Award at February 2001: £23,799

See: 1.2.3.2.C2 for details

1.7.3.C17 Case No. 11543

Award at February 2001: £22,906

See: 1.2.3.2.C3 for details

1.7.3.C18 Case No. 11321

Award at February 2001: £22,751

See: 1.2.3.2.C4 for details

1.7.3.C19 Case No. 10723

Name of case: Re Jones (SA)

Brief description of injuries: POST-TRAUMATIC STRESS DISORDER – SKIN – 14 PER CENT BURNS – SCARS

Reported: [1994] CLY 1571, 1699

JSB Category: 3(B); 7(B)(b); 8

Sex: Male

Age at injury: 34

Age at award: 39

Date of award: 13 April 1994

Tribunal: CICB, London

Amount of award then: £17,500

Award at February 2001: £21,393

Description of injuries: Firefighter suffered burns over 14 per cent body surface in flashover while trying to rescue people from fire – skin grafts under general anaesthetic required – burns so unsightly that wife and young son suffered acute psychiatric reaction due to the shock of seeing them and son required treatment; this in itself greatly distressed claimant – scarring on hands and wrists, with skin susceptible to breakage if knocked and acutely sensitive to cold – obvious scarring to neck on both sides, below hairline and above collar line of protective tunic – functional recovery good – development of post-traumatic stress disorder – distressing recollections of event – feelings of guilt and anger – period of counselling required.

Prognosis: Deemed permanently unfit to resume firefighting – prematurely retired.

Other points: Award includes unspecified amount for loss of congenial employment.

1.7.3.C20 Case No. 11452

Name of case: Stocks v Wadsworth

Brief description of injuries: SKIN – MULTIPLE SCALD SCARS

Reported: Kemp & Kemp, J3-018/1; [1997] CLY 2001

JSB Category: 8

Sex: Female

Age at injury: 8months

Age at award: 3

Date of award: 24 September 1997

Tribunal: Halifax County Court

Amount of award then: £17,500

Award at February 2001: £19,277

Description of injuries: Scalding to the lower face, scalp, neck, upper chest and arms – 5 to 6 per cent burns – scars were: 4cms by 4cms above the left elbow – 3cms by 2cms on the point of the elbow – 10cms by 3cms along the line of the clavicle – 7cms by 7cms below the chin – 6cms by 2cms on the left side of the neck.

Prognosis: Further improvement and surgery were thought unlikely.

1.7.3.C21 Case No. 10991

Award at February 2001: £17,503

See: 1.6.1.2.C18 for details

1.7.3.C22 Case No. 10047

Award at February 2001: £17,438

See: 1.2.3.6.2.1.C10 for details

1.7.3.C23 Case No. 11012
Award at February 2001: £17,407
See: 1.6.1.2.C19 for details

1.7.3.C24 Case No. 10028
Award at February 2001: £16,040
See: 1.2.3.2.1.C9 for details

1.7.3.C25 Case No. 10933
Name of case: Re Williams/Thorne
Brief description of injuries: ASSAULT – FACIAL SCARS – POST-TRAUMATIC STRESS DISORDER
Reported: Kemp & Kemp, J2-012; [1995] CLY 1684
JSB Category: 7(B)(b)(ii)
Sex: Male
Age at injury: 34
Age at award: 37
Date of award: 06 February 1995
Tribunal: CICB, Manchester
Amount of award then: £13,500
Award at February 2001: £16,013
Description of injuries: Plaintiff assaulted with kitchen knife – sustained two facial lacerations, together with puncture wound to left side of torso with major blood loss – kept in hospital five days – first laceration extended 10cm from left nostril along left cheekbone to left ear – second laceration extended 10cm from centre of lower lip to middle of right jaw – scarring was permanent, it had healed reasonably well but not capable of any revision – had pre-existing faded scar over his left eyebrow – the assault and scarring caused him severe anxiety and insomnia, with frequent flashbacks – victim feared he was going to die during assault and since assault had felt that his life had been damaged forever because of the scarring – developed exaggerated sensitivity, making him think that people made remarks about his face – was diagnosed as suffering from post-traumatic stress disorder, from which he would take long time to recover – had served in army for four years and had also worked as professional entertainer and singer, but was unemployed at time of assault and unable to make a claim for loss of earnings as such – was very keen to return to some form of work and was about to undergo further treatment for post-traumatic stress disorder at time of hearing.

1.7.3.C26 Case No. 11863
Award at February 2001: £15,775
See: 1.2.3.2.C6 for details

1.7.3.C27 Case No. 10326
Name of case: Re Sylvester
Brief description of injuries: FACE – SCAR – PSYCHIATRIC DISORDER
Reported: Kemp & Kemp, C5-021; [1992] CLY 1582
JSB Category: 3(A)(b)
Sex: Male
Age at injury: 17
Age at award: 23
Date of award: 13 January 1992
Tribunal: CICB, London
Amount of award then: £12,000
Award at February 2001: £15,399
Description of injuries: Six inch knife wound across left cheek and under ear – fears concerning his appearance lead to a psychiatric disorder which was controllable by medication – vulnerable to relapses.
Prognosis: Satisfactory healing – loss of self-esteem and depression.

1.7.3.C28 Case No. 10843
Award at February 2001: £15,304
See: 1.4.2.C9 for details

1.7.3.C29 Case No. 10465
Award at February 2001: £14,910
See: 1.4.3.C17 for details

Physical Damage to Skin

1.7.3.C30 Case No. 11865

Name of case: O (a minor) v Great Ormond Street Hospital for Children NHS Trust
Brief description of injuries: SKIN – SCARS
Reported: Kemp & Kemp, J3-020/1; [1999] CLY 1529
JSB Category: 8
Sex: Male
Age at injury: 10
Age at award: 13
Date of award: 01 July 1999
Tribunal: Central London County Court (infant settlement approval hearing)
Amount of award then: £14,000
Award at February 2001: £14,734

Description of injuries: 2 per cent superficial dermal burn on shoulders with blisters – treatment initially conservative due to claimant's serious clinical condition (neuro – surgery patient) – back extremely painful and daily dressings required – 2 months later, split skin graft deemed necessary; skin harvested from thigh and meshed to wound in back – claimant left with 2 dark and pale brown scarred patches on back, unpleasant and mottled in appearance, measuring 8 x 9cm and 10 x 6cm – skin on back tight and pulled, causing discomfort whenever claimant bent down or stretched arms – scarred areas itchy, disturbing sleep; claimant required cream to relieve itchiness – scar on donor site also itchy and tight, restricting claimant's ability to run and play football – both areas of scarring caused claimant significant embarrassment; claimant reluctant to change clothes in front of school – mates.

Prognosis: Embarrassment unlikely to abate as claimant moved into adolescence and adulthood – both scars likely to increase in proportion to claimant's overall body surface area – further plastic surgery would not improve appearance of scars.

1.7.3.C31 Case No. 10801
Award at February 2001: £14,398
See: 1.4.2.C11 for details

1.7.3.C32 Case No. 11662
Award at February 2001: £13,469
See: 1.6.1.2.C23 for details

1.7.3.C33 Case No. 10238
Award at February 2001: £13,292
See: 1.6.1.C7 for details

1.7.3.C34 Case No. 10466
Name of case: Hack v Heald
Brief description of injuries: SCARRING TO THE THIGH – RECONSTRUCTIVE SURGERY
Reported: Kemp & Kemp, J2-012/1, J2-015; [1992] CLY 1722
JSB Category: 8
Sex: Female
Age at injury: 52
Age at award: 55
Date of award: 27 August 1992
Tribunal: Kingston upon Thames County Court
Amount of award then: £9,750
Award at February 2001: £12,073

Description of injuries: Severe soft-tissue injury to the left thigh – able to cycle six miles a day to work – unable to continue hobbies of swimming, walking and keeping fit – eighteen months after the accident she underwent reconstructive surgery in an attempt to correct the severe contour deformity.

Prognosis: Unable to stand for long periods – left with a large scar and puckering – the wound had broken down on two occasions – the scar caused embarrassment.

1.7.3.C35 Case No. 10844
Award at February 2001: £11,933
See: 1.6.1.1.C15 for details

1.7.3.C36 Case No. 11109
Award at February 2001: £11,430
See: 1.2.3.2.C10 for details

1.7.3.C37 Case No. 10823
Award at February 2001: £11,347
See: 1.6.1.2.C27 for details

1.7.3.C38 Case No. 12057
Award at February 2001: £11,324
See: 1.2.3.2.C11 for details

1.7.3.C39 Case No. 11450

Name of case: Re Khan (Arbab)

Brief description of injuries: ARM – LEG – SCARS

Reported: Kemp & Kemp, J2-017; [1997] CLY 1999

JSB Category: 8

Sex: Male

Age at injury: 12

Age at award: 14

Date of award: 14 November 1996

Tribunal: CICB, York

Amount of award then: £10,000

Award at February 2001: £11,201

Description of injuries: Serious injuries to the right arm and both legs requiring plastic surgery – suffered nightmares – a 5cm by 7cm v-shaped scar on the arm – thirty or more scars to the right leg and ankle – five to ten scars on the left leg.

Prognosis: All the scars were very unsightly – several were hyperpigmented – and would be visible at a distance

1.7.3.C40 Case No. 11322

Award at February 2001: £11,091

See: 1.2.3.2.C12 for details

1.7.3.C41 Case No. 10179

Name of case: Re Kasprzyk,

Brief description of injuries: KNIFE ASSAULT – PERMANENT SCARRING TO THE FACE AND CHEST – 70 STITCHES

Reported: Kemp & Kemp, C5-027; [1991] CLY 1376

JSB Category: 7(B)(b)(iii)

Sex: Male

Age at injury: -

Age at award: 32

Date of award: 24 July 1991

Tribunal: CICB, London

Amount of award then: £8,500

Award at February 2001: £10,927

Description of injuries: Seventy stitches required after knife assault – multiple scars to the face and chest – taunted by threats to damage the other side of his face.

Prognosis: Permanent visible scarring – so embarrassed by the scars K did not visit his parents for two years.

1.7.3.C42 Case No. 11850

Award at February 2001: £10,534

See: 1.6.1.1.C17 for details

1.7.3.C43 Case No. 11847

Award at February 2001: £10,514

See: 1.6.1.C11 for details

1.7.3.C44 Case No. 11862

Award at February 2001: £10,417

See: 1.6.1.1.C18 for details

1.7.3.C45 Case No. 10155

Award at February 2001: £10,338

See: 1.2.3.2.C14 for details

1.7.3.C46 Case No. 10573

Award at February 2001: £9,787

See: 1.2.3.2.C15 for details

1.7.3.C47 Case No. 11451

Award at February 2001: £9,779

See: 1.6.1.C13 for details

1.7.3.C48 Case No. 10845

Award at February 2001: £9,704

See: 1.4.2.C18 for details

1.7.3.C49 Case No. 10475

Name of case: Costley (a minor) v Costley

Brief description of injuries: SCARRING – FOREARM

Reported: [1992] CLY 1731

JSB Category: 7(B)(a)(iv)

Sex: Female

Age at injury: 3

Age at award: 9

Date of award: 27 February 1992

Tribunal: Blackburn District Registry

Amount of award then: £7,500

Award at February 2001: £9,464

Description of injuries: Scald to the upper third of the right forearm.

Prognosis: Considerable scarring to the arm – wounds healed well – skin would never recover normality – disfigurement of a permanent nature – scarring was improving.

1.7.3.C50 Case No. 11964

Award at February 2001: £9,314

See: 1.2.3.2.C16 for details

1.7.3.C51 Case No. 10351

Name of case: Re MacLeod

Brief description of injuries: FACIAL SCAR – 4 INCHES

Reported: [1992] CLY 1607

JSB Category: 7(B)(b)(iii)

Sex: Male

Age at injury: -

Age at award: 30

Date of award: 08 April 1992

Tribunal: CICB

Amount of award then: £7,500

Award at February 2001: £9,294

Description of injuries: Left cheek slashed with a knife – residual scar.

Prognosis: Scar four inches long and half an inch wide – itched in cold weather.

1.7.3.C52 Case No. 10425

Name of case: Fryer v Smith

Brief description of injuries: FRACTURE OF LEFT FOREARM – CONTINUING PAIN – SIGNIFICANT SCARRING

Reported: Kemp & Kemp, H3-163; [1992] CLY 1681

JSB Category: 6(F)(d)

Sex: Male

Age at injury: 34

Age at award: 36

Date of award: 08 April 1992

Tribunal: Southampton County Court

Amount of award then: £7,500

Award at February 2001: £9,294

Description of injuries: Galeazzi-type fracture of the left forearm – underwent open reduction and internal fixation with plate and screws – absent from work for two months – light duties for six weeks.

Prognosis: 12-cm scar on the left forearm described as a significant cosmetic defect – discomfort in carrying out his duties – continuing pain.

1.7.3.C53 Case No. 10931

Name of case: Mason v Weeks

Brief description of injuries: DOG BITE – SCARRING TO FOREHEAD (HIDDEN BY HAIR)

Reported: [1995] CLY 1682

JSB Category: 7(B)(b)(iii)

Sex: Male

Age at injury: 5

Age at award: 10

Date of award: 12 November 1993

Tribunal: Bristol County Court

Amount of award then: £7,650

Award at February 2001: £9,292

Description of injuries: Rottweiler dog took a bite at plaintiff's head – plaintiff sustained severe laceration of forehead and scalp with loss of tissue from upper part of right side of forehead -under general anaesthetic, emergency operation was undertaken to close forehead and anterior scalp skin defect by means of scalp rotation flap – secondary defect at back of scalp, caused by rotation of flap, was healed by means of split skin graft taken from plaintiff's right thigh – required blood – a further operation was required for excision of secondary defect split skin graft as this had left him with noticeable bald area – scars produced by injury and treatment were originally red and uncomfortable and unsightly but matured to become pain-free and pale – there was a patch of residual numbness on his right forehead within the hair line – bore extensive scars within scalp and across forehead – scars healed soundly and hair fell naturally to camouflage them – all scars could be seen easily when the hair was brushed aside – superficial scar on the front of his right thigh from which the skin grafts were taken – now left with mature residual scars on scalp and forehead, some of which stretched and widened slightly.

Prognosis: It was possible that scalp scars would stretch and become wider with growth and surgical revision to narrow the scars may become necessary once the plaintiff had reached maturity – if and when plaintiff lost his hair with age, injury and operation scars on scalp might no longer be capable of being camouflaged and could become an understandable source of embarrassment.

1.7.3.C54 Case No. 11324

Award at February 2001: £9,283

See: 1.2.3.2.C17 for details

1.7.3.C55 Case No. 11323

Award at February 2001: £9,283

See: 1.2.3.2.C18 for details

1.7.3.C56 Case No. 10183

Name of case: Cartwright v Jones
Brief description of injuries: FRACTURED NOSE – FRACTURED ANKLE – SCAR TO KNEE
Reported: Kemp & Kemp, C5-034; [1991] CLY 1380
JSB Category: 7(A)
Sex: Female
Age at injury: 27
Age at award: 31
Date of award: 10 June 1991
Tribunal: Taunton District Registry
Amount of award then: £7,000
Award at February 2001: £8,978
Description of injuries: Fractured nose – fractured ankle – serious laceration to the knee – facial plaster for three days – leg plaster for five weeks – unable to work for three months.
Prognosis: Prominent scar to the knee – nose was a completely different shape – but not as such deformed – tenderness to the bridge of the nose was accentuated by wearing glasses.

1.7.3.C57 Case No. 10040

Award at February 2001: £8,937
See: 1.2.3.2.C20 for details

1.7.3.C58 Case No. 11832

Award at February 2001: £8,893
See: 1.4.3.1.C17 for details

1.7.3.C59 Case No. 10911

Award at February 2001: £8,623
See: 1.2.2.1.C19 for details

1.7.3.C60 Case No. 11848

Award at February 2001: £8,421
See: 1.6.1.C14 for details

1.7.3.C61 Case No. 11851

Award at February 2001: £8,334
See: 1.6.1.1.C19 for details

1.7.3.C62 Case No. 10467

Name of case: Coyle v Gateshead Metropolitan Borough Council
Brief description of injuries: SCARRING TO ANKLE AND THIGH
Reported: Kemp & Kemp, I3-023; [1992] CLY 1723
JSB Category: 8
Sex: Male
Age at injury: 9
Age at award: 11
Date of award: 12 December 1991
Tribunal: Gateshead County Court
Amount of award then: £6,500
Award at February 2001: £8,239
Description of injuries: Crush injury to the leg with skin loss to medial and lateral aspects of the ankle. Judge observed that there was no overwhelming logical reason why cosmetic awards should be higher for women than for men – the scarring was significant and ugly.
Prognosis: Permanent scarring at the donor site and at the point of injury – two scars to the right thigh – two scars to the ankle – lack of sensation in the scarred area of the ankle.

1.7.3.C63 Case No. 11797

Award at February 2001: £8,213
See: 1.2.3.2.C22 for details

1.7.3.C64 Case No. 10084

Award at February 2001: £8,177
See: 1.4.2.C20 for details

1.7.3.C65 Case No. 10156

Name of case: Re Elsdon
Brief description of injuries: ASSAULT – SCARRING ON LOIN – PSYCHOLOGICAL SYMPTOMS
Reported: Kemp & Kemp, C4-094; [1991] CLY 1353
JSB Category:
Sex: Male
Age at injury: 23
Age at award: 26
Date of award: 28 January 1991
Tribunal: CICB
Amount of award then: £6,000
Award at February 2001: £7,926
Description of injuries: Assault – 9.5cm scar on loin – smaller scars on chest and elbow – developed chronic post-traumatic stress disorder – absent from work for six weeks – scar hypersensitive and permanent – embarrassed by scar – no longer swam – anxious and reserved – lived in fear of another attack – disturbed sleep – anxious with strangers – avoids social contact – permanently tired and edgy-being treated by clinical psychologist.
Prognosis: Uncertain, although hope of some improvement.

1.7.3.C66 Case No. 11864

Award at February 2001: £7,861

See: 1.2.3.2.C23 for details

1.7.3.C67 Case No. 11446

Name of case: Hobart v McGiff and Stuart

Brief description of injuries: SHOULDER – ELBOW – SCARS

Reported: Kemp & Kemp, J2-022; [1997] CLY 1995

JSB Category: 8

Sex: Male

Age at injury: 6

Age at award: 14

Date of award: 19 May 1997

Tribunal: Central London County Court

Amount of award then: £7,000

Award at February 2001: £7,674

Description of injuries: Lacerations to the shoulder and elbow – shoulder wound required stitching in at least two layers – arm required stitching.

Prognosis: Elbow scar 7cms by 1cm – shoulder scar 10cms by 2cms – subject to maximum tension when the arm was at the side – the scar could be improved by plastic surgery – embarrassment would diminish.

1.7.3.C68 Case No. 10912

Name of case: Fotheringham v Murfitt and Scholey

Brief description of injuries: SKULL FRACTURE – SINGLE EPILEPTIC SEIZURE – MINOR SCAR

Reported: [1995] CLY 1663

JSB Category: 2(B)

Sex: Male

Age at injury: 16

Age at award: 21

Date of award: 21 March 1995

Tribunal: Oldham County Court

Amount of award then: £6,500

Award at February 2001: £7,580

Description of injuries: Plaintiff was injured when thrown from back of flatback lorry as it took corner – suffered depressed left temporal fracture with linear occipital fracture – the day after accident plaintiff experienced a self-limiting complex generalised epileptic seizure which lasted for about 30 seconds – did not have any further epileptic seizures at any stage – five years after accident plaintiff was not at any greater risk of epilepsy than any other member of the population – discharged from hospital eight days after accident – unable to ride motorcycle for two years – this affected his working and social life – had also been keen football player but had to cease because told that he should not head a football – accident occasioned a "real and significant" inconvenience to plaintiff's life – other injuries minor in comparison to head injury, consisting of cuts and abrasions which healed within few weeks – plaintiff was left with some relatively minor scarring which was not cosmetically disfiguring on his right arm.

1.7.3.C69 Case No. 11544

Award at February 2001: £7,549

See: 1.2.3.2.C24 for details

1.7.3.C70 Case No. 10969

Award at February 2001: £7,473

See: 1.5.1.C5 for details

1.7.3.C71 Case No. 11690

Award at February 2001: £7,405

See: 1.4.2.C22 for details

1.7.3.C72 Case No. 11833

Award at February 2001: £7,271

See: 1.4.3.1.C23 for details

1.7.3.C73 Case No. 12033

Award at February 2001: £7,227

See: 1.2.3.2.C25 for details

1.7.3.C74 Case No. 10358

Name of case: Allsop v White

Brief description of injuries: FACE – SCAR OVER EYE – MINOR FRACTURES

Reported: [1992] CLY 1614

JSB Category: 7(B)(a)(vi)

Sex: Female

Age at injury: 19

Age at award: 23

Date of award: 28 January 1992

Tribunal: Colchester County Court

Amount of award then: £5,500

Award at February 2001: £6,976

Description of injuries: Undisplaced fracture of the right ischium – multiple abrasions and contusions to both legs – bruising to lower ribs – horrific car accident – she was thrown forward and became covered in the blood of more seriously wounded passengers.

Prognosis: Worry caused by the obvious permanent scar above the right eye – could be masked by foundation cream but could appear spotty.

1.7.3.C75 Case No. 11828

Award at February 2001: £6,796

See: 1.4.1.1.C13 for details

1.7.3.C76 Case No. 11849

Name of case: Foot v Kenny Transport Ltd

Brief description of injuries: LEG – SCARS

Reported: (1999) 99 (2) QR 6; Kemp & Kemp, I3-024/1; [1999] CLY 1513

JSB Category: 6(K)(c)

Sex: Male

Age at injury: 56

Age at award: 58

Date of award: 01 July 1999

Tribunal: Lincoln County Court

Amount of award then: £6,500

Award at February 2001: £6,772

Description of injuries: Fracture dislocation of left ankle – X-rays revealed oblique fracture of lower third of left fibula, fracture of base of medial malleolus of left tibia and fracture of posterior aspect of lower end of left tibia; minimal displacement of ankle joint – fracture internally fixed with plates and screws, and leg immobilised in below – knee plaster – claimant in hospital 9 days; plaster taken off and one screw removed after 6 weeks; leg able to bear weight after 11 weeks; claimant returned to work after 16 weeks – fractures united soundly, but, after 8 months, pain and swelling after use or in cold weather persisted – claimant left with 8cm and 12cm scars which were sensitive to pressure – some loss of plantar flexion and dorsiflexion, as well as inversion and eversion of the hindfoot – some early loss of agility, but claimant made reasonably good recovery in activities and movements – still some discomfort from remaining screws 2 years after accident; claimant contemplating having them removed.

Prognosis: Some small risk of secondary arthritic change.

1.7.3.C77 Case No. 11860

Name of case: C (a minor) v Kay

Brief description of injuries: LEG – SCAR – NIGHTMARES

Reported: (1999) 99(2) QR 7; Kemp & Kemp, J4-023/1; [1999] CLY 1524

JSB Category: 8; 3(A)

Sex: Female

Age at injury: 10

Age at award: 15

Date of award: 01 July 1999

Tribunal: Bury County Court

Amount of award then: £6,500

Award at February 2001: £6,772

Description of injuries: Dog bite on right thigh above knee, sustained for several seconds – resultant wound very deep – claimant admitted to hospital, wound surgically cleaned and then stitched – some stitches removed 3 weeks after accident, but some subsequent difficulties and 2 further visits to clinic required to remove remaining sutures – some physiotherapy also prescribed – claimant left with ugly wound on anterior aspect of right thigh, U – shaped, 22 cm in length and appearing wider in several areas – psychological upset as a result of attack; claimant suffered regular nightmares, particularly in initial period following accident – claimant still suffering nightmares 5 years after incident, though with much less regularity – claimant felt inhibited from wearing shorts, skirts or short dresses and embarrassed when swimming or during lessons – psychological upset had improved a great deal, but claimant still frightened of large dogs.

Prognosis: Not stated

1.7.3.C78 Case No. 11467

Name of case: Re Dublin

Brief description of injuries: REPRODUCTIVE ORGANS FEMALE – MISCARRIAGE

Reported: (1997) 97 (1) QR 3; Kemp & Kemp, L8-220; [1997] CLY 2017

JSB Category: 5(F)

Sex: Female

Age at injury: 21

Age at award: 25

Date of award: 06 November 1996

Tribunal: CICB, London

Amount of award then: £6,000

Award at February 2001: £6,706

Description of injuries: Lacerations to the face requiring sutures – planned pregnancy miscarried due to the attack.

Prognosis: At the time of the hearing she had not been able to conceive another child.

1.7.3.C79 Case No. 11325

Award at February 2001: £6,603

See: 1.2.3.2.C28 for details

1.7.3.C80 Case No. 11691

Award at February 2001: £6,450

See: 1.4.2.C24 for details

1.7.3.C81 Case No. 11549

Award at February 2001: £6,331

See: 1.2.3.2.1.C22 for details

1.7.3.C82 Case No. 10976

Name of case: Lewis v Jukes

Brief description of injuries: ARM – DEEP LACERATION TO BICEPS MUSCLE – 2 OPERATIONS – SCARS

Reported: Kemp & Kemp, H3-164/2; [1995] CLY 1727

JSB Category: 6(F)(d)

Sex: Female

Age at injury: 21

Age at award: 24

Date of award: 15 May 1995

Tribunal: Stourbridge County Court

Amount of award then: £5,500

Award at February 2001: £6,324

Description of injuries: Plaintiff was dancing at nightclub when she was knocked and fell onto floor – left arm (non-dominant) landed on broken glass and she sustained deep four-inch laceration to medial aspect of left upper forearm – wound haemorrhaged profusely – admitted to hospital – large laceration of muscular tissue and biceps tendon was partly divided – brachial artery was visible – following day, under general anaesthetic, lacerated muscle tissue was sutured and skin wound left partially open – was elevated in Bradford sling and prescribed antibiotics – three days later, under local anaesthetic, underwent secondary suturing of skin wound – painful injury requiring five days in hospital and one month off work as payroll clerk – self-conscious about obvious cosmetic scarring – suffered numbness in skin distal to healed scar for some three to four inches – not prevented from carrying out any particular activity but she did not wear short sleeves – scar itched in sunny weather and was inflamed but this effect could be rectified with make-up.

1.7.3.C83 Case No. 11551

Award at February 2001: £6,316

See: 1.2.3.2.C29 for details

1.7.3.C84 Case No. 10468

Name of case: Kear v Torfaen Borough Council

Brief description of injuries: SCARRING TO THIGH

Reported: [1992] CLY 1724

JSB Category: 8

Sex: Female

Age at injury: 13

Age at award: 16

Date of award: 13 April 1992

Tribunal: Pontypool County Court

Amount of award then: £5,000

Award at February 2001: £6,196

Description of injuries: Gouging injury to the rear of the right thigh.

Prognosis: Left with an obvious scar to the back of the right thigh just above the knee – permanent cosmetic defect – surgical intervention would not improve the appearance – self-conscious of the scar.

1.7.3.C85 Case No. 10574

Award at February 2001: £6,178

See: 1.2.3.2.C30 for details

1.7.3.C86 Case No. 12007

Award at February 2001: £6,036

See: 1.2.3.2.C31 for details

1.7.3.C87 Case No. 10049

Name of case: Re Todd

Brief description of injuries: SCARRING

Reported: Kemp & Kemp, J2-025; [1990] CLY 1609

JSB Category: 8

Sex: Female

Age at injury: 20

Age at award: 22

Date of award: 19 October 1990

Tribunal: CICB, Newcastle

Amount of award then: £4,500

Award at February 2001: £5,940

Description of injuries: Lacerations on right forearm resulting in 3-inch irregular scar on middle of flexor aspect with hypersensitive skin all around this scar – also "T" shaped scar on ulnar side of lower forearm.

Prognosis: Would regain full movement of wrist but would be left with hypersensitivity – not likely to affect work or recreation in the future.

1.7.3.C88 Case No. 11447

Award at February 2001: £5,871

See: 1.4.2.C28 for details

1.7.3.C89 Case No. 10937

Name of case: Edwards v Blackmore

Brief description of injuries: LOSS OF 1 TOOTH – DAMAGE TO ANOTHER – FACIAL SCARS

Reported: Kemp & Kemp, C6-072; [1995] CLY 1688

JSB Category: 7(A)(f)(i)

Sex: Male

Age at injury: 32

Age at award: 36

Date of award: 03 April 1995

Tribunal: Torquay County Court

Amount of award then: £5,000

Award at February 2001: £5,772

Description of injuries: Plaintiff was punched and kicked in face on doorstep of his home in January 1991 – sustained a traumatic fracture of upper left first – longevity of upper left second premolar was also prejudiced – in January 1992, he lost remaining buccal aspect of first premolar and part of loose root had to be extracted – in February 1992 he lost substantial amount of palatal wall of upper left second premolar – composite resin filling was placed with pinned core retention to replace the cusp – bridge/crown treatment was expected to be required for second premolar within five years – in January 1994, plaintiff was admitted to hospital to have residual root of upper left first premolar removed by incision – residual root fragment was removed and gum was closed with stitches – plaintiff suffered a two-inch linear scar underlying the point of his chin requiring six stitches – this scar would be prominent for rest of his life – also suffered a smaller "C" shaped scar measuring one and a quarter inches radiating from left upper lip – at date of hearing this scar was only slightly visible – plaintiff suffered a cut to inner surface of left upper lip which tended to catch on left upper third canine – plaintiff who worked as a newsagent was too embarrassed by lacerations, abrasions, sutures to face and a black eye to return to work for three weeks.

1.7.3.C90 Case No. 11798

Award at February 2001: £5,754

See: 1.2.3.2.C35 for details

1.7.3.C91 Case No. 11201

Award at February 2001: £5,726

See: 1.4.2.C30 for details

1.7.3.C92 Case No. 11202

Award at February 2001: £5,621

See: 1.3.1.3.1.C26 for details

1.7.3.C93 Case No. 11448

Award at February 2001: £5,548

See: 1.4.2.C31 for details

1.7.3.C94 Case No. 10652

Award at February 2001: £5,533

See: 1.6.1.C17 for details

1.7.3.C95 Case No. 10743

Award at February 2001: £5,338

See: 1.2.1.C3 for details

1.7.3.C96 Case No. 10042

Award at February 2001: £5,280

See: 1.2.3.2.C39 for details

1.7.3.C97 Case No. 11545

Award at February 2001: £5,122

See: 1.2.2.1.C25 for details

1.7.3.C98 Case No. 10653

Award at February 2001: £4,957

See: 1.6.1.C18 for details

1.7.3.C99 Case No. 10356

Name of case: Re Hughes

Brief description of injuries: SCAR – FOREHEAD – 25 STITCHES

Reported: Kemp & Kemp, C5-053; [1992] CLY 1612

JSB Category: 7(B)(b)(iii)

Sex: Male

Age at injury: 24

Age at award: 27

Date of award: 22 August 1992

Tribunal: CICB, Birmingham

Amount of award then: £4,000

Award at February 2001: £4,953

Description of injuries: Forehead wounds requiring 25 stitches – severe bruising to the ribs and back.

Prognosis: Four-inch scar to the forehead – two-inch cross-shaped scar above the left eye – obvious at time of hearing and a source of embarrassment.

1.7.3.C100 Case No. 11318
Award at February 2001: £4,952
See: 1.2.3.2.C42 for details

1.7.3.C101 Case No. 11449
Award at February 2001: £4,952
See: 1.4.1.C21 for details

1.7.3.C102 Case No. 10575
Award at February 2001: £4,943
See: 1.2.3.2.C43 for details

1.7.3.C103 Case No. 10470
Name of case: Re McDevitt
Brief description of injuries: SCARRING TO FACE
Reported: [1992] CLY 1726
JSB Category: 7(B)(b)(iii)
Sex: Male
Age at injury: 21
Age at award: 22
Date of award: 07 October 1992
Tribunal: CICB, Birmingham
Amount of award then: £4,000
Award at February 2001: £4,918
Description of injuries: Laceration with a knife from the angle of the mouth to the lobe of the left ear.
Prognosis: Facial nerves were intact – left with a scar easily visible beyond normal conversational distance – it had faded to look like two scars.

1.7.3.C104 Case No. 10846
Award at February 2001: £4,755
See: 1.6.1.C21 for details

1.7.3.C105 Case No. 10654
Award at February 2001: £4,549
See: 1.6.1.C22 for details

1.7.3.C106 Case No. 11211
Award at February 2001: £4,497
See: 1.2.3.2.C47 for details

1.7.3.C107 Case No. 10180
Name of case: Re Bailey
Brief description of injuries: KNIFE ATTACK- FACIAL SCARRING – 27 STITCHES
Reported: [1991] CLY 1377
JSB Category: 7(B)(b)(c)
Sex: Male
Age at injury: 17
Age at award: -
Date of award: 25 September 1991
Tribunal: CICB
Amount of award then: £3,500
Award at February 2001: £4,473
Description of injuries: Attack with a "Stanley knife" – 10 cm laceration across an eyelid and temple required 27 stitches – visible scar.
Prognosis: The scar itched in the sun and in cold weather – B was conscious of the scarring.

1.7.3.C108 Case No. 10453
Name of case: Re Banfield
Brief description of injuries: STAB WOUND TO THE THIGH – SCARRING
Reported: [1992] CLY 1709
JSB Category: 6(K)(c)(iii)
Sex: Male
Age at injury: 28
Age at award: 32
Date of award: 07 July 1992
Tribunal: CICB, Birmingham
Amount of award then: £3,500
Award at February 2001: £4,337
Description of injuries: Severe stab wound through the left thigh – exit wound above the knee.
Prognosis: No damage to major nerves or vessels – residual perceived weakness of the upper leg.

1.7.3.C109 Case No. 10471

Name of case: Smith (Natalie) v Miller
Brief description of injuries: DOG BITE – SCARS ON ARM, LEG AND BACK
Reported: [1992] CLY 1727
JSB Category: 8
Sex: Female
Age at injury: 6
Age at award: 11
Date of award: 24 June 1992
Tribunal: Birmingham County Court
Amount of award then: £3,500
Award at February 2001: £4,322
Description of injuries: Nine dog bites to the left arm, left leg and back.
Prognosis: Left with five lasting scars – mostly pale and hardly noticeable – one scar on the inner thigh was raised and reddish in colour – the appearance of the scars would not improve.

1.7.3.C110 Case No. 11866

Name of case: H(a minor) v MHT Services Ltd
Brief description of injuries: HAND – SCARS
Reported: Kemp & Kemp, J3-034; [1999] CLY 1530
JSB Category: 8; 9
Sex: Female
Age at injury: 4 months
Age at award: 4
Date of award: 01 July 1999
Tribunal: Nottingham County Court
Amount of award then: £4,000
Award at February 2001: £4,167
Description of injuries: Burns to scalp and thumb of right hand – burns formed blisters which then burst, leaving residual scarring – one scar on crown of claimant's head, approximately 2in to right of centre line and above right ear, leaving a flat, hairless area of shiny skin, easily concealed, however, by claimant's natural hairstyle – other scar on dorsal aspect of claimant's right thumb – scar measured approximately 2mm x 6mm, appearing as a skin fold with a prominence of approximately 4mm at rest, flattening slightly on stretching – claimant had predisposition to poor scar formation – evidence that claimant was aware of presence of scar on hand and that it made her different from others.
Prognosis: Appearance of scar unlikely to change significantly as claimant grew.

1.7.3.C111 Case No. 10857

Award at February 2001: £4,160
See: 1.2.3.2.C50 for details

1.7.3.C112 Case No. 11548

Award at February 2001: £4,031
See: 1.2.3.2.C51 for details

1.7.3.C113 Case No. 10655

Award at February 2001: £4,013
See: 1.2.3.2.1.C28 for details

1.7.3.C114 Case No. 10046

Award at February 2001: £3,958
See: 1.2.3.5.C12 for details

1.7.3.C115 Case No. 11203

Name of case: Hill v Barnsley MDC
Brief description of injuries: LEG – SCARS
Reported: (1996) 96 (4) QR 7; Kemp & Kemp, I2-537; [1996] CLY 2294
JSB Category: 8(iv)
Sex: Male
Age at injury: 9
Age at award: 15
Date of award: 10 April 1996
Tribunal: Barnsley County Court
Amount of award then: £3,500
Award at February 2001: £3,945
Description of injuries: Laceration to the shin – permanent "poor quality" scar – 6cms by 2cms – of limited embarrassment.

1.7.3.C116 Case No. 11026

Award at February 2001: £3,732
See: 1.4.2.C41 for details

1.7.3.C117 Case No. 11799

Award at February 2001: £3,662
See: 1.2.3.2.C54 for details

1.7.3.C118 Case No. 11027

Award at February 2001: £3,594
See: 1.4.4.C41 for details

1.7.3.C119 Case No. 10440

Name of case: Patterson v Whitbread and Company

Brief description of injuries: DIVIDED TENDONS OF TWO RIGHT FINGERS – MILD SCARRING

Reported: [1992] CLY 1696

JSB Category: 6(I)

Sex: Female

Age at injury: 16

Age at award: 19

Date of award: 07 May 1992

Tribunal: Southport County Court

Amount of award then: £2,842

Award at February 2001: £3,509

Description of injuries: Laceration of the right hand – right ring- and middle-finger tendons divided – laceration explored and tendons repaired – left with a slightly numb lumpy scar – V-shaped scar in the palm of the hand.

Prognosis: Permanent mild cosmetic disability.

1.7.3.C120 Case No. 11546

Award at February 2001: £3,434

See: 1.2.3.2.C55 for details

1.7.3.C121 Case No. 11180

Name of case: Dix v MG Engineering Services

Brief description of injuries: FINGER – CRUSHED INDEX FINGER – SCAR

Reported: Kemp & Kemp, H6-046/1; [1996] CLY 2271

JSB Category: 6(I)(h)

Sex: Male

Age at injury: 45

Age at award: 47

Date of award: 14 May 1996

Tribunal: Llanelli County Court

Amount of award then: £3,000

Award at February 2001: £3,375

Description of injuries: Crushed index finger of the dominant right hand – two small chip fractures – left with a hyper-sensitive scar.

Prognosis: Some functional loss – unlikely to improve.

1.7.3.C122 Case No. 10847

Award at February 2001: £3,280

See: 1.6.1.C25 for details

1.7.3.C123 Case No. 10181

Name of case: Re Medland

Brief description of injuries: ASSAULT – SCARRING- 11 STITCHES

Reported: [1991] CLY 1378

JSB Category: 7(B)(b)(iv)

Sex: Male

Age at injury: 20

Age at award: -

Date of award: 26 June 1991

Tribunal: CICB

Amount of award then: £2,500

Award at February 2001: £3,207

Description of injuries: Unprovoked attack with a broken bottle – 5cm facial laceration required 11 stitches – permanent scarring.

Prognosis: Facial scar.

1.7.3.C124 Case No. 11867

Award at February 2001: £3,144

See: 1.4.2.C45 for details

1.7.3.C125 Case No. 10472

Name of case: Re Messum

Brief description of injuries: KNIFE WOUND TO THE BACK – 10 CM SCAR

Reported: [1992] CLY 1728

JSB Category: 8

Sex: Male

Age at injury: 16

Age at award: 18

Date of award: 30 April 1992

Tribunal: CICB, Birmingham

Amount of award then: £2,500

Award at February 2001: £3,098

Description of injuries: Ten cm knife wound to the back – extended through the muscle layers but did not affect the ribs or the chest wall – uneventful recovery.

Prognosis: Permanent scarring.

1.7.3.C126 Case No. 10473

Name of case: Ingless v Intransit (t/a Woodlands Medical Group (UK))

Brief description of injuries: SCARRING FROM LASER TREATMENT – TWO TO THREE REMEDIAL OPERATIONS

Reported: [1992] CLY 1729

JSB Category: 8

Sex: Male

Age at injury: 38

Age at award: 43

Date of award: 12 May 1992

Tribunal: Ilford County Court

Amount of award then: £2,500

Award at February 2001: £3,087

Description of injuries: Ugly scarring after negligent laser treatment to remove two tattoos.

Prognosis: Two or three operations required to reduce the scarring to a "less obtrusive" level – unable to afford remedial surgery – scarring would be permanent without further surgery.

1.7.3.C127 Case No. 10656

Award at February 2001: £3,047

See: 1.5.3.C1 for details

1.7.3.C128 Case No. 11939

Name of case: G (a minor) v Calderdale MBC

Brief description of injuries: HAND – TENDONS – SCAR

Reported: (1999) 99 (2) QR 7; Kemp & Kemp, H6-049/1; [1999] CLY 1603

JSB Category: 6(I); 8

Sex: Male

Age at injury: 9 years 11 months

Age at award: 12 years 4 months

Date of award: 01 July 1999

Tribunal: Bradford County Court

Amount of award then: £2,850

Award at February 2001: £2,969

Description of injuries: Fall onto broken glass, severing tendon of little finger of right, dominant, hand – wound stitched under local anaesthetic – arm then immobilised in plaster cast for 16 days – on removal of cast, claimant had full movement in hand – 3cm oblique scar at site of injury, lumpy, red and obvious for 4 months after accident – 2 years and 6 months later, scar had almost faded but still clearly visible – also light swelling at site of injury – claimant absent from school 2-3 days and missed 5-day school trip.

1.7.3.C129 Case No. 10935

Award at February 2001: £2,945

See: 1.2.3.2.C58 for details

1.7.3.C130 Case No. 11906

Award at February 2001: £2,863

See: 1.2.3.2.1.C29 for details

1.7.3.C131 Case No. 10657

Award at February 2001: £2,806

See: 1.4.1.C28 for details

1.7.3.C132 Case No. 10737

Name of case: May v Essex County Council

Brief description of injuries: FACIAL SCAR – EYEBROW

Reported: Kemp & Kemp, C5-068; [1994] CLY 1585

JSB Category: 7(B)(a)

Sex: Female

Age at injury: 12

Age at award: 14

Date of award: 05 May 1993

Tribunal: Colchester County Court

Amount of award then: £2,250

Award at February 2001: £2,743

Description of injuries: Claimant pushed by fellow pupil in classroom – struck head on projecting desk leg – sustained cut 8-9 cm long, requiring 7 stitches – bruising and swelling subsided after 4 weeks – scar remaining through left eyebrow, visible, but not prominent.

Other points: General damages figure an indication of appropriate amount – liability not established.

1.7.3.C133 Case No. 10134

Award at February 2001: £2,640

See: 1.2.3.2.C60 for details

1.7.3.C134 Case No. 11204

Award at February 2001: £2,583

See: 1.4.2.C47 for details

1.7.3.C135 Case No. 11011

Award at February 2001: £2,356

See: 1.6.1.C29 for details

1.7.3.C136 Case No. 11205

Name of case: Bridle v Hammacott
Brief description of injuries: THIGH – SCARS
Reported: Kemp & Kemp, J2-046; [1996] CLY 2296
JSB Category: 8(iv)
Sex: Male
Age at injury: 6
Age at award: 8
Date of award: 09 February 1996
Tribunal: Portsmouth County Court
Amount of award then: £2,000
Award at February 2001: £2,280
Description of injuries: Wound to the upper left thigh.
Prognosis: The scar could cause some cosmetic disability – made a good recovery.

1.7.3.C137 Case No. 11547

Award at February 2001: £2,157
See: 1.2.3.2.C62 for details

1.7.3.C138 Case No. 11949

Award at February 2001: £2,096
See: 1.2.3.2.C63 for details

1.7.3.C139 Case No. 11038

Award at February 2001: £2,072
See: 1.2.3.2.C64 for details

1.7.3.C140 Case No. 12067

Award at February 2001: £2,065
See: 1.6.1.C31 for details

1.7.3.C141 Case No. 11059

Award at February 2001: £2,065
See: 1.4.4.C54 for details

1.7.3.C142 Case No. 10493

Name of case: Re Cressey
Brief description of injuries: BITES TO THE FACE – NO SCARRING
Reported: Kemp & Kemp, K2-117; [1992] CLY 1749
JSB Category: 7(B)(b)(v)
Sex: Male
Age at injury: 26

Age at award: 28
Date of award: 17 December 1991
Tribunal: CICB
Amount of award then: £1,500
Award at February 2001: £1,901
Description of injuries: Two inch bite mark to the left angle of the jaw – bite to the left ear lobe.
Prognosis: No residual scarring – no bite marks visible on the face after six months.

1.7.3.C143 Case No. 11751

Award at February 2001: £1,887
See: 1.6.1.4.1.C7 for details

1.7.3.C144 Case No. 10497

Name of case: Bielby v Thorpe
Brief description of injuries: DOG BITE – NOSE – MINOR SCAR
Reported: [1992] CLY 1753
JSB Category: 7(B)(a)(iv)
Sex: Female
Age at injury: 43
Age at award: 45
Date of award: 28 May 1992
Tribunal: Burnley County Court
Amount of award then: £1,500
Award at February 2001: £1,852
Description of injuries: Bitten on the nose by a dog – laceration which healed to a Y-shaped scar.
Prognosis: Five months later the scar was easily visible but not very prominent.

1.7.3.C145 Case No. 11752

Award at February 2001: £1,842
See: 1.6.1.C36 for details

1.7.3.C146 Case No. 10870

Award at February 2001: £1,819
See: 1.6.1.C37 for details

1.7.3.C147 Case No. 11250

Award at February 2001: £1,664
See: 1.6.1.5.C27 for details

1.7.3.C148 Case No. 10280
Award at February 2001: £1,636
See: 1.2.3.2.1.C30 for details

1.7.3.C149 Case No. 11950
Award at February 2001: £1,563
See: 1.6.1.3.C37 for details

1.7.3.C150 Case No. 10503
Name of case: Hughes v Doncaster Borough Council
Brief description of injuries: FACIAL CUTS – TRIVIAL SCARS
Reported: Kemp & Kemp, K2-148; [1992] CLY 1759
JSB Category: 7(B)(a)(iv)
Sex: Female
Age at injury: 79
Age at award: 83
Date of award: 06 January 1992
Tribunal: Doncaster County Court
Amount of award then: £1,200
Award at February 2001: £1,522
Description of injuries: Lacerations above the left eye and to the bridge of the nose – grazed knees. Plaintiff fell out of her wheelchair when it got caught in a pothole – remained anxious when out in her wheelchair.
Prognosis: Made a good recovery but was left with two small scars.

1.7.3.C151 Case No. 11861
Award at February 2001: £1,465
See: 1.6.1.C38 for details

1.7.3.C152 Case No. 10361
Name of case: Re Rigby
Brief description of injuries: FACE – SCAR NEAR EYE
Reported: [1992] CLY 1617
JSB Category: 8(v)
Sex: Female
Age at injury: 24
Age at award: 26
Date of award: 08 April 1992
Tribunal: CICB, Liverpool
Amount of award then: £1,000
Award at February 2001: £1,239
Description of injuries: Laceration and bruising to the right eye – visible cosmetic scar 1 cm long under right eye.
Prognosis: Very conscious of the scar – it became tender in cold weather.

1.7.3.C153 Case No. 10852
Award at February 2001: £1,215
See: 1.6.1.5.C31 for details

1.7.3.C154 Case No. 11896
Award at February 2001: £1,158
See: 1.4.4.C69 for details

1.7.3.C155 Case No. 10118
Award at February 2001: £1,118
See: 1.4.2.C54 for details

1.7.3.C156 Case No. 11753
Award at February 2001: £1,024
See: 1.4.2.C57 for details

1.7.3.C157 Case No. 10882
Award at February 2001: £1,010
See: 1.4.2.C58 for details

1.7.3.C158 Case No. 10885
Award at February 2001: £966
See: 1.7.C3 for details

1.7.3.C159 Case No. 10122
Award at February 2001: £926
See: 1.4.1.1.C31 for details

SECTION 1.8
SPECIFIC INJURIES

1.8.1 ANIMAL BITES

1.8.1.C1 Case No.10081
Award at February 2001: £5,843
See: 1.4.3.C26 for details

1.8.1.C2 Case No. 10335
Name of case: Shields v Liverpool School of Tropical Medicine
Brief description of injuries: SNAKE BITE – PTSD
Reported: [1992] CLY 1591
JSB Category: 3(A)(c)
Sex: Female
Age at injury: 20
Age at award: 23
Date of award: 11 November 1991
Tribunal: Liverpool County Court
Amount of award then: £4,500
Award at February 2001: £5,708
Description of injuries: Bitten on left thumb by West African Carpet Viper – followed by post-traumatic stress disorder – plaintiff was aware that the bite was potentially life-threatening and that the antidote was derived from horses to which she was allergic – predisposed to anxiety.
Prognosis: Full physical recovery but persistent stress and nightmares.

1.8.1.C3 Case No. 10653
Award at February 2001: £4,957
See: 1.6.1.C18 for details

1.8.1.C4 Case No. 10900
Award at February 2001: £3,578
See: 1.5.4.C13 for details

1.8.1.C5 Case No. 12066
Award at February 2001: £3,097
See: 1.4.4.C47 for details

1.8.1.C6 Case No. 10163
Award at February 2001: £2,565
See: 1.4.3.C34 for details

1.8.1.C7 Case No. 10268
Name of case: Smith v Hurst
Brief description of injuries: MULTIPLE DOG BITES – FEAR OF DOGS
Reported: Kemp & Kemp, K2-082; [1991] CLY 1465
JSB Category:
Sex: Male
Age at injury: 54
Age at award: -
Date of award: 23 January 1991
Tribunal: Southampton District Registry
Amount of award then: £1,750
Award at February 2001: £2,312
Description of injuries: Attack by two Alsatian dogs – bite marks to both forearms, right buttock, back, lower right abdomen. and back of the left leg – very distressed – felt he was "fighting for his life" – wounds cleaned – no stitches required -left with slight scars – wounds became infected requiring treatment by elevating the arm – four months after the date of the accident he was signed off work for three weeks suffering depression.
Prognosis: At the time of the hearing he continued to have nightmares – nervous of large dogs.

1.8.1.C8 Case No. 10868
Award at February 2001: £1,944
See: 1.6.1.C35 for details

1.8.1.C9 Case No. 10870
Award at February 2001: £1,819
See: 1.6.1.C37 for details

1.8.1.C10 Case No. 10871

Award at February 2001: £1,783

See: 1.5.3.C3 for details

1.8.1.C11 Case No. 10500

Name of case: Grant v Measor

Brief description of injuries: DOG BITE – BRUISES AND GRAZES

Reported: Kemp & Kemp, K2-177; [1992] CLY 1756

JSB Category: 8(v)

Sex: Male

Age at injury: 36

Age at award: 38

Date of award: 24 July 1992

Tribunal: Clerkenwell County Court

Amount of award then: £1,000

Award at February 2001: £1,239

Description of injuries: Bitten by a dog – two puncture wounds of the right buttock – grazing to the thigh and elbow – bruised and sore little finger of the right hand – finger was painful and stiff for about four weeks – became wary of large dogs.

Prognosis: The injuries resolved.

1.8.1.C12 Case No. 10122

Award at February 2001: £926

See: 1.4.1.1.C31 for details

1.8.2 AMPUTATION

1.8.2.C1 Case No. 12020

Name of case: Re Schembri (CICB Quantum: 1999)

Brief description of injuries: LEG – ABOVE KNEE AMPUTATION

Reported: Kemp & Kemp, PRI-001; [2000] 4 CL 163

JSB Category: 6(K)(a)(iii)

Sex: Male

Age at injury: 44

Age at award: 50

Date of award: 19 November 1999

Tribunal: CICB, London

Amount of award then: £75,000

Award at February 2001: £89,502

Description of injuries: Assault – multiple stab wounds severed an artery to the left leg that led to an above knee amputation leaving a ten inch stump – the right leg was severely injured due to damage to the lower quadriceps and the cruciate ligament resulting in loss of power and instability – superficial stab wounds to the face, neck, abdomen and upper arm – a pre-existing psychological condition was exacerbated – S was an in-patient for thirteen weeks – his mobility was severely restricted.

Prognosis: Restriction to mobility would not improve – degenerative changes to the right leg would deteriorate when he was much older – he might require a wheelchair.

Other points: S suffered significant problems with his prosthesis which caused pain and falls.

1.8.2.C2 Case No. 10085

Award at February 2001: £75,662

See: 1.4.4.2.C1 for details

1.8.2.C3 Case No. 10820

Name of case: Ryan v Trans Manche Link

Brief description of injuries: LEG – BELOW-KNEE AMPUTATION

Reported: Kemp & Kemp, I2-201/2; [1994] CLY 1669

JSB Category: 6(K)(a)(iv)

Sex: Male

Age at injury: 37

Age at award: 39

Date of award: 19 July 1994

Tribunal: QBD

Amount of award then: £50,000

Award at February 2001: £66,614

Description of injuries: Claimant injured in course of work at site of Channel Tunnel – severely comminuted fractures of left tibia and fibula – bone grafting and external fixation carried out to England – claimant returned to his home in small farming community in Ireland – 14 months intense pain and extensive treatment – below-knee amputation then carried out – claimant had difficulties with wearing prosthesis – walking or driving limited to 20 minutes – development of lower back pain.

1.8.2.C4 Case No. 12045

Name of case: McFarlane v Clifford Smith & Buchanan

Brief description of injuries: LEG – BELOW KNEE AMPUTATION

Reported: Kemp & Kemp, PRI-002; [2000] 5 CL 189

JSB Category: 6(K)(iv)

Sex: Male

Age at injury: 17

Age at award: 28

Date of award: 26 September 1999

Tribunal: QBD

Amount of award then: £55,000

Award at February 2001: £63,116

Description of injuries: Complete dislocation of the tallus bone to the left foot – splintered displaced fracture of the left femur – moderately severe concussional head injury – operative treatment at the time – clawing of the toes throughout 1990/1991 – operative treatment to the Achilles tendon and a posterior capsulectomy of the left ankle – arthritis in the ankle joint – below-knee amputation of the left leg in 1995 – stump breakdown and abscess formation – below knee amputated – altered personality – impairment of memory and concentration – difficulty in renewing verbal learning – relatively poor speed of information processing.

Prognosis: Increased chance of osteoarthritis in remaining joints of both legs.

1.8.2.C5 Case No. 11433

Award at February 2001: £51,510

See: 1.6.1.2.C2 for details

1.8.2.C6 Case No. 10809

Award at February 2001: £40,504

See: 1.4.4.2.C2 for details

1.8.2.C7 Case No. 10433

Award at February 2001: £40,490

See: 1.4.4.2.C3 for details

1.8.2.C8 Case No. 11175

Award at February 2001: £36,392

See: 1.4.4.2.C4 for details

1.8.2.C9 Case No. 11689

Award at February 2001: £32,031

See: 1.6.1.5.2.C1 for details

1.8.2.C10 Case No. 10810

Award at February 2001: £28,421

See: 1.4.4.1.C4 for details

1.8.2.C11 Case No. 11010

Award at February 2001: £17,978

See: 1.4.4.2.C6 for details

1.8.2.C12 Case No. 11183

Name of case: Cutts v Mackie

Brief description of injuries: THUMB – TRAUMATIC AMPUTATION

Reported: Kemp & Kemp, H7-013; [1996] CLY 2274

JSB Category: 6(I)(s)

Sex: Female

Age at injury: 3

Age at award: 8

Date of award: 21 March 1996

Tribunal: Milton Keynes County Court

Amount of award then: £13,000

Award at February 2001: £14,915

Description of injuries: Traumatic part amputation of the left (non-dominant) thumb – thumb was pain free in use – tip remained tender.

Prognosis: Left with a loss of function in thumb and cosmetic defect which would be more noticeable as she grew.

1.8.2.C13 Case No. 10819

Name of case: Gee v Vantage Joinery

Brief description of injuries: THUMB – PART AMPUTATION

Reported: Kemp & Kemp, H7-013/1; [1994] CLY 1668

JSB Category: 6(I)(t); 8

Sex: Male

Age at injury: 21

Age at award: 25

Date of award: 26 October 1993

Tribunal: Bath County Court

Amount of award then: £11,000

Award at February 2001: £13,439

Description of injuries: Traumatic amputation of left (non-dominant) thumb at base of distal phalanx on circular saw – amputation tidied under general anaesthetic; remains of distal phalanx removed and skin closed – claimant sent home same day – healing good, but development of extreme hypersensitivity, especially on dorsal aspect, due to neuroma formation in radial nerve – neuroma excised over course of 4 operations, leaving 11cm scar in mid-forearm, lack of sensation in territory of radial nerve from mid-forearm to back of thumb, first web and second metacarpal – thumb tender if knocked – aching in cold weather – 35mm reduction in length of thumb interfered with strength of grip and manipulation of small objects – numbness at tip, extending onto flexor surface for about 1cm – forced abandonment of hobbies of cricket, snooker and weight training – claimant returned to work as wood machinist; not as fast a worker as prior to the accident – agreed medical evidence of 40 per cent loss of function in left hand – no embarrassment on claimant's part about deformity.

Prognosis: Condition unlikely to improve – no osteoarthritis anticipated.

1.8.2.C14 Case No. 11658

Name of case: Forbes v Scott Ltd

Brief description of injuries: THUMB – TRAUMATIC PARTIAL AMPUTATION

Reported: Kemp & Kemp, H7-013; [1998] CLY 1660

JSB Category: 6(I)(t)

Sex: Male

Age at injury: 31

Age at award: 35

Date of award: 23 January 1998

Tribunal: Newcastle upon Tyne County Court

Amount of award then: £10,000

Award at February 2001: £10,798

Description of injuries: Traumatic amputation of the terminal phalanx of the left thumb.

Prognosis: F was fit to return to his former occupation – unlikely that he would obtain work with his former employer.

1.8.2.C15 Case No. 10441

Award at February 2001: £9,878

See: 1.4.4.2.C7 for details

1.8.2.C16 Case No. 10842

Name of case: Hook v Yattendon Estates

Brief description of injuries: TOES – TWO AMPUTATIONS

Reported: Kemp & Kemp, I4-025; [1994] CLY 1691

JSB Category: 6(P)

Sex: Male

Age at injury: 42

Age at award: 52

Date of award: 07 October 1994

Tribunal: Reading County Court

Amount of award then: £7,000

Award at February 2001: £8,292

Description of injuries: Crush injury to fourth and fifth toes when caught in hydraulic towbar lift of tractor – both toes amputated – distal third of fifth metatarsal trimmed – 5 days in hospital – pre-existing osteoarthritis in right hip and pre-existing back pain both slightly exacerbated – off work (as farm labourer) 6 weeks; able to return to previous job thereafter – no osteoarthritis – special footwear unnecessary – continuing residual symptoms: limp, phantom pain, numbness in cold weather, difficulty climbing ladders.

Prognosis: No complications or deteriorations expected.

1.8.2.C17 Case No. 10628

Name of case: Cox v GKN Axles
Brief description of injuries: FINGER – LITTLE FINGER – AMPUTATION
Reported: Kemp & Kemp, H6-034; [1993] CLY 1523
JSB Category: 6(I)(m)
Sex: Male
Age at injury: 38
Age at award: 43
Date of award: 24 August 1993
Tribunal: Leeds County Court
Amount of award then: £5,500
Award at February 2001: £6,695
Description of injuries: Severe compound fracture of left (non-dominant) little finger when trapped in vice – fracture reduced but found to be unviable – amputation at level of proximal interphalangeal joint carried out – ongoing constant pain in stump for 5 months, disturbing sleep – further amputation at volar crease – 5 cm scar affecting ulnar border of left hand, swollen, itchy and tender – aching and stiffness in hand – stiffness of ring finger and distal inter-phalangeal joint, slightly limiting formation of full fist – difficulty carrying heavy objects and bags, and tendency to drop things – if site of amputation struck accidentally, claimant suffered excruciating pain which immobilised him for a few seconds.
Prognosis: No improvement or deterioration expected.

1.8.2.C18 Case No. 10984

Award at February 2001: £5,890
See: 1.4.4.2.C12 for details

1.8.2.C19 Case No. 10985

Award at February 2001: £5,772
See: 1.4.4.2.C13 for details

1.8.2.C20 Case No. 11424

Award at February 2001: £4,914
See: 1.4.4.C31 for details

1.8.2.C21 Case No. 12018

Name of case: Harding v Basingstoke and Deane BC
Brief description of injuries: FINGER – AMPUTATION OF TIP
Reported: Kemp & Kemp, H6-039; [2000] 4 CL 161
JSB Category: 6(I)(l)
Sex: Male
Age at injury: 59
Age at award: 64
Date of award: 17 November 1999
Tribunal: Salisbury County Court
Amount of award then: £4,500
Award at February 2001: £4,643
Description of injuries: Traumatic amputation of the tip of the ring finger of the non dominant left hand – the remains of the finger were amputated through the distal inter-phalangeal joint after three months – off work for four months.
Prognosis: The finger continued to feel stiff and painful at times – H had reduced grip.
Other points: The judge did not feel bound by the JSB Guidelines s 6(I)(l) which he stressed were only guidelines.

1.8.2.C22 Case No. 10631

Name of case: Scott v Higgins Potato Merchants
Brief description of injuries: FINGER – MIDDLE FINGER – PARTIAL AMPUTATION
Reported: Kemp & Kemp, H6-044; [1993] CLY 1526
JSB Category: 6(I)(p)
Sex: Male
Age at injury: 24
Age at award: 25
Date of award: 25 March 1993
Tribunal: Doncaster County Court
Amount of award then: £3,000
Award at February 2001: £3,704
Description of injuries: Left (non-dominant) hand trapped in potato tipper mechanism – crushing injury to middle finger – too badly damaged to be saved – primary amputation performed just proximal to distal interphalangeal joint; end 3 cm of finger lost – very painful for 2 weeks – 3 cm scar left – fingers swollen and hand unusable for 6-8 weeks – finger goes numb and tends to "freeze" in cold conditions – left hand reduced in strength, becomes sore when exerted, eg when operating motorcycle clutch or playing snooker – tendency to drop small items from left hand, eg coins – consciousness of cosmetic deformity – claimant now returned to work.
Other points: No evidence of current job being at risk, but judge accepted that prevailing economic climate created a general risk of redundancy, and that plaintiff would take longer to find a job if dismissed – risk nevertheless small – "accelerated receipt" of damages also taken into account.

1.8.2.C23 Case No. 11653

Name of case: Hickinson (a minor) v Chesterfield Transport Ltd

Brief description of injuries: FINGERS – AMPUTATION OF TIP OF MIDDLE FINGER

Reported: Kemp & Kemp, H6-049/1; [1998] CLY 1655

JSB Category: 6(I)(l)

Sex: Male

Age at injury: 12

Age at award: 14

Date of award: 16 March 1998

Tribunal: Chesterfield County Court

Amount of award then: £3,000

Award at February 2001: £3,209

Description of injuries: Amputation of the tip of the middle finger – parrot beak deformity of the finger tip.

Prognosis: Some risk of cold intolerance continuing.

1.8.2.C24 Case No. 11654

Name of case: Fraser v Doncaster MBC

Brief description of injuries: FINGERS – AMPUTATION OF TIP OF MIDDLE FINGER

Reported: Kemp & Kemp, H6-050/1; [1998] CLY 1656

JSB Category: 6(I)(l)

Sex: Male

Age at injury: 26

Age at award: 29

Date of award: 12 May 1998

Tribunal: Doncaster County Court

Amount of award then: £2,500

Award at February 2001: £2,630

Description of injuries: Traumatic amputation of the tip of the middle finger – F suffered from severe learning difficulties – unable to protect the injury or to appreciate that jarring the finger would exacerbate pain.

Prognosis: F was not expected to experience any serious long-term disability.

1.8.3 INJURY RESULTING IN DEATH

1.8.3.C1 Case No. 10897

Award at February 2001: £12,176

See: 1.7.1.C12 for details

1.8.3.C2 Case No. 10528

Name of case: Cooke and Rippin v Pruski

Brief description of injuries: PARAPLEGIA FOLLOWED BY DEATH

Reported: Kemp & Kemp, L5-011; [1992] CLY 1784

JSB Category: 2(A)(a)

Sex: Male

Age at injury: 16

Age at award: Deceased

Date of award: 27 October 1992

Tribunal: Nottingham County Court

Amount of award then: £9,000

Award at February 2001: £11,065

Description of injuries: Paraplegia followed by death. Died from bronchopneumonia secondary to tetraplegia and head injury.

1.8.3.C3 Case No. 10898

Award at February 2001: £6,538

See: 1.1.C11 for details

1.8.3.C4 Case No. 11694

Award at February 2001: £5,260

See: 1.7.1.C14 for details

1.8.3.C5 Case No. 10529

Award at February 2001: £740

See: 1.2.3.1.C39 for details

1.8.4 POISONING AND MEDICATION OVERDOSE

1.8.4.C1 Case No. 10901

Name of case: Knight v Tower Hamlets Health Authority

Brief description of injuries: POISONING – UNNECESSARY TREATMENT FOR CANCER

Reported: BPILS, XVIII 1088; [1994] CLY 1755

JSB Category:

Sex: Female

Age at injury: 75

Age at award: 78

Date of award: 21 March 1994

Tribunal: City and Mayor's County Court

Amount of award then: £10,000

Award at February 2001: £12,123

Description of injuries: Claimant negligently misdiagnosed as having terminal stomach cancer – likely correct diagnosis only benign ulcer with pyloric stenosis – unnecessarily prescribed morphine on daily basis for 22 months – disorientation – confusion – tiredness – debility – increased constipation – nausea – once-monthly bouts of vomiting spread over 2 days – development of addiction to drug – pain from constipation eased by drug – some elation caused by drug – claimant still able to hold a conversation, walk unaided (although some loss of confidence evident) and perform limited tasks, but did little except remain at home, in marked contrast to previously active life – loss of concentration, affecting reading and watching television – following reversal of diagnosis, claimant suffered withdrawal symptoms – prickly sensations – tremors – occasional hallucinations – mental recovery after 2 months – loss of confidence 3 months thereafter – similar symptoms due to unrelated Alzheimer's disease supervened thereafter – morphine did not have any long-term effects.

Other points: Court approved acceptance of a payment in of £21,000 on the postulated apportionment of £10,000 general damages.

1.8.4.C2 Case No. 12023

Name of case: R v Gardner

Brief description of injuries: POISONING – WRONG MEDICATION – NEUROLEPTIC MALIGNANT SYNDROME

Reported: Kemp & Kemp, PRL-001; [2000] 4 CL 166

JSB Category:

Sex: Male

Age at injury: 36

Age at award: 42

Date of award: 09 September 1999

Tribunal: Mayor's and City of London County Court

Amount of award then: £6,800

Award at February 2001: £7,037

Description of injuries: R, a patient under the Mental Health Act 1983, was treated by his GP with chlorpromazine at or in excess of 1,500 mg per day to control his erratic and agitated behaviour – the dose was considerably in excess of the recommended maximum – droperidol and zuclophenthixol were also prescribed – R became drowsy, over sedated and withdrawn – admitted to hospital three months later – he was noted as being physically unwell – hot and sweaty, with tremor – mute and confused – incontinent of urine – pyrexial and tachycardiac – diagnosed as suffering from neuroleptic malignant syndrome a potentially fatal condition – the neuroleptic medication was stopped and the condition was treated – discharged from hospital six months later. His condition remained reasonably stable thereafter.

1.8.4.C3 Case No. 11472

Name of case: Harvey v Fairscope

Brief description of injuries: RESPIRATORY ORGANS – CARBON MONOXIDE POISONING

Reported: Kemp & Kemp, PRL-005; [1997] CLY 2022

JSB Category: 5(A)

Sex: Female

Age at injury: 29

Age at award: 30

Date of award: 03 September 1997

Tribunal: Kingston County Court

Amount of award then: £5,000

Award at February 2001: £5,399

Description of injuries: Exposure to carbon monoxide fumes.

Prognosis: Symptoms fully resolved within three months of the correction to the boiler.

1.8.4.C4 Case No. 10692

Name of case: Patel v Patel

Brief description of injuries: POISONING – WRONG MEDICATION

Reported: [1993] CLY 1589

JSB Category:

Sex: Female

Age at injury: 47

Age at award: -

Date of award: 03 March 1993

Tribunal: Brentford County Court

Amount of award then: £3,000

Award at February 2001: £3,704

Description of injuries: Pharmacist accidentally transposed labels on bottles of 2 different drugs prescribed for claimant's severe asthmatic condition – claimant consequently took excessive dose of one medicine, 5 or 6 times over the prescribed amount – toxic side effects later in the evening – vomiting all night – 4 episodes of loose, watery diarrhoea – cramping pains in epigastrium – headache – pains in chest and back – taken to hospital following morning – shortness of breath – wheeziness – widespread rhonchi – poor air entry – crepitations in upper lobe area – tenderness in abdomen, especially in epigastric area – remained in hospital for 3 days, after which condition improved – unable to resume work until 3 months after discharge.

1.8.4.C5 Case No. 11271

Name of case: Stibbs v British Gas PLC

Brief description of injuries: CARBON MONOXIDE POISONING

Reported: Kemp & Kemp, L2-107; [1996] CLY 2364

JSB Category: 5(B)(h)

Sex: Female

Age at injury: 4

Age at award: 6

Date of award: 03 May 1996

Tribunal: Southend County Court

Amount of award then: £1,250

Award at February 2001: £1,406

Description of injuries: Carbon monoxide poisoning – poison cleared from her system within twenty-four hours.

Prognosis: No long-term effects were envisaged.

1.8.4.C6 Case No. 10499

Name of case: Re Hunt

Brief description of injuries: INHALATION OF CHEMICAL FUMES

Reported: [1992] CLY 1755

JSB Category:

Sex: Seven males

Age at injury: 23-44

Age at award: 27-47

Date of award: 13 December 1991

Tribunal: CICB, Manchester

Amount of award then: £1,000

Award at February 2001: £1,268

Description of injuries: Exposed to methyl bromide fumes – lethargy for about two months.

Prognosis: No reassurances were given of the unlikelihood of any lasting ill-effects for two years.

Other points: Individual awards ranged from £1,000, to maximum £1,500.

1.8.4.C7 Case No. 11259

Name of case: Moore v Mauri Products Ltd

Brief description of injuries: RESPIRATORY ORGANS – EXPOSURE TO DANGEROUS FUMES

Reported: Kemp & Kemp, K2-195; [1996] CLY 2351

JSB Category: 5(B)(h)

Sex: Male

Age at injury: 35

Age at award: 37

Date of award: 18 March 1996

Tribunal: Kingston upon Hull County Court

Amount of award then: £1,000

Award at February 2001: £1,135

Description of injuries: Exposure to dangerous fumes – severe difficulty breathing – panic – excessive vomiting – burning sensation to the face and lungs – at time of hearing a full recovery had been made.

Other points: Plaintiff was worried about the possibility of long-term damage to his lungs.

1.8.5 PARALYSIS

1.8.5.C1 Case No. 10534

Award at February 2001: £62,136

See: 1.4.3.C6 for details

1.8.5.C2 Case No. 10317

Award at February 2001: £54,115

See: 1.3.1.3.2.1.C1 for details

1.8.5.1 HEMIPARESIS

1.8.5.1.C1 Case No. 10312

Award at February 2001: £191,999

See: 1.2.3.8.C4 for details

1.8.5.1.C2 Case No. 11485

Name of case: Re Lawson

Brief description of injuries: HEAD – BRAIN DAMAGE – HEMIPARESIS

Reported: Kemp & Kemp, C2-034; [1998] CLY 1486

JSB Category: 2(A)(c)(ii)

Sex: Female

Age at injury: 20

Age at award: 25

Date of award: 02 September 1997

Tribunal: CICB, Durham

Amount of award then: £60,000

Award at February 2001: £73,023

Description of injuries: Brain damage causing left hemiparesis – laceration to the ear – undisplaced fractures of the maxilla – personality change – severe weakness to left side of body – required daily assistance from her parents.

Prognosis: Weakness in left side permanent – significant problems in obtaining future employment.

1.8.5.2 PARAPLEGIA

1.8.5.2.C1 Case No. 10700

Name of case: Sharpe v Woods

Brief description of injuries: VERY SEVERE MULTIPLE INJURIES "BETWEEN PARAPLEGIA AND TETRAPLEGIA" – CONSIDERABLE COSMETIC DISABILITY – FULL AWARENESS OF CONDITION

Reported: Kemp & Kemp, B2-002; [1994] CLY 1546

JSB Category: 1(b); 2(A); 7(B)(a); 3(A); 4(A)(e); 5(A)(g); 6(C)(a), 6(K)(b)

Sex: Female

Age at injury: 46

Age at award: 53

Date of award: 16 July 1993

Tribunal: Liverpool High Court

Amount of award then: £105,000

Award at February 2001: £163,709

Description of injuries: Road accident – devastating orthopaedic and cerebral injuries – head injury causing substantial emotional and intellectual impairment – permanent gross speech impediment – severe retrograde amnesia – memory deficit – reasoning ability impaired – ability to concentrate reduced – partially paralysed stiff right hand with limited function – fracture of right femur with substantial shortening of the leg and plantar flexion contracture of the foot – fracture of right pelvis and hip requiring surgical reduction, but which could not be carried out because of claimant's condition, and causing progressive osteoarthritis – fractured ribs – fractured temple – fractured jaw and right cheek, leaving "considerable cosmetic deformity" – partial third nerve palsy leaving right eye with permanent divergent squint, poor closure, fixed semi-dilated pupil and no useful vision, and necessitating eye patch to prevent excessive watering – proneness to depression, impaired will to overcome condition – effectively wheelchair-bound, though able to walk a very short distance with close attendance – unable to continue with work or activities, or live independently – everyday tasks only possible with constant care and attention – impairment of reasoning permanent, but claimant fully aware of extent of own injuries – embarrassment at speech impediment leading to social isolation – sense of being burden on family – regarded as being in a worse position than a paraplegic, but better than a tetraplegic.

Prognosis: Physical and mental impairments permanent.

1.8.5.2.C2 Case No. 11761

Name of case: Burns v Davies

Brief description of injuries: PARAPLEGIA

Reported: BPILS, VIII 54; [1999] CLY 1424

JSB Category: 1(b)

Sex: Male

Age at injury: 2

Age at award: 14

Date of award: 07 August 1998

Tribunal: QBD

Amount of award then: £106,000

Award at February 2001: £137,638

Description of injuries: Paraplegia – high level of lesion leaving no feeling or control below line across chest – poor trunkal balance – occasional spasms.

Prognosis: Life expectancy agreed to be 60 – significant deterioration expected at 40-45 – slight risk of development of syrinx, resulting in loss of sensation and movement in hands and arms – spasms likely to increase with age – prospects of marriage likely – fathering children still possible with medical assistance.

Other points: Claimant also suffered from asthma and had only one effective kidney.

1.8.5.2.C3 Case No. 10530

Name of case: Re Hosken

Brief description of injuries: PARAPLEGIA

Reported: Kemp & Kemp, A3-004; [1993] CLY 1421

JSB Category: 1(b)

Sex: Male

Age at injury: 33

Age at award: 39

Date of award: 15 April 1993

Tribunal: CICB

Amount of award then: £90,000

Award at February 2001: £135,736

Description of injuries: "All usual problems associated with a disability of that type"; – also frequent episodes of severe pain lasting several hours – urinary tract infection – pressure sores.

Prognosis: Life expectancy reduced to 35 years from date of hearing – permanent domestic care required.

1.8.5.2.C4 Case No. 10697

Name of case: Tate v West Cornwall and Isles of Scilly Health Authority

Brief description of injuries: PARAPLEGIA FOLLOWING NEGLIGENT TREATMENT FOR CIRCULATORY PROBLEMS IN LEG – LIFE EXPECTANCY 7 YEARS

Reported: Kemp & Kemp, A3-008; [1994] CLY 1543

JSB Category: 1(b)

Sex: Male

Age at injury: 64

Age at award: 70

Date of award: 07 January 1994

Tribunal: QBD

Amount of award then: £85,000

Award at February 2001: £125,960

Description of injuries: Claimant, with history of smoking – related circulation problems in leg, had above – knee amputation of right leg 15 years before date of trial; continued with employment and active lifestyle – circulatory problems developed in left leg 9 years later – chemical sympathectomy injection undergone, but treatment negligent – phenol injected into subarachnoid space damaged the cauda equina – paralysed from waist down, apart from slight residual power and sensation in left leg, and some sensation in buttocks, causing permanent discomfort – deemed paraplegic for practical purposes – double incontinence, proneness to bowel accidents – unable to be left unattended due to risk of such accidents – impotence – severe depression during hospitalisation – need to be turned 3 times per night – development of bedsore shortly after negligent treatment, for which no treatment provided, and sores exacerbated by placing of claimant in wheelchair – liability denied until 4 years later, when claimant admitted to defendant's spinal unit, but no treatment thought possible –

private surgery for sore eventually undertaken, proving successful.

Prognosis: Life expectancy of 7 years at date of trial, improved by fact that residual sensation in left leg would provide early warning of complications; no other health problems.

Other points: In view of claimant's age and pre-existing medical condition, judge indicated that he would have awarded general damages at lower end of scale – however, judge found that claimant had been detained unnecessarily for 4.5 years in hospitals and other institutions as a result of inadequate care by defendants – this reflected in general damages award.

1.8.5.2.C5 Case No. 10304

Name of case: Re Read

Brief description of injuries: PARAPLEGIA – LIFE EXPECTATION MUCH REDUCED

Reported: Kemp & Kemp, A3-012; [1992] CLY 1559

JSB Category: 1(a)

Sex: Female

Age at injury: 37

Age at award: 46

Date of award: 17 June 1991

Tribunal: CICB, London

Amount of award then: £75,000

Award at February 2001: £115,478

Description of injuries: Paraplegic at level T4 plus minor permanent disabling wrist injury.

Prognosis: Loss of amenity – injuries combined with pre-existing diabetes reduce life expectancy by 16 years (own medical consultant) or 4 years (Board's medical consultant).

1.8.5.2.C6 Case No. 11274

Name of case: Re L

Brief description of injuries: PARAPLEGIA

Reported: Kemp & Kemp, A4-017; [1997] CLY 1821

JSB Category: 1(b)

Sex: Male

Age at injury: 26

Age at award: 31

Date of award: 30 January 1997

Tribunal: CICB, Manchester

Amount of award then: £75,000

Award at February 2001: £97,833

Description of injuries: Severe injury to the spinal cord – not completely severed – profound depression – severe pain.

Prognosis: Many of the problems of paraplegia – continuing profound depression – confined to a wheelchair – award was assessed at the need for non-live-in care for twelve years – live-in care for the rest of his life.

Other points: Marriage broke down – care provided by a friend was assessed at lasting for six more years after the time of the hearing.

1.8.5.2.C7 Case No. 10537

Name of case: Michalski v Stabin Martin

Brief description of injuries: SPINE – "INCOMPLETE PARAPLEGIA"

Reported: Kemp & Kemp, E3-003; [1993] CLY 1429

JSB Category: 1(b); 3(A), 5(C), 5(E)(a), 5(H); 5(I)

Sex: Male

Age at injury: 59

Age at award: 65

Date of award: 18 January 1993

Tribunal: QBD

Amount of award then: £35,000

Award at February 2001: £47,058

Description of injuries: Burst fracture of body of first lumbar vertebra, with large fragment forced into spinal canal, causing permanent damage resulting in complete loss of power in one leg and partial loss of power in the other – complete loss of sexual function – bladder and bowel function impaired – painful urinary infections – asthma – agoraphobia – loss of self esteem – now using wheelchair as walking range confined to maximum of 25 yards.

Prognosis: Life expectancy reduced 5 years – hope for improvement in agoraphobia, bowel and bladder problems.

Other points: Neurologist described claimant as "incomplete paraplegic"; judge held that injuries were slightly less than complete paraplegia but considerably worse than the loss of one leg.

1.8.5.2.C8 Case No. 10528

Award at February 2001: £11,065

See: 1.8.3.C2 for details

1.8.5.3 QUADRIPLEGIA

1.8.5.3.C1 Case No. 10136

Name of case: Janardan v East Berkshire Health Authority

Brief description of injuries: QUADRIPLEGIA – ASPHYXIA AT BIRTH

Reported: [1990] 2 Med LR 1; Kemp & Kemp, A4-001/1, A4-109; BPILS, I 56, 58, 286.4, 286.7,582.4; XVII 1043; [1991] CLY 1333

JSB Category: 1(a)

Sex: Male

Age at injury: At birth

Age at award: -

Date of award: 01 July 1990

Tribunal: QBD

Amount of award then: £708,500

Award at February 2001: £1,278,206

Description of injuries: Cerebral palsy due to asphyxia at birth – mental faculties unimpaired – life expectancy 55.

Prognosis: Nursing attendance for the rest of life.

Other points: Award refers to General Damages sum.

1.8.5.3.C2 Case No. 11123

Name of case: Smith v Salford HA

Brief description of injuries: TETRAPLEGIA – TEMPORARY

Reported: [1994] 5 Med LR 321; 23 BMLR 137; BPILS, XI 9323; [1996] CLY 2214

JSB Category: 1(b)

Sex: Male

Age at injury: 39

Age at award: 46

Date of award: 01 July 1995

Tribunal: QBD

Amount of award then: £171,754

Award at February 2001: £263,516

Description of injuries: Temporary tetraplegia following negligent operation – neurological effects of the operation were disabling – plaintiff was unemployable – exacerbated pre-existing ankylosing spondylitis by one-third.

Other points: Ankylosing spondylitis contributed 30 per cent of disability – tetraparesis 60 per cent – depression 10 per cent.

1.8.5.3.C3 Case No. 10003

Name of case: O'Donnell v South Bedfordshire Health Authority

Brief description of injuries: SPASTIC QUADRIPLEGIA

Reported: Kemp & Kemp, A4-001/4; [1990] CLY 1578

JSB Category: 2(A)

Sex: Male

Age at injury: Birth

Age at award: 7

Date of award: 19 November 1990

Tribunal: QBD

Amount of award then: £105,000

Award at February 2001: £180,604

Description of injuries: Caesarean section abandoned when diagnosed as being dead in utero – born with spastic quadriplegia and cerebral palsy. Immobile and unable to speak – has some insight into his condition.

Prognosis: No improvement.

1.8.5.3.C4 Case No. 10002

Name of case: Thompson v South Tees Area Health Authority

Brief description of injuries: SPASTIC QUADRIPLEGIC

Reported: Kemp & Kemp, A4-003; BPILS, I 70.8, 286.6, 570.2, 593.3; [1990] CLY 1576

JSB Category: 2(A)

Sex: Female

Age at injury: Six months

Age at award: 9 years

Date of award: 10 April 1990

Tribunal: QBD

Amount of award then: £100,000

Award at February 2001: £178,283

Description of injuries: Intestinal obstruction due to intussesception – grossly dehydrated – cerebral anoxia led to spastic quadriplegia and severe mental handicap. Unable to crawl or sit unsupported – no speech – moaning, screaming and crying.

Prognosis: No improvement.

Other points: Sum of award included interest.

1.8.5.3.C5 Case No. 10302

Name of case: Re Tansley

Brief description of injuries: QUADRIPLEGIA – LIVE-IN CARER REQUIRED

Reported: Kemp & Kemp, A2-006/2; [1992] CLY 1557

JSB Category: 1(a)

Sex: Male

Age at injury: 39

Age at award: 44

Date of award: 01 January 1992

Tribunal: CICB, Liverpool

Amount of award then: £105,000

Award at February 2001: £171,365

Description of injuries: Quadriplegia exacerbating existing ankylosing spondylitis.

Prognosis: Unable to take required exercise to relieve ankylosing spondylitis – live-in carer required.

1.8.5.3.C6 Case No. 10000

Name of case: Bowden v Lane (dec'd)

Brief description of injuries: QUADRIPLEGIA

Reported: Kemp & Kemp, A2-007, A2-105; [1990] CLY 1577

JSB Category: 1

Sex: Female

Age at injury: 24

Age at award: 28

Date of award: 22 November 1990

Tribunal: QBD

Amount of award then: £100,000

Award at February 2001: £169,963

Description of injuries: Teacher at time of accident – fracture of C5 in road accident resulting in quadriplegia. Cannot feed herself, nor propel wheelchair – bladder emptied by catheter, and bowels by suppository and manual evacuation by nurse – some weak movement in shoulders and arms, but none below that level – some pain and discomfort in shoulders and lower limbs even though paralysed.

Prognosis: No improvement. Will never work again.

Specific Injuries

1.8.5.3.C7 Case No. 10303

Name of case: Wooding v Torbay District Council

Brief description of injuries: QUADRIPLEGIA – PARALYSIS AT LEVEL OF SHOULDERS

Reported: [1992] CLY 1558

JSB Category: 1(a)

Sex: Male

Age at injury: 16

Age at award: 22

Date of award: 17 March 1992

Tribunal: Exeter District Registry

Amount of award then: £105,000

Award at February 2001: £169,656

Description of injuries: Totally disabling fracture of the C5 vertebra and displacement of C4 vertebra.

Prognosis: . No worthwhile function in arms below shoulder level – appliance required to drain bladder – bowels evacuated manually – at risk of kidney and bladder infections and dysreflexia – no sexual function – dependent on carers for all everyday tasks – life expectancy reduced to 30 years from the date of the accident – permanently confined to a wheelchair.

1.8.5.3.C8 Case No. 10694

Name of case: Smith v Warrington Health Authority

Brief description of injuries: SPASTIC QUADRIPLEGIA – LIFE EXPECTANCY 45-50 YEARS

Reported: Kemp & Kemp, A4-004/1; BPILS, XVII 1258; [1994] CLY 1540

JSB Category: 1(a)

Sex: Female

Age at injury: at birth

Age at award: 16

Date of award: 18 July 1994

Tribunal: QBD

Amount of award then: £110,000

Award at February 2001: £168,503

Description of injuries: Profound brain damage suffered at birth due to admitted medical negligence – asymmetrical spastic quadriplegic cerebral palsy – generalised increase in limb muscle tone affecting legs more than arms.

Prognosis: Will never be able to live independently or work – special accommodation, care and equipment required – life expectancy of 45 to 50 years.

Other points: Approved settlement.

1.8.5.3.C9 Case No. 10531

Award at February 2001: £165,158

See: 1.2.3.8.C9 for details

1.8.5.3.C10 Case No. 10695

Name of case: Re Hughes (Ieuan Richard)

Brief description of injuries: QUADRIPLEGIA (INCOMPLETE TETRAPLEGIA) – LIFE EXPECTANCY 20 YEARS

Reported: Kemp & Kemp, A2-008; [1994] CLY 1541

JSB Category: 1(a)

Sex: Male

Age at injury: 35

Age at award: 40

Date of award: 08 December 1993

Tribunal: CICB, London

Amount of award then: £100,000

Award at February 2001: £152,575

Description of injuries: Assault – incomplete tetraplegia – all usual consequences of such an injury – daily spasms (temporarily relieved by 2 rhizotomy operations) – urinary tract infections – blocked suprapubic catheter, requiring cystoscopy.

Prognosis: Life expectancy 20 years from date of accident.

1.8.5.3.C11 Case No. 11477

Award at February 2001: £152,330

See: 1.2.3.8.C13 for details

1.8.5.3.C12 Case No. 11276

Name of case: Re Brewer

Brief description of injuries: TETRAPLEGIA – INCOMPLETE

Reported: [1997] CLY 1823

JSB Category: 1(b)

Sex: Female

Age at injury: -

Age at award: 52

Date of award: 01 July 1997

Tribunal: CICB

Amount of award then: £110,000

Award at February 2001: £150,907

Description of injuries: C5/6 fracture dislocation of the spine – C5 motor complete and sensory incomplete tetraplegia.

Prognosis: Life expectancy of 17 to 18 years from the time of the hearing – care to date was provided by her husband – commercial care would be required in the future.

1.8.5.3.C13 Case No. 10696

Name of case: Re McConnell

Brief description of injuries: QUADRIPLEGIA – SEVERE VISUAL HANDICAP – LIFE EXPECTANCY 40 YEARS

Reported: Kemp & Kemp, A2-006/3; [1994] CLY 1542

JSB Category: 1(a); 4(A)(c)

Sex: Female

Age at injury: 11 weeks

Age at award: 10

Date of award: 06 December 1993

Tribunal: CICB, Birmingham

Amount of award then: £90,000

Award at February 2001: £134,237

Description of injuries: Deliberate injuries to head – subdural haematoma causing brain damage – severe spastic quadriplegia – at date of hearing, aged 10, mental age approximately 9-12 months – limited understanding, some stimulation from music and television, able to recognise adoptive parents – unable to speak – unable to sit unaided – unable to walk – left arm and leg shortened and effectively useless – restricted, uncoordinated movement in right hand – unable to roll over when on ground – double incontinence – baby foods required – claimant wakes every 3 to 4 hours during sleep, requiring comforting – right hip dislocation suffered in past, requiring anti-convulsants, right femoral osteotomy and adductor tenotomy – left hip dislocated at time of hearing – hip and knee movements restricted – poor head control – serious, if not total, sight defect; registered as severely visually handicapped.

Prognosis: Intellectual impairment considered to be permanent, with no prospect of improvement – wheelchair required in future – will remain largely reliant on help and support of others – life expectancy 40 years (Board's finding).

1.8.5.3.C14 Case No. 11275

Name of case: Re J

Brief description of injuries: QUADRIPLEGIA

Reported: Kemp & Kemp, C2-014; [1997] CLY 1822

JSB Category: 1(a)

Sex: Male

Age at injury: Child

Age at award: 12

Date of award: 11 November 1996

Tribunal: CICB

Amount of award then: £80,000

Award at February 2001: £105,914

Description of injuries: Catastrophic head injury – gross cerebral oedema – bilateral cerebral infarct – possibility of major venous sinus thrombosis – multiple fractures.

Prognosis: There was significant neurological disability – microcephalic with severe spastic quadriplegia and gross mental retardation – medical evidence was that he had a 50 per cent chance of surviving for a further ten years – ten per cent chance of surviving for twenty years.

Other points: No reason to suppose that he would not have developed into a normal child had he not sustained the head injuries.

1.8.6 SEXUAL ABUSE

1.8.6.C1 Case No. 10016

Name of case: Re E, J, K and D (minors)

Brief description of injuries: PSYCHIATRIC DAMAGE; SEXUAL ABUSE

Reported: Kemp & Kemp, C4-224; [1990] CLY 1596

JSB Category: 3(A)

Sex: E – female; J – male; K – female; D – male

Age at injury: -

Age at award: 9, 11, 7 and 5 resp.

Date of award: 14 March 1990

Tribunal: CICB

Amount of award then: £57,500

Award at February 2001: £94,997

Description of injuries: E exhibited disturbed and sexualised behaviour and invited sexual advances – suffered from non-permanent physical changes to genitalia. J exhibited evidence of physical changes to anus. K exhibited sexualised behaviour and became enuretic – in need of regular psychotherapy. D was outwardly disturbed and exhibited destructive behaviour – in need of psychotherapy.

Prognosis: E was likely to continue being significantly disturbed in the future. J was in need of long-term psychotherapy – prone to depression – related in superficial way only. K had undoubtedly suffered a degree of irreversible emotional damage. D was likely to be emotionally affected for the rest of his life.

Other points: Award split: E: £17,500; J: £15,000; K: £12,500; D: £12,500

Specific Injuries

1.8.6.C2 Case No. 10569

Name of case: Re G

Brief description of injuries: SEXUAL ABUSE AND RAPE (2 SEPARATE CLAIMS)

Reported: Kemp & Kemp, C4-200; [1993] CLY 1462

JSB Category: 3(A)(a)

Sex: Female

Age at injury: (1) 7-14;(2) 14

Age at award: (1) 18;(2) 18

Date of award: 05 January 1993

Tribunal: CICB, London

Amount of award then: £50,000

Award at February 2001: £69,946

Description of injuries: (1) Daily sexual abuse over 7-year period by stepbrother – initially vaginal touching and oral sex – later full sexual intercourse – anal sex – threats of violence and death if facts revealed – abuse ended when abuser left home.(2) Evening in public house, first social evening after end of incidents related in (1) above – went back with man to his flat – rape with physical violence – released from flat – subsequent sexual assault by taxi driver taking her home.Incidents disclosed 1 year after attacks related in (2) above – subsequent depression – suicidal tendencies – strong emotional detachment (dissociation) – unable to continue with A-levels despite high academic achievement at GCSE level – acute trauma reaction diagnosed.

Prognosis: Prognosis uncertain – transferred to residential clinic for a period of 1 year at time of trial – unemployed since leaving school, prospects of being able to work poor in the short-term and possibly longer.

Other points: The award of £50,000 is inclusive of both claims.

1.8.6.C3 Case No. 10567

Name of case: Re G

Brief description of injuries: SEXUAL ABUSE – PSYCHIATRIC DAMAGE

Reported: Kemp & Kemp, C4-201; [1993] CLY 1460

JSB Category: 3(A)(a)

Sex: Female

Age at injury: 15 to 19

Age at award: 24

Date of award: 12 March 1993

Tribunal: CICB, London

Amount of award then: £50,000

Award at February 2001: £69,152

Description of injuries: Claimant in child care home (IQ of 68) – suffered extreme sexual abuse, accompanied by physical violence, for 4 years – forced anal, oral, and group sexual intercourse – voyeurism – exhibitionism – extreme degradation, including being urinated on, tied up and insertion of foreign objects – urinary tract infections, kidney infection and anal spasms – close relative of claimant subsequently murdered abusers when facts disclosed, bringing about severe behavioural reaction in claimant – several suicide attempts (swallowing glass, electrocution, strangulation) – apparent symptoms of psychosis including head-banging, window-butting, cutting and biting self – admitted to psychiatric hospital/

Prognosis: Prognosis guarded – no short-term plans for release from hospital – no realistic hope of future employment – unlikely to fulfil previous potential – considerable support and supervision required if ever placed in the community – only mildly mentally handicapped, but functioning at age range of 11 or 12/

1.8.6.C4 Case No. 10731

Name of case: Re A, M and T

Brief description of injuries: PSYCHIATRIC DAMAGE – SEXUAL ABUSE

Reported: Kemp & Kemp, C4-046; [1994] CLY 1579

JSB Category: 3(A), 3(B)

Sex: All female

Age at injury: A:5-12;M:7-14;T:10

Age at award: A:17;M:19;T:13

Date of award: 02 November 1993

Tribunal: CICB, London

Amount of award then: £50,000

Award at February 2001: £67,887

Description of injuries: Three sisters subjected to extensive sexual abuse for many years, mainly by father; also by grandfather and 2 men, also abused by father, at his instigation – digital penetration – masturbation by father in front of sisters while touching them – indecent photographs – A and T additionally subjected to full sexual intercourse – T additionally subjected to buggery – bribes or threats to ensure silence – all three suffered post-traumatic stress syndrome – acute and chronic traumatisation – daily intrusive memories – sleep disturbance – feelings of helplessness and powerlessness – loss of capacity to trust – low self-esteem – academic underachievement – over-idealisation of mother – abuse ceased in 1990 when A revealed truth, having previously kept silent to protect her sisters in mistaken belief that she was only victim – father convicted and imprisoned – father's maintenance of innocence and intention to appeal caused further distress, particularly to M and T, who had been made to feel responsible for abuse – A developed veneer of adjustment, in that she had steady boyfriend and sexual relationship and had developed maturely in other ways – symptoms of trauma, intrusive memories and sleep disturbance nevertheless present – academic performance particularly affected – M was considered too disturbed to give evidence at father's trial – acute sexual anxieties – cross-dressing – tomboyish behaviour – abnormal concern about development of secondary sexual characteristics – T became prematurely sexualised – had gone on to abuse younger siblings despite herself.

Other points: Award split: A: £15,000 M: £15,000 T: £20,000

1.8.6.C5 Case No. 11883

Name of case: Re H

Brief description of injuries: HIV – INFECTION DURING ASSAULT

Reported: (1999) 99 (4) QR 8; Kemp & Kemp, C4-028; [1999] CLY 1547

JSB Category: None

Sex: Male

Age at injury: 43

Age at award: 52

Date of award: 01 July 1998

Tribunal: CICB, London

Amount of award then: £50,000

Award at February 2001: £57,993

Description of injuries: Claimant infected with HIV virus during assault – 3 weeks later, admitted to hospital with headaches, fatigue, vomiting, diarrhoea and developing facial and trunkal rash – symptoms improved, but 12 months later, positive HIV test confirmed – claimant thereafter unable to continue working and took redundancy – claimant treated with various HIV drug treatments as they were developed, and was required to take a host of other drugs; suffered some side effects as a result – at time of trial, claimant suffering from diarrhoea, skin problems, general fatigue, peripheral neuropathy and relapsed depression (claimant had history of depression prior to diagnosis) – claimant responding to anti-retroviral therapy – claimant had not been involved in any sexual relationship since diagnosis as he had been unwilling to inform anybody that he had HIV due to the attached stigma.

Prognosis: Medical evidence before the Board stated that with further decline, HIV patients would suffer further HIV – related illnesses and ultimately develop a defining AIDS – related illness, a marker of severe immuno – suppression – with therapy, life expectancy can be 15-20 years, but difficult to predict in individual cases – confirmed at hearing that claimant's health would deteriorate and that he was 9 years into his HIV diagnosis at date of hearing.

Other points: Board informed that there were no previous comparable cases.

1.8.6.C6 Case No. 11776

Name of case: Re B

Brief description of injuries: SEXUAL ABUSE – PSYCHIATRIC DAMAGE

Reported: [1999] CLY 1439

JSB Category: 3(A)(a)

Sex: Female

Age at injury: 3-4 and 7-17

Age at award: 27

Date of award: 01 July 1999

Tribunal: CICB, York

Amount of award then: £50,000

Award at February 2001: £57,174

Description of injuries: Claimant physically abused by father between ages of 3 and 4 – beaten, locked in cupboards, kicked, hit with belt – claimant taken into care, returned to family when 7 – frequent sexual assaults by father thereafter – indecent touching, penetration with digits and foreign objects, oral sex, one occasion of full intercourse when 17 – claimant grossly traumatised – 47 admissions to psychiatric hospitals between ages of 19 and 26, both voluntary and under section – frequent overdoses – recurrent suicidal thoughts – self – mutilation to face, neck, legs and arm – deep, permanent scarring almost totally covering limbs – claimant formed relationship with schizophrenic and gave birth to one child, subsequently taken into care, prompting further episodes of self – harm – pregnant with second child at time of hearing, and further care proceedings anticipated when child born – claimant unable to have children thereafter.

Prognosis: Very poor – personality disorder untreatable – claimant unable to sustain herself in community without considerable support – prone to future episodes of self-harm.

1.8.6.C7 Case No. 11778

Name of case: Re S and B

Brief description of injuries: SEXUAL ASSAULT – PSYCHIATRIC DAMAGE

Reported: Kemp & Kemp, C4-210; [1999] CLY 1441

JSB Category: S: 3(A)(b), 3(B); 5(H) B: 3(B)(b)

Sex: S: Female B: Male

Age at injury: S:22;B:21

Age at award: S:27;B:26

Date of award: 24 September 1998

Tribunal: CICB, York

Amount of award then: £47,500

Award at February 2001: £54,270

Description of injuries: S and B, couple, attacked and both subjected to sexual assault lasting 3 hours – S: repeated anal and vaginal rape – forced to perform and receive oral sex – forced to masturbate – anal penetration with towbar, causing severe anal, rectal and peroneal injuries, requiring 6 months to heal – death threats; S in constant fear of life throughout assault – post-traumatic stress disorder, extreme for 16 months – flashbacks – frequent nightmares – avoidance of social situations – fear of being alone – personality change; quieter and less confident – interrupted sleep – avoidance of TV and newspaper reports – psychological inhibition of sexual function (not threatening to subsequent marriage to B) – exacerbation of symptoms annually on anniversary of assault – monthly therapy for 18 months.B: Lacerations to neck, leaving scars; facial and body bruising – forced to witness or participate in assault for 1.5 hours – forced to perform and receive oral sex – death threats – moderately severe post-traumatic stress disorder – flashbacks – nightmares – avoidance of social situations – therapy for 16 months – personality change from outgoing and confident to quiet, tearful and nervous – sexual function impaired – forced to leave job due to whispering campaign at work following extensive media coverage – further breakdown 2 years after attack; anti-depressants prescribed – fear of dark – ongoing hypervigilance and sleep disturbance – avoidance of TV and newspaper reports – premature vulnerability.

Prognosis: S: Permanently vulnerable to aggravation of condition by external triggers – inhibition of sexual function and exacerbation of symptoms on anniversary of assault unlikely to resolve – lifetime risk of incontinence from anal and rectal injuries.B: Continuing vulnerability to relapse on external triggers – sexual function likely to remain impaired.

Other points: Award split: S: £30,000 B: £17,500.

1.8.6.C8 Case No. 10017

Name of case: Re J and N

Brief description of injuries: PSYCHIATRIC DAMAGE; SEXUAL ABUSE

Reported: Kemp & Kemp, C4-225; [1990] CLY 1597

JSB Category: 3(A)

Sex: J – male; N – male

Age at injury: J-14;N-12

Age at award: J-19;N-17

Date of award: 14 August 1990

Tribunal: CICB

Amount of award then: £30,000

Award at February 2001: £43,104

Description of injuries: Abuse included frequent buggery, being photographed, given money and witnessing brother being buggered – touching and masturbation of both boys – suffered taunts – J suffered from significant reactive depression disorder – N was experiencing very real distress about the sexual abuse.

Prognosis: Continuing concern about sexual orientation

Other points: Award split: J: £17,500; N: £12,500

1.8.6.C9 Case No. 11777

Name of case: Re B

Brief description of injuries: SEXUAL ASSAULT – PSYCHIATRIC DAMAGE

Reported: [1999] CLY 1440

JSB Category: 3(A)(a)

Sex: Female

Age at injury: 33

Age at award: 37

Date of award: 12 January 1999

Tribunal: CICB, Manchester

Amount of award then: £35,000

Award at February 2001: £39,129

Description of injuries: Claimant victim of sexual assault – forced under threat of violence to remove clothes – oral and vaginal contact – attempted anal intercourse – attempt at strangulation – threats to kill – some short-term physical injuries – severe psychological injuries – anxiety, especially at night – fear of strangers, especially men – uncharacteristic anger and depression – flashbacks – nightmares – suicidal thoughts – episodes of self – harm – development of eating disorder and skin complaint – rape counselling, psychotherapy and other counselling undergone.

Other points: £35,000 approximately; total award of £50,000 included special damages estimated to total £15,000.

1.8.6.C10 Case No. 11784

Name of case: Re X

Brief description of injuries: SEXUAL ASSAULT – RAPE – PSYCHIATRIC DAMAGE

Reported: Kemp & Kemp, C4-207; [1999] CLY 1447

JSB Category: 3(A)(a)

Sex: Female

Age at injury: 29

Age at award: 34

Date of award: 23 September 1998

Tribunal: CICB, London

Amount of award then: £35,000

Award at February 2001: £38,873

Description of injuries: Claimant abducted at knifepoint and raped and sexually assaulted in empty building over a number of hours – claimant feared for her life – ongoing, severe psychiatric injury – still undergoing outpatient psychiatric treatment 6 years after attack, and inpatient treatment had been advised – unable to return to job as bank trader, or any other employment.

Other points: Award included sum of £4,500 for cost of inpatient psychiatric treatment.

1.8.6.C11 Case No. 10166

Name of case: Re AP

Brief description of injuries: GROSS SEXUAL ABUSE – PSYCHOLOGICAL DAMAGE – NOW DEPENDANT AND HIGHLY VULNERABLE

Reported: Kemp & Kemp, C4-209; [1991] CLY 1363

JSB Category: 3(A)(a)

Sex: Female

Age at injury: 7

Age at award: 15

Date of award: 04 September 1991

Tribunal: CICB, Liverpool

Amount of award then: £25,000

Award at February 2001: £33,566

Description of injuries: Gross sexual abuse by both parents, male family friend and younger brother – vaginal and anal intercourse – considerable psychological problems – had given birth to a child and required daily support from social services.

Prognosis: Described as highly vulnerable – at risk of forming relationships with potential physical and sexual abusers - unlikely to be able to form a stable relationship in the future.

1.8.6.C12 Case No. 10343

Name of case: Re X

Brief description of injuries: RAPE – PSYCHIATRIC DAMAGE – LOSS OF CONFIDENCE

Reported: [1992] CLY 1599

JSB Category: 3(A)(b)

Sex: Female

Age at injury: 39

Age at award: 42

Date of award: 08 May 1992

Tribunal: CICB, London

Amount of award then: £25,000

Award at February 2001: £32,355

Description of injuries: Domestic rape – hip and arm injuries from assault – loss of confidence, self-esteem, social life and activities.

Prognosis: Fearful of the future when her husband was released from prison.

1.8.6.C13 Case No. 10344

Name of case: Re X

Brief description of injuries: RAPE AND SEXUAL ASSAULT – POST-TRAUMATIC STRESS DISORDER

Reported: [1992] CLY 1600

JSB Category: 3(B)(b)

Sex: Female

Age at injury: 25

Age at award: 29

Date of award: 19 June 1992

Tribunal: CICB, London

Amount of award then: £25,000

Award at February 2001: £32,355

Description of injuries: Attacked by the lodger – felt guilt over her son having been forced to witness part of the attack – fear of being found by her attacker who had been acquitted – rape, buggery and imprisonment – post-traumatic stress disorder – extreme nervousness and fear for her safety – two suicide attempts followed by in-patient psychiatric hospital treatment – recent relapse at the time of the hearing.

Prognosis: Continuing psychiatric support required – anticipated return to work.

1.8.6.C14 Case No. 10927

Name of case: Re Y

Brief description of injuries: SEXUAL ABUSE – 2 YEARS – RAPE – BULIMIA – SCHOOL PHOBIA

Reported: Kemp & Kemp, C4-211; [1995] CLY 1678

JSB Category: 3(A)(a)

Sex: Female

Age at injury: 9-11

Age at award: 18

Date of award: 03 May 1995

Tribunal: CICB, Manchester

Amount of award then: £25,000

Award at February 2001: £29,986

Description of injuries: Was sexually abused by her stepfather between the ages of nine and 11 – initially abuse comprised indecent touching but progressed to rape – occurred approximately four times per week and involved aggressive vaginal penetration from behind – applicant was threatened that she would be killed if she told anyone about the abuse – threat was reinforced by her stepfather following her and then relating her movements to her – abuse ceased when the applicant visited Pakistan for six months and did not resume on her return – after gap of 18 months, her stepfather again raped and threatened her. The applicant then reported abuse and proceedings were taken against the stepfather resulting in his conviction – during this time applicant began to suffer symptoms including flashbacks, depression, low self-esteem and fear of going out – applicant became withdrawn and gained weight through bulimia – at time of criminal proceedings her distress was exacerbated by verbal abuse from other children at school – applicant became involved in solvent and alcohol abuse – she attended unit for children with disturbed behaviour – further, she developed a school phobia and ceased to attend school regularly – consequently, applicant left school with no academic qualifications, although prior to the abuse she had been doing well at school – had not been able to find employment – encountered problems in her sexual relationships, in particular frigidity, because of feelings of being defiled, which were likely to continue – continued to suffer from flashbacks and depression at time of hearing, although these were becoming less frequent.

1.8.6.C15 Case No. 11104

Name of case: Re Higgins

Brief description of injuries: SEXUAL ABUSE – POST-TRAUMATIC STRESS DISORDER

Reported: Kemp & Kemp, C4-213; [1996] CLY 2195

JSB Category: 3(A)(a)

Sex: Male

Age at injury: 2-14

Age at award: 26

Date of award: 29 August 1996

Tribunal: CICB, Manchester

Amount of award then: £25,000

Award at February 2001: £29,256

Description of injuries: Chronic form of post-traumatic stress disorder – sexual abuse – threats.

Prognosis: Psychological evidence stated that he was unlikely to ever fully recover.

Other points: He had committed a number of violent crimes – suffered a personality disorder related to the abuse.

1.8.6.C16 Case No. 10027

Name of case: Re R

Brief description of injuries: PSYCHIATRIC DAMAGE, SEXUAL ABUSE, STABBED IN CHEST

Reported: Kemp & Kemp, C4-215; [1990] CLY 1595

JSB Category: 5(A); 3(A)

Sex: Female

Age at injury: 13

Age at award: 18

Date of award: 01 July 1990

Tribunal: CICB, London

Amount of award then: £20,000

Award at February 2001: £28,199

Description of injuries: Stripped and sexually abused over some hours – stabbed through chest with sword, penetrating heart – left with operation scar that caused embarrassment due to unsightly nature – psychologically affected, but since abduction has shown improvement.

Prognosis: Has heart murmur which may require treatment.

1.8.6.C17 Case No. 11507

Name of case: Parrington v Marriot

Brief description of injuries: SEXUAL ABUSE – POST-TRAUMATIC STRESS DISORDER

Reported: Kemp & Kemp, C4-216; [1998] CLY 1509

JSB Category: 3(B)(b)

Sex: Female

Age at injury: 38

Age at award: 44

Date of award: 03 November 1997

Tribunal: Leicester County Court

Amount of award then: £25,000

Award at February 2001: £27,993

Description of injuries: Psychiatric disability after sexual abuse at work – at time of the hearing claimant had undergone 4 years of psychiatric counselling.

1.8.6.C18 Case No. 11506

Name of case: C v S

Brief description of injuries: SEXUAL ABUSE – POST-TRAUMATIC STRESS DISORDER

Reported: Kemp & Kemp, C4-217; [1998] CLY 1508

JSB Category: 3(B)(b)

Sex: Female

Age at injury: 9-12

Age at award: 17

Date of award: 14 November 1997

Tribunal: Norwich County Court

Amount of award then: £25,000

Award at February 2001: £27,993

Description of injuries: Sexual abuse – post-traumatic stress disorder.

Prognosis: A need for psychotherapy – possibility of sexual problems in the future.

1.8.6.C19 Case No. 11505

Name of case: Re F

Brief description of injuries: SEXUAL ABUSE – POST-TRAUMATIC STRESS DISORDER

Reported: Kemp & Kemp, C4-218; [1998] CLY 1507

JSB Category: 3(B)(b)

Sex: Female

Age at injury: 10-12

Age at award: 23

Date of award: 16 June 1998

Tribunal: CICB, London

Amount of award then: £25,000

Award at February 2001: £27,303

Description of injuries: Sexual abuse – post-traumatic stress disorder.

Prognosis: Always would be vulnerable to depression – post-traumatic stress disorder was long-term – psychotherapy would assist F to address the abuse.

1.8.6.C20 Case No. 11788

Name of case: Re B

Brief description of injuries: SEXUAL ASSAULT – RAPE – POST-TRAUMATIC STRESS DISORDER

Reported: [1999] CLY 1451

JSB Category: 3(A); 6(K)(iv), 8

Sex: Female

Age at injury: 16

Age at award: 23

Date of award: 01 July 1999

Tribunal: CICB, Birmingham

Amount of award then: £25,000

Award at February 2001: £27,006

Description of injuries: Claimant imprisoned and raped 3 times by distant relative – escaped by leaping from upstairs window – grossly comminuted fracture of right distal tibia, associated fractures to fibula and medial malleolus, requiring bone grafts and several operation to insert and remove metal plate and screws – permanent scars of 22 cm and 12 cm on leg and 10 cm on hip; claimant conscious of them and refused to wear shorts or skirts – leg still painful in cold weather or after walking about 1 mile 7 years after assault – ankle unstable, causing some difficulty in climbing stairs – psychological reaction to assault, diagnosed as a post-traumatic anxiety reaction (not full Post-traumatic stress disorder) – dietary problems causing weight loss – obsessive cleansing – washing self in disinfectant – nightmares once a month – flashbacks once a fortnight triggered by seeing violence on TV – anxiety when alone or in presence of males – feelings of shame – loss of confidence – reduced libido – symptoms ongoing at time of trial.

Prognosis: Greater than 50 per cent chance of osteoarthritis in leg in next 10-15 years – claimant would continue to undergo counselling and psycho-sexual counselling with husband.

1.8.6.C21 Case No. 10167

Name of case: Re B

Brief description of injuries: PERSISTENT SEXUAL ABUSE – ANXIETY – EARNING CAPACITY AFFECTED

Reported: Kemp & Kemp, C4-220; [1991] CLY 1364

JSB Category: 3(A)(b)

Sex: Female

Age at injury: 6

Age at award: 18

Date of award: 17 July 1991

Tribunal: CICB, London

Amount of award then: £20,000

Award at February 2001: £26,639

Description of injuries: Persistent sexual abuse by a male family member – physical injuries – depression, anxiety and sexual dysfunction – inability to persevere with any educational course- impact on earning ability.

Prognosis: It was hoped that symptoms would improve.

Other points: Award increased from £7,000 single member award

1.8.6.C22 Case No. 10168

Name of case: Re AP (a minor)

Brief description of injuries: REGULAR SEXUAL ABUSE BY BOTH PARENTS

Reported: Kemp & Kemp, C4-222; [1991] CLY 1365

JSB Category: 3(A)(b)

Sex: Male

Age at injury: 5

Age at award: 12

Date of award: 04 September 1991

Tribunal: CICB, Liverpool

Amount of award then: £20,000

Award at February 2001: £26,471

Description of injuries: Regular sexual abuse by both parents and older sister – oral sex and buggery and intercourse – three years behind at school.

Prognosis: He was coping well – difficulty informing relationships was likely to cause problems in the future.

1.8.6.C23 Case No. 10169

Name of case: Re L

Brief description of injuries: SERIOUS SEXUAL ABUSE – CHRONIC PSYCHIATRIC IMPAIRMENT

Reported: Kemp & Kemp, C4-223; [1991] CLY 1366

JSB Category: 3(A)(b)

Sex: Female

Age at injury: 12

Age at award: 17

Date of award: 15 November 1991

Tribunal: CICB, London

Amount of award then: £20,000

Award at February 2001: £26,265

Description of injuries: Serious sexual abuse by brother, father and grandfather – oral sex, digital penetration, masturbation and intercourse – became enuretic and encopretic following rejection by her mother – L had made three suicide attempts – thought to be attention seeking.

Prognosis: Severe chronic psychiatric impairment – emotionally damaged – employment prospects damaged.

Other points: Award was increased from £7,000 single member award.

1.8.6.C24 Case No. 10554

Name of case: Re M

Brief description of injuries: PSYCHIATRIC DAMAGE – POST-TRAUMATIC STRESS DISORDER

Reported: Kemp & Kemp, C4-044; [1993] CLY 1447

JSB Category: 3(B)(b)

Sex: Male

Age at injury: 3

Age at award: 7

Date of award: 19 February 1993

Tribunal: CICB, London

Amount of award then: £20,000

Award at February 2001: £25,625

Description of injuries: Boy found locked in bedroom next to murdered mother – believed to have witnessed at least part of murder – became increasingly withdrawn – post-traumatic stress – persistent bed-wetting and disturbed sleep – learning difficulties – hostility to those outside the family unit – some improvement appearing in learning difficulties.

Prognosis: Prognosis uncertain: memory of the violence clearly affecting thinking and behaviour, long-term effects difficult to assess.

1.8.6.C25 Case No. 10345

Name of case: Re B

Brief description of injuries: SEXUAL ASSAULT OVER MANY YEARS – SEVERE STRESS DISORDER AND MAL-ADAPTATION TO LIFE

Reported: [1992] CLY 1601

JSB Category: 3(B)(b)

Sex: Female

Age at injury: 4-24

Age at award: 26

Date of award: 19 August 1992

Tribunal: CICB, Leicester

Amount of award then: £20,000

Award at February 2001: £25,607

Description of injuries: Sexual interference – abuse began at age four years by father – progressed to full intercourse at age ten years and continued through to early twenties – two pregnancies resulted – first child kept – second child aborted – suicide attempt.

Prognosis: Continuing symptoms of stress disorder – mal-adaptation to life would endure.

Other points: Award increased from £12,000.

1.8.6.C26 Case No. 10170

Name of case: Re C

Brief description of injuries: PROLONGED SEXUAL ABUSE – STILL FEARFUL OF ADULTS

Reported: Kemp & Kemp, C4-227; [1991] CLY 1367

JSB Category: 3(A)(b)

Sex: Female

Age at injury: 9

Age at award: 15

Date of award: 05 July 1991

Tribunal: CICB, London

Amount of award then: £17,500

Award at February 2001: £23,140

Description of injuries: Prolonged sexual abuse by her father – digital interference, masturbation and full intercourse.

Prognosis: C was still nervous of adults -particularly men – she hoped to proceed to higher education.

Other points: Award was increased from £4,000 single member award.

1.8.6.C27 Case No. 11302

Name of case: Re GB, RB and RP

Brief description of injuries: SEXUAL ABUSE – POST-TRAUMATIC STRESS DISORDER

Reported: Kemp & Kemp, C4-228;[1997] CLY 1850

JSB Category: 3(B)(b)

Sex: Male

Age at injury: P1:13-15;P2:10-12;P3:13-16

Age at award: P1:31;P2:29;P3:31

Date of award: 13 August 1996

Tribunal: CICB, Liverpool

Amount of award then: £20,000

Award at February 2001: £23,111

Description of injuries: Physical sexual abuse – psychological and emotional manipulation – difficulties with relationships – severe/chronic post-traumatic stress disorder.

Other points: Sum awarded to each applicant. However, RP's award reduced by 50% under para.6(c) of the scheme – due to his current criminal record.

1.8.6.C28 Case No. 11303

Name of case: Re M

Brief description of injuries: SEXUAL ABUSE – POST-TRAUMATIC STRESS DISORDER

Reported: Kemp & Kemp, C4-229; [1997] CLY 1851

JSB Category: 3(B)(b)

Sex: Female

Age at injury: 11-21

Age at award: -

Date of award: 21 April 1997

Tribunal: CICB, Torquay

Amount of award then: £20,000

Award at February 2001: £22,613

Description of injuries: Sexual, emotional and physical abuse – repeated incidents of rape.

Prognosis: At continued risk of post-traumatic stress disorder – vulnerable to later severe depressive illness – might require long-term psycho-analytic psychotherapy in later life.

1.8.6.C29 Case No. 11508

Name of case: S v S
Brief description of injuries: SEXUAL ABUSE – POST-TRAUMATIC STRESS DISORDER
Reported: [1998] CLY 1510
JSB Category: 3(B)(b)
Sex: Female
Age at injury: 7-15
Age at award: 22
Date of award: 12 January 1998
Tribunal: Watford County Court
Amount of award then: £20,000
Award at February 2001: £22,138
Description of injuries: Psychiatric disability after sexual abuse – post-traumatic stress disorder of moderate severity.
Prognosis: She should be able to lead a relatively normal life by the time she was 25 – some psychotherapy might be required.

1.8.6.C30 Case No. 10346

Name of case: Re AT
Brief description of injuries: SEXUAL ABUSE – BUGGERY
Reported: [1992] CLY 1602
JSB Category: 3(A)(b)
Sex: Female
Age at injury: 14
Age at award: 19
Date of award: 05 June 1992
Tribunal: CICB, Leeds
Amount of award then: £17,000
Award at February 2001: £21,517
Description of injuries: Sexual abuse – suffered acts of buggery for a period of one year at age 14 years.
Prognosis: At serious risk of sexually abusive relationships.

1.8.6.C31 Case No. 10171

Name of case: Re P
Brief description of injuries: REPEATED SEXUAL ABUSE – FEELINGS OF GUILT – "BRAVE FACE"
Reported: Kemp & Kemp, C4-231; [1991] CLY 1368
JSB Category: 3(A)(b)
Sex: Female
Age at injury: 6
Age at award: 18
Date of award: 07 November 1991
Tribunal: CICB, Birmingham
Amount of award then: £16,500
Award at February 2001: £21,452
Description of injuries: Repeated sexual abuse by her father – threats – loss of family following disclosure of the abuse – feelings of guilt and distrust.
Prognosis: P put on " a brave face" – she had continued fears of her father and the discovery of her history by others – relatively isolated.

1.8.6.C32 Case No. 11957

Name of case: Re W (CICB Quantum: 1999)
Brief description of injuries: RAPE
Reported: Kemp & Kemp, C4-232; [2000] 1 CL 117
JSB Category: 3(A)(b)
Sex: Female
Age at injury: 12-18
Age at award: 25
Date of award: 07 June 1999
Tribunal: CICB, London
Amount of award then: £20,000
Award at February 2001: £21,284
Description of injuries: Rape by a family friend took place at least twice a week between the ages of twelve and eighteen – unreported until another victim made a complaint – the offender continued to live in the same locality – no depression – low self esteem and self blame – vulnerable to abusive and exploitative relationships with men – W did not derive sexual intimacy or pleasure from her private relationships.
Prognosis: It was hoped the situation would improve with therapy.

1.8.6.C33 Case No. 10172

Name of case: Re M
Brief description of injuries: PROLONGED SEXUAL ABUSE – RAPE – SEVERE EMOTIONAL DISTURBANCE
Reported: [1991] CLY 1369
JSB Category: 3(A)(b)
Sex: Female
Age at injury: 11
Age at award: 19
Date of award: 19 January 1991
Tribunal: CICB, Liverpool
Amount of award then: £15,000
Award at February 2001: £20,259
Description of injuries: Prolonged sexual abuse – rape and consensual sexual intercourse – intimidation by the assailant – severe emotional disturbance – some physical symptoms – extremely passive and dependent on her mother – little or no contact with her peers – bullied at school.
Prognosis: Sexual abuse would continue to affect her well into her adult life – caused academic and intellectual impairment.

1.8.6.C34 Case No. 11105

Name of case: Re B
Brief description of injuries: SEXUAL ABUSE – PSYCHIATRIC DISABILITY
Reported: Kemp & Kemp, C4-234; [1996] CLY 2196
JSB Category: 3(A)(b)
Sex: Female
Age at injury: 10-18
Age at award: 25
Date of award: 13 August 1996
Tribunal: CICB, London
Amount of award then: £17,500
Award at February 2001: £20,094

Description of injuries: Subjected to frequent rape – psychiatric disorder – she had formed a stable relationship – expecting her first child.

Other points: No medical evidence to support the allegations.

1.8.6.C35 Case No. 10178

Name of case: Re C and L (minors)
Brief description of injuries: LONG PERIOD OF SEXUAL ASSAULT – INTERCOURSE – BUGGERY
Reported: Kemp & Kemp, C4-252; [1991] CLY 1375
JSB Category: 3(A)(c)
Sex: Females
Age at injury: 13;12
Age at award: 17;16
Date of award: 03 May 1991
Tribunal: CICB (York)
Amount of award then: £15,000
Award at February 2001: £19,736

Description of injuries: C had been subjected to sexual intercourse, buggery, indecent assault and gross indecency by her brother and his friends – L had only one documented offence of indecent assault – her behavioural problems indicated that abuse had taken place over a lengthy period – both sisters had suffered from being removed from the family.

Prognosis: C complained of nightmares and an inability to form relationships with boys – L appeared to be obsessed with the abuse.

Other points: Award split: £10,000 for C. – £5,000 for L.

1.8.6.C36 Case No. 11304

Name of case: Re P
Brief description of injuries: SEXUAL ABUSE – POST-TRAUMATIC STRESS DISORDER
Reported: Kemp & Kemp, C4-235; [1997] CLY 1852
JSB Category: 3(B)(b)
Sex: Female
Age at injury: 12-18
Age at award: 32
Date of award: 03 July 1997
Tribunal:
Amount of award then: £17,500
Award at February 2001: £19,507

Description of injuries: Sexual abuse – post-traumatic stress disorder – alcohol abuse – received counselling for alcohol abuse – depressive mood-swings and nightmares continued.

1.8.6.C37 Case No. 10732

Name of case: Re R and R
Brief description of injuries: PSYCHIATRIC DAMAGE – SEXUAL ABUSE
Reported: Kemp & Kemp, C4-236; [1994] CLY 1580
JSB Category: 3(A)
Sex: One male, one female
Age at injury: -
Age at award: Boy:13;Girl:12
Date of award: 24 March 1994
Tribunal: CICB, London
Amount of award then: £15,000
Award at February 2001: £18,438

Description of injuries: Brother and sister abused by father from young age for several years until taken into care – both forced to carry out oral sex – boy forced to carry out mutual masturbation – girl subjected to digital penetration, penile penetration also suspected – further, undisclosed, abuse also suspected – boy displayed anxious, sexualised and aggressive behaviour in care – dissociation – auditory hallucination mechanisms developed to deal with trauma – girl similar symptoms, but less intense initially; more overtly sexualised – subsequent increase in dissociation and sleep disturbance and behaviour patterns similar to brother's – behaviour of both resulted in loss of 2 adoptive placements and reluctance of foster – parents to undertake adoption – academic under – achievement – belief that father still in contact with children and harassing them, particularly boy.

Prognosis: Prognosis for both poor – boy's symptoms generally deteriorating – suspected continued contact by father thought to be major factor in both boy's and girl's lack of recovery, and argued that this aggravated the initial abuse.

Other points: Sum awarded to each claimant.

1.8.6.C38 Case No. 12055

Name of case: Re F (CICB Quantum: 2000)

Brief description of injuries: SEXUAL ABUSE – PSYCHIATRIC INJURY

Reported: [2000] 6 CL 185

JSB Category: 3(A)(b)

Sex: Female

Age at injury: 9

Age at award: 13

Date of award: 14 December 1999

Tribunal: CICB, London

Amount of award then: £17,500

Award at February 2001: £18,317

Description of injuries: Sexual abuse by the stepfather on a daily basis – touching breasts and genital area – fingering and digital penetration – masturbation of the stepfather's penis – ejaculation over the girl's body – attempted intercourse on many occasions – she suffered thrush and an unnecessary appendectomy – F experienced powerful outbursts of aggression – unable to relate comfortably with male friends – GCSE results were below the expected grades due to the stress of her stepfather's trial.

Prognosis: It was not anticipated that she would make a complete recovery from the psychological and physical scarring.

1.8.6.C39 Case No. 10173

Name of case: Re V

Brief description of injuries: REGULAR SEXUAL ABUSE – INCLUDING BUGGERY

Reported: Kemp & Kemp, C4-237; [1991] CLY 1370

JSB Category: 3(A)(b)

Sex: Male

Age at injury: 9

Age at award: 18

Date of award: 05 February 1990

Tribunal: CICB

Amount of award then: £12,500

Award at February 2001: £18,206

Description of injuries: Sexual abuse by family friend – mutual masturbation, oral sex and buggery – inability to form relationships with girls – fear of being confined with older men.

Prognosis: Eventual return to normal life was not ruled out.

1.8.6.C40 Case No. 10733

Name of case: Re D and C

Brief description of injuries: PSYCHIATRIC DAMAGE – SEXUAL ABUSE

Reported: Kemp & Kemp, C4-238; [1994] CLY 1581

JSB Category: 3(A)

Sex: One male (D), one female (C)

Age at injury: D:6;C:4

Age at award: D:13;C:12

Date of award: 18 May 1994

Tribunal: CICB, Durham

Amount of award then: £15,000

Award at February 2001: £18,147

Description of injuries: Brother and sister repeatedly abused by stepfather – repeated buggery of both children – full sexual intercourse and cunnilingus with C – frequency of abuse unclear, though in C's case period of abuse was 2.5 years – resultant psychological and physical damage to both children – both received therapy from child and family psychiatric unit – assessment of severe abuse and necessity for extensive therapy.

Prognosis: No firm prognosis as to likely future psychological effect – medical evidence at time of hearing seemed to suggest a degree of stability – however, board took into account uncertainty of assessing long-term effects of psychological trauma.

Other points: Sum awarded to each claimant.

1.8.6.C41 Case No. 11295

Name of case: Re MRR

Brief description of injuries: SEXUAL ABUSE – PSYCHIATRIC DISABILITY

Reported: Kemp & Kemp, C4-239; [1997] CLY 1843

JSB Category: 3(A)(b)

Sex: Female

Age at injury: -

Age at award: 36

Date of award: 13 March 1996

Tribunal: CICB, Manchester

Amount of award then: £15,000

Award at February 2001: £17,300

Description of injuries: Systematically raped in a psychiatric institution – she suffered from pre-existing schizophrenia with moderate learning disability – her mental stability had decreased dramatically as a result of traumatization.

Other points: Her application was unsuccessful before single member (despite admissions by the assailant) – successful before the full board.

1.8.6.C42 Case No. 11305

Name of case: Re H

Brief description of injuries: SEXUAL ABUSE – POST-TRAUMATIC STRESS DISORDER

Reported: Kemp & Kemp, C4-240; [1997] CLY 1853

JSB Category: 3(B)(b)

Sex: Male

Age at injury: 11-13

Age at award: 17

Date of award: 18 March 1997

Tribunal: CICB, Nottingham

Amount of award then: £15,000

Award at February 2001: £16,850

Description of injuries: Sexual abuse by a female – distress, anger and confusion – suffered humiliation within the community – loss of schooling – lived in fear of his abuser who returned to the neighbourhood after serving her custodial sentence.

Prognosis: Unable to have normal adolescent experiences – further counselling required.

1.8.6.C43 Case No. 11509

Name of case: Re R

Brief description of injuries: SEXUAL ABUSE – POST-TRAUMATIC STRESS DISORDER

Reported: Kemp & Kemp, C4-241; [1998] CLY 1511

JSB Category: 3(B)(b)

Sex: Female

Age at injury: 8-12

Age at award: 21

Date of award: 26 March 1998

Tribunal: CICB, Torquay

Amount of award then: £15,000

Award at February 2001: £16,263

Description of injuries: Significant psychological damage from sexual abuse – change in personality – chaotic teenage years – R had stabilised in a supportive relationship – professional therapy required for 1 year.

1.8.6.C44 Case No. 10174

Name of case: Re H

Brief description of injuries: REGULAR SEXUAL ABUSE – POST-TRAUMATIC STRESS SYNDROME

Reported: [1991] CLY 1371

JSB Category: 3(A)(b)

Sex: Female

Age at injury: 11

Age at award: 18

Date of award: 30 October 1991

Tribunal: CICB, London

Amount of award then: £12,500

Award at February 2001: £16,126

Description of injuries: Regular abuse by her stepfather – masturbation and oral sex – visibly distracted and disturbed during her tenth and eleventh years at school – post-traumatic stress syndrome.

Prognosis: Continuing difficulties with her relationships with men – virtual loss of her relationship with her stepsister.

Other points: Mother blamed her for the abuse – mother died when she was 13 – she was forced to take on her mother's role.

1.8.6.C45 Case No. 10557

Name of case: Re Guin

Brief description of injuries: PSYCHIATRIC DAMAGE – POST-TRAUMATIC STRESS DISORDER

Reported: Kemp & Kemp, C4-061; [1993] CLY 1450

JSB Category: 3(B)(c)

Sex: Male

Age at injury: 39

Age at award: 46

Date of award: 15 January 1993

Tribunal: CICB

Amount of award then: £12,500

Award at February 2001: £15,786

Description of injuries: Claimant assaulted and received multiple injuries – physical recovery complete, but personality changes manifest – irritability – aggressive outbursts – lack of motivation – some memory impairment – family and social life affected – post-traumatic stress disorder diagnosed – claimant resigned from directorship of small company, attempted to set up another company but failed – employment history thereafter sporadic, but court found that claimant had been fit for work since April 1992, his current status as unemployed being simply due to the entry into receivership of company he had worked for since November 1991 until that date.

1.8.6.C46 Case No. 11306

Name of case: Re K

Brief description of injuries: RAPE – POST-TRAUMATIC STRESS DISORDER

Reported: Kemp & Kemp, C4-243; [1997] CLY 1854

JSB Category: 3(B)(b)

Sex: Female

Age at injury: Not specified

Age at award:

Date of award: 10 June 1997

Tribunal: CICB, London

Amount of award then: £13,500

Award at February 2001: £14,898

Description of injuries: Three rapes – assault causing facial injuries – post-traumatic stress disorder.

Prognosis: Dependence on alcohol and methadone under control – she was expected to recover from her symptoms within three to five years.

Other points: Fearful of the imminent release of her abuser from prison.

1.8.6.C47 Case No. 10018

Name of case: Re X

Brief description of injuries: PSYCHIATRIC DAMAGE AND RAPE

Reported: Kemp & Kemp, C4-244; [1990] CLY 1598

JSB Category: 3(A)

Sex: Female

Age at injury: 22

Age at award: 25

Date of award: 26 January 1990

Tribunal: CICB, Exeter

Amount of award then: £10,000

Award at February 2001: £14,533

Description of injuries: Raped at night in an alleyway – distrust of society in general – distrust of men in general – unease if travelling alone in daylight and fear if alone at night – consequent limitation on any job she might get – became timid and introverted.

Prognosis: Impact might or might not wane.

1.8.6.C48 Case No. 11307

Name of case: Re JW

Brief description of injuries: SEXUAL ABUSE – POST-TRAUMATIC STRESS DISORDER

Reported: Kemp & Kemp, C4-245; [1997] CLY 1855

JSB Category: 3(B)(b)

Sex: Male

Age at injury: 28

Age at award: 30

Date of award: 12 December 1995

Tribunal: CICB, Manchester

Amount of award then: £12,500

Award at February 2001: £14,401

Description of injuries: One episode of physical and sexual abuse by a male – post-traumatic stress disorder.

Prognosis: At the time of the hearing the prognosis was cautiously optimistic.

1.8.6.C49 Case No. 11512

Name of case: Re AB

Brief description of injuries: SEXUAL ABUSE – PSYCHIATRIC DISABILITY – DEPRESSION

Reported: Kemp & Kemp, C4-246; [1998] CLY 1514

JSB Category: 3(A)(b)

Sex: Female

Age at injury: 5

Age at award: 20

Date of award: 23 October 1997

Tribunal: CICB, Birmingham

Amount of award then: £12,500

Award at February 2001: £13,581

Description of injuries: Sexual assaults by a 14 year old male – withdrawnness – depression – fear of large numbers of people – psychologically vulnerable.

Other points: Award increased from £5,000 single member award.

1.8.6.C50 Case No. 11510

Name of case: Re D and D (minors)

Brief description of injuries: SEXUAL ABUSE – PSYCHIATRIC DISABILITY

Reported: Kemp & Kemp, C4-247; [1998] CLY 1512

JSB Category: 3(B)(b)

Sex: D1: Female / D2: Male

Age at injury: D1:4;D2:18 months

Age at award: D1:11;D2:8

Date of award: 17 December 1997

Tribunal: CICB, London

Amount of award then: £12,500

Award at February 2001: £13,538

Description of injuries: Sexual abuse by a male baby-sitter – physical assaults, cruelty and neglect by the foster carer – severe psychological damage – vulnerable children experienced severe trauma.

Prognosis: D1 Was at high risk of emotional breakdown in adulthood – for D2 the abuse would have disastrous repercussions in adolescence and adulthood.

Other points: Sum awarded to each applicant.

1.8.6.C51 Case No. 11511

Name of case: Re D

Brief description of injuries: SEXUAL ABUSE – PSYCHIATRIC DISABILITY

Reported: Kemp & Kemp, C4-248; [1998] CLY 1513

JSB Category: 3(B)(b)

Sex: Female

Age at injury: 18 months-4

Age at award: 9

Date of award: 16 February 1998

Tribunal: CICB, Torquay

Amount of award then: £12,500

Award at February 2001: £13,513

Description of injuries: Repeated penetrative abuse over a considerable period of time – severe psychological damage.

Prognosis: Significant psychological symptoms – prognosis poor due to the abuse starting at such an early age – effects would affect her throughout her life.

1.8.6.C52 Case No. 10177

Name of case: Re L

Brief description of injuries: SEXUAL ASSAULT – INTERCOURSE – CAPABLE OF STABLE RELATIONSHIPS

Reported: Kemp & Kemp, C4-249; [1991] CLY 1374

JSB Category: 3(A)(c)

Sex: Female

Age at injury: 7

Age at award: 26

Date of award: 09 January 1991

Tribunal: CICB, Leeds

Amount of award then: £10,000

Award at February 2001: £13,302

Description of injuries: Sexually assaulted by her father and his friend – sexual intercourse, mutual oral sex – made to have intercourse with her father's friend at age 13 – left home at 16.

Prognosis: L was able to have a stable relationship, marry and have children.

1.8.6.C53 Case No. 10019

Name of case: Re H

Brief description of injuries: PSYCHIATRIC DAMAGE AND RAPE

Reported: Kemp & Kemp, C4-250; [1990] CLY 1599

JSB Category: 3(A)

Sex: Female

Age at injury: 30

Age at award: 32

Date of award: 19 October 1990

Tribunal: CICB

Amount of award then: £10,000

Award at February 2001: £13,292

Description of injuries: Subjected to violent rape and was threatened with more violence – suffered from some vaginal soreness. Anxiety, depression, loss of self-esteem and enduring fear of all men and of going out – unable to form relationships.

1.8.6.C54 Case No. 10176

Name of case: Re T

Brief description of injuries: SEXUAL ABUSE OVER 12 MONTHS – INTERCOURSE

Reported: Kemp & Kemp, C4-251; [1991] CLY 1373

JSB Category: 3(A)(c)

Sex: Female

Age at injury: 11

Age at award: 18

Date of award: 08 March 1991

Tribunal: CICB

Amount of award then: £10,000

Award at February 2001: £13,178

Description of injuries: Sexual abuse over twelve months – mutual masturbation and intercourse – school record dropped considerably after the abuse – mother blamed T for the abuse.

Prognosis: At the time of the hearing T had two children – her relationship with her mother had improved – she hoped to take a course at college in the future.

1.8.6.C55 Case No. 10175

Name of case: Re K

Brief description of injuries: A SINGLE EPISODE OF BUGGERY – ANAL WARTS – PSYCHOLOGICAL PROBLEMS

Reported: Kemp & Kemp, C4-253; [1991] CLY 1372

JSB Category: 3(A)(c)

Sex: Female

Age at injury: 9

Age at award: 13

Date of award: 21 June 1991

Tribunal: CICB

Amount of award then: £10,000

Award at February 2001: £12,904

Description of injuries: Anal warts caused by a single assault of buggery – the same assailant had abused K's mother as a child causing her to display an ambivalent attitude to K – recurring problems with the warts included surgery – psychological problems.

Prognosis: At the time of the hearing K was still attending group therapy from time to time.

1.8.6.C56 Case No. 10347

Name of case: Re A

Brief description of injuries: SEXUAL ABUSE – TWO ACTS OF UNDER-AGE INTERCOURSE – "NAIVE" APPLICANT

Reported: Kemp & Kemp, C4-254; [1992] CLY 1603

JSB Category: 3(A)(c)

Sex: Female

Age at injury: 12

Age at award: 19

Date of award: 21 July 1992

Tribunal: CICB, Leeds

Amount of award then: £10,000

Award at February 2001: £12,456

Description of injuries: Two acts of under-age intercourse leading to the child's being psychologically affected – counselled for a number of years.

Prognosis: At first hearing child was adjudged to be at least partially willing to the assault – described as "naive" at the Appeal.

Other points: Damages figure decided on Appeal.

1.8.6.C57 Case No. 10559

Name of case: Fendwick v Chief Constable of the South Yorkshire Police

Brief description of injuries: PSYCHIATRIC DAMAGE – POST-TRAUMATIC STRESS DISORDER

Reported: Kemp & Kemp, C4-078; [1993] CLY 1452

JSB Category: 3(B)(b)

Sex: Male

Age at injury: 21

Age at award: 25

Date of award: 26 July 1993

Tribunal: Liverpool County Court

Amount of award then: £10,000

Award at February 2001: £12,282

Description of injuries: Claimant present at Hillsborough disaster – initially trapped in crush – escaped – returned to rescue trapped brother – part of group which carried 12 people, some dead, out of the stand onto the field – feared for safety of friend, but found him uninjured – later invited to take part in TV programme on the incident, but on arrival at studio became very distressed and was unable to take part – subsequently took excessive amount of Valium and admitted to hospital – personality change from carefree to snappy, irritable and more reclusive – withdrawnness – nightmares – flashbacks – judge held that claimant was suffering from post-traumatic stress disorder.

Prognosis: Syndrome likely to continue for the foreseeable future (judge's holding).

Other points: Claimant consumed amphetamines for a period of 6-12 months after disaster; judge inclined to view that this was a symptom of the syndrome.

1.8.6.C58 Case No. 10558

Name of case: Re Moore (Christine)

Brief description of injuries: PSYCHIATRIC DAMAGE – POST-TRAUMATIC STRESS DISORDER

Reported: Kemp & Kemp, F6-072; [1993] CLY 1451

JSB Category: 3(B); 5(J)(a); 8

Sex: Female

Age at injury: 34

Age at award: 39

Date of award: 17 September 1993

Tribunal: CICB, York

Amount of award then: £10,000

Award at February 2001: £12,176

Description of injuries: Punched in abdomen by husband, experiencing great pain, brief loss of consciousness and difficulty breathing – husband initially refused to call ambulance – claimant alarmed by concern evinced by ambulance and hospital staff, believing she was in danger of death – emergency laparotomy confirmed diagnosis of ruptured spleen – splenectomy – assault subsequently caused emotional stress, non-specific anxiety and evidence of post-traumatic stress disorder – embarrassment at reaction to laparotomy scar leading to inhibitions in displaying it in communal changing areas and in forming new relations with the opposite sex.

Prognosis: Counselling and medication unlikely to assist with psychological symptoms, but some small spontaneous improvement with the passage of time possible – claimant will require medication for rest of life to compensate for immunodeficiency due to loss of spleen.

1.8.6.C59 Case No. 10734

Name of case: Re D (a minor)
Brief description of injuries: PSYCHIATRIC DAMAGE – SEXUAL ABUSE
Reported: Kemp & Kemp, C4-256; [1994] CLY 1582
JSB Category: 3(A)
Sex: Male
Age at injury: 3-6
Age at award: 13
Date of award: 03 June 1994
Tribunal: CICB, Birmingham
Amount of award then: £10,000
Award at February 2001: £11,933

Description of injuries: Boy sexually abused by mother – repeated episodes of oral, bodily and genital contact – no evidence of coercion or injury – behaviour sexualised at school; touching and requesting oral sex from other pupils, due to corrupted behavioural norms – child fostered and successfully adopted – however, continuing sexualised behaviour, involving incidents of exposure and inappropriate touching of adults and children leading to isolation and difficulties in forming relationships.

Prognosis: Child, surprisingly, able to continue successfully in mainstream education – possibility of this continuing and child achieving employment and independence and coming to terms with history – child aware of abuse and likely to need assistance from educational psychologist and psychiatric counsellor in future.

1.8.6.C60 Case No. 11106

Name of case: Re F
Brief description of injuries: SEXUAL ABUSE – PSYCHIATRIC DISABILITY
Reported: Kemp & Kemp, C4-258; [1996] CLY 2197
JSB Category: 3(A)(b)
Sex: Female
Age at injury: 6-8
Age at award: 15
Date of award: 01 August 1996
Tribunal: CICB, Durham
Amount of award then: £10,000
Award at February 2001: £11,261

Description of injuries: Sexual abuse with threats – abandoned by mother – psychiatric disability.

Prognosis: Working well at school – likely to go to vocational further education – disruptive and sexualised behaviour.

Other points: Difficult to tell whether abandonment or abuse was the cause of her continuing problems.

1.8.6.C61 Case No. 10568

Name of case: Re Farley
Brief description of injuries: RAPE – PSYCHIATRIC DAMAGE
Reported: Kemp & Kemp, C4-257; [1993] CLY 1461
JSB Category: 3(A)(b)
Sex: Female
Age at injury: 20
Age at award: 22
Date of award: 19 January 1993
Tribunal: CICB, London
Amount of award then: £9,000
Award at February 2001: £11,226

Description of injuries: Claimant raped by minicab driver – bruised ribs – depression – anxiety – nightmares – weight loss – sexual dysfunction – break-up of relationship with boyfriend in period immediately after attack – off work for 1 month – subsequently married and condition improved by time of hearing – depression and anxiety still recurring – unable to remain at home alone.

1.8.6.C62 Case No. 11317

Name of case: Re O (a minor)
Brief description of injuries: SEXUAL ABUSE – POST-TRAUMATIC STRESS DISORDER
Reported: Kemp & Kemp, C4-259; [1997] CLY 1865
JSB Category: 3(B)(c)
Sex: Female
Age at injury: 7
Age at award: 12
Date of award: 04 April 1997
Tribunal: CICB, Nottingham
Amount of award then: £10,000
Award at February 2001: £11,025

Description of injuries: Prolonged sexual abuse by a male over a period of one year – post-traumatic stress disorder – symptoms of post-traumatic stress disorder still exhibited – she had suffered significant physical, psychological, social and emotional damage.

Other points: Board was concerned that symptoms might be attributable to her early home life rather than to abuse. Award of £6,000 (single member) increased to £10,000.

1.8.6.C63 Case No. 10020

Name of case: Re P

Brief description of injuries: PSYCHIATRIC DAMAGE AND SEXUAL ABUSE

Reported: Kemp & Kemp, C4-260; [1990] CLY 1600

JSB Category: 3(A)

Sex: Female

Age at injury: (7-12)

Age at award: 15

Date of award: 19 December 1989

Tribunal: CICB, Birmingham

Amount of award then: £7,500

Award at February 2001: £10,859

Description of injuries: Sexual abuse by grandfather – included oral and digital interference, touching of his person, and one incident of threatened intercourse. Disrupted but fully healed hymen – few manifestations of psychological stress – occasional nightmares, restlessness at night and reluctance to be medically examined.

Prognosis: Potential difficulties in establishing a normal relationship with men.

1.8.6.C64 Case No. 11514

Name of case: Re H

Brief description of injuries: SEXUAL ABUSE – PSYCHIATRIC DISABILITY

Reported: Kemp & Kemp, C4-261; [1998] CLY 1516

JSB Category: 3(A)(b)

Sex: Female

Age at injury: 8-14

Age at award: 20

Date of award: 28 October 1997

Tribunal: CICB

Amount of award then: £10,000

Award at February 2001: £10,798

Description of injuries: Sexual abuse – forced to watch the abuser masturbate and watch pornographic videos.

Prognosis: Effects of the abuse were potentially far-reaching – possibility of sexual dysfunction in future relationships.

1.8.6.C65 Case No. 11513

Name of case: Re Z

Brief description of injuries: SEXUAL ABUSE – PSYCHIATRIC DISABILITY

Reported: Kemp & Kemp, C4-262; [1998] CLY 1515

JSB Category: 3(A)(b)

Sex: Female

Age at injury: 3

Age at award: 15

Date of award: 03 November 1997

Tribunal: CICB, London

Amount of award then: £10,000

Award at February 2001: £10,791

Description of injuries: Physically and sexually abused – symptoms of psychiatric damage – phobia for toilets – difficulty forming friendships – nightmares.

1.8.6.C66 Case No. 11780

Name of case: H v Home Office

Brief description of injuries: SEXUAL ASSAULT – RAPE – PSYCHIATRIC DAMAGE – POST-TRAUMATIC STRESS DISORDER

Reported: Kemp & Kemp, C4-263; [1999] CLY 1443

JSB Category: 3(B)

Sex: Male

Age at injury: 27

Age at award: 31

Date of award: 23 November 1998

Tribunal: Bristol County Court

Amount of award then: £10,000

Award at February 2001: £10,468

Description of injuries: Claimant, serving prisoner, raped by another inmate – allegations made to prison authorities, but appropriate action not taken – subsequent second rape by same inmate – post-traumatic stress disorder of moderate severity for under 2 months – assault had some effect on claimant's sex life – residual fear of seeing people of same appearance as assailant.

1.8.6.C67 Case No. 11779

Name of case: Re S

Brief description of injuries: SEXUAL ABUSE – PSYCHIATRIC DAMAGE

Reported: Kemp & Kemp, C4-264; [1999] CLY 1442

JSB Category: 3(A)(b)

Sex: Female

Age at injury: 4-8

Age at award: 16

Date of award: 29 April 1999

Tribunal: CICB, London

Amount of award then: £10,000

Award at February 2001: £10,417

Description of injuries: Sexual abuse by grandfather between ages of 4 and 8 – digital interference, oral penetration, genital touching – development of obsessive sexual behaviour – problems in forming and maintaining relationships – no evidence of psychiatric condition.

Other points: Ambivalent evidence of further abuse by mother's new boyfriend – breakdown of family led to claimant being taken into care.

1.8.6.C68 Case No. 10570

Name of case: Re RED

Brief description of injuries: SEXUAL ABUSE- PSYCHIATRIC DAMAGE

Reported: Kemp & Kemp, C4-265; [1993] CLY 1463

JSB Category: 3(A)

Sex: Female

Age at injury: 11-18 months

Age at award: 5 years

Date of award: 03 December 1992

Tribunal: CICB, York

Amount of award then: £7,500

Award at February 2001: £9,267

Description of injuries: Abused by cohabitee of mother – forced oral sex and and buggery – mother aided and abetted – finding adoptive parents proved difficult due to child's behaviour.

Prognosis: Likely long-term effects – requirement of psychiatric support in later life highly probable (but see "Other Points" below).

Other points: Award of £7,500 appealed, but Board felt unable to adjust award in light of extreme youth of victim at time of abuse and behavioural improvements showing since placement of child with loving parents – Board indicated case could be reopened at a later date if expensive therapy in future needed.

1.8.6.C69 Case No. 11515

Name of case: Re SJY

Brief description of injuries: SEXUAL ABUSE – PSYCHIATRIC DISABILITY

Reported: Kemp & Kemp, C4-267; [1998] CLY 1517

JSB Category: 3(A)(c)

Sex: Female

Age at injury: 12-18

Age at award: 24

Date of award: 08 December 1997

Tribunal: CICB, Nottingham

Amount of award then: £8,500

Award at February 2001: £9,138

Description of injuries: Indecent assault – psychological damage.

Prognosis: The effects of the abuse had lasted a number of years – only susceptible to treatment in part – would continue to affect S into the future.

1.8.6.C70 Case No. 10736

Name of case: Re SNH (a minor)

Brief description of injuries: PSYCHIATRIC DAMAGE CAUSED BY SEXUAL ABUSE

Reported: Kemp & Kemp, C4-268; [1994] CLY 1584

JSB Category: 3(A)

Sex: Female

Age at injury: 3

Age at award: 6

Date of award: 17 January 1994

Tribunal: CICB, Lincoln

Amount of award then: £7,500

Award at February 2001: £9,130

Description of injuries: Claimant subjected to several instances of genital touching by male abuser, possibly in her bed – reluctant to talk, due to her age and threats of punishment from abuser – police and social services immediately involved – disruption to sleep – loss of appetite – reversion to bed-wetting – reluctance to associate with male adults – refusal to co-operate with medical examination to assess presence of physical damage – psychiatric assessment suggested that family and social service support had alleviated any acute problems.

Prognosis: Uncertainty as to whether future therapeutic intervention at various stages would be necessary as child grew up.

1.8.6.C71 Case No. 11781

Name of case: Re H (a minor)

Brief description of injuries: SEXUAL ASSAULT – PSYCHIATRIC DAMAGE – POST-TRAUMATIC STRESS DISORDER

Reported: [1999] CLY 1444

JSB Category: 3(B); 7(A)(f)

Sex: Male

Age at injury: 6-9 and 12

Age at award: 14

Date of award: 03 September 1998

Tribunal: CICB, London

Amount of award then: £8,500

Award at February 2001: £8,893

Description of injuries: Claimant suffered sexual abuse and threats to kill at gunpoint between ages of 6 to 9 made by relative – digital manipulation, oral sex – 3 years later, claimant beaten up at boys' club – injuries to mouth and broken tooth – claimant had received continuing psychological care – post-traumatic stress disorder lasting in excess of 1 year – flashbacks – intrusive thoughts – poor sleep – dissociation – insect phobia – experience of sexual abuse undoubtedly significant factor in emergence of these symptoms – social and emotional development affected.

Prognosis: Risk of social and emotional impairment continuing into adulthood.

Other points: Award comprised post-traumatic stress disorder: £7,500, oral damage: £1,000.

1.8.6.C72 Case No. 11107

Name of case: Re K

Brief description of injuries: RAPE – POST-TRAUMATIC STRESS DISORDER

Reported: Kemp & Kemp, C4-092; [1996] CLY 2198

JSB Category: 3(B)(c)

Sex: Female

Age at injury: 37

Age at award: 41

Date of award: 04 July 1996

Tribunal: CICB, London

Amount of award then: £7,500

Award at February 2001: £8,465

Description of injuries: Post-traumatic stress disorder – following rape at knife-point.

Prognosis: Prognosis uncertain – symptoms were generally expected to resolve – possible her condition would change into an enduring personality change.

Other points: Alcohol abuse was a complicating factor.

1.8.6.C73 Case No. 11311

Name of case: Re MP

Brief description of injuries: SEXUAL ABUSE – POST-TRAUMATIC STRESS DISORDER

Reported: Kemp & Kemp, C4-270; [1997] CLY 1859

JSB Category: 3(B)(c)

Sex: Male

Age at injury: 16

Age at award: 32

Date of award: 13 August 1996

Tribunal: CICB, Liverpool

Amount of award then: £7,500

Award at February 2001: £8,426

Description of injuries: One episode of sexual abuse by a male – post-traumatic stress disorder – continued to suffer post-traumatic stress disorder.

1.8.6.C74 Case No. 11782

Name of case: Re C

Brief description of injuries: SEXUAL ASSAULT – RAPE – PSYCHIATRIC DAMAGE

Reported: Kemp & Kemp, C4-271; [1999] CLY 1445

JSB Category: 3(A)

Sex: Female

Age at injury: 21

Age at award: 25

Date of award: 11 January 1999

Tribunal: CICB, London

Amount of award then: £8,000

Award at February 2001: £8,421

Description of injuries: Claimant was suffering from psychological and drinking problems following attack by a former boyfriend when she was violently raped by the driver of taxi in which she was travelling – bruising to thighs – stomach ache – urinary infection, resolved by antibiotics – difficulties with police interview process; claimant aggressive and intoxicated at times – initially willing to aid prosecution, but discouraged by tone of police advice and prosecution abandoned – development of symptoms of anger and short – temperedness, alcohol abuse continued – break – up of long-term relationship due to the effect of the rape – nightmares – depression – severe curtailment of social life – birth of son to claimant triggered end of drinking problems – claimant not suffering from depression at time of hearing.

Prognosis: Claimant believed social life would improve in time.

Other points: Pre-existing psychological problems and aggression exhibited by claimant, and her acknowledged alcoholism, taken into account.

1.8.6.C75 Case No. 11783

Name of case: Re H
Brief description of injuries: SEXUAL ABUSE – PSYCHIATRIC DAMAGE
Reported: [1999] CLY 1446
JSB Category: 3(A)(c)
Sex: Female
Age at injury: to 15
Age at award: 22
Date of award: 01 July 1999
Tribunal: CICB, Birmingham
Amount of award then: £8,000
Award at February 2001: £8,334

Description of injuries: Claimant sexually abused by mother's cohabitee and taken into care when 15 – male foster parent began also to sexually abuse the girl – touching of breasts and vagina when in bed, either under or over bedclothes – claimant would pretend to be asleep while this was done – female foster parent would frequently punch and slap claimant – claimant's head repeatedly banged against wall on one occasion – pushed down flight of stairs and kicked on another occasion – abuse from foster parents lasted for over a year while resident with them, and to a lesser extent when she had contact with them in the year thereafter – claimant received psychiatric care – continuing emotional difficulties, although these substantially contributed to by her earlier home life.

1.8.6.C76 Case No. 10571

Name of case: Re Saunders
Brief description of injuries: SEXUAL ASSAULT – BUGGERY – DEATH THREATS – PSYCHIATRIC DAMAGE
Reported: Kemp & Kemp, C4-275; [1993] CLY 1464
JSB Category: 3(A)
Sex: Female
Age at injury: 36
Age at award: 39
Date of award: 11 May 1993
Tribunal: CICB, London
Amount of award then: £6,500
Award at February 2001: £7,923

Description of injuries: Claimant suffered serious sexual assault lasting several hours while working as prostitute – attempted buggery – assault with intention to commit buggery – death threats – indecent assault – actual bodily harm – subsequent terror and depression – nightmares – loss of self - esteem – return to previous heroin use, having successfully withdrawn – at time of hearing still fearful of being alone or with a man, and still unable to form sexual relationships.

1.8.6.C77 Case No. 11971

Name of case: Re L (CICB Quantum: 1999)
Brief description of injuries: RAPE – POST-TRAUMATIC STRESS DISORDER
Reported: Kemp & Kemp, C4-274; [2000] 2 CL 142
JSB Category: 3(A)(c)
Sex: Female
Age at injury: 23
Age at award: 31
Date of award: 08 June 1999
Tribunal: CICB, Bath
Amount of award then: £7,500
Award at February 2001: £7,790

Description of injuries: Raped on two occasions and controlled by threats of violence – relocated and decided not to report the attacks out of fear – her symptoms included depression, haunting memories and nightmares – anxiety and irritability – mistrustful of men – unable to have a sexual relationship with her partner. At the appeal it was decided that her attacker was such a violent criminal that her decision not to report the incident was understandable – all her psychological problems could not be attributed to the rapes owing to threats having been made to her before they took place.

1.8.6.C78 Case No. 11980

Name of case: Re S (CICB Quantum: 1999)(Sexual Abuse)
Brief description of injuries: SEXUAL ABUSE – POST-TRAUMATIC STRESS DISORDER
Reported: Kemp & Kemp, PRC-011; [2000] 3 CL 164
JSB Category: 3(B)(c)
Sex: Male
Age at injury: 12
Age at award: 27
Date of award: 20 October 1999
Tribunal: CICB, Manchester
Amount of award then: £7,300
Award at February 2001: £7,541

Description of injuries: Sexually abused at the age of twelve by one of his carers in a local authority residential home – the penis was touched on two occasions – post-traumatic stress disorder – reliving the trauma through nightmares, while watching television programmes relating to sexual abuse and while attempting sexual intercourse – there was little intimacy in his relationship with his fiancee – S had difficulty in giving and receiving affection.

Prognosis: S's condition failed to respond to therapy – the prognosis was poor.

1.8.6.C79 Case No. 12032

Name of case: Re N (CICB Quantum: 2000)
Brief description of injuries: SEXUAL ABUSE
Reported: Kemp & Kemp, PRC-010; [2000] 5 CL 176
JSB Category: 3(A)(c)
Sex: Male
Age at injury: 7-12
Age at award: 19
Date of award: 27 January 2000
Tribunal: CICB
Amount of award then: £6,400
Award at February 2001: £6,607
Description of injuries: Sexual abuse by a family friend – mutual masturbation – oral sex – digital interference – penile penetration. Underwent psychotherapy for two years and counselling – continued to suffer anger and guilt.
Other points: £8,000 less 20 per cent reduction.

1.8.6.C80 Case No. 10572

Name of case: Re T
Brief description of injuries: SEXUAL ABUSE – CHILD – SEVERE CONDUCT DISORDER
Reported: Kemp & Kemp, C4-275; [1993] CLY 1465
JSB Category: 3(A)
Sex: Female
Age at injury: 8
Age at award: 12
Date of award: 12 February 1993
Tribunal: CICB, Nottingham
Amount of award then: £5,000
Award at February 2001: £6,196
Description of injuries: Single incident of sexual abuse by uncle (suspicion of further incidents) – penetration with digit and foreign object (walking stick) – forced to watch pornographic video – severe emotional disorder – severe conduct disorder – nocturnal enuresis – relationship difficulties with parents – pre-existing behavioural problems exacerbated to level of quite severe damage.
Prognosis: Prognosis poor.
Other points: Award increased on appeal from £2,000.

1.8.6.C81 Case No. 11108

Name of case: Re BR
Brief description of injuries: SEXUAL ASSAULT – DEPRESSION
Reported: Kemp & Kemp, C4-137; [1996] CLY 2199
JSB Category: 3(A)(c)
Sex: Female
Age at injury: 24
Age at award: 27
Date of award: 21 October 1996
Tribunal: CICB, London
Amount of award then: £5,000
Award at February 2001: £5,592
Description of injuries: Physical assault for four to five hours – sexual assault – rape threats – depression and anxiety – award made to reflect the assault and its consequences – not the background of domestic violence.
Other points: Developed asthma – phobia to public transport – loss of sexual libido.

1.8.6.C82 Case No. 11313

Name of case: Re W (a minor)
Brief description of injuries: SEXUAL ABUSE – POST-TRAUMATIC STRESS DISORDER
Reported: Kemp & Kemp, C4-278; [1997] CLY 1861
JSB Category: 3(B)(c)
Sex: Female
Age at injury: 13
Age at award: 18
Date of award: 19 February 1997
Tribunal: CICB, Bath
Amount of award then: £5,000
Award at February 2001: £5,548
Description of injuries: One episode of indecent assault – depression – loss of confidence.
Prognosis: Likely to experience adverse feelings on and off for the rest of her life.

1.8.6.C83 Case No. 11314

Name of case: Re W (a minor)
Brief description of injuries: SEXUAL ABUSE – POST-TRAUMATIC STRESS DISORDER
Reported: Kemp & Kemp, C4-279; [1997] CLY 1862
JSB Category: 3(B)(c)
Sex: Male
Age at injury: -
Age at award: 14
Date of award: 27 May 1997
Tribunal: CICB, Durham
Amount of award then: £5,000
Award at February 2001: £5,481
Description of injuries: Sexual abuse by a female – post-traumatic stress disorder – a profound depressive reaction.
Prognosis: The abuse continued to have a significant impact on all areas of his life.

1.8.6.C84 Case No. 11518

Name of case: H v Nottinghamshire CC

Brief description of injuries: SEXUAL ABUSE – CLAIMANT SUFFERED FROM DOWN'S SYNDROME

Reported: Kemp & Kemp, C4-280; [1998] CLY 1520

JSB Category: 3(B)(c)

Sex: Female

Age at injury: 25

Age at award: 29

Date of award: 05 January 1998

Tribunal: Nottingham County Court

Amount of award then: £5,000

Award at February 2001: £5,392

Description of injuries: Assault – apparently of a sexual nature – showed signs of psychological disturbance – post-traumatic stress disorder – signs of wariness and reluctance to be parted from her parents 2 years after the incident.

Prognosis: Severe anxiety reactions could be triggered by external factors.

Other points: H suffered from Down's Syndrome – she was unable to give a very clear account of the incident due to intellectual impairment.

1.8.6.C85 Case No. 11517

Name of case: Re R

Brief description of injuries: SEXUAL ABUSE – PSYCHIATRIC DISABILITY

Reported: [1998] CLY 1519

JSB Category: 3(A)(c)

Sex: Female

Age at injury: 36

Age at award: 40

Date of award: 27 January 1998

Tribunal: CICB, London

Amount of award then: £5,000

Award at February 2001: £5,392

Description of injuries: Serious sexual assault in claimant's own home – severe anxiety on being on her own – insomnia

Other points: Claimant had been traumatised by the assault – she believed that a prosecution of her assailant would be unsuccessful

1.8.6.C86 Case No. 11516

Name of case: Re D and K

Brief description of injuries: SEXUAL ABUSE – PSYCHIATRIC DISABILITY

Reported: Kemp & Kemp, C4-282; [1998] CLY 1518

JSB Category: D: 3(B)(c) K: 3(A)(c)

Sex: D: Male/K: Female

Age at injury: D:5-8;K:6

Age at award: D:10;K:11

Date of award: 23 February 1998

Tribunal: CICB, London

Amount of award then: £5,000

Award at February 2001: £5,365

Description of injuries: D: post-traumatic stress disorder following sexual abuse – K: depression and insecurity following sexual abuse.

Prognosis: D – sexual development and adult relationships were likely to be hindered as a result of the abuse – K was expected to have difficulties in forging relationships with boyfriends – and in exploring her sexuality in adulthood – likely to suffer ambivalent feelings towards her own children.

Other points: D was rejected by his mother and went to live with his aunt – K was abandoned by her mother – it was difficult for the Board to distinguish between the effects of the abandonment and the sexual abuse. Sum awarded to each child.

1.8.6.C87 Case No. 10021

Name of case: Re S

Brief description of injuries: SEXUAL ABUSE

Reported: Kemp & Kemp, C4-107; [1990] CLY 1601

JSB Category: 3(A)

Sex: Female

Age at injury: 16

Age at award: 20

Date of award: 19 November 1990

Tribunal: CICB, Leeds

Amount of award then: £3,500

Award at February 2001: £4,631

Description of injuries: Punched about the face, put in bath, had clothes ripped and covered in tomato sauce, washing-up liquid etc. – bruising to face and hands. Suffered personality change – was frightened to go out to work and needed accompanying everywhere – after two years was much better.

Prognosis: Residue of fear – suffered headaches, irritability and anxiety when reminded of assaults.

SECTION 1.9
ONSET OF DISEASE

1.9.C1 Case No. 11072

Name of case: Re Sanders

Brief description of injuries: HEMIPLEGIA

Reported: Kemp & Kemp, C2-002; [1996] CLY 2163

JSB Category: 1(b)

Sex: Female

Age at injury: 2

Age at award: 10

Date of award: 20 March 1996

Tribunal: CICB, Torquay

Amount of award then: £120,000

Award at February 2001: £176,261

Description of injuries: Totally blind – partially paralysed – risk of epilepsy 50% – at time of the hearing – totally blind – risk of epilepsy 10% right-sided hemiplegia.

Prognosis: Future uncertain.

1.9.1 CIRCULATORY DISEASE

1.9.1.C1 Case No. 10902

Name of case: Molinari v Ministry of Defence

Brief description of injuries: LEUKAEMIA

Reported: [1994] PIQR Q33; Kemp & Kemp, L3-091; [1994] CLY 1756

JSB Category:

Sex: Male

Age at injury: 20-29

Age at award: 39

Date of award: 06 December 1993

Tribunal: QBD

Amount of award then: £40,000

Award at February 2001: £52,810

Description of injuries: Claimant formerly civilian classified radiation worker at nuclear submarine base, during which time he was exposed to ionising radiation – 7 years after employment, diagnosed as suffering from acute lymphoblastic leukaemia – cessation of self-employment and commencement of treatment – chemotherapy – autologous bone marrow transplant, requiring further chemotherapy and doses of ionising radiation – in isolation 4 weeks – life threatening lung infection – many types of antibiotic and antifungal drugs taken – repeated lumbar punctures – insertion of lines into body for administration of drugs – hair loss – weight loss – loss of body image (claimant had been body – builder throughout adult life and this a significant factor in pride and self esteem) – constant nausea – loss of saliva – premature ageing – cramps in hands – painful joints – chemotherapy finally ended 1 month before trial.

Prognosis: 20 per cent chance of relapse – second relapse would be fatal – 5 or 6 years after bone marrow transplant, chance of relapse would have decreased to 1 per cent – antibiotics required for rest of life – unable to return to own double glazing business.

Other points: Defendant admitted liability and that exposure to radiation caused disease – claimant claimed provisional damages on 20 per cent chance of relapse – provisional award made.

1.9.2 FAILURE TO DIAGNOSE

1.9.2.C1 Case No. 11404

Award at February 2001: £61,340

See: 1.5.4.3.C2 for details

1.9.2.C2 Case No. 11759

Name of case: Bateman v Industrial Orthopaedic Society

Brief description of injuries: UNDIAGNOSED CANCER

Reported: (1998) 3 Medical Litigation 3; BPILS, XVII 1089; [1998] CLY 1762

JSB Category:

Sex: Female

Age at injury: 41

Age at award: Deceased

Date of award: 01 July 1997

Tribunal: QBD

Amount of award then: £22,500

Award at February 2001: £25,393

Description of injuries: Failure to diagnose and treat colorectal carcinoma – 2 operations and numerous medical investigations – back and abdominal pain – rectal bleeding – constipation – weight loss – claimant eventually died.

Other points: The judge considered Mills v British Rail Engineering Ltd [1992] PIQR Q130, [1991] CLY 1497 and Stratford v British Rail Engineering Ltd [1991] CLY 1498 – he decided that the award for general damages should be greater than in those cases due to the longer period of pain and suffering.

1.9.2.C3 Case No. 11757

Name of case: Burns (a minor) v Doncaster HA

Brief description of injuries: HEART – FAILURE TO DIAGNOSE CORONARY – AVOIDABLE SIDE-EFFECTS OF UNNECESSARY DRUGS

Reported: Kemp & Kemp, F6-010; [1998] CLY 1760

JSB Category:

Sex: Male

Age at injury: 0

Age at award: 16

Date of award: 20 October 1997

Tribunal: Doncaster County Court

Amount of award then: £10,000

Award at February 2001: £10,798

Description of injuries: 6 or 7 undiagnosed paroxysmal attacks of torsades de pointes – claimant mis-diagnosed as suffering from epilepsy – was in a drugged state due to high levels of carbamazepine prescribed for the epilepsy – claimant had not suffered any serious effects from the carbamazepine – no further attacks following the fitting of a pacemaker.

Other points: There was some educational retardation during his adolescent years.

1.9.2.C4 Case No. 10221

Name of case: Thomas v West Midlands HA

Brief description of injuries: FAILURE TO DIAGNOSE TORSION OF THE TESTIS – LOSS OF A TESTICLE

Reported: Kemp & Kemp, F5-060; [1991] CLY 1418

JSB Category: 5(E)

Sex: Male

Age at injury: 20

Age at award: 25

Date of award: 18 December 1990

Tribunal: Birmingham District Registry

Amount of award then: £7,000

Award at February 2001: £9,269

Description of injuries: Failure to diagnose torsion of the testis for 48 hours – loss of the left testicle – fixing of the right – pain and suffering for 48 hours.

Prognosis: Reproductive facility at hazard should the remaining testicle become diseased – no secondary effects.

1.9.2.C5 Case No. 11755

Name of case: Hirst (a minor) v Tameside and Glossop HA

Brief description of injuries: DIABETES – FAILURE TO DIAGNOSE

Reported: Kemp & Kemp, L8-081; [1998] CLY 1758

JSB Category:

Sex: Female

Age at injury: 3

Age at award: 12

Date of award: 19 January 1998

Tribunal:

Amount of award then: £6,000

Award at February 2001: £6,470

Description of injuries: Failure to diagnose diabetes insipidus for 3 years – H had made a full and permanent recovery.

1.9.3 GASTRO-INTESTINAL DISEASE

1.9.3.C1 Case No. 11400

Name of case: Miles v West Kent HA

Brief description of injuries: INTERNAL ORGANS – IRRITABLE BOWEL SYNDROME

Reported: [1997] 8 Med LR 191; BPILS, XVII 1109; [1997] CLY 1949

JSB Category: 5(D)(a)

Sex: Female

Age at injury: -

Age at award: -

Date of award: 01 July 1997

Tribunal: QBD

Amount of award then: £60,000

Award at February 2001: £73,971

Description of injuries: Negligent surgery during removal of the gall bladder – bile duct cut and clamped in two places – jaundice and infections.

Prognosis: Repair operation was required – caused wound pain – irritable bowel syndrome – changed personality.

1.9.4 INFECTIOUS DISEASE

1.9.4.C1 Case No. 11473

Name of case: Rubins v Employment Office

Brief description of injuries: BLOOD – HEPATITIS

Reported: Kemp & Kemp, L3-051; [1997] CLY 2023

JSB Category: 5

Sex: Female

Age at injury: Not stated

Age at award:

Date of award: 24 June 1997

Tribunal: Canterbury County Court

Amount of award then: £4,350

Award at February 2001: £4,641

Description of injuries: Symptoms of infectious Hepatitis A – anorexia

Prognosis: Fully recovered within six months of the date of the accident – no long term sequelae.

1.9.4.C2 Case No. 10483

Name of case: Foreman v Saroya

Brief description of injuries: HEPATITIS – COMPLETE RECOVERY

Reported: [1992] CLY 1739

JSB Category:

Sex: Female

Age at injury: -

Age at award: 41

Date of award: 13 January 1992

Tribunal: QBD

Amount of award then: £2,250

Award at February 2001: £2,854

Description of injuries: Contracted hepatitis – not A or B – disease contracted as a direct result of halothane anaesthetic being administered for dental work – on a previous occasion she had suffered the same reaction to the drug.

Prognosis: Told she was lucky to be alive – made a complete recovery.

1.9.4.C3 Case No. 10899

Name of case: Joyce v Mumin

Brief description of injuries: FOOD POISONING – SALMONELLA

Reported: Kemp & Kemp, L2-052; [1994] CLY 1751

JSB Category: 5(D)

Sex: Female

Age at injury: 20

Age at award: -

Date of award: 08 July 1994

Tribunal: Brentford County Court

Amount of award then: £2,250

Award at February 2001: £2,688

Description of injuries: Claimant found to have contracted salmonella from curry served in defendant's restaurant – diarrhoea – vomiting – stomach cramps – loss of nearly three-quarters of a stone in weight – claimant absent from work for 3 months.

1.9.4.C4 Case No. 12071

Name of case: Duffy v First Choice Holidays & Flights Ltd

Brief description of injuries: DIGESTIVE ORGANS – GASTROENTERITIS

Reported: [2000] 6 CL 201

JSB Category: 5(D)

Sex: Female

Age at injury: 23

Age at award: 25

Date of award: 13 January 2000

Tribunal: Guildford County Court

Amount of award then: £1,500

Award at February 2001: £1,549

Description of injuries: Acute gastroenteritis – central abdominal pain – watery stools – locally prescribed medication led to vomiting – difficulty in the administration of intravenous and intramuscular medication – recovery took about four weeks.

Other points: Award took into account the distress and disappointment of the spoilt honeymoon.

1.9.4.C5 Case No. 12072

Name of case: A (a child) v Milupa Ltd

Brief description of injuries: DIGESTIVE ORGANS – SALMONELLA

Reported: [2000] 6 CL 202

JSB Category: 5(D)

Sex: Male

Age at injury: 7 months

Age at award: 3

Date of award: 14 February 2000

Tribunal: Stourbridge County Court

Amount of award then: £1,300

Award at February 2001: £1,335

Description of injuries: A was fed milk which gave rise to salmonella food poisoning – acute for fourteen days – he lost two pounds in weight – re-hydrating fluids required – salmonella was present for six months – suffered intermittent symptoms on 10 – 12 occasions some of which could be due to unrelated childish ailments.

1.9.4.C6 Case No. 10512

Name of case: Barton v Ali Raj Tandoori Takeaway

Brief description of injuries: SALMONELLA POISONING – 1 MONTH

Reported: [1992] CLY 1768

JSB Category:

Sex: Male

Age at injury: 32

Age at award: 34

Date of award: 15 May 1992

Tribunal: Leeds County Court

Amount of award then: £750

Award at February 2001: £926

Description of injuries: Salmonella

Prognosis: Full recovery took one month.

1.9.5 NEUROLOGICAL DISEASE

1.9.5.C1 Case No. 10526

Name of case: Re Parkes

Brief description of injuries: MULTIPLE SCLEROSIS – ACCELERATION BY 10 YEARS

Reported: [1992] CLY 1782

JSB Category:

Sex: Male

Age at injury: 32

Age at award: 45

Date of award: 03 February 1992

Tribunal: CICB

Amount of award then: £275,000

Award at February 2001: £461,547

Description of injuries: Developed symptoms of multiple sclerosis following an assault – at time of hearing he had a severe level of disability resulting from the disease – Board accepted medical evidence that the assault had accelerated the development of the disease by ten years.

1.9.5.C2 Case No. 10144

Name of case: Re K

Brief description of injuries: TRIGGERING OF DORMANT MULTIPLE SCLEROSIS

Reported: [1991] CLY 1341

JSB Category: [None]

Sex: Female

Age at injury: 48

Age at award: 53

Date of award: 26 February 1991

Tribunal: CICB

Amount of award then: £19,800

Award at February 2001: £26,975

Description of injuries: Assault – hit head against a wall – triggered the symptoms of previously dormant multiple sclerosis – speech slurred – great difficulty in maintaining balance – neurological symptoms manifested within a day or two.

Prognosis: Never returned to work.

1.9.6 PSYCHIATRIC DISEASE

1.9.6.C1 Case No. 10008

Name of case: Re Gregory
Brief description of injuries: MODERATELY SEVERE PSYCHIATRIC INJURY
Reported: Kemp & Kemp, C2-028; [1990] CLY 1585
JSB Category: 3(A)
Sex: Male
Age at injury: 30
Age at award: 37
Date of award: 11 September 1990
Tribunal: CICB
Amount of award then: £55,000
Award at February 2001: £83,899
Description of injuries: Severe head injury with left parietal fracture – large intra-cerebral haematoma in left tempero-parietal region – smaller haematomas in right temporal and frontal region. Violent temper outbursts – increased irritability – mood swings – intolerance of frustration – significant short and long term memory loss – poor concentration – impaired verbal fluency – impairment of balance – hearing loss – other sensory impairment (smell and taste).

Prognosis: No improvement.

1.9.6.C2 Case No. 10063

Name of case: Fender v British Coal Corporation
Brief description of injuries: IMPOTENCE – DEPRESSION
Reported: Kemp & Kemp, F5-054; [1990] CLY 1641
JSB Category: 5(E)
Sex: Male
Age at injury: -
Age at award: -
Date of award: 15 November 1990
Tribunal: Court of Appeal
Amount of award then: £50,000
Award at February 2001: £74,780
Description of injuries: Impotence and resulting reactive depression.

1.9.6.C3 Case No. 10009

Name of case: Re T, G and J
Brief description of injuries: PSYCHIATRIC DAMAGE
Reported: Kemp & Kemp, C4-036, M4-070; [1990] CLY 1588
JSB Category: 3(A)
Sex: Female
Age at injury: 5, 3 and 2
Age at award: -
Date of award: 12 June 1990
Tribunal: CICB, London
Amount of award then: £45,000
Award at February 2001: £68,334
Description of injuries: Infants T, G and J aged 5, 3 and 2 at the time of their mother's murder by their father at which they were present – sustained psychiatric injuries.

Other points: Award split: T: £20,000; G: £20,000; J: £5,000

1.9.6.C4 Case No. 10165

Award at February 2001: £41,347

See: 1.2.3.8.C73 for details

1.9.6.C5 Case No. 10007

Name of case: Crompton v Peacock;
Brief description of injuries: MODERATELY SEVERE PSYCHIATRIC INJURY
Reported: Kemp & Kemp, C2-063; [1990] CLY 1581
JSB Category: 3(A)
Sex: Male
Age at injury: 18
Age at award: 22
Date of award: 13 November 1990
Tribunal: QBD
Amount of award then: £25,000
Award at February 2001: £34,840
Description of injuries: Severe head injury causing amnesia – some moderate facial scarring. Good recovery – left with significant intellectual impairment – reduced confidence and memory, occasional depression, irritability and bad temper – difficulty concentrating.

Prognosis: Found to have variation in the cognitive functions well above average – possible lifetime of frustration – suffers delayed career development to a lower level.

1.9.6.C6 Case No. 11521

Name of case: Lawrence v WW Martin (Thanet) Ltd

Brief description of injuries: PSYCHIATRIC – PARANOID PSYCHOSIS – SCHIZOPHRENIA

Reported: Kemp & Kemp, C4-025; [1998] CLY 1523

JSB Category: 3(B)(a); 6(B)

Sex: Male

Age at injury: 27

Age at award: -

Date of award: 13 August 1997

Tribunal: Canterbury County Court

Amount of award then: £30,000

Award at February 2001: £34,251

Description of injuries: Muscular sprain to the lower back – compensation neurosis – full blown paranoid psychosis (schizophrenia).

Prognosis: Incurable schizophrenia could be controlled by medication – back pain was likely to persist indefinitely – physical and mental condition made claimant unfit for work.

Other points: L's schizophrenia had been exacerbated by surveillance by W's enquiry agents.

1.9.6.C7 Case No. 10896

Name of case: Page v Smith

Brief description of injuries: CHRONIC FATIGUE SYNDROME

Reported: [1996] 1 AC 155; [1996] PIQR P364; [1995] 2 WLR 644; [1995] 2 All ER 736; [1995] 2 Lloyd's Rep 95; [1995] PIQR P239; [1995] RTR 210; [1995] 23 LS Gaz R 33; (1995) 145 NLJ Rep 723, HL; Kemp & Kemp, L8-210; BPILS, I98.8, 98.17, 105.1, VIII 61, 3403, XI 4580,

JSB Category:

Sex: Male

Age at injury: -

Age at award: 50

Date of award: 01 May 1994

Tribunal: QBD

Amount of award then: £20,000

Award at February 2001: £24,525

Description of injuries: Claimant, previously suffering from mild and sporadic Chronic Fatigue Syndrome (CFS, also known as ME), involved in road accident – exacerbation of CFS to status of being chronic and permanent – claimant sleeping a great deal – no longer any energy to relate to children – marital relationship suffering – general loss of interest in life – unable to continue in work (as teacher).

1.9.6.C8 Case No. 10323

Name of case: Benney v Carnon Consolidated Tin Mines

Brief description of injuries: PHOBIC SYMPTOMS – PHOBIC ATTACKS – LIFELONG

Reported: [1993] PIQR Q7; Kemp & Kemp, C4-048; [1992] CLY 1579

JSB Category: 3(A)(b)

Sex: Male

Age at injury: 32

Age at award: 39

Date of award: 01 April 1992

Tribunal: Truro County Court

Amount of award then: £18,000

Award at February 2001: £22,935

Description of injuries: Phobic symptoms – panic attacks – damaged employment prospects.

Prognosis: Unlikely to make a full recovery from the trauma – impairment of social interaction and sexual function – phobic symptoms would persist for life.

1.9.6.C9 Case No. 10555

Name of case: Re Slater

Brief description of injuries: PSYCHIATRIC DAMAGE – WITNESS TO MURDER

Reported: Kemp & Kemp, C4-050; [1993] CLY 1448

JSB Category: 3(A)(b), 3(B)(b)

Sex: Female

Age at injury: 33

Age at award: 38

Date of award: 26 January 1993

Tribunal: CICB, Leeds

Amount of award then: £17,500

Award at February 2001: £22,419

Description of injuries: Claimant's husband stabbed by assailant at front door – claimant dragged husband inside while assailant remained in garden, staring at her – husband died in her arms – deep and intense post-traumatic stress disorder – flashbacks – intrusive thoughts – acute distress and panic attacks on exposure to anything that stimulated memories of the event – anxiety – high tension – depressive thoughts – tearfulness – concentration and sleep poor – claimant had protected children to the neglect of herself.

Prognosis: Little or no progress possible without professional help.

1.9.6.C10 Case No. 10920

Name of case: Re Isaacs

Brief description of injuries: SEVERE PSYCHOLOGICAL PROBLEMS – IMPAIRED MEMORY – PERSONALITY CHANGE

Reported: Kemp & Kemp, C4-057; [1995] CLY 1671

JSB Category: 3(B)(b)

Sex: Male

Age at injury: 19

Age at award: 31

Date of award: 12 June 1995

Tribunal: CICB, Bristol

Amount of award then: £15,000

Award at February 2001: £17,503

Description of injuries: Assaulted by group of youths when working as barman – sustained a fracture to the skull together with bruising of his chest and legs – was headbutted in face, kicked and struck several times over head with beer glasses – detained in hospital for one week and thereafter had three months convalescing – four months after accident applicant attempted to return to bar work but after about three months he became apprehensive and scared – thereafter was unemployed for a period of approximately three years – in 1988 the applicant commenced employment as manager of public house but he still suffered serious psychological problems and was forced to give up that form of employment after three years – there was then another period of three years' unemployment but by October 1994 he had secured a job as assistant manager at a brasserie and had recently been promoted – at time of hearing, his memory impairment had not changed and he was suffering from headaches which were migrainous in nature associated with nausea and vomiting – these occurred about twice a month. The prognosis was that the headaches were unlikely to improve and could well form part of a post-traumatic syndrome that also included the memory and personality problems. The personality changes were also likely to persist, with severe mood swings and a tendency to be aggressive and rather depressive. As a result of the personality change, his marriage had collapsed. He was described as being forgetful, easily distracted, with poor concentration and easily upset. The overall prognosis was that the matters were unlikely to improve in the future – the head injuries gave rise to the following permanent changes: (i) severe memory impairment in that he could not remember simple events or assignments and would easily forget things; (ii) headaches associated with vomiting, blurred vision and photophobia about twice a month; and (iii) personality change in that he was now moody and short-tempered – all had an effect on the applicant's employment and his social/recreational lifestyle.

Prognosis: Overall prognosis was that matters were unlikely to improve in the future.

1.9.6.C11 Case No. 10010

Name of case: Re Simpson

Brief description of injuries: MODERATELY SEVERE PSYCHIATRIC DAMAGE

Reported: Kemp & Kemp, C4-071; [1990] CLY 1589

JSB Category: 3(A)

Sex: Female

Age at injury: 35

Age at award: 40

Date of award: 07 August 1990

Tribunal: CICB

Amount of award then: £10,000

Award at February 2001: £13,527

Description of injuries: Two lacerations towards the back of the head – subconjunctival haemorrhage in outer aspect of right eye – small puncture wound in corner of mouth – lacerations to both lips – broken partial denture – other lacerations and bruising to head.

Prognosis: Uncertain – expected to benefit from psychiatric treatment – at time of trial was suffering from anxiety depression.

1.9.6.C12 Case No. 11775

Name of case: Lancaster v Birmingham City Council

Brief description of injuries: PSYCHIATRIC DAMAGE

Reported: Kemp & Kemp, C4-076; [1999] CLY 1438

JSB Category: 3(A)

Sex: Female

Age at injury: 38-42

Age at award: 44

Date of award: 25 June 1999

Tribunal: Birmingham County Court

Amount of award then: £12,000

Award at February 2001: £12,529

Description of injuries: Claimant, in employ of defendants since 1971 in various technical/administrative/supervisory roles involving little contact with general public, transferred in 1993 to different post in Neighbourhood Housing Office, requiring demanding day – to – day contact with general public, without training or support – development of insomnia – diminished powers of concentration – self – esteem affected – development of severe anxiety state and depression – 2 long absences from work totalling 4 and 10 months in a period of just under 2 years from April 1994 – medication and cognitive therapy under the care of hospital psychiatrists – assigned to undemanding clerical tasks on return after second absence, but retired from work on grounds of mental ill health in 1997 – domestic life not affected.

Prognosis: Some improvement anticipated in condition at conclusion of litigation – medical prognosis that claimant would eventually be able to undertake part-time and full – time work of relatively straightforward and undemanding nature – judge found accordingly, but had regard also to claimant's future vulnerability on open labour market.

1.9.6.C13 Case No. 10735

Name of case: Re SKR

Brief description of injuries: EXACERBATION OF PRE-EXISTING PSYCHOLOGICAL DIFFICULTIES BY INDECENT ASSAULT

Reported: Kemp & Kemp, C4-255; [1994] CLY 1583

JSB Category: 3(A)

Sex: Female

Age at injury: 27

Age at award: -

Date of award: 13 January 1994

Tribunal: CICB, Manchester

Amount of award then: £10,000

Award at February 2001: £12,228

Description of injuries: Claimant, suffering from epilepsy, learning difficulties and schizo-affective disorder, living in sheltered accommodation integrated into the community – indecently assaulted by member of staff at day care centre – digital penetration – demand for her to touch assailant's genitals – subsequent deterioration of mental state, resulting in hospital admissions – moved to more secure environment – relapse into schizophrenic symptoms of hallucinations and delusions, far greater in frequency and severity than might otherwise have been expected – severe depression, requiring medication – aggressive and child-like, regressive, behaviour – independence skills suffered – alteration of type and frequency of medication necessitated – change in personality; sad, uninterested, less motivated, requiring prompting – loss of self-confidence – consultant psychiatrist's evidence that these changes and disabilities were significant and appeared to be related to the stressful event of the sexual assault.

Prognosis: Fear that recovery would be poor, prolonged and slow – some improvement detected in year leading up to hearing, but support and supervision level still higher than prior to the assault.

1.9.6.C14 Case No. 10560

Name of case: Waller and Waller v Canterbury and Thanet Health Authority

Brief description of injuries: PSYCHIATRIC DAMAGE – DEPRESSION

Reported: Kemp & Kemp, C4-085; [1993] CLY 1453

JSB Category: 3(A)

Sex: One male, one female (husband and wife)

Age at injury: husband:43;wife:44

Age at award: husband:46;wife:47

Date of award: 01 September 1993

Tribunal: Thanet County Court

Amount of award then: £8,500

Award at February 2001: £10,303

Description of injuries: Claimants' son's voluntary admission to psychiatric hospital with suicidal tendencies – disappeared from ward – hospital staff's search inadequate – claimants undertook own search of premises and discovered hanged body of son in disused building.(Husband): depression – tearfulness – sleep disturbance – intrusive mental images – apathy – forgetfulness – poor concentration – increase in frequency and severity of pre-existing headaches condition – declared unfit to work 9 months after incident, still unfit at time of trial.(Wife): tearfulness – sleep disturbance – low spirits – apathy – irritability – impatience – nightmares about miscarriages – intrusive mental images while awake – heavy drinking to aid sleep.

Prognosis: (Both claimants): receiving medication and counselling, prognosis of slow recovery over 1 or 2 years, 1 year at best.

Other points: Award is sum to each individual.

1.9.6.C15 Case No. 10011

Name of case: Re Inkersole

Brief description of injuries: PSYCHOLOGICAL

Reported: Kemp & Kemp, C4-088; [1990] CLY 1590

JSB Category: 3(A)

Sex: Male

Age at injury: 45

Age at award: 48

Date of award: 08 May 1990

Tribunal: CICB, London

Amount of award then: £7,000

Award at February 2001: £9,540

Description of injuries: Minor physical injuries – depressive anxiety state – became introspective, broody, oversensitive and inhibited – loss of libido – intolerance of anyone touching his head. Slow but gradual improvement although impossible to predict when symptoms will end – too fearful to continue security work, which he had enjoyed.

1.9.6.C16 Case No. 10562

Name of case: Re Grange

Brief description of injuries: PSYCHIATRIC DAMAGE

Reported: [1993] CLY 1455

JSB Category: 3(A); 6(A)(c)

Sex: Female

Age at injury: 42

Age at award: 45

Date of award: 16 February 1993

Tribunal: CICB, London

Amount of award then: £7,500

Award at February 2001: £9,294

Description of injuries: Claimant attacked in car during "poll tax" riot – car damaged, threats to overturn it and set it alight – exited car, struck on head and doused with petrol – no physical injuries, but after incident developed chronic neck, back and shoulder pain – requiring osteopathic treatment and physiotherapy – high anxiety – stress – insomnia – loss of weight (2.5 stones) – development of heavy smoking habit (40 to 50 cigarettes a day) – flashbacks – panic attacks (shakiness, tension, tearfulness) – loss of confidence at and interest in work (pub landlady), particularly when confronted with hostile situations – clumsiness – more mistake-prone – deterioration of relationship with husband – intolerance – shortness of temper – loss of high spirits – nervousness about travel in cars – continuing to attend physiotherapy sessions at time of hearing – frequent flashbacks and panic attacks ongoing at time of hearing.

1.9.6.C17 Case No. 10374

Name of case: Cartmel v Anderson

Brief description of injuries: SIGNIFICANT LOSS OF PERIPHERAL VISION – 3 YEAR ACCELERATION OF EXISTING PROBLEM WITH EYE – HEADACHES – LOSS OF CONFIDENCE

Reported: [1992] CLY 1630

JSB Category: 7(A)

Sex: Female

Age at injury: 70

Age at award: 74

Date of award: 02 December 1991

Tribunal: Burnley County Court

Amount of award then: £6,500

Award at February 2001: £8,239

Description of injuries: Severe headaches immediately after the accident – soft-tissue injury to the neck with pain in neck and shoulder – pain in right knee, abdomen, left arm, front and rear of left hip – intermittent postural vertigo – significant loss of peripheral vision – registered blind in 1986 but had sufficient peripheral vision to run her own home and garden with some confidence before the accident.

Prognosis: Loss of peripheral vision permanent – vertigo permanent – loss of confidence – pre-existing poor vision exacerbated by the accident – deterioration accelerated by two to three years.

1.9.6.C18 Case No. 10162

Name of case: Moores v Dixon

Brief description of injuries: NERVOUS SHOCK FOR 2 YEARS

Reported: Kemp & Kemp, C4-122; [1991] CLY 1359

JSB Category:

Sex: (1) Female; (2)Male; (3) Male

Age at injury: (1) 13;(2) -;(3) 12

Age at award: -

Date of award: 26 September 1991

Tribunal: Manchester County Court

Amount of award then: £6,250

Award at February 2001: £7,987

Description of injuries: Car crashed into house – (1) superficial wounds painful for a week or two – thought brothers had been killed – suffered severe frequent nightmares for 18 months but by time of trial only rarely – gradually diminishing over-vigilance for safety of brothers – but made complete recovery by date of trial.(2) Cut to nose – one stitch – did not sleep properly – excessively clingy – frequent nightmares – complete recovery by date of trial.(3) Suffered minor grazes only – but thought he was going to die in incident and thought sister had died – suffered severe nightmares initially – nightmares reducing in frequency and severity – ceased by time of trial – behaviour deteriorated – played truant – eventually suspended from school – within two years behaviour improved and back to pre-accident state.

Other points: Award split: (1) £2,500; (2) £1,500; (3) £2,250.

1.9.6.C19 Case No. 10012

Name of case: Re Claringbold

Brief description of injuries: PSYCHOLOGICAL

Reported: Kemp & Kemp, C4-100; [1990] CLY 1591

JSB Category: 3(A)

Sex: Male

Age at injury: 31

Age at award: 35

Date of award: 09 November 1990

Tribunal: CICB, London

Amount of award then: £5,000

Award at February 2001: £6,615

Description of injuries: Serious assault – drug overdose due to stress two months later – suffered regular depression – started to drink heavily – impaired sleep – wrist occasionally hurt in cold weather – social relationships affected – phobia against going out at night – precautions against burglary described as pathological – fear of repeat occurrence of crime – unable to be responsible for tasks involving keys or money.

Prognosis: Likely to remain disabled by his symptoms for some years.

1.9.6.C20 Case No. 11101

Name of case: Re Gensale

Brief description of injuries: PSYCHIATRIC DISABILITY

Reported: [1996] CLY 2192

JSB Category:

Sex: Female

Age at injury: 27

Age at award: 31

Date of award: 05 October 1995

Tribunal: CICB, London

Amount of award then: £5,000

Award at February 2001: £5,741

Description of injuries: Psychiatric disability following stabbing.

Prognosis: Largely recovered at the time of the hearing – hoped to return to her former work.

1.9.6.C21 Case No. 10565

Name of case: Re Hirst

Brief description of injuries: PSYCHIATRIC DAMAGE – DEPRESSION

Reported: Kemp & Kemp, K2-013; [1993] CLY 1458

JSB Category: 3(A)

Sex: Female

Age at injury: 28

Age at award: 33

Date of award: 29 January 1993

Tribunal: CICB, Leeds

Amount of award then: £3,500

Award at February 2001: £4,365

Description of injuries: Claimant suffered attempted strangulation by husband with chain-link dog lead – physical injuries quickly healed – subsequent depression – anti-depressants prescribed 5 months after incident

1.9.6.C22 Case No. 10336

Award at February 2001: £4,337

See: 1.7.2.C2 for details

Onset of Disease

1.9.6.C23 Case No. 11459

Name of case: Carpenter v Easton

Brief description of injuries: PSYCHIATRIC CONDITION – DEPRESSION

Reported: Kemp & Kemp, C4-114; [1997] CLY 2008

JSB Category: 3(B)(c)

Sex: Female

Age at injury: Not stated

Age at award:

Date of award: 18 July 1997

Tribunal: Weymouth County Court

Amount of award then: £3,750

Award at February 2001: £4,095

Description of injuries: Depression – eight months – post-traumatic stress disorder – twelve months.

Prognosis: Phobic Anxiety Neurosis would persist – cognitive behaviour therapy might help to settle the symptoms.

1.9.6.C24 Case No. 10013

Name of case: Hunt v Clancy

Brief description of injuries: PSYCHOLOGICAL

Reported: Kemp & Kemp, C4-118; [1990] CLY 1592

JSB Category: 3(A)

Sex: Male

Age at injury: 9

Age at award: 13

Date of award: 28 September 1990

Tribunal: Bow County Court

Amount of award then: £2,750

Award at February 2001: £3,658

Description of injuries: Attacked by alsatian dog, causing bruising, puncture wounds and cuts to left leg – cosmetically insignificant scars – left with continuing fear of dogs.

Prognosis: "Very possible" that phobia would continue for life and unlikely to disappear before adulthood.

1.9.6.C25 Case No. 10730

Name of case: Re Binney

Brief description of injuries: PSYCHIATRIC – AGGRAVATION OF BEHAVIOURAL PROBLEMS

Reported: Kemp & Kemp, C4-119; [1994] CLY 1578

JSB Category: 3(A)

Sex: Male

Age at injury: 10

Age at award: 15

Date of award: 20 October 1994

Tribunal: CICB, York

Amount of award then: £3,000

Award at February 2001: £3,554

Description of injuries: Assault by stepfather – thrown against various items of furniture, punched in back several times; severe grazing, bruising and swelling – claimant formerly attended school for children with behavioural problems; after assault, taken into care and separated from rest of family – aggravation of behavioural problems – refusal to attend school – fire-starting – sexual abuse of neighbour's 3 year old child.

1.9.6.C26 Case No. 10566

Name of case: Re Byrne

Brief description of injuries: PSYCHIATRIC DAMAGE-4-5 MONTHS

Reported: [1993] CLY 1459

JSB Category: 3(A)

Sex: Male

Age at injury: 39

Age at award: 43

Date of award: 18 June 1993

Tribunal: CICB, Durham

Amount of award then: £2,500

Award at February 2001: £3,050

Description of injuries: Assault – significant head injury – marked post-traumatic amnesia for 2 weeks – increased irritability – intolerance of noise – apathy – pain and joint stiffness in legs – loss of confidence in ability to drive – period of loss of amenity was of the order of 4 to 5 months after the incident.

1.9.6.C27 Case No. 10341

Award at February 2001: £2,516

See: 1.2.3.8.C92 for details

1.9.6.C28 Case No. 10015

Name of case: Re Cunningham
Brief description of injuries: PSYCHOLOGICAL
Reported: Kemp & Kemp, C4-129; [1990] CLY 1594
JSB Category: 3(A)
Sex: Male
Age at injury: 26
Age at award: 28
Date of award: 27 October 1989
Tribunal: CICB, Glasgow
Amount of award then: £1,500
Award at February 2001: £2,196

Description of injuries: During bank raid, had sawn-off shotgun pointed in his face with murderous threats. Became jumpy and security-conscious with anxiety – an incident involving loud noise caused hysteria.

Prognosis: When he sees balaclavas he has flashbacks. Otherwise full recovery.

1.9.6.C29 Case No. 12000

Name of case: A (a child) v Westminster Society For People With Learning Difficulties
Brief description of injuries: PSYCHIATRIC DAMAGE
Reported: Kemp & Kemp, PRC-019; [2000] 3 CL 184
JSB Category: 3(A)
Sex: Male
Age at injury: 16
Age at award: 17
Date of award: 13 October 1999
Tribunal: Central London County Court
Amount of award then: £1,500
Award at February 2001: £1,550

Description of injuries: A had profound and multiple disabilities – he was admitted to a respite home where his mother specifically asked that he was not to be given a bed-guard – a bed-guard was used and A's head was trapped between the bars for one hour – he suffered blistering, swelling and flattening of one ear – a line across his cheekbone was visible eighteen months later – difficult to assess his psychological reaction to the accident due to his disabilities – sleep disturbance for one year and increased attachment to his parents were noticeable.

Other points: Due to A's disabilities he would be unable to administer any award himself – a trust would be too cumbersome for the level of damages – it was ordered that the monies be paid to his mother on his attaining 18 years.

1.9.6.C30 Case No. 10164

Name of case: Lawrence v Bown & Bown
Brief description of injuries: DRIVING ANXIETY – FAILED TO MITIGATE BY UNDERGOING COUNSELLING
Reported: [1991] CLY 1361
JSB Category: 3
Sex: Male
Age at injury: 45
Age at award: 47
Date of award: 22 October 1991
Tribunal: Slough County Court
Amount of award then: £1,200
Award at February 2001: £1,528

Description of injuries: Vehicle struck in side – no physical injuries – no medical advice initially sought – nervous and apprehensive of driving – enjoyed driving previous 24 years – only drove when necessary – preferred to be driven – became anxious in vehicle even as passenger – condition not improving – failed to mitigate condition by declining to take counselling.

1.9.6.C31 Case No. 11710

Name of case: Marsh (a minor) v Igoe
Brief description of injuries: PSYCHIATRIC INJURY – STRESS
Reported: Kemp & Kemp, C4-132; [1998] CLY 1713
JSB Category: 3(A)(d)
Sex: Female
Age at injury: 4
Age at award: 6
Date of award: 05 March 1998
Tribunal: Birkenhead County Court
Amount of award then: £1,250
Award at February 2001: £1,337

Description of injuries: Road accident – no physical injury – psychiatric reaction to the accident – nightmares and enuresis – 20 months after the accident fear of motorways and travelling by bus persisted.

1.9.6.C32 Case No. 10053

Name of case: March v The Post Office

Brief description of injuries: NERVOUS SHOCK

Reported: [1990] CLY 1694

JSB Category: 3(B)

Sex: Male, Male

Age at injury: 7;5

Age at award: -;-

Date of award: 05 September 1990

Tribunal: Barrow-in-Furness County Court

Amount of award then: £750

Award at February 2001: £998

Description of injuries: Mother's vehicle hit by other car – two sons sustained severe shock – oldest boy had asthma condition and night terrors aggravated by the shock – younger boy suffered from recurring nightmares and vomiting for six to eight weeks.

Prognosis: Younger child's behavioural problems aggravated by the shock – both boys apprehensive about travelling by car.

1.9.6.C33 Case No. 10054

Name of case: Walley v Linney

Brief description of injuries: NERVOUS SHOCK – MINOR

Reported: [1990] CLY 1701

JSB Category: 3(B)

Sex: Female

Age at injury: 40

Age at award: 42

Date of award: 30 March 1990

Tribunal: Nuneaton County Court

Amount of award then: £700

Award at February 2001: £992

Description of injuries: Involved in motor accident – suffered no physical injuries but was upset by accident and still nervous about driving – drove to work on daily basis.

1.9.6.C34 Case No. 11898

Name of case: O (a minor) v Rowley

Brief description of injuries: PSYCHOLOGICAL REACTION (2 CLAIMANTS) – 2 YEARS

Reported: Kemp & Kemp, K2-251/1; [1999] CLY 1562

JSB Category: (1): 3(A)(2): 3(A)(d)

Sex: Both female

Age at injury: (1):2;(2):6

Age at award: (1):5;(2):9

Date of award: 25 March 1999

Tribunal: Willesden County Court

Amount of award then: £650

Award at February 2001: £681

Description of injuries: 2 claimants, sisters, involved in road accident – both claimants distressed, but did not require treatment – difficulty getting to sleep on night of accident – disturbed sleep for several days – increased awareness when travelling by car – occasional anxiety when car reversing or parking – diagnosis of mild psychological reaction, not amounting to post-traumatic stress disorder or any recognisable complaint – symptoms continued for 2 years after accident.

Other points: Sum awarded to each applicant.

1.9.6.C35 Case No. 10295

Name of case: Linell v Draper

Brief description of injuries: NERVOUS REACTION TO A TRAFFIC ACCIDENT

Reported: Kemp & Kemp, K2-265; [1991] CLY 1492

JSB Category: 3(A)

Sex: Male

Age at injury: 49

Age at award: 51

Date of award: 24 June 1991

Tribunal: Northampton County Court

Amount of award then: £400

Award at February 2001: £513

Description of injuries: Involved in a traffic accident – not a nervous person prior to the accident – he had difficulty in sleeping and nightmares.

Prognosis: At the time of the hearing L occasionally still felt nervous when driving.

1.9.6.C36 Case No. 10055

Name of case: Archer & Archer v Leighton

Brief description of injuries: DEPRESSION

Reported: [1990] CLY 1709

JSB Category: 3(B)

Sex: M,F

Age at injury: -

Age at award: -

Date of award: 10 July 1990

Tribunal: Manchester County Court

Amount of award then: £300

Award at February 2001: £407

Description of injuries: Damp and dry rot firm refused to remedy work under guarantee – plaintiffs unable to use their kitchen – suffered from strong smell – became edgy, argumentative and depressed.

1.9.6.C37 Case No. 10056

Name of case: James and Evand v Keenan

Brief description of injuries: NERVOUS SHOCK, SEVERAL DAYS

Reported: [1990] CLY 1710

JSB Category: 3(B)

Sex: Male, Male

Age at injury: 39;29

Age at award: -;-

Date of award: 16 October 1990

Tribunal: Manchester County Court

Amount of award then: £250

Award at February 2001: £330

Description of injuries: Driver and passenger respectively when stationary motor car struck in rear – both suffered bad shaking up – both took several days to get over the event.

1.9.6.C38 Case No. 10057

Name of case: Nicholson v Bolton

Brief description of injuries: NERVOUS SHOCK, 1 DAY

Reported: [1990] CLY 1712

JSB Category: 3(B)

Sex: Male

Age at injury: 48

Age at award: 49

Date of award: 02 January 1990

Tribunal: Bolton County Court

Amount of award then: £200

Award at February 2001: £288

Description of injuries: Road traffic accident in which another vehicle was pushed into head-on collision with plaintiff's car – plaintiff suffered shock – no medical report tendered – plaintiff lost no time from work – shock resolved within 24 hours.

1.9.6.1 PHYCHIATRIC DISEASE AFTER INJURY

1.9.6.1.C1 Case No. 10312

Award at February 2001: £191,999

See: 1.2.3.8.C4 for details

1.9.6.1.C2 Case No. 10305

Award at February 2001: £169,963

See: 1.2.3.6.2.1.C1 for details

1.9.6.1.C3 Case No. 10016

Award at February 2001: £94,997

See: 1.8.6.C1 for details

1.9.6.1.C4 Case No. 11869

Name of case: Gough v Consolidated Beryllium Ceramics Ltd

Brief description of injuries: LUNGS – BERYLLIOSIS – PERSONALITY CHANGE

Reported: Kemp & Kemp, F2-012/1; [1999] CLY 1533

JSB Category: 5(B)(a); 3(A)

Sex: Male

Age at injury: 21

Age at award: 38

Date of award: 11 December 1998

Tribunal: QBD

Amount of award then: £65,000

Award at February 2001: £77,167

Description of injuries: Development of chronic berylliosis from 19 months' exposure to beryllium dust in course of employment – breathlessness – chronic fatigue – claimant unable to work since December 1992 – emergency admission with pneumothorax in 1996; lung had collapsed by 50 per cent; pneumothraces a likely future occurrence in light of claimant's condition and medication – at time of trial, condition had worsened – oxygen therapy required 18 hours per day – claimant able to drive for 2 hours, walk short level distances and dress himself, but unable to walk up gradients, do light housework or wash own hair – claimant formerly keen sportsman, playing rugby to county standard and other sports; disease prevented him from continuing those pastimes and affected social life, which revolved around sporting activities – personality change; claimant formerly pleasant and relaxed; now constantly irritable and liable to snap at family members.

Prognosis: Claimant's life expectancy only 4 years – continued deterioration in health would require increasing levels of professional care – claimant would suffer a highly distressing death.

Other points: Judge found that case exceeded severity of conditions envisaged by JSB Guidelines in category 5(B)(a).

1.9.6.1.C5 Case No. 11978

Award at February 2001: £69,462

See: 1.2.3.1.C4 for details

1.9.6.1.C6 Case No. 10567

Award at February 2001: £69,152

See: 1.8.6.C3 for details

1.9.6.1.C7 Case No. 10731
Award at February 2001: £67,887

See: 1.8.6.C4 for details

1.9.6.1.C8 Case No. 11965
Award at February 2001: £63,416

See: 1.7.1.C7 for details

1.9.6.1.C9 Case No. 11776
Award at February 2001: £57,174

See: 1.8.6.C6 for details

1.9.6.1.C10 Case No. 11778
Award at February 2001: £54,270

See: 1.8.6.C7 for details

1.9.6.1.C11 Case No. 10317
Award at February 2001: £54,115

See: 1.3.1.3.2.1.C1 for details

1.9.6.1.C12 Case No. 10904
Award at February 2001: £50,605

See: 1.2.3.8.C62 for details

1.9.6.1.C13 Case No. 10319
Award at February 2001: £46,724

See: 1.2.3.8.C65 for details

1.9.6.1.C14 Case No. 11494
Award at February 2001: £46,413

See: 1.2.3.8.C66 for details

1.9.6.1.C15 Case No. 10017
Award at February 2001: £43,104

See: 1.8.6.C8 for details

1.9.6.1.C16 Case No. 11872
Name of case: Jeffrey v Cape Insulation Ltd

Brief description of injuries: LUNGS – MESOTHELIOMA – PRE-EXISTING BRONCHITIS AND EMPHYSEMA

Reported: (1999) 99 (2) QR 5; Kemp & Kemp, F2-030/1; [1999] CLY 1536

JSB Category: 5(B)

Sex: Male

Age at injury: 36

Age at award: 67

Date of award: 03 November 1998

Tribunal: QBD

Amount of award then: £38,000

Award at February 2001: £42,495

Description of injuries: Claimant exposed to asbestos dust for 8 months at age of 36 – 25 years later, development of right – sided chest pain – 2 years thereafter, development of shortness of breath on exertion, gradually increasing over time – 31 years after exposure, claimant diagnosed as suffering from asbestosis – within 2 years claimant assessed as 50 per cent disabled, 30 per cent of which attributable to asbestos – related illness, 20 per cent of which to smoking – related chronic bronchitis and emphysema – claimant forced to abandon working on allotment and county walking – able to climb stairs at home, but dyspnoeic at top – sleep disturbed, as lying down caused wheeziness and breathlessness – estimation of 3 hours' care per week needed from wife.

Prognosis: Slow deterioration expected – risk of mesothelioma developing – increased risk of developing lung cancer – loss of life expectancy estimated at 8 years, with asbestos – related conditions being responsible for the bulk of the reduction, smoking responsible for the remainder.

1.9.6.1.C17 Case No. 11090
Name of case: Re Swift

Brief description of injuries: HEAD – SEVERE PSYCHIATRIC DAMAGE

Reported: Kemp & Kemp, C4-018; [1996] CLY 2181

JSB Category: 3(A)(a)

Sex: Female

Age at injury: 35

Age at award: 40

Date of award: 30 July 1996

Tribunal: CICB, York

Amount of award then: £35,000

Award at February 2001: £42,198

Description of injuries: Depression – lack of confidence – small pontine haemorrhage – macula oedema of the left eye.

Prognosis: Within the JSB classification of "Severe Psychiatric Damage" – optimistic that she would work again before retirement age.

1.9.6.1.C18 Case No. 11777
Award at February 2001: £39,129

See: 1.8.6.C9 for details

1.9.6.1.C19 Case No. 11784

Award at February 2001: £38,873

See: 1.8.6.C10 for details

1.9.6.1.C20 Case No. 10149

Award at February 2001: £33,566

See: 1.1.C5 for details

1.9.6.1.C21 Case No. 10027

Award at February 2001: £28,199

See: 1.8.6.C16 for details

1.9.6.1.C22 Case No. 10321

Award at February 2001: £25,510

See: 1.2.3.8.C79 for details

1.9.6.1.C23 Case No. 10849

Award at February 2001: £25,147

See: 1.7.3.C13 for details

1.9.6.1.C24 Case No. 10784

Name of case: Vincent v London Electricity

Brief description of injuries: LUNGS – ASBESTOSIS – DEPRESSION – PROVISIONAL AWARD

Reported: Kemp & Kemp, F2-044; [1994] CLY 1633

JSB Category: 5(B); 3(A)

Sex: Male

Age at injury: 55 (date of diagnosis)

Age at award: 61

Date of award: 18 March 1994

Tribunal: QBD

Amount of award then: £20,000

Award at February 2001: £24,924

Description of injuries: Claimant former worker at power station for 10 years and exposed to asbestos – diagnosis of pleural plaques in 1988 – diagnosis of asbestosis and 5 per cent respiratory disability in 1993 – claimant with previous history of stress problems requiring occasional treatment with anti-depressants; personality described as obsessional and anxious – development of episodic depressive illness after diagnosis – claimant of firm belief that he was likely to die of asbestos-related cancer – belief that pains experienced in neck, chest and shoulder were symptoms of cancer, notwithstanding medical evidence that suggested symptoms were caused by cervical spondylosis and osteoarthritis – extreme anxiety leading to shortness of breath over and above relatively small degree of respiratory difficulty caused by asbestosis – breakdown of 36-year marriage due to obsession with illness – attempt at suicide.

Prognosis: Respiratory difficulty likely to increase to 20 per cent by age 70.

Other points: Judge made provisional award, ordering that claimant could make further application should he develop (1) asbestosis causing respiratory disability of over 25 per cent; (2) disabling pleural disease; (3) lung cancer or any other cancer proved to be due to asbestos; (4) mesothelioma.

1.9.6.1.C25 Case No. 12058

Award at February 2001: £24,913

See: 1.2.3.2.1.C6 for details

1.9.6.1.C26 Case No. 10800

Award at February 2001: £21,315

See: 1.4.1.1.C3 for details

1.9.6.1.C27 Case No. 10362

Award at February 2001: £21,015

See: 1.2.3.2.1.C8 for details

1.9.6.1.C28 Case No. 11105

Award at February 2001: £20,094

See: 1.8.6.C34 for details

1.9.6.1.C29 Case No. 10732

Award at February 2001: £18,438

See: 1.8.6.C37 for details

1.9.6.1.C30 Case No. 12055

Award at February 2001: £18,317

See: 1.8.6.C38 for details

1.9.6.1.C31 Case No. 10733

Award at February 2001: £18,147

See: 1.8.6.C40 for details

1.9.6.1.C32 Case No. 11295

Award at February 2001: £17,300

See: 1.8.6.C41 for details

1.9.6.1.C33 Case No. 11874

Name of case: Greenwood v Newalls Insulation Co Ltd

Brief description of injuries: LUNGS – PLEURAL PLAQUES – DEPRESSION

Reported: Kemp & Kemp, F2-058/1; [1999] CLY 1538

JSB Category: 5(B); 3(A)

Sex: Male

Age at injury: 24-26

Age at award: 60

Date of award: 30 July 1998

Tribunal: Sunderland County Court

Amount of award then: £16,000

Award at February 2001: £17,146

Description of injuries: Exposure to asbestos at work for 2 years – asbestos – related pleural plaques diagnosed in 1994, when claimant about 56 – agreed medical evidence that plaques asymptomatic, but claimant complained of chest pain and shortness of breath attributable to asbestos exposure – development of psychiatric illness as a result of diagnosis of pleural plaques – tendency to attribute all physical problems to asbestos exposure – depression – poor sleep – lack of enjoyment of life – fear of death.

Prognosis: 2 per cent risk of claimant developing pleural disease sufficient to cause a disability – 1 per cent risk of asbestosis – 3 per cent risk of mesothelioma – 1-2 per cent risk of lung cancer.

1.9.6.1.C34 Case No. 11875

Name of case: McCarthy v Abbott Insulation

Brief description of injuries: LUNGS – PLEURAL PLAQUES – ANXIETY – PRE-EXISTING EMPHYSEMA

Reported: Kemp & Kemp, F2-058/2; [1999] CLY 1539

JSB Category: 5(B); 3(A)

Sex: Male

Age at injury: 17-18

Age at award: 55

Date of award: 04 December 1998

Tribunal: Mayor's and City of London County Court

Amount of award then: £15,600

Award at February 2001: £16,554

Description of injuries: Development of benign, asymptomatic bilateral pleural plaques – no clinical or radiological evidence of asbestosis and no impairment of lung function or disablement had developed at time of trial – claimant suffering anxiety from having an asbestos – related condition – diagnosis made in course of investigations into claimant's long – standing smoking – related emphysema, which had rendered him unfit for work.

Prognosis: Future risks assessed at 2 per cent pleural thickening sufficient to cause disablement – 1 per cent risk of clinical and radiological evidence of asbestosis associated with disablement – 3 per cent risk of mesothelioma – 15 per cent risk of lung cancer – future life expectancy reduced from 20 years to 18 years as result of asbestos – related risks of malignant disease.

Other points: Award comprised: pleural plaques and anxiety: £5,500; future malignant risks: £8,100; future non-malignant disability: £2,000.

1.9.6.1.C35 Case No. 10018

Award at February 2001: £14,533

See: 1.8.6.C47 for details

1.9.6.1.C36 Case No. 11512

Award at February 2001: £13,581

See: 1.8.6.C49 for details

1.9.6.1.C37 Case No. 11510

Award at February 2001: £13,538

See: 1.8.6.C50 for details

1.9.6.1.C38 Case No. 11511

Award at February 2001: £13,513

See: 1.8.6.C51 for details

1.9.6.1.C39 Case No. 10019

Award at February 2001: £13,292

See: 1.8.6.C53 for details

1.9.6.1.C40 Case No. 11876

Name of case: Horne v Prescot (No 1) Ltd

Brief description of injuries: LUNGS – PLEURAL PLAQUES – ANXIETY

Reported: (1999) 99(2) QR 6; Kemp & Kemp, F2-063/1; [1999] CLY 1540

JSB Category: 5(B); 3(A)

Sex: Male

Age at injury: 16-23

Age at award: 64

Date of award: 01 July 1999

Tribunal: Mayor's and City of London County Court

Amount of award then: £12,500

Award at February 2001: £13,107

Description of injuries: Claimant exposed to asbestos for approximately 4 years – claimant suffered stroke when 60; when being X-rayed, calcified pleural plaques were identified – claimant considered himself to be breathless on exertion, but consultant considered his respiratory function to be better than average, any impairment not being attributable to the pleural plaques – claimant claimed that diagnosis made him unduly anxious, particularly because his brother had died of asbestosis and a close friend had died of mesothelioma 30 years earlier; this claim considered unreasonable by judge as claimant had not sought medical treatment for anxiety, and because risks of any future deterioration or development of other asbestos – related disease were very low.

Prognosis: Overall risk of claimant developing some form of lung disease 16 per cent – 10 per cent risk of developing mesothelioma – 1-2 per cent risk of lung cancer – 2 per cent risk of pleural thickening – 2 per cent risk of asbestosis – life expectancy reduced by 1 year as a result of asbestos exposure, having been reduced by 4 years by stroke.

1.9.6.1.C41 Case No. 10327

Name of case: Re Watts

Brief description of injuries: ASSAULT – PSYCHIATRIC DAMAGE – PERSONALITY CHANGE

Reported: [1992] CLY 1583

JSB Category: 3(A)(b)

Sex: Female

Age at injury: 51

Age at award: 57

Date of award: 07 May 1992

Tribunal: CICB, London

Amount of award then: £10,000

Award at February 2001: £12,409

Description of injuries: Severely beaten in unprovoked attack at work – bruised and in shock – loss of all ambition – suffering depression and an anxiety state – sexual impairment causing strained marital relationship, irritability and loss of sleep – full physical recovery – significant personality change.

Prognosis: No indication of further recovery likely.

1.9.6.1.C42 Case No. 10734

Award at February 2001: £11,933

See: 1.8.6.C59 for details

1.9.6.1.C43 Case No. 11000

Award at February 2001: £11,891

See: 1.6.1.3.1.C8 for details

1.9.6.1.C44 Case No. 11106

Award at February 2001: £11,261

See: 1.8.6.C60 for details

1.9.6.1.C45 Case No. 10568

Award at February 2001: £11,226

See: 1.8.6.C61 for details

1.9.6.1.C46 Case No. 10020

Award at February 2001: £10,859

See: 1.8.6.C63 for details

1.9.6.1.C47 Case No. 11514

Award at February 2001: £10,798

See: 1.8.6.C64 for details

1.9.6.1.C48 Case No. 11513

Award at February 2001: £10,791

See: 1.8.6.C65 for details

1.9.6.1.C49 Case No. 11850

Award at February 2001: £10,534

See: 1.6.1.1.C17 for details

1.9.6.1.C50 Case No. 10330

Name of case: Re Duff

Brief description of injuries: LACERATION – 4 STITCHES – PHOBIC ANXIETY

Reported: Kemp & Kemp, C4-082; [1992] CLY 1586

JSB Category: 3(A)(c)

Sex: Male

Age at injury: 33

Age at award: 36

Date of award: 20 August 1992

Tribunal: CICB, London

Amount of award then: £8,500

Award at February 2001: £10,526

Description of injuries: Laceration requiring four stitches – no specific advice for his psychological problems until fourteen months after the assault.

Prognosis: Developed an increased generalised anxiety and phobic response to the possibility of being assaulted.

Other points: Award increased from £2,500.

1.9.6.1.C51 Case No. 11862

Award at February 2001: £10,417

See: 1.6.1.1.C18 for details

1.9.6.1.C52 Case No. 11779

Award at February 2001: £10,417

See: 1.8.6.C67 for details

1.9.6.1.C53 Case No. 10853

Name of case: Harris v Readymix Drypack

Brief description of injuries: SKIN – DERMATITIS – PSYCHOLOGICAL REACTION

Reported: Kemp & Kemp, J4-013; [1994] CLY 1703

JSB Category: 3(A)

Sex: Female

Age at injury: 22

Age at award: 26

Date of award: 27 April 1994

Tribunal: Liverpool County Court

Amount of award then: £8,500

Award at February 2001: £10,139

Description of injuries: Claimant worked as quality control assistant, testing samples of cement, adhesives, concrete and routing – no gloves provided – development of rash on wrist, spreading to fingers and thumb, forearms, other areas of wrists and inside of upper arm – formation of bubble – like blisters, drying out to form flakes – claimant endeavoured to continue at work, but forced to go sick just over 2 years after first appearance of rash – return to work 3 months later caused immediate recurrence of symptoms – employment terminated – 2 further outbreaks in course of decorating at home – mental suffering as a consequence of condition – nervousness and social embarrassment when hands remarked upon – gradual slippage into depression – anti-depressants prescribed.

Prognosis: Hands had recovered since leaving work, but prognosis of further suffering from dermatitis, affecting future life and ability to gain work – claimant only able to do "clean" work in future, as even washing up and some domestic jobs sufficient to cause problems.

1.9.6.1.C54 Case No. 10570

Award at February 2001: £9,267

See: 1.8.6.C68 for details

1.9.6.1.C55 Case No. 11754

Award at February 2001: £9,166

See: 1.3.1.2.1.C7 for details

1.9.6.1.C56 Case No. 11515

Award at February 2001: £9,138

See: 1.8.6.C69 for details

1.9.6.1.C57 Case No. 10736

Award at February 2001: £9,130

See: 1.8.6.C70 for details

1.9.6.1.C58 Case No. 11984

Award at February 2001: £8,909

See: 1.3.1.2.1.C8 for details

1.9.6.1.C59 Case No. 10563

Award at February 2001: £8,643

See: 1.3.1.2.1.C11 for details

1.9.6.1.C60 Case No. 11782

Award at February 2001: £8,421

See: 1.8.6.C74 for details

1.9.6.1.C61 Case No. 11783

Award at February 2001: £8,334

See: 1.8.6.C75 for details

1.9.6.1.C62 Case No. 10308
Award at February 2001: £8,055
See: 1.2.3.1.C25 for details

1.9.6.1.C63 Case No. 10156
Award at February 2001: £7,926
See: 1.7.3.C65 for details

1.9.6.1.C64 Case No. 10571
Award at February 2001: £7,923
See: 1.8.6.C76 for details

1.9.6.1.C65 Case No. 11985
Award at February 2001: £6,973
See: 1.2.3.2.1.C20 for details

1.9.6.1.C66 Case No. 10159
Award at February 2001: £6,605
See: 1.1.C10 for details

1.9.6.1.C67 Case No. 11312
Name of case: Smith v Stickley
Brief description of injuries: PSYCHIATRIC – PHOBIC TRAVEL ANXIETY
Reported: Kemp & Kemp, C4-090; [1997] CLY 1860
JSB Category: 3(B)(c)
Sex: Male
Age at injury: 36
Age at award: 39
Date of award: 04 August 1997
Tribunal: Birmingham County Court
Amount of award then: £6,000
Award at February 2001: £6,511
Description of injuries: Modest physical injuries – phobic travel anxiety – full recovery from physical injuries within eighteen months – symptoms of phobic travel anxiety continued.

1.9.6.1.C68 Case No. 11877
Name of case: Greenhow v Rilmac Ltd
Brief description of injuries: LUNGS – PLEURAL PLAQUES – ANXIETY
Reported: Kemp & Kemp, F2-073/1; [1999] CLY 1541
JSB Category: 5(B)(g); 3(A)
Sex: Male
Age at injury: 20-22 and 25-27
Age at award: 54
Date of award: 01 July 1999
Tribunal: Kingston-upon-Hull County Court
Amount of award then: £6,000
Award at February 2001: £6,251
Description of injuries: Claimant suffered substantial exposure to asbestos during 2 periods of employment with defendants – in 1994, claimant became aware that many of his colleagues were suffering breathing problems due to asbestos exposure; concerned that his breathing was similarly affected, claimant underwent X-rays – pleural plaques revealed – plaques not the cause of claimant's breathlessness, but inevitably a degree of anxiety caused by diagnosis – risk of developing more serious asbestos – related condition in the future.

Prognosis: 10 per cent risk of pleural thickening – 5 per cent risk of developing asbestosis – 3 per cent risk of developing lung cancer – 5 per cent risk of developing mesothelioma – also increased risk of developing laryngeal and gastro-intestinal cancer.

Other points: Provisional award.

1.9.6.1.C69 Case No. 11517
Award at February 2001: £5,392
See: 1.8.6.C85 for details

1.9.6.1.C70 Case No. 11516
Award at February 2001: £5,365
See: 1.8.6.C86 for details

1.9.6.1.C71 Case No. 10564
Award at February 2001: £5,251
See: 1.2.3.5.C9 for details

1.9.6.1.C72 Case No. 11914
Award at February 2001: £4,708
See: 1.3.1.2.C98 for details

1.9.6.1.C73 Case No. 10955
Award at February 2001: £4,081
See: 1.3.1.1.C41 for details

1.9.6.1.C74 Case No. 11901
Award at February 2001: £3,511
See: 1.3.1.2.1.C30 for details

Onset of Disease

1.9.6.1.C75 Case No. 12027
Award at February 2001: £3,084
See: 1.6.1.3.1.C20 for details

1.9.6.1.C76 Case No. 10656
Award at February 2001: £3,047
See: 1.5.3.C1 for details

1.9.6.1.C77 Case No. 11906
Award at February 2001: £2,863
See: 1.2.3.2.1.C29 for details

1.9.6.1.C78 Case No. 10576
Award at February 2001: £2,682
See: 1.2.3.5.C18 for details

1.9.6.1.C79 Case No. 11900
Award at February 2001: £2,620
See: 1.7.2.C3 for details

1.9.6.1.C80 Case No. 11905
Award at February 2001: £2,604
See: 1.2.3.5.C19 for details

1.9.6.1.C81 Case No. 11890
Award at February 2001: £2,604
See: 1.2.3.1.C35 for details

1.9.6.1.C82 Case No. 10163
Award at February 2001: £2,565
See: 1.4.3.C34 for details

1.9.6.1.C83 Case No. 11709
Name of case: Kemp v Burden (No 1)
Brief description of injuries: HEAD – PSYCHOLOGICAL SYMPTOMS
Reported: Kemp & Kemp, C4-128; [1998] CLY 1712
JSB Category: 3(A)(d); 2(B)
Sex: Male
Age at injury: 41
Age at award: 43
Date of award: 15 October 1997
Tribunal: Milton Keynes County Court
Amount of award then: £2,250

Award at February 2001: £2,426
Description of injuries: Seatbelt bruising – knock to the head – psychological injury.
Prognosis: Spontaneous improvement to the psychological symptoms were expected within 6 months of the date of the hearing.

1.9.6.1.C84 Case No. 11233
Name of case: Howell v Bolton Hospitals NHS Trust
Brief description of injuries: NEEDLE STICK INJURY – ANXIETY
Reported: [1996] CLY 2325
JSB Category:
Sex: Female
Age at injury: 29
Age at award: 31
Date of award: 16 November 1995
Tribunal: Bolton County Court
Amount of award then: £2,000
Award at February 2001: £2,296
Description of injuries: Needle stick injury (hypodermic) – mixed anxiety depressive disorder – full recovery took place within a very short time – anxiety lasted for seven months.
Other points: Advised not to become pregnant until a course of hepatitis injections was complete.

1.9.6.1.C85 Case No. 10868
Award at February 2001: £1,944
See: 1.6.1.C35 for details

1.9.6.1.C86 Case No. 11244
Name of case: Dickinson v Burton
Brief description of injuries: PHOBIC ANXIETY DISORDER
Reported: Kemp & Kemp, C4-130; [1996] CLY 2336
JSB Category: 5
Sex: Female
Age at injury: 7
Age at award: 9
Date of award: 04 July 1996
Tribunal: Boston County Court
Amount of award then: £1,500
Award at February 2001: £1,693
Description of injuries: She was bitten on the stomach by a pony – developed a phobic anxiety disorder with horses – phobia was overcome following seven sessions of psychological counselling.

1.9.6.1.C87 Case No. 11255

Name of case: Re Dixon

Brief description of injuries: ANXIETY REACTION

Reported: Kemp & Kemp, C4-131; [1996] CLY 2347

JSB Category: 3(A)(d)

Sex: Female

Age at injury: 23

Age at award: 29

Date of award: 20 August 1996

Tribunal: CICB, Birmingham

Amount of award then: £1,210

Award at February 2001: £1,359

Description of injuries: Significant anxiety reaction.

Prognosis: Some possibility that some residual anxiety symptoms to alcohol might persist.

Other points: She was helped by counselling from Victim Support.

1.9.6.1.C88 Case No. 11732

Award at February 2001: £1,242

See: 1.3.1.1.C60 for details

1.9.6.1.C89 Case No. 11052

Name of case: Re Keith

Brief description of injuries: PSYCHIATRIC – ANXIETY AFTER ROBBERY – 5 MONTHS

Reported: Kemp & Kemp, K2-192; [1995] CLY 1806

JSB Category: 3(A)(d)

Sex: Female

Age at injury: 27

Age at award: 29

Date of award: 17 May 1995

Tribunal: CICB, Liverpool

Amount of award then: £1,000

Award at February 2001: £1,150

Description of injuries: Cashier in local betting shop – four months pregnant when armed robbery took place in which two men in masks with baseball bats demanded takings from shop till – suffered no physical injury, but complained of chronic morning sickness and nervousness throughout remainder of preganancy – also remained anxious about possibility that some damage had been done to foetus until she delivered a healthy baby boy.

1.9.6.1.C90 Case No. 10120

Award at February 2001: £1,098

See: 1.3.1.2.C200 for details

1.9.6.1.C91 Case No. 11930

Award at February 2001: £1,041

See: 1.3.1.2.1.C56 for details

1.9.6.1.C92 Case No. 11929

Award at February 2001: £1,039

See: 1.3.1.1.C64 for details

1.9.6.1.C93 Case No. 11470

Award at February 2001: £550

See: 1.5.5.C32 for details

1.9.6.1.C94 Case No. 10151

Name of case: Re C

Brief description of injuries: ASSAULT – SEXUAL PHOBIA

Reported: Kemp & Kemp, C4-226; [1991] CLY 1348

JSB Category: 3(B)

Sex: Female

Age at injury: 28

Age at award: 33

Date of award: 17 January 1991

Tribunal: CICB

Amount of award then: £18

Award at February 2001: £23

Description of injuries: Assault – left black eye – bruises of scalp, right cheek, right face, which was bleeding – finger marks on neck – bruises on hips and legs – pain in supra pubic area – nasal septal cartilage displaced and dislocated causing cosmetic deformity requiring septoplasty – developed post-traumatic stress disorder.

Prognosis: Severe headaches with migraine characteristics every six to eight weeks likely to be permanent – sexual phobia, expected never to marry or ever have sexual intercourse.

1.9.6.1.1 Psychological shock

1.9.6.1.1.C1 Case No. 10487

Award at February 2001: £2,152

See: 1.6.1.3.1.C23 for details

1.9.6.1.1.C2 Case No. 10505

Award at February 2001: £1,235

See: 1.6.1.3.1.C26 for details

1.9.6.1.1.C3 Case No. 10520

Name of case: Hart v Tenmat

Brief description of injuries: SHOCK – AGITATED WHEN DRIVING

Reported: [1992] CLY 1776

JSB Category:

Sex: Female

Age at injury: 39

Age at award: 40

Date of award: 24 September 1991

Tribunal: Salford County Court

Amount of award then: £450

Award at February 2001: £575

Description of injuries: Shock and shaking-up.

Prognosis: Remained agitated when driving several months later.

1.9.6.1.2 Post-traumatic stress disorder

1.9.6.1.2.C1 Case No. 10533

Name of case: Re V

Brief description of injuries: MULTIPLE INJURIES – POST-TRAUMATIC STRESS DISORDER

Reported: Kemp & Kemp, C4-011; [1993] CLY 1425

JSB Category: 3(A), 3(B), 6(B); 6(G)

Sex: Female

Age at injury: 45

Age at award: 50

Date of award: 25 October 1993

Tribunal: CICB

Amount of award then: £55,000

Award at February 2001: £75,500

Description of injuries: Beaten with hammer – threats of torture and death – lacerations and bruising to body and nose, including haematoma in both eyes – dislocated left elbow resulting in exacerbation of pre-existing loss of mobility – prolapsed disc in spine rendering symptomatic previously wholly asymptomatic cervical spondylosis – right-sided radiculopathy – paraesthesia in right arm and 2 fingers of right hand – symptoms of vertigo – post-traumatic stress disorder – depression – phobias – flashbacks – panic attacks.

Prognosis: Strong possibility of further deterioration in muscle power – possibility of further neck surgery being required – likelihood of enforced retirement from job as GP within 5 years – domestic help required – psychiatric treatment ongoing for at least 6 months after time of hearing – full mental recovery regarded as unlikely because of constant reminders from long-term physical injuries.

1.9.6.1.2.C2 Case No. 11493

Award at February 2001: £72,253

See: 1.6.1.1.C2 for details

1.9.6.1.2.C3 Case No. 11519

Name of case: Knott v Haden Maintenance Ltd

Brief description of injuries: SKIN – BURNS – POST-TRAUMATIC STRESS DISORDER

Reported: Kemp & Kemp, C4-012; [1998] CLY 1521

JSB Category: 3(B)(a)

Sex: Male

Age at injury: 39

Age at award: 47

Date of award: 16 June 1998

Tribunal: QBD

Amount of award then: £57,000

Award at February 2001: £66,964

Description of injuries: Superficial burns – severe and disabling post-traumatic stress disorder – significant anxiety disorder – marked social phobia – obsessional behaviour – depressive state – in need of specialist care by nurses or care workers – could not safely be left alone.

Prognosis: Claimant permanently disabled from working.

1.9.6.1.2.C4 Case No. 11560

Award at February 2001: £64,198

See: 1.2.3.6.1.C1 for details

1.9.6.1.2.C5 Case No. 10029

Award at February 2001: £62,810

See: 1.4.4.1.C1 for details

1.9.6.1.2.C6 Case No. 11503

Award at February 2001: £59,083

See: 1.5.1.1.C1 for details

1.9.6.1.2.C7 Case No. 11520

Name of case: Re Pallant

Brief description of injuries: PSYCHIATRIC – POST-TRAUMATIC STRESS DISORDER – TINNITUS

Reported: Kemp & Kemp, C2-045; [1998] CLY 1522

JSB Category: 3(B)(a); 4(B)(d)

Sex: Female

Age at injury: 53

Age at award: 65

Date of award: 19 November 1997

Tribunal: CICB

Amount of award then: £47,500

Award at February 2001: £56,080

Description of injuries: Severe and chronic post-traumatic stress disorder – severe headaches for 2 years – phobic behaviour – moderate intellectual and memory impairment – balance disturbance and tinnitus – claimant's complaints originally dismissed by the medical profession as eccentricities without organic cause.

Prognosis: Condition was unlikely to improve – required long-term therapeutic support and regular respite care.

1.9.6.1.2.C8 Case No. 10928

Name of case: Re Duke

Brief description of injuries: RAPE – POST-TRAUMATIC STRESS DISORDER – ONLY CAPABLE OF LIGHT WORK

Reported: Kemp & Kemp, C4-204; [1995] CLY 1679

JSB Category: 3(A)(a)

Sex: Female

Age at injury: 40

Age at award: 45

Date of award: 15 May 1995

Tribunal: CICB, York

Amount of award then: £40,000

Award at February 2001: £49,825

Description of injuries: Female violently raped and threatened with death – injuries on admission to hospital included fractures of transverse processes of lumbar vertebrae and bruising to head, neck and left loin – required counselling for rape – three years after incident, she suffered from continuing post-traumatic stress disorder, depression and recurrent physical symptoms, such as headaches and back pain – almost five years after incident there was little improvement in her psychological condition – experienced loss of libido and was capable of only the lightest work.

Prognosis: The prognosis was guarded.

1.9.6.1.2.C9 Case No. 10914

Name of case: Re Castle

Brief description of injuries: POST-TRAUMATIC STRESS DISORDER – DEPRESSION – CHARACTER CHANGE

Reported: Kemp & Kemp, H3-150; [1995] CLY 1665

JSB Category: 3(B)(a)

Sex: Male

Age at injury: 27

Age at award: 36

Date of award: 06 July 1995

Tribunal: CICB, Durham

Amount of award then: £36,750

Award at February 2001: £45,575

Description of injuries: Assaulted in course of an armed robbery when employed as security guard – hit over right shoulder, neck and head and kicked while on ground – sustained a comminuted fracture of left ulna requiring plating and bone grafting – good recovery was made from physical injuries but post-traumatic stress developed, requiring out-patient psychiatric treatment including drug therapy for depression – initially, suffered from nightmares and flashbacks of assault and then continued to suffer from depression, anxiety, irritability and generalised phobic anxiety state with poor self-esteem and feelings of inadequacy – gained weight substantially, harboured thoughts of suicide and, from being gregarious and happily married, became reclusive and saw marriage break down – had not worked since the accident except in voluntary capacity – had tried to obtain work as care assistant but without success.

1.9.6.1.2.C10 Case No. 11565

Name of case: Chapman v Bennett

Brief description of injuries: SPINE – POST-TRAUMATIC STRESS DISORDER

Reported: Kemp & Kemp, E3-004/2; [1998] CLY 1567

JSB Category: 6(B)(a)(ii), 6(I);5(A)(g); 3(B)

Sex: Male

Age at injury: 39

Age at award: 47

Date of award: 06 April 1998

Tribunal: QBD

Amount of award then: £38,000

Award at February 2001: £43,006

Description of injuries: Fracture of the spine at T12/L1 – fractured ribs – crushing injury to the left hand developed into algo-dystrophy – kyphotic collapse of T12 – moderately severe post-traumatic stress disorder – chronic moderately severe adjustment disorder – claimant was unable to pursue his work as a lorry driver and retained firefighter, or to practice sporting activities.

Prognosis: DSS assessed claimant as 73 per cent disabled.

1.9.6.1.2.C11 Case No. 10720

Name of case: Murby v Derby City Transport

Brief description of injuries: POST-TRAUMATIC STRESS DISORDER – SEVERE

Reported: Kemp & Kemp, C4-020; [1994] CLY 1568

JSB Category: 3(B)(a)

Sex: Male

Age at injury: 37

Age at award: 41

Date of award: 08 December 1993

Tribunal: Derby High Court

Amount of award then: £30,000

Award at February 2001: £38,581

Description of injuries: Claimant, bus driver, had his bus shunted from behind by another and driven into scaffolding which was supporting workmen – physical injuries (whiplash; blow to head causing headaches; blow to left knee causing swelling; lower back pain) resolved within weeks apart from residual postural neck ache – however, claimant developed severe post-traumatic stress disorder – nightmares – insomnia – sleep disturbance – sleepwalking – palpitations – sweating – muscular tension – panic attacks to point of nausea – unable to return to work as bus driver, or drive at all – acute symptoms when driven at low speeds for short journeys; otherwise unable to bear being driven at all – problems with alcohol consumption for a period – family and social life extremely restricted – personality change to obsessive, phobic disposition – only comfortable at home, or at day centre attended 3 times per week – ongoing out-patient psychiatric treatment involving drug therapy and counselling by occupational therapists and psychologists.

Prognosis: Symptoms slowly diminishing with time – claimant might eventually become fit for relatively simple, light work close to home, eg shelf stacking – permanently and substantially disadvantaged on open labour market.

1.9.6.1.2.C12 Case No. 11297

Name of case: Re Lawson

Brief description of injuries: POST-TRAUMATIC STRESS DISORDER

Reported: Kemp & Kemp, C4-021; [1997] CLY 1845

JSB Category: 3(B)(b)

Sex: Female

Age at injury: 28

Age at award: 34

Date of award: 26 February 1997

Tribunal: CICB

Amount of award then: £32,500

Award at February 2001: £38,238

Description of injuries: Stabbed while on duty – post-traumatic stress disorder.

Prognosis: At the time of the hearing symptoms of post-traumatic stress disorder had lessened – she would continue to feel vulnerable and unsafe.

Other points: Her earning capacity had been reduced.

1.9.6.1.2.C13 Case No. 10926

Name of case: Re CW

Brief description of injuries: SEXUAL ABUSE – EIGHT YEARS – SERIOUS LONG-TERM PSYCHIATRIC DAMAGE

Reported: Kemp & Kemp, C4-208; [1995] CLY 1677

JSB Category: 3(A)(a)

Sex: Female

Age at injury: -

Age at award: 22

Date of award: 10 May 1995

Tribunal: CICB, London

Amount of award then: £30,000

Award at February 2001: £36,444

Description of injuries: The applicant was sexually abused by her father and two brothers during the period between 1977 and 1985 – she was buggered by her father and had sexual intercourse with her two brothers – eventually the abuse was discovered and she was taken into care – notwithstanding fact that she was in care, she continued to be abused at hands of her father and two brothers – when she was 15 years old, she was victim of unlawful sexual intercourse at hands of man who was staying at small private residential unit to which she had been sent – ultimately left care and spent the late 1980s walking the streets, taking drugs, living rough and being alcohol-dependent – became a lesbian and was attacked by her brothers when they found out – in 1993, she formed a new lesbian relationship with another woman who was a prostitute – that relationship provided her with the most stability she had had for years – in 1995 she had started therapy with a psychotherapist – in 1995 she was still having nightmares about the abuse which had happened when she was a child.

Prognosis: The prognosis was very guarded – if her relationship with her current partner broke down, the likelihood was that there would be a significant turn for worse in terms of prognosis – Board was persuaded that an award should be made for the continuing cost of psychotherapy.

1.9.6.1.2.C14 Case No. 10721

Name of case: Hale v London Underground

Brief description of injuries: POST-TRAUMATIC STRESS DISORDER – SEVERE

Reported: [1994] CLY 1569

JSB Category: 3(B)(a)

Sex: Male

Age at injury: 39

Age at award: 44

Date of award: 04 November 1992

Tribunal: QBD

Amount of award then: £27,500

Award at February 2001: £35,725

Description of injuries: Claimant firefighter in attendance at King's Cross fire disaster – entered station several times, displaying great bravery – no physical injuries, but collapsed from exhaustion at scene and had to be helped above ground – development of post-traumatic stress disorder, but "bottled – up" at first; claimant threw himself into work, gaining 2 promotions – became difficult and irritable at home; relationship with wife and children deteriorated markedly – sexual relations with wife ceased – commenced counselling sessions 2 years after incident – soon after sought psychiatric help and revealed symptoms – nightmares, lessening in frequency somewhat – sleep disturbance – depression – short temper – headaches – general tension – medication prescribed – fear of going to work led to absenteeism some months later – medically retired from operational duty – took non-operational job, but unhappiness and spells of absenteeism continued – discharged altogether from brigade on grounds of disability – offered job as fire prevention officer – absenteeism continued – some success in post-traumatic stress disorder programme followed by relapse – fundamental underlying depression, requiring counselling, still persisting.

Prognosis: Prognosis that claimant would never make full recovery – prospects of real improvement in condition minimal, but perceptible improvement in attitude to life likely once he left fire service altogether in approximately 6 months from date of trial (judge's finding) – capacity to gain employment impaired, likely to take 2 years after departure from fire service – continued vulnerability to stress in limited field in which claimant could seek employment.

1.9.6.1.2.C15 Case No. 11523

Name of case: Easton v Ellis

Brief description of injuries: PSYCHIATRIC – POST-TRAUMATIC STRESS DISORDER – BACK – DEPRESSION

Reported: Kemp & Kemp, C4-026; [1998] CLY 1525

JSB Category: 3(A), 3(B)(a), 6(B)

Sex: Female

Age at injury: 32

Age at award: 36

Date of award: 16 January 1998

Tribunal: Pontypridd County Court

Amount of award then: £30,000

Award at February 2001: £34,021

Description of injuries: Soft-tissue injury to the back – chronic pain syndrome developed – deepening and worsening of pre-existing depressive illness.

Prognosis: Pain would be permanent – accident had made it virtually certain that claimant would not recover from the depressive illness.

1.9.6.1.2.C16 Case No. 11522

Name of case: Re Nixon

Brief description of injuries: PSYCHIATRIC – POST-TRAUMATIC STRESS DISORDER

Reported: Kemp & Kemp, J2-010; [1998] CLY 1524

JSB Category: 3(B)(a)

Sex: Male

Age at injury: 25

Age at award: 28

Date of award: 15 January 1998

Tribunal: CICB, York

Amount of award then: £30,000

Award at February 2001: £34,021

Description of injuries: Life threatening stab wounds – nightmares – personality change – behavioural change – alcohol abuse.

Other points: Police protection in hospital required until N's assailant was arrested (10 days).

1.9.6.1.2.C17 Case No. 11785

Name of case: Re DJH

Brief description of injuries: PSYCHIATRIC – POST-TRAUMATIC STRESS DISORDER

Reported: Kemp & Kemp, C4-028; [1999] CLY 1448

JSB Category: 3(B)(a)

Sex: Male

Age at injury: 51

Age at award: 54

Date of award: 01 July 1999

Tribunal: CICB, Nottingham

Amount of award then: £30,000

Award at February 2001: £32,787

Description of injuries: Claimant victim of serious assault – bruising to head and ribs – severe post-traumatic stress disorder – poor memory – irritability – claustrophobia – panic – palpitations – sweating – shaking – shallowness of breath – chest pains – nausea – lightheadedness – fear of flying – numbness or tingling – chills and hot flushes – every aspect of former life devastated; claimant "shell of his former self" – claimant undergoing psychiatric treatment at time of hearing.

Other points: Board took into account claimant's pre-morbid personality and history of pre-incident depression.

1.9.6.1.2.C18 Case No. 10344

Award at February 2001: £32,355

See: 1.8.6.C13 for details

1.9.6.1.2.C19 Case No. 10320

Award at February 2001: £32,331

See: 1.3.1.3.2.1.C3 for details

1.9.6.1.2.C20 Case No. 11786

Name of case: Day v Bell

Brief description of injuries: PSYCHIATRIC – POST-TRAUMATIC STRESS DISORDER

Reported: Kemp & Kemp, C4-031; [1999] CLY 1449

JSB Category: 3(B)(b); 7(B)(a)

Sex: Female

Age at injury: 43

Age at award: 45

Date of award: 19 June 1999

Tribunal: Norwich County Court

Amount of award then: £29,500

Award at February 2001: £32,099

Description of injuries: Claimant assaulted – threatened with shotgun, which she pushed away from her head shortly before assailant discharged it – struck on head with rubber mallet, causing cuts, grazing, swelling and bruising to nose, 1 inch laceration on right upper lip extending through mucosa and partially clipped right upper second incisor – 2 irregular lacerations to skull in right parietal region – physical injuries healed after 3 months leaving scars, not immediately obvious but noticeable for claimant – moderately severe post-traumatic stress disorder – anxiety – depression – claimant sectioned under Mental Health Act 1983 and detained for a few months – 10 months after assault, claimant received threatening letter, which she believed came from assailant – significant aggravation of post-traumatic stress disorder symptoms, continuing to time of trial – avoidance of place of assault (claimant moved away from area) – recurring thoughts about assault – avoidance of social contact and intimate relationships – severe distress – work history following assault only sporadic and unremunerative.

Prognosis: Claimant unlikely to be able to hold down any job requiring significant concentration or contact with public – claimant would always be vulnerable to post-traumatic stress disorder, but would cope with symptoms – claimant intending to take accountancy course at date of trial.

Other points: Award comprised: physical injuries: £4,500; post-traumatic stress disorder: £25,000.

1.9.6.1.2.C21 Case No. 11092

Name of case: Baynton v ICI

Brief description of injuries: POST-TRAUMATIC STRESS DISORDER

Reported: Kemp & Kemp, C4-034; [1996] CLY 2183

JSB Category: 3(B)(a)

Sex: Male

Age at injury: 49

Age at award: 54

Date of award: 03 October 1995

Tribunal: Manchester District Registry

Amount of award then: £25,000

Award at February 2001: £29,942

Description of injuries: Post-traumatic stress disorder – minor rib and nose injuries and lacerations – total change in him before and after the accident.

Prognosis: Post-traumatic stress disorder of such severity that he would never work again.

Other points: Symptoms would improve with appropriate specialist counselling – not readily obtainable in the north.

1.9.6.1.2.C22 Case No. 11091

Name of case: Re Dewar
Brief description of injuries: POST-TRAUMATIC STRESS DISORDER
Reported: Kemp & Kemp, C4-035; [1996] CLY 2182
JSB Category: 3(B)(a)
Sex: Male
Age at injury: 43
Age at award: 48
Date of award: 27 March 1996
Tribunal: CICB, Durham
Amount of award then: £25,000
Award at February 2001: £29,585
Description of injuries: Post-traumatic stress disorder – bruising to the trunk, arms and legs – medically discharged from the prison service.
Prognosis: Prolonged and disabling illness – permanent incapacity – unlikely to return to work.
Other points: Suffered from a genetic pre-disposition to a manic depressive disorder.

1.9.6.1.2.C23 Case No. 11103

Name of case: Re C
Brief description of injuries: POST-TRAUMATIC STRESS DISORDER
Reported: Kemp & Kemp, C4-212; [1996] CLY 2194
JSB Category: 3(A)(b)
Sex: Female
Age at injury: 10-12
Age at award: 16
Date of award: 11 April 1996
Tribunal: CICB, London
Amount of award then: £25,000
Award at February 2001: £29,357
Description of injuries: Sexual abuse – oral sex – buggery – full intercourse.
Prognosis: Doing well on a college course – future job prospects good.
Other points: Continued to feel angry, sad and anxious.

1.9.6.1.2.C24 Case No. 11104

Award at February 2001: £29,256
See: 1.8.6.C15 for details

1.9.6.1.2.C25 Case No. 11294

Name of case: Re AH
Brief description of injuries: POST-TRAUMATIC STRESS DISORDER
Reported: Kemp & Kemp, C4-214; [1997] CLY 1842
JSB Category: 3(B)(b)
Sex: Male
Age at injury: 6-12
Age at award: 41
Date of award: 13 August 1996
Tribunal: CICB, Liverpool
Amount of award then: £25,000
Award at February 2001: £29,256
Description of injuries: Severe/chronic post-traumatic stress disorder – childhood sexual abuse – very dependent on others – difficulty in dealing with men.
Other points: Difficulty in dealing with men affected his employment prospects.

1.9.6.1.2.C26 Case No. 11525

Name of case: Re Gibney
Brief description of injuries: PSYCHIATRIC – POST-TRAUMATIC STRESS DISORDER – FEAR OF AIDS
Reported: Kemp & Kemp, C4-037; [1998] CLY 1527
JSB Category: 3(B)(b)
Sex: Female
Age at injury: 48
Age at award: 54
Date of award: 22 October 1997
Tribunal: CICB, Birmingham
Amount of award then: £25,000
Award at February 2001: £28,011
Description of injuries: Two assaults 8 days apart – claimant stabbed with a hypodermic needle by drug addict who said she was HIV positive – in the second incident claimant was overpowered, kicked and punched – suspected cracked rib and bruising – post-traumatic stress disorder and depressive illness caused by the assaults.
Prognosis: Guarded – expected that a course of treatment might relieve some of her symptoms.

1.9.6.1.2.C27 Case No. 11507

Award at February 2001: £27,993
See: 1.8.6.C17 for details

1.9.6.1.2.C28 Case No. 11506

Award at February 2001: £27,993
See: 1.8.6.C18 for details

1.9.6.1.2.C29 Case No. 11505

Award at February 2001: £27,303

See: 1.8.6.C19 for details

1.9.6.1.2.C30 Case No. 11774

Award at February 2001: £27,303

See: 1.2.3.1.C14 for details

1.9.6.1.2.C31 Case No. 10539

Award at February 2001: £27,043

See: 1.6.1.1.C6 for details

1.9.6.1.2.C32 Case No. 11787

Name of case: Re C

Brief description of injuries: PSYCHIATRIC – POST-TRAUMATIC STRESS DISORDER

Reported: [1999] CLY 1450

JSB Category: 3(B); 2(B); 5(A)(g)

Sex: Male

Age at injury: 49

Age at award: 54

Date of award: 01 July 1999

Tribunal: CICB, London

Amount of award then: £25,000

Award at February 2001: £27,006

Description of injuries: Claimant victim of assault, leaving him with extensive bruising to chest, fractured rib, bruising to eyes and lacerations to left eyebrow and left cheek – claimant suffered second assault 3 months later, sustaining haematoma to back of head – following recovery from physical injuries, development of headaches and nervous depression – disturbed sleep – nightmares – ringing in ears – dizziness – hypertension – vertigo – panic attacks – fear of going into outside world; claimant described himself as "recluse" – inability to continue working – difficulty in sustaining personal relationships and coping with everyday tasks – post-traumatic stress disorder diagnosed 2 years after attack – also development of spondylosis, causing unsteadiness, weakness in right hand, inability to grip properly or walk significant distances – no obvious clinical explanation for this condition.

Prognosis: Prognosis uncertain; claimant had showed no predisposition to stress or depression prior to incident, but fact that claimant was still suffering from all symptoms 4 years after attack, and had not responded well to treatment despite significant efforts to resolve condition, suggested that illness might be permanent.

Other points: Award included unspecified award for future loss of earnings.

1.9.6.1.2.C33 Case No. 11958

Name of case: Re Long (CICB Quantum: 1999)

Brief description of injuries: POST-TRAUMATIC STRESS DISORDER

Reported: Kemp & Kemp, C4-060; [2000] 1 CL 118

JSB Category: 3(A)(a)

Sex: Female

Age at injury: 25

Age at award: 30

Date of award: 29 September 1999

Tribunal: CICB, Nottingham

Amount of award then: £25,000

Award at February 2001: £26,817

Description of injuries: A store manageress L was injured while attempting to arrest a shoplifter – shoplifter was joined by seven other youths who assaulted L and ran riot in the store – bruising to the back, eye, elbow and leg which resolved within weeks – on receiving notice of the date of the court hearing L fainted, had panic attacks and other psychological sequaelae – she suffered diminished self confidence, depression and anxiety – returned to work on a part time basis – a marginally distressing incident at work some months after her return led to her being unable to work – post-traumatic stress disorder was diagnosed – L ceased working two years after the assault. L was going to weekly therapy – her marriage had suffered and every aspect of her life had been touched.

1.9.6.1.2.C34 Case No. 10150

Name of case: Re Lloyd

Brief description of injuries: POST-TRAUMATIC STRESS DISORDER

Reported: Kemp & Kemp, C4-041; [1991] CLY 1347

JSB Category: 3(B)

Sex: Female

Age at injury: 49

Age at award: 54

Date of award: 10 April 1991

Tribunal: CICB

Amount of award then: £20,000

Award at February 2001: £26,787

Description of injuries: Assault – minor physical injury but thereafter post-traumatic stress disorder – extremely distressed – severe impaired sleep disturbance with reminiscent dreams – became overweight – loss of libido and sexual dysfunction – phobia about cars – agoraphobia/social phobia.

Prognosis: Not optimistic: symptoms might continue for foreseeable future.

1.9.6.1.2.C35 Case No. 11526

Name of case: James v London Electricity plc

Brief description of injuries: PSYCHIATRIC – POST-TRAUMATIC STRESS DISORDER – OBSESSIVE-COMPULSIVE DISORDER

Reported: Kemp & Kemp, C4-042; [1998] CLY 1528

JSB Category: 3(B)(b)

Sex: Female

Age at injury: 25

Age at award: 28

Date of award: 03 July 1998

Tribunal: Central London County Court

Amount of award then: £24,000

Award at February 2001: £26,217

Description of injuries: Post-traumatic stress disorder – severe depression and obsessive-compulsive disorder (OCD) – pre-existing vulnerable personality predisposed claimant to anxiety and phobias.

Prognosis: Further improvement to the OCD was expected with therapy treatment – remaining psychiatric problems would largely resolve within a further 2 or 3 years.

1.9.6.1.2.C36 Case No. 10322

Name of case: Re C

Brief description of injuries: TRUNK – 13 STAB WOUNDS – PTSD – VULNERABLE TO LUNG INFECTIONS

Reported: [1992] CLY 1578

JSB Category: 3(B)(b)

Sex: Female

Age at injury: 20

Age at award: 22

Date of award: 04 February 1992

Tribunal: CICB, Leeds

Amount of award then: £20,000

Award at February 2001: £26,122

Description of injuries: Thirteen stab wounds – severe shock – right-sided pneumothorax requiring a drain – operation to remove a portion of the knife blade – badly scarred from attack and from operative procedures – required re-admittance to hospital one month after the attack suffering from a large abscess and a collapsed lung.

Prognosis: Unlikely to fully recover from the post-traumatic stress disorder – liable to lung infection for life.

1.9.6.1.2.C37 Case No. 11301

Name of case: Re Croucher

Brief description of injuries: POST-TRAUMATIC STRESS DISORDER

Reported: Kemp & Kemp, C4-043; [1997] CLY 1849

JSB Category: 3(B)(b)

Sex: Male

Age at injury: 57

Age at award: 62

Date of award: 29 October 1996

Tribunal: CICB, London

Amount of award then: £22,500

Award at February 2001: £26,040

Description of injuries: Minor physical injuries – post-traumatic stress disorder – clinical depression – post-traumatic stress disorder worsened between 1992 and 1994.

Prognosis: At the time of the trial the prognosis was poor – full recovery from the post-traumatic stress disorder was thought to be unlikely in his lifetime.

Other points: Medically retired in 1992 – unlikely to work again.

1.9.6.1.2.C38 Case No. 11300

Name of case: Watson v CICB

Brief description of injuries: POST-TRAUMATIC STRESS DISORDER

Reported: Kemp & Kemp, B-026/1; E2-020; [1997] CLY 1848

JSB Category: 3(B)(b)

Sex: Female

Age at injury: 22

Age at award: 28

Date of award: 20 January 1997

Tribunal: CICB, Birmingham

Amount of award then: £22,500

Award at February 2001: £25,933

Description of injuries: Multiple stab wounds to the neck, breast, chest and abdomen – the liver, spleen and diaphragm required sutures – post-traumatic stress disorder – good recovery made from the wounds – very self-conscious of the scars – felt unable to cope with counselling for the post-traumatic stress disorder.

1.9.6.1.2.C39 Case No. 10554

Award at February 2001: £25,625

See: 1.8.6.C24 for details

1.9.6.1.2.C40 Case No. 11371

Award at February 2001: £25,264

See: 1.3.1.1.C7 for details

1.9.6.1.2.C41 Case No. 11539

Award at February 2001: £24,926

See: 1.7.3.C14 for details

1.9.6.1.2.C42 Case No. 10921

Name of case: Re Walsh

Brief description of injuries: PSYCHIATRIC DISORDER – POST-TRAUMATIC STRESS DISORDER

Reported: Kemp & Kemp, C4-047; [1995] CLY 1672

JSB Category: 3(B)(b)

Sex: Female

Age at injury: 30

Age at award: 37

Date of award: 20 June 1995

Tribunal: CICB, London

Amount of award then: £20,000

Award at February 2001: £23,646

Description of injuries: Plaintiff came upon her five-year-old son's completely blackened body being carried to her flat by neighbours – child had picked up a booby trapped incendiary device left in childrens' play park which had exploded when he picked it up – child's older brother witnessed him being engulfed in flames and trying to escape – child sustained extensive burns to most of his body and particularly his face – not known for some hours whether he would survive – from date of accident the child underwent continual skin grafting and reconstructive surgery which would continue until he was fully grown – the mother, who had no history of psychiatric illness, suffered a psychiatric disorder together with post-traumatic stress disorder – although by date of hearing, more than six years after the accident, she was no longer suffering from any psychiatric illness, she continued to display symptoms of mild post-traumatic stress disorder and high levels of anxiety.

Prognosis: Constant reminder of the accident because of presence of her disfigured child, and his need for repeated operations together with care and attention to skin grafts, meant that the mother was unlikely ever to be fully free of symptoms.

Other points: The brother, who had been a well-adjusted eight-year-old at the time of accident, also suffered from post-traumautic stress disorder which involved some behavioural problems – initially his symptoms were considered to be mild to moderate – however, as he grew older intrusive thoughts and efforts at avoidance increased together with levels of anxiety, suggesting that he was facing up to accident and associated guilt more than he had done previously. Award for brother £10,000.

1.9.6.1.2.C43 Case No. 11302

Award at February 2001: £23,111

See: 1.8.6.C27 for details

1.9.6.1.2.C44 Case No. 11163

Award at February 2001: £23,000

See: 1.3.1.3.1.C8 for details

1.9.6.1.2.C45 Case No. 10324

Award at February 2001: £22,625

See: 1.5.4.C1 for details

1.9.6.1.2.C46 Case No. 11303

Award at February 2001: £22,613

See: 1.8.6.C28 for details

1.9.6.1.2.C47 Case No. 11508

Award at February 2001: £22,138

See: 1.8.6.C29 for details

1.9.6.1.2.C48 Case No. 11537

Award at February 2001: £21,570

See: 1.2.3.6.2.1.C9 for details

1.9.6.1.2.C49 Case No. 10722

Name of case: Re Hawkins

Brief description of injuries: POST-TRAUMATIC STRESS DISORDER – MODERATELY SEVERE

Reported: Kemp & Kemp, C4-052; [1994] CLY 1570

JSB Category: 3(B)(b)

Sex: Male

Age at injury: 42

Age at award: 52

Date of award: 06 July 1994

Tribunal: CICB, Glasgow

Amount of award then: £17,500

Award at February 2001: £21,423

Description of injuries: Claimant member of ambulance service attending Lockerbie air disaster – post-traumatic stress disorder, found on the basis of evidence from claimant, his wife, his colleagues and extensive medical evidence to have been caused by the disaster – claimant forced to take early retirement from service.

1.9.6.1.2.C50 Case No. 10723

Award at February 2001: £21,393

See: 1.7.3.C19 for details

1.9.6.1.2.C51 Case No. 11790

Name of case: Re Ducker

Brief description of injuries: MULTIPLE INJURIES – POST-TRAUMATIC STRESS DISORDER

Reported: Kemp & Kemp, B2-030; [1999] CLY 1453

JSB Category: 3(B), 3(A); 6(K)(c)(i); 7(A)(c); 8

Sex: Male

Age at injury: 27

Age at award: 36

Date of award: 06 July 1999

Tribunal: CICB, London

Amount of award then: £20,000

Award at February 2001: £21,352

Description of injuries: Claimant suffered assault by gang – nasal fracture, leaving slight deformity and narrow airways – spiral fractures of lower third of right tibia extending to lower end and fracture to upper third of right fibula, both slightly comminuted – standing, joint movement and walking restricted, and pain, ankle stiffness and limp present, after plaster removed from leg – 8.5in scar on tibia with 10 degrees external torsion – ankle and calf size increased by 1in and 0.75in respectively – right ankle flexion 30 degrees less than normal at first, with subsequent improvement – subtalar movements 30 degrees of normal, mid tarsal movements 80 degrees of normal, also subsequently improving – infrequent lower leg pain, and wet weather discomfort, lasting 4 years after assault – claimant suffered from depression after the attack – flashbacks – sleep disturbance – depression exacerbated by being made redundant, coincidentally shortly after the assault – assault prevented claimant from taking up comparable work, and depression worsened by continuing unemployment – no significant employment obtained since assault – ongoing symptoms diagnosed as major depressive illness and post-traumatic stress disorder.

Prognosis: Full recovery from physical injuries at time of hearing, although running would never be normal and claimant would be unable to play sport – prognosis regarding psychological symptoms uncertain – conclusion of legal proceedings expected to assist with recovery, but claimant unlikely to fully recover from psychological effects.

1.9.6.1.2.C52 Case No. 10749

Award at February 2001: £21,315

See: 1.3.1.2.1.C1 for details

1.9.6.1.2.C53 Case No. 10724

Name of case: Gardner v Epirotiki Steamship Co

Brief description of injuries: POST-TRAUMATIC STRESS DISORDER – MODERATELY SEVERE

Reported: Kemp & Kemp, C4-053; [1994] CLY 1572

JSB Category: 3(B)(b)

Sex: Female

Age at injury: 14

Age at award: 20

Date of award: 26 May 1994

Tribunal: QBD

Amount of award then: £17,500

Award at February 2001: £21,315

Description of injuries: Claimant passenger aboard motor vessel when rammed by another vessel and sunk within 40 minutes – thrown off feet by impact – proceeded to muster point in main lounge – ship listed and lights went out; claimant slid along floor into pile of furniture; other passengers landed on top of her and she was trapped for a while – fear of death, and experienced breathing difficulties – escaped ship by climbing over deck rail and jumping 30 or 40 feet into sea – pulled underwater by vortex of sinking ship and engulfed in debris – surfaced and was eventually rescued – considerable distress after the experience, subsequently diagnosed as post-traumatic stress disorder – vivid nightmares, making her feel unwell – fitful sleep – flashbacks for 4 years – intrusive thoughts about incident, which claimant kept at bay by inward recitation of a monologue, which occasionally broke through into actual conversation and was exhausting to keep up, or by singing to herself – claimant stayed up late watching television or reading until overcome by sleep, rather than going to bed – concentration profoundly affected – significant depression – occasional suicidal thought – phobic about water, especially the sound of running water – dislike of crowds, and constant checking for emergency exits – education disrupted, with exam marks particularly disappointing, forcing change of plan from pursuing degree course to pursuing HND – underwent 15 month session of counselling 2 years before date of trial – counselling alleviated symptoms of post-traumatic stress disorder, but it remained moderately severe, with nightmares continuing, and allied to feelings of profound anxiety and depression, at date of trial.

Prognosis: 6 months' weekly counselling and end of litigation thought likely to bring about substantial recovery – claimant would always be vulnerable to stresses in the future – expected grades in HND exam likely to allow her to move on to a degree course, effectively 2 years late.

1.9.6.1.2.C54 Case No. 11350

Award at February 2001: £19,917

See: 1.3.1.2.1.C2 for details

1.9.6.1.2.C55 Case No. 11304

Award at February 2001: £19,507

See: 1.8.6.C36 for details

1.9.6.1.2.C56 Case No. 11527

Name of case: Re Gardner (a minor)

Brief description of injuries: PSYCHIATRIC – POST-TRAUMATIC STRESS DISORDER

Reported: Kemp & Kemp, C4-054; [1998] CLY 1529

JSB Category: 3(B)(b)

Sex: Male

Age at injury: 4

Age at award: -

Date of award: 19 February 1998

Tribunal: CICB, Durham

Amount of award then: £17,500

Award at February 2001: £19,152

Description of injuries: Claimant suffered post-traumatic stress disorder after witnessing a stabbing attack on his father – behavioural problems – significant impairment in academic development.

Prognosis: The consequences of serious psychiatric injury were likely to be indefinite.

1.9.6.1.2.C57 Case No. 10918

Name of case: Re McPherson

Brief description of injuries: POST-TRAUMATIC STRESS DISORDER – SYMPTOMS CONTINUING AFTER 5 YEARS

Reported: [1995] CLY 1669

JSB Category: 3(B)(b)

Sex: Male

Age at injury: 12

Age at award: 17

Date of award: 31 January 1995

Tribunal: CICB, London

Amount of award then: £15,750

Award at February 2001: £18,915

Description of injuries: Boy assaulted by a group of other boys – when bricks were thrown at him, he ran across the road to escape and was hit by car – suffered comminuted fractures to left tibia and fibula and a chip fracture of left elbow – made good recovery from these injuries and there was no growth disturbance – however, developed post-traumatic stress disorder as result of assault – for a long period after the assault suffered distressing intrusive thoughts and images of assault, avoided place where it happened (near his home) – also avoided feelings that he had about it and suffered disturbance of sleep and concentration and an increase in irritability and anger – disorder improved gradually without specific treatment (which he was unwilling to undergo) but at time of hearing he had by no means made a full recovery.

1.9.6.1.2.C58 Case No. 11528

Name of case: Pearson v British Midland Airways

Brief description of injuries: PSYCHIATRIC – POST-TRAUMATIC STRESS DISORDER

Reported: Kemp & Kemp, C4-056; [1998] CLY 1530

JSB Category: 3(B)(b)

Sex: Male

Age at injury: 31

Age at award: 40

Date of award: 09 February 1998

Tribunal: QBD

Amount of award then: £17,000

Award at February 2001: £18,582

Description of injuries: Post-traumatic stress disorder after assisting at a plane crash – avoidance and emotional numbing – claimant unprepared to recognise he had a problem – relationships suffered – job was lost due to poor performance.

Prognosis: Prognosis was hopeful – minor symptoms were expected to resolve slowly over the years – no future deterioration was predicted.

1.9.6.1.2.C59 Case No. 10726

Name of case: Re Seedin

Brief description of injuries: POST-TRAUMATIC STRESS DISORDER – MODERATE

Reported: Kemp & Kemp, E2-011; [1994] CLY 1574

JSB Category: 3(B)(c)

Sex: Male

Age at injury: 17

Age at award: 26

Date of award: 01 November 1994

Tribunal: CICB, London

Amount of award then: £15,000

Award at February 2001: £18,069

Description of injuries: Violent racial attack by gang – serious stab wound to back of neck; full physical recovery made, except for scar – marked subsequent psychological damage – loss of motivation – failure of subsequent exams – described as being like "an old man" – unable to hold down employment for any length of time because of difficulty with being with people – unable to pursue chosen career in Customs and Excise Service – proneness to pronounced mood swings – unable to use public lavatories, as unable to urinate when others present.

Prognosis: Prognosis unclear at date of assessment – claimant's condition improving gradually.

1.9.6.1.2.C60 Case No. 11305

Award at February 2001: £16,850

See: 1.8.6.C42 for details

1.9.6.1.2.C61 Case No. 11509
Award at February 2001: £16,263
See: 1.8.6.C43 for details

1.9.6.1.2.C62 Case No. 10933
Award at February 2001: £16,013
See: 1.7.3.C25 for details

1.9.6.1.2.C63 Case No. 10557
Award at February 2001: £15,786
See: 1.8.6.C45 for details

1.9.6.1.2.C64 Case No. 11981
Name of case: Re M (a child) (CICB Quantum: 1999)
Brief description of injuries: POST-TRAUMATIC STRESS DISORDER
Reported: Kemp & Kemp, PRC-007; [2000] 3 CL 165
JSB Category: 3(B)(b)
Sex: Male
Age at injury: 21 months
Age at award: 7
Date of award: 15 June 1999
Tribunal: CICB, London
Amount of award then: £15,000
Award at February 2001: £15,775

Description of injuries: Witnessed his mother being killed by his father – he saw her thrown out of the front door, have her head repeatedly banged against a brick wall and despite her struggles and bloodied state she was kicked severely about the head and body – M screamed and was distraught throughout the assault – he was found by his mother's side on police arrival – his mother died two days later – the father was convicted of manslaughter – M's father informed him of the death of his mother two years later. He suffered from post-traumatic stress disorder – mourned the loss of his "major love object", his mother, and of his father – suffered substantial regression of speech and language skills – exhibited disturbed behaviour at school from the age of about four – he would require lengthy psychotherapy to make sense of the information he had been given. M was assessed as having special care needs – he was made the subject of a care order and was up for adoption.

1.9.6.1.2.C65 Case No. 10947
Name of case: Thompson v Priest
Brief description of injuries: SIGNIFICANT WHIPLASH – DAILY HEADACHES – POST-TRAUMATIC STRESS DISORDER
Reported: Kemp & Kemp, E2-017; [1995] CLY 1698
JSB Category: 6(A)(b)(i)
Sex: Female
Age at injury: 73
Age at award: 75
Date of award: 25 November 1994
Tribunal: Plymouth County Court
Amount of award then: £12,750
Award at February 2001: £15,264

Description of injuries: Plaintiff was involved in road accident as passenger in car which was involved in a rear-end shunt and sustained a significant whiplash injury to her cervical spine, some less serious thoracic and lumbar injuries and bruising to chest – wore soft collar for three months and went to 51 sessions of physiotherapy over four-month period – at time of trial, physical symptoms were still evident and comprised of pain and stiffness in neck, especially after sitting for more than half an hour in one position, daily headaches and pain in right shoulder, which prevented carrying shopping with right hand – also suffered chronic fatigue and diagnosed as suffering from post-traumatic stress syndrome which resulted in frequent nightmares – feared travelling in any vehicle and suffered depression.

Prognosis: Claimant would suffer a marked impairment in her quality of life in her latter years.

1.9.6.1.2.C66 Case No. 10727
Award at February 2001: £15,095
See: 1.1.C6 for details

1.9.6.1.2.C67 Case No. 11306
Award at February 2001: £14,898
See: 1.8.6.C46 for details

1.9.6.1.2.C68 Case No. 10728
Award at February 2001: £14,724
See: 1.7.1.C11 for details

1.9.6.1.2.C69 Case No. 11307
Award at February 2001: £14,401
See: 1.8.6.C48 for details

1.9.6.1.2.C70 Case No. 10919

Name of case: Somwaru v London Electricity

Brief description of injuries: ELECTRIC SHOCK – POST-TRAUMATIC STRESS DISORDER – SOFT-TISSUE INJURY – PERSONALITY CHANGE

Reported: Kemp & Kemp, C4-066; [1995] CLY 1670

JSB Category: 3(B)(b)

Sex: Female

Age at injury: 45

Age at award: 50

Date of award: 29 November 1994

Tribunal: Wandsworth County Court

Amount of award then: £12,000

Award at February 2001: £14,337

Description of injuries: Plaintiff was electrocuted by redundant cable in cellar of her house – thrown to the ground and suffered straining to neck and across shoulders and minor fracture to sacrum – accelerated pre-existing lumbar spondylosis by six to 12 months – electric shock caused contractions of shoulder girdle muscles and some soft-tissue straining – after three years, there were minimal orthopaedic effects – main effect of accident was post-traumatic stress disorder – plaintiff had suffered significant personality change, becoming depressed, moody, tearful and difficult.

Prognosis: Prognosis was uncertain – plaintiff had not undergone any counselling prior to trial – it was possible that she might benefit from counselling in future, but she might continue to suffer from chronic post-traumatic stress disorder – was able to resume her work.

1.9.6.1.2.C71 Case No. 11093

Name of case: Griggs v Olympic Holidays Ltd (No 1)

Brief description of injuries: POST-TRAUMATIC STRESS DISORDER

Reported: Kemp & Kemp, C4-068; [1996] CLY 2184

JSB Category: 3(B)(c)

Sex: Female

Age at injury: 45

Age at award: 47

Date of award: 29 July 1996

Tribunal: Lincoln County Court

Amount of award then: £12,500

Award at February 2001: £14,235

Description of injuries: Post-traumatic stress disorder.

Prognosis: Likely to be long standing – the accident has not ruined her life but has taken the sparkle out of it.

Other points: Fear of heights and holidays since the accident.

1.9.6.1.2.C72 Case No. 11308

Name of case: Re Jenkins

Brief description of injuries: POST-TRAUMATIC STRESS DISORDER

Reported: Kemp & Kemp, C4-069; [1997] CLY 1856

JSB Category: 3(B)(b)

Sex: Male

Age at injury: 49

Age at award: 54

Date of award: 26 February 1997

Tribunal: CICB, Cardiff

Amount of award then: £12,500

Award at February 2001: £13,990

Description of injuries: Considerable facial bruising following an assault – serious psychological problems – sleep-pattern disturbance – unable to cope with stress – at time of hearing there was improvement through psychiatric treatment.

Prognosis: An excellent recovery was expected within six to twelve months.

1.9.6.1.2.C73 Case No. 11309

Name of case: Zammit v Stena Offshore Ltd

Brief description of injuries: POST-TRAUMATIC STRESS DISORDER

Reported: Kemp & Kemp, C4-070; [1997] CLY 1857

JSB Category: 3(B)(b)

Sex: Male

Age at injury: 31

Age at award: 34

Date of award: 20 March 1997

Tribunal: QBD (Garland)

Amount of award then: £12,500

Award at February 2001: £13,952

Description of injuries: Moderate post-traumatic stress disorder with depression and phobic disorders – followed an event involving a threat to his physical integrity – due to his phobias he could not return to his former employment of diving.

1.9.6.1.2.C74 Case No. 11760

Name of case: Re I, L and S

Brief description of injuries: POST-TRAUMATIC STRESS DISORDER

Reported: Kemp & Kemp, M4-052/1; [1998] CLY 1764

JSB Category: 3(B)(b)

Sex: I: Male L: Male S: Female

Age at injury: I:6;L:5;S:3

Age at award: I:12;L:11;S:9

Date of award: 15 July 1998

Tribunal: CICB, York

Amount of award then: £13,000

Award at February 2001: £13,830

Description of injuries: Loss of mother – post-traumatic stress disorder – claimant L witnessed the assault on his mother, claimant I heard it.

Prognosis: Social Services recommended continued monitoring – counselling offered from time to time.

Other points: Award split between applicants – I: £5,000; L £8,000.

1.9.6.1.2.C75 Case No. 11310

Name of case: Teague v Camden LBC

Brief description of injuries: POISONING – SOLVENTS – POST-TRAUMATIC STRESS DISORDER

Reported: Kemp & Kemp, C4-077; [1997] CLY 1858

JSB Category: 3(B)(c)

Sex: Male

Age at injury: 25

Age at award: 30

Date of award: 07 November 1996

Tribunal: Central London County Court

Amount of award then: £11,000

Award at February 2001: £12,353

Description of injuries: Exposure to high levels of solvents – he suffered hallucinations and temporary blindness – thought he was going to die – caused psychiatric injury – he could not return to his job due to the permanent consequences of post-traumatic stress disorder.

1.9.6.1.2.C76 Case No. 10559

Award at February 2001: £12,282

See: 1.8.6.C57 for details

1.9.6.1.2.C77 Case No. 10558

Award at February 2001: £12,176

See: 1.8.6.C58 for details

1.9.6.1.2.C78 Case No. 10929

Award at February 2001: £11,891

See: 1.2.3.2.1.C13 for details

1.9.6.1.2.C79 Case No. 10930

Name of case: Re Dewhurst

Brief description of injuries: ASSAULT – BROKEN NOSE – CHRONIC POST-TRAUMATIC STRESS DISORDER

Reported: Kemp & Kemp, C5-025; [1995] CLY 1681

JSB Category: 3(B)(c)

Sex: Female

Age at injury: 47

Age at award: 52

Date of award: 04 April 1995

Tribunal: CICB, Manchester

Amount of award then: £10,000

Award at February 2001: £11,579

Description of injuries: Claimant attacked in own home by ex-husband's new wife – during attack was punched and kicked about head and face – suffered lacerations and bruising, particularly of upper body, head and face – pre-existing symptoms of cervical scoliosis and discomfort were exacerbated for two years following attack – suffered damage to skeletal structure of nose giving rise to nasal deformity, facial pains and nasal congestion – was rendered prone to upper respiratory tract infection – despite two nasal operations, including septorhinoplasty, symptoms of facial pain and nasal and throat congestion were expected to be permanent – suffered post-traumatic anxiety which had become chronic; perpetuating factors being that she still lived in the house in which the attack took place and her assailant still lived locally – sleep was impaired and plaintiff still regularly visualised the attack, and in particular assailant's eyes (which she saw as her assailant looked through her letterbox) – recommended that her anxiety might improve if she could move to another area but she owned her home, had a substantial mortgage and could not afford to do so – did not like being left alone in her home, for example when her present husband worked night shifts.

Prognosis: Post-traumatic disorder of moderate severity would probably persist for foreseeable future.

1.9.6.1.2.C80 Case No. 11530

Name of case: Re Gambill (No 2)

Brief description of injuries: PSYCHIATRIC – POST-TRAUMATIC STRESS DISORDER

Reported: Kemp & Kemp, C4-079L [1998] CLY 1532

JSB Category: 3(B)(b)

Sex: Female

Age at injury: 32

Age at award: 36

Date of award: 12 August 1997

Tribunal: CICB, Liverpool

Amount of award then: £10,500

Award at February 2001: £11,426

Description of injuries: Claimant suffered severe shock and reactive depression on witnessing an horrific attack on her husband – lost her home (public house) due to her inability to continue working.

Prognosis: Return to pre-morbid state unlikely.

1.9.6.1.2.C81 Case No. 11126

Award at February 2001: £11,384

See: 1.3.1.2.1.C5 for details

1.9.6.1.2.C82 Case No. 11095

Name of case: Mackie v Rogerson

Brief description of injuries: POST-TRAUMATIC STRESS DISORDER

Reported: Kemp & Kemp, F3-013/2; [1996] CLY 2186

JSB Category:

Sex: Male

Age at injury: 38

Age at award: 45

Date of award: 01 March 1996

Tribunal: Newcastle upon Tyne County Court

Amount of award then: £10,000

Award at February 2001: £11,384

Description of injuries: Post-traumatic stress disorder – gunshot wounds to the abdomen.

Prognosis: There appeared to be no good physical reason why he should not carry out full heavy work.

Other points: Evidence pointed to the chronicity of his symptoms being caused by the circumstances of the attack – also his obsessional personality.

1.9.6.1.2.C83 Case No. 11094

Name of case: Allin v City and Hackney HA

Brief description of injuries: POST-TRAUMATIC STRESS DISORDER

Reported: [1996] Med LR 167; Kemp & Kemp, C4-080; [1996] CLY 2185

JSB Category: 3(B)(c)

Sex: Female

Age at injury: -

Age at award: -

Date of award: 01 April 1996

Tribunal: Mayor's and City of London County Court

Amount of award then: £10,000

Award at February 2001: £11,298

Description of injuries: Post-traumatic stress disorder – not referred for psychiatric treatment.

1.9.6.1.2.C84 Case No. 11283

Award at February 2001: £11,201

See: 1.1.C7 for details

1.9.6.1.2.C85 Case No. 11791

Name of case: S (a minor) v Hearnshaw

Brief description of injuries: POST-TRAUMATIC STRESS DISORDER

Reported: Kemp & Kemp, C4-081; [1999] CLY 1454

JSB Category: 3(B)(c)

Sex: Male

Age at injury: 4

Age at award: 9

Date of award: 02 February 1999

Tribunal: Mayor's & City of London County Court

Amount of award then: £10,500

Award at February 2001: £11,053

Description of injuries: Claimant suffered minor physical injuries (cuts and bruises to right side of body, particularly face, elbow, lower leg and ankle) and severe post-traumatic stress disorder for 2 years following road accident – double incontinence – loss of appetite – temporary growth retardation – nightmares – disturbed sleep, with consequent tiredness on following days – anti-social behaviour; spitefulness, possessiveness, proneness to tantrums – withdrawnness – difficulties with interaction – reduction in attention span – proneness to dreaming – educational achievement suffered; registered as a child with special needs – condition improved after 2 years, and at date of trial claimant described as "nearly out of the woods" – ongoing difficulties with getting to sleep (routinely staying awake until 11 pm) and peer relationships, some concentration problems and mild traffic phobia.

Prognosis: Claimant's difficulties with peer relationships expected to continue throughout adolescence and vulnerability to stress expected to continue – otherwise symptoms expected to resolve fully within next 7-8 years – physical injuries had not caused any lasting damage.

Other points: Award included £1,000 for physical injuries.

1.9.6.1.2.C86 Case No. 11317
Award at February 2001: £11,025
See: 1.8.6.C62 for details

1.9.6.1.2.C87 Case No. 11780
Award at February 2001: £10,468
See: 1.8.6.C66 for details

1.9.6.1.2.C88 Case No. 10922
Name of case: Re Johnston
Brief description of injuries: KIDNAP VICTIM – DEPRESSION – POST-TRAUMATIC STRESS DISORDER – AGORAPHOBIA
Reported: Kemp & Kemp, C4-086; [1995] CLY 1673
JSB Category: 3(B)(c)
Sex: Male
Age at injury: 50
Age at award: 55
Date of award: 24 July 1995
Tribunal: CICB, Liverpool
Amount of award then: £8,500
Award at February 2001: £9,805
Description of injuries: Plaintiff kidnapped for a period of two-and-a-half days and held for ransom by a gang – captors persistently threatened to kill and maim him – disguised themselves, which made him believe he would be killed whatever happened – during captivity, he was handcuffed, tied up and punched in left eye – was threatened with knives and told that parts of him would be amputated – was threatened with snakes and injected with horse tranquilliser – a black handgun was discharged within a foot of him causing him to believe for a few seconds that he had been shot – was required to make numerous telephone calls to business associates to raise the ransom – eventually escaped after a meeting was arranged with his associates – suffered a sub-conjunctival haemorrhage of left eye – experienced double-vision for short period, but his eye was symptom-free after eight months – suffered post-traumatic stress disorder – for 12 months after his ordeal up until the criminal trial of his kidnappers, his mood gradually worsened – unable to relax and would often burst into tears for no apparent reason – sleep and concentration were both severely disturbed – experienced vivid dreams about event – had feelings of guilt in relation to incident and had suicidal thoughts – became acutely aware of most minute noises around house – avoided watching the news or violence on television and stopped going out with friends – after 18 months was still suffering from severe post-traumatic stress disorder; he was diagnosed as agoraphobic and had severely disabling symptom levels. At the date of the award (three years after incident) condition had improved, although still suffered from anxiety, agoraphobia and disrupted sleep.

1.9.6.1.2.C89 Case No. 11096
Name of case: Barry and Morgan v Williams and Jones
Brief description of injuries: POST-TRAUMATIC STRESS DISORDER
Reported: [1996] CLY 2187
JSB Category: 3(B)(c)
Sex: Female
Age at injury: 26
Age at award: 32
Date of award: 18 April 1996
Tribunal: Llangefni County Court
Amount of award then: £8,500
Award at February 2001: £9,581
Description of injuries: Post-traumatic stress disorder – exacerbation of pre-existing psoriasis.
Prognosis: Neither "devastating" nor "mild" symptoms – high prospect of success of therapy in reducing her symptoms – possibility therapy could cause regression.

1.9.6.1.2.C90 Case No. 10561

Name of case: Re Delaney

Brief description of injuries: PSYCHIATRIC DAMAGE – POST-TRAUMATIC STRESS DISORDER – ALCOHOL ABUSE

Reported: Kemp & Kemp, C4-266; [1993] CLY 1454

JSB Category: 3(B); 6(I)(k)

Sex: Female

Age at injury: 41

Age at award: 43

Date of award: 26 April 1993

Tribunal: CICB, Manchester

Amount of award then: £7,500

Award at February 2001: £9,175

Description of injuries: Claimant, nurse, victim of sexual assault at hospital by intruder, feared for her life – beaten, bitten, rope put round neck, ring finger permanently distorted – symptoms of depression and anxiety became apparent – post-traumatic stress for period of 12 months – vivid nightmares – phobias, including one about paper towels (which were used to gag her during the attack) – memory loss – inability to go out alone – vomiting – diarrhoea – weight loss (2.5 stones) – miscarriage at 20 weeks after period of extreme alcohol abuse, and subsequent feelings of guilt – loss of trust in men, particularly her own teenage son – felt family life destroyed.

Prognosis: Initial prognosis was complete recovery approximately 1 month before date of hearing, but claimant still occasionally experiencing majority of symptoms at time of hearing and seeking counselling – claimant back in full-time work at time of hearing (but see below).

Other points: Claimant very bitter about employer's behaviour – had attempted a return to work 4 times but each time had been assigned to ward where attack took place – took total of 38 weeks off work – eventually re-allocated and down-graded – subsequently learned that she was the 22nd victim of assault on staff members in 4 months, and no extra security measures had been taken.

1.9.6.1.2.C91 Case No. 11781

Award at February 2001: £8,893

See: 1.8.6.C71 for details

1.9.6.1.2.C92 Case No. 10331

Name of case: Re H

Brief description of injuries: SEVERE POST-TRAUMATIC STRESS DISORDER

Reported: [1992] CLY 1587

JSB Category: 3(B)(c)

Sex: Male

Age at injury: 25

Age at award: 28

Date of award: 06 April 1992

Tribunal: CICB, London

Amount of award then: £7,020

Award at February 2001: £8,699

Description of injuries: Prison officer involved in a frightening incident during a prison riot – severe post-traumatic stress disorder.

Prognosis: Continued post-traumatic stress disorder.

Other points: Award increased from £3,520.

1.9.6.1.2.C93 Case No. 11107

Award at February 2001: £8,465

See: 1.8.6.C72 for details

1.9.6.1.2.C94 Case No. 11097

Name of case: Re Bidwell

Brief description of injuries: POST-TRAUMATIC STRESS DISORDER

Reported: Kemp & Kemp, C4-093; [1996] CLY 2188

JSB Category: 3(B)(c)

Sex: Male

Age at injury: 32

Age at award: 38

Date of award: 29 April 1996

Tribunal: CICB, London

Amount of award then: £7,500

Award at February 2001: £8,453

Description of injuries: Post-traumatic stress disorder – beaten and kicked around the face and trunk.

Prognosis: No long-term physical effects – the severity of the psychiatric conditions made the long-term prognosis guarded – a reasonable chance that cognitive behavioural therapy, anti-depressants and hypnotics could effect considerable progress.

1.9.6.1.2.C95 Case No. 11311

Award at February 2001: £8,426

See: 1.8.6.C73 for details

1.9.6.1.2.C96 Case No. 11792
Name of case: Re R
Brief description of injuries: POST-TRAUMATIC STRESS DISORDER
Reported: [1999] CLY 1455
JSB Category: 3(B)(c); 7(A)(f)
Sex: Male
Age at injury: 24
Age at award: 26
Date of award: 06 May 1999
Tribunal: CICB
Amount of award then: £7,600
Award at February 2001: £7,894

Description of injuries: Claimant assaulted – damage to tooth, requiring root filling – onset of some symptoms associated with post-traumatic stress disorder – poor concentration – affected sleep – constant flashbacks – anger – 2 years after attack, severe post-traumatic stress disorder diagnosed – claimant receiving cognitive therapy and taking Paroxetire for depression.

Prognosis: Although claimant had suffered from condition for over a year, it was not believed to be permanent.

Other points: Award of £1,000 made for damage to tooth, reduced to £100 due to its being the second injury sustained.

1.9.6.1.2.C97 Case No. 11970
Name of case: Re Crolla (CICB Quantum: 1999)
Brief description of injuries: POST-TRAUMATIC STRESS DISORDER – 4 1/2 YEARS
Reported: Kemp & Kemp, C4-096; [2000] 2 CL 141
JSB Category: 3(A)(c)
Sex: Male
Age at injury: 47
Age at award: 50
Date of award: 04 August 1999
Tribunal: CICB, Manchester
Amount of award then: £7,500
Award at February 2001: £7,795

Description of injuries: C was mugged, tied up and threatened with being set alight – he escaped but suffered a significant psychological reaction – he had to give up working as a pub landlord fifteen months after the attack – a quick recovery was made from physical injury – he suffered flashbacks and nightmares two or three times a week in the following year – loss of confidence manifested in nervousness, anxiety, mood swings and depression – loss of energy, disorganisation and disinterest in day to day life severely affected his personal relationships – poor libido, loss of appetite and weight loss – symptoms were attributed to post-traumatic stress disorder.

Prognosis: At the time of the hearing it was thought likely that treatment with anti-depressants and cognitive behaviour therapy should result in C becoming asymptomatic within 12 to 18months.

Other points: C had not followed an earlier recommendation to undergo therapy treatment.

1.9.6.1.2.C98 Case No. 11971
Award at February 2001: £7,790
See: 1.8.6.C77 for details

1.9.6.1.2.C99 Case No. 11980
Award at February 2001: £7,541
See: 1.8.6.C78 for details

1.9.6.1.2.C100 Case No. 10332
Name of case: Re Knight
Brief description of injuries: MODERATE POST-TRAUMATIC STRESS DISORDER
Reported: [1992] CLY 1588
JSB Category: 3(B)(c)
Sex: Male
Age at injury: 54
Age at award: 57
Date of award: 15 May 1992
Tribunal: CICB
Amount of award then: £6,000
Award at February 2001: £7,408

Description of injuries: Train driver involved in unarmed hold-up of his train – returned to work but was granted permission to apply for a review if his employment situation changed due to his experience – no physical injury but suffered moderate post-traumatic stress disorder.

Prognosis: From which he was unlikely to recover.

1.9.6.1.2.C101 Case No. 11145
Award at February 2001: £7,336
See: 1.3.1.2.1.C17 for details

1.9.6.1.2.C102 Case No. 11098

Name of case: Re Woods

Brief description of injuries: POST-TRAUMATIC STRESS DISORDER

Reported: Kemp & Kemp, C4-099; [1996] CLY 2189

JSB Category: 3(B)(c)

Sex: Male

Age at injury: 44

Age at award: 48

Date of award: 21 February 1996

Tribunal: CICB, Birmingham

Amount of award then: £6,000

Award at February 2001: £6,839

Description of injuries: Post-traumatic stress disorder – still not the man he was – well on the way to recovery.

Other points: Had to take work at a lower wage – redeployment refused.

1.9.6.1.2.C103 Case No. 11533

Name of case: Re R and S

Brief description of injuries: PSYCHIATRIC – POST-TRAUMATIC STRESS DISORDER

Reported: Kemp & Kemp, C4-103; [1998] CLY 1535

JSB Category: 3(B)(c)

Sex: R: Female /S: Male

Age at injury: R:6;S:3

Age at award: R:10;S:7

Date of award: 09 February 1998

Tribunal: CICB

Amount of award then: £6,000

Award at February 2001: £6,438

Description of injuries: Two children were present in the house when their grandmother was murdered by her husband – R experienced anxiety and concern for her mother and brother – S became increasingly disturbed once he was able to articulate his feelings – fell into rages if he felt his security was threatened – both children were doing well at school at time of hearing.

Other points: Sum awarded for each claimant.

1.9.6.1.2.C104 Case No. 10158

Name of case: Ross v Bowbelle and Marchioness

Brief description of injuries: MODERATE DEPRESSION AND POST-TRAUMATIC STRESS DISORDER

Reported: Kemp & Kemp, C4-097; [1991] CLY 1355

JSB Category: 3(B)

Sex: Female

Age at injury: 27

Age at award: 29

Date of award: 18 June 1991

Tribunal: Admiralty Registrar

Amount of award then: £5,000

Award at February 2001: £6,413

Description of injuries: Involved in collision on River Thames – moderate depression and post-traumatic stress disorder – tipped into the water within seconds – people on top of her – swam away with three friends one of whom did not survive – attempted unsuccessfully to rescue another passenger – swam to shore – no significant physical injuries – -unable to sleep – wept uncontrollably – upset until memorial service after which symptoms subsided a little – thought about disaster every day – slept badly – distressed, irritable and uncomfortable in group situations – lost social skills – increased alcohol and cigarette consumption – constant intrusive thoughts – guilt feelings because she did not save more people.

Prognosis: Still experiencing disaster on daily basis – suffering from increased arousal – found social situations difficult – likely to make a recovery within four years.

1.9.6.1.2.C105 Case No. 11099

Name of case: Veogent v Matrix Scaffolding

Brief description of injuries: POST-TRAUMATIC STRESS DISORDER

Reported: Kemp & Kemp, C4-104; [1996] CLY 2190

JSB Category: 3(B)(c)

Sex: Male

Age at injury: 33

Age at award: 35

Date of award: 15 July 1996

Tribunal: Southport County Court

Amount of award then: £5,500

Award at February 2001: £6,207

Description of injuries: Post-traumatic stress disorder – at the time of the hearing the only continuing symptom was a fear of heights.

Prognosis: He would be at a disadvantage in the labour market if he lost his current job.

1.9.6.1.2.C106 Case No. 11696

Award at February 2001: £6,170

See: 1.3.1.2.1.C20 for details

1.9.6.1.2.C107 Case No. 11534

Name of case: Shepherd v Iceland Group plc

Brief description of injuries: POST-TRAUMATIC STRESS DISORDER – SOFT-TISSUE INJURIES

Reported: Kemp & Kemp, E2-076/2; [1998] CLY 1536

JSB Category: 3(B)(c); 6(A), 6(D), 6(H), 6(L)

Sex: Female

Age at injury: 35

Age at award: 38

Date of award: 19 May 1998

Tribunal: Court of Appeal

Amount of award then: £5,500

Award at February 2001: £5,786

Description of injuries: Soft-tissue injury to the knees, neck, shoulder and wrists – psychiatric injury caused very serious distress, perpetuating physical symptoms – moderately severe depressive episode – organically based symptoms resolved within 6 weeks – depression was controlled.

1.9.6.1.2.C108 Case No. 10335

Award at February 2001: £5,708

See: 1.8.1.C2 for details

1.9.6.1.2.C109 Case No. 11313

Award at February 2001: £5,548

See: 1.8.6.C82 for details

1.9.6.1.2.C110 Case No. 11314

Award at February 2001: £5,481

See: 1.8.6.C83 for details

1.9.6.1.2.C111 Case No. 11315

Award at February 2001: £5,013

See: 1.3.1.2.1.C23 for details

1.9.6.1.2.C112 Case No. 11243

Name of case: Martin v Sealey

Brief description of injuries: POST-TRAUMATIC STRESS DISORDER

Reported: Kemp & Kemp, C4-123; [1996] CLY 2335

JSB Category: 3(B)(d)

Sex: P1 Male; P2 Female

Age at injury: P1:2;P2:4

Age at award: -

Date of award: 23 February 1996

Tribunal: Reading County Court

Amount of award then: £4,250

Award at February 2001: £4,844

Description of injuries: P1 Post-traumatic stress disorder / P2 Post-traumatic stress disorder – cut lip – P1 and P2 complete recovery from post-traumatic stress disorder – P2 had two very small permanent scars to the lip.

Other points: Award split – P1: £1,500; P2:£2,750.

1.9.6.1.2.C113 Case No. 10477

Award at February 2001: £4,706

See: 1.6.1.1.C25 for details

1.9.6.1.2.C114 Case No. 11316

Award at February 2001: £4,677

See: 1.6.1.1.C26 for details

1.9.6.1.2.C115 Case No. 10338

Award at February 2001: £4,644

See: 1.7.2.C1 for details

1.9.6.1.2.C116 Case No. 10924

Name of case: Re Simmonds

Brief description of injuries: ASSAULT – ANXIETY ATTACKS – PROGNOSIS GOOD

Reported: Kemp & Kemp, C4-110; [1995] CLY 1675

JSB Category: 3(B)(c)

Sex: Male

Age at injury: 30

Age at award: 33

Date of award: 25 October 1995

Tribunal: CICB, Birmingham

Amount of award then: £4,000

Award at February 2001: £4,593

Description of injuries: Claimant was postman assaulted by three youths when on delivery round – was punched to ground and held whilst contents of his postbags were stolen – bruising to face was only physical injury – plaintiff was previously anxiety-prone but in good health – after accident he experienced regular anxiety attacks, loss of confidence, nightmares, headaches and became introverted – he avoided social contact and felt insecure in public places – started taking anti-depressants and his alcohol consumption increased – suffered occasional loss of balance during anxiety attacks, one of which led to a fall which injured his knee cartilage – a minor operation was necessary but no long-term consequences ensued – off work for four weeks after assault and for six weeks after injuring his knee – left his employment with post office and became an estate agent.

Prognosis: At the time of the hearing he was still anxious in public places but the prognosis was good.

1.9.6.1.2.C117 Case No. 11536

Name of case: Re Bhatti

Brief description of injuries: PSYCHIATRIC – POST-TRAUMATIC STRESS DISORDER

Reported: Kemp & Kemp, C4-116; [1998] CLY 1538

JSB Category: 3(B)(c)

Sex: Male

Age at injury: 49

Age at award: 57

Date of award: 24 September 1997

Tribunal: CICB, London

Amount of award then: £3,500

Award at February 2001: £3,779

Description of injuries: Physical and psychological injuries suffered – multiple bruising – post-traumatic stress disorder.

Prognosis: Prognosis was fair for recovery within 2 years of the date of the incident.

1.9.6.1.2.C118 Case No. 10329

Name of case: Sheppard v Neville and Sagar

Brief description of injuries: POST-TRAUMATIC STRESS DISORDER

Reported: Kemp & Kemp, C4-117; [1992] CLY 1585

JSB Category: 3(B)(d)

Sex: Female

Age at injury: 34

Age at award: 36

Date of award: 20 May 1992

Tribunal: Bristol County Court

Amount of award then: £3,000

Award at February 2001: £3,704

Description of injuries: Minor scratches with bruising to the chest and arm – suffered nightmares and flash-backs to the assault – nervous anxiety and tearfulness.

Prognosis: Persistent post-traumatic stress disorder.

1.9.6.1.2.C119 Case No. 11102

Name of case: Firth v Zanussi

Brief description of injuries: POST-TRAUMATIC STRESS DISORDER

Reported: Kemp & Kemp, C4-120; [1996] CLY 2193

JSB Category: 3(A)(c)

Sex: Female (2)

Age at injury: 11 and 7

Age at award: -

Date of award: 27 March 1996

Tribunal: Pontefract County Court

Amount of award then: £3,000

Award at February 2001: £3,406

Description of injuries: Smoke inhalation – post-traumatic stress disorder – no signs of post-traumatic stress disorder at the time of the hearing.

1.9.6.1.2.C120 Case No. 11362

Award at February 2001: £3,320

See: 1.3.1.2.1.C32 for details

1.9.6.1.2.C121 Case No. 11902

Name of case: Balli v Mahmood

Brief description of injuries: POST-TRAUMATIC STRESS DISORDER – 4 YEARS

Reported: Kemp & Kemp, K2-055/1; [1999] CLY 1566

JSB Category: 3(B)

Sex: Female

Age at injury: 34

Age at award: 38

Date of award: 08 February 1999

Tribunal: Brentford County Court

Amount of award then: £2,750

Award at February 2001: £2,889

Description of injuries: Road accident – acute post-traumatic stress disorder – immediately after accident, claimant suffered palpitations, shallow breathing, trembling, shaky limbs, sensation of feeling hot – headaches – sleep disturbance – nightmares 5 or 6 times a week for 6 months – claimant would re-live experiences, suffering from increased heart rate, breathing difficulties, and butterflies in the stomach – symptoms resolved after 6 months, thereafter claimant suffered continuing phobic anxiety and avoidance – claimant would not drive for 1 year after the accident, preferring awkward routes by public transport and walking, and was very nervous as a passenger – upon resuming driving, claimant irritable and excessively vigilant – claimant felt unable to work for 6 months and became demotivated – claimant had intended to pursue a Master's degree before the time of the accident, but after the accident she found herself concentrating on limiting the amount of travel in her work – 4 years after accident, claimant had entirely recovered, except for continuing to avoid the scene of the accident and experiencing anxiety when being forced to drive through it.

1.9.6.1.2.C122 Case No. 11296

Name of case: Jukes v Ratcliff

Brief description of injuries: SEXUAL ASSAULT – POST-TRAUMATIC STRESS DISORDER

Reported: Kemp & Kemp, C4-276; [1997] CLY 1844

JSB Category: 3(B)(d)

Sex: Male

Age at injury: 20

Age at award: 23

Date of award: 16 April 1997

Tribunal: Canterbury County Court

Amount of award then: £2,500

Award at February 2001: £2,751

Description of injuries: Sexual assault without genital contact – severe attack of asthma – post-traumatic stress disorder – two-and-a-half years after the date of the assault he had still not got over it.

1.9.6.1.2.C123 Case No. 11465

Name of case: Re Bourne

Brief description of injuries: POST-TRAUMATIC STRESS DISORDER – VERY MILD

Reported: Kemp & Kemp, C4-126; [1997] CLY 2014

JSB Category: 3(B)(d)

Sex: Female

Age at injury: 44

Age at award: 47

Date of award: 23 May 1997

Tribunal: CICB, Birmingham

Amount of award then: £2,500

Award at February 2001: £2,741

Description of injuries: Very mild post-traumatic anxiety state.

Prognosis: No Comment made.

1.9.6.1.2.C124 Case No. 10340

Name of case: Re Beverley

Brief description of injuries: ASSAULT – POST-TRAUMATIC STRESS DISORDER – THREE YEARS

Reported: [1992] CLY 1596

JSB Category: 3(B)(d)

Sex: Male

Age at injury: 30

Age at award: 32

Date of award: 21 February 1992

Tribunal: CICB

Amount of award then: £2,000

Award at February 2001: £2,524

Description of injuries: Neck-tie tightened around the neck during attack – feared death – given counsel for symptoms of post-traumatic stress syndrome and depression for 16 weeks – embarrassing residual incurable vascular facial disorder was made worse in hot weather.

Prognosis: All symptoms should be resolved by three years from the date of the attack.

1.9.6.1.2.C125 Case No. 11892

Name of case: Davies v Edmonds

Brief description of injuries: BRUISING – POST-TRAUMATIC STRESS DISORDER

Reported: Kemp & Kemp, K2-162/1; [1999] CLY 1556

JSB Category: 5(A); 3(A)(d)

Sex: Female

Age at injury: 34

Age at award: 34

Date of award: 12 January 1999

Tribunal: Cardiff County Court

Amount of award then: £1,350

Award at February 2001: £1,421

Description of injuries: Road accident – minor seatbelt bruising – anti-inflammatories prescribed by GP on following day – claimant returned to GP 1 week later with continuing pain in right breast and chest, and similar medication prescribed – physical symptoms resolved after 2 weeks – claimant also suffered considerable stress at time of accident – mild re-experience phenomena for 24 hours – development of nervousness at travelling in cars, although claimant continued to make such journeys and to drive – irritability and anxiety for approximately 1 month – symptoms not significant enough to amount to a diagnosis of post-traumatic stress disorder, clinical depression or clinical anxiety; diagnosis of mild phobic response made.

Prognosis: Favourable

1.9.6.1.2.C126 Case No. 11711

Name of case: Rush v Mobil Oil Co Ltd

Brief description of injuries: POST-TRAUMATIC STRESS DISORDER

Reported: Kemp & Kemp, K2-208/2; [1998] CLY 1714

JSB Category: 3(B)(d)

Sex: Female

Age at injury: 26

Age at award: 27

Date of award: 17 October 1997

Tribunal: Oxford County Court

Amount of award then: £1,000

Award at February 2001: £1,078

Description of injuries: Post-traumatic stress following an accident – shaky, tearful – poor sleep for several nights – claimant recovered by time of hearing – heightened caution of HGVs.

1.9.6.1.2.C127 Case No. 11712

Name of case: Walkes (a minor) v Oxley

Brief description of injuries: POST-TRAUMATIC STRESS DISORDER

Reported: Kemp & Kemp, K2-238/1; [1998] CLY 1715

JSB Category: 3(A)(d)

Sex: Female

Age at injury: 3

Age at award: 8

Date of award: 24 February 1998

Tribunal: Croydon County Court

Amount of award then: £800

Award at February 2001: £858

Description of injuries: Mild bruising – cut nose – post-traumatic reaction – nightmares, anxiety, tantrums, "clingy" to her mother – full recovery made by time of the hearing.

1.9.6.1.3 DEPRESSION AFTER INJURY

1.9.6.1.3.C1 Case No. 10474

Award at February 2001: £109,834

See: 1.7.1.C2 for details

1.9.6.1.3.C2 Case No. 11082

Award at February 2001: £108,567

See: 1.2.3.8.C25 for details

1.9.6.1.3.C3 Case No. 10848

Award at February 2001: £89,339

See: 1.2.3.2.1.C1 for details

1.9.6.1.3.C4 Case No. 10410

Award at February 2001: £77,046

See: 1.3.1.3.1.C1 for details

1.9.6.1.3.C5 Case No. 11272

Award at February 2001: £70,465

See: 1.3.1.1.C1 for details

1.9.6.1.3.C6 Case No. 10535

Award at February 2001: £60,755

See: 1.2.3.2.1.C2 for details

1.9.6.1.3.C7 Case No. 10318

Name of case: Re R

Brief description of injuries: POST-TRAUMATIC STRESS DISORDER – SEVERE DEPRESSION

Reported: Kemp & Kemp, C4-017; [1992] CLY 1574

JSB Category: 3(B)(b)

Sex: Female

Age at injury: 42

Age at award: 46

Date of award: 12 December 1991

Tribunal: CICB, Bristol

Amount of award then: £35,000

Award at February 2001: £47,894

Description of injuries: Post-traumatic stress syndrome and depressive illness – advised not to work in a stressful occupation – doubtful if she would ever recover totally from depressive illness which was kept under control with medication.

Prognosis: Loss of career as a solicitor.

1.9.6.1.3.C8 Case No. 12006

Award at February 2001: £44,318

See: 1.2.3.1.C8 for details

1.9.6.1.3.C9 Case No. 10916

Name of case: Re DC

Brief description of injuries: MAJOR DEPRESSIVE DISORDER FOLLOWING TWO ASSAULTS

Reported: [1995] CLY 1667

JSB Category: 3(B)(a)

Sex: Male

Age at injury: 35-36

Age at award: 40

Date of award: 12 December 1994

Tribunal: CICB, South Sefton Magistrates' Court

Amount of award then: £30,000

Award at February 2001: £37,413

Description of injuries: Plaintiff suffered two assaults while employed as a prison officer – sustained minor injury to right knee in both incidents – first injury occurred when dealing with deliberate cell fire – he rescued an inmate from the fire and struck his knee with fire extinguisher while doing so – absent from work for about 22 weeks – second injury occurred when he was restraining an inmate – he was kicked and punched, injuring the same knee – did not return to work after this and was medically retired – the knee injury was diagnosed as being minor and likely to have caused moderate disability for a six-month period; however, he suffered severe post-traumatic stress disorder – had major depressive disorder, 25 per cent due to marital difficulties, but otherwise due to relevant assaults – in November 1992 had had symptoms of a psychotic breakdown which was believed to be single episode and not likely to cause continuing problems – it was likely that he would be handicapped with symptoms of post-traumatic stress disorder in long term as he suffered from intrusive recollections, depression and suicidal ideation – an employment consultant's report indicated that he had 50 per cent prospect (subject to his medical condition) of obtaining part-time casual work, a 33 per cent chance of obtaining full-time but undemanding low status work, a 10 per cent chance of re-directing his career to achieve basic or average earnings and a 70 per cent chance of obtaining occasional work of therapeutic value only – at date of hearing he was on waiting list to see a consultant with a view to revision of medication and possibility of having cognitive behaviour therapy.

1.9.6.1.3.C10 Case No. 10455

Award at February 2001: £37,034

See: 1.6.1.3.1.C2 for details

1.9.6.1.3.C11 Case No. 10636

Award at February 2001: £36,367

See: 1.6.1.1.C5 for details

1.9.6.1.3.C12 Case No. 11837

Award at February 2001: £33,087

See: 1.4.4.1.C2 for details

1.9.6.1.3.C13 Case No. 10320

Award at February 2001: £32,331

See: 1.3.1.3.2.1.C3 for details

1.9.6.1.3.C14 Case No. 10553

Award at February 2001: £31,722

See: 1.2.3.4.C4 for details

1.9.6.1.3.C15 Case No. 11846

Award at February 2001: £26,920

See: 1.6.1.1.C7 for details

1.9.6.1.3.C16 Case No. 10457

Award at February 2001: £25,510

See: 1.6.1.3.1.C4 for details

1.9.6.1.3.C17 Case No. 11561

Award at February 2001: £21,074

See: 1.2.3.4.C7 for details

1.9.6.1.3.C18 Case No. 11819

Award at February 2001: £18,737

See: 1.3.1.3.1.C9 for details

1.9.6.1.3.C19 Case No. 10751

Award at February 2001: £18,684

See: 1.3.1.2.1.C3 for details

1.9.6.1.3.C20 Case No. 11820

Award at February 2001: £18,513

See: 1.3.1.3.1.C10 for details

1.9.6.1.3.C21 Case No. 10785

Name of case: Aissani v HF Food Management (Holborn)

Brief description of injuries: LUNGS – ASTHMA – DEPRESSION

Reported: Kemp & Kemp, F2-056; [1994] CLY 1634

JSB Category: 5(C)(b); 3(A)

Sex: Male

Age at injury: about 26

Age at award: 30

Date of award: 21 June 1994

Tribunal: Central London County Court

Amount of award then: £15,000

Award at February 2001: £18,147

Description of injuries: Claimant employed in commercial kitchen – fumes in kitchen, exacerbated by faulty and inadequate extractor fans – development of asthma, bronchitis, wheezing and breathing problems – no previous history of asthma – depression – sleeping difficulties – dismissed on grounds of ill health after 3 year's employment; unemployed since then – medical advice not to work again in smoky or polluted atmospheres – after a year away from polluted atmosphere in kitchen, claimant still suffering considerable reduction in ventilatory capacity and breathlessness on exertion – inhaler required twice a day on regular basis.

Prognosis: Prognosis uncertain.

1.9.6.1.3.C22 Case No. 11568

Award at February 2001: £18,108

See: 1.3.1.3.1.C11 for details

1.9.6.1.3.C23 Case No. 11529

Award at February 2001: £16,347

See: 1.7.1.C10 for details

1.9.6.1.3.C24 Case No. 10929

Award at February 2001: £11,891

See: 1.2.3.2.1.C13 for details

1.9.6.1.3.C25 Case No. 10922

Award at February 2001: £9,805

See: 1.9.6.1.2.C88 for details

1.9.6.1.3.C26 Case No. 11532

Award at February 2001: £9,318

See: 1.2.3.1.C23 for details

1.9.6.1.3.C27 Case No. 10334

Award at February 2001: £6,366

See: 1.1.C12 for details

1.9.6.1.3.C28 Case No. 11100

Award at February 2001: £5,617

See: 1.2.3.2.1.C24 for details

1.9.6.1.3.C29 Case No. 11108

Award at February 2001: £5,592

See: 1.8.6.C81 for details

1.9.6.1.3.C30 Case No. 11913

Award at February 2001: £4,934

See: 1.3.1.2.1.C24 for details

1.9.6.1.3.C31 Case No. 10925

Name of case: Szulc v Howard

Brief description of injuries: ASSAULT – MODERATE DEPRESSIVE ILLNESS

Reported: Kemp & Kemp, C4-113; [1995] CLY 1676

JSB Category: 3(A)(c)

Sex: Female

Age at injury: 37

Age at award: 41

Date of award: 24 February 1995

Tribunal: Birmingham County Court

Amount of award then: £3,500

Award at February 2001: £4,098

Description of injuries: Female teacher was assaulted during the course of an attempted motor car theft by the defendant – punched in the face causing laceration of upper lip requiring two stitches – bruising was also sustained to plaintiff's coccyx when she fell during the assault – her menstrual cycle was affected and she suffered thrush as a result of a reaction to the drugs prescribed – she sustained psychiatric damage which had profound effect on her life – symptoms included apathy, loss of confidence, fatigue, panic attacks, recurring dreams and fear of further attack – diagnosed as suffering from depressive neurosis with anxiety and panic disorder – prior to incident she had been very active in the scouting movement, involving public speaking to large numbers of people – no longer able to play such a significant role in scouting, which she found upsetting – attempted to return to work on two occasions but found it "harrowing" – symptoms continued until date of trial, the prognosis being that with treatment there was a 70 per cent chance of full recovery, a 20 per cent chance of partial recovery and a 10 per cent chance of permanent symptoms – plaintiff had not had any treatment for her psychiatric injuries at the date of trial, preferring to deal with the matter within her own supportive family – the judge found that psychiatric injuries plaintiff suffered fell within the "moderate psychiatric damage" band in the JSB Guidelines.

1.9.6.1.3.C32 Case No. 10610

Award at February 2001: £3,742

See: 1.3.1.3.1.C30 for details

1.9.6.1.3.C33 Case No. 11224

Name of case: Bugden v Wills

Brief description of injuries: NECK – WHIPLASH – DEPRESSION

Reported: Kemp & Kemp, E2-118; [1996] CLY 2316

JSB Category: 6(A)(c)

Sex: Female

Age at injury: 33

Age at award: 37

Date of award: 26 May 1995

Tribunal: Salisbury County Court

Amount of award then: £2,500

Award at February 2001: £2,874

Description of injuries: Whiplash injury to the neck – depression – insomnia – complete recovery occurred by September 1992.

Other points: Plaintiff's horse was also injured and plaintiff suffered a psychological reaction to this.

1.9.7 RESPIRATORY DISEASE

1.9.7.C1 Case No. 10405

Name of case: Ambler v Hepworth

Brief description of injuries: LUNGS – MESOTHELIOMA – CLAIMANT DYING

Reported: Kemp & Kemp, F2-023; BPILS, I 344.1 [1992] CLY 1661

JSB Category: 5(B)(b)

Sex: Male

Age at injury: 30-39

Age at award: 46

Date of award: 02 June 1992

Tribunal: QBD, Leeds

Amount of award then: £37,500

Award at February 2001: £50,199

Description of injuries: Mesothelioma – breathlessness – first symptoms of sudden breathlessness developed in April 1991 – symptoms progressed slowly at first – then more rapidly eight months later.

Prognosis: At the time of the trial 120mg per day of morphine for pain relief due to chest wall pain.

1.9.7.C2 Case No. 10381

Award at February 2001: £21,452

See: 1.3.1.1.C10 for details

1.9.7.C3 Case No. 11154

Name of case: Barwise v Liverpool City Council

Brief description of injuries: LUNGS – ASTHMA-LIKE ILLNESS

Reported: Kemp & Kemp, F2-067; [1996] CLY 2245

JSB Category: 5(C)(d)

Sex: Female

Age at injury: 36

Age at award: 38

Date of award: 21 May 1996

Tribunal: Liverpool County Court

Amount of award then: £8,000

Award at February 2001: £8,999

Description of injuries: Restrictive airways dysfunction syndrome – asthma-like illness after a single exposure to a high level of irritating vapour.

1.9.7.C4 Case No. 10478

Award at February 2001: £4,445

See: 1.6.1.2.1.C10 for details

1.9.7.C5 Case No. 10491

Award at February 2001: £2,116

See: 1.2.2.1.C32 for details

1.9.7.1 ASTHMA

1.9.7.1.C1 Case No. 11150

Name of case: Venn v Hitachi Consumer Products (UK) Ltd

Brief description of injuries: LUNGS – ASTHMA

Reported: Kemp & Kemp, F2-055; [1996] CLY 2241

JSB Category: 5(C)(b)

Sex: Female

Age at injury: 30

Age at award: 35

Date of award: 06 June 1996

Tribunal: Cardiff County Court

Amount of award then: £16,000

Award at February 2001: £18,312

Description of injuries: Industrial asthma.

Prognosis: A case of sensitation rather than irritation – with retraining she would find alternative work at lower wages.

Other points: Pre-existing low IQ – poor reading ability – deafness from birth.

1.9.7.1.C2 Case No. 10785

Award at February 2001: £18,147

See: 1.9.6.1.3.C21 for details

1.9.7.1.C3 Case No. 11152

Name of case: Goodenough v Dunlop Ltd

Brief description of injuries: LUNGS – CHRONIC ASTHMA

Reported: Kemp & Kemp, F2-058; [1996] CLY 2243

JSB Category: 5(C)(b)

Sex: Male

Age at injury: 19

Age at award: 47

Date of award: 19 January 1996

Tribunal: Cardiff County Court

Amount of award then: £15,000

Award at February 2001: £17,456

Description of injuries: Fume inhalation causing 80 per cent of chronic asthma.

Prognosis: At risk of on-going asthma attacks which could be life-threatening – life expectancy reduced by about five years – improvement unlikely.

Other points: Reduced employment prospects.

1.9.7.1.C4 Case No. 11399

Name of case: Sola v Royal Marsden Hospital

Brief description of injuries: LUNGS – OCCUPATIONAL ASTHMA

Reported: Kemp & Kemp, F2-047; [1997] CLY 1948

JSB Category: 5(C)(b)

Sex: Female

Age at injury: 43

Age at award: 51

Date of award: 05 June 1997

Tribunal: Clerkenwell County Court

Amount of award then: £14,000

Award at February 2001: £15,470

Description of injuries: Occupational asthma following exposure to gluteraldehyde – clinical depression – nursing burn-out.

Prognosis: Retired on ill-health grounds in 1993 – only suffered asthmatic symptoms if she had contact with gluteraldehyde.

1.9.7.1.C5 Case No. 10786

Name of case: McCaffery v Lambeth London Borough Council

Brief description of injuries: LUNGS – ASTHMA IN THREE YOUNG CHILDREN

Reported: Kemp & Kemp, F2-078; [1994] CLY 1635

JSB Category: 5(C)(e)

Sex: All female

Age at injury: (1): 2 months-4 years 7 months;(2): 1 year-6 years 6 months;(3): 8 months-2 years 11 months

Age at award: (1):7;(2):9;(3):4

Date of award: 14 March 1994

Tribunal: Wandsworth County Court

Amount of award then: £6,075

Award at February 2001: £7,333

Description of injuries: 3 children ((1), (2) and (3)) growing up in damp accommodation held by their parents on secure tenancy.(1) Chest problems with wheezing and shortness of breath from age of 2 months – initial diagnosis of bronchitis and antibiotics prescribed – at age of 6 months, diagnosis changed to asthma and Nuelin liquid prescribed – 9 full blown attacks – health improved after being rehoused.(2) Frequent colds at age of 1 year leading to wheeziness – wheeziness sometimes evident even without cold symptoms – asthma diagnosed and anti-asthmatic drugs prescribed – health improved after being rehoused.(3) Chest problems at age of 8 months – development of wheeziness – antibiotics and Nuelin prescribed – immediate chest problems resolved – subsequent frequent chest problems treated with antibiotics or Nuelin.

Other points: Award split: (1): £2,700 (2): £2,475 (3): £900

1.9.7.1.C6 Case No. 10062

Name of case: Bygraves v London Borough of Southwark

Brief description of injuries: LUNGS – ASTHMA – 4 SEVERE ATTACKS

Reported: Kemp & Kemp, F2-062; [1990] CLY 1640

JSB Category: 5(C)

Sex: Male

Age at injury: -

Age at award: 5

Date of award: 19 September 1990

Tribunal: Wood Green Court Court

Amount of award then: £4,000

Award at February 2001: £5,321

Description of injuries: Developed asthma – suffered four severe asthma attacks – other upper respiratory tract infections.

1.9.7.1.C7 Case No. 10391

Name of case: Wand v Gozuboyok

Brief description of injuries: WHIPLASH – ASTHMA EXACERBATED

Reported: Kemp & Kemp, K2-044; [1992] CLY 1647

JSB Category: 6(A)(c)

Sex: Female

Age at injury: 25

Age at award: 27

Date of award: 21 January 1992

Tribunal: Croydon County Court

Amount of award then: £2,500

Award at February 2001: £3,171

Description of injuries: Whiplash injury to the neck – pain in the chest – generalised aching to the back and shoulders – stiffness to the neck – immediate thrusting pain to the chest – analgesics taken for four days – interfered with driving and keeping fit. Pre-existing asthma exacerbated by distress – pain in lifting children (worked as a nanny) – slightly more nervous when driving.

Prognosis: Some residual disability likely to settle.

1.9.7.1.C8 Case No. 11153

Name of case: Stone v Redair Mersey Agencies

Brief description of injuries: LUNGS – ASTHMA

Reported: Kemp & Kemp, F2-038/2, F2-066; [1996] CLY 2244

JSB Category: 5(C)(e)

Sex: Female

Age at injury: 21

Age at award: 25

Date of award: 07 March 1996

Tribunal: Liverpool County Court

Amount of award then: £2,000

Award at February 2001: £2,271

Description of injuries: Asthma – condition was exacerbated by the living conditions in the flat which the plaintiff leased.

Other points: Building in a state of disrepair – penetrating damp.

1.9.7.2 ASBESTOSIS

1.9.7.2.C1 Case No. 10060

Name of case: Leal v British Sugar

Brief description of injuries: LUNGS – ASBESTOSIS – CONDITION DETERIORATING

Reported: Kemp & Kemp, F2-043; [1990] CLY 1638

JSB Category: 5(B)

Sex: Male

Age at injury: -

Age at award: 49

Date of award: 16 February 1988

Tribunal: QBD

Amount of award then: £64,119

Award at February 2001: £130,184

Description of injuries: Asbestosis developed with the period (1972-1978) of exposure – breathlessness – bilateral pleural thickening.

Prognosis: Deterioration of breathing to grade 3 on the Medical Research Council Grade – expected to deteriorate further to grade 4 within 10 years.

1.9.7.2.C2 Case No. 10059

Name of case: Kent v Wakefield Metal Traders

Brief description of injuries: LUNGS – ASBESTOS – MESOTHELIOMA – CLAIMANT DYING

Reported: Kemp & Kemp, F2-018; BPILS, I 133, III 17.2; [1990] CLY 1637

JSB Category: 5(B)

Sex: Male

Age at injury: -

Age at award: 52

Date of award: 19 October 1990

Tribunal: QBD

Amount of award then: £45,000

Award at February 2001: £66,213

Description of injuries: Exposure to substantial quantities of asbestos dust – bouts of acute chest pain – breathlessness – blunting of left costrophenic angle and very minor pleural thickening on the left side – mesothelioma

Prognosis: Forced to retire after ill-health – unable to pursue pastimes – breathless after walking 20 to 25 yards or after negotiating flight of stairs – likely to die within weeks.

1.9.7.2.C3 Case No. 11392

Name of case: Tilley v Tucker

Brief description of injuries: LUNGS – ASBESTOSIS

Reported: Kemp & Kemp, F2-020; [1997] CLY 1941

JSB Category: 5(B)(b)

Sex: Male

Age at injury: 15

Age at award: 48

Date of award: 19 June 1996

Tribunal: Leicester County Court

Amount of award then: £42,000

Award at February 2001: £51,287

Description of injuries: Exposure to asbestos dust – 50 per cent respiratory disability due to pleural thickening – mild asbestosis – two cancer scares – at five per cent risk of developing cancer – pain with the pleural disease.

Prognosis: Significant pain with the pleural disease – likely to suffer increasingly severe disablement.

1.9.7.2.C4 Case No. 10210

Name of case: Jenkins v Darlington Insulation Co.

Brief description of injuries: LUNGS – ASBESTOS – 20% DISABILITY – 10% CHANCE OF MESOTHELIOMA – 20% CHANCE OF LUNG CANCER

Reported: Kemp & Kemp, F2-024; [1991] CLY 1407

JSB Category: 5(B)(c)

Sex: Male

Age at injury: -

Age at award: 55

Date of award: 05 July 1991

Tribunal: QBD

Amount of award then: £35,000

Award at February 2001: £48,640

Description of injuries: Asbestosis, pleural thickening and pleural plaques following nineteen years of exposure to asbestos – 20 per cent respiratory disability – grade 2 breathlessness – required anti-depressant drugs after diagnosis – obsessed with death, suffered a personality change.

Prognosis: The disease would progress to an inability to do other than very light work beyond age 60 – 10 per cent chance of developing mesothelioma – 20 per cent chance of developing lung cancer.

1.9.7.2.C5 Case No. 11621

Name of case: Ward v Newalls Insulation Co Ltd

Brief description of injuries: LUNGS – ASBESTOSIS

Reported: [1998] 1 WLR 1722; [1998] 2 All ER 690; [1998] PIQR Q41; 95(15) LSG 32; 142 SJLB 103; (1998) The Times, March 5, Kemp & Kemp, F2-025/2 ; [1998] CLY 1623

JSB Category: 5(B)(b)

Sex: Male

Age at injury: 20's

Age at award: 46

Date of award: 19 February 1998

Tribunal: CA

Amount of award then: £40,000

Award at February 2001: £46,192

Description of injuries: Asbestosis – severe bilateral pleural thickening – breathlessness, grossly reduced exercise performance and chest pain – sleep disturbance – persistent depressive reaction.

Prognosis: Symptoms would get worse – 50 per cent disabled – life expectancy reduced to 5-10 years.

Other points: Provisional damages were awarded on the basis that W did not develop either lung cancer or mesothelioma.

1.9.7.2.C6 Case No. 10783

Name of case: Fisher v Darlington Insulation

Brief description of injuries: LUNGS – ASBESTOSIS – PLEURAL THICKENING – SIGNIFICANT RISK OF MORE SERIOUS CONDITION

Reported: Kemp & Kemp, F2-018/5, F2-027; [1994] CLY 1632

JSB Category: 5(B)

Sex: Male

Age at injury: 17-38

Age at award: 63

Date of award: 26 May 1994

Tribunal: Not stated

Amount of award then: £35,000

Award at February 2001: £44,649

Description of injuries: Claimant worked as lagger from 1948-1969 and exposed to asbestos during that time – diagnosed with asbestosis – induced pleural thickening and mild asbestosis – by July 1991, claimant had respiratory disability of 20 per cent; increased to 30 per cent by June 1992 and 50 per cent from January 1994 – pre-existing heart problems; one episode of suspected heart attack – claimant elected to work to 65 on occasion of 60th birthday, but increasing shortness of breath forced him to take voluntary redundancy 13 months later – anxiety of claimant increased by fact that brother died of mesothelioma.

Prognosis: Prognosis that asbestosis would be progressively disabling, leading to complete disability and oxygen dependency in later life – 40 per cent risk of contracting lung cancer – 10 per cent risk of contracting mesothelioma – life expectancy reduced by 3 years due to pre-existing heart problems – life expectancy reduced a further 3 years, principally due to risk of contracting a malignancy, but also as effect of asbestosis – wife had resigned from part-time employment to help care for claimant – level of care required likely to increase yearly.

1.9.7.2.C7 Case No. 11149

Name of case: Spencer v Arco

Brief description of injuries: LUNGS – ASBESTOSIS – CORONARY HEART DISEASE

Reported: Kemp & Kemp, F2-018/6, F2-028; [1996] CLY 2240

JSB Category: 5(B)(c)

Sex: Male

Age at injury: 28

Age at award: 75

Date of award: 16 June 1995

Tribunal: Hull County Court

Amount of award then: £36,000

Award at February 2001: £44,334

Description of injuries: Asbestosis and coronary heart disease – asbestosis causing 60 per cent of his disability.

Prognosis: The risks of developing asbestos-related mesothelioma were relatively small.

Other points: Factors taken into account when assessing damages: current age and age at diagnosis (71 years) – his later years had been blighted by the disease.

1.9.7.2.C8 Case No. 10211

Name of case: Mulry v William Kenyon & Son

Brief description of injuries: LUNGS – ASBESTOS – BILATERAL PLEURAL PLAQUES – 10% CHANCE OF MESOTHELIOMA – 30%CHANCE OF LUNG CANCER

Reported: [1992] PIQR Q24; Kemp & Kemp, F2-035, F2-109; BPILS, I 42.1; [1991] CLY 1408

JSB Category: 5(B)(c)

Sex: Male

Age at injury: -

Age at award: 51

Date of award: 17 December 1990

Tribunal: QBD

Amount of award then: £25,000

Award at February 2001: £34,869

Description of injuries: Exposed to asbestos for most of his working life – bilateral pleural plaques – anxiety, loss of weight and concern for his future health and welfare.

Prognosis: 30 per cent risk of developing lung cancer – 10 per cent risk of developing mesothelioma – further 10 per cent risk of increased pleural thickening – 10 per cent risk of developing asbestosis – 10 per cent risk he would not be fit for his work at age 60.

1.9.7.2.C9 Case No. 11622

Name of case: Sutcliffe v Heywood Williams Group plc

Brief description of injuries: LUNGS – ASBESTOSIS

Reported: Kemp & Kemp, F2-035/1; [1998] CLY 1624

JSB Category: 5(B)(c)

Sex: Male

Age at injury: -

Age at award: 66

Date of award: 06 November 1997

Tribunal: QBD

Amount of award then: £30,000

Award at February 2001: £33,998

Description of injuries: Asbestosis or diffuse pleural fibrosis – chest pain, breathlessness and weight loss – chest wall pain as a result of surgery – some breathlessness on exertion.

Prognosis: Lifetime risk of developing mesothelioma.

Other points: Notional awards were made in respect of claimant's inability to do DIY, gardening and housework.

1.9.7.2.C10 Case No. 11873

Name of case: Godfrey v Gnitrow Ltd

Brief description of injuries: LUNGS – PLEURAL PLAQUES AND ASBESTOSIS

Reported: Kemp & Kemp, PRF-004; [1999] CLY 1537

JSB Category: 5(B)

Sex: Male

Age at injury: 15-20

Age at award: 61

Date of award: 24 June 1999

Tribunal: Oldham County Court

Amount of award then: £28,000

Award at February 2001: £30,360

Description of injuries: Claimant exposed to asbestos at work between 1953-1958 – admitted to hospital with pneumonia, and in course of investigations pleural plaques and asbestosis diagnosed – claimant recovered from pneumonia, but remained breathless – total respiratory disability estimated at 50 per cent, of which 40 per cent due to hyperventilation and 10 per cent due to asbestosis – pleural plaques asymptomatic – 25 per cent of hyperventilation symptoms due to claimant's anxiety at knowledge of his condition and fear of developing asbestos – related cancer – hyperventilation disability attributable to asbestos exposure thus 10 per cent, and total respiratory disability due to asbestos exposure 20 per cent.

Prognosis: Asbestosis likely to progress, but not possible to say at what rate – claimant might ultimately have 40 per cent respiratory disability due to asbestos – in absence of asbestosis, claimant would have normal life expectancy – if asbestosis did not worsen, claimant's life expectancy would reduce by 1-2 years – if asbestosis worsened, claimant's life expectancy could be reduced by 3-5 years – estimates all excluded the risk of claimant developing lung cancer, the risk of which was 3-5 per cent – risk of developing mesothelioma 10 per cent – risk of developing diffuse pleural thickening 2 per cent – provisional award made.

Other points: Provisional award.

1.9.7.2.C11 Case No. 10212

Name of case: Smith v Cape

Brief description of injuries: MESOTHELIOMA – LUNGS – ASBESTOS – CLAIMANT DYING

Reported: Kemp & Kemp, F2-039; [1991] CLY 1409

JSB Category: 5(B)(b)

Sex: Male

Age at injury: -

Age at award: 67

Date of award: 02 December 1991

Tribunal: QBD

Amount of award then: £22,500

Award at February 2001: £29,735

Description of injuries: Mesothelioma – severe breathlessness, niggling chest pain, poor appetite and loss of weight

Prognosis: Too ill to attend the trial – resident at an hospice.

1.9.7.2.C12 Case No. 11395

Name of case: Somerset v Simpkin Machin & Co Ltd
Brief description of injuries: LUNGS – ASBESTOSIS
Reported: Kemp & Kemp, F2-041; [1997] CLY 1944
JSB Category: 5(B)(d)
Sex: Male
Age at injury: 51
Age at award: 56
Date of award: 11 June 1997
Tribunal: Sheffield County Court
Amount of award then: £23,500
Award at February 2001: £26,587
Description of injuries: Asbestosis – 25 per cent loss of breathing function.
Prognosis: Reduced life expectancy of two to five years – lost amenity.
Other points: Damages were awarded on the basis that mesothelioma or bronchial cancer would not develop.

1.9.7.2.C13 Case No. 10784

Award at February 2001: £24,924
See: 1.9.6.1.C24 for details

1.9.7.2.C14 Case No. 11624

Name of case: Brown v Saunders Valve Co Ltd
Brief description of injuries: LUNGS – ASBESTOS EXPOSURE
Reported: Kemp & Kemp, F2-049; [1998] CLY 1626
JSB Category: 5(B)(d)
Sex: Male
Age at injury: -
Age at award: 74
Date of award: 08 April 1997
Tribunal: Cardiff County Court
Amount of award then: £18,500
Award at February 2001: £20,839
Description of injuries: Mixed dust fibrosis – reduced lung gas transfer – basal cracking – textural changes.
Prognosis: No risk of mesothelioma.
Other points: The judge decided that 25 per cent of J's 50 per cent disability was due to heavy smoking.

1.9.7.2.C15 Case No. 11625

Name of case: Little v VSEL Birkenhead Ltd
Brief description of injuries: LUNGS – ASBESTOSIS
Reported: Kemp & Kemp, F2-049/1; [1998] CLY 1627
JSB Category: 5(B)(d)
Sex: Male
Age at injury: 60
Age at award: 66
Date of award: 24 February 1998
Tribunal: Manchester County Court
Amount of award then: £18,500
Award at February 2001: £20,297
Description of injuries: Bilateral pleural plaques – mild asbestosis – associated anxiety.
Prognosis: Possibility that claimant might develop mesothelioma, diffuse pleural thickening or lung cancer.
Other points: Provisional award.

1.9.7.2.C16 Case No. 10213

Name of case: Eddleston v Sheffield HA
Brief description of injuries: LUNGS – ASBESTOS – PLEURAL THICKENING – 20% CHANCE OF MESOTHELIOMA
Reported: Kemp & Kemp, F2-051; [1991] CLY 1410
JSB Category: 5(B)(e)
Sex: Male
Age at injury: -
Age at award: 58
Date of award: 22 November 1990
Tribunal: QBD
Amount of award then: £14,500
Award at February 2001: £19,586
Description of injuries: Pleural thickening associated with exposure to asbestos dust – restrictive airways disease – a 40 per cent disability was likely by the time he was 65 – E suffered anxiety concerning his future health.
Prognosis: 20 per cent risk of developing mesothelioma or a carcinoma condition – reduction in life expectancy of three years
Other points: Award made on a provisional basis.

1.9.7.2.C17 Case No. 11151

Name of case: Urwin v Darlington Insulation
Brief description of injuries: LUNGS – ASBESTOSIS
Reported: Kemp & Kemp, F2-059; [1996] CLY 2242
JSB Category: 5(C)(c)
Sex: Male
Age at injury: -
Age at award: 72
Date of award: 09 August 1996
Tribunal: Newcastle upon Tyne County Court
Amount of award then: £15,000
Award at February 2001: £17,112
Description of injuries: Mild asbestosis causing 10 per cent of his disability.
Prognosis: Risk of asbestosis cancer and malignant mesothelioma 5-10 per cent.
Other points: Breathlessness more likely to be caused by pre-existing heart disease.

1.9.7.2.C18 Case No. 10214

Name of case: Lower v British Broadcasting Corp.
Brief description of injuries: LEGIONNAIRE'S DISEASE
Reported: Kemp & Kemp, L3-075; [1991] CLY 1411
JSB Category: 5(B)(e)
Sex: Male
Age at injury: 47
Age at award: 50
Date of award: 17 May 1991
Tribunal: QBD
Amount of award then: £12,500
Award at February 2001: £16,327
Description of injuries: Legionnaire's disease – severe pneumonia, complicated by respiratory failure – confusion, hallucinations, aggression, cardiac failure and diabetes – unable to work for eight months – diabetes was precipitated by the Legionnaire's disease, controlled by insulin and diet – lung function tests were normal.
Prognosis: Continuing disability was attributable to the Legionnaire's disease for two to three years – current symptoms were due more to the stresses of litigation.

1.9.7.2.C19 Case No. 10061

Name of case: Davies v Newalls Insulation Co.
Brief description of injuries: LUNGS – ASBESTOSIS
Reported: Kemp & Kemp, F2-071, [1990] CLY 1639
JSB Category: 5(B)
Sex: Male
Age at injury: -
Age at award: 50
Date of award: 23 July 1990
Tribunal: Cardiff County Court
Amount of award then: £5,000
Award at February 2001: £6,782
Description of injuries: Asbestosis in the form of pleural plaques.
Prognosis: Benign, but his two brothers died as a result of same exposure to asbestos.

1.9.7.2.C20 Case No. 10215

Name of case: Goodman v Ministry of Defence
Brief description of injuries: ASBESTOS – PLEURAL PLAQUES – 15% BREATHLESSNESS DUE TO ASBESTOS
Reported: Kemp & Kemp, 12-275,F2-043/1; [1991] CLY 1412
JSB Category: 5(B)(g)
Sex: Male
Age at injury: -
Age at award: 62
Date of award: 14 November 1990
Tribunal: QBD
Amount of award then: £4,800
Award at February 2001: £6,351
Description of injuries: Exposure to asbestos dust – plaques that were moderately marked – appreciably disabled – suffered anxiety proportionate to the extent of his injury.
Prognosis: Grade 3 breathlessness on the MRC scale – 85 per cent attributable to a heart condition and 15 per cent attributable to his exposure to asbestos dust.
Other points: Provisional damages.

1.9.7.2.C21 Case No. 10216

Name of case: Large v Ministry of Defence
Brief description of injuries: ASBESTOS – PLAQUES – SLIGHT BREATHLESSNESS
Reported: Kemp & Kemp, 12-277,F2-076; [1991] CLY 1413
JSB Category: 5(B)(g)
Sex: Male
Age at injury: -
Age at award: 53
Date of award: 14 November 1990
Tribunal: QBD
Amount of award then: £3,300
Award at February 2001: £4,366
Description of injuries: 20 years' exposure to asbestos dust – pleural plaques noticeable on X-ray – slightly disabled by breathlessness.
Prognosis: Currently anxious about his pleural condition.
Other points: Provisional damages.

1.9.7.2.C22 Case No. 10217

Name of case: Moore v Ministry of Defence
Brief description of injuries: ASBESTOS – BILATERAL PLEURAL PLAQUES
Reported: Kemp & Kemp, F2-077; [1991] CLY 1414
JSB Category: 5(B)(g)
Sex: Male
Age at injury: -
Age at award: 48
Date of award: 14 November 1990
Tribunal: QBD
Amount of award then: £2,800
Award at February 2001: £3,705
Description of injuries: Extensive and symptomless bilateral pleural plaque disease – immediate anxiety on learning of the radiological changes to his lungs.
Other points: Provisional damages.

1.9.7.2.C23 Case No. 10218

Name of case: Mears v Kitsons Insulations
Brief description of injuries: ASBESTOS – PLEURAL PLAQUES – 10% RISK OF MESOTHELIOMA – 5% RISK OF LUNG CANCER
Reported: Kemp & Kemp, F2-079; [1991] CLY 1415
JSB Category: 5(B)(h)
Sex: Male
Age at injury: -
Age at award: 60
Date of award: 22 March 1991

Tribunal: QBD
Amount of award then: £2,000
Award at February 2001: £2,618
Description of injuries: M was exposed to asbestos in his work – pleural plaque formation and pleural thickening attributable to asbestos exposure diagnosed in 1989.
Prognosis: 10 per cent risk of malignant mesothelioma and asbestosis of the lungs – 5 per cent risk of more diffuse pleural disease and lung cancer.
Other points: Provisional damages.

1.9.7.3 BERYLLIOSIS

1.9.7.3.C1 Case No. 11869

Award at February 2001: £77,167
See: 1.9.6.1.C4 for details

1.9.7.4 MALIGNANCY

1.9.7.4.C1 Case No. 11966

Name of case: Sandford v British Railways Board
Brief description of injuries: LUNGS – MESOTHELIOMA
Reported: Kemp & Kemp, PRF-001; [2000] 1 CL 126
JSB Category: 5(B)(a)
Sex: Male
Age at injury: 56
Age at award: 60 at death
Date of award: 09 September 1999
Tribunal: QBD
Amount of award then: £58,000
Award at February 2001: £66,994
Description of injuries: During 40 years working for BRB S was exposed to very extensive asbestos dust – he developed mesothelioma – symptoms began in August 1993 and he died on the 5 December 1997 – suffered an extensive period of illness for a mesothelioma victim – severe distress and pain, breathlessness, weakness, swelling of the chest, gastrointestinal symptoms, depression and paralysis of the legs – the massive tumour caused much embarrassment – S suffered considerable depression at the thought of his impending death.
Prognosis: Dead

1.9.7.4.C2 Case No. 11147

Name of case: Mulgrew v Upper Clyde Shipbuilders Ltd

Brief description of injuries: LUNGS – MESOTHELIOMA

Reported: Kemp & Kemp, F2-078; [1996] CLY 2238

JSB Category: 5(B)(b)

Sex: Male

Age at injury: 64

Age at award: 66

Date of award: 06 March 1996

Tribunal: Not stated

Amount of award then: £45,000

Award at February 2001: £55,957

Description of injuries: Mesothelioma – depression.

Prognosis: Poor – life expectancy of one year – last three months likely to be "distressing and degrading".

1.9.7.4.C3 Case No. 11148

Name of case: Johnson v Cawdor Industrial Holdings

Brief description of injuries: LUNGS – MESOTHELIOMA

Reported: [1996] CLY 2239

JSB Category: 5(B)(b)

Sex: Female

Age at injury: -

Age at award: Deceased

Date of award: 23 May 1996

Tribunal: Manchester County Court

Amount of award then: £45,000

Award at February 2001: £55,390

Description of injuries: Death from mesothelioma – deceased had undergone experimental chemotherapy which had unpleasant consequences.

Prognosis: Deceased -widow attended court.

Other points: Judge increased the set figure of damages to follow the Scottish case of Farrely v Yarrow Shipbuilders – defendants were not represented at court.

1.9.7.4.C4 Case No. 11955

Name of case: Worrall v Powergen plc

Brief description of injuries: LUNGS – MESOTHELIOMA

Reported: [1999] PIQR P103; [1999] Lloyd's Rep Med 177; 96(6) LSG 34; 99 (2) QR 8; (1999) The Times, February 10; Kemp & Kemp, F2-020/1, M2-056; BPILS, II 166.1, XI 3103, XV 33; [1999] CLY 1619

JSB Category: 5(B)

Sex: Male

Age at injury: 25 onwards

Age at award: Deceased

Date of award: 01 February 1999

Tribunal: QBD

Amount of award then: £45,000

Award at February 2001: £51,367

Description of injuries: Deceased exposed to asbestos in course of employment for just under 25 years – development of symptoms of mesothelioma from November 1995 – several biopsies and chest drains to relieve pleural effusions – pleurodesis and part of rib removed – revolutionary chemotherapy unsuccessful – tumour emerged through chest wall on left side with large portion being visible outside the body for several months before he died – claimant died in February 1997.

Other points: Award made with reference to Law Reform (Miscellaneous Provisions) Act 1934.

1.9.7.4.C5 Case No. 11870

Name of case: Rees v Mabco (102) Ltd

Brief description of injuries: LUNGS – MESOTHELIOMA

Reported: Kemp & Kemp, IT-431; [1999] CLY 1534

JSB Category: 5(B)(a)

Sex: Female

Age at injury: 73

Age at award: deceased

Date of award: 17 May 1999

Tribunal: Bristol County Court

Amount of award then: £45,000

Award at February 2001: £50,719

Description of injuries: Claimant contracted mesothelioma from inhaling asbestos dust from late husband's work overalls – progressive pain, disability, debility and breathlessness – 18 months after first symptoms appeared in February 1992, claimant in constant pain – only able to walk a few yards before becoming breathless – wholly reliant on care and services of children – claimant died in September 1993.

1.9.7.4.C6 Case No. 11620

Name of case: Rooker v Metro Cammell Ltd

Brief description of injuries: LUNGS – MESOTHELIOMA

Reported: Kemp & Kemp, F2-025/1; [1998] CLY 1622

JSB Category: 5(B)(b)

Sex: Male

Age at injury: -

Age at award: Deceased

Date of award: 05 December 1997

Tribunal: QBD

Amount of award then: £40,000

Award at February 2001: £46,287

Description of injuries: Mesothelioma consequent on being exposed to asbestos dust.

Prognosis: Deceased within 1 year of diagnosis.

1.9.7.4.C7 Case No. 10299

Name of case: Simpkins v British Rail Engineering Ltd.

Brief description of injuries: LUNGS – MESOTHELIOMA – DEATH OF CLAIMANT

Reported: Kemp & Kemp, F2-026; [1991] CLY 1496

JSB Category: 5(B)(b)

Sex: Male

Age at injury: 48

Age at award: 50 at death

Date of award: 05 December 1990

Tribunal: QBD

Amount of award then: £32,000

Award at February 2001: £45,547

Description of injuries: Mesothelioma was diagnosed in 1988 – mild abnormal liver function – between 2.5 to 4.5 litres of fluid drained from the lungs no fewer than twelve times – S was devastated by his illness and the prognosis for the future – he died on 5 April 1990.

1.9.7.4.C8 Case No. 11871

Name of case: O'Toole (deceased) v Iarnrod Eireann Irish Rail

Brief description of injuries: LUNGS – MESOTHELIOMA

Reported: Kemp & Kemp, F2-026/1; [1999] CLY 1535

JSB Category: 5(B)

Sex: Male

Age at injury: 53

Age at award: deceased

Date of award: 19 February 1999

Tribunal: QBD

Amount of award then: £40,000

Award at February 2001: £45,145

Description of injuries: Claimant developed mesothelioma as a result of asbestos exposure in course of employment – symptoms of breathlessness first noted in July 1986 – condition then deteriorated in fashion typical of the disease – increasing level of care required from wife – surgery undergone for draining of large pleural effusion and removal of much of pleura – radiotherapy – claimant died in November 1987.

1.9.7.4.C9 Case No. 11071

Name of case: Whittaker v BBA Groups

Brief description of injuries: CHEST – MESOTHELIOMA

Reported: Kemp & Kemp, F2-020/1; BPILS. I 366; [1995] CLY 1825

JSB Category: 5(B)(b)

Sex: Male

Age at injury: 66

Age at award: -

Date of award: 05 April 1995

Tribunal: Not stated

Amount of award then: £35,000

Award at February 2001: £43,246

Description of injuries: Plaintiff exposed to asbestos – liability was admitted – prior to November 1993 deceased had experienced good health – around this time began to complain of tiredness and some breathlessness – despite retirement in February 1994 there was no noticeable improvement in his symptoms – first saw doctor in July 1994 and later that month an X-ray examination revealed a right-sided pleural effusion – pleural effusion was aspirated – after further examination in August further aspiration was carried out followed by pleural biopsy which revealed malignant mesothelioma of pleura – diagnosis of a malignancy was made towards the end of August 1994 – by January 1995 was receiving morphine to kill pain; was waking up in night frequently despite painkillers; had profuse sweating and was very depressed – admitted to hospital March 1995 and died one week later (just two weeks before trial) – prior to going into hospital had required some gratuitous nursing care during last six months of 1994 and in 1995 required day and night care by his wife.

1.9.7.4.C10 Case No. 10300

Name of case: Mills v British Rail Engineering Ltd.

Brief description of injuries: LUNGS – MESOTHELIOMA -DEATH OF CLAIMANT

Reported: [1992] 1 PIQR Q130; Kemp & Kemp, F2-053, M2-075, M2-238; BPILS, I 238, 569.1, II 266; [1991] CLY 1497

JSB Category: 5(B)(c)

Sex: Male

Age at injury: 60

Age at award: 62 at death

Date of award: 04 July 1991

Tribunal: QBD

Amount of award then: £20,000

Award at February 2001: £26,639

Description of injuries: Extensive exposure to asbestos – first manifestation of mesothelioma in November 1989 – discomfort with symptoms like a cold – increasing breathlessness – lethargy – weight loss – collapsed lung – tumour blocking the main bronchus – M was given chemotherapy on three occasions – he was rendered a complete invalid requiring full-time nursing care – devastated by his illness and its prognosis – no actual pain until the last month of his life.

1.9.7.4.C11 Case No. 10301

Name of case: Stratford v British Rail Engineering Ltd

Brief description of injuries: LUNGS – MESOTHELIOMA – DEATH OF CLAIMANT

Reported: Kemp & Kemp, F2-045; [1991] CLY 1498

JSB Category: 5(B)(b)

Sex: Male

Age at injury: 72

Age at award: 72

Date of award: 11 October 1990

Tribunal: QBD

Amount of award then: £18,000

Award at February 2001: £24,511

Description of injuries: Mesothelioma diagnosed in 1988 – fluid was drained from his lungs – prescribed diamorphine to alleviate his extreme symptoms – he was in constant pain to the chest – he had difficulty walking, was unable to sleep well and felt constantly sick – drinking was difficult and he completely lost his appetite – he lost four stones in weight in ten weeks. S died a slow and agonising death in September 1988.

1.9.7.5 PLEURAL THICKENING AND PLAQUES

1.9.7.5.C1 Case No. 11393

Name of case: Smith v Dicks Eagle Insulation Ltd

Brief description of injuries: LUNGS – BILATERAL PLEURAL THICKENING – CLAIMANT SUFFERED FROM ASTHMA

Reported: Kemp & Kemp, F2-038; [1997] CLY 1942

JSB Category: 5(B)(c)

Sex: Male

Age at injury: -

Age at award: 49

Date of award: 11 July 1997

Tribunal: Central London County Court

Amount of award then: £27,000

Award at February 2001: £30,811

Description of injuries: Exposed to asbestos – benign symptomless bilateral pleural thickening – developed an obsessional compulsive disorder and acute phobic anxiety.

Prognosis: At risk of developing asbestosis (5%) – mesothelioma (10%) – lung cancer (30%) – phobia could be treated within four to six months.

Other points: Fitness for work compromised by breathlessness due to unrelated asthma and obesity.

1.9.7.5.C2 Case No. 11394

Name of case: Glendinning v Powergen PLC

Brief description of injuries: LUNGS – PLEURAL THICKENING

Reported: Kemp & Kemp, F2-040; [1997] CLY 1943

JSB Category: 5(B)(c)

Sex: Male

Age at injury: 26-56

Age at award: 77

Date of award: 15 January 1997

Tribunal: QBD

Amount of award then: £25,000

Award at February 2001: £28,995

Description of injuries: Exposed to asbestos dust for thirty years – 40 per cent respiratory disability due to pleural thickening.

Prognosis: Risk of further thickening (5%) – asbestosis (3%) – lung cancer (10%) – mesothelioma (10%).

1.9.7.5.C3 Case No. 11623

Name of case: Johnson v British Railways Board
Brief description of injuries: LUNGS – PLEURAL THICKENING
Reported: Kemp & Kemp, F2-048; [1998] CLY 1625
JSB Category: 5(B)(d)
Sex: Male
Age at injury: -
Age at award: -
Date of award: 04 December 1997
Tribunal: Swindon County Court
Amount of award then: £19,000
Award at February 2001: £20,911
Description of injuries: Bilateral diffuse pleural thickening – breathlessness – 20 per cent disabled.
Prognosis: 50 per cent risk claimant might develop mesothelioma, lung cancer or asbestosis.

1.9.7.5.C4 Case No. 11396

Name of case: Elford v Ministry of Defence
Brief description of injuries: LUNGS – SYMPTOMLESS PLEURAL PLAQUES
Reported: Kemp & Kemp, F2-052; [1997] CLY 1945
JSB Category: 5(B)(e)
Sex: Male
Age at injury: 30-55
Age at award: 57
Date of award: 24 April 1997
Tribunal: Portsmouth County Court
Amount of award then: £17,300
Award at February 2001: £19,429
Description of injuries: Symptomless pleural plaques.
Prognosis: Future risk of asbestos bilateral thickening (1-2%) – mesothelioma (5%) – laryngeal cancer (1-2%) – lung cancer (23%).
Other points: Plaintiff was a heavy smoker – risk of lung cancer was likely to decline at a rate of approximately 0.75% per annum.

1.9.7.5.C5 Case No. 11874

Award at February 2001: £17,146
See: 1.9.6.1.C33 for details

1.9.7.5.C6 Case No. 11875

Award at February 2001: £16,554
See: 1.9.6.1.C34 for details

1.9.7.5.C7 Case No. 11397

Name of case: Barker v Roberts
Brief description of injuries: LUNGS – PLEURAL PLAQUES
Reported: Kemp & Kemp, F2-050; [1997] CLY 1946
JSB Category: 5(B)(e)
Sex: Male
Age at injury: 23-25
Age at award: 69
Date of award: 20 March 1997
Tribunal: Oldham County Court
Amount of award then: £14,000
Award at February 2001: £15,686
Description of injuries: Large pleural plaques – extensive pleural disease – mild fibrotic changes.
Prognosis: Future risk of pleural disease (5%) – mesothelioma (5-10%) – normal life expectancy save for the risk of malignant tumours.
Other points: Disability was equally attributable to smoking and asbestos.

1.9.7.5.C8 Case No. 10404

Name of case: Cowan v Kitson Insulations
Brief description of injuries: LUNGS – PLEURAL PLAQUES
Reported: [1992] PIQR Q19; Kemp & Kemp, F2-110; BPILS I 42.1; [1992] CLY 1660
JSB Category: 5(B)(e)
Sex: Male
Age at injury: 17-26
Age at award: 50
Date of award: 18 October 1991
Tribunal: QBD
Amount of award then: £10,000
Award at February 2001: £12,806
Description of injuries: Routine examination showed calcified pleural plaques on both diaphragms – plaintiff sensibly aware of the risks to his future health – exposed to asbestos between 1959 and 1968. Condition No evidence of asbestosis.

1.9.7.5.C9 Case No. 11398

Name of case: Ford v Clarbeston Ltd

Brief description of injuries: LUNGS – PLEURAL PLAQUES

Reported: Kemp & Kemp, F2-075; [1997] CLY 1947

JSB Category: 5(B)(g)

Sex: Male

Age at injury: 32-49

Age at award: 58

Date of award: 23 May 1997

Tribunal: Bristol County Court

Amount of award then: £4,750

Award at February 2001: £5,207

Description of injuries: Bilateral pleural plaques after exposure to significant amounts of asbestos dust.

Prognosis: Future risk of mesothelioma (2%).

1.9.8 SKIN DISEASE

1.9.8.1 FUNGAL INFECTION

1.9.8.1.C1 Case No. 11474

Name of case: Wilcock v John Mace Ltd

Brief description of injuries: SKIN – RINGWORM

Reported: Kemp & Kemp, J6-013; [1997] CLY 2024

JSB Category:

Sex: Female

Age at injury: 32

Age at award: 35

Date of award: 15 May 1997

Tribunal: Sheffield County Court

Amount of award then: £1,200

Award at February 2001: £1,315

Description of injuries: Ringworm infection – distress.

Prognosis: No comment made.

Other points: Infection was caught from a kitten bought at the defendant's shop – plaintiff could not take oral medication due to her pregnancy.

1.9.8.2 DERMATITS

1.9.8.2.C1 Case No. 10255

Name of case: Pape v Cumbria County Council

Brief description of injuries: DERMATITIS – ECZEMA – 90 % ERYTHRODERMA

Reported: Kemp & Kemp, J4-011; [1991] CLY 1452

JSB Category:

Sex: Female

Age at injury: -

Age at award: 57

Date of award: 23 May 1991

Tribunal: QBD, Sheffield

Amount of award then: £22,000

Award at February 2001: £29,542

Description of injuries: Irritation to the hands developed in 1982 – strong cream prescribed – diagnosed as primary irritant dermatitis in 1983 – always wore gloves after the diagnosis – facial dermatitis developed in 1984 – required treatment with oral drugs – 1985 saw a rapid deterioration of her problems – eczemous dermatitis required intensive in-patient treatment (ten days) – steroid treatment ceased and she suffered a relapse developing eczemous dermatitis on her thighs and back – by November1985 P had developed 90 per cent erythroderma – skin red, inflamed and swollen – litchenified eczema, especially to the hands and feet – fissured, markedly thickened and cracked – often weeping – three weeks in hospital treated with systemic corticosteroids – corticosteroid treatment continued for five years – her condition gradually improved.

Prognosis: At the time of the hearing she suffered from chronic mild eczema to both hands and a little reddening to the face – she would be sensitive to sunlight for the foreseeable future – relied on others for her domestic cleaning.

1.9.8.2.C2 Case No. 10256

Name of case: Frost v Yorkshire Water Authority

Brief description of injuries: DERMATITIS – CONTACT WITH CHEMICALS – ALLERGY TO RUBBER

Reported: [1991] CLY 1453

JSB Category:

Sex: Male

Age at injury: 49

Age at award: 55

Date of award: 26 September 1990

Tribunal: Dewsbury County Court

Amount of award then: £9,200

Award at February 2001: £12,238

Description of injuries: Showered with effluent containing some toxic chemical – dermatitis condition appeared about a week later – the condition fluctuated from time to time, particularly in cold weather – chemicals caused an allergy to rubber.

Prognosis: Dryness of patches of his skin would continue indefinitely – he would have to use emollients on a long term basis – the allergy to rubber could get worse – if this happened he could be at a disadvantage in the labour market.

1.9.8.2.C3 Case No. 10844
Award at February 2001: £11,933
See: 1.6.1.1.C15 for details

1.9.8.2.C4 Case No. 10031
Name of case: Arkley v Alfred Ellis and Sons (Wakefield)
Brief description of injuries: DERMATITIS
Reported: [1990] CLY 1611
JSB Category: 6(I)
Sex: Male
Age at injury: 54
Age at award: 59
Date of award: 13 October 1989
Tribunal: QBD, Leeds
Amount of award then: £8,000
Award at February 2001: £11,711
Description of injuries: Dermatitis involving redness, weeping, cracking and scaling between fingers, spreading onto the backs of the hands.
Prognosis: As long as plaintiff continues to work as he was, he would suffer relapses into further periods of incapacity.

1.9.8.2.C5 Case No. 11013
Name of case: Davies v Gwent Health Authority
Brief description of injuries: SKIN – DERMATITIS
Reported: Kemp & Kemp, J4-014; [1995] CLY 1765
JSB Category: 6(I)
Sex: Female
Age at injury: -
Age at award: 46
Date of award: 11 September 1995
Tribunal: Cardiff County Court
Amount of award then: £8,000
Award at February 2001: £9,137
Description of injuries: Plaintiff was employed by defendants as catering assistant at Royal Gwent Hospital – developed dermatitis on both hands in January 1991 as result of undertaking wet work involving contact with detergents and bleach – continued to work until August 1991 – employment was terminated in March 1993 – plaintiff developed rash initially to her fingers, consisting of blistering, weeping, scaling and cracking – suffered from acute scaling and exuding eczema – rash spread to her left wrist and she had to wear gloves for all wet work at home and use emollient creams and occasionally topical steroids – plaintiff was likely to develop future hand dermatitis – pre-existing nickel sensitivity was not causative of injury but affected the chronicity of dermatitis – plaintiff was no longer able to work.

1.9.8.2.C6 Case No. 11014
Name of case: Williams v Gwent Health Authority
Brief description of injuries: SKIN – DERMATITIS
Reported: Kemp & Kemp, J4-015/1; [1995] CLY 1766
JSB Category: 6(I)
Sex: Female
Age at injury: -
Age at award: 55
Date of award: 11 September 1995
Tribunal: Cardiff County Court
Amount of award then: £7,000
Award at February 2001: £7,995
Description of injuries: Plaintiff was employed by defendants as catering assistant at Royal Gwent Hospital – developed dermatitis on both hands in December 1990 as result of undertaking wet work involving contact with detergents and bleach – continued to work until September 1991 and employment was terminated in November 1992 on basis of her dermatitis – she developed dry scaly skin rash which later blistered and wept – rash spread from fingers to back of hands, her forearms and wrists – plaintiff remained at risk of future hand dermatitis and would only remain free of further eruption on the basis of her avoiding wet work and contact with bleach and detergents – pre-existing nickel sensitivity was not causative of injury but affected the chronicity of dermatitis – plaintiff was no longer able to work.

1.9.8.2.C7 Case No. 11207
Name of case: Thomas v West Glamorgan AHA
Brief description of injuries: SKIN – INADEQUATE PROTECTION – DERMATITIS
Reported: Kemp & Kemp, J4-076; [1996] CLY 2298
JSB Category:
Sex: Female
Age at injury: 28
Age at award: 34
Date of award: 16 May 1996
Tribunal: Swansea County Court
Amount of award then: £6,000
Award at February 2001: £6,750
Description of injuries: Dermatitis to the hands
Prognosis: Plaintiff issued with rubber gloves at work that were too loose and too short – dermatitis likely to continue indefinitely – her hands needed protection from water and mild irritants.

1.9.8.2.C8 Case No. 11016

Name of case: Brown v Gwent Health Authority
Brief description of injuries: SKIN – DERMATITIS
Reported: Kemp & Kemp, J4-018; [1995] CLY 1768
JSB Category: 6(I)(c)
Sex: Female
Age at injury: -
Age at award: 27
Date of award: 11 September 1995
Tribunal: Cardiff County Court
Amount of award then: £5,000
Award at February 2001: £5,710
Description of injuries: Plaintiff was employed by defendants as catering assistant at Royal Gwent Hospital – developed dermatitis on both hands in March 1992 as result of undertaking wet work involving contact with detergents and bleach – developed rash on right hand red and dry with painful cracking which prevented her bending fingers – eventually spread to right wrist – rash was treated with emollient cream and moisturiser – plaintiff continued to work with protection of gloves to prevent further outbreaks.

1.9.8.2.C9 Case No. 11015

Name of case: Gray v Gwent Health Authority
Brief description of injuries: SKIN – DERMATITIS
Reported: Kemp & Kemp, J4-017; [1995] CLY 1767
JSB Category: 6(I)
Sex: Female
Age at injury: -
Age at award: 32
Date of award: 11 September 1995
Tribunal: Cardiff County Court
Amount of award then: £5,000
Award at February 2001: £5,710
Description of injuries: Plaintiff was employed by defendants as catering assistant at Royal Gwent Hospital – developed dermatitis on both hands in January 1992 as result of wet work involving detergents and bleach – developed soreness, swelling and cracking which affected back of hands and knuckles – condition required treatment with emollient and cortisone creams – plaintiff required some time off work in summer of 1992 but was able to return to work and continued in employment at date of trial – use of gloves successfully prevented further outbreaks.

1.9.8.2.C10 Case No. 11868

Name of case: Clarke v Vauxhall Motors Ltd
Brief description of injuries: HANDS – DERMATITIS
Reported: Kemp & Kemp, J4-020; [1999] CLY 1532
JSB Category:
Sex: Female
Age at injury: 50
Age at award: 55
Date of award: 19 January 1999
Tribunal: Wandsworth County Court
Amount of award then: £5,000
Award at February 2001: £5,263
Description of injuries: Development of irritant contact dermatitis in hands as a result of exposure to lubricants, oils and greases in course of employment.
Prognosis: Dermatitis expected to remain indefinitely, with increased susceptibility to other irritants in addition to those that caused the problem in the first place – risk of severe relapses for indefinite periods, placing future employability, both in present job and in a large spectrum of other jobs, at risk.

1.9.8.2.C11 Case No. 11951

Name of case: Meletti v Lane
Brief description of injuries: SKIN – DERMATITIS
Reported: Kemp & Kemp, J4-021; [1999] CLY 1615
JSB Category:
Sex: Female
Age at injury: 37
Age at award: 42
Date of award: 22 February 1999
Tribunal: Cardiff County Court
Amount of award then: £4,000
Award at February 2001: £4,203
Description of injuries: Claimant developed contact irritant dermatitis as a result of excessive and improper application of perming solution – claimant experienced burning sensation on back of neck, face and forehead at time of application – subsequent development of rash with flaking and weeping of skin – emollient creams prescribed – 10 months after accident, claimant had acute eczema at nape of neck extending to occipital protuberance – skin red, scaly and weepy – weeping, flaky skin resolved after 18 months, but claimant remained troubled by burning sensation on scalp, and discomfort when washing hair or feeling tense – subsequent diagnosis of "burning scalp syndrome" – no evidence of scalp disease, and claimant had fully recovered from dermatitis, but still suffering significant symptoms in the form of an anxiety reaction secondary to the original injury – judge held that both original dermatitis and secondary burning scalp syndrome were caused by accident.
Prognosis: Syndrome would resolve completely within 1 year of trial.

1.9.8.2.C12 Case No. 11952

Name of case: Fentum v William Baird plc

Brief description of injuries: SKIN – DERMATITIS

Reported: Kemp & Kemp, J4-022; [1999] CLY 1616

JSB Category:

Sex: Female

Age at injury: 51

Age at award: 52

Date of award: 08 June 1999

Tribunal: Exeter County Court

Amount of award then: £1,200

Award at February 2001: £1,246

Description of injuries: Claimant's hands came into contact with a new type of cleaning fluid at work due to faulty protective gloves – development of tingling, warm sensation in left hand for short periods, gradually becoming more severe – after 3 weeks, development of itchiness and rash on thumb and index finger, spreading to rest of hand – no cracking present – corticosteroid ointment prescribed, but hand worsened and became swollen and painful for 7-10 days over Christmas – sleepless nights, inconvenience and embarrassment as a result – claimant stopped carrying out cleaning tasks, but took no time off work – diagnosis of irritant contact dermatitis – further treatment with hydrocortisone; symptoms immediately began to improve – symptoms resolved completely within 2 months.

Prognosis: No further outbreaks anticipated provided claimant avoided contact with cleaning fluid.

1.9.8.3 PSORIASIS

1.9.8.3.C1 Case No. 11679

Award at February 2001: £39,233

See: 1.6.1.3.1.C1 for details

1.9.8.3.C2 Case No. 10693

Award at February 2001: £36,034

See: 1.3.1.1.C3 for details

INDEX

Abdominal injury, 342
Amputation, 462
Animal bites, 461
Arm or wrist and other injury, 282
Arm or wrist injury, 265
Breast injury, 340
Burns, 436
Buttock injury, 341
Circulatory disease, 497
Damage to head, 7
   Hair loss, 7
   Headaches, 11
   Head injury, 23
Damage to lower limbs, 362
   Leg or ankle injury, 362
Damage to spine, 116
   Neck injury, 116
Damage to trunk, 334
   Breast injury, 340
   Buttock injury, 341
   Abdominal injury, 342
   Pelvis and hip injury, 355

Damage to upper limbs, 252
   Shoulder injury, 252
   Arm or wrist injury, 265
   Arm or wrist and other injury, 282
   Hand injury, 300
Death, injury resulting in, 466
Failure to diagnose, 497
Gastro-intestinal disease, 499
General injury, 1
Hair loss, 7
Hand injury, 300
Head injury, 23
Headaches, 11
Injury cases, 1
   General injury, 1
Injury resulting in death, 466
Leg or ankle injury, 362
Neck injury, 116
Needle stick, 441
Neurolgical disease, 500

Onset of disease, 497
   Circulatory disease, 497
   Failure to diagnose, 497
   Gastro-intestinal disease, 499
   Neurolgical disease, 500
   Psychiatric disease, 501
   Respiratory disease, 544
   Pleural thickening and plaques, 555
   Skin disease, 557
Paralysis, 468
Pelvis and hip injury, 355
Physical damage to skin, 435
   Burns, 436
   Needle stick, 441
   Scarring, 442
Pleural thickening and plaques, 555

Poisoning and medication overdose, 467
Psychiatric disease, 501
Respiratory disease, 544
Scarring, 442
Sexual abuse, 474
Shoulder injury, 252
Skin disease, 557
Specific injuries, 461
   Animal bites, 461
   Amputation, 462
   Injury resulting in death, 466
   Poisoning and medication overdose, 467
   Paralysis, 468
   Sexual abuse, 474